Ur III PERIOD

(2112–2004 BC)

THE ROYAL INSCRIPTIONS OF MESOPOTAMIA

Volumes Published

ASSYRIAN PERIODS

1 Assyrian Rulers of the Third and Second Millennia BC (TO 1115 BC)
A. KIRK GRAYSON

2 Assyrian Rulers of the Early First Millennium BC I (1114–859 BC)
A. KIRK GRAYSON

3 Assyrian Rulers of the Early First Millennium BC II (858–754 BC)
A. KIRK GRAYSON

EARLY PERIODS

2 Sargonic and Gutian Periods (2334–2113 BC)
DOUGLAS FRAYNE

3/1 Gudea and His Dynasty
DIETZ OTTO EDZARD

3/2 Ur III Period (2112–2004 BC)
DOUGLAS FRAYNE

4 Old Babylonian Period (2003–1595 BC)
DOUGLAS FRAYNE

BABYLONIAN PERIODS

2 Rulers of Babylonia: From the Second Dynasty of Isin to the End of Assyrian Domination (1157–612 BC)
GRANT FRAME

SUPPLEMENTS

1 Royal Inscriptions on Clay Cones from Ashur Now in Istanbul
V. DONBAZ and A. KIRK GRAYSON

THE ROYAL INSCRIPTIONS OF MESOPOTAMIA

EARLY PERIODS / VOLUME 3/2

Ur III Period

(2112–2004 BC)

DOUGLAS FRAYNE

UNIVERSITY OF TORONTO PRESS

Toronto Buffalo London

Toronto Buffalo London
Reprinted in paperback 2014

ISBN 978-0-8020-4198-2 (cloth)
ISBN 978-1-4426-2376-7 (paper)

Printed on acid-free paper

Canadian Cataloguing in Publication Data

Frayne, Douglas

Ur III period (2112–2004 BC)

(The Royal Inscriptions of Mesopotamia. Early Periods ; 3/2)
Includes bibliographical references and index.
ISBN 978-0-8020-4198-2 (bound) ISBN 978-1-4426-2376-7 (pbk.)

1. Cuneiform inscriptions, Sumerian.2. Cuneiform inscriptions, Akkadian. 3. Sumerian language – Texts. 4. Akkadian language – Texts. 5. Ur (Extinct city) – Kings and rulers.6. Ur (Extinct city) – History – Sources. 7. Babylonia – Kings and rulers. 8. Babylonia – History – Sources. I. Title. II. Series.

PJ3826.F72 1997 935′.01 C96–932070–1

The cover illustration is from a panel of the Ur-Nammu Stele.
The drawing was done by Loretta James.

The research and publication of this volume
have been supported by
the Social Sciences and Humanities Research Council of Canada
and the University of Toronto.

To

my parents

Contents

List of Maps

Preface

Many people have helped in the preparation of this volume, and I would like to acknowledge their assistance here.

First, I must thank Professor A.K. Grayson for his ongoing efforts to sustain the Royal Inscriptions Project. The continued financial support of the Social Sciences and Humanities Research Council of Canada has made the research and publication of this volume possible, and is deeply appreciated.

I would also like to thank D.O. Edzard, Editor-in-Charge of Early Periods, for his careful reading of the preliminary manuscript and for his many suggestions which have greatly improved the volume. The care and time that N. Postgate and W. Sallaberger, the two readers of the volume, took in reading the manuscript are gratefully acknowledged; their comments resulted in numerous corrections and improvements. Of course, the author is responsible for any errors or omissions that may remain.

Many scholars have collated texts, provided information on new inscriptions, given permission to publish new texts, or by their discussions aided me in the preparation of this volume. Special thanks must go to D. Owen, who kindly allowed me to include the results of his investigation of the members of the Ur III royal family (from an unpublished manuscript) to appear in this volume. Similarly, W.W. Hallo graciously provided me with a copy of his unpublished update of his study of the *ensis* of the Ur III dynasty, and allowed me to incorporate this material in this book. H. Steible kindly provided me with copies of his collation notes of the Ur III inscriptions in the Iraq Museum. The list of inscriptions found in the section entitled "Königsinschriften des dritten Jahrtausends" in R. Borger's HKL 3 was of great assistance in compiling the volume, as, of course, were his companion volumes HKL 1 and 2. Other scholars who have given assistance include G. Algaze, B. André-Salvini, J. Aruz, J.A. Brinkman, P.-A. Beaulieu, R. Biggs, B. Bohen, F. Carroué, E. Carter, E. Castle, A. Cavigneaux, M. Civil, M. Cooper, V. Donbaz, A. Echalier, D. Fleming, I. Finkel, D. Foxvog, G. Frame, W.W. Hallo, P. Harper, A. Kilmer, J. Knudsen, J. Marzahn, P. Michalowski, J. Oelsner, M. Sigrist, Å. Sjöberg, P. Steinkeller, J. Stuckey, R.F.G. Sweet, S. Tinney, C.B.F. Walker, J. Westenholz, and C. Wilcke. I must also thank the RIM headquarters staff: L. Cooper, H. Grau, J. Ruby, and L. Wilding, for their aid in seeing this volume through to completion.

Toronto
December 1996 D.R.F.

Editorial Notes

The present monograph, containing Dr. D. Frayne's editions of royal inscriptions of the Third Dynasty of Ur and of contemporary rulers of a few other cities on the periphery of territory controlled by Ur in the last century of the third millennium BC, is the second part of volume 3 of the Early Periods series of the Royal Inscriptions of Mesopotamia publication project (RIME 3/2). The first part of volume 3 (RIME 3/1) contains Professor D.O. Edzard's editions of the inscriptions of the Second Dynasty of Lagash—the Gudea dynasty.

In keeping with the standard practice of this publication project, each text has been assigned a four-element designator of the type E3/2.1.2.3 in which the first element (E3/2) indicates the volume in the Early Periods series, the second element indicates the dynasty in the sequence treated in the volume (or, as in the present instance, in the part of the volume; dynasty 1 in this monograph is Ur III), the third element indicates the number of the ruler in the dynasty, and the fourth element indicates the text in the sequence adopted by the editor. The rationale for the ordering of the texts is given in the Introduction.

The number 6 has been used for the ruler of the dynasty (third element) in the case of inscriptions of the Third Dynasty of Ur that cannot confidently be attributed to any one of the five rulers of the dynasty (Unattributed Ur III, pp. 393–425). If a text cannot definitely be assigned to a particular ruler, a number in the 1000 range has been used for the fourth element of the designator. Text numbers in the 2000 range are used for the inscriptions of non-royal persons that mention members of ruling families.

The full score of texts with multiple exemplars are given on the microfiches in the envelope inside the back cover. If a text is attested in multiple exemplars, a catalogue of the exemplars is given in the introductory material that precedes the transliteration and translation in the body of the publication. Note that the abbreviation cpn in such a catalogue stands for collated, (collated from) photo, or not collated. Which of these three applies to a particular exemplar is noted in the table. The collation of many exemplars in the Iraq Museum (museum signature IM) has been prevented by political circumstances.

The manuscript was prepared on an Apple Macintosh IIsi computer, using Microsoft Word 5.1a with Cuneiform Oriental font, and the camera-ready copy was output on a 1200 dpi laser printer.

Toronto
August 1996

R.F.G. Sweet
Editor-in-Chief

Bibliographical Abbreviations

AAAS	Les annales archéologiques arabes syriennes. Damascus, 1951–
AASF	Annales Academiae Scientiarum Fennicae. Series B. Helsinki, 1909–
AASOR	The Annual of the American Schools of Oriental Research. New Haven, 1919–
AB	Assyriologische Bibliothek. Leipzig, 1881–
ABAW	Abhandlungen der Bayerischen Akademie der Wissenschaften, philosophisch-historische Klasse. Munich, 1835
AcOr	Acta Orientalia. Copenhagen, 1922–
Adams, Countryside	R.McC. Adams, The Uruk Countryside: The Natural Setting of Urban Societies. Chicago and London, 1972
Adams, Heartland	R. McC. Adams, Heartland of Cities: Surveys of Ancient Settlement and Land Use on the Central Floodplain of the Euphrates. Chicago, 1981
ADFU	Ausgrabungen der Deutschen Forschungsgemeinschaft in Uruk-Warka. Berlin and Leipzig, 1936–
AfK	Archiv für Keilschriftforschung, vols. 1–2. Berlin, 1923–25
AfO	Archiv für Orientforschung, vol. 3– (vols. 1–2 = AfK). Berlin, Graz, and Horn, 1926–
AHw	W. von Soden, Akkadisches Handwörterbuch, 3 vols. Wiesbaden, 1965–81
AJ	The Antiquaries Journal, Being the Journal of the Society of Antiquaries of London. London, 1921–
AJSL	American Journal of Semitic Languages and Literatures. Chicago, 1884–1941
Al-Fouadi, Enki's Journey	A.-H. Al-Fouadi, Enki's Journey to Nippur: The Journeys of the Gods. Ph.D. dissertation, University of Pennsylvania, 1969
Ali, Sumerian Letters	F.A. Ali, Sumerian Letters: Two Collections from the Old Babylonian Schools. Ph.D. dissertation, University of Pennsylvania, 1964
Alster, Death	B. Alster (ed.), Death in Mesopotamia. Papers Read at the XXVIe Rencontre assyriologique internationale (=Mesopotamia 8). Copenhagen, 1980
Amiet, Elam	P. Amiet, Elam. Auvers-sur-Oise, 1966
Andrae, AIT	W. Andrae, Die archaischen Ischtar-Tempel in Assur (=WVDOG 39). Leipzig, 1922
André-Leicknam, Naissance de l'écriture	B. André-Leicknam, Naissance de l'écriture cunéiformes et hiéroglyphes, 4e édition. Paris, 1982
ANET^3	J.B. Pritchard (ed.), Ancient Near Eastern Texts Relating to the Old Testament, 3rd edition. Princeton, 1969
AnOr	Analecta Orientalia. Rome, 1931–
AOAT	Alter Orient und Altes Testament. Neukirchen-Vluyn, 1968–
AoF	Altorientalische Forschungen. Berlin, 1974–
AOS	American Oriental Series. New Haven, 1935–
Arch.	Archaeologia, vols. 1–100. London, 1888–1966
Archi and Pomponio, Torino	A. Archi and F. Pomponio, Testi cuneiformi neo-sumerici da Drehem, n. 0001–0412 (=Catalogo del Museo Egizio di Torino, Serie Seconda-Collezioni 7). Milan, 1990
ArOr	Archiv Orientální. Prague, 1930–
ARRIM	Annual Review of the Royal Inscriptions of Mesopotamia Project. Toronto, 1983–91
AS	Assyriological Studies. Chicago, 1931–
ASJ	Acta Sumerologica. Hiroshima, 1979–
Attinger, Eléments	P. Attinger, Eléments de linguistique sumérienne. La construction de du_{11}/e/di "dire." Freiburg, 1993
AUWE	Ausgrabungen in Uruk-Warka Endberichte. Mainz am Rhein, 1987–
BA	Beiträge der Assyriologie und semitischen Sprachwissenschaft, vols. 1–10. Leipzig, 1890–1927
Bagh. Mitt.	Baghdader Mitteilungen. Berlin, 1960–
Banks, Bismya	E.J. Banks, Bismya, or the Lost City of Adab. New York and London, 1912
Barnett and Wiseman, Fifty Masterpieces	R.D. Barnett and D.J. Wiseman, Fifty Masterpieces of Ancient Near Eastern Art in the Department of Western Asiatic Antiquities in the British Museum. London, 1969
Barton, Haverford	G. Barton, Haverford Library Collection of Cuneiform Tablets or Documents from the Temple Archives of Telloh. Part I. Philadelphia and London, 1905

Barton, RISA	G.A. Barton, The Royal Inscriptions of Sumer and Akkad (=Library of Ancient Semitic Inscriptions 1). New Haven, 1929
Basmachi, Treasures	F. Basmachi, Treasures of the Iraq Museum. Baghdad, 1976
BBVO	Berliner Beiträge zum Vorderen Orient. Berlin, 1982–
BE	Babylonian Expedition of the University of Pennsylvania, Series A: Cuneiform Texts, vols. 1–14. Philadelphia, 1893–1914
BÉHÉ	Bibliothèque de l'École des Hautes Études, IVe section (sciences historiques et philologiques)
Benito, Enki	C. Benito, "Enki and Ninmaḫ" and "Enki and the World Order." Ph.D. dissertation, University of Pennsylvania, 1969
Bernhardt, TMH NF 4	I. Bernhardt, Sumerische literarische Texte aus Nippur. Band II: Hymnen, Klagelieder, Weisheitstexte und andere Literaturgattungen (=TMH NF 4). Berlin, 1967
Bezold, Cat.	C. Bezold, Catalogue of the Cuneiform Tablets in the Kouyunjik Collection of the British Museum, 5 vols. London, 1889–99
Biggs, Abū Ṣalābīkh	R.D. Biggs, Inscriptions from Tell Abū Ṣalābīkh (=OIP 99). Chicago and London, 1974
BIN	Babylonian Inscriptions in the Collection of J.B. Nies. New Haven, 1917–
BiOr	Bibliotheca Orientalis. Leiden, 1943–
BJVF	Berliner Jahrbuch für Vor- und Frühgeschichte. Berlin, 1961–
BM Guide	British Museum. A Guide to the Babylonian and Assyrian Antiquities, 3 editions. London, 1900, 1908, and 1922
Börker-Klähn, Bildstelen	J. Börker-Klähn, Altvorderasiatische Bildstelen und Vergleichbare Felsreliefs (=Bagh. For. 4). Mainz am Rhein, 1982
BNYPL	Bulletin of the New York Public Library. New York, 1897–
Boese, Weihplatten	J. Boese, Altmesopotamische Weihplatten, Eine sumerische Denkmalsgattung des 3. Jahrtausends v. Chr. Berlin and New York, 1971
Borger, EAK 1	R. Borger, Einleitung in die assyrischen Königsinschriften, Erster Teil: Das zweite Jahrtausend v. Chr. (=Handbuch der Orientalistik Ergänzungsband V/1/1). Leiden, 1961
Borger, HKL	R. Borger, Handbuch der Keilschriftliteratur, 3 vols. Berlin, 1967–75
Boson, TCS	G. Boson, Tavolette cuneiformi sumere, degli archivi di Drehem e di Djoha, dell'ultima dinastia di Ur. Milano, 1936
Braun-Holzinger, Weihgaben	E.A. Braun-Holzinger, Weihgaben der frühdynastischen bis altbabylonischen Zeit (=HSAO 3). Heidelberg, 1991
BRM	Babylonian Records in the Library of J. Pierpont Morgan, 4 vols. New Haven and New York, 1912–23
Buccellati, Amorites	G. Buccellati, The Amorites of the Ur III Period. Naples, 1966
Buccellati, Mozan 1	G. Buccellati and M. Kelly-Buccellati, Mozan I: The Soundings of the First Two Seasons (=Bibliotheca Mesopotamica 20). Malibu, 1988
Buchanan and Hallo, Early Near Eastern Seals	B. Buchanan and W.W. Hallo, Early Near Eastern Seals in the Yale Babylonian Collection. New Haven and London, 1981
CAD	The Assyrian Dictionary of the Oriental Institute of the University of Chicago. Chicago, 1956–
Cagni and Pettinato, MVN 4	L. Cagni, La collezione del Pontificio Istituto Biblico – Roma; G. Pettinato, La collezione della Collegiata dei SS. Pietro e Orso – Aosta (=MVN 4). Rome, 1976
Calmeyer, Datierbare Bronzen	P. Calmeyer, Datierbare Bronzen aus Luristan und Kirmanshah. Berlin, 1969
Calvot and Pettinato, MVN 8	D. Calvot, Textes économiques de Ṣelluš-Dagan du Musée du Louvre et du Collège de France; G. Pettinato, S.A. Picchioni, and F. Reshid, Testi economici dell'Iraq Museum-Baghdad (=MVN 8). Rome, 1979
Cameron, Iran	G.G. Cameron, History of Early Iran. Chicago, 1936
Carter and Schoville, Sign, Symbol, Script	M. Carter and K. Schoville, Sign, Symbol, Script: An Exhibition on the Origins of Writing and the Alphabet. Madison, 1984
Charpin, Le clergé d'Ur	D. Charpin, Le clergé d'Ur au siècle d'Hammurabi (XIXe–XVIIIe siècles av. J.-C.) (=Hautes études orientales 22). Geneva and Paris, 1986
Charpin and Durand, Documents Strasbourg	D. Charpin and J.-M. Durand, Documents cunéiformes de Strasbourg (=Recherche sur les grandes civilisations, Cahier no. 4). Paris, 1981
Chiera, SRT	E. Chiera, Sumerian Religious Texts (=Crozier Theological Seminary Babylonian Publications 1). Upland, 1924
Chiera, STA	E. Chiera, Selected Temple Accounts from Telloh, Yokha and Drehem. Cuneiform Tablets in the Library of Princeton University. Philadelphia, 1922
Christian, Altertumskunde	V. Christian, Altertumskunde des Zweistromlandes von der Vorzeit bis zum Ende der Achämenidenherrschaft I. Leipzig, 1940
Çığ and Kızılyay, ISET 1	M Çığ, H. Kızılyay, and S.N. Kramer, İstanbul Arkeoloji Müzelerinde bulunan Sumer edebî tablet ve parçaları 1 (=TTKY 6/13). Ankara, 1969
Çığ and Kızılyay, NRVN	M Çığ and H. Kızılyay, Neusumerische Rechts- und Verwaltungsurkunden aus Nippur – I (=TTKY 6/7). Ankara, 1965
Clay, BRM 3	A. Clay, Cuneiform Bullae of the Third Millennium B.C. New York, 1914

Clay, YOS 1	A. Clay, Miscellaneous Inscriptions in the Yale Babylonian Collection. New Haven, 1915
de Clercq, Collection	H.F.X. de Clercq and J. Ménant, Collection de Clercq, catalogue méthodique et raisonné, antiquités assyriennes, cylindres orientaux, cachets, briques, bronzes, bas-reliefs etc., 2 vols. Paris, 1888/1903
Collon, Cylinder Seals 2	D. Collon, Catalogue of the Western Asiatic Seals in the British Museum. Cylinder Seals II: Akkadian, Post Akkadian, Ur III Periods. London, 1982
Collon, First Impressions	D. Collon, First Impressions: Cylinder Seals in the Ancient Near East. London, 1987
Contenau, Antiquités orientales	G. Contenau, Les antiquités orientales: Sumer, Babylonie, Elam. Paris (no date)
Contenau, Manuel	G. Contenau, Manuel d'archéologie orientale, 4 vols. Paris, 1927–47
Contenau, Umma	G. Contenau, Umma sous la dynastie d'Ur. Paris, 1916
Cooper, SARI	J.S. Cooper, Sumerian and Akkadian Royal Inscriptions. New Haven, 1986
CRAIB	Comptes-rendus des séances de l'académie des inscriptions et belles-lettres. Paris, 1857–
Crawford, Ancient Near Eastern Art	V. Crawford, P. Harper, O. Muscarella, and B. Bodenstein, Ancient Near Eastern Art: The Metropolitan Museum of Art Guide to the Collections. New York, 1966
Cros, Tello	G. Cros, Nouvelles fouilles de Tello, Mission française de Chaldée. Paris, 1910
CRRA	Compte Rendu de la Rencontre Assyriologique Internationale. [various locations], 1950–
CT	Cuneiform Texts from Babylonian Tablets in the British Museum. London, 1896–
Delaporte, ITT 4	L. Delaporte, Textes de l'époque d'Ur (=ITT 4). Paris, 1912
Delaporte, Louvre 1	L. Delaporte, Musée du Louvre. Catalogue des cylindres, cachets et pierres gravées de style oriental, tome I: Fouilles et Missions. Paris, 1920
Delaporte, Louvre 2	L. Delaporte, Musée du Louvre. Catalogue des cylindres, cachets et pierres gravées de style oriental, tome II: Acquisitions. Paris, 1923
Delougaz, Private Houses	P. Delougaz, H. Hill, and S. Lloyd, Private Houses and Graves in the Diyala Region (=OIP 88). Chicago, 1967
van Dijk, Sagesse	J.J. van Dijk, La sagesse suméro-accadienne: recherches sur les genres littéraires des textes sapientaux avec choix de textes. Leiden, 1953
van Dijk, Sumerische Götterlieder 2	J.J. van Dijk, Sumerische Götterlieder. II Teil. Heidelberg, 1960
van Dijk, TLB 2	J.J. van Dijk, Textes divers (=TLB 2). Leiden, 1957
van Dijk, VAS 24	J.J. van Dijk, Literarische Texte aus Babylon (=VAS 24). Berlin, 1987
van Driel, Aššur	G. van Driel, The Cult of Aššur. Assen, 1969
Durand, Amurru 1	J.-M. Durand (ed.), Amurru 1: Mari, Ébla et les Hourrites, dix ans de travaux. Paris, 1996
DV	Drevnii Vostok. Erevan, 1973–
Ebeling, IAK	E. Ebeling, B. Meissner, and E.F. Weidner, Die Inschriften der altassyrischen Könige (=Altorientalische Bibliothek 1). Leipzig, 1926
Edzard, Rép. Géogr. 1	D.O. Edzard, G. Farber, and E. Sollberger, Die Orts- und Gewässernamen der präsargonischen und sargonischen Zeit. Wiesbaden, 1977
Edzard, Rép. Géogr. 2	D.O. Edzard and G. Farber, Die Orts- und Gewässernamen der Zeit der 3. Dynastie von Ur. Wiesbaden, 1974
Eichler, Tall al-Hamīdīya 2	S. Eichler, M. Wäfler, and D. Warburton, Tall al-Ḥamīdīya 2. Symposion, Recent Excavations in the Upper Khabur Region, Berne, December 9–11, 1986. Göttingen, 1990
Ellis, Foundation Deposits	R.S. Ellis, Foundation Deposits in Ancient Mesopotamia (=YNER 2). New Haven and London, 1968
Fales, Alfabeto	F.M. Fales (ed.), Prima dell'Alfabeto. Venice, 1989
Falkenstein, Gerichtsurkunden	A. Falkenstein, Die neusumerische Gerichtsurkunden. Erster Teil: Einleitung und systematische Darstellung. Zweiter Teil: Umschrift, Übersetzung und Kommentar. Dritter Teil: Nachträge und Berichtigung, Indizes und Kopien (=ABAW Neue Folge Heft, 39, 40 and 44). Munich, 1956 (I–II) and 1957 (III)
Falkenstein, Inschriften Gudeas	A. Falkenstein, Die Inschriften Gudeas von Lagaš I. Einleitung (=AnOr 30). Rome, 1966
FAOS	Freiburger altorientalische Studien. Wiesbaden and Stuttgart, 1975–
Ferrara, Nanna-Suen's Journey	A.J. Ferrara, Nanna-Suen's Journey to Nippur (=Studia Pohl: Series Maior 2). Rome, 1973
Essays Finkelstein	M. de Jong Ellis (ed.), Essays on the Ancient Near East in Memory of J.J. Finkelstein. Hamden, 1977
Fish, Catalogue	T. Fish, Catalogue of Sumerian Tablets in the John Rylands Library. Manchester, 1932
Forde, Dakota	N.W. Forde, Neo-Sumerian Texts from South Dakota University, Luther and Union Colleges. Lawrence, Kansas, 1987
Frank, Kunstgeschichte 1	C. Frank (ed.), Kunstgeschichte in Bildern I: Das Altertum; 2. Heft: Babylonisch-assyrische Kunst. Leipzig, 1912
Frankfort, Art and Architecture	H. Frankfort, The Art and Architecture of the Ancient Orient. Harmondsworth (paperback edition), 1970

Frankfort, Cylinder Seals	H. Frankfort, Cylinder Seals: A Documentary Essay on the Art and Religion of the Ancient Near East. London, 1939
Frayne, Correlations	D.R. Frayne, The Historical Correlations of the Sumerian Royal Hymns (2400–1900 B.C.). Ph.D. dissertation, Yale University, 1981
Frayne, Early Dynastic List	D.R. Frayne, The Early Dynastic List of Geographical Names (=AOS 74). New Haven, 1992
Frayne, RIME 2	D. Frayne, Sargonic and Gutian Periods (2334–2113 BC) (=RIME 2). Toronto, 1993
Frayne, RIME 4	D. Frayne, Old Babylonian Period (2003–1595 BC). Toronto, 1990
FuB	Forschungen und Berichte. Berlin, 1957–
Gadd, UET 1	C.J. Gadd, L. Legrain, and S. Smith, Royal Inscriptions. London, 1928
Gelb, Amorite	I.J. Gelb, Computer-aided Analysis of Amorite (=AS 21). Chicago, 1980
Gelb, Hurrians	I.J. Gelb, Hurrians and Subarians (=SAOC 22). Chicago, 1944
Gelb, MAD 2^{2}	I.J. Gelb, Old Akkadian Writing and Grammar, 2nd edition. Chicago, 1961
Gelb, MAD 3	I.J. Gelb, Glossary of Old Akkadian. Chicago, 1957
Gelb, Nuzi Personal Names	I.J. Gelb, P. Purves, and A. MacRae, Nuzi Personal Names (=OIP 57). Chicago, 1943
Gelb and Kienast, Königsinschriften	I.J. Gelb and B. Kienast, Die altakkadischen Königsinschriften des dritten Jahrtausends v. Chr. (=FAOS 7). Stuttgart, 1990
de Genouillac, FT	H. de Genouillac. Fouilles de Telloh. 2 vols. Paris 1934–36
de Genouillac, ITT 2	H. de Genouillac, Textes de l'époque d'Agadé et de l'époque d'Ur (=ITT 2). 2 parts. Paris, 1910–11
de Genouillac, ITT 3	H. de Genouillac, Textes de l'époque d'Ur (=ITT 3). Paris, 1912
de Genouillac, ITT 5	H. de Genouillac, Époque présargonique, époque d'Agadé, époque d'Ur (=ITT 5). Paris, 1921
de Genouillac, TCL 2	H. de Genouillac, Tablettes de Dréhem publiées avec inventaire et tables (=TCL 2). Paris, 1911
de Genouillac, TCL 5	H. de Genouillac, Textes économiques d'Oumma de l'époque d'Our (=TCL 5). Paris, 1922
de Genouillac, TCL 15	H. de Genouillac, Textes religieux sumériens du Louvre 1. Paris, 1930
de Genouillac, Trouvaille	H. de Genouillac, La trouvaille de Dréhem. Étude avec un choix de textes de Constantinople et Bruxelles. Paris, 1911
de Genouillac, TRS	H. de Genouillac, Textes religieux sumériens du Louvre (=TCL 15 and 16). Paris, 1930
George, House Most High	A.R. George, House Most High: The Temples of Ancient Mesopotamia. Winona Lake, Indiana, 1993
Gerardi, Bibliography	P. Gerardi, A Bibliography of the Tablet Collections of the University Museum (=OPBF 8). Philadelphia, 1984
Gibson and Biggs, Bureaucracy	McC.G. Gibson and R. Biggs (eds.), The Organization of Power: Aspects of Bureaucracy in the Ancient Near East (=SAOC 46). Chicago, 1987
Gibson and Biggs, Seals	McC.G. Gibson and R.D. Biggs, Seals and Sealing in the Ancient Near East (=Bibliotheca Mesopotamica 6). Malibu, 1977
Goetze, YOS 10	A. Goetze, Old Babylonian Omen Texts. New Haven and London, 1947
Gomi, Hirose	T. Gomi, Y. Hirose, and K. Hirose, Neo-Sumerian Administrative Texts of the Hirose Collection. Potomac, Maryland 1990
Gomi, John Rylands	T. Gomi, Ur III Texts in the John Rylands University Library of Manchester. Manchester, 1981
Gomi and Sato, British Museum	T. Gomi and S. Sato, Selected Neo-Sumerian Administrative Texts from the British Museum. Abiko, Japan, 1990
Gordon Festschrift	See Studies Gordon 1.
Gordon, Smith College	C. Gordon, Smith College Tablets: 110 Cuneiform Texts Selected from the College Collection. Northampton, 1952
Grayson, ARI	A.K. Grayson, Assyrian Royal Inscriptions, 2 vols. Wiesbaden, 1972–76
Grayson, RIMA 1	A.K. Grayson, Assyrian Rulers of the Third and Second Millennia BC (T0 1115 BC). Toronto, 1987
Green, Eridu	M.W. Green, Eridu in Sumerian Literature. Ph.D. dissertation, University of Chicago, 1975
Greengus, OBTI	S. Greengus, Old Babylonian Tablets from Ishchali and Vicinity (=Uitgauen van het Nederlands Historisch-Archaeologisch Instituut te Istanbul 44). Leiden, 1979
Grégoire, MVN 10	J.-P. Grégoire, Inscriptions et archives administratives cunéiformes, 1e partie (=MVN 10). Rome, 1981
Gurney and Kramer, OECT 5	S.N. Kramer and O.R. Gurney, Sumerian Literary Texts in the Ashmolean Museum. Oxford, 1976
Hackman, BIN 5	G.G. Hackman, Temple Documents of the Third Dynasty of Ur from Umma (=BIN 5). New Haven, 1937
Halén, Handbook	H. Halén, Handbook of Oriental Collections in Finland. London and Malmö, 1978
Hall, Sculpture	H.R. Hall, Babylonian and Assyrian Sculpture in the British Museum. Paris and Brussels, 1928

Hall, Season's Work	H.R. Hall, A Season's Work at Ur, Al-ʿUbaid, Abu Shahrain (Eridu), and Elsewhere, Being an Unofficial Account of the British Archaeological Mission to Babylonia, 1919. London, 1930
Hall, UE 1	H.R. Hall, et al., Al-ʿUbaid. A Report on the Work Carried Out at Al-ʿUbaid for the British Museum in 1919 and for the Joint Expedition in 1922–3. Oxford, 1927
Hallo, Ensi's	W.W. Hallo, The Ensi's of the Ur III Dynasty. M.A. dissertation, University of Chicago, 1953
Hallo, Ensi's2	W.W. Hallo, The Ensi's of the Ur III Dynasty (reworking of M.A. dissertation). Unpublished manuscript, n.d.
Hallo Festschrift	See Studies Hallo.
Hallo, Royal Titles	W.W. Hallo, Early Mesopotamian Royal Titles, a Philologic and Historical Analysis (=AOS 43). New Haven, 1957
Handcock, Mesopotamian Archaeology	S.P. Handcock, Mesopotamian Archaeology: An Introduction to the Archaeology of Babylonia and Assyria. London, 1912
Harper Memorial 1	R.H. Harper, F. Brown, and G.F. Moore (eds.), Old Testament and Semitic Studies in Memory of William Rainey Harper, vol. 1. Chicago, 1908
Harper, Susa	P.O. Harper, J. Aruz, and F. Tallon (eds.), The Royal City of Susa: Ancient Near Eastern Treasures in the Louvre. New York, 1992
Hehn, Gottesidee	J. Hehn, Die biblische und die babylonische Gottesidee, die israelitische Gottes-ausfassung im Lichte der altorientalischen Religionsgeschichte. Leipzig, 1913
Herzfeld, Persian Empire	E. Herzfeld, The Persian Empire: Studies in Geography and Ethnography of the Ancient Near East. Wiesbaden, 1968
Heuzey, Catalogue Louvre	L. Heuzey, Catalogue des antiquités chaldéennes, sculpture et gravure à la pointe. Paris, 1902
Heuzey, Origines	L. Heuzey, Les origines orientales de l'art. Paris, 1891–1915
Heuzey, Villa royale	L. Heuzey, Une villa royale chaldéenne vers l'an 4000 avant notre ère d'après les levés et les notes de M. de Sarzec. Paris, 1900
Hilprecht, BE 1	H.V. Hilprecht, Old Babylonian Inscriptions Chiefly from Nippur, 2 vols. Philadelphia, 1893/96
Hilprecht, Explorations	H.V. Hilprecht, Explorations in Bible Lands during the 19th Century. Philadelphia, 1903
Hommel, Geschichte	F. Hommel, Geschichte Babyloniens und Assyriens. Berlin, (1885–) 1888
Hrouda, Isin 1	B. Hrouda (ed.), Isin-Išān Baḥrīyāt I. Die Ergebnisse der Ausgrabungen 1973–1974 (=Bayerische Akademie der Wissenschaften philosophisch-historische Klasse NF 79). Munich, 1977
Hrouda, Isin 2	B. Hrouda (ed.), Isin-Išān Baḥrīyāt II. Die Ergebnisse der Ausgrabungen 1975–1978 (=Bayerische Akademie der Wissenschaften philosophisch-historische Klasse NF 87). Munich, 1981
Hrouda, Isin 3	B. Hrouda (ed.), Isin-Išān Baḥrīyāt III. Die Ergebnisse der Ausgrabungen 1983–1984 (=Bayerische Akademie der Wissenschaften philosophisch-historische Klasse NF 94). Munich, 1987
Hrouda, Isin 4	B. Hrouda (ed.), Isin-Išān Baḥrīyāt IV. Die Ergebnisse der Ausgrabungen 1986–1989 (=Bayerische Akademie der Wissenschaften philosophisch-historische Klasse NF 105). Munich, 1992
HSAO	Heidelberger Studien zum Alten Orient. Heidelberg, 1986–
HUCA	Hebrew Union College Annual. Cincinnati, 1924–
Hunger, Kolophone	H. Hunger, Babylonische und assyrische Kolophone (=AOAT 2). Neukirchen-Vluyn, 1968
Hunger, SbTU 1	H. Hunger, Spätbabylonische Texte aus Uruk, vol. 1 (=ADFU 9). Berlin, 1976
ILN	The Illustrated London News. London, 1842–
Iraq Museum Guide 1	A Guide to the Iraq Museum Collections. Baghdad, 1937
Iraq Museum Guide 2	A Guide to the Iraq Museum Collections. Baghdad, 1942
ITT	Inventaire des tablettes de Tello conservées aux Musée Impérial Ottoman. 5 vols. Paris, 1910–21
Jacobsen, AS 6	T. Jacobsen, Philological Notes on Eshnunna and Its Inscriptions (=AS 6). Chicago, 1934
Jacobsen, Cylinder Seals	H. Frankfort and T. Jacobsen, Stratified Cylinder Seals from the Diyala Region (=OIP 72). Chicago, 1955
Jacobsen, Gimilsin Temple	T. Jacobsen, The Gimilsin Temple and the Palace of the Rulers at Tell Asmar (=OIP 43). Chicago, 1940
Jacobsen, Harps	T. Jacobsen, The Harps That Once ... Sumerian Poetry in Translation. New Haven, 1987
Jacobsen, Jerwan	T. Jacobsen, Sennacherib's Aqueduct at Jerwan (=OIP 24). Chicago, 1935
Jacobsen, SKL	T. Jacobsen, The Sumerian King List (=AS 11). Chicago, 1939
Jacobsen, Treasures	T. Jacobsen, The Treasures of Darkness: A History of Mesopotamian Religion. New Haven and London, 1976
JANES	Journal of the Ancient Near Eastern Society of Columbia University. New York, 1968–
Janneau, Dynastie	Ch.-Guill. Janneau, Une dynastie chaldéenne: les rois d'Ur. Paris, 1911

JAOS	Journal of the American Oriental Society. New Haven, 1893–
Jastrow, Bildermappe	M. Jastrow, Bildermappe mit 273 Abbildungen samt Erklärungen zur Religion Babyloniens und Assyriens. Giessen, 1912
Jastrow, Civilization	M. Jastrow, The Civilization of Babylonia and Assyria: its Remains, Language, History, Religion, Commerce, Law, Art and Literature. Philadelphia and London, 1915
JBAA	Journal of the British Archaeological Association. London, 1845–
JCS	Journal of Cuneiform Studies. New Haven and Cambridge, Mass., 1947–
JEA	The Journal of Egyptian Archaeology. London, 1914–
Jean, ŠA	C.-F. Jean, Šumer et Akkad, contribution à l'histoire de la civilisation dans la Basse-Mésopotamie. Paris, 1923
Jensen, KB 3/1	P. Jensen, et al., Historische Texte altbabylonischer Herrscher. Berlin, 1892
JEOL	Jaarbericht van het Vooraziatisch-Egyptisch Genootschap "Ex Oriente Lux." Leiden, 1933–
Jeremias, HAOG^{2}	A. Jeremias, Handbuch der altorientalischen Geisteskultur. 2nd edition. Lepizig, 1929
JNES	Journal of Near Eastern Studies. Chicago, 1942–
Johns, Ur-Engur	C.H.W. Johns, Ur-Engur: A Bronze of the Fourth Millennium in the Library of J. Pierpont Morgan. New York, 1908
Jones and Snyder, SET	T. Jones and J. Snyder, Sumerian Economic Texts from the Third Ur Dynasty: A Catalogue and Discussion of Documents from Various Collections. Minneapolis, 1961
Jordan, Uruk-Warka	J. Jordan, Uruk-Warka nach den Ausgrabungen durch die Deutsche Orient-Gesellschaft (=WVDOG 51). Leipzig, 1928
JSOR	Journal of the Society of Oriental Research, vols. 1–16. Chicago and Toronto, 1917–32
Kärki, KDDU	I. Kärki, Die Königsinschriften der dritten Dynastie von Ur (=Studia Orientalia 58). Helsinki, 1986
Kärki, SAKAZ 1	I. Kärki, Die sumerischen und akkadischen Königsinschriften der altbabylonischen Zeit, I: Isin, Larsa, Uruk (=Studia Orientalia 49). Helsinki, 1980
Kang, SETDA	S. Kang, Sumerian Economic Texts from the Drehem Archive: Sumerian and Akkadian Cuneiform Texts in the Collection of the World Heritage Museum of the University of Illinois, vol. 1. Urbana, 1972
Kang, SETUA	S. Kang, Sumerian Economic Texts from the Umma Archive: Sumerian and Akkadian Cuneiform Texts in the Collection of the World Heritage Museum of the University of Illinois. vol. 2. Urbana, 1973
Keiser, BIN 2	C.E. Keiser and J.B. Nies, Historical Religious and Economic Texts and Antiquities (= BIN 2). New Haven, 1920
Keiser, BIN 3	C.E. Keiser, Neo-Sumerian Account Texts from Drehem (=BIN 3). New Haven and London, 1971
Keiser, BRM 3	C.E. Keiser, Cuneiform Bullae of the Third Millennium B.C. New York, 1914
Keiser, Patesis	C.E. Keiser, Patesis of the Ur Dynasty. New Haven, 1919 (=YOR 4). Reprint New York, 1980
Keiser, YOS 4	C.E. Keiser, Selected Temple Documents of the Ur Dynasty. New Haven, 1919
Kessler, Nordmesopotamien	K. Kessler, Untersuchungen zur historischen Topographie Nordmesopotamiens nach keilschriftliche Quellen des 1. Jahrtausends v. Chr. (=Beihefte zum Tübinger Atlas des Vorderen Orients, Reihe B, Nr. 26). Wiesbaden, 1980
King, Early History	L.W. King, A History of Sumer and Akkad: An Account of the Early Races of Babylonia from Prehistoric Times to the Foundation of the Babylonian Monarchy. London, 1910
King and Hall, EWA	L.W. King and H.R. Hall, Egypt and Western Asia in the Light of Recent Discoveries. London, 1907
Klein, Three Šulgi Hymns	J. Klein, Three Šulgi Hymns: Sumerian Royal Hymns Glorifying King Šulgi of Ur. Ramat-Gan, 1981
Koldewey, WEB^{4}	R. Koldewey, Das wieder erstehende Babylon, Die bisherigen Ergebnisse der deutschen Ausgrabungen. 4th edition. Leipzig, 1925
Kramer Anniversary	B. Eichler (ed.), Kramer Anniversary Volume: Cuneiform Studies in Honor of Samuel Noah Kramer (=AOAT 25). Neukirchen-Vluyn, 1976
Kramer, FTS	S.N. Kramer, From the Tablets of Sumer. Twenty-five Firsts in Man's Recorded History. Indian Hills, 1956
Kramer, ISET 2	S.N. Kramer, İstanbul Arkeoloji Müzelerinde Bulunan: Sumer Edebî Tablet ve Parçaları 2 (=TTKY 6/13^{a}). Ankara, 1976
Kramer, SLTN	S.N. Kramer, Sumerian Literary Texts from Nippur in the Museum of the Ancient Orient at Istanbul (=AASOR 23). New Haven, 1944
Kramer, Sumerians	S.N. Kramer, The Sumerians, Their History, Culture and Character. Chicago and London, 1963
Kraus, Role of Temples	F. Kraus, The Role of Temples from the Third Dynasty of Ur to the First Dynasty of Babylon. Translation by B. Foster (=MANE 2/4). Malibu, California. 1990
Krecher, Sumerische Kultlyrik	J. Krecher, Sumerische Kultlyrik. Wiesbaden, 1966

Kutscher, Brockmon Tablets	R. Kutscher, The Brockmon Tablets of the University of Haifa: Royal Inscriptions (=Shay Series of the Zinman Institute of Archaeology). Haifa, 1989
Laessøe, Shemshāra	J. Laessøe, The Shemshāra Tablets: A Preliminary Report. Copenhagen, 1959
Lafont, Documents	B. Lafont, Documents administratifs sumériens provenant du site de Tello et conservés au Musée du Louvre (=Recherche sur les Civilisations; Mémoire 61). Paris, 1985
Lafont and Yıldız, TCT	B. Lafont and F. Yıldız, Tablettes cunéiformes de Tello au Musée d'Istanbul datant de l'époque de la III e Dynastie d'Ur I (=PIHANS vol. 65). Leiden, 1989
Landsberger Festschrift	H.G. Güterbock and T. Jacobsen (eds.), Studies in Honor of B. Landsberger on His Seventy-fifth Birthday, April 21, 1965 (=Assyriological Studies 16). Chicago, 1965
Langdon, Babylonian Liturgies	S. Langdon, Babylonian Liturgies: Sumerian Texts from the Early Period and from the Library of Ashurbanipal, for the Most Part Transliterated and Translated, with Introduction and Index. Paris, 1913
Langdon, TAD	S. Langdon, Tablets from the Archives of Drehem, with a Complete Record of the Origin of the Sumerian Calendar. Paris, 1911
Larsen, City-State	M.T. Larsen, The Old Assyrian City-State and Its Colonies (=Mesopotamia 4). Copenhagen, 1976
Lau, OBTR	R.J. Lau, Old Babylonian Temple Records (=Columbia University Oriental Studies 3). New York, 1906
Layard, Discoveries	A.H. Layard, Discoveries in the Ruins of Nineveh and Babylon; With Travels in Armenia, Kurdistan and the Desert: Being the Result of a Second Expedition Undertaken for the Trustees of the British Museum. London, 1853
Legrain, PBS 13	L. Legrain, Historical Fragments. Philadelphia, 1922
Legrain, PBS 14	L. Legrain, The Culture of the Babylonians from Their Seals in the Collections of the Museum. Philadelphia, 1925
Legrain, PBS 15	L. Legrain, Royal Inscriptions and Fragments from Nippur and Babylon. Philadelphia, 1926
Legrain, TRU	L. Legrain, Le temps des rois d'Ur, recherche sur la société antique, d'après des textes nouveaux (=BÉHÉ 199). Paris, 1912
Legrain, UE 10	L. Legrain, Seal Cylinders. London and Philadelphia, 1951
Legrain, UET 3	L. Legrain, Business Documents of the Third Dynasty of Ur, 2 vols. London, 1937/1947
Festschrift Lehmann-Haupt	K. Regling and H. Perch (eds.), Festschrift zu C.F. Lehmann-Haupts Sechzigstem Geburtstage. Vienna and Leipzig, 1921
Lehmann-Haupt, Mat.	C.F. Lehmann-Haupt, Materialien zur älteren Geschichte Armeniens und Mesopotamiens. Berlin, 1907
Leichty, Šumma Izbu	E. Leichty, The Omen Series Šumma Izbu (=TCS 4). Locust Valley, 1970
Lenormant, Choix	F. Lenormant, Choix de textes cunéiformes inédits ou incomplètement publiés. Paris, 1873–75
Lenormant, Études accadiennes	F. Lenormant, Études accadiennes, 3 vols. (=Lettres assyriologiques, seconde série). Paris, 1873–80
Lesko, Women's Earliest Records	B.S. Lesko, Women's Earliest Records From Ancient Egypt and Western Asia. Proceedings of the Conference on Women in the Ancient Near East, Brown University, Providence, Rhode Island, November 5–7, 1987. Atlanta, 1989
Levine and Young, Mountains and Lowlands	L.D. Levine and T.C. Young (eds.), Mountains and Lowlands: Essays in the Archaeology of Greater Mesopotamia (=Bibliotheca Mesopotamica 7). Malibu, 1977
Lieberman, Sumerian Loanwords	S.J. Lieberman, The Sumerian Loanwords in Old Babylonian Akkadian, vol. 1: Prolegomena and Evidence. Missoula, Montana, 1977
Limet, Anthroponymie	H. Limet, L'anthroponymie sumerienne dans les documents de la 3e dynastie d'Ur. Paris, 1968
Limet, Textes sumériens	H. Limet, Textes sumériens de la IIIe Dynastie d'Ur (=Documents du Proche-Orient Ancien, Épigraphie 1). Brussels, 1976
Limper, AUWE 2	K. Limper, Uruk: Perlen, Ketten, Anhänger; Grabungen 1912–1985 (=AUWE 2). Mainz am Rheim, 1988
Loding, UET 9	D. Loding, Economic Texts from the Third Dynasty (=UET 9). Philadelphia, 1976
Luckenbill, Adab	D.D. Luckenbill, Inscriptions from Adab (=OIP 14). Chicago, 1930
Luckenbill, ARAB	D.D. Luckenbill, Ancient Records of Assyria and Babylonia, 2 vols. Chicago, 1926–27
Ludwig, Išme-Dagan	M.-Ch. Ludwig, Untersuchungen zu den Hymnen des Išme-Dagan von Isin. Wiesbaden, 1990
MAM	Mission Archéologique de Mari
MANE	Monographs on the Ancient Near East. Malibu, 1979–
MAOV	Mitteilungen des Akademisch-Orientalischen Vereins zu Berlin. Berlin, 1887–
Margolis, STD	E. Margolis, Sumerian Temple Documents. New York, 1915
MARI	Mari, Annales de Recherches Interdisciplinaires. Paris, 1982–
McCown, Nippur 1	D.E. McCown, R.C. Haines, and D. Hansen, Nippur I: Temple of Enlil, Scribal Quarter and Soundings (=OIP 78). Chicago, 1967.

McCown, Nippur 2	D.E. McCown, R.C. Haines, and R.D. Biggs, Nippur II: The North Temple and Sounding E (=OIP 97). Chicago, 1978
McNeil, Messenger Texts	R.C. McNeil, The "Messenger Texts" of the Third Ur Dynasty. Ph.D. dissertation, University of Pennsylvania, 1970
MCS	Manchester Cuneiform Studies, vols. 1–9. Manchester, 1951–64
MDOG	Mitteilungen der Deutschen Orient-Gesellschaft. Berlin, 1898–
van der Meer, OECT 4	P. van der Meer, Syllabaries A, B1 and B with Miscellaneous Lexicographical Texts from the Herbert Weld Collection (=OECT 4). Oxford and London, 1938
Ménant, Babylone	M.J. Ménant, Babylone et la Chaldée. Paris, 1875
Ménant, Glyptique	M.J. Ménant, Les pierres gravées de la Haute-Asie, recherches sur la glyptique orientale, 2 vols. Paris, 1883/86
Merhav, Treasures	R. Merhav (ed.), Treasures of the Bible Lands: The Elie Borowski Collection. Tel Aviv, 1987
Messerschmidt, VAS 1	L. Messerschmidt and A. Ungnad, Vorderasiatische Schriftdenkmäler der königlichen Museen zu Berlin. Heft 1. Leipzig, 1907
de Meyer, Tell ed-Dēr 3	L. de Meyer (ed.), Tell ed-Dēr: Soundings at Abū Habbah (Sippar). Louvain, 1980
de Meyer, Tell ed-Dēr 4	L. de Meyer (ed.), Tell ed-Dēr IV: Progress Reports (Second Series). Louvain, 1984
Michalowski, Correspondence	P. Michalowski, The Royal Correspondence of Ur. Ph.D. dissertation, Yale University, 1976
Michalowski, Lamentation	P. Michalowski, The Lamentation over the Destruction of Sumer and Ur (=Mesopotamian Civilizations 1). Winona Lake, 1989
MIFAO	Mémoires publiés par les membres de l'Institut français d'Archéologie orientale de Caire. Cairo, 1902–
MJ	Museum Journal of the University Museum, University of Pennsylvania, vols. 1–24. Philadelphia, 1910–35
MMAB	Metropolitan Museum of Art Bulletin. New York, 1905–
Molina, Montserrat	M. Molina, Tablillas administrativas neosumerias de la Abadía Montserrat (Barcelona): Copias cuneiformes (=MVN 18). Rome, 1993
Moortgat, Kunst	A. Moortgat, Die Kunst der alten Mesopotamien. Die klassische Kunst Vorderasiens. Cologne, 1967
Moortgat, VAR	A. Moortgat, Vorderasiatische Rollsiegel: Ein Beitrag zur Geschichte der Steinschneidekunst. Berlin, 1940
de Morgan, MDP 1	J. de Morgan, G. Jéquier, et G. Lampre, Recherches archéologiques. Fouilles à Suse en 1897–1898 et 1898–1899 (Mémoires de la Délégation en Perse: 1). Paris, 1900
de Morgan, MDP 7	J. de Morgan, Recherches archéologiques, deuxième série (=Mémoires de la Délégation en Perse: 1). Paris, 1905
MSL	B. Landsberger, et al. (eds.), Materials for the Sumerian Lexicon. Rome, 1937–
Muscarella, Bronze and Iron	O.W. Muscarella, Bronze and Iron: Ancient Near Eastern Artifacts in the Metropolitan Museum of Art. New York, 1988
MVAG	Mitteilungen der Vorderasiatisch-Aegyptischen Gesellschaft, vols. 1–44. Berlin and Leipzig, 1896–1939
MVN	Materiali per il vocabolario neosumerico. Rome, 1974–
Myhrman, BE 3/1	Sumerian Administrative Documents Dated in the Reigns of the Kings of the Second Dynasty of Ur from the Temple Archives of Nippur Preserved in Philadelphia. Philadelphia, 1910
NABU	Nouvelles assyriologiques brèves et utilitaires. Paris, 1987–
Nashef, Rép. Géogr. 5	Kh. Nashef, Die Orts- und Gewässernamen der mittelbabylonischen und mittelassyrischen Zeit. Wiesbaden, 1982
Nassouhi, Guide sommaire	E. Nassouhi, Musées des Antiquités de Stamboul, Antiquités Assyrio-Babyloniennes, Guide sommaire. Istanbul, 1926
Nesbit, SRD	W. Nesbit, Sumerian Records from Drehem. New York, 1914
Nestmann, Excavations	C. Nestmann, Excavations at Bismya. Ph.D. dissertation, University of Chicago, 1949
Nies, UDT	J. Nies, Ur Dynasty Tablets: Texts Chiefly from Tello and Drehem Written during the Reigns of Dungi, Bur-Sin, Gimil-Sin, and Ibi-Sin (=AB 25), Leipzig, 1919
Nikol'skiy, DV 5	M.V. Nikol'skiy, Dokumenty chozyaystvennoi otčetnosti drevney Chaldei iz sobraniya N.P. Lichačeva, Čast' II: Epocha dinastiy Ura. Moscow, 1915
Nöldeke and Lenzen, UVB 11	A. Nöldeke and H. Lenzen, Elfter vorläufiger Bericht über die von der Deutschen Forschungsgemeinschaft unternommenen Ausgrabungen in Uruk-Warka. Berlin, 1940
Nöldeke et al., UVB 8	A. Nöldeke, A. von Haller, H. Lenzen, and E. Heinrich, Achter vorläufiger Bericht über die von der Deutschen Forschungsgemeinschaft unternommenen Ausgrabungen in Uruk-Warka. Berlin, 1937
Nöldeke et al., UVB 10	A. Nöldeke, E. Heinrich, and H. Lenzen, Zehnter vorläufiger Bericht über die von der Deutschen Forschungsgemeinschaft unternommenen Ausgrabungen in Uruk-Warka. Berlin, 1939
OECT	Oxford Editions of Cuneiform Texts. London, 1923–
OIC	Oriental Institute Communications. Chicago, 1922–

OIP	Oriental Institute Publications. Chicago, 1924–
OLZ	Orientalistische Literaturzeitung. Berlin and Leipzig, 1898–
OPBF	Occasional Publications of the Babylonian Fund, Philadelphia, 1976–
OPKF	Occasional Publications of the Samuel Noah Kramer Fund. Babylonian Fund. Philadelphia, 1990–
Oppenheim, Eames Collection	A.L. Oppenheim, Catalogue of the Cuneiform Tablets of the Wilberforce Eames Babylonian Collection in the New York Public Library. Tablets of the Time of the Third Dynasty of Ur (=AOS 32). New Haven, 1948
Oppert, EM 1	J. Oppert, Expédition scientifique en Mésopotamie exécutée par ordre du gouvernement de 1851 à 1854 par Mm. Fulgence Fresnel, et al. Tome 1: Relation du voyage et résultats de l'expédition. Paris, 1863
OrAnt	Oriens Antiquus, Rivista del Centro per le Antichità e la Storia dell'Arte del Vicino Oriente. Rome, 1962–
OrSuec	Orientalia Suecana. Uppsala, 1952–
Orthmann (ed.), Der alte Orient	W. Orthmann (ed.), Der alte Orient (=Propyläen Kunstgeschichte 14). Berlin, 1975
Owen, MVN 3	D. Owen, The John Frederick Lewis Collection (=MVN 3). Rome, 1975
Owen, MVN 11	D. Owen, Selected Ur III Texts from the Harvard Semitic Museum. Rome, 1982
Owen, MVN 15	D. Owen, Neo-Sumerian Texts from American Collections (=MVN 15). Rome, 1991
Owen, NATN	D. Owen, Neo-Sumerian Archival Texts Primarily from Nippur in the University Museum, the Oriental Institute and the Iraq Museum. Winona Lake, 1982
Parrot, Architecture	A. Parrot, Le palais, architecture (=MAM 2/1). Paris, 1958
Parrot, Documents	A. Parrot, Le palais, documents et monuments (=MAM 2/3). Paris, 1959
Parrot, Sumer	A. Parrot, Sumer. Paris, 1960
Parrot, Tello	A. Parrot, Tello, vingt campagnes de fouilles (1877–1933). Paris, 1948
Parrot, Trésor	A. Parrot, Le " Tresor" d'Ur (=MAM 4). Paris, 1968
PBS	Publications of the Babylonian Section, University Museum, University of Pennsylvania, 15 vols. Philadelphia, 1911–26
Peters, Nippur	J.P. Peters, Nippur, or Explorations and Adventures on the Euphrates. The Narrative of the University of Pennsylvania Expedition to Babylonia in the Years 1888–1890, 2 vols. New York and London, 1897
Pettinato, MVN 6	G. Pettinato, Testi economici di Lagaš del Museo di Istanbul Parte I: La. 7001–7600 (=MVN 6). Rome, 1977
Pettinato and Waetzoldt, MVN 1	G. Pettinato and H. Waetzoldt, La collezione Schollmeyer (=MVN 1). Rome, 1974
Pézard and Pottier, Catalogue	M. Pézard and E. Pottier, Musée du Louvre, Catalogue des antiquités de la Susiane (mission J. de Morgan), 2nd edition. Paris, 1926
PIHANS	Publications de l'Institut historique-archéologique néerlandais de Stamboul
Pinches, Amherst Tablets	T.G. Pinches, The Amherst Tablets, Being an Account of the Babylonian Inscriptions in the Collection of the Right Hon. Lord Amherst of Hackney. London, 1908
Poebel, PBS 5	A. Poebel, Historical and Grammatical Texts. Philadelphia, 1914
Pohl, TMH NF 1/2	A. Pohl, Rechts- und Verwaltungsurkunden der III. Dynastie von Ur (=TMH NF 1/2). Leipzig, 1937
Porada, Corpus	E. Porada, Corpus of Ancient Near Eastern Seals in North American Collections, 1: The Collection of the Pierpont Morgan Library (=Bollingen Series 14). Washington, 1948
Porter, Travels	R. Ker Porter, Travels in Georgia, Persia, Armenia, Ancient Babylonia, etc. during the years 1817, 1818, 1819, and 1820, 2 vols. London, 1821–22
Potts, Dilmun	D.T. Potts (ed.), Dilmun: New Studies in the Archaeology and Early History of Bahrain (=BBVO 2). Berlin, 1983
PSBA	Proceedings of the Society of Biblical Archaeology, vols. 1–40. London, 1878–1918
1 R	H.C. Rawlinson and E. Norris, The Cuneiform Inscriptions of Western Asia, vol. 1: A Selection from the Historical Inscriptions of Chaldaea, Assyria, and Babylonia. London, 1861
$4 R^2$	H.C. Rawlinson and T.G. Pinches, The Cuneiform Inscriptions of Western Asia, vol. 4: A Selection from the Miscellaneous Inscriptions of Assyria, 2nd edition. London, 1891
RA	Revue d'assyriologie et d'archéologie orientale. Paris, 1886–
Raaflaub, Anfänge	K. Raaflaub, Anfänge politischen Denkens in der Antike: Die nahöstlichen Kulturen und die Griechen. Munich, 1993
Radau, BE 29/1	H. Radau, Sumerian Hymns and Prayers to God Nin-Ib from the Temple Library of Nippur (=BE 29/1). Philadelphia, 1911
Radau, EBH	H. Radau, Early Babylonian History down to the End of the Fourth Dynasty of Ur. New York and London, 1900
Rashid, Gründungsfiguren	A.A Rashid, Gründungsfiguren im Iraq (=Prähistorische Bronzefunde I/2). Munich, 1983
Rashid, TIM 6	F. Rashid, Administrative Texts from the Ur III Dynasty (=TIM 6). Baghdad, 1971
Reisner, Telloh	G.A. Reisner, Templurkunden aus Telloh (=Mittheilungen aus den Orientalischen Sammlungen 16). Berline, 1901
RHA	Revue hittite et asianique. Paris, 1930–

RIME	Royal Inscriptions of Mesopotamia, Early Periods. Toronto, 1990–
RLA	Reallexikon der Assyriologie. Berlin, 1932–
RLV	Reallexikon der Vorgeschichte, vols. 1–15. Berlin, 1924–32
RO	Rocznik Orientalistyczny. Kraków, Lwów, Warszawa, 1914–
Römer, Bilgameš und Akka	Willem H. Ph. Römer, Das sumerische Kurzepos "Bilgameš und Akka" (=Alter Orient und Altes Testament 209/1). Neukirchener-Vluyn, 1980
Römer, SKIZ	Willem H. Ph. Römer, Sumerische 'Königshymnen' der Isin-Zeit. Leiden, 1965
Roth, Law Collections	M.T. Roth, Law Collections from Mesopotamia and Asia Minor. Atlanta, 1995
RP NS	Records of the Past, Being English Translations of the Ancient Monuments of Egypt and Western Asia, New Series, 6 vols. London, 1888–
RSO	Rivista degli studi orientali. Rome, 1907–
RT	Receuil de travaux relatifs à la philologie et à l'archéologie égyptiennes et assyriennes, vols. 1–40. Paris, 1870–1923
Rutten, Encyclopédie	M. Rutten, Encyclopédie photographique de l'art. 2 vols. Paris, 1935–36
Sallaberger, Kalender	W. Sallaberger, Der kultische Kalender der Ur III-Zeit, 2 parts. (=Untersuchungen zur Assyriologie und Vorderasiatische Archäologie 7/1–2). Berlin, 1993
Salonen, Hausgeräte 2	A. Salonen, Die Hausgeräte der alten Mesopotamier nach sumerisch-akkadischen Quellen. Teil II: Gefässe (=AASF B 144). Helsinki, 1966
Salonen, Puzriš-Dagan-Texte	M. Çığ, H. Kızılyay, and A. Salonen, Die Puzriš-Dagan-Texte der Istanbuler Archäologischen Museen. Teil I: Nrr. 1–725. Helsinki, 1954
SAOC	Studies in Ancient Oriental Civilizations. Chicago, 1930–
de Sarzec, Découvertes	E. de Sarzec, Découvertes en Chaldée par Ernest de Sarzec, ouvrage accompagné de planches, publié par les soins de Léon Heuzey, avec le concours de Arthur Amiaud et François Thureau-Dangin pour la partie épigraphique, 2 vols. Paris, 1884/1912
Sauren, MVN 2	H. Sauren, Wirtschaftsurkunden des Musée d'Art et d'Histoire in Genf. Rome, 1974
Sauren, New York Public Library	H. Sauren, Les tablettes cunéiformes de l'époque d'Ur des collections de la New York Public Library. Louvain-la-Neuve, 1978
Sauren, Topographie Umma	H. Sauren, Topographie der Provinz Umma nach den Urkunden der Zeit der III. Dynastie von Ur. Teil I: Kanäle und Bewässerungsanlagen. Ph.D. dissertation, Heidelberg, 1966
Sauren, WMAH	H. Sauren, Wirtschaftsurkunden aus der Zeit der III. Dynastie von Ur im Besitz des Musée d'Art et d'Histoire in Genf (=Seminario di Semitistica Ricerche 6). Naples, 1969
Schäfer and Andrae, Kunst	H. Schäfer and W. Andrae, Die Kunst des alten Orients (=Propyläen Kunstgeschichte 1–2). Berlin 1925–30
Scheil, MDP 2	V. Scheil, Textes élamites-sémitiques, 1e série. Paris, 1900
Scheil, MDP 4	V. Scheil, Textes élamites-sémitiques, 2e série. Paris, 1902
Scheil, MDP 6	V. Scheil, Textes élamites-sémitiques, 3e série. Paris, 1905
Scheil, MDP 10	V. Scheil, Textes élamites-sémitiques, 4e série. Paris, 1908
Scheil, MDP 14	V. Scheil, Textes élamites-sémitiques, 5e série. Paris, 1913
Scheil, MDP 28	V. Scheil, Mélanges épigraphiques. Mémoires de la Mission Archéologique en Perse. Paris, 1939
Scheil, Sippar	V. Scheil, Une saison de fouilles à Sippar (=MIFAO 1/1). Cairo, 1902
Schneider, Drehem- und Djoḫatexte	N. Schneider, Die Drehem- und Djoḫatexte im Kloster Montserrat (Barcelona) in Autographie und mit systematischen Wörterverzeichnissen herausgegeben (=AnOr 7). Rome, 1932
Schneider, Keilschriftzeichen	N. Schneider, Die Keilschriftzeichen der Wirtschaftsurkunden von Ur III nebst ihren charakterischsten Varianten. Rome, 1935
Schneider, Strassburg	N. Schneider, Die Drehem- und Djoḫa- Urkunden der Strassburger Universitäts- und Landesbibliothek (=AnOr 1). Rome, 1931
Schneider, Zeitbestimmungen	N. Schneider, Die Zeitbestimmungen der Wirtschaftsurkunden von Ur III (=AnOr 13). Rome, 1936
Schroeder, KAH 2	O. Schroeder, Keilschrifttexte aus Assur: historischen Inhalts, Zweites Heft (=WVDOG 35). Leipzig, 1922
SD	Studia et documenta ad iura Orientis Antiqui pertinentia. Leiden, 1936–
SEL	Studi epigrafici e linguistici sul Vicino Oriente antico. Verona, 1984–
Shileiko, ZVO 25	V.K. Shileiko, Zapiski Vostočnogo Otdyeleniya Russkogo Arkheologičeskogo Obščestva 25. 1921
Sigrist, AUCT 1	R.M. Sigrist, Neo-Sumerian Account Texts in the Horn Archaeological Museum (=Institute of Archaeology Publications; Assyriological Series 6 = Andrews University Cuneiform Texts 1). Berrien Springs, Michigan 1984
Sigrist, AUCT 2	R.M. Sigrist, Neo-Sumerian Account Texts in the Horn Archaeological Museum (=Institute of Archaeology Publications; Assyriological Series 5 = Andrews University Cuneiform Texts 2). Berrien Springs, Michigan, 1988

Sigrist, AUCT 3	R.M. Sigrist, C. Gavin, D. Stein, and C. Menard, Neo-Sumerian Account Texts in the Horn Archeological Museum. (=Institute of Archaeology Publications Assyriological Series 6 = Andrews University Cuneiform Texts 3). Berrien Springs, Michigan, 1988
Sigrist, Drehem	M. Sigrist, Drehem. Bethesda, Maryland, 1992
Sigrist, MVN 13	R.M. Sigrist, D. Owen, and G. Young, The John Frederick Lewis Collection. Part II (=MVN 13). Rome, 1984
Sigrist, Rochester	M. Sigrist, Documents from Tablet Collections in Rochester, New York. Bethesda, Maryland, 1991
Sigrist, ROM	R.M. Sigrist, Neo-Sumerian Texts from the Royal Ontario Museum. I: The Administration at Drehem. Bethesda, Maryland, 1995.
Sigrist, Syracuse	M. Sigrist, Textes économiques Néo-Sumériens de l'Université de Syracuse. Paris, 1983
Sigrist, TPTS	R.M. Sigrist, Tablettes du Princeton Theological Seminary; époque d'Ur III (=OPKF 10). Philadelphia, 1990
Sigrist and Gomi, Comprehensive Catalogue	R.M. Sigrist and T. Gomi, The Comprehensive Catalogue of Published Ur III Tablets. Bethesda, Maryland, 1991
Sigrist and Vuk, Franciscanum	M. Sigrist and T. Vuk, Inscriptions cunéiformes (=Studium Biblicum Franciscanum Museum 4). Jerusalem, 1987
Sjöberg Festschrift	See Studies Sjöberg.
Sjöberg and Bergmann, Temple Hymns	Å.W. Sjöberg and E. Bergmann, The Collection of the Sumerian Temple Hymns (=TCS 3). Locust Valley, New York, 1969
Smick, Cuneiform Documents	E.B. Smick, Cuneiform Documents of the Third Millennium in the John F. Lewis Collection in the Public Library of Philadelphia. Ph.D. dissertation, Dropsie College, 1951
SMS	Syro-Mesopotamian Studies. Malibu, 1977–
Snell, MVN 9	D. Snell, The E.A. Hoffman Collection and other American Collections. Rome, 1979
Snell and Lager, YOS 18	D.C. Snell and C.H. Lager, Economic Texts from Sumer. New Haven and London, 1991
Sollberger, Correspondence	E. Sollberger, The Business and Administrative Correspondence under the Kings of Ur (=TCS 1). Locust Valley, New York, 1966
Sollberger, MVN 5	E. Sollberger, The Pinches Manuscript (=MVN 5). Rome, 1978
Sollberger, UET 8	E. Sollberger, Royal Inscriptions Part 2. London, 1965
Sollberger and Kupper, IRSA	E. Sollberger and J.R. Kupper, Inscriptions royales sumériennes et akkadiennes. Paris, 1971
Solyman, Götterwaffen	T. Solyman, Die Entstehung und Entwicklung der Götterwaffen im alten Mesopotamien und ihre Bedeutung. Beirut, 1968
Southesk, Catalogue	J. Southesk, Catalogue of the Collection of Antique Gems Formed by James Ninth Earl of Southesk K.T. Edited by his daughter Lady Helena Carnegie in two volumes. London, 1908
Spar, Met.Mus.1	I. Spar (ed.), Cuneiform Texts in the Metropolitan Museum of Art, Volume I: Tablets, Cones and Bricks of the Third and Second Millennia B.C. New York, 1988
Speiser, Origins	E. Speiser, Mesopotamian Origins. The Basic Population of the Near East. Oxford, 1930
Speleers, Catalogue	L. Speleers, Catalogue des intailles et empreintes orientales des Musées Royaux du Cinquantenaire. Brussels, 1917
Speleers, Recueil	L. Speleers, Recueil des inscriptions de l'Asie antérieure des Musées Royaux du Cinquantenaire à Bruxelles. Textes sumeriens, babyloniens et assyriens. Brussels, 1925
Spycket, Statuaire	A. Spycket, La statuaire du Proche-Orient ancien (=Handbuch der Orientalistik 7/1/2/ B 2). Leiden and Cologne, 1981
Spycket, Statues	A. Spycket, Les statues de culte dans les textes mésopotamiens des origines à la Ire dynastie de Babylone (=Cahiers de la Revue Biblique 9). Paris, 1968
Stamm, Namengebung	J.J. Stamm, Die akkadische Namengebung (=MVAG 44). Leipzig, 1939
Steible, ASBW	H. Steible, Die altsumerischen Bau- und Weihinschriften. Teil 1: Inschriften aus "Lagaš." Teil II: Kommentar zu den Inschriften aus "Lagaš" (=FAOS 5: 1–2). Stuttgart, 1982.
Steible, NSBW	H. Steible, Die neusumerischen Bau- und Weihinschriften, 2 vols. (=FAOS 9:1–2). Stuttgart, 1991
Steinkeller, Sale Documents	P. Steinkeller, Sale Documents of the Ur-III-Period (=Freiburger altorientalische Studien 17). Stuttgart, 1989
Steinkeller, Texts Baghdad	P. Steinkeller and J.N. Postgate, Third-Millennium Legal and Administrative Texts in the Iraq Museum, Baghdad. Winona Lake, 1992
Stephens, YOS 9	F.J. Stephens, Votive and Historical Texts from Babylonia and Assyria. New Haven, 1937
Steve Festschrift	See Studies Steve
StOr	Studia Orientalia (Societas Orientalis Fennica). Helsinki, 1925–
Strommenger and Hirmer, Mesopotamien	E. Strommenger and M. Hirmer, Fünf Jahrtausende Mesopotamien: die Kunst von den Anfängen um 5000 v. Chr. bis zu Alexander. Munich, 1962
Studies Artzi	J. Klein and A. Skaist (eds.), Bar-Ilan Studies in Assyriology dedicated to Pinḥas Artzi. Ramat-Gan, 1990

Studies Gordon 1	H.A. Hoffner (ed.), Orient and Occident: Essays presented to Cyrus H. Gordon on the Occasion of his Sixty-fifth Birthday (=AOAT 22). Neukirchen-Vluyn, 1973
Studies Hallo	M.E. Cohen, D.C. Snell, and D.B. Weisberg (eds.), The Tablet and the Scroll: Near Eastern Studies in Honor of William W. Hallo. Bethesda, Maryland, 1993
Studies Sjöberg	H. Behrens, et al. (eds.), Dumu-e_2-dub-ba-a: Studies in Honor of Åke W. Sjöberg (=Occasional Publications of the Samuel Noah Kramer Fund 11). Philadelphia, 1989
Studies Steve	L. de Meyer, H. Gasche, and F. Vallat (eds.), Fragmenta Historiae Elamicae: Mélanges offerts à M.J. Steve. Paris, 1986
Tallqvist, Götterepitheta	K.L. Tallqvist, Akkadische Götterepitheta (=StOr 7). Helsinki, 1938
TAPS	Transactions of the American Philosophical Society Held at Philadelphia for Promoting Useful Knowledge. Philadelphia, 1771–
TAVO	Beihefte zum Tübinger Atlas des Vorderen Orients. Wiesbaden, 1977–
TCL	Textes cunéiformes du Musée du Louvre, Département des Antiquités Orientales. Paris, 1910–
TCS	Texts from Cuneiform Sources. Locust Valley, New York, 1966–
Thureau-Dangin, RTC	F. Thureau-Dangin, Recueil de tablettes chaldéennes. Paris, 1903
Thureau-Dangin, SAK	F. Thureau-Dangin, Die sumerischen und akkadischen Königsinschriften (=VAB 1). Leipzig, 1907
TIM	Texts in the Iraq Museum. Baghdad, 1964–
TLB	Tabulae cuneiformes a F.M.Th. de Liagre Böhl collectae. Leiden, 1954–
TMH	Texte und Materialien der Frau Professor Hilprecht Collection of Babylonian Antiquities im Eigentum der Universität Jena
TSBA	Transactions of the Society of Biblical Archaeology. London, 1872–93
TTKY	Türk Tarih Kurumu Yayınlarından. Ankara
TUAT	O. Keiser (ed.), Texte aus der Umwelt des Alten Testaments. Gütersloh, 1982–
UCP	University of California Publications in Semitic Philology, vols. 1–24. Berkeley, 1907–63
UE	Ur Excavations. Oxford, London, and Philadelphia, 1926–
UET	Ur Excavations, Texts. London, 1928–
UMB	The University Museum Bulletin. Philadelphia
Unger, Katalog	E. Unger, Kaiserlich Osmanische Museen, Katalog der babylonischen und assyrischen Sammlung III: Geräte. Constantinople, 1918
Unger, Naram-Sin	J.P. Naab and E. Unger, Pir Hüseyin'de Naram-Sin Stelinin Keşfi. Die Entdeckung der Stele des Naram-Sin in Pir Hüseyin. Istanbul, 1934
Unger, SuAK	E. Unger, Sumerische und akkadische Kunst. Breslau, 1926
UVB	Vorläufiger Bericht über die von (dem Deutschen Archäologischen Institut und der Deutschen Orient-Gesellschaft aus Mitteln) der Deutschen Forschungsgemeinschaft unternommenen Ausgrabungen in Uruk-Warka. Berlin, 1930–
VAB	Vorderasiatische Bibliothek. Leipzig, 1907–16
Van Buren, Found.	E.D. Van Buren, Foundation Figurines and Offerings. Berlin, 1931
Van De Mieroop, BIN 10	M. Van De Mieroop, Sumerian Administrative Documents from the Reigns of Išbi-Erra and Šū-ilišu. New Haven and London, 1987
VAS	Vorderasiatische Schriftdenkmäler der Königlichen Museen zu Berlin. Leipzig and Berlin, 1907–
VDI	Vestnik drevney istorii. Moscow, 1937–
Waetzoldt and Yıldız, MVN 16	H. Waetzoldt and F. Yıldız, Die Umma-Texte aus den Archäologischen Museen zu Istanbul. Band II (Nr. 601–1600). Rome, 1994
Walker, CBI	C.B.F. Walker, Cuneiform Brick Inscriptions in the British Museum, the Ashmolean Museum, Oxford, the City of Birmingham Museums and Art Gallery, the City of Bristol Museum and Art Gallery. London, 1981
Ward, Seals	W.H. Ward, The Seal Cylinders of Western Asia. Washington, 1910
Watson, Birmingham	P. Watson, Catalogue of Cuneiform Tablets in Birmingham City Museum, Vol. 1: Neo-Sumerian Texts from Drehem. Vol. 2: Neo-Sumerian Texts from Umma and other Sites. Warminster, England, 1986 and 1993
von Weiher, Nergal	E. von Weiher, Der babylonische Gott Nergal (=AOAT 11). Neukirchen-Vluyn, 1971
Wetzel, Königsburgen	F. Wetzel and R. Koldewey, Die Königsburgen von Babylon. Teil II: Die Hauptburg und der Sommerpalast Nebukadnezars im Hügel Babil (=WVDOG 55). Leipzig, 1932
Whiting, Letters	R. Whiting, Old Babylonian Letters from Tell Asmar (=AS 22). Chicago, 1987
Wiggermann, Protective Spirits	F.A.M. Wiggermann, Mesopotamian Protective Spirits: The Ritual Texts (=Cuneiform Monographs 1). Groningen, 1992
Wilcke, Kollationen	C. Wilke, Kollationen zu den sumerischen Literarischen Texten aus Nippur in der Hilprecht-Sammlung Jena. Berlin, 1976
Wilcke, Lugalbandaepos	C. Wilcke, Das Lugalbandaepos. Wiesbaden, 1969
Wilhelm, Hurrians	G. Wilhelm, The Hurrians. Warminster, 1989
Wilhelm, Hurriter	G. Wilhelm, Gründzüge der Geschichte und Kultur der Hurriter. Darmstadt, 1982
Winckler, KB 3/1	H. Winckler, et al., Historische Texte altbabylonischer Herrscher. Berlin, 1892

Winckler, AOF	H. Winckler, Altorientalische Forschungen. Leipzig, 1893–1905
Winckler, Untersuchungen	H. Winckler, Untersuchungen zur altorientalischen Geschichte. Leipzig, 1889
Winckler and Böhden, ABK	H. Winckler and E. Böhden, Altbabylonische Keilschrifttexte zum Gebrauch bei Vorlesungen. Leipzig, 1892
Wiseman and Forman, Seals	D.J. Wiseman and W. and B. Forman, Cylinder Seals of Western Asia. London, 1959
WO	Die Welt des Orients. Wuppertal, Stuttgart, and Göttingen, 1947–
Woolley, UE 2	C.L. Woolley, The Royal Cemetery. London and Philadelphia, 1934
Woolley, UE 4	C.L. Woolley, The Early Periods. London and Philadelphia, 1955
Woolley, UE 5	C.L. Woolley, The Ziggurat and Its Surroundings. London and Philadelphia, 1939
Woolley, UE 6	C.L. Woolley, The Buildings of the Third Dynasty. London and Philadelphia, 1974
Woolley, UE 8	C.L. Woolley, The Kassite Period and the Period of the Assyrian Kings. London, 1965
Woolley, UE 9	C.L. Woolley, The Neo-Babylonian and Persian Periods. London, 1962
Woolley and Mallowan, UE 7	C.L. Woolley and M. Mallowan, The Old Babylonian Period. London and Philadelphia, 1976
Woolley and Moorey, Ur	C.L. Woolley, Ur "of the Chaldees," revised and updated by P.R.S. Moorey. London, 1982
WVDOG	Wissenschaftliche Veröffentlichungen der Deutschen Orient-Gesellschaft. Leipzig and Berlin, 1901–
WZJ	Wissenschaftliche Zeitschrift der Friedrich Schiller Universität Jena. Jena, 1951–
WZKM	Wiener Zeitschrift für die Kunde des Morgenlandes. Vienna, 1887–
Yang, Sargonic Archive	Z. Yang, A Study of the Sargonic Archive from Adab. Ph.D. dissertation, University of Chicago, 1986
Yang, Sargonic Inscriptions	Z. Yang, Sargonic Inscriptions from Adab (=Institute for the History of Ancient Civilizations, Period Publications on Ancient Civilizations 1). Changchun, 1989
Yıldız, MVN 14	F. Yıldız, H. Waetzoldt, and H. Renner, Die Umma-texte aus den Archäologischen Museen zu Istanbul Nr. 1–600 (=MVN 14). Rome, 1988
Yıldız and Gomi, PDT 2	F. Yıldız and T. Gomi, Die Puzriš-Dagan-Texte der Istanbuler archäologischen Museen. Teil II: Nr. 726–1379 (=FAOS 16). Stuttgart, 1988
Yıldız and Gomi, Umma-Texte	F. Yıldız and T. Gomi, Die Umma-texte aus den Archäologischen Museen zu Istanbul. Band III (Nr. 1601–2300) (= İstanbul Arkeoloji Müzeleri bulunan Umma metinleri). Bethesda, Maryland, 1993
YNER	Yale Near Eastern Researches. New Haven and London, 1967–
YOS	Yale Oriental Series, Babylonian Texts. New Haven, 1915–
YOSR	Yale Oriental Series Researches. New York, 1912–
ZA	Zeitschrift für Assyriologie und verwandte Gebiete. Berlin, 1886–
Zadok, Elamite Onomasticon	R. Zadok, The Elamite Onomasticon. Naples, 1984
ZDMG	Zeitschrift der Deutschen Morgenländischen Gesellschaft. Leipzig and Wiesbaden, 1879–
ZDMG Suppl. 1	Zeitschrift der Deutschen Morgenländischen Gesellschaft. Supplementa I. XVII. Deutscher Orientalistentag vom 21. bis 27. Juli 1968 in Würzburg. 2 parts. Wiesbaden, 1969
Zervos, L'art	C. Zervos, L'art de la Mésopotamie de la fin du quatrième millénaire au XVe siècle avant notre ère. Paris, 1935
Zettler, Inanna Temple	R. Zettler, The Ur III Inanna Temple at Nippur. Ph.D. dissertation, University of Chicago, 1984
Zettler, Ur III Temple	R. Zettler, The Ur III Temple of Inanna at Nippur: The Operation and Organization of Urban Religious Institutions in Mesopotamia in the Late Third Millennium B.C. (= BBVO 11). Berlin, 1992

Other Abbreviations

AS	Amar-Suena
c	collated
cm	centimetre(s)
col(s).	column(s)
dia.	diameter
DN	divine name
dupl.	duplicate
E	east
ED	Early Dynastic
ed(s).	editor(s)
ex(s).	exemplar(s)
fig(s).	figure(s)
frgm(s).	fragment(s)
GN	geographical name
IS	Ibbi-Sîn
km(s)	kilometre(s)
MB	Middle Babylonian
n	not collated
N	north
NA	Neo-Assyrian
n(n).	note(s)
NB	Neo-Babylonian
no(s).	number(s)
NS	New Series
OB	Old Babylonian
obv.	obverse
OS	Old Series
p	collated from photo
p(p).	page(s)
pl(s).	plate(s)
PN	personal name
reg.	registration
rev.	reverse
RN	royal name
S	south
Š	Šulgi
ŠS	Šū-Sîn
UN	Ur-Nammu
W	west
var(s).	variant(s)
vol(s).	volume(s)

+	Between object numbers indicates physical join
(+)	Indicates fragments from same object but no physical join

Object Signatures

When the same signature is used for more than one group, the first group in this list is meant unless otherwise indicated. For example, "A" always means the Chicago collection unless stated otherwise.

A	1) Asiatic collection of the Oriental Institute, Chicago
A	2) Signature of tablets in the Birmingham City Museum, Birmingham, England
A	3) Signature of tablets in the Robert Hull Fleming Museum, University of Vermont, Burlington, Vermont
AO	Collection of Antiquités Orientales of the Musée du Louvre, Paris
As	Excavation numbers of the Chicago excavations at Ešnunna (Tell Asmar)
Ash	Collection of the Ashmolean Museum, Oxford
Ass	Prefix of excavation numbers from the German excavations at Aššur
AUAM	Signature of tablets in the Horn Archaeological Museum of Andrews University, Berrien Springs, Michigan
BCM	Birmingham City Museum, Birmingham, England
BLMJ	Bible Lands Museum, Jerusalem
BM	British Museum, London
BT	William and Sylvia Brockmon Collection of Cuneiform Tablets at the University of Haifa (now housed in the Bible Lands Museum, Jerusalem)
CBS	Babylonian Section of the University Museum, Philadelphia
Cfc	Signature of tablets in the Collège de France, Cabinet d'Assyriologie, Paris
Crozer	Crozer Museum, Crozer Seminary, Rochester, New York
E	Excavation numbers from the Iraqi excavations at Eridu (Abū Šaḫrain)
EAH	E.A. Hoffman Collection (on loan to Yale Babylonian Collection, New Haven)
EŞ	Eşki Şark Eserleri Müzesi of the Arkeoloji Müzeleri, Istanbul
FLP	John Frederick Lewis collection of the Free Library of Philadelphia
FM	Fitzwilliam Museum, Cambridge University, Cambridge, England
FMNH	Field Museum for Natural History, Chicago
Haverford Library	Signature of tablets in the Library of Haverford College, Haverford, Pennsylvania
Hirose	Signature of tablets in the collection of Mr. and Mrs. Hirose, Tokyo
HS	Hilprecht collection of Babylonian Antiquities of Fr. Schiller University, Jena
HSM	Harvard Semitic Museum, Cambridge, Massachusetts
HTS	Hartford Theological Seminary, Hartford, Connecticut
IB	1) Excavation numbers of the Munich expedition to Isin (Išān Baḫrīyāt)
IB	2) Signature of the cuneiform tablets in the Pontifical Biblical Institute, Rome
IM	Iraq Museum, Baghdad
Kelsey	Kelsey Museum of the University of Michigan, Ann Arbor, Michigan
L	Lagash collection of the Arkeoloji Müzeleri, Istanbul
Lager	Collection C.H. Lager, New Haven, and Hamilton, New York
LB	Tablets in the Liagre Böhl collection of the University of Leiden
M	Prefix of excavation numbers from the French excavations at Mari (Tell Harīrī)
MA	1) Signature of objects in the State Hermitage, St. Petersburg, Russia
MA	2) Signature of tablets in the collection of Pietro e Orso di Aosta (published by Pettinato in MVN 4)
MAH	Musée d'Art et d'Histoire, Geneva
ME	Prefix of excavation numbers from the French excavations at Mari (Tell Harīrī)
MLC	J. Pierpont Morgan collection of the Yale Babylonian Collection, New Haven
MLC	J. Pierpont Morgan collection, New York
MM	Signature of objects in the collection of the Museo Montserrat, Barcelona
MMA	Metropolitan Museum of Art, New York
MNB	Musées Nationaux of the Musée du Louvre, Paris
MOA	Museum of Anthropology, University of British Columbia, Vancouver
MSBF	Musée du Studium Biblicum Franciscanum, Jerusalem

MVFG	Museum für Vor- und Frühgeschichte, Berlin
N	1) Nippur collection of the University Museum, Philadelphia
N	2) Signature of objects in the Gulbenkian Museum of Oriental Art, University of Durham, Durham, England
N-T	Excavation numbers of inscribed objects from the American excavations at Nippur
NBC	James B. Nies collection of the Yale Babylonian Collection, New Haven
NCBT	Newell Collection of Babylonian Tablets of the Yale Babylonian Collection, New Haven
Ni	Nippur collection of the Arkeoloji Müzeleri, Istanbul
O	Objects in the Section du Proche Orient of the Musées Royaux du Cinquantenaire, Brussels
PD	Puzriš-Dagan collection of the Arkeoloji Müzeleri, Istanbul
Pinches	Manuscript of cuneiform copies originally prepared by T.G. Pinches (see E. Sollberger as MVN 5)
PTS	Princeton Theological Seminary
RC	Signature of tablets in the Rosicrucian Egyptian, Oriental Museum, San José, California
ROM	Royal Ontario Museum, Toronto
Sb	Susa collection of the Musée du Louvre, Paris
Sch.	Schollmeyer Collection
Si	Sippar collection of the Arkeoloji Müzeleri, Istanbul
Ste-Anne	Signature of tablets in the Monastery of Sainte-Anne, Jerusalem
TG	Excavation numbers from the French excavations at Girsu (Telloh)
TH	Prefix of excavation numbers from the French excavations at Mari (Tell Harīrī)
TTN	Signature of tablets in the Toruń Scientific Society (Towarzystwo Naukowe Toruńskie), Toruń, Poland
U	1) Prefix of excavation numbers from the British-American excavations at Ur (Tell al Muqayyar)
U	2) Signature of tablets in the National and University Library, Prague
UCBC	University of California Babylonian Collection
UCPHMA	University of California Phoebe Hearst Museum of Anthropogy
UM	University Museum, Philadelphia
Um	Umma collection of the Arkeoloji Müzeleri, Istanbul
VA	Vorderasiatisches Museum, Berlin
W	Excavation numbers of the German excavations at Uruk (Warka)
WH	Excavation numbers of the Iraqi excavations at Tell al-Wilāyah
WHM	World Heritage Museum, University of Illinois, Urbana, Illinois
YBC	Yale Babylonian Collection, New Haven

Table I: List of Deities Appearing in the Inscriptions

UN = Ur-Nammu **Š = Šulgi** **AS = Amar-Suena** **ŠS = Šū-Sîn** **IS = Ibbi-Sîn**

Deity	King	RIM number	RIM page number	Type of inscription	Object
Adad	Š	1.2.38	144–46	Label(?)	Tablet copy of stele inscription
An	UN	1.1.5	27	Building	Bricks
Annunītum	ŠS	1.4.20	330–31	Building	Door sockets
Baba	IS	1.5.2004	381–82	Votive	Eyestone
Damgalnuna	Š	1.2.17	126	Building	Foundation tablet
Enki	UN	1.1.31	68–69	Canal	Door socket(?)
	UN	1.1.32	69	Building	Door socket
	Š	1.2.1	111	Building	Foundation tablet
	AS	1.3.15	260–62	Building	Bricks
Enlil	UN	1.1.24	59–61	Building	Bricks, foundation tablets, and canephors
	UN	1.1.25	61	Building	Door sockets
	UN	1.1.26	62	Canal	Cones
	UN	1.1.38	75–76	Building	Foundation tablet
	UN	1.1.39	76–77	Canal	Cones
	UN	1.1.40	77–78	Canal	Cones
	Š	1.2.18	126–27	Building	Bricks
	Š	1.2.54	156–57	Votive(?)	Tablet copy of statue(?) inscription
	AS	1.3.3	248	Building	Brick
	AS	1.3.5	249–50	Building	Door socket
	AS	1.3.6	250–51	Building	Door socket
	ŠS	1.4.3	301–306	Votive	Tablet copy of statue inscription
	ŠS	1.4.5	308–12	Votive	Tablet copy of statue inscription
Ennugi	Š	1.2.19	127–28	Building	Brick
Gatumdu	IS	1.5.2015	390–91	Votive	Bead
Geštinana	Š	1.2.62	163	Votive	Earring
Gilgameš	UN	1.1.47	82–83	Votive	Vase
Ḫaniš, see Šul-lat and Ḫaniš					
Id (see also Nārum)	Š	1.2.29	137	Building	Foundation tablet
Igalim	Š	1.2.55	157–58	Votive	Statuette
Inanna	UN	1.1.15	37–38	Building	Bricks
	UN	1.1.16	39	Building	Door sockets
	UN	1.1.27	63	Canal	Cone
	UN	1.1.33	69–71	Building	Bricks
	UN	1.1.34	71–72	Building	Foundation tablets and canephors
	Š	1.2.6	116	Building	Foundation tablets and canephors
	Š	1.2.20	128–30	Building	Bricks
	Š	1.2.21	130	Building	Door sockets
[Inanna]	Š	1.2.22	131	Label(?)	Clay sealings
[Inanna]	Š	1.2.2044	227	Votive	Vase
	AS	1.3.13	258–59	Building	Bricks
[Inanna]	ŠS	1.4.1	295–300	Votive	Tablet copy of statue inscription(?)
[Inanna]	ŠS	1.4.18	328–29	Building	Foundation tablet
	Unattributed	1.6.1015	403	Votive	Statuette fragment
[Inanna] Ninkununa	Unattributed	1.6.1037	418–19	Votive	Bowl fragment
Inšušinak	Š	1.2.31	138–39	Building	Bricks
	Š	1.2.32	139–140	Building	Foundation tablets and canephors
Iškur	Š	1.2.38	144–46	Label(?)	Tablet copy of stele inscription
Lamma	Š	1.2.2030	215–16	Votive	Stone wig(?)
	AS	1.3.2009	284	Building	Bead
Laṣ	Š	1.2.26	134–35	Building(?)	Tablet copy

Deity	King	RIM number	RIM page number	Type of inscription	Object
Meslamta-eʾa	Š	1.2.64	164–65	Votive(?)	Tablet copy
	Š	1.2.2033	219	Votive	Mace-head
	Š	1.2.2034	223	Votive	Mace-head
	Š	1.2.2038	223	Votive	Seal
	Š	1.2.2039	223–24	Votive	Seal
	Š	1.2.2040	224	Votive	Seal
	IS	1.5.2014	390	Votive	Mace-head
	Unattributed	1.6.1018	406	Votive	Mace-head
Nanna	UN	1.1.2	22–24	Building	Bricks and door sockets
	UN	1.1.3	24	Label	Cup
	UN	1.1.4	25–26	Building	Bricks
	UN	1.1.11	31–34	Building	Bricks
	UN	1.1.12	35	Building	Bricks
	UN	1.1.17	39–41	?	Cones
	UN	1.1.18	41–42	Votive	Foundation tablet
	UN	1.1.19	42–43	Canal	Bricks and tablet copy
	UN	1.1.28	63–65	Canal	Cones
	UN	1.1.41	78–79	Votive	Vessel
	UN	1.1.42	79	Votive	Vessel
	UN	1.1.45	81	Votive	Mace-head
	Š	1.2.50	153–54	Weight	Weight Stone
	Š	1.2.51	154	Weight	Weight Stone
	Š	1.2.52	154–55	Weight	Weight Stone
	Š	1.2.56	158–59	Votive	Statue
[Nanna(?)]	AS	1.3.7	251	Building	Foundation tablet
	AS	1.3.9	253–55	Building	Door sockets
	AS	1.3.16	262–64	Building	Bricks and door sockets
	AS	1.3.17	264–65	Building	Foundation tablets and canephor
	ŠS	1.4.21	331–32	Building	Door socket
	IS	1.5.2	370–71	Votive	Tablet copy of inscription on vessel
	IS	1.5.3	371–73	Votive	Tablet copy of inscription on vessel
	IS	1.5.4	373–74	Votive	Tablet copy of inscription on figurine
	IS	1.5.5	374	Votive	Bead
	Unattributed	1.6.1017	405–406	Votive	Mace-head
[Nanna(?)]	Unattributed	1.6.1024	410	Weight	Weight stone
[Nanna(?)]	Unattributed	1.6.1025	411	Weight	Weight stone
	Unattributed	1.6.1036	418	Votive	Vessel
Nanše	Š	1.2.9	118–19	Building	Foundation tablets and tauriform figurine
	Š	1.2.10	119–20	Building	Cones
	Š	1.2.61	162	Votive	Mace-head
	UN	2.2.1	429–30	Votive	Vessel
Nārum (see also Id)	Š	1.2.29	137	Building	Foundation tablet
Nergal	Š	1.2.23	132	Building	Foundation tablet
	Š	1.2.24	132–33	Building	Foundation tablet
	Š	1.2.25	133–34	Building	Tablet copy
[Nergal(?)]	Š	1.2.26	134–35	Building(?)	Tablet copy
	Atal-šen	7.2.1	461–62	Building	Foundation tablet
Nimintaba	Š	1.2.4	114–15	Building	Foundation tablets and canephors
Ninazu	Š	1.2.28	136–37	Building	Bricks
NinDARa	Š	1.2.2031	216–18	Votive	Statue
	IS	1.5.2005	382–83	Votive	Statuette
Ninegal	UN	1.1.14	37	Building	Door sockets
Ningal	UN	1.1.13	36	Building	Door sockets
	UN	1.1.43	79–80	Votive	Plaque
	Š	1.2.53	155	Weight	Weight Stone
	Š	1.2.58	160–61	Votive	Bead
	AS	1.3.8	252–53	Building	Door sockets and steles
Ningirsu	Š	1.2.12	121–22	Building	Cones
	Š	1.2.15	124–25	Building	Foundation tablet
Ningišzida	Š	1.2.2037	222	Votive	Seal
	Š	1.2.2042	225–26	Votive	Bowl
Ningublaga(?)	UN	1.1.46	81–82	Votive	Mace-head

Deity	King	RIM number	RIM page number	Type of inscription	Object
Ninḫursaga	UN	1.1.36	73–74	Building	Foundation tablet
	Š	1.2.16	125	Building	Bricks
	Š	1.2.30	137–38	Building	Foundation tablets and canephors
	Š	1.2.59	161	Votive	Bead
	Unattributed	1.6.1014	402–403	Votive(?)	Statue fragment
Nininduba	Š	1.2.2043	226	Votive(?)	Tablet copy
Ninkununa	UN	1.1.15	37–38	Building	Bricks
	Unattributed	1.6.1037	418–19	Votive	Vessel
Ninlil	UN	1.1.37	74–75	Building	Door sockets
	Š	1.2.60	161–62	Votive	Bead
[Ninlil]	ŠS	1.4.4	307–308	Votive	Tablet copy of statue inscription
	ŠS	1.4.5	308–312	Votive	Tablet copy of statue inscription
Ninmarki	Š	1.2.13	122–23	Building	Foundation tablets, canephors, and stone
	Š	1.2.14	123–24	Building	Cone
	Š	1.2.2032	218–19	Votive	Statuette
NinSAR	Š	1.2.2	112	Building	Foundation tablet
Ninsiʾana	Š	1.2.7	117	Building	Foundation tablet
	AS	1.3.14	259–60	Building	Foundation tablets and canephor
Ninsuna	UN	1.1.6	28–29	Building	Door socket
	UN	1.1.23	58–59	Building	Foundation tablet
	Š	1.2.57	159–60	Votive ([i]n-na-[ba])	Statue
Ninsuna(?)	Unattributed	1.6.1016	404–405	Votive(?)	Tablet copy
Ninšagepada	UN	1.1.7	29	Building	Foundation tablet
Ninšubur	Š	1.2.8	117–18	Building	Foundation tablet
Nintinuga	Unattributed	1.6.1006	396–97	Building	Tablet copy
Ninurima	Š	1.2.5	115	Building	Foundation tablet
NinuruamuDU	Š	1.2.2036	221–22	Votive	Mace-head
Ninutula	UN	1.1.8	29–30	Building	Door socket
Nissaba	Unnamed ruler of Girsu	2.3.1001	430–31	Votive(?)	Bowl
Nungal	AS	1.3.2008	283	Building	Stone tablet
PIRIG.GAL	Tiš-atal	7.3.1	463–64	Building	Foundation tablet and lion pegs
Šara	UN	1.1.44	80	Votive	Vessel
[Šara]	Š	1.2.2044	227	Votive	Vase
	ŠS	1.4.16	326–27	Building	Door sockets and stone blocks
	ŠS	1.4.17	327–28	Building	Door sockets and stone blocks
[Šara]	ŠS	1.4.18	328–29	Building	Foundation tablet
	ŠS	1.4.2017	358	Votive	Vase
	ŠS	1.4.2018	358–59	Votive	Axe
Tišpak	Šū-ilīia	3.1.1	435	Royal seal	Seal impression
Ulmašītum	Unattributed	1.6.1003	394	Building	Foundation tablet
Utu	UN	1.1.35	72–73	Building	Bricks
[Utu]	Unattributed	1.6.1030	414	Votive	Vase

Table II: List of Members of the Ur III Royal Family

UN = Ur-Nammu Š = Šulgi AS = Amar-Suena ŠS = Šū-Sîn IS = Ibbi-Sîn

PN	Relation-ship to king	King	RIM number	RIM page number	Type of inscription	Object	Chart
Abī-simtī	Wife	AS	—	267	—	—	AS Family no. 1
Amar-Damu	Son	Š	—	168	—	—	Š Family no. 24
Amat-Sîn	Wife	Š	—	167	—	—	Š Family no. 3
		Š	1.2.67	171	Servant seal	Seal impression	—
		Š	1.2.68	172	Servant seal	Seal impression	—
Amir-Šulgi	Son	AS	—	268	—	—	AS Family no. 22
Aḫuni	Son	AS	—	268	—	—	AS Family no. 21
Aḫu-Wer	Son	Un-known	—	422	—	—	Unattributed Family no. 2
Atu	Son	Un-known	—	422	—	—	Unattributed Family no. 1
Babati	Uncle	ŠS	—	337	—	—	ŠS Family no. 8
		ŠS	1.4.32	340–41	Presentation seal (in-na-[ba])	Seal impression	—
		ŠS	1.4.33	341–42	Servant seal	Tablet copy	—
(Babati's son Aḫam-arši)		ŠS	1.5.7	376–77	Personal seal	Seal impression	—
(Babati's son Girini-isa)		ŠS	1.5.8	377	Personal seal	Seal impression	—
Bamu	Son	AS	—	268	—	—	AS Family no. 23
Baqartum	Daughter	Š	—	167	—	—	Š Family no. 11
		Š	1.2.86	182–83	Servant seal	Seal	—
Dada	Son	AS	—	268	—	—	AS Family no. 24
Dadagu	Daughter	Š	—	167	—	—	Š Family no. 12
Dagān-DUni	Son	Š	—	168	—	—	Š Family no. 25
Damiqtum	Mother(?)	UN	—	85	—	—	UN Family no. 1
Ea-niša	*Lukur*	Š	—	167	—	—	Š Family no. 5
		Š	1.2.72	174–75	Votive	Bead	—
		Š	1.2.73	175	Servant seal	Seal impression	—
		Š	1.2.74	175–76	Servant seal	Seal impression	—
		Š	1.2.75	176–77	Servant seal	Seal impression	—
		Š	1.2.76	177	Servant seal	Seal impression	—
		Š	1.2.77	177–78	Servant seal	Seal impression	—
		Š	1.2.78	178	Servant seal	Seal impression	—
		Š	1.2.79	178	Servant seal	Seal impression	—
		Š	1.2.80	179	Servant seal	Seal impression	—
		Š	1.2.81	179–80	Votive	Tablet copy of statue inscription(?)	—
En-maḫgal-ana	Daughter	AS	—	267	—	—	AS Family no. 6
		AS	1.3.19	269	Label	Bowl	—
En-nirgal-ana	Daughter	UN	—	85	—	—	UN Family no. 4
		UN	1.1.54.1	87–88	Votive	Cone	—
		UN	1.1.54.2	87–88	Votive	Bowl	—
En-nirzi-ana	Daughter	Š	—	168	—	—	Š Family no. 13
		Š	1.2.87	183	Servant seal	Seal impression	—

PN	Relation-ship to king	King	RIM number	RIM page number	Type of inscription	Object	Chart
En-uburzi-ana	Daughter	Š	—	168	—	—	Š Family no. 14
Eštar-ilšu	Son	Š	—	168	—	—	Š Family no. 26
Etel-pû-Dagān	Son	Š	—	168	—	—	Š Family no. 27
Geme-Eanna	Daughter	AS	—	267	—	—	AS Family no. 7
Geme-Enlila	Wife	IS	—	375	—	—	IS Family no. 1
Geme-Nanna	Daughter	AS	—	267	—	—	AS Family no. 8
Geme-Ninlila	*Lukur*	Š	—	167	—	—	Š Family no. 6
		Š	1.2.82	180	Presentation seal (in-na-ba)	Seal	—
Geme-Ninlila	Daughter	ŠS	—	337	—	—	ŠS Family no. 4
Ibbi-Ištarān	Son	AS	—	268	—	—	AS Family no. 25
Inim-Nanna	Son	AS	—	268	—	—	AS Family no. 26
Ir-Nanna	Son	AS	—	268	—	—	AS Family no. 27
Kubātum	Wife	ŠS	—	336	—	—	ŠS Family no. 1
		ŠS	1.4.28	337–38	Label	Bead	—
Liwwir-miṭṭašu	Daughter	Š	—	168	—	—	Š Family no. 15
Lu-duga	Son	Š	—	168	—	—	Š Family no. 28
Lugal-azida	Son	Š	—	168	—	—	Š Family no. 29
Lugal-ezen	Son	Un-known	—	422	—	—	Unattributed Family no. 3
Lu-Nanna	Son	Š	—	168	—	—	Š Family no. 30
Lu-Sunzida	Son	Š	—	168	—	—	Š Family no. 31
Lu-Šulgi	Son	AS	—	268	—	—	AS Family no. 28
Lu-Utu	Son	Un-known	—	422	—	—	Unattributed Family no. 4
Mamma-niša	Daughter	Un-known	—	422	—	—	Unattributed Family no. 5
		Un-known	1.6.1042	422–23	Servant seal	Seal	—
Mammētum	Daughter	IS	—	375	—	—	IS Family no. 3
		IS	1.5.6	376	Servant seal	Seal impression	—
Mansum	Son	AS	—	268	—	—	AS Family no. 29
Nabi-Enlil	Son	Š	—	168	—	—	Š Family no. 32
Nabi-Sîn	Son	Un-known	—	422	—	—	Unattributed Family no. 6
Nabi-Šulgi	Son	AS	—	268	—	—	AS Family no. 30
Nabiʾum	Son	Š	—	168	—	—	Š Family no. 33
Na-DI	Son	Š	—	168	—	—	Š Family no. 34
Nanna-maba	Son	AS	—	268	—	—	AS Family no. 31
Ninegale-si	Daughter	Un-known	—	422	—	—	Unattributed Family no. 7
Nin-ḫedu	Daughter	AS	—	267	—	—	AS Family no. 9
		AS	1.3.20	269–70	Servant seal	Seal impression	—
Nin-kala	*Lukur*	Š	—	167	—	—	Š Family no. 7
		Š	1.2.83	180–81	Label(?)	Bowl	—
	Lukur	Š	1.2.84	181	Votive	Tablet copy of statue inscription(?)	—
Ninlile-manag	Daughter	AS	—	267	—	—	AS Family no. 10
Ninlil-tukultī	Daughter	AS	—	267	—	—	AS Family no. 11

PN	Relation -ship to king	King	RIM number	RIM page number	Type of inscription	Object	Chart
Nin-TUR.TUR-mu	Daughter	Š	—	168	—	—	Š Family no. 16
		Š	1.2.88	184	Votive	Bead	—
Pakinana	Daughter	AS	—	267	—	—	AS Family no. 12
Peš-TUR.TUR	Daughter	Š	—	168	—	—	Š Family no. 17
Puzur-Eštar	Son	Š	—	168	—	—	Š Family no. 35
Puzur-Ninsuna	Son	Un-known	—	422	—	—	Unattributed Family no. 8
Puzur-Sîn	Son	Un-known	—	422	—	—	Unattributed Family no. 9
Puzur-uša	*Lukur*	AS	—	267	—	—	AS Family no. 2
SI.A-tum	Wife	UN	—	85	—	—	UN Family no. 2
		UN	1.1.51	85–86	Servant seal	Seal impression	—
SI.A-tum	Mother	Š	—	167	—	—	Š Family no. 1
		Š	1.2.66	170–71	Votive(?)	Bead	—
Simat-Ea	*Lukur*	Š	—	167	—	—	Š Family no. 8
Simat-Enlil	Daughter	Š	—	168	—	—	Š Family no. 18
		Š	1.2.89.1	184–85	Label	Bowl	—
		Š	1.2.89.2	184–85	Label	Vessel	—
Simat-Eštar	Daughter	Š	—	168	—	—	Š Family no. 19
Simat-Ištarān	Daughter	AS	—	267	—	—	AS Family no. 13
Šāt-Erra	Daughter	ŠS	—	337	—	—	ŠS Family no. 5
		ŠS	1.4.31	339–40	Servant seal	Seal impression	—
Šeleppūtum	Daughter	AS	—	267	—	—	AS Family no. 15
Šulgi-rāmā	Son	AS	—	268	—	—	AS Family no. 34
Šulgi-simtī	Wife and *lukur*	Š	—	167	—	—	Š Family no. 4
		Š	1.2.69	172–73	Servant seal	Seal impression	—
		Š	1.2.70	173	Servant seal	Seal impression	—
		Š	1.2.71	174	Servant seal (?)	Seal impression	—
Šulgi-simtī	Daughter	IS	—	375	—	—	IS Family no. 2
Šū-Enlil	Son	Š	—	168–69	—	—	Š Family no. 36
		Š	1.2.94	187–88	Princely seal	Seal impression	—
Šū-Sîn (the future king)	Son	AS	—	268	—	—	AS Family no. 32
Šūqur[tum]	*Lukur*	Š	—	167	—	—	Š Family no. 10
		Š	1.2.85	182	Label	Vessel	—
Šū-Šulgi	Son	AS	—	268	—	—	AS Family no. 33
Tabūr-Haṭṭum	Daughter	ŠS	—	337	—	—	ŠS Family no. 6
Taddin-Eštar	Daughter	AS	—	267	—	—	AS Family no. 16
		AS	1.3.21	270	Presentation seal (in-na-ba)	Bowl	—
Tarām-Šulgi	Daughter	Š	—	168	—	—	Š Family no. 22
Tarām-Uram	Daughter-in-Law	UN	—	85	—	—	UN Family no. 3
		UN	1.1.52	86	Votive(?)	Tablet copy	—
		UN	1.1.53	87	Servant seal(?)	Seal impression	—
	Wife(?)	Š	—	167	—	—	Š Family no. 2
Teṣin-Mamma	Daughter	AS	—	267	—	—	AS Family no. 17
Ti'āmat-bāštī	*Lukur*	ŠS	—	336	—	—	ŠS Family no. 2
		ŠS	1.4.29	338	Label	Bead	—
Tūlid-Šamšī	?	?	1.2.92	186–87	Servant seal	Seal impression	—
		?	1.2.93	187	Servant seal	Seal impression	—

PN	Relation-ship to king	King	RIM number	RIM page number	Type of inscription	Object	Chart
*Udad-zenat	*Lukur*	AS	—	267	—	—	AS Family no. 3
Ur-Baba	Son	AS	—	268	—	—	AS Family no. 35
		AS	1.3.22	271	Princely seal	Seal impression	—
Ur-Enlila	Brother	ŠS	—	337	—	—	ŠS Family no. 7
Ur-Ištarān	Son	AS	—	268	—	—	AS Family no. 36
Ur-nigingar	Son	Š	—	169	—	—	Š Family no. 38
Ur-Ninsuna	Son	AS	—	268	—	—	AS Family no. 37
Ur-saga	Son	AS	—	268	—	—	AS Family no. 38
Ur-Suena	Son	Š	—	169	—	—	Š Family no. 39
		Š	1.2.95	188–89	Servant seal	Seal impression	—
		Š	1.2.96	189	Servant seal	Seal impression	—
		Š	1.2.97	189–90	Servant seal	Seal impression	—
Watartum, see SI.A-tum							
ZagaANbi	*Lukur*	AS	—	267	—	—	AS Family no. 4
[x]-natum	*Lukur*	AS	—	267	—	—	AS Family no. 5

Table III: List of Ur III Period Governors

UN = Ur-Nammu **Š = Šulgi** **AS = Amar-Suena** **ŠS = Šū-Sîn** **IS = Ibbi-Sîn**

PN	City	King	RIM number	RIM page number	Type of inscription	Object
Aa-kala	Umma	AS	—	277	—	—
	Umma	AS	1.3.2007	282	Personal seal	Seal impression
	Umma	ŠS	—	345	—	—
	Umma	ŠS	1.4.2012	354	Personal seal	Seal impression
(Aa-kala's wife Ninḫilia)	Umma	ŠS	1.4.2013	355	Personal seal	Seal impression
	Umma	ŠS	1.4.2014	355–56	Personal seal	Seal impression
Abba, see Itūr-ilum						
Aḫḫū'a	Puš	Š	—	194	—	—
Aḫuma	Puš	Š	—	194	—	—
	Puš	AS	—	276	—	—
(Aḫḫū'a's son PN)	Puš	Unknown	1.6.1044	424	Personal seal	Seal impression
Ahum-bāni	Kiš	AS	—	275	—	—
Alla	Girsu/Lagaš	Š	—	192	—	—
	Girsu/Lagaš	Š	1.2.2019	207–208	Servant seal	Seal impression
Allamu, see Ursagamu						
Aman-ilī, see Ir-Nanna						
Amur-Sîn	TiWA(A.ḪA)	Š	—	195	—	—
Apillaša	Kazallu	AS	—	274–75	—	—
	Kazallu	ŠS	—	343	—	—
	Kazallu	ŠS	1.4.2004	348–49	Personal seal	Seal impression
Arši-aḫ	Babylon	Š	—	192	—	—
	Babylon	AS	—	272	—	—
Bamu	Ešnunna	Š	—	192	—	—
Dada	Nippur	ŠS	—	344	—	—
	Nippur	ŠS	1.4.2007	350–51	Personal seal	Seal impression
	Nippur	ŠS	1.4.2008	351–52	Servant seal	Seal impression
	Nippur	ŠS	1.4.2009	352	Servant seal	Seal
	Nippur	IS	—	379	—	—
	Nippur	IS	1.5.2007	384–85	Personal seal	Seal impression
	Nippur	IS	1.5.2008	385	Servant seal	Seal impression
	Nippur	IS	1.5.2009	385–86	Servant seal	Seal impression
	Nippur	IS	1.5.2010	386	Servant seal	Seal impression
Dada	TiWA(A.ḪA)	AS	—	277	—	—
Dadaga	Umma	ŠS	—	345	—	—
	Umma	IS	—	379	—	—
	Umma	IS	1.5.2012	387–88	Personal seal	Seal impression
(Dadaga's son Gududu)	Umma	IS	1.5.2013	388–89	Personal seal	Seal impression
Dadani	Šarrākum	AS	—	277	—	—
Ea-bāni	Ereš	Š	—	191	—	—
Ea-bāni, see Pišaḫ-ilum						
Enlil-zišagal	TiWA(A.ḪA)	ŠS	—	345	—	—
Ennam-Šulgi, see Lu-Nanna						
Gudea	Kutha	AS	—	273–75	—	—
Gudea	Girsu/Lagaš	AS	1.3.2002	279	Servant seal	Seal impression
	Girsu/Lagaš	ŠS	—	343	—	—
	Girsu/Lagaš	ŠS	1.4.2003	348	Servant seal	Seal impression
Gududu, see Dadaga						
Ḫabaluge	Adab	Š	—	191–93	—	—
	Adab	Š	1.2.2004	197–98	Votive	Bowl
	Adab	Š	1.2.2005	198–99	Servant seal	Seal impression
	Adab	AS	—	272	—	—
	Adab	ŠS	—	343	—	—

PN	City	King	RIM number	RIM page number	Type of inscription	Object
Ḫala-Lamma, see Lu-girizal						
Ḫašḫamer	Iškun-Sîn	UN	1.1.2001	88–89	Personal seal	Seal
Ibni-ilum	Kazallu	AS	—	273	—	—
Igi-Ana-ezu	Puš	Š	—	194	—	—
Ikšudum	Puš	AS	—	276	—	—
Illalum	Šarrākum	AS	—	277	—	—
Imlik-Ea	Marad	AS	—	276	—	—
Ir-Nanna (also known as Irmu)	Girsu/Lagaš	AS	—	274–75	—	—
	Girsu/Lagaš	ŠS	—	343	—	—
	Girsu/Lagaš	ŠS	1.4.13	323–24	Building	Door socket
	Girsu/Lagaš	ŠS	1.4.2002	346–47	Personal seal	Seal impression
	Girsu/Lagaš	IS	—	378	—	—
	Girsu/Lagaš	IS	1.5.2003	381	Personal seal	Seal impression
(Ir-Nanna's wife Aman-ilī)	Girsu/Lagaš	IS	1.5.2004	381–82	Votive	Eyestone
Iṣṣur-ilum, see Itūr-ilum						
Itūrīia	Ešnunna	ŠS	—	343	—	—
	Ešnunna	ŠS	1.4.12	322–23	Building	Brick
	Ešnunna	IS	—	378	—	—
(Itūrīia's son Šū-ilīia) For Šū-ilīia, ruler of Ešnunna, see 3.1.1	Ešnunna	IS	1.5.2002	380	Personal seal	Seal impression
Itūr-Ilum	Babylon	Š	—	192	—	—
	Babylon	Š	1.2.2006	199	Servant seal	Seal impression
(Itūr-ilum's son Iṣṣur-ilum)	Babylon	Š	1.2.2007	199–200	Personal seal	Seal impression
(Itūr-ilum's son Abba)	Babylon	Š	1.2.2008	200	Personal seal	Seal impression
Izarriq	Kazallu	Š	—	193	—	—
Kalamu	Ešnunna	Š	—	193	—	—
	Ešnunna	Š	1.2.2009	201	Servant seal	Seal impression
	Ešnunna	AS	—	273–75	—	—
Ku-Nanna	Šuruppak	ŠS	—	345	—	—
Lišānum, see Šū-ilī						
Lišānum	Marad	AS	—	276	—	—
Lu-balasag	Šuruppak	AS	—	277	—	—
Lu-banda	Šarrākum	Š	—	194	—	—
	Šarrākum	Š	1.2.2026	212–13	Servant seal	Seal impression
Lugal-ḫedu	Šuruppak	Š	—	194	—	—
Lugal-kuzu	Puš	AS	—	276	—	—
Lugal-magure	Ur	ŠS	1.4.15	325–26	Building	Door socket
Lugal-melam	Nippur	AS	—	276	—	—
	Nippur	AS	1.3.2003	279–80	Personal seal	Seal impression
	Nippur	AS	1.3.2004	280–81	Servant seal	Seal impression
	Nippur	ŠS	—	344	—	—
Lugal-pa'e	Išīm-Šulgi	Š	—	193	—	—
Lu-girizal	Girsu/Lagaš	Š	—	191–92	—	—
	Girsu/Lagaš	Š	1.2.2010	201–202	Votive	Bowl
(Lu-girizal's son Nammaḫni-du)	Girsu/Lagaš	Š	1.2.2011	202–203	Building	Foundation tablet
(Lu-girizal's daughter Ḫala-Lamma)	Girsu/Lagaš	Š	1.2.2012	203	Votive	Statuette
Lu-girizal	Girsu/Lagaš	Š	1.2.2013	204	Servant seal	Seal impression
	Girsu/Lagaš	Š	1.2.2014	204–205	Servant seal	Seal impression
	Girsu/Lagaš	Š	1.2.2015	205	Servant seal	Seal impression
	Girsu/Lagaš	Š	1.2.2016	205–206	Servant seal	Seal impression
	Girsu/Lagaš	Š	1.2.2017	206	Servant seal	Seal impression
Lu-Nanna	Simudar	ŠS	—	344	—	—
	Simudar	ŠS	1.4.2010	352–53	Personal seal	Seal impression
	Simudar	ŠS	1.4.2011	353–54	Servant seal	Seal impression

PN	City	King	RIM number	RIM page number	Type of inscription	Object
(Lu-Nann's son Ennam-Šulgi)	Simudar	IS	1.5.2011	387	Personal seal	Seal impression
Lu-Utu, see Ur-Ašgi II						
Nammaḫni-du, see Lu-girizal						
Namzi-tara	Nippur	ŠS	1.4.2005	349–50	Personal seal	Seal impression
	Nippur	ŠS	1.4.2006	350	Personal seal	Seal impression
Nanna-zišagal	Šarrākum	AS	—	277	—	—
Nanna-zišagal	Girsu/Lagaš	AS	—	273–74	—	—
NE.NE	Marad	ŠS	—	344	—	—
	Marad	IS	—	379	—	—
Ninḫilia, see Aa-kala						
Nita-saga, see Ur-Ašgi II						
Nūr-Dagān	Sippar	AS	—	276	—	—
Pišaḫ-ilum	Kutha	IS	—	378	—	—
(Pišaḫ-ilum's son Ea-bāni)	Kutha	IS	1.5.2006	383–84	Personal seal	Seal impression
Puzur-Tutu	Babylon	IS	—	378	—	—
Sîn-abušu	Ur	IS	—	389	—	—
Ṣilluš-Dagān	Simurrum	Š	—	194	—	—
	Simurrum	AS	—	276	—	—
	Simurrum	AS	1.3.2005	281	Servant seal	Seal impression
	Simurrum	ŠS	—	344	—	—
	Simurrum	ŠS	1.4.2011	353–54	Servant seal	Seal impression
	Simurrum	Š	1.6.1046	425–26	Personal seal	Seal impression
Šamaš-bāni	Sippar	ŠS	—	344	—	—
Šarakam	Girsu/Lagaš	AS	—	274–75	—	—
Šarrum-bāni	Apiak	AS	—	272	—	—
Šarrum-ilī	Uruk	Š	—	195	—	—
	Uruk	AS	—	277	—	—
$ši_x$(SIG_4)teli	Babylon	AS	—	272	—	—
Šū-ilī	Marad	Š	—	—	—	—
(Šū-ilī's son Lišānum)	Marad	Š	—	193	—	—
	Marad	Š	1.2.2021	209	Personal seal	Seal impression
Šū-ilīia, see Itūrīia						
Šū-Mamma	Kazallu	AS	—	273–75	—	—
Šū-Tirum	Apiak	AS	—	272	—	—
Ugula	Kiš	AS	—	273–74	—	—
Ur-Ašgi I	Adab	Š	—	192	—	—
	Adab	Š	1.2.2001	195–96	Votive	Bowl
	Adab	Š	1.2.2002	196–97	Servant seal	Seal impression
	Adab	Š	1.2.2003	197	Servant seal	Seal impression
Ur-Ašgi II (probably grandson of Ur-Ašgi I)	Adab	ŠS	—	343	—	—
(Ur-Ašgi II' s son Lu-Utu)	Adab	ŠS	1.4.2001	346	Personal seal	Seal impression
	Adab	IS	—	378	—	—
(Ur-Ašgi II's son Nita-saga)	Adab	IS	1.5.2001	379–80	Personal seal	Seal impression
Ur-Baba	Ereš	AS	—	272	—	—
Ur-Guedina	Ešnunna	Š	—	191	—	—
Ur-Ḫendursag	Šulgi-Utu	Š	1.2.2028	213–14	Personal seal	Seal impression
Urkiʾum	Susa	Š	—	194	—	—
Ur-Lamma	Girsu/Lagaš	Š	—	191–93	—	—
	Girsu/Lagaš	Š	1.2.2018	206–207	Servant seal	Seal impression
	Girsu/Lagaš	AS	—	273	—	—
Ur-Lisi	Umma	Š	—	195	—	—
	Umma	Š	1.2.2029	214–15	Personal seal	Seal impression
	Umma	AS	—	277	—	—
	Umma	AS	1.3.2006	281–82	Personal seal	Seal impression
Ur-mes	Šarrākum	AS	—	277	—	—

PN	City	King	RIM number	RIM page number	Type of inscription	Object
Ur-Nanibgal	Nippur	Š	—	193	—	—
	Nippur	Š	1.2.2022	209–210	Personal seal	Seal impression
	Nippur	Š	1.2.2023	210–11	Votive	Seal
	Nippur	Š	1.2.2024	211	Servant seal	Seal impression
Ur-nigin-gar	Šuruppak	Š	—	194	—	—
	Šuruppak	Š	1.2.2027	213	Servant seal	Seal impression
Ur-Ninkura	Šuruppak	AS	—	277	—	—
	Šuruppak	ŠS	—	345	—	—
Ur-Ninmug	Ereš	Š	—	191	—	—
(Ursagamu's son Allamu)	Kutha(?)	Š	1.2.2020	208–209	Personal seal	Seal impression
Ur-Suena	Urum(ÚR×Ú.KI)	Š	—	195	—	—
Watarum	Marad	Š	—	193	—	—
Zarriq	Susa	Š	—	194	—	—
Zarriq(um)	Susa	AS	—	277	—	—
Zarriqum	Aššur	AS	1.3.2001	278	Building	Plaque
[PN] governor of Nippur	Nippur	—	1.6.1043	423	Votive	Vase
[x]-kala	Ur	ŠS	1.4.14	324–25	Building	Door socket
Son of governor of Adab	Adab	—	1.6.1045	424–25	Votive	Vase

UR III PERIOD

(2112–2004 BC)

Introduction

The time period covered by the inscriptions in this volume extends from the accession of the first king of the Ur III dynasty, Ur-Nammu, to the end of the reign of the fifth and last king of the dynasty, Ibbi-Sîn. According to J.A. Brinkman's chronology (found in the appendix: "Mesopotamian Chronology of the Historical Period," in A.L. Oppenheim's Ancient Mesopotamia), this corresponds to 2112 to 2004 BC. This dating follows the so-called "Middle Chronology." More recently, P. Huber, in a volume edited by P. Åström entitled High, Middle or Low, has argued (pp. 16–17) that the "Long Chronology" is the chronological scheme that is most likely to be correct. If this is true, then Ur-Nammu's reign would have begun in 2167 BC. For the time being, however, we have retained the dates given in the appendix to Oppenheim's book.

In addition to inscriptions of kings of the Ur III dynasty, we have included inscriptions of contemporaneous rulers who controlled states such as Mari and Urkiš that were on the periphery of Mesopotamia.

A large majority of the inscriptions in this volume are written in Sumerian. A few are in Akkadian, and one text, the Tiš-atal inscription (E3/2.7.3.1) is in Hurrian.

For the most part, our sources are building inscriptions; they appear on bricks, cones, foundation tablets, and canephors. These texts do not generally provide us with much historical information. While a handful of Old Babylonian tablet copies of statue inscriptions of king Šū-Sîn do provide us with accounts of his campaign against Simaški, we have only one or two scraps of inscriptions that may refer to campaigns of Šulgi. This is particularly surprising in view of the fact that most of the year names of the latter half of Šulgi's long (forty-eight-year) reign commemorate military victories. Perhaps it is only through the accident of discovery that we have not yet found more of Šulgi's stele and statue inscriptions.

We have attempted in the cases of kings Ur-Nammu, Amar-Suena, Šū-Sîn, and Ibbi-Sîn to present the texts in a roughly chronological order. In the case of Šulgi, however, the fact that we have so many inscriptions that cannot be connected with year names prompted us to organize the Šulgi inscriptions typologically. For a study of the typology of the Ur III inscriptions, see W.W. Hallo, "The Royal Inscriptions of Ur: A Typology," HUCA 33 (1962) pp. 1–43. Šulgi's building inscriptions have been ordered geographically, proceeding from south to north.

Lists of year names of the various Ur III kings and the Ešnunna ruler Šū-ilīya have been given in the introductory remarks for each king. Reflections in the contemporary archival texts of the events commemorated in the year names have, in many cases, been noted.

We have given an overall alphabetized list of deities appearing in the dedicatory sections of the inscriptions in Table I: List of Deities Appearing in the Inscriptions (pp. xxxiii–xxxv).

In addition to inscriptions of members of the royal family — these appear in the main sequence immediately after the inscriptions of the king himself — we have also included charts giving references in the archival texts to members of the royal family. An overall alphabetized list of all members of the Ur III royal family is found in Table II: List of Members of the Ur III Royal Family (pp. xxxvii–xxxix). The inclusion of this material was made possible through D. Owen's kind permission to cite entries from his unpublished manuscript entitled "The Royal Family of Ur: Preliminary List of Sources." Of course, any errors or omissions in this connection are the sole responsibility of the author.

As an addition to the normal RIM corpus, we have also included seal inscriptions of Ur III period city governors (ensis). These appear in the 2000 series in this volume. As with inscriptions mentioning members of the royal family, we have prepared charts listing the names of city governors attested in Ur III archival texts. References to governors of Elam and other eastern regions have not been included. I am thankful to W.W. Hallo who kindly provided me with an unpublished list of Ur III period governors that was an update of his MA dissertation "The Ensis of the Ur III Dynasty." While we have not striven for absolute completeness in these charts, it is hoped that they will be of use to the reader. In the charts of city governors we have given the dates of the relevant tablets in the following manner: 1 ii Š 47, for example, refers to the first day of the second month of Šulgi's 47th year. Further, we have used the sigla (t) for tablet, and (s) for seal inscriptions, in order to differentiate between governors' names appearing in the actual text of an archival text (t), from names found in seal inscriptions on the tablets (s). References to regnal years of the kings use the following abbreviations: UN = Ur-Nammu, Š = Šulgi, AS = Amar-Suena, ŠS = Šū-Sîn, and IS = Ibbi-Sîn. An overall alphabetized list of governors of the Ur III period is found in Table III: List of Ur III Period Governors (pp. xli–xliv).

In our transliterations of Akkadian texts we have used the character ś to indicate the phoneme which was probably pronounced /s/ in pre-Ur III times, but which had shifted, by the end of the Ur III period, to /š/.

In the bibliographies the designation "study" is used as a kind of grab-bag term to indicate a reference that does not fit into the categories of photo, copy, transliteration, edition, or the like. Thus a bibliographic reference to an individual item in Hallo's catalogue of the Ur III inscriptions (such as the siglum Ur-Nammu 1) is listed in our bibliography as a "study."

UR

E3/2.1

An important preliminary consideration in any discussion of the dynasty founded by Ur-Nammu is the relative chronology of the Ur III and Lagaš II dynasties. The conventional view on this subject was put forward by E. Sollberger in an article entitled "Sur la chronologie des rois d'Ur et quelques problèmes connexes" (AfO 17 [1954–57] p. 35); he set the defeat of the Lagašite ruler Namḫani, an event that seemed to be alluded to in a broken passage of the prologue of the "Ur-Nammu Law Code," as year two of Ur-Nammu (Nammaḫni 3 = Ur-Nammu 2). Civil now interprets the passage as referring to Ur-Nammu's *installation!* (íl) of Namḫani as governor at Lagaš. Falkenstein (Inschriften Gudeas p. 13) modified the synchronism slightly by setting Nammaḫni 2 = Ur-Nammu 2. However, a basic difficulty with these proposed synchronisms has been pointed out by P. Steinkeller in a communication entitled "The Date of Gudea and His Dynasty" (JCS 40 [1988] pp. 47–53). Steinkeller observes (p. 49): "The assumption that the Second Dynasty of Lagaš came to an end at the very beginning of Ur-Nammu's reign results in a gap of twenty-eight years between the reigns of Šulgi and Gudea." Steinkeller notes that this hiatus is simply too long to accommodate the tenures of office of various Lagašite officials, whose careers, he demonstrated, spanned the period from Gudea to Šulgi.

In a second study (S. Monaco, "Two notes on ASJ 10, 1988," ASJ 12 [1990] pp. 89–105), Monaco provides a table of important synchronisms relevant to the question of Ur III and Lagaš II connections. He notes (p. 100) the following data:

> Namḫani was a contemporary of UrNammu (UrNammu's Law Code)
> Urabba was a contemporary of both UrNammu (*RTC* 261, 263, 265, *AOAT* 25, 81 nr. 10) and Utuḫegal (*RTC* 264 'mu ur-ab-ba ensi': year formula not belonging to UrNammu reign as demonstrated by T. Maeda)
> Urmama, having ruled between Urabba and Namḫani, was a contemporary of UrNammu
> Nammaḫni, having ruled before Urabba, was a contemporary of Utuḫegal
> Utuḫegal was a contemporary of the Gutean king Tirigan (*IRSA* II k3a)
> UrNammu, šagina of Ur, was a contemporary of Utuḫegal (*IRSA* II k3c)
> Lugalannatum, ruler of Umma, was a contemporary of the Gutean king Si'um (*IRSA* II j5)
> Nammaḫni, ruler of Umma, was a contemporary of the Gutean king Yarlagan (*IRSA* II j4)

Monaco further proposes that the PN nam-ḫa-ni, which, as noted, appears in the prologue of the "Ur-Nammu Law Code" as the name of a governor of

Lagaš, is to be kept separate from the PN nam-maḫ-ni which appears in a number of inscriptions from Girsu (Steible, NSBW 1 pp. 374–90). Monaco does, however (pp. 97–98), equate the (earlier) Nammaḫni of Girsu with the ruler Nammaḫni of Umma; the latter is named in a royal inscription that is edited as E2.11.12.1 in RIME 2. Nammaḫni of Umma apparently consolidated his hold over Girsu by his marriage to the daughter of the governor Ur-Baba of Lagaš (see Steible, NSBW 1 p. 380 Nammaḫni 7).

A second important study on the chronology of the Lagaš II dynasty has been published by T. Maeda ("Two Rulers by the Name Ur-Ningirsu in Pre-Ur III Lagash," ASJ 10 [1988] pp. 19–35). Maeda has convincingly argued that the year name: mu éš-gána-lugal šà gír-su.KI-ke_4 ba-ta-è "The year the royal field-measuring rope was brought out in Girsu" (Thureau-Dangin, RTC no. 267) is to be attributed to Utu-ḫegal of Uruk. The year name is undoubtedly to be connected with three royal inscriptions from Girsu (see Frayne, RIME 2 pp. 280–83 E2.13.6.1–3) that deal with Utu-ḫegal's arbitration of a new boundary for the territory of the gods Nanše and Ningirsu. The fact that the year name was used at Girsu is suggestive of a brief period of Urukean hegemony over Girsu. Another year name noted by Maeda (ASJ 10 [1988] pp. 28–29) deals with the oracular designation of the lú-maḫ priest of Inanna (Thureau-Dangin, RTC no. 234; Delaporte, ITT 4 no. 7562). Since we have no other examples of Lagašite year names mentioning the goddess Inanna, it is highly probable that this year name (as Maeda, p. 31, suggests) is also to be assigned to Utu-ḫegal.

An indication of the particularly close ties that existed between Uruk and Lagaš in late Lagaš II times is found in an important study by F. Carroué ("La Situation Chronologique de Lagaš II: Un Élément du Dossier," ASJ 16 [1994] pp. 47–75). Carroué (p. 57) argues that the references in the Lagaš II dynasty texts to the king (lugal), queen (nin), and prince (dumu-lugal) refer to the royal family of Uruk. He suggests, as a working hypothesis, that the enormous expenditures recorded in the archive of Lagaš texts denoted in his study as "textes A" could be explained by seeing them as disbursements for the marriage of the prince Ur-Ningirsu of Lagaš to a daughter of the king of Uruk.

Another important datum for the chronology of the late Lagaš II period is provided by an inscription of the Ummaite governor Lugal-ana-tuma (Frayne, RIME 2 p. 268 E2.11.13.1). It records Lugal-ana-tuma's construction of the E-gidru temple at Umma. Of importance is the remark in the inscription (lines 4–7) that the temple construction took place "thirty-five years after (the territory of) Umma was divided up" (umma.KI ba-ba-a 35 mu zal-la-ba). The allusion is likely to an attack of the late Sargonic ruler Dudu against Umma (see Frayne, RIME 2 p. 210); this offensive is recorded in an archival text published by C. Wilcke (AfO 25 [1974–77] p. 84 no. 1 lines 7–9). Another, likely contemporaneous assault was made by Dudu on Girsu; booty from the attack was dedicated by Dudu in Nippur (see Frayne, RIME 2 E2.1.10.2). The likely intent of this raid was to quell the revolt of the Lagašite ruler Puzur-Mama; for the career of this independent ruler see K. Volk, "Puzur-Mama und die Reise des Königs," ZA 82 [1992] pp. 22–29.

Now, it is noteworthy that roughly thirty-five Lagašite year names are known that can be placed in the time period between the accession of Ur-Ningirsu and the time of the Ummaite governor Lugal-ana-tuma. This can be compared with the thirty-five years given as being the span of time from the attack (of Dudu?) on Umma to the reign of Lugal-ana-tuma. We may also note that the five kings of the Uruk IV dynasty are assigned a total reign of thirty years in the Sumerian King List.

The status of Ur during the period of the Lagaš II dynasty is unclear. For the most part, it seems not to have had really independent rulers (see Hallo, JCS 20 [1966] pp. 136–38); the one inscription of a possibly autonomous governor, Lu-saga (Frayne, RIME 2 pp. 299–301 E2.15.1.1), may date to the time of confusion that followed the death of Šar-kali-šarrī. Evidence pointing to possible domination of Ur by Uruk is suggested by an inscription recording a dedication to the goddess Ningal of Ur by Kuda, *sanga* priest of Inanna. As noted in RIME 2 p. 277, this name may refer to the Kuda who appears as the third king of the Uruk IV dynasty. Certainly, there is unequivocal evidence that Ur formed part of Uruk's domain during the first years of Utu-ḫegal's reign; in a votive inscription from Ur (Frayne, RIME 2 pp. 295–96, E2.13.6.2001) Ur-Nammu, military governor of Ur, dedicates a stele for the life of Utu-ḫegal, king of Uruk.

On the other hand, the find at Ur of stone vases (Gadd, UET 1 no. 25) which name a certain En-ane-pada, daughter of governor Ur-Baba of Lagaš, as *en* of Nanna suggests that, for a time, Ur was under the domination of Lagaš. Now, the year name found in Legrain, UET 3 no. 291: mu ^{d}lugal-ba-gára é-a ku_4-ra ús-sa "The year after the god Lugal-bagara entered his temple," has been assigned by some scholars to Gudea of Lagaš, and seen as evidence of Lagašite control over Ur. However, F. Carroué (in a forthcoming study) will show that this year name should be attributed to Šulgi (see discussion under Šulgi year name 13b, p. 100). Further, the handful of royal inscriptions of Gudea found at Ur (Gadd, UET 1 nos. 27 and 28) may simply be stray pieces from Girsu. The fact that the Girsu calendar was employed at Ur before Š 30 is notable, but what specific conclusions we are to draw from this fact are unclear.

Ur-Nammu

E3/2.1.1

The Sumerian King List credits Ur-Nammu, the founder of the Ur III dynasty, with a reign of eighteen years. This is the same figure given in the Ur-Isin king lists published by E. Sollberger (JCS 8 [1954] pp. 135–36; cf. A.K. Grayson, RLA 6/2 p. 90 §3.2).

The origins of Ur-Nammu and his dynasty are not clear. According to C. Wilcke (CRRA 19 [1974] pp. 192–93 n. 67), Ur-Nammu was possibly the brother of Utu-ḫegal of Uruk. Indeed, offerings connected with (the deceased) Utu-ḫegal (as family ancestor?) are noted in an Ur III archival text dated to the time of Šū-Sîn. The tablet in question records a disbursement of reeds for the temple of Utu-ḫegal in Uruk (see Waetzoldt and Yıldız, MVN 16 no. 1496 lines 1–5). According to W. Sallaberger (in an article to appear in AoF 23 [1996]), a certain Damiqtum was possibly the mother of Ur-Nammu (see also the discussion in Šulgi — Royal Family item 1 below).

As for the origins of Ur-Nammu himself, we may note that his name is composed with the theophoric element Nammu. Evidence of the archaic zà-mì hymns from Abū Ṣalābīkh (Biggs, Abū Ṣalābīkh p. 50 lines 140–41) suggests that the goddess Nammu's cult city was located at eš:šu.(KI); it is a town that is listed in the aforementioned hymnic cycle between the cities of Ennegi(r) and KI.KAL, the latter two GNs being towns that lay not far northwest of Ur. A reference to eš-šu.(KI) may be seen in the literary composition "Lamentation over the Destruction of Sumer and Ur"; it occurs in the variant spelling: aš-šu (see Michalowski, Lamentation pp. 48–49 line 196): aš-šu.KI é íd-dè lá-a-ri a-e ba-da-ab-bu "Aššu, the estate that stretches out along the river, was deprived of water." Aššu is listed in the lament between the cities of Gaʾeš and Kiʾabrig. In all likelihood, then, Eššu/Aššu was a small town in the general vicinity of Ur.

Civil (Orientalia NS 54 [1985] p. 27 n. 1), noting the writing na-am-ma for LAGAB×ḪAL in Proto-Ea 53 (MSL 14 p. 33), prefers to read the divine name conventionally rendered ᵈnammu as ᵈnamma, seeing it as possibly deriving from a reduplicated form *namnam. If Civil's reading of the divine name be correct, then we should, by extension, read the royal name as Ur-Namma. Civil (Orientalia NS 54 [1985] p. 27 n. 1) does, in fact, quote phonetic writings of the RN that support this hypothesis. The designation Ur-Nammu which appears in this volume is thus merely conventional; the reader should bear in mind that the name may very well be Ur-Namma.

As yet, no year list has appeared for Ur-Nammu; thus the following catalogue of year names is organized in only rough chronological order. Three studies of the Ur-Nammu year names have appeared. One, authored by F.R. Kraus, is entitled "Zur Chronologie der Könige Ur-Nammu und Šulgi von Ur," Orientalia NS 20 (1951) pp. 385–98. A second investigation was published by E. Sollberger ("Sur la chronologie des rois d'Ur et quelques problèmes connexes," AfO 17 [1954–56] pp. 10–14). Finally, a tentative ordering of the Ur-Nammu year names was given in Frayne, Correlations pp. 72–138.

Ur-Nammu's year names, with one exception, are attested only on tablets from Telloh, ancient Girsu. Now, historical sources indicate that Ur-Nammu did not control Girsu when he acceded to the throne of Ur. It was only after his (presumed) defeat of Namḫani, the last ruler of the Lagaš II Dynasty, that he was able to incorporate the Lagašite territories into his own domains. As a consequence of these two facts, the extant corpus of Ur-Nammu year names is restricted to dates which belong to the last half of the reign; in all, eight year names can be assigned to the period of the king's control over Girsu. Events of the early part of the reign may be alluded to in two Ur-Nammu compositions: (a) Ur-Nammu Hymn C (AO 5378: de Genouillac, TRS no. 12; edition by G. Castellino, ZA 53 [1959] pp. 118–31) and (b) Ni 4375 (Çığ and Kızılyay, ISET 1 p. 177 = pl. 119); the latter is an Old Babylonian copy of an Ur-Nammu inscription that is edited as inscription E3/2.1.1.1 in this volume. A detailed study of the Ur-Nammu year names is planned by the author in a separate publication.

I. Year Names and Events of the Reign

(a) [mu ur-^{d}nammu lugal "The year Ur-Nammu (became) king."]

While this year name is as yet unattested, its reconstruction (based on parallels provided by accession year names of other kings) is reasonably certain. By issuing his own year names and royal inscriptions Ur-Nammu proclaimed his independence from his erstwhile lord, Utu-ḫegal of Uruk. During his first regnal years Ur-Nammu controlled a small kingdom that encompassed the city of Ur on the Euphrates River, and, in all likelihood, the settlements of Kuʾar and Eridu on the Eridu canal. In inscriptions dating to this time period the king appears with the simple title "king of Ur."

(b) [mu en ^{d}nanna maš-e ba-pà-da "The year the *en* of the god Nanna was chosen by omens."]

Ur-Nammu installed his daughter as *en* of the god Nanna under the priestly name En-nirgal-ana (see inscription E3/2.1.54). While the year name dealing with the priestess's oracular designation is, as yet, unattested, the fact that the act of designating the *en* of Nanna always provided a year name during the Ur III period makes the reconstruction of the year name (b) highly likely.

(c) mu KIB.KIB še-la[gaš].KI giš bí-ra-a "The year the ... threshed the grain of Lagaš." Ni 1453 (museum number kindly provided by E. Sollberger): V. Scheil, RT 19 (1897) p. 61 and V. Scheil, RA 14 (1917) p. 163. See also Radau, EBH p. 281 and E. Sollberger, AfO 17 (1954–56) p. 13 (j).

The events commemorated in year name (c) apparently date to the time when Ur-Nammu ruled at Ur and Utu-ḫegal at Uruk. The year name, in all likelihood, alludes to a raid made by the forces of Ur-Nammu on the neighbouring territory of Lagaš. As a consequence of the incursion, grain from the Lagaš region was evidently taken back to Ur. A reference to the raid is probably found in three Utu-ḫegal cone inscriptions that were edited as inscriptions E2.13.6.1–3 in RIME 2. The first of these reads: "For the goddess Nanše, the mighty lady, the lady of the boundary, Utu-ḫegal, king of the four quarters, restored into her (Nanše's) hands the border of Lagaš on which the man of Ur had laid a claim." It is highly likely that the "man of Ur" named in these two Utu-ḫegal inscriptions was none other than Ur-Nammu. In addition to its commemoration in the cone inscriptions, Utu-ḫegal's demarcation of a new boundary for the Lagaš region was apparently solemnized in a year name used at Girsu (AO 3363: Thureau-Dangin, RTC no. 267): mu éš-gána-lugal šà-gír-su.KI ba-ta-è "The year the royal field-measuring rope was brought out in Girsu." According to T. Maeda (ASJ 10 [1988] p. 31), the king mentioned in this year name is likely to have been Utu-ḫegal. By fixing a new boundary for Lagaš, Utu-ḫegal was acting in a role analogous to that played much earlier by King Me-salim of Kiš (see Sollberger and Kupper, IRSA IC7i, I 1–12 and Cooper, SARI La 3.2–3, 5.1). In that case the dispute was between the rival city states of Umma and Girsu. A memory of Utu-ḫegal's authority over the

Girsu region at this time may possibly be seen in the appearance of the PN Ḫengal in the so-called "Rulers of Lagaš" text edited by Sollberger (JCS 21 [1967] p. 291 lines 189 and 191).

(d) The expulsion of the Gutians.

Line 90 of the hymn Ur-Nammu C reads:

> gu-ti-um.KI lú-x-a-ke_4 šu-ùri-na mu-du_8
>
> The bloody (for ùri[n] = *dāmu*[*m*], see Krecher, Sumerische Kultlyrik p. 158) hand of the Gutians, the ..., I tied.

A comparable section of the hymn found on Ni 4375 (iv 1′–5′) gives:

> ^{d}[ur-^{d}nammu] lugal-[...] gu-t[i-um.KI] lú-x-[x] kur-ba im-m[i-...]
>
> (I), [Ur-Nammu], king of [...], Guti[um ...], the ... ones, in their mountain [I ...].

These passages, then, allude to Ur-Nammu's campaigns against the Gutians. It may be that there is some connection between Ur-Nammu's attacks on the Gutians and the well-known account of Utu-ḫegal's expulsion of the Gutians, but this is uncertain. An alternate explanation would see a reference here to the attacks (which apparently took place late in the reign) against a coalition of eastern forces including the Elamites (see inscriptions E3/2.1.1.29–30).

(e) (i) The (first) construction of the "wall of Ur."

According to the evidence of the hymn Ur-Nammu C, Ur-Nammu built a structure named the "wall of Ur." The relevant passage (Ni 4375 iii′ 10′–14′) reads:

> ^{d}u[r-^{d}nammu] nam-lu[gal ...] numun-na[m-en-na] u[ri_5.KI-ma bàd-b[i mu-dù]
>
> (I), U[r-Nammu], who [...] king[ship], offspring of [*en*]-sh[ip], [built] the "wall of U[r]."

The construction of the "wall of Ur" is also recorded in the royal inscription that is edited as inscription E3/2.1.1.4 in this volume. The fact that the king appears in the relevant inscription with the simple title "king of Ur" securely dates the text to an early period of the reign, probably before the king's trip to Nippur. As pointed out in our discussion of E3/2.1.1.4, the wall commemorated in the royal inscription was likely the temenos wall and may not have included the actual city wall. The building of a (later?) structure also named "the wall of Ur" was commemorated in year name (p); see the discussion in § (p) below for the details.

(e) (ii) The construction of the temples of Enki at Eridu, of Ninsuna at Kuʾar, and of Inanna-Ninkununa at Ur.

While the date of Ur-Nammu's first construction of Enki's temple in Eridu and his building of Ninsuna's temple at Kuʾar (for the reading of the goddess Ninsuna's name as Ninsuna rather than the conventional Ninsun, see the comments of Jacobsen, JCS 41 [1989] p. 74) cannot be determined with precision, we can state with assurance that the work must have begun at a very early period in the reign, certainly before Ur-Nammu's trip to Nippur. In both relevant inscriptions (E3/2.1.1.10 and E3/2.1.1.6 respectively), Ur-Nammu appears with the simple title "king of Ur." Work on the Inanna/Ninkununa shrine at Ur also apparently began before the king's trip to Nippur; in the brick inscription dealing with the temple's construction (E3/2.1.1.15) the king appears again with the simple title "king of Ur."

(f) Ur-Nammu's trip to Nippur.

The evidence for Ur-Nammu's trip to Nippur comes from a passage in the hymn Ur-Nammu C (lines 93–107). While the poor state of preservation of Ur-Nammu C prevents a translation of the passage as a whole, it is clear that the cited excerpt described festivities that took place at Nippur. We may note, for example, lines 101–102 in Castellino's edition:

> uru-a KI.KAŠ.GAR-e mu-⌜da⌝-a[n-...]
> e-ne-di ḫúl-la gar-ra-šè gá-x-x-[...]
>
> In the city (Nippur) I(?) [...] a banquet,
> for the joyous games I ...

During the course of the celebrations Ur-Nammu poured out libations to the god Enlil (line 106: ᵈen-líl-ra tin làl ba-an-na-dé), and in return for these offerings Enlil was asked to bless the king (line 107): sipa ur-ᵈnammu-me-en ti nì-ba-mu ḫé-a "I am shepherd Ur-Nammu, may life be my reward."

We may ask, then, what occasion prompted this remarkable banquet in Nippur. An answer to the question is suggested by an earlier event that took place during the reign of King Lugal-zage-si of Uruk. Lugal-zage-si's well-known votive inscription to Enlil is inscribed on a large number of stone fragments that were found in the area of the Ekur temple. Commenting on these vessel fragments Westenholz (RLA 7 [1987] p. 156) writes:

> The occasion for the dedication of such a large number of cups or vases is likely to have been the coronation in Nippur of L[ugal-zage-si] as "King of the Land" ... Each cup could then represent one of the ensis who acknowledged his suzerainty; cf. Sargon's remark about the 50 ensis allied with L[ugal-zage-si].

Now, it is clear, as revealed by the titulary used by Ur-Nammu, that a highly significant change in the king's status occurred during the period when the Nanna temple was under construction in Ur. In the cone inscription commemorating the construction of the temenos wall (E3/2.1.1.11) Ur-Nammu appears with the simple titles "mighty man, king of Ur," whereas in the corresponding brick inscription (E3/2.1.1.12) the king has added the titles "lord of Uruk, and king of the lands of Sumer and Akkad." The last epithet was likely adopted by the king only after his trip to Nippur, when, on the death of Utu-ḫegal, his claim to exercise hegemony in the lands of Sumer and Akkad was duly recognized by the authorities in Nippur.

Of interest is the fact that the account of Ur-Nammu's trip to Nippur in Ur-Nammu C finds parallels in two other literary compositions, namely "Nanna-Suen's Journey to Nippur" (edition A.J. Ferrara, Nanna-Suen's Journey) and the hymn Ur-Nammu D (see W.W. Hallo, JCS 20 [1966] pp. 139–41).

The former composition describes a trip that Nanna-Suen made to Nippur; on his arrival in the religious capital, the moon god presented various gifts and offerings to Enlil. A banquet was then celebrated; on its conclusion Nanna-Suen petitioned Enlil to grant the kingship and abundance of the land to him. Enlil apparently consented to Nanna's request, since the composition ends with a blessing of the unnamed king.

Now, there are striking parallels between lines found in the hymn Ur-Nammu C and "Nanna-Suen's Journey to Nippur." In the former text, for example, lines 104–105 read:

> kar-geštin-na ᵈen-líl-lá-šè má na-an-ga-mu-ni-in-ús!
> kar-za-gìn-na ᵈnanna-ka má na-an-ga-mu-ni-in-ús!

Both at the "wine quay" of the god Enlil I moored the ship
(And) at the "shining quay" of the god Nanna I moored the ship.

These lines may be compared with lines found in "Nanna-Suen's Journey to Nippur" (lines 254–57):

kar-za-gìn kar-^{d}en-líl-lá-šè
^{d}nanna ^{d}EN.ZU-e GIŠ.má na-ga-àm-mi-in-ús
kar-babbar kar-^{d}en-líl-lá-šè
^{d}aš-ím-bábbar-e GIŠ.má na-ga-àm-mi-in-ús

Both at the "luminous quay" of the god Enlil,
the god Nanna-Suen moored the ship,
(And) at the "luminous quay" of the god Enlil,
The god Ašimbabbar moored the ship.

Furthermore, as noted by C. Wilcke (CRRA 19 p. 187–88 n. 12 and by the same author in K. Raaflaub, Anfänge pp. 38–39 and nn. 49–51), there is a remarkable similarity between the benison found in "Nanna-Suen's Journey to Nippur" and an excerpt from the hymn Ur-Nammu D. The former passage (line numbers 349–352 in Ferrara's edition, transliteration and translation following Wilcke) reads:

lugal-mu bára-za ^{d}en-líl-lá
^{d}nanna-(ar) ^{d}EN.ZU-(e) u_4-imin ḫé/ši-(bí)-a-ù-tu
bára-kù-(za) ama(/ama!)-gal ^{d}nin-líl-lá
(en) ^{d}aš-ím-babbar-(e) u_4-imin(u+ia) ḫé/⌜ši⌝-(⌜bí⌝!)-aù-tu

My lord, for your dais, (O child) of the god Enlil,
The god Nanna-Suen, (in) seven days you have truly fashioned (it)!
For your shining dais, (child) of the great mother the goddess Ninlil,
The god, lord Ašimbabbar, (in) seven days you have truly fashioned (it)!

The corresponding section of the hymn Ur-Nammu D, on the other hand (lines 7–13 according to the numbering of W.W. Hallo, JCS 20 [1966] pp. 139–41), reads:

lugal-mu bára-za ^{d}en-líl-le en-^{d}aš-ím-babbar
šul-^{d}EN.ZU bára-za ^{d}en-líl-le en-^{d}aš-ím-babbar
lugal šà-zi-ta nam-tar-ra nam-nir-ra sag íl
ur-^{d}nammu šul igi-íl-la kur-[gal] ^{d}en-líl-le
^{d}nu-nam-nir-re ki-en-gi ⌜ki-uri-a⌝ gá-e mu-en-suḫ-en
nibru.KI-a ḫur-sag nam-ti-⌜la-ka⌝ nam-mu im-mi-in-du_{10}
sag-ki-zalag-ga-ni mu-un-ši-bar ⌜nam⌝-lugal ⌜ma⌝-an-⌜sum⌝

Oh my lord (Suen), for your throne has the god Enlil, oh lord the god Ašimbabbar,
Oh youth god Suen, for your throne has god Enlil, oh lord god Ašimbabbar,
(It is me) the king whose fate has been destined from the true womb, who carries (his) head proudly,
(It is me) Ur-Nammu, the young man selected by the [great] mountain, the god Enlil,
(It is) me, whom the god Nunamnir has chosen in the land of Sumer and Akkad.

> In Nippur, in (the temple) of the mountain of life, he has made my destiny favourable.
> He has looked approvingly at me, has given kingship to me.

Now, while a number of features of the Yale exemplar of Ur-Nammu D enumerated by Hallo clearly indicate that the original redaction of the Yale version took place in post-Ur III times, possibly around the time of Išme-Dagān of Isin, the subsequent discovery of a Nippur tablet (UM 29-16-93) inscribed with a version of the hymn that entirely omits the anachronistic features found in the Yale tablet, suggests that that Nippur version was indeed a product of the Ur III period. If this be true, then the evidence presented in this study would suggest a specific date of composition during the reign of Ur-Nammu.

As noted by Sallaberger (Kalender 1 pp. 53–54), four archival texts from the times of Šulgi and Amar-Suena record offerings to Enlil and Ninlil as gifts from the god Su᾿en. Sallaberger (Kalender 1 p. 54) writes: "Man denkt dabei an einen Ritus, wie er im Mythos 'Nannas Fahrt nach Nippur' uberliefert ist: Nanna bringt Gaben zu seinem Vater Enlil und erhält dafür als Geschenk das Gedeihen des Landes zugesichert." A further allusion to this practice in Ur III times is found in the hymn Šulgi F (lines 13-16; see Michalowski, Lamentation p. 97; cf. Wilcke, CRRA 19 p. 201 n. 131):

> ià du_{10}-a-bi gára du_{10}-a-bi
> ^{d}nanna-a nì-mu-a a-a-ni ^{d}en-lil-ra tùr kù-ta
> mu-na-ni-in-ku_4-ku_4
> má nisag-g[á-k]e_4-si um-sá
> ^{d}en-líl-ra nibru.KI tùm-dè

> The god Nanna took the first quality butter and cheese from the pen, the yearly produce, for his father, the god Enlil, he loaded it on the ship of first fruit offerings in order to bring (them) to the god Enlil (in) Nippur ...

(g) [**mu é-^{d}nanna ba-dù-a** "The year the temple of the god Nanna was built."]

Ur-Nammu's rebuilding of the E-temen-ni-guru temple complex at Ur was arguably the most notable achievement of the king and we would expect that such a vast undertaking would have been commemorated in an (as yet unattested) year name. This hypothesis is supported by the occurrence of a temporal clause found in two royal inscriptions (E3/2.1.1.18 and E3/2.1.1.47): u_4 é-^{d}nanna mu-dù-a "when he built the temple of the god Nanna." An examination of the corpus of royal inscriptions and year names for the Ur III and Isin-Larsa/Old Babylonian period reveals that, in a majority of cases, temporal clauses in royal inscriptions can be correlated with year names; for several examples, see Frayne, Correlations pp. 509–13. In addition to the various royal inscriptions and a possible year name, the completion(?) of work on the Nanna temple in Ur is apparently alluded to in line 109 of the hymn Ur-Nammu C: é-kiš-nu-gál ḫur-sag-sig_7(collated)-ga-gin_7 ki-gal-la bí-gub "I set E-kišnugal like a yellow mountain, on its platform."

(h) **mu ur-^{d}nammu lugal-e sig-ta IGI.NIM-šè gìr si bí-sá-a** "The year Ur-Nammu, the king, put the 'road' in order from below to above." AO 3891, AO 3332, AO 3331: Thureau-Dangin, RTC nos. 261–263 and L. 7983: Delaporte, ITT 4 no. 7983.

The ordering of year names (h) to (i) follows the scheme proposed by Waetzoldt (in NABU 1990 p. 4 no. 6); years (h) to (i) correspond to years 4–5 in his list. Waetzoldt writes:

> Die Reihenfolge der Jahresdaten Urnammus ist noch immer nicht fixiert. RTC 264, IV 1 ff. gestattet m. E. zu bestimmen, wieviele Jahre zwischen dem "Jahr Urabba (wurde)

> Stadtfürst" (IV 5) und dem "Jahr (nachdem) der Sohn Urnammus zum En-Priester Inannas (IV 6) bestimmt wurde", fehlen. Nach den Spuren ist RTC 264 IV 1 zu lesen: ⸢šu-nígin⸣ 42 ù[zl!?]. Diese Zwischensumme entspricht genau 1/3 der Endsumme in IV 3 šu-nígin 126 ùz GIŠ.KU. Demnach haben wir in RTC 264 aller Wahrscheinlichkeit nach eine Abrechnung über die Lieferung von Ziegen in 3 Jahren vor uns. Zwischen dem Jahr mu Ur-ab-ba énsi und mu en-^{d}inanna ... fehlt folglich nur 1 weiterer Jahresname. In Frage kommt dafür besonders mu Ur-^{d}Nammu lugal-e sig-ta igi-nim-šè gìri si bí-sa-a (RTC 263; dort auch Urabba énsi; 262).

If Waetzoldt's scheme be correct, then year name (h) would be the first Ur-Nammu year name that is actually attested in archival texts from Girsu. A possible allusion to the event commemorated in the year name may be found in the hymn Ur-Nammu C (line 19): [u]r-^{d}[na]mmu lugal-úri.KI-ma nam-du_{10} tar-ra-DU/ gìr si mu-un-da-ab-sá "[U]r-[Na]mmu, king of Ur, a favourable destiny having been determined (for him) — ... put the 'road' in order." The line of the hymn is somewhat obscure; if Ur-Nammu indeed be the subject, we would expect to find an ergative marker -ke_4 after lugal-úri.KI-ma.

The "putting in order" of the road is also alluded to (in a restored passage) in the prologue of the Ur-Nammu Law Code. The translation of the relevant section follows that given by M. Roth (Roth, Law Collections p. 16), who, in turn, followed suggestions of M. Civil. It reads:

> At that time, [I regulated] the river-boat traffic on the banks of the Tigris River, on the banks of the Euphrates River, on the banks of all rivers. [I secured safe roads for] the couriers(?); I [built] the (roadside) house. [I planted] the orchard, the king, placed a gardener in charge of them.

The lines are comparable to a section of the hymn Šulgi A (lines 28–33; transliteration Klein, Three Šulgi Hymns pp. 190–91) that similarly recorded measures to ensure the safe passage of travellers:

> gìr ḫu-mu-gur kaskal-kalam-ma-ke_4 si ḫé-em-sá-sá
> danna ḫu-mu-gi é-gal-la ḫé-bí-dù
> zà-ba $kiri_6$ ḫé-bí-gub ki-ní-dúb-bu ḫé-bí-gar
> ki-bé lú-zu-a ḫé-em-mi-tuš
> sig-ta du igi-nim-ta du-e
> á-$šed_x$(MÙŠ.DI)-bi-šè ní ḫé-eb-ši-te-en-te-en
>
> I ... the roads, I put the highways of the land in order.
> I established mile-(markers) and set them in "great houses."
> I planted gardens by their side, established resting-places
> there.
> I settled in those places experienced (men).
> (As for he) who comes from "above," (or he) who comes
> from "below,"
> May they refresh themselves in their cool *shade*.

Of interest is the fact that both the Ur-Nammu (if restored correctly) and the Šulgi passages refer to the establishment of way-stations for travelers and the planting of gardens beside them.

Now, as revealed by the prologue of the Ur-Nammu Law Code, the putting in order of the roads of the land was but one of several reforms instituted by Ur-Nammu:

(h) (i) The return of the Magan trade to Ur

Inscriptions E3/2.1.1.17–18, which allude to the construction of the temple of the god Nanna in Ur, refer to Ur-Nammu's restoration of the Magan trade to Ur for the god Nanna.

(h) (ii) The promulgation of the "Ur-Nammu Law Code"

The king's establishment of justice in the land is alluded to in the hymn Ur-Nammu C (line 38): nì-si-sá pa-è bí-ak nì-érim sá bí-du$_{11}$ "I made justice manifest, I overtook the evildoer." This line may well allude to Ur-Nammu's promulgation of his famous "law code"; its prologue and concluding formula are edited as inscription E3/2.1.1.20 in this volume. Now, the historical allusions found in the prologue of the "law code" enable us to determine, at least in general terms, its probable date of composition. Most valuable for this purpose are lines 79–84: ki-⌈SAR⌉-ra má-má-gan.KI-na ^{d}nanna á-^{d}nanna lugal-⌈gá⌉-ta ḫé-mi-gi$_{4}$ "By the might of the god Nanna, my lord, I returned to (the) ki-SAR-ra Nanna's Magan ship." As noted, the restoration of the Magan trade occurred a short time after the building of Nanna's temple at Ur.

(h) (iii) The incorporation of new territories into the Ur III kingdom

Lines 125–134 of the prologue of the "Ur-Nammu Law Code" gives a list of various northern regions, once subservient to Anšan, that were liberated by the king of Ur. The list corresponds to a remarkable degree with the toponyms found in the so-called "Ur-Nammu Cadastre," a text that is edited as inscription E3/2.1.1.21 in this volume. The following chart gives the details:

Ur-Nammu Law Code (E3/2.1.1.20)	Ur-Nammu Cadastre (E3/2.1.1.21)
line 126: GIŠ.ÚḪ.KI(Umma)	Ex. 3 frgm. 11 col. ii′: Cities in the Umma region are listed
line 127: már-da.KI (Marad)	Ex. 2 iv 29–30: ki-sur-ra-^{d}lugal-már-da-ke$_{4}$ már-da.KI-ke$_{4}$(?) "the boundary of the god Lugal-marada of Marad"
line 127: GÍR-kal.KI =? Irkal. See Frayne (Early Dynastic List p. 26) for a suggestion that the city GÍR-kal was located on the Kazallu canal a short distance northwest of ancient Apiak	Ex. 1 ii 20–21: ki-sur-ra-^{d}mes-lam-ta-è-a a-pi$_{5}$-ak.KI-e "Boundary of the god Meslamtaea of Apiak"
line 128: ka-za-lu.KI (Kazallu)	Ex. 1 i 5: I$_{7}$.ka-zal-lu.KI "the Kazallu canal"
line 129: ú-ṣa-ru-um.KI (Uṣarum)	Ex. 1 ii 24: ú!(Text: MA)-ṣa-ru-um

(i) mu en-^{d}inanna-unu.KI-a dumu-ur-^{d}nammu lugal-a maš-e ba-pà-da "The year the *en* of the goddess Inanna of Uruk, offspring of Ur-Nammu, was chosen by omens." AO 3330: Thureau-Dangin, RTC no. 264.

If the ordering of Ur-Nammu year names proposed by Waetzoldt be correct, then the year name dealing with the installation of the *en* of the goddess Inanna should immediately follow year name (h). Now, it is clear that Ur-Nammu did not control Uruk when he acceded to the throne of Ur. His adoption, part way through his reign, of the title "lord of Uruk" (en-unu.KI-ga) attests to his having gained control over Inanna's cult city. The epithet is found in only two royal inscriptions: E3/2.1.1.12 and E3/2.1.1.46; thus it apparently was not retained as part of the standard royal titulary. This fact, then, suggests that the two aforementioned inscriptions date to the time shortly after the king's annexation of Uruk. Just as one of Ur-Nammu's first acts after his accession at Ur was his installation of his daughter as *en* of the god Nanna, so year name (i) tells us that a family member was inaugurated as *en* at Uruk shortly after Uruk's incorporation.

(j) mu GIŠ.gigir-^{d}nin-líl ba-dím-ma "The year the chariot of the goddess Ninlil was fashioned." AO 3364: Thureau-Dangin, RTC no. 266; L 7544, 7546 and 7550: Delaporte, ITT 4 nos. 7544, 7546 and 7550.

While Sollberger (AfO 17 [1954–56] p. 15) assigned year name (j) as year three of Šulgi, the fact that all the early year names of Šulgi can now be otherwise accounted for makes its ascription to Ur-Nammu a much more likely proposition. Proof that a cult chariot of the goddess Ninlil existed in Ur III times at Nippur is found in archival texts that refer to offerings for Ninlil's chariot at Nippur (see AO 5501: de Genouillac, TCL 2 no. 5501 col. ii line 20 [dated to Š 47] and PD 1173: Yıldız and Gomi, PDT 2 no. 1173 col. ii line 16 [dated to AS 1]; these references are cited from Sallaberger, Kalender 1 p. 100). We have placed the year name dealing with the chariot of the goddess Ninlil following year name (i) based on comparative evidence from the reliefs of the Ur-Nammu stele; one of the registers depicts a large chariot (Ninlil's chariot?) set in a swamp-like setting (= her cult centre Tummal?). I intend to examine the details of this hypothesis in a separate study of the Ur-Nammu year names.

(k) [mu é]-⸢^{d}⸣nin-súna [úri.KI]-⸢a⸣ ba-dù-a "[The year the temple] of the goddess Ninsuna [of Ur] was built." AO 3329: Thureau-Dangin, RTC no. 265.

While no royal name appears in year name (k), it has always been ascribed by scholars to Ur-Nammu. The construction of Ninsuna's temple in Ur is commemorated in a stone foundation tablet which is edited as inscription E3/2.1.1.23 in this volume. The titulary of the king found in this inscription clearly dates the construction to the time after the king's trip to Nippur. We follow Waetzoldt (NABU 1990 p. 4 no. 6) in placing year name (k) shortly after year name (i).

(l) [mu é-^{d}en-líl-lá ba-dù-a "The year the temple of the god Enlil was built."]

While this postulated year name of Ur-Nammu dealing with the construction of the temple of Enlil has not yet appeared from archival sources, various data point to its probable existence. A temporal clause in inscription E3/2.1.1.28 (lines 8–9) reads: u_4 é-^{d}en-líl-lá in-dù-a "when he built the temple of the god Enlil" and, as noted, temporal clauses in royal inscriptions almost invariably allude to actual year names. The construction of Enlil's temple in Nippur was, along with the building of the Nanna temple in Ur, a major achievement of Ur-Nammu's reign; the deed was recorded in two building inscriptions (E3/2.1.1.24–25) and alluded to in two canal inscriptions (E3/2.1.1.26 and 28). Not surprisingly, a royal hymn dedicated to the god Enlil was composed to memorialize the Ekur's construction. The hymn is known from five tablet copies: (a) Ni 2430: Chiera, SRT no. 11, edition G. Castellino, ZA 53 (1959) pp. 106–18; (b) AO 6316: de Genouillac, TRS no. 38, edition Å. Sjöberg, OrSuec 10 (1961) pp. 3–5; (c) CBS 15168 (+) N 7926 (+) N 6876: transliteration, M. Civil, Orientalia NS 54 (1985) pp. 36–37; (d) IM 61500: edition, M. Civil, Orientalia NS 54 (1985) pp. 33–36); (e) VAT 17417: van Dijk, VAS 24 no. 42, utilized by Klein in his new edition of Ur-Nammu G (ASJ 11 [1989] pp. 44–56).

Of interest is the fact that exemplar (d) was apparently an Ur III copy; its existence demonstrates that hymns praising the kings of Ur had entered the literary canon at Nippur already in Ur III times. This fact accords well with the evidence discussed by W.W. Hallo in his article "On the Antiquity of Sumerian Literature," JAOS 83 (1963) pp. 167–76; Hallo edits there an Ur III catalogue of royal hymns. He notes that some of the incipits found in the Yale tablet can be identified with well-known royal hymns.

(m) ⸢mu⸣ I_7.EN.ÉREN.NUN [ba]-al "The year the Iturungal canal was [d]ug." AO 4308: Thureau-Dangin, in Cros, Tello p. 185.

While no royal name is found in year name (m), there can be little doubt of its attribution to Ur-Nammu, since the digging of the Iturungal canal is recorded in two of the king's inscriptions (E3/2.1.1.26–27). The canal name is found in two writings: (a) I_7.EN.ERÉN.NUN (E3/2.1.1.26 line 9) and (b) I_7.EN.ŠEŠ.GAL (E3/2.1.1.27 line 8); similar variants occur in the copies of the Utu-ḫegal inscription dealing with the expulsion of the Gutians: (a) I_7.ÉREN.NUN.NA (=RA 10 [1913] p. 99 rev. 3) and (b) I_7.EN.ÙRU.GAL (= RA 9 [1912] p. 113 iii 12). Lexical evidence cited by Edzard (see RLA 5/3, sub Iturungal) indicates pronunciations: *i-tu-ru-un-gal, i-su-ru-(en)-gal*, and *i-dar-en-gal* for this canal name. The first reading is conventional, and has been employed here. For the latest detailed discussion of the various writings of the canal name Iturungal and a study of the location of the canal's watercourse, see F. Carroué, "L'Iturungal et le Sud Sumérien," ASJ 15 (1993) pp. 11–69.

Cones dealing with Ur-Nammu's digging of the Iturungal canal were found at Didiqqah, Tell al-Madāʾin (ancient Bad-tibira), and Uruk. This accords well with Jacobsen's tracing of the route of the Iturungal canal (Iraq 22 [1960] p. 177): "The line of its course was picked up in the Survey of Central Sumer at Bismayah (Adab), from where it continued southward over Jidr, past Bzeikh (Zabalam), over Jokha (Umma), Umm-el-Aqarib, Mansuriyah to Madinah (Bàd-tibira). Here it veered west over Able and Senkerah (Larsa) to junction with the Euphrates again."

The fact that inscription E3/2.1.1.26 mentions Ur-Nammu's building of the Enlil temple in its opening lines securely dates the digging of the Iturungal canal to the time shortly after the Ekur's construction.

(n) mu nin-dingir-ᵈiškur maš-e pà-da "The year the *nin-dingir* priestess of the god Iškur was chosen by omens." AO 3358: Thureau-Dangin, RTC no. 257; L 7771: Delaporte, ITT 4 no. 7771; L 39705: M. Çığ, in Kramer Anniversary pp. 78 and 81 no. 10.

This unplaced year name of early Ur III date was assigned "probablement" to Ur-Nammu by Thureau-Dangin (RA 5 [1898] pp. 70–71 n. 5); to Šulgi by Kraus (Orientalia NS 20 [1951] p. 392); and to Ur-Nammu by Sollberger (AfO 17 [1954–56] p. 12). Again, since all the early Šulgi year names can now be accounted for, year name (n) is likely to belong to Ur-Nammu. The year name attests to the king's concern for the cult of the god Iškur; while the god's cult city is not named in the year name, it is likely to have been Karkar. Several Ur III archival texts record offerings to the god Iškur at Karkar; for the references, see Edzard, Rép. Géogr. 2 p. 92 and Sallaberger, Kalender 1 p. 226. Evidence points to a location of ancient Karkar on the Iturungal canal south of the cities of Adab and Šarrākum. It has been plausibly located at modern Tell Jidr (see Powell, JNES 39 [1980] pp. 47–52 and Frayne, Early Dynastic List p. 37). We may also note in this connection, that inscription E3/2.1.1.36, records construction work at the city of Šarrākum just north of Karkar, and year name (q) commemorates the digging of a canal that likely flowed in the vicinity of Šarrākum or Adab.

(o) mu uš-é-ᵈnin-gublaga ki ba-a-gar "The year the foundations of the temple of the god Ningublaga were laid." AO 3365: Thureau-Dangin, RTC 271; L 7268, 7662, and 7665: Delaporte, ITT 4 nos. 7268, 7662, and 7665; L 6737: de Genouillac, ITT 5 no. 6737.

Year names (o)–(q) appear in three Louvre tablets that were assigned by Thureau-Dangin to a specific group of tablets, his "cinquième série" (see the discussion in RTC on pp. vi–vii). In all likelihood, RTC 269–71 bear year names of Ur-Nammu that are to be placed at the very end of his reign. RTC 272–86, on the other hand, are year names from the first eleven years of Šulgi. The details have been set out in the following list.

RTC number	Year Name
269	wall of Ur (Ur-Nammu/or Šulgi?)
270	digging of Nintu canal (Ur-Nammu?)
271	foundations of Ningublaga temple (Ur-Nammu?)
272	Š 7 (associated by Thureau-Dangin with the coronation of the king)
273	Š 1 Šulgi king

RTC number	Year Name
274	Š 5 foundations of Ninurta temple
275	Š 6 year after the foundations of the Ninurta temple
276	year names Š 5–7
277	Š 7 round-trip of the king
278	Š 7 round-trip of the king
279	Š 7 round-trip of the king
280	Š 7 round-trip of the king
281	Š 8 boat of Ninlil
282	Š 9 year after the boat of Ninlil
283	Š 9 year after the boat of Ninlil
284	Š 10 é-ḫur-sag of the king
285	year names Š 10–11
286	Š 11 Ištarān of Dēr

Tablets of Thureau-Dangin's "cinquième série" belong to a Lagaš archive dealing with textiles that has been discussed in detail by H. Limet in an article entitled "Au début du règne de Šulgi," RA 65 (1971) pp. 15–21.

No royal name appears in year name (o). Whereas Kraus (Orientalia NS 20 [1951] p. 392) assigned the formula to Šulgi, Sollberger (AfO 17 [1954–56] p. 12) preferred an ascription to Ur-Nammu. We have followed Sollberger's attribution in this study.

Evidence from Isin-Larsa/Old Babylonian times points to the existence of a temple of Nin-gublaga at Ur in the SM area immediately to the south of the Gipar-ku (see Charpin, Le clergé d'Ur p. 330). The location of the Ur III temple is unknown.

(p) mu bàd-uri$_5$.KI-ma ba-dù-a "The year the 'wall of Ur' was built." AO 3360: Thureau-Dangin, RTC no. 269 and L 7547: Delaporte, ITT 4 no. 7547.

While, as noted, inscription E3/2.1.1.4 commemorates the building of a structure known as the "wall of Ur," the titulary found in that inscription indicates an early date for the text, certainly before Ur-Nammu's trip to Nippur. The fact that year name (p) belongs to a group of texts that, for the most part, dates to the first ten years of Šulgi, argues that year name (p) should be placed either at the very end of the reign of Ur-Nammu or at the beginning of Šulgi's reign. The idea that there was construction work on the "wall of Ur" late in the reign of Ur-Nammu is supported by a passage from the literary composition "Death of Ur-Nammu" which reads (line 147; see Kramer, JCS 21 [1967] pp. 115 and 119): bàd-úri.KI-ma [n]u-mu-un-til-la-ni "(the wail) for the wall of Ur that he (Ur-Nammu) had not finished." Year name (p) apparently refers to a different building of the "wall of Ur" from the one commemorated in inscription E3/2.1.1.4.

(q) mu i$_7$-a-^{d}nin-tu ba-al "The year the A-Nintu canal was dug." AO 3362: Thureau-Dangin, RTC 270; L 8066: Delaporte, ITT 4 no. 8066; L. 6708: de Genouillac, ITT 5 no. 6708.

Sollberger (AfO 17 [1954–56] pp. 12–13), following Thureau-Dangin (RA 5 [1982] p. 70 n. 5), assigned year name (q) to Ur-Nammu. Again, the fact that this year name appears in a group of texts (RTC nos. 269–286) that date, in the main, to the first ten years of Šulgi, argues that it should be placed either at the very end of the reign of Ur-Nammu, or at the beginning of the reign of Šulgi. The canal named in year name (q) is composed with the divine name Nintu, one of the names of the birth goddess Ninḫursaga. Now, we know that Ur-Nammu built the sacred precinct of the goddess Ninḫursaga at Keš/Šarrākum (see E3/2.1.1.36), and for that reason we have tentatively assigned year name (q) to Ur-Nammu.

(r) Ur-Nammu's campaigns in the Diyālā region; the death of Ur-Nammu

Two inscriptions of Ur-Nammu (E3/2.1.1.29–30) describe wars the king waged in regions to the northeast of Sumer. In the first text (E3/2.1.1.29), the king's antagonist is named to be the Elamite king Kutik-Inšušinak and the locale of hostilities is said to have been highland Elam. As a consequence of the battle the territories of "Awal, Kismar, Maškan-šarrum, the [la]nd of Ešnunna, the [la]nd of Tutub, the [lan]d of Simudar, the [lan]d of Akkad" were apparently liberated from the yoke of the Elamites. In the second inscription (E3/2.1.1.30) Ur-Nammu's foes are said to have been both the Elamites and the Gutians, and the area of conflict described as "the district of Guti and Simudar." Now, there is a distinct Sumerian literary tradition of Ur-Nammu having fallen on the field of battle; a passage from literary composition "Death of Ur-Nammu" (Kramer, JCS 21 [1967] pp. 113 and 118, line 59) reads: [ki]-lul-la ur-^{d}nammu dug-gaz-gin$_7$ ba-ni-in-tag$_4$-aš "In the place of slaughter they abandoned Ur-Nammu like a broken pitcher." If we were to see the Gutians as the agents of Ur-Nammu's destruction, this would harmonize with Wilcke's contention (C. Wilcke, CRRA 19 [1974] pp. 181–82, now followed by Klein, CRRA 33 [1987] p. 105) that the hymn Šulgi D+X describes a war that the young Šulgi waged against Gutium in order to avenge the murder of his father.

II. Another Year Name Sometimes Attributed to Ur-Nammu

The year name found on AO 3350: Thureau-Dangin, RTC no. 191: mu I$_7$.giš-šub-ba ba-ba-al-la "The year the canal 'brick mold' was dug," was assigned by Sollberger (AfO 17 [1954–56] p. 13) to Ur-Nammu. However, the fact that the tablet in question belongs to a group that Thureau-Dangin (RTC p. IV) assigned to pre-Ur III times would argue against Sollberger's attribution, and we have not listed it in our series of possible Ur-Nammu year names.

1

A clay tablet from Nippur provides a copy of an apparent monumental inscription of Ur-Nammu.

COMMENTARY

The tablet, which bears the museum number Ni 4375 (Istanbul), was found in excavations of the old expedition of the University of Pennsylvania to Nippur. The rulings of the tablet break the text into sections of varying length; they probably correspond to section divisions of an original monument. As noted, the text records deeds that may date to an early period of the reign of Ur-Nammu: (1) the king's carrying out the rites of *en*-ship; (2) the determining of a new boundary (or boundaries) for Ur; (3) the defeat of the Gutians; and (4) the construction of the wall of Ur.

For the restoration of iv 12′, cf. de Genouillac, TCL 15 no. 12, line 113: numun-nam-en-na-me-en. Lines 7′–9′ of col. iv are taken to be one clause despite the ruling after line 8′. Lines given in the RIM transliteration and translation columns correspond to the line divisions on the tablet.

BIBLIOGRAPHY

1969 Çığ and Kızılyay, ISET 1 pl. 119 (p. 177) (copy)

TEXT

Col. iv Lacuna 1′) x [...]	Lacuna iv 1′) ...
2′) ^{d}[ur-^{d}nammu] 3′) lugal [...] 4′) gu-t[i-um.KI ...] 5′) lú-x-[...] 6′) kur-ba im-m[i-x-(x)]	iv 2′–6′) (I), [Ur-Nammu], king [...], Guti[um ...], the ..., in its mountain [I ...].
7′) en lug[al ...] 8′) ⸢dusu⸣-ta [...]	iv 7′–9′) (I), the lord, the ki[ng], from corvée [...] stopped.
9′) gá-la x [... dag] 10′) ^{d}u[r-^{d}nammu] 11′) nam-lu[gal ...] 12′) numun-na[m-en-na] 13′) u[ri$_5$.KI-ma] 14′) bàd-b[i mu-dù]	iv 10′–14′) (I), U[r-Nammu], who [...] king[ship], offspring of [*en*]-sh[ip], [built] the wall of U[r].
15′) ^{d}u[r-^{d}nammu] 16′) x x [...] Lacuna	iv 15′–16′) (I), U[r-Nammu] ... Lacuna
Col. v Lacuna 1′) [^{d}u]r-⸢^{d}nammu⸣ 2′) ⸢x x⸣ nam-en-né 3′) šu ḫé-bí-du$_7$	Lacuna v 1′–3′) (I), [U]r-Nammu, ... seed, carried out *en*-ship perfectly.
4′) nam-tar-ra x x ⸢NI!⸣ 5′) é(Text: GÁ)-kiš-[nu-gál]-⸢la⸣(?) 6′) é(Text: GÁ)-e x [...] x 7′) ⸢kalam/un⸣ [...] x 8′) igi [...] x ⸢x⸣	v 4′–5′) Destiny, ..., the E-kiš[nugal], v 6′–8′) at the temple, the land/people ...
9′) lu[gal ...] [z]i(?) ak 10′) mu-m[u x]-peš-⸢e⸣(?)	v 9′–10′) (I), the k[ing...], [li]fe(?), m[y] name ....
11′) ^{d}ur-⸢^{d}nammu⸣ 12′) in-dub-ki-en-gi-⸢ra⸣ 13′) KA ba-gi-na-ba	v 11′–13′) (I), Ur-Nammu, after having confirmed the (new) border of the land of Sumer,
14′) [x] x x x x KI-a-ke$_4$ Lacuna	v 14′) ... Lacuna
Col. vi Lacuna 1′) [...] x 2′) [...] x 3′) [...] x 4′) [...] x-me-[e]n	Lacuna vi 1′–4′) ..., [a]m I.
5′) [...]-ba 6′) [...] ⸢x⸣-me-en	vi 5′–6′) ..., ..., am I.
7′) [^{d}ur]-⸢^{d}⸣nammu 8′) [... ki-e]n-gi-ra 9′) [...] x-me-en	vi 7′–9′) [Ur]-Nammu, [... of the land of S]umer, ..., am I.
10′) [...] x -da 11′) [... me]-⸢en⸣ Lacuna	vi 10′–11′) ..., am I. Lacuna

2

For the early period of Ur-Nammu's reign we have evidence of the king's building activities in only three cities: Ur, Kuʾar (probably modern Rejībah), and Eridu. Inscriptions dating to this period are edited in this volume as inscriptions E3/2.1.1.2–8. The most noteworthy accomplishment of this time was the king's rebuilding of the temple of the god Nanna, patron deity of his capital city.

The reconstruction of the Nanna temple complex can be divided into two phases. The earlier phase involved the construction of the ziqqurrat core and rooms immediately to its northwest. In the bricks and door sockets commemorating this work, which are edited as this inscription, the king appears with the simple title "king of Ur." A second phase of the construction saw the erection of the great temenos wall E-temen-ni-guru. This latter work is commemorated in E3/2.1.1.11–12.

CATALOGUE A

Ex.	Museum number	Excavation number	Registration number	Ur provenance	Dimensions (cm)	Lines preserved	cpn
Bricks							
1	BM 90002	—	1979-12-20, 3	From the lower story of the ziqqurrat	28.5×28×5	1–4	c
2	BM 90003	—	1979-12-20, 4	As ex. 1	32×32×6	1–4	c
3	BM 90020	—	51-1-1, 289	As ex. 1	29×28.5×5.5	1–4	c
4	BM 90790	—	1979-12-20, 352	As ex. 1	29.5×23.5×5.5	1–4	c
5	BM 90791+90793	—	1979-12-20, 353	As ex. 1	27.5×18.5×6.5	1–4	c
6	BM 90801	—	1979-12-20, 358	As ex. 1	23×18×6	1–4	c
7	BM 114226	—	1919-10-11, 4657	—	29.2×29.2×7.6	—	n
8	BM 114227	—	1919-10-11, 4658	As ex. 1	29×20.5×5	1–4	c
9	BM 114229	—	1919-10-11, 4660	As ex. 1	29.5×29.5×5	1–4	c
10	BM 114230	—	1919-10-11, 4661	As ex. 1	29.5×29.5×6	1–4	c
11	BM 114236	—	1919-10-11, 4667	As ex. 1	29×29×5.5	1–4	c
12	BM 114237	—	1919-10-11, 4668	As ex. 1	30×29.5×6	—	c
13	BM 114239	—	1919-10-11, 4670	As ex. 1	11.4×6.3×5.7	—	c
14	BM 114244	—	1919-10-11, 4675	As ex. 1	16×13.5×7	1–4	c
15	BM 114246	—	1919-10-11, 4677	As ex. 1	30×29.5×6	1–4	c
16	BM 114254	—	1919-10-11, 4685	As ex. 1	29.5×29.5×5.5	1–4	c
17	BM 137357	—	1919-10-11, 5362	As ex. 1	29.5×17×6	1–4	c
18	BM 137495	—	1919-10-11, 116	From the ziqqurrat	31.5×31×6	1–4	c
19	CBS 15338	U 65(?)	—	—	29.5×29×6	1–4	n
20	CBS 16527	U 3132	—	No provenance given	25×14×5.5	1–4	n
21	Museo Barracco, Rome	—	—	—	—	1–4	n
22	Museo di Antichità di Torino	—	—	—	—	1–4	p
23	AO 26688	—	—	—	24.2×24.2×4.8	1–4	c
24	YBC 2384	—	—	—	30.5×29.5×6.5	1–4	c
25	BM 90904 (=BM 12032) (frgm. of bitumen)	—	—	—	7.6×6.35	1–3	c
26	Private collection	—	—	—	6.5×2.2×5.5	2–3	n

CATALOGUE B

Ex.	Museum number	Excavation number	Level	Provenance	UE publication	Lines preserved	Dimensions (cm)	cpn
Door sockets								
27	BM 90846	From Loftus's or Taylor's excavations	—	From the lower story of the ziqqurrat	—	1–4	50×28×20	c
28	CBS 15323	U 422	post-Ur III?	By the later door of room 17 of the E-nun-maḫ, SE end	6 p. 52	—	—	n
29	BM 115026	U 423	Ur III	Against the SW door jamb of room 11 of the E-nun-maḫ	6 p. 51	1–4	46×36×20	c
30	—	—	Ur III	SE side of ziqqurrat, by entry steps to temenos platform	5 pp. 26–27	—	—	n
31	IM 672	U 1357	—	P.R. room 5	—	—	72×49×27	n
32	IM 916	U 2675		Doorway EE to 7 LL		—	—	n
33	University Museum, no number	U 2749	Ur III	NW side of terrace, room immediately west of room 3	5 p. 31	1–4	55×42×19	c
34	IM 929	U 2749A	Ur III	NW side of terrace, room 6	—	—	—	n
35	IM 931	U 2750	Ur III	NW side of terrace, room 5	—	—	—	n
36	IM 938	U 2768	Ur III	NW side of terrace, room 1	5 p. 31	—	—	n
37	IM 940	U 2771	Ur III	NW side of terrace, room 3	5 p. 31	—	—	n
38	IM 941	U 2772	Ur III	NW side of terrace, room 2	5 p. 31	—	—	n
39	IM 963	U 2855	—	Found at "corner of drain in front of E-dublal-maḫ"	—	—	—	n
40	—	—	OB	Giparku, room A. 3	7 p. 44	—	—	n
41	—	—	OB	Giparku, room C. 25	7 p. 58	—	—	n
42	—	—	OB	Giparku, room C. 26	7 p. 58	—	—	n
43	—	—	Kassite	E-mu-ri-na-ba-ak	5 p. 50	—	—	n
44	—	—	Kassite	NW side of ziqqurrat, near room 13	5 p. 53	—	—	n
45	IM 1007	U 3032	Kassite	Ningal temple of Kurigalzu	5 p. 55	—	—	n
46	IM 1028	U 3103	—	ES 11	—	—	—	n
47	IM 1057	U 3172	Kassite	Ningal temple of Kurigalzu, room 6	5 p. 56	—	—	n
48	IM 1087	U 3261	NB	Ningal temple, room 6	5 p. 64	—	—	n
49	—	—	NB	Ningal temple, room 2	5 p. 63	—	—	n
50	—	—	NB	Ningal temple, room 1	5 p. 63	—	—	n
51	—	—	NB	E-gipar, room 5	9 p. 20	—	—	n
52	Philadelphia	—	—	—	—	1–4	—	c
Among the above are the following:								
A	IM—	U—	—	—	—	—	Stone: 44×33×21 Inscription: 8.5×6	p
B	IM—	U—	—	—	—	—	Stone: 45 ×35×22 Inscription: 10.2×7.5	p
C	IM—	U—	—	—	—	—	Stone: 26 ×27×9 Inscription: 9.6×7.3	p
D	IM—	U—	—	—	—	—	Stone: 70 ×40×25 Inscription: 10.7×7.8	p
E	IM—	U—	—	—	—	—	Stone: 35×60 Inscription: 9×7.2	p
F	IM—	U—	—	—	—	—	Stone: 35×60 Inscription: 9×7.2	p

COMMENTARY

Exs. 1–18 were collated by C.B.F. Walker. Ex. 3 comes from the excavations of Loftus, exs. 7–17 from those of Hall, and exs. 18–20 from those of Woolley. Door sockets A–F, part of the Iraq Museum's collections, were last seen near the Mosul dig house. Behrens (JCS 37 [1985] p. 230) lists CBS 15338 (ex. 19) as having the excavation number U 65; according to the Ur registry book, the object in question is a clay figurine. Ex. 28's museum number is known only from a note of Woolley in UE 6 p. 90. The piece could not be located in Philadelphia. Information on ex. 46 was kindly provided by H. Steible. The text is arranged in one column of four lines.

BIBLIOGRAPHY

1861 1 R I 1 (exs. 1–6, composite copy)
1863 Oppert, EM 1 p. 261 (exs. 1–6, translation)
1872 Smith, TSBA 1 p. 35 (exs. 1–6, translation)
1874 Lenormant, Études accadiennes 2 p. 303 (exs. 1–6, translation)
1875 Ménant, Babylone p. 74 (exs. 1–6, translation)
1879 Lenormant, Bullettino della Commissione Archeologica di Roma pp. 25–32 and pl. 6 (ex. 21, copy, edition)
1892 Winckler, KB 3/1 pp. 76–77 Ur-gur 1 (exs. 1–6, edition)
1899 Bezold, Cat. 5 p. 2233 (exs. 1–6, study)
1905 King, CT 21 pl. 4 BM 90801 (ex. 6, copy)
1907 Thureau-Dangin, SAK pp. 186–87 Ur-engur a (exs. 1–6, edition)

1922 BM Guide p. 60 nos. 33–34 (exs. 1–2, study)
1925 Woolley and Legrain, MJ 16 p. 296 (ex. 33, photo)
1928 Gadd, UET 1 p. xxiv (study)
1929 Barton, RISA pp. 270–71 Ur-Nammu 1 (exs. 1–6, edition); pp. 272–73 Ur-Nammu 12 (ex. 52, edition)
1936 Boson, Aegyptus 15 p. 420 (ex. 22, photo, edition)
1937 Stephens, YOS 9 no. 115 (ex. 24, study)
1962 Hallo, HUCA 33 p. 24 Ur-Nammu 1 (exs. 1–6, 22, 24, study)
1971 Sollberger and Kupper, IRSA IIIA1b (exs. 1–6, 22, 24, translation)
1981 Grégoire, MVN 10 no. 24 (ex. 26, copy)
1981 Walker, CBI no. 12 (exs. 1–18, study)
1985 Behrens, JCS 37 pp. 230–31 (exs. 19–20, study)
1986 Kärki, KDDU p. 1 Urnammu 1 (exs. 1–18, 22, 24, 52, edition)
1991 Steible, NSBW 2 pp. 93–94 Urnammu 1 (exs. 1–26, 29, 33, 52, edition)

TEXT

1) ur-^{d}nammu
2) lugal-uri$_5$.KI-ma
3) lú é-^{d}nanna
4) in-dù-a

1–2) Ur-Nammu, king of Ur,
3–4) the one who built the temple of the god Nanna.

3

A copper hemispherical cup in the Ligabue Collection bears a five-line inscription of Ur-Nammu that is identical to the previous inscription.

COMMENTARY

The copper cup is said to have come from Luristan. The inscription was collated from the published photo.

BIBLIOGRAPHY

1989 Fales, Alfabeto p. 91 no. 13 (photo, edition)

TEXT

1) ur-^{d}nammu
2) lugal-uri$_5$.KI-ma
3) lú é-
4) ^{d}nanna
5) in-dù-a

1–2) Ur-Nammu, king of Ur,
3–5) the one who built the temple of the god Nanna.

E3/2.1.1.2.4 52 in-ni-dù.

4

As part of construction work at his capital city, Ur-Nammu built the great wall named the "wall of Ur." The deed is commemorated in an eight-line stamped brick inscription that also mentions the construction of Nanna's temple. Although commentators have generally taken this inscription to refer to the city wall of Ur, the findspots of the bricks suggest that it was the wall of the sacred temenos (see commentary below). The fact that Ur-Nammu appears in this inscription without the title "king of the lands of Sumer and Akkad" indicates a date for this text in the early period of his reign.

CATALOGUE

Ex.	Museum number	Excavation number	Registration number	Ur provenance	Dimensions (cm)	Lines preserved	cpn
1	BM 90004	—	1979-12-20, 5	—	36.5×36.5×8.5	1–8	c
2	BM 90009	—	1979-12-20, 9	—	37.5×36.5×9	1–8	c
3	BM 90011	—	1979-12-20, 11	—	37×36.5×10	1–8	c
4	BM 90012	—	1979-12-20, 12	—	37.5×28.5×9.5	1–8	c
5	BM 90797	—	1979-12-20, 356	Ur	28×26×8.5	2–4, 6–8	c
6	BM 114228	—	1919-10-11, 4659	From the E-ḫursag area	38.1×37.5×7.5	1–8	c
7	BM 114231	—	1919-10-11, 4662	As ex. 6	25×21×9	1–8	c
8	BM 114232	—	1919-10-11, 4663	As ex. 6	37×26×8.5	1–8	c
9	BM 114233+114235	—	1919-10-11, 4664+ 1919-10-11, 4666	As ex. 6	36×34×10	1–8	c
10	BM 114238	—	1919-10-11, 4669	As ex. 6	17×15×6.5	2–4, 6–8	c
11	BM 114240	—	1919-10-11, 4671	As ex. 6	31×27.5×9	1–4	c
12	BM 114241	—	1919-10-11, 4672	As ex. 6	37×26×8.5	1–8	c
13	BM 114242	—	1919-10-11, 4673	As ex. 6	37.5×36.5×10	1–8	c
14	BM 114245	—	1919-10-11, 4676	As ex. 6	20.5×15×7.5	1–3, 6–8	c
15	BM 114248	—	1919-10-11, 4679	As ex. 6	19×17×9	3–4, 7–8	c
16	BM 114249	—	1919-10-11, 4680	As ex. 6	12×12×8	1–7	c
17	BM 114250	—	1919-10-11, 4681	As ex. 6	14×11.5×7	3–4, 6–8	c
18	BM 114251	—	1919-10-11, 4682	As ex. 6	24×18×10	1–4	c
19	BM 114253	—	1919-10-11, 4684	As ex. 6	27×26×9	3–4, 6–8	c
20	BM 137417	—	1979-12-18, 52	As ex. 6	29.5×21.5×9	1–8	c
21	IM 22	U 32(?)	—	Hall's excavations in the E-ḫursag area	37×37×10	—	n
22	CBS 15327	U 2624a	—	—	37×37×9	—	n
23	CBS 16461	U 2624b	—	Drain, top west corner of ziqqurrat	34×34×8.5	—	n
24	CBS 16530	U 2624c	—	—	36×36×8.5	—	c
25	IM 66434	2nd season of the Iraqi excavations	—	From the wall of the E-ḫursag palace	—	1–8	n

COMMENTARY

Exs. 1–20 were collated by C.B.F. Walker. Bezold (Cat. 5 p. 2233) mentions a duplicate of this inscription, not listed by Walker, with the registration number no. 51-1-1, 303; it apparently came from Loftus's excavations at Ur. We expect that exs. 1–5, which predate the Woolley excavations, would have come from the soundings of Loftus or Taylor. Exs. 6–15 come from Hall's excavations, apparently from the E-ḫursag palace, since Woolley (AJ 6 [1926] p. 382) has noted that the bricks of the walls of that structure were stamped with this inscription. Ex. 21 is known from notes on the IM brick collection which were shown to the author in 1985; the putative excavation number of the piece, U 32, does not agree with the Ur registry book; the latter source states that the piece is an earring. The text is arranged in two columns: col. i has lines 1–4, col. ii lines 5–8.

As noted, this inscription has generally been taken to refer to the construction of the city wall of Ur. Now, the fact that a cone inscription of Išme-Dagān from Isin (see Frayne RIME 4 pp. 31–32 E4.1.4.5) that deals with the construction of the "great wall of Isin" (bàd-gal-ì-si-in.KI-na), but for which several exemplars were actually found *in situ* in the temenos wall at Isin (for a photo of some of these findspots, see Hrouda, Isin 4, pl. 18.1), raises the possibility that the "wall of Ur" named in inscription 3 might refer to the temenos wall at Ur. If we examine the findspots of the bricks with inscription 3, we find that several came from the area of the E-ḫursag palace. An examination of the map given by Woolley in UE 6 pl. 53 reveals that the Ur III temenos wall was situated in the area between the E-ḫursag palace of Ur-Nammu and Šulgi and the "Royal Cemetery." Woolley (UE 6 p. 55) notes:

> The platform of Ur-Nammu's Temenos was contained by a heavy wall of mud bricks (0.23 m. × 0.15 m. × c. 0.09 m.) faced with burnt bricks, the face sharply battered and relieved by shallow buttresses. ... It is only on the SE front of the E-ḫur-sag salient that the wall is at all well preserved. The burnt-brick facing is in good condition and stands to a height of 1.50 m.; the bricks bear no stamp but are characteristic of the Third Dynasty.

It seems likely, then, that bricks inscribed with the "wall of Ur" inscription came from the temenos wall in the area of the E-ḫursag. As to the extent of the temenos wall, Woolley (UE 6 p. 55) notes:

> The Ziggurat with its separate terrace crowded with buildings, and the great Nannar courtyard, both described in Volume V of this series, E-nun-maḫ and E-ḫur-sag, described in the foregoing pages, the Gig-Par-Ku founded by Bur-Sin and rebuilt by Enannatum (see UE VII), Dublal-maḫ (see UE VIII), and another large building now completely destroyed, formed the complex of religious structures dedicated to the service of Nannar; they stood apart from the other buildings of the city and the area which they occupied was known as E-gish-shir-gal, the Temenos of the Moon-god. It is probable that from very early times the Temenos was thus distinguished and surrounded by a wall; certainly this was the case from the beginning of the Third Dynasty until the final desertion of the city ...

A cone inscription of Ibbi-Sîn that also deals with the "wall of Ur" likely came from the same temenos wall beside the E-ḫursag palace. For the details, see the discussion to E3/2.1.5.1.

BIBLIOGRAPHY

1861 1 R I 3 (exs. 1–5, composite copy)
1872 Smith, TSBA 1 p. 35 (exs. 1–5, translation)
1874 Lenormant, Études accadiennes 2 p. 303 (exs. 1–5, translation)
1875 Ménant, Babylone p. 74 (exs. 1–5, translation)
1892 Winckler, KB 3/1 pp. 76–77 Ur-gur 2 (exs. 1–5, edition)
1899 Bezold, Cat. 5 p. 2233 (exs. 1–5, study)
1905 King, CT 21 pl. 2 90009 (ex. 2, copy)
1907 Thureau-Dangin, SAK pp. 186–87 Ur-engur b (exs. 1–5, edition)
1922 BM Guide p. 60 nos. 35–38 (exs. 1–4, study)
1926 Woolley, AJ 6 p. 382 (provenance)
1928 Gadd, UET 1 p. xxiv (study)
1929 Barton, RISA pp. 270–71 Ur-Nammu 2 (exs. 1–5, edition)
1930 Hall, Season's Work p. 106 (ex. 2, photo)
1962 Hallo, HUCA 33 p. 25 Ur-Nammu 9 (exs. 1–5, study)
1962 al-Ṣīwānī, Sumer 18 p. 189 (Arabic section) (ex. 25, provenance, copy, edition)
1971 Sollberger and Kupper, IRSA IIIA1c (exs. 1–5, translation)
1976 Basmachi, Treasures p. 205 no. 6 (ex. 25, study)
1981 Walker, CBI no. 18 (exs. 1–20, study)
1985 Behrens, JCS 37 p. 231 (exs. 22–24, study)
1986 Kärki, KDDU p. 5 Urnammu 9 (exs. 1–20, 25, edition)
1991 Steible, NSBW 2 pp. 102–104 Urnammu 9 (exs. 1–20, 22–25 edition)

TEXT

1) ^{d}nanna
2) lugal-a-ni
3) ur-^{d}nammu
4) lugal-uri$_5$.KI-ma-ke$_4$
5) é-a-ni
6) mu-na-dù
7) bàd-uri$_5$.KI-ma
8) mu-na-dù

1–2) For the god Nanna, his lord,

3–4) Ur-Nammu, king of Ur,

5–8) built his temple (and) built the wall of Ur.

E3/2.1.1.4.8 .3 mu-na-mu-MU.

5

Ur-Nammu built shrines at Ur to the chief gods of Uruk: An and Inanna. This reverence for the gods of Uruk by a king who, at the time the construction work on these temples began, did not yet control Uruk can be explained by the fact that Ur-Nammu likely came from an Uruk family.

An eight-line brick inscription deals with the planting of a garden and the erection of a shrine or dais for the god An.

CATALOGUE

Ex.	Museum number	Excavation number	Registration number	Ur provenance	Dimensions (cm)	Lines preserved	cpn
1	BM 90296	—	1979-12-20, 183	—	27.5×24.5×5.5	1–8	c
2	BM 119273	U 3081	1927-10-3, 268	E-gipar of Nabonidus room 3	31×19.5×7	1–8	c
3	BM 119275	U 3081	1927-10-3, 270	As ex. 2	30.5×30.5×6	1–8	c
4	BM 137398	—	1979-12-18, 33	—	30.5×30.5×6.5	1–8	c
5	BM 137418	—	1979-12-18, 53	—	16×14×8.2	2–8	c
6	CBS 16462	U 3081a	—	As ex. 2	—	—	n
7	CBS 16531a	U 3081b	—	As ex. 2	—	—	n
8	CBS 16531b	U 3081c	—	As ex. 2	—	—	n
9	CBS 16532	U 3081d	—	As ex. 2	—	—	n
10	UM 35-1-397	—	—	—	—	—	n

COMMENTARY

Exs. 1–5 were collated by C.B.F. Walker. The text is arranged in one column of eight lines.

BIBLIOGRAPHY

1872 Smith, TSBA 1 p. 35 (ex. 1, translation)
1873–75 Lenormant, Choix no. 60 (ex. 1, copy)
1874 Lenormant, Études accadiennes 2 p. 309 (ex. 1, translation)
1875 Ménant, Babylone p. 74 (ex. 1, translation)
1891 4R² 35 (ex. 1, copy)
1892 Winckler, KB 3/1 pp. 78–79 Ur-gur 9 (ex. 1, edition)
1899 Bezold, Cat. 5 p. 2241 (ex. 1, study)
1905 King, CT 21 pl. 9 90296 (ex. 1, copy)
1907 Thureau-Dangin, SAK pp. 186–87 Ur-engur f (ex. 1, edition)
1922 BM Guide p. 60 no. 41 (ex. 1, study)
1928 Gadd, UET 1 no. 41 (exs. 2–3, copy, edition)
1929 Barton, RISA pp. 270–71 Ur-Nammu 6 (ex. 1, edition)
1962 Hallo, HUCA 33 p. 25 Ur-Nammu 5 (exs. 1–3, study)
1971 Sollberger and Kupper, IRSA IIIA1j (exs. 1–3, translation)
1981 Walker, CBI no. 15 (exs. 1–5, study)
1985 Behrens, JCS 37 p. 231 (exs. 6–10, study)
1986 Kärki, KDDU p. 3 Ur-Nammu 5 (exs. 1–10, edition)
1991 Steible, NSBW 2 pp. 98–99 Urnammu 5 (exs. 1–10, edition)

TEXT

1) an lugal-dingir-re-ne
2) lugal-a-ni
3) ur-^{d}nammu
4) lugal-uri$_5$.KI-ma-ke$_4$
5) GIŠ.kiri$_6$-maḫ
6) mu-na-gub
7) bára ki-sikil-la
8) mu-na-dù

1–2) For the god An, king of the gods, his lord,

3–4) Ur-Nammu, king of Ur,

5–8) planted for him a lofty garden (and) built for him a shrine/dais in a pure place.

E3/2.1.1.5.6.3,9 mu-na-KAS$_4$-gunû(=LAK 487).

6

A door socket records Ur-Nammu's construction of a temple for the goddess Ninsuna. It may have come from the region of ancient Ku'ar.

COMMENTARY

The door socket measures 49×33 cm. It was found at the site Gadd denoted in UET 1 p. xi as "Radhibah." The piece was given the excavation number U 6336. Its museum number is BM 118547; the inscription, which is arranged in one column of four lines, was collated.

The GN "Radhibah" supplied by Gadd is, in all likelihood, simply a variant spelling of the site name which appears variously in Woolley's UE volumes as Reijibeh (UE 4 p. 10), Rajībah (UE 7 p. 10), and Reijebeh (UE 9 pp. 104 and 130); see Steinkeller, NABU 1995 pp. 82–83 no. 91.

Now, a mound named Rajībah is designated as sites 4–5 on the map of E. Wright published on p. 299 of Adams, Heartland; the site is located about eleven km northwest of Eridu and fifteen km southwest of Ur.

Because of the particular location of Rajībah, the door socket from "Radhibah" may well be connected with the temple of the goddess Ninsuna of the town KI.KAL that is named in various Ur III archival texts (Keiser, BIN 3 no. 607 line 3; Langdon, TAD no. 49 line 15; and Kang, SETDA no. 7 line 10). Concerning one of the Ur III archival texts that mention KI.KAL (TAD no. 49), W. Sallaberger (Kalender 1, p. 224) writes: "Eine mehrere Kultorte umfassende Feier, in die auch Ku'ara eingebunden ist, sind die 'Bade-Riten in Reinen Fluss' (sizkur$_2$ a-tu$_5$-a i$_7$-kù-[ga]; TAD 49): hier sind die Orte Uruk, KI.KAL, Ku'ara, Eridu und Ur angeführt, die vielleicht in dieser Reihenfolge von einer Kultprozession besucht werden." If Sallaberger's hypothesis is correct, then we would expect that ancient KI.KAL was situated not far upstream from Eridu on the Eridu canal, somewhere between the cities of Eridu and Uruk. This location would provide an excellent fit with the site of modern Rajībah. Now, Steinkeller has shown (NABU 1995 pp. 82–83 no. 91) that in Ur III times, in addition to her connection with the city of Uruk, Ninsuna apparently was the chief goddess at Ku'ar. This fact emerges from a study of the offerings noted for Ku'ar in various Ur III texts; the documents were analysed by Sallaberger in Table 77 of his Kalender 2. We are inclined, therefore, to posit that KI.KAL and Ku'ar may have been two quarters of a city conglomeration (sometimes subsumed in Ur III texts by the designation Ku'ar) that is marked by the modern mounds of Rejībah Jinub and Rejībah Shamal. If our understanding is correct, the original situation was one in which the god Asarluḫi and his wife Nin-damgal-ana were the chief gods of Ku'ar, and the gods Ninsuna and Lugalbanda were patron deities of the neighbouring mound of KI.KAL.

Of further interest in this connection is the appearance (in Schneider, Drehem- und Djoḫatexte no. 99 line 6) of an unnamed goddess with the epithet ama-KI.KAL.KI "mother of KI.KAL"; this very likely refers to the goddess Ninsuna. Also noteworthy is the fact that the city name KI.KAL is attested already in Early Dynastic times; it appears as ^{d}KAL.KI in the archaic zà-mì hymns from Abū Ṣalābīkh (Biggs, Abū Ṣalābīkh p. 50 line 149). This understanding accords well with the mention in the following line of the zà-mì hymn of the divine epithet ama-unu(?)-ga "mother of Uruk." Furthermore, the designation of the goddess of ^{d}KAL.KI in the zà-mì hymns (line 151) as ^{d}lamma-sa$_6$-ga agrees with the equation of the same goddess with Ninsuna (in a local[?] variant at Uruku/Al Hibā) in an inscription of Ur-Ningirsu I of Lagaš (Steible, NSBW 1 pp. 127–28 Ur-Ningirsu I. 6, 1′ 2′–3′:[^{d}la]mma-sa$_6$-ga/ [^{d}ni]n-súna). Of interest is the appearance (in line 147 of the zà-mì hymns) of a GN gán-gal; it occurs immediately preceding the hymn to the city ^{d}KI.KAL. Bearing in mind that the term KI.KAL is given the pronunciations kankal and kikla and equated with Akkadian *kankallu*, *kagallu*, *kigallu*, and *kiklû* (see Ur$_5$-ra = *ḫubullu*(*m*) I lines 168–75), the writing gán-gal in line 147 of the zà-mì hymns could plausibly be seen as a variant spelling for kankal. A reference to KI.KAL may possibly appear in the place name KAL.KI in an Ur III period copy of an (as yet) unattributed Ur III royal inscription (see E3/2.1.6.1016, col. ii′ lines 3 and 5). Further, a reflection of the toponym KI.KAL.KI may be seen in the name of the temple of the god Lugalbanda, Ninsuna's consort, at Kullab: é-kankal(KI.KAL) *bīt* ^{d}*lugal-bàn-da šá kul-*⌊*a*⌋*ba*$_4$ (CTL no. 470; see George, House Most High p. 19).

BIBLIOGRAPHY

1928 Gadd, UET 1 no. 33 (copy, edition)
1929 Barton, RISA pp. 360–61 Ur-Nammu 1 (edition)
1962 Hallo, HUCA 33 p. 24 Ur-Nammu 2 (study)
1986 Kärki, KDDU p. 1 Ur-Nammu 2 (edition)
1991 Steible, NSBW 2 pp. 94–95 Urnammu 2 (edition)

TEXT

1) ur-^{d}namm[u]
2) lugal-uri$_5$.⸢KI⸣-ma
3) ⸢lú⸣ é-^{d}nin-súna
4) ⸢in-dù⸣-a

1–2) Ur-Nammu, king of Ur,

3–4) the one who built the temple of the goddess Ninsuna.

7

A foundation tablet from Ur records Ur-Nammu's construction of the temple of the goddess Ninšagepada.

COMMENTARY

The tablet is made of limestone and measures 10.5×8×2.3 cm. It was found in the filling of the mausolea of Šulgi and Amar-Suena against the outer footing of the NE wall, and was given the excavation number U 16528 and museum number UM 31-43-249. The inscription was collated. The simple title "king of Ur" dates this inscription to the early period of Ur-Nammu's reign. The text is arranged in one column of six lines.

BIBLIOGRAPHY

1965 Sollberger, UET 8 no. 19 (copy, study)
1966 Falkenstein, BiOr 23 p. 166 (study)
1986 Kärki, KDDU p. 25 Urnammu 39 (edition)
1991 Steible, NSBW 2 pp. 143–44 Urnammu 38 (edition)

TEXT

1) ^{d}nin-šà-ge-[pà]-da
2) nin-a-ni
3) ur-^{d}[nammu]
4) lugal-uri$_5$.KI-ma-ke$_4$
5) [é-a]-ni
6) [mu-n]a-[dù]

1–2) For the goddess Ninšage[pa]da, his lady,

3–4) Ur-[Nammu], king of Ur,

5–6) [bu]il[t] her [temple].

8

A four-line inscription on a door socket records the construction of the temple of Ninutula.

COMMENTARY

This inscription was incised on a door socket last seen near the Mosul dig house. The simple title "king of Ur" indicates that the piece dates to the early period of the reign; the door socket, in all likelihood, came from Ur. The inscription measures 7×7.8 cm; the dimensions of the door socket itself are not known. The text is arranged in one column of four lines.

As far as can be determined, the cult of Ninutula is not otherwise attested for the city of Ur in Ur III times.

TEXT

1) ur-^{d}nammu
2) lugal-uri$_{5}$.KI-ma
3) lú é-^{d}nin-utul-ka
4) ⌈in-dù-a⌉

1–4) Ur-Nammu, king of Ur, the one who built the temple of Ninutula.

9

A stele fragment found in excavations at Ur gives Ur-Nammu's name and the title "king of Ur."

COMMENTARY

The fragment with this inscription was found in the courtyard in front of the Edublalmaḫ and given the excavation number U 3215. It bears the museum number CBS 16676. The inscription, which is arranged in one column of two lines, was collated.

Although this piece has traditionally been assigned as part of the "Ur-Nammu Stele," a mineralogical analysis of the stone (by R. Walsh and R. Giegenack, kindly communicated to the author by J. Canby, June 3, 1994) indicates that its sulphur content is too high to be a piece of the same monument. This accords well with the fact that the simple titulary "king of Ur" found on this piece dates the inscription to the very beginning of the reign whereas the "Ur-Nammu stele" likely dates to the time after the king's adoption of the title "king of the lands of Sumer and Akkad."

BIBLIOGRAPHY

1928 Gadd, UET 1 no. 44a (copy, edition)
1929 Barton, RISA pp. 362–63 Ur-Nammu 10 (a) (conflated edition)
1962 Hallo, HUCA 33 p. 27 Ur-Nammu 29 (study)
1974 Woolley, UE 6 pl 43a (top register, centre) (photo)
1986 Kärki, KDDU p. 18–19 Urnammu 29 (conflated edition)
1987 Canby, Expedition 29 p. 55 fig. 3 (photo)
1991 Braun-Holzinger, Weihgaben p. 340 Stele 25 (study)
1991 Steible, NSBW 2 p. 135 Urnammu 29 (conflated edition)

TEXT

1) ur-^{d}nammu
2) lugal-uri$_{5}$.KI-ma

1–2) Ur-Nammu, king of Ur.

10

As noted in the introductory comments for Ur-Nammu, the city of Eridu was an important cult centre that was held by Ur during the earliest years of the king's reign. The king's construction of Enki's temple there is commemorated in a six-line brick inscription.

CATALOGUE

Ex.	Museum number	Eridu provenance	Dimensions (cm)	Lines preserved	cpn
1	—	From the surface of the ziqqurrat	—	1–6	n
2	IM —	As ex. 1	Stamp: 12×10 Brick: 31.5×31.5×7.3	1–6	n
3	BCM 285′35	—	Stamp: 11.9×9.8 Brick: 31.5×30×7.5	1–6	c

COMMENTARY

According to Safar, Sumer 3 (1947) p. 235, approximately a dozen examples of this stamped brick were found at Eridu. The simple title "king of Ur" dates this inscription to the early part of Ur-Nammu's reign. The text is arranged in one column of six lines.

BIBLIOGRAPHY

1919 Thompson, Arch. 70 pp. 115–16 (ex. 1, copy, edition)
1947 Safar, Sumer 3 p. 236 (Arabic section) (ex. 2, copy)
1962 Hallo, HUCA 33 p. 25 Ur-Nammu 4 (exs. 1–2, study)
1979 George, Iraq 41 p. 122 (ex. 3, study)
1981 Walker, CBI no. 14 (ex. 3, study)
1981 Safar, Mustafa, and Lloyd, Eridu pp. 65 and 229 fig. 108 (ex. 2, provenance, copy, edition)
1986 Kärki, KDDU p. 3 Urnammu 4 (exs. 1–3, edition)
1991 Steible, NSBW 2 pp. 97–98 Urnammu 4 (exs. 1–3, edition)

TEXT

1) ur-^{d}nammu
2) lugal-uri$_{5}$.KI-ma
3) lú é-
4) ^{d}en-ki
5) eridu.KI-ga
6) mu-dù-a

1–2) Ur-Nammu, king of Ur,

3–6) the one who built the temple of the god Enki in Eridu.

11

As noted, a second phase of Ur-Nammu's construction of the Nanna temple complex at Ur saw the erection of the great temenos wall E-temen-ni-guru. The work was apparently begun before the king's trip to Nippur and continued after the king's return. In the cone inscription commemorating the construction, Ur-Nammu appears with the simple titles "mighty king, king of Ur"; in the corresponding brick inscription, on the other hand, the king has added the titles "lord of Uruk, king of the lands of Sumer and Akkad."

Numerous clay cones with an inscription recording the erection of the E-temen-ni-guru were found in the temenos wall surrounding the ziqqurrat. For a photo showing some of the cones *in situ*, see UE 5 pl. 15a.

CATALOGUE

Ex.	Museum number	Excavation number	Registration number	Ur provenance	Dimensions (cm)	Lines preserved	cpn
1	BM 30051	—	59-10-14, 85	—	7.7×5.9	1–10	c
2	BM 30052	—	59-10-14, 86	—	5.2×4.1	1–10	c
3	BM 30053	—	59-10-14, 87	—	3×5.2	2–4	c
4	BM 30054	—	59-10-14, 88	—	4.5×4.3	1–10	c
5	BM 30055	—	59-10-14, 89	—	6.5×4.4	1–10	c
6	BM 30057	—	59-10-14, 91	—	5.8×4.2	6–8	c
7	BM 30068	—	56-9-3, 1482	—	3.3×4.8	2–10	c
8	BM 30075	—	56-9-3, 1489	—	8.5×5.5	1–10	c
9	BM 30076	—	56-9-3, 1490	—	7.3×4.8	1–10	c
10	BM 30077	—	56-9-3, 1491	—	4.6×5.9	1–10	c
11	BM 30078	—	56-9-3, 1492	—	8.7×4.6	1–10	c
12	BM 30079	—	56-9-3, 1493	—	7×4	1–8	c
13	BM 30080	—	56-9-3, 1494	—	6×5.5	1–10	c
14	BM 30081	—	56-9-3, 1495	—	9.5×3.9	1–10	c
15	BM 30082	—	56-9-3, 1497	—	6×3.8	1–3, 5–10	c
16	BM 30083	—	56-9-3, 1498	—	5.5×3.8	3–8	c
17	BM 30085	—	56-9-3, 1500	—	5×3.8	1–9	c
18	BM 30087	—	56-9-3, 1502	—	4.7×4.1	1–3	c
19	BM 30090	—	56-9-3, 1496	"From the mounds south of the great temple"	6×4.6	1–10	c
20	BM 90911	—	—	—	4×4.5	2–9	c
21	IM 96	U 201	—	Surface	6.5×6	—	n
22	—	U 228	—	TTB, top soil	7 long	—	n
23	IM 103	U 243a	—	Outside south corner of TTB 11	14×5.5	—	n
24	IM 114	U 297	—	Loose in TTB 24	11×7	nearly complete	n
25	IM 115	U 300	—	TTB 25	12×6.5	—	n
26	IM 380	U 328	—	E-nun-maḫ area	5.5×5	—	n
27	IM 90906	U 331	—	E-nun-maḫ area	3×5	—	n
28	IM 123	U 345	—	E-nun-maḫ area	11.5×5	—	n
29	IM 134	U 436	—	TTB 8 by aqueduct	8×6	1–10	n
30	IM 135	U 437	—	TTB 6	7.5×6	nearly complete	n
31	IM 177	U 527	—	TTB 21	8×6	—	n
32	IM 376	U—	—	—	—	—	n
33	IM 377	U—	—	—	—	—	n
34	IM 386	U 529	—	E-nun-maḫ area	3×4	—	n
35	IM 387	U 530	—	E-nun-maḫ area	8×4	—	n
36	IM 388	U 531	—	E-nun-maḫ area	4.5×5	—	n
37	IM 389	U 533	—	E-nun-maḫ area	3×3	—	n
38	IM 392	U—	—	—	—	—	n
39	Ash 1935-774	U 551	—	In mud packing at S end of TTB 55	12×6	—	n
40	IM 239	U 747	—	Near gate in temenos wall on NW	10×5.5	—	n
41	IM 240	U 748	—	As ex. 39	7×6	—	n
42	IM 566A	U 1116a	—	—	—	—	n
43	IM 566B	U 1116b	—	—	—	—	n
44	IM 566C	U 1116c	—	—	—	—	n
45	IM 566D	U 1116d	—	—	—	—	n
46	IM 378	U 2437	—	—	—	—	n
47	BM 119017	U 2648	1927-10-3, 12	In a mud brick of the great Nanna courtyard, room 23	14.2×5.3	1–10	c
48	BM 119019	U 2648A	1927-10-3, 14	—	14.5×5.7	1–10	c
49	IM 906A	U 2648B	—	—	11×5	—	n
50	IM 906B	U 2648C	—	—	15×5.5	—	n
51	BM 119020	U 2648D	1927-10-3, 15	—	16.6×5.3	1–10	c
52	BM 119018	U 2648E	1927-10-3, 13	—	15.4×6.2	1–10	c
53	IM 1039	U 3134	—	40 exs. from the terrace of E-temen-ni-guru	—	—	n
54	IM 1351	U—	—	—		—	n
55	IM 2222 (= IM 49857/5)	U—	—	—	—	—	n
56	IM 2412/1	U—	—	—	—	—	n
57	IM 2412/12	U—	—	—	—	—	n
58	IM 90907	U 6081	—	"Dim-tab-ba" temple range "loose surface soil"	—	—	n
59	IM 90964 (formerly IM 3568)	U 7713a	—	Near temenos wall, under pavement (Nebuchadnezzar) of E-nun-maḫ, N corner of temenos	—	1–10	n
60	IM 3568/1	U 7713b	—	Trial trench D	—	—	n
61	IM 3568/2	U 7713c	—	—	—	1–10	n
62	IM 3568/3	U 7713d	—	—	—	—	n
63	IM 3568/4	U 7713d	—	—	—	—	n
64	IM 3568/5	U 7713e	—	—	—	—	n
65	IM 3568/6	U 7713f	—	—	—	—	n
66	IM 3568/7	U 7713h	—	—	—	—	n
67	IM 3568/8	U 7713i	—	—	—	—	n

Ex.	Museum number	Excavation number	Registration number	Ur provenance	Dimensions (cm)	Lines preserved	cpn
68	IM 3568/9	U 7713j	—	—	—	—	n
69	IM 3568/10	U 7713k	—	—	—	—	n
70	IM 3568/11	U 7713l	—	—	—	—	n
71	IM 3568/12	U 7713m	—	—	—	—	n
72	IM 3568/13	U 7713n	—	—	—	—	n
73	IM 3568/14	U 7713o	—	—	—	—	n
74	IM 3568/15	U 7713p	—	—	—	—	n
75	IM 3568/16	U 7713q	—	—	—	—	n
76	IM 3568/17	U 7713r	—	—	—	—	n
77	IM 3568/18	U 7713s	—	—	—	—	n
78	IM 3568/19	U 7713t	—	—	—	—	n
79	IM 3568/20	U 7713u	—	—	—	—	n
80	IM 3568/21	U 7713v	—	—	—	—	n
81	IM 90910	U 7717	—	Loose in soil in the area of the Larsa houses on the SW side of the temenos	—	—	n
82	IM 3574	U 7779	—	Under Nebuchadnezzar floor of E-nun-maḫ	—	—	n
83	IM 9226	U—	—	—	—	—	n
84	IM 22866A	U—	—	—	—	—	n
85	IM 22866B	U—	—	—	—	—	n
86	IM 22866C	U—	—	—	—	—	n
87	IM 22866D	U—	—	—	—	—	n
88	IM 22866E	U—	—	—	—	—	n
89	IM 22866F	U—	—	—	—	—	n
90	IM 22866G	U—	—	—	—	—	n
91	IM 22866H	U—	—	—	—	—	n
92	IM 22866I	U—	—	—	—	—	n
93	IM 22866J	U—	—	—	—	—	n
94	IM 22866K	U—	—	—	—	—	n
95	IM 22866L	U—	—	—	—	—	n
96	IM 22866M	U—	—	—	—	—	n
97	IM 22907	U—	—	—	—	—	n
98	IM 90904	U 10102	—	"Top filling" of the Royal Cemetery area or ziqqurrat courtyard	—	—	n
99	IM 90905	U 10102	—	As ex. 98	—	—	n
100	IM 90908	U 10102	—	As ex. 98	—	—	n
101	IM 90909	U 10102	—	As ex. 98	—	—	n
102	IM 90919	U 10102	—	As ex. 98	—	—	n
103	IM 90920	U 10102	—	As ex. 98	—	—	n
104	IM 90921	U 10102	—	As ex. 98	—	—	n
105	IM 90922	U 10102	—	As ex. 98	—	—	n
106	IM 90937	U 10102	—	As ex. 98	—	—	n
107	IM 90903	U 13604a	—	Larsa rubbish filling over the Royal Cemetery area and by the town wall	—	—	n
108	IM 90912	U 13604b	—	As ex. 107	—	—	n
109	IM 90913	U 13604c	—	As ex. 107	—	—	n
110	IM 90914	U 13604d	—	As ex. 107	—	—	n
111	IM 90917	U 13604e	—	As ex. 107	—	—	n
112	IM 90918	U 13604f	—	As ex. 107	—	—	n
113	IM 90930	U 13604g	—	As ex. 107	—	—	n
114	IM 90929	U 18769	—	"Between 250 and 300 m below the modern surface" of the extension of the Royal Cemetery area	—	—	n
115	IM 90923	U 18786	—	As ex. 114 on level 1700′	—	1–10	n
116	BM 124352	U rb	—	—	12×6.4	1–10	c
117	BM 124353	U sb	—	—	8.6×5.7	1–10	c
118	BM 124354	U tb	—	—	8×5.2	1–10	c
119	BM 124355	U ub	—	—	9×5.6	1–10	c
120	IM 90926	U—	—	—	—	—	n
121	IM 90927	U—	—	—	—	—	n
122	IM 90928	U—	—	—	—	—	n
123	IM 90931	U—	—	—	—	—	n
124	IM 90932	U—	—	—	—	—	n
125	IM 90936	U—	—	—	—	—	n
126	IM 90938	U—	—	—	—	—	n
127	IM 90939	U—	—	—	—	—	n
128	IM 90940	U—	—	—	—	—	n
129	IM 90942	U—	—	—	—	—	n
130	IM 90945	U—	—	—	—	—	n
131	IM 90946	U—	—	—	—	—	n
132	IM 90947	U—	—	—	—	—	n
133	IM 90948	U—	—	—	—	—	n
134	IM 90949	U—	—	—	—	—	n
135	IM 90950	U—	—	—	—	—	n
136	IM 90951	U—	—	—	—	—	n
137	IM 90952	U—	—	—	—	—	n
138	IM 90953	U—	—	—	—	—	n
139	IM 90954	U—	—	—	—	—	n
140	IM 92792	U—	—	—	—	—	n
141	IM 92793	U—	—	—	—	—	n

Ex.	Museum number	Excavation number	Registration number	Ur provenance	Dimensions (cm)	Lines preserved	cpn
142	IM 92797	U—	—	—	—	—	n
143	IM 92798	U—	—	—	—	—	n
144	IM 92800	U—	—	—	—	—	n
145	IM 92803	U—	—	—	—	—	n
146	IM 92804	U—	—	—	—	—	n
147	IM 92805	U—	—	—	—	—	n
148	IM 92806	U—	—	—	—	—	n
149	UM 33-35-194	—	—	—	12×4.3	1–10	c
150	UM 33-35-195	—	—	—	—	—	n
151	UM 35-1-149	—	—	—	8×5.8	1–10	c
152	UM 35-1-150	—	—	—	7.3×5.9	1–10	c
153	UM 35-1-151	—	—	—	7.4×5.9	1–10	c
154	UM 35-1-152	—	—	—	9.5×4	1–10	c
155	UM 84-3-1	—	—	—	14.5×5.5	1–10	c
156	CBS 19704	—	—	—	15×6.5	1–10	c
157	CBS 13148	—	—	—	9×6.6	1–10	c
158	MAH 19351	—	—	—	7.5×5.7	1–10	c
159	FMNH 156003	—	—	—	—	—	n
160	BCM 63'76	—	—	—	—	—	n
161	BCM 64'76	—	—	—	—	—	n
162	Ash 1925-663	—	—	—	—	—	n
163	FM E. 3.48	—	—	—	—	—	n

COMMENTARY

Exs. 1–6 come from Taylor's excavations; exs. 7–19 from those of Loftus; and exs. 21–154 from those of Woolley. For a list of the IM exemplars, see D. Edzard, Sumer 13 (1957) p. 176 and H. Steible, NSBW 2 pp. 120–22. Cones with the U numbers U vb–yb, zb, ac–za, and ad–ed, in all 36 fragments (see Sollberger, UET 8 p. 36 to no. 46), must be contained in the group of exs. 117–45; individual identifications are not possible at present.

BIBLIOGRAPHY

1861 1 R I 4 (ex. 19, copy)
1872 Smith, TSBA 1 p. 35 (ex. 19, translation)
1874 Lenormant, Études accadiennes 2 p. 304 (ex. 19, translation)
1875 Ménant, Babylone p. 74 (ex. 19, translation)
1890 Winckler and Böhden, ABK no. 20 (ex. 19, copy)
1892 Winckler, KB 3/1 p. 76 Ur-gur 3 (ex. 19, edition)
1899 Bezold, Cat. 5 p. 2233 (exs. 1, 3, 8, 9, 19, study)
1905 King, CT 21 pl. 8 BM 30051 (ex. 1, copy; exs. 3, 8, 9, variants)
1907 Thureau-Dangin, SAK pp. 188–89 Ur-engur h (ex. 1, edition)
1910 King, Early History pl. 33 facing p. 314 (lower right) (ex. 19, photo)
1928 Gadd, UET 1 p. xxiv (study)
1929 Barton, RISA pp. 272–73 Ur-Nammu 8 (exs. 1, 19, edition)
1957 Edzard, Sumer 13 p. 176 (various IM exs., study)
1962 Hallo, HUCA 33 p. 27 Ur-Nammu 25 (exs. 1, 19, various IM exs., ex. 159, study)
1965 Sollberger, UET 8 pp. 35–36 no. 46 (exs. 27, 47–48, 51–52, 58–81, 98–112, 114–48, study)
1969 Sauren, WMAH p. xxiii (ex. 158, study)
1979 George, Iraq 41 p. 122 nos. 24–25 (exs. 160–61, study)
1981 Grégoire, MVN 10 nos. 17–18 (exs. 39, 162, study; ex. 39, copy)
1985 Kärki, KDDU pp. 13–14 Urnammu 25 (exs. 1, 3, 8, 9, 19, various IM exs., exs. 158–61, edition)
1991 Steible, NSBW 2 pp. 120–23 Urnammu 25 (exs. 1–163, edition)

TEXT

1) ^{d}nanna 2) amar-bàn-da-an-na 3) dumu-sag- 4) ^{d}en-líl-lá 5) lugal-a-ni	1–5) For the god Nanna, impetuous calf of the god An, first-born son of the god Enlil, his lord,
6) ur-^{d}nammu 7) nita-kala-ga 8) lugal-uri$_{5}$.KI-ma-ke$_{4}$	6–8) Ur-Nammu, mighty man, king of Ur,
9) é-temen-ní-gùru-ni 10) mu-na-dù	9–10) built his E-temen-ni-guru ("House, Foundation Platform which Bears Terror") for him.

Variants for E3/2.1.1.11:
2.57 amar-bàn-da-ŠEŠ.KI.
6.81 Omits line.
9.19 Copy in 1 R I 4 restored (incorrectly): é-temen-ní-gùru/ ⌜é-ki-ág-gá-ni⌝; original has é-temen-ní-gùru-ni (collated).

12

A thirteen-line brick inscription records Ur-Nammu's construction of the temenos wall E-temen-ni-guru.

CATALOGUE

Ex.	Museum number	Excavation number	Registration number	Ur provenance	Dimensions (cm)	Lines preserved	cpn
1	BM 90000	—	1979-12-20, 1	From the centre of the ruins	23×15	1–12	c
2	BM 124349	—	1933-10-13, 2	—	23×15×7.5	1–12	c
3	CBS 16458	U 3133a	—	—	—	—	n
4	CBS 16528a	U 3133b	—	—	—	—	n
5	CBS 16528b	U 3133c	—	—	—	—	n
6	UM 35-1-394	—	—	—	—	—	n
7	UM 35-1-395	—	—	—	—	—	n
8	UM 35-1-396	—	—	—	—	—	n
9	FM E. 206.1934	—	—	—	—	—	n

COMMENTARY

Exs. 1–2 were collated by C.B.F. Walker. As noted, Ur-Nammu appears with the title "lord of Uruk" in only this text and inscription E3/2.1.1.46; both inscriptions probably date to the time shortly after the incorporation of Uruk into the realm of Ur. The text is arranged in one column of thirteen lines.

BIBLIOGRAPHY

1861 1 R I 5 (ex. 1, copy)
1872 Smith, TSBA 1 p. 35 (ex. 1, translation)
1874 Lenormant, Études accadiennes 2 p. 306 (ex. 1, translation)
1875 Ménant, Babylone p. 74–75 (translation)
1892 Winckler, KB 3/1 pp. 78–79 Ur-gur 4 (edition)
1899 Bezold, Cat. 5 p. 2233 (ex. 1, study)
1905 King, CT 21 pl. 7 BM 90000 (ex. 1, copy)
1907 Thureau-Dangin, SAK pp. 186–87 Ur-engur c (ex. 1, edition)
1922 BM Guide p. 60 no. 32 (ex. 1, study)
1928 Gadd, UET 1 p. xxiv (exs. 3–5, study)
1929 Barton, RISA pp. 270–71 Ur-Nammu 3 (ex. 1, edition)
1939 Woolley, UE 5 p. 31 (provenance)
1962 Hallo, HUCA 33 p. 25 Ur-Nammu 10 (ex. 1, study)
1965 Szlechter, Studia et documenta historiae et juris 31 pl. after p. 496 (ex. 9, copy)
1971 Sollberger and Kupper, IRSA IIIA1d (ex. 1, translation)
1981 Walker, CBI no. 19 (exs. 1–2, study)
1985 Behrens, JCS 37 p. 232 no. 12 (exs. 3–8, study)
1985 Kärki, KDDU p. 6 Urnammu 10 (exs. 1–2, edition)
1991 Steible, NSBW 2 pp. 104–105 Urnammu 10 (exs. 1–9, edition)

TEXT

1) ^{d}nanna
2) dumu-sag-
3) ^{d}en-líl-lá
4) lugal-a-ni

1–4) For the god Nanna, first-born son of the god Enlil, his lord,

5) ur-^{d}nammu
6) nita-kala-ga
7) en-unu.KI-ga
8) lugal-uri$_5$.KI-ma
9) lugal-ki-en-gi-ki-uri-ke$_4$

5–9) Ur-Nammu, mighty man, lord of Uruk, king of Ur, king of the lands of Sumer and Akkad,

10) é-temen-ní-gùru
11) é-ki-ág-gá-ni
12) mu-na-dù
13) ki-bé mu-na-gi$_4$

10–13) built for him the E-temen-ni-guru, his beloved temple, (and) restored it.

13

Woolley (UE 7 p. 40) reports the find of twelve door sockets incised with an Ur-Nammu inscription dedicated to the goddess Ningal. Of these, ten have been identified. All exemplars came from the Gipar-ku at Ur. Many of these door sockets were reused by Amar-Suena in his reconstruction of that structure.

CATALOGUE

Ex.	Museum number	Excavation number	Registration number	Material	Dimensions (cm)	Lines preserved	cpn
1	BM 118548	U 6353	1927-5-27, 4	Diorite	—	—	n
2	BM 118550	U 6353	1927-5-27, 6	Diorite	21×23×16	1–8	c
3	CBS 16567	U 6353	—	Diorite	27×26×15	1–8	c
4	IM 1133	U 6353	—	Limestone	—	—	n
5	IM 1134	U 6353	—	Limestone	—	—	n
6	IM 1137	U 6353	—	Limestone	—	—	n
7	IM 1132	U 6364	—	Black limestone	—	—	n
8	IM 1136	U 6364	—	Limestone	—	—	n
9	IM 1138	U 6364	—	Limestone	—	—	n
10	IM 1139	U 6364	—	Limestone	—	—	n

COMMENTARY

According to Woolley and Mallowan's account in UE 7 pp. 40–63, door sockets bearing this inscription were found in rooms A.3, C.1, C.25, and C.26 of the Gipar-ku. One of the IM door sockets was last seen near the dig house at Mosul. Exs. 7–10 are known from notes kindly provided by H. Steible. The text is arranged in one column of eight lines.

BIBLIOGRAPHY

1926 Woolley, AJ 6 p. 366 (provenance)
1928 Gadd, UET 1 no. 35 (exs. 1–2, copy, edition)
1929 Barton, RISA pp. 360–61 Ur-Nammu 3 (exs. 1–2, edition)
1962 Hallo, HUCA 33 p. 26 Ur-Nammu 19 (exs. 1–2, study)
1971 Sollberger and Kupper, IRSA IIIA1i (exs. 1–2, translation)
1986 Kärki, KDDU p. 10 Urnammu 19 (exs. 1–2, edition)
1991 Steible, NSBW 2 pp. 112–13 Urnammu 19 (exs. 1–6, edition

TEXT

1) ^{d}nin-gal
2) nin-a-ni
3) ur-^{d}nammu
4) nita-kala-ga
5) lugal-uri$_5$.KI-ma
6) lugal-ki-en-gi-ki-uri-ke$_4$
7) gi$_6$-par$_4$-kù-ga-ni
8) mu-na-dù

1–2) For the goddess Ningal, his lady,

3–6) Ur-Nammu, mighty man, king of Ur, king of the lands of Sumer and Akkad,

7–8) built her shining Gipar for her.

14

An inscription found on three door sockets from the Gipar-ku at Ur records Ur-Nammu's construction of a temple for the goddess Ninegal. The text is arranged in one column of eight lines.

CATALOGUE

Ex.	Museum number	Excavation number	Registration number	Ur provenance	Object	Dimensions (cm)	Lines preserved	cpn
1	CBS 16564	U 6354	—	Gipar-ku, room A.5	Diorite door socket	46×44×22	1–8	c
2	BM 115025	—	—	—	Diorite door socket frgm.	56×33×23	1–8	c
3	IM 1135	U 6354	—	Gipar-ku F.14	Limestone door socket	—	—	n

BIBLIOGRAPHY

1926 Woolley, AJ 6 p. 366 (findspot)
1928 Gadd, UET 1 no. 38 and pl. G (ex. 1, photo, copy, edition)
1929 Barton, RISA pp. 362–63 Ur-Nammu 5 (ex. 1, edition)
1962 Hallo, HUCA 33 p. 26 Ur-Nammu 18 (ex. 1, study)
1976 Woolley and Mallowan, UE 7 p. 45 (ex. 1, provenance)
1984 Gerardi, Bibliography p. 192 (ex. 1, study)
1986 Kärki, KDDU p. 10 Urnammu 18 (ex. 1, edition)
1991 Steible, NSBW 2 p. 112 Urnammu 18 (exs. 1–3, edition)

TEXT

1) ^{d}nin-é-gal
2) nin-a-ni
3) ur-^{d}nammu
4) nita-kala-ga
5) lugal-uri$_{5}$.KI-ma
6) lugal-ki-en-gi-ki-uri-ke$_{4}$
7) é-a-ni
8) mu-na-dù

1–2) For the goddess Ninegal, his lady,

3–6) Ur-Nammu, mighty man, king of Ur, king of the lands of Sumer and Akkad,

7–8) built her temple for her.

15

Two inscriptions deal with Ur-Nammu's construction of a shrine of the goddess Inanna at Ur. The work apparently began before the king's trip to Nippur as is evidenced by the brick inscription (E3/2.1.1.15); in it the king appears with the simple title "king of Ur." The door socket inscription (E3/2.1.1.16), on the other hand, was apparently issued after the king's return, since it employs an updated titulary for the monarch. The combined evidence of the two inscriptions suggests that the Inanna temple at Ur was completed sometime around year (f) of Ur-Nammu.

A parallel to these two Ur-Nammu inscriptions is provided by two inscriptions of Šulgi (E3/2.1.2.31–32). In the first text, the brick inscription, the king's name appears without the prefixed DINGIR sign. In the second text, inscribed on foundation tablets and canephores, the king's name appears with the prefixed divine determinative. The Ur-Nammu and Šulgi inscriptions, then, provide evidence that an extended period of time was necessary to complete the rebuilding of a temple; in both cited cases the titulary of the king was altered as work on the edifice progressed. Of further note is the textual variation allowed in inscriptions dealing with one structure. In both examples cited, the temple name is absent from the brick inscription but present on the companion door socket or foundation tablet inscription.

CATALOGUE

Ex.	Museum number	Excavation number	Registration number	Ur provenance	Dimensions (cm)	Lines preserved	cpn
1	BM 114234	—	1919-10-11, 4665	—	30.5×23.5×7	1–7	c
2	BM 114243	—	1919-10-11, 4674	—	31×30.5×6	1–7	c
3	BM 114247	—	1919-10-11, 4678	—	30.5×24×6.5	1–7	c
4	BM 137416	—	1979-12-18, 51	—	29.5×27.5×6.5	1–7	c
5	CBS 15346	—	—	—		—	n
6	CBS 16459	U 2878a	—	Loose		—	n
7	CBS 16529	U 2878b	—	Loose		—	n

COMMENTARY

Exs. 1–4 were collated by C.B.F. Walker. Exs. 1–3 come from Hall's excavations at Ur, but unfortunately more precise information on their findspots is unavailable. In all likelihood, Ninkununa's temple was situated somewhere within the Ur III temenos. The inscription is arranged in one column of seven lines.

Although the name of Inanna's shrine does not appear in this brick inscription, the name is known from the companion door socket inscription to have been èš-bur "shrine of the bowls."

Inanna's epithet in this inscription: nin-kù-nun-na, suggests that this particular cult of the goddess was an import from Eridu. According to Green (Eridu p. 210): "A temple of Inanna at Eridu occurs in Temple List 296: é-[ ] = [É 18 š]*a Eridu*. This should be restored as é-[kù-nun-na] according to é-kù-nun-na urú-zé-eb.KI-ba-za ⌜é⌝ nam tar-re-da dúr-zu bí-in-gar 'you have made your residence at your Ekunna at Eridu, the temple where fates are to be decided' (Inanna D 63f.)." At the time work on the the èš-bur temple was begun by Ur-Nammu, the king likely did not yet control Uruk. While he may have wished to honour Inanna, the fact that her chief cult city was in the hands of his brother(?) at this time may have constrained Ur-Nammu. A parallel situation may be seen in Ur-Nammu's care for the cult of another Uruk goddess, Ninsuna, through his construction of her temple at the cult centre of KI.KAL/Kuʾar. The fact that Ninkununa is named together with Nimin-taba in An:*Anum* but does not appear with that goddess in a section of the Abū Ṣalābīkh god list that evidently deals with deities at Ur (lines 74–80 in Alberti's edition in SEL 2 [1985] p. 8) would argue in favour of seeing Ninkununa as an Ur III import. Certainly, the practice of transferring cults from Eridu to Ur is well attested for later (Old Babylonian) times; see the discussion in chapter 5 of Charpin, Le Clergé d'Ur, in this connection. For Ur III archival references to Ninkununa at Ur, see Sallaberger, Kalender 1 p. 208. For an Ur III votive inscription dedicated to Ninkununa, see inscription E3/2.1.6.1037. A prebend to this goddess is known from Old Babylonian times (NBC 5369: Grice, YOS 5 no. 135; see Charpin, Le Clergé d'Ur p. 186).

BIBLIOGRAPHY

1928 Gadd, UET 1 no. 39 (copy, edition)
1929 Barton, RISA pp. 362–63 Ur Nammu 6 (edition)
1962 Hallo, HUCA 33 p. 25 Ur-Nammu 6 (study)
1981 Walker, CBI no. 16 (exs. 1–4, study)
1985 Behrens, JCS 37 p. 231 no. 10 (exs. 5–7, study)
1986 Kärki, KDDU p. 4 Urnammu 6 (exs. 1–7, edition)
1991 Steible, NSBW 2 pp. 99–100 Urnammu 6 (exs. 1–7, edition)

TEXT

1) ᵈinanna 2) nin-kù-nun-na 3) nin-a-ni	1–3) For the goddess Inanna/ Ninkununa, his lady,
4) ur-ᵈnammu 5) lugal-uri₅.KI-ma-ke₄	4–5) Ur-Nammu, king of Ur,
6) é-a-ni 7) mu-na-dù	6–7) built her temple for her.

16

Two door sockets that were reused in the Neo-Babylonian levels of the Giparku at Ur bear an inscription commemorating Ur-Nammu's construction of Inanna/Nin-kununa's Ešbur shrine. The text is arranged in one column of ten lines.

CATALOGUE

Ex.	Museum number	Excavation number	Registration number	Ur provenance	Dimensions (cm)	Lines preserved	cpn
1	BM 119008	U 2736	1927-10-3, 3	Room 6 of the E-gipar of Nabonidus	50×41×24	1–10	c
2	IM —	U 6744	—	SE corner of the E-gipar of Nabonidus	—	1–10	n

BIBLIOGRAPHY

1925 Woolley, AJ 5 pp. 379 and 382 (provenance)
1928 Gadd, UET 1 nos. 36–37 (exs. 1–2, copy, edition)
1929 Barton, RISA pp. 274–75 Ur-Nammu 14 and pp. 362–63 Ur-Nammu 4 (ex. 1, edition)
1962 Hallo, HUCA 33 p. 26 Ur-Nammu 17 (exs. 1–2, study)
1986 Kärki, KDDU pp. 9–10 Urnammu 17 (exs. 1–2, edition)
1991 Steible, NSBW 2 p. 111 Urnammu 17 (exs. 1–2, edition)

TEXT

1) ^{d}inanna
2) nin-kù-nun-na
3) nin-a-ni
4) ur-^{d}nammu
5) nita-kala-ga
6) lugal-uri$_5$.KI-ma
7) lugal-ki-en-gi-ki-uri-ke$_4$
8) èš-bur
9) é-ki-ág-a-ni
10) mu-na-dù

1–3) For the goddess Inanna/Nin-kununa, his lady,

4–7) Ur-Nammu, mighty man, king of Ur, king of the lands of Sumer and Akkad,

8–10) built for her the Ešbur ("House of Jars"), her beloved temple.

17

Two inscriptions (E3/2.1.1.17–18) allude to Ur-Nammu's construction of the temple of the god Nanna, and probably date to the time around the construction of the temple. One of these, a fourteen-line cone inscription, deals with the return of the Magan trade to the ki-SAR-a. Two of the cones bearing this inscription were found at Diqdiqqah, a small mound on the outskirts of Ur, and a possible site for the ki-SAR-a.

E3/2.1.1.16.2.1 nin-nun-na.

CATALOGUE

Ex.	Museum number	Excavation number	Registration number	Provenance	Dimensions (cm)	Lines preserved	cpn
1	BM 30086	—	56-9-3,1501	—	5.2×4.5	1–2, 8–10	c
2	BM 119041	U 2520	1927-10-3, 36	Diqdiqqah	7×3.8	11–14	c
3	BM 119029	U 2701	1927-10-3, 24	Diqdiqqah	6.2×4.6	4–7, 11–14	c
4	CBS 16231	U 6019	—	Lower surface soil of EH site (Ur)	13.5×6	1–14	c
5	IM 92814	U 7722	—	SM site (Ur)	—	—	n
6	AO 15306 (Musée de Belfort)	T 31(?)	—	—	—	1–14	p

COMMENTARY

Ex. 1 comes from Loftus's soundings at Ur, exs. 2–3 from Woolley's excavations at Diqdiqqah, and exs. 4–5 from Woolley's excavations at Ur. The text follows Gadd's copy (UET 1 no. 50), which is a restored text. Steible (NSBW 2 p. 124) indicated that UET 1 no. 50 is a copy of ex. 4, but the copy does not correspond to the text that was collated in Philadelphia. Ex. 6 apparently came from Telloh; it is now housed in the Musée de Belfort, France. Its text was collated from photos kindly provided by A. Cavigneaux. As far as can be determined, the text is arranged in two columns: col. i contains lines 1–10, and col. ii lines 11–14.

The reading and meaning of ki-SAR-a in line 13 is not entirely clear. In addition to this text, we find a ki-SAR-ra mentioned in connection with the Magan trade in the prologue to the Ur-Nammu Law Code (see E3/2.1.1.20 line 79) and a ki-sur-ra in association with the same trade in the inscription edited as E3/2.1.1.18 (col. i line 3) in this volume. Jacobsen, Iraq 22 (1960) p. 242, translated the word ki-SAR-a in inscription 16 as "registry place," apparently understanding SAR to be connected with Akkadian *šaṭāru*(*m*) "to write." Sollberger and Kupper, IRSA p. 136, gave a translation "phare" (lighthouse), taking the phrase ki-SAR-a as ki-mú-a "place d'embrasement" (place of burning).

Heimpel (ZA 77 [1987] p. 32 n. 35) notes that an Ur III archival text (King, CT 7 pl. 16 col. i line 20) refers to a field that was offered to the ki-SAR-a. Heimpel suggests that the ki-SAR-a was perhaps a mooring place for ships where traders exchanged their goods. His suggestion that it represents a *locality* (Örtlichkeit) is supported by the evidence of the zà-mì collection of hymns from Abū Ṣalābīkh edited by R. Biggs (Abū Ṣalābīkh pp. 45–56). In this composition each new hymn normally begins with the name of a locality and ends with praise for the tutelary deity of that place. In particular, it is worth noting that lines 39–40 of the zà-mì hymns deal with a (toponymn?) ki-SAR, apparently located in the general vicinity of Ur, whose deity was the goddess Ningal. Of interest, in this connection is the apparent link between the goddess Ningal and sailors. Oppenheim, JAOS 74 (1954) p. 8, notes:

> Another way to show the sailor's gratitude to Ningal — this goddess was apparently considered the "Notre Dame de la Garde" of Ur — consisted in the dedication of silver models of sea-going boats ...

The goddess Nanše at Lagaš apparently played a similar role (as protectress of sailors) at Lagaš (see B. Alster, in Potts, Dilmun p. 50). It may be that the ki-SAR of the Abū Ṣalābīkh zà-mì hymns is to be connected with the ki-SAR-a of this inscription, both seen to refer to a place (possibly modern Diqdiqqah) where ships from the Persian Gulf trade tied up.

BIBLIOGRAPHY

1928 Gadd, UET 1 no. 50 (exs. 1–4, provenance; ex. 4, copy, edition)

1929 Barton, RISA pp. 364–65 Ur-Nammu 15 (ex. 4, edition)

1960 Jacobsen, Iraq 22 pp. 184–85 (exs. 1–4, edition, study)

1962 Hallo, HUCA 33 p. 27 Ur-Nammu 26 (exs. 1–4, study)

1965 Sollberger, UET 8 p. 26 no. 12 (ex. 5, study)

1971 Sollberger and Kupper, IRSA IIIA1f (exs. 1–4, translation)

1976 Woolley and Mallowan, UE 7 p. 83 n. 4 (exs. 1–4, provenance)

1984 Gerardi, Bibliography p. 192 (ex. 4, study)

1986 Kärki, KDDU pp. 14–15 Urnammu 26 (exs. 1–4, edition)

1987 Heimpel, ZA 77 pp. 32, 34, and 78–79 (translation, study)

1991 Steible, NSBW 2 pp. 124–26 Urnammu 26 (exs. 1–5, edition)

TEXT

1) dnanna
2) dumu-sag-
3) den-líl-lá
4) lugal-a-ni

1–4) For the god Nanna, first-born son of the god Enlil, his lord,

5) ur-^{d}nammu
6) nita-kala-ga
7) lugal-uri$_5$.KI-ma
8) lugal-ki-en-gi-ki-uri-ke$_4$
9) lú é-^{d}nanna
10) in-dù-a
11) nì-ul-lí-a-ke$_4$ pa mu-na-è
12) gaba-a-ab-ka-ka
13) ki-SAR-a nam-ga-eš$_8$ bí-sá
14) má-má-gan šu-na mu-ni-gi$_4$

5–10) Ur-Nammu, mighty man, king of the lands of Sumer and Akkad, the one who built the temple of the god Nanna,

11) brought into being the ancient state of affairs.

12–13) On the shore he had trade reach (the) ki-SAR-a

14) (and) returned the ships of Magan into his (Nanna's) hands.

18

A stone foundation tablet records Ur-Nammu's return of the Magan trade to the god Nanna.

COMMENTARY

The tablet is made of limestone and measures 15.1×11.5×2.35 cm. It bears the museum number BM 104744 and the registration number 1912-7-6, 8. Its original provenance is not known. The inscription was collated.

If the restoration of the proper name of col. ii line 5 (⸢a-ba-^{d}nanna⸣ [x x]-ni) is correct, then there might be a connection with the canal name a-ba-^{d}nanna-gin$_7$ of inscription 19 line 19. In col. iv line 12, ḫé-a is a writing for ḫé-ak.

BIBLIOGRAPHY

1922 BM Guide p. 85 no. 62 (study)
1991 Steible, NSBW 2 pp. 149–52 and pls. 13–14 Urnammu 47 (photo, edition)

TEXT

Col. i
1) ^{d}nanna
2) lugal-a-ni
3) ⸢ki⸣-sur-⸢ra⸣
4) má-⸢má-gan.na⸣
5) an-né
6) ^{d}⸢en-líl-le⸣
7) sag-šè ì-[x]-ri[g$_7$-ga]
8) ur-[^{d}]⸢nammu⸣
9) ni[ta-kala-g]a
10) lugal-⸢uri$_5$.KI⸣-m[a]
11) lugal-[ki-en]-gi-[ki-uri-ke$_4$]
12) u$_4$ é-⸢^{d}⸣[na]nn[a]
13) ⸢mu⸣-dù-⸢a⸣

i 1–2) For the god Nanna, his lord,

i 3–7) the boundary for the ships of Magan, which the gods An and Enlil gra[nted (to him) as a gift],

i 8–11) Ur-Nammu, [might]y ma[n], king of Ur, king of the [land of Su]mer [and Akkad],

i 12–13) when he built the temple of the god [Na]nn[a],

E3/2.1.1.17.11.5 pa mu-na-ni-è (from Sollberger).

Col. ii
1) di-nì-gi-[na]-
2) ^{d}utu-ta
3) ⸢KA mu⸣-na-gi-in
4) ⸢šu-na mu⸣-ni-[g]i$_{4}$
5) ⸢a-ba-^{d}nanna⸣ [x x]-ni
6) [a m]u-na-ru
7) [l]ú á-nì-⸢ḫul-dím⸣-ma
8) [íb-ši]-ág-ge$_{26}$-a
9) l[ú ki-gub-ba]-bi
10) [í]b-kúru-a
11) ^{d}nanna
Col. iii
1) ⸢lugal⸣(?) ⸢x x⸣ [x] ⸢x(?)⸣
Rest of column is illegible
Col. iv
1) [ḫ]é-in-ti-e
2) uru-ni-da
3) sag-ki-⸢ni⸣
4) ḫa-ba-da-[gíd-dè]
5) GIŠ.g[u-za-ni-ta]
6) saḫar-r[a ḫé-em-ta-tuš]
7) ur[u-ni]
8) g[i-suḫur$_{x}$(KA)-ta]
9) ḫé-⸢ta⸣-[DAG].⸢DAG-ge⸣
10) ⸢nam⸣-[ti-il]
11) [nì-gi]g-⸢ga-ni⸣
12) [ḫ]é-⸢a⸣

ii 1–3) by the ju[st] verdict of the god Utu, confirmed it (the boundary) for him.

ii 4) (Ur-Nammu) returned (the boundary) to him (the god Nanna).

ii 5–6) "Who [*is like*(?)] Nanna ...," his ..., he [de]dicated to him.

ii 7–8) As for the [o]ne who [gi]ves orders to do evil [against it],

ii 9–10) (or) w[ho] alters the [place where] it [stands],

ii 11) (may) the god Nanna

iii 1) king ...

iv 1) [M]ay he live.

iv 2–4) May he (the god) *frown* at his city.

iv 5–6) [From his th]rone [may he make him sit] i[n] the dust.

iv 7–9) May he tear down [his] ci[ty] from (its) summit shrine.

iv 10–12) [M]ay li[fe] become a [ma]lady for him.

19

A twenty-line cone inscription deals with Ur-Nammu's draining of a swamp in the vicinity of Ur.

CATALOGUE

Ex.	Museum number	Excavation number	Registration number	Ur provenance	Dimensions (cm)	Lines preserved	cpn
Cones							
1	BM 30056	(Taylor's excavations)	59-10-14, 90	—	10×4.5×4.5	13–20	c
2	—	U 7778	—	TTD	—	7–12	n
3	IM 92781	U 10101	—	Top filling of the Royal Cemetery	10×8.5	1–8, 13–17	n
4	IM 92782	U 11673a	—	Royal Cemetery	7.5×12.5	8–20	n
5	—	U 11673b	—	NE city wall, central section	—	—	n
6	IM 92783	U 15024	—	Royal Cemetery area "near surface"	15×7	1–5, 11–20	n
7	BM 123119	U 17821	1932-10-8, 3	LH (= Larsa houses [?]) in the mixed rubbish in front of the IIIrd Dyn. wall	3×4.4	1–5, 7–17	c
8	BM 138346	—	1935-1-13, 749	—	9.6×7	1–20	c
9	IM 92771	—	—	—	—	1–20	n
10	IM 92772	—	—	—	—	13–20	n
11	IM 92768	—	—	—	—	7–12	n
Tablet copy							
12	IM 85462	U 7746	—	No. 7 Quiet Street, rms. 5–6	11×6.5	1–20	n

COMMENTARY

The exemplars designated by Sollberger as U ob and U pb are likely to be found among the cones numbered IM 92771, 92772, and 92786.

The text is arranged in two columns: col. i lines 1–12, and col. ii lines 13–20.

The name of the canal in this text, "Who is like the god Nanna," may appear in the previous inscription, E3/2.1.1.18 ii 5.

BIBLIOGRAPHY

1928 Gadd, UET 1 nos. 284–85 (exs. 2, 12, copy, conflated edition)
1962 Hallo, HUCA 33 p. 27 Ur-Nammu 27 (exs. 2, 12, study)
1965 Sollberger, UET 8 p. 33 (exs. 3–7, study)
1971 Sollberger and Kupper, IRSA IIIA1h (exs. 2–7, translation)
1986 Kärki, KDDU pp. 15–16 Urnammu 27 (exs. 2–7, edition)
1991 Steible, NSBW 2 pp. 126–30 Urnammu 27 (exs. 1–12, edition)

TEXT

1) ^{d}nanna
2) dumu-sag-
3) ^{d}en-líl-lá
4) lugal-a-ni

1–4) For the god Nanna, first-born son of the god Enlil, his lord,

5) ur-^{d}nammu
6) nita-kala-ga
7) lugal-uri$_5$.KI-ma
8) lugal-ki-en-gi-ki-uri-ke$_4$

5–8) Ur-Nammu, mighty man, king of Ur, king of the lands of Sumer and Akkad,

9) sug-peš-dù-a
10) sug ḫé-me-àm

9–10) in a swamp planted with date palms — it was a veritable swamp —

11) a-šà-bi
12) ŠÁR.GAL GÁNA-àm
13) a-ta
14) ḫa-mu-na-ta-DU

11–14) he brought forth from the water a field that had an area of 3,600 *bur* (= 233.28 km^2).

15) e-bi 4 da-na 260 nindan
16) ḫé-na-AK

15–16) He made its canal four *dana* (= 43.2 km) and 260 *nindan* (= 1560 m) in length.

17) uri$_5$.KI-e gi$_{16}$-sa-aš
18) hé-mi-AK

17–18) He laid it out for perpetuity in Ur.

19) e-ba a-ba-^{d}nanna-gin$_7$
20) mu-bi

19–20) The name of that canal is: "Who (is) like the god Nanna?"

20

In 1954 S. Kramer published a Nippur tablet in Istanbul that was inscribed with an Old Babylonian copy of a Sumerian law code. Since Ur-Nammu's name occurred twice in the text, Kramer assigned it to the first Ur III king. More

---

Variants for E3/2.1.1.19:
4.12 lugal-a-ni-⌜ir⌝.
6.7 Omits line.
12.7,12 ŠÁR.GAL <GÁNA>-àm.
14. 1 ⌜ḫa⌝-mu-na-ta-è
15. 6 270 nindan (collation Steible).
17. 4 uri$_5$.KI-a; a over an erased ma.
18. 6 [ḫé]-mi-na.

recently, however, some scholars have suggested that the composition might belong instead to Šulgi. Geller has summarized the arguments pro and con in his review of Gibson and Biggs, Bureaucracy (ZA 81 [1991] pp. 145–46):

> The second problem in this volume is the re-assigning of the so-called Ur-Nammu Law Code to Šulgi, since Steinkeller states categorically that "Shulgi's authorship of the code is virtually assured" (p. 19, 21). The attribution of the Code to Šulgi began as a tentative suggestion by J.J. van Dijk (Or. 50 [1981] 93f.), which was then more staunchly advocated by S.N. Kramer (Or. 52 [1983] 453ff.). The argument runs as follows: the clauses of the Ur-Nammu Code prologue are expressed in the first person, rather than in the third person as originally translated by Kramer (Or. 23 [1954] 40—51) and J.J. Finkelstein (JCS 22 [1969] 66ff.), which is now confirmed by the discovery of a Sippar duplicate (F. Yıldız, Or. 50 [1981] 87ff.). Van Dijk, apud Yıldız, suggests that Šulgi could have been author of the Code, based upon the following passage: u$_4$ An-né ^{d}En-líl-le ^{d}Nanna-ar nam-lugal-Úri.ki-ma [mu-na]-sum-mu-uš-a-ba u$_4$-ba Ur-^{d}Nammu-ke$_4$ dumu tu-da ^{d}Nin-súna-ka ama-a-tu ki-ág-gá-ni-ir nig-si-sá-ni-šè ..., which we would translate as, "after An and Enlil granted the kingship of Ur to Nanna, then to Ur-Nammu, natural son of Ninsuna, her beloved offspring, for him to put things right ... ." The suggestion is here that the form Ur-^{d}Nammu-ke$_4$ is an indirect object, in contrast to the first person perspective of the remainder of the prologue. Kramer (Or. 52, 454) reinforces the argument by re-reading line 24 of the Code as [^{d}Ur-]⸢^{d}⸣Nammu-r[a], further suggesting that Ur-Nammu was an indirect object. The essence of the argument is therefore grammatical, and specifically the analysis of the syntax of the name "Ur^{d}Nammu-ke$_4$": is it a locative-terminative construction, or simply an agentive subject? Either case would be difficult if the king, as author, speaks in the first person. The only likely candidate to refer to Ur-Nammu in the prologue would be his son Šulgi, who would then be the author of the Code.
>
> One can immediately recognize the attractions of the argument, which supports a Šulgi-centric view of the Ur III period in which that king dominated the political landscape, and his authorship of the Code would reinforce this view. Nevertheless, a lot has been read into the grammar of a single damaged passage, in the face of several cogent arguments against Šulgi's authorship: van Dijk, first of all, already recognized certain parallels between the Code of Ur-Nammu and the Ur-Nammu hymns (Or. 50, 93^{20a} and 95^{30}), while one might have expected similarities with Šulgi's own hymns. An alternative suggestion might be that the Ur-Nammu Code was pseudepigraphic, i.e. composed in Šulgi's reign but merely ascribed to Ur-Nammu, in which case both the events described and the laws ought to refer to Ur-Nammu's period. Otherwise, it would be impossibly complicated to determine which part of the Code actually referred to UrNammu, and which to Šulgi's own time (*pace* Kramer Or. 52, 453).
>
> Furthermore, Steinkeller's attempt to disassociate Ur-Nammu from the conquests described in the prologue of the Code can be discounted, since the historical evidence is ambiguous, and Steinkeller himself cites evidence to the contrary recently supplied by C. Wilcke (p. 20).
>
> Finally, the strongest evidence against Šulgi's authorship is the fact that while Ur-Nammu's name appears at least three times in this Code (ll. 24, 36, 104), Šulgi's own name is completely absent, although it is extremely unlikely that Šulgi would have omitted reference to himself in such a prominent context.

Further, Wilcke (in Raaflaub, Anfänge p. 37 n. 45), in arguing against the attribution of the composition to Šulgi, notes that the ba-an-si-sá measure of 5 sìla that the author of the law code claims to have instituted has left no traces in the archival texts of Šulgi and his successors.

The prologue of the law code contains a narrative not unlike that of a royal inscription, and, as noted, is a valuable source for the history of the early Ur III period. For that reason the prologue (and the concluding formula, but not the laws) have been included in this volume. Since Kramer's original edition, three additional exemplars of the "law code" have been published; exs. 1–2 provide parts of the text of the prologue and ex. 4 of the concluding formula.

Ex. 5 is tentatively identified as being a piece of a monumental copy of the Ur-Nammu Law Code. Support for this hypothesis comes from the comparative evidence provided by the "Ur-Nammu Stele"; one of its registers depicts Ur-Nammu pouring an oblation before a seated god. The scene is strikingly similar to one found on a limestone relief fragment now in the Louvre, here designated as ex. 5 (= Sb 7), that was found in excavations by de Morgan at Susa (de Morgan, MDP 1 pl. 3a). The Louvre piece is clearly the top of a stele; an excellent colour photo of the object was published in a catalogue for a recent Metropolitan Museum of New York exhibition of Susa treasures (Harper, Susa p. 170, fig. 110). Commenting on the piece Harper (Susa p. 169) writes:

> On the front surface of the stele is a scene comparable to many representations in Mesopotamian art of the late third millennium B.C. The enthroned god, perhaps Shamash, facing to the left, holds in his right hand a rod and circlet. The god is approached by a male figure, probably a Mesopotamian ruler, whose head is now missing. In the right hand this figure holds a vessel with a long, almost vertical spout, from which a libation is poured onto an altar. ... Similar imagery appears on the great stone stele of Ur-Nammu (2112–2095) also found at Ur and now in Philadelphia (fig. 47).

The Louvre fragment, along with other great monuments of Mesopotamian art (among these the so-called "Victory Stele" of Narām-Sîn and Ḫammu-rāpi's Law Code) was found in trench 7 of de Morgan's excavations on the Acropole mound at Susa. This fact led Harper (Susa p. 171) to conclude that the stele fragment was a piece of booty from Mesopotamia; in all likelihood, it came not from Ur, as Harper suggests, but rather from Sippar. Further, Harper (Susa p. 169) notes: "The composition of the scene on the Susa stele resembles the imagery at the summit of the diorite Code of Laws of Hammurabi (ca. 1792–1750 B.C.)." If our hypothesis be correct, Sb 7 would be a piece from the top of a monumental copy of the "Ur-Nammu Law Code" that once stood in Sippar.

Because of the relatively small overlap between texts no score has been prepared.

CATALOGUE

Ex.	Museum number	Excavation number	Provenance	Lines preserved	cpn
1	Ni 3191	—	Nippur	(Prologue) 8–18, 24–42, 46, 49–51, 71–96, 104–36, 140–52, 161–70	p
2	Si 277	—	Sippar	(Prologue) 125–79	p
3	IM 85688+85689	U 7739+U 7740	Ur	Laws only	—
4	BM 54722+	—	Sippar	Laws and col. iii′ 9′–23′ = (concluding formula) 1–15	n
5	Sb 7	—	Susa	Relief only, no text (see commentary)	p

COMMENTARY

The line count follows that given by Kramer for ex. 1, which was followed by Yıldız in her edition of ex. 2 and by Römer in his translation in TUAT I/1 pp. 17–23. We have given the column numbers of ex. 1 in the transliteration column to facilitate comparison with Kramer's copy. In order to accommodate both the evidence of ex. 2 as well as maintaining Kramer's original numbering, a somewhat skewed line count is given (following Römer) for lines 150–60. We have benefited greatly in this edition from the transliteration and translation of the text (following suggestions of Civil) given by M. Roth, in Law Collections pp. 15–17.

For the expression ki-SAR-ra of line 79, see the discussion to E3/2.1.1.17 line 13 above. For the expression ḫaš-dab$_5$ of lines 94–95, see Römer, Bilgameš und Akka pp. 52–53 and Michalowski, JCS 30 (1978) p. 116 to line 4. Kramer, in his edition of ex. 1 (Orientalia NS 23 p. 45), read lines 75–78: nam-ḫa-ni énsi-lagaš.KI-ke$_4$ ḫé-m[i-ug]$_5$ "... killed (Namḫani), the governor of Lagash." Roth (Law Collections), following Civil, read the verb: ⌈ḫé-mi-íl⌉ and translated the passage: "I promoted Namḫani to be governor of the city of Lagash." The verb, according to a collation of V. Donbaz, should indeed be read ⌈íl⌉. The text of lines 125–79 is a conflation of the texts found on exs. 1–2. For the translation of the verb forms of lines 162 ff., see Attinger, Eléments p. 196. For the term gi-suḫur$_x$ (KA) of line 6 of the concluding formula, see Civil, RA 61 (1967) pp. 63–66. The Sumerian term suḫur is equivalent to Akkadian *šaḫūru*(*m*), which AHw translates as "Gipfelbau." According to a Seleucid period tablet (Weissbach, WVDOG 59 p. 54 line 42), the seventh and highest stage of the ziqqurrat at Babylon had a chapel (*kiṣṣu*[*m*]) and *šaḫūru*(*m*) "summit shrine." For literature on the term "summit shrine," see Weidner, AfO 18 (1957–58) pp. 354–55; Börker-Klähn, ZA 70 (1980) pp. 258–72 and van Driel, Aššur pp. 24–28.

BIBLIOGRAPHY

1952 Kramer, UMB 17/2 fig. 13 (ex. 1, obv. copy)
1953 Klíma, ArOr 21 pp. 442–47 (ex. 1, study)
1953 Kramer, Scientific American 188/1 pp. 26–27 (ex. 1, obv. copy, photo)
1953 Szlechter, RA 47 pp. 1–10 (ex. 1, study)
1954 Kramer and Falkenstein, Orientalia NS 23 pp. 40–51 and pls. 4–7 (ex. 1, photo, copy, edition, study)
1955 Szlechter, RA 49 pp. 169–77 (ex. 1, edition)
1956 Kramer, FTS p. 49 fig. 25 (ex. 1, obv. copy); pp. 118–19 figs. 24 and 26 (ex. 1, photos)
1958 Kunderewicz, Czasopismo prawno-historyczne 10 pp. 9ff. (ex. 1, translation)
1965 Gurney and Kramer, in Landsberger Festschrift pp. 13–19 (ex. 3, copy, edition)
1967 Szlechter, RA 61 pp. 105–26 (ex. 3, edition)
1968–69 Finkelstein, JCS 22 pp. 66–82 (ex. 3, photo; exs. 1, 3, edition)
1969 Finkelstein, in ANET^3 pp. 523–25 (exs. 1, 3, translation)
1976 Kramer, ISET 2 pls. 128–29 (ex. 1, copy)
1978 Green, BiOr 35 p. 180 (ex. 1, study)
1979 Haase, Keilschriftlichen Rechtssammlungen 2 pp. 6–9 (exs. 1, 3, translation)
1981 Yıldız, Orientalia NS 50 pp. 87–97 and pls. 2–4 (ex. 2, copy, edition)
1982 Römer, TUAT I/1 pp. 17–23 (exs. 1–3, translation)
1983 Kramer, Orientalia NS 52 pp. 453–56 (study)
1983 van Dijk, Orientalia NS 52 p. 457 (study)
1987 Steinkeller, in Gibson and Biggs, Bureaucracy pp. 19–21 and nn. 1 and 10 (study)
1989 Michalowski and Walker, Studies Sjöberg pp. 386–96 (ex. 4, copy, edition)
1995 Roth, Law Collections pp. 13–22 (exs. 1–3, edition)

TEXT

Col. i

Lacuna	Lacuna
6) [...] x	6–9) Too broken for translation.
7) [...] x	
8) [... B]I	
9) [...] AN	
10) [ur]-⌈^{d}⌉!nam[mu]	10–13) (I) [Ur]-Nam[mu], [m]ighty [man], [king of U]r, [king of the la]nd of Su[mer and Akkad],
11) [nita-k]ala-g[a]	
12) [lugal-u]ri$_5$.K[I-ma]	
13) [lugal-k]i-en-[gi ki-uri]	
14) [...] AN [...]	14–23) Too broken for translation.
15) [...] x x [...]	
16) [...] x [...]	
17) [...] x x [...]	
18) [...] x šu [...]	
19) [...] x x [...]	

20) [...]
21) [...] x [...]
22) [...] x x [...]
23) [...] x x [...]
24) [... ka]lam-ma-š[è]
25) [x] x itu-da
26) 1.30 še gur
27) 30 udu
28) 30 sìla ì-nun
29) sá-du$_{11}$-šè
30) mu-na-ni-gar

24–30) for the [la]nd, I established ninety *gur* (= c. 2,700 litres) grain, thirty sheep, thirty *sila* (= c. 30 litres) butter as regular deliveries for him (the god Nanna?).

31) u$_4$ an-né
32) ^{d}en-líl-le
33) ^{d}nanna-ar
34) ⸢nam-lugal⸣-uri$_5$.KI-ma
35) ⸢mu-na-sum⸣-mu-uš-a-ba

31–35) When the gods An and Enlil granted to the god Nanna the kingship of Ur,

36) ⸢u$_4$-ba⸣ ur-^{d}nammu-<<ke$_4$>>
37) dumu tu-da-
38) ^{d}nin-súna-ka
39) ⸢émedu⸣(AMA.A.TU)
40) ki-ág-gá-ni-ir
41) nì-si-sá-ni-šè
42) [nì-g]e-[na]-ni-šè
43) ⸢x⸣ [...] x x x
44) [...] x

36–44) at that time, for (me) Ur-Nammu, the son born of the goddess Ninsuna, for her beloved house-born slave, according to his (the god Nanna's) principles of equity (and) [tr]u[th] ...

Col. ii
45) [x] x x [...]
46) [x] mu [...]
47) [s]i(?) x [...]
48) ba x [...]
49) 2 x [...]
50) 2 x [...]
51) x [...]
Lacuna

45–51) Too broken for translation.
Lacuna

71) [...] AN [...]
72) [x] x x [x] x

71–72) Too broken for translation.

73) ⸢x x⸣-7-bi
74) ⸢ḫu⸣-mu-un-da-an-⸢x⸣

73–74) its seven ... I ... beside him.

75) nam-ḫa-ni
76) énsi-
77) lagaš.KI-ke$_4$
78) ḫé-m[i]-⸢íl⸣

75–78) I *promoted* Namḫani (to be) governor of Lagaš.

79) ki-⸢SAR⸣-ra
80) má-má-gan.KI-na
81) ^{d}nanna
82) á-^{d}nanna
83) lugal-⸢gá⸣-ta
84) ḫé-mi-gi$_4$

79–84) By the might of the god Nanna, my lord, I returned to (the) ki-SAR-ra Nanna's Magan ship.

85) uri$_5$.KI-ma
86) ḫa-ba-zálag

85–86) I made it shine in Ur.

87) u$_4$-ba
88) a-šà *ni-is-qum*
89) ì-gál-la-àm
90) nam-gàraš
91) má-laḫ$_5$-ga[l]
92) ì-gál-la-⸢àm⸣

87–92) At that time the *nisku*-people had control of the fields, the chief sea-captain had control of trade,

Col. iii
93) [utu]l$_4$-e
94) [gu$_4$-dab$_5$ udu]-dab$_5$
95) [anše]-dab$_5$

93–97) [the herdsm]an had control over those who [*held back* cattle], *held back* [sheep] and [*held back*] asses.

96) [ì-gál-la]-àm
97) [...] x
Lacuna

Lacuna

103) [...] x
104) [u$_4$-ba ur-^{d}]nammu
105) [nita-kala]-ga
106) [lugal-uri$_5$.K]I-ma
107) [lugal-ki-en-gi]-ki-uri
108) [á-^{d}]nanna
109) [lugal-g]á-ta
110) [inim g]i(?)-na
111) [^{d}utu]-ta
112) [nì-s]i(?)-sá
113) [kalam-ma ḫ]u-mu-ni-⸢gar⸣
114) [...] x
115) [...]
116) [x]-⸢x⸣ ḫé-mi-gi$_4$

103–16) ... [At that time, I, Ur]-Nammu], [migh]ty [man], [king of Ur, king of the land of Sumer] and Akkad, by [the might of the god] Nanna, [m]y [lord], and by the [tr]ue [command of the god Utu], did indeedestablish [ju]stice [in the land]. I did indeed return [...]

117) nam-gàraš
118) má-laḫ$_4$-gal
119) utul$_4$-e
120) gu$_4$-dab$_5$ udu-dab$_5$
121) anše-⸢dab$_5$⸣
122) uri lú-gi[r$_5$-ra] [...]
123) ki-en-g[i ki-uri-a]
124) šu-ba b[a-an-bar]

117–24) Freedom was established for those conducting trade (free from) the chief sea-captain, for those who *held back* cattle, *held back* sheep, and *held back* asses (free from) the herdsman, and for the Akkadians and foreign[ers](?) in the land of Sum[er and Akkad].

125) u$_4$-ba
126) umma.KI
127) már-da.KI GÍR-kal.KI
128) ka-za-lu.KI
128a) ù maš-kán-bi
129) ú-ṣa-ru-um.KI
130) nì an-š[a]-an.KI-a nam-ìr ḫé-eb-ak-e

125–30) At that time, Umma, Marad, GIRkal, Kazallu, Uṣarum — those (cities) which had been subjugated by An[š]an —

131) á-^{d}nanna
132) lugal-gá-ta
133) ama-ar-gi$_4$-bi
134) ḫu-mu-gar

131–34) by the might of the god Nanna, my lord, I established their freedom.

135) [URU]DU.ba-rí-ga
136) ḫu-mu-gub
137) 1.00 sìla-àm ḫé-ge-en

135–37) I established a [cop]per *bariga* vessel and standardized it as 60 *sila* (= c. 60 litres) capacity.

138) URUDU.ba-an ḫu-mu-dím
139) 10 sìla-àm ḫé-ni-ge-en

138–39) I fashioned a copper *ban* measure and standardized it as ten *sila* (= c. 10 litres) capacity.

Col. iv
140) URUDU.ba-an-si-sá-lugal-la
141) ḫu-mu-dím
142) 5 s[ìla ḫé]-ni-ge-en

140–42) I fashioned a royal *ban* measure of current value (made) of copper and standardized it as five *s[ila]* (= c. 5 litres) (capacity).

143) 1 sìla zabar
144) ḫu-mu-dím
145) 1 ma-na-a
146) ḫé-ni-ge-en

143–46) I fashioned a bronze measure of one *sila* (= c. 1 litre) and standardized it as one mina.

147) 1 gín kù na$_4$
148) zà 1 ma-na-⸢e⸣
149) ḫé-ni-ge-en

147–49) I standardized weight stones from the pure one shekel weight to the one mina weight.

Variants for E3/2.1.1.20:
128a. 1 ù maš-gan-bi may be omitted (text broken away)
130.1 Probably omits nam-ìr ḫé-ab-ak-e (text broken away).
143.2 zabar-1-sìla. Ex. 2 puts lines 147–49 before lines 143–46.
145.2 1 ma-na-àm.
147.2 na$_4$-1-gín-kù.
148.2 zà-1-ma-na-e.

150) u_4-ba
151) gú-I_7.idigna
152) gú-I_7.buranun
153) gú-íd-dù-a-bi
154) add[ir(PAD.[x x x x si ḫé-em-mi-sá-sá]
155–56) É×KASKAL(?) šà [...]
157) x ḫé-em-mi-in-[dù]
158–60) GIŠ.$kiri_6$ ḫ[é-b]í-í[b-gub]
161) šandana lugal-e ḫé-éb-tuk
162) nu-síg lú-nì-tuku-ra
163) ba-ra-an-gar
164) nu-mu-un-kúš lú-á-tuku-ra
165) ba-ra-na-an-gar
166) lú 1 gín-e
167) [l]ú 1 ma-na-ra
168) ba-ra-n[a]-an-gar
169) lú-1-udu-ra
170) lú-1-gu_4-e
171) ba-ra-na-an-gar
172) GÍR.NÍTA.GÍR.NÍTA-mu-ne
173) ama-mu-[n]e šeš-šeš-mu-ne
174) su-a-[su-a-ne]-ne
175) ki ḫa-b[a-ni-gar]-re-eš
176) á-[ág-gá-n]e-ne-a
176a) ba-ra-b[a-gu]b(?)-bé-en
176b) kin ba-ra-ba-ni-gar
177) nì-érim
178) nì-á-zi
179) i-^{d}utu ug-gu ḫé-ni-dé
180) nì-si-sá
181) kalam-ma ḫu-mu-ni-gar
The laws follow.
Concluding formula
1) [lú mu]-⸢sar-ra⸣-ba šu bí-íb-ùr-ru-a mu-ni bí-⸢íb⸣-sar-re-a
2) [áš-bal]-⸢ba⸣-ke_4-eš lú-kúr šu ba-an-zi-⸢zi-a⸣
3) [lú mu-s]ar-⸢ra-ba⸣ šu bí-íb-ùr-ru-a mu-nu x x in-na-ab-x
4) [lú-b]i lugal ḫé-a en ḫé-a énsi ḫé-⸢àm⸣
5) [...] ZA(?) DU x x ra ḫé-éb-t[a]-⸢an⸣-gi(?)
6) [uru-n]i gi-⸢suḫur$_x$(KA)⸣-ta ḫé-eb-ta-DAG.DAG-ge
7) [uru]-ni uru-^{d}en-líl nu-še-ga ḫé-a
8) [abul]a-uru-na-ke_4 ⸢gál⸣ [ḫé]-TAK_4.TAK_4
9) [...] x guruš uru-na igi-nu-du_8 ḫé-me-eš
10) [...] ki-sikil uru-na ù nu-ku_4-⸢dè(?)⸣-⸢e-eš⸣
11) [...]-uru-na-ke_4 ^{d}en-ki ^{d}⸢iškur⸣ ^{d}ez[inu]
12) [inim]-maḫ-^{d}en-líl-lá-⸢ka⸣ [x] x x ḫé-[...]
13) [...] uš bar si ⸢ra⸣ b[a]-x-an-né ḫ[é-...]
14) [...] x x x [x x] x x x [...]
15) [...] ⸢ri⸣ [...]
Lacuna

150–54) At that time, I [put in order] ri[ver-boat traffic] on the banks of the Tigris, on the banks of the Euphrates, and on the banks of all the rivers.

155–61) [I established] *road stations* in [...]. I [*built*] ... (and) [planted] orchards beside them. (I), the king, placed gardeners in charge of them.

162–71) The orphan was not handed over to the rich (man). The widow was not handed over to the mighty (man). The man of one shekel was not handed over to the man of one mina. The man of one sheep was not handed over to the man of one ox (Text: the man of one ox was not handed over to the man of one sheep).

172–75) I did indeed [settle] them [there] — my generals, my mothers, my brothers, and their fam[ili]es,

176–76a) (and) I will not impose the[ir] o[rders] (that is, orders on them).
176b) I did not impose toil there.
177–79) I banished there evil, violence, and (any cause for) complaint.

180–81) I established justice in the land.

The laws follow.
Concluding formula
1–3) As for the [one] who erases this [in]scription (and) writes his (own) name there, or who because of its [curse] incites another to do so, or [who] erases its [ins]cription and *writes his* (own) name,

4) [th]at [man], whether he be king, lord, or governor,
5) may he ... from ...
6) May [h]is [city] be torn down from (its) summit shrine.
7) May his [city] not find favour with the god Enlil.
8) May the [gat]es of his city be flung open.
9–12) May the ... young men of his city become blind. (May) the young women of his city not fall asleep. May the gods Enki, Iškur, and Ez[inu] ... the ... ... of his city, at the lofty [command] of the god Enlil.
13–15) Too broken for translation.
Lacuna

Variants for E3/2.1.1.20:
153.2 gú-íd dù-a-bi.
161.1 šandana lugal-<e>.
164.2 nu-mu-k[úš].

21

A cadastre text known from two Old Babylonian tablet copies edited by F. Kraus indicates that Ur-Nammu defined boundaries for the new provinces of his realm. Many of the territories described therein, to judge from the evidence of inscription E3/2.1.1.20 (lines 125–34), were lands that had recently been liberated from Elamite control. In addition to their mention in the Ur-Nammu Law Code, some of the new lands, in particular those in the Diyālā region, are named as territories emancipated from the Elamites in inscription E3/2.1.1.29.

It is not absolutely certain, albeit probable, that eleven fragments of an original stone monument now housed in Philadelphia that were published by L. Legrain as PBS 15 nos. 28–30, 32, and 33–39 are fragments of the monument which served as forerunner for the Old Babylonian tablet copies. Duplication of text is found in only a few lines; See ex. 1 iv lines 11–12: *ki-rí*-LUM-ta / *ḫi-bar-rí-tum*-šè, with ex. 3 frgm. 5 lines 1′–2′: [*ki-rí*]-⌈LUM⌉-t[a] / [*ḫi-ba-rí*]-*tum*-[šè], and ex. 1 iv 25–26: ka I₇.*ši-ma-at* / -ᵈ*èr-ra*-ta(Text: šè), with ex. 3 frgm. 9 line 1′: [... I₇.*ši-ma-at*]-ᵈ*èr*-⌈*ra* -šè⌉.

CATALOGUE

Ex.	Fragment number	Museum number	PBS 15 number	Dimensions (cm)	cpn
OB tablet copies					
1	—	Ni 2464	—	—	n
2	—	Ni 2438	—	—	n
Ur III stone fragments					
3	1	CBS 9557	28	16×10×8.3	c
3	2	CBS 13893	29	7×5.9×4.5	c
3	3	CBS 9560	30	12×3.8×6	c
3	4	CBS 9561	32	6×2×5	c
3	5	CBS 19928	34	11×13.7×5.9	c
3	6	CBS 13899	35	5.2×4.5×2	c
3	7	CBS 9564	36	8.7×4.5	c
3	8	CBS 9908	37	6×4.5×3.2	c
3	9	CBS 9559	38	12×8.3×5.5	n
3	10	CBS 9558	39	16.2×11	n
3	11	MMA 41.160.184	—	12.7×16.9×22.86	c

COMMENTARY

An examination of the stone pieces in Philadelphia reveals that PBS 15 nos. 31 and 33, which Legrain thought might be parts of the same monument edited as this inscription, likely come from one (or more) different steles.

BIBLIOGRAPHY

1926 Legrain, PBS 15 nos. 28–30, 32, and 34–39 (ex. 3, frgms. 1–10, copy, partial transliteration)
1955 Kraus, ZA 51 pp. 45–75 (exs. 1–2, copy, edition, study)
1963 Goetze, JCS 17 p. 4 (exs. 1–2, study)
1984 Carter and Schoville, Sign, Symbol, Script p. 15 fig. 22 no. 46 (ex. 3, frgm. 11, photo)

TEXT

Ex. 1
Col. i

1) [a]n-za-gàr-^{d}nu-muš-da-ka-ta
2) bára-^{d}nu-muš-da-ka-šè
3) á-IM.ùlu-bi

i 1–3) From the "Tower of the god Numušda" to the "Shrine of the god Numušda": its southern side.

4) bára-^{d}nu-muš-da-ka-ta
5) I$_{7}$.ka-zal-lu.KI-ka-šè
6) [á-I]M.*sa$_{12}$-dì-um*-ma-bi

i 4–6) From the "Shrine of the god Numušda" to the Kazallu canal: its eastern [side].

7) [I$_{7}$.k]a-zal-lu.KI-ka-ta
8) ḫur-sag-[(x)] x x-ka-šè
9) á-I[M.mir-ra-b]i

i 7–9) From the [K]azallu [canal] to the "... mountain": [it]s [northern] side.

10) x [...-t]a
11) an-za-gàr-^{d}[n]u-[muš]-[d]a-[k]a-šè
12) á-IM.mar-dú-bi

i 10–12) [Fr]om [GN] to the "Tower of the god [N]u[mušd]a": its western side.

13) a-šà-^{d}nu-muš-da kiri$_{8}$-tab.KI-kam
14) ^{d}nu-muš-da-ra
15) KA in-na-gi-in
16) ur-^{d}nammu lugal-e

i 13–16) (These are) the fields of the god Numušda of Kiritab, Ur-Nammu, the king, determined (the boundary) for the god Numušda.

---

17) an-za-gàr-^{d}nu-muš-da-ka-ta
18) bára-^{d}nu-muš-da-ka-šè
19) bára-^{d}nu-muš-da-ka-ta
20) an-za-gàr-ḫur-sag-gá-šè
21) an-za-gàr-ḫur-sag-gá-ta
22) I$_{7}$.še-er-ús-sa-šè
23) I$_{7}$.še-er-ús-sa-ta
24) é-duru$_{5}$-*i-bí-lum*-ma-šè
25) é-duru$_{5}$-*i-bí-lum*-ma-ta
26) I$_{7}$.áb-gal-šè
27) I$_{7}$.áb-gal-e ù-bal-e
28) ka I$_{7}$.*ur-ša-tum*-ta
29) 9;20 U[Š] ù-ta-DU
30) RI ki-sur-ra-kam
31) á-IM.mir-ra-bi

i 17–31) From the "Tower of the god Numušda" to the "Shrine of the god Numušda"; from the "Shrine of the god Numušda" to the "Tower of the Mountain"; from the "Tower of the Mountain" to the Šer-ussa canal; from the Šer-ussa canal to Ibillum village; from Ibillum village to the Abgal canal; after (you) cross over the Abgal canal; from the source of the Ušartum (canal you) go 560 UŠ (= c. 2,016,000 m); (it is) *this side* of the boundary: its northern side.

Col. ii

1) RI ki-sur-ra-t[a]
2) me-en-*ì-lí*-šè
3) á-IM.*sa$_{12}$-dì-um*-ma-bi

ii 1–3) From *this side* of the boundary to Me-en-ili: its eastern side.

4) me-en-*ì-lí*-ta
5) gú-I$_{7}$.áb-gal ka-I$_{7}$
6) DINGIR-*ba-ni*-šè
7) I$_{7}$.áb-gal-e ù-bal-e
8) ka I$_{7}$.*i-da-um*-ma-ta (Text: šè)
9) I$_{7}$.IM.NI-a-šè
10) á-IM.ùlu-bi

ii 4–10) From Me-en-ili to the bank of the Abgal canal (at) the source of the Ilum-bāni canal; after (you) cross over the Abgal canal; from (Text: to) the source of the Ida'um canal to the IM.NI-a canal: its southern side.

11) I$_{7}$.IM.NI-a-ta
12) NAGAR.BI-šè
13) NAGAR.BI-ta
14) uru-ambar-šè
15) uru-ambar-ta
16) ḫur-sag-šè
17) ḫur-sag-ta
18) á-ḫur-sag-gá a-ba-a-šè
19) ^{d}an-za-gàr-^{d}nu-muš-da-šè

ii 11–19) From the IM.NI-a canal to NAGAR.BI; from NAGAR.BI to the "Swamp City"; from "Swamp City" to the "Mountain"; from the "Mountain" to the *back* side of the "Mountain"; to the "Tower of the god Numušda": <its western side>.

20) ki-sur-ra ^{d}mes-lam-ta-è-a
21) a-pi$_{5}$-ak.KI-e
22) KA ba-an-gi-in

ii 20–23) Boundary of the god Meslamtaea of Apiak. Ur-Nammu, the king, determined it.

---

23) ur-^{d}nammu lugal-e
24) *ú*(Text: MA)-*ṣa-ru-um* [g]ú-
25) I$_7$.zubi IGI.NIM
26) *ḫi-ba-rí-tum*-ma-ka-ta(over erased šè)
27) ú(Text: MA)-*ṣa-ru-um* libir-šè
28) ú(Text: MA)-*ṣa-ru-um* libir-ta
29) ^{d}geštin-an-na
30) *ḫi-ba-rí-tum*-ma-ka-šè
31) ^{d}geštin-an-na
32) *ḫi-ba-rí-tum*-m[a-ka-ta]

ii 24–32) From Uṣarum on the bank of the Zubi canal above Ḫibarītum to "Old Uṣarum"; from "Old Uṣarum" to Geštin-ana (by) Ḫibarītum; [from] Geštin-ana (by) Ḫibarītum

Col. iii
1) da-x-[...-šè]
2) da-[...-ta]
3) x [...-šè]
4) x [...] x-ta
5) k[á-^{d}geštin-an-na-k]a-šè
6) á-[I]M.mi[r]-r[a-b]i

iii 1–6) [to] G[N$_1$]; [from] G[N$_1$ to] G[N$_2$]; from G[N$_2$] to K[a-geštin-ana]: [i]ts north[ern] side.

7) ká-^{d}geštin-an-na-ka-ta
8) *rí-ig-mu-úš-dan*-šè
9) *rí-ig-mu-úš-dan*-ta
10) I$_7$.ir-ni-na-šè
11) á-IM.mar-dú

iii 7–11) From Ka-geštin-ana to Rigmuš-dān; from Rigmuš-dān to the Irnina canal: its western side.

12) gú-I$_7$.ir-ni-na
13) a-ba-a-šè
14) *ḫi-rí-tum*-šè
15) *ḫi-rí-tum*-ta
16) *ḫur-ši-tum*-šè
17) *ḫur-ši-tum*-ta
18) *šar-ru-la-ba*-šè
19) *šar-ru-la-ba*-ta
20) *nam-zi-um*-šè
21) *nam-zi-um*-ta
22) I$_7$.ir-ni-na ù-bal-e
23) k[a(?)] ⸢I$_7$⸣.*ši-ma-at-*
24) [...] x-t[a]
25) a-zar-šè
26) a-zar-ta
27) bára-^{d}EN.ZU-šè
28) bára-^{d}EN.ZU-ta
29) gú-I$_7$.zubi-šè
30) á-IM.ùlu-bi

iii 12–30) To the *back side* of the bank of the Irnina canal to Ḫirītum; from Ḫirītum to Ḫuršītum; from Ḫuršītum to Šarru-labba; from Šarru-labba to Namzium; from Namzium (you) cross over the Irnina canal; from the s[ource] of the Šimat-... canal to Azar; from Azar to the "Shrine of the god Sîn"; from the "Shrine of the god Sîn" to the bank of the Zubi canal: its southern side.

Col. iv
1) [g]ú-I$_7$.zubi
2) a-ba-a-šè
3) pu-uš.KI-šè
4) pu-uš.K[I]-t[a]
5) kun ⸢I$_7$⸣.[i]r-[ni-na-šè]
6) I$_7$.ir-ni-na ù-bal-e-
7) kun I$_7$.ir-ni-na-ta
8) a-šà-^{d}EN.ZU-šè
9) a-šà-^{d}EN.ZU-ta
10) *ki-rí*-LUM-šè
11) *ki-rí*-LUM-ta
12) *ḫi-ba-rí-tum*-šè
13) *ḫi-ba-rí-tum*-ta
14) *ú*(Text: MA)-*ṣa-ru-um*-šè
15) I$_7$.zubi-IGI.NIM
16) *ḫi-ba-rí-tum*-ma-
17) ka-šè
18) á-IM.*sa$_{12}$-dì*-

iv 1–19) To the *back side* of the [b]ank of the Zubi canal to Puš; from Puš to the mouth of the [I]r[nina] canal; after (you) cross over the Irnina canal; from the mouth of the Irnina canal to the "Field of the god Sîn"; from the "Field of the god Sîn" to KiriLUM; from KiriLUM to Ḫibarītum; from Ḫibarītum to Uṣarum on the bank of the Zubi canal above Ḫibarītum: its eastern side.

19) *um*-ma-bi
20) ki-sur-ra ^{d}EN.ZU-kam
21) [x] x.KI-e
22) [KA ba-an-g]i-[i]n
23) u[r-^{d}]nammu
24) lugal-e

iv 20–24) Boundary of the god Sîn of GN. U[r]-Nammu, the king, [deter]mined it.

---

25) ka I_7.*si-ma-at*
26) ^{d}*èr-ra*-ta(Text: šè)

iv 25–26) From the source of the Šimat-Erra canal

Ex. 2

Col. i
1) ki-gal ki-sur-r[a]
2) kiš.KI ka-zal-[lu.K]I
3) ur$_5$-bi-da-[t]a(?)
4) gú I_7.me-[^{d}e]n-[líl]

i 1–4) [F]rom Kigal on the common boundary of Kiš and Kazal[lu] [to(?)] the bank of the Me-[E]n[lil] canal (at) the source of the ... canal;

5) ka ⸢I_7⸣.x [x x]

i 5) at the source of the ... canal;

6) IGI.NIM x [...]
7) 170 [x]
8) ⸢x x⸣-da-ti-[... šè(?)]

i 6–8) Too broken for translation.

9) I_7.me-^{d}en-[líl-lá]
10) ù-b[al-e]
11) ka I_7.[...-ta]
12) é-duru$_5$-PA.T[E.SI ...]
13) gú I_7.[edin-maḫ-šè]
14) é-duru$_5$-PA.T[E.SI ...]
15) gú I_7.edin-ma[ḫ-ta]

i 9–15) After (you) cross over the Me-En[lila] canal; [from] the source of the ... canal (to) Eduru-en[si] on the bank of the [Edin-maḫ] canal; [from] E-duru-en[si] on the bank of the Edin-ma[ḫ] canal to the bank of the ... canal.

16) gú I_7.a-x-x
17) x [...]
18) x ga(?) AN x [...]
19) sig-t[a(?)] x x
20) la-ba-d[a]-ti-la-aš-šè(?)
21) gú I_7.a-x-li(?)-ta(?)
22) x x [(x)] x

i 16–22) Too broken for translation.

Col. ii
1) LAGAR.DINGIR.[I]GI(?)-šè
2) LAG[AR].DINGIR.[I]GI(?)-ta

ii 1–2) To LAGAR.DINGIR.[I]GI; from LAGAR.DINGIR.[I]GI

3–15) Traces

ii 3–15) Traces

16) [á-IM].mar-dú-bi

ii 16) its western [side]

17–23) Traces

ii 17–23) Traces

Col. iii
1) KI.KAL-edin-[š]è
2) KI.KAL-edin-ta
3) é-kur-re-šè
4) é-kur-re-ta
5) é-^{d}nin-SAR-ka-šè
6) é-^{d}nin-SAR-ka-[t]a
7) KA.IGI-šè
8) KA.IGI-ta
9) dingir-bir-šè
10) dingir-bir-ta
11) e-gibil-š[è]
12) e-gibil-ta
13) NAGAR.BI 4-kam-ma-šè
14) NAGAR.BI 4-kam-ma-[t]a
15) ^{d}geštin-an-ka-šè
16) ^{d}geštin-an-ka-ta
17) uru-maš-tab-šè
18) uru-maš-tab-ta
19) ^{d}nin-ḫur-saga-ka-š[è]
20) á-IM.ùlu-bi

iii 1–20) [T]o Dunni-edin; from Dunni-edin to Ekur; from Ekur to E-Nin-SAR; [fr]om E-Nin-SAR to KA.IGI; from KA.IGI to Dingir-bir; from Dingir-bir to the new canal; from the new canal to NAGAR.BI.4; from NAGAR.BI.4 to (x) of Geštin-ana; from (x) of Geštin-ana to Uru-maš-tab; from Uru-maš-tab to (x) of Ninḫursaga: its southern side.

21) ^{d}nin-ḫur-saga-ka-ta
22) USAR-x-GABA-an-na-šè
23) USAR-x-GABA-an-na-ta
24) *še-ri-im-tum*-šè
25) *še-ri-im-tum*-ta
26) KÍSIM-ur-már-da.KI-ka-šè
27) KÍSIM-ur-már-da.KI-ka-ta
28) du$_{6}$-lugal-uru-ka-šè
29) du$_{6}$-lugal-uru-ka-ta
Col. iv
1) me-en-*ì-lí*-šè
2) me-en-*ì-lí*-ta
3) é-TU-ni-ga-an-na-šè
4) é-TU-ni-ga-an-na-ta
5) an-za-gàr-dumu-lugal-ka-šè
6) an-za-gàr-dumu-lugal-ka-ta
7) ba-rí-šè
8) ba-rí-ta
9) bu-ul-šè
10) bu-ul-ta
11) é-duru$_{5}$-BI.BI-an-na-šè
12) é-duru$_{5}$-BI.BI-an-na-ta
13) an-za-gàr-ḫu-wu-um-ma-šè (Text: BI)
14) an-za-gàr-ḫu-wu-um-ma-ta (Text: BI)
15) I$_{7}$.saḫar-šè
16) I$_{7}$.saḫar-ta
17) du$_{6}$-gu-zu-ma-ka-šè
18) du$_{6}$-gu-zu-ma-ka-ta
19) pa$_{5}$ ìr-šum-ma-šè
20) pa$_{5}$ ìr-šum-ma-ta
21) ki-gal-šè
22) ki-gal-ta
23) ki-gal 2-kam-ma-šè
24) ki-gal 2-kam-ma-ta
25) ki-gal ki-sur-ra
26) ka-zal-lu.KI
27) ù kiš.KI-ka-šè
28) á-IM.mar-dú-bi

iii 21 – iv 28) From (x) of Ninḫursaga to USAR-x-GABA-ana; from USAR-x-GABA-ana to Šerimtum; from Šerimtum to KISIM-urmarda; from KISIM-urmarda to Du-lugal-uru; from Du-lugal-uru to Me-en-ili; from Me-en-ili to E-TU-niga-ana; from E-TU-niga-ana to the "Tower of the Prince"; from the "Tower of the Prince" to Bari; from Bari to Bul; from Bul to BI.BI-ana village; from BI.BI-ana village to the "Tower of Huwum"; from the "Tower of Huwum" to the Saḫar canal; from the Saḫar canal to Du-Guzuma; from Du-Guzuma to the Iršumma canal; from the Iršumma canal to Kigal; from Kigal to the second Kigal; from the second Kigal to the Kigal of the boundary of Kazallu and Kiš: its western side.

29) ki-sur-ra-^{d}lugal-már-da-ke$_{4}$
30) már-da.KI-ke$_{4}$(?)
31) KA ba-an-gi-in
32) ur-^{d}nammu lugal-e

iv 29–32) The boundary of the god Lugal-marda of Marad. Ur-Nammu, the king, determined it.

---

33) *tu-lá-um*-ta

iv 33) From Tula'um.

Ex. 3 Frgm. 1
Lacuna
1′) [I$_{7}$].*e-ur-tum*-šè
2′) ⸢á⸣-IM.mir-ra-bi
3′) ⸢I$_{7}$⸣.*e-ur-tum*-ta
4′) [...] x [šè]
Lacuna

1′–2′) To the Eʾurtum [canal]: its northern side.

3′–4′) From the Eʾurtum canal to [...].
Lacuna

Ex. 3 Frgm. 2
Col. i′
Lacuna
1′) [...]-x-an-dùl/ [...]-ti-a-ta
2′) [...] x-^{d}nanna-[...]-šè
Lacuna

i′ 1′–2′) From [...]-x-andul-[...]-tia [to] [...]-x-Nanna-[...]
Lacuna

Col. ii′
Lacuna
1′) ere[š.KI-ta]
2′) ki-[...-šè]

ii′ 1′–3′) [From] Er[eš to] Ki-[...]; [from] K[i-...] to [...]

3′) ki-[...-ta]	Lacuna
Lacuna	
Ex. 3 Frgm. 3	Ex. 3 Frgm. 3
Lacuna	Lacuna
1′) ⸢^{d}⸣nin-ḫur-sa[g]/ sa[ḫar ...]	1′) [From/to] Ninḫursaga-sa[ḫar ...].
Lacuna	Lacuna
Ex. 3 Frgm. 4	Ex. 3 Frgm. 4
Lacuna	Lacuna
1′) [*ki-rí*]-⸢LUM⸣-t[a]	1′–2′) Fr[om] [Kiri]LUM to [Ḫibarī]tum.
2′) [*ḫi-ba-rí*]-*tum*-[šè]	Lacuna
Lacuna	
Ex. 3 Frgm. 5	Ex. 3 Frgm. 5
Col. i′	
Lacuna	Lacuna
1′) [...] x	Too broken for translation.
2′) [...] ki ki/ [(x x)]-⸢šè⸣	Lacuna
Lacuna	
Col. ii′	
Lacuna	Lacuna
1′) é-^{d}aš-ŠIR-gi$_4$-x	ii′ 1′) (To/from) E-Ašgi.
Lacuna	Lacuna
Ex. 3 Frgm. 6	Ex. 3 Frgm. 6
Lacuna	Lacuna
1′) [...] ⸢A⸣ KU x/ [(x x)]-ka	1′–2′) ... : i[ts] southern side.
Space	Lacuna
2′) ⸢á⸣-IM.ùlu-b[i(?)/ [...] UD DA	
Lacuna	
Ex. 3 Frgm. 7	Ex. 3 Frgm. 7
Col. i′	
Lacuna	Lacuna
1′) [... I$_7$.*ši-ma-at*]-^{d}*èr*-⸢*ra*-šè⸣	i′ 1′–2′) to the [Šimat]-Erra canal: its northern side.
2′) [á-I]M.mir-[r]a-⸢bi⸣	Lacuna
Lacuna	
Col. ii′	
Lacuna	Lacuna
1′) [...]	ii′ 1′–2′) ... : its eastern side
2′) á-[sa_{12}]/-*d*[*ì-um*-ma-bi]	Lacuna
Lacuna	
Ex. 3 Frgm. 8	Ex. 3 Frgm. 8
Col. i′	
Lacuna	Lacuna
1′) [...] x	i′ 1′–3′) Too broken for translation.
2′) [...]	Lacuna
3′) [...] x	
Lacuna	
Col. ii′	
Lacuna	Lacuna
1′) á-[IM.mar]/-d[ú-bi]	ii′ 1′–2′) [Its] [wes]te[rn] side. To URU-x.
2′) URU-x [...-šè]	Lacuna
Lacuna	
Ex. 3 Frgm. 9	Ex. 3 Frgm. 9
Col. 1′	
Lacuna	Lacuna
1′) [...] x	i′ 1′–4′) Too broken for translation.
2′) [...] ša/ [...] x-šè	Lacuna
3′) [...] x ša/ [...] x -ta	
4′) [...] x nagar/ [...] x [(x)]-⸢šè⸣	
Lacuna	

Col. ii′
Lacuna
1′) a-[giš ... -šè]
2′) a-giš [...-ta]
3′) ki x [...-šè]
4′) ki [x ...-ta]
5′) ki [.. -šè]
6′) [ki ...-ta]
Lacuna

Lacuna
ii′ 1′–6′) Too broken for translation.
Lacuna

Ex. 3 Frgm. 10
Col. i′
Lacuna
1′) [...]
2′) [...] x-i[n-la]/-[(x)] UḪ.ME-⸢šè⸣
3′) [... x]-[i]n-la/-[(x) UḪ.ME]-ta
4′) [...] x [(x x x)]-⸢šè⸣
Lacuna

Ex. 3 Frgm. 10

Lacuna
i′ 1′–4′) Too broken for translation.
Lacuna

Col. ii′
Lacuna
1′) g[ú ...]/ ⸢nun(?)-ta⸣
2′) ki-gal kur-ú-sal-la-šè
3′) [...]
Lacuna

Lacuna
ii′ 1′–3′) From the ba[nk] of the ...-nun [canal] to Kigal-kur-usalla.
Lacuna

Col. iii′
1′) ⸢gú⸣ [...-šè]
2′) g[ú ...]
Lacuna

iii′ 1′–2′) [To] the bank [of the ... canal]. [From] the b[ank of the ... canal ...].
Lacuna

Ex. 3 Frgm. 11
Col. i′
Lacuna
1′) Traces
2′) [...] x-li/ [...] x-lá-ta
3′) [...]-ni-šè
4′) [...]-ni-ta
5′) [...]-gala-/ [(x)]-ka-šè
6′) Traces
Lacuna

Ex. 3 Frgm. 11

Lacuna
i′ 1′–6′) Too broken for translation.
Lacuna

Col. ii′
Lacuna
1′) Traces
2′) du$_{6}$-GIŠ-ab-ba-šè
3′) du$_{6}$-GIŠ-ab-ba-ta
4′) na:es$_{5}$-rú-a-šè
5′) na:eš$_{5}$-rú-a-t[a]
6′) na-rú-a-x-[x]/ x [...]
Lacuna

Lacuna
ii′ 1′–6′) From Du-GIŠ-aba; from Du-GIŠ-aba to Na'eš-rua; fr[om] Na'eš-rua to Narua-...
Lacuna

Col. iii′
Lacuna
1′) Traces
2′) gána-DU$_{6}$.D[U-šè]
3′) gána-DU$_{6}$.D[U-ta]
4′) GI[Š ...]
Lacuna

Lacuna
iii′ 1′–4′) To Gana-DU$_{6}$.D[U]; [from] Gana-DU$_{6}$.D[U] to GI[Š-...].
Lacuna

22

A large limestone stele, whose various fragments were found by Woolley on and around the ziqqurrat terrace, for the most part in the Kassite level of the Edublalmaḫ, bears an inscription that records the digging of various canals by an unnamed king of Ur. While an attribution of the monument to Ur-Nammu on the basis of the fragment UET 1 no. 44a must now be abandoned (see commentary to E3/2.1.1.9 above), an assignment of the other stele fragments to Ur-Nammu is still likely; one of the canals named in the text, the Nanna-gugal canal (i 9″), also figures in Ur-Nammu inscription E3/2.1.1.28.

COMMENTARY

The extant inscribed portion is found on the fragments U 3328 (frgm. 1) and U 3265 (frgm. 2), now both numbered CBS 16676; they form a band between the third and fourth registers of the "reverse" of the stele. The bibliography gives only a sample of photos, depictions or discussions of this famous monument; for a complete list, see Börker-Klähn, Bildstelen pp. 155–56. The inscription was kindly collated by S. Tinney.

BIBLIOGRAPHY

1925 Woolley, AJ 5 pp. 398–40 and pls. 46–48 (photos, study)
1927 Legrain, MJ 18 pp. 74–98 (photo, study)
1928 Gadd, UET 1 no. 44 (copy, edition)
1929 Barton, RISA pp. 362–63 Ur-Nammu 10 (b) (edition)
1933 Legrain, RA 30 pp. 111–15 (photos, study)
1935 Zervos, L'art p. 228 (photos)
1940 Christian, Altertumskunde pl. 424 figs. 1–2 (photos)
1961 Parrot, Sumer figs. 279–82 (photos)
1962 Hallo, HUCA 33 p. 27 Ur-Nammu 29 (study)
1967 Moortgat, Kunst pls. 194–95, 198–99 and 201 (photos)
1974 Woolley, UE 6 pp. 75–81 and pls. 41–45 (photos, study)
1975 Orthmann (ed.), Der alte Orient pls. 115, 116a–b, and p. 203 (photos, drawing)
1980 Amiet, Art of the Ancient Near East fig. 404 (photo)
1982 Börker-Klähn, Bildstelen pp. 39–44 and 155–56 no. 94; figs. 94 g, i, and pl. g (photos, study, drawing)
1986 Kärki, KDDU pp. 18–20 Urnammu 29 (edition)
1991 Braun-Holzinger, Weihgaben p. 340 Stele 25 (study)
1991 Steible, NSBW 2 pp. 134–38 Urnammu 29 (edition)

TEXT

Frgms. 1+2 Col. i
1′) [...]
2′) [...U]NU
3′) [...] IM
4′) [...] x [...]
Lacuna

i 1′–4′) Too broken for translation.
Lacuna

1″) ⸢mu⸣-[ba-al]

i 1″) he (Ur-Nammu) dug.

2″) I$_7$.[...]
3″) [...]
4″) ⸢mu⸣-ba-a[l]

i 2″–4″) He du[g] the ... canal.

5″) I$_7$.[x (x)]-na
6″) ⸢I$_7$⸣.[x x]-maḫ-
7″) ^{d}nanna
8″) mu-ba-al

i 5″–8″) He dug the ... canal, the great ... canal of the god Nanna.

9″) I$_7$.^{d}nanna-gú-gal
10″) ⸢i$_7$-ki-sur-ra⸣-
11″) [^{d}]⸢nin-gír⸣-su
12″) ⸢mu⸣-ba-al

i 9″–12″) He dug the Nanna-gugal canal, the boundary canal of the god Ningirsu.

13″) I$_7$.gú-bi-eridu.KI-ga
14″) I$_7$.gú-[x]-úr(?)-
15″) ^{d}nin-⸢gír-su⸣
16″) mu-ba-a[l]
Lacuna

i 13″–16″) He du[g] the Gubi-eriduga canal, the ... canal of the god Ningirsu.
Lacuna

Frgms. 1+2 Col. ii
1′) [...] ⸢KI⸣
2′) [x gi$_6$-p]ar$_4$-⸢ka⸣(?)
3′) ⸢x⸣-da
4′) [ḫu]-mu-da-gi$_4$

ii 1′–4′) He *returned* with ... in the [*gip*]*ar*.

5′) lú á(Text: DA)-nì-ḫul-d[ím-ma]
6′) [íb-ši-ág-ge$_{26}$-a]
7′) [mu-sar-ra]-ba
8′) [šu bí]-íb-[ùr-re-a]
Lacuna

ii 5′–8′) As for the one who [gives] orders to do ev[il against (this monument), who erases] its [inscription]
Lacuna

1″) ⸢x⸣ [x (x)] ⸢x⸣ [x]
2″) ⸢x⸣ [x (x)]-⸢x⸣-ga
3″) lu[gal(?) x (x)]-⸢GI⸣
4″) [...]
5″) luga[l-...]

ii 1″–5″) Too broken for translation.

6″) [^{d}nanna]
7″) lugal-[mu]
8″) ⸢^{d}⸣[nin-gal]
9″) nin-⸢x⸣ [x (x)] ⸢x x⸣ [x (x)]
10″) nam [ḫa-ba-da-]
11″) ⸢kuru$_5$⸣(?)-[ne]

ii 6″–11″) [May the god Nanna, my] lord, and the goddess [Ningal], the lady of ..., cu[rse him].

23

A foundation tablet of Ur-Nammu records the construction of the temple of the goddess Ninsuna at Ur. As noted, the deed may be correlated to a year name of early Ur III date found on a tablet from Girsu (Thureau-Dangin, RTC no. 265).

COMMENTARY

The tablet is made of limestone and measures 10.4×7.2×1.7 cm. It was found by Hall outside the east corner of the E-ḫursag. If this findspot indicates the actual location of the Ninsuna temple, then its proximity to the royal palace would recall the fact that, according to the literary tradition, Ninsuna was Ur-Nammu's mother. The tablet bears the museum number BM 114187 and the registration number 1919-10-11, 277. The inscription was collated. Lines 1–7 are found on the obverse of the tablet, lines 8–9 on the reverse. For an archival text of Old Babylonian date referring to the E-maḫ at Ur, see Figulla, Iraq 15 (1953) p. 89.

BIBLIOGRAPHY

1923 Hall, JEA 9 p. 185 and pl. 37 no. 4 (provenance, photo [of obverse only])
1928 Gadd, UET 1 no. 47 and pl. H (photo [of obverse only], copy, edition)
1929 Barton, RISA pp. 364–65 Ur-Nammu 13 (edition)
1930 Hall, Season's Work pp. 162–63 (provenance, photo [of obverse only])
1962 Hallo, HUCA 33 p. 26 Ur-Nammu 15 (study)
1986 Kärki, KDDU pp. 8–9 Urnammu 15 (edition)
1991 Steible, NSBW 2 pp.109–110 Urnammu 15 (edition)

TEXT

1) ^{d}nin-súna
2) dingir-ra-ni
3) ur-^{d}nammu
4) nita-kala-ga
5) lugal-uri$_{5}$.KI-ma
6) lugal-ki-en-gi-ki-uri-ke$_{4}$
7) é-maḫ
8) é-[ki-ág-gá-n]i
9) mu-na-dù

1–2) For the goddess Ninsuna, his (personal) goddess,
3–6) Ur-Nammu, mighty man, king of Ur, king of the lands of Sumer and Akkad,

7–9) built for her the E-maḫ ("Exalted House"), [he]r [beloved] temple.

24

A five-line inscription found on bricks, foundation tablets, and bronze canephors records Ur-Nammu's construction of the temple of the god Enlil in Nippur.

CATALOGUE

Ex.	Museum number	Excavation number	Registration number	Nippur provenance	Object	Dimensions (cm)	Lines preserved	cpn
Bricks								
1	BM 80151	—	Bu 91-5-9, 264	—	Brick	14×13×3	1–5	c
2	BM 90374	—	51-10-9, 69	—	Brick	17×15.5×6.5	2–5	c
3	BM 90396	—	51-10-9, 86	—	Brick	15.5×14×6.5	3–5	c
4	BM 90792	—	1979-12-20, 354	—	Brick	17×14.4×6.5	1–4	c
5	BM 90794+ unnumbered frgm.	—	51-10-9, 70	—	Brick	27×21×7	1–5	c
6	BM 90795	—	1979-12-20, 355	—	Brick	19.5×19.5×6.5	1–4	c
7	BM 90796	—	51-10-9, 79+80	—	Brick	21.5×14.5×6.5	1–5	c
8	BM 90799	—	51-10-9, 84R	—	Brick	22×21.5×7	2–5	c
9	BM 90802	—	1979-12-10, 359	—	Brick	25×24.5×6.5	1–5	c
10	BM 114298	—	1919-10-11, 4442	—	Brick	31.5×31.5×7.5	1–5	c
11	BM 137358	—	1919-10-11, 5363	—	Brick	24.5×20×7	1–4	c
12	CBS 8638	—	—	—	Brick	11×9	—	n
13	CBS 8647	—	—	—	Brick	20×25×7	—	n
14	CBS 8648	—	—	—	Brick	31×31×7.5	—	n
15	UM 84-26-35	—	—	—	Brick	—	—	c
16	UM 84-26-36	—	—	—	Brick	30.5×30 ×7.5	—	c
17	UM 84-26-37	—	—	—	Brick	31×31×6	—	c
18	UM 84-26-38	—	—	—	Brick	31.5×31.5×8.5	—	c
19	HS 1991	—	—	—	Brick frgm.	6.5×5.5×1.3	3–5	c
20	HS 2014	—	—	—	Gypsum cast of brick	30.5×31×7.5	1–4	c
21	EŞ 8926	—	—	—	Brick	31.2×16×17 Stamp: 11.8×9.8	1–5	c
22	EŞ 8927	—	—	—	Brick	31.2×25×6.5 Stamp: 11.8×9.8	1–5	c
23	EŞ 8928	—	—	—	Brick	—	—	n
24	EŞ 8929	—	—	—	Brick	31×26 ×7 Stamp: 11.7×9	1–5	c
25	YBC 2382	—	—	—	Brick	31.5×31.8×6.5	1–5	c
26	Ash 1967-1504	—	—	—	Brick	16×15×6.5	1–5	c
27	Finland	—	—	—	Brick	—	—	n
28	IM 45765	—	—	—	Brick	—		n
29	IM 56105	2 N-T 46	—	—	Brick	—	—	n
29a	—	2 N–T 487	—	From the surface	Brick	—	—	n
30	MMA 59.41.86	6 N–T 1125	—	From the surface	Brick	30.9×31.4×7.5	1–5	c
31	IM 66951	8 N–T 20	—	From the surface	Brick	20.5 × 15.5×6.8	—	n
32	VA 14656	W 12117	—	—	Brick	—	1–6	c
33	VA 14656	—	—	—	Brick	—	1–6	c
34	VA 5393	—	—	Purchased	Brick	13.5×14×3.6	1–6	c

Ex.	Museum number	Excavation number	Registration number	Nippur provenance	Object	Dimensions (cm)	Lines preser	cpn
Foundation boxes and their deposits								
35a	MLC 2628	—	—	—	Bronze canephor	33 high, 5.2 wide	1–5	c
35b	MLC 2628	—	—	—	Stone tablet	12.5×8×2.7	1–5	c
36b	CBS 9332	—	—	SE side of ziqqurrat	Soapstone tablet	12×7.7×1.7	1–5	c
37a	(USA?)	5 N 200	—	Beneath SE tower flanking entrance to Ekur	Bronze canephor	—	1–5	n
37b	—	5 N 200	—	As ex. 37a	Stone tablet	—	1–5	n
37c	A 30791	5 N-T 681	—	As ex. 37a	Brick	Stamp: 10.4×9	1–5	c
38a	IM 59586	5 N 201	—	Beneath SW tower flanking entrance to Ekur	Bronze canephor	35.6 high, 12.8 wide	1–5	p (partial 1–3)
38b	—	5 N 202	—	As ex. 38a	Stone tablet	—	1–5	n
38c	A 30791	5 N-T 683	—	As ex. 38a	Brick	—	1–5	c
39a	IM 61402/1	6 N—	—	Beneath the north corner of the Ekur enclosure wall	Bronze canephor	33.1 high, 14.6 wide	1–5	n
39b	—	6 N—	—	As ex. 39a	Stone tablet	—	1–5	n
39c	A 31068	6 N-T 1127	—	As ex. 39a	Brick	30.5×30.7×8	1–5	c
39d	Kelsey 63.6.111	6 N-T 1126	—	As ex. 39a	Brick	38x39	1–5	c
40b	IM 59590	—	—	—	Steatite tablet	—	—	n

COMMENTARY

Exs. 1–11 were collated by C.B.F. Walker. Ex. 1 was purchased by Budge in Baghdad; exs. 2–3, 5, and 7–8 come from Layard's soundings at Nippur in 1850. Exs. 12–24 and 33b come from the old University of Pennsylvania expedition to Nippur and exs. 29–31 and 37–39 from the more recent American expedition. The latter (exs. 37–39) come from foundation boxes which were found beneath the gateway of the temple courtyard, or from under the north corner of the temple enclosure wall. In the catalogue for this inscription the foundation boxes and contents are listed in sets: ex. 37a refers to the inscribed canephor; ex. 37b to the inscribed foundation tablet; and ex. 37c to the inscribed brick that formed one of the sides of the foundation box. The text is arranged in one column of five lines.

BIBLIOGRAPHY

1853 Layard, Discoveries p. 557 (exs. 2–3, 5, 7–9, provenance)
1861 1 R I 9 (exs. 2, 4–9, conflated copy)
1872 Smith, TSBA 1 p. 35 (exs. 2, 4–9, translation)
1874 Lenormant, Études accadiennes 2 p. 309 (exs. 2, 4–9, translation)
1875 Ménant, Babylone p. 75 (exs. 2, 4–9, translation)
1892 Winckler, KB 3/1 pp. 78–79 Ur-gur 8 (exs. 2, 4–9, edition)
1896 Hilprecht BE I/2 no. 122 (ex. 36b, study)
1899 Bezold, Cat. 5 p. 2233 (exs. 2, 4–9, study)
1905 King, CT 21 pl. 4 BM 90802 (ex. 9, copy)
1907 Thureau-Dangin, SAK pp. 186–87 Ur-engur g (exs. 2, 4–9, edition)
1908 Johns, Ur-Engur frontispiece, pl. 20 and pp. 20–23 (ex. 35a, photo, study)
1923 Clay, BRM 4 no. 44 and pl. 1 (ex. 35b, photo, copy, study)
1929 Barton, RISA pp. 272–73 Ur-Nammu 7 (exs. 2, 4–9, edition); pp. 274–75 Ur-Nammu 16 (ex. 36b, edition)
1937 Stephens YOS 9 no. 114 (ex. 25, study)
1956 Haines, ILN August 18 p. 266 fig. 13 (ex.?, photo); fig. 14 (exs. 38a-c, photo of findspot); fig. 15 (exs. 37a, 38a, photo)
1958 Haines, ILN September 6 p. 389 fig. 17 (exs. 39a–b, photo)
1959 Crawford, Archeology 12/2 pp. 77–78 (exs. 39a–b, photo of objects and findspot)
1961 Parrot, Sumer p. 238 fig. 292D (ex. 38b or 40b, photo)
1962 Hallo, HUCA 33 p. 24 Ur-Nammu 3 (exs. 2, 4–9, 25, 37–38, study)
1969 Oelsner, WZJ 18 p. 53 no. 17 (ex. 19, edition; ex. 20, study)
1969 Biggs and Buccellati, AS 17 p. 5 (ex. 31, study)
1975 Orthmann (ed.), Der alte Orient fig. 65 (ex. 38b or 39b, photo)
1976 Basmachi, Treasures fig. 100 (extreme right) and p. 400 (ex. 38a, photo)
1976 Schlossman, Ancient Mesopotamian Art pp. 16–24 and pls. 5–8 (exs. 35a–b, photo, edition, study)
1978 Halén, Handbook p. 109 no. 393 (ex. 27)
1981 Walker, CBI no. 13 (exs. 1–11, 26, study)
1981 Grégoire, MVN 10 no. 16 (ex. 26, copy)
1983 Rashid, Gründungsfiguren, pp. 24–25 and pls. 21–23 nos. 120–23 (exs. 37a–39a, study, drawing [except 37a])
1984 Zettler, Inanna Temple p. 21 n. 2 (exs. 29a, 37–38, study)
1985 Behrens, JCS 37 p. 231 no. 8 (exs. 12–18, study)
1985 Kärki, KDDU p. 2 Urnammu 3 (exs. 1–11, 19–20, 25–27, 30, 32, 35–36, edition)
1988 Sigrist, in Spar, Met. Mus. 1 p. 159 no. 116 (ex. 30, copy, edition)
1992 Steible, NSBW 2 pp. 95–97 Urnammu 3 (exs. 1–20, 25–26, 30, 32, 35, 36, 37a–39a, 40b, edition)

TEXT

1) ur-^{d}nammu 2) lugal-uri$_5$.KI-ma 3) lugal-ki-en-gi-ki-uri	1–3) Ur-Nammu, king of Ur, king of the lands of Sumer and Akkad,
4) lú é-^{d}en-líl-lá 5) in-dù-a	4–5) the one who built the temple of the god Enlil.

25

A ten-line door socket inscription records Ur-Nammu's construction of Enlil's temple in Nippur.

CATALOGUE

Ex.	Museum number	Excavation number	Nippur provenance	Dimensions (cm)	Lines preserved	cpn
1	Istanbul(?)	—	12.2 m below surface, underneath W corner of SE buttress of ziqqurrat	Stone: 41×25×18 Inscription: 19.7× 7.5	1–10	p
2	IM --	—	—	65×35×17	1–10	p

COMMENTARY

The text of ex. 1 was entered from a photograph labelled as OBI No. 121 that was found bound in the RIM copy of BE 1/2. Since this door socket could not be located in Philadelphia, we have assumed that it is housed in Istanbul.

Ex. 2 is a door socket that was last seen at the dig house in Mosul. Its IM number is unknown.

The text is arranged in one column of ten lines.

BIBLIOGRAPHY

1896 Hilprecht, BE 1/2 no. 121 (ex. 1, copy)
1900 Radau, EBH p. 222 (ex. 1, edition)
1907 Thureau-Dangin, SAK pp. 188–89 Ur-engur k (ex. 1, edition)
1962 Hallo, HUCA 33 p. 26 Ur-Nammu 16 (ex. 1, study)
1986 Kärki, KDDU p. 9 Urnammu 16 (ex. 1, edition)
1992 Steible, NSBW 2 p. 110 Urnammu 16 (edition)

TEXT

1) ^{d}en-líl 2) lugal-kur-kur-ra 3) lugal-a-ni	1–3) For the god Enlil, lord of the foreign lands, his lord,
4) ur-^{d}nammu 5) nita-kala-ga 6) lugal-uri$_5$.KI-ma 7) lugal-ki-en-gi-ki-uri-ke$_4$	4–7) Ur-Nammu, mighty man, king of Ur, king of the lands of Sumer and Akkad,
8) é-kur 9) é-ki-ág-gá-ni 10) mu-na-dù	8–10) built for him the Ekur, his beloved temple.

26

Inscriptions E3/2.1.1.26–28 deal with canals dug by Ur-Nammu. The first of these, a cone inscription, records Ur-Nammu's digging of the Iturungal canal. As noted, year name (m), found on a tablet from Girsu, commemorates the digging of this canal. The text is arranged in one column of eleven lines.

CATALOGUE

Ex.	Museum number	Excavation number	Registration number	Provenance	Dimensions (cm)	Lines preserved	cpn
1	IM 92779	U 872	—	Diqdiqqah, loose	12×6	—	n
2	IM 779	U 1595	—	Diqdiqqah	5.5×5	—	n
3	IM 780	U 1596	—	Diqdiqqah	5.1×4.4	—	n
4	—	U 1597	—	Diqdiqqah	8×5.3	—	n
5	IM 790	U 1632	—	Diqdiqqah	9.2×6	—	n
6	BM 116986	U 1649	1924-9-20, 249	Diqdiqqah	7×5.4	1–11	c
7	IM 3569	U 7724	—	SM loose	—	—	n
8	IM 45472	—	—	—	—	—	n
9	IM —	U qa	—	—	—	—	n
10	IM —	U ra	—	—	—	—	n
11	IM —	U sa	—	—	—	—	n
12	EŞ 13539	—	—	—	—	—	n
13	IM —	E(ridu) 733	—	Eridu	4×5	1–3, 9–11	n
14	BCM 287'35	—	—	—	—	—	n
15	VA 15448	W 13201	—	Uruk	4.8×5.3	1–11	c
16	McGill Ethnological Collections, RM 15	—	—	Diqdiqqah or Ur(?)	9×5.5	1–5, 8–11	c

BIBLIOGRAPHY

1928 Gadd, UET 1 no. 46 (exs. 1–5, conflated copy, edition)
1929 Barton, RISA pp. 362–65 Ur-Nammu 12 (exs. 1–5, edition)
1947 Kraus, in Halil Edhem Memorial Volume p. 113 no. d (ex. 12, study)
1956 Oberhuber, Innsbrucker Keilschrifttexte pp. 6–7 and pl. 1 no. 1 (ex. 13, copy, edition)
1957 Edzard, Sumer 13 p. 176 (exs. 2–3, 5, 7–8, study)
1960 Jacobsen, Iraq 22 pp. 182–83 (exs. 1–5, edition)
1962 Hallo, HUCA 33 p. 27 Ur-Nammu 23 (exs. 1–5, 7–8, 12–13, study)
1965 Sollberger, UET 8 p. 26 no. 11 (exs. 6, 9–11, study)
1979 George, Iraq 41 p. 122 to II B 26 (ex. 14, study)
1986 Kärki, KDDU pp. 12–13 Urnammu 23 (exs. 1–13, edition)
1987 Marzahn, AoF 14/1 pp. 33–34 no. 14 and pl. 1 (ex. 15, photo [second cone from right], transliteration)
1989 Frayne, ARRIM 7 p. 7 no. 5 (ex. 16, photo, study)
1991 Steible, NSBW 2 pp. 117–18 Urnammu 23 (exs. 1–15, edition)
1993 Carroué, ASJ 15 pp. 15–16 (transliteration, study)

TEXT

1) ^{d}en-líl
2) lugal-kur-kur-ra
3) lugal-a-ni
4) ur-^{d}nammu
5) lugal-uri$_{5}$.KI-ma
6) lugal-ki-en-gi-ki-uri-ke$_{4}$
7) é-a-ni
8) mu-na-dù
9) I$_{7}$.EN.ÉREN.NUN
10) i$_{7}$-nidba-ka-ni
11) mu-na-ba-al

1–3) For the god Enlil, lord of the foreign lands, his lord,

4–6) Ur-Nammu, king of Ur, king of the lands of Sumer and Akkad,

7–8) built for him his temple.

9–11) He dug for him the Iturungal canal, his canal of offerings.

E3/2.1.1.26.9.1 I$_{7}$.EN.x.NUN

27

A ten-line cone inscription deals with Ur-Nammu's digging of the Iturungal canal for the goddess Inanna.

COMMENTARY

The cone was found in the area called al-Mada'in (ancient Badtibira) near the mounds al-Masāfit or al-Šuwailāt. It measures 7.5 cm in length and 6.5 cm in diameter (at the wide end) and 3.5 cm (at the narrow end). The text is in the Iraq Museum; its museum number is not known. The text is arranged in one column of ten lines.

BIBLIOGRAPHY

1989–90 Al-Rawi, Sumer 46 pp. 84–85 (copy, edition)

TEXT

1) ^{d}inanna
2) [n]in-é-an-na
3) nin-a-ni
4) ur-^{d}nammu
5) nita-kala-ga
6) lugal-uri$_5$.KI-ma
7) [lu]gal-ki-en-gi$_4$-ki-uri-ke$_4$
8) I$_7$.EN.ŠEŠ.GAL
9) I$_7$.ki-ág-ni
10) [m]u-na-ba-al

1–3) For the goddess Inanna, [la]dy of Eanna, his lady,

4–7) Ur-Nammu, mighty man, king of Ur, king of the lands of Sumer and Akkad,

8–10) dug for her the Iturungal canal, her beloved canal.

28

A thirty-two-line cone inscription from Girsu records Ur-Nammu's digging of the Nanna-gugal canal; the watercourse apparently served as a boundary between the regions of Lagaš and Ur/Larsa (see Jacobsen, Iraq 22 [1960] p. 178). The canal is also mentioned in E3/2.1.1.22 col. i, line 9″. This inscription indicates that the canal was dug shortly after the reconstruction of the Enlil temple in Nippur.

CATALOGUE

Ex.	Museum number	Excavation number	Provenance	Dimensions (cm)	Lines preserved	Text arrangement	cpn
1	AO 4194	TG —	Tello, Tell H, 1.65 m. deep	13.4×8	1–32	col. i: 1–18 col. ii: 19–32	c
2	AO 12776	TG 2528	—	9.2×8.7	1–17	col. i: 1–17; col. ii broken away	c
3	AO 15304	TG —	—	15.7×7.5	1–32	col. i: 1–16 col. ii: 17–32	c

Ex.	Museum number	Excavation number	Provenance	Dimensions (cm)	Lines preserved	Text arrangement	cpn
4	AO 15305	TG —	—	15×17.5	1–32	col. i: 1–17 col. ii: 18–32	c
5	IM 20864	—	—	—	1–32	col. i: 1–17 col. ii: 18–32	n
6	IM 22847	—	—	—	—	—	n
7	IM 23089	—	—	—	—	—	n

COMMENTARY

Exs. 2 and 4 are edited here for the first time through the kind permission of B. André-Salvini. Variants d) and e) given in Steible, NSBW 2 p. 132, could not be identified among the collated exemplars of this inscription.

BIBLIOGRAPHY

1904 Thureau-Dangin, RA 6 pp. 79–82 (ex. 1, copy, edition)
1907 Thureau-Dangin, SAK pp. 188–89 Ur-engur i (ex. 1, edition)
1810 Cros, Tello p. 138 (ex. 1, provenance); pp. 167–70 (ex. 1, copy, edition)
1929 Barton, RISA pp. 272–73 Ur-Nammu 9 (ex. 1, edition)
1957 Edzard, Sumer 13 p. 176 (exs. 5–7, study)
1960 Aynard, RA 54 p. 16 (ex. 1–4?, study)
1960 Jacobsen, Iraq 22 p. 178 (ex. 1, edition)
1962 Hallo, HUCA 33 p. 27 Ur-Nammu 28 (exs. 1–4, 5–7, study)
1971 Sollberger and Kupper, IRSA IIIA1g (exs. 1–4, 5–7, translation)
1980 Sauren, ASJ 2 pp. 141–52 (exs. 1–4, 5–7, study)
1986 Kärki, KDDU pp. 16–18 Urnammu 28 (exs. 1–4, 5–7 edition)
1992 Steible, NSBW 2 pp. 130–34 Urnammu 28 (exs. 1–7 edition)

TEXT

1) ^{d}nanna
2) dumu-sag-^{d}en-líl-lá
3) lugal-a-ni
4) ur-^{d}nammu
5) nita-kala-ga
6) lugal-uri$_{5}$.KI-ma
7) lugal-ki-en-gi-ki-uri.KI-ke$_{4}$
8) u$_{4}$ é-^{d}en-líl-lá
9) in-dù-a
10) i$_{7}$-da
11) ^{d}nanna-gú-gal mu-bi
12) i$_{7}$-ki-sur-ra-kam
13) mu-ba-al
14) kun-bi a-ab-ba-ka ì-lá
15) di-nì-gi-na-
16) ^{d}utu-ta
17) bar bí-tam
18) KA bí-gi-in
19) lú
20) ^{d}nanna-a
21) in-da$_{5}$-kúru-a
22) lugal ḫé-a
23) énsi ḫé-a
24) lú-áš-du$_{11}$-ga-
25) ^{d}nanna-gin$_{7}$
26) ḫé-na
27) ki-tuš-^{d}nanna-ka
28) ḫé-éb-GIBIL

1–3) For the god Nanna, first-born son of the god Enlil, his lord,

4–7) Ur-Nammu, mighty man, king of Ur, king of the lands of Sumer and Akkad,

8–9) when he built the temple of the god Enlil,

10–13) dug the canal named "Nanna-gugal," the boundary canal.

14) He extended its mouth into the "sea."

15–18) By the just verdict of the god Utu he cleared up (previous claims to the area) and confirmed (the boundary).

19–21) As for the one who alters (that which belongs) to the god Nanna,

22–23) whether he be king or governor,

24–26) may he be like one cursed by the god Nanna.

27–28) May the dwelling of god Nanna be renewed,

Variants for E3/2.1.1.28:
6.3 lugal-uri$_{5}$.<KI>-ma-ke$_{4}$.
8.1 u$_{4}$ <é>-^{d}en-líl-lá.
9.3 in-dù-<a>.
14.3 kun-<bi> a-ab-ba-ka-NI ì-lá.

29) uru-ni gi-suḫur$_{x}$(KA)-ta
30) hé-ta-DAG.DAG-ge
31) nam-ti-il nì-gig-ga-ni
32) ḫé-a

29–30) May [h]is [city] be torn down from its summit shrine.
31–32) May life become a malady for him.

29

An Old Babylonian tablet copy of an Ur-Nammu inscription records a campaign against the Elamite king Kutik-Inšušinak.

COMMENTARY

The Ur-Nammu inscription is found on rev. cols. v′–vi′ of the tablet IB 1537. The tablet was found at Isin in the probe near the northern enclosure wall, 138 N, 61.50 W, +8.10. The inscription was not collated.

The toponyms in this text may be compared with the cities of Marad, GIRkal, Kazallu, and Uṣarum named in the Ur-Nammu Law Code. The mention of the city of Akkad v′ 22′ is an important new datum.

BIBLIOGRAPHY

1987 Wilcke, in Hrouda, Isin 3 pp. 109–11 and pl. 44 (photo, edition, study)

TEXT

Column v′
Lacuna
1′) [x x] ⌈ur-^{d}nammu⌉
2′) nita-kala-ga
3′) lugal-úri-KI-ma
4′) lugal-ki-en-gi-ki-uri
5′) nam-ti-la-ni-šè
6′) a mu-na-ru
7′) u$_{4}$-ba ^{d}en-líl-l[e]
8′) NIM-ra
9′) NÍG(?).Á.TAG(?).GA
10′) ḫa-mu-ne-sum(?)
11′) ma-da-kur-NIM.KI-ma
12′) mè-šè ní-ba
13′) ḫu-mu-ši-DU
14′) lugal-bi(?)
15′) PUZUR$_{4}$-^{d}MÙŠ.EREN-ke$_{4}$
16′) a-wa-al.KI
17′) ki-is-ma-ar.KI
18′) maš-kán-LUGAL.KI
19′) [m]a-da éš-nun-na.KI
20′) [m]a-da tu-tu-úb.KI
21′) [ma-d]a sí-mu-dar.KI
22′) [ma-d]a a-ga-dè.KI
23′) ⌈LÚ⌉.L[Ú ...]
Lacuna

Lacuna
v′ 1′–6′) [...] (I), Ur-Nammu, mighty man, king of Ur, king of the lands of Sumer and Akkad, dedicated (this object) for my (Text: his) life.

v′ 7′–10′) At that time the god Enlil gave(?) ... to the Elamites.

v ′11′–13′) In the territory of highland Elam they drew up against one another for battle.

v′ 14′–23′) Their(?) king, Kutik-Inšušinak — Awal, Kismar, Maškan-šarrum, the [la]nd of Ešnunna, the [la]nd of Tutub, the [lan]d of Simudar, the [lan]d of Akkad, the peop[le ...] —
Lacuna

Column vi′

Lacuna		Lacuna
1′)	[...] x ⸢LUGAL⸣	vi′ 1′–5′) ..., I took as booty ... and forty-five (plus) asses.
2′)	[x] x-ús-a	
3′)	⸢x+45⸣ anše-bi	
4′)	nam-ra-aš	
5′)	ḫa-mu-ak	
6′)	^{d}en-líl	vi′ 6′–10′) I brought (the booty) to the god Enlil, my lord, in Nippur, (and) marked it for him (Enlil).
7′)	lugal-mu	
8′)	nibru.KI-šè	
9′)	ḫé-na-la$ḫ_5$	
10′)	zà ḫé-na-$šu_4$	
11′)	nì-egir-bi	vi′ 11′–14′) The remainder I presented as a gift to my troops.
12′)	ugnim-mu	
13′)	nì-ba-a	
14′)	ḫa-ba-ni-gar	

30

A royal inscription known from an apparent Ur III copy on a clay cylinder from Nippur describes a campaign of a king of Ur against the Elamites and Gutians. While Ur-Nammu's name is found twice (in a restored text) in the inscription, the contexts in which it appears are so broken that an attribution of the text as a whole to Ur-Nammu is uncertain; for lack of more precise information we have edited the text at this point.

CATALOGUE

Frgm.	Museum number	Excavation number	cpn
1	A 33656a	6 N-T 908a	c
2	A 33657	6 N-T 909	c
3	—	6 N-T 908	c
4	—	6 N-T 908	c

COMMENTARY

The cylinder fragments were found in area SB 76 at Nippur in the general area of the Inanna temple, more specifically, in the fill underlying the lower Parthian temple (level II). The main fragment (frgm. 1) has a preserved height of 14.6 cm and an original diameter (calculated by triangulation) of about 10.6 cm.

BIBLIOGRAPHY

1985 Civil, Orientalia NS 54 pp. 27–32 and pl. VI (after p. 320) (photo, edition)

TEXT

Frgm. 1
Col. i′
Lacuna
1′) [...] x
2′) [...] x [...] x
3′) [...] x
4′) [...] ⌜TÚG⌝(?)
5′) [...]
6′) [...] x
7′) [...] ⌜ḫa⌝
8′) [...] x
9′) [...] x [...^{d}]nammu
Lacuna
Col. ii′
Lacuna
1′) Traces
2′) ⌜ig⌝-gal NIM-a-ta
3′) zà-šušin.KI-na-šè
4′) lugal-ra
5′) gu$_4$ mu-na-gi$_4$-gi$_4$
6′) udu ⌜mu⌝-na-gi$_4$-gi$_4$
7′) é[n]si-énsi-NIM-a-ke$_4$
8′) mušen téš-bi nunuz zuḫ-zuḫ-gin$_7$
9′) ne-ra ní-ba mu-na-ak-ke$_4$
10′) sag NIM ù-tu-d[a]
11′) Traces
Lacuna
Col. iii′
1′) u$_4$-b[a ...]
2′) ur ⌜šu⌝-s[i(?) ...]
3′) gìr a-ba-[x]-n[á]
4′) gú-tar-lá dumu gu-tim-um-ma-ra
5′) inim-an-na-ke$_4$
6′) šu nu-mu-ni-íb-tag
7′) gizkim ^{d}en-líl-lá
8′) na-me nu-[m]u-da-gál
9′) n[a]m-lugal-šè
10′) [a i]m-ma-⌜tu$_5$⌝
11′) [a]ga ba-an-⌜x-x⌝-né-éš-[a]
12′) Traces
Lacuna
Col. iv′
1′) ne-[...] mi-[...]
2′) ù a-n[e ...] mi-ni-í[l]
3′) a-na bí-in-ak-bi
4′) ma-⌜da⌝ gu-tim-um.KI
5′) sí-mu-⌜dar⌝.KI
6′) sig-ba ugnim ki ba-ni-tag
7′) tu-li-um.K[I]
8′) kar má-gur$_8$ nu-z[u(?)]
9′) me-te NI [...]
Lacuna
Col. v′
Lacuna
1′) na[m-...]
2′) nam [...] su[d ...]
3′) ur-⌜^{d}⌝[nammu]

Frgm. 1

Lacuna
i′ 1′–9′) Too broken for translation.
Lacuna

Lacuna
ii′ 1′–6′ ... from the great gate of Elam to the border of Susa, for the king (he/they) killed bulls, killed sheep.

ii′ 7′–9′ All the governors of Elam, like birds stealing eggs together, committed murder against him.

ii′ 10′–11′) The persons bor[n] in Elam, ...
Lacuna

iii′ 1′–6′) At that time [... *like*] a ... dog(?), after he lay at his feet, Gutarla, the Gutian, by the word of An had not been chosen.

iii′ 7′–8′) Of Enlil's signs there were none.

iii′ 9′–10′) For the kingsh[i]p, he (Gutarla[?]) took a ritual ba[th].
iii′ 11′–12′) The [c]rown which they had [...]
Lacuna

iv′ 1′–3′) ... but he carried(?) [...] all he had done about it.

iv′ 4′–6′) The district of Guti and Simudar had troops established in the South.

iv′ 7′–9′) Tuliʾum, the harbour which is not su[itable](?) for *magur* boats, the proper thing [...]
Lacuna

Lacuna
v′ 1′–3′) Too broken for translation.

Frgm. 2
Col. i′
1) [... u]ri$_5$.⸢KI⸣-ma
2) [... -g]i
3) [...] ⸢x⸣-ni
4) [...] ⸢a⸣-ba
Lacuna
Col. ii′
1) zi-šà-gá[l (x)] kù-^{d}en-[líl-lá]
2) an-t[a ...]
3) x [...]
Lacuna

Frgm. 2

i′ 1–4) Too broken for translation.
Lacuna

ii′ 1–3) Too broken for translation.
Lacuna

Frgm. 3
Lacuna
1′) [...] AN lugal dumu [...]
2′) [...] x lú mu-ši-ak
3′) [... i]m-mi-x-e an-šè x
Lacuna

Frgm. 3
Lacuna
1′–3′) Too broken for translation.
Lacuna

Frgm. 4
Lacuna
1′) [...] x
2′) [...] x
Lacuna

Frgm. 4
Lacuna
1′–2′) Too broken for translation.
Lacuna

31

Inscriptions E3/2.1.1.31–38 are building inscriptions, and E3/2.1.1.39–40 canal inscriptions, which date to the time after the king's trip to Nippur but which cannot be correlated to specific year names of the king. They are edited here in a geographical (south to north) order.

The first of this group of inscriptions, an inscribed stone, bears an eight-line inscription commemorating Ur-Nammu's construction of Enki's temple in Eridu.

COMMENTARY

The stone measures 40×18×20 cm. Its dimensions, in particular its thickness, are too large for the object, as Kärki suggested, to have been a foundation tablet. Perhaps the piece was a small door socket. The stone was found outside the ruins of the ziqqurrat near the eastern corner of Abū Šaḫrain. It now bears the museum number IM 52374.

The text is arranged in one column of eight lines.

BIBLIOGRAPHY

1947 Safar, Sumer 3 p. 236 (Arabic section) fig. 1b (copy)
1962 Hallo, HUCA 33 p. 25 Ur-Nammu 12 (study)
1981 Safar, Mustafa, and Lloyd, Eridu pp. 65 and 228–29, fig. 108 no. 1 (provenance, copy, edition)
1986 Kärki, KDDU p. 7 Urnammu 12 (edition)
1991 Steible, NSBW 2 pp. 106–107 Urnammu 12 (edition)

TEXT

1) ^{d}en-ki
2) lugal-a-ni
3) ur-^{d}nammu
4) nita-kala-ga
5) lugal-uri$_{5}$.KI-ma
6) lugal-ki-en-gi-ki-uri-ke$_{4}$
7) é-a-ni
8) mu-na-dù

1–2) For the god Enki, his lord,

3–6) Ur-Nammu, mighty man, king of Ur, king of the lands of Sumer and Akkad,

7–8) built for him his temple.

32

A door socket with an eight-line inscription records Ur-Nammu's construction of Enki's temple in Eridu.

COMMENTARY

The door socket, which is now on temporary loan to the Ashmolean Museum, came from a private collection; the piece had originally been a gift from the Turkish Governor of Baghdad in 1918. The stone apparently came from Eridu.

The text is arranged in one column of eight lines. For mar-uru$_{5}$ of line 1, see B. Eichler, in Studies Hallo pp. 90–94. In line 1 we have made a simple emendation KI to na.

BIBLIOGRAPHY

1982 Gurney, Iraq 44 pp. 143–44 (photo, edition)
1986 Kärki, KDDU p. 27 Urnammu 44 (edition)
1991 Steible, NSBW 2 pp. 148–49 Urnammu 46 (edition)

TEXT

1) ^{d}en-ki mar-uru$_{5}$-an-na(Text: KI)-ra
2) lugal-a-ni
3) ur-^{d}nammu
4) nita-kala-ga
5) lugal-uri$_{5}$.KI-ma
6) lugal-ki-en-gi-ki-uri-ke$_{4}$
7) é-a-ni
8) mu-na-dù

1–2) For the god Enki, the storm of heaven, his lord,

3–6) Ur-Nammu, mighty man, king of Ur, king of the lands of Sumer and Akkad

7–8) built for him his temple.

33

An eight-line brick inscription records Ur-Nammu's building of Inanna's temple in Uruk.

CATALOGUE

Ex.	Museum number	Excavation number	Registration number	Provenance	Dimensions (cm)	Lines preserved	cpn
Bricks							
1	BM 90006	—	51-1-1, 279	"In the buttress of the ruin called Bowarieh"	31.5×31	1–8	c
2	BM 90007	—	1979-12-20, 7	Uruk	31.5×32×7.5	1–8	c
3	BM 90010	—	1979-12-20, 10	Uruk	31.5×31×7	1–8	c
4	BM 90014	—	95-5-14, 9	Uruk	32×32×7	1–8	c
5	BM 90015	—	1979-12-20, 14	Uruk	32×32×7.5	1–8	c
6	BM 90019	—	51-1-1, 303	Uruk	31.5×31.5×7	1–8	c
7	BM 90021	—	1979-12-20, 18	Uruk	32×32.5×7.5	1–8	c
8	VA 16456	—	—	Uruk	32×20.3×7.8 Inscription: 12.5×13	1–8	c
9	VA 14656	W 1162	—	Uruk, Pa XVI 3	28.2×19.5 Inscription: 8.3×10	1–8	c
10	VA 14656	—	—	Uruk	32×32×8.2 Inscription: 10.1×8.4	1–8	c
11	VA 14656	—	—	Uruk	31.7×32 Inscription: 11×8.8	1–8	c
12	VA 14656	—	—	Uruk	32×31.8	1–8	c
13	VA 14656	—	—	Uruk	32.5×32.4 Inscription: 11×9.2	1–8	c
14	VA 14656	W 1830	—	Uruk	31.5×31×6.8 Inscription: 10.5×8.8	1–8	c
15	VA 14656	—	—	Uruk	31×31.6 Inscription: 10.2×8.9	1–8	c
16	EŞ 8854	—	—	Uruk	29×18×7	5–8	c
17	EŞ 9625	—	—	Uruk	31×31×7.5 Inscription 10×8.8	1–8	c
18	—	—	—	Found at WS 078	—	—	n
19	—	—	—	Found at WS 369	—	—	n
Tablet copy							
20	MLC 2075	—	—	—	9.1×5×3	1–8, plus colophon	c

COMMENTARY

Exs. 1–7, which were collated by C.B.F. Walker, come from Loftus's excavations at Uruk. Exs. 8–17 result from Jordan's excavations at the same site. Exs. 8–15, in Berlin, are all subsumed under the museum number VA 14656. Only two of these, ex. 9 (W 1162) and ex. 14 (W 1830), bear visible excavation numbers. The other exemplars mentioned by Schott (UVB 1 p. 50) are: W 1460, W 1981c, W 1981a, and W 1981b; see Jordan, UVB 1 for the details. Ex. 20 is a late, possibly Neo-Babylonian, copy. It contains a colophon on rev. 3–8; its text is given here through the kind courtesy of W.W. Hallo: *ki-⸢i pi-i⸣* SIG$_4$.[AL].ÙR.RA LIBIR.RA *šá é-an-na* ^{d}AMAR.UTU-ÙRI-*ir* A ^{m}*ib-ni-*^{d}*iš-⸢tar⸣ uš-bal-ki-it* "According to the text of a old baked brick of Eanna. Marduk-nāṣir, son of Ibni-Ištar, copied it." For another occurrence of *ušbalkit* in a colophon, see Hunger, Kolophone p. 122 no. 416 line 3.

The text is arranged in two columns: col. i has lines 1–4 and col. ii has lines 5–8.

BIBLIOGRAPHY

1861 1 R I 6 (ex. 1, copy)
1863 Oppert, EM 1 p. 264 (ex. 1, translation)
1872 Smith, TSBA 1 p. 35 (ex. 1, translation)
1874 Lenormant, Études accadiennes 2 p. 306 (ex. 1, translation)
1875 Ménant, Babylone p. 75 (ex. 1, translation)
1892 Winckler, KB 3/1 pp. 78–79 Ur-gur 5 (ex. 1, edition)
1899 Bezold, Cat. 5 p. 2233 (exs. 1–3, study)
1905 King, CT 21 BM 90006, 90015 pl. 3 (exs. 1, 5, copy)
1907 Thureau-Dangin, SAK pp. 186–87 Ur-engur d (ex. 1, edition)
1913 Jordan, MDOG 51 p. 50 (exs. [8–17], study)
1922 BM Guide p. 60 nos. 42–47 (exs. 1–5, 7, study)
1929 Barton, RISA pp. 270-71 Ur-Nammu 4 (exs. 1, 5, edition)
1930 Jordan, UVB 1 pp. 25, 50, and pl. 24 nos. 2–3 (some of exs. 8–17, provenance, copy, edition)
1962 Hallo, HUCA 33 p. 25 Ur-Nammu 7 (exs. 1, 5, [8–17], 20, study)
1972 Adams, Countryside p. 217 (exs. 18–19, study)
1981 Walker, CBI no. 17 (exs. 1–7, study)
1986 Kärki, KDDU p. 4 Urnammu 7 (exs. 1–7, [8–17], 18–20, edition)
1991 Steible, NSBW 2 pp. 100–101 Urnammu 7 (exs. 1–7, [8–17], 18–20, edition)

TEXT

1) ^{d}inanna
2) nin-a-ni
3) ur-^{d}nammu
4) nita-kala-ga
5) lugal-uri$_5$.KI-ma
6) lugal-ki-en-gi-ki-uri-ke$_4$
7) é-a-ni
8) mu-na-dù

1–2) For the goddess Inanna, his lady,

3–6) Ur-Nammu, mighty man, king of Ur, king of the lands of Sumer and Akkad,

7–8) built her temple for her.

34

A ten-line inscription of Ur-Nammu commemorates his building of Inanna's Eanna temple in Uruk. The text is inscribed on stone foundation tablets and bronze canephores that were found in foundation boxes from various points in the Eanna precinct. Some of these were obtained through scientific excavations, while others came from illicit diggings. The same text is found on a door socket.

CATALOGUE

Ex.	Museum number	Excavation number	Registration number	Uruk provenance	Object	Dimensions (cm)	Lines preserved	Text arrangement	cpn
Excavated pieces									
1a	VA 10938 (now lost)	W 13936a	—	Under the casement wall of Sargon II, SW of ziqqurrat, Od XVI$_3$ +21.78 (see UVB 5 pl. 3)	Bronze canephor	27.3 high	1–10	col. i: 1–7; col. ii: 8–10	n
1b	VA 10945	W 13936b	—	As ex. 1a	Steatite foundation tablet	12×6.9×1.8	1–10	obv.: 1–8; rev.: 9–10	c
2b	VA 15450	W 16956	—	Qa XVI$_5$	Steatite foundation tablet	3.2×3×1.3	5–8	obv.: 5–6; rev.: 7–8	c
3a	IM 45428	W 17922a	—	Qa XV$_4$	Bronze canephor	26.5 high	1–10	col. i: 1–7; col. ii: 8–10	p
3b	IM 45429	W 17922b	—	As ex. 3a	Steatite foundation tablet	6.9×10.5	1–10	obv.: 1–7 rev.: 8–10	p (obv. only)
4	IM —	W —	—	Beside the door of rm. 216 of the enclosure wall, NW side of the ziqqurrat, Oe XV$_4$	Door socket	—	—	—	n
Purchased pieces									
5b	MLC 2629	—	—	—	Stone foundation tablet	11.5×5.8×2.2	1–10	obv.: 1–7; rev.: 8–10	c
6a	BM 113896	—	—	—	Bronze canephor	27 high	1–10	col. i: 1–7; col. ii: 8–10	c
6b	BM 113866	—	1919-7-12, 615	—	Steatite foundation tablet	—	1–10	obv.: 1–7; rev.: 8–10	c
7a	Burrell Collection, Glasgow Art Gallery 28/75	—	—	—	Bronze canephor	27 high	1–10	—	n
8a	MMA 47.49	—	—	—	Bronze canephor	26.8 high 8.8 wide	1–10	col. i: 1–7; col. ii: 8–10	c
9b	Erlenmeyer Collection	—	—	—	Basalt foundation tablet	6×11×23	1–10	obv.: 1–7; rev.: 8–10	p (obv. only)

COMMENTARY

In this and following cases, foundation tablets and canephors from one foundation box are listed under one catalogue number, with the foundation tablet designated as ex. a, and the canephor as ex. b. The provenance of ex. 1 is given as quadrant OeXVI4 in UVB 8 p. 22, but is marked as coming from quadrant OdXV3 in the plan in UVB 5 pl. 3. Ex. 2b was given an attribution "unbekannt" by Marzahn (AoF 14/1 p. 40). However, the preserved text is almost certainly a duplicate of this text. Ex. 2b cannot be a duplicate of the Šulgi or Amar-Suena Eanna inscriptions. For the findspot of ex. 4, see UVB 8 pl. 6; the door socket is marked as a small circle beside the doorway leading from room 216.

BIBLIOGRAPHY

1922 BM Guide p. 85 nos. 63–64 (exs. 6a–b, study)
1923 Clay, BRM 4 no. 44 (ex. 5b, copy)
1931 Van Buren, Found. fig. 18 and p. 22 (ex. 6a, photo, study)
1934 Nöldeke, et al., UVB 5 p. 19 and pl. 17 (exs. 1a–b, provenance; ex. 1b, photo, edition)
1935 Zervos, L'art p. 225 (ex. 6a, photo)
1937 Nöldeke, et al., UVB 8 p. 22 (ex. 4, provenance, study)
1940 Nöldeke and Lenzen, UVB 11 pp. 10–11 (exs. 3a–b, provenance)
1957–58 Wells, AfO 18 p. 164 (ex. 7a, study)
1949 Wilkinson, MMAB NS 7/7 p. 192 [photo on right] (ex. 8a, photo)
1962 Hallo, HUCA 33 pp. 25–26 Ur-Nammu 13 (study)
1962 Strommenger and Hirmer, Mesopotamien pl. 146b (ex. 6a, photo)
1976 Basmachi, Treasures fig. 100 and p. 400 (exs. 3a–b, photo, study)
1983 Rashid, Gründungsfiguren p. 27 and pls. 24–25 nos. 124–27 (exs. 1a, 3a, 6a, 7a, 8a, study, drawing, except 1a)
1986 Kärki, KDDU pp. 7–8 Urnammu 13 (exs. 1, 3–6, edition)
1987 Marzahn, AoF 14/1 pp. 32–33 no. 12 (ex. 1a, copy, edition, study; ex. 1b study); pp. 39–40 no. 19 (ex. 2b, copy, edition, study)
1988 Christie's (London), Ancient Near Eastern Texts from the Erlenmeyer Collection p. 48 (ex. 9b, photo, translation)
1988 Muscarella, Bronze and Iron pp. 305–313 no. 436 (ex. 8a, photo, study)
1991 Steible, NSBW 2 pp. 107–108 Urnammu 13 (exs. 1, 3–9, edition)

TEXT

1) ^{d}inanna
2) nin-é-an-na
3) nin-a-ni
4) ur-^{d}nammu
5) nita-kala-ga
6) lugal-uri$_{5}$.KI-ma
7) lugal-ki-en-gi-ki-uri-ke$_{4}$
8) é-a-ni
9) mu-na-dù
10) ki-bé mu-na-gi$_{4}$

1–3) For the goddess Inanna, lady of Eanna, his lady,

4–7) Ur-Nammu, mighty man, king of Ur, king of the lands of Sumer and Akkad,

8–10) built and restored her temple for her.

35

An eight-line brick inscription records Ur-Nammu's building of Utu's temple in Larsa.

E3/2.1.1.34.9.9b mu-na-dù(Text: NI).

CATALOGUE

Ex.	Museum number	Excavation number	Registration number	Larsa provenance	Dimensions (cm)	Lines preserved	cpn
1	BM 90001	—	1979-12-20, 2	—	32.5×32×7–	1–8	c
2	BM 90008	—	1979-12-20, 8	—	33.5×32×7.5	1–8	c
3	BM 90013	—	1979-12-20, 13	—	33×32×7	1–8	c
4	BM 90016	—	1979-12-20, 15	—	32×32×7.5	1–8	c
5	BM 90018	—	1979-12-20, 17	—	32.5×32×7.5	1–8	c
6	BM 90722+90800	—	·1979-12-20, 324	—	32.5×32.5×7.5	1–8	c
7	IM —	L 7089	—	From the surface, between bench-mark 22 and the oven area on the west slope of the tell	—	—	n
8	IM —	L 7090	—	—	—	—	n
9	IM 77967	L 7425	—	—	—	—	n
10	VA 14656	W 3772 (photo W775)	—	Ruins south-east of the Šamaš-temple	19.8×22×5.3	1–8	c

COMMENTARY

Exs. 1–6, which come from Loftus's excavations at Larsa, were collated by C.B.F. Walker. Exs. 7–9 come from the French expedition directed by J.-L. Huot. Ex. 10, from Senkereh, was brought in to the German expedition to Warka on January 20, 1929, and assigned the find number W 3772. On it the last sign of line one is indistinct; we have assumed that it is an UTU sign; a reading of line 1 as ^{d}[en]-⌈ki⌉ is also conceivable. However, an Ur-Nammu inscription dealing with an Enki temple in Larsa is otherwise unattested.

The text is arranged in one column of eight lines.

BIBLIOGRAPHY

1861 1 R 1 7 (exs. 1–6, conflated copy)
1872 Smith, TSBA 1 p. 35 (exs. 1–6, translation)
1874 Lenormant, Études accadiennes 2 p. 307 (exs. 1–6, translation)
1875 Ménant, Babylone p. 75 (exs. 1–6, translation)
1892 Winckler, KB 3/1 pp. 78–79 Ur-gur 6 (exs. 1–6, edition)
1899 Bezold, Cat. 5 p. 2233 (exs. 1–6, study)
1905 King, CT 21 pl. 5 90001 (ex. 1, copy)
1907 Thureau-Dangin, SAK pp. 186–87 Ur-engur e (exs. 1–6, edition)
1922 BM Guide p. 60 nos. 48–52 (ex. 1, study)
1929 Barton, RISA pp. 270–71 Ur-Nammu 5 (exs. 1–6, edition)
1962 Hallo, HUCA 33 p. 25 Ur-Nammu 11 (exs. 1–6, study)
1971 Arnaud, Syria 48 p. 292 (exs. 7–8, study)
1976 Arnaud, Syria 53 p. 48 (ex. 9, study)
1981 Walker, CBI no. 20 (exs. 1–6, study)
1985 Kärki, KDDU pp. 6–7 Urnammu 11 (exs. 1–6, edition)
1991 Steible, NSBW 2 p. 106 Urnammu 11 (exs. 1–6, edition)

TEXT

1) ^{d}utu
2) lugal-a-ni
3) ur-^{d}nammu
4) nita-kala-ga
5) lugal-uri$_5$.KI-ma
6) lugal-ki-en-gi-ki-uri-ke$_4$
7) é-a-ni
8) mu-na-dù

1–2) For the god Utu, his lord,

3–6) Ur-Nammu, mighty man, king of Ur, king of the lands of Sumer and Akkad,

7–8) built his temple for him.

36

A foundation tablet with a nine-line inscription records Ur-Nammu's construction of a temple for the goddess Ninḫursaga.

COMMENTARY

The tablet is made of basalt and measures 12.23×5.58×2.2 cm. The piece was purchased by the old expedition of the University of Pennsylvania to Nippur; its original provenance is not known. The tablet bears the museum number CBS 841 and was collated. Lines 1–8 are found on the obverse, line 9 on the reverse.

In view of the inscription, the tablet likely originally came from the ancient city of Šarrākum (URU.SAG.RIG$_7$), since the evidence of a Sumerian lamentation edited by Wilcke (ZA 62 [1972] pp. 49–61) indicates that Keš(i) was the sanctuary or sacred precinct at URU.SAG.RIG$_7$. He notes (p. 55):

> Neu ist hier die Nennung von Aruru als Stadtgöttin von Urusagrig/Āl-Šarrāki und die Verbindung dieser Stadt mit Keši, das nach dem Parallelismus zu den beiden folgenden Abschnitten das Heiligtum oder der Heilige Bezirk von Urusagrig war.

For the reading of the logogram URU.SAG.RIG$_7$ as Šarrākum, see Frayne, Early Dynastic List pp. 28 and 32.

BIBLIOGRAPHY

1893 Hilprecht, BE 1/1 no. 14 (copy)
1900 Radau, EBH pp. 222–23 (edition)
1907 Thureau-Dangin, SAK pp. 188–89 Ur-engur m (edition)
1929 Barton, RISA pp. 274–75 Ur-Nammu 15 (edition)
1962 Hallo, HUCA 33 p. 26 Ur-Nammu 14 (study)
1986 Kärki, KDDU p. 8 Urnammu 14 (edition)
1991 Steible, NSBW 2 pp. 108–109 Urnammu 14 (edition)

TEXT

1) ^{d}nin-ḫur-saga
2) nin-a-ni
3) ur-^{d}nammu
4) nita-kala-ga
5) lugal-uri$_5$.KI-ma
6) lugal-ki-en-gi-ki-uri-ke$_4$
7) [é-k]èš.KI
8) [é]-ki-ág-gá-ni
9) mu-na-dù

1–2) For the goddess Ninḫursaga, his lady,

3–6) Ur-Nammu, mighty man, king of Ur, king of the lands of Sumer and Akkad,

7–9) built for her the [K]eš [temple], her beloved [temple].

37

An inscription found on two door sockets from Nippur records Ur-Nammu's construction of a storehouse for the goddess Ninlil.

The text is arranged in one column of eight lines.

CATALOGUE

Ex.	Museum number	Registration number	Dimensions (cm)	Lines preserved	cpn
1	BM 90826	80-11-12, 2172	Stone: 41×25×18 Inscription: 19.7×7.5	1–10	c
2	BM 103352	1911-4-8, 42	24×17	1–10	c

BIBLIOGRAPHY

1861 1 R I 8 (ex. 1, copy)
1872 Smith, TSBA 1 p. 35 (ex. 1, translation)
1874 Lenormant, Études accadiennes 2 p. 308 (ex. 1, translation)
1875 Ménant, Babylone p. 75 (ex. 1, translation)
1892 Winckler, KB 3/1 pp. 78–79 Ur-gur 7 (ex. 1, edition)
1899 Bezold, Cat. 5 p. 2233 (ex. 1, study)
1905 King, CT 21 pl. 6 BM 90826 (ex. 1, copy)
1907 King and Hall, EWA p. 188 (ex. 1, photo)
1907 Thureau-Dangin, SAK pp. 188–89 Ur-engur l (ex. 1, edition)
1922 BM Guide p. 60 nos. 31 and 55 (exs. 1–2, study)
1929 Barton, RISA pp. 272–73 Ur-Nammu 11 (ex. 1, edition)
1962 Hallo, HUCA 33 p. 26 Ur-Nammu 21 (ex. 1, study)
1985 Kärki, KDDU p. 11 Urnammu 21 (ex. 1, edition)
1992 Steible, NSBW 2 p. 114 Urnammu 21 (exs. 1–2, edition)

TEXT

1) ^{d}nin-líl
2) nin-a-ni
3) ur-^{d}nammu
4) nita-kala-ga
5) lugal-uri$_{5}$.KI-ma
6) lugal-ki-en-gi-ki-uri-ke$_{4}$
7) é-šu-tum-ki-ág-gá-ni
8) mu-na-dù

1–2) For the goddess Ninlil, his lady,

3–6) Ur-Nammu, mighty man, king of Ur, king of the lands of Sumer and Akkad,

7–8) built her beloved storehouse for her.

38

A nine-line steatite tablet from Nippur found in the (old) excavations at Nippur records Ur-Nammu's construction of the "wall of Nippur." This could refer to either the actual city wall or the temenos wall (see discussion to E3/2.1.1.4 above). Lines 1–7 are on the obverse, lines 8–9 on the reverse.

The old University of Pennsylvania expedition to Nippur uncovered a lengthy section of the northeast city wall. Hilprecht and Fisher attributed at least one phase of the wall to the time of Ur-Nammu because its bricks were the same size as those used by Ur-Nammu in the Ekur ziqqurrat. Hilprecht and Fisher's hypothesis is supported by the find of this foundation tablet inscription, if it does refer to the city wall.

COMMENTARY

The foundation tablet, whose exact Nippur provenance is not known, measures 12×7.8×1.1 cm and bears the museum number HS 1965. The inscription was collated.

BIBLIOGRAPHY

1969 Oelsner, WZJ 18 p. 53 no. 18 (study)
1984 Zettler, Inanna Temple p. 16 (study)
1986 Kärki, KDDU p. 26 Urnammu 42 (edition)
1992 Steible, NSBW 2 pp. 147–48 Urnammu 45 (edition)

TEXT

1) ^{d}en-líl
2) lugal-kur-kur-ra
3) lugal-a-ni
4) ur-^{d}nammu
5) nita-kala-ga

1–3) For the god Enlil, lord of the foreign lands, his lord,

4–5) Ur-Nammu, mighty man

6) lugal-uri$_5$.KI-ma
7) lugal-ki-e[n-]gi-ki-uri-k[e$_4$]
8) bàd-nibru.[KI]
9) mu-na-dù

6–7) king of Ur, king of the lands of Sumer and Akkad,
8–9) built the wall of Nippur for him.

39

A cone inscription from Diqdiqqah and Uruk records Ur-Nammu's digging of the "Ur canal."

The text is arranged in one column of ten lines.

CATALOGUE

Ex.	Museum number	Excavation number	Registration number	Provenance	Dimensions (cm)	Lines preserved	cpn
1	BM 30065	—	56-9-3, 1479	—	12.7×5.3	1–6, 8–10	c
2	BM 30084	—	56-9-3, 1499	—	5.7×5.2	1–4, 6–7	c
3	BM 30088	—	56-9-3, 1503	—	3.5×3.7	1, 3–6	c
4	—	U 169	—	Ur, TTB 16	9.8×3.3	—	n
5	IM 100	U 229	—	Ur, TTB outside main wall at W end of SS	8.3×5.5	—	n
6	IM 176	U 520	—	"Found near Murshid's water engine"	8 long	—	n
7	IM 384	U 522	—	—	9 long	—	n
8	IM 385	U 526	—	—	—	—	n
9	IM 238	U 722	—	TTB/SS	9×5.5	—	n
10	—	U 872	—	Ur, surface	12×6	—	n
11	IM 288	U 917	—	"Found near Murshid's water engine"	9×3	—	n
12	IM 741	U 1516	—	Diqdiqqah	13.6×7	—	n
13	—	U 1517	—	Diqdiqqah	10.9×6	—	n
14	BM 117142	U 1597	1924-9-20, 391	Diqdiqqah	7.5×5.5	1–10	c
15	BM 119054	U 2595	1927-10-3, 49	Diqdiqqah	8×4.5	1–10	c
16	BM 119026	U 2795	1927-10-3, 29	Diqdiqqah	12×3.7	7–10	c
17	IM 90961	U 6307	—	Ur, "Dim-tab-ba" temple range, "loose surface soil"	—	—	n
18	IM 90916 (formerly IM 3565A)	U 7701	—	Ur, "loose in soil" in the Larsa houses, on the SW side of the temenos	—	—	n
19	IM 90916	U 7701	—	—	—	—	n
20	IM 90965	U 10135a	—	Ur, area of Royal Cemetery	—	—	n
21	IM 92788	U 13613a	—	Ur, "Larsa filling rubbish" over the Royal Cemetery area, at "1.5 metres"	—	—	n
22	IM —	U 13613b	—	Ur, NE city wall, central section	—	—	n
23	IM —	U pa	—	—	—	—	n
24	IM 22868	U—		—	—	—	n
25	IM 90955	U—	—	—	—	—	n
26	IM 90969	U—	—	—	—	—	n
27	IM 92799	U—	—	—	—	—	n
28	UCPHMA 9-1777	—	—	—	11×6	1–10	n
29	VA 15447	W 6434	—	Uruk	11.1×6.6	1–10	c

COMMENTARY

Exs. 1–3 come from Loftus's excavations. They may have come from Ur or Larsa. It is not certain whether exs. 2, 7–9, and 11 belong to this inscription or E3/2.1.1.40. They are arbitrarily listed here. Ex. 28 was kindly collated by D. Foxvog.

BIBLIOGRAPHY

1928 Gadd, UET 1 no. 45 (exs. 4, 6, 9–16, conflated copy, edition)
1929 Barton, RISA pp. 362–63 Ur-Nammu 11 (exs. 4, 6, 9–16, edition)
1957 Edzard, Sumer 13 p. 176 (exs. 5, 7, 9, 12, 18, 24, study)
1960 Jacobsen, Iraq 22 p. 182 (edition)
1962 Hallo, HUCA 33 p. 26 Ur-Nammu 22 (exs. 4–6, 9–13, 15–16, 18, 24, study)
1965 Sollberger, UET 8 p. 26 no. 10 (exs. 17–23, study)
1978 Foxvog, RA 72 p. 41 (ex. 28, study)
1986 Kärki, KDDU pp. 11–12 Ur-Nammu 22 (exs. 4–6, 9–13, 15–16, 18, 24, 28, edition)
1987 Marzahn, AoF 14/1 p. 33, no. 13 and pl. 1 (ex. 29, transliteration, photo)
1991 Steible, NSBW 2 pp. 114–16 Urnammu 22 (exs. 1–29, edition)
1993 Carroué, ASJ 15 pp. 15–17 (transliteration, study)

TEXT

1) ^{d}en-líl
2) lugal-kur-kur-ra
3) lugal-a-ni
4) ur-^{d}nammu
5) nita-kala-ga
6) lugal-uri$_5$.KI-ma
7) lugal-ki-en-gi-ki-uri-ke$_4$
8) i$_7$-uri$_5$.KI-ma
9) i$_7$-nidba-ka-ni
10) mu-na-ba-al

1–3) For the god Enlil, lord of the foreign lands, his lord,

4–7) Ur-Nammu, mighty man, king of Ur, king of the lands of Sumer and Akkad,

8–10) dug the Ur canal, his canal for offerings, for him.

40

A nine-line cone inscription deals with Ur-Nammu's digging of the I-nun canal. The text is arranged in one column of nine lines.

CATALOGUE

Ex.	Museum number	Excavation number	Registration number	Provenance	Dimensions (cm)	Lines preserved	cpn
1	IM 22908(?)	U 918	—	"Found near Murshid's water engine"	11.5×5.5	—	n
2	BM 116984	U 1634	1924-9-20, 247	Diqdiqqah	9.2×6.7	1–9	c
3	BM 119027	U 2521	1927-10-3, 22	Diqdiqqah	7.3×5	1–5, 7–9	c
4	BM 119042	U 2521	1927-10-3, 37	Diqdiqqah	9.2×5.1	1–9	c
5	BM 119055	U 2521	1927-10-3, 50	Diqdiqqah	4.7×5	4–6, 8–9	c
6	IM 3572A	U 7771	—	Ur, Royal Cemetery area (Trial Trench E), "1 metre from top"	—	—	n
7	IM 92794	U 7771	—	As ex. 6	—	—	n
8	IM 92795	U 10135b	—	By PG 827!(5 m. below surface)	—	—	n
9	IM 90963	U 13001	—	NE city wall, central section	—	—	n
10	IM 90967	U 13602	—	—	—	—	n
11	IM 90968	U 13603a	—	"Larsa rubbish filling" over Royal Cemetery area	—	—	n
12	—	U 13603b	—	Rīm-Sîn's Enki temple, "by wall, loose"	—	—	n
13	BM 116985	U na	1924-9-20, 248	—	7.7×7.5	1–9	c
14	IM—	U oa	—	—	—	—	n
15	IM 90943	—	—	—	—	—	n
16	IM 90944	—	—	—	—	—	n
17	IM 90962	—	—	—	—	—	n
18	UM 35-1-148	—	—	—	—	—	n
19	New York Public Library D-28	—	—	—	11.1×5.7	1–9	c
20	FM E.64.1935	—	—	—	—	1–9	n

E3/2.1.1.39 .2.1 omits.
E3/2.1.1.39.2. 3 omits.
E3/2.1.1.39.5. 2 omits.

BIBLIOGRAPHY

1928 Gadd, UET 1 no. 42 (ex. 1, copy; exs. 1–5, edition)
1929 Barton, RISA pp. 362–63 Ur-Nammu 9 (exs. 1–5, edition)
1940 BNYPL 44 p. 808 no. 25 (ex. 19, study)
1957 Edzard, Sumer 13 p. 176 (exs. 1, 6, study)
1960 Jacobsen, Iraq 22 p. 183 (edition)
1962 Hallo, HUCA 33 p. 27 Ur-Nammu 24 (exs. 1–6, 19, study)
1965 Sollberger, UET 8 p. 26 no. 9 (exs. 7–9, 11–14, study)
1965 Szlechter, Studia et documenta historiae et juris 31 p. 496 (ex. 20, copy)
1971 Sollberger and Kupper, IRSA IIIA1e (exs. 1–6, 19, translation)
1986 Kärki, KDDU p. 13 Urnammu 24 (exs. 1–6, 19, edition)
1991 Steible, NSBW 2 pp. 118–19 Urnammu 24 (exs. 1–20, edition)

TEXT

1) ^{d}nanna
2) lugal-a-ni
3) ur-^{d}nammu
4) nita-kala-ga
5) lugal-uri$_5$.KI-ma
6) lugal-ki-en-gi-ki-uri-ke$_4$
7) i$_7$-nun
8) i$_7$-ki-ág-ni
9) mu-na-ba-al

1–2) For the god Nanna, his lord,

3–6) Ur-Nammu, mighty man, king of Ur, king of the lands of Sumer and Akkad,

7–9) dug for him the I-nun, his beloved canal.

Votive and Seal Inscriptions
(a) Of the King
41–50

41

A vessel fragment found in excavations at Ur bears a votive inscription of Ur-Nammu for the god Nanna.

COMMENTARY

The fragmentary stone vessel was found in the E-nun-maḫ and given the excavation number U 7799, museum number IM 3576.

The text is arranged in one column.

BIBLIOGRAPHY

1928 Gadd, UET 1 no. 286 (copy, edition)
1962 Hallo, HUCA 33 p. 28 Ur-Nammu 30 (study)
1986 Kärki, KDDU pp. 20–21 Urnammu 30 (edition)
1991 Braun-Holzinger, Weihgaben p. 183 G 336 (edition)
1991 Steible, NSBW 2 pp. 138–39 Urnammu 30 (edition)

E3/2.1.1.40.2.1 Copy: lugal-a-ni-šè; original not collated.
E3/2.1.1.40.7.2 i$_7$ (Text: ENGUR)-nun
E3/2.1.1.40.8.2 i$_7$ (Text: ENGUR)-nun

TEXT

1) ⸢^{d}⸣nan[na]
2) [l]ugal-a-ni
3) [u]r-^{d}n[ammu]

1–2) For the god Nan[na], his [l]ord,

3) [U]r-N[ammu]

42

A fragment of an alabaster vessel from Ur was dedicated to the god Nanna by Ur-Nammu.

COMMENTARY

The alabaster vessel fragment, which measures 6.2×5.8×1.4 cm, was found in room 10 of the E-nun-maḫ and given the excavation number U 252. The signs are carved in a very big size reminiscent of Sargonic period inscriptions from Ur. The piece bears the museum number CBS 14943. The text is arranged in one column. The inscription was collated.

BIBLIOGRAPHY

1974 Woolley, UE 6 pp. 50 and 87 (provenance, study)
1991 Braun-Holzinger, Weihgaben p. 185 G 342 (edition)
1991 Steible, NSBW 2 p. 147 Urnammu 44 (edition)

TEXT

1) ^{d}n[anna]
2) lugal-⸢a⸣-[ni]
3) u[r-^{d}nammu]
Lacuna

1–2) For the god N[anna], [his] lord,

3) U[r-Nammu]
Lacuna

43

A plaque bears a votive inscription of Ur-Nammu for the goddess Ningal.

COMMENTARY

The "oolite" (limestone) plaque was found in room C. 26 of the Gipar-ku and given the excavation number U 6366. It measures 6 cm in height, with a diameter of 32 cm, and bears the museum number IM 1174.

The text is arranged in one column of eight lines.

BIBLIOGRAPHY

1928 Gadd, UET 1 no. 34 (copy, edition)
1929 Barton, RISA pp. 360–61 Ur-Nammu 2 (edition)
1962 Hallo, HUCA 33 p. 28 Ur-Nammu 31 (study)
1986 Kärki, KDDU p. 21 Urnammu 31 (edition)
1991 Braun-Holzinger Weihgaben p. 184 G 337 (edition)
1991 Steible, NSBW 2 p. 139 Urnammu 31 (edition)

TEXT

1) ^{d}nin-gal
2) nin-a-ni
3) ur-^{d}nammu
4) nita-kala-ga
5) lugal-uri$_5$.KI-ma
6) lugal-ki-en-gi-ki-uri-ke$_4$
7) nam-ti-la-ni-šè
8) a mu-na-ru

1–2) For the goddess Ningal, his lady,

3–6) Ur-Nammu, mighty man, king of Ur, king of the lands of Sumer and Akkad,

7–8) dedicated (this plate) to her for his life.

44

A fragment of marble vessel from Umma bears a votive inscription of Ur-Nammu.

COMMENTARY

The marble fragment, a purchased piece, which measures 11.5×8.6×2.5 cm, is said to have come from Jōkhā; it bears the museum number YBC 2156. The completely flat fragment bears no traces of a rim. The text is arranged in one column of six preserved lines. The inscription was collated.

BIBLIOGRAPHY

1915 Clay, YOS 1 no. 16 (copy, translation, study)
1929 Barton, RISA pp. 274–75 Ur-Nammu 17 (edition)
1962 Hallo, HUCA 33 p. 28 Ur-Nammu 32 (study)
1986 Kärki, KDDU p. 21 Urnammu 32 (edition)
1991 Braun-Holzinger, Weihgaben p. 184 G 338 (edition)
1991 Steible, NSBW 2 pp. 139–40 Urnammu 32 (edition)

TEXT

1) ⸢^{d}⸣šára
2) [lu]gal-a-ni
3) [u]r-^{d}nammu
4) [n]ita-kala-ga
5) [lu]gal-uri$_5$.KI-ma
6) [lug]al-ki-e[n-g]i-ki-⸢uri⸣-[ke$_4$]
Lacuna

1–2) For the god Šara, his [lo]rd,

3–6) [U]r-Nammu, mighty [m]an, [ki]ng of Ur, [ki]ng of the land of S[um]er and Akkad
Lacuna

45

A mace-head found in excavations at Ur was dedicated by Ur-Nammu to the god Nanna.

COMMENTARY

The white marble mace-head, which measures 12 cm in diameter and 9.5 cm in height, is complete. It was found in room 11 of the E-nun-maḫ, below the Kurigalzu floor level, and was given the excavation number U 208. It bears the museum number IM 97. The text is arranged in one column of eight lines.

BIBLIOGRAPHY

1923 Woolley, AJ 3 pl. 32 (top left) (photo)
1928 Gadd, UET 1 no. 32 and pl. F (photo, copy, edition)
1937 Iraq Museum Guide 1 p. 70 fig. 57 (photo)
1942 Iraq Museum Guide 2 p. 110 fig. 91 (photo, copy, translation)
1962 Hallo, HUCA 33 p. 28 Ur-Nammu 33 (study)
1968 Solyman, Götterwaffen pls. 29–30 figs. 215–16 (photos)
1974 Woolley, UE 6 p. 85 (provenance)
1975–76 Basmachi, Treasures fig. 95 (photo)
1986 Kärki, KDDU p. 22 Urnammu 33 (edition)
1991 Braun-Holzinger, Weihgaben pp. 59–60 K 78 (edition)
1991 Steible, NSBW 2 p. 140 Urnammu 33 (edition)

TEXT

1) ⌈d⌉[nan]na
2) lugal-a-ni
3) ur-dnammu
4) ⌈nita⌉-kala-ga
5) lugal-uri$_5$.KI-ma
6) lugal-ki-en-gi-ki-uri-ke$_4$
7) [nam-ti]-la-ni-šè
8) ⌈a⌉ [mu]-na-ru

1–2) For the god [Nan]na, his lord,

3–6) Ur-Nammu, mighty man, king of Ur, king of the lands of Sumer and Akkad

7–8) [de]dicated (this mace) to him for his (own) [li]fe.

46

A mace-head fragment found in excavations at Ur bears a votive inscription of Ur-Nammu for a god whose name is not entirely preserved; the DN is likely to be restored as Ningublaga.

COMMENTARY

The calcite mace-head, which measures 9.5 cm in height and 11.5 cm in width, with an original diameter of about 15 cm, was found in room 11 of the E-nun-maḫ, below the Kurigalzu floor level, and was given the excavation number U 267. The top section is largely broken away. It bears the museum number BM 116433 (1923-11-10, 18). The text is arranged in one column of nine lines. The preserved text is arranged in one column.

BIBLIOGRAPHY

1928 Gadd, UET 1 no. 49 (copy, edition)
1962 Hallo, HUCA 33 p. 28 Ur-Nammu 34 (study)
1986 Kärki, KDDU p. 22 Urnammu 34 (edition)
1991 Braun-Holzinger, Weihgaben p. 60 K 79 (edition)
1991 Steible, NSBW 2 p. 141 Urnammu 34 (edition)

TEXT

1) ⸢^{d}⸣[nin]-⸢gublaga⸣
2) lugal-a-ni
3) ur-⸢^{d}nammu⸣
4) nita-⸢kala-ga⸣
5) ⸢en-unu.KI-ga⸣
6) lugal-u[ri$_5$.KI-ma]
7) lugal-⸢ki-en⸣-[gi]-ki-⸢uri-ke$_4$⸣
8) ⸢nam⸣-ti-la-ni-šè
9) ⸢a⸣ mu-na-ru

1–2) For the god [Nin]⸢gublaga⸣, his lord,

3–7) Ur-Nammu, mighty man, lord of Uruk, king of U[r], king of the land of Su[mer] and Akkad,

8–9) dedicated (this mace) to him for his (own) life.

47

A votive inscription of Ur-Nammu incised on the foot of a marble vase dedicates the piece to the god Gilgameš of the city Ennegi(r).

COMMENTARY

The vase fragment was found in a "tomb" in the mausolea of Šulgi and Amar-Suena (tomb-chamber 2 of Amar-Suena's SE mausoleum according to the catalogue in UE 6). The piece bears the excavation number U 16530 and the museum number IM 14322. The text is arranged in one column of fifteen lines. The inscription was not collated.

For the identification of the GN EN.DÌM.GIG of line 2 and its tentative localization at modern Išan Khaiber, see Frayne, BiOr 401/2 col. 96 and Carroué, ASJ 15 (1993) pp. 35–40. For the characterization of Ennegi(r) as a city of the dead, we may note the comments of Lambert (in Alster, Death p. 61):

> The latter section [of the Sumerian Temple Hymns dealing with Ešnunna] does not refer to the underworld and will receive no further attention here. The former [referring to Ennegi] is full of infernal things. The town Enegi is first described as "big pipe, pipe of Ereškigal's underworld," where the "pipe" is the clay tube down which offerings to the dead of a liquid kind were poured. It is next described as "Kutha of Sumer", presumably contrasting it with Nergal's Kutha, which was in Akkad, "where mankind gathers", i.e. at their deaths. The city of the god of the underworld partakes of the character of the underworld, just as Eridu in some sense is the Apsû. Egidda, temple of Enegi is now described in the words: "your shadow has stretched over the princes of the underworld (kur) in the underworld (kur)". This again implies that Enegi, as the city of the god of the underworld, is metaphorically the underworld.

For Gilgameš as lord of the underworld, cf. lines 80–82 of the literary composition "The Death of Gilgameš" (ms. Cavigneaux):

^{d}bìl-ga-mes gi[di]m-bi-ta ki-ta ug$_5$-ga
GÌR.NÍTA kur-ra ḫé-ak-⸢e⸣ IGI.DU gidim ḫé-nam
di-da mu-un-ku$_5$-da ka-aš-b[a-x-b]ar-re

Gilgameš, with the shades, (is) dead in the nether (region).
May he serve as general of the underworld, may he be the leader of the shades.
He will decide legal cases, he will render decisions.

BIBLIOGRAPHY

1965 Sollberger, UET 8 no. 21 (copy, study)
1971 Sollberger and Kupper, IRSA IIIA1k (translation)
1974 Woolley, UE 6 pp. 29 and 101 (provenance)
1986 Kärki, KDDU p. 26 Urnammu 41 (edition)
1988 Römer, TUAT 2/4 pp. 463–64 § 3 (translation)
1991 Braun-Holzinger, Weihgaben p. 217 Ständer 9 (edition)
1991 Steible, NSBW 2 pp. 144–45 Urnammu 40 (edition)

TEXT

1) ᵈbìl-ga-mes 2) EN.DÍM.GIG.KI 3) lugal-a-ni	1–3) For the god Gilgameš of Ennegi(r), his lord,
4) ur-ᵈnammu 5) nita-kala-ga 6) lugal-uri$_5$.KI-ma 7) lugal-ki-en-gi-ki-uri-ke$_4$	4–7) Ur-Nammu, mighty man, king of Ur, king of the lands of Sumer and Akkad,
8) u$_4$ é-ᵈnanna 9) mu-dù-a	8–9) when he built the temple of the god Nanna,
10) nam-ti-la-ni-šè 11) a mu-na-ru	10–11) dedicated (this vase) to him for his (own) life.
12) lú mu-sar-ra-ba 13) šu bí-íb-ùr-a 14) ᵈ⌈bìl⌉-ga-mes-e 15) nam ḫa-ba-da-ku$_5$-e	12–15) As for the one who erases this inscription, may the god Gilgameš curse him.

48

A bowl fragment found in excavations at Ur preserves part of an apparent votive inscription of Ur-Nammu.

COMMENTARY

The white calcite bowl fragment was found in the Isin-Larsa area, "house II (= no. 3 Straight Street?), main court, below pavement II," and was given the excavation number U 16533, museum number UM 31-43-253. It measures 4×3.5×1.7 cm with an original diameter of 16 cm and a rim thickness of 1.5 cm. The preserved text is arranged in one column. The inscription was collated.

BIBLIOGRAPHY

1965 Sollberger, UET 8 no. 20 (copy, study)
1986 Kärki, KDDU p. 25 Urnammu 40 (edition)
1991 Braun-Holzinger, Weihgaben p. 184 G 340 (edition)
1991 Steible, NSBW 2 p. 144 Urnammu 39 (edition)

TEXT

Lacuna	Lacuna
1′) [...] 2′) ⌈ur⌉-[ᵈnammu] 3′) nita-[kala-ga] 4′) lugal-u[ri$_5$.KI-ma]	1′–4′) [...], Ur-[Nammu, mighty] man, king of U[r]
Lacuna	Lacuna

49

A fragment of a limestone bowl bears a dedicatory inscription of Ur-Nammu.

COMMENTARY

The shallow limestone bowl fragment with a slightly thickened edge, was found in room 10 of the E-nun-maḫ under the Kurigalzu level, and given the excavation number U 246, museum number CBS 14939. It measures 8.8×7.3 cm with a height of 2.5 cm, and an original diameter of 18 cm. The width of the rim is 1 cm. The text is arranged in one column of fifteen lines. The inscription, which is on the base, was collated.

BIBLIOGRAPHY

1974 Woolley, UE 6 p. 86 (provenance)
1991 Braun-Holzinger, Weihgaben p. 184 G 341 (edition)
1991 Steible, NSBW 2 p. 146 Urnammu 42 (edition)

TEXT

Lacuna
1′) nin-⸢a⸣-[ni]
2′) ur-^{d}na[mmu]
3′) ⸢nita⸣-kala-g[a]
4′) lugal-ur[i$_5$].KI-m[a]
5′) [...] x [...]
Lacuna

Lacuna
1′) [For DN], [his] lady,
2′–5′) Ur-Na[mmu], mighty man, king of U[r], ...
Lacuna

50

A bead fragment found in excavations at Ur is inscribed with the name and titles of Ur-Nammu.

COMMENTARY

The fragment, about half of a large ball of black obsidian, measures 2.4×2 cm. It was found in room 9 of the E-nun-maḫ, and given the excavation number U 404, museum number BCM 69′76. The inscription is arranged in two columns: col. i has lines 1–2 and col. ii has line 3.

BIBLIOGRAPHY

1979 George, Iraq 41 pp. 132–33, no. 23 (copy, edition)
1986 Kärki, KDDU pp. 26–27 Urnammu 43 (edition)
1991 Braun-Holzinger, Weihgaben p. 366 P 7 (edition)
1991 Steible, NSBW 2 pp. 146–47 Urnammu 43 (edition)

TEXT

1) [ur-^{d}nam]mu
2) [nita-kala]-ga
3) lugal-uri$_5$.KI-ma

1–3) [Ur-Nam]mu, [migh]ty [man], king of Ur.

Votive and Seal Inscriptions (b) Of the Royal Family 51–54

Inscriptions E3/2.1.1.51–54 name members of Ur-Nammu's family.

Ur-Nammu — Royal Family

Item	Royal Name	RIM Number	Bibliography
Mother(?)			
1	*da-mi-iq-tum*	—	See W. Sallaberger, AoF 23 (1996) (forthcoming); Sallaberger cites occurrences of Damiqtum in connection with the cult of Ur-Nammu in the texts published by Neumann and Hruška (AcOr 62 [1994] pp. 240-41 no. I 870 line 4) and Owen (MVN 15 no. 162 lines 17 and 39)
Wife			
2	SI.A-*tum*	E3/2.1.1.51	Sollberger, RA 61 (1967) p. 69; Steinkeller, ASJ 3 (1981) pp. 77–78; Michalowski, ASJ 4 (1982) p. 132 and Van De Mieroop in Lesko, Women's Earliest Records p. 58
Daughter-in-Law			
3	*tá-ra-am*-ÚRI.KI-*am* daughter of general Apil-kīn of Mari	E3/2.1.1.52–53	Civil, RA 56 (1962) p. 213; Sallaberger, AoF 23 (1996) (forthcoming)
Daughter			
4	en-nir-gál-an-na	E3/2.1.1.54	Sollberger, AfO 17 (1954–56) p. 23 and n. 65

51

A clay sealing bears the impression of a servant of SI.A-tum, the wife of Ur-Nammu (see Ur-Nammu — Royal Family item 2 above).

COMMENTARY

The impression measures 6×4.1 cm; it comes from Ur, but its excavation number is unknown. The piece bears the museum number BM 134880 and the registration number 1953-4-11, 277. No date is preserved on the sealing. The text is arranged in two columns: col. i has lines 1–3 and col. ii has lines 4–6. The inscription was collated.

Since the reading Watartum proposed by Sollberger (RA 61 p. 69) for the PN of line 1 has never been established, we have retained here the non-committal reading SI.A-*tum*.

BIBLIOGRAPHY

1967 Sollberger, RA 61 p. 69 (edition)
1971 Sollberger and Kupper, IRSA IIIA1n (translation)
1982 Michalowski, ASJ 4 (1982) pp. 131–32 (study)
1986 Kärki, KDDU p. 24 Urnammu 36b (edition)
1989 Van De Mieroop, in Lesko, Women's Earliest Records p. 58 (study)
1991 Steible, NSBW 2 p. 146 Urnammu 41 (study)

TEXT

1) SI.A-*tum*
2) dam-ur-^{d}nammu
3) lugal-uri$_5$.KI-ma
4) lugal-kù-zu
5) nu-bànda
6) ir$_{11}$-zu

1–3) SI.A-tum, wife of Ur-Nammu, king of Ur:

4–6) Lugal-kuzu, lieutenant, (is) your servant.

52

An OB Sammeltafel from Nippur contains an abbreviated copy of a dedicatory inscription of Tarām-Uram, a daughter of the Mari ruler Apil-kīn, and daughter-in-law (é-gi$_4$-a) of Ur-Nammu (see Ur-Nammu — Royal Family item 3 above).

COMMENTARY

The inscription appears on obv. vii of the tablet N 2230+N 4006. The inscription was collated. The Sumerian term é-gi$_4$-a of line 6′ corresponds to Akkadian *kallatu*(*m*). According to CAD the word *kallatu*(*m*) "denotes a young woman who was acquired by the master of a household as a wife for his son living in this household."

BIBLIOGRAPHY

1962 Civil, RA 56 p. 213 (copy, edition)
1971 Sollberger and Kupper, IRSA IIIE1a (translation)
1985 Civil, Orientalia NS 54 pp. 38 and 41 (copy, edition)
1986 Kärki, KDDU pp. 24–25 Urnammu 38 (edition)

TEXT

Lacuna
1′) x x
2′) nin-a-ni-ir
3′) *tá-ra-am*-ÚRI.KI-*am*
4′) dumu-munus *a-pil-ki-in*
5′) lugal-ma-rí.KI-ka
6′) é-gi$_4$-a
7′) ur-^{d}nammu
8′) lugal-⸢uri$_5$.KI-ma⸣
Lacuna

Lacuna
1′–2′) [For the goddess DN], her lady,

3′–5′) Tarām-Uram, daughter of Apil-kīn, king of Mari,

6′–8′) é-gi$_4$-a of Ur-Nammu, king of Ur,
Lacuna

53

A cylinder seal in Philadelphia bears the inscription of a servant(?) of Tarām-Uram (see Ur-Nammu — Royal Family item 2 above).

COMMENTARY

The seal is made of limestone and measures 2.9×1.6 cm; it was purchased in Baghdad in 1890, and now bears the museum number CBS 5005. The inscription was collated. The inscription was read incorrectly by Legrain and Sollberger; the correct reading was kindly pointed out to the author by P. Steinkeller. The text is arranged in one column of three lines.

BIBLIOGRAPHY

1925 Legrain, PBS 14 no. 237 (photo, edition, study)

1971 Sollberger and Kupper, IRSA IIJ3a (translation)

TEXT

1) puzur$_4$-^{d}EN.ZU
2) ENGAR(?) *tá-ra-am*-ŠEŠ.
3) AB.KI

1) Puzur-Sîn,
2–3) *farmer* of Tarām-Uram.

54

A votive inscription of En-nirgal-ana, daughter of Ur-Nammu and *en* of the god Nanna, which is incised on a stone cone and a fragment of a shallow limestone bowl, dedicates the pieces to the goddess Ningal for the life of Ur-Nammu (see Ur-Nammu — Royal Family item 4 above).

CATALOGUE

Ex.	Museum number	Excavation number	Ur provenance	Object	Dimensions (cm)	Lines preserved	cpn
1	CBS 14938	U 209	E-nun-maḫ, room 11	Stone cone frgm.	Height: 9 Base dia.: 9.5 Rim dia.: 5	1–12	c
2	CBS 14940	U 249+U 270	E-nun-maḫ, room 11, under pavement TTB 16–17 (Kurigalzu level)	Joined frgms. of a shallow white limestone dish	U 249: 8.5×6.5×1.8 U 270: 5.5×5×1.5	7–12	c

COMMENTARY

According to Woolley (UE 6 pp. 86–87), U 249 joins U 270; the two pieces were listed separately by Steible. The texts, as far as can be determined, are arranged in one column.

BIBLIOGRAPHY

1928 Gadd, UET 1 no. 48 (exs. 1–2, conflated copy, edition)
1929 Barton, RISA pp. 364–65 Ur-Nammu 14 (exs. 1–2, edition)
1954–56 Sollberger, AfO 17 p. 23 and n. 65 (exs. 1–2, study)
1962 Hallo, HUCA 33 p. 28 Ur-Nammu 35 (exs. 1–2, study)
1971 Sollberger and Kupper, IRSA IIIA1l (exs. 1–2, translation)
1974 Woolley, UE 6 pp. 85–87 (exs. 1–2, provenance, study)
1986 Kärki, KDDU pp. 22–23 Urnammu 35 (exs. 1–2, edition)
1991 Braun-Holzinger, Weihgaben p. 184 G 339 (ex. 2, edition) and pp. 216–17 Ständer 8 (ex. 1, edition)
1991 Steible, NSBW 2 pp. 142–43 Ur-Nammu 35 (exs. 1–2, edition) and pl. 24 (exs. 1–2, copy, edition)

TEXT

1) ⸢^{d}⸣nin-gal
2) [ni]n-a-ni
3) [na]m-ti-
4) ⸢ur⸣-^{d}nammu
5) [nita-k]ala-ga
6) [luga]l-uri$_{5}$.KI-ma
7) [lugal]-ki-en-gi-ki-uri
8) ad-da-na-šè
9) en-nir-gál-an-na
10) [e]n-^{d}nanna
11) [dum]u-ki-ág-ni
12) ⸢a⸣ mu-na-ru

1–2) For the goddess Ningal, his [la]dy,

3–8) for the [li]fe of Ur-Nammu, [m]ighty [man], [king] of the lands of Sumer and Akkad, her father,

9–11) En-nirgal-ana, [*e*]*n* of the god Nanna,

12) dedicated (this object) to her.

Votive and Seal Inscriptions
(c) Of City Governors
2001

A cylinder seal bears the inscription of Ḫašḫamer, governor of Iškun-Sîn.

COMMENTARY

The seal is made of greenstone and measures 5.28×3.03 cm. According to D. Collon, Cylinder Seals 2 p. 168, the seal was "Presented by C.D. Cobham, H.M. Commissioner at Larnaka, through C.T. Newton; obtained at Babylon some time before 1820 by John Hine, Medical Officer to H.M. Consulate at Baghdad, and handed, on his death in 1860, to Mr Cobham." The seal bears the museum number BM 89126 and the registration number 80-10-9, 1. The text is arranged in two columns: col. i has lines 1–3 and col. ii has lines 4–7. The inscription was collated.

BIBLIOGRAPHY

1820 Dorow, "Die Assyrische Keilschrift erläutert durch zwei noch nicht bekannt gewordene Jaspis Cylinder aus Nineveh und Babylon ... ," Morgenlaendische Altertümer, fasc. I pl. II fig. II (drawing)
1822 Porter, Travels 2 pl. LXXIX no. 6 (drawing)
1861 1 R I 10 (copy)
1872 Smith, TSBA 1 p. 35 (translation)
1874 Lenormant, Études accadiennes 2 p. 312 (translation)
1875 Ménant, Babylone p. 75 (translation)
1880 Ménant, Empreintes pp. 44–45 no. 55 (copy)
1883 Ménant, Glyptique 1 pp. 129–31 fig. 73 and pl. IV no. 2 (photo, copy, study)
1892 Winckler, KB 3/1 pp. 80–81 Ur-gur 10 (edition)
1900 BM Guide [1] p. 137 no. 24 and pl. XXIII no. 1 (photo, study)
1905 King, CT 21 pl. 6 BM 89126 (copy)
1907 Thureau-Dangin, SAK pp. 188–89 Ur-engur n (edition)
1908 BM Guide [2] pp. 157–58 no. 27 (photo, study)
1910 King, Early History pl. opposite p. 246 (middlephoto)
1910 Ward, Seals pp. 13 and 109, fig. 303a (copy, study)
1920 Thompson, Arch. 70 pl. XI opposite p. 152, no. 6 (photo)
1922 BM Guide [3] pp. 232–33 no. 2 (photo, study)
1929 Barton, RISA pp. 274–75 Ur-Nammu 18 (edition)
1935 Zervos, L'art p. 253 (photo)
1959 Wiseman and Forman, Seals no. 40 (photo)
1962 Hallo, HUCA 33 p. 28 Ur-Nammu 36 (study)
1962 Strommenger and Hirmer, Mesopotamien pl. 128 and p. 80 (photo, study)
1969 Barnett and Wiseman, Fifty Masterpieces no. 41 (photo, translation, study)
1971 Sollberger and Kupper, IRSA IIIA1m (translation)
1982 Collon, Cylinder Seals 2 no. 469 (photo, edition, study)
1986 Kärki, KDDU pp. 23–24 Urnammu 36a (edition)
1987 Winter, in Gibson and Biggs (eds.), Bureaucracy p. 95 Ia and pl. 1a (photo, study)
1991 Steible, NSBW 2 p. 143 Urnammu 36 (study)

TEXT

1) ur-^{d}nammu
2) nita-kala-ga
3) lugal-uri$_5$.KI-ma
4) ḫa-áš-ḫa-me-er
5) énsi-
6) *íš-ku-un*-^{d}EN.ZU
7) ir$_{11}$-zu

1–3) Ur-Nammu, mighty king, king of Ur:

4–7) Ḫašḫamer, governor of Iškun-Sîn, (is) your servant.

Šulgi

E3/2.1.2

The Weld-Blundell exemplar of the Sumerian King List assigns Šulgi a reign of forty-six years; source Su_{3+4} (sigla are those used by Jacobsen in SKL) gives forty-eight years, and source P_5 fifty-eight years. In the Ur-Isin king lists published by E. Sollberger (JCS 8 [1954] pp. 135–36) Šulgi is credited with a reign of forty-eight years, and this figure is generally accepted by scholars to be correct. Two year lists are available for the king. The first, Ni 394, of likely Old Babylonian or later date, was published by H. Hilprecht as BE 1/2 no. 125. It contains the names of Š 5 (or Š 6 — see discussion below) down to Š 43. The second year list, IB 542a+b+, a fragmentarily preserved multicolumn tablet from Isin that originally may have listed the year names of Ur-Nammu, Šulgi, and Amar-Suena, was edited by C. Wilcke in a study entitled "Neue Quellen aus Isin zur Geschichte der Ur-III-Zeit," Orientalia NS 54 [1985] pp. 299–303. It gives the names of Š 4–5 (or Š 5–6) and Š 19–24. Of note is the fact that some of the year names of the Isin list are clearly variants to those found in the Nippur date list.

The year names of Šulgi have been studied by F.R. Kraus in an article entitled "Zur Chronologie der Könige Ur-Nammu und Šulgi von Ur," Orientalia NS 20 (1951) pp. 385–98 and by E. Sollberger in a study called "Sur la chronologie des rois d'Ur et quelques problèmes connexes," AfO 17 (1954–56) pp. 14–17. A more recent discussion is found in Frayne, Correlations pp. 139–253.

It is unfortunate that relatively few changes are detectable in the titulary of Šulgi that would allow us to date the king's inscriptions. A prime index for dating purposes is the presence or absence of the prefixed divine determinative in the writing of the royal name. Now, the first unequivocal occurrence of the divine determinative before the king's name is found in the year name Š 21a. We suspect, however, that the king was already deified by year Š 20, since the royal name is preceded by the DINGIR sign in brick inscriptions from Tell al-ʿUbaid that were likely connected with the introduction of a new cult statue of Ninḫursaga there; the introduction of Ninḫursaga's statue is commemorated in the year name Š 20b. However, it may be that the king was deified already by Š 12b. F. Carroué (in a forthcoming study which he kindly communicated to me in advance of its publication) argues that the year name: mu ^{d}nin-gír-su é-ba-gára é-a-na!-ku$_4$-<ra> "The year the god Ningirsu was brought into his Bagara temple" (Brooklyn Museum 74.71.2 = Owen, MVN 15 no. 125 rev. line 3′) should be seen as a variant year name for Š 12. Now, in inscription E3/2.1.2.15, which deals with Šulgi's construction of the Bagara temple, Šulgi's name is written *with* the prefixed DINGIR sign. If inscription E3/2.1.2.15 dates to year 12, as seems likely, then it would appear that the king had already adopted the divine determinative by Š 12. More data are needed to clarify this question.

Another significant change in the royal titulary apparently took place by Š 27. The provisional formula for that year found on L 7129 = Pettinato, MVN 6 no. 128 rev. lines 10–13 (no month name recorded) reads: mu ^{d}šu[l-gi ni]ta-kala-ga lugal-an-ub-da-límmu-ba-ke$_4$ si-mu-ur$_4$-um.KI a-rá-2-kam-aš mu-ḫul-a mu-ús-sa-bi "The year Šu[lgi], mighty [ma]n, king of the four quarters, destroyed Simurrum, the year after (this)." Of note is the appearance for the first time in a Šulgi year name of the title "king of the four quarters." While the Akkadian equivalent of the title: LUGAL *ki-ib-ra-tim ar-ba-im* was employed in royal inscriptions that clearly predate Š 21 (as, for example, in E3/2.1.2.23 and 27 where Šulgi's name is rendered without the prefixed *dingir* sign), its Sumerian rendition is so far attested only in inscriptions that date to Š 27 and later. Its presence or absence in *Sumerian* texts, then, is a second important index for dating purposes. Perhaps the adoption of the new title was in some way connected with Enlil's granting of "supreme power" to Šulgi, as commemorated in the year name Š 23.

In the following discussion the Šulgi hymns are designated by the sigla given in Klein, Three Šulgi Hymns pp. 36–43; Klein's scheme follows that which was originally provided by A. Falkenstein in ZA 50 (1952) pp. 62–63.

I. Year Names and Events of the Reign

(1) mu šul-gi lugal "The year Šulgi (became) king." AO 3336: Thureau-Dangin, RTC no. 273.

Šulgi's father apparently met an untimely death in battle against the Gutians, and it is likely that Šulgi ascended to the throne of Ur at a young age. The events of Šulgi's accession served as inspiration for the court poets at Nippur; at least two lengthy literary compositions deal with events connected with the inauguration of the new king.

The hymn Šulgi F was first recognized by W.H.P. Römer (in an article entitled "Königshymnen der Isinzeit und Königsinvestitur," ZDMG Suppl. 1 [1969] pp. 133–36) to be a composition celebrating the coronation of king Šulgi. Römer's conclusions were reiterated by C. Wilcke in an article entitled "Eine Schicksalentscheidung für den toten Urnammu," CRRA 17 (1970) p. 89 n. 1. A passage in the hymn (primary source AO 8845: de Genouillac, TRS no. 86 obv. lines 13–18, with restorations from HS 1460: Bernhardt, TMH NF 4 no. 11 lines 78–83) describes how the god Nanna asks Enlil to choose Šulgi to be the new king in Sumer and Akkad:

[a]-a-^{d}en-líl en du_{11}-ga nu-gi_4-gi_4
[a]-a-dingir-re-e-ne me ki-bé gar-gar
uru-ni igi mi-x-ni-íl úri.KI-ma [nam] bí-in-⸢tar⸣
x lugal-si-sá šà-kù-ge pà-da-gá
⸢lugal⸣ sipa šul-gi sipa-zi ḫi-li gùr-ru-àm
nam-du_{10} tar-mu-ni-íb kur ḫa-ma-a[b-GAM.GAM-e]

Oh [fa]ther Enlil, lord (whose) word cannot be countermanded,
[Fa]ther of the gods who puts the *me*s in their (proper) place,
I have looked in his (var.: my) city, I have determined the destiny of Ur,
The upright king who was called by me in the pure heart,
It is the king, shepherd Šulgi, the true shepherd endowed with beauty,
Decree a good destiny (for him) in order that he might make the foreign land(s) bow down to me.

A later passage in the hymn (found on Ni 626: Kramer, SLTN no. 78 rev. cols. i–ii) describes a coronation ceremony in which various royal insignia — the men-kù "pure crown," gidru-u_4-sù-rá "sceptre of long days," GIŠ.gu-za-suḫuš-gi-na "throne with a secure foundation," and GIŠ.eškiri "nose-rope" are all mentioned — were presented to Šulgi. J. Klein has proposed that the hymn deals with an actual coronation of Šulgi in Ur (Klein, TAPS 71 [1981] pp. 11 and 25).

A second Šulgi composition, Šulgi D+X (edition by Klein, Three Šulgi Hymns, Šulgi D: pp. 50–123 and Šulgi X: pp. 124–66) appears to narrate events connected with the accession and coronation of Šulgi in Nippur. Concerning the *Sitz im Leben* of this composition, C. Wilcke (CRRA 19 [1974] p. 197 n. 84) writes:

> Er [Klein] möchte Šulgi D in die Mitte von Šulgi's Regierungszeit setzen, da die Datenformeln erst nach seinem 23. Jahr Feldzüge überliefern. Aber der Königsname trägt nicht das Gottesdeterminative und Šulgi ist (nur) sipa-zi-ki-en-gi-ra; er will seine Stadt rächen und Vergeltung für die Zerstörungen in Sumer nehmen (s.o. Anm. 73). Diese räumliche Beschränkung (s. auch die Städte-Reihe in Anm. 85) und das Motiv der Rache passen m.E. nur zum Regierungsanfang von Šulgi, da wir aus UT wissen, dass die Herrschaft seines Vaters Urnammu mit einer Katastrophe endete. J. Kleins Argument, der Sieg hätte in einem Jahresnamen festgehalten werden müssen, uberzeugt nicht. Auch kein späterer Jahresname berichtet einen Sieg über die Gutäer. Es ist aber sehr gut denkbar, dass der Sieg nicht im Jahresdatum festgehalten wurde, weil es ein wichtigeres religiös-politisches Ereignis gab, nämlich Regierungsantritt und Krönung; s. auch E. Sollberger, AfO 17, S. 15 mit Anm. 18 zum Jahresdatum 2.

As noted by Wilcke, a passage in the poem describes the god Enlil's blessing of Šulgi in Nippur after the king's return from the Gutian battlefield; in all likelihood it refers to an investiture ceremony that took place in the religious capital. In the following passage (pp. 88–89, lines 384–97 in Klein's edition, which is quoted here) the god Enlil addresses Šulgi with the following words:

lugal nam gi$_4$-rí-íb-tar^{ar} nam-dul$_{10}$ gú-mu-rí-íb-tar^{ar}
šul-gi nam gi$_4$-rí-íb-tar^{ar} nam-dul$_{10}$ gú-mu-rí-íb-tar^{ar}
nam-ur-sag nam-šè gú-mu-rí-íb-tar^{ar}
nam-en-nam-lugal-la-u$_4$!-sù-da!′nam-šè gú-mu-rí-íb-tar^{ar}
ní-me-lám-ma gú hu-mu-ni-ús
igi-huš-zu lú nam-ba-gub
aga$_x$(TÙN)-nam-lugal-lá-zu-ù dalla ḫé-im-è
gidri-zu nì-nam-nun-na ḫé-em
pa-mul-bi an-dùl-le-éš ḫu-mu-ù-ak
šà-za šà-húl-la hé-in-gál nam-ba-kúš-U-dè-èn
lugal-zi-šà-gál-unken-za hé-me-en
nam-ti-[l]a?-zu gu-gim ḫé-[m]ú-mú še-gim hé-mú-mú
[m]es-zi-[gi]m? [ki?]-dagal-e ḫé-[mú-m]ú
[x] x nar! [x x x x] x [x x x]
(end of hymn missing)

Oh King, let me decree the fate for you, let me decree a good fate for you!
Oh Šulgi, let me decree the fate for you, let me decree a good fate for you!
Let me decree for you heroship as (your) fate!
Let me decree for you long lasting *en*-ship and kingship as (your) fate!
May you lift (your) head with a terrifying splendour!
May no man stand before your fierce gaze!
May your royal crown radiate!
May your scepter be of princeship,

May its "shining branches" become a (refreshing) shade!
May joy be placed in your heart, may you never grow weary!
May you be the "life-giving-king" of your assembly!
May your life flourish like herbs, may it flourish like grain!
Like a fertile *mes*-tree may you grow high? on a wide [place?]!

(2) mu šul-gi lugal-uri$_5$.KI-ma-ke$_4$ GIŠ.gu-za-za-gìn ^{d}en-líl-ra ì-na-ku$_4$-ra "The year Šulgi, king of Ur, brought in a lapis-lazuli throne for the god Enlil." 6N-T382: A. Goetze, Iraq 22 (1969) p. 156 and pl. XX.

The relative placement of this year name within Šulgi's reign is not entirely certain. It is likely that four or five year names are to be assigned to the gap at the beginning of the Nippur (Hilprecht) date list; the year name dealing with Enlil's throne could be either Š 2 or 3; it has arbitrarily been placed here as Š 2.

(3) mu é-muḫaldim-^{d}nin-šubur ba-dù-a "The year the temple kitchen of the god(dess) Ninšubur was built." Ni 6: M. Çığ, in Kramer Anniversary pp. 78 and 82 no. 11; V. Scheil, RT 19 (1897) p. 55, no. 6.

Year name (3), of likely Ur III date, should be assigned to either Ur-Nammu or Šulgi, since all the year names of the remaining Ur III kings have been accounted for. It may provide the name of the year Š 3. A temple or shrine of the goddess Ninšubur named é-šà-te-zu "House which knows how to soothe the heart" is mentioned in rev. 6′ of the the short hymn Šulgi M (Ni 2999: Kramer, SLTN no. 76). It is possible, albeit uncertain, that this is the name of the temple kitchen of Š 3. Whether there is any connection with a foundation tablet from Uruk dealing with the goddess Ninšubur (see E3/2.1.2.8) is unclear.

(4) Not yet attested?

(5) mu uš-é-^{d}nin-urta ki ba-a-gar "The year the foundations of the temple of the god Ninurta were laid." AO 3339 and AO 3333: Thureau-Dangin, RTC nos. 274 and 276; L 8121: Delaporte, ITT 4 no. 8121.

F. Kraus (Orientalia NS 20 [1951] pp. 389–90) has provided convincing arguments that the year name dealing with the laying of the foundations of the temple of Ninurta should be assigned to Šulgi.

The event recorded in this year name may be commemorated in the short *tigi* hymn Šulgi T. The text is known from an Old Babylonian Sammeltafel copy of Ninurta compositions (CBS 11325+11348+11362+11367: Radau, BE 29/1 no. 1; edition by Å Sjöberg, in Kramer Anniversary pp. 411–19 and 425–26; Šulgi T is found in col. iii lines 6–36 = lines 91–119 of Sjöberg's edition). The composition mentions (in a restored text) the laying of the foundations of Ninurta's temple in Nippur (lines 97–99 edition Sjöberg, slightly modified here):

lugal-mu uru-za èš-nibru.KI tir x [...]
é-šu-me-ša$_4$ ki šu mu-r[a-ab gá-gá]
en nam-lugal-e šu mu-ra-ab-du-[du$_7$-e]

My king, in your city, shrine Nippur ...
He (Šulgi[?]) is laying Ešumeša on the ground for you,
He is carrying out kingship perfectly for you, Oh Lord.

Of further interest in this connection is the discovery at Nippur of a brick, of probable Ur III date (no royal name appears in the extant text), bearing an inscription dedicated to the god Ninurta. Strangely enough, it was found in a wall of the Inanna temple at Nippur. Its inscription is edited as E3/2.1.6.1005 in this volume.

(6a) ⌈mu BÀD.GAL.AN⌉.[KI ki-bé gi$_4$-a] "The year Dēr(?) [was restored]." Ni 394: Hilprecht, BE 1/2 no. 125 obv. line 1′.

Kraus (Orientalia NS 20 [1951] p. 390) read the traces of the year name as [m]u [B]À[D.G]A[L.A]N.[K]I [...] and saw a reference to the city of Dēr. Since so little of the year name is preserved, the restoration is not entirely certain. However, if we bear in mind the fact that temporal clauses in royal inscriptions can often be matched with year names, Kraus's restoration is supported by the occurrence of a temporal clause in a foundation tablet inscription found at Susa (but almost certainly originally from Dēr) that reads in part (see E3/2.1.2.63 col. ii lines 1–5):

[u$_4$ é]-ki-ág-gá-ni	[When] he [b]uilt his (Ištarān's[?])
[mu]-na-dù-a	beloved temple for him and restored
BÀD.AN.KI	Dēr, his beloved city ...
uru-ki-ág-gá-ni	
ki-bé mu-na-gi$_4$-a	

The inscription probably dates to Ur III times; we have tentatively assigned it to Šulgi (see E3/2.1.2.63).

The particular writing of the city name Dēr as BÀD.GAL.AN.KI in the Nippur date list, as far as can be determined, is unique to that list (it is also found there in the name of Š 11). Dēr is normally written BÀD.KI or BÀD.AN.KI in archival texts and royal inscriptions. In the Nippur list the writing BÀD.GAL.AN.KI is probably an anagraphic writing for BÀD.AN.GAL.KI. Weidner has shown that the deity AN.GAL, which appears in a number of sources connected with the city Dēr, is "ohne Zweifel mit ^{d}KA.DI [=Ištarān] identisch." He cites thirteen data supporting this hypothesis (see AfO 9 [1933–34] pp. 98–99).

Further, Sjöberg (Temple Hymns p. 13) notes dingir-gal (DINGIR.GAL = *ilu rabû*) as an epithet of Ištarān. He cites in this connection Weidner, AfK 2 (1924–25) p. 15 col. iii 8a, where the correct reading of KAV no. 63 line 20 and KAV 47 col. ii line 13: [...]...-ra-an ^{d}GAL ^{d}*il*-⌈*tar*⌉-*an* has been pointed out by Lambert (ZA 59 [1969] pp. 100–103); cf. Landsberger and Bauer, ZA 37 (1927) p. 73 with n. 2 and Unger, RLA 2 pp. 199–201 where K. 1354, 38 (unpublished) is noted: *šá* URU *di-ri šá* ^{d}KA.DI DINGIR.GAL. For the reading of ^{d}KA.DI see Weidner, AfO 16 (1952–53) p. 24 where the (erroneous) reading Sataran is proposed; Lambert, AfO 18 (1957–58) p. 44 line 43: ^{d}*iš-ta-ra-an*; Litke, ms. An: *Anum* p. 214 note to line 287, where the gloss ^{di}š-ta-ra-^{an}KA.DI in YBC 2401 is noted; and finally (and conclusively), Lambert, ZA 59 (1969) pp. 100–103. For the reading of BÀD.AN.KI as Dēri, see van der Meer, OECT 4 pl. XXXII no. 153 col. iii 6–8 (Proto-Diri 514–16): [BÀD.AN].KI = *di*-[*e-ri*], [BÀD.A]N.KI = *da-a*-[*ri*], [BÀD].AN.KI = *du-ur-ì-lí*.

For the location of ancient Dēr at modern Tell ʿAqr, a site which lies to the west of the modern Jawi River about one kilometre west of modern Badrāyā, see the comments of S. Smith in JEA 18 (1932) pp. 28–32 — Smith examined the mound briefly in 1930. Excavations at the neighbouring ruin of Tell Baḥrām were carried out in 1955 by F. Safar (see Sumer 7 [1951] pp. 53ff. [Arabic section]). Safar (p. 53) suggests that the modern name Badrāyā derives from the elements *be+dara*. In this case *be* is to be analysed as a reduced form of Aramaic *bēt* "house"; it was apparently prefixed to the ancient name of the city. A survey of the neighbouring sites of Tell Baḥrām and Tell Qirawī in the vicinity of Badrāyā was conducted by B. Hrouda in spring 1971 (see Bagh. Mitt. 6 [1973] pp. 7–18).

(6b) mu-ús-s[a uš]-é-^{d}nin-urta ki-a b[í-gar] "The year aft[er the foundations] of the temple of the god Ninurta were laid." IB 542a+b+: Wilcke, Orientalia NS 54 (1985) pp. 300–301.

In the fragmentary Ur III period date list from Isin studied by Wilcke (Orientalia NS 54 [1985] pp. 299–303) a mu-ús-sa formula to that for Š 5 is given as the name of Š 6. Furthermore, as noted by Wilcke, the same sequence of year names is found on the tablet AO 3333 (Thureau-Dangin, RTC no. 276 obv. i lines 18–20): (a) mu uš-é-^{d}nin-urta, (b) mu-ús-sa uš-é-^{d}nin-urta, and (c) mu lugal-e šu in-nígin.

In this case, the evidence of the Lagaš tablets is at variance with the evidence of the Nippur date list, as can be seen in the table below.

Nippur Date List	RTC 276
[...]	mu uš-é-^{d}nin-urta
1′ ⸢mu BÀD.GAL.AN⸣.[KI ki-bé gi$_{4}$-a]	mu-ús-sa uš-é-^{d}nin-urta
2′ mu gìr-nibru.⸢KI⸣ [si bí-sá-a]	mu lugal-e šu in-nígin
3′ mu lugal-e úri.KI-[ta]	

The year name of the Nippur date list dealing with the [restoration] of Dēr is not attested in any of the Lagaš tablets. They give a different year name; it is a mu-ús-sa formulation to the year name dealing with the laying of the foundations of the Ninurta temple. In order to account for the apparent discrepancy between the year names of the Nippur list and the Lagaš tablets, Wilcke (Orientalia NS 54 [1985] p. 301) has suggested that lines 2′–3′ of the obverse of the Nippur date list might be combined to give one year name: *mu gìr-nibru.⸢KI⸣ [(...)] lugal-e úri.KI-t[a šu in-nígin] "The year the Nippur road [(...)] (and) the king [made a round trip] fr[om] Ur." We have followed Wilcke's suggestion in the list given in this study.

(7a) mu gìr-nibru.⸢KI⸣ [si bí-sá-a] "The year the Nippur road [was put in order]." Ni 394: Hilprecht, BE 1/2 no. 125 obv. line 2′.

This year name, or more accurately, part of a year name, has not yet been found in any archival texts; it occurs only in the Nippur date list. The end of the line can be restored, with a reasonable degree of certainty, on the basis of Ur-Nammu year (h): mu ur-^{d}nammu lugal-e sig-ta IGI.NIM-šè gìr si bí-sá-a "The year Ur-Nammu, the king, set the 'road' in order from below to above." The setting in order of the road between Ur and Nippur apparently entailed the establishment of way-stations for travellers, as is described in the hymn Šulgi A (transliteration following Klein, Three Šulgi Hymns pp. 190–91 lines 28–33; translation by the author):

gìr ḫu-mu-gur kaskal-kalam-ma-ke$_{4}$ si ḫé-em-sá-sá
danna ḫu-mu-gi é-gal-la ḫé-bí-dù
zà-ba GIŠ.kiri$_{6}$ ḫé-bí-gub ki-ní-dúb-bu ḫé-bí-gar
ki-bé lú-zu-a ḫé-em-mi-tuš
sig-ta du IGI.NIM-ta du-e
á-šed$_{10}$(MÙŠ.DI)-bi-šè ní ḫé-eb-ši-te-en-te-en

I ... the roads, I put the highways of the land in order.
I established mile-(markers) and set them in "great houses."
I planted gardens by their side, established resting-places there.
I settled in those places experienced (men).
(As for he) who comes from "above," (or he) who comes from "below,"
May they refresh themselves in their cool *shade*.

In line 29, the Sumerian word dana, a measure of length equivalent to about 10 km, is commonly, if not accurately, rendered in English by the term "mile." The fact that the text refers to the danas as being set *in* "great houses" indicates that we are not dealing with the danas as actual distances, but rather more likely, they refer to milestones. We have followed Klein in taking the words dana and é-gal of line 29 to be plural. One might argue that the reference here is to one central mile marker in the palace at Ur (so W.

Sallaberger in RIM reader's comments), but this would not account for the hymn's clear connection between these danas and é-gals and the gardens and rest-stops for the traveller.

(7b) mu lugal-e úri.KI-[ta] "The year the king [from] Ur." Ni 394: Hilprecht BE 1/2 no. 125, obv. line 3′. A more complete version of the year name is found on AO 3893 (Thureau-Dangin, RTC no. 277): mu lugal-e uri$_{5}$.KI-ta nibru.KI-šè ⸢in⸣-nígin "The year the king made a round trip between Ur and Nippur." Further examples of the name of Š 7 are catalogued in Schneider, Zeitbestimmungen p. 13 nos. 3a–c.

Šulgi's famous run between the cities of Ur and Nippur is celebrated in the hymn Šulgi A. A brief synopsis of events connected with the run is found in lines 38–41 (transliteration Klein, Three Šulgi Hymns pp. 192–93; translation by the author):

ka-tar-mu kur-kur-ra si-il-le-dè
du$_{10}$-tuku-me-en usu-mu íb-zi-ge-en kas$_{4}$-e káb di-dè
nibru.KI-ta sig$_{4}$-úri.KI-ma-šè
danna-aš-gin$_{7}$ šu-nigin-ta šà-mu ḫa-ma-ab-du$_{11}$

That praise of me break out in the foreign lands,
I, the speedy one, summoned my strength to test my running.
From Nippur to the brick-work of Ur,
My heart prompted me to make a round trip, as if it were (only) one "mile."

Šulgi's famous run is also commemorated in inscription E3/2.1.2.54, an Old Babylonian copy of an apparent Ur III inscription; it may have once been inscribed on a Nippur statue that depicted the king as a racer. Further, a handful of passages in Sumerian literature refer to Šulgi as a sprinter; he is invariably described in metaphorical language that compares him to a swift horse. In the hymn Šulgi A, for example, Šulgi boasts (in line 17, quoted from Klein, Three Šulgi Hymns pp. 188–89): ANŠE.KUR.RA ḫar-ra-an kun sù-sù-me-en "I am a horse, waving its tail on the highway." In line three of the literary letter of Aba-indasa to Šulgi (Ali, Sumerian Letters pp. 53 and 58), Aba-indasa addresses Šulgi in the following terms: ANŠE.KUR.RA-ḫur-sag-gá umbin-ḫu-rí-in.MUŠEN-na "O horse of the mountain, (with) the claws of an eagle." Of further interest is an entry in the omen series *šumma izbu* (Leichty, Šumma Izbu p. 206 line 41) which reads: DIŠ *iz-bu-um ki-ma* ANŠE.KUR.RA *a-mu-ut* ^{d}*šul-gi* "If an anomaly is like a horse — omen of Šulgi who ruled the four quarters."

(8) mu má-^{d}nin-líl-lá ba-du$_{8}$ "The year the boat of Ninlil was caulked." Ni 394: Hilprecht, BE 1/2 no. 125, obv. line 4′.

The construction of Ninlil's boat served as inspiration for the creation of the royal hymn Šulgi R, whose introductory section reads as follows (edition and translation quoted from J. Klein, "Šulgi and Išme-Dagan: Originality and Dependence in Sumerian Royal Hymnology," in Studies Artzi pp. 102–103 and 112–13 lines 1–8):

[má-g]ur$_{8}$ ^{d}en-ki-ke$_{4}$ kar-ḪI-gál nam-šè ma-ra-ni-in-⸢tar ar⸣
[a]-⸢a⸣(?) ^{d}en-líl-le igi-zu mu-ù-ši-bar^{ar}
nin-zu-ù ^{d}nin-líl-le ù-tu-zu bí-in-du$_{11}$
ú-a-zi lugal šul-gi-da á-zu mu-da-an-ág
géštu-dagal-la-kam sá-gal mu-ù-ši-in-p[à]d
sipda-dè u$_{4}$-gi$_{6}$-a ù nu-mu-ù-ši-in-ku$_{4}$-ku$_{4}$
igi-gál tuku giš-ḫur-re kin-gá kù-zu-nì-nam-ma-k[e$_{4}$]
GIŠ.tir-gal-gal-la erin(?)-gal ma-ra-an-ni-[in-ku$_{5}$(?)]

Oh barge, Enki decreed for you a quay of abundance as
(your) fate,
Father Enlil looked upon you with true benevolence,
Your lady, Ninlil, ordered your construction,
To the faithful provider, the king Šulgi, she gave instructions
concerning to you,
He of the intelligence wide took great counsel about you,
The shepherd, day and night sleeps not,
The wise one, who is proficient in planning, the omniscient
one,
In the huge cedar forest he caused large *cedars* to be felled
for you.

Ninlil's boat was used in Ur III times to transport cult statues of the divine pair, Enlil and Ninlil, during their annual pilgrimage to Tummal (see S. Oh'e, "An Agricultural Festival in Tummal in the Ur III Period," ASJ 8 [1986] pp. 121–32 and Sallaberger, Kalender 1 pp. 131–33). The celebration of the Tummal festival itself is alluded to in Šulgi R (lines 58–59, edition Klein, Studies Artzi p. 107):

má-gur$_8$(?) kar-me-te-a-gi$_6$-a a-ne-sud ì-im-[me]
GIŠ.gi-tum-ma-al.KI-^{d}en-líl-lá-ke$_4$ á mu-sù-sud-e

The barge, *The-Quay-the-Ornament-of-the-Current*, is
joyfully prancing (on the water),
It is sailing to the canebrake of Enlil's Tummal.

This same cult vessel figures in the name of ŠS 9; it is designated there as the cult boat of Enlil and Ninlil.

(9) mu ^{d}nanna kar-zi-da é-a ba-ku$_4$ "The year the god Nanna of Karzida was brought into (his) temple." Ni 394: Hilprecht, BE 1/2 no. 125 obv. line 5′.

As far as can be determined, this year name appears only in the Hilprecht date list and has not yet been found in archival texts. The available tablets (all from Girsu) use a mu-ús-sa formulation to the name of Š 8.

(10) mu é-ḫur-sag-lugal ba-dù "The year the 'Mountain House' of the king was built." Ni 394: Hilprecht, BE 1/2 no. 125 obv. line 6′.

The construction of "Mountain House," the royal palace of Šulgi at Ur, is commemorated in inscription E3/2.1.2.3. Bricks bearing this text came from a large rectangular structure that lay on the southeast side of the Nanna temple temenos. For a recent discussion of this building, see Moorey, Iraq 46 (1984) p. 18. The construction of the "Mountain House" is clearly alluded to in two passages of the hymn Šulgi B. It is described there as being an IM.SAG.(KI), a term of uncertain translation. The first passage (lines 198–220, transliteration from an unpublished ms. quoted by the kind permission of G. Haayer, its author) reads:

IM.SAG.KI é-gal gi-né-dam
sag-dù gi-(diš)-ninda uru.KI dù-dù-ù-dè
IM.SAG.KI-mu a-ba-da-ab-gál-la-àm

To make firm the IM.SAG, the palace,
To plant the wedge and measuring line (in) the city,
(With respect to) my IM.SAG, who can compare with me?

A second passage in the hymn sings the praises of the "Mountain House" (lines 377–79, edition Castellino, Two Šulgi Hymns [BC] pp. 68–69; lines 380–82, in the ms. of G. Haayer, which is quoted here):

[šu]l-gi-me-en é-mu é-ḫur-sag é-gal-é-gal-bi-im
[é-gal]-nam-lugal-la-gá zà-mí-gal-gal-la-kam

I, Šulgi, my house, the "Mountain House," is a superlative palace.
These are the great songs of praise of the [palace] of my kingship.

According to G. Castellino, the occasion which prompted the creation of the hymn Šulgi B itself was the dedication of "Mountain House." He writes (Two Šulgi Hymns [BC] p. 10):

> What the cause and motive was for the particular celebration, for once we are not left to guess. Šulgi himself tells us in the last section of the composition where he celebrates the completion and dedication of the royal palace, the é-ḫur-sag, connected with the é-^{d}en-líl-lá, that we know through Woolley's excavations.

For bibliography on the "Mountain House," see George, House Most High p. 100 no. 474. The building is named in a handful of Sumerian literary compositions. It serves, for example, as the locus of the disputation in the literary debate "Tree and Reed" (line 30, quoted in van Dijk, Sagesse p. 35 and Castellino, Two Šulgi Hymns (BC) p. 240; see also W.W. Hallo, HUCA 33 [1962] p. 29 n. 214). E-ḫursag is named in a hymn to the god Nanna (Å. Sjöberg, JCS 29 [1977] p. 9 rev. 18′), and temple hymn nine in the "Collection of Sumerian Temple Hymns" (Sjöberg and Bergmann, Temple Hymns p. 24) sings the praises of this edifice. For a cautionary note on the significance of these literary references to E-ḫursag, see B. Alster and H. Vanstiphout, ASJ 9 (1987) pp. 41–42 n. 10. Wilcke (CRRA 19 p. 190 n. 51) notes archival texts that deal with the repair of the E-ḫursag in AS 1 and IS 16.

(11) mu ^{d}ištarān BÀD.GAL.AN.KI é-a ba-ku$_4$ "The year the god Ištarān of Dēr was brought into (his) temple." Ni 394: Hilprecht, BE 1/2 no. 125 obv. line 7′.

As noted above, the writing BÀD.GAL.AN of the Nippur date list is unusual. In the examples of the name for Š 11 found on archival tablets from Girsu (for a list, see Sigrist and Gomi, Comprehensive Catalogue p. 99 sub SH11) Dēr appears in the normal writing BÀD.AN.KI.

(12a) mu nu-^{umuš}muš-da ka-zal-lu.KI é-a ba-ku$_4$ "The year the god Numušda of Kazallu was brought into (his) temple." Ni 394: Hilprecht, BE 1/2 no. 125 obv. line 8′.

(12b) mu $^{\langle d \rangle}$lugal-ba-gára é-a-na! ku$_4$-<ra> "The year the god Ningirsu was brought into his Bagara temple." Brooklyn Museum 74.71.2 = Owen, MVN 15 no. 125 rev. line 3′.

As noted above, F. Carroué, in a forthcoming study of local variants at Lagaš of the Šulgi year names, will argue that Lagaš tablets dated with a year name dealing with the introduction of the god Ningirsu into this Bagara temple should be assigned to the reign of Šulgi, rather than to the time of Gudea, as had been done previously. Carroué provides evidence that this year name should be assigned as a variant (at Lagaš) to the name Š 12a found in the Nippur date list. Šulgi's construction of Ningirsu's Bagara temple is commemorated in inscription E3/2.1.2.15; it most likely commemorates the construction work recorded in year name Š 12b.

(13a) mu é-ḫal-bi lugal ba-dù "The year the royal 'ice (lit: frost)-house' was built." Ni 394: Hilprecht, BE 1/2 no. 125 line 9′.

In the expression é-ḫal-bi, ḫal-bi is a phonetic writing for the Sumerian logogram ḫalba/i/u "frost" which is found in the spellings MÙŠ×A.DI, ZA.MÙŠ.DI, ZA.MÙŠ-*gunû*, LÁ+LÁ+ḪAL, LÁ+LA+GIŠGAL, A.MÙŠ.DI, ZA.MÙŠ-*gunû*.DI, GIŠ.MÙŠ×A.DI, GIŠ.A.MÙŠ-*gunû*.DI, and GIŠ.ZA.MÙŠ-*gunû* (see Lieberman, Sumerian Loanwords p. 305); cf. AHw p. 313 sub *ḫalpium* "eine Art Brunnen" and *ḫalpû*(*m*) I "Frost." The translation "ice-house" follows normal English usage; technically é-ḫal-bi should be translated "frost-house." According to Wilcke (CRRA 19 p. 190 note 51, citing Reisner, Telloh no. 173 and Chiera, STA no. 30 line 27), an é-ḫal-bi was located in Lagaš. An archival text noted by Wilcke and dated to Š 42 (Legrain, UET 3 no. 845) refers to materials for the repair of an é-ḫal-bi at Ur. It is likely that this latter structure is the one whose construction is noted in the name of Š 13. For discussions on "ice-houses" in Old Babylonian texts, see P. Charlier, "Les glaciers à Mari," Akkadica 54 (1987) pp. 1–10; I. Cornelius, "Ice and Ice-Houses in the Mari Texts," Journal of Northwest Semitic Languages 13 (1987) pp. 23–32; and F. Joannès, "L'eau et la glace," in Charpin and Durand, Florilegium marianum 2 pp. 137–50. Ice-houses are attested from these sources for the cities of Mari, Terqa, and Saggarātum. For a royal inscription of Zimrī-Līm of Mari recording the construction of an "ice-house," see Frayne, RIME 4 p. 625 E4.6.12.3.

(13b) mu lugal-ba-gára é-a ku₄-ra ús-sa "The year after 'the king of the Bagara (temple)' (= Ningirsu) entered (his) temple." U 8846 = Legrain, RA 30 (1933) p. 119; Legrain, UET 3 no. 291; Gadd, UET 1 no. 283.

As will be pointed out in Carroué's forthcoming study of the Šulgi year names from Lagaš, year Š 13b, a mu-ús-sa formulation to year Š 12b, is so far attested only on the one cited tablet from Ur. The earlier attribution of this year name to Gudea (see Sollberger, AfO 17 [1954–56] p. 34 and Falkenstein, Inschriften Gudeas p. 9) was taken as possible evidence of domination over the area of Ur by the Lagaš II dynasty. However, with the realization that this year name belongs to Šulgi, not Gudea, the primary argument supporting the theory of Lagaš control over Ur in pre-Ur III times vanishes.

(14) mu ᵈnanna-nibru.KI é-a ba-ku₄ "The year the god Nanna of Nippur was brought into (his) temple." Ni 394: Hilprecht, BE 1/2 no. 125 line 10′.

(15) mu en-nir-zi-an-na en-ᵈnanna máš-e ì-pà "The year En-nirzi-ana, *en* of the god Nanna, was chosen by omens." Ni 394: Hilprecht, BE 1/2 no. 125 obv. line 11′.

A tablet dated to Š 38 (Legrain, UET 3 no. 1320) bears the seal impression of a servant of En-nirzi-ana; its inscription appears as E3/2.1.2.87 in this volume.

(16) mu ná-ᵈnin-⸢líl-lá ba-dím⸣ "The year the bed of Ninlil was built." Ni 394: Hilprecht, BE 1/2 no. 125 obv. line 12′.

(17) mu en-nir-zi-an-na en-ᵈnanna ba-ḫun-gá "The year En-nirzi-ana, the *en* of the god Nanna, was installed." Ni 394: Hilprecht, BE 1/2 no. 125 obv. line 13′.

(18) mu *lí-wir*(GÌR)-*mi-ṭa-šu* dumu-munus-lugal nam-nin mar-ḫa-ši.KI ba-íl "The year Liwwir-miṭṭašu, daughter of the king, was elevated to the queenship of Marḫaši." Ni 394: Hilprecht, BE 1/2 no. 125 obv. line 14′.

For the reading wir for the GÌR sign in the personal name, see Sollberger, AfO 17 (1954–56) pp. 21–22 n. 55; cf. Gelb, MAD 3 p. 192 citing AD.DA-*na-wir*(PIRIG) in CT 7 pl. 34 18409 rev. 6. The second component of the princess's name has been interpreted as Akkadian *miṭṭu*(*m*) "mace"; thus Liwwir-miṭṭašu's name would mean "May-His(that is, the king's)-Mace-Shine." A parallel to the name is found in the PN Tabūr-ḫaṭṭum "The-Rule (literally: Sceptre)-Has-Remained-Firm." Tabūr-ḫaṭṭum appears in a handful of archival texts (see Michalowski, JAOS 95 [1975] pp. 718–19) as a "daughter-in-law" (é-gi$_4$-a) of the governor of Ḫamazi. In all likelihood she was an Ur III princess. A second parallel to the name Liwwir-miṭṭašu can be seen in the name of Ibbi-Sîn's daughter, Tukīn-ḫaṭṭi-migriša "She-Established-the-Rule (literally: Sceptre)-of-Her-Favourite"; it appears in the year name for IS 5. It may be that the names of these princesses were not their actual birth names, but rather ceremonial names adopted (for political reasons) on the occasion of their betrothal. It seems more than a coincidence that words symbolic of the power of the Ur III empire, such as "sceptre" or "mace," occur specifically in the names of these three princesses, who ended up as wives of foreign rulers.

For other examples of diplomatic marriages in the Ur III period, the reader may consult W. Röllig, "Hierat, politische," RLA 4 p. 283 nos. 6–9. An example not cited in Röllig's study has been noted by P. Steinkeller. He describes (ZA 72 [1982] p. 241 n. 16) a text that records the expenditure of various animals "for the house of Tarām-Šulgi, the king's daughter, the wife of Šudda-bāni, the man (i.e., the ruler) of Pašime" (é *tá-ra-am-*^{d}šul-gi dumu-SAL lugal dam šu-da-ba-ni lú ba-šim.e.KI-ka-šè). Pašime was an eastern state located in what is modern-day Iran; it bordered on the Persian Gulf.

As it turns out, the diplomatic marriages of the Ur III period were in many cases "liaisons dangereuses"; the consequences of these unions were often disastrous. We may note the following interesting couplets: (a) Š 30: marriage of the king's daughter to the governor of Anšan — Š 34: destruction of Anšan by Šulgi; (b) marriage of Šū-Sîn's daughter Kunšī-mātum to the ruler of Simānum (Šulgi, year unknown) — war against Simānum (Šū-Sîn 3); (c) marriage of Ibbi-Sîn's daughter to the governor of Zabšali (IS 5) — loss of Susa to the Simaškian rulers presumed to have controlled Zabšali, as evidenced by the complete cessation of documents dated with Ibbi-Sîn's year names at Susa.

(19) mu EZEN×KASKAL(?).KI ki-bé ba-ab-gi$_4$ "The year EZEN×KASKAL(?).KI was restored." Ni 394: Hilprecht, BE 1/2 no. 125 obv. line 15′. **[m]u BÀD.KI k[i-bé gi$_4$-a]** "The [ye]ar Dūrum(?) was re[stored]." IB 542a+b+: C. Wilcke, Orientalia NS 54 (1985) p. 301. **mu EZEN×(x).KI ki-bé gi$_4$-a** "The year EZEN×(x).KI was restored." U. 3538: L. Legrain, UET 3 no. 292.

Because of the variation in the spelling of the GN in this year name some uncertainty exists as to exactly which toponym is referred to. Unfortunately, the copy of the one contemporary exemplar (Legrain, UET 3 no. 292) does not clearly indicate what sign, if any, is inscribed inside the EZEN sign.

(20a) mu dumu-úri.KI-ma lú-giš-gíd-šè KA ba-ab-kešda "The year the citizens of Ur were conscripted as lancers." Ni 394: Hilprecht, BE 1/2 no. 125 obv. line 16′.

The conscription of lancers commemorated in the name of Š 20 is almost certainly to be seen as a prelude to the event commemorated in the name of the following year (Š 21b), namely the destruction of the city of Dēr. Now, a conscription of troops for an attack against some rebel city, conceivably but not certainly Dēr (in this case the reference is to archers, not lancers), is alluded to in the hymn Šulgi B (lines 99–100, edition Castellino, Two Šulgi Hymns (BC) pp. 40–41; lines 98–99, ms. Haayer):

> GIŠ.kak-ban-ta KA-kešda-gá na-me
> im-ri-a 1-ta lú na-ma-ta-è-e
>
> As for my conscription with bow (and) *arrow*, nobody
> — (the levy) being one (member) per family — evaded it.

(20b) mu ^{d}nin-ḫur-saga-gá nu-tur é-a-na [b]a-an-ku$_4$ "The year the goddess Ninḫursaga of Nutur was [b]rought into her temple." IB 542a+b+: C. Wilcke, Orientalia NS 54 (1985) p. 302; cf. Wilcke in Hrouda, Isin 3 p. 83 note *.

The name of Š 20b can be connected with the divine name Ninḫursaga-nutur which is found in a handful of Ur III archival texts (Holma, Cuneiform Tablets no. 27 rev. line 1; Sollberger, JCS 23 [1970–71] p. 28 no. 4 line 2; Sigrist, AUCT 1 no. 209 line 9) and in the literary composition "Lamentation over the Destruction of Sumer and Ur" (pp. 48–49 line 207 of Michalowski, Lamentation): ^{d}nin-ḫur-saga é-nu-tur-ra-ke$_4$ u$_4$ ḫul ba-an-da-dal "An evil storm swept over Ninḫursaga at Enutura." Now, the various cult centres mentioned in the adjoining lines of the lament can be shown to have been situated in the general environs of Ur, and in all likelihood Ninḫursaga's Nutur shrine lay in this same general area. This hypothesis is supported by the evidence of an archival text from the Zion Research Library, Boston (Owen and Young, JCS 23 [1970] pp. 106 and 114 no. 31) that mentions the goddess Ninḫursaga of Nutur followed by the god Ningišzida of Gišbanda (there the GN is written niš-bàn-da.KI). Now, a location for ancient Gišbanda on the ancient Euphrates a little upstream from Ur has been proposed by the author (see D. Frayne, BiOr 45 [1988] col. 349) and F. Carroué (ASJ 15 [1993] p. 50). Ancient Nutur, in turn, may plausibly be equated with the mound marked by modern Tell al-ʿUbaid. H.R. Hall uncovered a temple oval of Early Dynastic date at the site, from which a marble foundation tablet incised with a building inscription of an Early Dynastic king of Ur, A-ane-pada, was found. The inscription clearly indicates that the temple oval was dedicated to the goddess Ninḫursaga; since the oval was the largest structure found at Tell al-ʿUbaid, we might logically infer that the goddess Ninḫursaga was the tutelary deity of the city. Of interest, then, in view of the name of Š 20b, is evidence that Šulgi undertook building activities at Tell al-ʿUbaid. Hall (UE 1 p. 14) writes:

> Above it (the ED temple) had been built a tiered platform of large oblong crude bricks, above which is a pavement(?) of burnt bricks, measuring 11 1/2 by 8 by 2 1/2 in. (29.2 by 20.3 by 6.3 cm), stamped by King Dungi or Šulgi.

The relevant brick inscription is edited as E3/2.1.2.45 in this volume. It is not unlikely that the construction work by Šulgi at Tell al-ʿUbaid was undertaken to prepare the site for the introduction of Ninḫursaga's new cult statue.

Similar conclusions concerning the location of Ninḫursaga's cult centre at Nutur/Al-ʿUbaid were reached by W. Sallaberger in Kalender 1 p. 59 n. 246 and by Steinkeller in ASJ 17 (1995) p. 280.

(21a) mu ^{d}nin-urta énsi-gal-^{d}en-líl-lá-ke$_4$ é-^{d}en-líl ^{d}nin-líl-lá-ke$_4$ eš-bar-kin ba-an-du$_{11}$-ga ^{d}šul-gi lugal-uri$_5$.KI-ma-ke$_4$ GÁNA nì-kas$_7$ šuku-é-^{d}en-líl ^{d}nin-líl-lá-ke$_4$ si bí-sá-a "The year the god Ninurta, the great 'field-manager' of the god Enlil, pronounced an oracle in the temples of the gods Enlil and Ninlil, (and) Šulgi, king of Ur, put in order the fields (and) accounts, the sustenance of the temples of (var. in Isin date list: for) the gods Enlil and Ninlil." 5N-T 490: A. Goetze, Iraq 22 (1960) pp. 151–53. For slightly variant forms of this year name, see C. Wilcke, Orientalia NS 54 (1985) p. 302 no. 21 and Hilprecht, BE 1/2 no. 125 obv. lines 17′–19′.

The normal translation of énsi as "governor" would not suffice here to indicate Ninurta's prominent role as the god of agriculture; on this question, see Steinkeller, in Gibson and Biggs, Seals p. 51 n. 37. For the term *iššakku(m)* as "a member of a class of priviliged farmers," see CAD I sub *iššaku*.

For an apparently abbreviated form of the year name, see A.572-1982 (Birmingham City Museum = Wellcome R37892): Watson, Birmingham 2 no. 3 lines 10–12: mu nì-kas$_7$-ak al-la-ta: "From the year of the accounting of the 'hoe' land ..."; cf. PTS 551: Sigrist, PTS no. 562: mu nì-kas$_7$-ak al-la-ka mu-2-kam-ús-sa-a-bi; and Colgate 14: Snell and Lager, YOS 18 no. 96: mu-nì-kas$_7$-

ak al-la-ka mu-4-kam-ús-sa-bi. Concerning this year name dealing with the "hoe-land," see the comments of Sallaberger, OLZ 89 (1994) p. 540.

A probable allusion to the events commemorated in the name of Š 21a is found in Šulgi inscription E3/2.1.2.57. It reads in part (line 1′): ⸢ù á-šuku!⸣-[ra-ke$_4$] si m[u-sá-a] "[when (PN) ...] and put the sustenance provisions in [order]." If the correlation holds true, it would indicate that Šulgi dedicated a statue to the goddess Ninsuna sometime around Š 21a.

(21b) [mu BÀ]D.AN.KI ba-ḫul "The year [D]ēr was destroyed." IB 542a+b+: C. Wilcke, Orientalia NS 54 (1985) p. 302 no. 21a.

An attack against Dēr, possibly the one which figures in the year name Š 21b, is found in the hymn Šulgi C (lines 27′–34′, transliteration from ms. Tinney corresponding to Castellino, Two Šulgi Hymns [BC] pp. 260–63 rev. lines 23–30; see the photo on pl. 23 of Castellino's book):

gú-i$_7$-dur-ùl-lá gú-i$_7$-*ṭa-ba-na*-ka
ní ku$_4$-kur-mu ki ba-ni-ús
sag-maḫ-mu a ⸢peš$_{10}$⸣ DU.DU ⸢gìr?⸣ [(x x)] nu-DI
ki-bala-e ù-ma-ti-a-ta
sig$_4$-bi úr-ba mu-⸢bù-bù-uš⸣
uru mu-sì-ga-mu ki-bé-e n[am-g]i$_4$-gi$_4$
é-mu-gul-a-mu du$_6$-ra(var. du$_6$-du$_6$-⸢rá⸣) ⸢ša?⸣-m[u-u]n-šid
BÀD.AN.KI gú-érim-gál nam-ba-d[a-x]-[ta]g$_4$

Along the banks of the Diyālā and Ṭaban rivers
My fearful aura and *wave* ... were cast there.
(translation uncertain)
After I arrived at the rebellious land,
They (the troops?) ripped out its brickwork by its foundations.
May the city which I have smitten not [be] restored!
The houses which I destroyed were counted as ruin heap(s).
Dēr — all the enemy (troops) — I did indeed leave abandoned.

Two lines later in the hymn Šulgi claims: nita-zi á-maḫ sum-ma-me-e[n] "I am the true male, the one granted supreme power," a fact that ties in well with the name of Š 23: "The year the king was given supreme power."

The campaign against Dēr is likely commemorated in a royal inscription (E3/2.1.2.35) that is found on a Sammeltafel of Šulgi inscriptions. The relevant lines (obv. col iii′ 0–9) read:

[GU$_7$ I$_7$.*tur-ùl*]	[The banks of the River
ù I$_7$.*ṭa-ba-an*	Diyālā] and the River Ṭaban
iš-bi-ir-ma!	he smashed, and in a swamp
ù in <*a*>-*pá-ri-im*	he annihilated (the enemy).
kà-ma-ra-ma	The land *which he in-*
íš-ku-un	*undated*—he smashed his
ma-ta-a-am	(the enemy's) weapon.
u(Text: *i*)-*ṭe$_4$*^{te}-*eb*-<*bu*>-*ma*	
ù GIŠ.TUKUL-*šu*	
iš-bi-ir	

Šulgi took measures to consolidate his hold on the newly conquered territories in the basins of the Diyālā and Taban rivers. Chief among these was the construction of two new fortresses named for the king: Šulgi-Nanna and Išīm-Šulgi. According to an Ur III archival text (Legrain, UET 3 no. 75 line 6) Šulgi-Nanna lay on the banks of the Diyālā River. On the other hand, a location for Išīm-Šulgi in the general Diyālā region has been indicated (see R. Harris, JCS 9 [1955] p. 45).

(22a) ⌜mu-ús-sa ᵈnin-urta⌝ [...] "The year after Ninurta ..." Ni 394: Hilprecht, BE 1/2 no. 125 rev. line 1.

(22b) [mu-ú]s-sa BÀD.AN.KI ba-ḫul "[The year af]ter Dēr was destroyed." IB 542a+b+: C. Wilcke, Orientalia NS 54 (1985) p. 302 no. 22. Compare also CBS 8351: D. Owen, NATN no. 119 and CBS 10088: D. Owen, NATN no. 351.

(23) mu ᵈšul-gi lugal-e ⌜á⌝-maḫ ᵈen-lí[l su]m-ma-ni [x] x x [x x] x x "The year Šulgi, the king — Enli[l gra]nted him supreme power ... ." IB 542a+b+: C. Wilcke, Orientalia NS 54 (1985) p. 302 no. 23: "The year the king [was given] supreme power." Cf. Ni 394: Hilprecht, BE 1/2 no. 125 rev. line 2: **mu lugal á-maḫ** "The year the king (was given) supreme power."

For the reading of the year name, see Kraus, Orientalia NS 20 (1951) p. 387. Of interest is the fact that a majority of Šulgi year names following Š 23 refer to military campaigns of the king; in contrast, no year names preceding Š 23 (with the exception of Š 21b and 22b) mention any wars waged by Šulgi.

(24) mu kára-ḫar.KI ba-ḫul "The year Karaḫar was destroyed." Ni 394: Hilprecht, BE 1/2 no. 125 rev. line 3.

(25) mu si-mu-ru-um.KI ba-ḫul "The year Simurrum was destroyed." Ni 394: Hilprecht, BE 1/2 no. 125, rev. line 4.

For an extensive bibliography on the location of Simurrum/Zabban, see Kh. Nashef, Rép. Géogr. 5 pp. 279–80. According to Nashef (p. 280), Simurrum/Zabban comprised: "etwa die Hügellandschaft zwischen Kifrī und Qarā Tepe." I intend to examine the question of the location of Simurrum in a separate study, and to posit a location of the strategic city beside the modern Mount Zangan at or near the point where the modern Pungla River joins the modern Sirwān River.

(26) mu si-mu-ru-um.Ki a-rá-2-kam-ma-aš ba-ḫul "The year Simurrum was destroyed for a second time." Ni 394: Hilprecht, BE 1/2 no. 125 rev. line 5.

(27) mu ḫa-ar-ši.KI ba-ḫul "The year Ḫarši was destroyed." Ni 394: Hilprecht, BE 1/2 no. 125 rev. line 6.

(28) mu en eridu.KI-ga ba-ḫun-gá "The year the *en* of Eridu was installed." Ni 394: Hilprecht, BE 1/2 no. 125 rev. line 7.

A fuller form of this year name is found on a tablet from Nippur, CBS 9161: Owen, NATN no. 235 which reads: mu en-nam-šita-ᵈšul-gi-ra-ke$_4$ ba-gub ba-ḫun "The year En-nam-šita-Šulgirake-bagub was installed (as *en*)." She is attested as late as x AS 7 in an archival text from Drehem (AUAM 73.0687: Sigrist, AUCT 1 no. 948 obv. line 3). An archival text probably related to her installation is U 7162 (Legrain, UET 3 no. 296 dated to xi^2 Š 27), which records various copper objects (line 3): nam-en en-eridu.KI-kam "(for) the office of *en* of the *en* of Eridu."

(29) mu-ús-sa en eridu.KI-ga ba-ḫun-gá "The year after the *en* of Eridu was installed." Ni 394: Hilprecht, BE 1/2 no. 125 rev. line 8.

(30) mu dumu-munus lugal énsi an-ša-an.KI-ke$_4$ ba-tuk "The year the daughter of the king was married to the governor of Anšan." Ni 394: Hilprecht, BE 1/2 no. 125 rev. line 9.

(31) mu kára-ḫar.KI a-rá-2-kam-ma-aš ba-ḫul "The year Karaḫar was destroyed for the second time." Ni 394: Hilprecht, BE 1/2 no. 125 rev. line 10.

(32) mu si-mu-ru-um.KI a-rá-3-kam-ma-aš ba-ḫul "The year Simurrum was destroyed for the third time." Ni 394: Hilprecht, BE 1/2 no. 125 rev. line 11.

According to W.W. Hallo ("Simurrum and the Hurrian Frontier," RHA 36 [1978] p. 74): "The third defeat of Simurrum may have involved Šulgi's crowning military achievement, to judge from the Old Babylonian omen tradition." The ruler of Simurrum conquered by Šulgi is known to have been a certain Tappa(n)-Daraḫ; Hallo has examined various Ur III and later sources that refer to this ruler. Three omens published by Goetze ("Historical Allusions in Old Babylonian Omen Texts," JCS 1 [1947] pp. 259–60 nos. 25–27) deal with the capture of Tappa(n)-Daraḫ, namely: (a) Goetze, YOS 10 no. 22 line 17: DIŠ KÁ É.GAL *ši-rum i-bi-ir* ⌜*a*⌝*-mu-ut* ^{d}*šul-gi ša* ^{m}*tap-pá-*^{d}*da-ra-aḫ ik-mu-ú* "If tissue (is) across the 'palace gate,' it is an omen of Šulgi, who took Tappa(n)-Daraḫ prisoner"; (b) Goetze, YOS 10 no. 24 line 35: DIŠ KÁ É.GAL *ši-ra-am ú-du-uḫ a-mu-ut* ^{d}*šul-gi ša tap-<pá>-*^{d}*da-ra-aḫ ik-mu-ú* "If the 'palace gate' is covered with tissue, it is an omen of Šulgi, who took Tap<pa>(n)-Daraḫ prisoner"; and (c) YOS 10 no. 24 line 40: DIŠ i-na ŠÀ KÁ É.GAL *ši-rum ku-bu-ut-ma ša-ki-in a-mu-ut* ^{d}*šul-gi ša tap-pá-an-*^{d}*da-ra-aḫ ik-mu-ú* "If in the middle of the 'palace gate' a heavy mass of tissue is located, it is an omen of Šulgi, who took Tappa(n)-Daraḫ prisoner." As noted by Hallo, a PN *tap-pá-da-ra-aḫ* is found in a Drehem tablet dated to Š 34 (LB 2217: Hallo, TLB 3 no. 14 line 3), and a daughter Tappa(n)-Daraḫ is mentioned in a text dated to Š 33 (MM 25: Schneider, Drehem- und Djoḫatexte no. 53 = Molina, Montserrat no. 53 line 22: gìr dumu-munus *tap-pá-da-ra-aḫ*). Tappa(n)-Darah's wife appears in a tablet dated to Š 33 (Montserrat 40: Schneider, Drehem- und Djoḫatexte no. 40 = Molina, Montserrat no. 40, line 4: dam *tap-pá-da-ra-aḫ*); later references noted by Hallo (RHA 36 [1978] p. 75) date to the time of Šū-Sîn. Further, an omen known from a Middle Assyrian copy dated by Nougayrol to the time and library of Tiglath-pileser I refers to the defeat of Tappa(n)-Daraḫ: (BM 122643: [Thompson copy] in Walker, CT 51 pl. 53 rev. lines 14–15): [... *tab*]*-ba-gar ù*(!) *rab-si-si* MAN.MEŠ *šá* x [...] / [...] x *su-nu-ti-ma* ŠEŠ.ŠEŠ-*šú* GAZ "[...Tab]ba-gar and(!) Rabsisi, kings of ... [...], he [...] and brother killed brother." In addition, a chronicle text from Seleucid Uruk retains a memory of Šulgi's attack against Tappa(n)-Daraḫ: (W 22289: Hunger, SbTU 1 no. 2 lines 3–5): [x ^{d}š]ul-gi LUGAL ŠEŠ.UNU.KI A ^{m}ur-^{d}nammu/ [*šar*]*-ru-tu* KUR.KUR *ka-la-ši-na i-pu-uš* / [*tab*]*-ban-ga-ár u* ^{m}*rab-si-si* LUGAL.MEŠ *šá* KUR SU.BIR$_4$.KI *i-be-el* "Šulgi, king of Ur, son of Ur-Nammu, exercised [ki]ngship over all the lands; [Tab]bangar and Rabsisi, kings of the land of Subartu, he overpowered."

(33) mu-ús-sa si-mu-ru-um.KI a-rá-3-kam-ma-aš ba-ḫul "The year after Simurrum was destroyed for the third time." Ni 394: Hilprecht, BE 1/2 no. 125 rev. line 12.

(34) mu an-ša-an.KI ba-ḫul "The year Anšan was destroyed." Ni 394: Hilprecht, BE 1/2 no. 125 rev. line 13.

As noted, the evidence of the name of Š 34 indicates that Šulgi's war against Anšan took place a scant four years after the marriage of his daughter to the governor of the city. A reference to what must have been an earlier campaign of Šulgi against Anšan is found in an undated tablet from Nippur (Ni 1956: Çığ and Kızılyay, NRVN no. 7); it contains the temporal clause "when Šulgi destroyed Anšan" (u$_4$ an-śa-an.KI šul-gi mu-ḫul). The appearance of Šulgi's name here without the prefixed divine determinative and the writing of GN Anšan with the sibilant ś instead of š clearly point to a date of Šulgi's first campaign against Anšan sometime before Š 21.

(35) mu-ús-sa an-ša-an.KI ba-ḫul "The year after Anšan was destroyed." Ni 394: Hilprecht, BE 1/2 no. 125 rev. line 14.

(36) mu ^{d}nanna kar-zi-da.KI a-rá-2-kam-aš é-a ba-⌜ku$_4$⌝ "The year Nanna of Karzida entered his temple for a second time." Ni 394: Hilprecht, BE 1/2 no. 125 rev. line 15.

(37) mu bàd-ma-da ba-dù "The year the wall of the land was built." Ni 394: Hilprecht, BE 1/2 no. 125 rev. line 16.

Three letters in the corpus of literary letters known as the "Royal Correspondence of Ur" (nos. 9–11 in Michalowski's edition in his Yale dissertation, the so-called "Puzur-Šulgi letters") deal with Šulgi's building of the "wall of the land" (bàd ma-da). Michalowski (Correspondence p. 84) comments:

> The only fact, however, which may be utilized in the ordering of the (literary) letters is the building of the bad mada in Š 36 (here Š 37). The Puzur-Šulgi correspondence deals with a wall named Bad-igi-ḫursaga, "The Wall Facing the Highland." There can be little doubt that these two names refer to the same fortifications.

The Puzur-Šulgi letters make it clear that troops working on the wall had to contend with attacks by Tidnumite nomads as the work progressed. In letter 10 in Michalowski's edition, for example, Šulgi writes to Puzur-Šulgi as follows (Michalowski, Correspondence p. 199):

> The wall is to be finished in the period of one month! (And) there are to be no (further) inquiries pertaining to these building activities! And now the Tidnum have come down from the mountain(s).

Šulgi may have responded militarily to these Tidnumite attacks. This is suggested by a tablet dated to xi Š 38 (ROM 270 925.62.254: Sigrist, ROM no. 14) that records the disbursement (line 10) "for soldiers of the king" (mu aga-ús-lugal-ka-šè) said to be (line 13) "on the campaign" (šà-kaskal-la). While the text does not name the particular campaign, the date of the tablet is suggestive of some connection with the building of the wall. Also of note is a tablet dated to Š 40 (YBC 11456; Michalowski, Correspondence p. 81) that gives a record of "Amorite booty" (nam-ra-ak mar-dú).

mu é-^{d}nergal ba-dù "The year the temple of the god Nergal was built." BM 27564 (reference courtesy M. Sigrist).

As far as can be determined, BM 27564 is a unique attestation of this unplaced Ur III year name. Since the tablet belongs to an archive of BM tablets (including at least BM 27556–27568) that date to the period Š 30–38, we would expect that the year name dealing with the Nergal temple would date to this same general period. As noted, reflections of both cultic and buildings activities can often be seen in Ur III archival texts, and these documents should be examined in connection with the question of the date of BM 27564. Of interest, then, are two archival tablets of the Šulgi-simtī archive: RC 884: Jones and Snyder, SET no. 41 dated to ix Š 35 (collations Carnahan and Hillard, ASJ 15 [1993] p. 199); and MM 34: Schneider, Drehem- und Djhoḫatexte no. 59 = Molina, Montserrat no. 59 dated to iv Š 36. The first tablet (lines 1–3) records a number of goats at the quay of Kutha for the god Meslamta-e'a, and the second lists various sacrifices for Meslamta-e'a and his spouse Allatum. The combined evidence of the tablets suggests that some notable event took place at Kutha around Š 36. Furthermore, a Šulgi hymn may have been composed to celebrate the construction of the new Nergal temple. The relevant composition, Šulgi U, is known from a single tablet, Ash 1911.236, which according to Langdon (Babylonian Liturgies pp. v–vi) came from Nippur. It was published in copy by Langdon as Babylonian Liturgies no. 195; a transliteration and translation were provided by van Dijk in Sumerische Götterlieder 2 pp. 13–15. Of interest for the present discussion are lines 30–38 (transliteration van Dijk):

ur-sag un-e ḫaš-ḫaš dingir kur-ra nigin
ki-bal-e x-da ba-ni-x-du$_{11}$
^{d}nergal un-e ḫaš-ḫaš dingir kur-ra nigin
[k]i-dab$_{5}$-ba-zu éren téš-bi-šè ḫul m[i-ni-...]
an-ša$_{4}$-an.KI ti-da-nu-um-m[a ...]
^{d}nergal ki-dab$_{5}$-ba-<zu> éren téš-bi-š[è ḫul mi-ni-...]

Oh hero who *smashes* the people, oh god who goes about
the foreign land,
To ... the foreign land it was decreed.
Oh Nergal, who *smashes* the people, oh god who goes about
the foreign land(s),
(In) the place where you stride the (enemy) troops all
together [fall upon] bad times,
Anšan and Tidānum [...]
Nergal, (in) the place where <you> stride, the (enemy)
troops all together [fall upon] bad times.

An interesting parallel to this particular passage in Šulgi U is found in the literary composition in-nin-me-ḫuš-a "Inanna and Mount Ebiḫ," a work for which an original Old Akkadian date of creation has been proposed by some scholars. The relevant section describes the perambulations of the war goddess Inanna (lines 24–27, ms. Edzard):

in-nin$_{9}$-me-en an nígin-na-mu-dè ki nígin-na-mu-dè
^{d}inanna-me-en an nígin-na-mu-dè ki nígin-na-mu-dè
NIM.KI su-bir$_{4}$.KI-a nígin-na-mu-dè
kur-lu$_{5}$-lu$_{5}$-bi-a nígin-na-mu-dè

As I, Innin, go about heaven, go about earth,
As I, Inanna, go about heaven, go about earth,
As I go about Elam and Subartu ...

The fact that the specific lands named in the epic coincide exactly with the regions named in historical sources as targets of the Sargonic king Narām-Sîn indicates that it was this monarch in particular whose deeds were immortalized in the poem. In a similar fashion the mention of Nergal's traversing of the enemy lands of Anšan and Tidanum in Šulgi U is likely to be associated with campaigns of Šulgi against those territories. The defeat of Anšan was commemorated in the name of Š 34 and, as noted, the evidence of the Puzur-Šulgi letters points to armed conflicts with the Tidnumites around Š 37. These data, then, would argue for a date of composition of the hymn Šulgi U sometime around year Š 37; a connection with the year name recording the construction of Nergal's temple is a distinct possibility.

A handful of inscriptions of Šulgi deal with the Emeslam temple in Kutha. Two of these (E3/2.1.2.23–24), which are foundation tablets, clearly date to the first half of the reign, since Šulgi's name appears in them without the prefixed divine determinative. Another text (E3/2.1.2.25), known from a later tablet copy, is unfortunately broken at the point where the king's name appears and thus we are unable to determine whether or not a DINGIR sign preceded Šulgi's name.

(38) mu-ús-sa mu bàd-ma-da ba-dù "The year after the wall of the land was built." Ni 394: Hilprecht, BE 1/2 no. 125 rev. line 17.

(39) mu é-*puzur$_{4}$-iš-^{d}da-gan*-na ba-dù "The year Puzriš-Dagān was built." Ni 394: Hilprecht, BE 1/2 no. 125 rev. line 18. An interesting variant to this year name is found on the tablet WHM 626: Kang, SETDA no. 105 and Pinches, Amherst Tablets p. 52 no. 29: mu *puzur$_{4}$-iš-^{d}da-gan* é-^{d}šul-gi ba-dù "The year Puzriš-Dagān, the house/temple of divine Šulgi was built." On the question of the meaning of the expression "the house of Šulgi," see the comments of Wilcke in CRRA 19 pp. 190–91 n. 51.

The name of Š 39 is to be connected with Šulgi's foundation of the great cattle yards at Puzriš-Dagān = modern Drehem. Puzriš-Dagān was apparently preceded in this role by the settlement called Esagdana Nibru, which, according to C. Wilcke (CRRA 35 [1992] p. 322 tab. 7), lay near, or even at, Puzriš-Dagān. The actual utilization of Puzriš-Dagān as the royal cattleyard apparently commenced in 1 i Š 43.

(40) mu-ús-sa é-*puzur*$_4$*-iš-*^{d} *da-gan*-na ba-dù "The year after Puzriš-Dagān was built." Ni 394: Hilprecht, BE 1/2 no. 125 rev. line 19.

(41) mu-ús-sa é-*puzur*$_4$*-iš-*^{d} *da-gan-na* ba-dù [mu-ús-sa-a-bi] "The year after Puzriš-Dagān was built, [the year after this]." Ni 394: Hilprecht, BE 1/2 no. 125 rev. line 20.

(42) mu ša-aš-ru.KI ⸢ba-ḫul⸣ "The year Šasru was destroyed." Ni 394: Hilprecht, BE 1/2 no. 125 rev. line 21.

(43) mu en-ubur-zi-an-na en-^{d}nanna maš-e ì-pà "The year En-uburzi-ana, *en* of the god Nanna, was chosen by omens." YBC 1051: Keiser, YOS 4 no. 110.

(44) mu si-mu-ru-um.KI ù lu-lu-bi.KI a-rá-10-LAL-1-kam-aš ba-ḫul "The year Simurrum and Lullubu were destroyed for the ninth time." AO 5487: de Genouillac, TCL 2 pl. VIII.

A possible reflection of the campaign against Lullubu may be seen in a tablet from Ur — unfortunately undated — (U. 11669: Legrain, UET 3 no. 1763) that mentions (lines 10–11) "female slaves taken as booty, (namely) [Lullu]beans" (géme nam-ra-aš-ak [lu-lu]-bu.KI-na-ke$_4$-ne). For this text and this particular restoration, see Maeda, ASJ 14 (1992) p. 157.

45) mu ^{d}šul-gi nita-kala-ga lugal-uri$_5$.KI-ma lugal-an-ub-da-límmu-ba-ke$_4$ ur-bí-lum.KI si-mu-ru-um.KI lu-lu-bu.KI ù kára-ḫar.KI-ra AŠ-eš šu du$_{11}$-ga šu-tibir-ra im-mi-ra "The year Šulgi, mighty man, king of Ur, king of the four quarters, having overtaken Urbillum, Simurrum, Lullubu, and Karaḫar as a single group, struck them down." BM 12231: King, CT 5 pl. 18.

The events which provided the name of Š 45 are alluded to in a handful of Ur III economic tablets. In this case a clear distinction must be made between tablets dated to Š 45 and those of AS 2 — both mention the defeat of Urbillum. The two can be distinguished in the "Treasure Archive" at Drehem. Sallaberger, Kalender 1 p. 8 n. 19, has shown that the dates for AS 2 in this archive always include the RN Amar-Suena. If the RN is absent, then the year name (in tablets from this archive) must be assigned as Š 45. A Drehem tablet dated to 17 vii Š 44 (Musées Royaux d'Art et d'Histoire O.70: de Genouillac, Trouvaille no. 86 = Limet, Texts sumériens no. 39 rev. line 6) describes various metal objects that are designated as "booty of Urbillum" (nam-ra-ak ur-bíl-lum.KI-ma). A Drehem tablet dated to xi Š 45 (FLP 1248: Sigrist, Owen and Young, MVN 13 no. 423) records (line 27) a disbursement said to be "part of the booty of Urbillum" (šà-nam-ra-ak ur-bíl-lum.KI). A further record of Urbillum booty is found in a tablet dated to xii Š 45 (AUAM 73.1377+73.0717: Sigrist, AUCT 2 nos. 326+336, see Sallaberger, Kalender 1 p. 16 n. 50). Already by i Š 47 an economic tablet (NBC 2150: Keiser, BIN 3 no. 18) mentions (lines 6–7) revenue of the territory of Urbillum (maš-da-ri-a ma-da ur-bí-lum.KI-ka).

(46) mu ^{d}šul-gi nita-kala-ga lugal-uri$_5$.KI-ma lugal-an-ub-da-límmu-ba-ke$_4$ ki-maš.KI ḫu-ur$_5$-ti.KI ù ma-da-bi u$_4$-AŠ!-a mu-ḫul "The year Šulgi, mighty man, king of Ur, king of the four quarters, destroyed Kimaš, Ḫurti, and their lands in a single day." Haverford Library 80: Barton, Haverford 1 pl. 35 col. xii lines 7–14.

The events commemorated in the name of Š 46 are alluded to in a temporal clause in inscription E3/2.1.2.33 (lines 7–10): *ì-nu ma-at ki-maš*.KI *ù ḫu-ur-tim*.KI *ù-ḫa-li-qú-na* "when he destroyed the land of Kimaš and Hurtum." Further, nine Ur III tablets — they are arranged chronologically as tablets (a)–(i) in this study — refer to Šulgi's campaign against Kimaš and Ḫumurti. The citations given are those collected by P. Michalowski (Correspondence p. 82), T. Maeda (ASJ 14 [1992] p. 157), and M. Cooper (personal communication). The references are as follows. Tablet (a), Legrain, TRU no. 144 dated to 27 iv Š 45, refers to troops (érin) of Kimaš (see Maeda, ASJ 14 [1992] p. 157 where érin should be read for u_4). Tablet (b), NCBT 1624 (information courtesy W.W. Hallo), dates to v Š 45 and contains the remark "when Kimaš was destroyed" (u_4 ki-maš.KI ba-ḫul). Tablet (c), dated to ii Š 46 (YBC 504: Keiser, YOS 4 no. 74), contains the note (lines 2–3) "banquet when Kimaš was destroyed" (kaš-dé-a u_4 ki-maš.KI ba-ḫul). Tablet (d), dated to ii Š 46 (HSM 911.10.231: Michalowski, Correspondence p. 82), contains the expression "offering during the (course of) the campaign, when the weapon was called/chosen" (siskur šà-kaskal-la u_4 GIŠ.tukul ba-pa [instead of the usual pà]-da). Tablet (e), dated to iii Š 46 (Hirose no. 50: Gomi, Hirose no. 50), records (lines 1–2) various cattle of the troops of Kimaš (érin ki-maš.KI). Tablet (f), dated to 14 iv Š 46 (AUAM 73.1571: Sigrist, AUCT 1 no. 683), contains the remark (lines 3–4) "banquet when Ḫurti was destroyed" (kaš-dé-a ḫu-ur_5-ti.KI ba-ḫul). Tablet (g), dated to 14 iv Š 46 (Kelsey 89217: Owen, MVN 15 no. 201), records (line 18) various cattle as being "part of the booty of Ḫurti" (šà nam-ra-ak ḫu-ur_5-ti.KI). Tablet (h), dating to 24 iv Š 46 (ROM 295 925.62.283a: Sigrist, ROM no. 44), registers (lines 4–5) disbursements for "the banquet in the temple of the god Enlil, when Ḫurti was destroyed for the second time" ($gizbun_x$[KI.KAŠ] šà-é-^{d}en-líl mu ḫu-ur_5-ti.KI a-rá-2-kam-aš ba-ḫul). For the expression KI.KAŠ "banquet," see Waetzoldt, NABU 1991 no. 71. Finally, tablet (i), dated to v Š 46 (A 5080 [Chicago], reference courtesy W.W. Hallo), indicates that the governor of Kimaš himself was captured during the campaign (u_4 énsi-ki-maš.KI im-ma-dab_5-ba). We may also note an archival tablet dated to xii Š 47 (Boson, TCS no. 363) that records (line 4) a disbursement of shoes for Bazamu, the governor of Ḫurti.

As pointed out by Hallo (RHA 36 [1978] p. 76), an echo of Šulgi's defeat of Kimaš may possibly be found in the later omen and chronicle tradition. He notes the apodosis of a Middle Assyrian omen (BM 122643: Walker CT 51 pl. 53 no. 152) that refers (rev. line 14′) to a certain Rabsisi (rab-si-si). This person is almost certainly to be connected with the ^{m}*rab-si-si* mentioned in a Seleucid chronicle from Uruk (W 22289: Hunger, SbTU 1 no. 2 line 5) in a passage that deals with Šulgi. Furthermore, Hallo suggests connecting this Rabsisi with the "Rašiši, man of Kimaš" named in a Drehem tablet dating to 4 vii AS 5 (Boson, TCS no. 140 = Archi and Pomponio, Torino no. 67 line 5).

(47) mu ^{d}šul-gi nita-kala-ga lugal-uri_5.KI-ma ⌜lugal⌝-an-ub-da-límmu-ba-ke_4 ki-maš.KI ḫ[u-u]r_5-ti.KI ⌜ù⌝ ma-da-[bi] u_4-⌜AŠ⌝-a mu-ḫul-a mu-ús-sa-a-bi "The year after Šulgi, mighty man, king of Ur, king of the four quarters, destroyed Kimaš, Ḫ[ur]ti, and [their] lands in a single day." Musées Royaux d'Art et d'Histoire O.639: Speleers, Receuil no. 84 = Limet, Texts sumériens no. 86 rev. col. viii lines 6–14.

Šulgi's Campaign against Simaški

A handful of archival texts noted by Maeda (ASJ 14 [1992] p. 157 sub *Shulgi 47 — to these can be added A 2952 cited in Michalowski, Correspondence p. 82 sub Š 48), all dating to Š 47, contain the remark "booty of Simaški" (nam-ra-ak LÚ.SU). In addition, a tablet dated to the same year (FLP 978: Sigrist, MVN 13 no. 672), also noted by Maeda, records (lines 5–6) a disbursement of leather shoes "(for) Šū-Enlil, the prince, when he smote(?) Simaški" (*šu-^{d}en-líl* dumu-lugal u_4 LÚ.SU.KI.A mu-TAG.TAG-a). These archival texts are an invaluable source; they provide evidence for an episode of Ur III history that, due to the fact that it does not figure in a year name, would otherwise be unknown.

(48) mu ḫa-ar-ši.KI ki-maš.KI ḫu-ur-ti.KI ù ma-da-bi u_4-AŠ-a ba-ḫul "The year Ḫarši, Kimaš, Ḫurti, and their territories were destroyed in a single day." AO 5485: de Genouillac, TCL 2 pl. VIII.

A small group of archival texts alludes to Šulgi's campaign against Ḫarši. We may first note the booty (nam-ra-ak) lists: (a) AO 5485: de Genouillac, TCL 2 pl. VIII line 1, dated to vii Š 48; (b) PTS 473: Sigrist, PTS no. 60, dated to vii Š 48; (c) YBC 1531 (see D. Owen, JCS 33 [1981] p. 252), dated to vii Š 48 (information courtesy P. Michalowski); and (d) AUAM 73.0568: Sigrist AUCT 2 no. 364 rev. 8 (undated). Also to be noted is a Drehem tablet (PD 538: Salonen, Puzriš-Dagan-Texte no. 538), dated to viii Š 48, that records (lines 1–2) the receipt of "forty able-bodied young men from Ḫarši" (40 guruš-sig_7-a lú-ḫa-ar-ši.KI); they were, in all likelihood, prisoners of war from that city. Another tablet (Private collection: Goetze, JCS 11 [1957] p. 77), dated to the viii Š 48, refers (lines 1–3) to cattle that are described as being "part of the revenue brought from the campaign" (šà máš-da-ri-a kaskal-ta ir-ra). They are further described as being "deliveries of the soldiers (belonging) to Huba'ā" (aga-ús lú-ḫu-ba-a mu-DU). Ḫuba'ā is well known as a general of Šulgi (see Michalowski, in Gibson and Biggs, Bureaucracy p. 58).

II. The death of Šulgi.

The abundance of archival material from the end of Šulgi's reign enables us to determine with some precision the date of the death of the king. This specific question has been addressed in a study by P. Michalowski entitled "The Death of Šulgi," Orientalia NS 46 (1977) pp. 220–25. Michalowki summarized the then available data and published a tablet (HSM 911.10.131), dated to 2 xi Š 48, that recorded a delivery of animals for the libation place (ki-a-nag) of Šulgi; the text proves that by this date Šulgi had died. Michalowski also suggested that Šulgi's queen Šulgi-simtī (and Geme-Ninlila) may have been buried with Šulgi. Offerings to the throne of the deified king are found commencing with 3 xi Š 48 (Cfc 56: Calvot and Pettinato, MVN 8 no. 113).

Of particular interest is a tablet in the Birmingham City Museum (A.1135-1982: Watson, Birmingham 1 no. 132), dated to xi Š 48 (no day date indicated), that contains the remark (line 5): "when divine Šulgi ascended to heaven" (u_4 ^{d}šul-gi an-na ba-a-e_{11}-da-a). The importance of this intriguing text has been noted by a number of scholars, among them M. Yoshikawa (ASJ 9 [1987] p. 321), H. Waetzoldt (OLZ 83 [1988] col. 30 note to text 132), C. Wilcke (Münchner Beitrage zur Völkerkunde 1 [1988] pp. 244-45), W.W. Hallo, Studies Tadmor pp. 158–59, Horowitz and Watson, ASJ 13 [1991] pp. 410–17, and P. Steinkeller (NABU 1992 p. 3 no. 4). Steinkeller writes: "As argued by Wilcke, this datum proves the existence of a popular belief (or more likely official theological position) that, at the termination of his earthly existence, Šulgi joined the ranks of the denizens of heaven." Various scholars (they are cited in the previous notes) have found a parallel to this "ascension of Šulgi" in an early Isin period tablet from Isin. The tablet in question (Van De Mieroop, BIN 10 no. 190) contains the remark (lines 10–12) "(for) the great [la]mentation, when the king (Išbi-Erra) ascended to heaven" ([é]r-gu-la u_4 lugal an-šè ba-a-da<ba-a-e_{11}-da>). Šulgi may have been honoured by being assigned a home in the celestial heavens. A "star of Šulgi" is attested in the star section of the Old Babylonian Forerunner to Ur_5-ra = *ḫubullum* (see Reiner and Civil, MSL 11 p. 133 col. viii line 41: mul ^{d}šulgi).

The combined evidence of the Harvard and Birmingham tablets cited here indicates that Šulgi died on either the first or second day of xi Š 48.

Building Inscriptions
1–34

The building inscriptions of Šulgi are edited here according to their provenance — the sites are listed in a south-to-north order. For each site, inscriptions in which Šulgi's name is written without the prefixed divine determinative precede those in which the king's name appears with the DINGIR sign.

1

An eight-line Sumerian inscription deals with Šulgi's building of the temple of the god Enki.

COMMENTARY

The tablet with this inscription, BM 17827, is a purchased piece; its provenance is unknown. Lines 1–6 are on the obverse, lines 7–8 on the reverse. The inscription was collated.

BIBLIOGRAPHY

1897 Winckler, AoF 1/6 p. 547 no. 8 (copy)
1889 King CT 3 pl. 1 BM 17287 (copy)
1907 Thureau-Dangin, SAK pp. 192–93 Dun-gi m (edition)
1929 Barton, RISA pp. 278–79 Shulgi 13 (edition)
1962 Hallo, HUCA 33 p. 30 Šulgi 10 (study)
1986 Kärki, KDDU p. 33 Šulgi 10 (edition)
1991 Steible, NSBW 2 p. 163 Šulgi 10 (edition)

TEXT

1) $^{\ulcorner d \urcorner}$en-ki
2) lugal-a-ni
3) šul-gi
4) nita-kala-ga
5) lugal-uri$_5$.KI-ma
6) lugal-ki-en-gi-ki-uri-ke$_4$
7) é-a-ni
8) mu-na-dù

1–2) For the god Enki, his lord,

3–6) Šulgi, mighty man, king of Ur, king of the lands of Sumer and Akkad,

7–8) built for him his temple.

2

An eight-line Sumerian inscription found at Ur deals with Šulgi's construction of NinSAR's temple.

COMMENTARY

The inscription is incised on a steatite tablet that measures 9.5×6.2 cm. The piece was found in room 19 of the E-nunmaḫ and given the excavation number U 222. It bears the museum number IM 2. Lines 1–7 are found on the obverse, line 8 on the reverse.

As far as can be determined, there is no evidence from Ur III or Old Babylonian archival texts for a cult of NinSAR at Ur. She is, on the other hand, well attested in Early Dynastic and Ur III texts from Nippur (see Sallaberger, Kalender 1 p. 104). The goddess and her temple appear in three informative passages: (a) the Canonical Temple List (see George, House Most High p. 13) line 115 which gives the name of her temple at Nippur: é-šu-luḫ-ḫa-túm-ma; (b) the metrological tablet in Jena (Bernhardt and Kramer, Orientalia NS 44 [1975] p. 98 line 40) that again mentions her temple in Nippur; and (c) the god list An:*Anum* (1: 328; ms. Litke, where she appears as the wife of Nergal). In all these references NinSAR appears two entries after a mention of the god Ennugi. It is not unlikely, then, that her temple at Nippur was situated in the general vicinity of the Ennugi temple. Now, Šulgi is known to have built the temple of Ennugi at Nippur (see E3/2.1.2.19) and we would not be surprised if the neighbouring NinSAR temple were also rebuilt. However, the findspot of the Ur inscription would seem to indicate that there was an (otherwise unattested) cult of NinSAR at Ur.

Although line 2 was copied: gír-lá é-kúr-ra-ra by Gadd, the expected reading é-kur-ra is compatible with the photo published as pl. J in Gadd, UET 1.

BIBLIOGRAPHY

1928 Gadd, UET 1 no. 58 and pl. J (photo, copy, edition)
1929 Barton, RISA pp. 366–67 Shulgi 10 (edition)
1962 Hallo, HUCA 33 p. 30 Šulgi 16 (study)
1986 Kärki, KDDU p. 36 Šulgi 16 (edition)
1991 Steible, NSBW 2 p. 169 Šulgi 16 (edition)

TEXT

1) ^{d}nin-SAR
2) gír-lá-é-kur-ra-ra
3) šul-gi
4) nita-kala-ga
5) lugal-uri$_5$.KI-ma
6) lugal-ki-en-gi-ki-uri-ke$_4$
7) é-a-ni
8) mu-na-dù

1–2) For the goddess NinSAR, butcher of the Ekur,

3–6) Šulgi, mighty man, king of Ur, king of the lands of Sumer and Akkad,

7–8) built her temple for her.

3

An inscription found on bricks at Ur records Šulgi's construction of E-ḫursag, the royal palace at Ur. The text is arranged in one column of seven lines. As noted, the name of Š 10 also commemorates this deed.

CATALOGUE

Ex.	Museum number	Excavation number	Registration number	Provenance	Dimensions (cm)	Lines preserv	cpn
1	BM 90277	—	1979-12-20, 170	Ur	27.5×25.5	1–7	c
2	BM 90278	—	1979-12-20, 171	Ur	35×34×8	1–7	c
3	BM 90804	—	1979-12-20, 360	Ur	31×25×7	1–7	c
4	BM 114252	—	1919-10-11, 4683	Ur, from the SE portion of the E-ḫursag palace	26×21×9	1–5	c
5	BM 114255	—	1919-10-11, 4686	As ex. 4	32.5×28.5×9	1–7	c
6	BM 114256	—	1919-19-11, 4687	As ex. 4	35×35×8	1–7	c
7	BM 114257	—	1919-10-11, 4688	As ex. 4	10×8×6	3–7	c
8	BM 114258	—	1919-10-11, 4689	As ex. 4	35.5×35×8	1–7	c
9	BM 114301	—	1919-10-11, 4690	As ex. 4	35.5×35×8.5	1–7	c
10	BM 114302	—	1919-10-11, 4691	As ex. 4	29×23.5×7.5	1–7	c
11	BM 114303	—	1919-10-11, 4692	As ex. 4	22.5×20×8	1–7	c
12	BM 114304	—	1919-10-11, 4693	As ex. 4	19×18.5×8	1–7	c
13	BM 114305	—	1919-10-11, 4694	As ex. 4	36×35.5×8.5	1–7	c
14	BM 114306	—	1919-10-11, 4695	As ex. 4	36×36×9	1–7	c
15	CBS 16464	—	—	Ur —	—	—	n
16	CBS 16535a	U 2880a	—	Loose, from Diqdiqqah	—	—	n
17	CBS 16535b	U 2880b	—	Loose, from Diqdiqqah	—	—	n
18	CBS 16536a	U 2880c	—	Loose, from Diqdiqqah	—	—	n
19	IM 66433	—	—	Foundation box near the NW corner of the E-ḫursag palace	—	—	n

COMMENTARY

Exs. 1–14 were collated by C.B.F. Walker. Three foundation boxes were uncovered during excavations of the palace. One, near the south corner, contained a bronze canephore (U 1000) and steatite tablet (U 1001; dimensions 8×5 cm); both were uninscribed. A second foundation box near the east corner also also contained a bronze canephore and a steatite tablet; again, both were uninscribed. A third foundation box found near the NW corner contained a bronze canephore (IM 66434; dimensions 24 cm high, 8.5 cm diameter) and a steatite tablet (IM 6643x); both pieces were uninscribed.

A brick stamp fragment from Nippur (see McCown, Nippur 1 pl. 148 and facing page no. 8) mentions a building named: [...]-ḫur-sag; it has been taken to refer to the E-ḫursag. If this were a reference to the palace at Ur, then the Nippur brick stamp would be a stray piece. In view of its provenance, the inscription should probably be restored [é-IM]-ḫur-sag and connected with the ziqqurrat of that name attested as a Nippur landmark (see George, House Most High p. 105 no. 529).

BIBLIOGRAPHY

1861 1 R 2 II 2 (exs. 1–2, conflated copy)
1872 Smith, TSBA 1 pl. 36 (exs. 1–2, translation)
1874 Lenormant, Études accadiennes 2 p. 313 (translation)
1875 Ménant, Babylone p. 76 (exs. 1–6, translation)
1892 Winckler, KB 3/1 pp. 80–81 Dungi 2 (exs. 1–2, edition)
1899 Bezold, Cat. 5 p. 2233 (exs. 1–2, study)
1906 King, CT 21 pl. 11 BM 90277, 90278 (exs. 1–2, copy)
1907 Thureau-Dangin, SAK pp. 190–91 Dun-gi b (exs. 1–2, edition)
1922 BM Guide p. 60 no. 59 (exs. 1–2, study)
1923 Woolley AJ 3 p. 318 and pl. 32 fig. 2 (provenance, photo)
1925 Woolley and Legrain, MJ 16 p. 301 (photo)
1928 Gadd, UET 1 p. xxxiv (study)
1929 Barton, RISA pp. 276–77 Shulgi 2 (exs. 1–2, edition)
1962 Hallo, HUCA 33 p. 29 Šulgi 5 (exs. 1–2, study)
1962 al-Ṣīwānī Sumer 18 p. 188 [Arabic section] (ex. 19, copy, edition)
1968 Ellis, Foundation Deposits pp. 63–64 (study)
1981 Walker, CBI no. 22 (exs. 1–14, transliteration, study)
1985 Behrens, JCS 37 p. 232 no. 14 (exs. 15–18, study);
1986 Kärki, KDDU pp. 30–31 Šulgi 5 (exs. 1–14, 19, edition); p. 158 Anonym 21 (ex. 20, edition)
1991 Steible, NSBW 2 pp. 158–60 Šulgi 5 (exs. 1–19, edition)

TEXT

1) šul-gi
2) nita-kala-ga
3) lugal-uri$_5$.KI-ma
4) lugal-ki-en-gi-ki-uri-ke
5) é-ḫur-sag
6) é-ki-ág-gá-ni
7) mu-dù

1–4) Šulgi, mighty man, king of Ur, king of the lands of Sumer and Akkad,

5–7) built his beloved E-ḫursag ("Mountain House").

6 10 é-ki-ág-a-ni.

4

An eight-line Sumerian inscription records Šulgi's building of the temple of the goddess Nimintaba at Ur.

CATALOGUE

Ex.	Museum number	Excavation number	Registration number	Ur provenance	Object	Dimensions (cm)	Lines preserved	cpn
1a	IM 1376	U 6158	—	In situ in a foundation box below the wall of the temple	Copper canephor	23.5 high	—	n
1b	BM 118560	U 6157	—	As ex. 1	Steatite foundation tablet	—	1–8	p
2a	IM 1376	U 6301	—	As ex. 1	Copper canephor	24.5 high	—	n
2b	CBS 16217	U 6300	—	As ex. 1	Steatite foundation tablet	—	1–8	p
3a	IM 1376	U 6303	—	As ex. 1	Copper canephor	24.5 high	—	n
3b	IM 1157	U 6302	—	As ex. 1	Steatite foundation tablet	6.8×10.8	1–8	p
4a	CBS 16216	U 6305	—	As ex. 1	Copper canephor	—	1–8	c
4b	IM 1158	U 6304	—	As ex. 1	Steatite foundation tablet	5.9×10.6×2.1	1–8	c

COMMENTARY

In the northwest sector of the EH site at Ur, Woolley excavated the partially preserved remains of an Ur III period temple. Five foundation boxes were uncovered from the thick northeast wall of the structure, each of which yielded a matched set of copper canephor and steatite foundation tablet. Four of the five sets bore inscriptions; one set: U 6968a = CBS 16219 and U 6968b were uninscribed. Ex. 4b was collated by H. Steible.

For the cult of Nimintaba at Ur, cf. the comments of the author (Frayne, BiOr 45 no. 3/4 p. 352), who writes:

> Entry 80 (of the Abū Ṣalābīkh god list = Alberti, SEL 2 [1985] p. 8 item 80): ^{d}nin-TAB.TAB should probably be read ^{d}nin-min$_{6}$-tab and seen as the equivalent of the later ^{d}nimin-tab-ba (see W.G. Lambert, Or NS 54 [1985] p. 200 quoting An = *Anum* 1 270: ^{d}nin.min.tab.ba). We know that an Ur III period temple to this goddess was built by Sulgi (UET 1, no. 59). Charpin has demonstrated (p. 146 in Le clergé d'Ur) that a temple to this goddess probably stood in Old Babylonian times, although no remains of the Old Babylonian period have actually survived. Beneath the Ur III period level were found plano-convex bricks and a mace-head of Early Dynastic date of a daughter of AN.BU, the latter possibly the king of Mari (see M. Geller in Eblaitica Essays on the Ebla Archives and Eblaite Language, p. 145). These facts led Woolley to posit a pre-Ur III temple of Nimintaba on the same site.

Charpin (Le clergé d'Ur p. 147) notes that the beginning of a hymn to this goddess is known from an Old Babylonian tablet copy (U 7765). Unfortunately, too little of the text is preserved to determine if it might deal with Šulgi and Nimintaba.

BIBLIOGRAPHY

1926 Woolley, AJ 6 pp. 392–93 and pl. LVIII (exs. 1–4, provenance)
1926 Woolley, ILN March 20 p. 513 and fig. 7 (exs. 1a and 4a, photo)
1928 Gadd, UET 1 no. 59 and pl. J (ex. 2b, photo, copy, edition)
1929 Barton, RISA pp. 366–67 Shulgi 11 (partial edition)
1931 Van Buren, Found. p. 25 and figs. 17, 19 (exs. 1a and 4a, photos, study)
1937 Iraq Museum Guide1 p. 82 and fig. 67 (ex. 3b, photo, copy, translation) and p. 83 fig. 68 (exs. 1a, 2a, photo)
1942 Iraq Museum Guide 2 p. 108 fig. 88 (ex. 3b, photo, copy, translation) and p. 109 fig. 89 (exs. 1a and 2a, photo)
1962 Hallo, HUCA 33 p. 30 Šulgi 18 (exs. 1–4, study)
1968 Ellis, Foundation Deposits p. 63 (exs. 1–4, provenance, study)
1974 Woolley, UE 6 pp. 40–41, 98 and pls. 47c and 48a (exs. 1–4, provenance, exs. 1a-b, 4a, photos)
1983 Rashid, Gründungsfiguren p. 32 and pls. 31–32 nos. 143, 146–147 (exs. 1a, 2a, 3a, 4a, study; exs. 1a, 2a or 3a, 4a, drawing)
1984 New York Times, April 18 p. A14 (ex. 2b, photo)
1986 Charpin, Le clergé d'Ur pp. 144 and 146 (exs. 1–4, edition)
1986 Kärki, KDDU p. 37 Šulgi 18 (exs. 1–4, edition)
1991 Steible, NSBW 2 pp. 170–71 Šulgi 18 (exs. 1–4, edition)

TEXT

1) [d]nimin-tab-ba
2) nin-a-ni
3) šul-gi
4) nita-kala-ga
5) lugal-uri$_5$.KI-ma
6) lugal-ki-en-gi-ki-uri-ke$_4$
7) é-a-ni
8) mu-na-dù

1–2) For the goddess Nimintaba, his lady,

3–6) Šulgi, mighty man, king of Ur, king of the lands of Sumer and Akkad,

7–8) built her temple for her.

5

An eight-line foundation tablet deals with Šulgi's construction of the goddess Ninurima's temple in Karzida (Ga'eš).

COMMENTARY

The inscription is found on a soapstone tablet that measures 8.6×5×1.88 cm. The provenance of this purchased piece is unknown; it probably came from Ur or its vicinity. The piece now bears the museum number CBS 842. The text is arranged in two columns: col. i has lines 1–6 and col. ii lines 7–8. The inscription was collated.

According to the god list An:*Anum* III line 38 (ms. Litke), Ninurima was the spouse of the god Alammuš, the latter the vizier of the god Sîn. For the deities Ninurima and Alamuš in Ur, see Sallaberger, Kalender 2 p. 106 Table 62a and Kalender 1 p. 184 n. 868.

BIBLIOGRAPHY

1893 Hilprecht BE 1/1 no. 16 (copy)
1907 Thureau-Dangin, SAK pp. 192–93 Dun-gi k (edition)
1929 Barton, RISA pp. 278–79 Shulgi 11 (edition)
1962 Hallo, HUCA 33 p. 30 Šulgi 17 (study)
1986 Kärki, KDDU pp. 36–37 Šulgi 17 (edition)
1991 Steible, NSBW 2 pp. 169–70 Šulgi 17 (edition)

TEXT

1) [d]nin-ur[i$_5$].KI-ma
2) nin-a-ni
3) šul-gi
4) nita-kala-ga
5) lugal-uri$_5$.KI-ma
6) lugal-ki-en-gi-ki-uri-ke$_4$
7) é-kar-zi-da-ka-ni
8) mu-na-dù

1–2) For the goddess Ninur[i]ma, his lady,

3–6) Šulgi, mighty man, king of Ur, king of the lands of Sumer and Akkad,

7–8) built her Karzida temple for her.

6

An eleven-line inscription found on foundation tablets and bronze canephors deals with Šulgi's building of the temenos wall of Eanna.

CATALOGUE

Ex.	Museum number	Excavation number	Uruk provenance	Object	Dimensions (cm)	Lines preserved	cpn
1	BM 90897 (=BM 12025)	—	—	Steatite tablet	—	1–11	c
2	Museo Barracco, Rome, no. 44	—	—	Bronze canephor	—	1–11	c
3a	IM 45614	W 17303	Oa XIV 3, foundation box on west side of doorway	Bronze canephor	Length: 24.5 Max. width: 6.8	1–11	p (partial)
3b	IM 45615	W 17304	As ex. 3a	Steatite tablet	—	1–11	p
4a	VA 15192	W 17945a	Oa XIV 3, foundation box on east side of doorway	Bronze canephor	Length: 24.6 Max. width: 7.3	1–11	c
4b	VA 15192	W 17945b	As ex. 4a	Diorite tablet	7.4×5.4×1.5	1–11	c

COMMENTARY

The inscription of ex. 2 was kindly collated by B. Cifola.

BIBLIOGRAPHY

1861 1 R II 3 (ex. 1, copy)
1872 Smith, TSBA 1 p. 36 (ex. 1, translation)
1874 Lenormant, Études accadiennes 2 p. 314 (ex. 1, translation)
1875 Ménant, Babylone p. 76 (ex. 1, translation)
1892 Winckler, KB 3/1 pp. 80–81 Dungi 3 (ex. 1, edition)
1905 King, CT 21 pls. 10–11 (ex. 1, copy)
1907 Thureau-Dangin, SAK pp. 192–93 Dun-gi n (ex. 1, edition)
1910 King, Early History, pl. 29 opposite p. 288 [top left] (ex. 1, photo [obv. only])
1929 Barton, RISA pp. 278–81 Shulgi 14 (ex. 1, edition)
1931 Van Buren, Found. p. 24 and fig. 20 (ex. 2, photo, study)
1939 Nöldeke, et al., UVB 10 p. 18 and pl. 22 (exs. 3a–b, photos)
1940 Nöldeke and Lenzen, UVB 11 p. 18 (exs. 4a–b, provenance)
1961 Federici, Bollettino dei Musei Comunali di Roma 8 pp. 1–9 (ex. 2, study)
1962 Hallo, HUCA 33 p. 30 Šulgi 11 (exs. 1, 3, study)
1983 Rashid, Gründungsfiguren p. 30 nos. 140–41 (exs. 3a, 4a, study, ex. 3a, drawing)
1986 Kärki, KDDU pp. 33–34 Šulgi 11 (exs. 1–3b, edition)
1987 Marzahn, AoF 14/1 pp. 34–35 no. 15 (exs. 3–4, copy, transliteration, study)
1991 Steible, NSBW 2 pp. 163–64 Šulgi 11 (exs. 1, 3–4, edition)

TEXT

1) ^{d}inanna 2) nin-é-an-na 3) nin-a-ni	1–3) For the goddess Inanna, lady of Eanna, his lady,
4) šul-gi 5) nita-kala-ga 6) lugal-uri$_5$.KI-ma 7) lugal-ki-en-gi-ki-uri-ke$_4$	4–7) Šulgi, mighty man, king of Ur, king of the lands of Sumer and Akkad,
8) é-an-na 9) ki-bé mu-na-gi$_4$	8–9) restored Eanna ("House of Heaven") for her
10) bàd-gal-bi 11) mu-na-dù	10–11) (and) built for her its great wall.

7

A steatite foundation tablet deals with Šulgi's construction of the temple of the goddess Ninsi'ana.

COMMENTARY

The provenance of this steatite tablet, which measures 7×4.7×1.4 cm, is unknown. It was given the museum number MNB 1970. The inscription was collated from the published photo. Lines 1–5 are on the obverse, lines 6–8 on the reverse.

For the divine name of line 1, see the comments of Sollberger, Correspondence p. 166, and Steinkeller, Sale Documents p. 244 notes to line 18. We may also note that Beaulieu (Orientalia NS 64 [1995] pp. 201–202) cites line 8 from MLC 1890: ^{d}nin-si$_4$-an-na *an-tu$_4$ be-el-⸢tu$_4$⸣ mu-nam-<me>-rat* AN-*e* "Ninsiana: Antu: the mistress who illuminates heaven." The DN Ninsi'ana likely means "(divine) lady of the twilight (literally: of 'the redness of heaven')," an apparent epithet of the planet Venus.

For an inscription of Amar-Suena dealing with the goddess Inanna/Ninsi'ana at Uruk, see E3/2.1.3.14. In view of the parallels between the Šulgi and Amar-Suena texts, we have edited the Šulgi inscription with those dealing with Uruk.

BIBLIOGRAPHY

1991 Steible, NSBW 2 p. 210 and pls. XV–XVI Šulgi 67 (photo, edition)

TEXT

1) ^{d}nin-^{d}si$_4$-an-na	1–2) For the goddess Ninsi'ana, his lady
2) nin-a-ni	
3) ^{d}šul-gi	3–6) Šulgi, mighty man, king of Ur, king of the lands of Sumer and Akkad,
4) nita-kala-ga	
5) lugal-uri$_5$.KI-ma	
6) lugal-ki-en-gi-ki-uri-ke$_4$	
7) é-a-ni	7–8) built her temple for her.
8) mu-na-dù	

8

A fragment of a foundation tablet bears the first six lines of a probable building inscription of Šulgi for the goddess Ninšubur.

COMMENTARY

The steatite tablet fragment (top of tablet) measures 6×6.55×1.7 cm. The piece was purchased; its original provenance, in view of the inscription, is likely to have been Uruk. The piece was given the museum number BM 26256 and registration number 98-5-14, 74. The extant text is arranged in one column. The inscription was collated. As noted, a correlation of this royal inscription with the name of Š 3 is likely.

BIBLIOGRAPHY

1922 BM Guide p. 85 no. 65 (study)
1981 Steible, NSBW 2 p. 216 Šulgi 74 (edition)

TEXT

1) ᵈnin-šubur-	1–3) For the goddess Ninšubur of Uruk, his lady,
2) unu.KI-ga	
3) nin-a-ni	
4) šul-gi	4–6) Šulgi, mighty man, [king of U]r
5) nita-kala-ga	Lacuna
6) [lugal-u]ri$_5$.[KI-ma]	
Lacuna	

9

An eleven-line Sumerian inscription incised on foundation tablets and a tauriform figurine records Šulgi's construction of Nanše's E-šeššeše-gara temple in Girsu.

CATALOGUE

Ex.	Museum number	Girsu provenance	Object	Dimensions (cm)	Lines preserved	cpn
1	MNB 1371	From a foundation box on Tell M	Bronze tauriform figurine	25.6 high 10 wide	1–7	c
2	MNB 1363	As ex. 1	Stone foundation tablet	6.1×9.3×1.3	1–11	c
3	Was in Mercer's private collection; present whereabouts unknown (not in Royal Ontario Museum)	—	Stone foundation tablet	—	1–11	n
4	Kelsey Museum, Ann Arbor, Michigan	—	Stone foundation tablet	—	—	n
5	John Frederick Lewis Collection, Free Library of Philadelphia	—	Stone foundation tablet	—	—	n

BIBLIOGRAPHY

1884–1912 de Sarzec, Découvertes 1 p. 247 (exs. 1–2, provenance); Découvertes 2 pl. 28 no. 6 (ex. 1, photo); pl. 29 no. 4 (ex. 2, photo); p. XXXIII (exs. 1–2, edition)
1888 Hommel, Geschichte p. 335 (ex. 1, drawing)
1889 Amiaud RP NS 2 p. 109 XI Inscriptions of Dungi, King of Ur no. 2 (ex. 2, translation)
1892 Winckler and Böhden, ABK no. 33 (ex. 2, copy)
1902 Heuzey, Catalogue Louvre pp. 310–13 no. 162 (ex. 1, study, drawing)
1907 Thureau-Dangin, SAK pp. 190–91 Dun-gi h (ex. 2, edition)
1910 King, Early History p. 256 fig. 62 (ex. 1, drawing)
1910 Toscanne, RA 7 p. 59 n. 1 (ex. 2, transcription in Neo-Assyrian characters)
1912 Frank, Kunstgeschichte 1 p. 48 no. 3 (ex. 1, photo)
1912 Handcock, Mesopotamian Archaeology p. 250 fig. 40 c (ex. 1, drawing)
1912 Jastrow, Bildermappe pl. 25 no. 78 (ex. 1, photo)
1914 Meissner, Alte Orient 15 p. 54 fig. 95 (ex. 1, photo)
1915 Jastrow, Civilization pl. LXIII opposite p. 410 (ex. 1, photo)
1925 Schäfer and Andrae, Kunst 2 pl. p. 471 [middle photo] (ex. 1, photo)
1926 Mercer, JSOR 10 p. 284 and pl. facing p. 286 no. 7 (ex. 3, copy, edition)
1927 Contenau, Antiquités Orientales p. 17 and pl. 27b (ex. 1, photo)
1929 Barton, RISA pp. 278–79 Shulgi 9 (ex. 5, edition); pp. 366–67 Shulgi 9 (ex. 4, edition)
1931 Van Buren, Found. pp. 25–26 (ex. 1, study)
1935–36 Rutten, Encyclopédie fig. 245 (ex. 1, photo)
1948 Parrot, Tello p. 204 fig. 44c (ex. 1, drawing)
1962 Hallo, HUCA 33 p. 30 Šulgi 13 i–iv (exs. 1–4, study)
1968 Ellis, Foundation Deposits p. 64 (ex. 1, study)
1983 Rashid, Gründungsfiguren p. 28 and pl. 27 no. 132 (ex. 1, study, drawing)
1986 Kärki, KDDU pp. 34–35 Šulgi 13 (exs. 1–3, edition)
1991 Steible, NSBW 2 pp. 165–66 Šulgi 13 (exs. 1–4, edition)

TEXT

1) ^{d}nanše
2) nin-uru$_{16}$
3) nin-in-dub-ba
4) nin-a-ni
5) šul-gi
6) nita-kala-ga
7) lugal-uri$_5$.KI-ma
8) lugal-ki-en-gi-ki-uri-ke$_4$
9) é-šeš-šeš-e-gá-ra
10) é-ki-ág-gá-ni
11) mu-na-dù

1–4) For the goddess Nanše, the mighty lady, the lady of the border, his lady,

5–8) Šulgi, mighty man, king of the lands of Sumer and Akkad,

9–11) built for her the E-šeššeše-gara ("House Established by the Brothers"), her beloved temple.

10

A variant of the preceding inscription is found in an eight-line cone version.

CATALOGUE

Ex	Museum number	Excavation number	Dimensions (cm)	Lines preserved	cpn
1	VA 3119	—	12.4 long, 6 dia.	1–8	c
2	VA 15449	W 5766	8.7 long, 4 dia.	1–8	c
3	AO 557	—	14.8 long, 6.2 dia.	1–8	c
4	AO 842	—	14 long, 6.3 dia.	1–8	c
5	AO 843	—	15 long, 6 dia.	1–8	c
6	AO 11924	TG 1027	11.5 long, 6.8 dia.	1–8	c
7	AO 11925	TG 70	10.2 long, 6.7 dia.	1–8	c
8	AO 11926	—	10.8 long, 5.4 dia.	1–8	c
9	AO 21049	—	13.2 long, 5.3 dia.	1–8	c
10	AO 21050	—	11 long, 6.2 dia.	1–8	c
11	AO 21051a	—	8.7 long, 5.4 dia.	1–8	c
12	AO 21051b	—	8 long, 5.5 dia.	1–8	c
13	AO 21051c	—	8.1 long, 5.8 dia.	1–8	c
14	EŞ 420	—	—	—	n
15	EŞ 5557	—	—	—	n
16	EŞ 5558	—	—	—	n
17	EŞ 5559	—	—	—	n
18	EŞ 5560	—	—	—	n
19	EŞ 5561	—	—	—	n
20	EŞ 5562	—	—	—	n
21	EŞ 13531	—	—	—	n
22	EŞ 13532	—	—	—	n
23	New York Public Library, Eames Collection FF-1	—	14 long, 6.6 dia.	1–8	c
24	FLP 2640	—	—	—	n
25	YBC 16435	—	10.9 long, 6.4 dia.	1–8	c
26	IM 20866	—	—	—	n
27	IM 22846	—	—	—	n
28	IM 22851	—	—	—	n
29	IM 23088–1	—	—	—	n
30	IM 23088–2	—	—	—	n
31	IM 23088–3	—	—	—	n
32	IM 23088–4	—	—	—	n
33	IM 23088–5	—	—	—	n
34	IM 23088–6	—	—	—	n
35	IM 23088–7	—	—	—	n
36	IM 23088–8	—	—	—	n
37	IM 23088–9	—	—	—	n
38	IM 23088–10	—	—	—	n
39	IM 23088–11	—	—	—	n
40	IM 23088–12	—	—	—	n

E3/2.1.2.9.10.4: line omitted according to transliteration of Barton (RISA pp. 366–67, Shulgi 9).

Ex	Museum number	Excavation number	Dimensions (cm)	Lines preserved	cpn
41	IM 23576–A	—	—	—	n
42	IM 23576–B	—	—	—	n
43	IM 23576–C	—	—	—	n
44	IM 49858–1	—	—	—	n
45	IM 49858–2	—	—	—	n
46	IM 49858–3	—	—	—	n

COMMENTARY

Ex. 2 was found at Uruk, in the northeast zone of the city. The other exemplars, as far as can be determined, came from Girsu. Exemplars noted by Steible that could not be identified with Louvre cones are TG 624+1258, 2322, 4155, and 4158. The supposed variants listed by Edzard in Sumer 13 (1957) p. 179 for IM 20866 are lines that are actually found in the tablet, not cone, version.

BIBLIOGRAPHY

1884–1912 de Sarzec, Découvertes 2 pl. 38 [middle right] (photo)

1907 Messerschmidt, VAS 1 no. 24 (ex. 1, copy)

1936 de Genouillac, FT 2 p. 129 and pl. XLVI (ex. 6, copy)

1940 Schwartz, BNYPL 44 p. 808 no. 18 (ex. 23, study)

1947 Kraus, in Halil Edhem Memorial Volume p. 112 (exs. 14–22, study)

1951 Smick, Cuneiform Documents p. 54 and pl. XCIII no. 73 (ex. 24, copy, study)

1957 Edzard, Sumer 13 pp. 176, 179 (exs. 26–46, study)

1960 Aynard, RA 54 pp. 16–17 (exs. 3–13, study)

1962 Hallo, HUCA 33 p. 31 Šulgi 22 (exs. 1, 3–23, 26–46, study)

1986 Kärki, KDDU p. 39 Šulgi 22 (exs. 1, 3–23, edition)

1991 Steible, NSBW 2 pp. 174–75 Šulgi 22 (exs. 1–24, 26–46, edition)

TEXT

1) ^{d}nanše
2) nin-in-dub-ba
3) nin-a-ni
4) šul-gi
5) nita-kala-ga
6) lugal-uri$_5$.KI-ma-ke$_4$
7) é-šeš-šeš-gar-ra-ka-ni
8) mu-na-dù

1–3) For the goddess Nanše, lady of the border, his lady,

4–6) Šulgi, mighty man, king of Ur,

7–8) built for her the E-šeššeše-gara ("House Established by the Brothers").

11

Two inscriptions commemorate Šulgi's building of the temple of the god Ningirsu at Girsu. The first is found on copper canephors and a stone foundation tablet.

CATALOGUE

Ex.	Museum number	Object	Dimensions (cm)	Lines preserved	cpn
1	EŞ 489	Copper canephor	23.3×7.8	1–11	n
2	EŞ 490	Copper canephor	25.8×7.5	1–11	n
3	EŞ —	Copper canephor	23.3×7.8	—	n
4a	AO 27907 (=AO 426)	Copper canephor	24 ×7.5	1–11	c
4b	AO 27910	Stone foundation tablet	—	1–11	c

COMMENTARY

This inscription is found on both canephors and a foundation tablet. Exs. 1 and 2 were kindly collated by V. Donbaz. According to Donbaz, EŞ 1524, which is listed by Rashid as an example of this inscription, bears a Gudea inscription.

BIBLIOGRAPHY

1888–1912 de Sarzec, Découvertes 1 pp. 72 and 246–47 (provenance); Découvertes 2 pl. 28 no. 1 (ex. 4a, photo); pl. 29 no. 3 (ex. 4b photo); p. XXXIII (exs. 4a–b, translation)
1888 Hommel, Geschichte p. 335 fig. in text (ex. 4a, photo)
1889 Amiaud, RP NS 2 p. 109 XI Inscriptions of Dungi, King of Ur no. 1 (ex. 4b, translation)
1892 Heuzey, Origines pp. 102–103 (exs. 4a–4b, study)
1900 Koldewey, MDOG 5 pp. 16–17 (ex. 4a, study)
1902 Heuzey, Catalogue Louvre pp. 309–10 no. 161 (ex. 4a, study)
1907 Thureau-Dangin, SAK pp. 192–93 Dun-gi i (ex. 4b, edition)
1908 Johns, Ur-Engur pls. xb and xii (ex. 4a, photos)
1912 Frank, Kunstgeschichte p. 47 no. 8 (ex. 4a, photo)
1912 Jastrow, Bildermappe pl. 25 no. 78 (ex. 4a, photo)
1915 Jastrow, Civilization pl. lxiii upper left (exs. 4a–b, photo)
1925 Schäfer and Andrae, Kunst 1 p. 470 [left-most figure] (ex. 4a, photo)
1926 Nassouhi, Guide sommaire pl. IVc (ex. 2, photo)
1926 Unger, SuAK fig. 53 (ex. 1, photo)
1927 Unger, RLV 8 pl. 141 (exs. 1–3, photo)
1929 Barton, RISA pp. 278–79 Shulgi 10 (ex. 4b, edition)
1930 Schäfer and Andrae, Kunst 2 pl. 498 [left-most photo] (ex. 4a, photo)
1931 Van Buren, Found. p. 23 (ex. 4a, study); p. 24 (exs. 1–3, study)
1962 Hallo, HUCA 33 p. 30 Šulgi 15 (exs. 1–4, study)
1971 Sollberger and Kupper, IRSA IIIA2i (exs. 1–4, translation)
1983 Rashid, Gründungsfiguren, p. 28 and pls. 25–26 nos. 128–30 (exs. 1–3, 4a, study, drawing)
1986 Kärki, KDDU p. 36 Šulgi 15 (exs. 1–4, edition)
1991 Steible, NSBW 2 pp. 167–68 Šulgi 15 (exs. 1–4, edition)

TEXT

1) ^{d}nin-gír-su
2) ur-sag-kala-ga-
3) ^{d}en-líl-lá
4) lugal-a-ni
5) ^{d}šul-gi
6) nita-kala-ga
7) lugal-uri$_{5}$.KI-ma
8) lugal-ki-en-gi-ki-uri-ke$_{4}$
9) é-ninnu
10) é-ki-ág-gá-ni
11) mu-na-dù

1–4) For the god Ningirsu, mighty hero of the god Enlil, his lord,

5–8) Šulgi, mighty man, king of Ur, king of the lands of Sumer and Akkad,

9–11) built for him E-ninnu, his beloved temple.

12

Cones with a ten-line inscription recording Šulgi's construction of the E-ninnu temple were found in excavations at Girsu; the text is a variant of the previous inscription.

CATALOGUE

Ex.	Museum number	Dimensions (cm)	Lines preserved	cpn
1	EŞ 419	14.9×7.2	—	n
2	AO 768	14×6.8	1–10	c
3	AO 840	12.1×7.4	1–10	c
4	AO 841	11.5×6.2	1–10	c
5	AO 15302	16.6×6.4	1–10	c
6	AO 21046	17×7	1–10	c

Ex.	Museum number	Dimensions (cm)	Lines preserved	cpn
7	AO 21048c	6.4×6	1–10	c
8	AO 210xx	16.5×6.6	1–10	c
9	IM 22849	—	—	n

BIBLIOGRAPHY

1907 Thureau-Dangin, SAK pp. 190–91 Dun-gi d (edition)
1929 Barton, RISA pp. 276–77 Shulgi 4 (edition)
1947 Kraus, in Halil Edhem Memorial Volume p. 112 no. 18 (ex. 1, study)
1957 Edzard, Sumer 13 p. 176 (ex. 9, study)
1960 Aynard, RA 54 p. 16 (exs. 2–8, study)
1962 Hallo, HUCA 33 p. 31 Šulgi 23 (exs. 1–9, study)
1986 Kärki, KDDU pp. 39–40 Šulgi 23 (exs. 1–9, edition)
1991 Steible, NSBW 2 p. 176 Šulgi 23 (exs. 1–9, edition)

TEXT

1) ^{d}nin-gír-su 2) ur-sag-kala-ga- 3) ^{d}en-líl-lá 4) lugal-a-ni	1–4) For the god Ningirsu, mighty hero of the god Enlil, his lord,
5) ^{d}šul-gi 6) nita-kala-ga 7) lugal-uri$_5$.KI-ma 8) lugal-ki-en-gi-ki-uri-ke$_4$	5–8) Šulgi, mighty man, king of Ur, king of the lands of Sumer and Akkad,
9) é-a-ni 10) mu-na-dù	9–10) built his temple for him.

13

Šulgi's building of a temple for the goddess Ninmarki in Girsu is recorded in two inscriptions (E3/2.1.2.13–14).

CATALOGUE

Ex.	Museum number	Object	Dimensions (cm)	Lines preserved	Line arrangement	cpn
1	See commentary	Black stone	—	1–9	obv. (?) 1–9	n
2	Was in the private collection of Mercer	Foundation tablet	—	1–9	obv. 1–6 rev. 7–9	n
3	Private collection in UK	Foundation tablet	6.7×4.7	1–9	obv. 1–6 rev. 7–9	p
4	YBC 2387	Bronze canephore	—	1–9	—	c

COMMENTARY

The whereabouts and exact nature of ex. 1 are uncertain. According to Rawlinson (1 R 2 II no. 4 — caption) the incription was incised on "a black stone" that was said to have come from Tell Eed about 23 km northeast of Uruk. Thureau-Dangin (SAK p. 190 Dun-gi e) interpreted this to be a reference to a door socket. Apparently, the object did not enter the BM, since Bezold (Cat. 5 p. 2233) mentions only a paper squeeze. According to C.B.F. Walker (letter of Feb. 17, 1987), the squeeze has been lost. Walker reports that a black foundation tablet bearing this inscription was brought to the BM in February 1987. If Rawlinson's copy is correct in giving the inscription in one column without a break, then it is unlikely that it is the stone shown to Walker, since the latter had six lines on the obverse and three lines on the reverse. The contents of the presented tablet, here designated as ex. 3, were entered in the score from a photo kindly provided by Walker. It could be the tablet published by Mercer, which we have been unable to locate in Toronto. Thus, the omission of the DINGIR sign of line 3 in the Mercer copy (it is found in the other three exemplars) could not be confirmed. It has not been included in the critical apparatus. Exs. 1–2 are entered in the score from the published copy. Ex. 4 was kindly collated by P.-A. Beaulieu.

The question of the reading of the divine name of line 1 has engendered considerable scholarly debate. Sollberger originally (ZA 50 [1952] p. 10 n. 1) read the name (following Thureau-Dangin, RA 15 [1918] p. 27): ^{d}nin-mar-ki. He later opted (AfO 17 [1954–56] pp. 34–35 and n. 126) for a reading: ^{d}nin-ki:mar. The latter proposal, as Whiting (ZA 75 [1985] p. 1) notes: "was either ignored, taken with a certain amount of skepticism, or rejected wholeheartedly."

Falkenstein, (Inschriften Gudeas p. 106 n. 7) drew attention to a passage in "The Lamentation Over the Destruction of Sumer and Ur" which, according to a Langdon copy (PBS 10/4 no. 6 obv. line 9), read: ^{d}nin-mar-ki-ra-ke$_4$ gú-ab-⌈ba⌉-[ka ...]. However, as W. Sallaberger informs me in RIM readers' notes, the supposed -ke$_4$ of Langdon's copy (collated from photo) is to be read: èš and the line: ^{d}nin-mar-ki-ra èš-gú-ab-⌈ba⌉-[ka izi im-ma-da-an-te] "[Fire approached] Ninmarki (-ra is dative) [in] the shrine Gu'aba."

Whiting, in ZA 75 (1985) pp. 1–3, in turn, argued for a reading ^{d}nin-mar.KI, taking the KI to be the determinative for place. However, the writing of the divine name ^{d}nin-MAR.GI$_4$ found in a Fara god list (see Krebernik, ZA 76 [1986] p. 199) if equated with Ninmarki, would argue against Whiting's proposal. A full discussion by Sallaberger of the correct reading of ^{d}nin-mar-ki's name will be found in his forthcoming article on this goddess which is to appear in RLA.

BIBLIOGRAPHY

1861 1 R 2 II (ex. 1, copy)
1872 Smith, TSBA 1 p. 36 (ex. 1, translation)
1874 Lenormant, Études accadiennes 2 p. 76 (ex. 1, translation)
1875 Ménant, Babylone p. 76 (ex. 1, translation)
1892 Winckler, KB 3/1 pp. 80–81 Dungi 4 (ex. 1, edition)
1899 Bezold, Cat. 5 p. 2233 (ex. 1, study)
1907 Thureau-Dangin, SAK pp. 190–91 Dun-gi e (ex. 1, edition)
1925 Dougherty, AASOR 5 p. 34 n. 42 (ex. 4, study)
1928 Mercer, JSOR 12 pp. 146–47, 149 no. 33 (ex. 2, copy, edition)
1929 Barton, RISA pp. 276–77 Shulgi 5 (ex. 1, edition)
1931 Van Buren, Found. p. 24 and fig. 21 (ex. 4, photo, study)
1962 Hallo, HUCA 33 p. 31 Šulgi 21 (exs. 1–2, study)
1983 Rashid, Gründungsfiguren p. 34 and pl. 34 no. 168 (ex. 4, study, drawing)
1986 Kärki, KDDU pp. 38–39 Šulgi 21 (exs. 1–2, 4, edition)
1991 Steible, NSBW 2 pp. 173–74 Šulgi 21 (exs. 1–2 and 4, edition)

TEXT

1) ^{d}nin-mar-ki
2) nin-a-ni
3) ^{d}šul-gi
4) nita-kala-ga
5) lugal-uri$_5$.KI-ma
6) lugal-ki-en-gi-ki-uri-ke$_4$
7) é-munus-gi$_{16}$-sa
8) gír-su.KI-ka-ni
9) mu-na-dù

1–2) For the goddess Ninmarki, his lady,

3–6) Šulgi, mighty man, king of Ur, king of the lands of Sumer and Akkad,

7–9) built her E-munus-gisa of Girsu for her.

14

A nine-line cone inscription similar to the previous inscription records Šulgi's construction of the goddess Ninmarki's E-munus-gisa temple.

COMMENTARY

The cone, which measures 10×4.8 cm, bears the museum number AO 12777. The text is arranged in one column of nine lines. The inscription was collated.

BIBLIOGRAPHY

1960 Aynard, RA 54 p. 17 (transliteration)
1962 Hallo, HUCA 33 p. 31 Šulgi 24 (study)
1986 Kärki, KDDU p. 40 Šulgi 24 (edition)
1991 Steible, NSBW 2 p. 177 Šulgi 24 (edition)

TEXT

1) ⸢^{d}nin-mar-ki⸣
2) ⸢munus-sa$_{6}$⸣-ga
3) ⸢dumu-sag-^{d}nanše⸣
4) ^{d}šul-gi
5) nita-kala-ga
6) lugal-uri$_{5}$.KI-ma
7) lugal-ki-en-gi-ki-uri-ke$_{4}$
8) é-munus-gi$_{16}$-sa-ka-ni
9) ⸢mu-na-dù⸣

1–3) For the goddess Ninmarki, the gracious lady, the first-born child of the goddess Nanše,

4–7) Šulgi, mighty man, king of Ur, king of the lands of Sumer and Akkad,

8–9) built her E-munus-gisa for her.

15

A stone foundation tablet records Šulgi's construction of Ningirsu's temple of Bagara (at Lagaš — modern Tell al-Hibā).

COMMENTARY

The inscription is found on Ash 1922-9, a steatite tablet that measures 7.6×5.4×1.4 cm. The piece was acquired through purchase; it presumably originally came fom Tell al-Hibā. Lines 1–8 are found on the obverse, lines 9–10 on the reverse. The inscription was collated.

BIBLIOGRAPHY

1981 Grégoire, MVN 10 no. 20 (copy)
1991 Steible, NSBW 2 p. 211 Šulgi 68 (edition)

TEXT

1) ^{d}nin-gír-⸢su⸣
2) ur-sag-kala-ga
3) ^{d}en-líl-lá
4) lugal-a-ni
5) ^{d}sul-gi
6) nita-kala-ga
7) lugal-uri$_{5}$.KI-ma
8) lugal-ki-en-gi-ki-uri-ke$_{4}$

1–4) For the god Ningirsu, mighty hero of the god Enlil, his lord,

5–8) Šulgi, mighty man, king of Ur, king of the lands of Sumer and Akkad,

9) é-ba-gára-ka-ni
10) mu-na-dù

9–10) built his temple of Bagara for him.

16

A Sumerian brick inscription from Adab records Šulgi's dedication of a weir to the goddess Ninḫursaga. The text is arranged in one column of nine lines.

CATALOGUE

Ex.	Museum number	Dimensions (cm)	RIM photo	Lines preserved	cpn
1	A 1143 (Chicago)	30.7×30.7×6.6	—	1–9	c
2	A 1141 (Chicago)	32×15.5×7	—	1–9	c
3	A 1142 (Chicago)	32.2×15.5×6.6	—	1–9	c
4	A 1140 (Chicago)	30.5×30.5	—	1–9	c
5	EŞ 3229	—	—	1–9	c
6	EŞ 3232	31×31×6.5	357	1–9	c
7	EŞ 3233	29.2×29.5	—	—	n
8	EŞ 3234	—	—	—	n
9	EŞ —	32.4×32×7	363	1–9	c

COMMENTARY

Although the inscription deals with the construction of a weir, the bricks themselves were found in an enclosure wall that apparently surrounded a small ziqqurrat. For a photo of this enclosure wall, which was located on Mound V, the "Temple Mound," at Adab, see Banks, Bismya p. 133.

BIBLIOGRAPHY

1912 Banks, Bismya p. 134 (ex. 1, copy); p. 344 (ex. 2, photo)
1930 Luckenbill, Adab nos. 37–39 (exs. 1–3, copy)
1962 Hallo, HUCA 33 p. 29 Šulgi 8 (exs. 1–3, study)
1986 Kärki, KDDU p. 32 Šulgi 8 (exs. 1–3, edition)
1986 Yang, Sargonic Archive p. 21 (exs. 1–3, provenance)
1991 Steible, NSBW 2 p. 162 Šulgi 8 (exs. 1–3, edition)

TEXT

1) ^{d}nin-ḫur-saga
2) nin-a-ni
3) šul-gi
4) nita-kala-ga
5) lugal-uri$_5$.KI-ma
6) lugal-ki-en-gi-ki-uri-ke$_4$
7) GIŠ.kéš-rá
8) ki-ág-ni
9) mu-na-dù

1–2) For the goddess Ninḫursaga, his lady,

3–6) Šulgi, mighty man, king of Ur, king of the lands of Sumer and Akkad,

7–9) built her beloved weir for her.

E3/2.1.2.16.2.1 ^{d}nin-a-ni.

17

An eight-line Sumerian inscription from Nippur records Šulgi's construction of the temple of the goddess Damgalnuna in that city.

COMMENTARY

The tablet was found in Season X of the old American expedition to Nippur, out of place in the rubbish at the foot of the mound, about 1 m above the surface of the plain. It measures 8.35×5.6×1.6 cm and bears the museum number HS 1963. Lines 1–6 are on the obverse, lines 7–8 on the reverse. The inscription was collated.

For archival texts referring to the goddess Damgalnuna at Nippur, see Sallaberger, Kalender 2 p.190 Register, sub ^{d}dam-gal-nun-na.

BIBLIOGRAPHY

1896 Hilprecht, BE 1/2 no. 123 (copy)
1900 Radau, EBH p. 224 (edition)
1907 Thureau-Dangin, SAK pp. 192–93 Dun-gi l (edition)
1929 Barton, RISA pp. 278–79 Shulgi 12 (edition)
1962 Hallo, HUCA 33 p. 29 Šulgi 9 (study)
1969 Oelsner, OLZ 18 p. 53 no. 19 (study)
1986 Kärki, KDDU pp. 32–33 Šulgi 9 (edition)
1991 Steible, NSBW 2 pp. 162–63 Šulgi 9 (edition)

TEXT

1) ^{d}dam-gal-nun-na
2) nin-a-ni
3) šul-gi
4) nita-kala-ga
5) lugal-uri$_{5}$.KI-ma
6) lugal-ki-en-gi-ki-uri-ke$_{4}$
7) é-nibru-KI-ka-ni
8) mu-na-dù

1–2) For the goddess Damgalnuna, his lady,

3–6) Šulgi, mighty man, king of Ur, king of the lands of Sumer and Akkad,

7–8) built her Nippur temple for her.

18

Two bricks from Nippur bear a Sumerian inscription that commemorates the construction of a weir for the god Enlil. The text is arranged in one column of eight lines.

CATALOGUE

Ex.	Museum number	Excavation number	Nippur provenance	Lines preserved	cpn
1	IM 56106	2 N-T 738	TB, level II, Locus 31, floor 1	3–8	p
2	IM —	5 N-T 683	SB, level II, Locus 8, floor 4	1–8	p

COMMENTARY

Ex. 2 was collated by R. Biggs from a field copy; ex. 1 from the excavation photo 46790. In both exemplars the second parts of lines 5 and 6 are written with the indented section above the beginning section of the line. This is opposite to the normal practice.

BIBLIOGRAPHY

1976 Basmachi, Treasures p. 205 no. 5 (ex. 1, study)
1992 Zettler, Ur III Temple p. 12 n. 22 (exs. 1–2, study)

TEXT

1) ^{d}en-líl
2) lugal-a-ni
3) šul-gi
4) nita-kala-ga
5) lugal-uri$_5$.KI-ma
6) lugal-ki-en-gi-ki-uri-ke$_4$
7) GIŠ.kéš-rá-a-ni
8) mu-na-dù

1–2) For the god Enlil, his lord,

3–6) Šulgi, mighty man, king of Ur, king of the lands of Sumer and Akkad,

7–8) built for him his weir.

19

A foundation deposit found in excavations of the Inanna temple at Nippur yielded a brick fragment with the first six lines (arranged in one column) of a probable building inscription of Šulgi for the god Ennugi. The same foundation deposit yielded an uninscribed canephor and a stone plano-convex "brick."

CATALOGUE

Ex.	Museum number	Excavation number	Nippur provenance	Object	Dimensions (cm)	Lines preserved	cpn
1a	IM —	5 N-T 688	Locus 86, under southwest tower of northwest gate	Inscribed brick	12.5×12.5 Inscription: 9×11.5	1–6	c
1b	ROM 961.162.1	5 N 251	As ex. 1a	Bronze canephor	31 high	Uninscribed	—
1c	ROM 961.162.2	5 N 251	As ex. 1a	Stone plano-convex "brick"	9×6.5×3.9	Uninscribed	—

COMMENTARY

Ex. 1a was collated from a cast housed at the Oriental Institute at the University of Chicago. The inscription is published here through the kind permission of E. Carter and J.A. Brinkman.

According to the Canonical Temple List (see George, House Most High pp. 12 and 137 no. 938), the name of Ennugi's temple (at Nippur) was é-rab-ri-ri "House of the Shackle which Holds in Check."

BIBLIOGRAPHY

1992 Zettler, Ur III Temple p. 41 n. 28 (study)

TEXT

1) ^{d}en-nu-gi$_4$
2) lugal-a-ni
3) šul-gi
4) nita-kala-g[a]
5) lugal-[uri$_5$.KI-ma]
6) lu[gal-ki-en-gi-ki-uri-ke$_4$]
Lacuna

1–2) For the god Ennugi, his lord,

3–6) Šulgi, might[y] man, king [of Ur], ki[ng of the lands of Sumer and Akkad]
Lacuna

20

An eight-line Sumerian inscription stamped on bricks records Šulgi's construction of Inanna's temple at Nippur. The bricks came from foundation boxes from various points in the temple. The text is arranged in one column of eight lines.

CATALOGUE

Ex.	Museum number	Excavation number	Nippur provenance	Object	Dimensions (cm)	Photo	Rashid number	Lines preserved	cpn
1a	A 30792 (Chicago)	5N-T685	Locus 55, under south wall	Stamped brick	31×31×7.5	—	—	1–8	c
1b	MMA 59.4.1	5N 202	Locus 55	Copper (see Muscarella, Bronze and Iron p. 311 n. 1) canephor	31.3 high 9 wide	ILN 1956 p. 268 fig. 9 3rd from left	138	—	—
1c	—	5N 202	Locus 55	Stone plano-convex "brick"	9.8×6.1×2.5	—	—	—	—
2a	—	5N-T686	Locus 56, under northeast tower flanking doorway, in southeast wall of Locus 28	Stamped brick	31×31×7.5	—	—	1–8	n
2b	IM 59588	5N 203	Locus 56	Copper canephor	30.1 high 11.7 wide	ILN 1956 p. 268 fig. 9 2nd from left	134	—	—
2c	—	5N 203	Locus 56	Stone plano-convex "brick"	8.7×5.45	—	—	—	—
3a	Kelsey 63.6.64	5N-T687	Locus 57, under southwest tower flanking doorway, in southeast wall of Locus 28	Stamped brick	39×39	—	—	1–8	c
3b	IM 59587	5N 204	Locus 57	Copper canephor	25.8 high 8.3 wide 4.9 thick	ILN 1956 p. 268 fig. 9 left-most	133	—	—
3c	—	5N 204	Locus 57	Stone plano-conve "brick"	7.35×5.65×2.1	—	—	—	—
4a	—	—	Locus 87, under northwest tower of northwest gate	Brick	—	—	—	—	n
4b	IM 59589	5N 204	Locus 87	Copper canephor	31.4 high 8.8 wide	ILN 1956 p. 268 fig. 9 4th from left	135	—	—

Ex.	Museum number	Excavation number	Nippur provenance	Object	Dimensions (cm)	Photo	Rashid number	Lines preserved	cpn
4c	—	5N 204	Locus 87	Stone plano-convex "brick"	10.3×6.2×3.2	—	—	—	n
5a	A 31069	6N-T1128	Locus 127, under southwest tower of doorway in southeast wall of Locus 118	Inscribed brick	31×31×6.15	—	—	1–8	c
5b	USA (Chicago)	6N 250	Locus 127	Copper canephor	31.7×9×5	ILN 1958 p. 389 fig. 19 left	137	—	—
5c	—	6N 250	Locus 127	Stone plano-convex "brick"	9.8×6.5×3.1	—	—	—	—
5d	—	6N 250	Locus 127	Wood fragments	—	—	—	—	—
6a1	MMA 59.41.87	6N-T1129	Locus 128, under northeast tower flanking doorway in southeast wall of Locus 118	Inscribed brick	—	—	—	1–8	c
6a2	IM 61766	6N-T1130	Locus 128	Inscribed brick	—	—	—	1–8	n
6b	IM 61403/1	6N 300	Locus 128	Bronze canephor	29.7 high 11.5 wide 5.2 thick	ILN 1958 p. 389 fig. 19 right	136	Un-inscribed	—
6c	—	6N 300	Locus 128	Stone plano-convex "brick"	8.6×3.7×3.3	—	—	Un-inscribed	—
6d	—	6N 300	Locus 128	Wood pins(?)	—	—	—	—	—

COMMENTARY

During the 1955–56 (5 N) season of the American excavations at Nippur five foundation boxes were unearthed in the area of the Inanna temple (yielding exs. 1–4 here; one of the five bears the inscription E3/2.1.2.19). All foundation boxes contained uninscribed bronze canephors and brick-shaped stone tablets. The attribution of the deposits to Šulgi was based on the inscription found on the bricks that made up the sides of the foundation boxes. R. Ellis (Foundation Deposits p. 66) notes:

> The Nippur deposits were each closed with three baked bricks, two laid side by side over the cavity, and the third covering their joint.

Then in the 1957–58 (6 N) season two more foundation boxes (yielding exs. 5–6 here) were found.

In the catalogue for this inscription the foundation boxes and contents are listed in sets: ex. Na refers to the inscribed or stamped brick; ex. Nb to the uninscribed canephor; ex. Nc to the uninscribed stone "brick"; and ex. Nd to the wood fragments. The heading "photo" in the chart refers to the photos published by Haines in ILN August 1956 p. 268 fig. 9 or in ILN September 6 1958 p. 389 fig. 19. The heading "Rashid no." refers to the number assigned the pegs in Rashid, Gründungsfiguren. For other foundation pegs possibly representing Šulgi, see Ellis, Foundation Deposits p. 65 n. 144.

In exs. 5a and 6a1 the written en sign of line 6 is written upside down. A score has been prepared for this inscription. Information on ex. 3a was kindly provided by P. Michalowski.

BIBLIOGRAPHY

1955 Haines, Sumer 11 p. 107 (ex. 1, provenance)
1956 Haines, ILN August 18 p. 268 fig. 9 (exs. 1b, 2b, 3b, 4b, photo)
1958 Haines, ILN September 6 p. 389 fig. 19 (exs. 5b and 6b, photo)
1958–60 Crawford, MMAB 18 p. 250 fig. 9 (ex. 1b, photo)
1966 Crawford, Ancient Near Eastern Art p. 13 fig. 18 (ex. 1b, photo)
1968 Ellis, Foundation Deposits pp. 64–65 and 67–69 (exs. 1b–6b, study)
1983 Rashid, Gründungsfiguren pp. 28–30 and pls. 27–30 nos. 133–39 (exs. 1b, 2b, 3b, 4b, 5b, 6b, study, drawing)
1984 Anonymous, MMAB 41/4 p. 36 no. 45 (ex. 1b, photo)
1987 Zettler, JCS 39 p. 219 n. 33 (edition, study)
1988 Muscarella, Bronze and Iron pp. 305–13 no. 435 (ex. 1b, photo, study)
1988 Sigrist, in Spar, Met. Mus. 1 p. 160 and pl. 121 no. 117 (ex. 6a1, copy, edition)
1991 Steible, NSBW 2 pp. 216–17 Šulgi 75 (ex. 6a1, edition)
1992 Zettler, Ur III Temple p. 239 no. 1 (edition)

TEXT

1) ^{d}inanna
2) nin-a-ni
3) šul-gi
4) nita-kala-ga

1–2) For the goddess Inanna, his lady,

3–6) Šulgi, mighty man, king of Ur, king of the lands of Sumer and Akkad,

5) lugal-uri$_5$.KI-ma	
6) lugal-ki-en-gi-ki-uri-ke$_4$	
7) é-dur-an-ki-ka-ni	7–8) built her E-dur-anki ("House, Bond of Heaven and Underworld") for her.
8) mu-na-dù	

21

A Sumerian inscription incised on door sockets commemorates Šulgi's construction of Inanna's E-duranki temple in Nippur. The text is arranged in one column of eleven lines.

CATALOGUE

Ex.	Museum number	Excavation number	Nippur provenance	Object	Dimensions (cm)	Lines preserved	cpn
1	CBS 14549	—	—	Diorite door socket	—	1–11	p
2	IM 54540	3 N 407	Locus 2	Basalt(?) door socket	38.5×28.5×14.5	1–11	c
3	ROM 961.162	5 N-T 678	Locus 13	Granite(?) door socket	34×19×14 Inscription: 15×5.1	1–11	c
4	—	5 N-T 679	Locus 16	Door socket	—	1–11	n
5	—	5 N-T 680	Locus 21	Door socket	30.8×26.3×30	1–11	n
6	—	6 N-T1146	Locus 120	Door socket	—	—	n
7	—	6 N-T 1147	Locus 141	Door socket	—	—	n

COMMENTARY

Ex. 2 was collated by H. Steible, who kindly communicated a transliteration to the author.

BIBLIOGRAPHY

1924 Legrain, MJ 15 pp. 77–79 (ex. 1, photo, edition)
1926 Legrain, PBS 15 no. 42 (ex. 1, copy, edition)
1929 Barton, RISA pp. 276–77 Shulgi 6 (ex. 1, edition)
1952 McCown, Archeology 5 p. 74 (ex. 2, photo)
1962 Hallo, HUCA 33 p. 32 Šulgi 20 (exs. 1–2, study)
1971 Sollberger and Kupper, IRSA IIIA2g (exs. 1–2, translation)
1986 Kärki, KDDU p. 38 Šulgi 20 (exs. 1–2, edition)
1987 Zettler, JCS 39 p. 219 n. 33 (edition, study)
1991 Steible, NSBW 2 pp. 172–73 Šulgi 20 (exs. 1–2, edition)
1992 Zettler, Ur III Temple p. 239 no. 3 (edition)

TEXT

1) ^{d}inanna	1–2) For the goddess Inanna, his lady,
2) nin-a-ni	
3) šul-gi	3–6) Šulgi, mighty man, king of Ur, king of the lands of Sumer and Akkad,
4) nita-kala-ga	
5) lugal-uri$_5$.KI-ma	
6) lugal-ki-en-gi-ki-uri-ke$_4$	
7) é-dur-an-ki-ka-ni	7–9) built her E-duranki (temple) for her and restored it.
8) mu-na-dù	
9) ki-bé mu-na-gi$_4$	
10) nam-ti-la-ni-šè	10–11) He dedicated it for his (own) life.
11) a mu-na-ru	

22

Two clay sealings from the area of the Inanna temple at Nippur bear an inscription that likely duplicates E3/2.1.2.20 or 21.

CATALOGUE

Ex.	Museum number	Excavation number	Nippur provenance	Object	Dimensions (cm)	Lines preserved	cpn
1	—	5 N-T 595	From the clay bin in the chancery courtyard, (Locus 78)	Clay sealing	11.3×6	3–6	n
2	—	6 N-T 688	SB 76 (from the fill of the Parthian platform)	Clay sealing	5.5×4.5	4, 6	n

COMMENTARY

Although 34 clay sealings were found in the clay bin of locus 78 of the Inanna temple, only one (here ex. 1) bore an inscription that was sufficiently preserved to warrant a copy by Zettler in his article in JCS 39.

Zettler describes the particular form and function of these clay sealings as follows (JCS 39 [1987] pp. 214 and 219):

> The flattened bases of a number of sealings from the bin which had been broken off a knob and hook (the "base" of the sealing is identified as such in the sections given in fig. 9 and is shown in fig. 6) show a raised casing and inscription. The cuneiform signs are in mirror-image, which indicates that the clay had been pressed against a cut inscription. That inscription was carved on the face of the plaque to which the knob was affixed. A portion of the casing of the inscription and several signs are visible on the sealing and positive of 5 NT 595 (fig. 8). As that sealing shows, the inscription was cut above the knob and vertically; that is, it was placed so that the cuneiform characters within cases were arranged from top to bottom and the cases from right to left. The inscription is not well-preserved on any of the sealings from the bin, but is on a sealing found in secondary context. ... What remains of the inscription is sufficient to identify it, and the examples from the bin in Locus 1, as duplicates either of Sulgi's inscription for Inanna found on baked bricks or of that on pivot stones used in the temple.

A clay sealing similar to these Nippur "door-bell" fragments was published by Hilprecht in Explorations p. 517. The Hilprecht piece is impressed with an inscription of Šar-kali-šarrī (see Frayne, RIME 2 pp. 197–98, E2.1.5.10).

BIBLIOGRAPHY

1987 Zettler, JCS 39 pp. 214–21 and figs. 5–8 and 10 (exs. 1–2, photo, copy, study)

TEXT

1) [^{d}inanna]
2) [nin-a-ni]
3) [šul-g]i
4) [nita-kala-g]a
5) [lugal-u[ri_5.([ŠEŠ].AB)].[KI]-ma
6) [lugal-ki]-en-[gi-ki-u]ri-ke_4
Lacuna

1–2) [For the goddess Inanna, his lady],

3–6) [Šulg]i, [mig]hty [man], [king of U]r, [king of the lands] of Su[mer] and Ak[kad]
Lacuna

23

An eleven-line Akkadian inscription incised on a foundation tablet records Šulgi's construction of Nergal's E-meslam temple at Kutha.

COMMENTARY

The steatite tablet, which is reported to have come from Nineveh, measures 7.6×5.1 cm and bears the museum number AO 22992. Lines 1–7 are found on the obverse, lines 8–11 on the reverse. The inscription was collated from an unpublished Louvre photo through the courtesy of B. André-Salvini.

BIBLIOGRAPHY

1873 Lenormant, Choix no. 61 (copy)
1876 Schrader, ZDMG 29 pp. 37–39 (copy, translation)
1888 Amiaud, ZA 3 pp. 94–95 and pl. opposite p. 95 (copy [including typescript copy], study)
1907 Thureau-Dangin, SAK pp. 190–91 Dun-gi g (edition)
1929 Barton, RISA pp. 278–79 Shulgi 8 (edition)
1961 Gelb, MAD 2^2 p. 16 § 1a (study)
1962 Hallo, HUCA 33 p. 29 Šulgi 4i (study)
1971 Sollberger and Kupper, IRSA IIIA2m (translation)
1971 von Weiher, Nergal p. 6 (edition)
1986 Kärki, KDDU p. 29 Šulgi 4a (edition)
1990 Gelb and Kienast, Königsinschriften pp. 339–40 Ur 2 (edition)
1991 Steible, NSBW 2 pp. 156–57 Šulgi 4a (edition)

TEXT

1) šul-gi
2) *da-núm*
3) LUGAL URI$_5$.KI
4) *ù* LUGAL
5) *ki-ib-ra-tim*
6) *ar-ba-im*
7) *ba*DÍM
8) é-⸢mes⸣-lam
9) É [^{d}KIŠ].ERI$_{11}$.GAL
10) *be-*[*lí*]*-šu*
11) ⸢*in*⸣ [GÚ.DU$_8$].A.KI

1–6) Šulgi, the mighty, king of Ur and of the four quarters,

7–11) builder of E-meslam ("House, Warrior of the Netherworld"), temple of the god [N]ergal, his lo[rd], in [Kuth]a.

24

An eight-line Sumerian inscription records Šulgi's building of Nergal's E-meslam temple at Kutha.

COMMENTARY

The tablet bearing this inscription, BM 35389 (no registration number known), was purchased from Spartali. The original provenance of this Neo-Babylonian copy is unknown. The tablet measures 5.5×4.8×1.5 cm. Lines 1–5 are on the obverse, lines 6–8 and the colophon on the reverse. The inscription was collated.

BIBLIOGRAPHY

1887 Winckler, MAOV 1 p. 16 no. 1 (copy)
1890 Winckler and Böhden, ABK no. 35 (copy)
1900 King, CT 9 pl. 3 BM 35389 (copy)
1907 Thureau-Dangin, SAK pp. 190–92 Dun-gi f (edition)
1929 Barton, RISA pp. 276–77 Shulgi 7 (edition)
1962 Hallo, HUCA 33 p. 29 Šulgi 4ii (study)
1968 Hunger, Kolophone p. 127 no. 442 (edition [colophon only])
1971 Sollberger and Kupper, IRSA IIIA2l (translation)
1971 von Weiher, Nergal pp. 6–7 (edition [without colophon])
1986 Kärki, KDDU p. 30 Šulgi 4b (edition)
1991 Steible, NSBW 2 pp. 157–58 Šulgi A! 4b (edition)

TEXT

1) šul-gi
2) nita-kala-ga
3) lugal-uri$_5$.KI-ma
4) lugal-ki-en-gi-ki-uri
5) é-mes-lam
6) é-^{d}mes-lam-ta-è-a
7) gú-du$_8$-a.KI
8) mu-dù-a

Colophon
1) *ša* ÚGU NA$_4$.NA.RÚ.A LIBIR.RA
2) *ša é-mes-lam qé-reb* GÚ.DU$_8$.A.KI
3) IM.GÍD.DA ^{md}EN-TIN-*iṭ* DUB.⌈SAR⌉

1–4) Šulgi, mighty man, king of Ur, king of the lands of Sumer and Akkad,

5–8) who built the E-meslam, temple of the god Meslamta-eʾa in Kutha.

Colophon
1–2) That which (was written) on an old foundation inscription of E-meslam, in Kutha.
3) Long-tablet of Bēl-uballiṭ, the scr[ibe].

25

A Šulgi inscription known from a later tablet copy gives an Akkadian account, in a more detailed version than that found in E3/2.1.2.23–24, of the king's construction of the E-meslam temple in Kutha.

COMMENTARY

The inscription is found on obv. cols. i′–ii′ of BM 78681+139969, a tablet purchased by Budge. Previously only BM 78681 had been published.

The join of the two tablet fragments was made by R.K. Uprichard; I. Finkel kindly notified the author of the join, provided a copy of the tablet, and graciously allowed its appearance in this volume in advance of his own study. Of course, any errors in the interpretation of the new piece are the responsibility of the author. It is edited here through the kind permission of the trustees of the British Museum and is herafter cited as the Pinches Sammeltafel of Šulgi inscriptions.

The curvature of the tablet indicates that at least two columns preceded the preserved text.

Line i′ 14 is restored [*in u*]-*mi-šu* following the reading found in RIME 2 p. 112 E2.1.4.9 line 19 (Clay, YOS 1 no. 10 line ii 1). For the goddess Laṣ, Nergal's wife, see Lambert, RLA 6 pp. 506–507, sub Laṣ.

BIBLIOGRAPHY

1963 Pinches, CT 44 pl. 1 no. 2 (BM 78681, copy)
1990 Gelb and Kienast, Königsinschriften pp. 291–92 Fragment C 7 (BM 78681, edition)

TEXT

Obv. col. i′
1) [*a-na* ^{d}KIŠ.ERI$_{11}$].GAL
2) [*be-lí*]-*šu*

i′ 1–2) [For the god Ner]gal, his [lord],

3) [(^{d})šul]-gi
4) [*da*]-*núm*
5) [LUGAL ŠEŠ.U]NU.KI-*ma*
6) LUGAL
7) [*ki-ib-r*]*a-tim*
8) [*ar-ba*]-*i-im*
9) [*ì-nu* ^{d}]*en-líl*
10) [*ṣé-r*]*a-at*
11) [NI].^{ši}SI$_{11}$
12) [*qá-ti-i*]*s-su*
13) [*i-d*]*ì*^{di}-*nu*
14) [*in u*]-*mi-šu*
15) [*é-mes*]-*lam*
16) [*bi*]-*ta-am*(Text:RA)
17) [*ša i*]-*ra-mu*
18) [*i*]*n* GÚ.DU$_{8}$.A.KI
19) [*ib*]-*ni-šum*
20) [LUGAL] *in* LUGAL-*rí*
21) [*ma*]-*na*-⸢*ma*⸣
Lacuna
1′) [^{d}EN.KI]
2′) [i$_{7}$-*šu*]
Col. ii′
1) *sà-kí*(Text: ZI)-*kà-am*
2) *li-im-du*-[*ud*]
3) ^{d}*en*-⸢*líl*⸣(?)
4) *na-aB-ru-tim*
5) *ba-ni-šu*
6) *a i-dì-š*[*u*]*m*
7) ^{d}⸢INANNA⸣
8) *be-la-at ì*-[*l*]*i*
9) *a tam-gur*$_{4}$^{gur}-*r*[*a*](?)-*šu*
10) ^{d}UTU
11) DI.KU$_{5}$-*šu*
12) *a ù-šu-ši-ir*
13) ^{d}KIŠ.ERI$_{11}$.GAL
14) *ù* ^{d}*la-aṣ*
15) LÚ *šu*$_{4}$-*a*-⸢*ti*⸣
16) ŠU.NÍGIN DINGIR.[DINGIR]
17) *á-ni*-⸢*ù*⸣-[*ut*]
18) SUḪUŠ-[*šu*]
19) *li*-[*sú-ḫu*]
20) ⸢*ù*⸣(?) [...]
Lacuna

i′ 3–5) [Šul]gi, the [mi]ghty, [king of U]r,

i′ 6–8) king of the [fou]r [quar]ters,

i′ 9–13) [when the god] Enlil entr[usted] [in]to his [hands] the [nose-r]ope of the [peo]ple,

i′ 14–19) [at that ti]me he [bu]ilt for him [E-mes]lam, the [tem]ple [which he l]oves, [i]n Kutha.

i′ 20–21) [No king] whosoever
Lacuna

i′ 1′ – ii′ 2) (May the god Ea) block up [his canal] with silt.

ii′ 3 –6) May the god *Enlil* of ... not grant to him a ...

ii′ 7–9) May the goddess Inanna, lady of the go[d]s, not grant his prayers.

ii′ 10–12) May the god Šamaš not make his legal case proceed correctly.

ii′ 13–20) As for that man, may the gods Nergal and Laṣ, (and) all thos[e] god[s](mentioned above), te[ar] out [his] foundation *and*
Lacuna

26

A second Akkadian inscription found on the Pinches Sammeltafel of Šulgi inscriptions (see E3/2.1.2.25) describes various apotropaic figures: *laḫmu*s ("long-haired-heroes"), *umu*s (possibly "lion-dragons") (see Wiggermann, Protective Spirits p. 170), and *Anzu* birds ("lion-headed eagles"), which once stood guard at the doorways of the shrines of the goddess Laṣ (and Nergal[?]) in Kutha.

COMMENTARY

The inscription is found on rev. cols. i–ii of BM 78681+139969. For the various types of apotropaic monsters, see Wiggermann, JEOL 27 (1983) pp. 90–105; ibid., Babylonian Prophylactic Figures: The Ritual Texts; ibid., Protective Spirits; ibid., "Mischwesen. A" RLA 8/3–4 pp. 222–46, and Green, "Mischwesen. B" RLA 8/3–4 pp. 246–64.

The *papāḫu(m)* seems to have been a room in the temple situated between the temple courtyard (*kisallu*[*m*]) and the *kummu(m)* (see Charpin, Iraq 45 [1983] pp. 56–63). The *kummu(m)* was the innermost room of the temple, likely the god's bedroom. For an actual stone doorway lion of roughly Ur III date (Gudea), see Boehmer, Bagh. Mitt. 16 (1983) pp. 141–45 no. 142, and Kessler, Bagh. Mitt. 16 (1983) pp. 149–50 and pl. 23.

BIBLIOGRAPHY

1963 Pinches, CT 44 pl. 1 no. 2 (BM 78681, copy)
1990 Gelb and Kienast, Königsinschriften pp. 291–92 Fragment C 7 (BM 78681, edition)

TEXT

Rev. col. i
7′) *u_4-mu-um á-ni-um*
8′) *e-ṣi-ip da-ma*
9′) *na-ki-ri*
10′) *^{d}šul-gi*
11′) *zi-ik-ru-ù-a*
12′) *śum-śu*
13′) ^{d}ANZU.MUŠEN *ù pa-paḫ*
14′) *ša i-mi^{ta}-tim*
Rev. col. ii
Lacuna
1′) *š*[*a* KÁ ^{d}x]
2′) *š*[*a i-mi-tim*]
3′) *la-a*[*ḫ-mu-um á-ni-um*]
4′) *ba-la-*⌈*tam*⌉ [... *śum-śu*]
5′) *ša* KÁ ^{d}[...]
6′) *ša šu-me-*[*lim*]
7′) *la-aḫ-mu-um á*[*-ni-um*]
8′) *i-te-ak-ri-*x [...]
9′) *^{d}la-aṣ iś-dè^{ti}-*⌈x x⌉
10′) *śum-śu ša* KÁ-*pa-p*[*a*]*ḫ*
11′) *^{d}la-aṣ ša šu-me-l*[*i*]*m*
12′) *la-aḫ-mu-um á-ni-*[*u*]*m*
13′) TAB-*la-su* IGI.SIG$_5$-*śu* <*śum-śu*>
14′) *ša* KÁ *pa-paḫ-^{d}la-*⌈*aṣ*⌉
15′) *ša i-mi-tim*

rev. i 7′–12′) This *lion-dragon* — "My words *gather* the blood of the enemies of Šulgi" (is) its name.

rev. i 13′–14′) The lion-headed eagle *of the bridge* of the cella, on the right (side).

Lacuna
rev. ii 1′–2′) O[f the doorway of the god DN] o[n] the [right side].
rev. ii 3′–6′) [This] long-hai[red "hero"] — "[...] life" (is) [its name]: of the doorway of the god [DN], on the le[ft] (side).

rev. ii 7′–11′) T[his] long-haired "hero" — "... the goddess Laṣ with ..." (is) its name: of the doorway of goddess Laṣ, on the left (side).

rev. ii 12′–15′) Th[i]s long-haired "hero" — "... *his chosen* one" (is) <its name>: of the doorway of the cella of the goddess Laṣ, on the right (side).

27

A ten-line Akkadian inscription deals with Šulgi's building of the temple of the god Tišpak in Ešnunna.

COMMENTARY

The stamped baked brick bearing this inscription, which measures 35×35.7 cm, was found reused in the pavement of the bathroom of a Larsa period private house at Tell Asmar (E 16:3), and was given the excavation number As

31–765. It bears the museum number A 8997 (Chicago). The text is arranged in one column of ten lines. The inscription was collated.

BIBLIOGRAPHY

1934 Jacobsen, AS 6 pp. 20–23 (copy, photo, edition)
1961 Gelb, MAD 2^2 p. 16 § 1a (study)
1962 Hallo, HUCA 33 p. 29 Šulgi 3 (study)
1967 Delougaz, Private Houses p. 195 and pl. 38 B (provenance)
1971 Sollberger and Kupper, IRSA IIIA2k (translation)
1986 Kärki, KDDU p. 29 Šulgi 3 (edition)
1990 Gelb and Kienast, Königsinschriften p. 339 Ur 1 (edition)
1991 Steible, NSBW 2 pp. 155–56 Šulgi 3 (edition)

TEXT

1) šul-gi
2) *da-núm*
3) LUGAL URI$_5$.KI
4) *ù* LUGAL
5) *ki-ib-ra-tim*
6) *ar-ba-im*
7) *ba*DÍM
8) *é-sikil*
9) É-^{d}⌈*tišpak*⌉
10) *in iš-nun*.KI

1–6) Šulgi, the mighty, king of Ur and king of the four quarters,

7–10) builder of E-sikil, temple of the god Tišpak in Ešnunna.

28

A Sumerian brick inscription commemorates Šulgi's building of the E-sikil temple in Ešnunna. The text is arranged in one column of nine lines.

CATALOGUE

Ex.	Museum number	Excavation number	Ešnunna provenance	Dimensions (cm)	Lines preserved	cpn
1	IM 23839	As 31–736	From the pavement of the bathroom of a Larsa period private house (E 16:3)	35×37×8	1–9	n
2	—	As 31–737	As ex. 1	—	—	n

BIBLIOGRAPHY

1934 Jacobsen, AS 6 pp. 20–21 (copy, edition)
1962 Hallo, HUCA 33 p. 29 Šulgi 7 (study)
1967 Delougaz, Private Houses p. 195 and pl. 38 B (provenance)
1971 Sollberger and Kupper, IRSA IIIA2j (translation)
1986 Kärki, KDDU p. 32 Šulgi 7 (edition)
1991 Steible, NSBW 2 p. 161 Šulgi 7 (edition)

TEXT

1) ^{d}nin-a-zu
2) lugal-a-ni
3) šul-gi
4) nita-kala-ga
5) lugal-uri$_5$.KI-ma

1–2) For the god Ninazu, his lord,

3–6) Šulgi, mighty man, king of Ur, king of the lands of Sumer and Akkad,

6) lugal-ki-en-gi-ki-uri-ke$_4$	
7) é-sikil 8) é-ki-ág-gá-ni 9) mu-na-dù (Text: NI)	7–9) built for him E-sikil, his beloved temple.

29

A fragmentarily preserved stone foundation tablet mentions Šulgi and the river-god; in all likelihood it recorded the construction of the god's temple. The tablet came from the mound marked by modern Tell ed-Dēr; the Ur III name of the site is unknown.

COMMENTARY

The tablet bears the museum number BM 17288 and the registration number 94-1-15, 2. The preserved text is on the obverse of the tablet. Objects with registration numbers in the 94-1-15 series form part of the 1891 "find" of tablets from Tell ed-Dēr. For an account of their discovery, see Budge, By Nile and Tigris pp. 261–62. The possibility of the construction of an Ur III period temple at Tell ed-Dēr is supported by archaeological evidence. According to H. Gasche (in de Meyer, Tell ed-Dēr 4 pp. 59–62), levels at Tell ed-Dēr date back at least to Ur III times.

BIBLIOGRAPHY

1897 Winckler, AoF 1/6 p. 547 no. 7 (copy)
1898 King, CT 3 pl. 1 BM 17288 (copy)
1900 Radau, EBH p. 252 (edition)
1907 Thureau-Dangin, SAK pp. 192–93 Dun-gi o (edition)
1922 BM Guide p. 85 no. 66 (study)
1929 Barton, RISA pp. 280–81 Shulgi 15 (edition)
1962 Hallo, HUCA 33 p. 30 Šulgi 14 (study)
1971 Sollberger and Kupper, IRSA IIIA2h (translation)
1986 Kärki, KDDU p. 35 Šulgi 14 (edition)
1990 Gelb and Kienast, Königsinschriften p. 340 Ur 3 (edition)
1991 Steible, NSBW 2 p. 167 Šulgi 14 (edition)

TEXT

1) *a-na* 2) ^{d}ÍD 3) *be-lí-šu*	1–3) For the god Id/Nārum, his lord,
4) šul-gi 5) *da-núm* 6) LUGAL [U]RI$_5$.KI 7) ⌜*ù*⌝ [LUG]AL 8) [*ki-ib-ra-tim*] 9) [*ar-ba-im*] Lacuna	4–9) Šulgi, king of [U]r and [kin]g of [the four quarters] Lacuna

30

A nine-line inscription found on bronze canephors and steatite foundation tablets records Šulgi's construction of the temple of the goddess Ninḫursaga at Susa.

CATALOGUE

Ex.	Museum number	Susa Excavation number (Sb)	Dimensions (cm)	Lines preserved	cpn
Bronze canephors					
1	Sb 2883	7621	23.4×8	2–9	c
2	Sb 2885	7624	24.2×8.2	1–9	c
3	Sb 11461 = AO 7618	7618	25.5×8	2–9	c
4	Sb 11462	—	25.5×8.2	1–9	c
5	Sb 11463	—	25×8	1–9	c
6	Sb 11464	7622	22×8.3	1–2, 4–9	c
7	Sb 11465	7623	25×8	1–9	c
8	Sb 11466	7625	25×8	1–9	c
Steatite foundation tablets					
9	Sb 2884	7636	7.8×4.3	1–9	c
10	Sb 2886	—	7×4.8	1–9	n
11	Sb 6847	—	6.8×5.1	1–9	c
12	Sb 6848	7640	7.1×4.7	1–9	c
13	Sb 6849	—	7.2×4.7	1–9(?)	n
14	Sb 6850	—	7.65×4.8	1–9(?)	n
15	Sb 6851	7638	7.15×4.8	1–9(?)	n
16	Sb 6852	7639	6.7×4.6	1–9	c
17	Sb 6853	—	7.6×4	1–9(?)	n

COMMENTARY

All exemplars were found during the French excavations in the acropolis area at Susa. Information on the museum numbers was kindly provided by A. Echalier through the generous permission of B. André-Salvini.

BIBLIOGRAPHY

1966 Amiet, Elam p. 238 (ex. 2, photo)
1970 Lambert, RA 64 pp. 70–71 no. 4 (ex. 11, photo, edition)
1983 Rashid, Gründungsfiguren p. 33 nos. 150–57 (exs. 1–8, study); pl. 33 no. 151 (ex. 2, drawing)
1986 Kärki, KDDU p. 69 Šulgi 72 (edition)
1991 Steible, NSBW 2 pp. 215–16 Šulgi 73 (exs. 1–8, 11, edition)

TEXT

1) dnin-ḫur-saga
2) šušin.KI-na
3) nin-a-ni
4) dšul-gi
5) nita-kala-ga
6) lugal-uri$_5$.KI-ma
7) lugal-ki-en-gi-ki-uri-ke$_4$
8) é-a-ni
9) mu-na-dù

1–3) For the goddess Ninḫursaga of Susa, his lady,

4–7) Šulgi, mighty man, king of Ur, king of the lands of Sumer and Akkad,

8–9) built her temple for her.

31

An eight-line Sumerian brick inscription records Šulgi's construction of the temple of the god Inšušinak at Susa.

CATALOGUE

Ex.	Museum number	Dimensions (cm)	Lines preserved	cpn
1	Sb —	—	1–4	p
2	Sb —	—	1–8	p
3	Sb 14726	28×23×4	1–8	n
4	Sb 14277	25.5×15×5.5	2 lines	n
5	Sb 14728	20×12×6.5	2 lines	n
6	Sb 14729	20×28×6	7 lines	n

COMMENTARY

The bricks were found in the French excavations of the Inšušinak temple on the acropolis of Susa. Information on exs. 3–6 was kindly provided by A. Echalier with the permission of B. André-Salvini.

Of note is the fact that Šulgi's name appears without the prefixed divine determinative in this brick inscription dealing with the Inšušinak temple whereas, in the corresponding inscription incised on canephors and foundation tablets (E3/2.1.2.32) the DINGIR sign does appear.

BIBLIOGRAPHY

1902 Scheil, MDP 4 p. 8 and pl. 1 no. 4 (ex. 1, photo, edition)
1905 Scheil, MDP 6 p. 20 and pl. 6 no. 1 (ex. 2, photo, edition)
1907 Thureau-Dangin, SAK pp. 190–91 Dun-gi c (ex. 2, edition)
1929 Barton, RISA pp. 276–77 Shulgi 3 (ex. 2, edition)
1962 Hallo, HUCA 33 p. 29 Šulgi 6 (exs. 1–2, study)
1971 Sollberger and Kupper, IRSA IIIA2n (exs. 1–2, translation)
1986 Kärki, KDDU p. 31 Šulgi 6 (exs. 1–2, edition)
1991 Steible, NSBW 2 pp. 160–61 Šulgi 6 (exs. 1–2, edition)

TEXT

1) šul-gi
2) nita-kala-ga
3) lugal-uri$_5$.KI-ma
4) lugal-ki-en-gi-KI-uri-ke$_4$
5) ^{d}NIN-šušin.KI-ra
6) é-a-ni
7) mu-na-dù
8) ki-bé mu-na-gi$_4$

1–4) Šulgi, mighty man, king of Ur, king of the lands of Sumer and Akkad,

5–7) built for the god Inšušinak his temple.

8) He restored it for him.

32

A nine-line inscription found on bronze canephors and foundation tablets deals with Šulgi's construction of the temple of the god Inšušinak at Susa.

CATALOGUE

Ex.	Museum number	Susa Excavation number	Dimensions (cm)	Lines preserved	cpn
Bronze canephors					
1	Sb 2879	7617	25×8.45	1–9	n
2	Sb 2881	7615	24×8.5	1–9	c
3	Sb 11455	7610	24.5×7.9	1–3, 7–9	c
4	Sb 11456	7611	24×8	1–9	c
5	Sb 11457	7612	26×8.5	1–9	c
6	Sb 11458	7613	25.6×8	1–9	c

Ex.	Museum number	Susa Excavation number	Dimensions (cm)	Lines preserved	cpn
7	Sb 11459	7614	25.9×7.7	1–9	c
8	Sb 11460	7616	22.5×7.8	1–9	c
Steatite foundation tablets					
9	Sb 2880	7632	5.85×4.3	1–9	c
10	Sb 2882	7633	5.8×4.2	1–9	n
11	Sb 6854	—	5.9×4.1	1–9	c
12	Sb 6855	7631	6×3.5×1.2	1–9	c
13	Sb 6856	7626	6.2×3.75×1.2	1–9	c
14	Sb 6857	7630	6.3×4.2	1–9	c
15	Sb 6858	—	6.1×4.4×0.8	1–9	c
16	Sb 6859	7629	5.5×4.5	1–9	c
17	Sb 6860	7628	5.85×3.4×1.1	1–9	c

COMMENTARY

Information on the excavation and museum numbers of these pieces was kindly provided by A. Echalier with the permission of B. André-Salvini.

BIBLIOGRAPHY

1905 de Mecquenem, in de Morgan, MDP 7 pp. 61–63 (exs. 1–8, provenance); pl. 11 (exs. 1a, 5a or 6a, photo)
1905 Scheil, MDP 6 pp. 21–22 and pl. 6 no. 2 (ex. ?, photo)
1907 Thureau-Dangin, SAK pp. 192–93 Dun-gi p (edition)
1926 Pézard and Pottier, Catalogue p. 108 no. 236 (exs. 1–8, study)
1929 Barton, RISA pp. 280–81 Shulgi 16 (edition)
1948 Parrot, Tello p. 205 fig. 44d (drawing)
1961 Parrot, Sumer pl. 292c (ex. ?, photo)
1962 Hallo, HUCA 33 p. 30 Šulgi 12 (exs. 1–8, study)
1982 André-Leicknam, Naissance de l'écriture p. 232 (ex. 2a, photo)
1983 Rashid, Gründungsfiguren pp. 33–34 nos.158–65 (exs. 1–8, study); pl. C no. 158 (ex. 1a, photo); pl. 33 nos. 158, 162 (exs. 1a, 5a, drawing)
1986 Kärki, KDDU p. 34 Šulgi 12 (exs. 1–8, edition)
1991 Steible, NSBW 2 pp. 164–65 Šulgi 12 (exs. 1–8, edition)

TEXT

1) ^{d}NIN-šušin
2) lugal-a-ni
3) ^{d}šul-gi
4) nita-kala-ga
5) lugal-uri$_5$.KI-ma
6) lugal-ki-en-gi-ki-uri-ke$_4$
7) a-ar-ke$_4$-éš
8) é-ki-ág-gá-ni
9) mu-na-dù

1–2) For the god Inšušinak, his lord,

3–6) Šulgi, mighty man, king of Ur, king of the lands of Sumer and Akkad,

7–9) built for him A᾿arkeš, his beloved temple.

33

A brick in Berlin bears a fourteen-line building inscription of Šulgi in Akkadian that alludes to his destruction of the lands of Kimaš and Ḫurtum. As noted in the introductory comments for Š 46, this event was commemorated in the name of Š 46.

E3/2.1.2.32.1.8 ^{d}NIN-šušin-ke$_4$.

COMMENTARY

The brick, which is thought to have come from Susa, is in the collection of the Museum für Vor- und Frühgeschichte, Berlin. The text is arranged in one column of fourteen lines.

BIBLIOGRAPHY

1967 von Schuler, BJVF 7 pp. 293–95 and pl. 3 (edition, photo)
1970 Westenholz, AfO 23 p. 27 (study)
1971 Sollberger and Kupper, IRSA IIIA2p (translation)
1986 Kärki, KDDU pp. 68–69 Šulgi 71 (edition)
1990 Gelb and Kienast, Königsinschriften pp. 341–42 Ur 5 (Šulgi 71) (edition)
1991 Steible, NSBW 2 pp. 206–207 Šulgi 63 (edition)

TEXT

1) dšul-gi
2) DINGIR *ma-ti-šu*
3) *da-núm*
4) LUGAL URI$_5$.KI
5) LUGAL *ki-ib-ra-tim*
6) *ar-ba-im*
7) *ì-nu*
8) *ma-at ki-maš*.KI
9) *ù ḫu-ur-tim*.KI
10) *ù-ḫa-li-qú-na*
11) *ḫi-ri-tám*
12) *iš-ku-un*
13) *ù bí-ru-tám*
14) *ib-ni*

1–6) Šulgi, god of his land, the mighty, king of Ur, king of the four quarters,

7–10) when he destroyed the land of Kimaš and Ḫurtum,

11–14) set out a moat and heaped up a pile of corpses.

34

A nine-line Sumerian inscription on a foundation tablet records Šulgi's construction of the temple of the god Šullat and Ḫaniš (a god with a compound name comparable, for example, to *kṯr-w-ḫss* or *šḥr-w-šlm* at Ugarit). His cult centre is unknown.

COMMENTARY

The inscription is incised on a black soapstone tablet that measures 11×6.7 cm, with a thickness that varies from 1.7 to 2.3 cm. The tablet is a purchased piece of unknown provenance; it bears the museum number A 3700 (Chicago). The text is arranged in one column of nine lines.

BIBLIOGRAPHY

1950 Gelb, ArOr 18 1/2 pp. 189–98 and pl. 2 (edition, photo)
1962 Hallo, HUCA 33 p. 31 Šulgi 19 (study)
1971 Sollberger and Kupper, IRSA IIIA2o (translation)
1986 Kärki, KDDU pp. 37–38 Šulgi 19 (edition)
1991 Steible, NSBW 2 pp. 171–72 Šulgi 19 (edition)

TEXT

1) ^{d}*šu-ul-la-at*
2) *ù* ^{d}*ḫa-ni-iš*
3) lugal-a-ni
4) šul-gi
5) nita-kala-ga
6) lugal-uri$_{5}$.KI-ma
7) lugal-ki-en-gi-ki-uri-ke$_{4}$
8) é-a-ni
9) mu-na-dù

1–3) For the god Šullat and Ḫaniš, his lord,

4–7) Šulgi, mighty man, king of Ur, king of the lands of Sumer and Akkad,

8–9) built his temple for him.

Inscriptions Recounting Military Campaigns 35–37

35

An Akkadian inscription known from a later Sammeltafel copy records the campaign of a king in the Diyālā region. The fact that all the other inscriptions on the Sammeltafel, as far as can be determined, deal with Šulgi, strongly suggests that this inscription as well should be attributed to that king.

COMMENTARY

The inscription is found on obv. col. iii′ and rev. col. i of the Pinches Sammeltafel of Šulgi inscriptions.

Obv. iii′ lines 1–2 likely refer to the smashing of river levees; by this stratagem Šulgi was apparently able to entrap the (unnamed) enemy forces in a morass (obv. iii′ lines 3–5). A comparison may be made with the name of year 38 of Ḫammu-rāpi, which records the destruction of Ešnunna by a flood. While the year name has generally been taken to refer to a natural disaster, an alternative view would see it as consequence of a military action. The verb in obv. iii′ line 7 is taken to be derived from *ṭebû*(*m*) "to sink," taken, in an emended text, to be in the D-stem. A parallel to obv. iii′ lines 10–12 is found in lines 43–47 of the Cruciform Monument (Sollberger, JEOL 20 [1967–68] p. 55): [*an-ša-a*]*n*.KI [*ù*] [*ši*$_{4}$*-rí-ḫu-um*].KI *lu* SAG.GIŠ.RA *lu e-be-el* "[Anša]n [and Širiḫum] I did [indeed] conquer and rule."

BIBLIOGRAPHY

1963 Pinches, CT 44 pl. 1 no. 2 (BM 78681, copy)
1990 Gelb and Kienast, Königsinschriften pp. 291–92 Fragment C 7 (BM 78681, edition)

TEXT

Obv. col. ii′
Lacuna
1′) [GU$_{7}$ I$_{7}$-*tur-ùl*]

obv. col. ii′
Lacuna
obv. ii′ 1′) [The banks of the River Diyālā]

Obv. col. iii′	
1) *ù* I_7.*ṭa-ba-an*	obv. iii′ 1–2) and the River Ṭaban he smashed,
2) *iš-bi-ir-ma!*	
3) *ù in* <*a*>-*pá-ri-im*	obv. iii′ 3–5) and in a swamp he annihilated (the enemy).
4) *kà-ma-ra-ma*	
5) *íš-ku-un*	
6) *ma-ta-a-am*	obv. iii′ 6–9) The land *which he inundated*—he smashed his (the enemy's) weapon.
7) *ú*(Text: *i*)-*ṭe*$_4^{te}$-*eb*-<*bu*>-*ma*	
8) *ù* GIŠ.TUKUL-*šu*	
9) *iš-bi-ir*	
10) URU.KI.URU.KI	obv. iii′ 10–12) He conquered (their) cities and ruled (them).
11) *en*-<*a*>-*ra-am* (Text: AḪ)	
12) *i-be-el*	
13) GÌR.NITA.	obv. iii′ 13–16) He appointed his generals ...
14) GÌR.NITA	Lacuna
15) ⸢*íš*⸣-*tá-kà-an*	
16) [...]-x-⸢*šu*⸣	
Lacuna	
Rev. col. i	
Lacuna	Lacuna
1′) [SUḪUŠ]-⸢*šu*⸣	rev. i 1′–2′) May they (the gods ...) tear out his [foundation]
2′) *li-sú-ḫu*	
3′) *ù* ŠE.NUMUN-*šu*	rev. i 3′–4′) and destroy his progeny.
4′) *li-íl-qù-tá* (Text: Á)	
5′) DUMU.NITA *ù* MU	rev. i 5′–6′) May they not grant to him heir or offspring.
6′) *a i-dì-nu-šum*	

36

An inscription found on an Old Babylonian Sammeltafel of royal inscriptions (for the most part they belong to Šulgi) records the capture of an enemy king. Unfortunately, the readings of the captive ruler's name as well as the name of his city are illegible.

COMMENTARY

The inscription is found on col. x 1′–10′ of N 2230+N4006. For more details on the Sammeltafel see E3/2.1.2.2049.

TEXT

Col. x	
1′) ⸢x x x⸣ ḫi-a	x 1′–3′) I took various ... as plunder.
2′) nam-ra-aš	
3′) ḫa-da-ak	
4′) NE(?)-ÉŠ ⸢lugal⸣	x 4′–7′) I took PN, king of GN, as a bound captive
5′) ⸢x x⸣.KI	
6′) LÚ×GÁNA-*tenû*.A	
7′) ḫa-ni-dab_5	
8′) šu-mu ba-ra-ba-ta-è	x 8′) and did not let him escape.
9′) lú <á-nì>-ḫul-<dím-ma>	x 9′–10′) As for the one who g[ives] <ev>il <orders> to ...
10′) íb-[ši-ág-ge_{26}-a]	
Lacuna	Lacuna

37

A second inscription on the aforementioned Old Babylonian Sammeltafel of royal inscriptions mentions a number of toponyms in Elam; it probably commemorated a campaign (of Šulgi?) in the east.

COMMENTARY

The inscription is found on col. xiv 1′–14′ of N 2230+N4006.

TEXT

Col. xiv	
Lacuna	Lacuna
1′) x [... .KI]	xiv 1′) [(PN governor) of GN].
2′) da-wa-a-[x] 3′) PA.<TE.SI> 4′) za-ul.KI	xiv 2′–4′) Dawa-[x], go<vernor> of Zaʾul.
5′) [x] x 6′) [PA].<TE.SI> 7′) [ḫu-ú]ḫ-nu-ri!.KI	xiv 5′–7′) [x] x, [go]<vernor> of [Ḫu]ḫnuri.
8′) [(x) x]-ma-at 9′) [PA].<TE.SI> 10′) [x]-x-lá-ka	xiv 8′–10′) [(x) x]-ma-at, [go]<vernor> of [x]-x-lá-ka.
11′) [...]-x-a 12′) [GÌR].NÍTA 13′) [...]-al.KI 14′) [sa]-bu-um.<KI>	xiv 11′–14′) [...]-x-a, [ge]neral of [...]-al, [Sa]bum
Lacuna	Lacuna

Stele Inscription
38

An Old Babylonian school copy of a Šulgi stele inscription was found in excavations at Tell Harmal.

COMMENTARY

The inscription is found on IM 53977, a clay tablet that measures 6.7×8.6×3 cm. The inscription is bilingual, with (syllabic) Sumerian and Akkadian versions. The two renditions are mixed together in an irregular manner that would appear not to respect the line divisions of an original monument.

The extant Sumerian version is given in column two, the Akkadian version in column three, and a reconstructed version in "normal" (logographic) Sumerian in column one. For clarity of presentation the reconstructed text is not enclosed in square brackets as would normally be the case.

In van Dijk's copy in TIM 9 no. 35, the indented end of his lines 15, 20, and 22 are assigned a separate (consecutive) line number. We have followed Kienast in counting these run-on lines as one line. Thus lines 15, 19, and 22 in this edition correspond to lines 15–16, 20–21, and 24–25 in van Dijk's copy. The line count and content of the translation follow the Akkadian version with some minor restorations from the Sumerian version. In order to more clearly connect the Akkadian line count with the translation, both line numbers have been displayed in bold font. The inscription was not collated.

BIBLIOGRAPHY

1955 van Dijk, Sumer 11 pl. 16 no. 10 (copy)
1962 Hallo, HUCA 33 p. 34 Šulgi 54 (study)
1976 van Dijk, TIM 9 no. 35 (copy)
1986 Kärki, KDDU pp. 59–61 Šulgi 54 (edition)
1990 Gelb and Kienast, Königsinschriften pp. 344–47 Ur C 1 (Šulgi 54) (edition)
1991 Steible, NSBW 2 p. 201 Šulgi 54 (study)

TEXT

(Reconstructed) Logographic Sumerian		(Extant) Syllabic Sumerian		Akkadian	Translation
—	1)	—	**1)**	*si-ma-at da-ri-a-tim* *si-ma-at ta-na-da-*⸢*a*⸣-[*tim*]	**1)** "(A monument) befitting eternity, suitable for praise."
^{d}IŠKUR lugal na-rú-a	2)	^{d}⸢IŠKUR⸣ lú-gal na-DI-a KU GÁ AM	**2)**	⸢*a*⸣-[*na* ^{d}IŠKUR *be*]-*li na-ri-i*[*m*]	**2)** For the god Adad, owner of (this) stele,
^{d}šul-gi	3)	^{d}šul-gi	**4)**	^{d}šul-gi	**4–6)** Šulgi, mighty man, king of Ur, king of the lands of Sumer and Akkad, son of Ur-Nammu (dedicated this stele).
nita-kala-ga	3)	ni-in-ta ka-la-ak-ka	**5)**	*zi-ka-ru-um da-a*[*n*]-*nu-um*	
lugal-uri$_5$.KI-ma	3)	lú-gal ú-ri-ma	**5)**	*šar ú-ri-im*	
lugal ki-en-gi-<ki>-uri	3–4)	lú-g[al]-ki-ì-ki <ki>-ú-ri	**5)**	*šar ma-at šu-mé-ri-im*	
	4)		**6)**	*ù a-ka-di-im*	
dumu-ur-^{d}nammu	4)	du-⸢mu úr⸣-na-⸢am⸣-<<⸢na-am⸣>>-mi	**6)**	*ma-ru* ur-na-am-ma	
lú á nì-ḫul-dím-ma	7)	lu a ni-im-ḫu-lu-di-(erasure)-ma	**8)**	*ša i-na i-da-at le-mu-tim*	**8–9)** As for the one who gives orders to bewitch me,
íb-ši-<ág>-ge$_{26}$-a	7)	ib-ši-<ág>-gi$_6$-ia	**8)**	*up-ša-še*$_{20}$*-e-ia ú-wa-ru*	
nì-dím-ma-mu	9)	ni-im-[d]i-im-ma-mu	**9)**	*ša i-pu-šu*	**9)** who obliterates my handiwork,
íb-zé-re-a	9)	ib-sì(Text: TE)-re-ia	**9)**	*ú-pa-sa-su*	
é-nì-GA-ra	10)	e-ni-⸢im-x⸣-ra	**11)**	[*ša*] ⸢*a-na*⸣ É.NÍG.GA (Text: ŠA)	**11)** who has it brought into a storehouse,
ì-ni-íb-ku$_4$-ku$_4$-dè(?)-a	10)	e-ni-im-ku-ku-ti-e	**11)**	*ú-še-ri-bu-ú*	
lú giš-ḫur	12)	l[ú] [ni]-⸢iš-ḫu-ur⸣	**13)**	*ša ú-ṣa-ra-at*	**13)** who erases the inscription of my stele in the place where I inscribed it,
na-rú-a	12)	⸢na-DI⸣-a	**13)**	*na-ri-ia*	
ki-šúš-šúš-a-mu	12)	ki-su-su-sa-mu	**13)**	*a-šar ú-ṣa-ru*	
šu íb-zi-x-e-dè-a	12)	šu ib-zi-⸢x⸣-e-le-ia	**13)**	*ú-pa-ša-ṭú*	

Logographic Sumerian		Syllabic Sumerian		Akkadian	Translation
lú mu-sar-ra-ba	14)	lú mu-sa-ra-ba	**15)**	*ša šu-mi ša-⸢aṭ-ra-am⸣*	**15)** who erases my name
ki-sar-ra-ba	14)	ki-sa-ra-ba	**15)**	*a-šar ša-aṭ-ru*	where it was written (or)
šu íb-ùr-e-a	14)	šu ib-ùr(Text: TE)-re-ia	**15)**	*i-pa-ši-ṭú ù-ma-ṭú-ú*	*abridges* (it),
mu-ni	14)	mu-ni im-im-áš-re-	**15)**	*ù* MU.NI.IM-šu	**15)** and writes his (own)
bí-íb-sar-re-a		ia	**15)**	*i-ša-ṭà-ru*	name,
áš-bal-a-ba-ke$_4$-eš	16)	a-áš-pa-la-ba-ke	**17)**	*aš-šum er-re-tim*	**17)** (or) who because of
lú-kúr	16)	lú-gu-ur	**17)**	*ša-na-am*	(this) curse instructs
šu ba-an-zi-zi-a	16)	šu ba-an-di-zi-⸢ia⸣(!)	**17)**	*ú-ša-ḫa-a-zu-ú*	another to do so —
lú-bi	18)	lú-bi	**19)**	*a-wi-lum šu-ú*	**19–21)** that man, whether
lugal ḫé-a	18)	lú-gal ḫe-a	**19)**	*lu ša-ar-ru-um*	he be king, *en* priest,
en ḫé-a	18)	in ⸢he⸣-a	**19)**	*lu e-nu-um*	governor, noble, or any
énsi ḫé-a	18)	ì-(Text: DÙ)-in-si ḫe-a	**19)**	*lu i-ši-a-ku-um*	man endowed with life,
ra-bu-um ḫé-a	18)	*ra-bu-um* ḫe-a	**19)**	*ù lu ra-bu-um*	
nam-lú-u$_{18}$-lu	20)	n[a-am-l]u-le	**21)**	*ù lu a-wi-lu-tum*	
mu-ni zi-gál-le	20)	mu-un zi-ga-l[e]	**21)**	*ša a-na ši-ki-in na-pí-iš-⸢tim⸣*	
sa$_4$-a ḫé-a	20)	<mu-ni> ša ḫe-a	**21)**	[*šu*]*-ma-am na-bi-at*	
^{d}en-líl lugal kur-kur-ra-ke$_4$ en ḫé-gál-la	22)	⸢^{d}en-líl⸣ lú-gal- kur-ku-ra-ke i-ḫi-gál-la	**22)**	⸢x⸣ [^{d}*en-líl be-el ma-ta*]*-tim ù ḫe-gá-al*!*-l*[*i-i*]*m*	**22)** may the god Enlil, lord of the lands and of abundance ...
...			**23)**	a gá-ra-am ku-ga in [...] (interpretation unclear; could be Syllabic Sumerian)	**23)** ...

Label Inscriptions 39–49

The "Label Inscriptions" of Šulgi are edited here according to their provenance — the sites are listed in order from south to north.

39

A standard inscription of Šulgi is found on bricks from Ur, and a brick stamp from Diqdiqqah. The text is arranged in one column of four lines.

CATALOGUE

Ex.	Museum number	Excavation number	Registration number	Provenance	Dimensions (cm)	Lines preserved	cpn
Bricks							
1	BM 90005	—	1979-12-20, 6	Ur, "From mounds in the centre of the ruins"	34.5×20.5×9	1–4	c
2	BM 90017	—	1979-12-20, 16	As ex. 1	32.5×20.5×8	1–4	c
3	BM 90276	—	1979-12-20, 169	As ex. 1	20×27×8	1–4	c
4	BM 90379	—	51-10-9, 89R	As ex. 1	13×11×4.5	3–4	c
5	CBS 16463	U 2881a	—	—	35×18×8.5	—	n
6	CBS 16533	U 2881b	—	—	36×36×8	—	n

Ex.	Museum number	Excavation number	Registration number	Provenance	Dimensions (cm)	Lines preserved	cpn
7	UM 84-26-32	—	—	—	29.5×20.5×8	—	n
8	UM 84-26-33	—	—	—	29.5×29.5×7	—	n
9	UM 84-26-34	—	—	—	31×29×6.5	—	n
Brick stamp							
10	IM 92925	U 7847	—	Diqdiqqah	—	1–4	n

BIBLIOGRAPHY

1861 1 R 2 II 1 (exs. 1–4, composite copy)
1872 Smith, TSBA 1 p. 36 (exs. 1–4, translation)
1875 Ménant, Babylone p. 76 (exs. 1–4, translation)
1892 Winckler, KB 3/1 pp. 80–81 Dungi 1 (exs. 1–4, edition)
1899 Bezold, Cat. 5 p. 2233 (exs. 1–3, study)
1905 King, CT 21 pl. 10 BM 90005 (ex. 1, copy)
1907 Thureau-Dangin, SAK pp. 190–91 Dun-gi a (exs. 1–4, edition)
1922 BM Guide p. 60 nos. 57–58 (exs. 1–2, study)
1928 Gadd, UET 1 p. xxiv (exs. 5–6, study)
1929 Barton, RISA pp. 274–75 Shulgi 1 (exs. 1–4, edition)
1962 Hallo, HUCA 33 p. 28 Šulgi 1i, iv (exs. 1–6, study)
1965 Sollberger, UET 8 no. 24 (ex. 10, copy, study)
1971 Sollberger and Kupper, IRSA IIIA2b (exs. 1–6, translation)
1981 Walker, CBI no. 21 (exs. 1–4, study)
1985 Behrens, JCS 37 p. 232 no. 13 (exs. 5–9, study)
1986 Kärki, KDDU pp. 27–28 Šulgi 1b (exs. 1–6, 10, edition)
1991 Steible, NSBW 2 pp. 153–54 Šulgi 1a (exs. 1–10, edition)

TEXT

1) ᵈšul-gi
2) nita-kala-ga
3) lugal-uri₅.KI-ma
4) lugal-ki-en-gi-ki-uri

1–4) Šulgi, mighty man, king of Ur, king of the lands of Sumer and Akkad.

40

A vase inscription from Ur dates to the early part of Šulgi's reign.

COMMENTARY

The inscription is found on a rimmed calcite bowl that measures 12.7×5.4×1.1 cm. It was found in room 12 of the E-nun-maḫ according to the catalogue in UE 6 (no findspot given in the Field Catalogue) and was given the excavation number U 296. It bears the museum number BM 116441 and the registration number 1923-11-10, 26. The text is arranged in one column. The inscription was collated.

BIBLIOGRAPHY

1965 Sollberger, UET 8 no. 22 (copy, study)
1971 Sollberger and Kupper, IRSA IIIA2a (translation)
1986 Kärki, KDDU p. 27 Šulgi 1a (edition)
1991 Braun-Holzinger, Weihgaben p. 186 G 349 (edition)
1991 Steible, NSBW 2 pp. 201–202 Šulgi 55 (edition)

TEXT

1) ⸢d⸣(erasure) šu[l-gi]
2) nita-ka[la-ga]
3) lugal-[uri₅.KI-m[a]

1–3) Šu[lgi], mig[hty] man, king [of Ur].

41

An alabaster vessel fragment from Ur bears a short inscription of Šulgi.

COMMENTARY

The fragment, which measures 4.9×4.5×1.1 cm, was found in room 10 of the E-nun-maḫ under the Kurigalzu level and given the excavation number U 269. It bears the museum number CBS 14944. The preserved text is arranged in one column. The inscription was collated.

BIBLIOGRAPHY

1974 Woolley, UE 6 p. 50 (provenance)
1991 Braun-Holzinger, Weihgaben p. 188 G 361 (edition)
1991 Steible, NSBW 2 p. 215 Šulgi 72 (edition)

TEXT

1) [š]ul-g[i]
2) [ni]ta-kala-g[a]
3) [lu]gal-ur[i$_5$].⸢KI-ma⸣
Lacuna

1–3) [Š]ulg[i], mighty [m]an, [ki]ng of U[r]
Lacuna

42

A standard inscription of Šulgi is found on five drainpipes from Ur. The text is arranged in one column of four lines.

CATALOGUE

Ex.	Museum number	Excavation number	Registration number	Provenance	Dimensions (cm)	Lines preserved	cpn
1	CBS 16525	U 6337a	—	Ur, below the "Šulgi pavement, square T 9" of the Nimin-taba temple	30.8×20.5	1–4	c
2	IM 1259	U 6337b	—	As ex. 1	—	1–4	p
3	IM—	U 6337c	—	As ex. 1	—	1–4	p
4	BM 118730	U 6337d	1927-5-27, 258	As ex. 1	31.3×21.7	1–4	c
5	BM 118729	U 6637e	1927-5-27, 257	As ex. 1	30.8×22	1–4	c

COMMENTARY

Exs. 2–3 are entered in the score from the photo in UE 6 pl. 48c.

BIBLIOGRAPHY

1926 Woolley, AJ 6 pl. LXIa (exs. 1–3, photo)
1962 Hallo, HUCA 33 p. 28 Šulgi 1ii (exs. 1–4, study)
1965 Sollberger, UET 8 no. 23 (exs. 1–5, conflated copy, study)
1974 Woolley, UE 6 pl. 48c (exs. 1–3, photo)
1986 Kärki, KDDU p. 28 Šulgi 1c (exs. 1–5, edition)
1991 Steible, NSBW 2 p. 154 Šulgi 1b (exs. 1–5, edition)

TEXT

1) ^{d}šul-gi
2) nita-kala-ga
3) lugal-uri$_5$.KI-ma
4) lugal-an-ub-da-límmu-ba

1–4) Šulgi, mighty man, king of Ur, king of the four quarters.

43

A fragment of a bowl bears a label inscription of Šulgi.

COMMENTARY

The black steatite bowl fragment, which measures 6.2×3.8 cm, was found in the E-nun-maḫ area, under the pavement of rooms 16–17 Kurigalzu level(?) (or room 11 according to the catalogue in UE 6) and given the excavation number U 280. It bears the museum number BM 116448 and the registration number 1923-11-10, 34. The preserved text is arranged in one column. The inscription was collated.

The bowl was originally inlaid on the side and bottom with small discs of shell; two pieces remain.

BIBLIOGRAPHY

1965 Sollberger, UET 8 no. 26 (copy, study)
1974 Woolley, UE 6 p. 88 (provenance)
1986 Kärki, KDDU p. 66 Šulgi 65 (edition)
1991 Braun-Holzinger, Weihgaben pp. 186–87 G 351 (edition)
1991 Steible, NSBW 2 p. 203 Šulgi 57 (edition)

TEXT

1) ⌜^{d}⌝šul-gi
2) [ni]ta-kala-ga
3) lugal-[uri$_5$.KI-ma]

1–3) Šulgi, mighty [m]an, king [of Ur].

44

A stone fragment gives the name and titles of Šulgi.

COMMENTARY

The fragment was found in the ziqqurrat courtyard and was given the excavation number U 10615. It bears the museum number IM 92931. The preserved text is found in one column. The inscription was not collated.

BIBLIOGRAPHY

1965 Sollberger, UET 8 no. 28 (copy, study)
1986 Kärki, KDDU pp. 66–67 Šulgi 67 (edition)
1991 Braun-Holzinger, Weihgaben p. 187 G 353 (edition)
1991 Steible, NSBW 2 p. 204 Šulgi 59 (edition)

TEXT

1) ^{d}šul-gi
2) nita-kala-ga
3) lugal-uri$_5$.KI-ma
4) lugal-[...]
Lacuna

1–4) Šulgi, mighty man, king of Ur, king of [...]
Lacuna

45

A standard inscription of Šulgi — the text is arranged in one column of four lines — is found on a brick from an Ur III platform that was raised over the Early Dynastic temple oval at Tell al-ʿUbaid. The text is arranged in one column of four lines. As indicated in the introductory remarks for the year Š 20, it likely came from a structure dedicated to the goddess Ninḫursaga of E-nutur.

COMMENTARY

The brick bears the museum number BM 114208 and was given the registration number 1919-10-11,2608. It measures 29.2×20.3×6.3 cm. The inscription was collated from the UE photo.

BIBLIOGRAPHY

1927 Hall, UE 1 pp. 14, 65, 127 and pl. 12 no. 7 (ex. 1, provenance, photo, study)
1930 Hall, Season's Work p. 107 fig. 81 centre (ex. 1, photo)
1962 Hallo, HUCA 33 p. 28 Šulgi 1iii (ex. 1, study)
1971 Sollberger and Kupper, IRSA IIIA2b (translation)
1981 Walker, CBI no. 21 (ex. 1, study)
1986 Kärki, KDDU pp. 27–28 Šulgi 1b (ex. 1, edition)
1991 Steible, NSBW 2 pp. 153–54 Šulgi 1a (edition)

TEXT

1) ^{d}šul-gi
2) nita-kala-ga
3) lugal-uri$_5$.KI-ma
4) lugal-ki-en-gi-ki-uri

1–4) Šulgi, mighty man, king of Ur, king of the lands of Sumer and Akkad.

46

A fragment of a clay jar from Girsu bears a label inscription of Šulgi.

COMMENTARY

The jar fragment, which measures 11.8×8.9 cm, was found in excavations of de Genouillac, and given the excavation number TG 1382 and the museum number AO 12227. The text is arranged in one column of two lines. The inscription was collated.

BIBLIOGRAPHY

1936 de Genouillac, FT 2 pl. XLIV (copy)
1962 Hallo, HUCA 33 p. 32 Šulgi 30 (study)
1986 Kärki, KDDU p. 43 Šulgi 30 (edition)
1991 Braun-Holzinger, Weihgaben p. 185 G 343 (transliteration)
1991 Steible, NSBW 2 p. 187 Šulgi 30 (edition)

TEXT

1) gurun-dug
2) ^{d}šul-gi lugal

1–2) Fruit-jar of king Šulgi.

47

A four-line standard inscription of Šulgi is found on a brick from Tell al-Wilāyah (the ancient name of site is unknown; see the discussion in E3/2.1.6.1042).

COMMENTARY

The brick, which measures 31×31×6.2 cm, was found in the "basin on north side of mound," and given the museum number IM 61278.

BIBLIOGRAPHY

1960 Madhlūm, Sumer 16 p. 91 and pl. 11B [Arabic section] (photo, edition, study)
1971 Sollberger and Kupper, IRSA IIIA2c (translation)
1986 Kärki, KDDU p. 28 Šulgi 1c (edition)
1991 Steible, NSBW 2 p. 154 Šulgi 1b (edition)

TEXT

1) ^{d}šul-gi
2) nita-kala-ga
3) lugal-uri$_5$.KI-ma
4) lugal-an-ub-da-límmu-ba

1–4) Šulgi, mighty man, king of Ur, king of the four quarters.

48

A metal mace-head from Nippur bears a label inscription of Šulgi.

COMMENTARY

The mace-head, which measures 5 cm in diameter and 12 cm in length including the stem, with a stem diameter of 1.65 cm, was found during the first season of the old series of excavations of the University of Pennsylvania at Nippur. It bears the museum number CBS 2489. The preserved text is arranged in one column of four lines.

BIBLIOGRAPHY

1991 Braun-Holzinger, Weihgaben p. 90 MW 13 (transliteration)

TEXT

1) šul-gi
2) nita-kala-ga
3) lugal-uri$_5$.KI-ma
4) ⸢lugal⸣-[ki]-⸢en⸣-[gi-ki]-uri
Lacuna

1–4) Šulgi, mighty man, king of Ur, king of the [lands] of Su[mer] and Akkad
Lacuna

49

A bronze axe from Susa bears the standard four-line inscription of Šulgi.

COMMENTARY

The axe, which measures 12.3×11 cm was found in Chantier 1 of the Ville Royale, in a sarcophagus. It is made of bronze (Sn 7.08; Pb 1.4%). The piece bears the museum number Sb 5634. The inscription, which is arranged in one column, was collated from the published photo.

BIBLIOGRAPHY

1953 de Mecquenem, RA 47 pp. 80–82 no. 4a (edition, drawing)
1958 Deshayes, Syria 35 p. 287 and fig. 3 (photo, translation)
1962 Hallo, HUCA 33 p. 28 Šulgi 1v (study)
1966 Amiet, Elam p. 243 fig. 176 (photo, study)
1969 Calmeyer, Datierbare Bronzen p. 38 §18a (study)
1971 Sollberger and Kupper, IRSA IIIA2b (translation)
1986 Kärki, KDDU pp. 27–28 Šulgi 1b (edition)
1987 Tallon, Métallurgie susienne I p. 138 Type B 2 no. 195 (study)
1991 Braun-Holzinger, Weihgaben p. 90 MW 12 (edition, study)
1991 Steible, NSBW 2 pp. 153–54 Šulgi 1a (edition)

TEXT

1) ^{d}šul-gi
2) nita-kala-ga
3) lugal-uri$_5$.KI-ma
4) lugal-ki-en-gi-ki-uri

1–4) Šulgi, mighty man, king of Ur, king of the lands of Sumer and Akkad.

Weight Stones 50–53

A granite duck weight from J.E. Taylor's excavations at Ur is now housed in the British Museum, registration number 56-9-8, 42, museum number BM 91434. While Lenormant's copy indicates a reading šul-gi for line 2, according to C.B.F. Walker (letter of 16 Dec. 1994): "... I am inclined to agree with his [Berriman's] comment that the rest of the inscription is illegible. Thus I could only read: 10 ma-na/x-x-AN? x x. ... I do not believe that you can safely associate the weight with Shulgi on the basis of the presently surviving inscription ..."

50

A weight stone in the Louvre is incised with an inscription of Šulgi.

COMMENTARY

The form of the weight stone is a four-sided pyramid with a rounded top; it has a symbol of the moon god (a crescent) on its top. The piece measures 6.2 cm in height with a width of 4.5 cm and a thickness of 3.6 cm. It weighs 248 g. The weight stone was formerly in the Collection de Clercq; it is now housed in the Louvre, museum number AO 22187. The inscription was collated from the published photo.

BIBLIOGRAPHY

1903 de Clercq, Collection 2 pp. 83–85 and pl. VIII no. 3 (photo, copy, edition)
1907 Thureau-Dangin, SAK pp. 194–95 Dun-gi s (edition)
1907 Weissbach, ZDMG 61 p. 394 (translation, study)
1929 Barton, RISA pp. 280–81 Shulgi 19 (edition)
1962 Hallo, HUCA 33 p. 34 Šulgi 51i (study)
1971 Sollberger and Kupper, IRSA IIIA2d (translation)
1982 André-Leicknam, Naissance de l'écriture p. 213 no. 152 (photo, study)
1986 Kärki, KDDU pp. 52–53 Šulgi 51 (i) (edition)
1991 Steible, NSBW 2 p. 200 Šulgi 51 (study)

TEXT

1) ^{d}nanna
2) lugal-a-ni
3) ^{d}šul-gi
4) nita-kala-ga
5) lugal-uri$_5$.KI-ma

1–2) For the god Nanna, his lord,

3–6) Šulgi, mighty man, king of Ur, king of the four quarters,

6) lugal-an-ub-da-límmu-ba-ke_4
7) maš ma-na
8) [m]u-na-gi-i[n]

7–8) confirm[ed] (this weight stone to be) one-half mina.

51

A two-mina weight stone of Šulgi is housed in Istanbul.

COMMENTARY

The duck weight weighs 999 g. Since the piece could not be located in Istanbul, its EŞ number is unknown. To judge from Bezold's transliteration, the text is arranged in one column of eight lines.

BIBLIOGRAPHY

1896 Bezold, ZA 11 p. 85 (transliteration)
1900 Radau, EBH p. 249 n. 2 (study)
1907 Weissbach, ZDMG 61 p. 394 no. 2 (study)
1918 Unger, Katalog no. 170 (study)
1962 Hallo, HUCA 33 p. 34 Šulgi 51ii (study)
1986 Kärki, KDDU p. 53 Šulgi 51 (ii) (edition)

TEXT

1) ^{d}nanna
2) lugal-a-ni
3) ^{d}šul-gi
4) nita-kala-ga
5) lugal-uri_5.KI-ma
6) lugal-an-ub-da-límmu-ba
7) min ma-na
8) mu-na-gi-in

1–2) For the god Nanna, his lord,

3–6) Šulgi, mighty man, king of Ur, king of the four quarters,

7–8) confirmed (this weight stone to be) two minas.

52

A diorite duck weight from Ur bears an inscription of Šulgi.

COMMENTARY

The duck weight, which measures 14 cm in length, was found at the south corner of the ziqqurrat terrace and given the excavation number U 7825. It now bears the museum number IM 3580. The piece weighs 2478 g. The text was arranged in one column of eight lines. The inscription was collated from the published photo.

BIBLIOGRAPHY

1927 Woolley, MJ 18 p. 137 right (photo)
1928 Gadd, UET 1 no. 287 (copy, edition)
1962 Hallo, HUCA 33 p. 34 Šulgi 51iii (study)
1962 Strommenger and Hirmer, Mesopotamien pl. 155 and p. 84 (photo, study)
1974 Woolley, UE 6 p. 99 and pl. 48b (photo, study)
1976 Basmachi, Treasures fig. 98 and p. 400 (photo, study)
1980 Amiet, Sumer, Assur, Babylone no. 106 (photo, translation)
1986 Kärki, KDDU p. 53 Šulgi 51 (iii) (edition)

TEXT

1) ^{d}nanna
2) lugal-a-ni
3) ^{d}šul-gi
4) nita-kala-ga
5) lugal-uri$_{5}$.KI-ma
6) lugal-an-ub-da-límmu-ba-ke$_{4}$
7) 5 ma-na
8) mu-na-gi-in

1–2) For the god Nanna, his lord,

3–6) Šulgi, mighty man, king of Ur, king of the four quarters,

7–8) confirmed (this weight stone to be) five minas.

53

A duck weight of Šulgi from Ur was dedicated to the goddess Ningal.

COMMENTARY

The duck weight, which measures 15×6 cm, was found in the Gipar-ku and given the excavation number U 6954. It bears the museum number BM 118552. The text is arranged in one column of six lines. The inscription was collated.

BIBLIOGRAPHY

1928 Gadd, UET 1 no. 55 (copy, edition)
1929 Barton, RISA pp. 364–65 Shulgi 6 (edition)
1962 Hallo, HUCA 33 p. 34 Šulgi 52 (study)
1986 Kärki, KDDU p. 54 Šulgi 52 (edition)
1991 Steible, NSBW 2 p. 200 Šulgi 52 (study)

TEXT

1) ^{d}nin-gal
2) nin-a-ni
3) ^{d}šul-gi
4) nita-kala-ga
5) lugal-uri$_{5}$.KI-ma
6) lugal-an-ub-da-límmu-ba

1–2) For the goddess Ningal, his lady,

3–6) Šulgi, mighty man, king of Ur, king of the four quarters (confirmed this weight-stone).

Votive Inscriptions
(a) Of the King
54–65

(i) Statue Inscriptions
54–57

54

An Old Babylonian tablet from Nippur contains copies of apparent statue inscriptions of Šulgi (on the obverse) and of Išme-Dagān (on the reverse). As noted, the Šulgi text is likely to be connected with the king's famous run between Ur and Nippur that is commemorated in the name of Š 7.

COMMENTARY

The Šulgi inscription appears on the obverse and lines 1–2 of the reverse of Ni 2432 (Istanbul). Normally Ur III statue inscriptions end with a dedicatory clause a mu-na-ru (see, for example E3/2.1.4.3 vi 33), followed by a curse formula (see E3/2.1.4.3 vi 34–vii 16). In this tablet the curse formula appears only after the second inscription, which concerns Išme-Dagān. As noted by Klein, Studies Artzi, pp. 77–79, the text shows a number of orthographic peculiarities thought to belong to a pre-Old Babylonian (Ur III?) scribal tradition.

In line 1 we have taken u_4 to be equivalent to Akk. *ūmu(m)* "storm." In line 2 we understand Sum. mir-ru as equivalent to Sum. mir = Akk. *meḫû(m)* "violent storm." In line 7 we take muš-idim-ma to be Akk. *kurṣindu(m)* "a kind of snake." Since *kurṣindu(m)* also denotes "plate(s) of armour" we have tentatively translated "snake *with scales*." Line 16 finds a parallel in Šulgi C lines 134–35 (ms. Klein): ur-sag-ga[l]-galkal[am-m]a-ke_4-ne/ kala-ga l[ú]-Á.TUKU kur-kur-ta [i]gi-sag-gá-na "The great heroes of the land, the mighty, the strong m[en] who were selected from all the lands." Line 17 is comparable to line 49 of the same tablet (Išme-Dagān text) á-na bad-rá-a-ba gá-gá-da-na sù-bi-šè mu-ul_4-ul_4-re "when he makes his limbs(?) spread wide he speeds far away." In line 21 we have taken sag ... sum to be equivalent to Akk. *ḫâšû(m)* "to move quickly," rather than *paqādu(m)* "to entrust." In line 21 we read sá ... gar *malāku(m)* "to come to a decision," rather than di ... gar "to establish justice." If the reading of the sign ⌜sig⌝ in line 28 is correct, it would recall line 75 of Šulgi A: ^{d}utu é-a-ni-šè igi ì-gá-gá-dè "(Before) sunset (lit. [Before] Utu set his face toward his house)."

BIBLIOGRAPHY

1924 Chiera, SRT no. 13 (copy)
1957 Kramer, ZA 52 p. 82 notes to no. 13 (study)
1965 Römer, SKIZ pp. 18–20 (edition [of comparable Išme-Dagān text])
1981 Klein, Three Šulgi Hymns p. 42 n. 81 and pp. 239–40 (partial edition, study)
1983 Frayne, JAOS 103 pp. 744–45 (study)
1985 Klein, Beer-Sheva 2 pp. 7*–38* (edition, study)
1990 Klein, in Studies Artzi pp. 77–79 (partial translation)
1990 Ludwig, Išme-Dagan pp. 75–89 (edition)

1) ^{d}en-líl u_4-è ÉŠ x KA [...]	1) The god Enlil, the storm(?) coming forth ...,
2) mir-ru-gal-^{d}a-nun-ke_4-ne [...]	2) violent storm of the Anuna gods ...,
3) ^{d}šul-gi ušum ní-gù[ru ...]	3) (for) Šulgi, the fearso[me] serpent ...,
4) lugal šu-du_{11}-ga-ni-ir IG[I](?) x x [...]	4) (for) the king, his (Enlil's) creation, ... [(the god Enlil) did such-and-such].
5) ne-gal-gal x [...]	5) (Enlil[?]) who [*possesses*] great *strength* ...

6) za-pa-ág-ni an-ki [x (x)]-bi-a gá(?) [...]
7) é-kur-gal muš-idim-ma me-x [...]
8) dur-an-ki giri$_{11}$-zal-a me-ul ba-til n[am-...]
9) sig$_4$ nun ki-gar-ra-ba GIŠ.ísimu.SAR-bi u$_4$ sù-sù-u$_5$
10) ^{d}šul-gi bala-nam-ḫé ba-tu-da šà-ta <nam>-gal mu-tar
11) un ka téš-a sì-ì
12) sù-ud-bi lugal-šár-ra-ba-ke$_4$
13) du$_{10}$-tuku u$_4$-mar-uru$_5$ zà-še-ni nu-til-e
14) kas$_4$ á-dam-á-dam-ta è-a
15) ḫu-luḫ-e kas$_4$-kas$_4$-e ḫuš-sà-à[m]
16) un-ta igi-sag$_5$(ŠID)-gá <lú>-ù-su-bi sag x [...]
17) á-AN-bad-rá-a bar-ra-ni-šè [...]
18) ^{d}šul-gi nì-gir$_5$-re(?) an-úr(?)-ta gá-gá-gá-d[am]
19) nam-a-nun-gál-la-né-eš á na-[x-n]i-ŠU.PEŠ$_5$(?).ŠU.PEŠ$_5$(?)-e
20) nu-kúš-ù kaskal-e bí-x-[...]-DI.DI
21) sag-gi$_6$-ga(Text: I)-a lugal-na-me sag nu-sum sá ⌜gal⌝-éš na-an-gar
22) u$_4$ giri$_{17}$-zal-a-aš è-a dungu(IM.DIRI) šeg$_x$(IM.A)-ka(?) gar-ra
23) nibru.KI ki-ùr-ta na-kas$_4$
24) èš-úri.KI é-temen-ní-gùru-šè
25) ^{d}nanna únu(Text: GUR$_8$.UNUG) kin-nim bur-nun su$_8$-ga-né sá-ul nam-mi-in-du$_{11}$
26) u$_4$-ne-[a]-a [u$_4$]-ḪI nam im-mi-in-tar!
27) IM.GÁNA.[U]Ḫ.[ME.U I]M.dal-ḫa-mun šu bar-àm
28) ^{d}utu-⌜e⌝(?) ⌜sig⌝(?)-ge-éš nam-ši-x
29) a-ne é-kur-za-gìn-šè na-gur(?)
30) u$_4$-ti-la-šè ur-sag-e-ne-e
31) ^{d}šul-gi-ra na[m]-maḫ-gal-gal-a-ni a-re-éš pà-dé-dè
32) x-alan(?)-u$_4$-sù-rá mu-da-rí-ka-na
33) mul-an-né-éš(?) bí-in-gùn(?)
34) a-a-^{d}en-líl <inim>-maḫ-di nu-kúr-r[a]
35) igi-du$_{10}$ nì-giri$_{17}$-zal si-a-ni-šè(Text: TÚG) nam-nun-na mu-ni-in-gub

6) whose roar [*covers*] heaven and earth ...,
7) (in) great Ekur, the snake *with scales* ...,
8) (in) Duranki, where the primordial *mes* ... in joy,
9) for the sapling (Šulgi) of the brickwork founded by the prince, whose days (of life) are long,
10) (for) Šulgi, who was born for a prosperous reign, (Enlil) determined, (even) from birth, a great <destiny> (namely, to be):
11) (one) who makes the people obedient,
12) king of their (the people's) multitudes, *forever*,
13) a runner, the (devastating) flood-storm, whose shoulders (or hips[?]) keep going,
14) who surpasses *all men* (lit.: [all] the villagers) in the race,
15) who is frightful in (his) turbulence and rush,
16) who (among the heroes) chosen by the people (is) their strong <man> ...,
17) (when) he makes (his) limbs(?) spread wide [*he hastens*] to *his outer limits.*
18) Šulgi ... from the *horizon* ...,
19) because of his noble strength, (his) arms ...
20) the untiring one, who ... at the road.
21) Among all the black-headed (people) no king had (ever) moved (so) quickly; (thus) he (Šulgi) reached a great decision.
22) On a day that came forth for rejoicing, that was appointed for rain clouds,
23–24) (Šulgi) ran from Ki-ur (of) Nippur to the E-temen-ni-guru (of) shrine Ur.
25) Having set up (before) the god Nanna the princely bowls (in) the dining hall (for) the morning meal, he (Šulgi) did indeed provide there the ancient regular offerings.
26) On that day, a [day] *of darkness* was *decreed.*
27) A storm wind from the south, a whirlwind, was unleashed.
28) As the sun *was low* (in the sky) ...
29) He (Šulgi) *returned* to shining Ekur.
30–31) In order that heroes might forever sing the praises of the great distinguished (deeds) of Šulgi,
32–33) (Šulgi) made (this inscription[?]) gleam like the stars of heaven on an everlasting ... image of himself (with) enduring fame.
34) (Before) father Enlil, whose lofty <command> is immutable,
35) before his (Enlil's) happy face which is filled with joy, (Šulgi) set up (this statue) in a noble fashion.

55

A statuette from Telloh, known from two fragments, one in Paris and the other in Istanbul, bears a votive inscription of Šulgi to the god Igalim.

COMMENTARY

The green steatite statuette is formed by the join of AO 36 (frgm. 1) + EŞ 438 (frgm. 2); the connection between the two pieces was discovered by C. Suter, who communicated the results of her research at the 202nd Annual Meeting of the American Oriental Society on March 31, 1992. The statuette measures 17.2 cm in height and 5.1 cm at the widest point. The inscription was collated. Notes on the statuette were kindly provided to the author by C. Suter in advance of her own publication of the joined fragments. Lines 1–9 are found in col. i, line 10 in col. ii. The Paris fragment was collated.

BIBLIOGRAPHY

1884–1912 de Sarzec, Découvertes 1 p. 156 (frgm. 1, study); pp. 341–42 and Découvertes 2 pl. 21bis no. 3 (frgm. 2, photo, study)
1902 Heuzey, Catalogue Louvre no. 101 (frgm. 1, study)
1926 Nassouhi, Guide sommaire p. 29 § A–1 (ex. 1, study)
1948 Parrot, Tello p. 222 (frgm. 1, study); p. 222 and n. 354 and fig. 46h (frgm. 2, study, drawing)
1960 Strommenger, Bagh. Mitt. 1 p. 69 n. 433 (frgm. 1, study); p. 69 n. 435 (frgm. 2, study)
1974 Barrelet, CRRA 19 p. 96 F 90 and F 91 (frgms. 1–2, study); pl. I no. F 91 (frgm. 1, photo); p. 130 (frgm. 1, copy, edition [by Durand])
1981 Spycket, Statuaire p. 206 n. 107 (frgm. 1, study); p. 206 n. 108 and pl. 141 (frgm. 2, photo, study)
1991 Braun-Holzinger, Weihgaben p. 272 St 147 (frgm. 2, study); p. 274 St 154 (frgm. 1, edition)
1991 Steible, NSBW 2 pp. 211–12 and pls. XVII–XVIII Šulgi 69 (frgm. 1, photo, edition)
1991–93 Suter, JCS 43–45 pp. 63–70 (frgms. 1–2, photo, edition, study)

TEXT

1) ^{d}i[g]-alim
2) dumu-k[i-á]g-
3) ^{d}n[in-gír-s]u-ka
4) [lu]gal-[a]-ni
5) ^{d}šu[l-g]i
6) [ni]ta-[k]ala-ga
7) [lu]gal-[ŠEŠ].⌜AB⌝.[KI-ma]
8) [lu]gal-ki-en-g[i]-ki-uri-k[e$_4$]
9) nam-ti-la-[ni-šè]
10) [a] mu-n[a-ru]

1–4) For the god I[g]alim, be[lov]ed son [of] the god N[ingirs]u, [h]is [lo]rd,

5–8) Šu[lgi], [mi]ghty [m]an, [k]ing [of] [U]r, [ki]ng of the lands of Sum[e]r and Akkad,

9–10) [dedicated] (this statuette) for hi[s] (own) life.

56

An eleven-line Sumerian dedicatory inscription of Šulgi appears on a statue of the king which was found in the Nimin-taba temple at Ur.

COMMENTARY

The text is incised on a diorite statue fragment which measures 26 cm in height. It was found in room 3 of the Nimin-taba temple, near the temenos wall (EH sq. T/10, beside the socle U 6276 to which it probably belongs) and given the excavation number U 6306. The statue fragment represents a standing male figure; the head, left half of the upper body, and lower part of the body are now missing. The statue fragment bears the museum number IM 1173. The inscription, which was collated from the published photo, is inscribed on the back of the statue. For the reading of ii 4, see Steible, NSBW 2 p. 178, n. 2.

BIBLIOGRAPHY

1926 Woolley, AJ 6 pl. 51 c (photo)
1928 Gadd, UET 1 no. 52 (copy, edition)
1929 Barton, RISA pp. 364–65 Shulgi 3 (edition)
1962 Hallo, HUCA 33 p. 31 Šulgi 25 (study)
1967 Moortgat, Kunst pl. 178 (photo)
1968 Spycket, Statues p. 61 (study)
1974 Spycket, in CRRA 19 p. 95 F 89 (study)
1974 Woolley, UE 6 p. 41 and pl. 47b (photo, study)
1975 Orthmann (ed.), Der alte Orient pls. 63a+b (photos)
1976 Basmachi, Treasures fig. 65 (photo)
1981 Spycket, Statuaire p. 205 n. 106 (study)
1986 Kärki, KDDU pp. 40–41 Šulgi 25 (edition)
1989 Zettler, in Behrens, et al. (eds.) Studies Sjöberg p. 69 fig. 2 (photo)
1991 Braun-Holzinger, Weihgaben pp. 272–73 St 150 (edition, study)
1991 Steible, NSBW 2 pp. 177–78 Šulgi 25 (edition)

TEXT

Col. i
1) ^{d}nanna
2) [lu]gal-a-ni
3) [š]ul-gi
4) [ni]ta-kala-ga
5) [lu]gal-uri$_{5}$.KI-ma
6) [lugal-ki]-⌜en⌝-[gi-ki-uri-ke$_{4}$]
Lacuna(?)
Col. ii
1) nam-ti-la-ni-šè
2) a mu-na-ru
3) alan-ba
4) ^{d}nanna bàd-[(x)-m]u
5) [mu-bi-im]

i 1–2) For the god Nanna, his [lo]rd,

i 3–6) [Š]ulgi, mighty [ma]n, [k]ing of Ur, [king of the lands] of Su[mer and Akkad]
Lacuna(?)

ii 1–2) dedicated (this statue) for his (own) life.

ii 3–5) [The name] of this statue [is]: "The god Nanna is my (...) fortress."

57

A diorite statue was dedicated by Šulgi to the goddess Ninsuna of Ur.

COMMENTARY

The diorite statue fragment, which measures 14×9 cm, was found in room ES 2 of the Gipar-ku of Nabonidus, the "museum of Bel-Shalti-Nannar," and given the excavation number U 2770. It bears the museum number IM 939. Although Hallo (HUCA 33 [1962] p. 31 Šulgi 27) referred to a published photo of this inscription, the citation actually refers to the statue edited as E3/2.1.2.56 in this volume. The extant text is apparently arranged in one column. It was not available for collation purposes.

Bearing in mind the frequent correlations between temporal clauses in royal inscriptions and year names, line 1′ may possibly refer to the putting in order of "the sustenance fields (and) accounts of the temple of the gods Enlil and Ninlil" mentioned in the year name Š 21 (see discussion of Šulgi year names above).

BIBLIOGRAPHY

1925 Woolley, AJ 5 p. 383 (provenance)
1928 Gadd, UET 1 no. 53 (copy, edition)
1929 Barton, RISA pp. 364–65 Shulgi 4 (edition)
1962 Hallo, HUCA 33 p. 31 Šulgi 27 (study)
1962 Woolley, UE 9 p. 17 (provenance)
1986 Kärki, KDDU p. 41 Šulgi 27 (edition)
1991 Braun-Holzinger, Weihgaben p. 273 St 151 (edition)
1991 Steible, NSBW 2 pp. 183–84 Šulgi 27 (edition)

TEXT

Lacuna
1′) ⸢ù á-šuku!⸣-[ra-ke$_4$] si m[u-sá-a]
2′) ^{d}šul-g[i]
3′) nita-kala-g[a]
4′) lugal-ur[i$_5$].KI-ma
5′) lugal-an-ub-da-límmu-ba-ke$_4$
6′) ^{d}nin-súna-u[r]i$_5$.KI-m[a-ra]
7′) [i]n-na-[ba]

Lacuna
1′) [(when) the ...] and the sustenance fields were put in [order],
2′–3′) Šulg[i], might[y] man,
4′–5′) king of U[r], king of the four quarters,
6′–7′) [presented] (this statue) to the goddess Ninsuna o[f] U[r].

(ii) Beads
58–60

The bead inscriptions of Šulgi are edited according to the alphabetical order of the names of the divine recipients. The beads may have originally formed parts of necklaces which once graced statues of the goddesses. These were designated in the ancient texts as ḫùl(KIB), NA$_4$.ḫar-gú-gil or NA$_4$.ad-gú = Akkadian *ḫullu*(*m*). An earring (nì-géštu) for a statue of Amar-Suena is mentioned in an archival text from Umma (see Kang, SETUA no. 119).

58

A carnelian bead bears an eight-line inscription of Šulgi dedicated to the goddess Ningal.

COMMENTARY

The bead was found at Susa and measures 5.8×2.7 cm. The piece bears the museum numbers Sb 6627 and AO 9063. Lines 1–5 are found in column i and lines 6–8 in col. ii.

BIBLIOGRAPHY

1905 Scheil, MDP 6 p. 22 (copy, edition)
1907 Thureau-Dangin, SAK pp. 194–95 Dun-gi y (edition)
1911 Janneau, Dynastie p. 38 (copy, edition)
1923 Delaporte, Louvre 2 p. 179 A. 815 (edition)
1928 Barton, RISA pp. 282–83 Shulgi 26 (edition)
1962 Hallo, HUCA 33 p. 33 Šulgi 43 (study)
1986 Kärki, KDDU p. 49 Šulgi 43 (edition)
1991 Braun-Holzinger, Weihgaben p. 367 P 11 (edition)
1991 Steible, NSBW 2 pp. 197–98 Šulgi 43 (edition)

TEXT

1) ^{d}nin-gal
2) ama-ni-ir
3) ^{d}šul-gi
4) dingir-kalam-ma-na
5) lugal-uri$_5$.KI-ma

1–2) For the goddess Ningal, his mother,
3–5) Šulgi, god of his land, king of Ur,

6) lugal-an-ub-da-límmu-ba-ke_4
7) nam-ti-la-ni-šè
8) a mu-na-ru

6) king of the four quarters,
7–8) dedicated (this bead) for his (own) life.

59

A carnelian bead bears a seven-line inscription of Šulgi dedicated to the goddess Ninḫursaga.

COMMENTARY

The bead, which measures 2.9×0.6 cm, is housed in the Metropolitan Museum of Art in New York and bears the museum number MMA 41.160.334. It is edited here for the first time through the kind permission of P.O. Harper, Curator, Department of Ancient Near Eastern Art. Lines 1–6 are in col. i and line 7 in col. ii. The inscription was collated.

BIBLIOGRAPHY

1962 Hallo, HUCA 33 p. 33 Šulgi 44 (study)
1986 Kärki, KDDU p. 49 Šulgi 44 (study)
1991 Steible, NSBW 2 p. 198 Šulgi 44 (study)

TEXT

1) ^{d}nin-ḫur-saga
2) nin-a-ni
3) ^{d}šul-gi
4) nita-kala-ga
5) lugal-uri_5.KI-ma
6) [l]ugal-ki-en-[g]i-ki-uri-ke_4
7) a mu-na-[ru]

1–2) For the goddess Ninḫursaga, his lady,

3–6) Šulgi, mighty man, king of Ur, [k]ing of the lands of Su[m]er and Akkad,

7) dedi[cated] (this bead).

60

A carnelian bead bears an eight-line inscription of Šulgi dedicated to the goddess Ninlil.

COMMENTARY

The bead, which measures 7 cm in length with a maximum diameter of 0.5 cm, is numbered Q a 37 in the Southesk collection. Its original provenance is unknown. It was first examined by Lehmann-Haupt in a dealer's shop in Arbela in 1899 and subsequently purchased by the Earl of Southesk. Lines 1–5 are arranged in col. i, lines 6–8 in col. ii. The inscription was not collated. The a of line 8 is misssing from the copy given in Lehmann-Haupt, Mat. pp. 5–6 no. 1.

BIBLIOGRAPHY

1906 Lehmann-Haupt, Mat., pp. 5–6 no. 1 (copy, edition)
1908 Southesk, Catalogue II p. 57 (copy, transliteration)
1962 Hallo, HUCA 33 p. 33 Šulgi 45 (study)
1986 Kärki, KDDU pp. 49–50 Šulgi 45 (edition)
1991 Braun-Holzinger, Weihgaben p. 367 P 13 (edition)
1991 Steible, NSBW 2 p. 198 Šulgi 45 (edition)

TEXT

1) ^{d}nin-líl 2) nin-a-ni	1–2) For the goddess Ninlil, his lady,
3) ^{d}šul-gi 4) nita-kala-ga 5) lugal-uri$_{5}$.KI-ma 6) lugal-ki-en-gi-ki-uri-ke$_{4}$	3–6) Šulgi, mighty man, king of Ur, king of the lands of Sumer and Akkad
7) nam-ti-la-ni-šè 8) a mu-na-ru	7–8) dedicated (this bead) for his (own) life.

(iii) Mace-head

61

A mace-head that was once part of a private collection bears a dedicatory inscription of Šulgi for the goddess Nanše. It may have come from her temple in Girsu.

COMMENTARY

This mottled marble mace-head measures 7 cm in height, with a maximum diameter of 6 cm. The extant text is arranged in one column. Its present whereabouts are unknown.

BIBLIOGRAPHY

1909 Toscanne, RA 7 p. 59 (copy, edition)
1911 Janneau, Dynastie pp. 8–9 (copy, edition)
1929 Barton, RISA pp. 282–83 Shulgi 27 (edition)
1954 Cocquerillat, RA 45 p. 22 no. 13 (study)
1962 Hallo, HUCA 33 p. 33 Šulgi 39 (study)
1986 Kärki, KDDU p. 47 Šulgi 39 (edition)
1991 Braun-Holzinger, Weihgaben pp. 60–61 K 82 (edition)
1991 Steible, NSBW 2 pp. 193–94 Šulgi 39 (edition)

TEXT

1) ^{d}nanše 2) nin-a-ni	1–2) For the goddess Nanše, his lady,
3) šul-g[i] 4) nita-ka[la-ga] 5) lugal-[uri$_{5}$.KI-ma] Lacuna	3–5) Šulgi, mighty man, king of [Ur] Lacuna

(iv) Other Objects 62–65

The objects are edited in alphabetical order according to the name of the divine recipient.

62

A gold earring was dedicated to the goddess Geštinana by Šulgi.

COMMENTARY

The gold earring, which measures 4.9×2.8 cm, was in the Foroughi Collection in Teheran; its present whereabouts are unknown. The inscription was collated from the published photo.

We may note here, in connection with the translation of line 2, the contention of P. Steinkeller (ASJ 3 [1981] p. 78): "that, after SI.A-tum (Šulgi's mother) had died, Šulgi established her official cult, in which she was venerated as one of the personifications of Geštinanna." Also to be noted are various references in the archival sources to forms of Geštinana: geštinana-ama-lugal (WHM 647: Kang, SETUA no. 258, line 12); geštinana-nin (IB 119: Cagni and Pettinato, MVN 4 no. 98 line 7); geštinana-lugal (IB 119: Cagni and Pettinato, MVN 4 no. 98 line 9 and YBC 13727, P. Michalowski, ASJ 4 [1982] p. 140 no. 2 line 6). The references cited come from Sallaberger, Kalender 1 p. 44.

The text is arranged in the following format:

First Lobe	1) ^{d}geštin-an-na 2) dumu-ni	3) šul-gi 4) nita-kala-ga
Second Lobe	5) lugal-uri$_5$.KI-ma	6) lugal-ki-en-gi-ki-uri-ke$_4$
Third Lobe	7) nam-ti-la-ni-šè	8) a mu-na-ru

BIBLIOGRAPHY

1973 Amiet and Lambert, RA 67 pp. 159–62 § II (photo, copy, edition)
1981 Steinkeller, ASJ 3 p. 78 (edition)
1986 Kärki, KDDU pp. 69–70 Šulgi 73 (edition)
1991 Steible, NSBW 2 pp. 212–14 Šulgi 70 (edition)

TEXT

1) ^{d}geštin-an-na
2) dumu-ni
3) šul-gi
4) nita-kala-ga
5) lugal-uri$_5$.KI-ma
6) lugal-ki-en-gi-ki-uri-ke$_4$
7) nam-ti-la-ni-šè
8) a mu-na-ru

1) To the goddess Geštinana,
2–6) her offspring, Šulgi, mighty man, king of Ur, king of the lands of Sumer and Akkad,
7–8) dedicated (this earring) for his (own) life.

63

A Sumerian votive inscription, known from a stone tablet fragment found at Susa, mentions the restoration of the city of Dēr. While no royal name is extant in the text, Šulgi's various connections with the city of Dēr (see the discussion to Šulgi year 6a) argue for an attribution of the inscription to Šulgi.

COMMENTARY

The present whereabouts of this tablet fragment are unknown. The tablet may have originally accompanied a cult object dedicated by the king. If so, it would be comparable to the [im-sa]r-ra "inscribed tablet" which likely was once affixed to a statue of the Larsa king Sîn-iddinam (see the comments of van Dijk, JCS 19 [1965] p. 5). The inscription was presumably dedicated to the god Ištarān.

BIBLIOGRAPHY

1902 Scheil, MDP 4 p. 3 and pl. 1 no. 3 (photo, edition)
1907 Thureau-Dangin, SAK pp. 174–75 XVII Herrscher von Dêr 1 Unbekannter Fürst (edition)
1929 Barton, RISA pp. 166–67 Dur-ili (Der) 1. Unknown Ruler (edition)

TEXT

Col. i (missing)
Col. ii
1) [u_4 é](?)-ki-ág-gá-ni
2) [mu]-na-dù-a
3) BÀD.AN.KI
4) uru-ki-ág-gá-ni
5) ki-bé mu-na-gi_4-a
6) nam-ti-la-ni-⌜šè⌝
7) a mu-na-[ru]

ii 1–2) [When] he [b]uilt his Ištarān's[?]) beloved [temple](?) for him
ii 3–5) and restored Dēr, his beloved city,
ii 6–7) he dedi[cated] (this object) for his (own) life.

64

A Sumerian inscription that mentions the E-meslam temple in a broken context is found on the Pinches Sammeltafel of Šulgi inscriptions (see E3/2.1.2.25). It likely gives the text of a votive inscription of Šulgi.

COMMENTARY

The inscription is found on rev. col. iii of BM 78681+139969. Because the tablet is broken, the nature of the object dedicated by Šulgi is unclear. The fact that it is described as being made of gold and silver (iii 11′) and is said to be "fashioned by Šulgi" (iii 13′–14′) suggests that it was some kind of movable cult object. If we were to examine the archival sources to find a possible connection with this inscription, then a Drehem text (FLP 1076: Sigrist, MVN 13 no. 682) dated vi Š 46 would come to mind. It records a royal dedication (line 7: a-ru-a lugal) of a golden *assammû* vessel (lines 1–2: [an]-za-am-kù-babbar) to the god Meslamta-eʾa, "lord of Kutha" (lugal-gu-du$_8$-a.KI). According to CAD A/2 p. 340 sub *assamû* the object in question was "a large drinking vessel, usually made of metal."

The epithets found in the first section of the text would accord well with an identification of the divine recipient as being Meslamta-eʾa. It would also conform with the fact that most of the other inscriptions on the Sammeltafel are dedicated to Nergal. For the epithet of iii 5′ we may note Meslamta-eʾa's designation *māḫira lā īšû* "who has no rival"; for iii 6′–8′, cf. the phrase *dā ʾiku lemnūti* "who kills the evil-doer" (for both terms, see Tallqvist, Götterepitheta p. 375). For lines 15′–16′, cf. E3/2.1.3.6 lines 15–16: ki-sískur-ra-ka-na nu-šilig-ge "(which) never cease in his place of offerings."

TEXT

Lacuna
Rev. col. iii
1′) [...] x x [...]
2′) [...] [a]ḫ(?) [...]
3′) [...] x um [(x)]
4′) [...] sag-b[i](?)
5′) [...] x am(?)-gi$_4$-a Gloss: [*l*]*a im-ma-ḫa-ru*
6′) [lú]-ḫul
7′) [sa]g-bi
8′) [im-m]i-ra
9′) [lugal-a-n]i-ir
10′) [...]-ni-in-dib
11′) [kù-GI] kù-babbar
12′) [é-mes]-lam-ma
13′) [(^{d})šul-g]i-re
14′) [bí]-in-dím-e-a
15′) [x] x-ga-ni
16′) [gá-la nu]-dag-e-dè
17′) [nam-n]ir-ba
18′) [u$_4$-sù-r]á-aš
19′) [bí]-in-gub
20′) [gú]-du$_8$.a.KI
21′) [...] BI
22′) [...] x
Lacuna

Lacuna
iii 1′–3′ [For the god Meslamta-eʾa(?)] who ...
iii 4′–5′) whose ... cannot be withstood,
iii 6′–8′) who smites the [he]ad of the evil-[doer],
iii 9′) for [h]is [lord],
iii 10′) ...
iii 11′–14′) the [gold] (and) silver of [E-mes]lam which [Šulg]i fashioned
iii 15′–19′) he set up in a n[oble] manner, [fore]ver, in order that his ... might not [ce]ase.
iii 20′–22′) [Ku]tha ...
Lacuna

65

A copper half-figure of a bird, with the head missing, bears an Akkadian inscription that mentions king Šulgi.

COMMENTARY

The provenance of this object is unknown; it bears the museum number CBS 15501. The object measures 13 cm in height and 10 cm in width. The inscription was collated from the published photo. The preserved text is arranged in one column.

Since the text does not begin with the royal name, it apparently is not a label inscription. Because it does not contain the phrase *ana balāṭ* "for the life" before Šulgi's name, it apparently is not an object dedicated for the life of the king. Our expectation, then, was that it was a piece dedicated by Šulgi to some god or goddess.

BIBLIOGRAPHY

1914 Poebel, PBS 5 no. 41 (photo, copy)
1961 Gelb, MAD 2[2] p. 16 § 1a (study)
1962 Hallo, HUCA 33 p. 32 Šulgi 36 (study)
1986 Kärki, KDDU p. 46 Šulgi 36 (edition)
1990 Gelb and Kienast, Königsinschriften p. 341 Ur 4 (Šulgi 36) (edition)
1991 Braun-Holzinger, Weihgaben p. 379 Varia 13 (edition)
1991 Steible, NSBW 2 pp. 191–92 Šulgi 36 (edition)

TEXT

Lacuna
1′) [...] ⌜x⌝ [...]
2′) [...] NE.IGI
3′) [(ᵈ)šu]l-g[i]
4′) [*da-núm*]
5′) [LUGAL U]RI₅.KI
6′) [*ù*] LUGAL
7′) [*ki-ib*]-*ra-tim*
8′) [*ar-ba*]-*im*
9′) [...] ⌜x⌝
Lacuna

Lacuna
1′–2′) [To the god/goddess ...] ...

3′–9′) [Šu]lgi, [the mighty, king of U]r [and] the [fou]r [quar]ters, ...
Lacuna

Votive and Seal Inscriptions (b) Of the Royal Family and Their Servants 66–97

The names of Šulgi's wives (noted in Sumerian as either dam or nin), his *lukur*s (normally translated as "consort" but in some cases to be interpreted as "wife"), and many of his children, are known from the extensive Ur III archival texts at our disposal.

The following register is based on an unpublished catalogue of D. Owen entitled "The Royal Family of Ur [Preliminary List of Sources]." It replaces the earlier study by N. Schneider, "Die 'Königskinder' des Herrscherhauses von Ur III," Orientalia NS 12 (1943) pp. 185–91. I am thankful to Dr. Owen for his kind permission to cite the attestations to the Ur III royal family collected by him in this volume. The same roster (with references restricted to the Drehem texts) is given in Sigrist, Drehem p. 361, n. 41.

In most cases in this list (and others given for the succeeding Ur III kings) a prince or princess has been assigned to a particular ruler on the basis of the earliest attestation of the name of the prince or princess. We should, however, bear in mind Jacobsen's comments (in JCS 7 [1953] p. 37 n. 6) in this connection:

> Though we have here spoken in terms of a "carry over" of titles from one reign to another we are actually inclined to go a step farther and to assume that titles such *as dumu lugal(ak)* and *dumu-munus lugal(ak)* are to be analyzed — like German "Königssohn" and "Königstochter" — as "son of *a* king" and "daughter of *a* king" not as "son of *the* king" and "daughter of *the* king." They should therefore be translated simply "prince" and "princess."

Thus, in some cases the earliest attested reference to the name of a prince or princess (during the reigns of Amar-Suena, Šū-Sîn, or Ibbi-Sîn) may not be a reliable index for determining his or her filiation. Clearly, what is offered here is a *tentative* assignment of the royal children.

The names of what may be six *lukur*s of Šulgi are found on a tablet in the Kelsey Museum (Kelsey 89203) that was edited by P. Michalowski in ASJ 4 (1982) pp. 133–36. In the following chart, line numbers corresponding to those found in the Kelsey tablet are given in parentheses after the name of the particular *lukur* (if they are found in the Kelsey tablet).

In the chart, Van De Mieroop = M. Van De Mieroop, "Women in the Economy of Sumer," in Lesko, Women's Earliest Records pp. 58–61. Where they are known, the items' dates are included in parentheses (day, month, year) after the attestations and bibliography.

Šulgi — Royal Family

Item	Royal Name	RIM Number	Attestations (A) and Bibliography (B)
Mother			
1	SI.A-*tum*	**E3/2.1.2.66**; see also E3/2.1.1.51	(B): Sollberger, RA 61 (1967) p. 69; Steinkeller, ASJ 3 (1981) pp. 77–78; Michalowski, ASJ 4 (1982) p. 132 and Van De Mieroop p. 58
Wives			
2	*Tá-ra-am*-ÚRI.KI-*am* (Tarām-Uram), daughter of Apil-kīn of Mari, and "daughter-in-law" of Ur-Nammu	**E3/2.1.1.52–53**	(B): Civil, RA 56 (1962) p. 213; Sallaberger, AoF 23 (1996)
3	GÉME-^{d}EN.ZU (Amat-Sîn) **"wife" (dam)**	**E3/2.1.2.67–68**	(B): Michalowski, JCS 28 (1976) pp. 169–72; Steinkeller, ASJ 3 (1981) p. 81; and Van De Mieroop p. 59
4	^{d}*šul-gi-sí-im-ti* **"queen" (nin)** (19); see also below under "*Lukur*s"	**E3/2.1.2.69–71**	(B): Kang, SETDA pp. 263–67; Michalowski, Orientalia NS 46 (1977) pp. 222–23; Steinkeller, ASJ 3 (1981) pp. 78–80; Van De Mieroop p. 58; Sallaberger, Kalender 1 pp. 18–20
***Lukur*s "consorts"**			
5	*é-a-ni-ša* (20)	**E3/2.1.2.72–81**	(B): Steinkeller, RA 73 (1979) p. 190; Grégoire, RA 73 (1979) pp. 190–91; Michalowski, JCS 31 (1979) p. 176 n. 16 and Van De Mieroop p. 58
6	géme-^{d}nin-líl-lá (16)	**E3/2.1.2.82**	(B): Gomi, Orient 12 (1976) pp. 1–14; Michalowski, Orientalia NS 46 (1977) pp. 222–23; Michalowski, JCS 31 (1979) pp. 171–76; Powell, RA 75 (1981) pp. 93–94; Michalowski, ASJ 4 (1982) p. 135; and Van De Mieroop p. 59
7	nin_9-kal-la (17)	**E3/2.1.2.83–84**	(B): Michalowski, JCS 31 (1979) p. 172 n. 8; Van De Mieroop, Orientalia NS 55 (1986) pp. 147–48; Maekawa, ASJ 9 (1987) pp. 104–109; and Van De Mieroop p. 59
8	*simat*(ME)-*é-a* (18)	—	(B): Michalowski, ASJ 4 (1982) p. 135; and Van De Mieroop p. 59
9	^{d}*šul-gi-sí-im-ti* (19) also **"queen" (nin)**; see above sub "Wives"	—	—
10	*šu-qur-*[*tum*]	**E3/2.1.2.85**	(B): Steinkeller, ASJ 3 (1981) p. 84 n. 44; and Van De Mieroop p. 59
Daughters			
11	*ba-qàr-tum*	**E3/2.1.2.86**	—
12	[d]a-da-gu [dumu]-munus-^{d}šul-gi	—	(A): Sauren, WMAH no. 207 lines 6–7 (- - ŠS 3)

Item	Royal Name	RIM Number	Attestations (A) and Bibliography (B)
Daughters (continued)			
13	en-nir-zi-an-na	**E3/2.1.2.87**	(B): Sollberger, AfO 17 (1954–56) p. 23; cf. year name Š 17
14	en-ubur-zi-an-na	—	(B): Sollberger, AfO 17 (1954–56) p. 23; cf. year name Š 43
15	*li-wir-ti-ṭa-šu*	—	Year name Š 18
16	nin-TUR.TUR-mu	**E3/2.1.2.88**	(A): Sigrist, Rochester no. 165 col. i line 18 (25 i to 13 ii Š 42)
17	péš-TUR.TUR	—	(A): Sigrist, MVN 13 no. 657 line 5 (- ii Š 46)
18	*simat*(ME)-^{d}*en-líl*	**E3/2.1.2.89**	—
19	*simat*(ME)-*eš*$_4$-*tár*	—	(A): Fish, Catalogue no. 470 line 4 (24 v Š 42 or AS 6)
20	*ša-at*-^{d}EN.ZU	**E3/2.1.2.90–91**	(A): de Genouillac, Trouvaille no. 85 line 3 (- ii Š 47) (wetnurse mentioned); Owen, MVN 11 no. 204 line 4 (seal) (- xii IS 2); Çığ and Kızılyay, NRVN no. 157 (seal) (- xii IS 3); (B): Kutscher, Tel Aviv 11 (1984) pp. 183–88 and Maekawa, ASJ 14 (1992) p. 200
21	*ša-at*-^{d}šul-gi		(A): Sollberger, MVN 5 no. 95 line 9 (9 i Š 43)
22	*ta-ra-am*-^{d}šul-gi	—	(A): Steinkeller, ZA 72 (1982) p. 241 n. 16 (- viii Š 48)
23	PN, wife of the ruler of Anšan	—	Year name for Š 30
Sons			
24	amar-^{d}da-mu	—	(A): Owen, MVN 15 no. 180 line 7 (- - Š 46)
25	^{d}da-gan-DU-ni		(A): Keiser, BIN 3 no. 491 lines 23–24 (- v Š 43)
26	*eš*$_4$-*tár-il-šu*	—	(A): Sollberger, MVN 5 no. 101 (15 iv Š 46); Sigrist, MVN 13 no. 794 line 10 (22 xii Š 46)
27	*e-te-al-pù*-^{d}*da-gan*		(A): Owen, MVN 11 no. 110 rev. line 10 (- vii -); Obermark, JCS 40 (1988) p. 244 no. 8 line 5 (- i Š 35)
28	lú-du$_{10}$-ga		(A): Owen, MVN 15 no. 162 line 44 (- vi Š 33); Kang, SETUA no. 221 line 3 (- xii Š 42 or AS 6); Schneider, Drehem-und Djoḫatexte no. 125 = Molina, Montserrat no. 125 line 10 (- - AS 1)
29	lugal-á-zi-da; according to Kutscher, Tel Aviv 11 (1984) p. 183, lugal-á-zi-da was the (half?) brother of Šāt-Sîn		(A): Keiser, BIN 3 no. 418 lines 9–10 (- ii Š 46); Holma and Salonen, StOr 9/1 no. 21 line 3 (12 iii Š 44); Fish, Catalogue no. 80 line 6 (29 x Š 44); Nikol'skiy DV 5 no. 530 line 3 (24 iii min Š 44); Sauren, WMAH no. 97 = Sauren, MVN 2 no. 97 line 17 (14 ii Š 46); Riedel, RA 10 (1913) p. 208 BM 103413 col. iii line 18 (13 xi diri AS 4)
30	lú-^{d}nanna		(A): Legrain, TRU no. 24 line 5 (- - Š 44); ibid., no. 28 line 10; (- iv Š 44); Schneider, Strassburg no. 105 lines 9–10 (26 v AS 7)
31	lú-^{d}sún-zi-da		(A): Delaporte, ITT 4 no. 8048 line 6 (- v Š 43)
32	*na-bí*-^{d}*en-líl*		(A): Sauren, WMAH no. 238 = Sauren, MVN 2 no. 238 lines 1–3 (25 xii -); Böhl Collection no. 120 line 2 (unpublished) (- x -);
33	*na-bí-um*		(A): Jones and Snyder, SET no. 5 line 2 (9 xii Š 41)
34	*na*-DI	—	(A): de Genouillac, Trouvaille no. 81 = Limet, Textes sumériens no. 81 obv. line 7 (25 v Š 45)
35	*puzur*$_4$-*éš*$_4$-*tár*	—	(A) Lafont, Documents no. 180 line 17 (5 xi min -) (no title)
36	*šu*-^{d}*en-líl*, general at Uruk and Dēr	**E3/2.1.2.94**	(A): Gomi, Hirose no. 24 line 3 (15 ii Š 44); de Genouillac, Trouvaille no. 85 = Limet, Textes sumériens no. 39 line 2 (17 vii Š 45); Sigrist, PTS no. 130 line 9 (- v Š 46); Sigrist, MVN 13 no. 672 line 5 (- i min Š 47); Grégoire, MVN 10 no. 139 line 3 (3 vi Š 47); Sigrist, PTS no. 60 line 10 (- vii Š 48); Sauren, MVN 2 no. 163 line 6 (27 ix Š 48); Sigrist, AUCT 1 no. 712 line 9

Item	Royal Name	RIM Number	Attestations (A) and Bibliography (B)
Sons	(continued)		
36	*šu-^{d}en-líl*		(16 vii AS 7); (B): Michalowski, Mesopotamia 12 (1977) pp. 83–84; ibid., SMS 2/3 p. 9 n. 31; and Sallaberger, in an article to appear in AoF 23 (1996)
37	*šu-eš$_{4}$-tár*	—	(A): Szachno-Romanowicz, RO 11 p. 96 no. 1 rev. line 5 (30 xi Š 43); Langdon, RA 19 (1922) p. 192 no. 7 line 4 (28 iii Š 44); Langdon, TAD no. 61 line 10 (- vii AS 3)
38	ur-nìgin-gar, general at Uruk	—	(A): Hackman, BIN 5 no. 11 line 5 (- - Š 32); YBC 3644 line 11 (- - Š 42); (B): Michalowski, Mesopotamia 12 (1977) p. 88 n. 29
39	ur-^{d}EN.ZU, general at Uruk and Dēr	**E3/2.1.2.95–97**	(A): Scheil, RA 13 (1916) p. 20 (- - Š 48); de Genouillac, Trouvaille no. 74 (- i AS 1); Hackman, BIN 5 no. 316 (no date); (B) Michalowski, Mesopotamia 12 (1977) p. 84 n. 3

1. Mother and Grandmother

An agate tablet from Nippur studied by Sollberger (RA 61 [1967] p. 69; see E3/2.1.2.66 below) names a certain SI.A-*tum* as an important Ur III lady; Sollberger compared the name with the PN SI.A-*tum* found on a seal inscription which is edited as inscription E3/2.1.1.51 in this volume. The latter text names SI.A-*tum* as the wife of Ur-Nammu, and Sollberger took the SI.A-tum of the agate inscription to refer to Ur-Nammu's wife as well. Sollberger's reading of the traces of the last line in Hilprecht's copy of the inscription as: a[ma] t[u-d]a-ni [a-ma-na-ru] cannot be confirmed or refuted, since the relevant line is now broken away. Of further note are two archival texts which are to be cited by Sallaberger in his forthcoming article in AoF 23 (1996). The first text (Karlsuniversität I 870 = Neumann and Hruška, ArOr 62 [1994] pp. 240–41) dated to v Š 37, refers to reed bundles as regular deliveries for the cults of the Ur III royal family, namely: Ur-Nammu (line 2); *da-mi-iq-tum* (line 4); and the unnamed father of Ur-Nammu (ab-ba-^{d}ur-^{d}nammu, line 8). We would expect, then, that the PN Damiqtum refers to Ur-Nammu's mother. Also of note is a second tablet (Elmira 2: Owen, MVN 15 no. 162) that refers to ur-^{d}nammu (line 3); ^{d}geštin-an-na-SI.A-tum (line 6); ^{d}geštin-an-na-lugal (line 9), and *da-mi-iq-tum* (line 17).

2. Wives

(a) Tarām-Uram

Although she is not actually attested in Ur III archival texts as the wife (dam) of Šulgi, Sallaberger (in a forthcoming article to appear in AoF 23 [1996]) provides persuasive arguments that Tarām-Uram, the daughter of Apil-kīn of Mari and the é-gi$_{4}$-a "daughter-in-law" of Ur-Nammu — see E3/2.1.1.52–53 — was Šulgi's first wife and mother of the royal heir Amar-Suena.

(b) Amat-Sîn

The first wife (dam) of Šulgi who is actually attested in the archival record is a certain Amat-Sîn; seal inscriptions of two of her servants are known (see E3/2.1.2.67–68). The fact that Šulgi's name appears in the first seal inscription mentioning Amat-Sîn without the prefixed divine determinative indicates that the seal (and presumably Amat-Sîn's marriage to Šulgi) dated to sometime before Š 21.

(c) Šulgi-simtī

According to Sallaberger (Kalender 1 p. 18 n. 59) a second change in the reigning queen probably occurred around the years Š 29–30. The new queen, Šulgi-simtī, first appears by name alone in an archival text dated to iv Š 32

(Sauren, MVN 2 no. 308). Sallaberger (Kalender 1 p. 18) notes an archival text dated to Š 32 (Calvot and Pettinato, MVN 8 no. 97) in which she appears for the first time with the title "queen" (line 11: gìr nin *dšul-gi-sí-im-ti*).

Šulgi-simtī is generally thought to have been a queen of "foreign" origin. This conjecture is based on the fact that offerings for the cults of the non-Sumerian goddesses Bēlat-Šuḫnir and Bēlat-Terraban appear for the first time in Ur III economic texts in a group of tablets connected with Šulgi-simtī; this particular archive dates to the time shortly after the queen's own appearance in the archival record. The aforementioned goddesses' names apparently derive from their respective cult cities. The fact that the cults of Bēlat-Šuḫnir and Bēlat-Terraban are attested at Ešnunna (see Jacobsen, Gimil-Sin Temple p. 143 no. 6; p. 144 no. 8) suggests a possible Diyālā link for these deities. It would also accord well with the fact that the first cities named in Šulgi's year names as being conquered by the king (apart from the city of Dēr) are the cities of Karaḫar and Simurrum. These cities probably lay on the Alwand and Upper Diyālā rivers, respectively. Bēlat-Terraban's name might possibly be linked with the GN *ti-ri-qa-an*.KI (bearing in mind the frequent alternation between g and b found, for example, in Sumerian) which appears in a Middle Babylonian boundary stone of Nazi-Maruttaš (Scheil, MDP 2 p. 87 i 24). The *kudurru* informs us that the town of Tiriqan lay on the bank of the Ṭaban river (see Nashef, Bagh. Mitt. 13 [1982] p. 122–23).

While Šulgi-simtī apparently served as queen down to the end of Šulgi's reign, she appears with only the title *lukur* (which is commonly translated as "consort") in seal inscriptions of her servants (E3/2.1.2.69–71). In noting this fact Steinkeller (ASJ 3 [1981] p. 81) writes: "This particular distribution (of Sumerian titles dam and nin) suggests that sometime around the middle of Šulgi's reign, lukur replaced dam as the term for 'king's wife.'"

66

A flat agate bead bears eight lines of a votive inscription in which SI.A-tum (likely Ur-Nammu's wife and Šulgi's mother) dedicates the bead for the life of Šulgi (see Šulgi — Royal Family item 1 above).

COMMENTARY

The bead, which measures 4.4×4.3×0.8 cm, bears the museum number CBS 8598. It was found at Nippur in a chamber on the edge of the canal outside the great SE wall of the ziqqurrat. The text is arranged in one column on the obverse. The reverse bears an inscription of Kurigalzu (BE 1/1 no. 43).

As Steible (NSBW 2 p. 196) points out, Sollberger's suggested reading of line 8 as a[ma]-t[u-d]a-ni is not supported by the collation. Further, not even the NI sign at the end of line 8, as given by Steible, was visible when the tablet was collated by the author.

BIBLIOGRAPHY

1893 Hilprecht, BE 1/1 no. 15 (copy)
1907 Thureau-Dangin, SAK pp. 192–93 Dun-gi r (edition)
1929 Barton, RISA pp. 280–81 Shulgi 18 (edition)
1962 Hallo, HUCA 33 p. 33 Šulgi 41 (study)
1967 Sollberger, RA 61 p. 69 (study)
1971 Sollberger and Kupper, IRSA IIIA2s (translation)
1986 Kärki, KDDU p. 48 Šulgi 41 (edition)
1991 Braun-Holzinger, Weihgaben p. 366 P 9 (edition)
1991 Steible, NSBW 2 pp. 195–96 Šulgi 41 (edition)

TEXT

1)	^{d}inanna	1–2) For the goddess Inanna, her lady,
2)	nin-a-ni	
3)	nam-ti-	3–4) for the life of Šulgi,
4)	šul-gi	
5)	nita-kala-ga	5–6) mighty man, king of Ur,
6)	lugal-uri$_5$.KI-ma-ka-šè	
7)	SI.A-*tum*	7–8) SI.A-tum ...
8)	⌜x x (x)⌝	Lacuna
Lacuna		

67

Two tablets (the first dated to xii Š 28 and the second to x Š 28) bear the impression of a seal of a servant of Sulgi's wife, Amat-Sîn (see Šulgi — Royal Family item 3 above).

CATALOGUE

Ex.	Museum number	Lines preserved	cpn
1	HSM 911.10.460	1–5	n
2	University of Iowa (no. 1 in edition of Rochberg and Zimansky)	1–5	n

COMMENTARY

The probable identity of the two exemplars of this seal inscription was pointed out by Sallaberger (Kalender 1 p. 18 n. 59). Lines 1–3 are found in col. i, lines 4–6 in col. ii.

The reading of the PN of line 1 in Akkadian as Amat-Sîn is based on the evidence of the seal inscription which follows in this volume.

BIBLIOGRAPHY

1976 Michalowski, JCS 28 pp. 169–71 (ex. 1, copy, edition)
1979 Rochberg-Halton and Zimansky, JCS 31 pp. 130 and 133 (ex. 2, copy, transliteration)
1986 Kärki, KDDU p. 58 Šulgi 53b (ex. 1, edition)
1989 Van De Mieroop, in Lesko, Women's Earliest Records p. 59 (study)

TEXT

1)	GÉME-^{d}EN.ZU	1–3) Amat-Sîn, wife of Šulgi, king of Ur:
2)	dam-šul-gi	
3)	lugal-uri$_5$.KI-ma	
4)	*šu-ku-bu-*[*um*]	4–6) Šū-Kūbum, the dispatch-rid[er], (is) yo[ur] servant.
5)	rá-gab[a]	
6)	ir$_{11}$-z[u]	

68

Impressions of a seal of a second servant of Amat(?)-Sîn are found on two tablets in the Aleppo Museum (see Šulgi — Royal Family item 3 above).

COMMENTARY

The seal impressions are found on the tablets numbered 11 and 12 in Touzalin's dissertation on the Aleppo Museum tablets (see bibliography); they were not collated. Both tablets are from Umma and are dated to the month ezen-^{d}nin-a-zu, but unfortunately no year name is given. I am grateful to M. Cooper for pointing out this seal inscription and for providing me with information about it.

The PN of line 1 was read ⸢*ša-at*⸣-^{d}EN.ZU by Touzalin (pp. 143ff). However, Kutscher (Tel Aviv 11 [1984] p. 185 n. 3) notes: "Dr. Sigrist informs me that the faint impressions were read from photographs of the tablets, and the restoration *ša-at-* is very doubtful."

In view of the fact that Šāt-Sîn is otherwise attested as being a princess, not a queen, we have offered a tentative suggestion for a reading of line 1 as ⸢*a-ma-at*⸣-^{d}EN.ZU; it is taken to be a reference to the queen GÉME-^{d}EN.ZU in E3/2.1.2.67.

BIBLIOGRAPHY

1982 Touzalin, L'administrative palatiale à l'époque de la troisième dynastie d'Ur, textes inédits du Musée d'Alep. Ph.D. dissertation, Université de Tours. M 4042 nos. 11–12 (edition)

TEXT

1) ⸢*a-ma-at*⸣-^{d}EN.ZU
2) dam-^{d}šul-gi
3) nita-kala-ga
4) lugal-uri$_{5}$.KI-ma
5) *it-ra-ak-ì-lí*
6) rá-gaba
7) ir$_{11}$-zu

1–4) Amat-Sîn, wife of Šulgi, mighty man, king of Ur:

5–7) Itrak-ilī, dispatch-rider, (is) your servant.

69

Šulgi-simtī, nin "queen" and *lukur* of Šulgi, is named in seal impressions of three of her servants (see Šulgi — Royal Family item 4 above).

The royal name actually occurs in two forms, Šulgi-simtum and Šulgi-simtī.

COMMENTARY

The first servant seal of Šulgi-simtī is impressed on a tablet that was in the Kelekian collection. Its present whereabouts are unknown. The tablet is dated to vi Š 32. Lines 1–4 are found in col. i, lines 5–8 in col. ii.

BIBLIOGRAPHY

1915 Scheil, RT 37 pp. 130–31 (copy, edition)
1963 Goetze, JCS 17 p. 35 (edition)
1971 Sollberger and Kupper, IRSA IIIA2z (translation)
1981 Steinkeller, ASJ 3 p. 78 (study)
1989 Kärki, KDDU pp. 58–59 Šulgi 53c (edition)

TEXT

1) ^{d}šul-gi
2) [n]ita-kala-ga
3) [l]ugal-⸢uri$_5$⸣.KI-ma
4) [lu]gal-an-ub-da-límmu-ba
5) ^{d}*šul-gi-sí-im-t*[*um*]
6) lukur-kaskal-la-ka-ni
7) maš-gu-la
8) sukkal ir$_{11}$-z[u]

1–4) Šulgi, mighty [m]an, [k]ing of Ur, [k]ing of the four quarters:

5–6) Šulgi-simt[um] (is) his travelling companion:

7–8) Maš-gula, the vizier, (is) yo[ur] servant.

70

A seal impression of a second servant of Šulgi-simtī is found on a tablet (dated to viii Š 48) from Puzriš-Dagan now housed in Istanbul (see Šulgi — Royal Family item 4 above).

COMMENTARY

The tablet is number 530 in the Puzriš-Dagan group of tablets in Istanbul. It measures 4.2×3.3×1.8 cm. Ur-lugal-edin(a)ka is attested as stockyard manager for Šulgi-simtī during Š 45 and Š 47 (see Sallaberger, Kalender 1 p. 21 and n. 79).

BIBLIOGRAPHY

1954 Salonen, Puzriš-Dagan-Texte no. 530 (transliteration)

TEXT

1) ^{d}*šul-gi-sí-im-ti*
2) lukur ki-ág-lugal
3) ur-^{d}lugal-edin-ka
4) dub-sar
5) dumu ku$_5$-da-[x]
6) [ir$_{11}$-zu]

1–2) Šulgi-simtī, *lukur* beloved of the king:

3–6) Ur-lugal-edin(a)ka, scribe, son of Kuda-[x], [(is)] your servant].

71

A Drehem tablet and its envelope dated to –/xii/ Š 43 bear the impressions of a seal of a third servant of Šulgi-simtī (see Šulgi — Royal Family item 4 above).

COMMENTARY

The impression, which is found on MM 54 (the tablet) and MM 1101 (the envelope), was not collated. I am thankful to W. Sallaberger for this reference.

According to Sallaberger (Kalender 1 p. 21 and n. 77) Bēlī-ṭāb was stockyard manager for Šulgi-simtī during Š 33 and 37.

BIBLIOGRAPHY

1932 Schneider, Drehem and Djohatexte no. 144 (conflated copy of tablet and envelope)
1993 Molina, Montserrat no. 144 (copy of tablet and envelope)

TEXT

1) *be-lí*-DU_{10} kurušda
2) [d]*šul-gi-<sí>-im-tum-ma*

1–2) Bēlī-ṭāb, stockyard manager of Šulgi-simtum.

72

Šulgi's *lukur* Ea-niša is known from a votive inscription, seal inscriptions of her servants, and is mentioned in various archival texts (see Šulgi — Royal Family item 5 above).

COMMENTARY

The first inscription mentioning Ea-niša is incised on a long bead of banded agate. The piece, which was purchased in Teheran, was formerly in the collection of R. Schmidt in Solothurn, Switzerland. It is now housed in the Bible Lands Museum, Jerusalem, where it bears the museum number BLMJ no. 1340. Lines 1–7 are found in column i, lines 8–12 in col. ii. The inscription was kindly collated by J. Westenholz.

BIBLIOGRAPHY

1947 Pohl, Orientalia NS 16 pp. 464–65 (copy, edition)
1962 Hallo, HUCA 33 p. 33 Šulgi 42 (study)
1971 Sollberger and Kupper, IRSA IIIA2t (translation)
1979 Steinkeller, RA 73 p. 190 (study)
1986 Kärki, KDDU pp. 48–49 Šulgi 42 (edition)
1987 Lambert, in Merhav, Treasures no. 28 (photo [partial], study)
1991 Braun-Holzinger, Weihgaben pp. 366–67 P 10 (edition)
1991 Steible, NSBW 2 pp. 196–97 Šulgi 42 (edition)

TEXT

1) ^{d}⸢inanna⸣
2) nin-é-an-[na]
3) nin-a-ni
4) nam-ti-
5) ^{d}šul-⸢gi⸣
6) nita-kala-⸢ga⸣
7) lugal-uri$_{5}$.KI-ma
8) lugal-ki-en-
9) ⸢gi⸣-ki-⸢uri⸣-ka-šè
10) ⸢*é*⸣*-a-ni-ša*
11) lukur-ra-ni
12) a mu-na-ru

1–3) For the goddess Inanna, lady of Eann[a], his lady,

4–9) for the life of Šulgi, mighty man, king of Ur, king of the lands of Sumer and Akkad,

10–12) Ea-niša, his *lukur*, dedicated (this bead).

73

A seal impression on a tablet in the Hartford Theological Seminary gives the name of a servant of Ea-niša (see Šulgi — Royal Family item 5 above).

COMMENTARY

The impression is found on HTS 104. Lines 1–4 are found on col. i, lines 5–6 on col. ii.

The reading of the PN in line 3 is uncertain. In the seal impression found on the tablet published by Owen as NATN no. 510 the spelling na-si-im appears as an apparent variant to the na-DI of the main text (reference courtesy W. Sallaberger). This would suggest a reading of na-silim for na-DI.

BIBLIOGRAPHY

1966 Sollberger, Correspondence no. 27 (edition)
1979 Steinkeller, RA 73 p. 190 (transliteration)

TEXT

1) *é-a-ni-ša*
2) lukur ki-ág-lugal
3) na-DI
4) lú [...]
5) dumu ur-èš-bar-ra
6) [ir$_{11}$-zu]

1–2) Ea-niša, beloved *lukur* of the king:

3–6) NaDI, the ..., son of Ur-ešbara, (is) [your servant].

74

A second seal inscription of a servant of Ea-niša is known from two exemplars (see Šulgi — Royal Family item 5 above).

CATALOGUE

Ex.	Museum number	Dimensions (cm)	Lines preserved	cpn
1	Buffalo Museum of Science no. C517b	4.03×3.85 (tablet) 2.18×3.7 (impression)	1–5	c
2	State Hermitage MA 9612	—	—	n

COMMENTARY

Lines 1–2 are found in col. i, lines 3–5 in col. ii. Ex. 1 was kindly collated by S. Paley.

The father's name of line 4 is very likely to turn out to be the same as that found in line 5 of the previous inscription. As Steinkeller (RA 73 [1979] p. 190) points out, it is unclear whether the father's name of line 4 is to be corrected to ur-ab-ba(!)-[dingir]-ra or to ur-èš-ba-an-ra.

BIBLIOGRAPHY

1914 Hussey, Bulletin of the Buffalo Society of Natural Sciences 11 pp. 137–38 and pl. 8 no. 6 (ex. 1, copy, study)
1921 Shileiko, ZVO 25 p. 136 (ex. 2, copy)
1979 Steinkeller, RA 73 p. 190 (exs. 1–2, transliteration)
1986 Kärki, KDDU p. 59 Šulgi 53d (exs. 1–2, edition)

TEXT

1) *é-a-ni-ša*
2) lukur ki-ág-lugal
3) na-DI
4) dumu ur-ab-ba-dingir-ra
5) ir_{11}-zu

1–2) Ea-niša, beloved *lukur* of the king:

3–5) NaDI, son of Ur-aba-dingira, (is) your servant.

75

A tablet in the Ashmolean Museum bears the impression of a seal that was granted to Ea-niša by Šulgi (see Šulgi — Royal Family item 5 above).

COMMENTARY

The tablet bears the museum number Ash 1971-346. It is dated to iii–iv Š 44, and comes from Ur. Lines 1–4 are found in column i, lines 5–7 in col. ii.

BIBLIOGRAPHY

1979 Grégoire, RA 73 pp. 190–91 (edition)
1986 Kärki, KDDU p. 62 Šulgi 56b (edition)

TEXT

1) ^{d}šul-gi
2) nita-kala-ga
3) lugal-uri_5.KI-ma-<ke_4>

1–3) Šulgi, mighty man, king of Ur,

4) lugal-an-ub-da-límmu-ba
5) *é-a-ni-š*[*a*]
6) lukur-kaskal-la-k[a]-ni-ir
7) in-na-ba

4) king of the four quarters:
5–7) to Ea-niš[a], his travelling companion, he presented (this seal).

76

The impression of a seal of a servant of Ea-niša is found on a tablet envelope in the Smithsonian Institution (see Šulgi — Royal Family item 5 above).

COMMENTARY

The tablet envelope, which bears the museum number SI 344992, was not collated. A reference to the text was kindly provided by W. Sallaberger.

BIBLIOGRAPHY

1991 Owen, MVN 15 no. 357 (copy, transliteration)

TEXT

1) *é-a-ni-ša*
2) lukur ki-ág-lugal
3) é-nun-kù
4) má-laḫ$_4$ ir$_{11}$-zu

1–2) Ea-niša, *lukur*, beloved of the king:
3–4) Enun-ku, the sailor, (is) your servant.

77

The impression of a seal of a servant of Ea-niša is found on a tablet in the Yale collections (see Šulgi — Royal Family item 5 above).

COMMENTARY

The impression is found on YBC 11864, a tablet from Umma dating to Š 39. A transliteration of the inscription was kindly made available to the author by R. Meyer. It is edited here through the permission of W.W. Hallo.

TEXT

1) ^{d}šul-gi
2) nita-kala-ga
3) lugal-ur[i$_5$.KI-ma]

1–3) Šulgi, mighty man, king of U[r]:

4) *é-a-ni-*[*ša*]
5) lukur ki-ág-a-ni
6) lú-^{d}nin-š[ubur]
7) dub-sar ir$_{11}$-[zu]

4–5) Ea-ni[ša], his beloved *lukur*:

6–7) Lu-Ninš[ubur], scribe, (is) [your] servant.

78

Impressions of seals of three servants of Ea-niša appear on tablets in the Horn Archaeological Museum (see Šulgi — Royal Family item 5 above).

COMMENTARY

The first seal impression is found on AUAM 73.0833, a tablet with a probable Drehem provenance that dates to xii Š 45. The text is arranged in one column.

BIBLIOGRAPHY

1988 Sigrist, AUCT 3 no. 321 (copy, transliteration)

TEXT

1) *é-a-ni-ša*
2) lukur ki-ág-lugal
3) in-zu-zu
4) ⸢ir$_{11}$⸣-[zu]

1–2) Ea-niša, beloved *lukur* of the king:

3–4) Inzuzu (is) [your] servant.

79

The impression of a seal of a second servant of Ea-niša (see Šulgi — Royal Family item 5 above) appears on AUAM 73.2212, an uninscribed (and therefore undated) clay bulla. The text is arranged in one column.

BIBLIOGRAPHY

1988 Sigrist, AUCT 3 no. 322 (copy, transliteration)

TEXT

1) *é-a-ni-ša*
2) lukur ki-ág-lugal
3) lú-^{d}nammu dub-sar
4) dumu ur-^{d}KA.DI
5) ir$_{11}$-zu

1–2) Ea-niša, beloved *lukur* of the king:

3–5) Lu-Nammu, scribe, son of Ur-Ištarān, (is) your servant.

80

A tablet from Umma in the Horn Archaeological Museum bears the impression of a seal of a gardener of Ea-niša (see Šulgi — Royal Family item 5 above). The inscription is arranged in one column.

COMMENTARY

The impression, which is found on AUAM 73.1039, was not collated.

BIBLIOGRAPHY

1988 Sigrist, AUCT 3 no. 412 (copy, transliteration)

TEXT

1) lú-^{d}na-rú-a
2) nu-GIŠ.kiri$_6$
3) *é-a-ni-ša*

1–3) Lu-Narua, gardener of Ea-niša.

81

An Old Babylonian Sammeltafel of copies of Šulgi inscriptions gives the text, written in an abbreviated form, of an inscription of Ea-niša (see Šulgi — Royal Family item 5 above).

COMMENTARY

The inscription is found on obv. iii lines 2–13 (according to Civil's line numbering) of N 2230+N 4006. The inscription was collated.

BIBLIOGRAPHY

1985 Civil, Orientalia NS 54 pp. 38 and 41 (copy, edition)

TEXT

Lacuna
1′) [nam-ti]
2′) ⸢^{d}šul⸣-<gi>
3′) nita-<kala-ga>
4′) lugal-<uri$_5$>.KI-<ma>

Lacuna
1′–4′) [for the life] <of> Šul<gi>, <mighty> man, king <of Ur>,

5′) lugal-<an-ub>-da-límmu-ba-ka-šè
6′) *é-a-ni-ša*
7′) lukur-kaskal-la
8′) lukur-ki-ág-gá-ni-e
9′) lugal-a-ni
10′) mu-tu
11′) mu-ud-na-ni
12′) igi-ni-šè in-gu[b]
Lacuna

5′) king of the four <quarte>rs:
6′–10′) Ea-niša, his travelling companion (and) beloved *lukur*, formed (a statue) of her lord,
11′–12′) (and) se[t] up (a statue of) her husband (Šulgi) before her(self).
Lacuna

82

A tablet in the State Hermitage Museum (Moscow) dated to vi Š 46 provides us with the seal inscription of Geme-Ninlila, probably a *lukur* of Šulgi (see Šulgi — Royal Family item 6 above).

COMMENTARY

The seal impression is found on State Hermitage MA 14933. A transliteration of the seal was kindly provided by M. Powell. Lines 1–4 are found in col. i, lines 5–7 in col. ii.

BIBLIOGRAPHY

1981 Powell, RA 75 pp. 93–94 (translation)

TEXT

1) ^{d}šul-gi
2) nita-kala-ga
3) lugal-uri$_5$.KI-ma
4) lugal-an-ub-da-límmu-ba-ke$_4$
5) géme-^{d}nin-líl-lá
6) ki-ág-gá-ni-ir
7) in-na-ba

1–3) Šulgi, mighty man, king of Ur,
4) king of the four quarters,
5–7) granted (this seal) to Geme-Ninlila, his beloved.

83

P. Michalowski (JCS 31 [1979] p. 172 n. 8 and ASJ 4 [1982] p. 136) has shown that a certain Nin-kala, who appears in various Ur III archival texts, was likely a member of Šulgi's family, possibly one of his *lukur*s (see Šulgi — Royal Family item 7 above). Two inscriptions mention Nin-kala. The first is inscribed on a bowl.

COMMENTARY

The bowl fragment was found in the Šulgi and Amar-Suena mausoleum at Ur (courtyard of Šulgi's mausoleum according to the catalogue in UE 6). It was given the excavation number U 16539 and bears the museum number IM 9425. The text is arranged in one column.

BIBLIOGRAPHY

1965 Sollberger, UET 8 no. 25 (copy [by Legrain])
1986 Kärki, KDDU pp. 65–66 Šulgi 64 (edition)
1991 Braun-Holzinger, Weihgaben p. 186 G 350 (edition)
1991 Steible, NSBW 2 p. 202 Šulgi 56 (edition)

TEXT

1) [^{d}]šul-gi
2) ⌈dingir⌉-kalam-ma-na
3) lugal-uri$_5$.KI-ma
4) lugal-an-ub-da-límmu-ba
5) nin$_9$-kal-la
6) ⌈dumu⌉-nibru.KI
7) [ki]-⌈ág⌉-gá-ni⌉
Lacuna

1–4) For Šulgi, god of his land, king of Ur, king of the four quarters,

5–7) Nin-kala, citizen of Nippur, his [be]loved
Lacuna

84

An Old Babylonian Sammeltafel of Šulgi inscriptions gives, according to a probable textual restoration, a copy of an inscription of Nin-kala (see Šulgi — Royal Family item 7 above).

COMMENTARY

The inscription is found on obv. ii lines 1–6 of N 2230+N 4006. The inscription was collated. For the reading of the caption, see Frayne, RIME 2 p. 20 Sargon E2.1.1.6 colophon 2 line 2.

BIBLIOGRAPHY

1985 Civil, Orientalia NS 54 pp. 38 and 40 (copy, edition)

TEXT

Lacuna
1′) [nin$_9$-ka]l-la
2′) dumu-nibru.KI
3′) ki-ág-gá-ni
4′) alan-na-n[i]
5′) mu-dím
Colophon
1) ⌈murgu⌉ šul-[g]i

Lacuna
1′–3′) [Nin-ka]la, citizen of Nippur, his beloved,

4′–5′) fashioned a statue of him (Šulgi).

Colophon
1) (Inscription) on the shoulder of Šul[g]i.

85

A calcite vessel found in excavations at Ur bears the inscription of Šuqur[tum], a *lukur* of Šulgi (see Šulgi — Royal Family item 10 above).

COMMENTARY

The vase was found in room 11 of the E-nun-maḫ. It consists of the join of three pieces: U 248+257+260. Joined together, the vase forms a tall cylindrical vessel, with a height of 29.8 cm, a base diameter of 11.2 cm, and a vessel thickness of 1.4 cm. The vase bears the museum number BM 116430. The text is arranged in one column of fourteen lines. The inscription, which is found on the top third of the vase, was collated.

BIBLIOGRAPHY

1928 Gadd, UET 1 no. 57 (copy, edition)
1929 Barton, RISA pp. 366–67 Shulgi 8 (edition)
1962 Hallo, HUCA 33 p. 42 Family 1 (study)
1971 Sollberger and Kupper, IRSA IIIA2r (translation)
1986 Kärki, KDDU pp. 64–65 (Familie 1 =) Šulgi 61 (edition)
1991 Braun-Holzinger, Weihgaben pp. 187–88 G 357 (edition)
1991 Steible, NSBW 2 pp. 208–209 Šulgi 65 (edition)

TEXT

1) šul-g[i]
2) nita-kala-g[a]
3) lugal-ur[i$_5$].KI-m[a]
4) lugal-ki-e[n]-gi-ki-uri-[(x)]
5) *šu-qur-[tum]*
6) lukur-ki-ág-gá-ni
7) lú mu-sar-ra-ba
8) šu bí-íb-uru$_{12}$-a
9) mu-ni bí-íb-sar-a
10) ^{d}nin-súna
11) dingir-mu
12) ^{d}lugal-bàn-da
13) lugal-mu
14) nam ḫa-ba-da-kuru$_5$-ne

1–4) Šulg[i], mighty man, king of U[r], king of the lands of [S]umer and Akkad:

5–6) Šūqur[tum] (is) his beloved *lukur*.

7–9) As for the one who erases this inscription (and) writes his (own) name there,

10–14) may the goddess Ninsuna, my (personal) deity, and the god Lugalbanda, my lord, curse him.

86

A seal in the Louvre collection belonged to a daughter of an Ur III king, likely Šulgi (see Šulgi — Royal Family item 11 above).

COMMENTARY

The haematite seal measures 1.4×0.6 cm. The piece was purchased in 1894 and given the museum number AO 2418. The text is arranged in one column of four lines. The inscription was collated.

BIBLIOGRAPHY

1923 Delaporte, Louvre 2 A. 255 (photo, edition)
1931 Contenau, Manuel 2 p. 791 fig. 553 (photo)
1954–56 Sollberger, AfO 17 p. 21 and n. 53 (study)

TEXT

1) *ba-qàr-tum* 2) dumu-munus-lugal	1–2) Baqartum, daughter of the king:
3) ᵈ*šul-gi-ì-lí* 4) ir₁₁-zu	3–4) Šulgi-ilī (is) your servant.

87

The name of Š 15 commemorates the oracular designation of En-nirzi-ana as *en* of the god Nanna (see Šulgi — Royal Family item 13 above). Five impressions of a seal of a servant of this priestess, who likely was a daughter of Šulgi, are found on a clay sealing from Ur.

COMMENTARY

The clay bulla, which measures 3.8×3.6 cm, was given the excavation number U 7024. It dates to i Š 37. Its present whereabouts are not known. Lines 1–3 are found in col. i, lines 4–6 in col. ii. The inscription was collated from the published photo.

BIBLIOGRAPHY

1937 Legrain, UET 3 no. 1320 (copy)
1951 Legrain, UE 10 no. 403 (photo, edition)
1962 Hallo, HUCA 33 p. 42 Family 3 (study)
1986 Kärki, KDDU p. 59 (Familie 3 =) Šulgi 53e (edition)

TEXT

1) en-nir-zi-an-na 2) en-ᵈnanna	1–2) En-nirzi-ana, *en* of the god Nanna:
3) gìr-né-ì-sa₆ 4) dub-sa[r] 5) dumu ḫé-sa₆-g[e] 6) ir₁₁-⌜zu⌝	3–6) Girine-isa, scrib[e], son of Hesag[e], (is) your servant.

88

An inscribed bead was dedicated by Šulgi to the goddess Ninlil on his own behalf and for his daughter nin-TUR.TUR-mu (see Šulgi — Royal Family item 16 above).

COMMENTARY

The present whereabouts of this bead are unknown; we have reproduced W.W. Hallo's transliteration of the piece.

BIBLIOGRAPHY

1919–24 Bromski, RO 2 pp. 188–89 (copy)
1957 Hallo, Royal Titles p. 32 and n. 4 (partial transliteration, study)
1962 Hallo, HUCA 33 p. 22 n. 196 (partial transliteration); p. 33 Šulgi 46 (study)
1971 Sollberger and Kupper, IRSA IIIA2f (translation)
1978 Wilcke, ZA 68 p. 219 discussion to lines 129ff. (edition)
1986 Kärki, KDDU p. 50 Šulgi 46 (edition)
1991 Braun-Holzinger, Weihgaben p. 367 P 14 (edition)
1991 Steible, NSBW 2 pp. 199–200 Šulgi 46 (edition)

TEXT

1) ^{d}nin-líl
2) nin-a-ni
3) šul-gi
4) nita-kala-ga
5) lugal-uri_5.KI-ma
6) lugal-ki-en-gi-ki-uri-ke_4
7) nam-ti-la-ni-šè
8) ù nam-ti-
9) nin-TUR.TUR-mu
10) dumu-ki-ág-gá-na-šè
11) a mu-na-ru
12) lú mu-sar-ra-b[a]
13) šu bí-íb-uru_{12}-[a]
14) nin-mu
15) ^{d}nin-líl-ke_4
16) nam ḫa-ba-da-ku_5-re_6

1–2) To the goddess Ninlil, his lady,

3–6) Šulgi, mighty man, king of Ur, king of the lands of Sumer and Akkad,

7) for his (own) life,
8–10) and for the life of Nin-TUR.TUR-mu, his beloved child,

11) he dedicated (this bead).
12–13) As for the one who erases th[is] inscription,

14–16) may my lady, the goddess Ninlil, curse him.

89

An inscription found on two stone vessels from Ur mentions Šulgi's daughter Simat-Enlil (see Šulgi — Royal Family item 18 above).

CATALOGUE

Ex.	Museum number	Excavation number	Registration number	Ur provenance	Object	Dimensions (cm)	Lines preserved	cpn
1	BM 118553	U 6355	1927-5-27, 26	Room C 25 of the Gipar-ku	Granite bowl	—	1–6	c
2	BM 116442	U 254	1923-11-10, 27	E-nun-maḫ, room 11	Calcite vessel	8.8×7.4×1	1–6	c

COMMENTARY

Ex. 1 is a reused bowl; it bears an earlier inscription of Narām-Sîn. See RIME 2, E2.1.4.41. The texts of this inscription are arranged in one column of six lines.

BIBLIOGRAPHY

1928 Gadd, UET 1 nos. 24B and 51 (exs. 1–2, copy, edition); pl. E (ex. 1, photo)

1929 Barton, RISA pp. 364–65 Shulgi 1 and 2 (exs. 1–2, edition)

1960 Sollberger, Iraq 22 pp. 77–78 and 86–87 no. 102 (study)

1962 Hallo, HUCA 33 p. 42 Family 2 (exs. 1–2, study)

1971 Sollberger and Kupper, IRSA IIIA2q (exs. 1–2, translation)

1974 Woolley, UE 6 pp. 51 and 87 (ex. 2, study); p. 98 (ex. 1, study)

1986 Kärki, KDDU p. 65 (Familie 2 =) Šulgi 62 (exs. 1–2, edition)

1991 Braun-Holzinger, Weihgaben p. 188 G 358 (ex. 1, edition); p. 188 G 359 (ex. 2, study)

1991 Steible, NSBW 2 pp. 209–10 Šulgi 66 (exs. 1–2, edition)

TEXT

1) ^{d}šul-gi
2) nita-kala-ga
3) lugal-uri$_5$.KI-ma
4) lugal-an-ub-da-límmu-ba
5) *simat*(ME)-^{d}*en-líl*
6) dumu-munus-a-ni

1–4) Šulgi, mighty man, king of Ur, king of the four quarters:

5–6) Simat-Enlil (is) his daughter.

90

An archival text from Drehem dated to ii Š 47 (de Genouillac, Trouvaille no. 85 = Limet, Textes sumériens no. 37, line 3) names Tarīš-mātum as the wet-nurse of (or for) a certain Šāt-Sîn, the latter designated as a princess (dumu-munus-lugal). Šāt-Sîn is also attested (but not named as princess) in a handful of tablets dating from viii Š 37 (Salonen, Puzriš-Dagan-Texte no. 593 line 8) to xii IS 2 (Owen, MVN 11 no. 155 line 4); for a complete list, see Kutscher, Tel Aviv 11 (1984) pp. 183–88 and note further the comments of Maekawa, ASJ 14 (1992) p. 200 (see Šulgi — Royal Family item 20 above). The impression of a seal of a servant of the princess is found on a tablet from Nippur.

COMMENTARY

The tablet, which is dated to xii IS 3, and which bears the museum number Ni 2094, was not collated.

For the reading lú-aslag$_x$(TÚG) in line 4, see Steinkeller, Sale Documents p. 171.

BIBLIOGRAPHY

1965 Çığ and Kızılyay, NRVN no. 157 (copy)
1984 Kutscher, Tel Aviv 11 p. 186 (edition, study)
1992 Maekawa, ASJ 14 p. 200 (study)

TEXT

1) *ša-a*[*t*]-^{d}EN.ZU
2) dumu-munus-lugal
3) a-a-zi-mu
4) lú-aslag$_{X}$(TÚG) ir$_{11}$-zu

1–2) Šāt-Sîn, daughter of the king,

3–4) Aa-zimu, the fuller, (is) your servant.

91

A partially preserved impression found on a Drehem tablet dated to xi IS 2, gives part of a seal inscription of "Šāt-Sîn, *daughter* [of the king]" (see Šulgi — Royal Family item 20 above).

COMMENTARY

The seal impression, which is found on the tablet HSM 911.10.405, was not collated.

BIBLIOGRAPHY

1982 Owen, MVN 11 no. 204 (copy)
1984 Kutscher, Tel Aviv 11 p. 185 (study)

TEXT

1) *ša-at*-^{d}EN.ZU
2) ⌈dumu-munus⌉-[lugal]
Lacuna

1–2) Šāt-Sîn, *daughter* [of the king]
Lacuna

92

Three archival texts (PD 555: Salonen, Puzriš-Dagan-Texte no. 555 [no date]; PD 1210: Yıldız and Gomi, PDT 2 no. 1210 [xi Š 47]; and Cfc 158: Calvot and Pettinato, MVN 8 no. 115 [Š 48]) refer to a certain Tūlid-Šamši as *nin-dingir* priestess of the god Nanna/Suen. None of these sources indicate her father or mother. We would expect, however, that she was a member of the royal family. Seal inscriptions of two of her servants are known. The first is found on a tablet in the Princeton Theological Seminary.

COMMENTARY

The tablet bears the museum number PTS 531. It dates to v AS 3.

BIBLIOGRAPHY

1990 Sigrist, PTS no. 381, seal no. 125 (transliteration)

TEXT

1) *tu-li-id*-UTU$^{\check{s}i}$
2) nin-dingir-^{d}nanna
3) a-a-u_4-sù-šè
4) rá-gaba ir_{11}-zu

1–2) Tūlid-Šamšī, *nin-dingir* priestess of the god Nanna:
3–4) Aa-usuše, dispatch-rider, (is) your servant.

93

A seal inscription of a second servant of Tūlid-Šamšī is found on a tablet from Nippur.

COMMENTARY

The tablet bears the museum number CBS 8105; it dates to AS 1 (month name broken). The text is arranged in one column.

BIBLIOGRAPHY

1982 Owen, NATN no. 36 (copy)

TEXT

1) *tu-li-id*-UTU$^{\check{s}i}$
2) nin-dingir-⌜^{d}nanna⌝
3) ir_{11}-é(?)-x-x-x
4) ir_{11}-zu

1–2) Tūlid-Šamšī, *nin-dingir* priestess of the god Nanna:
3–4) PN (is) your servant.

94

A seal impression on a clay bulla names Šū-[Enlil], general of Uruk, as son of Šulgi (see Šulgi — Royal Family item 36 above).

COMMENTARY

The impression is found on MLC 2357, an undated clay bulla which is housed in the Yale collections. Lines 1–4 are found in col. i, lines 5–8 in col. ii. The inscription was collated.

Schneider (Orientalia NS 12 [1943] p. 187), followed by Sollberger (AfO 17 [1954–56] pp. 20–21), Goetze (JCS 17 [1963] p. 14), and Michalowski, (Mesopotamia 12 [1977] p. 83) restored the PN of line 5 as Šū-[Sîn]. This reading, in turn, was one of the pieces of "evidence" that led to the theory by which, contrary to the testimony of the Sumerian King List, Šulgi, not Amar-Suena was the father of Šū-Sîn. However, as noted in the introductory remarks for Šū-Sîn in this volume, data point unequivocally to the fact that Šū-Sîn was the son of Amar-Suena, not Šulgi. Steinkeller (ASJ 3 [1981] p. 83 n. 33) tried to explain the apparent discrepancy of the seal inscription published as BRM 3 no. 52 by translating Sumerian dumu of line 8 as "grandson" or "descendant." A much simpler explanation will be offered by W. Sallaberger in an article to appear in AoF 23 (1996); I am thankful to W. Sallaberger who kindly communicated a draft of this article to me in advance of its publication. Sallaberger indicates that the PN of line 8 should be restored as *šu-*[d]*en-*[*líl*]. Šū-Enlil is a son of Šulgi well attested in archival texts dating to the end of Šulgi's reign (see Šulgi — Royal Family item 36).

BIBLIOGRAPHY

1920 Keiser, BRM 3 no. 52 (copy)
1962 Hallo, HUCA 33 p. 42 Family 5 (study)
1963 Goetze, JCS 17 p. 15 (transliteration)
1971 Sollberger and Kupper, IRSA IIIA2x (translation)
1977 Michalowski, Mesopotamia 12 p. 83 (study)
1986 Kärki, KDDU p. 61 (Familie 5 =) Šulgi 55 (edition)
1987 Winter, in Gibson and Biggs, Bureaucracy p. 96 IIi (study)
1990 Pomponio, SEL 7 p. 7 (edition, study)

TEXT

1) [d]šul-gi
2) nita-kala-ga
3) lugal-uri$_5$.KI-ma
4) lugal-an-ub-da-límmu-ba
5) *šu-*[d]*en-*[*líl*]
6) GÌR.NÍTA
7) unu.KI-[ga]
8) dumu-ni-[im]

1–4) Šulgi, mighty man, king of Ur, king of the four quarters:

5–8) Šū-En[lil], general of Uruk, (is) his son.

95

An impression of a seal of Ur-Suena, general of Uruk and Dēr, is found on a tablet dated to Š 48 (no month name preserved). According to the tablet AM 1 dated to Š 44 (see Dhorme, RA 9 [1912] p. 42), Ur-Suena was a son of Šulgi (see Šulgi — Royal Family item 39 above).

COMMENTARY

The present whereabouts of the tablet with this seal impression are unknown. Lines 1–3 are found in col. i, lines 4–6 in col. ii.

For the important official Rīṣ-ilum of line 5, see the comments of P. Michalowski, SMS 2/3 (1978) p. 7; P. Steinkeller, RA 74 (1980) p. 6; and Oh'e, ASJ 5 (1983) p. 120.

BIBLIOGRAPHY

1916 Scheil, RA 13 pp. 20–21 (copy, edition)
1977 Michalowski, Mesopotamia 12 p. 84 n. 3 (study)

TEXT

1) ur-^{d}EN.ZU	1–4) Ur-Suena, general of Uruk and Dēr:
2) GÌR.NÍTA	
3) unu.KI-ga	
4) ù BÀD.AN.KI	
5) *ri-iṣ*-DINGIR	5–6) Rīṣ-ilum (is) his dispatch rider.
6) rá-gaba-ni	

96

An impression of a seal of a servant of Ur-Suena is found on a letter order from Umma (see Šulgi — Royal Family item 39 above).

COMMENTARY

The impression is found on the tablet NBC 1934.

BIBLIOGRAPHY

1937 Hackman, BIN 5 no. 316 (copy)
1966 Sollberger, Correspondence no. 264 (edition)
1977 Michalowski, Mesopotamia 12 p. 84 n. 3 (study)

TEXT

1) ur-^{d}EN.ZU	1–3) Ur-Suena, general of Uruk and [D]ēr:
2) GÌR.NÍTA-unu.KI-ga	
3) ù [B]ÀD.AN.KI-⸢ka⸣	
4) ur-^{d}en-ki	4–5) Ur-Enki, city elder, (is) your servant.
5) ab-ba uru ir$_{11}$-zu	

97

The impression of a seal of a third servant of Ur-Suena is found on a tablet from Drehem dated to i AS 1 (see Šulgi — Royal Family item 39 above).

COMMENTARY

The tablet is number 0 68 in the collection of the Musées Royaux d'Art et d'Histoire (Brussels). Lines 1–3 are found in col. i, lines 4–6 in col. ii. The inscription was collated from the published photo.

BIBLIOGRAPHY

1911 de Genouillac, Trouvaille no. 74 (copy)
1917 Speleers, Catalogue pp. 140–41 no. 68 (photo, edition)
1977 Michalowski, Mesopotamia 12 p. 84 n. 3 (study)

TEXT

1) ur-^{d}EN.ZU	1–4) Ur-Suena, general of Uruk and Dē[r]:
2) GÌR.NÍTA	
3) unu.KI-ga	
4) ù BÀD[AN.KI]	
5) *ma-š*[*um*]	5–6) Maš[um] (is) [your] servant.
6) ir$_{11}$-[zu]	

Votive and Seal Inscriptions (c) Of City Governors 2001–2029

The extensive archival texts of Ur III date provide us with the names of many city governors for the reign of Šulgi. The list of governors' names summarized in the following chart derives from the data found in Keiser, Patesis; Hallo, Ensi's and from an unpublished update kindly communicated by Hallo and cited as Hallo, Ensi's^{2} in this study; A. Goetze, JCS 17 (1963) pp. 1–31; Edzard, Rép. Géogr. 2; D. Owen, JCS 33 (1981) pp. 244–70; ibid., JAOS 108 (1988) pp. 111–22; ibid., BiOr 49 (1992) pp. 445–47; T. Maeda, ASJ 14 (1992) pp. 162–63; and ibid., ASJ 16 (1994) pp. 156–62. The names of governors appearing in seal inscriptions edited in this volume are marked with an asterisk (*). Names appearing in seal inscriptions are marked with (s); those named in tablets with (t). Dates, where they are attested, follow in parentheses (day, month).

Since so many tablets impressed with seal inscriptions mentioning Ur-Lisi, governor of Umma, are known, they have not been included in the chart.

Year	Adab	Babylon	Ereš	Ešnunna	Girsu/Lagaš
28	—	—	—	—	**lú-giri$_{17}$-zal*** de Genouillac, ITT 2 no. 4312 (s) (- xi) (**E3/2.1.2.2014**)
29	—	—	—	—	—
30	—	—	—	—	—
31	—	—	—	**ur-gú-edin-na** As 31 T. 333, see Jacobsen, AS 6 p. 2; Hallo, Ensi's p. 15 (t)	—
32	—	—	—	—	**lú-giri$_{17}$-zal*** Thureau-Dangin, RTC no. 422 (s)(- -) (**E3/2.1.2.2013**); Delaporte, ITT 4 no. 7220 (s) (- xii) (**E3/2.1.2.2015**)
33	—	—	***é-a-ba-ni*** Owen, MVN 3 no. 136 line 6 (t) (- iv); Watson, Birmingham 1 no. 134 line 35 (t) (- xiii)	—	**ur-^{d}lamma*** Thureau-Dangin, RTC no. 420 (s) (x–xiii) (**E3/2.1.2.2018**); Thureau-Dangin, RTC no. 421 (s) (iv–ix) (**E3/2.1.2.2018**); Delaporte, ITT 4 no. 7152 (s) (- -) (not edited); Thureau-Dangin, in Cros, Tello p. 185 AO 4237 (s) (- i) (not edited)
34	—	—	—	—	—
35	—	—	—	—	—
36	—	—	—	—	**ur-^{d}lamma** Delaporte, ITT 4 no. 7165b (s) (- iv)(not edited); Delaporte, ITT 4 no. 7264 (- vii) (s) (not edited); Delaporte, ITT 4 no. 7162 (s) (- -) (not edited)
37	—	—	**ur-^{d}nin-mug** Owen, MVN 3 no. 152 line 45 (t) (- iii)	—	—
38	**ḫa-ba-lu$_{5}$-ge*** Owen, MVN 3 no. 250 line 1 (s) (14 -) (**E3/2.1.2.2005**)	—	—	—	**ur-^{d}lamma** Delaporte, ITT 4 no. 7214 (s)(- x) (not edited)
39	**ur-^{d}ašaš$_{7}$-gi$_{4}$*** Owen, MVN 3 no. 166 (s) (- viii) (**E3/2.1.2.2003**); **ḫa-ba-lu$_{5}$-ge*** Owen, MVN 3 no. 172 (s) (- viii) and no. 165 (s) (- ix) (**E3/2.1.2.2005**)	—	—	—	—

Year	Adab	Babylon	Ereš	Ešnunna	Girsu/Lagaš
40	**ḫa-ba-lu$_5$-ge*** Owen, MVN 3 no. 183 (s) (25 vii); no. 184 (s) (- -) and no. 327 (s) (- -) (**E3/2.1.2.2005**)	—	—	—	**lú-giri$_{17}$-zal*** Thureau-Dangin, RTC no. 423 (s) (- -) (**E3/2.1.2.2017**); Gomi and Sato, British Museum no. 14 (s)(- iv) (**E3/2.1.2.2016**); **al-la*** Thureau-Dangin, RTC 424 (s) (- iv) (**E3/2.1.2.2020**); for other duplicates of the seal inscription, see (**E3/2.1.2.2020**)
41	**ur-^{d}ašas$_7$-gi$_4$*** Owen, MVN 3 no. 188 (s) (- x) (**E3/2.1.2.2003**)	—	—	—	—
42	—	***ar-ši-aḫ*** A 4653, see Hallo, JCS 14 (1960) p. 109 no. 7 line 5 (t) (- xi) (a dating to AS 6 is possible); A 5329 see Hallo, JCS 14 (1960) p. 109 no. 8 line 6 (t) (- xi) (a dating to AS 6 possible)	—	—	—
43	—	***ar-ši-aḫ*** de Genouillac, TCL 2 no. 4679 line 3 (t) (- iii) ***i-túr*-DINGIR** YBC 16573 lines 5–7 (**E3/2.1.2.2008**)	—	—	—
44	—	**ab-ba** Oppenheim, Eames Collection, Eames L 6 = Sauren, New York Public Library no. 215 lines 5–6 (t) (ii min)	—	—	**ur-^{d}lamma** Salonen, Puzriš-Dagan-Texte no. 425 line 10 (t) (v–vi); Thureau-Dangin, RTC no. 305 col. iv line 10 (t) (xii–xiii); Barton, Haverford 1 pl. 10 no. 309 line 2 (t) (- -)
45	—	***ar-ši-aḫ*** MLC 2601 (- v)	—	**ba-mu** Yıldız and Gomi, PDT 2 no. 1246 line 3 (t) (- x)	—
46	—	***ar-ši-aḫ*** de Genouillac, Trouvaille no. 78 line 15 (t) (- -)	—	**ba-mu** Fish, Catalogue no. 119 (t) (- vii)	**ur-^{d}lamma** Limet, RA 62 (1968) p. 6 no. 7 line 7 (t) (- xi); Delaporte, RA 8 (1911) p. 185 no. 3 line 5 (t) (- xi)

Year	Adab	Babylon	Ereš	Ešnunna	Girsu/Lagaš
47	**ḫa-ba-lu₅-ge** A 3111 (Chicago); see Hallo, Ensi's p. 5 (t) (- v); Legrain, UET 3 no. 15 rev. line 8′ (- -) (t)	—	—	**kal-la-mu** de Genouillac, TCL 2 no. 5493 lines 5–6 (t) (- ix)	**ur-ᵈlamma** Legrain, TRU no. 117 (xii–xiii)
48	—	—	—	**kal-la-mu** A 2952 (Chicago), see Hallo, Ensi's p. 15 (t) (- x); Weidner, RSO 9 (1921–23) p. 472 Peiser 367 (now in Böhl Collection, date lost, Hallo, [JCS 14 (1960) p. 90] suggests Š 48 or 49)	—

Year	Išīm-Šulgi	Kazallu	Kutha	Marad	Nippur
33	—	***i-za-rí-iq*** Keiser, YOS 4 no. 75 line 6 (t) (- iii)	—	—	—
34	—	—	—	—	—
35	—	—	—	—	—
36	—	—	—	—	**ur-ᵈnanibgal** Zettler, Ur III Temple p. 294 6 NT 606+668, 687–88 and 902 (= IM 61716) rev. vi lines 8′–10′ (t) (- -)
37	—	—	—	***wa-a-tá-ru-um*** Keiser, Patesis p. 22; see Hallo, Ensi's p. 29	—
38	—	—	—	—	—
39	—	—	—	—	—
40	—	—	—	—	—
41	—	—	—	—	—
42	—	—	—	—	—
43	—	—	—	—	—
44	—	—	—	—	**ur-ᵈnanibgal** Schneider, Orientalia 18 (1925) pl. II no. 6 line 9 (t) (19 vii)
45	—	—	**nam-zi-tar-ra** Owen, ASJ 15 (1993) p. 137 line 3 (t) (9 vii)	—	**ur-nanibgal*** Zettler, Ur III Temple p. 295 (A 31226) (s) (- ii) **(E3/2.1.2.2024)**
46	—	—	—	—	—
47	—	—	—	—	—
48	**lugal-pa-è** (HTS no. 139), see Sollberger, JCS 10 (1956) p. 24 no. 12 (t); Sigrist, AUCT 2 no. 281 line 3 (t) (- viii)	—	—	***li-ša-num**** (s) (undated)	—

Year	Puš	Simurrum	Susa	Šarrākum	Šuruppak
31	—	—	—	—	**lugal-ḫé-du₇** As 31 T. 333, see Hallo, Ensi's p. 42 (t)
32	—	—	—	—	—
33	—	—	***ur-ki-um*** Thureau-Dangin, RTC no. 329 line 3 (t) (- iv)	—	—
34	—	—	—	—	—
35	—	—	—	—	—
36	—	—	—	**lú-bàn-da** Deimel, Orientalia 6 (1923) p. 60 no. 12 (Wengler 50) line 11 (t) (- -)	—
37	—	—	—	—	—
38	—	—	—	**lú-bàn-da*** Oppenheim, Eames Collection, Eames S 10 = Sauren, New York Public Library no. 281A (s) (- xi) **(E3/2.1.2.2026)**	—
39	—	—	—	—	**ur-nìgin-gar-ra*** Pettinato and Waetzoldt, MVN 1 no. 198 (s)(- iv) **(E3/2.1.2.2027)**
40	***a-ḫu-a*** Keiser, BIN 3 no. 336 lines 8–9 (t) (6 iv)	—	***za-rí-iq*** Rashid, TIM 6 no. 6 line 4 (t) (- xi) (Susa not mentioned)	—	—
41	—	—	***za-rí-iq*** Sigrist, AUCT 1 no. 954 line 3 (t) (- vii)	—	—
42	—	—	—	—	—
43	—	—	—	—	—
44	—	***ṣi-lu-uš-ᵈda-gan*** Owen, MVN 3 no. 200 line 2 (t) (30 i) (no indication of status)	—	—	—
45	—	—	—	—	—
46	**igi-an-na-⌈é⌉-zu** Nies, UDT no. 154 line 14 (t) (22 ii)	—	—	—	—
47	***a-ḫu-ma*** de Genouillac, TCL 2 no. 5501 col. iv (= rev. ii) line 22 (t) (22 ii); ***a-ḫu!-ma*** (collated) Oppenheim, Eames Collection, I 10 (Bab. 21) = Sauren, New York Public Library no. 353 lines 4–5 (t) (- ii); A 4504 (Chicago); see Hallo, Ensi's p. 38 (11 v)	—	—	—	—
48	—	—	—	—	—

Year	TiWA (A.ḪA)	Uruk	Umma	Urum (ÚR×Ú)
33	—	—	—	—
34	—	—	**ur-ᵈli₉-si₄** Scheil, RT 19 (1897) p. 62–63 (t) (- -); cf. MLC nos. 1311 and 1312 (t); HTS nos. 55–57 (t); see Hallo, Ensi's² p. 59	—
35	—	—	**ur-ᵈli₉-si₄** WHM no. 380, see Hallo Ensi's² p. 59 (t) (- vi)	—
36	—	—	—	—
37	—	—	—	—
38	—	—	—	—
39	—	—	—	—
40	—	—	—	—
41	—	—	**ur-ᵈli-si₄** YBC 379 (s) (- -)	—
42	—	—	**ur-ᵈli₉-si₄** NCBT 1556 (t) (- viii), see Hallo, Ensi's² p. 59; Oppenheim, Eames Collection, Eames I 13 = Sauren, New York Public Library no. 164 line 2 (t) (- xi)	—
43	***a-mur-*ᵈEN.ZU** de Genouillac, Trouvaille no. 80 line 3 (t) (24 iii)	—	—	**ur-ᵈEN.ZU** Boson, Aegyptus 17 (1937) p. 58 no. 121 = Archi and Pomponio, Torino no. 211 rev. line 1 (t) (- viii)
44	—	—	—	**ur-ᵈEN.ZU** de Genouillac, TCL 2 no. 5487 line 3 (t) (- x)
45	—	—	—	
46	***a-mur-*ᵈEN.ZU** de Genouillac, Trouvaille no. 78 line 15 (t) (- -)	—	—	
47	—	—	**ur-ᵈli₉-si₄** Keiser, YOS 4 no. 86 lines 4–5 (t) (- i)	
48	—	***šar-ru-um-ì-lí*** (HSM 911.3.108); see Michalowski, Mesopotamia 12 (1977) p. 93 line 2 (t) (- x)	**ur-ᵈli₉-si₄** Oppenheim, Eames Collection, Eames W 29 = Sauren, New York Public Library no. 291 lines 5–6 (t) (- i); Schneider, Orientalia 47–49 (1930) no. 60 lines 4–5	

2001

Tablets dated to Š 29 and 31 refer to a certain Ur-Ašgi as governor of Adab. A votive inscription of the governor, now only partially preserved, was dedicated to the goddess Ninḫursaga for the life of Šulgi.

COMMENTARY

The inscription is formed by the join of three chlorite vase fragments, A 199 (frgm. 1) + LB 934 (frgm. 2) + A 202 (frgm. 3). Fragments 1 and 3 are in the Oriental Institute of the University of Chicago and fragment 2 in the De Liagre Böhl Collection of the Netherlands Institute for the Near East, Leiden. Van Dijk said that fragment 2 was diorite, but it is clearly chlorite. Fragment 1 was found 70 cm below the surface in a small room eight metres from the west corner of the temple tower on Mound V (see Banks, Bismya p. 257). The text is arranged in one column. The inscription was collated.

BIBLIOGRAPHY

1912 Banks, Bismya p. 257 (frgm. 3, copy, study)
1930 Luckenbill, Adab no. 36 (frgm. 3, copy)
1949 Nestmann, Excavations fig. 40 (frgms. 1 and 3, photo)
1957 van Dijk, TLB 2 no. 14 (frgm. 2, copy)
1962 Hallo, HUCA 33 p. 32 Šulgi 33 (frgm. 2, study); p. 41 Anonymous 3 (frgms. 1 and 3, study)
1986 Kärki, KDDU p. 44 Šulgi 33 (frgm. 2, edition); p. 151 Anonym 3 (frgms. 1, 3, edition)
1986 Yang, Sargonic Archive p. 23 no. 4 (frgm. 3, study)
1989 Yang, Sargonic Inscriptions p. 110 (frgm. 3, study)
1991 Braun-Holzinger, Weihgaben p. 185 G 346 (frgm. 2, edition); pp. 196–97 G 410 (frgm. 3, edition)
1991 Steible, NSBW 2 pp. 189–90 Šulgi 33 (frgm. 2, edition); pp. 349–50 Adab 2 (frgm. 3, edition)

TEXT

1)   ᵈnin-ḫur-saga
2)   nin-a-ni
3)   nam-t[i]-
4)   ᵈšul-g[i]
5)   nita-kala-ga
6)   lugal-uri₅.KI-˹ma˺
7)   lugal-ki-en-gi-ki-[uri-ka-šè]
8)   ur-ᵈašaš₇-g[i]
9)   [énsi]
10) [adab.KI]
11) [a mu-na-ru]

1–2) To the goddess Ninḫursaga, his lady,

3–5) for the li[fe] of Šulgi, mighty man,

6–7) king of Ur, king of the lands of Sumer [and Akkad],

8–11) Ur-Ašgi, [governor of Adab, dedicated (this vase)].

2002

The impression of a seal of a servant of the Adab governor Ur-Ašgi is found on a tablet found at Ur (but according to Steinkeller, Sale Documents p. 251 originally from Adab) dated to Š 29.

COMMENTARY

The impression is found on U 6746, a tablet that was found in the SE corner of the E-gipar-ku at Ur. According to the catalogue in Legrain, UET 3/2 p. 284 listing the distribution of the objects, the piece should be in the British Museum.

BIBLIOGRAPHY

1928 Gadd, UET 1 no. 79 (copy of seal inscription, edition)
1947 Legrain, UET 3 no. 19 (copy of tablet and seal inscription)
1951 Legrain, UE 10 no. 426 (photo, transliteration, study [of seal and seal inscription])
1958 Kraus, BiOr 15 p. 72 (study of tablet)
1989 Steinkeller, Sale Documents pp. 251–53 no. 67 (edition)

TEXT

1) ur-^{d}[^{aš}aš$_7$-gi$_4$]
2) énsi
3) adab.KI
4) a-a-kal-la
5) egir ir$_{11}$-zu

1–3) Ur-[Ašgi], governor of Adab:

4–5) Aa-kala, "retainer" (is) your servant.

2003

Tablets dated to Š 39 and 41 (see Owen JCS 33 [1981] p. 247) bear impressions of a seal of a servant of Ur-Ašgi. The text is arranged in one column.

CATALOGUE

Ex.	Museum number	MVN 3 number	Date
1	FLP 218	166	viii Š 39
2	FLP 250	188	x Š 41
3	FLP 1349	355	—
4	FLP 1362	365	—
5	FLP 1377	378	—

BIBLIOGRAPHY

1975 Owen, MVN 3 nos. 188, 355, and 378 (exs. 2–3, 5, copy)

TEXT

1) ur-^{daš}aš$_7$-gi$_4$
2) énsi-adab.KI
3) ur-pap-mu-ra
4) dub-sar
5) ir$_{11}$-zu

1–2) Ur-Ašgi, governor of Adab:

3–5) Ur-Papmura, scribe, (is) your servant.

2004

Tablets dated to Š 38–40 (see D. Owen [JCS 33 [1981] p. 247) bear impressions of a seal of a servant of the Adab governor Ḫabaluge. For a discussion of the Sumerian PN ḫa ba-lu$_5$-gé = Akkadian *liwwir* "May he shine," see A. Alberti, NABU 1990 pp. 101–102 no. 123. Ḫabaluge is also mentioned in two tablets (A 3111 and UET 3 no. 15; see Hallo, Ensi's p. 5) that date to Š 47.

A fragment of a stone bowl in Berlin was dedicated by governor Ḫabaluge for the life of Šulgi.

COMMENTARY

The dark-brown bowl fragment measures 12 cm in length and 4.5 cm in height, with a rim thickness of 0.9–1.3 cm, and an original diameter of about 21.5 cm. It bears the museum number VA 3324. The text is arranged in one column. The inscription was collated. For the reading of line 8, see Steible, NSBW 2 p. 188 n. 1.

BIBLIOGRAPHY

1907 Messerschmidt, VAS 1 no. 25 (copy)
1962 Hallo, HUCA 33 p. 32 Šulgi 31 (study)
1971 Sollberger and Kupper, IRSA IIIC1a (translation)
1986 Kärki, KDDU p. 43 Šulgi 31 (edition)
1991 Braun-Holzinger, Weihgaben p. 185 G 344 (edition)
1991 Steible, NSBW 2 p. 188 Šulgi 31 (edition)

TEXT

1) dingir-maḫ
2) nin-a-ni
3) nam-ti-
4) dšul-gi
5) nita-kala-ga
6) lugal-uri5.KI-ma
7) lugal-an-ub-da-límmu-ba-ka-šè
8) [ḫa-ba-l]ú-gé
9) [éns]i-
10) [adab.KI]
11) [a mu-na-ru]

1–2) For the goddess Dingirmah, his lady,

3–7) for the life of Šulgi, mighty man, king of Ur, king of the four quarters,

8–11) [Ḫabal]uge, [govern]or of [Adab, dedicated (this bowl)].

2005

Impressions of a seal of a servant of Ḫabaluge are found on eight tablets in the Free Library of Philadelphia collection.

CATALOGUE

Ex.	Museum number	MVN 3 number	Date
1	FLP 217	165	x Š 39
2	FLP 224	172	vii Š 39
3	FLP 242	183	vii Š 40
4	FLP 243	184	— Š 40
5	FLP 808	250	— Š 38
6	FLP 1158	327	Š 40 (?)
7	FLP 1350	356	—
8	FLP 1380	381	—

COMMENTARY

The text is arranged in one column.

BIBLIOGRAPHY

1975 Owen, MVN 3 no. 250 (ex. 5 copy)
1986 Yang, Sargonic Archive p. 44 (transliteration)
1989 Yang, Sargonic Inscriptions p. 26 (edition)

TEXT

1) ḫa-ba-lu$_5$-gé
2) énsi-adab.KI
3) amar-šúba(MÙŠ.ZA)
4) dub-sar ir$_{11}$-zu

1–2) Ḫabaluge, governor of Adab:
3–4) Amar-šuba, scribe, (is) your servant.

2006

An impression of a seal of a servant of Itūr-ilum, governor of Babylon, is found on a tablet in the Horn Archaeological Museum.

COMMENTARY

The impression is found on AUAM 73.3155, a tablet dated to the sixth month at Drehem (year not recorded). The text is arranged in one column.

BIBLIOGRAPHY

1988 Sigrist, AUCT 3 no. 366 (copy)

TEXT

1) *i-túr*-DINGIR
2) énsi-
3) KÁ.DINGIR.KI-ma!(Copy: KA)
4) lugal-dalla
5) dub-sar ir$_{11}$-zu

1–3) Itūr-ilum, governor of Babylon:
4–5) Lugal-dalla, scribe, (is) your servant.

2007

The impression of a seal of a son of Itūr-ilum is found on a tablet in the Yale collections.

COMMENTARY

The impression is found on NBC 1316, an undated tablet. Lines 1–3 are found in column i, lines 4–6 in col. ii. The inscription was collated.

BIBLIOGRAPHY

1920 Keiser, BIN 2 no. 30 (copy, edition)

TEXT

1) *i-túr*-DINGIR 2) énsi- 3) KÁ.DINGIR.KI	1–3) Itūr-ilum, governor of Babylon:
4) *i-ṣ̣ur*-DINGIR 5) dub-sar 6) dumu-ni	4–6) Iṣṣur-ilum, scribe, (is) his son.

2008

A seal impression on a tablet in the Yale collections names a certain Abba as son of Itūr-ilum. Abba is further attested as governor of Babylon in a tablet dated to Š 44 (Oppenheim, Eames Collection, Eames L 6 = Sauren, New York Public Library no. 215).

COMMENTARY

The impression is found on YBC 16573, which dates to Š 43. Lines 1–4 are found in col. i, lines 5–8 in col. ii. The seal inscription was collated.

BIBLIOGRAPHY

1920 Keiser, BIN 2 p. 48 (edition)
1962 Hallo, HUCA 33 p. 34 Šulgi 53i (study)
1971 Sollberger and Kupper, IRSA IIIA2y (translation)
1986 Kärki, KDDU p. 54 Šulgi 53a (i) (edition)

TEXT

1) ^{d}šul-gi 2) nita-kala-ga 3) lugal-uri$_5$.KI-ma 4) [lugal-an-ub-da-límmu-ba]	1–4) Šulgi, mighty man, king of Ur, [king of the four quarters]:
5) ab-ba dub-[sar] 6) dumu *i-túr*-DINGIR 7) énsi KÁ.DINGIR.KI-ma 8) ir$_{11}$-zu	5–8) Abba, scri[be], son of Itūr-ilum, governor of Babylon, (is) your servant.

2009

Tablets dating to Š 47–48 and AS 1, 4, and 7 attest to a certain Kalamu as governor of Ešnunna. A seal impression of a servant of Kalamu is found on an undated tablet from Nippur. It has been arbitrarily listed here under Šulgi.

COMMENTARY

The tablet bears the museum number CBS 14177. The text is arranged in one column. The inscription was collated.

BIBLIOGRAPHY

1922 Legrain, PBS 13 no. 31 (copy, transliteration)
1925 Legrain, PBS 14 no. 285 (photo, edition)
1929 Barton, RISA pp. 152–53 Kallamu 1 (edition)
1934 Jacobsen, AS 6 p. 3 (partial edition)
1953 Hallo, Ensi's p. 16 (partial edition)

TEXT

1) kal-la-mu
2) énsi-
3) áš-nun-na.KI-ka
4) lú-dEN.ZU dub-sar
5) dumu é-ki-gal-la
6) ir_{11}-zu

1–3) Kalamu, governor of Ešnunna:

4–6) Lu-Suena, scribe, son of E-kigala, (is) your servant.

2010

Lu-girizal, governor of Lagaš, is attested in tablets dating to the last half of Šulgi's reign.

A fragment of a stone bowl found in excavations at Girsu was dedicated by Lu-girizal for the life of Šulgi.

COMMENTARY

This fragment of a large shallow grey alabaster bowl has a double fluted rim. The rim of the bowl measures 5.7 cm in height (originally about 6 cm) with an original diameter of 22 cm and a thickness of 1.3 cm. It was found at Tell K at Telloh together with G 277 and G 406, and bears the museum number AO 191. Since Šulgi's name appears without the prefixed DINGIR sign, the inscription must date to sometime before Š 21. The text is arranged in one column. The inscription was collated.

BIBLIOGRAPHY

1897 Heuzey, RA 4 p. 90 fig. 2 (copy)
1900 Heuzey, Villa royale p. 4 no. 2 (copy)
1907 Thureau-Dangin, SAK pp. 194–95 Dun-gi v (edition)
1929 Barton, RISA pp. 280–81 Shulgi 22 (edition)
1948 Parrot, Tello p. 221 n. 344 (study)
1962 Hallo, HUCA 33 p. 32 Šulgi 32 (study)
1971 Sollberger and Kupper, IRSA IIIB4a (translation)
1986 Kärki, KDDU pp. 43–44 Šulgi 32 (edition)
1991 Braun-Holzinger, Weihgaben p. 185 G 345 (edition)
1991 Steible, NSBW 2 p. 189 Šulgi 32 (edition)

TEXT

1) ^{d}nin-gír-su 2) ur-s[ag-kal]a-ga- 3) ^{d}e[n-l]íl-lá 4) lugal-a-n[i]	1–4) For the god Ningirsu, [migh]ty he[ro] of the god E[nl]il, hi[s] lord,
5) nam-ti- 6) šul-g[i] 7) ni[t]a-ka[la-ga] 8) [l]ugal-uri$_5$.KI-ma-ka-šè	5–8) for the life of Šulg[i], mi[ghty] m[a]n, [k]ing of Ur,
9) lú-giri$_{17}$-zal 10) énsi- 11) ⌜lagaš.KI⌝-[ke$_4$] 12) [a mu-na-ru]	9–12) Lu-girizal, governor of Lagaš, [dedicated (this bowl)].

2011

A limestone tablet was dedicated to the goddess Inanna by a son of Lu-girizal.

COMMENTARY

The tablet, found in excavations at Girsu, measures 10.9×6.9×0.5 cm, and was given the excavation number TG 1459. It bears the museum number AO 16650. Lines 1–9 are found on the obverse of the tablet, lines 10–12 on the reverse. The inscription was collated.

For the date of the Lu-girizal of this tablet, see Steible, NSBW 2 p. 336 sub Lu-girizal 1. For the name Nin-anše-la, which, like Ninkununa, is probably a surname of Inanna and not an epithet, see Pettinato, ZA 60 (1970) p. 212 S. 133, and Sallaberger, Kalender 1 p. 128 n. 597.

BIBLIOGRAPHY

1947 Nougayrol, RA 41 pp. 24–25 (photo, edition)
1948 Parrot, Tello pl. 22 b+c (photo)
1968 Sollberger, RA 62 pp. 138–39 (study)
1971 Sollberger and Kupper, IRSA IIIB4b (translation)
1991 Steible, NSBW 2 Lu-girizal 1 pp. 335–36 (edition)

TEXT

1) ^{d}inanna 2) ^{d}nin an-šè lá-a 3) nin-⌜un⌝-gal- 4) dingir-re-ne 5) nin-a-ni	1–5) For the goddess Inanna/Nin-anše-la, exalted lady of the gods, his lady,

6) nam-⸢maḫ⸣-ni-du$_{10}$
7) ⸢dumu(?)⸣-lú-giri$_{17}$-zal
8) [é]nsi-
9) ⸢lagaš⸣.KI-ka-ke$_{4}$
10) mu-tu
11) é-a-ni
12) mu-na-dù

6–10) Nammaḫni-du, *son* of Lu-girizal, [g]overnor of Lagaš, formed (this statue).

11–12) He built her (Inanna's) temple for her.

2012

A diorite statuette of a standing female figure was dedicated by Ḫala-Lamma, daughter of governor Lu-girizal, to the goddess Lamma-TAR-sirsira.

COMMENTARY

The statuette was found in excavations at Girsu and bears the museum number AO 44. Lines 1–6 are found in col. i, lines 7–12 in col. ii. The text was collated.

As Steible (NSBW 2 p. 185) points out, we would expect a dedicatory verb after line 12. Unfortunately, the fact that a large hole is found immediately to the right of col. ii prevents us from determining exactly how the inscription ended.

BIBLIOGRAPHY

1884–1912 de Sarzec, Découvertes 2 pl. 21 no. 4 (photo)
1892 Winckler and Böhden, ABK no. 34 (copy)
1907 Thureau-Dangin, SAK pp. 194–95 Dun-gi w (edition)
1929 Barton, RISA pp. 282–83 Shulgi 24 (edition)
1948 Parrot, Tello pp. 221 and 233 fig. 46g (study, drawing)
1962 Hallo, HUCA 33 p. 32 Šulgi 28 (study)
1971 Sollberger and Kupper, IRSA IIIB4c (translation)
1981 Spycket, Statuaire pp. 210–11 and n. 133 (study)
1986 Kärki, KDDU pp. 41–42 Šulgi 28 (edition)
1991 Braun-Holzinger, Weihgaben p. 274 St 153 (edition)
1991 Steible, NSBW 2 pp. 184–85 Šulgi 28 (edition)

TEXT

1) [^{d}lamma-TAR-s]ír-[sí]r-ra
2) [ama-^{d}]ba-ba$_{6}$
3) [nin-a]-ni
4) [nam-t]i-
5) [^{d}šu]l-gi
6) [nita-ka]la-ga
7) lugal-uri$_{5}$.KI-ma
8) lugal-ki-en-<gi>-ki-uri-ka-šè
9) ḫa-la-^{d}lamma
10) dumu-lú-giri$_{17}$-zal
11) énsi-
12) ⸢lagaš.KI-ka⸣-ke$_{4}$
Lacuna

1–3) [To the goddess Lamma-TAR-s]ir-[si]r, [mother of the goddess] Baba, her [lady],

4–8) for the [lif]e of [Šu]lgi, [migh]ty [man], king of Ur, king of the lands of Su<mer> and Akkad,

9–12) Ḫala-Lamma, daughter of Lu-girizal, governor of Lagaš (dedicated this statuette).
Lacuna

2013

An impression of a seal of a servant of Lu-girizal is found on a tablet from Girsu dated to Š 32 (no month date preserved).

COMMENTARY

The tablet bears the museum number AO 3545; the inscription was collated. Lines 1–3 are found in col. i, lines 4–7 in col. ii.

BIBLIOGRAPHY

1903 Thureau-Dangin, RTC no. 422 (copy)
1907 Thureau-Dangin, SAK pp. 148–49 Galu-ka-zal c (edition)
1920 Delaporte, Louvre 1 p. 17 and pl. 11 no. 3 T. 148 (photo, edition)
1929 Barton, RISA pp. 266–67 Lukani 2 (edition)

TEXT

1) lú-giri$_{17}$-zal
2) énsi-
3) lagaš.KI
4) ur-^{d}[nanše]
5) dub-sa[r]
6) dumu a[l-la]
7) ir$_{11}$-[zu]

1–3) Lu-girizal, governor of Lagaš:

4–7) Ur-[Nanše], scrib[e], son of A[lla], (is) [your] servant.

2014

An impression of a seal of Aba-kala, servant of Lu-girizal, is found on a tablet from Girsu dated to xi Š 29. The PN of line 4 is restored from the tablet.

COMMENTARY

The tablet bears the museum number L 4312 (Istanbul). Lines 1–3 are found in col. i, lines 4–6 in col. ii.

BIBLIOGRAPHY

1910 de Genouillac, ITT 2/1 pl. 62 no. 4312 (copy)
1929 Barton, RISA pp. 266–67 Lukani 3 (edition)

TEXT

1)	lú-$giri_{17}$-zal	1–3) Lu-girizal, governor of Lagaš:
2)	énsi-	
3)	lagaš.KI	
4)	ab-b[a-kal-la]	4–6) Ab[a-kala], *sanga* priest of URU×KAR, (is) [your] servant.
5)	sanga-URU×KÁR.[KI]	
6)	ir_{11}-[zu]	

2015

An impression of a seal of a servant of Lu-girizal (reading of a restored text) is found on a tablet (dated to Š 32) and its envelope (dated to Š 33).

COMMENTARY

The tablet together with its envelope bear the museum number L 7220 (Istanbul). The tablet measures 9.5×5.4 cm. Lines 1–4 are found in col. i, lines 5–7 in col. ii.

For Sumerian ka-gur_7, cf. Akkadian *kagurrû(m)* "official in charge of grain stores."

BIBLIOGRAPHY

1912 Delaporte, ITT 4 p. 24 no. 7220 (edition)
1977 Pettinato, MVN 6 no. 216 (transliteration)

TEXT

1)	lú-[$giri_{17}$-zal]	1–3) Lu-[girizal], governor of Lagaš:
2)	énsi-	
3)	lagaš.KI	
4)	ur-^{d}lamma	4–7) Ur-Lamma, official in charge of the grain stores of the goddess Ninmarki, (is) your servant.
5)	ka-gur_7-	
6)	^{d}nin-mar-ki-ka	
7)	ir_{11}-zu	

2016

An impression of a seal of Ur-kisal, servant of Lu-girizal, is found on a tablet in the British Museum.

COMMENTARY

The tablet bears the museum number BM 13016. The tablet is dated to iv Š 40. Lines 1–4 are found in col. i, lines 5–7 in col. ii.

BIBLIOGRAPHY

1990 Gomi and Sato, British Museum no. 14 (transliteration)

TEXT

1) lú-giri$_{17}$-zal
2) énsi-
3) [lagaš.KI]
4) ur-kisal
5) dub-[sar]
6) du[mu ...]
7) ir$_{11}$-[zu]

1–3) Lu-girizal, governor of [Lagaš]:

4–7) Ur-kisal, sc[ribe], so[n] of [...], (is) [your] servant.

2017

An impression of a seal of Lu-URU×KAR, servant of Lu-girizal, is found on a tablet in Paris.

COMMENTARY

The impression is found on AO 3546. The tablet is dated to iv Š 40. Lines 1–3 are found in col. i, lines 4–7 in col. ii.

BIBLIOGRAPHY

1903 Thureau-Dangin, RTC no. 423 (copy)
1920 Delaporte, Louvre 1 p. 19 T. 179 (edition)

TEXT

1) lú-giri$_{17}$-zal
2) énsi-
3) lagaš.KI
4) lú-URU×KÁR.[KI]
5) dub-sar
6) dumu ur-^{d}ni[n-bára]
7) ir$_{11}$-⌈zu⌉

1–3) Lu-girizal, governor of Lagaš:

4–7) Lu-URU×KAR, scribe, son of Ur-Ni[n-bara], (is) your servant.

2018

Lu-girizal was followed by Ur-Lamma as governor of Lagaš. Here we edit the seal inscription of his servant Ur-nigin-gar (RTC 420 [dating to x–xiii Š 35 and iv–ix Š 35]) as being representative of the servant seals of the governor.

This and other servant seals of Ur-Lamma are listed in the chart given below.

No.	Owner of Seal	Published	Date
1	ur-nìgin-gar dub-sar dumu lú-⸢an⸣-[né]; see below	Thureau-Dangin, RTC nos. 420–21	Š 32
2	ur-^{d}ba-ba$_{6}$ dub-sar dumu ur-dun	Delaporte, ITT 4 p. 15 and pl. 7 no. 7152	Š 33
3	^{d}utu [bar-ra] dumu [...]	Thureau-Dangin, in Cros, Tello p. 185 AO 4237	Š 33
4	ur-^{d}ba-ba$_{6}$ dub-sar dumu lu$_{5}$-a-mu sanga ^{d}giš-bar-è	Delaporte, ITT 4 pp. 17–18 and pls. 1 and 9 no. 7165b	iv Š 33
5	ba-zi dub-sar dumu na-DI	Delaporte, ITT 4 p. 29 no. 7264	vii Š 36
6	lú-^{d}utu dub-sar dumu ba-zi	Delaporte, ITT 4 p. 17 and pl. 7 no. 7162	Š 36
7	na-ba-s[a$_{6}$] dub-[sar] ir$_{11}$-[zu]	Delaporte, ITT 4 p. 23 no. 7214	Š 38

COMMENTARY

Impressions of a seal of Ur-nigin-gar, servant of Ur-Lamma, are found on two tablets, AO 3548 and AO 3549, that are dated to Š 32. Lines 1–3 are found in col. i, lines 4–7 in col. ii. The seal inscription was collated.

BIBLIOGRAPHY

1884–1912 de Sarzec, Découvertes 1 p. 307 fig. M (copy)
1902 Heuzey, RA 5 p. 139 fig. N (copy)
1903 Thureau-Dangin, RTC nos. 420–21 (copy)
1907 Thureau-Dangin, SAK pp. 148–49 Ur-lama (edition)
1910 Ward, Seals fig. 39a (copy)
1913 Hehn, Gottesidee fig. 11 (copy)
1920 Delaporte, Louvre 1 p. 14 and pl. 10, T. 116 (photo, edition)
1929 Barton, RISA pp. 266–67 Ur-Lama 1 (edition)
1929 Jeremias, HAOG2 fig. 187 (copy)

TEXT

1) ur-^{d}lamma
2) énsi-
3) lagaš.KI
4) ur-nìgin-ga[r]
5) dub-sar
6) dumu lú-⸢an-né⸣
7) ir$_{11}$-[zu]

1–3) Ur-Lamma, governor of Lagaš:

4–7) Ur-nigin-gar, scribe, son of Lu-ane, (is) [your] servant.

2019

Tablets dated to Š 40 bear a seal inscription of a servant of the Lagaš governor Alla. Lines 1–3 are found in col. i, lines 4–6 in col. ii.

CATALOGUE

Ex.	Museum number	Publication	MVN 6 no.	Date	cpn
1	AO 3550	Thureau-Dangin, RTC no. 424	—	iv Š 40	c
2	L 7226 (Istanbul)	Delaporte, ITT 4 no. 7226	222	ii Š 40	n
3	L 7491 (Istanbul)	Delaporte, ITT 4 no. 7491	464	—	n
4	L 7497 (Istanbul)	Delaporte, ITT 4 no. 7497	470	i Š 40	n
5	MAH 16522	Sauren, WMAH no. 10	—	– Š 40	n
6	MAH 15870	Sauren, WMAH no. 11	—	– Š 40	n

BIBLIOGRAPHY

1903 Thureau-Dangin, RTC no. 424 (ex. 1, copy)
1907 Thureau-Dangin, SAK pp. 148–49 Al-la (ex. 1, edition)
1912 Delaporte, ITT 4 pp. 25, 53–54 nos. 7226, 7491, and 7497 (exs. 2–4, study)
1920 Delaporte, Louvre 1 T. 116 (ex. 1, photo, edition; exs. 2–4, study)
1929 Barton, RISA pp. 268–69 Alla 1 (ex. 1, edition)
1969 Sauren, WMAH nos. 10–11 (exs. 5–6, edition)
1974 Sauren, MVN 2 nos. 10–11 (exs. 5–6, copy)
1977 Pettinato, MVN 6 nos. 222 and 470 (exs. 2 and 4, transliteration)

TEXT

1) al-la
2) énsi-
3) lagaš.KI
4) ur-^{d}nin-mar-ki
5) dumu lú-^{d}utu
6) ir_{11}-zu

1–3) Alla, governor of Lagaš:

4–6) Ur-Ninmarki, son of Lu-Utu, (is) your servant.

2020

A seal inscription found on an undated tablet from Girsu names a certain Allamu as son of governor Ur-sagamu. A governor Ur-sagamu, possibly the same person named in this inscription, is attested in Legrain, UET 3 no. 1438 col. iii lines 8–9 as governor of Kutha.

COMMENTARY

The seal inscription mentioning Allamu and Ur-sagamu is found on the tablet L 1001 (Istanbul; no year date known). Lines 1–4 are found in col. i, lines 5–9 in col. ii.

BIBLIOGRAPHY

1897 Scheil, RT 19 p. 50 no. 9 (copy [in typescript], translation)
1911 de Genouillac, ITT 2/2 p. 55 Appendice and pl. 87 no. 1001 (copy)
1929 Barton, RISA pp. 286–87 Shulgi 38 (edition)
1962 Hallo, HUCA 33 p. 34 Šulgi 53ii (study)
1986 Kärki, KDDU p. 55 Šulgi 53a (ii) (edition)
1989 Lafont and Yıldız, TCT 1 p. 261 no. 1001 (transliteration)
1992 Owen, BiOr 49 p. 444 (transliteration)

TEXT

1) ᵈšul-gi
2) nita-kala-ga
3) lugal-uri$_5$.KI-ma
4) lugal-an-ub-da-límmu-ba
5) al-la-mu
6) dumu ur-sa$_6$-ga-mu
7) énsi
8) [... .KI]
9) ir$_{11}$-zu

1–4) Šulgi, mighty man, king of Ur, king of the four quarters:

5–9) Allamu, son of Ur-sagamu the governor, (is) your servant.

2021

An impression of a seal of the Marad governor Lišānum is found on a tablet envelope fragment from Nippur.

COMMENTARY

The fragment, whose date is broken away, bears the museum number CBS 14193. Lines 1–3 are found in col. i, lines 4–8 in col. ii. The inscription was collated.

BIBLIOGRAPHY

1922 Legrain, PBS 13 no. 28 (copy, transliteration, study)
1925 Legrain, PBS 14 no. 286 (photo, edition)
1929 Barton, RISA pp. 302–303 Lishalu 1 (edition)
1962 Hallo, HUCA 33 p. 34 Šulgi 53iv (study)
1963 Goetze, JCS 17 p. 26 no. 63 (edition)
1986 Kärki, KDDU p. 55 Šulgi 53a (iv) (edition)
1987 Winter, in Gibson and Biggs, Bureaucracy p. 95 IIb and pl.1b (photo, study)

TEXT

1) ᵈšul-gi
2) nita-kala-ga
3) lugal-uri$_5$.KI-ma
4) *li-ša-núm*
5) dumu *šu-ì-li*
6) énsi-
7) már-da.KI
8) ir$_{11}$-zu

1–3) Šulgi, mighty man, king of Ur:

4–8) Lišānum, son of Šū-ilī, governor of Marad, (is) your servant.

2022

Ur-Nanibgal, son of Lugal-engardu, and governor of Nippur, is attested in tablets dating to the period Š 36–44.

Impressions of a seal of Ur-Nanibgal in which he acknowledges Šulgi as sovereign are found on three undated Nippur tablets. The text is arranged with lines 1–4 in col. i and lines 5–11 in col. ii.

CATALOGUE

Ex.	Museum number	cpn
1	HS 1346	n
2	Ni 1199 (Istanbul)	n
3	CBS 9540	n

BIBLIOGRAPHY

1937 Pohl, TMH NF 1/2 Siegel 139* (ex. 1, copy)
1965 Çığ and Kızılyay, NRVN no. 249 and p. 115 no. 50 (ex. 2, photo, copy)
1972 Hallo, JNES 31 p. 93 and n. 52 (exs. 1–2, study)
1982 Owen, NATN no. 273 (ex. 3, copy)
1984 Zettler, AfO 31 p. 3 and n. 11 (exs. 1–3, study)
1987 Winter, in Gibson and Biggs, Bureaucracy p. 96 IIo (study)
1989 Steinkeller, Sale Documents pp. 248–51 nos. 66*–66*** (exs. 1–3, edition)

TEXT

1) ᵈšul-gi
2) nita-kala-ga
3) lugal-uri$_5$.KI-ma
4) [l]ugal-[ki-en-gi]-⸢ki⸣-[ur]i
5) ur-ᵈnanibgal
6) énsi-
7) nibru.KI
8) dumu lugal-engar-du$_{10}$
9) énsi-
10) nibru.KI-⸢ka⸣
11) [ir$_{11}$-zu]

1–4) Šulgi, mighty man, king of Ur, [k]ing [of the lands of Sumer and Akk]ad:

5–7) Ur-Nanibgal, governor of Nippur,

8–11) son of Lugal-engardu, governor of Nippur, (is) [your servant].

2023

A votive seal was dedicated by Ur-Nanibgal to the god Nuska for the life of Šulgi.

COMMENTARY

The white agate seal, which measures 3.4 cm in length and 2.2 cm in diameter, was formerly in the Collection de Clercq. It is now housed in the Louvre, museum number AO 22312. Lines 1–9 of the text are found in col. i, lines 10–16 in col. ii. The inscription was collated from the published photo.

BIBLIOGRAPHY

1888 de Clerq, Collection 1 pp. 67–68 and pl. 10 no. 86 (photo, copy, edition)
1907 Thureau-Dangin, SAK pp. 196–97 Dun-gi a′ (edition)
1929 Barton, RISA pp. 284–85 Shulgi 31 (edition)
1939 Frankfort, Cylinder Seals p. 145 and n. 2 (study); pl. XXVj (photo)
1962 Hallo, HUCA 33 p. 33 Šulgi 49 (study)
1971 Sollberger and Kupper, IRSA IIIA2v (translation)
1972 Hallo, JNES 31 p. 93 and n. 51 (study)
1982 André-Leicknam, Naissance de l'écriture p. 87 no. 46 (photo, study)
1986 Kärki, KDDU pp. 51–52 Šulgi 49 (edition)
1991 Braun-Holzinger, Weihgaben pp. 356–57 S 8 (edition)
1991 Steible, NSBW 2 p. 200 Šulgi 49 (study)

TEXT

1) ^{d}nuska
2) sukkal-maḫ-
3) ^{d}en-líl-lá
4) lugal-a-ni
5) nam-ti-
6) [^{d}]šul-gi
7) nita-kala-ga
8) lugal-uri$_{5}$.KI-ma
9) lugal-ki-en-gi-ki-uri-ka-šè
10) ur-^{d}nanibgal
11) énsi-
12) nibru.KI
13) dumu lugal-engar-du$_{10}$
14) énsi-
15) nibru.KI-ka-ke$_{4}$
16) a mu-na-ru

1–4) To the god Nuska, grand-vizier of the god Enlil, his lord,

5–9) for the life of Šulgi, king of Ur, king of the lands of Sumer and Akkad,

10–12) Ur-Nanibgal, governor of Nippur,

13–15) son of Lugal-engardu, governor of Nippur,

16) dedicated (this seal).

2024

The impression of a seal of a servant of Ur-Nanibgal is found on a tablet from Nippur.

COMMENTARY

The impression is found on the tablet A 31226 (Chicago); it bears the excavation number 6 NT 630 and dates to ii Š 45. Lines 1–6 are arranged in one column.

Impressions of seals of two other servants of Ur-Nanibgal (which are not edited here) are discussed by Zettler in AfO 31 (1984) p. 3 n. 13.

BIBLIOGRAPHY

1992 Zettler, Ur III Temple p. 295 6 NT 630 (transliteration)

TEXT

1) u[r-^{d}]nanibgal
2) énsi-nibru.[KI]
3) lugal-mè-a
4) sukkal-kas$_{4}$
5) ugula-uku-uš
6) ir$_{11}$-zu

1–2) U[r]-Nanibgal, governor of Nippur:

3–6) Lugal-mea, minister-(in-charge-of)-the-dispatch-runners, overseer of the gendarmerie, (is) your servant.

2025

A seal of Ur III date of an *en* of the god Enlil was found in excavations at Nippur. W.W. Hallo (JNES 31 [1972] p. 92) has proposed that the lady Inannaka who is named as the wife of the *en* in this seal inscription is to be identified with the Inannaka who appears as the author of a letter-prayer to the goddess Nintinuga; the letter-prayer is known from seven Old Babylonian tablet copies (for an edition, see Ali, Sumerian Letters pp. 137–40). Inannaka was the daughter of Enlil-amaḫ, prefect of the Inanna temple; her father served during the reign of Šulgi.

COMMENTARY

The lapis lazuli seal, which measures 2.3 cm in length and 1.9 cm in width, was found in a drain in the northeast corner of Locus 38, one of the rooms of Level IV of the Inanna temple. It was given the excavation number 5 N 236. The drain had been cut down from the Parthian platform, so its attribution to level IV is only a guess. The seal bears the museum number A 30568. The text is arranged in one column; the inscription was collated.

BIBLIOGRAPHY

1956 Haines, ILN August 18 p. 269 fig. 18 (photo)
1958 CAD E p. 178 2a (transliteration)
1972 Hallo, JNES 31 p. 92 and nn. 32–33 (study)
1984 Zettler, AfO 31 p. 6 and n. 33 (edition, study)

TEXT

1) KA-kù-ga-ni
2) en ^{d}en-líl-lá
3) ^{d}inanna-ka
4) dam-ni

1–2) KA-kugani, *en* of the god Enlil:

3–4) Inannaka (is) his wife.

2026

The impression of a seal of a servant of Lu-banda, governor of Šarrākum, is found on a tablet from Umma dated xi Š 38.

COMMENTARY

The tablet is no. S 10 in the Eames Collection, part of the New York Public Library's collections. Lines 1–3 are found in col. i, lines 4–7 in col. ii. The tablet was collated.

BIBLIOGRAPHY

1948 Oppenheim, Eames Collection p. 136 S 10 (partial transliteration, translation)
1978 Sauren, New York Public Library no. 281A (copy)

TEXT

1)	lú-bàn-da	1–3) Lu-banda, governor of Šarrākum:
2)	énsi-	
3)	URU.SAG.RIG$_7$.KI	
4)	ur-sa$_6$-ga	4–5) Ur-saga, scribe,
5)	dub-sar	
6)	dumu da-⸢da⸣	6–7) son of Dada: (is) your servant.
7)	ir$_{11}$-zu	

2027

The impression of a seal of a servant of Ur-nigin-gar, governor of Šuruppak, is found on a tablet from Umma dated iv Š 39.

COMMENTARY

The tablet is no. 105 in the Missionsmuseum der Franziskaner of Werl, Germany. Lines 1–3 are found in col. i, lines 4–6 in col. ii.

BIBLIOGRAPHY

1974 Pettinato and Waetzoldt, MVN 1 no. 198 (copy)

TEXT

1)	ur-nìgin-gar	1–3) Ur-nigin-gar, governor of Šuruppak:
2)	énsi-	
3)	šuruppak.KI	
4)	*a-bu*-[x]	4–6) Abu[x], scribe, (is) your servant.
5)	dub-sar	
6)	ir$_{11}$-zu	

2028

A fragment of a tablet envelope that was found in excavations at Girsu bears the impression of a seal of a governor of the city Šulgi-Utu. No date is visible on the published photo.

COMMENTARY

The envelope bears the museum number AO 4164. Lines 1–3 are found in col. i, lines 4–7 in col. ii. The inscription was collated from the published photo.

BIBLIOGRAPHY

1907 Thureau-Dangin, SAK pp. 196–97 Dun-gi d′ (edition)
1910 Thureau-Dangin, in Cros, Tello p. 185 AO 4164 (copy)
1920 Delaporte, Louvre 1 p. 20 and pl. 12 T. 185 (photo, edition)
1929 Barton, RISA pp. 284–85 Shulgi 34 (edition)
1962 Hallo, HUCA 33 p. 34 Šulgi 53v (study)
1986 Kärki, KDDU pp. 55–56 Šulgi 53a (v) (edition)
1987 Winter, in Gibson and Biggs, Bureaucracy p. 96 III (study)
1991 Steible, NSBW 2 p. 200 Šulgi 53 v (study)

TEXT

1) dšul-gi
2) nita-kala-ga
3) lugal-uri₅.KI-ma
4) ur-dḫendur-sa[g]
5) énsi-
6) dšul-g[i]-dutu.⌜KI⌝
7) ir₁₁-zu

1–3) Šulgi, mighty man, king of Ur:

4–7) Ur-Ḫendursa[g], governor of Šulg[i]-Utu, (is) your servant.

2029

Tablets dated to Š 33–AS 7 mention Ur-Lisi as governor of Umma. Impressions of the seal of the governor are found on innumerable tablets and clay sealings. Only a sample are listed in the catalogue.

CATALOGUE

Ex.	Museum number	YOS 4 no.	cpn
1	YBC 528	86	c
2	YBC 1482	141	c
3	YBC 1381	142	c
4	YBC 1755	164	c

COMMENTARY

For other examples of this seal inscription, see Bergamini, Mesopotamia 26 (1991) pp. 112–13. The text is arranged with lines 1–4 in col. i and lines 5–8 in col. ii.

BIBLIOGRAPHY

1919 Keiser, YOS 4 nos. 86, 141–42, and 164 (exs. 1–4, copy)
1929 Barton, RISA pp. 300–301 Ur-Negun 1 (exs. 1–4, edition)
1962 Hallo, HUCA 33 p. 34 Šulgi 53vi (study)
1986 Kärki, KDDU p. 56 Šulgi 53a (vi) (exs. 1–4, edition)
1987 Winter, In Gibson and Biggs, Bureaucracy p. 96 IIn (study)
1991 Bergamini, Mesopotamia 26 pp. 112–13 (study)

TEXT

1) ^{d}šul-gi
2) nita-kala-ga
3) lugal-uri$_5$.KI-ma
4) lugal-an-ub-da-límmu-ba
5) ur-^{d}li$_9$-si$_4$
6) énsi-
7) umma.KI
8) ir$_{11}$-zu

1–4) Šulgi, mighty man, king of Ur, king of the four quarters:

5–8) Ur-Lisi, governor of Umma, (is) your servant.

Votive Inscriptions (c) Of Private Individuals Dedicated for the Life of the King 2030–2048

Within each section the texts are listed in alphabetical order according to the divine name at the head of the inscription.

(i) Statues and Statuettes 2030–2032

2030

A stone wig, presumably for a statue, was dedicated by a servant of Ur-Ningirsu for the life of Šulgi.

COMMENTARY

The stone wig, which measures 5.7 cm in height, was acquired through purchase and given the museum number BM 91075 (formerly BM 12218) and registration number 78-12-12, 1. The text is arranged in one column. The inscription was collated from the published photo. For the translation "cup-bearer" for Sumerian zabar-dab$_5$, see Charpin, Le clergé d'Ur pp. 236–37; M. Stol, JCS 34 (1982) pp. 153–54 and n. 85; B. Lafont, NABU 1987 no. 94; Sallaberger, Kalender 1 p. 211 n. 997 and p. 231 n. 1103; and Molina Martos, Aula Orientalis 10 (1992) p. 88.

BIBLIOGRAPHY

1889 Winckler, Untersuchungen p. 157 no. 9 (copy)
1892 Jensen, KB 3/1 p. 68–69 § II Inschrift Bau-ninan's (edition)
1898 King, CT 5 pl. 2 BM 12218 (copy)
1907 Thureau-Dangin, SAK pp. 194–95 Dun-gi x (edition)
1910 King, Early History pl. XIX opposite p. 206 (bottom left) (photo)
1928 Hall, Sculpture pl. VIII no. 7 (photo)

1929 Barton, RISA pp. 282–83 Shulgi 25 (edition)
1948 Parrot, Tello p. 233 fig. 46f (drawing)
1960 Wiseman, Iraq 22 pl. XXII b (photo)
1962 Hallo, HUCA 33 p. 32 Šulgi 29 (study)
1971 Sollberger and Kupper, IRSA IIIA2u (translation)
1981 Spycket, Statuaire p. 212 n. 141 (study)
1986 Kärki, KDDU pp. 42–43 Šulgi 29 (edition)
1991 Steible, NSBW 2 pp. 185–87 Šulgi 29 (edition)

TEXT

1) ⸢^{d}⸣lamma
2) nin-a-ni
3) [n]am-ti-
4) ⸢^{d}⸣šul-gi
5) nita-kala-ga
6) lugal-uri$_5$.KI-ma-ka-šè
7) ^{d}ba-ba$_6$-nin-àm
8) zabar-dab$_5$-
9) ur-^{d}nin-gír-su
10) en-ki-ág-^{d}nanše-ka-ke$_4$
11) ḫi-li-nam-munus-ka-ni
12) mu-na-dím

1–2) For the goddess Lamma, his lady,

3–6) for the [l]ife of Šulgi, mighty man, king of Ur,

7–10) Baba-ninam, the *cup-bearer* of Ur-Ningirsu, beloved *en* of the god Nanše,

11–12) fashioned her ladylike wig for her.

2031

A stone statue, possibly from Girsu, was dedicated to the god NinDARa, spouse of the goddess Nanše, for the life of Šulgi.

COMMENTARY

The statue is carved in a black mottled stone that is identified as being hornblendplagioclase or a basic hornfels. The lower body of a standing figure is preserved; it measures 26 cm in height. The statue belongs to the Eames collection of antiquities of the Rare Books and Manuscripts Division, New York Public Library. It is currently on loan to the Metropolitan Museum of Art, New York (MMA L. 1983 95a-b). The lines are arranged as follows: col. i, lines 1–14; col. ii, lines 15–35; col. iii, lines 36–61; and col. iv, lines 62–87. The line count given here follows that of Steible in NSBW 2 pp. 178–83 Šulgi 26. It restores lines 5–6 of Civil's edition as one line (line 5). Hence, for all line numbers after line 5, the line count is one less than that given in Civil's edition. The inscription was collated. I am thankful to W. Sallaberger for communicating numerous collations of C. Wilcke, some of which were incorporated in Steible's edition of the text.

BIBLIOGRAPHY

1962 Hallo, HUCA 33 p. 31 Šulgi 26 (study)
1986 Kärki, KDDU p. 41 Šulgi 26 (study)
1989 Civil, in Studies Sjöberg pp. 49–60 and 63 (copy, edition, study)
1989 Zettler, in Studies Sjöberg, pp. 65–77 and figs. 1a–d (photos, study)
1991 Braun-Holzinger, Weihgaben pp. 273–74 St 152 (edition)
1991 Steible, NSBW 2 pp. 178–83 Šulgi 26 (edition)

TEXT

1) ^{d}ni[n]-DAR-a
2) [lu]gal-uru$_{16}$
3) ⸢x⸣ [...]
4) [lugal-a-ni]

1–4) For the god Ni[n]DARa, mighty [lo]rd, ..., [his lord],

5) [nam-ti-]
6) [^{d}šul-gi]
7) [nit]a-kala-[ga]

5–7) [for the life of Šulgi], might[y ma]n,

8) lu[g]al-uri$_{5}$.KI-ma
9) lugal-ki-en-gi-ki-uri-ka-šè

8–9) ki[n]g of Ur, king of the lands of Sumer and Akkad,

10) ^{d}šul-gi-ki-ur$_{5}$-sa$_{6}$-kalam-ma-ka
11) lú-giš-tag-ga-né
12) alan-a-ni
13) mu-tu

10–13) Šulgi-kiursa-kalama, his official in charge of offerings, formed a statue of him (Šulgi).

14) alan-ba
15) ^{d}šul-gi
16) ⸢á-sum⸣-m[a]
17) [^{d}]nin-DAR-⸢a⸣
18) [z]i-šà-⸢gál⸣-uru-⸢na⸣
19) [m]u-[b]i

14–19) The name of this statue is "Šulgi, who has been given strength by the [god] NinDARa, is the [b]reath of life of his city."

20) ⸢x x⸣ [x]
21) ⸢x-a(?)/za(?)-x-x⸣ [(x)]
22) ⸢KA⸣-bur-[r]a
23) ki-an-na-ka áb-ba šu-tùm

20–23) (When) ... to handle the cows in "An's place."

24) u$_{4}$-ezem-ma-ka
25) é-^{d}nin-mar-ki-ka
26) sag kisal-la dab$_{5}$-ba

24–26) On the festival day, in Ninmarki's temple, to take hold of the *first-fruit offerings* in the courtyard:

27) 5 dida (KAS.Ú.SA)
28) 7 dug kaš
29) 0.1.1 zì-lugal
30) 1 gada ga-dul$_{9}$
31) 1 gada gu-za
32) GIŠ.DAR.DÙ-GIŠ.eren ù KAB.RA-GIŠ.eren
33) 7 ma-na a-rá-2-àm
34) 10.00 lá 10 (=590) ku$_{6}$-al-dar-ra
35) 1 mun gur-lugal
36) 1 naga gur
37) ⸢dug⸣-sìla-⸢IGI+x⸣
38) [x] x [...]
39) [...]
40) ⸢ku$_{6}$ ab-ba⸣(?)
41) ⸢ḫar⸣-kù-[babbar]
42) ⸢1⸣(?) dug ì-⸢Ù⸣-⸢x⸣
43) nì-ba gašam-[k]am

27–43) five (jugs) of *beer extract,* seven jugs of beer, one UL one *ban* royal flour, one linen cover, one linen cover for a throne, cedar sprouts and cedar tops, twice seven *mina*s of them, 590 split fish, one royal *gur* of salt, one *gur* soda, quart jugs ..., one ..., *fish of the sea* ... [silver] rings, one(?) jug ... oil — these are the allotments for the artisans.

44) gír-su.KI še ⸢íl⸣-la-⸢da!⸣(?)
45) má-šu-du$_{7}$-a
46) gú-ab-ba.KI-ta du$_{8}$-dam
47) nam-lú-pi-lu$_{5}$-da
48) é-ta-izi-lá-a
49) gašam-kam

44–49) In Girsu (at the time when) the grain is transported, the fully equipped boat which is to be caulked (on its return) from Gu'abba — it is the charge of the "master of ceremonies" and the one who brings fire out from the temple (for: lit. of) the artisans.

50) bal-u$_{4}$-10-
51) ù igi-3-gál
52) é-ki-ès-sá.KI-ga
53) é-gír-su.KI-ka igi-3-gál
54) má èš-gi$_{6}$-zal
55) ù má kar-e tag-da-bi
56) nì-⸢ba⸣(?) 5/6 (or2/3?)-ša-bi
57) má úsur(LAL.SAR)-pára-šè du-a-bi
58) nì-dab$_{5}$-bi lú [n]u-d[a-tu]ku

50–58) A term of office of ten days, and a one-third (prebend) in the temple of Ki-es, one-third in the temple of Girsu, (when) the boat stays at the "night shrine," and when the boat ties up at the quay, five-sixths of that, as the boat comes to Uṣar-para — [n]o one will have a claim to those provisions.

59) ú[r]-gu$_{4}$-udu ⸢é-gal⸣ é sag
60) ù bára-^{d}nin-[gí]r-[su-k]a

59–60) Legs of beef (and) mutton of the palace and storehouse and of the shrine of the god Nin[gi]r[su].

61) nam-šita$_{4}$
62) KI.UD kur$_{6}$ a-gúb-bi
63) é-sag-udu-é-gal
64) úr-udu-ama-siki

61–73) The office of *šita*, the *open area* for food allotments and holy water, the storehouse of the palace sheep, legs of wool-bearing mother sheep, five *sila* of ghee, six royal (*sila*) of dates, ten (*sila*)

65) 5 sìla ì-nun
66) 0.1.0 zú-lum-lugal
67) [...] 0.0.1 ga-à[r]
68) 0.0.1 z[ì]
69) 10 ⸢sìla⸣-geštin
70) [x] [GI]Š.pèš še-[er-gu]
71) ⸢4⸣ GIŠ.ḫašḫur še-[er-gu]
72) nì-kaskal gú-[ab-ba.KI]-⸢šè⸣
73) nì-dab$_5$-gašam-kam

of *cheese*, ten *sila* of fl[our], ten *sila* of wine, [N] strings of dates, four stri[ngs] of apples — provisions for the journey to Gu᾿aba, provisions of the artisans.

74) a-šà ambar-tur
75) a-šà ki-mu-ra
76) a-šà giš-gi-bànda
77) a-šà a-geštin-na
78) a-šà ⸢x⸣-gi$_4$-a
79) gìr-gin-na-gašam-kam

74–79) The field Ambar-tur, the field Kimura, the field Gišgi-banda, the field A-geština the field ...-gi᾿a — (this is) the list (of fields) of the artisans.

80) udu é DU.DU
81) máš inim-ma
82) nì-dab$_5$-gašam-kam

80–82) The sheep of the ... temple and the goats of the "word" are provisions for the artisans.

83) u$_4$-ul-lí-a-šè
84) lú giš udun ì-na-SUM-da
85) lú-ba ^{d}lamma-a-ni ḫé-me
86) mu-mu ḫé-pà-dè
87) èn-mu ḫé-<tar>-re

83–87) In the future, may I truly be the protective deity of the one who puts wood in the oven for him (Šulgi). May he invoke my name. May he take care of me.

2032

A statuette was dedicated by the priest Ur-Ningirsu to the goddess Ninmarki for the life of Šulgi.

COMMENTARY

The statue was acquired through purchase from "General Ironsides." The piece now bears the museum number UCPHMA 9-16476 as a result of the renaming of the former Lowie Museum in Berkeley to the Phoebe A. Hearst Museum of Anthropology. Information on the statuette, including a transliteration of the text, was kindly provided by D. Foxvog. It is edited here through the kind permission of the Phoebe A. Hearst Museum of Anthropology, University of California at Berkeley.

According to A. Cavigneaux (RA 85 [1991] p. 65), two Drehem tablets — one dated to Š 46 (Boson, TCS no. 217) and the other with date broken away (Sch. 225; Pettinato and Waetzoldt, MVN 1 no. 144) — apparently refer to this same personage under his priestly title EN.ME.ZI.AN.NA. For the title, see the discussion of Cavigneaux (RA 85 [1991] pp. 63–66) and cf. Proto-Diri 384: EN.ME.AD.KÙ *e-nu-um ša* ^{d}ad-kù (see van der Meer, OEC 4 pl. XXIX col. vii line 52). Cf. also Diri IV 58: EN.ME.AD.KÙ = *e-nu šá* ^{d}*é-a* (cited in CAD E p. 178, lexical section). For the god ^{d}ad-kù, see Biggs, Abū Ṣalābīkh no. 82, obv. col. ii line 7′; cf. A. Alberti, SEL 2 (1985) p. 7 no. 29. The god appears in the aforementioned god list among deities of the Lagaš-Umma region. The priest Ur-Ningirsu of line 9 also appears in the inscriptions edited as E3/2.1.5.2005 and E3/2.2.1–2 in this volume.

For inscriptions dealing with Šulgi's building of Ninmarki's E-munus-gisa temple, see E3/2.1.2.13 and 14.

BIBLIOGRAPHY

1991 Braun-Holzinger, Weihgaben p. 275 St 158 (study [erroneous reference to non-existent publication])

TEXT

1) ^{d}nin-mar-ki
2) nin munus-⸢gi$_{16}$⸣-sa
3) nin-a-ni
4) nam-ti-
5) ⸢^{d}⸣[šul]-gi
6) n[ita-kal]a-ga
7) l[uga]l-⸢uri$_{5}$.KI⸣-ma
8) lugal an-ub-da-límmu-ba-⸢ka-šè⸣
9) u[r-^{d}nin-gír-su]
10) E[N.ME.ZI.AN.NA]
11) še[nnu(ME.[AD.KÙ)]
12) e[n ki-ág]-⸢^{d}⸣[nanše-ka]
13) ⸢a⸣ [mu-na-ru]

1–3) For the goddess Ninmarki, lady, ("Bejewelled Woman"), his lady,

4–8) for the life of [Šul]gi, [migh]ty m[an], k[in]g of Ur, king of the four quarters,

9–13) U[r-Ningirsu], E[N.ME.ZI.AN.NA], *še*[*nnu*] priest, [beloved] *e*[*n* priest of the] goddess [Nanše], d[edicated] (this statuette).

(ii) Mace-heads 2033–2036

2033

A mace-head was dedicated to the god Meslamta-eʾa for the life of Šulgi.

COMMENTARY

The mace-head is made of bright reddish beige-flecked stone and measures 11 cm in height and 14.6 cm in diameter, with an internal diameter of 3.7 cm. The inscription is carved deeper than is usually the case. The provenance (and registration number) of this mace-head is unknown. It bears the museum number BM 91074 (formerly BM 12217). The text is arranged in one column. The inscription was collated. The text dates to the time before the deification of the king.

BIBLIOGRAPHY

1898 King, CT 5 pl. 2 BM 12217 (copy)
1907 Thureau-Dangin, SAK pp. 192–93 Dun-gi q (edition)
1910 King, Early History pl. XIX opposite p. 206 [top left] (photo)
1929 Barton, RISA pp. 280–81 Shulgi 17 (edition)
1962 Hallo, HUCA 33 p. 32 Šulgi 37 (study)
1968 Solyman, Götterwaffen p. 130 no. 211 (photo, study)
1986 Kärki, KDDU p. 46 Šulgi 37 (edition)
1991 Braun-Holzinger, Weihgaben p. 60 K 80 (edition)
1991 Steible, NSBW 2 p. 192 Šulgi 37 (edition)

TEXT

1) ^{d}mes-lam-ta-è-a
2) dingir-a-ni
3) lú-nimgir-ke$_{4}$
4) nam-ti-
5) šul-gi-šè
6) a mu-na-ru

1–2) To the god Meslamta-eʾa, his (personal) deity,

3–6) Lu-nimgir, dedicated (this mace) for the life of Šulgi.

2034

A second mace-head was dedicated to the god Meslamta-e'a for the life of Šulgi.

COMMENTARY

The mace-head, a purchased piece of unknown provenance, is made of dark-green steatite and measures 4 cm in diameter and 3.1 cm in height with an internal hole of 0.8–11 cm. It appears in the shape of a sphere. It bears the museum number NBC 6105. The text is arranged in one column. The inscription was collated.

BIBLIOGRAPHY

1937 Stephens, YOS 9 no. 21 (copy)
1962 Hallo, HUCA 33 p. 32 Šulgi 38 (study)
1986 Kärki, KDDU p. 46–47 Šulgi 38 (edition)
1991 Braun-Holzinger, Weihgaben p. 60 K 81 (edition)
1991 Steible, NSBW 2 p. 193 Šulgi 38 (edition)

TEXT

1) ⸢d⸣mes-lam-ta-è-a
2) [lu]gal-a-ni
3) ⸢nam⸣-ti-
4) dšul-gi
5) nita-kala-ga
6) lugal-uri$_5$.KI-ma
7) lugal-an-ub-⸢da⸣-límmu-ba-ka-šè
8) DINGIR-*ba-ni*
9) dumu-*ḫa*-⸢*sí*⸣-*is*-É.⸢MUNUS⸣-ke$_4$
10) ⸢a mu⸣-na-ru

1–2) To the god Meslamta-e'a, his [lo]rd,

3–7) for the life of Šulgi, mighty man, king of Ur, king of the four quarters,

8–10) Ilum-bāni, son of Hasīs-E.MUNUS, dedicated (this mace).

2035

A circular rock crystal fragment, possibly a mace-head, was dedicated for a king of Ur, almost certainly Šulgi.

COMMENTARY

The present whereabouts of the rock crystal fragment, which was formerly in the J. de Morgan Collection in Paris, are unknown. It is not in the Louvre. The preserved text is arranged in one column.

BIBLIOGRAPHY

1910 Toscanne, RA 7 p. 60 (copy [including typescript copy], edition)
1929 Barton, RISA pp. 282–83 Shulgi 28 (edition)
1962 Hallo, HUCA 33 p. 41 Anonymous 9 (study)
1986 Kärki, KDDU p. 154 Anonym 9 (edition)
1991 Braun-Holzinger, Weihgaben p. 61 K 84 (edition)
1991 Steible, NSBW 2 pp. 207–208 Šulgi 64 (edition)

TEXT

Lacuna	Lacuna
1′) ⸢^{d}⸣[šul-gi]	1′–3′) [for] (the life of) Šulgi, [mighty] man, king o[f Ur],
2′) nita-[kala-ga]	
3′) lugal-[uri$_5$].KI-m[a-ka-šè]	
4′) ḫa-ZI-[x]	4′–5′) PN [fashioned] (this object).
5′) mu-[na-dím]	

2036

A mace-head from Susa was dedicated for the life of Šulgi.

COMMENTARY

The mace-head is made of black and grey marble and measures 11.5 cm in height and 8.5 cm in diameter. It was found in excavations at Susa and given the museum number Sb 2745. It depicts two lions in low relief. The text is arranged in one column. The inscription was collated from the published photo.

A goddess named ninuruamuunDU appears in an Old Babylonian god list (AO 5376: de Genouillac, TCL 15 pl. XXVIII line 224) and in An: *Anum* 4 line 35: ^{d}⸢nin-uru⸣-mu-un-DU (ms. Litke); see Steible, NSBW 2 pp. 194–95.

Comparative evidence from Ur suggests that this mace-head may have been a votive offering given in gratitude for the safe return of the merchants named in the inscription. Oppenheim (JAOS 74 [1954] pp. 7 and 8 n. 9) notes: "The contexts suggest that returning sailors were wont to offer the deity in gratitude a share of their goods. ... Another way to show the sailor's gratitude to Ningal — this goddess was apparently considered the 'Notre Dame de la Garde' of Ur — consisted in the dedication of silver models of sea-going boats ... " A similar role was apparently played by the goddess Nanše at Lagaš (see B. Alster, in Potts, Dilmun p. 50).

BIBLIOGRAPHY

1909 Scheil, RT 31 pp. 135–36 (copy, edition)
1913 Scheil, MDP 14 pp. 22–23 (edition, drawing)
1929 Barton, RISA pp. 282–83 Shulgi 29 and pp. 286–87 Shulgi 37 (edition)
1954 Oppenheim, JAOS 74 p. 14 (study)
1962 Hallo, HUCA 33 p. 33 Šulgi 40 (study)
1966 Amiet, Elam p. 244 fig. 177 (photo, translation)
1986 Kärki, KDDU pp. 47–48 Šulgi 40 (edition)
1991 Braun-Holzinger, Weihgaben p. 61 K 83 (edition)
1991 Steible, NSBW 2 pp. 194–95 Šulgi 40 (edition)

TEXT

1) ^{d}nin-uru-a-mu-DU	1–2) To the goddess NinuruamuDU, his lady,
2) nin-a-ni	
3) nam-ti-	3–4) for the life of Šulgi,
4) šul-gi	
5) nit[a]-kala-ga	5–6) mighty ma[n], k[in]g of Ur,
6) l[ug]al-uri$_5$.KI-[m]a-ka-šè	

7) nin-kisal-šè
8) ur-nigin-mu
9) ga-⌜eš$_8$⌝-a-ab-ba-ka-ke$_4$
10) a mu-na-ru

7–9) Ninkisalše(and) Urniginmu, the sea-faring merchants,

10) dedicated (this mace).

(iii) Cylinder Seals 2037–2040

2037

A cylinder seal found in excavations at Girsu was dedicated to the god Ningišzida for the life of Šulgi.

COMMENTARY

The white marble seal, which measures 4×2.5 cm, was found in sounding VII of Cros's excavations in the necropolis of Tell H at Girsu and given the museum number AO 4359. Lines 1–5 are found in col. i, lines 6–8 in col. ii.

The inscription was collated from the published photo.

Line 5 stretches the full width of the two columns of seal inscription.

BIBLIOGRAPHY

1907 Thureau-Dangin, SAK pp. 196–97 Dun-gi f′ (edition)
1909 Toscanne, RT 31 pp. 125–26 § F (copy, edition)
1910 Cros, Tello p. 143 (translation, drawing)
1911 Janneau, Dynastie p. 10 fig. III (drawing)
1920 Delaporte, Louvre 1 p. 13 and pl. 5 T. 111 (photo, edition)
1929 Barton, RISA pp. 284–85 Shulgi 36 (edition)
1960 Parrot, Sumer p. 249 fig. 309 (photo)
1962 Hallo, HUCA 33 p. 33 Šulgi 48 (study)
1986 Kärki, KDDU p. 51 Šulgi 48 (edition)
1991 Braun-Holzinger, Weihgaben p. 356 S 7 (edition)
1991 Steible, NSBW 2 p. 200 Šulgi 48 (study)

TEXT

1) ^{d}nin-giš-zi-da
2) lugal-a-ni
3) nam-ti-
4) ^{d}šul-gi
5) nita-kala-ga-<<ka>>-šè
6) nì-kal-la
7) sipa udu-niga(ŠE)-ke$_4$
8) a mu-na-ru

1–2) For the god Ningišzida, his lord,

3–5) for the life of Šulgi, mighty man,

6–7) Nikala, the shepherd of the fattened sheep,

8) dedicated (this seal).

2038

A cylinder seal was dedicated to the god Meslamta-eʾa for the life of Šulgi.

COMMENTARY

The dolomite (magnesian limestone) seal measures 4.17×2.64 cm. The seal was acquired through purchase and given the museum number BM 116719, registration number 1925-1-10, 17. The seal inscription was not finished; the name of the person who dedicated the seal is missing. Lines 1–6 are found in col. i, line 7 in column ii. The inscription was collated from the published photo.

BIBLIOGRAPHY

1971 Sollberger and Kupper, IRSA p. 145 n. 1 to IIIA2w (study)
1982 Collon, Cylinder Seals 2 no. 471 (photo, edition, study)
1986 Kärki, KDDU p. 70 Šulgi 74 (study)
1991 Braun-Holzinger, Weihgaben p. 357 S 9 (edition)

TEXT

1) ^{d}mes-lam-ta-è-a
2) lugal-a-ni
3) nam-ti-
4) ^{d}šul-gi
5) dingir-kalam-ma-na
6) lugal-uri$_5$.KI-ma
7) lugal-an-ub-<da>-límmu-ba-ka-šè

1–2) To the god Meslamta-eʾa, his lord,

3–7) for the life of Šulgi, god of his lands, king of Ur, king of the four quar[ter]s.

2039

A second cylinder seal, which probably came from the Lagaš area, was dedicated to the god Meslamta-eʾa for the life of Šulgi.

COMMENTARY

The calcite seal, which measures 5.35×3.35 cm, was acquired through purchase; it bears the museum number BM 89131 and the registration number 7-11-15, 2. The text is arranged in one column. The inscription was collated from the published photo.

A dative ending rather than the attested -ke$_4$ would be expected in line 3.

BIBLIOGRAPHY

1873–75 Lenormant, Choix no. 62 (copy)
1880 Ménant, Empreintes pp. 45–46 no. 56 (copy)
1885 Pinches, JBAA p. 398 pl. 1, 3 (...)
1891 4 R 2 p. 35 no. 2 (copy)
1905 King, CT 21 pl. 9 BM 89131 (copy)
1907 Thureau-Dangin, SAK pp. 194–95 Dun-gi z (edition)

1910 King, Early History pl. XXII facing p. 246 (bottom) (photo [of impression])
1910 Ward, Seals p. 164 no. 436 (drawing)
1922 BM Guide p. 233 no. 3 (study)
1929 Barton, RISA pp. 284–85 Shulgi 30 (edition)
1939 Frankfort, Cylinder Seals p. xxxi § XXV c and pl. 25c (photo [of seal design], study)
1948 Gadd, Iraq 10 p. 98 n. 1 (study)
1962 Hallo, HUCA 33 p. 33 Šulgi 47 (study)
1971 Sollberger and Kupper, IRSA IIIA2w (translation)
1982 Collon, Cylinder Seals 2 p. 169 and pl. LII no. 470 (photo, edition)
1986 Kärki, KDDU pp. 50–51 Šulgi 47 (edition)
1987 Collon, First Impressions pp. 133–34 no. 567 (photo, study)
1988 Römer, TUAT 2/4 pp. 464–65 (translation)
1991 Braun-Holzinger, Weihgaben p. 356 S 6 (edition)
1991 Steible, NSBW 2 p. 200 Šulgi 47 (study)

TEXT

1) ^{d}mes-lam-ta-è-⌈a⌉
2) lugal-á-zi-da-
3) lagaš.KI-ke$_4$(sic!)
4) nam-ti-il
5) ^{d}šul-gi nita-kala-ga
6) lugal-uri$_5$.KI-ma-ka-šè
7) ki-lu$_5$-la gu-za-lá
8) dumu ur-ba-gára-ke$_4$
9) mu-na-dím kišib-ba
10) lugal-mu ⌈gèštu⌉ nì-sa$_6$-ga-ka-ni
11) ga-an-ti-il
12) mu-bi

1–3) For the god Meslamta-eʾa, the king (who is) the right arm of Lagaš,

4–6) for the life of Šulgi, mighty man, king of Ur,

7–8) Kilula, the chair-bearer, son of Ur-Bagara,

9) fashioned (this seal) for him.

10–12) The name of this seal (is): “My king, let me live by his benevolent wisdom.”

2040

A third cylinder seal was dedicated to the god Meslamta-eʾa for the life of Šulgi.

COMMENTARY

The rock crystal seal measures 3.1×1.8 cm. It was likely acquired by Earl Percy, 7th Duke of Northhumberland, and now bears the museum number N 2421 in the Near Eastern seal collection of the Gulbenkian Museum of Oriental Art, University of Durham. The text is arranged in one column. The inscription was collated from the published photo.

For the PN of line 6, see Limet, Anthroponymie p. 111.

BIBLIOGRAPHY

1979 Lambert, Iraq 41 pp. 29–30 and pl. XI no. 90 (photo, edition, study)
1986 Kärki, KDDU p. 70 Šulgi 75 (edition)

TEXT

1) ^{d}mes-lam-ta-è-a
2) lugal-a-ni
3) nam-ti-^{d}šul-gi-
4) ka-šè
5) ur-^{d}EN.ZU
6) [dumu] ú-ú
7) a mu-na-ru

1–2) To the god Meslamta-eʾa, his lord,

3–4) for the life of Šulgi,

5–7) Ur-Suena, [son] of U-u, dedicated (this seal).

Inscriptions on Bowls, Vases, and Plates 2041–2048

2041

A fragment of a white calcite bowl found at Ur bears a dedicatory inscription, possibly to the goddess Nungal, for the life of Šulgi.

COMMENTARY

The findspot and the museum number of this bowl fragment, which was found in Season XII are unknown. It was given the excavation number U 18807. The text is arranged in one column. The inscription was not collated.

If line 1′ has been restored correctly, then the epithet ⸢nin⸣-⸢é⸣-[kur]-⸢ra⸣ would apparently apply to the goddess Nungal; cf. E3/2.1.3.2008 lines 1–2: ^{d}⸢nun⸣-gal / nin-é-kur-ra. According to Civil (Studies Hallo p. 75, § 2.1) é-kur in connection with Nungal is to be translated as "prison."

In the first sign of line 8′ Sollberger may have mistaken a crack for a wedge, and thus copied the sign as the end of an apparent AN sign. We have read the line (with due reserve): ⸢ba!⸣-zi-ge$_4$ taking into account the commonly attested Sumerian PN ba-zi-ge (see Limet, Anthroponymie p. 390).

BIBLIOGRAPHY

1965 Sollberger, UET 8 no. 105 (copy, study)
1986 Kärki, KDDU p. 68 Šulgi 70 (edition)
1991 Braun-Holzinger, Weihgaben p. 187 G 356 (edition)
1991 Steible, NSBW 2 pp. 205–206 Šulgi 62 (edition)

TEXT

Lacuna
1′) ⸢nin⸣-⸢é⸣-[kur]-⸢ra⸣
2′) nin-a-ni
3′) nam-ti-
4′) ^{d}šul-gi
5′) nita-kal[a]-ga
6′) lug[al-ur]i$_5$.KI-ma
7′) lugal-ki-en-gi-ki-uri-ka-šè
8′) ⸢ba⸣(?)-zi-ge$_4$
Lacuna

Lacuna
1′–2′) lady of the *pris*[*on*](?),
3′–7′) for the life of Šulgi, migh[ty] man, kin[g] of [U]r, king of the lands of Sumer and Akkad,
8′) ⸢Ba⸣zige
Lacuna

2042

A green diorite bowl fragment bears a dedicatory inscription to the god Ningišzida for the life of Šulgi.

COMMENTARY

The bowl fragment was found at Diqdiqqah and was given the excavation number U 16008. It bears the museum number BM 122936 and the registration number 1931-10-10, 4. The text is arranged in one column.

BIBLIOGRAPHY

1965 Sollberger, UET 8 no. 29 (copy, study)
1986 Kärki, KDDU p. 67 Šulgi 68 (edition)
1991 Braun-Holzinger, Weihgaben p. 187 G 354 (edition)
1991 Steible, NSBW 2 pp. 204–205 Šulgi 60 (edition)

TEXT

1) ^{d}nin-gi[š]-zi-da
2) dingir-ra-ni
3) nam-ti-
4) ^{d}šul-gi
5) nita-kala-ga
6) lu[gal-uri$_5$.KI-ma]
Lacuna

1–2) To the god Ningi[š]zida, his (personal) deity,

3–6) for the life of Šulgi, mighty man, ki[ng of Ur]
Lacuna

2043

A section of the Pinches Sammeltafel of Šulgi inscriptions (see E3/2.1.2.25) gives a copy of a dedicatory inscription to the goddess Nininduba for the life of Šulgi. We do not know on what object this text was originally inscribed.

COMMENTARY

The inscription, which was collated, is found on rev. col. ii lines 16′–20′ of BM 78681+139969.

BIBLIOGRAPHY

1963 Pinches, CT 44 pl. 1 no. 2 (BM 78681 [only], copy)

TEXT

1) ^{d}nin-in-dub-ba
2) [n]in-a-ni-ir
3) [nam]-ti-
4) [^{d}]šul-gi
5) [nita]-kala-ga
Lacuna

1–2) To the goddess Nininduba, his [l]ady,

3–5) for the [li]fe of Šulgi, mighty [man]
Lacuna

2044

A white marble vase was dedicated, probably to the god Šara, for the life of Šulgi.

COMMENTARY

The vase fragment, which measures 12×9×2 cm, forms part of a large vessel. The piece was acquired through purchase and given the museum number YBC 2158; it likely came from Umma. The text is arranged in one column. The inscription was collated.

BIBLIOGRAPHY

1915 Clay, YOS 1 no. 17 (copy, edition)
1929 Barton, RISA pp. 282–83 Shulgi 23 (edition)
1962 Hallo, HUCA 33 p. 32 Šulgi 34 (study)
1986 Kärki, KDDU pp. 44–45 Šulgi 34 (edition)
1991 Braun-Holzinger, Weihgaben p. 186 G 347 (edition)
1991 Steible, NSBW 2 p. 190 Šulgi 34 (edition)

TEXT

1) [^{d}šára]
2) [nir-gál-an-na]
3) ⸢dumu⸣-ki-ág-^{d}i[nanna]
4) lugal-a-n[i]
5) ⸢nam⸣-t[i]-
6) ^{d}šul-gi
7) nita-k[ala-ga]
8) lugal-⸢ŠEŠ⸣.AB.KI-ma
9) lugal-an-ub-da-límmu-ba-ka-šè
10) ⸢lú⸣-^{d}⸢nanna⸣
11) dumu-*šu-èr-ra*
12) dam-gàr-ke$_{4}$
13) ⸢x⸣ [...]
14) [a mu-na-ru]

1–4) [For the god Šara, distinguished one of the god An], beloved son of the goddess I[nanna], hi[s] lord,

5–9) for the lif[e] of Šulgi, mi[ghty] man, king of Ur, king of the four quarters,

10–14) Lu-Nanna, son of Šū-Erra, the merchant, [dedicated] (this) ...

2045

A vase found at Ur was dedicated for the life of Šulgi.

COMMENTARY

The black steatite vase fragment, probably a piece of a large bowl, was found in the SW temenos wall and given the excavation number U 652. It bears the museum number BM 116449 and the registration number 1923-11-10, 35. The text, as far as preserved, is arranged in one column.

BIBLIOGRAPHY

1965 Sollberger, UET 8 no. 30 (copy, study)
1986 Kärki, KDDU pp. 67–68 Šulgi 69 (edition)
1991 Braun-Holzinger, Weihgaben p. 187 G 355 (edition)
1991 Steible, NSBW 2 p. 205 Šulgi 61 (edition)

TEXT

Lacuna
1′) [...] ⸢x⸣ [...]
2′) [nam]-ti-
3′) [(^{d})šul]-gi
4′) [nita-ka]la-g[a]
5′) [lugal]-⸢uri$_5$⸣.[KI-ma]
Lacuna

Lacuna
1′) ...
2′–5′) [for] the [li]fe of [Šul]gi, [migh]ty [man], [king of] Ur
Lacuna

2046

A steatite plate from Ur was dedicated for the life of Šulgi.

COMMENTARY

The steatite plate fragment was found in room A 31 of the Larsa level of the Gipar-ku and given the excavation number U 6736. It bears the museum number IM 1151. The text is arranged in one column. The inscription was not collated.

BIBLIOGRAPHY

1928 Gadd, UET 1 no. 54 (copy, edition)
1929 Barton, RISA pp. 364–65 Shulgi 5 (edition)
1957 Hallo, Royal Titles p. 61 (transliteration)
1962 Hallo, HUCA 33 p. 32 Šulgi 35 (study)
1968 Kärki, KDDU p. 45 Šulgi 35 (edition)
1991 Braun-Holzinger, Weihgaben p. 186 G 348 (edition)
1991 Steible, NSBW 2 p. 191 Šulgi 35 (edition)

TEXT

Lacuna
1′) nam-ti-
2′) ^{d}šul-gi
3′) dingir-kalam-ma-na-ka-šè
4′) lugal-uri$_5$.KI-ma
5′) lugal-an-ub-da-límmu-ba-ka-šè
6′) [(x)] ⸢x x x⸣ [...]
Lacuna

Lacuna
1′–6′) for the life of Šulgi, god of his land, king of Ur, king of the four quarters, ...
Lacuna

2047

A small onyx vessel was dedicated for the life of Šulgi.

COMMENTARY

The vessel, which measures 2.5×2×0.4 cm, was found in the second campaign of Cros at Girsu, and bears the museum number AO 4392 The inscription was collated.

BIBLIOGRAPHY

1991 Braun-Holzinger, Weihgaben p. 188 G 360 (edition)
1991 Steible, NSBW 2 p. 214 and pl. XII (bottom) Šulgi 71 (photo, edition)

TEXT

Lacuna
1′) [nam]-⌜ti⌝-
2′) [^{d}]šul-gi-šè
3′) [x]-sa$_{6}$-ga
4′) [n]u-kiri$_{6}$
5′) [a mu]-⌜na⌝-[ru]

Lacuna
1′–2′) For the [l]ife of Šulgi,

3′–5′) [x]saga, the [g]ardener, [dedicated] (this vessel) to him/her.

2048

A vase fragment found at Ur bears part of a votive inscription for Šulgi.

COMMENTARY

The vase fragment, which measures 5×3 cm was found on the surface at Ur and given the excavation number U 2996. It bears the museum number IM 998. The inscription is known only from a translation given in the Ur registry book; it reads as follows: "[To the god DN], his king(?), for the life of Šulgi, mighty man, king of Ur, [...]-ra-ke$_{4}$ ..."

Miscellaneous Inscriptions 2049–2059

An Old Babylonian Sammeltafel from Nippur gives the texts, in an abbreviated writing, of a number of short Sumerian inscriptions belonging principally to Šulgi. We have followed Civil's line count in this edition, with the minor modification of giving primed numbers (N′), since the exact extent of the original tablet is unknown.

Inscription on Sammeltafel	**Tablet Lines**	**RIM number E3/2.**	**Comments**
1	i 6′–13′	1.2.2049	—
2	ii 1′–7′	1.2.84	*Lukur* Nin-kala
3	ii 8′–16′	1.2.2050	—
4	iii 3′–13′	1.2.81	*Lukur* Ea-niša
5	iv 5′–13′	1.2.2051	—
6	v 4′–11′	1.2.2052	—
7	v 12′–15′	1.2.2053	—
8	vi 1′–8′	1.2.2054	—
9	vi 9′–17′	1.2.2055	—
10	vii 5′–12′	1.1.52	Tarām-Uram, é-gi$_4$-a of Ur-Nammu
11	viii 1′	Unedited	—
12	viii 2′–5′	Unedited	—
13	viii 6′–8′	Unedited	—
14	viii 9′	Unedited	—
15	ix 1′–10′	1.2.2056	—
16	x 1′–10′	1.2.36	Military Campaign
17	xi 1′–5′	Unedited	Colophon mentions Gilgameš
18	xi 6′–9′	1.2.2057	—
18	xii 1′–6′	1.2.2058	
19	xiii 1′–2′	Unedited	—
20	xiii 3′–11′	1.2.2059	—
21	xiv 1′–14′	1.2.37	Military Campaign

COMMENTARY

The tablet bears the museum number N 2230+N 4006. The inscriptions were collated. The bibliography given applies for all the inscriptions edited below.

BIBLIOGRAPHY

1985 Civil, Orientalia NS 54 pp. 37–45 (copy, edition)

2049

TEXT

Col. i
1′–5′) Lacuna
6′) [...]-da [...]
7′) ^{d}šul-<gi>
8′) lugal-<úri>.KI-<ma>
9′) lugal-<an-ub>-da-límmu-ba
10′) zi ma-da
11′) ⸢x⸣ [x] NE
12′) [...] ⸢x⸣
13′) [...] ⸢x⸣-ni
(Line ruling, end of inscription)

i 1′–5′) Lacuna
i 6′) ...
i 7′–9′) Šul<gi>, king of <Ur>, king of the four <quar-t>ers,

i 10′–13′) ...

2050

TEXT

Col. ii
8′) ^{d}<DN>
9′) nin-<a-ni>
10′) nam-ti-il
11′) ^{d}šul-<gi>
12′) nita-<kala-ga>
13′) lugal-<úri>.KI-<ma>
14′) [...]-da-límmu-ba-ka-šè
15′) [x kala]m(?)-ma
16′) Traces
Lacuna

ii 8′–9′) For the goddess <DN>, <his> lady,

ii 10′–14′) for the life of Šul<gi>, <mighty> man, king <of Ur>, [<king>] of the four <quart>ers,

ii 15′) PN
ii 16′) Traces
Lacuna

2051

TEXT

Col. iv
1′–4′) Lacuna
5′) ^{d}šul-<gi>
6′) téš(?)-bi-da-na-⸢x⸣
7′) ⸢u_4⸣ a [x]-⸢x⸣
8′) ^{d}en-[líl]-lá
9′) luga[l-ú]ri.KI-ma
10′) ⸢^{d}⸣[e]n-líl
11′) ⸢x⸣-[n]i-šè
12′) ⸢x⸣ [x] ⸢á(?)⸣-daḫ
13′) [...] ⸢x⸣
Lacuna

iv 1′–4′) Lacuna
iv 5′) Šul<gi>
iv 6′) ...
iv 7′–8′) when the ... of the god En[lil],

iv 9′) the kin[g of U]r,
iv 10′–13′) the god [E]nlil, for [h]is ..., ... [*h*]*elper*, ...
Lacuna

2052

TEXT

Col. v
1′) [^{d}šul-<gi>]
2′) [nita <kala-ga>]
3′) [lugal <úri>.KI-<ma>]
4′) ⸢lugal⸣ <an-ub>-da-[límmu-ba]
5′) ^{d}ŠEŠ.<KI>-z[i x (x)]
6′) x-bi-a-⸢x⸣
7′) zabar-dab$_5$
8′) SÌLA.ŠU.DU$_8$-⸢maḫ⸣
9′) ugula maš-šu-gíd-gíd-dè-ne
10′) ir$_{11}$-zu
Colophon
11′) kišib ^{d}nanna-zi-⸢x-(x)⸣

v 1′–4′) [Šul<gi>, <mighty> man, king <of Ur>, king of the four <quart>ers]:

v 5′–10′) Nanna-z[i x (x)], ..., cup-bearer (and) chief steward, overseer of the extispicy priests, (is) your servant.

Colophon
v 11′) Seal of Nanna-zi-⸢x-(x)⸣

2053

TEXT

Col. v
12′) ^{d}<nin-líl>
13′) nin-<a-ni>
14′) nam-<ti-il>-
15′) [^{d}]šul-<gi>
Lacuna

v 12′–13′) For the goddess <Ninlil>, <his> lady,

v 14′–15′) for the l[ife] of Šul<gi>
Lacuna

2054

TEXT

Col. vi
1′) [^{d}en-líl]
2′) [lugal]
3′) ⸢kur-kur-ra-ke$_4$⸣
4′) ^{d}nin-<líl>
5′) nin-kur-kur-ra-ke$_4$
6′) nam ḫa-ba-da-kuru$_5$-ne
Colophon
7′) mu-sar-ra
8′) ⸢x-x⸣-na

vi 1′–3′) May [the god Enlil, lord of the lands],

vi 4′–5′) (and) the goddess Nin<lil>, lady of the lands,
vi 6′) curse him.
Colophon
vi 7′–8′) Inscription on his ...

2055

TEXT

Col. vi
9′) ⸢^{d}⸣<DN>
10′) ⸢nin⸣-<a-ni>
11′) ^{d}šul-<gi>
12′) nita-<kala-ga>
13′) lugal-<úri>.KI-<ma>
14′) lugal-<ki-en>-gi(?)-<ki-uri>-ke$_4$
15′) nam-<ti-la-ni-šè>
16′) [a m]u-<na-ru>
17′) alan-ba
18′) [...]
19′) [mu-bi-im]

vi 9′–10′) To the goddess <DN> <his> lady,

vi 11′–14′) Šul<gi>, <mighty> man, king <of Ur>, king <of the lands of Sum>er and <Akkad>,

vi 15′) <for his own> li<fe>,
vi 16′) [d]e<dicated> (this statue) to her.
vi 17′–19′) [The name of] this statue [is ...].

2056

TEXT

Col. ix
0′) [^{d}DN]
1′) [n]in-<a-ni>
2′) šul-<gi>
3′) nita-<kala-ga>
4′) lugal-<úri>.KI-<ma>
5′) lugal-<ki-en>-gi-ki-uri>-ke$_4$
6′) nam-<ti-la-ni-šè>
7′) a mu-<na-ru>
Colophon
8′) egir-bi na
9′) 2-kam-ma-bi
10′) šu-bi gin$_7$-nam

ix 0′–1′) [For the goddess DN], <his> [l]ady,

ix 2′–5′) Šul<gi>, <mighty> man, king <of Ur>, king <of the lands of Su>mer and <Akkad>,

ix 6′–7′) de<dicated> (this object) <for his own> li<fe>.
Colophon
ix 8′–10′) Behind it (are) two stone ... which are the same.

2057

TEXT

Col. xi
6′) ⸢^{d}⸣<DN>
7′) ⸢nin⸣-<a-ni>
8′) [šu]l-<gi>
9′) [nit]a-<kala-ga>
Lacuna

xi 6′–7′) For the goddess <DN>, <his> lady,

xi 8′–9′) [Šu]l<gi>, <mighty> man
Lacuna

2058

TEXT

Col. xii
1′) ⸢šul⸣(?)-<gi>
2′) nita-<kala-ga>
3′) lugal-<úri>.KI-<ma>
4′) lugal-<ki-en>-gi-<ki-uri>-ke$_4$
5′) alan-lú-ḫu-gi(?)-na
6′) lú igi-ni-šè
Lacuna

xii 1′–4′) Šul<gi>(?), <mighty> man, king <of Ur>, king of the <lands of Su>mer and <Akkad>,
xii 5′) a ... statue,
xii 6′) the one who ... before him
Lacuna

2059

TEXT

Col. xiii
3′) ^{d}<DN>
4′) nin-<a-ni>
5′) nam-<ti-il>-
6′) šul-<gi>
7′) nita-<kala-ga>
8′) lugal-<úri>.KI-<ma>
9′) lugal-<ki-en>-gi-<ki-uri>-ka-šè
10′) ur-⸢x⸣-[...]
11′) k[i-..]
Lacuna

xiii 3′–4′) To the goddess <DN>, <his> lady,
xiii 5′–7′) for the li<fe> of Šul<gi>, <mighty> man,
xiii 8′–9′) king <of Ur>, king <of the lands of Su>mer <and Akkad>
xiii 10′–11′) PN, ...
Lacuna

Amar-Suena

E3/2.1.3

Conflicting numbers are found in the various manuscripts of the Sumerian King List for the length of Amar-Suena's reign. The Weld-Blundell prism's figure of nine years is proven to be correct by the evidence of two date lists: (a) CBS 10799: Hilprecht, BE 1/2 no. 127 + small unpublished fragment (AS 1–9); and (b) IB 542a+b+ obv. col. ii′ (AS 3–9); for the latter list, see C. Wilcke, Orientalia NS 54 (1985) pp. 299–303, where a general discussion of the tablet is given. In a recent article (RA 88 [1994] pp. 97–119) Lafont has assembled various data that would seem to indicate that years AS 8 and ŠS 1 are to be taken as equivalent years and that Amar-Suena reigned eight years, not nine. In this case, the fact that list (c): NBC 2141 = Clay, YOS 1 no. 26 gives the names for only AS 1–8 cannot be used as solid proof for an eight-year reign, since the tablet may simply have been drawn during Amar-Suena's eighth year. Its evidence flatly contradicts the information provided by lists (a) and (b). Also of interest, as was first pointed out by Oppenheim (Eames Collection sub G 28, O 30 and Bab. 9), then McGuinness (in Chapter III "Evidence for a Co-Regency during the Third Dynasty" in his unpublished dissertation Studies in Neo-Sumerian Administrative Machinery [University of Minnesota, 1976] pp. 117–27), followed by Waetzoldt (Mesopotamia 5–6 [1970–71] pp. 321–23), and finally Pomponio (SEL 7 [1990] pp. 6–7), is the fact that a handful of archival texts from Umma and Drehem dated to AS 6–8 are impressed with seals dedicated to the divine Šū-Sîn (as king of Ur). This practice, as far as can be determined, is unparalleled in Ur III times and, with the scanty historical sources at our disposal, a ready explanation for the phenomenon (a co-regency?) escapes us. It may be connected with Lafont's theory that the years AS 8 and ŠS 1 are equivalent; clearly, a full discussion of these issues is beyond the scope of the present study.

Sallaberger (Kalender 1 p. 105) and Wilcke (RLA 7 [1987] p. 120) have pointed out that a reorganization of the cult at Nippur during the year ŠS 1 saw the appearance in the offering lists of a new sequence of deities, namely Šū-Sîn (the reigning king), Sîn, and Šulgi. In these lists the god Sîn's name appears in the very spot where we would expect to find a reference to Amar-Suena. The reasons why Šū-Sîn apparently chose to honour the memory of his grandfather, but not his father, remain unclear.

The names of AS 1–8 are catalogued here according to their form in date list (c); the name of AS 9 comes from date list (a).

Amar-Suena, in contrast to his illustrious father, remains a somewhat enigmatic figure. As for his genealogy, we may note that the Sumerian King List names Amar-Suena as being Šulgi's son: ^{d}amar-^{d}EN.ZU dumu ^{d}šul-gi-ke$_{4}$ (Jacobsen, SKL p. 122). Further, Šulgi appears as Amar-Suena's father in the so-called "Weidner Chronicle" (see now F.N.H. Al-Rawi, "Tablets from the Sippar Library: I. The 'Weidner Chronicle': A Supposititious Royal Letter concerning a Vision," Iraq 52 [1990] p. 10: "Amar-Suena, his [Šulgi's] son, altered the great bulls and the [sheep] sacrifices of the New Year Festival of Esagil"). According to Sallaberger (in an article to appear in AoF 23 [1996]), Amar-Suena was likely the offspring of Šulgi and Tarām-Uram; the latter was the daughter of the ruler Apil-kīn of Mari. She was apparently betrothed to Šulgi during the reign of Ur-Nammu (see E3/2.1.1.52).

Now, in the later historical tradition there is a faint remembrance of Amar-Suena as an "Unheilsherrscher," a figure characterized as "the calamitous ruler who by his impiety brings destruction upon his land" (Michalowski in Essays Finkelstein p. 156). The omen tradition, in its Old Babylonian (A. Goetze, JCS 1 [1947] p. 261) and now Neo-Assyrian (I. Starr, JCS 29 [1977] pp. 160–62) versions, records the king's untimely death as the result of a foot infection. A second source, an apparent Old Babylonian literary composition known from two tablets from Ur (Sollberger, UET 8 nos. 32–33; see A. Falkenstein, "Wahrsagung in der sumerischen Überlieferung," CRRA 14 [1966] p. 50; Green, Eridu pp. 58–65; Michalowski in Essays Finkelstein pp. 155–57; and Pomponio, SEL 7 [1990] pp. 13–14), describes the king's repeated efforts, frustrated by his inability to receive favourable omens from the gods, to rebuild the Enki temple in Eridu. In UET 8 no. 33 mention is made (in a broken context, namely line 7′) of a revolt in the land: kalam-e ba-da-an-bal kur-ra ⌜x⌝ "The homeland revolted, the foreign land ..." As is not unexpected, the corpus of Amar-Suena royal inscriptions makes no mention of a calamity taking place during the king's reign, and it is difficult to ascertain what veracity, if any, the literary traditions cited above might hold.

Amar-Suena's reign is noteworthy for the installations of several new *en*s; fully four of the king's nine year names commemorate the inauguration of these priestly officials. Further, we suspect that there was even a fifth, the first installation of the *en* of Nanna of Karzida, dating to, but not commemorated in, the name of AS 2.

I. Year Names and Events of the Reign

(1) mu ^{d}amar-^{d}EN.ZU lugal "The year Amar-Suena (became) king."

We know that Šulgi died on either the first or second day of xi Š 48, and there is evidence that his son, Amar-Suena, was already active in Nippur during the following month. An archival text dated to xii Š 48 (AUAM 73.1375: Sigrist, AUCT 1 no. 506) records the votive gift of the new king (a-ru-a l[ugal]) of large amounts of gold — 22 minas in total — to the gods Enlil, Ninlil, and Ninurta in Nippur. The gift may possibly be connected with ceremonies in Nippur for the accession of the new king. The performance of these pious acts in Nippur by Amar-Suena was a crucial element in the legitimization of the new king. Amar-Suena was the first Ur III king to adopt an epithet compounded with Enlil's name: "supporter of the temple of the god Enlil" (sag-ús-é-^{d}en-líl-ka) as part of his standard titulary. Further, inscription E3/2.1.3.3 records his construction work on the shrine E-kura-igi-gal, part of the Enlil temple complex. For previous examples of Ur III building inscriptions connected with the Enlil temple we must look all the way back to the time of Ur-Nammu.

(2) mu ur-bí-lum.KI ba-ḫul "The year Urbillum was destroyed."

A possible reference from archival sources to Amar-Suena's campaign against Urbillum is found in a Drehem tablet dated to xii AS 1 (Gomi, John Rylands no. 68) that records (the general) Niridagal's receipt of some wooden object on the occasion of an unspecified campaign (1 GIŠ.gam-x-x nir-ì-da-gal u_4 kaskal-šè). Two booty (nam-ra-ak) texts may also be connected with the campaign noted in the name of AS 2; they are: (a) AUAM 73.3190: Sigrist AUCT 2 no. 284 dated to vii AS 2 and (b) AUAM 73.0529: Sigrist AUCT 1 no. 28 dated to vii AS 3. While neither text specifies the origin of the booty, the dates of the tablets (as was pointed out by T. Maeda, ASJ 14 [1992] p. 158) suggest a possible connection with Amar-Suena's Urbillum campaign.

The installation of the *en* of the god Nanna at Karzida.

An archival text from Drehem (Yıldız and Gomi, PDT 2 no. 767) records deliveries of various animals over the whole twelve-month period of AS 2;

they are subsumed three times in the text under the rubric: nì-dab$_5$ en-^{d}nanna-kar-zi-da ḫun-e-da "provisions to install the *en* of the god Nanna of Karzida." Also of interest is mention in col. i line 10 of the same text of *siskur* offerings for the *ki-utu* rite(?) for the *en* (sískur-ki-^{d}utu-en-na). We might expect, then, that the name of AS 2 would have commemorated the installation of the new *en* of Nanna of Karzida. However, AS 2 was named instead for the king's campaign against Urbillum. W. Sallaberger (ZA 82 [1992] pp. 132–33) has argued that Yıldız and Gomi, PDT 2 no. 767 lists provisions specifically for En-aga-zi-ana, the priestess who appears by name in inscription E3/2.1.3.17. Since the *en* who appears in the name for AS 9 bears a different cognomen, Sallaberger's suggestion is plausible.

(3a) mu ^{d}gu-za-^{d}en-líl-lá ba-dím "The year the deified throne of the god Enlil was fashioned."

For references in the archival texts to this throne of Enlil (it is mentioned in tablets dating from AS 4 on) see Sallaberger, Kalender 1 p. 99 and n. 429.

(3b) mu en-maḫ-gal-an-na en-^{d}nanna máš-e ì-pà "The year En-maḫ-gal-ana, *en* of the god Nanna (at Ur), was chosen by omens." NBC 286 (unpublished, reference courtesy M. Sigrist).

Only one example of this year name has, as yet, come to light. We have very tentatively placed the year name as a variant to the standard name for AS 3a. Another (more likely) possibility is that it is simply a mistake for the name of AS 4.

(4) mu en-maḫ-gal-an-na en-^{d}nanna ba-ḫun "The year En-maḫ-gal-ana, *en* of the god Nanna (of Ur), was installed."

En-maḫ-gal-ana's name appears, with no indication of her father's name, in a label inscription incised on a bowl; the inscription is edited as E3/2.1.3.19 in this volume. Sollberger (AfO 17 [1954–56] p. 24) proposed that En-maḫ-gal-ana was to be identified with the daughter of Šulgi who was designated under the priestly name En-ubur-zi-ana, as is recorded in the year name for Š 43. According to his theory, she was installed under the different name En-maḫ-gal-ana some nine years after her oracular designation. However, such a lengthy period of time between the oracular designation and the installation of a priestess, as well as the change in the sacerdotal name, is unparalleled in Ur III times. Since it was the standard practice at this time for the reigning king to install his own daughter as *en*, it is highly likely, as Woolley (UE 7 p. 50) suggests, that En-maḫ-gal-ana was the daughter of Amar-Suena and not the daughter of Šulgi, as some scholars following Sollberger (cf. Steible, NSBW 2 p. 300 Ur 6) have indicated. Amar-Suena's rebuilding of the *gipar* at Ur, which is commemorated in inscription E3/2.1.3.8, may have been undertaken for En-maḫ-gal-ana's installation. A Drehem text dated to AS 3 — no month name is preserved (Langdon, TAD no. 47) — records various offerings to the god Nanna at Ur and may (following Sallaberger, Kalender 1 p. 208 n. 987) be connected with En-maḫ-gal-ana's installation. Obv. col. ii lines 11-12, for example, record cattle: mu-en-šè "for the *en*," and lines 13–15 note various cattle: ki-en-na-šè "for the '(resting) place' of the (former) *en*."

The first campaign against Šašrum and Šuruthum. Four archival texts, all of which date to AS 4, allude to Amar-Suena's victory over the cities of Šašrum and Šuruthum. The tablets in question are: (a) BM 103435: Riedel, RA 10 (1913) p. 209, dated to vii AS 4, which notes (rev. lines 25–26): "when Amar-Suena destroyed Šašrum and Šuruthum" (u$_4$ ^{d}amar-^{d}EN.ZU-ke$_4$ ša-aš-ru-um.KI ù šu-ru-ut-ḫu-um.KI ḫul-a); (b) AO 5545: de Genouillac, TCL 2 pl. 35, dated to 29 viii AS 4, which records (obv. line 4): "part of the delivery of the booty of Šašru and Šuruthum" (šà mu-DU nam-ra-ak ša-aš-ru.KI ù šu-ru-ut-ḫu-um.KI); (c) de Genouillac, Trouvaille no. 2, dated to viii AS 4, which contains the remark (rev. line 6): "when Amar-Suena destroyed Šašrum and Šuruthum" (u$_4$ ^{d}amar-^{d}EN.ZU-ke$_4$ ša-aš-ru-um.KI ù šu-ru-ut-ḫu-um.KI mu-ḫul-a); and (d), dated to viii (Umma), known from four copies: (i) YBC 1472: Keiser, YOS 4 no. 67; (ii) unknown collection: Scheil, RA 15 (1918) pp. 61–62 = Scheil, RA 24 (1927) pp. 44–45; (iii) University of Hiroshima no. 14: Yoshikawa, ASJ 7 (1985) pp. 191–92; and (iv) Ligabue Collection: Fales, Alfabeto no. 33, which records various personnel noted (lines 5–7) as "booty dedicated to the god Šara, (from) the city Šariphum" (nam-ra-ak a-ru-a dšára URU.ša-rí-ip-hu-um-ma.KI). The GN Šariphum was taken by Edzard (Rép. Géogr. 2 p. 177) to be a variant spelling of Šarithum; in this he is apparently followed by Yoshikawa (ASJ 7 [1985] p. 192). Three other tablets dated to AS 4 (see Maeda, ASJ 14 [1992] p. 158) record booty from a campaign of Amar-Suena, but unfortunately do not specify its provenance. The dates of the tablets, however, suggest some connection with the war against Šašrum and Šuruthum. The expectation is that this attack would have supplied the name for AS 5. Instead, the installation of the new *en* of Inanna was used to name that year. The expedition of AS 4 was the first of two campaigns directed against these cities; the second was commemorated in the name of AS 6.

(5) mu en-unu$_6$-gal-^{d}inanna unu.KI ba-hun "The year (the *en*) En-unu-gal-ana of Uruk was installed."

A possible reflection of this year name is to be seen in Amar-Suena's fashioning of a bronze *argibillu* for the goddess Inanna that is commemorated in inscription E3/2.1.3.13. Also of note is an archival text dated to xii AS 4 (no day date; AUAM 73.0696: Sigrist, AUCT 1 no. 78) that records a royal dedication (a-ru-a lugal) of a bronze basket (ma-sá-ab urudu) for the goddess Inanna of Uruk. Both the basket and the *argibillu* were possibly new fittings for the goddess's *gipar*.

(6) mu ša-aš-ru-um.KI a-rá-2-kam ba-hul "The year Šaš(šu)rum was destroyed for a second time." MLC 2448: Keiser, BRM 3 no. 166. The year list YOS 1 no. 26, which is normally cited in this study, gives an abbreviated form of this year name: **mu ša-aš-ru.KI ba-hul** "The year Šaš(šu)ru was destroyed."

Unfortunately, we have no steles or statue inscriptions of Amar-Suena describing either of his campaigns against Šaššuru, comparable, for example, to the Šū-Sîn inscriptions chronicling that king's conquest of Simaški. We do, however, have evidence from archival sources dating to AS 5, namely: (a) booty (nam-ra-ak) lists; (b) rosters of (royal) deliveries (mu-túm-[lugal]) from soldiers (érin); and (c) tribute rolls (gún ma-da and gún) that shed some light on this campaign (for these texts in general, see Steinkeller, "The Administrative and Economic Organization of the Ur III State: The Core and the Periphery," in Gibson and Biggs, Bureaucracy pp. 19–41 and Maeda, "The Defense Zone during the Rule of the Ur III Dynasty," ASJ 14 [1992] pp. 135–72).

One step in the conquest of the northeast regions seems to have been the taking of the city of Rašap. The two known booty lists for AS 5 (both dated to 20 i; see Sigrist, Drehem p. 108, who cites: [a] NBC 6541: Kieser, BIN 3 no. 532 and [b] PD 120: Salonen, Puzriš-Dagan-Texte no. 120) mention booty of a city whose name appears in the texts either as URU.MES.LAM.TA.È.A or URU.dNERGAL. Steinkeller (Vicino Oriente 6 [1986] p. 37) and Frayne (Early Dynastic List p. 56) have connected this city with the toponym dra-sa-ap found as entry 33 in the Early Dynastic geographical list from Ebla and Abū Ṣalābīkh. I have proposed (Early Dynastic List p. 55 map 6) a location for Rašap a little to the southwest of ancient Awal on the road that proceeded up the Diyālā valley and then headed northwest following the back of the Jebel Ḥamrīn, that is, along the so-called "Kirkūk Corridor."

If Laessøe (Shemshāra p. 70) and Hallo (RHA 36 [1978] p. 77) are correct in equating ancient Šaššurum with modern Shemshara in the area of the Lower Zab, then our expectation would be that the defeat of Arrapha (probably marked by the modern mound named ʿArafah, about 3 km north-west of Qalʿat Kirkūk [see N. Hannoon, Studies in the Historical Geography of

Northern Iraq during the Middle and Neo-Assyrian Periods, Ph.D dissertation, University of Toronto 1986, pp. 369–70]), would have occurred during the campaign commemorated in the name of AS 6. Of interest, then, is an archival text dated to v AS 5 (Puzriš-Dagan no. 166: Salonen, Puzriš-Dagan-Texte no. 166) that mentions (lines 7–8 and 14) the general Ḫašip-atal in connection (line 11) with deliveries of the "soldiers of Arrapḫa" (érin ar-ra-ap-ḫu-um.KI). For Ḫašip-atal as general, see the comments of Steinkeller in Gibson and Biggs, Bureaucracy p. 39 n. 63.

A reflection of the campaign against Šaššurum may possibly be found in an archival text dated to xii AS 5 (MA 15: Cagni and Pettinato, MVN 4 no. 263); it contains the remark (line 2): "one goat for the standard (in the form of) the weapon, (when) it went on the campaign" (1 máš šu-nir GIŠ.tukul kaskal-šè gen-na). The practice of convening troops in front of an ensign is attested in a passage of an inscription of Eannatum of Lagaš (see Steible, ASBW 1 p. 147, Eʾannatum 2 iii 17–20): "He (Eannatum) defeated the governor of the emblem of URU×A, who went at the head of the (mustered troops)" (šu-nir URU×A.KI-ka énsi-bi sag mu-gub-ba TÙN.ŠÈ bi-sè).

(7) mu ḫu-úḫ-nu-ri.KI ba-ḫul "The year Ḫuḫnuri was destroyed." A fuller form of the year name appears in Schneider, Zeitbestimmungen p. 28 no. 7q: mu ^{d}amar-^{d}EN.ZU lugal-e bí-tum-ra-bí-um.KI ià-ab-ru.KI ma-da-ma-da-bi ù ḫu-úḫ-nu-ri.KI mu-ḫul "The year Amar-Suena, the king, destroyed Bītum-rabiʾum, Iabru, and their territories, together with Ḫuḫnuri."

The author intends to examine, in a separate study, the possibility that the name of AS 7 refers not to the Ḫuḫnuri in Elam, as is generally assumed, but rather to a similarly named GN located somewhere in the foothills of the Zagros Mountains between modern Kifrī and Ṭāwūq.

An archival text from Umma dated to vi AS 6 (P[inches] 67: Sollberger, MVN 5 no. 46) may be connected with the campaign against Ḫuḫnuri. It notes (lines 1–3): "one goat from Alulu, (when) the standard went on the campaign" (1 máš šu-nir kaskal-šè gen-na). A further allusion to the Ḫuḫnuru campaign may be seen in an archival text dated to 25 vii AS 6 (Sollberger, MVN 5 no. 115) that records (line 5) various disbursements "for the soldiers coming (back) from the campaign" (mu aga_x-ús kaskal-ta ir-ra-ne-šè). If the Ḫuḫnuri campaign extended into AS 7, as seems probable, then a second reference to it is likely found in the tablet, Legrain, TRU no. 334, dated to 10 viii AS 7. It records various disbursements "for the lieutenants and royal body guard coming (back) from the campaign" (nu-bànda ù gàr-du ... kaskal-ta ir-ra-ne-šè). An archival text dated to 10 vi AS 8 (NBC 2421: Keiser, BIN 3 no. 402) alludes to a banquet that may have been held to honour the heroes of the campaign against Ḫuḫnuri. The text reads, in part (obv. lines 1–3, rev. line 1): "one grain-fed sheep (for) the 'Seven-Heroes Hill'; the 'heroes,' the men of Ḫuḫnuri, ate its meat ... in the field 'Amar-Suena is the Ploughman of Enlil'" (1 udu-niga du_6-^{d}ur-sag-imin uzu-bi gàr-du lú ḫu-uḫ-nu-ri.KI-e-ne ba-ab-kú ... šà-a-šà ^{d}amar-^{d}EN.ZU-engar-^{d}en-líl-lá). Here we take the mention of the "men of Ḫuḫnuri" as a reference to the champions who took part in the war against Ḫuḫnuri. A second text, that is undated (AO 5556: de Genouillac, TCL 2 pl. 38), refers (lines 4–5) to a banquet held (at the field) "Amar-Suena is the Ploughman of Enlil" (kaš-dé-a ^{d}amar-^{d}EN.ZU-engar-^{d}en-líl-lá). It may allude to the feast mentioned in NBC 2421, or perhaps to another celebration held in the same spot.

(8) mu en eridu.KI ba-ḫun "The year the *en* of Eridu was installed." The full form of the *en*'s name is known from other examples of the year name (see Schneider, Zeitbestimmungen p. 29 8Ba) to have been En-nune-Amar-Suenra-kiag "*En*: the prince (Enki) loves Amar-Suena."

Two archival texts can be connected with Amar-Suena's installation of the new *en* of Eridu. The first, a summary tablet (Collection Béghin, Versailles no. 2: Grégoire, MVN 10 no. 230), one of whose sections presents records pertaining to AS 7 (see col. ii line 17: mu ḫu-úh-nu-ri.KI), notes quantities of wood (col. i lines 14–15) "placed on the boat in order to install the *en* of Eridu" (en-eridu.KI ḫun-e-dè má-a gá-ra). A second text, a Drehem tablet dated to x AS 7 (AUAM 73.0687: Sigrist, AUCT 1 no. 948), records various golden rings issued (line 2) "(when) the *en* returned to Eridu" (en eridu.KI mu-gi_4). The text mentions (lines 3–4) the former *en* of Eridu named en-nam-šita-dšul-gi-ra-ke_4 ba-gub; she was the *en* installed by Šulgi and appears in the year name for Š 27.

As noted, the later literary tradition points to a special devotion of Amar-Suena for the cult of the god Enki of Eridu. This concern is amply attested in contemporary sources — royal inscriptions, year names, and archival texts. Amar-Suena's rebuilding of Enki's E-abzu temple at Eridu was, in all likelihood, the completion of the construction project begun by Ur-Nammu. The building of the temple complex was arguably Amar-Suena's most noteworthy achievement. The work is commemorated in a frequently attested thirteen-line brick inscription (E3/2.1.3.15). The bricks come from a handful of sites in addition to Eridu. Curiously, many of the localities that have yielded these bricks are quite distant from Eridu itself. Part of the refurbishing of Enki's temple may have entailed the setting up of a new gate adorned with lion figures, for two lion torsos of probable Ur III date were found at and near Eridu. Spycket (Statuaire, pp. 221–22) writes:

> Le *grand lion*, découvert en 1853 par Taylor à Abu-Shahrein/Eridu et re-découvert en 1947 par les fouilles irakiennes, est taillé dans un bloc de basalte gris, haut de lm,65, qui a commandé l'attitude assise du fauve, ramassé sur son train arrière, tandis que les pattes antérieures suivent la ligne verticale de la pierre (Pl. 148) ... Des fragments d'un autre lion en même matière ont été signalés sur un tell voisin d'Abu-Shahrein et Fuad Safar a pensé légitimement que l'entrée d'un temple de la IIIe dynastie d'Ur était flanquée de ces lions, pratique que généraliseront les dynasties suivantes (ci-dessous, p. 288 ss.).

The lions found by Safar or their propotypes are alluded to in a number of Sumerian literary compositions. Green (Eridu p. 216) writes:

> Thc lion-faced gate, apparently the main gate of the temple, is also called the great gate (ká-gu-la, UrLEr 8) and the place of fate-determining (ki nam tar-re-ba, IEr 3:1; ki nam tar-ra, UrLEr 8). Inanna is greeted there by Isimud when she visits the *abzu*, and she is given beer to drink: igi-pirig-gá-ka kaš hu-mu-[na-nag-nag] (Inanna-Enki I ii 11); igi-pirig-gá-ka kaš mu-na-nag-nag (ibid. I ii 23). It is not clear whether or not the welcoming banquet is set up for Inanna at this place. The guardians Kahegal and Igihegal stand at the lion-faced gate; and it apparently is there that the *kiškanû*-trees, sacred to Eridu, stand, perhaps as part of the architecture (see chapter 6, pp. 186–92, chapter 10, pp. 357–58). Other literary references to lions and lion-faced aspects of Eridu are: abzu igi-pirig-gá me al nu-di-dam "at the *abzu*, the lion-faced (place), whose *me*'s are not to be coveted" (Hymn to thc Hoe 43): ká-zu ur-maḫ lú šu ti-a kun_4-zu pirig lú-ra e_{11}-dè "your gate is a lion laying hold of a man; your doorsill is a lion coming down on a man" (praise addressed to the Eengurra, ErH 31f.); é da-engur-ra pirig abzu-šà-ga "temple at the edge of the *engur*, lion in the midst of the *abzu*" (epithets of the Eengurra, ibid. 57).

The construction work on the temple seems to be but one (albeit the major) element of a royal agenda for the god Enki that certainly included the rebuilding of the god's temple and the installation of his new *en*; a third element may have been the fashioning of Enki's cult boat. Amar-Suena was able to accomplish only the first two tasks; the fabrication of the cult boat of Enki was left to his successor, Šū-Sîn, who named the first year after his accession for that event.

(9) [mu] ⌜en⌝-^{d}nanna [...] "The year the *En*: Nanna ..." The full year name can be restored from U 6731 = Legrain, UET 3 no. 1499: **mu en-^{d}nanna-^{d}amar-^{d}EN.ZU-ra-ki-ág en-^{d}nanna-kar-zi-da-ka ba-ḫun** "The year En-Nanna-Amar-Suenara-kiag-(ana) ("[Heavenly] *en*: Nanna loves Amar-Suena"), *en* of the god Nanna of Karzida, was installed."

As noted, En-Nanna-Amar-Suenara-kiag-(ana) was apparently the second *en* of Nanna installed during the reign of Amar-Suena. A handful of archival texts can likely be connected with the *en*'s inauguration; they are discussed here in chronological order. The first text (private collection: Owen, MVN 15 no. 365), dated to 14 xi AS 8, notes (lines 1–4): "1 fattened ox, *siskur* offering for the *ki-utu* ritual of the *en* in E-gula (E-gula here perhaps means 'the old house') (on the occasion) when En-Nanna-Amar-Suenra-kiag-ana, *en* of Gaʾeš, was installed" (1 gu$_4$-niga sískur ki-^{d}utu-en-na šà-é-gu-la u$_4$ en-^{d}nanna-^{d}amar-^{d}EN.<ZU>-ra-ki-ág-an-na en-ga-eš.KI ba-ḫun-gá). A second archival text (WHM 198: Kang, SETDA no. 165), dated to 29 xi AS 8, records (lines 1–2): "1 fattened ox for the *ki-utu* ritual of the *en* of Gaʾeš" (1 gu$_4$-niga ki-^{d}utu en ga-eš.KI-šè). A third tablet (NBC 331; Keiser, BIN 3 no. 352), dated to xi AS 8 (no day date recorded), notes (lines 1–2): "7 oxen to install the *en*" (7 gu$_4$ en ḫun-dè). A fourth tablet dated to the 5 i AS 9 (ROM 65 925.62.4: Sigrist, ROM no. 82), notes (lines 5–6) a royal offering in connection with a trip(?) of the *en* of Nanna to Eridu(?) (máš-da-ri-a-lugal en-^{d}nanna nun.KI DU-ni). Finally, a Drehem tablet dated to 16 i AS 9 (de Genouillac, Trouvaille no. 4) records the receipt of various animals for the en of Nanna of Gaʾeš (line 7: en-^{d}nanna ga-eš.KI).

We may also note in this connection a tablet (MAH 363: Sauren, WMAH no. 164 = Sauren, MVN 2 no. 164), dated to 7 x AS 9, that records (lines 2–3) a "royal offering for the (resting) place of the *en* of Nanna" (máš-da-ri-a-lugal ki-en ^{d}nanna-šè). This last text likely refers to an offering for the former *en* whom En-Nanna-Amar-Suenra-kiag-(ana) replaced.

II. Other Events of the Reign

(i) The digging of the Amar-Suena canal

A major undertaking of Amar-Suena was the digging of a new canal that was named for the king: "Canal established by Amar-Suena" (i$_7$-^{d}amar-^{d}EN.ZU-ke$_4$ gar/gá-ra). While no year name commemorating its excavation is known, a number of archival texts do record work on this canal. Sauren (Topographie Umma p. 97) indicated that the canal was dug during the years AS 2–5, but the relevant dossier of texts does, in fact, extend as far as ŠS 6, as can be seen from the following survey:

Year	Source
AS 2	Hackman, BIN 5 no. 263
AS 2	Fish, MCS 3 (1953) p. 54 105547
AS 3	Boson, TCS no. 33
AS 3	Fish, MCS 3 (1953) p. 54 112944
AS 3	de Genouillac, TCL 5 no. 5674 viii 6
AS 5	Jones and Snyder, SET no. 261
AS 5	Deimel, Orientalia 15 (1925) pp. 63–64 IB 69
AS 9	Schneider, Drehem- und Djoḫatexte p. 61 no. 213
AS 9	Fish, MCS 3 (1953) p. 87 105516
ŠS 2	de Genouillac, TCL 5 no. 5676 x 3, 5

ŠS 2	Lutz, UCP 9 (1928–31) p. 235 no. 21
ŠS 4	Nikol'skiy, DV 5 no. 111
ŠS 6	Fish, Catalogue no. 617

C. Wilcke (ZA 62 [1972] p. 57) has proposed, based on the evidence from Ur III archival texts, that the Amar-Suena canal was a side branch of the Euphrates river system, and that it joined the watercourse that flowed between the cities of Šarrākum and Umma (the ancient Iturungal) at a point roughly halfway between those two cities. If one accepts the location of the ancient city of Šarrākum at modern Umm al-Ḥafriyāt that has been proposed by the author (Frayne, Early Dynastic List p. 36), then the confluence of the Amar-Suena canal and Iturungal should be placed somewhere between the ancient cities of Adab (modern Bismāyā) and Karkar (possibly modern Tell Jidr; see M. Powell, "Karkar, Dabrum and Tall Ğidr: An Unresolved Geographical Problem," JNES 39 [1980] pp. 47–52). It happens that the one extant literary letter of Amar-Suena to Šulgi (Kramer, ISET 2 pl. 115 Ni 3083 1′–8′) deals with "the maintaining of waterworks in the region of Karkar" (Michalowski in Essays Finkelstein p. 155), that is, in the very same area where the Amar-Suena canal once flowed. Could it be that the task alluded to in the literary letter was to see to completion a major canal project that was a final directive of Amar-Suena's father? The fact that work on the canal had begun already by AS 2 would certainly support this idea. The actual course of the Amar-Suena canal can be determined with some precision by plotting the various small towns and cities that have yielded the standard nine-line (E3/2.1.3.1)and *abzu* (E3/2.1.3.15) inscriptions of Amar-Suena. The sites are shown in Map 1. Nissen (in Adams, Countryside p. 217) writes:

> Bricks with inscriptions of Amarsuena were found at eight sites, including all duplicates of the known building inscription of the construction of the Abzu of Enki in Eridu (*SAK* 196 3c) in five, and duplicates of the short inscription which only gives the titles of the ruler (*SAK* 196 3b) in three. It is interesting that these bricks were found not only at major towns like Uruk (surface find made in 1967 in the area of the Sinkashid Palace), Adab (*OIP* 14, 40, and 42), Bad-Tibira (*Iraq* 22:198), and Kisurra (*MDOG* 17, 15), but also at smaller sites, WS–039, 097, 100, 131, 242, and 439. As has been discussed in chapter 3, all the latter sites lie along the western branch of the Euphrates.

Map 1 reveals a system of canals that comprised three main watercourses in the land of Sumer: (a) the channel of the Euphrates from Bad-tibira in the southeast to Nippur in the northwest; (b) a connecting branch between the Euphrates river and Iturungal canal (the Amar-Suena canal proper); and, in all likelihood, (c) part of the Iturungal canal.

(ii) The construction of the Dublalmaḫ at Ur

Inscription E3/2.1.3.9, which is found on door sockets from Ur, records the king's (re)construction of the Edublalmaḫ at Ur. An archival text (de Genouillac, Trouvaille no. 11), dated to x AS 5 line 2, mentions (line 2) a "banquet (for?) the Dublalmaḫ" (kaš-dé-a-dub-lá-maḫ). It may possibly refer to festivities held for the dedication of the new structure.

III. The death of Amar-Suena

An archival text (W[alker Art Center] 94: Jones and Snyder, SET no. 66), dated to 26 ii AS 9, records (line 5): "2 sheep for the throne of Amar-Suena" (2 udu GIŠ.gu-za-^{d}amar-^{d}EN.ZU). A second tablet (Nesbit, SRD no. 20) dated to the same month, but without a day date, similarly mentions (lines 1–5) offerings for the throne of Amar-Suena. Sallaberger (Kalender 1 p. 147) has

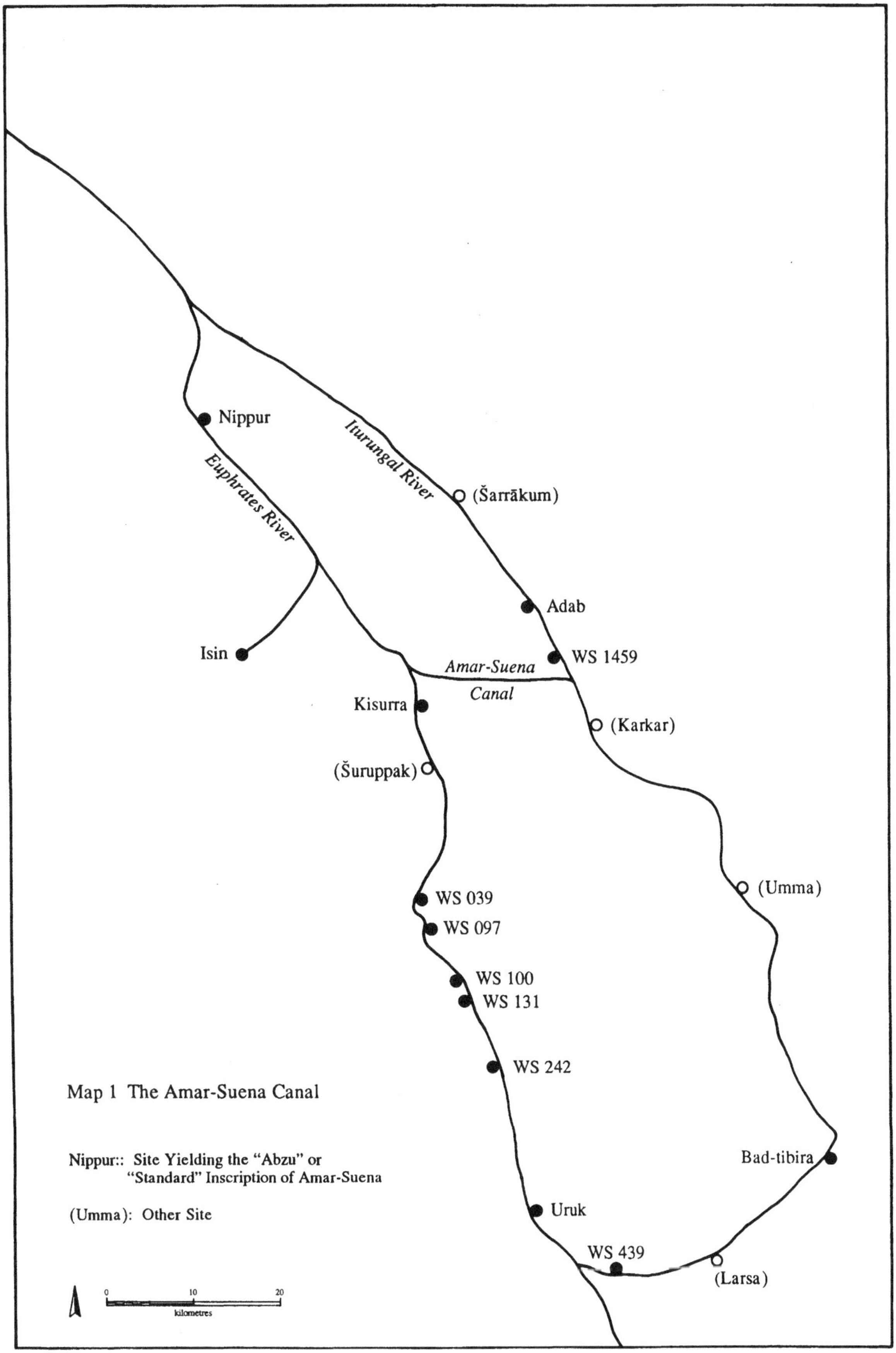
Nippur
Iturungal River
Euphrates River
(Šarrākum)
Adab
Isin
WS 1459
Amar-Suena Canal
Kisurra
(Karkar)
(Šuruppak)
(Umma)
WS 039
WS 097
WS 100
WS 131
WS 242
Bad-tibira
Uruk
WS 439
(Larsa)
Nippur:: Site Yielding the "Abzu" or "Standard" Inscription of Amar-Suena
(Umma): Other Site
0
10
20
kilometres

Map 1 The Amar-Suena Canal

pointed out that offerings to the royal seat of the Ur III king were made only after the ruler's death. This fact, then, enables us to fix the date of Amar-Suena's death somewhere within the roughly two-month period that extended from 1 i AS 9 to 26 ii AS 9. The fact that AS 9 bears a year name of the king indicates that Amar-Suena was alive on the very first day of that year. Amar-Suena's successor, Šū-Sîn, appears for the first time with his name written with the prefixed divine determinative in an archival text dated to 1 viii AS 9 (HS 1225: Pohl, TMH NF 1/2 no. 225), although, as noted, seals dedicated to Šū-Sîn as king of Ur predate this. By xii AS 9 *ki-a-nag* offerings were being made for the deceased Amar-Suena (PD 384: Salonen, Puzriš-Dagan-Texte no. 384 line 4 and T. Gomi, Orient 12 [1976] p. 7).

As noted, the omen tradition discloses that Amar-Suena's death apparently resulted from a serious foot infection (Goetze, YOS 10 no. 25 line 32: [*šumma šumēlam si-ip-p*]*i* KÁ *ši-lum ip-lu-uš-ma uš-te-eb-ri a-mu-ut* amar-^{d}EN.ZU [*ša še-nu-um* ... *a-na še*]*-pi-im iš-ša-ak-nu-šum i-na ni-ši-ik še-ni-im i-mu-tu* "[If on the left side] a cavity pierces the 'doorframe' of the 'palace gate' and is permanent, it is an omen of Amar-Suena, [to whose f]oot [a ... shoe] was fitted [and who] died from the 'bite' of a shoe").

1

The standard nine-line inscription of Amar-Suena is known from both stamped and inscribed bricks from numerous sites.

CATALOGUE

Ex.	Museum number	Excavation number	Registration number	Provenance	Dimensions (cm)	Lines preserved	cpn
Bricks							
1	EŞ 1333	—	—	Sippar	19×16.5×6	1–7	c
2	EŞ 6682	—	—	Fara	24×27×6.5	1–9	c
3	EŞ 6683	—	—	Fara	31×19×7	6–9	c
4	EŞ 8962	—	—	Nippur	30.5×30×7	—	n
5	EŞ 8963	—	—	Nippur	32×18×6.5	—	n
6	EŞ 8967	—	—	Nippur	31×30×6	1–9	c
7	BM 90023	—	1979-12-20, 20	Eridu	32.5×32.5×7	1–9	c
8	BM 90025	—	1979-12-20, 22	Eridu	32.5×32.5×7	1–9	c
9	BM 90030	—	1979-12-20, 27	Eridu	32×32×7	1–9	c
10	BM 90034	—	1979-12-20, 29	Eridu	32.5×16.5×7	1–9	c
11	BM 90037	—	59-10-14, 46	Eridu	32.5×16.5×7.5	1–9	c
12	BM 90040	—	59-10-14, 8	Eridu	30×15.5×7	1–9	c
13	BM 90042	—	1979-12-20, 33	—	32×15.5	1–9	c
14	BM 90043	—	1979-10-20, 34	Eridu	31×31×7	1–9	c
15	BM 90348	—	59-10-14, 4	Eridu	21×18×7	1–8	c
16	BM 90349	—	59-10-14, 5	Eridu	13.5×12×6.5	1–6	c
17	BM 90352	—	1979-12-20, 210	—	30×29×8	1–9	c
18	BM 90372	—	59-10-14, 10	Eridu	21×15×7.5	1–9	c
19	BM 90399	—	1979-12-20, 230	—	15×19×7	9	c
20	BM 90767	—	59-10-14, 338	—	33×26.5×7	1–9	c
21	BM 114265	—	1919-10-11, 4696	Ur	31.5×31.5×6	1–9	c
22	BM 114266	—	1919-10-11, 4697	Ur	24×15.5×6.5	1–6	c
23	BM 114267	—	1919-10-11, 4698	Ur	32×23×7	1–9	c
24	BM 114268	—	1919-10-11, 4699	Ur	15.5×15×6	1–5	c
25	BM 114269	—	1919-10-11, 4700	Ur	14.5×14×6	1–7	c
26	BM 114270	—	1919-10-11, 4701	Ur	19.5×15×6	1–8	c
27	BM 114272	—	1919-10-11, 4703	Ur	33×33×6.5	1–9	c
28	BM 114273	—	1919-10-11, 4704	Ur	20.5×15×6.5	1–9	c
29	BM 114274	—	1919-10-11, 4705	Ur	28×13.5×6.5	1–9	c
30	BM 114275	—	1919-10-11, 4706	Ur	32×30×7	1–9	c
31	BM 122941	—	1931-10-10, 9	Ur	34×16.5×7	1–9	c
32	BM 132804	—	1959-11-17, 98	—	5×4.5×2	1	c
33	BM 137344	U 975	1935-1-13, 4	Ur, TTB 7	9.5×8.5×6	7–8	c
34	BM 137348	U 3135	1935-1-13, 8	Ur, no provenance given in registry book	30.5×29.5×6.5	1–9	c
35	BM 137359	—	1919-10-11, 5364	Ur	33×29.5×6	1–9	c
36	BM 137382	—	1979-12-18, 17	—	32.5×32.5×7	1–9	c
37	BM 137403	—	1979-12-18, 38	—	32.5×32.5×5.8	1–9	c
38	BM 137419	—	1979-12-18, 54	—	32.5×21.5×7.5	1–9	c
39	BM 137423	—	1979-12-18, 58	—	17×16.5×7.5	1–9	c
40	VA 3040	—	—	Kisurra, NW area of mound	—	1–9	c
41	—	—	—	Tell el-Laḫm, from the top of a well	—	1–9	n
42	—	—	—	Isin	—	1–6	p
43	—	—	—	Badtibira	—	1–9	p
44	—	—	—	Badtibira	—	1–4	n
45	"Some badly-effaced half bricks"	—	—	Badtibira	—	—	n
46	A 1133	—	—	Adab	30.8×30.6×6.8	1–9	c
47	A 1135	—	—	Adab	30.6×20.4×5.6	1–9	c
48	AO —	—	—	Girsu, "nécropole du Tell H"; see Cros, Tello p. 121 plan E point *b*	32×32	1–9	n
49	Ash 1924-625	—	—	Isin(?)	30.5×30.5×7.5	1–9	c
50	Ash 1980-126	—	—	—	23×16×5.5	1–9 (face) 2–6 (edge)	c
51	Private collection	—	—	—	—	1–7	n

Ex.	Museum number	Excavation number	Registration number	Provenance	Dimensions (cm)	Lines preserved	cpn
52	CBS 15331	—	—	Ur	17×8.5×7	—	n
53	CBS 15339	U 73	—	Ur	32×32×6.5	—	p
54	CBS 16537a	U 3135a	—	Ur	33×32×7	—	n
55	CBS 16537b	U 3135b	—	Ur	32×16×7.5	—	n
56	—	2 N-T 734b	—	Nippur	30×15×7	—	n
57	UM 84-26-2	—	—	—	33×33×7	—	n
58	UM 84-26-3	—	—	—	31×30×6.5	—	n
59	UM 84-26-4	—	—	—	32×32×6.5	—	n
60	UM 84-26-5	—	—	—	31×31×7	—	n
61	Bibliothèque Nationale et Universitaire de Strasbourg no. 146	—	—	—	—	1–9	n
62	MSBF —	—	—	—	Inscription: 6.5×13	1–9	n
63	IM —	IB 205	—	Isin	—	—	n
64	IM —	IB 206	—	As ex. 63	—	—	n
65	IM —	IB 262	—	As ex. 63	—	—	n
66	IM —	IB 293	—	As ex. 63	—	—	n
67	IM —	IB 294	—	As ex. 63	—	—	n
68	IM —	IB 593	—	As ex. 63	—	—	n
69	IM —	IB 687	—	As ex. 63	—	—	n
70	IM —	IB 689(?)	—	As ex. 63	—	—	n
71	IM —	IB —	—	Isin, in the foundation box in the approach to the cella of Gula in the Gula temple	—	—	n
72	IM —	IB — numerous exs.	—	Isin, from various points in the Gula temple, Nordabschnitt II and Südostabschnitt	—	—	n
73	IM—	IB — 17 exs.	—	From the "castle"	—	—	n
74	—	— 3 exs.	—	From various sites along the ancient Euphrates from Larsa to Šuruppak (see map 1)	—	—	n
Clay vessel fragment							
75	A 438	—	—	Adab	18.5×12	3–9	c
Brick stamps							
76	BLMJ —	—	—	—	9.5×6.5	3–9	n
77	Pittsburgh Theological Seminary 03-45	—	—	—	—	—	n

COMMENTARY

Exs. 7–39 were collated by C.B.F. Walker. The text is arranged in one column.

BIBLIOGRAPHY

1861 1 R 3 XII 2 (exs. 7–20, conflated copy)
1872 Smith, TSBA 1 p. 40 (exs. 7–20, translation)
1874 Lenormant, Études accadiennes 2 p. 321 (exs. 7–20, translation)
1875 Ménant, Babylone p. 93 (exs. 7–20, translation)
1892 Winckler, KB 3/1 pp. 88–89 Bur-Sin 3 (exs. 7–20, edition)
1894 Scheil, RT 16 pp. 184 and 186 (ex. 1, study)
1899 Bezold, Cat. 5 p. 2234 (exs. 7–10, 12–13, 15–20, study)
1902 Scheil, Sippar p. 140 (ex. 1, study)
1903 Andrae, MDOG 17 p. 15 (ex. 40, study)
1905 King, CT 21 pl. 24 90034 (ex. 10, copy)
1907 Messerschmidt, VS 1 no. 26 (ex. 40, copy)
1907 Thureau-Dangin, SAK pp. 196–97 Pûr-sin b (exs. 7 and 40, edition)
1910 Thureau-Dangin, in Cros, Tello p. 140 (ex. 48, study)
1912 Banks, Bismya p. 343 (ex. 46, photo)
1920 Thompson, Arch. 70 p. 142 (ex. 41, translation, study)
1922 BM Guide p. 60 nos. 75–84 (exs. 7–14, study)
1925 Woolley and Legrain, MJ 16 p. 302 (ex. 53, photo)
1925–26 Dougherty, AASOR 7 fig. 40 (ex. 42, photo) and figs. 41–42 (exs. 43–44, photos)
1928 Gadd, UET 1 p. xxiv (ex. 34, study)
1929 Barton, RISA pp. 286–87 Bur-Sin 2 (exs. 7 and 10, edition)
1930 Luckenbill, Adab nos. 40–41 (exs. 46–47 copy)
1960 Crawford, Iraq 22 p. 198 (ex. 45, study)
1962 Hallo, HUCA 33 pp. 34–35 Amar-Sin 2 (exs. 1, 7, 10, 40–44, 46–47, study)
1971 Sollberger and Kupper, IRSA IIIA3b 1b (exs. 1, 7, 10, 40–44, 46–47, translation)
1972 Nissen, in Adams, Countryside p. 217 (ex. 74, study)
1977 Edzard and Wilcke, in Hrouda, Isin 1 p. 85, C 6 b (exs. 63–70, study)
1981 Charpin and Durand, Documents Strasbourg no. 146 (ex. 61, copy)
1981 Grégoire, MVN 10 nos. 21–22 (exs. 49 and 51, copy)
1981 Walker, CBI no. 23 (exs. 7–39, study)
1981 Walker and Wilcke, in Hrouda, Isin 2 p. 92, C 6 b (exs. 71–72, study)
1985 Behrens, JCS 37 pp. 232–33 Amarsuen 2 (exs. 52–60 study)

1986 Kärki, KDDU pp. 71–72 Amarsuena 2 (exs. 1, 7–44, 46–49, 53, 63–72, edition)
1986 Yang, Sargonic Archive p. 38 no. 5 (exs. 46–47 study)
1987 Vuk, in Sigrist and Vuk, Franciscanum pp. 38–39 and pl. 13 fig. 1 (ex. 62, photo, copy, edition)
1991 Steible, NSBW 2 pp. 218–21 Amarsuen 2 (exs. 7–44, 46–49, 51–70, 74, edition)
1992 Sommerfeld, in Hrouda, Isin 4 pp. 145–47 (ex. 73, study)
1994 Curtis, ASJ 16 p. 113 no. 24 (ex. 76, copy)

TEXT

1) ^{d}amar-^{d}EN.ZU
2) nibru.KI-a
3) ^{d}en-líl-le
4) mu-pà-da
5) sag-ús-
6) é-^{d}en-líl-ka
7) nita-kala-ga
8) lugal-uri$_5$.KI-ma
9) lugal-an-ub-da-límmu-ba

1–9) Amar-Suena, the one called by name by the god Enlil in Nippur, supporter of the temple of the god Enlil, mighty man, king of Ur, king of the four quarters.

2

A clay vessel fragment from Adab bears the end of the standard nine-line inscription of Amar-Suena.

COMMENTARY

The vessel fragment, which measures 18.5×12 cm, bears the museum number A 438 (Chicago). The text is arranged in one column. The inscription was collated.

BIBLIOGRAPHY

1930 Luckenbill, Adab no. 42 (copy)
1986 Yang, Sargonic Archive p. 38 no. 5 (study)
1991 Steible, NSBW 2 pp. 218–21 Amarsuen 2 (edition)

TEXT

1) [^{d}amar-^{d}EN.ZU]
2) [nibru.KI-a]
3) ^{d}en-líl-le
4) mu-pà-da
5) sag-ús-
6) é-^{d}en-líl-ka
7) nita-kala-ga
8) lugal-uri$_5$.KI-ma
9) lugal-an-ub-da-límmu-ba

1–9) [Amar-Suena, the one called by name] by the god Enlil [in Nippur], supporter of the temple of the god Enlil, mighty man, king of Ur, king of the four quarters.

Variants for E3/2.1.3.1:
2–3.53 ^{d}en-líl-le nibru.KI.a.
7.14, 52, 53, 59, 60 lugal-kala-ga.

3

Four of Amar-Suena's inscriptions (E3/2.1.3.3–7) record construction work at Nippur. The first of these, which is stamped on a brick, deals with the construction of the shrine E-kura-igi-gal.

COMMENTARY

The brick was found in locus 3, level IV, of the Inanna temple and given the excavation number 5 N-T 690. The inscription was collated from a cast in the Oriental Institute of the University of Chicago; the original is in the Iraq Museum. Its museum number is unknown. The stamped area of the inscription, as determined from the cast, measures 16×6 cm. The text is arranged in one column. The inscription is published here through the kind permission of E. Carter and J.A. Brinkman.

For other references to the E-kura-igi-gal see George, House Most High p. 117 no. 683 and Sallaberger, Kalender 1 p. 53 n. 223.

BIBLIOGRAPHY

1992 Zettler, Ur III Temple p.12 n. 22

TEXT

1) ⌈^{d}en-líl⌉
2) lugal-kur-kur-⌈ra⌉
3) lugal-ni-ir
4) ^{d}amar-^{d}EN.ZU
5) nibru.KI-a
6) ^{d}en-líl-le
7) mu pà-da
8) sag-ús-
9) é-^{d}en-líl-ka
10) lugal-kala-ga
11) lugal-uri$_{5}$.KI-ma
12) lugal-an-ub-da-límmu-ba-ke$_{4}$
13) <é>-⌈kur⌉(?)-⌈ra⌉(?)-igi-gál
14) ⌈é⌉(?)-u$_{6}$-nir-⌈x⌉
15) [é]-⌈ki-ág⌉-gá-ni
16) mu-[na]-dù

1–3) For the god Enlil, lord of the foreign lands, his lord,

4–9) Amar-Suena, the one called by name by the god Enlil in Nippur, supporter of the temple of the god Enlil,

10–12) mighty king, king of Ur, king of the four quarters,

13–16) built [for him] <E>kura-igi-gal, the ziqqurrat *structure*, his beloved [temple].

4

In his second season of excavations at Nippur, Peters unearthed a small shrine built on a baked brick platform. It lay about seventy-seven metres southeast of the exterior wall of Enlil's ziqqurrat. Baked bricks bearing a two-line inscription of Amar-Suena came from the walls of the shrine.

CATALOGUE

Ex.	Museum number	Dimensions (cm)	Lines preserved	cpn
1	CBS 8653	17×8.5×7	1–2	c
2	HS 1967	12.2×6.3×8	1–2	c
3	EŞ 8971	10.7×9×6.8	1–2	c
4	EŞ 8979(?)	12.5×8.5×6.5	1–2	p
5	EŞ no number	14×7×9	1–2	c

COMMENTARY

Ex. 1 was collated by H. Behrens. The text is arranged in one column.

BIBLIOGRAPHY

1893 Hilprecht, BE 1/1 no. 22 (ex. 1, copy)
1897 Peters, Nippur 2 foldout facing p. 142 (findspot); p. 146 (study)
1907 Thureau-Dangin SAK pp. 196–97 Pûr-sin a (ex. 1, edition)
1929 Barton, RISA pp. 286–87 Bur-Sin 1 (ex. 1, edition)
1962 Hallo, HUCA 33 p. 34 Amar-Sin 1 (ex. 1, study)
1969 Oelsner, WZJ 18 no. 20 (ex. 2, edition)
1971 Sollberger and Kupper, IRSA IIIA3a (exs. 1–2, translation)
1984 Zettler, JNES 43 p. 232 (exs. 1–2, study)
1986 Kärki, KDDU pp. 70–71 Amarsuena 1 (exs. 1–2, edition)
1991 Steible, NSBW 2 p. 218 Amarsuen 1 (exs. 1–2, edition)

TEXT

1) ^{d}amar-^{d}EN.ZU
2) lugal-kala-ga

1–2) Amar-Suena, mighty king.

5

A seventeen-line diorite door socket was found in the "small shrine" of Enlil.

COMMENTARY

The door socket, which is in the shape of an irregular cube about 19 cm on each side, was found in the northwest wall of room 1 of the "small shrine" of Enlil (see Zettler, JNES 43 [1984] p. 233). It bears the museum number CBS 8838. Lines 1–11 are found in col. i, lines 12–17 in col. ii. The inscription was collated.

BIBLIOGRAPHY

1893 Hilprecht, BE 1/1 no. 20 (copy)
1897 Peters, Nippur 2 p. 146 (study)
1900 Radau, EBH pp. 270–71 (edition)
1907 Thureau-Dangin, SAK pp. 198–99 Pûr-sin f (edition)
1929 Barton, RISA pp. 290–91 Bur-Sin 7 (edition)
1962 Hallo, HUCA 33 p. 36 Amar-Sin 9 (study)
1984 Zettler, JNES 43 p. 236 (edition)
1986 Kärki, KDDU pp. 81–82 Amarsuena 9 (edition)
1991 Steible, NSBW 2 pp. 234–35 Amarsuen 9 (edition)

TEXT

1)	ᵈen-líl	1–3) For the god Enlil, lord of the foreign lands, his lord,
2)	lugal-kur-kur-ra	
3)	lugal-a-ni-ir	
4)	ᵈamar-ᵈEN.ZU	4–12) Amar-Suena, the one called by name by the god Enlil in Nippur, supporter of the temple of the god Enlil, mighty man, king of Ur, king of the four quarters,
5)	nibru.KI-a	
6)	ᵈen-líl-le	
7)	mu pà-da	
8)	sag-ús-	
9)	é-ᵈen-líl-ka	
10)	nita-kala-ga	
11)	lugal-uri₅.KI-ma	
12)	lugal-an-ub-da-límmu-ba-ke₄	
13)	uš-kù	13–17) set (with this door socket) the shining foundations of the god Enlil at Amar-Suena's place of rejoicing.
14)	ᵈen-líl-lá	
15)	ki-šà-ḫúl-la-	
16)	ᵈamar-ᵈEN.ZU-ka-ka	
17)	mu-na-an-gub	

6

A second diorite door socket was found in the "small shrine" of Enlil.

COMMENTARY

The door socket measures 33×28×23 cm. Its present location is unknown; it may be in Istanbul. The text is arranged in one column. The door socket, which apparently was reused, bears an earlier inscription of Lugal-kigine-dudu; see Steible, ASBW 2 p. 298 Lugalkiginnedudu 1.

In line 13 we have translated ì-nun, as "ghee" (= clarified butter) following CAD sub *himētu*; AHw gives "Butter."

BIBLIOGRAPHY

1893 Hilprecht, BE 1/1 no. 21 (copy)
1897 Peters, Nippur 2 p. 146 (study)
1900 Radau, EBH pp. 271–72 (edition)
1907 Thureau-Dangin, SAK pp. 198–201 Pûr-sin g (edition)
1929 Barton, RISA pp. 290–91 Bur-Sin 8 (edition)

1962 Hallo, HUCA 33 p. 36 Amar-Sin 10 (study)
1971 Sollberger and Kupper, IRSA IIIA3f (translation)
1984 Zettler, JNES 43 p. 237 (edition)
1986 Kärki, KDDU pp. 82–83 Amarsuena 10 (edition)
1991 Steible, NSBW 2 pp. 235–36 Amarsuen 10 (edition)

TEXT

1)	ᵈen-líl	1–3) For the god Enlil, lord of the foreign lands, his beloved lord,
2)	lugal-kur-kur-ra	
3)	lugal-ki-ág-gá-ni-ir	
4)	ᵈamar-ᵈEN.ZU	4–9) Amar-Suena, the one called by name by the god Enlil in Nippur, supporter of the temple of the god Enlil,
5)	ᵈen-líl-le	
6)	nibru.KI-a	
7)	mu pà-da	
8)	sag-ús-	
9)	é-ᵈen-líl-ka	

10 lugal-kala-ga
11) lugal-uri$_5$.KI-ma
12) lugal-an-ub-da-límmu-ba-ke$_4$
13) é làl ì-nun
14) ù geštin
15) ki-sískur-ra-ka-na
16) nu-šilig-ge
17) mu-na-an-dù

10–12) mighty king, king of Ur, king of the four quarters,

13–17) built for him the temple in which date syrup, ghee and wine never cease in his place of offerings.

7

Six inscriptions of Amar-Suena (E3/2.1.3.7–12) record building activities of the king in Ur.

The first of these texts commemorates the building of the temenos wall E-temen-ni-guru.

COMMENTARY

The tablet, which measures 6.7×2.6×1.7 cm, was found in room 13 of the E-nun-maḫ and given the excavation number U 220. It bears the museum number BM 116452 and registration number 1923-11-10, 38. The inscription was collated.

BIBLIOGRAPHY

1965 Sollberger, UET 8 no. 41 (copy)
1986 Kärki, KDDU p. 156 Anonym 17 (edition)
1991 Steible, NSBW 2 pp. 248–49 Amarsuen 19 (edition)

TEXT

Obv.
Lacuna
1′) [mu-pà-d]a
2′) [sag-ú]s-
3′) [é-^{d}en-l]íl-ka
4′) [nita/lugal-k]ala-ga
5′) [lugal-u]ri$_5$.[KI]-ma
6′) [lugal-a]n-ub-[da-l]ímmu-ba-ke$_4$
Rev.
1) [é-temen-n]í-gùru
2) [é-ki]-ág-gá-ni
3) [uri$_5$].[K]I-ma
4) [mu-na]-dù

Lacuna
obv. 1′) [the one call]ed [by name by the god Enlil in Nippur]
obv. 2′–3′) [suppor]ter [of the temple of the god Enl]il,
obv. 4′–6′) [mi]ghty [king], [king of U]r, [king] of the [f]our quar[ters],

rev. 1–4) built [for him] the [E-temen-n]i-guru, his [be]loved [temple] in U[r].

8

Door sockets and steles with a ten-line inscription commemorating Amar-Suena's construction of Ningal's *gipar* were found at various points in the Gipar-ku at Ur.

CATALOGUE A

Ex.	Museum number	Excavation number	Registration number	Ur provenance	Material	Dimensions (cm)	Lines preserved	cpn
Door sockets								
1	BM 116418	U 295	1923-11-10, 3	Surface soil above TTB 25	—	36×25×19	1–10	c
2	—	U 901	—	In N doorbox of "Bursin" gate, temenos wall NE	Basalt	50×30×42	—	n
3	IM 1149	U 1727	—	Brought in from the desert from a spot about ½ mile south of the outermost mounds	Dark limestone	27×16×12	—	n
4	BM 119009	U 3031	1927-10-3, 4	—	Diorite	46×34×21	1–10	c
5	CBS 16565	U 6334	—	Gipar-ku	Diorite(?)		1–10	c
6	CBS 16568	U 6357	—	Gipar-ku	Diorite(?)		1–10	c
7	BM 118456	U 615x	1927-5-27, 2	—	—	Inscr.: 20.7×9.5	1–10	c
8	IM 1140	U 6357	—	Gipar-ku	Diorite	—	—	n
9	IM 1141	U 6357	—	Gipar-ku	Dark limestone	—	—	n
10	IM 1142	U 6357	—	Gipar-ku	Light limestone	—	—	n
11	IM 1143	U 6357	—	Gipar-ku	Light limestone	—	—	n
12	IM 1144	U 6357	—	Gipar-ku	Dark limestone	—	—	n
13	IM 1145	U 6357	—	Gipar-ku	Limestone	—	—	n
14	IM 1008	U 3037	—	Gipar-ku room 6	Diorite	—	—	n
15	IM 1150	U 6357	—	Gipar-ku	Diorite	—	—	n
16	IM 92940	U 10613	—	Ziqqurrat courtyard	Diorite	—	1–10	n
Steles								
17	IM 1387	U 6970	—	Gipar-ku, room B 7	Limestone	130×90×22	—	n
18	IM 1388	U 6971	—	As ex. 18	"Mosul marble" (gypsum)	—	—	n
19	IM 1389	U 6972	—	As ex. 18	"Mosul marble" (gypsum)	—	—	n

CATALOGUE B

Ex.	Museum number	Material	Dimensions (cm)	Lines preserved	cpn
A	IM —	Greyish-white granite(?)	48×54×34	1–10	p
B	IM —	Bluish-grey granite(?)	—	1–10	p
C	IM —	Bluish-grey granite(?)	46×37×17	4–6	p
D	IM —	Bluish-grey granite(?)	54×40×28	5–9	p

COMMENTARY

The following findspots for the door sockets are noted by Woolley and Mallowan in their description of the Gipar-ku in UE 7 pp. 40–63: A 5, by the door to A 6; room A 8, below the floor in the east corner; room A 9, against the NW jamb of the door; room A 20, against the SW jamb of the door from A 16; room A 22, north door; room A 24 against the SE door; room A 33, by the inner face of the door jamb; room A 35, by the inner face of the door jamb; room C 1, door in NW wall, SW jamb; room C 19, against the jamb of the entrance-door; room C 20, against the jamb of the entrance-door; room C 28, against the SE door-jamb.

Ex. 7, previously uncited, was identified in the basement of the British Museum. It is cited here through the courtesy of the trustees of the British Museum. Ex. 14 is known from notes of H. Steible which he kindly communicated to the author. The four IM door sockets of Catalogue B were last seen near the Mosul dig-house.

The text is arranged in one column of ten lines.

BIBLIOGRAPHY

1925 Woolley and Legrain, MJ 16 p. 295 (ex. 4, photo)
1926 Woolley, AJ 6 pp. 371–72 and pl. 46 b (exs. 17–19, provenance, photo)
1928 Gadd, UET 1 no. 67 (exs. 1–6, copy, edition); pl. J (ex. 5, photo)
1929 Barton, RISA pp. 366–67 Bur-Sin 1 (exs. 1–6, edition)
1962 Hallo, HUCA 33 p. 36 Amar-Sin 13 (exs. 1–6, study)
1965 Sollberger, UET 8 no. 31 (ex. 16, copy)
1976 Woolley and Mallowan, UE 7 pp. 50–51, 226, and pl. 6b (exs. 17–19, provenance, photo)
1982 Börker-Klähn, Bildstelen p. 48 (exs. 17–19, study)
1986 Kärki, KDDU pp. 85–86 Amarsuena 13 (exs. 1–6, 16, edition)
1991 Braun-Holzinger, Weihgaben pp. 340–41 Stelen 26–28 (exs. 17–19, study)
1991 Steible, NSBW 2 pp. 242–43 Amarsuen 13 (exs. 1–6, 8–13, 15–16, edition)

TEXT

1) ^{d}nin-gal
2) nin-a-ni-ir
3) ^{d}amar-^{d}EN.ZU
4) nita-kala-ga
5) lugal-uri$_5$.KI-ma
6) lugal-an-ub-da-límmu-ba-ke$_4$
7) gi$_6$-par$_4$-kù é-ki-ág-gá-ni
8) mu-na-dù
9) nam-ti-la-ni-šè
10) a mu-na-ru

1–2) For the goddess Ningal, his lady,

3–6) Amar-Suena, mighty man, king of Ur, king of the four quarters,

7–8) built the Gipar-ku, her beloved temple (some texts read: built her Gipar-ku) for her (and)
9–10) dedicated it for his (own) life.

9

Three door sockets found at Ur deal with Amar-Suena's construction of the Dublalmaḫ.

CATALOGUE

Ex.	Museum number	Excavation number	Registration number	Ur provenance	Object	Dimensions (cm)	Lines preserved	cpn
1	CBS 15885	U 1165	—	Reused in the NB gateway abutting on the SW side of the ziqqurrat close to its south corner	Diorite door socket	31.7×17.2×20	4–45	c
2	IM—	U 3224	—	Room 30 of the E-dublalmaḫ	Diorite(?) door socket	—	1–49	p
3	BM 119006	U 3224	1927-10-3, 1	Room 30 of the E-dublalmaḫ(?)	Door socket	24×28×17	1–49	c

COMMENTARY

Ex. 3 was inadvertently omitted from the edition of H. Steible. A comparison of ex. 3 with the photos published in UET 1 pls. K–L reveals that the BM door socket must be a different piece. The text is arranged in one column that wraps around the stone.

In line 5, the translation of ki-šu-tag is uncertain. We would expect that ki-šu-tag would refer to a place of offerings, but this particular translation is hard to justify by lexical means. In view of the fact that Sumerian šu ... tag corresponds (among various equivalents) to Akkadian

Variants for E3/2.1.3.8:
3.16 ^{d}EN:ZU written with EN sign upside down.
4.16 -ga written over erasure.
7.1,6,A,B gi$_6$-pàr-kù-ga-ni.
7.4,5,7,D gi$_6$-par$_4$-kù é-ki-ág-gá-ni.

lapātu(*m*), and *lapātu*(*m*), which can mean "to apply water" (see CAD L p. 86 § g), we have translated, with all due reserve, "a place of libations." Other interpretations of ki-šu-tag are possible; we may compare, for example, the description of Ur in the inscription of En-ane-du (Frayne, RIME 4 p. 300 E4.2.14.20 line 13: ki-šu-tag-za-⸢na⸣-ru "[the place] where lyres play"). Alternately, we could translate ki-šu-tag as "place of anointing" based on SIG$_7$.ALAN = *nabnītu* VII 212–14 (Finkel and Civil, MSL 16 p. 111): 212 šu-[ùr] = *ma-ša-a-du*; 213 šu-[x] = [*ma-ša-a-du*]; 214 šu-tag-[g]a = [*ma-ša-a-du*], where we would note *muššudu*(*m*) "to rub (with date syrup or ghee)." In line 35 the exact translation of GIŠ.šu-kár is uncertain. It corresponds to *unūtu*(*m*) "tool, implement, utensil, piece of furniture" (see AHw p. 1422 sub *unūtu*[*m*]).

BIBLIOGRAPHY

1925 Woolley and Legrain, MJ 16 p. 297 (ex. 2, photo [partial])
1928 Gadd, UET 1 pls. K-L no. 71 (ex. 2, photo; exs. 1–3, edition)
1929 Barton, RISA pp. 290–92 Bur-Sin 9 (exs. 1–3, edition)
1962 Hallo, HUCA 33 p. 36 Amar-Sin 12 (exs. 1–3, study)
1971 Sollberger and Kupper, IRSA IIIA3c (exs. 1–3, translation)
1986 Kärki, KDDU pp. 84–85 Amarsuena 12 (exs. 1–3, edition)
1991 Steible, NSBW 2 pp. 238–42 Amarsuen 12 (exs. 1–3, edition)

TEXT

1) ^{d}nanna	1–2) For the god Nanna, his beloved lord,
2) lugal-ki-ág-gá-ni-ir	
3) dub-lá-maḫ	3–8) — the Dublalmaḫ, which from ancient times had been a *place of libations*(?), whose daily(?) provisions had fallen (into limbo) (and) whose house had not been (re)built —
4) u$_4$-ul-lí-a-ta	
5) ki-šu-tag	
6) šuku-UD šub-ba	
7) ì-me-a-na-an-na	
8) é-bi nu-dù-àm	
9) ^{d}amar-^{d}EN.ZU	9–18) Amar-Suena, beloved of the god Nanna, the one called by name by the god Enlil in Nippur, supporter of the temple of the god Enlil, mighty man, king of Ur, king of the four quarters,
10) ki-ág-^{d}nanna	
11) nibru.KI-a	
12) ^{d}en-líl-le	
13) mu pà-da	
14) sag-ús-	
15) é-^{d}en-líl-ka	
16) nita-kala-ga	
17) lugal-uri$_5$.KI-ma	
18) lugal-an-ub-da-límmu-ba-ke$_4$	
19) dub-lá-maḫ	19–25) — the Dublalmaḫ, the house "wonder of the land," his place of judgment, his net (from which) no enemies of Amar-Suena escape —
20) é-u$_6$-di-kalam-ma	
21) ki-di-ku$_5$-da-ni	
22) sa-bar-a-ni	
23) lú-NE.RU-	
24) ^{d}amar-^{d}EN.ZU-ka	
25) nu-è	
26) é-bi mu-na-dù	26–27) that house he built and made manifest for him.
27) pa mu-na-an-è	
28) kù-GI kù-babbar NA$_4$.za-gìn-na	28–29) He adorned it for him with gold, silver and lapis-lazuli.
29) mí mu-na ni du$_{11}$	
30) ^{d}amar-^{d}EN.ZU-ke$_4$	30–31) With this Amar-Suena prolongs his life-span.
31) u$_4$ im-da-ab-sù-re$_6$	
32) lú é a-ba-sumun	32–37) As for the one who, after the house has become old, (re)builds it (and) does not alter the place where its inscription and wooden fixture stand,
33) ù-un-dù	
34) mu-sar-ra-bi	
35) ù GIŠ.šu-kár-bi	
36) ki-gub-ba-bé	
37) nu-ub-da-ab-kúr-re-a	
38) igi-^{d}nanna-ka	38–39) may he find favour with the god Nanna.
39) ḫé-en-sa$_6$	

40) lú mu-sar-ra-ba
41) šu bí-íb-ùr-re-a
42) ù GIŠ.šu-kár-bi
43) ki-gub-<ba>-bi-šè
44) nu-ub-ši-íb-gi$_4$-gi$_4$-a
45) muš-^{d}nanna
46) ḫé-en-gar
47) numun-na-ni
48) ^{d}nanna
49) ḫé-eb-til-le

40–44) As for the one who erases its inscription and does not restore its wooden fixture to its (proper) place,

45–49) may the snake of the god Nanna be set (against) him. May the god Nanna bring his progeny to an end.

10

A twenty-four-line inscription found on bricks records Amar-Suena's fashioning of a statue. The bricks may have originally come from the socle which once supported the statue.

CATALOGUE

Ex.	Museum number	Excavation number	Registration number	Ur provenance	Object	Dimensions (cm)	Lines preserved	cpn
1	BM 90036	—	59-10-14, 6	From the south and eastern line of mounds at Mugheir	Stamped brick	30×30.5×6	1–24	c
2	BM 90039	—	59-10-14, 8	As ex. 1	Stamped brick	32×32×7	1–24	c
3	BM 90353	—	59-10-14, 45	As ex. 1	Stamped brick	33×15.5×8	1–24	c
4	BM 90811	—	59-10-14, 7	As ex. 1	Stamped brick	32×31.5×7.5	1–24	c
5	CBS 16466	U 2861	—	E-dublamaḫ, first room, pavement of level of Išme-Dagān	Stamped brick	—	—	n

COMMENTARY

Exs. 1–5 were collated by C.B.F. Walker. Lines 1–13 are found in col. i, lines 14–24 in col. ii.

BIBLIOGRAPHY

1861 1 R 5 XIX (ex. 4, copy)
1872 Smith, TSBA 1 pp. 40–41 (ex. 4, translation)
1875 Ménant, Babylone p. 93 (ex. 4, translation)
1892 Winckler, KB 3/1 pp. 88–89 Bur-Sin 1 (ex. 4, edition)
1899 Bezold, Cat. 5 p. 2234 (exs. 1–4, study)
1905 King, CT 21 pls. 25–26 (ex. 4, copy; ex. 2, variants)
1907 Thureau-Dangin, SAK pp. 198–99 Pûr-sin d (ex. 4, edition)
1922 BM Guide p. 61 nos. 85–86 (exs. 1–2, study)
1928 Gadd, UET 1 p. xxiv (ex. 5, study)
1929 Barton, RISA pp. 286–89 Bur-Sin 3 (ex. 4, edition)
1962 Hallo, HUCA 33 p. 35 Amar-Sin 3 (exs. 1–5, study)
1971 Sollberger and Kupper, IRSA IIIA3e (exs. 1–5, translation)
1981 Walker, CBI no. 24 (exs. 1–4, transliteration, study)
1986 Kärki, KDDU pp. 72–74 Amarsuena 3 (exs. 1–5, edition)
1991 Steible, NSBW 2 pp. 221–25 Amarsuen 3 (exs. 1–5, edition)

TEXT

1) ^{d}amar-^{d}EN.ZU
2) nibru.KI-a
3) ^{d}en-líl-le
4) mu pà-da-
5) sag-ús-
6) é-^{d}en-líl-ka

1–6) Amar-Suena, the one called by name by the god Enlil in Nippur, supporter of the temple of the god Enlil,

7) lugal-kala-ga
8) lugal-uri$_5$.KI-ma
9) lugal-an-ub-da-límmu-ba-me
10) ⌈alan⌉-ba
11) ^{d}amar-^{d}EN.ZU ki-ág-uri$_5$.KI-ma
12) mu-bi-im
13) alan-ba
14) lú ki-gub-ba-bi
15) íb-da-ab-kúr-re-a
16) bára-si-ga-bi
17) ì-bù(KA×ŠU)-re-a
18) ^{d}nanna
19) lugal-uri$_5$.KI-ma-ke$_4$
20) ^{d}nin-gal
21) ama-uri$_5$.KI-ma-ke$_4$
22) nam ḫa-ba-an-da-kuru$_5$-ne
23) numun-na-ni
24) ḫé-eb-til-le-ne

7–9) mighty king, king of Ur, king of the four quarters, am I.

10–12) The name of this statue is: "Amar-Suena is the beloved of Ur."

13–16) As for the one who alters the place where this statue stands (or) who rips out its pedestal,

17–22) may the god Nanna, lord of Ur, (and) the goddess Ningal, mother of Ur, curse him.

23–24) May they bring his offspring to an end.

11

A clay drum-shaped object bears a Neo-Babylonian copy of an inscription of Amar-Suena. Although the text has often been considered to be simply a variant of E3/2.1.3.10, it differs sufficiently from it to warrant a separate edition here.

COMMENTARY

The description of the object given is quoted from G. Frame in RIMB 2 p. 246 B.6.32.2016: "The clay object (BM 119014; 1927-10-3, 9) was found in the 'museum' of En-nigaldi-nanna in the gipāru of the time of Nabonidus and was given the Ur excavation number U 2757. Woolley indicates that the piece was found in room ES 2 of the building in AJ 5 [1925] p. 383 and in 'room 5' (= ES 5?) in UE 9 p. 17; see UE 9 pl. 65 for a plan of the building. The object measures 10.8 cm in height and 6.8 cm in diameter. The colophon (col. iv) is written in contemporary Babylonian script, while the remainder of the inscription is written in an archaizing script. Since the passage on the top of the object is written in an archaizing script, it may well be a copy of an older inscription just like cols. i–iii; ... The inscription of Amar-Suen appears to be based upon Amar-Suen inscription no. 3 (see Steible, NSBW 2 pp. 221–25); however, if so, the individual who copied the inscription for Sîn-balāssu-iqbi, Nabû-šuma-iddin, either made a bad job of copying the text or had a different or damaged version of it in front of him. The copy made by Nabû-šuma-iddin includes several errors [the royal name, for example, is rendered amar-^{d}EN.ZU instead of the expected ^{d}amar-^{d}EN.ZU] and differs markedly from Amar-Suen no. 3."

Lines 1–11 are found in col. i, lines 12– 21 in col. ii, and lines 22–29 in col. iii. Col. iv contains the colophon. The inscription was collated by G. Frame.

BIBLIOGRAPHY

1925 Woolley, AJ 5 pp. 383–84 and pl. XL no. 1 (provenance, photo, translation)
1925 Woolley and Legrain, MJ 16 p. 34 (photo)
1928 Gadd, UET 1 no. 172 (photo, copy, edition [of colophon])
1962 Woolley, UE 9 pp. 14, 17, and 111 and pl. 29 (provenance, photo, study)
1965 Brinkman, Orientalia NS 34 p. 250 (study)
1965 Woolley, UE 8 pp. 4 and 102 (study)
1968 Hunger, Kolophone no. 73 (edition [of colophon])
1971 Sollberger and Kupper, IRSA IIIA3e n. 1 (translation)
1980 Edzard, RLA 6/1–2 pp. 64–65 (translation [of colophon])
1982 Woolley and Moorey, Ur p. 231 (photo)
1991 Steible, NSBW 2 pp. 221–25 Amarsuen 3 Text B (edition)

TEXT

1) amar-⸢^{d}EN.ZU⸣
2) nibru.KI
3) ^{d}en-líl-le
4) mu pà-da
5) sag-ús-
6) é-^{d}en-líl-ka
7) lugal-kala-ga
8) lugal-uri$_{5}$.KI-ma
9) lugal-an-ub-da-límmu-ba

1–9) Amar-Suena, the one called by name by the god Enlil in Nippur, supporter of the temple of the god Enlil, mighty king, king of Ur, king of the four quarters,

10) alan
11) mu-pà-da-^{d}EN.ZU
12) ki-ág-uri$_{5}$.KI-ma
13) mu-na-ni-in-dù

10–13) built the statue (named) "Called by the god Sîn, beloved of Ur,"

14) alan
15) ^{d}nin-gal
16) ni[n-uri$_{5}$.KI-ma-ka]

14–16) (and) a statue of the goddess Ningal, la[dy of Ur].

17) [lú]
18) alan-ne
19) kù(Text: KÙ reversed)-gi(Text: BÙLUG)-gá
20) é-nì-ga-ke$_{4}$
21) in-bù(KA×ŠU)-NI

17–21) [As for the one] who removes *these* statues *of my gold* from a storehouse,

22) ^{d}nanna
23) lugal-
24) uri$_{5}$.KI-ma-ke$_{4}$
25) ^{d}nin-gal
26) nin-uri$_{5}$.KI-ma-ke$_{4}$
27) nam ḫa-da-kuru$_{5}$-ne

22–27) may the god Nanna, lord of Ur, (and) the goddess Ningal, lady of Ur, curse him.

28) numun(Text: MU)-na-ni
29) ḫé-eb-ku$_{4}$-ku$_{4}$-ne

28–29) May they ... his *progeny*.

Colophon
1) GABA.RI ⸢SIG$_{4}$⸣.AL.ÙR.RA
2) *nap-pal-ti* ÚRI.KI
3) *ep-šet amar-*^{d}EN.ZU LUGAL *ú-ri*
4) *ina ši-te-ʾ-ú ú-ṣu-ra-a-ti*
5) *é-giš-nu$_{11}$-gal* ^{md}EN.ZU-TIN-*su*-⸢*iq-bi*⸣
6) GÌR.NÍTA ⸢URI$_{5}$⸣.KI *iš-te-*⸢*ʾ-ú*⸣
7) ^{md}AG-MU-SUM.NA DUMU ^{m}MU-^{d}*pap-sukkal*
8) LÚ.GALA ^{d}EN.(erasure).ZU
9) *a-na ta-mar-*(erasure)-*ti*
10) *i-mur-ma iš-ṭur*

Colophon
1–10) Copy from a baked brick from the debris of Ur, the work of Amar-Suen, king of Ur, (which) Sîn-balāssu-iqbi, viceroy of Ur, had *discovered* while looking for the ground-plan of Ekišnugal. Nabû-šuma-iddin, son of Iddin-Papsukkal, the lamentation-priest of the god Sîn, saw (it) and wrote (it) down for display.

Top
1) [(x)] ^{d}BÁRA ^{d}*en-líl* x
2) [...] ⸢AN⸣ ME
3) [...]-⸢*ú*(?)⸣
4) [...] x

Top
1–4) No translation warranted.

12

A ten-line brick inscription records Amar-Suena's construction of a watchtower.

COMMENTARY

The brick bearing this inscription, which measures 26×26×6.5 cm, was found at Diqdiqqah and given the excavation number U 7704. It bears the museum number BM 120520 and the registration number 1928-10-9, 3. The text, which was stamped on the brick, is arranged in one column on the edge.

BIBLIOGRAPHY

1928 Gadd, UET 1 no. 288 (copy, edition)
1962 Hallo, HUCA 33 p. 35 Amar-Sin 4 (study)
1981 Walker, CBI no. 25 (transliteration)
1986 Kärki, KDDU pp. 74–75 Amarsuena 4 (edition)
1991 Steible, NSBW 2 p. 225 Amarsuen 4 (edition)

TEXT

1) ^{d}amar-^{d}EN.ZU
2) lugal-kala-ga
3) lugal-uri$_5$.KI-ma
4) lugal-an-ub-da-límmu-ba-ke$_4$
5) ki-en-nu-gá-uri$_5$.KI-ma
6) mu-na-dù
7) [ki]-en-nu-gá-ba
8) [^{d}am]ar-^{d}EN.ZU
9) [ki-á]g-^{d}nanna
10) [m]u-bi-im

1–4) Amar-Suena, mighty king, king of Ur, king of the four quarters,

5–6) built the watchtower of Ur.

7–10) The [na]me of this [w]atchtower (is) "[Am]ar-Suena (is) the [bel]oved of the god Nanna."

13

Two royal inscriptions record activities of Amar-Suena in Uruk. The first, a seventeen-line brick inscription, deals with the fashioning of a bronze *argibillu* for the goddess Inanna.

CATALOGUE

Ex.	Museum number	Excavation number	Uruk provenance	Dimensions (cm)	Lines preserved	cpn
1	—	W 433	Area of Eanna, SW enclosure, surface find	16.5×7.8	3–12	p
2	—	W 877	Area of Eanna, surface find	—	Face: 3–9 Side: 2–14	n
3	—	W 1253a	Area of Eanna, surface find	—	Face: 1–8 Side: 1–9	n
4	—	W 1253c (Warka photo 785)	Area of Eanna, surface find	—	Side: 4–16	n
5	—	W 3210	Qc XV 3	23.8×22×6.2	Face: 1–11 Side: 9–17	c
6	VA 14657	W 4268	Area of Eanna	29.5×29.8×5.8	Face: 1–17 Side: 9–17	c
7	VA 14657	W 4557	Qd XV 1, entrance room to Inanna temple	24.6×28.5×7.2	Face: 2–17 Side: 9–17	c
8	VA 14657	W—	—	28×15.2×6.1	Face: 2–14	c
9	EŞ 9650	W—	—	19×14×6.5	Face: 12–17 Side: 1–7	c
10	EŞ 9648	W—	—	17×10×7	—	n

COMMENTARY

As far as can be determined, the text is arranged in one column.

The exact nature of the *argibillu* is unknown (see CAD A/2 sub *argibillu* and Steible, NSBW 2 pp. 244–45 sub Amarsuen 14). In view of the element gibil in the word, we might expect that it was a loan into Akkadian from Sumerian x-gibil "new-x," which was subsequently loaned back into Sumerian. However, no clear Sumerian etymology is apparent. The object (variant spelling ri-gi$_4$-bil-lu) is commonly written with the GIŠ "wood" determinative, but in our text it is apparently made of (or plated with) bronze. The expression GIS.ig-ar-gi-bil-lu "door(s) of an *argibillu*" found in Gadd, UET 3 no. 272 rev. col. v line 10, indicates that an *argibillu* could have doors. *Argibillu* appear as parts of vehicles and ploughs in various Pre-Sargonic texts.

BIBLIOGRAPHY

1928 Jordan, Uruk-Warka p. 49 and pl. 107b and c (ex. 1, photo, copy, edition)
1930 Schott, UVB 1 pp. 25, 50, and pl. 24 d (exs. 1–7, edition, conflated copy)
1962 Hallo, HUCA 33 p. 36 Amar-Sin 14 (exs. 1–7, study)
1971 Sollberger and Kupper, IRSA IIIA3g (exs. 1–7, translation)
1986 Kärki, KDDU pp. 86–87 Amarsuena 14 (exs. 1–7, edition)
1991 Steible, NSBW 2 pp. 244–45 Amarsuen 14 (exs. 1–7, edition)

TEXT

1) ^{d}inanna
2) nin-mè
3) dam-ki-ág-gá-ni-ir
4) ^{d}amar-^{d}EN.ZU
5) ^{d}en-líl-le
6) nibru.KI-a
7) mu-pà-da
8) sag-ús-
9) é-^{d}en-líl-ka
10) lugal-kala-ga
11) lugal-uri$_5$.KI-ma
12) lugal-an-ub-da-límmu-ba-ke$_4$
13) *ar-gi-bil-lu*-zabar-
14) é-gi$_6$-pàr-ra-ka-ni
15) mu-na-an-dím
16) nam-ti-la-ni-šè
17) a mu-na-ru

1–3) For the goddess Inanna, lady of battle, his beloved spouse,

4–12) Amar-Suena, the one called by name by the god Enlil in Nippur, supporter of the temple of the god Enlil, mighty king, king of Ur, king of the four quarters,

13–15) built for her her bronze *argibillu* of the *gipar*.

16–17) He dedicated it to her for his (own) life.

14

A nine-line inscription known from two foundation tablets and a bronze canephor found at Uruk records Amar-Suena's construction of a temple for the goddess Inanna under her surname Ninsiʾana.

CATALOGUE

Ex.	Museum number	Registration number	Object	Dimensions (cm)	Lines preserved	cpn
1	BM 91014 = BM 12156	92-12-13, 10	Stone tablet	7×4.8	1–9	c
2	BM 91017	92-12-13, 8	Bronze canephor	20.6 long 7.2 wide	1–9	c
3	EAH 26	—	Black stone tablet	7.4×4.9	1–9	c

COMMENTARY

In the edition of Steible, the DINGIR sign at the beginning of line 2 was inadvertently omitted. Ex. 2, which is housed at Yale, was kindly collated by G. Beckman. For an inscription of Šulgi dedicated to Ninsiʾana, see E3/2.1.2.7.

BIBLIOGRAPHY

1898 King, CT 3 pl. 1 BM 12156 (ex. 1, copy)
1900 Radau, EBH pp. 273–74 (ex. 3, copy, edition)
1907 Thureau-Dangin, SAK pp. 200–201 Pûr-sin h (exs. 1, 3, edition)
1910 King, Early History pl. 26 facing p. 272 (ex. 2, photo); pl. 29 facing p. 288 (ex. 1, photo)
1921 Bezold, in Festschrift Lehmann-Haupt pp. 115–16 (ex. 2, transliteration)
1929 Barton, RISA pp. 292–93 Bur-Sin 10 (exs. 1, 3, edition)
1931 Van Buren, Found. pl. 12 fig. 22 (ex. 2, photo)
1962 Hallo, HUCA 33 p. 35 Amar-Sin 7 (exs. 1–3, study)
1983 Rashid, Gründungsfiguren p. 35 and pl. 35 no. 171 (ex. 2, study, drawing)
1986 Kärki, KDDU pp. 77–78 Amarsuena 7 (exs. 1–3, edition)
1991 Steible, NSBW 2 p. 231 Amarsuen 7 (exs. 1–3, edition)

TEXT

1) ^{d}inanna
2) ^{d}nin-^{d}si$_{4}$-an-na
3) nin-a-ni-ir

1–3) For the goddess Inanna/ Ninsiʾana, his lady,

4) ^{d}amar-^{d}EN.ZU
5) nita-kala-ga
6) lugal-uri$_{5}$.KI-ma
7) lugal-an-ub-da-límmu-ba-ke$_{4}$

4–7) Amar-Suena, mighty man, king of Ur, king of the four quarters,

8) é-a-ni
9) mu-na-dù

8–9) built her temple for her.

15

A thirteen-line brick inscription records Amar-Suena's construction of Enki's temple in Eridu.

CATALOGUE

Ex.	Museum number	Excavation number	Registration number	Provenance	Dimensions (cm)	Lines preserved	cpn
Bricks							
1	BM 90024	—	1979-12-20, 21	Ur	23.5×13.5×7.5	1–13	c
2	BM 90026	—	1979-12-20, 23	Ur or Eridu	26×26	1–13	c
3	BM 90027	—	1979-12-20, 24	Ur	26.5×26×6.5	1–13	c
4	BM 90035	—	1979-12-20, 30	Ur	26×26.5×6.5	1–13	c

Ex.	Museum number	Excavation number	Registration number	Provenance	Dimensions (cm)	Lines preserved	cpn
5	BM 90038	—	1979-12-23, 31	Ur	26.5×26.5×7	1–13	c
6	BM 90044	—	1979-12-20, 35	Ur	27.5×14.5×7.5	1–13	c
7	BM 90056	—	1979-12-20, 45	Ur	25.5×26.5×7	1–13	c
8	BM 90058+90821	—	1979-12-20, 47	Ur	26.5×26×7.5	1–13	c
9	BM 90061	—	1979-12-20, 49	Ur	25.5×26×6.5	1–9	c
10	BM 90279	—	1979-12-20, 172	Eridu	27×26.5×6.5	1–13	c
11	BM 90717	—	1979-12-20, 322	—	25.5×25×5.5	2–13	c
12	BM 90813	—	1979-12-20, 364	Ur or Eridu	26×25.5×6	1–13	c
13	BM 114216	—	1919-10-11, 4647	Eridu	26×13.5×7.5	1–13	c
14	BM 114217	—	1919-10-11, 4648	Eridu	26×25.5×7	1–13	c
15	BM 114218	—	1919-10-11, 4649	Eridu	27×26×6.5	1–13	c
16	BM 114219	—	1919-10-11, 4650	Eridu	27.5×27×7	1–13	c
17	BM 114220	—	1919-10-11, 4651	Eridu	26.5×16.5×7	7–13 (on face) 1–9 (on edge)	c
18	BM 114221	—	1919-10-11, 4652	Eridu	25.5×25×7	1–13	c
19	BM 114222	—	1919-10-11, 4653	Eridu	26.5×26×6	1–13	c
20	BM 114223	—	1919-10-11, 4654	Eridu	27.5×18×7.5	1–13	c
21	BM 114224	—	1919-10-11, 4655	Eridu	27.5×27×7.5	1–13	c
22	BM 114225	—	1919-10-11, 4656	Eridu	27×26.5×6.5	1–13	c
23	BM 114297	—	1919-10-11, 4741	Eridu	10×9.5×7	11–13	c
24	BM 114343	—	1918-10-12, 678	Eridu	27×13.5×7	1–13	c
25	BM 114344	—	1918-10-12, 679	Eridu	26×26×7	1–13	c
26	BM 137338	—	1919-10-11, 5360	Eridu	9.5×6.5×6.5	1–7	c
27	BM 137339	—	1919-10-11, 5361	Eridu	9×8.5×6.5	9–13	c
28	BM 137387	—	1979-12-18, 22	Ur or Eridu	8.5×5×6.5	1–7	c
29	BM 137420	—	1979-12-18, 55	Ur or Eridu	25.5×18×6.5	1–13	c
30	BM 137421	—	1979-12-18, 56	Ur or Eridu	27×26.5×6.5	1–13	c
31	BM 137422	—	1979-12-18, 57	Ur or Eridu	27×26×6.5	1–13	c
32	—	—	—	Eridu	—	—	n
33	YBC 2376	—	—	—	27×7.5×3.4	6–13	c
34	YBC 16948	—	—	—	27.7×7.4×7.2	1–13	c
35	IM 52380	—	—	Eridu	26.5×26.5×5	1–13	n
36	CBS 15329	—	—	Ur	24.5×24×7	1–13	n
37	CBS 15334	U 111(?)	—	Ur	25×24×7	1–13	n
38	UM 84-26-6	—	—	Ur(?)	25×25×7	1–13	n
39	CBS 16465	U 2891	—	Ur	26×25×7	1–13	n
40	CBS 16538	—	—	Ur	27×27×6.5	1–13	n
41	Baghdad	—	—	—	—	—	—
42	Collection of Prof. K. Galling, Tübingen	—	—	Eridu	—	—	n
43	UCPHMA 9-7953	—	—	—	9.5×9×3	10–13	n
44	LB 1308a	—	—	—	—	—	n
45	Collection E.S. David, New York	—	—	—	—	—	n
46	Robert Hull Fleming Museum of the University of Vermont, A 14948	—	—	—	19.5×5	1–13	n
47	Collection B. Hechich, Rome	—	—	—	—	1–8	n
48	Uruk Survey, 5 exs.	—	—	—	—	—	n
49	MOA 4.29	—	—	Eridu	26.3×26.2×6.7	1–13	c
50	MOA 4.30	—	—	Eridu	26.4×22×7.3	1–11	c
Bitumen fragments with impressions of the stamp							
51	BM 90900 (= 12028)	—	56-9-8, 402	—	18.4×16.5	1–8 (lines 2–3 reversed)	c
52	BM 90901(= 12029)	—	—	—	13.9×13.3	10–13	c
53	BM—	—	56-9-8, 400	Ur or Eridu	—	—	n
54	BM—	—	56-9-8, 401	Ur or Eridu	—	—	n
55	BM—	—	56-9-8, 403	Ur or Eridu	—	—	n

COMMENTARY

Exs. 1–12 and 28–31 come from either Loftus's excavations at Ur or Taylor's excavations at Ur and Eridu. Exs. 13–27 come from Hall's excavations at Eridu. Exs. 32 and 35 come from Eridu. Exs. 51–55 come from Taylor's excavations at Ur or Eridu. The BM exemplars were collated by C.B.F. Walker. The text is arranged in one column.

BIBLIOGRAPHY

1861 1 R 3 XII 1 (exs. 1–12, conflated copy)
1863 Oppert, EM 1 p. 269 (exs. 1–12, translation)
1872 Smith, TSBA 1 p. 40 (exs. 1–12, translation)
1874 Lenormant, Études accadiennes 2 p. 322 (exs. 1–12, translation)
1875 Ménant, Babylone p. 93 (exs. 1–12, translation)
1892 Winckler, KB 3/1 pp. 88–89 Bur-Sin 2 (exs. 1–12, edition)
1899 Bezold, Cat. 5 p. 2234 (exs. 1–12, study)
1905 King, CT 21 pl. 27 (ex. 7, copy)
1907 Thureau-Dangin, SAK pp. 196–99 Pûr-sin c (exs. 1–12, edition)
1910 King, Early History pl. 32 facing p. 310 (ex. 7, photo)
1920 Thompson, Arch. 70 pp. 115–16 (ex. 32, copy, edition)
1922 BM Guide p. 60 nos. 75–84 (exs. 1–9, 13, study)
1928 Gadd, UET 1 p. xxiv (ex. 39, study)
1929 Barton, RISA pp. 288–89 Bur-Sin 4 (exs. 1–12, edition)
1930 Hall, Season's Work p. 218 (exs. 13–27, provenance; exs. 13–14, photo)
1937 Stephens, YOS 9 no. 116 (ex. 33, study)
1947 Safar, Sumer 3 pl. opposite p. 235 (Arabic section) (ex. 35, copy)
1962 Hallo, HUCA 33 p. 35 Amar-Sin 5 (exs. 1–12, 33, 35, study)
1962 Matouš, Bulletin of the College of Arts 5 [Baghdad] pp. 1–4 (ex. 41, study)
1967 Borger, HKL 1 p. 228 to CT 21 pl. 27 (ex. 42, study)
1971 Sollberger and Kupper, IRSA IIIA3h (exs. 1–12, 33, 35, translation)
1972 Nissen in Adams, Countryside p. 217 (ex. 48, study)
1976 Basmachi, Treasures p. 205 no. 8 (ex. 35, study)
1978 Foxvog, RA 72 p. 46 (ex. 43, copy)
1979 Hallo, RA 73 pp. 88–89 no. 2 (exs. 42–45, study)
1981 Safar, et al., Eridu pp. 228–29 no. 3 (ex. 35, copy, edition)
1981 Walker, CBI no. 26 (exs. 1–31, 51–55, study)
1982 Lewis and Jewell, ASJ 4 p. 54 no. 11 (ex. 46, study)
1985 Behrens, JCS 37 p. 233 no. 18 (exs. 36–40, study)
1986 Kärki, KDDU pp. 75–76 Amarsuena 5 (exs. 1–33, 35, 42–45, 48, 51–55, edition)
1987 Sigrist and Vuk, Franciscanum pp. 40–41 (ex. 47, copy, edition)
1990 Peters and Frayne, ARRIM 8 pp. 54–56 nos. 8–9 (exs. 49–50, copy, edition)
1991 Steible, NSBW 2 pp. 226–28 Amarsuen 5 (exs. 1–48, 51–55, edition)

TEXT

1) ᵈamar-ᵈEN.ZU
2) ᵈen-líl-le
3) nibru.KI-a
4) mu-pà-da

1–4) Amar-Suen, the one called by name by the god Enlil in Nippur,

5) sag-ús-
6) é-ᵈen-líl-ka
7) lugal-kala-ga
8) lugal-uri$_5$.KI-ma
9) lugal-an-ub-da-límmu-ba-ka

5–9) supporter of the temple of the god Enlil, mighty king, king of Ur, king of the four quarters,

10) ᵈen-ki
11) lugal-ki-ág-gá-ni-ir

10–11) for the god Enki, his beloved lord,

12) abzu-ki-ág-gá-ni
13) mu-na-dù

12–13) built his beloved Abzu for him.

16

A twenty-eight-line inscription found stamped on bricks and incised on door sockets records Amar-Suena's construction of a *gipar* for the god Nanna of Karzida. Since no priestly name appears in this text, it is unclear whether this inscription should be connected with the installation of the *en* of Nanna that took place in AS 2 or in AS 9.

Variants for E3/2.1.2.15:
2–3.6, 8, 13, 15, 17, 19, 20, 31, 46 nibru.KI.a ᵈen-líl-le.
9.32, 35 lugal-an-ub-da-límmu-ba-ke$_4$.
13.46 mu-na(Text: KI)-dù.

CATALOGUE

Ex.	Museum number	Excavation number	Registration number	Provenance	Dimensions (cm)	Lines preserved	cpn
Bricks							
1	EŞ 8965	—	—	Ur	31×31×7.4	1–28	c
2	EŞ 8964	—	—	Ur	31×31×7.4	15–28	n
3	EŞ 8966	—	—	Ur	26×26×6.5	—	n
4	BM 137386	—	1929-12-18, 21	—	31×13.5×7.5	15–28	c
Door sockets							
5	—	W 17715	—	Uruk, NB temple in Qd/Qe XV 5, reused in northeast foundation box	37×38.5	1–28	p
6	—	W—	—	Uruk, NB temple in Qd/Qe XV 5, reused in southwest foundation box	—	1–28	n
7	NBC 11412	—	—	—	12.5×9.1×3.2 (frgm.)	11–17	c
8	BM 116453	U 874	1923-11-10, 39	Ur, in the area west of the E-nun-maḫ	—	21–24	n

COMMENTARY

A hand copy of EŞ 8965 was kindly provided to the author by V. Donbaz. A comparison of the Donbaz copy and the type-font copy published by Scheil (the latter in RT 20 [1898] pp. 67–68) leaves no doubt that EŞ 8965 is the piece published by Scheil. Scheil's copy is defective in line 9 (-le for -ka) and line 28 (mu-na-dù for a mu-na-[ru]). On EŞ 8965 and the other brick exemplars two stamps are impressed on the sides of the bricks, one containing lines 1–14 and the other lines 15–28. The faces of the bricks were left blank. As Walker (CBI no. 27) notes, only the second stamp (lines 15–28) survives on BM 137386. In the door socket inscriptions, the text, as far as can be determined, is arranged in one column. Ex. 5 appears in Warka photos 5259–63. Further information on ex. 6 is not available. Ex. 7 is edited here through the kind permission of W.W. Hallo. Ex. 8 was described by Sollberger as being a piece of a diorite disc; it is more likely to be a fragment of a door socket.

BIBLIOGRAPHY

1898 Scheil, RT 20 pp. 67–68 (ex. 1, transcription in Neo-Assyrian characters, edition)
1900 Radau, EBH p. 269 n. 11 (ex. 1, partial edition)
1907 Thureau-Dangin, SAK pp. 198–99 Pûr-sin e (ex. 1, edition)
1929 Barton, RISA pp. 288–89 Bur-Sin 5 (ex. 1, edition)
1939 Falkenstein in Nöldecke, et al., UVB 10 pp. 18–19, pls. 23a and 28 (ex. 5, photo, copy, edition)
1956 Falkenstein in Lenzen, UVB 12–13 p. 25 (ex. 6, translation)
1962 Hallo, HUCA 33 p. 35 Amar-Sin 6 (ex. 1, study); Amar-Sin 11 (ex. 5, study)
1965 Sollberger, UET 8 no. 8 (ex. 8, copy, study)
1971 Sollberger and Kupper, IRSA IIIA3d (ex. 1, edition, variants from E3/2.1.3.15 noted)
1981 Walker, CBI no. 27 (exs. 1, 4–5, edition)
1986 Kärki, KDDU pp. 83–84 Amarsuena 11 (exs. 1, 4–6, edition)
1991 Steible, NSBW 2 pp. 229–30 Amarsuen 6 (ex. 1, edition); pp. 236–38 Amarsuen 11 (exs. 4–6, edition); pp. 250–51 Amarsuen 21 (ex. 8, edition)

TEXT

1) ^{d}nanna
2) kar-zi-da
3) lugal-ki-ág-gá-ni-ir
4) ^{d}amar-^{d}EN.ZU
5) nibru.KI-a
6) ^{d}en-líl-le
7) mu pà-da
8) sag-ús-
9) é-^{d}en-líl-ka
10) dingir-zi
11) ^{d}utu-kalam-ma-na
12) lugal-kala-ga

1–3) For the god Nanna of Karzida, his beloved lord,

4–12) Amar-Suena, the one called by name by the god Enlil in Nippur, supporter of the temple of the god Enlil, true god, sun-god of his land, mighty king,

Variants for E3/2.1.3.16:
1. 1 Copy Scheil and Donbaz: ^{d}ŠEŠ.
3. 1 Copy Scheil: ki-ág-ga-ni-ir; copy Donbaz: ki-ág-gá-ni-ir.
5–6. 5 $^{⌈d⌉}$en-líl-le [ni]bru.KI ([EN.L]ÍL.KI)-a
9. 1 Copy Scheil: é-^{d}en-líl-le; copy Donbaz: é-^{d}en-líl-ka.
15. 5 kar-zi-da-a.

13) lugal-uri$_5$.KI-ma 14) lugal-an-ub-da-límmu-ba-ke$_4$	13–14) king of Ur, king of the four quarters,
15) kar-zi-da 16) u$_4$-ul-lí-a-ta 17) gi$_6$-par$_4$-bi nu-dù-àm 18) en nu-un-ti-la-àm	15–18) in Karzida, from ancient times no *gipar* had been built (and) no *en* had dwelt (there).
19) ^{d}amar-^{d}EN.ZU 20) ki-ág-^{d}nanna-ke$_4$ 21) gi$_6$-par$_4$-kù-ga-ni 22) mu-na-dù	19–22) Amar-Suena, beloved of the god Nanna, built his holy *gipar* for him (Nanna).
23) en-ki-ág-gá-ni 24) mu-na-ni-ku$_4$	23–24) He brought in his beloved *en*.
25) ^{d}amar-^{d}EN.ZU-ke$_4$ 26) u$_4$ im-da-ab-sù-re$_6$	25–26) (By this) Amar-Suena prolongs his life-span.
27) nam-ti-la-ni-šè 28) a mu-na-ru	27–28) He dedicated (this structure) to him (Nanna) for his (own) life.

17

A twenty-seven-line inscription found on foundation tablets and a canephor records Amar-Suena's construction of a *gipar* for the god Nanna of Karzida.

CATALOGUE

Ex.	Museum number	Registration number	Object	Dimensions (cm)	Lines preserved	cpn
Foundation tablets						
1	AO 3143	—	Steatite tablet	3.5×15.7×1.3	1–27	c
2	IM 54537	—	Black stone tablet	4.6×6.5×1	1–27	c
3	BM 114684	1920-10-11, 1	Black stone tablet	5.9×9.3×1.9	1–27	c
4	Collection of V. Scheil	—	Schist tablet	5.3×4×0.5	1–27	n
5	—	—	—	23×23×3	1–11	n
6	Mede;hausmuseet Stockholm 1957:4	—	Purchased lapis lazuli tablet	4.5×2.3×1.5	2–27	p
Bronze canephor						
7	AO 3142	—	Bronze canephor	22×7.25	1–27	c

COMMENTARY

All exemplars were acquired through purchase; their original provenance is not known. Although Steible (NSBW 2 p. 229) listed ex. 6 as an example of a different inscription — it was assigned by him as Amarsuen 6 — collation of the canephor reveals that it belongs to this text (Steible's Amarsuen 8) instead. The present whereabouts of exs. 4–5 are unknown; they are entered in the scores from Scheil's copy and transliteration, respectively. Scheil gave a transliteration for only lines 1–11 for ex. 5; it is not clear whether or not more is actually preserved on the tablet. Because of the unusual line breaks, exs. 2, 5 and 6 are almost certainly forgeries. Generally speaking, exs. 1 and 6 agree in their variants as opposed to the other exemplars. Ex. 2 was collated by H. Steible. Exs. 1, 3, and 4, likely genuine tablets, contain lines 1–15 on the obverse, and lines 16–27 on the reverse.

Since En-aga-zi-ana appears by name in this text, the reference is likely to the *en* who, according to Sallaberger (ZA 82 [1992] p. 132), was installed in AS 2.

Variants for E3/2.1.2.16:
20.1 Copy Scheil:^{d}ŠES; copy Donbaz:^{d}⌈ŠEŠ-(x)⌉, where (x) might be a KI sign.
23.1 Copy Scheil: en(Text: TÚG)-ki-ág-ga-ni; copy Donbaz: en-ki-ág-ga-ni.
27.4 nam-ti-la-<ni>-šè.
28.1 Copy Scheil: mu-na-dù; copy Donbaz: a mu-na-[ru].

BIBLIOGRAPHY

1900 Scheil, RT 22 pp. 38–39 (ex. 1, edition)
1902 Heuzey, Catalogue Louvre pp. 313–14 no. 163 (ex. 7, study)
1907 Thureau-Dangin, SAK pp. 200-201 Pûr-sin i (ex. 1, edition)
1908 Johns, Ur-Engur p. 16 and pl. XI a (ex. 7, photo, study)
1912 Scheil, RT 34 p. 111 no. XV (ex. 5, edition)
1921 Gadd, CT 36 pl. 2 (ex. 3, copy)
1926 Thureau-Dangin, RA 23 p. 32 (ex. 1, copy)
1927 Scheil, RA 24 pp. 45–46 (ex. 4, copy)
1929 Barton, RISA pp. 288–89 Bur-Sin 6 (ex. 3, edition); pp. 292–93 Bur-Sin 11 (ex. 1, edition)
1931 Van Buren, Found. pp. 28–29 (ex. 7, study)
1954–56 Sollberger, AfO 17 p. 28 (ex. 1, partial edition)
1959 Edzard, Sumer 15 p. 25 and pl. 4 after p. 28 no. 9 (ex. 2, copy, study)
1962 Hallo, HUCA 33 p. 36 Amar-Sin 8 (exs. 1–2, study)
1971 Sollberger and Kupper, IRSA IIIA3d (exs. 1–3, translation)
1983 Rashid, Gründungsfiguren p. 35 and pl. 35 no. 170 (ex. 7, study, drawing)
1986 Kärki, KDDU pp. 78–81 Amarsuena 8 (exs. 1–5, edition)
1991 Steible, NSBW 2 pp. 231–34 Amarsuen 8 (exs. 1–5, edition); pp. 229–30 (ex. 7, edition [as Amarsuen 6])
1991–92 Pedersen, Medelhausmuseet Bulletin 26–27 pp. 4, 11–13 (ex. 6, photo, copy, edition, study)

TEXT

1) ^{d}nanna- 2) kar-zi-da 3) lugal-a-ni-ir	1–3) For the god Nanna of Karzida, his lord,
4) ^{d}amar-^{d}EN.ZU 5) nibru.KI-a 6) ^{d}en-líl-le 7) mu pà-da 8) sag-ús- 9) é-^{d}en-líl-ka 10) dingir-zi-kalam-ma-na 11) lugal-uri$_{5}$.KI-ma 12) lugal-an-ub-da-límmu-ba-ke$_{4}$	4–12) Amar-Suena, the one called by name by the god Enlil in Nippur, supporter of the temple of the god Enlil, true god of his land, king of Ur, king of the four quarters,
13) u$_{4}$-ul-lí-a-ta 14) kar-zi-da 15) gi$_{6}$-par$_{4}$ nu-dù 16) en nu-un-tìl-a	13–16) from ancient times, in Karzida no *gipar* had been built and no *en* had dwelt (there).
17) ^{d}amar-^{d}EN.ZU 18) dumu-ki-ág-^{d}nanna-ke$_{4}$ 19) ^{d}nanna 20) ki-ág-gá-ni-ir 21) kar-zi-da-a 22) gi$_{6}$-par$_{4}$ mu-na-dù	17–22) Amar-Suena, beloved son of the god Nanna, for the god Nanna, his beloved, built the *gipar* in Karzida
23) en-àga-zi-an-na 24) en-ki-ág-gá-ni 25) mu-un-na-ni-in-ku$_{4}$	23–25) and brought in En-aga-zi-ana, his beloved *en*.
26) ^{d}amar-^{d}EN.ZU-ke$_{4}$ 27) nam-ti íb-sù-re$_{6}$	26–27) (By this) Amar-Suena prolongs his life-span.

Variants for E3/2.1.3.17:
2.2 kar-zi!-da(Text: GUR).
9.5 <é>-^{d}en-líl-ka.
10.3 dingir-zi-kalam-ma-<na>.
12.2 lugal(Text: LÚ)-⸢an⸣-ub-da-límmu-ba(Text: UD)-ke$_{4}$.
14.1 kar-zi-da-⸢a⸣; **14**.6 ⸢kar-zi-da-a⸣.
15.1 nu-dù-[àm]; **15**.6 nu-[dù-àm].
16.1 nu-un-ti-à[m]; **16**.6 nu-un-ti-àm
18.2 dumu-ki-ág-^{d}EN.ZU.
25.2–4 mu-un-na-ni-<in-ku$_{4}$>.
27.2 nam(Text: ŠE)-ti bi-sù-u$_{5}$ **27**.6 ⸢nam-ti⸣ [íb]-⸢sù-ù⸣(?)

Votive and Seal Inscriptions
(a) Of the King

18

A fragment of a steatite bowl bears a votive inscription of Amar-Suena.

COMMENTARY

The fragment of the rim of a bowl, which measures 4.8×4.5 cm, was found loose in the E-ḫursag area, and given the excavation number U 6967. It bears the museum number CBS 16209. The text, as far as preserved, is arranged in one column. The inscription was collated.

BIBLIOGRAPHY

1928 Gadd, UET 1 no. 29 (copy, edition)
1962 Hallo, HUCA 33 p. 41 Anonymous 2 (study)
1986 Kärki, KDDU pp. 150–51 Anonym 2 (edition)
1991 Braun-Holzinger, Weihgaben pp. 188–89 G 362 (edition)
1991 Steible, NSBW 2 pp. 249–50 Amarsuen 20 (edition)

TEXT

Lacuna
1′) [sag-ús]-
2′) ⌜é⌝-^{d}e[n-líl-ka]
3′) lugal-kala-g[a]
4′) lugal-ur[i$_{5}$].KI-[ma]
5′) ⌜lugal⌝-[an-ub-da-límmu-ba-ke$_{4}$]
Lacuna

Lacuna
1′–5′) [supporter] of the temple of the god E[nlil], might[y] king, king of U[r], king [of the four quarters]
Lacuna

Votive and Seal Inscriptions
(b) Of the Royal Family
19–22

The names of Amar-Suena's wife, various *lukur*s "spouses," and several of his children are attested from archival texts and dedicatory inscriptions of the Ur III period. In particular, a tablet in the Metropolitan Museum in New York (MMA 11.217.29; see Sigrist in Spar, Met. Mus. 1 no. 17) gives the names of twelve princesses, some of whom were likely daughters of Amar-Suena.

The following summary, which is based on D. Owen's MS. "The Royal Family of Ur [Preliminary List of Sources]" (see p. 166 above), gives the RIM numbers of inscriptions that mention members of Amar-Suena's family.

Amar-Suena — Royal Family

Item	Royal Name	RIM number	Attestations (A) and Bibliography (B)
Wife			
1	*a-bí-sí-im-ti*	—	(B) Steinkeller, ASJ 3 (1981) pp. 79–80 and Sallaberger, Kalender 1 p. 61 n. 259; the latter author cites the following bibliography: Å Sjöberg, OrSuec 21 (1972) p. 109; E. Sollberger, JCS 30 (1978) pp. 99 ff.; Th. Jacobsen, JCS 7 (1953) pp. 45–47; R.M. Whiting, JCS 28 (1976) p. 182; C.B.F. Walker, JCS 35 (1983) pp. 92–96; B.R. Foster, SEL 2 (1985) pp. 37–41.
Lukurs			
2	puzur$_4$-ú-ša	—	(A) Nikol'skiy, DV 5 no. 484 line 2 (24 ix AS 5)
3	*ú-da-ad-zé-na-at*	—	(A) Keiser, BIN 3 no. 134 line 2 (1 iv AS 7); (B) Steinkeller, ASJ 3 (1981) p. 84 n. 44 no. 6
4	za-ga-AN-bi(?)	—	(A) Gordon, Smith College no. 24 line 1 (22 i AS 8); (B) Steinkeller, ASJ 3 (1981) p. 84 n. 44 no. 7; Michalowski, ASJ 4 (1982) pp. 137 and 141 no. 6
5	[x]-*na-tum*	—	(A) Sollberger, MVN 5 no. 113 rev. 1 (5 vii AS 5); (B) Steinkeller, ASJ 3 (1981) p. 84 n. 44 no. 8
Daughters			
6	en-maḫ-gal-an-na, *en* of the god Nanna	**E3/2.1.3.19**	—
7	géme-é-an-na, daughter-in-law of Irmu, the grand-vizier	—	(A) Spar, Met. Mus. 1 no. 17 line 32 (1 vii AS 4); Sigrist, MVN 13 no. 635 line 11 (5 iv AS 6); (B) Michalowski, in Gibson and Biggs, Bureaucracy p. 58 n. 15
8	géme-^{d}nanna	—	(A) Spar, Met. Mus. 1 no. 17 line 16 (1 vii AS 4); NBC 782, see McNeil, Messenger Texts p. 135 no. 2 line 9
9	nin-ḫé-du$_7$, wife of Ḫašib-atal, the general	**E3/2.1.3.20**	(A) Spar, Met. Mus. 1 no. 17 line 28 (1 vii AS 4); (B) Michalowski, in Gibson and Biggs, Bureaucracy p. 59 n. 16
10	^{d}nin-líl-le-ma-an(var.: na!)-ág	—	(A) Sigrist, AUCT 2 no. 367 line 2 (- i AS 6); Schneider, Drehem- und Djoḫatexte no. 99 = Molina, Montserrat no. 99 line 3 (6 v AS 4)
11	^{d}NIN.LÍL-*tu-kúl-ti*	—	Spar, Met. Mus. 1 no. 17 line 12 (1 vii AS 4)
12	pa$_4$-ki-na-na	—	(A) Spar, Met. Mus. 1 no. 17 line 20 (1 vii AS 4)
13	*simat* (ME)-^{d}*ištarān* (KA.DI)	—	(A) Salonen, Puzriš-Dagan-Texte no. 171 line 4 (30 ii AS 2); Kang, SETDA no. 154 line 11 (3 xi AS 4); Scheil, RA 17 (1920) p. 209 HE 217 line 3 (- iii AS 6); Jean, ŠA clv line 2 (- - AS 7); Legrain, TRU no. 303 line 5 (- viii AS 9); Schneider, Orientalia 47–49 (1930) no. 37 line 4 (- v ŠS 4); (B) Michalowski, SMS 2/3 p. 11; Sallaberger, Kalender 1 pp. 59–60
14	*ša-at-^{d}ma-mi* (married to the sukkal-maḫ, son: Šū-Adad)	—	(A) Fish, MCS 3 (1953) p. 25 HSM 7869 = Owen, MVN 11 no. 192 line 4 (- viii AS 2) (marriage to sukkal-maḫ); Jean, ŠA vii lines 4–5 (5 vi AS 5); Spar, Met. Mus. 1 no. 17 line 24 (1 vii AS 4)
15	*še-lu-pu-tum*	—	(B) Klein, ZA 80 (1990) pp. 20–39
16	*tá-din-eš$_4$-tár*	**E3/2.1.3.21**	(A) Spar, Met. Mus. 1 no. 17 line 8 (1 vii AS 4); (B) Michalowski, JCS 31 (1979) p. 172 and ASJ 4 (1982) p. 135; Sigrist, RA 80 (1986) p. 185; Steible, NSBW 2 p. 252
17	*te-ṣi-in-ma-ma!* (Text: IB)	—	(A) Spar, Met. Mus. 1 no. 17 line 35 (1 vii AS 4)

Item	Royal Name	RIM number	Bibliography (B) and Attestations (A)
Princesses who were wives of high officials			
18	Wife of Lugal-magure	—	(A) Spar, Met. Mus. 1 no. 17 line 38 (1 vii AS 4)
19	Wife of Lu-Nanna, son of Ur-nigin-gar	—	(A) Spar, Met. Mus. 1 no. 17 line 47 (1 vii AS 4)
20	Wife of Šarrum-bāni	—	(A) Spar, Met. Mus. 1 no. 17 line 44 (1 vii AS 4)
Sons			
21	*a-ḫu-ni*	—	(A) Sigrist, AUCT 2 no. 40 line 2 (24 vii AS 1); Boson, TCS no. 336 lines 3–4 (10 iv AS 2); Keiser, BIN 3 no. 224 line 2 (10 ix ŠS 2); Sigrist, AUCT 3 no. 454 line 3 (1 x ŠS 3); Sigrist, AUCT 3 no. 213 line 2 (4 vii ŠS 4); Fish, Catalogue no. 434 line 6 (24 viii ŠS 5)
22	*a-mi-ir-*^{d}*šul-gi*	—	(A) Schneider, Orientalia 47–49 (1930) no. 23 line 2 (26 i AS 3); Sigrist, AUCT 1 no. 418 line 2 (animals for wedding of Amir-Šulgi at the estate of Dada) (25 viii AS 2)
23	ba-a-mu	—	(A) NBC 779, see McNeil, Messenger Texts p. 135 no. 1
24	da-da	—	(A) Forde, Dakota no. 58 col. vi line 23 (- xii AS 5); Sigrist, AUCT 3 no. 484 line 8 (- v AS 8); Sigrist, JCS 31 (1979) p. 166 line 8 (8 v AS 8)
25	*i-bí-*^{d}*ištarān* (KA.DI)	—	(A) Watson, Birmingham 1 no. 78 line 7 (16 xi AS 3)
26	inim-^{d}nanna	—	(A) de Genouillac, TCL 2 no. 5563 rev. line 1 (30 i AS 1) (for wedding of inim-^{d}nanna); Fish, Catalogue no. 218 line 5 (20 ii AS 1); Keiser, BIN 3 no. 68 line 5 (30 x AS 3); Legrain, TRU no. 330 line 5 (- xii AS 3); Fish, Catalogue no. 323 line 4 (30 vi AS 5); Sigrist, AUCT 3 no. 363 line 3 (- viii AS 7); Sollberger, MVN 5 no. 122 line 3 (22 ix ŠS 1)
27	ir_{11}-^{d}nanna	**See under Šū-Sîn E3/2.1.4.13**	(A) Schneider, Strassburg no. 111 lines 4–5 and 10–11 (2 iv AS 7)
28	lú-^{d}šul-gi	—	(A) Chiera, STA no. 8 col. v lines 4–5 (ii x AS 5)
29	ma-an-sum	—	(A) Barton, Haverford 1 pl. 36 no. 75 line 6 (- - AS 1)
30	*na-bí-*^{d}*šul-gi*	—	(A) Chiera, STA no. 8 col. v line 15 (ii x AS 5)
31	^{d}nanna-ma-an-ba	—	(A) Freedman, JANES 9 (1977) p. 21 no. 3 line 4 (17 ii AS 5)
32	^{d}*šu*-^{d}EN.ZU, the future king	—	(A) not all attestations given may refer to the prince: de Genouillac, TCL 2 no. 5563 line 3 (30 i AS 1) (no title); Langdon, TAD no. 68 line 8 (22 i AS 2) (named as judge); Owen, JCS 24 (1971) p. 152 no. 15 line 4 (- iii AS 2) (named as prince); Salonen, Puzriš-Dagan-Texte no. 171 rev. line 3 (named as prince); Legrain, TRU no. 294 line 7 (27 iii Š 46 or AS 3) (named as cup-bearer); Salonen, Puzriš-Dagan-Texte no. 355 line 1 (20 x AS 4) (no title); Nikol'skiy, DV 5 no. 476 line 31 (29 ix AS 5) (n o title); Sigrist, MVN 13 no. 812 line 10 (29 ix AS 5) (no title); de Genouillac, TCL 2 no. 5504 col. i line 11 (9 x AS 5) (no title); Nikol'skiy, DV 5 no. 459 line 13 (9 xi AS 5) (no title); de Genouillac, Trouvaille no. 13 line 6 (27 x AS 6 or Š 44) (no title); King, CT 32 pl. 26 col. iv line 2 (30 v AS 7) (no title); Pohl, TMH NF 1/2 no. 225 line 3 (1 viii AS 9) (no title)
33	*šu*-^{d}šul-gi	—	(A) Sollberger, MVN 5 no. 116 line 9 (9 iii AS 7)
34	^{d}šul-gi-*r*[*a*]*-ma*	—	(A) de Genouillac, Trouvaille no. 88 = Limet, Textes sumériens no. 35 line 4 (- iv AS 7)
35	ur-^{d}ba-ba_{6}	**E3/2.1.3.22**	(A) de Genouillac, ITT 2 no. 954 = Lafont and Yıldız, TCT 1 no. 954 (seal lines 5–6) (- - -); Owen, MVN 3 no. 232 line 3 (animals for wedding of Ur-Baba) (- x AS 6)
36	ur-^{d}ištarān(KA.DI)	—	(A) Lafont, Documents no. 53 col. iv lines 2 and 10 (- - AS 8); Kang, SETDA no. 153 line 3 (- vii AS 4); Legrain, TRU no. 370 lines 13–14 (- - -)
37	ur-^{d}nin-súna	—	(A) Fish, MCS 5 (1955) p. 32 AOTc 317 line 3 (- vii AS 7); Sauren, WMAH no. 237 = Sauren, MVN 2 no. 237 lines 17–19 (20 xii -)
38	ur-sa_{6}-ga	—	(A) Barton, Haverford 2 pl. 67 no. 32 col. ii line 6 (- - AS 1)

19

A black stone bowl is inscribed with the name of En-maḫ-gal-ana, *en* of the god Nanna (see Amar-Suena — Royal Family item 6 above).

COMMENTARY

The dark stone bowl was found in room A 31 of the Giparku and given the excavation number U 6726. It bears the museum number BM 118555, and the registration number 1927-5-27, 28. The text is arranged in one column. The inscription was collated.

As noted in the introductory comments for Amar-Suena, En-maḫ-gal-ana, in all likelihood, was the daughter of Amar-Suena.

BIBLIOGRAPHY

1928 Gadd, UET 1 no. 64 (copy, edition)
1954–56 Sollberger, AfO 17 p. 24 n. 69 (study)
1962 Hallo, HUCA 33 p. 42 Family 4 (study)
1976 Woolley and Mallowan, UE 7 pp. 50 and 225 (provenance)
1986 Kärki, KDDU p. 65 (Familie 4 =) Šulgi 63 (edition)
1991 Braun-Holzinger, Weihgaben p. 191 G 373 (edition)
1991 Steible, NSBW 2 p. 300 Ur 6 (edition)

TEXT

1) en-maḫ-gal-an-na
2) en-^{d}nanna

1–2) En-maḫ-gal-ana, *en* of the god Nanna.

20

A tablet in the Iraq Museum bears the impression of a seal of a servant of the princess Nin-ḫedu. According to the Metropolitan tablet published by Sigrist, she may have been a daughter of Amar-Suena (see Amar-Suena — Royal Family item 9 above).

COMMENTARY

The inscription is found on IM 13358, an unpublished tablet. A transliteration of the text was kindly provided by D. Owen.

According to the tablet Legrain, TRU no. 110 line 7, Nin-ḫedu, likely this same princess, was the "daughter-in-law" (é-gi$_4$-a) of Ḫašib-atal. Ḫašib-atal is named as the general connected with Arrapḫa in Salonen, Puzriš-Dagan-Texte no. 166. Alternately, a Ḫašib-atal is named as "man" (= "ruler?") of Marḫaši in Keiser, BIN 3 no. 12 lines 3–4.

TEXT

1)	nin-ḫé-du$_{7}$	1–2) Nin-ḫedu, daughter of the king:
2)	dumu-munus-lugal	
3)	ur-gu kurušda	3–4) Urgu, the cattle-fattener, (is) your servant.
4)	ir$_{11}$-zu	

21

This inscription, found on a fragment of a limestone vessel from Ur, indicates that the piece was presented by Amar-Suena to his daughter Taddin-Eštar (see Amar-Suena — Royal Family item 16 above).

COMMENTARY

The cylindrical limestone vessel, which measures 8 cm in height and 5 cm in width, was found in the E-nun-maḫ room 11 and given the excavation number U 908, museum number BM 116437, and registration number 1923-11-10, 23. The text, as far as preserved, seems to be arranged in one column; no traces of the supposed col. i noted by Sollberger in his copy of UET 8 no. 42 could be found when the inscription was collated.

BIBLIOGRAPHY

1965 Sollberger, UET 8 no. 42 (copy)
1974 Woolley, UE 6 pp. 51 and 93 (study)
1986 Kärki, KDDU pp. 156–57 Anonym 18 (edition)
1991 Braun-Holzinger, Weihgaben p. 189 G 363 (edition)
1991 Steible, NSBW 2 pp. 251–52 Amarsuen 22 (edition)

TEXT

1′)	[...] ⸢x⸣	1′–4′) ... [Amar]-Suena, [ki]ng of U[r], [ki]ng of the four quarters, ...
2′)	[amar]-⸢^{d}EN.ZU⸣	
3′)	[lu]gal-u[ri$_{5}$].⸢KI⸣-ma	
4′)	[lug]al-⸢an-ub⸣-[da]-límmu-ba-ke$_{4}$	
5′)	[...]	5′–7′) Too broken for translation.
6′)	[x] EN.DÍM.KI	
7′)	⸢ki x⸣ GIŠ(?) x [x]	
8′)	⸢*tá-dì-in*-^{d}INANNA⸣	8′–10′) granted (this vase) to Taddin-Eštar, his beloved [d]aughter.
9′)	[d]umu-ki-ág-gá-ni-ir	
10′)	in-na-ba	

22

Ur-Baba, a son of Amar-Suena, is named in a seal impression on an undated clay bulla fragment from Girsu (see Amar-Suena — Royal Family item 35 above).

COMMENTARY

The impression is found on L 954, which is conserved in Istanbul.

BIBLIOGRAPHY

1897 Scheil, RT 19 p. 49 (copy [in typescript], translation)
1900 Radau, EBH p. 274 (edition)
1907 Thureau-Dangin, SAK pp. 200–201 Pûr-sin 1 (edition)
1910 de Genouillac, ITT 2/1 no. 954 (translation); pl. I no. 954 (photo)
1929 Barton, RISA pp. 292–93 Bur-Sin 13 (edition)
1962 Hallo, HUCA 33 p. 43 Family 6 (study)
1971 Sollberger and Kupper, IRSA IIIA3j (translation)
1986 Kärki, KDDU p. 90 (Familie 6 =) Amarsuena 19 (edition)
1989 Lafont and Yıldız, TCT no. 954 (transliteration)

TEXT

1) [^{d}a]mar-^{d}EN.ZU
2) [ni]ta-kala-ga
3) [lu]gal-uri$_{5}$.KI-ma
4) lugal an-[ub]-da-límmu-[ba]
5) ur-^{d}⸢ba-ba$_{6}$⸣
6) dumu-ni

1–4) [A]mar-Suena, mighty [m]an, [k]ing of Ur, king of the four quar[ters]:

5–6) Ur-Baba (is) his son.

Votive and Seal Inscriptions (c) Of City Governors 2001–2007

The names of various city governors who served under Amar-Suena are known from Ur III archival texts and seal inscriptions. The data summarized in the following chart derives from the researches of Keiser, Patesis; Hallo, Ensi's and Ensi's^{2}; Goetze, JCS 17 (1963) pp. 1–32; Edzard, Rép. Géogr. 2; Owen, JCS 33 (1981) pp. 244–70; ibid., JAOS 108 (1988) pp. 111–22; ibid., BiOr 49 (1992) cols. 441–48; T. Maeda, ASJ 14 (1992) pp. 162–63; and ibid., ASJ 16 (1994) pp. 157–62.

The names appearing in inscriptions edited in this volume are indicated with an asterisk (*). Names found in seal inscriptions are indicated with (s); those mentioned in tablets are marked with (t).

We have not listed the innumerable impressions of the seals of the Umma governors Ur-Lisi and Aa-kala.

Year	Adab	Apiak	Aššur	Babylon	Ereš
1	**ḫa-ba-lu$_5$-ge** Fish, Catalogue no. 227 line 5 (t) (28 iv); Salonen, Puzriš-Dagan-Texte no. 438 line 3 (t) (- v)	—	***za-ri-qum**** (general) **(E3/2.1.3.2001)**	—	—
2	**ḫa-ba-lu$_5$-ge** Legrain, UET 3 no. 18 rev. lines 8–9 (t) (- -); Keiser, YOS 4 no. 64 lines 7–8 (t) (- iii)	—	—	***ar-ši-aḫ*** de Genouillac, Trouvaille no. 31 line 3 (t) (- i); Schneider, Orientalia 47–49 (1930) no. 62 lines 3–4 (t) (- i)	—
3	**ḫa-ba-lu$_5$-ge** Dhorme, RA 9 (1912) p. 48 SA no. 102 (t) (- ix); see Hallo, Ensi's^2 p. 3 no. 28	—	—	—	—
4	—	***šu-ti-ru-um*** Schneider, Orientalia 47–49 (1930) no. 80 line 10 (t) (- ix)	—	***ar-ši-aḫ*** Boissier, Babyloniaca 8 (1924) pl. IV Pupil no. 7 line 3 (t) (- i); Salonen, Puzriš-Dagan-Texte no. 557 rev. col. iii line 14 (t) (i-xii)	—
5	**ḫa-ba-lu$_5$-ge** Schneider, Orientalia 47–49 (1930) no. 27 lines 33–34 (t) (- ii); Fish, Catalogue no. 301 rev. line 3 (t) (- ii); A 5005 (Chicago), see Hallo Ensi's p. 6. ibid., Ensi's^2 p. 4 no. 33 (t) (- ix); A 4486 (Chicago), see Hallo Ensi's p. 6; ibid., Ensi's^2 p. 4 no. 34 (t) (- x)	***šar-ru-um-ba-ni*** Nies, UDT no. 127 lines 8–9 (t) (- iii); A 5911 (Chicago), see Hallo, Ensi's p. 4; ibid., Ensi's^2 p. 1 no. 7b (t) (- iii)	—	***ar-ši-aḫ*** de Genouillac, TCL 2 no. 5504 rev. i line 16 (Babylon not mentioned) (t) (9 x); Fish, Catalogue no. 335 line 5 (t) (13 xi)	—
6	**ḫa-ba-lu$_5$-ge** Keiser, YOS 4 no. 62 line 2 (t) (- i)	—	—	***ar-ši-aḫ*** A 5329 (Chicago) rev. line 1 (t) (- xi); A 4653 (Chicago) obv. line 5 (- xi). For both, see Hallo JCS 14 (1960) p. 109 nos. 7 and 8	—
7	—	***šar-ru-um-ba-ni*** YBC 13087, see Goetze, JCS 17 (1963) p. 15 no. 10 (AS 7 or 8) (t)	—	***ar-ši-aḫ*** Keiser, YOS 4 no. 65 lines 6–7 (t) (9 xi); Salonen, Puzriš-Dagan-Texte no. 424 line 8 (t) (xi); ibid., no. 477 line 5 (t) (- xi); YBC 13087, see Goetze, JCS 17 (1963) p. 26 no. 62 (t) (AS 7 or 8)	**ur-^{d}ba-ba$_6$** YBC 13087, see Owen, JAOS 108 (1988) p. 116 and n. 8 (t) (AS 7 or 8)
8	—	***šar-ru-um-ba-ni*** Nies, UDT 1 no. 128 lines 5–6 (t) (29 i)	—	***ši$_x$*(SIG$_4$) *-te-li*** de Genouillac, TCL 2 no. 5491 line 4 (t) (- iii)	—
9	—	—	—	***ši$_x$*(SIG$_4$) *-te-li*** Jones and Snyder, SET no. 11 line 3 (t) (13 xi)	—

Year	Ešnunna	Girsu/Lagaš	Kazallu	Kiš	Kutha
1	**kal-la-mu** HTS no. 132, see Hallo, Ensi's^{2} p. 16 no. 6 (t) (- vii)	**ur-^{d}lamma** Speleers, Receuil no. 109 (t) (- viii); Reisner, Telloh no. 60 rev. 6–7 (- ix–x)	***ib-ni*-DINGIR** Keiser, Patesis p. 16 YBC 9825 (t) (- ix)	—	**nam-zi-tar-ra** Sigrist, AUCT 2 no. 270 lines 5–6 (t) (- vi); de Genouillac, Trouvaille no. 72 line 5 = Limet, Textes sumériens no. 63 line 5 (t) (- viii); HTS no. 125 , see Hallo, Ensi's^{2} p. 25 no. 19 (t) (- vi)
2	**kal-la-mu** de Genouillac, TCL 2 no. 5533 rev. line 6 (t) (Ešnunna not mentioned) (- ix)	**ur-^{d}lamma** Keiser, BIN 3 no. 373 (t) (- iv); YBC 12560, see Hallo, JCS 14 (1960) p. 108 no. 3 rev. 4′ (t) (30 v); Langdon, TAD no. 19 lines 10–11 (t) (- viii); Hackman, BIN 5 no. 128 lines 11–12 (t)	***šu-ma-ma*** Sigrist, AUCT 2 no. 315 line 17 (t) (- viii)	—	**gù-dé-a** YBC 1774, see Hallo, Ensi's^{2} p. 25 no. 21 (t) (11 viii); de Genouillac, TCL 2 no. 5533 rev. i (t) (1 ix)
3	—	**ur-^{d}lamma** de Genouillac, Trouvaille no. 29 line 4 (t)(- iii); A 431 rev. 1 (Chicago), see Hallo, JCS 14 (1960) p. 107 no. 4 rev. 1 (t) (- iii); NBC 506, see Hallo, JCS 14 (1960) p. 107 no. 5 lines 5–6 (t) (- vii); HTS 133, see Hallo Ensi's^{2} p. 20 no. 44 (t) (- vii) **^{d}nanna-zi-šà-gál** Salonen, Puzriš-Dagan-Texte no. 537 line 10 (t) (30 vi)	***šu-ma-ma*** Sigrist, MVN 13 no. 443 line 3 (30 xi)	**ugula (PA)** de Genouillac, TCL 2 no. 5617 lines 4–5 (t) (- xi)	**gù-dé-a** de Genouillac, Trouvaille no. 25 obv. col. ii line 2 (t) (- -); Sigrist, Rochester no. 38 line 4 (t) (- -); de Genouillac, TCL 2 no. 4686 rev. line 3 (t) (21 vi) = de Genouillac, RA 7 (1909) p. 189 rev. line 3 (t) (21 vi); A 5596 (Chicago), see Hallo, JCS 14 (1960) p. 108 no. 6 lines 5–6 (t) (- ix); Yıldız and Gomi, PDT 2 no. 1197 line 11 (t) (- vi)

Year	Ešnunna	Girsu/Lagaš	Kazallu	Kiš	Kutha
4	**kal-la-mu** Keiser, YOS 4 no. 61 lines 5–6 (t) (- vi)	**^{d}nanna-zi-šà-gál** Sigrist, PTS no. 88 line 5 (t) (29 i); Sigrist, AUCT 1 no. 209 line 11 (20 i); Salonen, Puzriš-Dagan-Texte no. 211 line 7 (t) (30 ii); de Genouillac, Trouvaille no. 79 rev. i (t) (- ii); Schneider, Strassburg no. 12 rev. lines 2–3 (t) (- viii); Owen and Young, JCS 23 (1971) p. 113 no. 22 rev. line 1 (t) (- x); Dhorme, RA 9 (1912) p. 59 SA no. 125 line 4 (t) (- x); de Genouillac, TCL 2 no. 4687 rev. line 2 (t) (- ix); Salonen, Puzriš-Dagan-Texte no. 557 rev. col. iii line 4 (t) (- i–xii) **^{d}šára-kam** Salonen, Puzriš-Dagan-Texte no. 557 rev. col. iii line 7 (t) (- i–xii) **ir$_{11}$-mu** de Genouillac, TCL 2 no. 5504 obv. col. i line 1 (t) (9 x); Owen, Mesopotamia 8–9 (1973–74) p. 152 no. 8 rev. 1 (t) (- x)	—	**ú-gu-la** de Genouillac, TCL 2 no. 5490 line 7 (t) (- viii); Dhorme, RA 9 (1912) p. 60 SA 129 line 14 (t) (29 xi)	**gù-dé-a** HTS 126, see Hallo, Ensi's[2] p. 25 no. 26 (t) (- viii); Sigrist, AUCT 2 no. 273 rev. i (t) (- viii); NBC 181, see Hallo, Ensi's[2] p. 25 no. 27 (t) (- xii)
5	**kal-la-mu** de Genouillac, TCL 2 no. 5504 rev. i line 18 (t) (- x)	—	***šu-ma-ma*** Kang, SETDA no. 70 line 7 (- iv); de Genouillac, TCL 2 no. 5504 rev. i line 23 (t) (9 x) ***á-pi$_5$-la-ša*** de Genouillac, TCL 2 no. 5504 obv. i line 12 (t) (9 x)	—	**gù-dé-a** Mississippi 1, see Goetze, JCS 17 (1963) p. 21 no. 36 (t); Fish, Catalogue no. 313 rev. 2 (Kutha not mentioned) (t) (27 iv); Snell and Lager, YOS 18 no. 10 line 6 (t) (27 v); Keiser, BIN 3 no. 340 lines 6–7 (t) (- vi, - xii) Schneider, Orientalia 18 (1925) pl. VI no. 20 line 10 (t) (12 viii)

Year	Ešnunna	Girsu/Lagaš	Kazallu	Kiš	Kutha
5	—	—	—	—	**gù-dé-a** Buccellati, Amorites pl. vii no. 18, col. iv line 25 = Forde, Dakota no. 58 col. iv line 25 (t) (- xii) (Kutha not mentioned), tablet erroneously cited by Goetze, JCS 17 (1963) p. 21 sub no. 36 as "Nebraska"
6	—	**^{d}šára-kam** Keiser, YOS 4 no. 70 lines 9–10 (t) (- xiii)	***šu-ma-ma*** Sigrist, AUCT 2 no. 114 line 6 (t) (- xii)	—	—
7	**kal-la-mu** Fish, Catalogue no. 362 line 4 (t) (- vi); Langdon, TAD no. 45 lines 2–3 (t) (- vi); YBC 13087, see Goetze, JCS 17 (1963) p. 26 (AS 7 or 8) (t) (- -)	**^{d}šára-kam** YBC 13087, see Goetze, JCS 17 (1963) p. 29 no. 78 (AS 7 or 8) (- -) (t)	***šu-ma-ma*** MLC 84, see Hallo, JCS 14 (1960) p. 109 no. 9 line 11; (t) (30 iv); YBC 13807 (AS 7 or 8) (t), see Goetze, JCS 17 (1963) pp. 27–28 no. 69 ***á-pi$_5$-la-ša*** MLC 84, see Hallo, JCS 14 (1960) p. 109 no. 9 line 25 (t) (30 iv); Sigrist, MVN 13 no. 694 line 42 (t) (30 iv)	—	**gù-dé-a** NCBT no. 1688, see Hallo, JCS 14 (1960) p. 110 no. 10 rev. 1 (t) (- vii); Sigrist, AUCT 2 no. 375 rev. i (t) (30 vii); YBC 13087 see Goetze, JCS 17 (1963) p. 21 no. 36 (AS 7 or 8) (t)
8	—	**ir$_{11}$-mu** Dhorme, RA 9 (1912) p. 61 SA 182 line 4 (t) (- xii); Legrain, TRU no. 37 (t) (- viii–ix) **gù-dé-a** Lafont and Yıldız, TCT 1 no. 839 (s) (- iii) **(E3/2.1.4.2002)**; ibid., no. 858 (s) (-vii) **(E3/2.1.3.2002)**	***a-pi$_5$-la-ša*** NCBT no. 1471, see Hallo, JCS 14 (1960) p. 110 no. 11 line 6 (t) (11 v); de Genouillac, TCL 2 no. 5489 line 4 (t) (13 iv) **i-ti-ti** Salonen, Puzriš-Dagan-Texte no. 516 line 9(t) (- v)	***a-ḫu-um-ba-ni*** Keiser, YOS 4 no. 78 line 6 (-ix)	**gù-dé-a** Hussey, JAOS 32 (1913) p. 172 no. 5 rev. line 6 (t) (21 ix)
9	—	—	—	—	**gù-dé-a** Holma and Salonen, StOr 9 no. 30 line 12 (t) (26 viii)

Year	Marad	Nippur	Puš	Simurrum	Sippar
1	—	**lugal-me-lám** Keiser, YOS 4 no. 68 line 5 (t) (3 xi)	***a-ḫu-ma*** Schneider, Orientalia 47–49 (1930) no. 485 col. ii lines 4–5 (t) (-viii); Legrain, TRU no. 71 (t) (9 ix)	—	—
2	—	—	***ik-šu-dum*** de Genouillac, TCL 5 no. 6041 obv. col. ii lines 11–12 (t) (- -)	—	—
3	***im-lik-é-a*** A 3155 (Chicago), see Hallo, JCS 14 (1960) p. 110 no. 13 line 4 (t) (- iii)	—	—	—	—
4	***li-ša-núm*** Edgerton, AJSL 38 (1921–22) p. 141 line 4 (t) (29 iv); Schneider, Orientalia 47–49 (1930) no. 78 lines 5–6 (- viii); NCBT no. 1535, see Hallo, Ensi's² p. 38 no. 28 (t) (- ix)	**lugal-me-lám** Schneider, Orientalia 47–49 (1930) no. 121 lines 13–14 (t) (29 xii); Riedel, RA 10 (1913) p. 208 BM 103413 rev. col. i line 7 (t) (19 xii)	—	—	***nu-úr-ᵈda-gan*** Schneider, Drehem- und Djoḫatexte no. 128 lines 6–7 (t) (-viii)
5	***li-ša-núm*** de Genouillac, TCL 2 no. 5504 rev. i line 17 (Marad not mentioned) (t) (19 x)	**lugal-me-lám** Boson, Aegyptus 17 (1937) no. 101 = Archi and Pomponio, Torino no. 144 line 3 (t) (- ix)	***a-ḫu-ma*** Sigrist, Syracuse no. 476 rev. line 3 (- xii) **lugal-kù-zu** Salonen, Puzriš-Dagan-Texte no. 314 line 7, for the reading pu-uš.KI instead of Salonen's gír-su.KI, see the collation of Picchioni, OrAnt 14 (1975) p. 158 note to PD 314 (t) (10 xi)	—	***ik-šu-dum*** de Genouillac, TCL 2 no. 5504 obv. col. ii line 17 (Sippar not mentioned) (t) (9 x)
6	—	—	***a-ḫu-ma*** Owen, MVN 3 no. 230 line 5 (- vi)	***ṣi-lu-uš-ᵈda-gan**** Keiser, BIN 3 no. 627 (- ii) (s) **(E3/2.1.3.2005)**	—
7	—	**lugal-me-lám** YBC 13087, see Goetze, JCS 17 (1963) p. 21 no. 37 (t) (dates to AS 7 or 8)	—	—	***nu-úr-ᵈda-gan*** Weidner, RSO 9 (1921–23) p. 472 no. 367 lines 6–7 (t) (-v); Hallo, TLB 3 no. 27 line 6 (t) (- v); Sigrist, MVN 13 no. 854 line 17 (t) (- v); YBC 13087, see Goetze, JCS 17 (1963) p. 26 no. 60 (t) (dates to AS 7 or 8)
8	—	—	—	—	—
9	***im-lik-é-a*** A 3155 (Chicago), see Hallo Ensi's p. 30; ibid., Ensi's² p. 39 no. 32 (t) (2 iii)	**lugal-me-lám** Fish, Catalogue no. 400 line 2 (t) (27 xi); Pohl, TMH NF 1/2 Siegel no. 103* (s) (-xi-xii) **(E3/2.1.3.2004)**	—	—	***nu-úr-ᵈda-gan*** Owen, MVN 11 no. 211 line 25 (t) (27 v)

Year	Susa	Šarrākum	Šuruppak	Ti-WA (A.ḪA)	Umma	Uruk
1	—	—	—	—	—	—
2	—	**^{d}nanna-zi-šà-gál** A 5107 (Chicago), see Hallo, Ensi's p. 10	***a-ḫu-a*** Lutz, UCP 9/2 p. 177 no. 13 lines 6–7 (t) (- viii)	—	—	—
3	***za-rí-iq*** Yıldız and Gomi, PDT 2 no. 1266 rev. line 2 (t) (19 xii)	**ur-mes** de Genouillac, TCL 2 no. 4685 line 4 (t) (- v)	**ur-^{d}nin-kur-ra** Fish, Catalogue no. 281 rev. 1 (t) (29 ix)	—	—	—
4	***za-rí-iq*** Salonen, Puzriš-Dagan-Texte no. 557 obv. col. ii line 19 (t) (- xii)	—	—	—	**ur-^{d}li$_{9}$-si$_{4}$** Schneider, Orientalia 47–49 (1930) no. 79 lines 6–7 (t) (- ix); Szachno-Romanowicz, RO 11 (1935) p. 97 no. 6 lines 2–3 (t) (- xi)	—
5	***za-rí-qùm*(LUM)** Oppenheim, Eames Collection, Eames G 16 = Sauren, New York Public Library no. 366 lines 3–4 (- -)	**ur-mes** de Genouillac, TCL 2 no. 5504 obv. col. ii line 4 (Šarrākum not mentioned) (t) (9–10 -); Forde, Dakota no. 58 obv. iii line 6 (t) (10 i)	**lú-bala-sa$_{6}$-ga** A 4553 (Chicago), see Hallo, Ensi's[2] p. 55 no. 38 (t) (- v); A 5140 (Chicago), see Hallo, Ensi's[2] p. 55 no. 39 (t) (-ix)	**ur-^{d}EN.ZU** Salonen, Puzriš-Dagan-Texte no. 314 lines 8–9 (t) (10 xi)	**ur-li$_{9}$-si$_{4}$** A 5922 (Chicago), see Hallo, Ensi's[2] p. 61 no. 46 (t) (- viii); Legrain, TRU no. 49 (t) (5 ix); Nikol'skiy, DV 5 no. 502 line 5 (t) (13 ix)	—
6	—	—	—	—	—	—
7	—	**ur-mes** Keiser, YOS 4 no. 76 lines 5–6 (t) (- v); YBC 13087, see Goetze, JCS 17 (1963) p. 20 no. 29 (AS 7 or 8) ***ì-làl-lum*** Margolis, STD no. 7 lines 3–4 (t) (- xi) **da-da-ni** Keiser, BIN 3 no. 379 lines 5–6 (t) (-xi)	**lú-bala-sa$_{6}$-ga** YBC 13087 see Goetze, JCS 17 (1963) p. 27 no. 65 (dates to AS 7 or 8)	**^{d}en-líl-zi-šà-gál** de Genouillac, Trouvaille no. 76 lines 4–5 (t) (- xii)	**ur-^{d}li$_{9}$-si$_{4}$** NBC 381 obv. line 5, see Hallo Ensi's[2] p. 62 no. 57 (t) (- viii); Keiser, BIN 3 no. 133 line 3 (t) (-viii)	—
8	—	**da-da-ni** HTS 142, see Sollberger, JCS 10 (1956) p. 24 note to no. 12 (t) ***ì-làl-lum*** A 5036 (Chicago), see Hallo, Ensi's p. 13; ibid., Ensi's[2] p. 9 no. 8 (t) (- xi)	**ur-^{d}nin-[kur-ra]** de Genouillac, Trouvaille no. 28 rev. 1 (t) (- ix); Keiser, BIN 3 no. 352 lines 4–5 (t) (- xi); Langdon, TAD no. 50 lines 21–22 (t) (viii AS 8–i AS 9)	**da-da** Speleers, Recueil no. 112 line 4 (t) (25 iii)	**a-a-kal-la** Waetzoldt and Yıldız, MVN 16 no. 627 rev. lines 1–2 (t) (- vi); Schneider, Orientalia 47–49 (1930) no. 382 lines 143–44 (t) (-xii)	***šar-ru-um-ì-lí*** Michalowski, Mesopotamia 12 (1977) p. 94 C line 3 (t) (- ix)
9	***za-rí-iq*** Scheil, RT 37 (1915) p. 134 line 2 (t) (- vi)	—	—	—	**a-a-kal-la** Boson, TCS no. 143 rev. lines 1–2 (t) (10 viii)	—

2001

A stone plaque was dedicated by Zarriqum, general of Aššur, to the goddess Bēlat-ekallim for the life of Amar-Suena.

COMMENTARY

The rectangular limestone plaque, which measures 33×43 cm, was found in the Ištar temple of Tukultī-Ninurta I, reused in the flooring of the altar room, and was given the excavation number Ass 21982 and the museum number EŞ 7070. The inscription, which appears above the central hole in the plaque, was collated from the published photo.

Line 6 is written in two lines. The text as a whole is written in one column.

BIBLIOGRAPHY

1912 Jordan, MDOG 49 p. 31 (provenance)
1914 Andrae, MDOG 54 pp. 16–17 (edition)
1922 Andrae, AIT pp. 106–107 and pl. 64c (photo, copy, edition)
1922 Schroeder, KAH 2 no. 2 (copy)
1926 Ebeling, IAK 2 no. 1 (edition)
1926 Luckenbill, ARAB I §§ 19–20 (translation)
1942 Poebel, JNES 1 p. 258 (study)
1952 Falkenstein, JAOS 72 pp. 43–44 (study)
1956 Hallo, JNES 15 pp. 220–25 (study)
1961 Borger, EAK 1 pp. 2 and 4 n. 2 (study)
1961 Gelb, MAD 2^2 p. 16 § 1 a (study)
1962 Hallo, HUCA 33 p. 36 Amar-Sin 15 (study)
1963 Hansen, JNES 22 p. 149 (study)
1971 Boese, Weihplatten p. 208 AR 2 and pl. XXXV, 2 (study, drawing)
1971 Sollberger and Kupper, IRSA IIIF1a (translation)
1972 Grayson, ARI 1 pp. 3–4 (translation)
1976 Larsen, City-State pp. 32–33 (study)
1979 Kutscher, RA 73 pp. 81–82 (study)
1986 Kärki, KDDU pp. 87–88 Amarsuena 15 (edition)
1987 Grayson, RIMA 1 p. 9 (edition)
1990 Gelb and Kienast, Königsinschriften p. 342 Ur 6 (edition)
1991 Braun-Holzinger, Weihgaben pp. 316–17 W 31 (edition)
1991 Steible, NSBW 2 pp. 245–46 Amarsuen 15 (edition)

TEXT

1) É ^{d}NIN.É.GAL^{lim} 2) *be-la-ti-šu*	1–2) The temple of Bēlat-ekallim, his lady,
3) *a-na ba-la-aṭ* 4) ^{d}AMAR.^{d}EN.ZU 5) *da-nim* 6) LUGAL.⸢URI$_5$⸣.KI.MA 7) *ù* LUGAL 8) *ki-ib-ra-tim* 9) *ar-ba-im*	3–9) for the life of Amar-Suena, the mighty, king of Ur, and king of the four quarters,
10) *za-ri-qum* 11) GÌR.NÍTA 12) ^{d}*a-šùr*.KI 13) IR$_{11}$-*su*!	10–13) Zarriqum, general of Aššur, his servant,
14) *a-na ba-la-ṭi-šu* 15) *i-pu-uš*	14–15) built for his (own) life.

2002

A tablet dated to iii AS 8 bears the impression of a seal of a servant of Gudea, governor of Lagaš.

COMMENTARY

The impression is found on L 839 (Istanbul) and probably on L 858 (Istanbul). Lines 1–3 are found in col. i, lines 4–6 in col. ii.

BIBLIOGRAPHY

1910 de Genouillac, ITT 2/1 p. 31 no. 839 (translation)
1989 Lafont and Yıldız, TCT 1 no. 839 (transliteration)
1992 Owen, BiOr 49 p. 447 n. 29 (study)

TEXT

1) gù-dé-a 2) énsi- 3) lagaš.KI	1–3) Gudea, governor of Lagaš:
4) lú-[...] 5) sag-[...] 6) [ir$_{11}$-zu]	4–6) Lu-[...], ... , [(is) your servant].

2003

Tablets dated to AS 1, 4, 5, 7, and 9 mention a certain Lugal-melam as governor of Nippur.

Lugal-melam may have begun his career as sukkal "vizier" of the governor of Nippur; see Keiser, BIN 3 no. 491 (dated to Š 43) line 59: kišib lugal-me-lám sukkal énsi-nibru.KI "seal of Lugal-melam, vizier of the governor of Nippur." The unnamed Nippur governor is almost certainly Ur-Nanibgal, who is attested for the years Š 36–44 or 45 (see Zettler, AfO 31 [1984] p. 3.)

A seal inscription of the governor is known from a small fragment of an undated tablet envelope from Nippur.

COMMENTARY

The seal inscription is found on HS 1334. The reading follows that given by Waetzoldt in OrAnt 15 (1976) p. 327. Lines 1–4 are found in col. i and lines 5–11 in col. ii.

For the term dub-sar-zà-ga denoting, in all likelihood, a high administrative official, see Meissner, OLZ 25 (1922) cols. 243–44; Landsberger, OLZ 26 (1923) col. 73; Landsberger and Gurney, AfO 18 (1957–58) p. 83; and Charpin, ARM 26/2 p. 140 and n. 6. Charpin notes: "Reste à savoir si le dub-sar-zà-ga est vraiment un 'secrétaire de cadastre' ce qui n'est pas aussi sûr qu'il y paraît. Dans la série proto-Lu (MSL XII p. 34), on trouve la séquence dub-sar / dub-sar-zag-ga / dub-sar-maḫ, dub-sar-lugal (47–50), mais les fonctionnaires du cadastre sonts énumérés plus lion: dub-sar-a-šà-ga et sa_{12}-du_5 (61–62). On se rappellera d'ailleurs que Landsberger comprenait le dub-sar-zag-ga comme un 'public secretary of high officials' (réf. apud F.R. Kraus, Edikt p. 139)."

BIBLIOGRAPHY

1937 Pohl, TMH NF 1/2 Siegel no. 134* (copy)
1976 Waetzoldt, OrAnt 15 p. 327 collation to no. 134* (transliteration)

TEXT

1) [^{d}amar-^{d}EN.Z]U
2) [lugal-kala-ga]
3) [lugal-ur]i_5.KI-ma
4) [lugal]-an-ub-da-límmu-ba
5) lugal-⸢me⸣-[lám]
6) énsi-nibru.KI
7) [d]ub-sar-⸢zà⸣-ga
8) dumu [...]-^{d}en-líl
9) dub-[sar]-gi_6-⸢pàr⸣-
10) n[ibru].KI-ka
11) ir_{11}-[x] x [x]

1–4) [Amar-Suena, mighty king, king of U]r, [king] of the four quarters:

5–11) Lugal-melam, governor of Nippur, son of [...]-Enlil, ... scr[ibe] of the *gipar* of Ni[ppur], (is) [your(?)] servant.

2004

Impressions of a seal of a servant of governor Lugal-melam, named Lugal-magure, are found on tablets from Nippur that date to the period AS 9–ŠS 1. For Lugal-magure's seal dedicated to Šū-Sîn, see E3/2.1.4.2008.

CATALOGUE

Ex. no.	Museum number	TMH NF 1/2 no.	Date
1	HS 1226	226	xi AS 9
2	HS 1227	227	xi AS 9
3	HS 1228	228	xii AS 9
4	HS 1229	229	xii AS 9
5	HS 1231	231	- ŠS 1
6	HS 1240	240	- ŠS 1
7	HS 1241	241	—

BIBLIOGRAPHY

1937 Pohl, TMH NF 1/2 Siegel no. 103* (exs. 1–5, combined copy)

TEXT

1) lugal-me-lám
2) énsi-
3) nibru.KI

1–3) Lugal-melam, governor of Nippur:

4) lugal-má-gur$_8$-re
5) dub-sar
6) ir$_{11}$-zu

4–6) Lugal-magure, scribe, (is) your servant.

2005

An important official named Ṣilluš-Dagān is mentioned (generally without title) in a handful of archival texts dating to the period Š 43 to IS 1 (see A. Goetze, JCS 17 [1963] pp. 13–14 no. 7). A seal impression on a tablet envelope indicates that he was govenor of Simurrum.

COMMENTARY

The seal impression is found on NBC 5613. The tablet and envelope date to ii AS 6. Lines 1–3 are found in col. i, lines 4–6 in col. ii. The inscription was collated.

BIBLIOGRAPHY

1962 Hallo, HUCA 33 p. 42 Anonymous 14 (study)
1971 Keiser, BIN 3 no. 627 (copy)
1978 Hallo, RHA 36 pp. 77–78 (study)
1981 Buchanan and Hallo, Early Near Eastern Seals no. 679 (photo, edition)

TEXT

1) *ṣi-lu-uš-^{d}da-gan*
2) énsi-
3) si-mu-ru-um.KI-ma
4) *i-bí-*^{d}IŠKUR
5) dub-sar
6) ir$_{11}$-zu

1–3) Ṣilluš-Dagān, governor of Simurrum:

4–6) Ibbi-Adad, scribe, (is) your servant.

2006

Ur-Lisi is attested as governor of Umma in tablets dating to AS 1–8. The seal of the governor, in which he acknowledges Amar-Suena as his lord, is found on numerous tablets and bullae. The seal impression, in which he appears simply as "governor of Umma" (see Bergamini, Mesopotamia 26 [1991] p. 113), is not edited in this volume.

COMMENTARY

Here we note one bulla, MLC 2310, as being representative of the numerous exemplars of this seal impression. In it lines 1–4 are found in col. i, and lines 5–8 in col. ii. Among other exemplars of this seal impression we may note Keiser, BRM 3 no. 16; Yıldız, MVN 14 p. 19 no. 154c; Yıldız and Gomi, Umma-Texte pp. 32–33 nos. 157 a–h; and Parr, JCS 24 (1971–72) p. 135–36 (BM 111374). For a complete list, see Bergamini, Mesopotamia 26 p. 112.

BIBLIOGRAPHY

1920 Keiser, BRM 3 no. 44 (copy)
1962 Hallo, HUCA 33 p. 37 Amar-Sin 18ii (study)
1971–72 Parr, JCS 24 p. 135 (edition)
1986 Kärki, KDDU p. 89 Amarsuena 18 (ii) (edition)
1987 Winter in Gibson and Biggs, Bureaucracy p. 96 IIIg (study)
1991 Bergamini, Mesopotamia 26 p. 112 (study)

TEXT

1) ^{d}amar-^{d}EN.ZU
2) nita-kala-ga
3) lugal-uri$_5$.KI-ma
4) lugal-an-ub-da-límmu-ba
5) ur-^{d}li$_9$-si$_4$
6) énsi-
7) umma.KI
8) ir$_{11}$-zu

1–4) Amar-Suena, mighty man, king of Ur, king of the four quarters:

5–8) Ur-Lisi, governor of Umma, (is) your servant.

2007

Aa-kala is attested as governor of Umma in tablets dating from AS 8 and 9 (and ŠS 1–6). The seal of the governor, in which he acknowledges Amar-Suena as his lord, is found on numerous tablets and bullae. For his seal used during the reign of Šū-Sîn, see E3/2.1.4.2012.

COMMENTARY

Here we note one bulla, MLC 2334, as being representative of the many exemplars of this seal inscription. In it lines 1–4 are found in col. i, and lines 5–8 in col. ii. For other examples, see Yıldız, MVN 14 p. 12 no. 11 and Yıldız and Gomi, Umma-Texte p. 26 no. 16.

BIBLIOGRAPHY

1920 Keiser, BRM 3 no. 47 (copy)
1962 Hallo, HUCA 33 p. 37 Amar-Sin 18i (study)
1986 Kärki, KDDU p. 89 Amarsuena 18 (i) (edition)
1987 Winter in Gibson and Biggs, Bureaucracy p. 96 IIIa (study)
1990 Maeda, ASJ 12 p. 74 (transliteration)

TEXT

1) ^{d}amar-^{d}EN.ZU
2) lugal-kala-ga
3) lugal-uri$_5$.KI-ma
4) lugal-an-ub-da-límmu-ba
5) a-kal-la
6) énsi-
7) umma.KI
8) ir$_{11}$-zu

1–4) Amar-Suena, mighty king, king of Ur, king of the four quarters:

5–8) Aa-kala, governor of Umma, (is) your servant.

Votive and Seal Inscriptions
(d) Of Private or Unnamed Individuals
2008–2009

2008

A stone tablet from Susa was dedicated for the life of Amar-Suena.

COMMENTARY

Lines 1–10 are found on the obverse, lines 11–17 on the reverse.

As noted in our discussion for E3/2.1.2.2041, Civil, in Studies Hallo p. 75 § 2.1, argues for a translation of "prison" for é-kur when used in connection with the goddess Nungal.

BIBLIOGRAPHY

1939 Scheil, MDP 28 pp. 3–4 no. 1 (copy, edition)
1962 Hallo, HUCA 33 p. 36 Amar-Sin 16 (study)
1971 Sollberger and Kupper, IRSA IIIA3i (translation)
1986 Kärki, KDDU p. 88 Amarsuena 16 (edition)
1988 Römer, TUAT 2/4 p. 465 (translation)
1991 Steible, NSBW 2 pp. 246–47 Amarsuen 16 (edition)

TEXT

1) ^{d}⸢nun⸣-gal
2) nin-é-kur-ra
3) nin-lú-ti-ti
4) nin-a-ni-⸢ir⸣
5) nam-⸢ti⸣-
6) ^{d}amar-^{d}⸢EN.ZU⸣
7) ⸢nibru⸣.KI-[a]
8) ⸢^{d}en-líl-le⸣
9) mu pà-da
10) sag-ús-
11) é-^{d}e[n-líl]-ka
12) ⸢nita⸣-kala-ga
13) lugal-uri$_5$[K]I-[m]a
14) lugal-an-ub-d[a]-límmu-ba-ka-[šè(?)]
15) *puzur$_4$-ì-lí*
16) šabra-é-UG-ti-ke$_5$
17) ⸢a⸣ mu-⸢na⸣-ru

1–4) For the goddess Nungal, lady of the prison, lady who causes people to live, his lady,

5–14) for the life of Amar-Suena, the one called by name by the god Enlil in Nippur, supporter of the temple of the god E[nlil], mighty man, king of Ur, king of the four quarte[rs],

15–17) Puzur-ilī, chief administrator of the temple UG-ti, dedicated to her (this object).

2009

A brown and white agate bead was dedicated to the goddess Lamma for the life of Amar-Suena.

COMMENTARY

The bead, which measures 3.8×2.6×0.3 cm, was acquired through purchase and given the museum number NBC 2530 (not YBC 2530 as reported by Steible).

The Ur-Lamma of line 8 may possibly refer to the Lagaš governor of that name, although this is uncertain. The text is arranged in one column. The inscription was collated.

BIBLIOGRAPHY

1916 Scheil, RA 13 p. 180 (copy, edition)
1920 Keiser, BIN 2 no. 17 (copy, edition)
1962 Hallo, HUCA 33 p. 36 Amar-Sin 17 (study)
1986 Kärki, KDDU pp. 88–89 Amarsuena 17 (edition)
1991 Braun-Holzinger, Weihgaben p. 368 P 15 (edition)
1991 Steible, NSBW 2 pp. 247–48 Amarsuen 17 (edition)

TEXT

1) ^{d}lamma
2) nin-a-ni-ir
3) nam-ti-
4) ^{d}amar-^{d}EN.ZU
5) lugal-kala-ga
6) lugal-uri$_5$.KI-ma-ka-šè
7) ḫa-la-^{d}ba-ba$_6$
8) dam-ur-^{d}lamma
9) dub-sar-ke$_4$
10) a mu-na-ru

1–2) For the goddess Lamma, her lady,

3–6) for the life of Amar-Suena, mighty king, king of Ur,

7–10) Ḫala-Baba, wife of Ur-Lamma, the scribe, dedicated (this bead).

Šū-Sîn

E3/2.1.4

Conflicting numbers are found for the length of Šū-Sîn's reign in the various manuscripts of the Sumerian King List. The Weld-Blundell prism's figure of nine years is proven to be correct by the evidence of various date lists; see Ungnad, RLA 2 pp. 135 and 144–45. The names of years ŠS 1–9 are registered here according to their fullest form as found in Schneider, Zeitbestimmungen pp. 30–36.

I. Year Names and Events of the Reign

(1) mu ^d*šu*-^dEN.ZU lugal-àm "The year Šū-Sîn (became) king."

While the Sumerian King List explicitly names Šū-Sîn as the son of Amar-Suena, some scholars have argued (erroneously) that the two kings were, in fact, brothers. Falkenstein, in editing a hymn to the divine Šū-Sîn (WO 1 [1947] pp. 43–50 — the text discussed is Chiera, SRT no. 23), interpreted the address of the queen Abī-simtī to Šū-Sîn: du_5-mu-^dšul-gi-ra-mu "my son of Šulgi" to mean that Abī-simtī was Šulgi's wife and mother of Šū-Sîn. In this he was followed by Jacobsen (JCS 7 [1953] p. 36) and Sollberger (AfO 17 [1954–56] p. 22), although both scholars subsequently changed their views (see Sollberger, JCS 30 [1978] pp. 99–100 and Jacobsen, Harps pp. 85–86 and 95–96). Jacobsen (Harps p. 85) now describes the setting of the hymn in the following manner:

> For the song I call "The First Child," one can easily imagine King Shu-Suen, accompanied by a lord-in-waiting, sitting in a room next to one in which his queen Kubātum is giving birth with the assistance of Shu-Suen's mother, the dowager queen Abī-simtī; also his great relief at hearing his wife's happy hailing of the newborn child. This fits in with the opening address by Shu-Suen praising Kubātum — and with filial deference also his mother — for being now clear of obligation to produce offspring, having proved that she is fertile. She has started a family, which Shu-Suen likens to beginning weaving cloth by placing the warp on the loom; Abī-simtī, mother of a large family, he likens to the clothbeam with its finished cloth. Kubātum then thanks him for gifts he has given her — or perhaps promised — and ends her thanks with a traditional formula for hailing the king.

A supposed piece of "evidence" supporting the argument that Šū-Sîn was the son of Šulgi is the seal published by Keiser as BRM 3 no. 52. As noted in our discussion of the seal inscription (which benefited greatly from comments of W. Sallaberger as RIM reader, see E3/2.1.2.94), the PN Šū-^dEN.[x] of the seal inscription is almost certainly to be restored as Šū-En[lil] not Šū-S[în].

A crucial piece of evidence in the debate concerning Šū-Sîn's father was Whiting's publication (JCS 28 [1976] pp. 173–82) of a seal inscription in which Abī-simtī is named as the mother of Šū-Sîn. Subsequently, Steinkeller (ASJ 3 [1981] pp. 79–80) pointed out that Abī-simtī is called nin "queen" during the reign of Amar-Suena. From this it follows, first, that Abī-simtī was the wife of Amar-Suena, and second, that Šū-Sîn was Amar-Suena's son, not his brother. While Steinkeller thought that Abī-simtī appeared as nin "queen" only during the reign of Amar-Suena, a handful of tablets from the reign of Šū-Sîn published since his article appeared (for a list see Sallaberger, Kalender 1 p. 45 n. 190) refer to Abī-simtī as nin "queen." The tablets in question: Um 713, Um 916, and Um 960, have now been published; see Waetzoldt and Yıldız, MVN 16 under the cited numbers. This new information, however, does not change the fact that Abī-simtī was Amar-Suena's queen. Meanwhile, the idea that Šū-Sîn was the son of Amar-Suena, not his brother, has been supported by evidence given by B. Lafont (RA 77 [1983] p. 70) and F. Pomponio (SEL 7 [1990] pp. 8–10); the latter scholar has listed five arguments in favour of seeing Šū-Sîn as Amar-Suena's son. Certainly, all the known references to Šū-Sîn as "prince" (dumu-lugal) date to the time of Amar-Suena; for a list, see the chart "Amar-Suena — Royal Family," item 32 on p. 268.

As part of an apparent program of legitimization, Šū-Sîn had several new statues of himself set up at the very beginning of his reign. Sallaberger (Kalender 1 p. 106) writes:

> Šū-Suʾen scheint sich am Anfang seiner Herrschaft darum bemüht zu haben überall im Reich, und zwar nur im Kernland, seine Statuen aufstellen zu lassen.

The texts mentioning these statues may be summarized as follows:

Date	Text	Statue Designation	Place Where Statue Stood
- AS 9	de Genouillac, ITT 2 no. 795	alan-^{d}*šu*-^{d}EN.ZU	Not mentioned, probably Girsu
ix AS 9	de Genouillac, ITT 5 no. 6968	alan	Kisura
xi^{2} AS 9	Thureau-Dangin, RTC 390	alan-^{d}*šu*-^{d}EN.ZU	NE-du$_8$-ḫu-lí.KI
xi^{2} AS 9	Lafont, Documents no. 377	alan-^{d}*šu*-^{d}EN.ZU	NE-<du$_8$>-ḫu-NE.KI
vi ŠS 1	Sollberger, AnSt 33 (1983) pp. 73–74	URUDU.alan lug[al]	—

For general discussions of the statues of Šū-Sîn, see Sollberger, "A Statue for Šū-Suen," AnSt 33 (1983) pp. 73–74; Lafont, "Deux notes sur les règnes de Šu-Sîn et Ibbi-Sîn," RA 77 (1983) pp. 69–71; Michalowski, in Gibson and Biggs, Bureaucracy p. 65 n. 42; Lafont, Documents p. 101 no. 377; and Sallaberger, Kalender 1 p. 106 and n. 480.

(2) mu ^{d}*šu*-^{d}EN.ZU lugal-uri$_5$.KI-ma-ke$_4$ má dàra-abzu ^{d}en-ki in-dím "The year Šū-Sîn, king of Ur, fashioned the boat called 'ibex of the abzu' of the god Enki."

In the entire corpus of Ur III year names, only three dates commemorate the fashioning of cult boats (Š 9, ŠS 2, and ŠS 8). In the case of Š 9, as noted in the introductory notes for Šulgi, the hymn Šulgi R was composed to celebrate the fabrication of Ninlil's boat. It is of interest, then, that a Sumerian composition is known that deals with the construction of Enki's boat and which bears striking similarities to the hymn Šulgi R. The text is known from a very late tablet copy from Kuyunjik (4 R^{2} no. 25 col. i). While Klein (in Studies Artzi p. 91) stated that this composition "was composed not earlier than the MB period," the evidence he uses to support this assertion is not persuasive. The appearance of the deities Asarluḫi, Damgalnuna, Sirsir, and Nimildu, for example, is hardly proof of a late date, since three of these four deities occur with some frequency in Ur III archival sources. In view of the late date of the copy and the specialized subject matter of the composition, its Sumerian text is remarkably good. It is certainly superior to the standards typically found in Sumerian compositions whose origins we would place in Middle Babylonian times. The Kuyunjik copy, then, is much more likely to be derived from an Old Babylonian forerunner than from a Middle Babylonian or later original composition as Klein proposes. A section of the composition is quoted here (lines 22–30 of Klein's edition in Studies Artzi pp. 94–95) to provide the reader with an idea of the style of the work:

GIŠ.má ^{d}en-ki-ke$_{4}$ nam-tar-ra-àm
^{d}dam-gal-nun-na mí-zi du$_{11}$-ga-àm
^{d}asar-lú-ḫi mu-du$_{10}$-ga sa$_{4}$-àm
^{d}sirsir má-laḫ$_{5}$-eridu.KI-ga-ke$_{4}$
^{d}nin-íldu nagar-gal-an-na-ke$_{4}$
šu-kù-ga-ne-ne-a mí-zi mu-ni-in-du$_{11}$-ga
GIŠ.má igi-zu-ta ḫé-gál ḫé-du
GIŠ.má egir-zu-ta giri$_{17}$-zal-la ḫé-du
šà-zu-ta šà-ḫúl-la ḫé-em-me-ak

The boat — it has been blessed by Enki,
It has been taken care of by Damgalnunna,
(And) given a good name by Asarluḫi,
Sirsir the (divine) sailor of Eridu,
(And) Ninildu, the chief carpenter of heaven,
Constructed it carefully with their holy hands.
Oh boat, may prosperity walk before you!
Oh boat, may abundance walk behind you!
May your heart be filled with joy!

Of course, since no royal name appears in the extant text, any connection with Šū-Sîn's building of Enki's boat cannot, for the present, be demonstrated.

A possible literary reflection of the events of AS 8 – ŠS 2, a period that saw the completion of construction work on the Enki temple in Eridu and, in all likelihood, a journey by the god Enki in his new *magur* boat, may be seen in the literary composition "Enki's Journey to Nippur." An edition of this 129-line work has been provided by Al-Fouadi (Al-Fouadi, Enki's Journey). The composition describes the building of Enki's temple in Eridu followed by an account of Enki's pilgrimage by boat to Nippur. We may also note the lengthy literary composition "Enki and the World Order" (see Benito, Enki pp. 77–160 and Wilcke, Kollationen pp. 9–12), which could conceivably have an Ur III date of composition.

(3) mu ^{d}*šu*-^{d}EN.ZU lugal-uri$_{5}$.KI-ma-ke$_{4}$ si-ma-núm.KI mu-ḫul "The year Šū-Sîn, king of Ur, destroyed Simānum."

A description of Šū-Sîn's campaign against Simānum is found in a passage in "Collection B" of Šū-Sîn's royal inscriptions (E3/2.1.4.1 iii 26 – v 23). This particular episode of Ur III history has been elucidated by P. Michalowski in a study entitled "The Bride of Simanum," JAOS 95 (1975) pp. 716–19. According to Michalowski's reconstruction of events, sometime during the reign of Šulgi, Šū-Sîn's daughter, Kunšī-mātum, was given as a "daughter-in-law" (é-gi$_{4}$-a) to the ruling house at Simānum.

Kunšī-mātum was likely resident in Simānum during the latter part of Šulgi's reign down to ŠS 2. Michalowski (JAOS 95 [1975] pp. 717–18) has assembled a small group of texts that name three members of the ruling family at Simānum during this period, namely Pušam and his two sons Arib-atal and Ipḫuḫa. Michalowski notes: "As our lady [Kunšī-mātum] is referred to in one instance as the é-gi$_{4}$-a of his son Arib-atal we may suggest that she was actually intended as a bride for Pušam's other son Ipḫuḫa, who might have been the younger of the two brothers. Arib-atal would have nominally been her guardian for bureaucratic or perhaps protocol reasons in the absence of his father when the document PDT 572 was composed." Of interest in this connection is an archival tablet that was published after Michalowski's study. The tablet in question comes from Drehem and is dated to iv ŠS 1 (AUAM 73.1044 = Sigrist, AUCT 3 no. 294). It records various cattle withdrawn (line 11): "(for) Kunšī-mātum, daughter-in-law of Arib-atal, king of Šimānum" (*ku-un-ši-ma-tum* é-g[i$_4$-a] *ar-ba-tal* lugal *ši-ma-núm*.KI). During the year ŠS 2, an insurrection at Simānum apparently ousted Pušam from power. Šū-Sîn's response to the revolt was swift: Simānum was attacked (as recorded in both the year name for ŠS 2 and the aforecited royal inscription) and Pušam and Kunšī-mātum were both restored to their former positions. As noted by Civil (JCS 21 [1967] p. 36), a reflection in the archival record of the campaign against Simānum is found in four tablets dated to vi ŠS 8 (Pohl, TMH NF 1/2 nos. 300–304), which register the "soldiers of Simānum" (érin si-ma-núm.KI).

We are fortunate in possessing, in addition to the aforementioned Nippur tablets, an archival text from Drehem that lists soldiers from cities that were, according to Maeda's interpretation (ASJ 14 [1992] p. 137), conquered during Šū-Sîn's campaign against Simānum and Ḫabūra. The text (Birmingham A.651-1982: Watson, Birmingham 1 no. 4) is dated to iii ŠS 3. It mentions four (or possibly five) cities: Nineveh (ni-nú-a.KI, line 8); Talmuš (tal-muš.KI, line 4; for the reading tal-muš instead of *ri-muš, see Kessler, Nordmesopotamien p. 17 n. 87, where Assyrian Talmusi is noted), Ḫabūra (ḫa-bu-ra.KI, line 2), and ú-ra(?)-e (line 6) = ? ú-ra-um.KI (A 4567, line 2: D. Owen, JAOS 108 [1988] p. 119). Line 6 reads: ⸢ma⸣-ri-ma-nu-um mar-dú; if we were to assume the omission of a da sign and of the KI postpositioned determinative, a connection with the GN that appears in Ur III sources as ma-ar-da-ma-an.KI would be conceivable, especially in view of the fact that this city is frequently mentioned together with Ḫabūra. The same GN occurs in the spelling ma-ri-da-ba-an.KI in a year name of Narām-Sîn of Akkad (Ni 2451: Unger, Naram-Sin p. 47 and pl. 5 no. 9). The writing prompts an emendation of the Watson text to read: ⸢ma⸣-ri-<da>-ma-nu-um.<KI>.

While the location of Nineveh is, of course, fixed, the situation of the other cities is uncertain; in all likelihood they lay in the Tigris basin northwest of Nineveh (see Map 2). Talmuš has been located by Jacobsen (Jerwan p. 39) at modern Jerahīyah, about 40 km northwest of Nineveh, and by Kessler (TAVO map BIV10) at modern Gir-e pan, slightly to the northwest of Jerahīyah. Ḫabūra, in turn, may tentatively be located at or near the confluence of the modern Ḫābūr River, an eastern tributary of the Tigris (see Kessler, Nordmesopotamien p. 21 Map 1), with the Tigris. A likely candidate for its location is the modern tell of Basorin, a large mound located just north of the junction of the eastern Ḫabūr River and the Tigris (see Algaze, Breuninger, Lightfoot, and Rosenberg, Anatolica 17 [1991] p. 198 fig. 19a site 16). For a (later) campaign of Šamšī-Adad against the cities of Ḫaburātum and Širwun, see Birot, MARI 4 p. 231 and Joannès, in Durand, Amurru 1 p. 347. The location of ú-ra(?)-e is unknown.

The ultimate goal of Šū-Sîn's campaign was the conquest of the city of Simānum. This important city appears in an Old Akkadian source (HS 1954+1955+2499+2506: Foster, ARRIM 8 [1990] p. 27 ii 4) as (A)simānum, and in Ur III texts written Simānum or Šimānum. In late texts it apparently occurs in the spelling Sinān(u). The first occurrence may be in a Middle Assyrian tablet (TR 2069A+2908: H.W.F. Saggs, Iraq 30 [1968] pl. LI; edition K. Deller and C. Saporetti, OrAnt 9 [1970] pp. 295–96) whose line 15, according to the collation of D. Kennedy, reads: <ša> URU.si!-na!-nu!. A later reference to Sinān (in the form Sinas) is likely found in an account of Procopius of Caesarea (Buildings II iv 14; reference courtesy A. Harrak) in which the Byzantine historian lists the town as one of the fortresses in the region of Amida, that is, modern Diyarbakır. It is further mentioned (as Sinan) in the Arab geographer Yāqūt's treatise Muʿjam al-Buldān (edition Beirut 1979 vol. III p. 260; reference courtesy A. Harrak). The toponym may plausibly be connected with the modern GN Sinan. It marks an important town situated in the area of the Batman river, a tributary of the Tigris. For a map

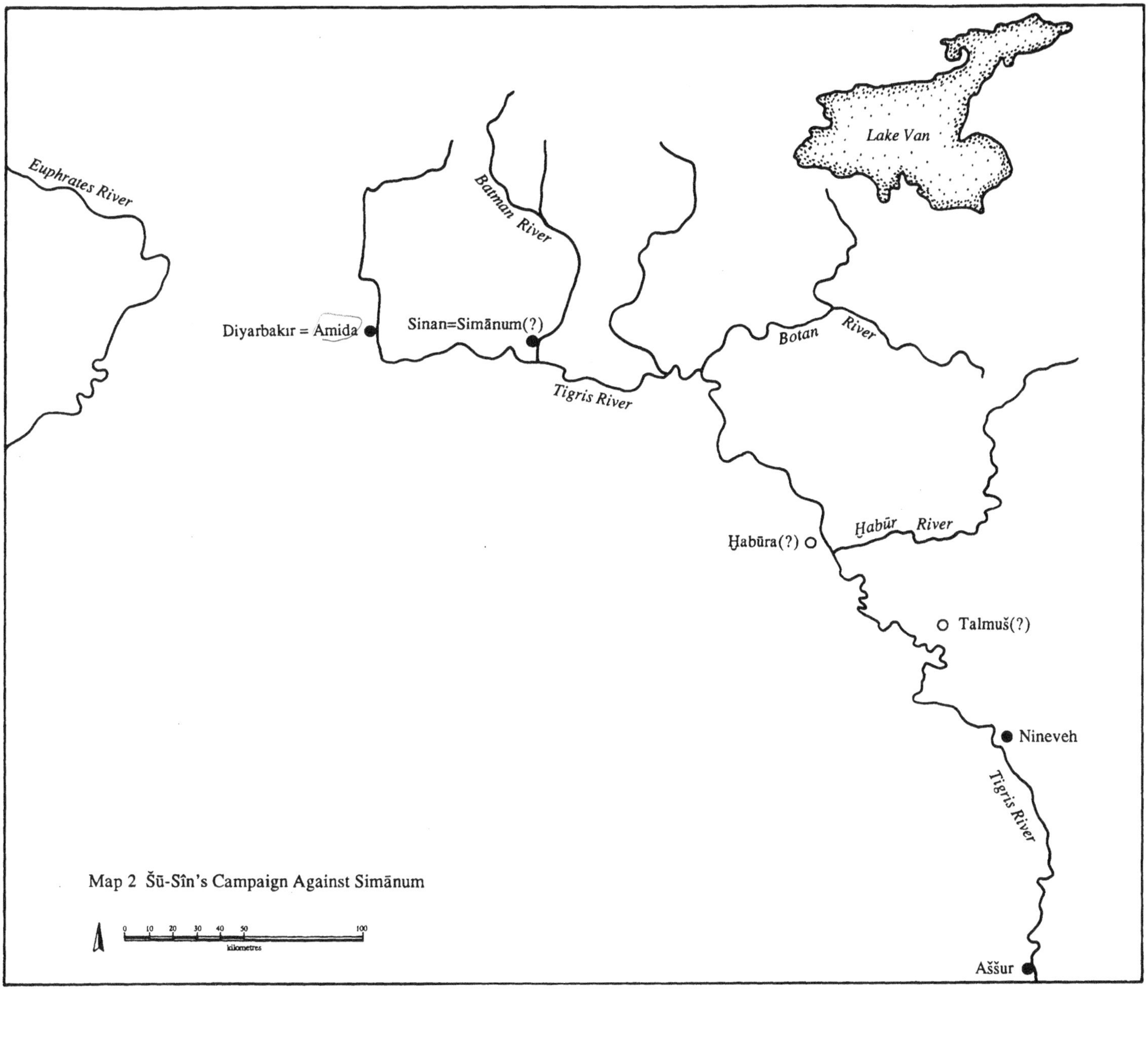

Map 2 Šū-Sîn's Campaign Against Simānum

showing ancient sites in the area of the Batman River, see Algaze, Breuninger, Lightfoot, and Rosenberg, Anatolica 17 (1991) pp. 212–13 figs. 2a–2b.

Šū-Sîn's Campaign against the Amorite Lands of Tidnum and Iam'adī'um

Shortly after the first mention of the land of Simānum in the Sammeltafel of Šū-Sîn inscriptions, the text, according to the placement and reading of the fragment Ni 4394 suggested by Wilcke (NABU 1990 pp. 25–26 no. 33), refers to Šū-Sîn's war against the lands: *ti-id-nu*-[*um* (x).K]I and *ià-a-ma-d*[*ì-um*]. Now, according to Gelb (Amorite pp. 24 and 607, no. 3623), the gentilic *ià-à-ma-dì-um* is to be analysed as JA-M'AD-IJ-UM and connected with the GN Jam'ad = Iamḫad. For a brief discussion of this interesting hypothesis the reader is referred to the comments of Wilcke, NABU 1990 p. 26 no. 33 and Owen, in Studies Hallo, p. 182.

Gelb's hypothesis is supported to some degree by the existence of a tablet fragment (Ni 9654) whose reverse gives the text of a royal inscription listing various cities that lay within the territory encompasssed by the later Old Babylonian state of Iamḫad; Ebla and Mukiš, for example, are noted. Now, before the identification of the ethnica Tidnum and Iam'adī'um in Ni 4934 we had no concrete evidence that Šū-Sîn actually campaigned in the far western regions. For that reason, the author of this volume edited the reverse of Ni 9654 as a probable inscription of Narām-Sîn (see Frayne, RIME 2 pp. 162–63 E2.1.4.1004). Although this attribution is now clearly to be abandoned, we may note that Šū-Sîn, in pursuing his western campaign, was clearly emulating the actions of his Sargonic forebear. It seems reasonably certain that the reverse of Ni 9654 gives part of a description of Šū-Sîn's attack on the lands of Tidnum and Iama'dī'um. The piece is edited as inscription E3/2.1.4.2 in this volume.

(4) mu ^{d}*šu*-^{d}EN.ZU lugal-uri$_{5}$.KI-ma-ke$_{4}$ bàd mar-dú *mu-ri-iq-ti-id-ni-im* mu-dù "The year Šū-Sîn, king of Ur, built the Amorite wall called 'It keeps Tidnum at a distance.'"

It is clear that construction of the wall named Murīq-Tidnim was closely connected with Šū-Sîn's campaigns against the lands in the west. An apparent allusion to the two interconnected events is found in a passage in a Šū-Sîn inscription (E3/2.1.4.17, lines 20–26): u$_{4}$ bàd-mar-dú *mu-ri-iq ti-id-ni-im* mu-dù-a ù gìr-mar-dú ma-da-né-e bí-in-gi$_{4}$-a "when he built the Amorite wall (called) 'It keeps Tidnim at a distance' and returned the 'foot' of the Amorites to their land." Further, an allusion to Šū-Sîn's victory over the Tidnumites is found in the literary composition known as the "Letter of Lugal-nisage to a King" (see Ali, Sumerian Letters pp. 92–98 Letter B 8). Lines 3–4 give epithets of the unnamed royal addressee of the letter:

> i-^{d}utu ab-sín-ta íb-ta-an-zi-ge
> ti-id-nu-um.KI-e šu bí-in-gar šibir-bi mu-un-dab$_{5}$-bé
>
> (To him) who removed (any cause for) complaint from the furrows (of the land),
> Who *avenged* Tidnum and took its staff.

Since two kings of the Ur III dynasty are known to have campaigned against Tidnum — Šulgi, in the period around Š 38–40 and Šū-Sîn, around ŠS 3–4 — it remains to determine which of the two kings the "Lugal-nisage" letter might allude to. Michalowski (Correspondence pp. 20–23) has demonstrated that the letter is part of a group of letters in "Collection B" that name various officials who, as far as can be determined, served at Nippur during the reigns of Amar-Suena and Šū-Sîn. This fact, then, allows us to identify the king of the Lugal-nisage letter as being Šū-Sîn.

Šū-Sîn's attack on the Tidnumites may have been a response to enemy provocations. Just as the Puzur-Šulgi correspondence that was noted above in our introductory remarks for Šulgi informs us that workers had to contend with attacks by Tidnumites as the construction of Šulgi's wall progressed, so the Šarrum-bāni letters indicate that labourers on Šū-Sîn's wall had to fend off Amorite raids. The following passage in one of the Šarrum-bāni letters (Michalowski, Correspondence pp. 225 and 229, lines 1–16) is informative:

> ᵈ*šu*-ᵈEN.ZU lugal-mu-ra ù-na-a-du₁₁
> *šar-ru-um-ba-ni* gal-zu-unken-na ìr-zu na-ab-bé-a
> bàd-gal *mu-ri-iq-tidnim*-e dím-e-dè kin-gi₄-a-aš mu-e-gi₄
> igi-zu mu-e-gar-ma
> mar-dú ma-da-aš mu-un-šub-šub-bu
> bàd dù-ù-dè gíri-bi ku₅-ru-dè
> I₇.idigina I₇.buranun-bi-da
> gú-gìr-bi a-šà-e nam-bí-ib-šú-šú a-šè mu-e-da-ág
> zi-zi-da-mu-dè
> gú-I₇.áb-gal-ta en-na ma-da-sí-mu-dar.KI-ra-šè
> [...]-bi ì-zi-dè
> bàd-bi 26 danna-àm dím-e-da-mu-dè
> dal-ba-na ḫur-sag-min-a-bi inim di-di-da-mu-dè
> dím-me-mu-šè mar-dú ḫur-sag-gá-ka íb-tuš-a géštu mu-ši-in-ak
> si-mu-ur₄.KI nam-tab-ba-ani-šè im-ma-da-[gi]n
> dal-ba-na ḫur-sag ebiḫ.KI-ke₄ GIŠ.tukul sìg-ge-⌜dè⌝ im-ma-ši-gin
>
> To Šū-Sîn, my king, speak,
> thus says Šarrum-bāni, the high commissioner, your servant:
> You have sent me as an envoy in order to built the great wall *Muriq Tidnim.*
> I am presenting to you (how matters stand).
> The Mardu are descending upon the land.
> You have instructed me to build the wall, to cut off their path
> (so that) they may not overwhelm the field(s) by a breach
> between the Tigris and Euphrates.
> At the time of my departure
> from the bank of the Abgal canal to the territory of Simudar
> its [...] has been raised.
> As a result of my building activities the wall is (now) 26 danna long.
> When I sent for word (to the area) between the two mountains
> it was brought to my attention that the Mardu were camped in the mountains.
> Simurrum had come to their aid.
> (Therefore) I proceeded to (the area) "between" the mountain range(s) of Ebiḫ in order to do battle.

This letter is important, because it indicates that the high state official Šarrum-bāni, who is attested in a handful of Drehem texts, was the officer in charge of overseeing the construction of the wall. Of interest, then, is an archival text dated to the ŠS 3 (Owen, MVN 3 no. 257) that Michalowski has interpreted as possibly referring to activities connected with the building of Murīq-Tidnim. The text reads in part (lines 1–6; see Michalowski, Correspondence pp. 53–54):

> 87.3.2 še-gur
> éren ugnim-ma
> ì-íl-la-ne
> šu ba-an-ti
> šà dub šar-ru-um-ba-ni
> lú-ᵈutu-ra ba-an-na-zi

> Illane received 87 2/3 bushels of barley for the "worker troops." Issued from the account of Šarrum-bāni to Lu-Utu.

Concerning this archival text, Michalowski (Correspondence pp. 54–55) writes:

> We may then possibly speculate that this document refers to the issue of grain at Drehem to the troops and workers destined for work on the Muriq-Tidnim wall.
>
> As Šarrum-bani may have already been at the building site in his absence subordinates would have taken care of the rations for the men who were leaving to join him. Assuming the normal ration of sixty sìla of barley for a grown man per month this expenditure would provide for four hundred and thirty eight persons for that period.
>
> In conclusion, this text may not only provide us with an indirect reference to the building of the Mardu wall but also with evidence that by the fourth month of ŠS 3 Šarrum-bani was already directing these activities in the field.

In the letter giving Šū-Sîn's reply to Šarrum-bāni, the king of Ur expresses some impatience with the progress of the work on the wall. He informs Šarrum-bāni that, because of this delay, he is to be replaced by Babati, the royal comptroller. A possible indication that work on the wall may not have been proceeding as originally planned may possibly be seen in the fact that the year name dealing with the construction of Murīq-Tidnim does not appear with any currency in archival sources until the seventh month of ŠS 4, that is, relatively late in the year.

Two archival texts can plausibly be connected with the events that transpired around ŠS 3–4. The first (Um 655; see Sallaberger, Kalender 1 p. 275), dated to iii ŠS 4, registers "one sheep (for) the standard (in the form of the weapon) going on the campaign" (1 udu šu-nir GIŠ.tukul kaskal-šè gen-na). The second (VAT 6946: Schneider, Orientalia 47–49 [1930] no. 38), dated to v ŠS 4, records (lines 5–6) the arrival of an Amorite emissary at Nippur ([u$_{4}$] kur-mar-dú-ta [l]ú im-gin-na-a). The same tablet also mentions (lines 11–12) the arrival of an envoy from Ṣilluš-Dagān (⌜lú-kin-gi$_{4}$⌝-a *ṣi-lu-uš-*^{d}*da-gan*). As noted, the latter is known from various sources (see E3/2.1.3.2005) to have been the governor of Simurrum.

The fashioning of the statue KA-gìr-^{d}inanna ^{d}*šu*-^{d}EN.ZU.

A handful of archival texts dated to the period ŠS 4–IS 1 mention offerings at Nippur for a cult object, apparently a statue, named ^{d}inanna-KA-gìr ^{d}*šu*-^{d}EN.ZU. The dossier of texts known to the author that refer to this object is given below.

Tablet	Publication	Statue reference	Date
NBC 6640	Keiser, BIN 3 no. 571	line 55: ^{d}inanna-KA-gìr ^{d}*šu*-^{d}EN.ZU	xii ŠS 4
Crozer 57	Sigrist, Rochester no. 88	rev. 5′: ^{d}inanna KA-gìr-^{d}*šu*-^{d}EN.ZU	27 i ŠS 6
Lager 25	Snell and Lager, YOS 18 no. 18	line 28: ^{d}inanna KA-gìr-^{d}*šu*-^{d}EN.ZU	25 iii ŠS 7
BM 103407	King, CT 32 pls. 41–43	ii 26: ^{d}inanna KA-gìr-^{d}*šu*-^{d}EN.ZU	4 xiii IS 1
BM 103409	King, CT 32 pl. 50	rev. 4: ^{d}inanna-kaskal-^{d}*šu*-^{d}EN.ZU	—

Various evidence points to the likelihood that the statue named ^{d}inanna KA-gìr-^{d}*šu*-^{d}EN.ZU was inscribed with the text which we have edited as inscription E3/2.1.4.1 in this volume. We may note the following data:

Item	**Statue KA-gìr-^{d}inanna ^{d}*šu*-^{d}EN.ZU**	**Royal Inscription**
Deity to whom dedicated	Inanna	Inanna
Subject Matter	Military Campaigns? (KA-gìr)	Campaigns against Simānum, Ḫabūra, and the Amorites
Earliest Possible Date	xii ŠS 4	ŠS 4

Because of the appearance of Inanna's name in ^{d}inanna KA-gìr-^{d}*šu*-^{d}EN.ZU, Sallaberger (Kalender 1 p. 103 n. 458) suggested that the statue in question depicted the goddess Inanna as helper of the king in battle. If our textual reconstruction of E3/2.1.4.1 is correct in placing the fragment Ni 13222 (ex. 7) at the end of the inscription, then the fact that it contains a concluding formula alluding to a statue of the king (line 11″: [a]lam-gá "my statue") would indicate that the text of E3/2.1.4.1 was inscribed on a royal image. It seems likely, then, that ^{d}inanna KA-gìr-^{d}*šu*-^{d}EN.ZU was a statue of Šū-Sîn that was dedicated to the goddess Inanna.

(5) mu-ús-sa ^{d}*šu*-^{d}EN.ZU lugal-uri$_{5}$.KI-ma-ke$_{4}$ bàd mar-dú *mu-ri-iq-ti-id-ni-im* mu-dù "The year after Šū-Sîn, king of Ur, built the Amorite wall called 'It keeps Tidnum at a distance.'"

(6) mu ^{d}*šu*-^{d}EN.ZU lugal-uri$_{5}$.KI-ma-ke$_{4}$ na-rú-a-maḫ ^{d}en-líl ^{d}nin-líl-ra mu-ne-dù "The year Šū-Sîn, king of Ur, fashioned a lofty stele for the gods Enlil and Ninlil."

The "lofty stele" of ŠS 6 is mentioned in inscription E3/2.1.4.8; in all likelihood, the text as a whole — most of it is now missing — described the creation of the stele. An allusion to cleansing(?) rituals (ki-^{d}utu) for this stele may possibly be seen in an archival text from Drehem (PD no. 528: Salonen, Puzriš-Dagan-Texte no. 528) dated to iv ŠS 6, which contains the remark (lines 18–19): nar!-munus-me-⌜eš⌝ u$_{4}$ ki-^{d}utu na-rú-a-maḫ in-ke$_{4}$-eš-ša-a(in.ak.eš.a) "Lady singers (who received the aforementioned cattle) when they performed the *ki-utu* ritual (by?) the lofty stele."

(7) mu ^{d}*šu*-^{d}EN.ZU lugal-uri$_{5}$.KI-ma-ke$_{4}$ ma-da za-ab-ša-li.KI mu-ḫul "The year Šū-Sîn, king of Ur, king of the four quarters, destroyed the land of Zabšali."

Šū-Sîn's campaign against the lands of Zabšali and Simaški is commemorated in four royal inscriptions: (a) "Collection A" Statue Inscription 1 = E3/2.1.4.3 and E3/2.1.4.4, and (b) "Collection A" Statue Inscription 2 = E3/2.1.4.5 and E3/2.1.4.6.

(8) mu ^{d}*šu*-^{d}EN.ZU lugal-uri$_{5}$.KI-ma-ke$_{4}$ má-gur$_{8}$-maḫ ^{d}en-líl ^{d}nin-líl-ra mu-ne-dím "The year Šū-Sîn, king of Ur, fashioned a lofty *magur* boat for the gods Enlil and Ninlil."

Šū-Sîn's fashioning of a new cult boat for the gods Enlil and Ninlil is commemorated in inscription E3/2.1.4.9. As noted by Sallaberger (Kalender 1 pp. 136–44), the new boat was provided for the observance of the Tummal festival. If the celebrations connected with the new boat actually took place during the latter part of ŠS 7, then two archival texts may be connected with this event. The first (Nesbit 29: Nesbit, SRD no. 29), dated to 1(?) ŠS 7, records offerings to Enlil and Ninlil in Tummal on the occasion of a royal entry (lugal-ku$_{4}$-ra). The second (PD 545: Salonen, Puzriš-Dagan-Texte no. 545), dated to 13 viii ŠS 7, notes disbursements in Tummal for the "... *tigi* harp of the holy mound" (tigi$_{x}$[É.BALAG]-gi$_{4}$ du$_{6}$-kù-ga). The evidence of the latter text accords well with the fact that musical and choral offerings were important features of the Tummal festival.

(9) mu ^{d}*šu*-^{d}EN.ZU lugal-uri$_5$.KI-ma-ke$_4$ é-^{d}šára umma.KI mu-dù "The year Šū-Sîn, king of Ur, built the temple of the god Šara in Umma."

Šū-Sîn's construction of Šara's temple in Umma named é-šà-ge-pà-da is recorded in three royal inscriptions (E3/2.1.4.16–18). In addition, a handful of Ur III archival records from Umma deal with the building of the temple. The temple's foundations were apparently laid in ŠS 2. One tablet (AO 5680: de Genouillac, TCL 5 no. 5680), dated to ŠS 2, lists (v 28–34) various aromatic woods "(for) filling in the foundations of the temple of Šara" (é-^{d}šára-ka temen si-ga). Another text (BM 105548: Fish, MCS 8 p. 95) dated to the same year records (lines 1–3) bitumen as "provisions (for) the foundations of the temple of Šara" (nì-dab$_5$ temen é-^{d}šára). The date and subject matter of the BM tablet allows us, then, to see a connection with two other Umma tablets. The first (Um 676: Sallaberger, Kalender 1 p. 275), dated to ŠS 1, records offerings "(on the occasion when) the boat from Madga arrived" (sízkur má máda-ga-ta gin-na). The second (Um 745: Sallaberger, Kalender 1 p. 275) contains the same remark, but is dated to ŠS 2. Now, Madga is well known as a source of bitumen in ancient times, and thus the arrival of the Madga boats during ŠS 1 and 2 can be connected with deliveries of bitumen for the Šara temple then under construction. Of comparative interest is an archival text dated to AS 1 (WMAH 16104: Sauren, WMAH no. 3) that records "bitumen from Madga for the storehouse on the bank of the canal." Three Umma tablets noted by Kraus (Kraus, Role of Temples p. 5 citing Keiser, YOS 4 nos. 178, 176, and 177) inform us that masons (šitim) were busy at work on the walls of the Šara temple during the years ŠS 2, 5, and 7. Of further interest is an undated text in the Yale collections, possibly a school exercise tablet, that records various quantities of bricks for building the temples of Šara and Ninura. The tablet was first published by L. Legrain ("Quelques textes anciens," RA 32 [1935] 128–29) and is now properly edited by S. Dunham ("Bricks for the Temples of Šara and Ninurra," RA 76 [1982] 27–41). In all likelihood, the tablet forerunner of this text was in some way connected with Šū-Sîn's building of the Šara temple at Umma. Of course, for all these citations we bear in mind Sallaberger's observation (Kalender 1 p. 85) that a second temple to Šara, in addition to the one in Umma (named é-maḫ and located in KI.AN), is referred to in various Ur III archival sources.

II. The Death of Šū-Sîn

Offerings for the throne of Šū-Sîn commence with 4 x ŠS 9 (Sallaberger, Kalender 1 p. 147); we can be sure that by this date the king had died.

Of interest, in connection with the death of Šū-Sîn, is the large summary tablet MM 154: Schneider, Drehem- und Djoḫatexte no. 108. It records disbursements during x ŠS 9 made first at the beginning of the month for Ibbi-Sîn's successive coronations in the cities of Nippur, Uruk, and Ur; and second (according to Sigrist's interpretation given in the article "Le deuil pour Šū-Sin," in Studies Sjöberg pp. 499–505), at the end of the month for the king's attendance with his wife Geme-Ninlila at Uruk for the funeral of his father. While some of the activities noted by Sigrist may well be connected with the funeral of the king, Sallaberger (Kalender 1 p. 113 n. 509) cautions: "Nicht alle in AnOr 7 108 vermerkten Ausgaben haben etwas mit der Klage um Šū-Su'en und der Krönung Ibbi-Su'ens zu tun, wie M. Sigrist, Fs. Sjöberg 499–505, angenommen hatte, da sich viele montalichen oder jährlichen Festen zuordnen lassen." A second tablet (PD 563: Salonen, Puzriš-Dagan-Texte no. 563) noted by Sigrist records various offerings for one day (21 x ŠS 9) during the period of the Montserrat tablet.

1

A compilation of Šū-Sîn inscriptions, designated by its editor, M. Civil, as "Collection B," is known from a large Sammeltafel from Nippur (ex. 1). The first inscription on the Sammeltafel (also known from six other tablet duplicates) commemorates the king's dedication of an image of the king to the goddess Inanna. As noted in the introductory remarks for Šū-Sîn, this text may have been inscribed on the statue named ^d^inanna-KA-gìr-*šu*-^d^EN.ZU.

CATALOGUE

Ex.	Museum number	Tablet lines preserved	Text lines preserved	cpn
1	UM 29-15-556+UM 29-16-611+N 3152+N 3180+	i 25–48	i 25–48	c
	N 4240+N 4241+Ni 4394+N 5144+N 6718	ii 1–23, 28–38, 42–52	ii 1–23, 28–38, 42–52	c
		iii 19–48	iii 19–48	
		iv 19–48	iv 19–48	
		v 1–6, 19–34, 40–48	v 1–6, 19–34, 40–48	
		vi 40–43	vi 40–43	
	Among these:			
	Ni 4394	col. i′ 1′–9′	ii 42–49	n
		col. ii′ 1″–10″	iii 36–45	n
	Ni 6718	1–11	ii 42–52	
2	Ni 9654	obv. i 1′–8′	i 47–48, ii 1–16	n
		obv. ii 1′–6′	iv 14–17, 19–28	
		rev. 1′–11′	See E3/2.1.4.2	
3	Ni 9656	obv. i 1′–15′	i 39–40, 42–43, 46,	n
		rev. i′ 1′–13′	vii(?) 1′–13′	
4	Ni 13221	obv. 1′–10′	iii 20–29	n
5	IM 85674	obv. i 1′–12′	iv 1′–12′	n
6	Ni 9662	obv. i′ 1′–6′	ii 36–37, 39, 42, 44–45	n
		obv. ii′ 1′–6′	iv 44–48,	
		obv. iii′ 1′–8′	vi(?) 1′–8′	
7	Ni 13222	obv. 1′–9′	vii(?) 1″–9″	n
		rev. 1′–8′	vii(?) 10″–17″	

COMMENTARY

The line count established by Civil, which is based on the column divisions of ex. 1, is used in this edition. Ex. 5 was assigned the arbitrary excavation number U h by Sollberger.

Two recent discoveries are important for establishing the text of this important inscription. First, Wilcke (NABU 1990 pp. 25–26 no. 33) has shown that the fragment Ni 4394, which was essentially unplaced in Civil's edition, is to be set in the lacuna between cols. ii–iii; the signs found on the second column of the fragment provide the beginnings of lines iii 36–45 in this edition. Second, S. Tinney has discovered that the previously unpublished fragment N 6718 contains lines near the bottom of col. ii (lines ii 42–52 in this edition). We are thankful to Dr. Tinney for kindly communicating a transliteration and photo of the fragment to the author in advance of his publication of the piece. The fragment is edited here through the permission of Å. Sjöberg.

It is probable that ex. 7 belongs to this inscription.

We have given here the translation of Civil with modifications suggested by Wilcke. The edition benefited greatly from RIM readers' comments of W. Sallaberger, who read the text with C. Wilcke in 1989–90.

We have followed the convention of placing some line numbers in parentheses following Civil; he notes (JCS 21 [1967] p. 24): "to make comparison easier, the text of these sources (B, C, and F) has been arbitrarily cut into short lines, easily recognizable in the reconstruction because the corresponding line numbers are in parentheses."

BIBLIOGRAPHY

1959–60 Edzard, AfO 19 pp. 28–32 and pl. 4 (ex. 3, copy, edition; ex. 6, copy, transliteration)
1962 Hallo, HUCA 33 p. 39 Šu-Sin 20ii (ex. 1, study)
1965 Sollberger, UET 8 no. 34 (ex. 5, copy)
1967–69 Civil, JCS 21 pp. 24–38 (exs. 1, 2, 4, copy; exs. 1–6, edition)

1969 Çığ and Kızılyay, ISET 1 p. 89 (exs. 2, 6, copy); p. 216 (exs. 4, 7, copy)
1986 Kärki, KDDU pp. 118–30 Šusuen 20b (exs. 1–6, edition)
1990 Wilcke, NABU 4 p. 25–26 no. 33 (study)
1991 Steible, NSBW 2 p. 271 Šūsuen 20 B (study)
1993 Owen, in Studies Hallo p. 182 (study)

TEXT

Col. i	
Lacuna of 24 lines	Lacuna of 24 lines
25) [...]-lá	i 25–27) Too broken for translation
26) [...]-ni	
27) [...]-⸢x⸣-a-ba	
28) [nin mè]-šen-šen-na	i 28–29) [Lady of battle (and)] combat, butting [l]ike a [bull],
29) [am-g]in$_7$(?)-du$_7$-du$_7$	
30) [in-ni]n(?) nam-ur-sag-šè	i 30–31) [Inn]in, [b]orn to be a warrior,
31) [t]u-da	
32) ⸢x⸣ GIŠ.tukul ti mar-uru$_5$	i 32–33) [p]resented with a ..., a mace, arrows (and) a quiver,
33) [s]ag-éš RIG$_7$-a	
34) [m]ud$_5$-me-gar dul$_4$(Text: dul$_4$ without *šeššig*)-dul$_4$-la	i 34–36) the one covered with [as]tounding qualities, the first [da]ughter of the god Sîn, holding the fifty [*m*]*es*,
35) [du]mu-gal-^{d}EN.ZU-na	
36) [m]e-ninnu šu-du$_8$	
37) ⸢kù⸣-^{d}inanna-ke$_4$	i 37–39) the holy goddess Inanna — for Šū-Sîn, her beloved spouse
38) ^{d}*šu*-^{d}EN.ZU	
39) ⸢MÍ⸣.ÚS ki-ág-gá-ni-ir	
40) kur gú-érim-gál	i 40–45) — in order to sweep like a huge onrushing flood over its population — (namely) the enemy country which in disobedience to him, (engages) in battle (and) hostilities
41) nu-še-ga-na	
42) mè giš-giš-šè-lá-a-ba	
43) a-ma-ru ùlu(GIŠGAL)-maḫ	
44) zi-ga-gin$_7$	
45) un-ba ùr-ùr-dè	
46) á-tuku ḫul-gál	i 46–48) in order to smite its powerful ones, mischievous (and) inimical,
47) érim-DU-bi-ne	
48) [t]u$_{10}$-tu$_{10}$-bé ak-dè	
Col. ii	
1) sag-gi$_6$ zi-gál	ii 1–3) in order to destroy the memory of its famous black-headed people,
2) mu-tuku-ba	
3) mu-bi ḫa-lam-e-dè	
4) ḫur-sag-gal-gal	ii 4–6) in order to subdue its great far-reaching mountain ranges —
5) á-sù-rá-bi	
6) gú ki-šè gá-gá-dè	
7) ^{d}inanna ^{d}en-líl-le	ii 7–13) the god Enlil made Inanna ... as the helper for Šū-Sîn, mighty king, king of Ur, king of the four quarters.
8) ^{d}*šu*-^{d}EN.ZU	
9) lugal-kala-ga	
10) lugal-úri.KI-ma	
11) lugal-an-ub-da-límmu-ba-ra	
12) á-daḫ-a-na	
13) mu-na-ni-in-ku$_4$-ku$_4$	
14) mìn-na-ne-ne	ii 14–16) The two of them descended from above(?) to his right (and) left.
15) zi-da-gùb-bu-na	
16) ⸢an-ta mu-è⸣-e[š]	
17) lugal-[^{d}*šu*]-^{d}EN[.ZU]	ii 17–19) The king [Šū]-Sîn [...]
18) [...]	
19) [...]	
20) é-kur za-gìn	ii 20–23) the pure Ekur
21) [...]	
22) [...]	
23) [...]	
24) ⸢inim(?)-^{d}en-líl⸣	ii 24) By the order of the god Enl[il ...]

25) ⌈^{d}⌉ [nin-líl-lá-ta]
26) ^{d}[...]
27) x [...]
28) ⌈x⌉ [...]
29) zà [...]
30) ^{d}[...]
31) ^{d}[...]
32) sig-[...]
33) x [...]
34) NI [...]
35) kur [...]
36) x [...]
37) [lugal-bi]

ii 25–37) Too broken for translation

38) [mè šen-še]n-ba
39) ⌈x⌉ [^{d}e]n-líl
40) ^{d}nin-líl-lá-ta

ii 38–40) [B]y the ... of the [god E]nlil, (and) the goddess Ninlil,

41) ^{d}*šu*-^{d}EN.ZU
42) lugal-kala-ga
43) lugal-úri.KI-ma
44) lugal-an-ub-da-límmu-ba-ke$_4$
45) TÙN.KÁR bí-sè-sè

ii 41–45) Šū-Sîn, mighty king, king of Ur, king of the four quarters, was victorious (in those battles).

46) kur ⌈bala⌉(?) [x x]
47) ⌈gú⌉(?)-[érim-gál]
48) x [...]

ii 46–48) The rebellious land, all [the enemy ...]

Col. iii
Lacuna of 18 lines

19) ⌈lugal⌉ x [x x]
20) [a-m]a-ru
21) ki-bal-a ùr-ùr

iii 19–21) (Šū-Sîn) ... , [the fl]ood which overwhelms the disobedient king (and) the rebel land,

22) á-ág-gá-ni
23) kur tuk$_4$-tuk$_4$-e

iii 22–23) whose orders make the foreign country tremble,

24) kala-ga-ni
25) sag-bi-šè è-a

iii 24–25) whose strength is outstanding —

26) dumu-munus-a-ni
27) si-ma-núm.KI-e
28) ⌈nam-é⌉-gi$_4$-a-bi-šè
29) [...]-sum

iii 26–29) his daughter was given as a bride to Simānum.

30) [si-ma-nú]m.KI
31) [ḫa-bu-r]a.KI
32) [ù ma-da-m]a-da-bi
33) [lugal-da gú-ér]im
34) [ba-an-da-ab]-gál
35) [dumu-munus-a]-ni
36) é [ki-tuš-a-ni]-ta
37) ság [im-ta]-eš

iii 30–37) [Simānu]m, [Ḫabūr]a, (and) [the surrounding district]s, rebe[lled against the king].They ch[as]ed his [daughter] away from [her] residence.

38) mar-dú l[ú(?) x x] x [...] x
39) *ti-id-nu*-[*um*.KI]
40) *ià-a-ma-d*[*ì-um*.K]I
41) im-m[a-na-d]a-

iii 38–41) The Amorites, the ... on[es], the Tidnu[m]ites and the Iam'ad[eans] came fo[rth] (to do battle).

42) lugal-b[i]
43) mè šen-š[en-ba gaba]

iii 42–45) The[ir] kings co[nfront]ed (him) in battles and comb[at].

44) im-m[a-d]a-r[i]-eš
45) r[i]-eš
46) [á ^{d}en]-líl
47) [lugal-n]a-ta
48) [mè šen-šen]-ba

iii 46 – iv 1) By the [strength] of the [god En]lil, [h]is [lord, he was victorious] in those [battles and combat].

Col. iv 1) [TÙN.KÁR bí-sè-sè]	
Lacuna	Lacuna
1′) [x] pà [...]	iv 1′) ...
2′) [š]ul-^{d}utu [...]	iv 2′) The hero Utu [...]
3′) dumu-munus-a-[ni]	iv 3′) [his] daughter.
4′) si-ma-núm.KI 5′) ḫa-bu-ra.K[I] 6′) ù ma-da-ma-da-bi 7′) lugal-da gú-érim-gál ba-an-da-ab-gál 8′) dumu-munus-a-ni 9′) é-ki-tuš-a-ni-ta 10′) [s]ág im-ta-eš-àm	iv 4′–10′) Simānum, Ḫabūra, and the surrounding districts, rebelled against the king. They [ch]ased his daughter away from her residence.
11′) ^{d}*šu*-^{d}EN.ZU lugal-kala-ga 12′) [lu]gal-úri.KI-ma	iv 11′–12′) Šū-Sîn, mighty king, [ki]ng of Ur
Lacuna	Lacuna
14) ḫur [...] 15) am TAR [...] 16) ⸢x⸣ [...]	iv 14–16) Too broken for translation.
17) du$_{10}$-tuku-bi ⸢LÚ×GÁNA *tenû*-a⸣ 18) [mi-ni-(in)]-da[b$_{5}$]	iv 17–18) He took their runners as prisoners,
19) nam-lu-ùlu(GIŠGAL)-ba 20) saḫar im-mi-⸢dul⸣	iv 19–20) and *covered* their men with dust.
21) si-ma-núm.KI 22) ḫa-bu-ra.KI 23) ù [m]a-da-ma-da-bi 24) sag-du-bi 25) tíbir im-mi-ra	iv 21–25) He smote the heads of Simānum, Ḫabūra, and the surrounding districts.
26) dumu-munus-a-ni 27) é-ki-tuš-a-ni-a 28) im-ma-ši-in-gi$_{4}$	iv 26–28) He returned his daughter to her residence.
29) si-ma-núm.KI 30) ḫa-bu-ra.KI 31) ù ma-da-ma-da-bi 32) nam-ìr(?)-da-ni-šè 33) sag-šè mu-ni-rig$_{7}$	iv 29–33) He assigned to her service Simānum, Ḫabūra, and the surrounding districts.
34) sag-érim-gál 35) nam-ra-aš-ak-ni 36) ^{d}en-líl ^{d}nin-líl-r[a] 37) ki-sur-r[a] 38) nibru.KI-ka [(x)] 39) si-ma-nú[m.KI] 40) ki m[u-ne]-gar 41) [... mu-n]e-dù	iv 34–41) He settled the enemy people, his booty, (namely) Simānum, for the god Enlil and the goddess Ninlil, on the frontier of Nippur, (and) built for them [a town].
42) [...-t]a mu-ne- 43) [x-t]a-an-gub	iv 42–43) He set (them) apart for them (Enlil and Ninlil).
44) uru.KI-ba 45) ^{d}*šu*-^{d}EN.ZU 46) dingir-bi im	iv 44–46) The god of their town was Šū-Sîn.
47) u$_{4}$-nam-tar-ra-ta 48) lugal-na-me Col. v 1) sag-nam-ra-aš-ak-ni-ta 2) ^{d}en-líl ^{d}nin-líl-ra 3) ki-sur-ra 4) nibru.KI-ka 5) uru.KI 6) ki nu-ne-gar	iv 47 – v 6) Since the days of decreeing the fates, no king has established a town for the god Enlil and the goddess Ninlil on the frontier of Nippur, with the people he had captured;

7) ^{d}*šu*-^{d}EN.ZU
8) lugal-kala-ga
9) lugal-úri.KI-ma
10) lugal-an-ub-da-límmu-ba-ke$_4$
11) si-ma-núm.KI

v 7–11) (but) Šū-Sîn, mighty king, king of Ur, king of the four quarters, [established] Simānum ...

12–18) Lacuna

v 12–18) Lacuna

19) ^{d}en-l[íl ^{d}nin-líl-ra]
20) ki-s[ur-ra]
21) ni[bru.KI-ka]
22) si-ma-nú[m.KI]
23) ki mu-ne-[gar]

v 19–23) [for] the god Enl[il] (and) [the goddess Ninlil] on the fron[tier] of Nipp[ur] established Simānum.

---

24) u$_4$-bi-t[a]
25) mar-dú lú-ḫa-lam-m[a]
26) dím-ma-ur-ra-gin$_7$
27) ur-bar-ra-gin$_7$
28) tùr ⸢x⸣ [x] ⸢x⸣

v 24–28) Since that time, the Amorites, a ravaging people, with the instincts of a beast, like wolves, ... the stalls.

---

29) lú [še nu]-zu
30) lú [...]-ga
31) [....] silim-ma
32) [...]-da
33) ⸢bára(?)⸣-[...]-ke$_4$
34) ⸢mu⸣-[un]-sì-sì

v 29) A people [who do not know grain],
v 30–34) Too broken for translation

35–39) Lacuna

v 35–39) Lacuna

40) u$_4$ uru.KI
41) an-ta nam-m[i-...]

v 40–41) Then the town(s) ...

---

42) ḫur-sag-gal-ga[l]
43) ḫu-rí-in-g[in$_7$]
44) gú ki-[šè]
45) ba-an-da-ab-[gar]

v 42–45) the big mountains were subdued as if by an eagle;

---

46) uru.KI á-dam
47) ki gar-gar-ra-b[i]
48) du$_6$-du$_6$-rá mi-ni-[gar]

v 46–48) the towns, the population, (and) their settlements, were turned into ruins.

Col. vi

Ex. 6 (Ni 9662) obv. iii′ is probably to be placed in col. vi; it is edited immediately below

Lacuna

1′) š[*u*-^{d}EN.ZU] lu[gal-...]
2′) géštu-[...]
3′) géštu-ma[ḫ(?) ...]
4′) lugal en [...]
5′) ^{d}*šu*-^{d}EN.[ZU ...]
6′) nam-ma [...]
7′) é-x [...]
8′) x [...]

Lacuna

1′–8′) Š[ū-Sîn] ki[ng ...], intelligence, supre[me] intelligence, king, lord [...] Šū-S[în] ...

Lacuna

Lacuna

Col. vi of ex. 1 is edited at this point

40) ⸢x x⸣
41) x-šè mi DU DI(?)

vi 40–43) Too broken for translation.

---

42) ub-da-an-na-ke$_4$
43) [x] ⸢x⸣ URU in-ne-eš

44–48) Lacuna

vi 44–48) Lacuna

Col. vii

Ex. 3 rev. i′ is edited immediately below

Lacuna

1′) [...] x ḪI x [...]
2′) [...] ga(?) x [...]
3′) [ÉN]SI.ÉN[SI]
4′) [^{d}*šu*]-^{d}EN.ZU lu[gal ...]
5′) [x (x)] uru(?) [...]

Lacuna

1′–7′) ..., the governors, [Šū-Sîn, the ki[ng ...], ... Šū-Sîn, the kin[g ...], his great might ...

6′) ^{d}*šu*-^{d}EN.ZU luga[l ...]
7′) á-gal-bi [...]
8′) u$_{4}$-ba (x) x ur-sag x [...]
9′) inim-^{d}en-líl-lá-t[a]
10′) sig$_{4}$-é-kur-ra [...]
11′) mè šen-šen-na [...]
12′) ki-x-gi$_{4}$ a x [...]
13′) ⸢x an-ki-a⸣ [...]
Lacuna
Ex. 7 is likely to be placed at the end of the inscription (in col. vii[?])
Lacuna
1″) [G]IŠ.g[u-za suḫus-gi-na]
2″) [k]alam-ma ḫ[é-x]
3″) mu-ni kur-kur-[ra]
4″) [ḫ]é-⸢x⸣
5″) [i]gi-dingir-gal-gal-ne-šè
6″) ḫúl-ḫúl!-la-ni
7″) [ḫ]é-dib-dib-e
8″) ⸢é⸣-kur-za-gìn
9″) ^{d}en-líl-lá-ka
10″) [g]ú an-šè ḫé-ni-zi
11″) [a]lam-gá
12″) [k]i-gub-bi
13″) [íb]-da-ab-kúr a
14″) [...-x]-na-ni
15″) [b]í-íb-DU-a
16″) [nì-dím]-ma-mu
17″) [íb-ze-r]e-a
Lacuna

8′–11′) At that time, ..., the hero, ... b[y] the decree of the god Enlil, the brickwork of the Ekur in battles and combat ...

12′–13′) ...
Lacuna

Lacuna
1″–2″) May a th[rone with a secure foundation ...] in the [l]and.
3″–4″) May his name [*be invoked*] in the foreign lands.
5″–7″) May he stride joyously [b]efore the great gods.

8″–10″) May he hold his head (literally: neck) high in the shining Ekur of the god Enlil.

11″–13″) (As for the one who) alters the [pl]ace where (this) statue of me stands,

14″–15″) who .... his ...

16″–17″) who [destr]oys my [handiwo]rk
Lacuna

2

An Old Babylonian tablet copy of a Sumerian inscription, found on the reverse of ex. 2 of the previous inscription, recounts campaigns of an unnamed king (he most likely was Šū-Sîn) in the area of modern Syria.

COMMENTARY

The inscription is found on the reverse of Ni 9654. The extant text lists various western cities that lay within the territory encompassed by the later Old Babylonian state of Iamḫad; Ebla and Mukiš, for example, are noted. It is uncertain whether Ni 9654 should be placed somewhere in col. vi or vii of E3/2.1.4.1 or whether it belongs to a separate inscription. We have provisionally edited the text here as a independent composition.

BIBLIOGRAPHY

1967 Civil, JCS 21 pp. 27 and 37–38 (copy [by Kramer]; transliteration)
1969 Çığ and Kızılyay, ISET 1 p. 89 (copy)
1986 Kärki, KDDU pp. 130–31 Šusuen 20b Zusäztliche Inschrift (edition)
1987 Heimpel, ZA 78 p. 79 no. 36 (study)

TEXT

Lacuna
1′) GÁ x x [...] P[U ...]
2′) ⸢ma⸣-ḫa-z[u-um.KI ...]
3′) pu-u[š.KI ...]
4′) x [x x x] da aš(?) gi(?) KU x [(x)]
5′) e[b-l]a.KI ma-rí.KI tu-tu-ul.KI ma-x [(x)]
6′) ur-gi$_4$-iš.KI mu-x-⸢gi$_4$⸣-iš EZEN(x X?).NI-^{d}IŠKUR
7′) x-x-la.KI a-bar-nu-um.KI
8′) ù kur GIŠ.erin-ku$_5$ ma-da-ma-d[a-bi]
9′) kur šubur-r[a] gaba-gaba-a-ab-[ba I]GI.NIM-ma x [x]
10′) ù má-gan.KI ma-da-[ma-da-bi] kur x [...]
11′) bal-a-ri a-[ab-ba ...]
Lacuna

Lacuna
1′–5′) ..., Māḫāz[um], Pu[š], ... E[bl]a, Mari, Tuttul,

6′–11′) Urkiš, Mukiš, ..., ..., Abarnum, and the land where the cedars are cut down, along with their provinces. The land of Subartum on the shores of the [Up]per Se[a], and Magan, along with [its] province[s] ... the other side of the se[a ...]
Lacuna

3

A set of three Šū-Sîn statue inscriptions, designated by M. Civil as "Collection A," is known from two Old Babylonian tablet copies. Two of the inscriptions (E3/2.1.4.3–4) commemorate the king's victory over Simaški.

CATALOGUE

Ex.	Museum number	Tablet lines preserved	Text lines preserved	cpn
1	BT 4+HS 2009+2985	i 1–37	i 1–37	c
		ii 1–34, 39–43	ii 1–34, 39–43	
		iii 1–30, 32, 35–36	iii 1–30, 32, 35–36	
		iv 1–34	iv 1–34	
		v 1–35	v 1–35	
		vi 1–35	vi 1–35	
		vii 1–16	vii 1–16	
		vii 17–18	Colophon 1	
		vii 19–29	Caption 1	
		vii 30	Colophon 2	
		vii 31–34	Caption 2	
		vii 35–37		
		xiv 7–10	Colophon summarizing all the inscriptions found on ex. 1	
2	N 6264	—	v 27–29 vi 23–29	c

COMMENTARY

Ex. 1 is a Sammeltafel formed by the join of two fragments, B(rockmon) T(ablets) 4 (= fragment 2, the left piece) +HS 2009 (= fragment 1, the right piece). It contains eight columns on the obverse and six columns on the reverse. The fragment in the Brockmon Collection, which is now housed in the Bible Lands Museum, Jerusalem, was kindly collated by J. Westenholz; the fragment in Jena by the author. I have also benefited from the collations of Oelsner published in Studies Sjöberg pp. 407–408; further, W. Sallaberger kindly communicated to me collations and comments on the text that resulted from a reading of the inscription by Sallaberger and Wilcke in 1989–90.

The first text, "Statue Inscription 1," is found on obv. cols. i–vii of ex. 1. So little is preserved of ex. 2 that a score was not prepared for this fragment.

BIBLIOGRAPHY

1959–60 Edzard, AfO 19 pp. 1–8, 14–20 and pls. 1–2 (ex. 1, frgm. 1, photo, copy, edition)
1962 Hallo, HUCA 33 p. 39 Šu-Sin 20i (ex. 1, frgm. 1, study)
1967–69 Civil, JCS 21 p. 38 (ex. 2, study)
1971 Sollberger and Kupper, IRSA IIIA4e (ex. 1, frgm. 1, translation [partial]); IIIA4f (ex. 1, frgm. 1, translation [partial])
1986 Kärki, KDDU pp. 106–10 Šusuen 20a Inschriften 1–2 (ex. 1, frgm. 1, edition)
1989 Kutscher, Brockmon Tablets pp. 71–82, 89–91, 122, and 126 (ex. 1, copy, edition); p. 114 (ex. 1, frgm. 2, photo)
1989 Oelsner, in Studies Sjöberg pp. 407–408 (partial copy, study)
1990 Steinkeller, NABU pp. 10–11 no. 13 (study)
1991 Steible, NSBW 2 p. 271 Šūsuen 20 A (study)

TEXT

Col. i

1) [^{d}en]-líl
2) [lugal-ku]r-kur-ra
3) [lugal]-⸢a⸣-ni-ir

i 1–3) For the [god En]lil, [lord of the lan]ds, his [lord],

4) ^{d}⸢*šu*⸣-^{d}EN.ZU
5) mu-pà-da-
6) an-na
7) ki-⸢ág⸣-
8) ^{d}en-líl-lá
9) lugal ^{d}en-líl-le
10) šà-ga-na
11) in-pà
12) sipa-kalam-ma
13) ù an-ub-da-límmu-ba-šè
14) lugal-kala-ga
15) lugal-úri.KI-ma
16) lugal-an-ub-da-límmu-ba-ra

i 4–16) Šū-Sîn, called by name by the god An, beloved of the god Enlil, king whom the god Enlil chose in his (own) heart as shepherd of the land and of the four quarters, mighty king, king of Ur, king of the four quarters.

17) u$_4$ ^{d}en-líl-le
18) nam-ti
19) zi-sù-gál
20) ⸢aga⸣-men
21) gidru u$_4$-sù-rá
22) GIŠ.gu-za-nam-lugal
23) suḫuš-gi-na
24) m[u-ḫ]é-gál-la
25) GIŠ.tukul-a-ma-ru
26) ní-gal mu-ru
27) á-an-kár
28) á-mè
29) á-nam-ur-sag-gá
30) ní-me-lám-bi
31) an-né [ús-sa]
32) za-pa-á[g-b]i
33) ki-bal-a dul$_9$-dul$_9$-la
34) bal-a-ri
35) a-ab-ba sig-ga-ta
36) [a-a]b-ba IGI.NIM-ma-šè
37) i$_7$ [...]

i 17–37) When the god Enlil [granted to Šū-Sîn] a long life-span, a crown (and) tiara, a sceptre of long days, a royal throne, a firm foundation, ye[ars] of [ab]undance, a weapon — the flood — which casts terror, the *a*ʾ*ankara* weapon, the arm of battle, the arm of valour whose awesome radiance [reaches up] to heaven, whose roa[r] covers the rebellious land across from the Lower Sea to the Upper Sea, the river ...

Lacuna of about 9 lines

Lacuna of about 9 lines

Col. ii

1) ḫur-sag-gal-gal
2) kur-ki-sù-rá
3) nam-lú-ùlu
4) en-en bára-bára-bi
5) ^{d}*šu*-^{d}EN.ZU
6) lugal-mu-pà-da-an-na-ra
7) gìr-né šu-GAM.GAM-e

ii 1–7) That the people, lords, and enthroned ones of the great mountains, distant land(s), bow down at the feet of Šū-Sîn, the king called by name by the god An,

8) ^{d}en-líl
9) en du$_{11}$-ga-na
10) sag-dù-dù-e
11) ^{d}*šu*-^{d}EN.ZU
12) lugal šà-kù-ge-pà-da-ni-ir
13) mu-na-an-sum-ma-a
14) u$_{4}$-ba
15) simaški(LÚ.SU).KI
16) ma-da-ma-da
17) za-ab-ša-li.KI
18) zà-an-ša-an.KI-ta
19) a-ab-ba IGI.NIM-ma-šè
20) buru$_{5}$-gin$_{7}$ zi-ga-bi
21) ni-bu-ul-m[a-at.KI]
22) ⸢x⸣-[x-x-a]m.KI
23) si-ig-rí-iš.KI
24) a-lu-mi-da-tim.KI
25) ga-ar-tá.KI
26) a-za-ḫa-ar.KI
27) bu-ul-ma.KI
28) nu-šu-uš-ma-ar.KI
29) nu-uš-ga-ne-lu-um.KI
30) zi-zi-ir-tum.KI
31) a-ra-ḫi-ir.KI
32) ša-ti-lu.KI
33) ti-ir-mi-um.KI
34) ⸢ù⸣
35) [...]
36) [...]
37) [...]
38) [...]
39) [...]-⸢da⸣
40) ⸢im-ma-da⸣-
41) ⸢è-eš⸣
42) [lugal]-⸢bi⸣
43) [mè šen-š]en-ba

Col. iii

1) gaba mu-na-da-ri-eš
2) ^{d}*šu*-^{d}EN.ZU
3) lugal-kala-ga
4) lugal-úri.KI-ma
5) lugal-an-ub-da-límmu-ba-ke$_{4}$
6) á-^{d}en-líl
7) lugal-na-ta
8) inim-^{d}nin-líl
9) nin-ki-ág-gá-na-ta
10) mè šen-šen-ba
11) TÙN.KÁR bí-in-sè-sè
12) sag-ur-sag-bi
13) gú-gur$_{x}$(ŠE.UR$_{4}$) bí-in-du$_{11}$
14) du$_{10}$-tuku-bi
15) šu-si-ga bí-in-du$_{11}$
16) kala-ga si-ga-bi
17) ur-re-éš mu-ug$_{7}$-ug$_{7}$
18) sag-zi sag-lul-bi
19) numun-e-éš mu-gar-gar
20) ad$_{6}$-nam-lú-ùlu(GIŠGAL)-bi
21) zar-re-éš mu-du$_{8}$-du$_{8}$

ii 8–13) (is) what the god Enlil, whose word *is outstanding*, granted to Šū-Sîn, the king chosen in his pure heart.

ii 14–20) At that time, Simaški (which comprises) the lands of Zabšali, whose surge is like (a swarm) of locusts, from the border of Anšan to the Upper Sea.

ii 21–39) Nibulm[at], ..., Sigriš, Alumidatum, Garta, Azaḫar, Bulma, Nušušmar, Nušgalenum, Zizirtum, Araḫir, Šatilu, Tirmiʾum, and ...

ii 40–41) came forth (to do battle).

ii 42 – iii 1) Their [kings], confronted him (Šū-Sîn)in [battles and com]bat.

iii 2–5) Šū-Sîn, mighty king, king of Ur, king of the four quarters,

iii 6–11) by the might of the god Enlil, his lord, and at the command of the goddess Ninlil, his beloved lady, was victorious in those battles and combats.

iii 12–13) He cut down their *assinnu*s.

iii 14–15) He enfeebled their runners.

iii 16–17) He killed both strong and weak.

iii 18–19) He sowed the heads of the just and the iniquitous (alike) like seeds.

iii 20–21) He piled up the corpses of the people into a heap.

22) en-en bára-bára-bi

23) LÚ×KÁR-a mi-ni-in-dab₅-dab₅

24) énsi-gal-gal

25) ma-da-ma-da

26) za-ab-ša-li.KI

27) ù

28) énsi-énsi-

29) uru.KI-uru.KI

30) mè-a mu-da-an-gur-re-ša

31) [en-en bára-bára-bi]

32) LÚ×KÁR mi-ni-in-dab₅-dab₅-ba-na

33) [...]

34) [...]

35) ⸢igi⸣-ᵈ⸢en⸣-líl

36) [ᵈnin-l]íl-lá-šè

Col. iv

1) b[í ...]

2) na[m-guruš]

3) šu mè-ta

4) im-ma-ta-šub-bu-⸢ša⸣-a

5) uru.KI-uru.KI-bi-šè

6) mušen-gin₇ zi-bi ba-ab-de₆-⸢a⸣

7) šu-ni la-[ba]-ta-⸢è⸣

8) uru.KI-uru.KI-[bi]-šè

9) anzu.[MUŠEN-gin₇] a-⸢ne⸣

10) še₁₄(ŠID) bí-[i]n-g[i]

11) uru.KI á-dam ki-gar-gar-⸢ra⸣-bi

12) du₆-du₆-rá mi-ni-in-gar

13) bàd-bi

14) mu-gul-gul

15) nam-guruš uru.KI-uru.KI-ba

16) sá ba-ni-⸢in⸣-du₁₁-[g]a-a

17) igi-b[i i]m-m-[ma]-an-du₈-du₈

18) GIŠ.kiri₆ ᵈen-[l]íl

19) ᵈnin-líl-⸢lá⸣

20) ù

21) [GIŠ.ki]ri₆ dingir-[gal]-⸢gal⸣-e-ne-[ka]

22) ⸢gìri⸣-šè im-mi-in-sè

23) ù nam-g[éme]

24) uru.KI-uru.KI-[ba]

25) sá ba-ni-⸢in⸣-in-du₁₁-⸢ga⸣

26) é-uš-b[ar]

27) ᵈen-líl

28) ᵈnin-líl-lá

29) ù

30) é-dingir-gal-⸢gal⸣-e-ne-ka

31) sag-⸢šè⸣ im-mi-[in-r]ig₇

32) ⸢gu₄⸣ udu máš anše-bi

33) mu-u[n-la-ḫa]

34) é-⸢ᵈen⸣-líl

Col. v

1) [ᵈnin-líl]

2) [ù]

3) [é-dingir-gal-gal-e-ne-ka]

4) [giš] i[m-ma]-⸢ni⸣-[i]n-tag

5) [kù]-GI kù-babbar

6) [nì-dím]-dím-ma

7) ⸢KUŠ⸣.⸢LU.ÚB.ŠIR over LU.ÚB.ŠIR⸣-gal-gal-[(x)]

8) mi-ni-in-si-s[i]

iii 22–23) Their lords and enthroned ones he took as bound captives.

iii 24–26) The great governors of the lands of Zabšali

iii 27–30) and the governors of the cities whom he had brought back from battle he took as bound captives.

iii 31 – iv 1) [Their lords and enthroned ones] which he took as his bound captives he [brought(?)] [...] before the god Enlil and the goddess [Ninl]il.

iv 2–7) The [m]en who had evaded battle and who, like birds, saved their lives (by fleeing) to their cities, did not escape his hand.

iv 8–10) Against [their] cities he himself screeched like the Anzu bird.

iv 11–12) He turned their established cities and villages into (ruin) heaps.
iv 13–14) He destroyed their walls.

iv 15–17) He blinded the men of those cities, whom he had overtaken,

iv 18–22) and established them as domestic (servants) in the orchards of the god Enlil, the goddess Ninlil and of the great gods.

iv 23–25) And the [wom]en of [those cities], whom he had overtaken,

iv 26–31) he offered as a present to the weaving mills of the god Enlil, the goddess Ninlil and of the great gods.

iv 32 33) Their cattle, sheep, goats, and asses he [led away]
iv 34 – v 4) and [offer]ed them in the temples of [the god E]nlil, [the goddess Ninlil and the temples of the great gods].

v 5–8) He filled leather sacks with [go]ld (and) silver, and [items fash]ioned (from them).

9) uru[du]
10) AN.NA-bi
11) zab[ar]
12) nì-dím-ma-bi
13) anše-bar-e bí-in-lá-lá

v 9–13) He loaded cop[per], its tin, bronze (and) items fashioned from them on pack-asses.

14) é-^{d}en-líl
15) ^{d}nin-líl-lá
16) ù
17) é-dingir-gal-gal-e-ne-ke$_4$
18) gi$_{26}$-sa-aš
19) im-mi-in-ak

v 14–19) He (thereby) provided treasure for the temples of the god Enlil, the goddess Ninlil, and of the great gods.

20) ⸢^{d}⸣*šu*-^{d}EN.ZU
21) lugal-mu-pà-da-an-na-ke$_4$
22) á-maḫ-sum-ma
23) ^{d}en-líl-lá-ke$_4$

v 20–23) [Š]ū-Sîn, king called by name by the god An, granted supreme power by the god Enlil,

24) u$_4$-da eger-bi-šè
25) a-ar-bi
26) ka-ta nu-šub-bu-dè
27) šu-a bal-e-dè

v 24–27) in order that from this day until forever its/their fame not fall from (men's) lips (but rather) be handed down,

28) ⸢bu⸣-ul-ma.KI
29) ma-da-simaš-ki-ka
30) ⸢UD⸣-da-bé-eš
31) ⸢NE⸣-ni in-šub

v 28–31) Bulma in the land of Simaški he ...-ly *threw down* ...

32) ⸢nam⸣-lú-ùlu(GIŠGAL)
33) munus-nita
34) zi-gál mu-tuku-bi
35) [x] GIŠ.tukul mi-ni-in-⸢gaz⸣

v 32–35) Its [pe]ople, men and [wo]men, those possessing life (and) having a name, he crushed with weapons.

Col. vi
1) [x]-e im-mi-in-pà-da

vi 1) ... which he found

2) ki-gal á-ra
3) á-kala-ga
4) nam-gìr-ra-ni
5) ⸢u$_4$⸣-ul-lí-a-aš
6) nu-⸢ÙR-ÙR⸣-a
7) zà-ba ⸢im⸣-mi-in-⸢x⸣

vi 3–7) in order that his might and strength forever not be wiped out, he ...

8) [na]m-l[ú-ùlu] ḫa-[bu-ra].KI
9) ù
10) [mar]-⸢da⸣-ma-an.KI
11) ^{d}*šu*-^{d}EN.ZU
12) [lu]gal ⸢sipa-sag-gi$_6$-ga-ke$_4$⸣
13) ⸢nam-ir$_{11}$⸣-da-ni-šè
14) ba-ni-zi
15) túg-ba bí-d[ul$_4$]

vi 8–15) (As for) the [pe]ople of Ḫa[būra] and [Mar]daman, Šū-Sîn, [ki]ng of the black-headed people, raised servitude for them (and) co[vered] (them with it) as with a garment.

16) kù-GI kù-babbar
17) ba-al-e-dè
18) im-ma-ta-an-gar

vi 16–18) In order to mine silver (and) gold he set them (to work) there (in Zabašali) from there (Bulma).

19) u$_4$-ba
20) ^{d}*šu*-^{d}EN.ZU
21) lugal-kala-ga
22) lugal-úri.KI-ma
23) lugal-an-ub-da-límmu-ba-ke$_4$
24) kù-[GI]
25) [ma]-da-ma-da
26) simaški(LÚ.SU).KI-ka
27) nam-ra-aš aka-ni
28) alan-na-ni-šè
29) mu-dím

vi 19–29) At that time, Šū-Sîn, mighty king, king of Ur, king of the four quarters, fashioned into an image of himself the [si]lver of the [l]ands of Simaški which he had taken as booty.

30) ^{d}en-líl
31) lugal-a-ni-ir
32) nam-ti-la-ni-šè

vi 30–33) He dedicated it to the god Enlil, his lord, for his (own) life.

33) a-mu-na-ru
34) lú á-nì-ḫul-dím-ma
35) [ib-ši-á]g-ge$_{26}$-a

vi 34–35) (As for) the one who would give [or]ders to do evil (against this statue),

Col. vii
1) mu-s[ar-r]a-ba
2) šu bí-íb-[ùr]-ùr-a

vii 1–2) who would erase its insc[ription]

3) [mu]-ni
4) [bí]-íb-sar-re-a

vii 3–4) who would write his (own) [name],

5) nì-dím-ma-mu
6) íb-ze-re-a

vii 5–6) who would destroy my handiwork,

7) lú-ba

vii 7) that man,

8) ^{d}e[n-l]íl
9) lugal-kur-kur-⌈ra⌉-ke$_{4}$
10) ^{d}nin-líl
11) nin-dingir-ré-e-ne-ke$_{4}$
12) nam ḫa-ba-an-da-[ku$_{5}$-r]e$_{6}$-ne

vii 8–12) may the god E[nl]il, lord of the lands, (and) the goddess Ninlil, lady of the gods, [cu]rse him.

13) ^{d}[nin-urta]
14) ur-sag-k[ala-ga]-
15) ^{d}en-líl-[lá]
16) maškim-bi ḫé-a

vii 13–16) May the god [Ninurta], m[ighty] warrior of the god Enlil, act (as) its (the curse's) [bail]iff.

Colophon 1
17) mu-sar-ra
18) ki-gal-ba

Colophon 1
vii 17–18) Inscription on its socle.

Caption 1
19) ^{d}*šu*-^{d}EN.[ZU]
20) ki-á[g]-
21) ^{d}en-lí[l-lá]
22) lugal ^{d}e[n-líl]-le
23) [šà-ga]-né
24) in-⌈pà⌉
25) sipa-kala-⌈ma⌉
26) ù an-ub-da-límmu-ba-šè
27) lugal-kala-ga
28) lugal-úri.KI-ma
29) lugal-an-ub-da-límmu-ba

Caption 1
vii 19–29) Šū-Sî[n], belov[ed] of the god Enl[il], king whom the god E[nlil] chose in his (own) [heart] as shepherd of the land and of the four quarters, mighty king, king of Ur, king of the four quarters.

Colophon 2
30) mu-sar-ra gìri-na

Colophon 2
vii 30) Inscription on his foot.

Caption 2
31) zi-rí-in-gu
32) én[si]
33) ma-[da]
34) za-ab-ša-[li].KI

Caption 2
vii 31–34) Ziringu, go[vernor] of the la[nd] of Zabša[li].

Colophon 3
35) mu-sar-ra
36) zà zi-rí-in-gu
37) lugal LÚ×KÁR

Colophon 3
vii 35–37) Inscription on the shoulder of Ziringu, the king (taken) as a bound captive.

Summary Colophon for all the inscriptions on ex. 1
7) dub-mu-sa[r-ra]
8) 3 dub-alan
9) ^{d}*šu*-^{d}EN.ZU
10) ù ki-gal 2-bi

Summary Colophon for all the inscriptions on ex. 1
xiv 7–10) A tablet of the inscript[ions] of three inscriptions of statues of Šū-Sîn and their two pedestals.

4

A variant version of Šū-Sîn "Statue Inscription 1," with a dedication to the goddess Ninlil instead of Enlil, is known from an Old Babylonian tablet copy.

COMMENTARY

The text is found on the obverse of the tablet UM 29-16-42, which measures 9.2×12×3 cm. The inscription was collated by S. Tinney.

The reverse of the tablet contains, in addition to the end of this inscription, a text of Enlil-bāni of Isin (see Frayne, RIME 4 p. 84 E4.1.10.8; Kärki, SAKAZ 1 pp. 31–32 Enlilbāni 6).

BIBLIOGRAPHY

1972 Sjöberg, JCS 24 pp. 70–73 (photo, edition)
1986 Kärki, KDDU pp. 134–36 Šusuen 27 (edition)
1991 Steible, NSBW 2 p. 271 Šūsuen 20 C (study)

TEXT

Col. i
1′) AN x [x (x)]
2′) šu nu-bal-x
3′) nitalam$_{4}$-ni
4′) en ^{d}nu-nam-nir-re
5′) nì-al-du$_{11}$-ga-ni
6′) nu-un-ši-⸢íb⸣-kéš-re
7′) ^{d}nin-líl
8′) nun kur-kur-ra diri-ga
9′) nin-ki-ág-
10′) ^{d}*šu*-^{d}⸢EN⸣.Z[U-n]a-ke$_{4}$
11′) u$_{4}$ nam-ti
12′) zi-sù-[g]ál
13′) aga men [gidru]-u$_{4}$-sù-rá
14′) GIŠ.gu-za-n[am]-lugal
15′) suḫuš-gi-na
16′) mu-⸢ḫé-gál⸣-[la]
17′) GIŠ.tukul a-ma-ru
18′) ní-gal mu-šub
19′) á-an-kára
20′) á-mè
21′) á-nam-ur-sag-gá
22′) ní-me-lám-bi
23′) an-né ús-sa
24′) ⸢za⸣(?)-pa-ág-bi
25′) ki-bal-a dul$_{4}$-dul$_{4}$-lu

i 1′–2′) ... [...] does not change.

i 3′–6′) Her husband, lord Nunamnir, does not withhold her request.

i 7′–10′) The goddess Ninlil, *princess*, supreme over the lands, lady beloved of Šū-Sîn,

i 11′–25′) when (for Šu-Sîn) a long life-span, a crown (and) tiara, [a sceptre] of long days, a r[o]yal throne, a firm foundation, years of abundance, a weapon — the flood — which casts terror, the *a'ankara* weapon, arm of battle, the arm of combat whose awesome radiance reaches up to heaven, whose roar covers the rebellious land,

Col. ii
1′) gìri [...]
2′) ^{d}nin-l[íl x x]
3′) ^{d}*šu*-^{d}EN.ZU-[x x]
4′) ki-nitalam$_{4}$-[na-ta]
5′) ^{d}nin-líl a x x

ii 1′) ... [...]
ii 2′–6′) Ninl[il] asked [for] Šū-Sîn [from her] spouse (Enlil) Ninlil ...

6′) al im-ma-an-du$_{11}$
7′) ^{d}nin-líl dam-ki-ág-
8′) ^{d}en-líl-lá
9′) nitlam$_{4}$-ni en ^{d}nu-nam-nir-re
10′) gal-bi túm-ma-e

ii 7′–10′) For Ninlil, beloved spouse of Enlil, her husband, lord Nunamnir, is one who performs great (deeds).

11′) ^{d}*šu*-^{d}EN.ZU
12′) ìr-ki-ág-
13′) ^{d}en-líl-lá
14′) lugal ^{d}en-líl-le šà-ga-na
15′) in-pà

ii 11′–15′) To Šū-Sîn, beloved servant of Enlil, king whom the god Enlil chose in his (own) heart, <shepherd of the land>

Blank line

Blank line

16′) ù an-ub-da-límmu-ba
17′) lugal-kala-ga lugal-úri.KI-ma
18′) lugal-an-ub-da-límmu-ba
19′) ìr-ki-ág-gá-ni-ir
20′) mu-na-an-sum-ma-a

ii 16′–20′) and of the four quarters, mighty king, king of Ur, king of the four quarters, his beloved servant, (the god Enlil) had given (the above-mentioned requests),

21′) u$_{4}$-ba simaški(LÚ.SU).KI
22′) ma-da-ma-da-za-ab-ša-li.KI
23′) zà (Text: ù)-an-ša-an.KI-ta

ii 21′–23′) at that time, Simaški (which comprises) the lands of Zabšali, from the border of Anšan,

Col. iii
1′) x [...]
2′) IM [...]

iii 1′–2′) Too broken for translation.

3′) alan-[na-ni]
4′) PI(?) x x [...]
5′) mu-[dím]

iii 3′–5′) He [fashioned] an image of [himself] ...

6′) ^{d}nin-líl
7′) nin-a-ni-ir
8′) nam-ti-la-ni-šè
9′) a mu-na-ru

iii 6′–9′) (and) dedicated to the goddess Ninlil, his lady, for his (own) life.

5

Šū-Sîn's "Statue Inscription 2" is known from two Old Babylonian tablet copies. It gives Akkadian accounts of the events commemorated in inscriptions E3/2.1.4.3–4.

CATALOGUE

Ex.	Museum number	Dimensions (cm)	Tablet lines preserved	Text lines preserved	cpn
1	BT 4 (frgm. 1)	23×17	obv. viii 1–16, 18–26	1–16, 18–26	c
	+HS 2009 (frgm. 2)		rev. i 1–30	37–66	
	+HS 2985 (frgm. 3)		rev. i 31–33	Colophon	
			rev. i 34–36	Caption 1	
			rev. i 37–38	Colophon 1	
			rev. ii 1–8	Caption 2	
			rev. ii 9–13	Colophon 2	
			rev. ii 14–16	Caption 3	
			rev. ii 17–18	Colophon 3	
			rev. ii 19–21	Caption 4	
			rev. ii 22–23	Colophon 4	
			rev. ii 24–26	Caption 5	
			rev. ii 27–28	Colophon 5	
			rev. ii 29–31	Caption 6	
			rev. ii 32–34	Colophon 6	
			rev. iii 1–3	Caption 7	
			rev. iii 4–5	Colophon 7	

Ex.	Museum number	Dimensions (cm)	Tablet lines preserved	Text lines preserved	cpn
			rev. iii 6–8	Caption 8	n
			rev. iii 9–10	Colophon 8	
			rev. iii 11–12	Notation 1	
			rev. iii 13–15	Caption 9	
			rev. iii 16–17	Colophon 9	
			rev. iii 18–20	Caption 10	
			rev. iii 21–22	Colophon 10	
			rev. iii 23–25	Caption 11	
			rev. iii 26–27	Colophon 11	
			rev. iii 28–30	Caption 12	
			rev. iii 31–32	Colophon 12	
			rev. iv 1–10	Notation 2	
			rev. iv 11–15	Concluding colophon	
2	Ni 2760	—	obv. a 21–30	obv. 1–10	n
			obv. b 21–30	obv. 11–20	
			rev. 1′–23′	rev. 1′–23′	
			rev. 24′–26′	Colophon	

COMMENTARY

Ex. 1 is dedicated to the god Enlil, ex. 2 to the goddess Ninlil. Since the two texts, with the exception of the name of the divine recipient, are virtually identical, they have been edited together here in full, with ex. 1 in col. 2 and ex. 2 in col. 1; the translation follows the line numbering of ex. 1. Because complete texts have been given, no critical apparatus has been provided. The line count of the translation follows the consecutive line numbering of ex. 1. Ex. 2 is written on the bottom third of the obverse of Ni 2760 in two columns, and on the reverse of the same tablet in one column. We have assumed that all the captions and colophons on ex. 1 are written in Akkadian, with the exception of Caption 2, which is clearly in Sumerian.

BIBLIOGRAPHY

1959–60 Edzard, AfO 19 pp. 9–14, 21–28, and pls. 1–2 (ex. 1, frgm. 2, photo, copy, edition); pl. 3 (ex. 2, copy)

1962 Hallo, HUCA 33 p. 39 Šu-Sin 20i (ex. 1, frgm. 2, study)

1976 Kramer, ISET 2 pls. 126–27 (ex. 2, copy)

1986 Kärki, KDDU pp. 110–18 Šusuen 20a Inschriften 3–5 (ex. 1, frgm. 2, edition)

1989 Kutscher, Brockmon Tablets pp. 82–89, 91–92, 97–98, 114–15, 122–23, and 126–27 (ex. 1, frgms. 1–2, photo, copy, edition)

1989 Oelsner, in Studies Sjöberg pp. 408–409 (ex. 1, frgm. 3, copy, study)

1990 Gelb and Kienast, Königsinschriften pp. 347–54 Ur C 2 (Šusîn 20) (exs. 1–2, edition)

TEXT

Ex. 2	Ex. 1	
Obv.	Obv. viii	
1) ^{d}*nin-líl*	1) ^{d}⌈*en*⌉*-líl*	1–2) The god Enlil (var. Ninlil) granted to him,
2) *i-dì-šum-ma*	2) *i-dì-šum-ma*	
3) *a-na*	3) *a-na*	3–14) to Šū-Sîn, the mighty, king of Ur and king of the four quarters, favourite of the gods Enlil and Sîn, the lands of Simaški.
3) ^{d}*šu*-^{d}EN.ZU	4) ^{d}*šu*-^{d}EN.ZU	
4) *da-nim*	5) *da-nim*	
5) LUGAL URI$_5$.KI.MA	6) LUGAL URI$_5$.KI	
6) *ù* LUGAL	7) *ù* LUGAL	
6) *ki-ib-ra-tim*	8) *ki-ib-ra-tim*	
7) *ar-ba-im*	9) *ar-ba-im*	
8) *mì-gir*	10) *mì-gir*	
8) ^{d}*en-líl*	11) ^{d}*en-líl*	
8) *ù*	12) ⌈*ù*⌉	
8) ^{d}EN.ZU	13) [...]	
9) ⌈*ma*⌉*-ta-at si-*[*m*]*aš-ki-im*.KI	14) [...] x x *si-maš-ki-im*.KI	

Ex. 2

10) [*ù*]-*ḫa-li-iq*
11) *ma-at za-ab-ša-li*.KI
12) *ma-at si-ig-*<*rí*>*-iš*.KI
13) *ma-at ni-bu-ul-ma-*<*at*>.KI
14) *ma-at a-lu-mi-da-tim*.KI
15) *ma-at ga-ar-ta*.KI
16) *ma-at ša-ti-lu*.KI
17) ŠU.NIGIN 6 *ma-*⸢*tá-tim*⸣
18) *a-za-ḫa-ar*.K[I]
19) *bu-ul-ma*.<KI>
20) *nu-šu-uš-ma-*<*ar*.KI>

Lacuna

Rev.

Lacuna

1′) [...] ⸢x⸣-*at* [...]
2′) *i-*⸢*na*⸣ [...] x *ù* ⸢x⸣ [...]
3′) *ù-ḫa-l*[*i-i*]*q* ⸢x⸣

4′) *in-*⸢*da-sú*⸣ [*ni-iš* ...]
5′) *ù ni-iš* [...]
6′) *a-na na-*[ʾ*à-ši-im*]
7′) SA.DÚ [...]
8′) *ù* ⸢ᵈx⸣ [...]
9′) *ù* ⸢x x x⸣ [...]
10′) ᵈ⸢*en*(?)-*líl*(?)⸣ [...]
10′) ŠÁR.RA [...]
11′) *ù* ᵈ*nin-urta* [...]
11′) MAŠKIM [...]
12′) *in* ⸢*dam-qù-ti*⸣-[*im*]
13′) *i-na* [K]Ù.GI [...]
14′) *š*[*a iš*]-*lu*-[*lu*]
15′) ALAN-⸢*šu*⸣
15′) *i*[*b-ni-ma*]
16′) *a-na*
16′) ⸢ᵈ*en*⸣-[*líl*]
16′) [...]
17′) ⸢*a-na*⸣
17′) [*na*]-ʾ*à*-[*ši-šu*]
18′) ⸢*iš*(?)⸣-*ru*(?)-[*uk*]
19′) *ša ṭup-*⸢*pá-am*⸣
19′) [...]
20′) *ù* ⸢x⸣-[...]
21′) ᵈ*en-líl*
21′) ⸢*ù*⸣ [...]
22′) SUḪUŠ-*sú*
22′) ⸢*li*(?)⸣-[...]
23′) *ù* ŠE.NUMUN-*šu*
23′) ⸢*li-il*⸣-*qú-tá*

Colophon

1) MU.SAR.RA in-da-su
2) ÉNSI *za-ab-ša-li*.KI
3) ŠÀ É ᵈNIN.LÍL É.GU.LA

Ex. 1

15) *ù-ḫa-li-iq*
16) MA.⸢DA⸣-*za-ab-*⸢*ša*⸣-*li*.KI
17) [...]
18) [*ma-at ni-bu*]-⸢*ul-ma*⸣-*at*.⸢KI⸣
19) *ma-at a-lu-mi-*[*da-t*]*im*.KI
20) [*ma-at ga*]-*ar-*[*ta*.KI]
21) [*ma-a*]*t ša-*[*ti-l*]*u*.KI
22) Š[U].⸢NIGIN⸣ 6 MA.D[A]
23) *a-za-ha-ar*.[KI]
24) *bu-ul-*⸢*ma*⸣.KI
25) *nu-šu-uš-ma-ar*.KI
26) [*n*]*u-uš-g*[*a-n*]*e-*[*l*]*u-um*.KI
27) [*z*]*i-zi-ir-*[*t*]*um*.KI
28) [*a*]-⸢*ra-ḫi*⸣-[*ir*.KI]
29) [...]
30) ⸢x⸣ [...]
31) ⸢x⸣ [...]
32) [...]
33) [...]
34) [...]
35) [...]
36) [...]

rev. i

37) *i*[*n-da-sú* ...]
38) *ù* [...]
39) *a-na n*[*a-*ʾ*à-ši-im*]
40) SA.D[Ú-*e* ...]
41) *ù* ⸢ᵈ⸣ [...]
42) *ù* ⸢ᵈ(?)⸣[...]
43) ᵈ[...]
44) ŠÁR [...]
45) *ù* [ᵈ*nin-urta*]
46) ⸢MAŠKIM⸣ [...]
47) *in* [...] x [...]
48) *i-na* [KÙ.GI]
49) *ša i*[*š-lu-lu*]
50) ALAN-[*šu*]
51) *ib-ni-*[*ma*]
52) *a-na*
53) ᵈ*en-líl*
54) *be-lí-šu*
55) *a-na*
56) *na-*ʾ*à-ši-šu*
57) A.MU.NA.RU
58) *ša ṭup-pá-am*
59) *šu-a-ti*
60) *ù-ša-sà-ku*
61) ᵈ*en-líl*
62) [*ù*] ᵈNIN.LÍL-*tum*
63) ⸢SUḪUŠ⸣-*sú*
64) *li-sú-ḫa*
65) *ù* ŠE.NUMUN-*šu*
66) ⸢*li-il*⸣-*qú-*⸢*tá*⸣

Colophon

1) MU.SAR.RA
2) ÚR in-da-su
3) LUGAL-LÚ×KÁR

15–22) He destroyed the land Zabšali, the land Sig<ri>š, the land Nibulmat, the land Alumidatum, the land Garta, (and) the land Šatilu — altogether six lands.

23–25) Azaḫar, Bulma, Nušušmar,

26) [N]ušg[an]e[l]um,
27) [Z]izir[t]um,
28) [A]raḫir
29–36) Too broken for translation.

37–40) Indasu, *in order to save his* (*own*) *life and the life of* ... (fled to) the mountains.

41–47) Too broken for translation.

48–57) From the [g]old which he took as [bo]oty, he fashioned an image of himself [and] dedicated it to the god Enlil, his lord, for his (own) life.

58–66) As for the one who removes this inscription, may the gods Enlil and Ninlil tear out his foundations and destroy his progeny.

Colophon

Ex. 1: Inscription on the *flank* of Indasu, the king taken as captive.

Ex. 2: Inscription (on) Indasu, governor of Zabšali, which is in the temple of Ninlil, the "Old Temple."

Ex. 1

Caption 1
1) in-da-sú
2) ÉNSI
3) za-ab-ša-li.KI

Caption 1
1–3) Indasu, governor of Zabšali.

Colophon 1
1) MU.SAR.RA
2) ZAG.GA.NA

Colophon 1
1–2) Inscription on his shoulder.

Caption 2
1) ^{d}*šu*-^{d}EN.ZU
2) ki-ág-^{d}en-líl-lá
3) lugal ^{d}en-líl-le
4) ki-ág šà-ga-na
5) in-pà
6) lugal-kala-ga
7) lugal-uri$_{5}$.KI-ma
8) lugal-an-ub-da-límmu-ba

Caption 2
1–8) Šū-Sîn, beloved of the god Enlil, the king whom the god Enlil lovingly chose in his (own) heart, mighty king, king of Ur, king of the four quarters.

Colophon 2
1) MU.[SA]R.RA
2) ⸢MURGU x⸣-KI
3) LÚ in-da-sú
4) LUGAL-LÚ×KÁR
5) GÌR AN-ÚS-SA

Colophon 2
1–5) In[scr]iption *on the shoulder*, the "man" of Indasu, the king taken captive, with (Šū-Sîn's) foot trampling him.

Caption 3
1) ti-ti
2) ÉNSI
3) nu-šu-uš-ma-ar.KI

Caption 3
1–3) Titi, governor of Nušušmar.

Colophon 3
1) MU.SAR.RA
2) ZAG.ZI.DA.NA

Colophon 3
1–3) Inscription on his right shoulder.

Caption 4
1) s[a-a]m-ri
2) [EN]SI
3) [X]-⸢X⸣-li-[x].⸢KI⸣

Caption 4
1–3) S[a]mri, [gov]ernor of ... .

Colophon 4
1) [MU.S]AR.RA
2) GÌ[RI.N]A

Colophon 4
1–2) [Ins]cription on h[is] foo[t].

Caption 5
1) nu-[x]-li
2) ÉNSI
3) a-lu-⸢mi-id-da⸣-tim

Caption 5
1–3) Nu-[x]-li, governor of Alumidatum.

Colophon 5
1) MU.SAR.RA
2) GABA.[NA]

Colophon 5
1–2) Inscription [on his] chest.

Caption 6
1) bu-ni-⸢ir⸣-ni
2) É[N]SI
3) [s]i-ig-rí-iš.KI

Caption 6
1–3) Bunirni, go[ver]nor of [S]igriš.

Colophon 6
1) [M]U.SAR.RA
2) ZAG.GÙB.BU
3) EGER.RA.NA

Colophon 6
1–3) [In]scription on the left shoulder, behind him.

Caption 7
1) ba-ri-ḫi-za
2) ÉNSI
3) a-ra(?)-ḫi-ir.KI

Caption 7
1–3) Bariḫiza, governor of Araḫir.

Colophon 7
1) MU.SAR.RA
2) EGER.ZAG.GÙB.BU.NA

Colophon 7
1–2) Inscription behind his left shoulder.

Ex. 1

Caption 8

1) wa-bur-tum
2) [É]NSI
3) [lu(?)]-lu-bi-im.[KI]

Caption 8

1–3) Waburtum, [go]vernor of [Lul]lubum.

Colophon 8

1) M[U.SAR.R]A
2) ZAG.GÙB.BU.⌈NA⌉

Colophon 8

1–2) I[nscript]ion on his left shoulder.

Notation 1

1) 6 LÚ-ŠU-DU$_8$-A-ME-EŠ A-AB-SAR
2) 6 LÚ-EN-NU-UN-BI NU-UB-SAR

Notation 1

1–2) (Depictions of) six men taken captive, which are inscribed. (Depictions of) their six watchmen, which are not inscribed.

Caption 9

1) ne-ni-íb-zu
2) ÉNSI
3) zi-zi-ir-tum.KI

Caption 9

1–3) Nenibzu, governor of Zizirtum.

Colophon 9

1) MU.SAR.RA
2) EGER.ZI.DA.NA

Colophon 9

1–2) Inscription behind the right side.

Caption 10

1) ti-ru-⌈bi⌉-ú
2) ÉNSI
3) nu-uš-ga-ne-[l]u-um.KI

Caption 10

1–3) Tirubi'u, governor of Nušgane[l]um.

Colophon 10

1) [M]U.⌈SAR.RA⌉
2) [EG]ER.ZAG.⌈ZI⌉.DA.NI

Colophon 10

1–2) [In]scription [be]hind his right shoulder.

Caption 11

1) ⌈x⌉-am-ti
2) ÉNSI
3) ga-ar-ta.KI

Caption 11

1–3) ⌈x⌉-am-ti, governor of Garta.

Colophon 11

1) MU.SAR.RA
2) ZAG.SI.ZI.DA.NI

Colophon 11

1–2) Inscription (on) the top of his right shoulder.

Caption 12

1) dun-gá-at
2) [É]NSI
3) ni!-[bu-ul]-m[a-at.KI]

Caption 12

1–3) Dungat, [go]vernor of Ni[bul]m[at].

Colophon 12

1) MU.SAR.RA
2) [ZA]G.S[I.ZI.D]A.NI

Colophon 12

1–2) Inscription (on) the [t]o[p] of his [ri]ght] ... si]de.

Notation 2

1) [4 LÚ-ŠU-DU$_8$-A-ME]-EŠ [A-A]B-SAR
2) [4 LÚ-EN-N]U-UN-BI [NU-UB-SAR]
3) [IGI-NA] EGER-RA-NA
4) Z[I-D]A-⌈GÙB-BU⌉-NA
5) IR [...]
6) ⌈x⌉ [...]
7) ⌈x⌉ [...]
8) ⌈x⌉ [...]
9) [...]
10) [...] ⌈x⌉

Notation 2

1) [They a]re four captives; [they are] inscribed.
2) (They are) [(his) four wat]ch-men; [they are not inscribed].
3–4) [In front of him], behind him, on his ri[gh]t and left.
5–10) Too broken for translation.

Concluding Colophon

1) M[U.SA]R.RA
2) [LUG]AL-⌈LÚ×KÁR⌉-ME-EŠ
3) *ù* ⌈^{d}*šu*⌉-^{d}EN.ZU
4) [LÚ] in-da-su
5) [GÌ]R AN-ÚS-SA

Concluding colophon

1–5) In[scrip]tion on the [kin]gs taken captive (and) on Šū-Sîn, [who tra]mpled Indasu.

6

An Old Babylonian Sammeltafel copy of a votive inscription of Šū-Sîn mentions his campaign against Zabšali.

COMMENTARY

The tablet, which was found in excavations at Nippur, bears the museum number CBS 12694 and measures 30.5×20×6.5 cm. The Šū-Sîn inscription is found on col. i lines 1′–15′; the remainder of the tablet gives an inscription of Ur-Ninurta (see Frayne, RIME 4 p. 66 E4.1.6.2). The inscription was collated.

Poebel (PBS 4 p. 138) erroneously attributed this inscription to Ur-Ninurta. While no royal name is actually preserved in the extant text, scholars have agreed that it should be attributed to Šū-Sîn. The divine name is broken away at the beginning of the text. Since the other inscription on the Sammeltafel refers to the goddess Ninlil, it is not unlikely that this inscription was also dedicated to that goddess.

BIBLIOGRAPHY

1914 Poebel, PBS 5 no. 68 (copy)
1949 Falkenstein, ZA 49 p. 81 n. 3 (study)
1959–60 Edzard, AfO 19 pp. 2–3 n. 26 (partial edition)
1965 Sollberger, UET 8 p. 9 no. 37 (study)
1966 Falkenstein, BiOr 23 p. 166 no. 37 (study)
1971 Sollberger and Kupper, IRSA IIIA4g (translation)
1972 Pettinato, Mesopotamia 7 p. 63 n. 93 (edition)
1986 Kärki, KDDU pp. 131–32 Šusuen 21 (edition)
1991 Steible, NSBW 2 pp. 275–76 Šusuen A26 (edition)

TEXT

Lacuna
1′) [*šu*-^{d}EN.ZU]
2′) [lugal-kala]-ga
3′) [lugal-úri].KI!-ma
4′) [lug]al-an-ub-⌈da⌉-límmu-ba-ke$_4$
5′) u$_4$ ma-da-za-[a]b-ša-li.KI!
6′) ù ma-d[a-m]a-da-
7′) simaški(LÚ.SU).KI-ka
8′) mu-ḫul-a
9′) máš-gal
10′) gú-un an-ša-an.KI-na
11′) mu-un-túm-<ma>-na
12′) *tám-ši-lum*-bi
13′) mu-na-an-dím
14′) nam-ti-la-ni-šè
15′) a mu-na-ru

Lacuna
1′–4′) [Šū-Sîn], [migh]ty [king], [king of U]r, [ki]ng of the four quarters,

5′–8′) when he destroyed the land of Za[b]šali and the lands of Simaški,

9′–13′) fashioned for her(?) an image of a great goat — tribute of Anšan which had been brought to him.

14′–15′) He dedicated it for his (own) life.

7

Šū-Sîn's "Statue Inscription 3" is known from an Old Babylonian tablet copy (which also gives the texts of E3/2.1.4.3 and E3/2.1.4.5) and from the original statue base.

CATALOGUE

Ex.	Museum number	Excavation number	Nippur provenance	Dimensions (cm)	Tablet lines preserved	Text lines preserved	cpn
1	BT 4 (frgm. 1)+ HS 2009(frgm. 2)+HS 2985 (frgm. 3)	—	—	23×17	"Shoulder Inscription" rev. v 25–31 rev. vi 1–3 Colophon 1 rev. vi 4–6 "Socle Inscription" rev. iv 13–34 rev. v 1–21 Colophon 2 rev. v 22–24	"Shoulder Inscription" 1–10 Colophon 1 1–3 "Socle Inscription" 1–43 Colophon 2 1–3	c
2	?	6 N 351	Inanna temple, locus SB 53, reused as a door socket in the main gate of the Parthian temple (L II)	Original dia. ca. 63	"Socle Inscription" 1–2, 11–19, 20–22	"Socle Inscription" 1–2, 11–19, 20–22	p

COMMENTARY

Here we have given first the "Shoulder Inscription" followed by the "Socle Inscription." The reverse order is actually found on the tablet copy. Ex. 2 is the base of a diorite statue. Presumably the "Shoulder Inscription" was incised on a part of the statue that is now broken away.

For the term *ma-la-kum*$_{x}$ (GÚM) of Socle Inscription line 5 (which is to be normalized either as *malākum/mālakum/ malāqum* or *mālaqum*, since *parasu[m]* is not found as a nominal formation in Akkadian), see the comments of Charpin, Le clergé d'Ur p. 323, where he notes:

> *malakum* est compris comme un morceau de viande par le *CAD* ("a cut of meat", M/1 p. 153b). De façon plus précis, J.-M. Durand a pu montrer sur la base de *ARMT* XII 206 qu'un mouton était divisé en 10 *malaku* (*ARMT* XXI, p. 67).

BIBLIOGRAPHY

1959–60 Edzard, AfO 19 pp. 14, 26–27, and pl. 2 (ex. 1, frgm. 2, photo, copy, edition)

1962 Hallo, HUCA 33 p. 39 Šu-Sin 20i (ex. 1, frgm. 2, study)

1989 Civil, in Studies Sjöberg pp. 60–61 and 64 (ex. 2, photo, edition)

1989 Kutscher, Brockmon Tablets pp. 87–89, 92–93, 97–98, 123, and 127 (ex. 1, copy, edition); p. 115 (ex. 1, frgm. 1, photo)

1991 Braun-Holzinger, Weihgaben p. 275 St 156, p. 288 fig. 4 (ex. 2, drawing, study)

TEXT

Shoulder inscription
1) ^{d}*šu*-^{d}EN.ZU
2) ki-ág-^{d}en-⸢líl⸣-lá
3) lugal ^{d}en-líl-le
4) šà-ga-na
5) in-pà

Shoulder Inscription
1–5) Šū-Sîn, beloved of the god Enlil, the king whom the god Enlil chose in his (own) heart,

6) lugal-kala-⌜ga⌝
7) lu[gal]-ú[ri].KI-⌜ma⌝
8) lugal-an-ub-da-límmu-ba

6–8) mighty king, ki[ng] of U[r], king of the four quarters,

9) nam-ti-la-ni-šè
10) a mu-n[a-ru]

9–10) for his (own) life, ded[icated] (this statue).

Colophon 1
1) mu-sar-ra
2) zag-zi-da-ni
3) alan-na$_4$

Colophon 1
1–3) Inscription on the right shoulder of a stone statue.

Socle inscription
1) 2 sìla ninda
2) 2 sìla làl
3) 1 sìla kurun
4) 1 sìla kaš
5) 1 *ma-la-kum*$_x$(GÚM) udu
6) [nì-d]ab$_5$ itu-da-ka
7) [GI]Š.banšur
8) ^{d}en-líl
9) lugal-[gá-ta]
10) ⌜1⌝ gín ⌜x (x)⌝
11) 1 sìla ì-du$_{10}$-ga
12) nì-dab$_5$ itu-da-ka
13) é-^{d}nin-líl
14) nin-gá-t[a]

Socle inscription
1–14) Two *sila* of bread, two *sila* of date-syrup, one *sila* of wine, one *sila* of beer, one cut of mutton, the monthly [assi]gnment (for) the table of the god Enlil, [my] lord, (and) one shekel of [...], one *sila* of good oil, the monthly assignment (for) the temple of the goddess Ninlil, my lady,

15) ^{d}*šu*-^{d}EN.ZU
16) ki-ág-^{d}en-líl-lá
17) lugal ^{d}en-líl-le
18) ki-ág šà-ga-na
19) in-pà
20) lugal-kala-ga

15–20) Šū-Sîn, beloved of the god Enlil, the king whom the god Enlil lovingly chose in his (own) heart, mighty king,

21) lugal-úri.KI-ma
22) lu[ga]l-an-ub-[da-límmu-ba]-ke$_4$

21–22) king of Ur, ki[ng] of the [four] quarters,

23) ì-ba

23) made as a donation.

24) lú u$_4$-na-me
25) nì-⌜dab$_5$⌝-e
26) ì-⌜ku$_5$⌝-re$_6$-[a]

24–26) (As for) the one who in the future *cuts off* the provisions,

27) lú-bi
28) lugal ḫé-a
29) en ḫé-a
30) énsi ḫé-a
31) sanga ḫé-a
32) gudu$_4$ máš-e pà-da ⌜ḫé-a⌝

27–32) that man, whether he be king, *en* priest, governor, *sanga* priest, or an anointed priest chosen by oracular means,

33) lú-ba
34) ^{d}en-líl
35) ^{d}nin-líl-e
36) nam ḫa-ba-da-kuru$_5$-ne

33–36) that man — may the god Enlil and the goddess Ninlil curse him.

37) DUMU.NITA na-an-ni-TUK.TUK-ne
38) mu-ni kalam-ma na-an-ni-gá-gá-ne

37–38) May they cause him to get no male heir; may they see that he has no descendant in the land.

39) lú inim (Text: SAG)-bi
40) nu-ub-da-ab-kúr-r[e-a]
41) igi-^{d}e[n-l]íl
42) ^{d}ni[n-l]íl-lá-ka
43) ḫé-en-sa$_6$

39–43) As for the one who does not alter its (the statue's) words, may he find favour in the eyes of the gods E[nl]il and Ni[nl]il.

Colophon
1) mu-sar-ra
2) ki-gal ^{d}[*šu*-^{d}EN].ZU
3) alan-na$_4$-kam

Colophon
1–3) Inscription on the socle of [Šū-S]in. Belonging to a stone statue.

8

An inscription found on col. ix (= rev. ii) of the large Sammeltafel of Šū-Sîn inscriptions published by Civil and edited as E3/2.1.4.1 in this volume commemorates the fashioning of a lofty stele (na-rú-a-maḫ) in Nippur, probably for the god Enlil. As noted, the deed provided the name for ŠS 6.

CATALOGUE

Ex.	Museum number	Tablet lines preserved	Text lines preserved	cpn
1	UM 29-15-556+UM 29-16-611+N 3152+N 3180+ N 4240+N 4241+Ni 4394+N 5144+N 6435+N 6718	ix 5–17	ix 5–17	c

COMMENTARY

The line count follows that established by Civil in his *editio princeps*. Very little of this inscription is preserved. Lines 17–19 are restored from the partial parallel provided by E3/2.1.4.9 xiii 17–20.

BIBLIOGRAPHY

1962 Hallo, HUCA 33 p. 39 Šu-Sin 20ii (study)
1967 Civil, JCS 21 pp. 24–38 (copy, edition)
1986 Kärki, KDDU pp. 122 and 127 Šusuen 20b (edition)

TEXT

Col. ix
1–4) Lacuna
5) ⸢u_4-ul un-ki-gar-ra-ta⸣
6) ⸢na-rú-a-maḫ⸣
7–10) Illegible traces
11) [lugal-n]a-me
12) nu-[mu-na]-an-dím

---

13) ^{d}*šu*-^{d}EN.ZU
14) lugal-kala-ga
15) lugal-uri_5.KI-m[a]
16) lugal-an-u[b-da-límmu-ba]
17) [^{d}en-líl]
18) [lugal-a-ni-ir]
19) [mu-na-dím]
Lacuna

ix 1–4) Lacuna
ix 5–6) Since the ancient time when the people were (first) established, a lofty stele
ix 7–10) Too broken for translation
ix 11–12) [n]o [king] built [for him (Enlil[?])].

---

ix 13–19) (But) Šū-Sîn, mighty king, king of Ur, king of the [four] qua[rters, fashioned it for the god Enlil, his lord]
Lacuna

9

An inscription found on cols. x–xiv (= rev. iii–vii) of the Sammeltafel of Šū-Sîn inscriptions published by Civil and edited as E3/2.1.4.1 in this volume celebrates the king's fashioning of Enlil and Ninlil's cult boat. As noted, the event provided the name for ŠS 8.

CATALOGUE

Ex.	Museum number	Tablet lines preserved	Text lines preserved	cpn
1	UM 29-15-556+UM 29-16-611+N 3152+ N 3180+N 4240+N 4241+Ni 4394+N 5144+ N 6435+N 6718	x 3–18 xi 1–18, 23–34 xii 4–19, 22–32 xiii 4–20 xiv 1–14	x 3–18 xi 1–18, 23–34 xii 4–19, 22–32 xiii 4–20 xiv 1–14	c
2	Ni 9662	rev. i′ 1′–7′ rev. ii′ 1′–3′ rev. ii′ 4′–5′	Unplaced Concluding formula Colophon	n

COMMENTARY

The line count follows the *editio princeps* of Civil.

N 6435 was identified as a fragment of ex. 1 by S. Tinney, who kindly communicated a transliteration of the piece to the author. It joins ex. 1 in col. xiv. Ex. 2 concludes with a colophon indicating both the type of cult object which bore this inscription and the place where it stood. The object in question was read GIŠ.alan!? "statue" by Civil (JCS 21 [1967] p. 35). The sign, as copied, does not seem to be an alan sign; while it does share some features of a balag sign, the reading of the sign is uncertain.

Since there is no overlap between exs. 1 and 2, a score has not been provided for this inscription.

BIBLIOGRAPHY

1959–60 Edzard, AfO 19 pp. 28–29 and pl. 2 (ex. 2, copy, edition)
1967 Civil, JCS 21 pp. 24–38 (ex. 1, copy; exs. 1–2, edition)
1986 Kärki, KDDU pp. 122–24 and 127–29 Šusuen 20b (exs. 1–2, edition)
1993 Sallaberger, Kalender 1 p. 142 (study)

TEXT

Col. x	
1–2) Lacuna	x 1–2) Lacuna
3) ⌜^{d}⌝[nin-líl] 4) nin-dingir-re-n[e] 5) nin-a-ni-i[r]	x 3–5) For the goddess [Ninlil], queen of the gods, his lady,
6) ^{d}*šu*-^{d}EN.Z[U] 7) ki-⌜ág⌝- 8) ^{d}en-líl-[lá] 9) lugal-^{d}en-líl-[le] 10) šà-ga-na ⌜in-pà⌝-[(da)]	x 6–10) Šū-Sîn, beloved of the god Enlil, the king whom the god Enlil lovingly chose in his (own) heart
11) ⌜sipa⌝-kalam-ma 12) lugal-an-ub-da-límmu-⌜ba-šè⌝	x 11–12) as shepherd of the land (and) king for the four quarters,
13) u$_{4}$ ^{d}en-líl-le 14) an-úr-ta 15) an-pa-aš 16) [s]ig-ta IGI.NIM-šè 17) an-ki-nígin-na	x 13–18) when the god Enlil, from the horizon to the zenith, from the [lo]wlands to the highlands, the whole universe (of) people (who) are taken care of (by the god) ...

18) [u]n-sag sè-[ga]
19–48) Lacuna
Col. xi
1) [n]am-gal ḫúl-[la-da]
2) nin ki-ág-gá-[ni]
3) ^{d}nin-líl-da
4) má-gur$_{8}$-maḫ
5) íd-maḫ-e ḫé-du$_{7}$
6) kar-AB-e
7) kar-^{d}nin-líl-lá-kam
8) men-dalla-bi
9) [ki]-tuš-tum-ma-al.KI
10) ⸢^{d}⸣nin-líl-lá-kam
11) ⸢x x⸣ [x] x⸣-ka
12) lugal-[b]i
13) ^{d}en-líl-[le]
14) nin-[bi]
15) ^{d}nin-l[íl-le]
16) pa-bi mu-u[n-è-eš]
17) gissu dag[al ...]
18) ⸢i$_{7}$-da⸣ [...]
19–22) Lacuna
23) ⸢x⸣
24) AN [...]
25) kin-gal [...]
26) mi-ni-in-[...]
27) NA$_{4}$.nír-sag-kal
28) NA$_{4}$.gug-gi-rin
29) NA$_{4}$.za-gìn-sù-ág
30) šu-gal ba-ni-in-du$_{7}$
31) GIŠ.gizzal$_{x}$(BI.GIŠ)
32) GIŠ.gi-m[uš]
33) GIŠ.⸢zi⸣-[gan]
34) ⸢GIŠ⸣.[šu-kár]
35–48) Lacuna
Within this lacuna ex. 2, rev. i′ is likely to be placed; it is edited immediately below
Lacuna
1′) [...]
2′) [...]
3′) x ⸢^{d}⸣ x [...]
4′) má-gur$_{8}$ [...]
5′) zà [...]
6′) UD x [...]
7′) x [...]
Lacuna
Col. xii
1–3) Lacuna
4) túl-dagal [x x x]
5) GIŠ.má-gur$_{8}$ [x x x]
6) im-ma-ni-i[n-ši-gá]l
7) giš-gi-tum-ma-al.KI
8) ^{d}en-líl-lá-šè
9) ki-šà-ḫúl-la-^{d}nin-líl-⸢lá⸣-šè
10) ^{d}en-líl ^{d}nin-líl-da
11) mu-dì-ni-in-u$_{5}$
12) šìr-kù nam-šub
13) mu-na-an-tuku
14) NAR.É.BALAG [nì]-du$_{10}$-ge
15) si mu-na-ab-sá

x 19–48) Lacuna

xi 1–3) rejoicing in the great joy over the queen, the goddess Ninlil.

xi 4–10) The great *magur* boat (is) fit for the largest rivers; the AB-e quay is the quay of the goddess Ninlil; its bright crown is the Tummal [dw]elling of the goddess Ninlil.

xi 11–16) The ..., [it]s king, the god Enlil, (and) [its] queen, the goddess Ninl[il], made sh[ine forth],

xi 17–18) (in) its br[oad] shadow, on the river

xi 19–22) Lacuna
xi 23–24) Too broken for translation.

xi 25–26) [did] a great work ...

xi 27–30) He decorated it perfectly with precious (and) selected *nir*-stone, red carnelian, (and) radiant lapis-lazuli.

xi 31) The oars,
xi 32) the puntin[g poles],
xi 33) the rud[der],
xi 34) the [equipment],
xi 35–48) Lacuna

Lacuna
1′–7′) ..., the *magur* boat, ...
Lacuna

xii 1–3) Lacuna
xii 4–6) He placed the *magur* boat ... [in] the wide basin ...

xii 7–11) Toward the canebrake of the god Enlil's Tummal, toward the goddess Ninlil's place of joy, the god Enlil, together with the goddess Ninlil, sailed.

xii 12–13) He had sacred songs (and) incantations sung to him.
xii 14–15) For him, the *tigi* harp, the sweet-toned instrument, was correctly tuned.

16) i_7-bi
17) i_7 nin mu-túm
18) zal-le mu-p[à-d]a
19) un-e ⸢x x⸣ [x]
20–21) Lacuna
22) [má-gur_8]-bi
23) [tum-m]a-al-e
24) [im-ma]-ti-a-ta
25) [^{d}]nin-líl
26) [nin me]-gal-gal-la-ra
27) [x]-ma-ni kù-kù-ga-àm
28) [x] ba-an-daḫ
29) [á-á]g-gá-ni gal-gal-la-àm
30) [im-mi]-ni-in-tab-tab
31) [...]-maḫ-àm
32) [...-i]n-gar

Col. xiii

1–3) Lacuna
4) nam-ti-la-ni-šè
5) ⸢a⸣ mu-ne-ru
6) má-gur ur_5-gin_7 dib-ba
7) u_4-na-me
8) lugal-na-me
9) ^{d}en-líl
10) ^{d}nin-líl-ra
11) ⸢nu⸣-[mu-ne]-dím
12) ^{d}*šu*-^{d}EN.ZU
13) [lu]gal-kala-ga
14) lugal-úri.KI-ma
15) [lu]gal-an-ub-da-
16) límmu-ba-ke_4
17) [^{d}e]n-líl
18) [lugal]-a-ni-ir
19) [^{d}ni]n-líl
20) [nin-a-n]i-ir
21–48) Lacuna

Col. xiv

1) GIŠ.[$gizzal_x$]
2) GIŠ.gi-m[uš]
3) GIŠ.zi-gan
4) GIŠ.šu-kár
5) nì-dím-dím-ma-mu
6) ib-zi-[i]r-zi-re-a
7) é-nì-ga-ra
8) ì-íb-ku_4-ku_4-[a]
9) azak-ka
10) [k]i(?)-gar im-ma-ni-íb-g[ar]
11) [m]á-gur_8-ma[ḫ]
12) [^{d}e]n-líl
13) [^{d}ni]n-líl-r[a]
14) u_4 ⸢du_8⸣-du_8-a
15) íb-pà [...]
16) GIŠ.[...]
17) GIŠ.šu-[kár]
18) nì-dím-dím-m[a-mu]
19) má-kúr-ra [...]
20) [x] x ⸢x⸣ ⸢má⸣ [...]
Lacuna

xii 16–18) The canal was called nin-mu-túm-zal-le.

xii 19) The people ...

xii 20–21) Lacuna

xii 22–32) After its [boat] arrived at Tummal, for Ninlil, the [lady] of the great [*mes*], whose ... are pure, ... were added, whose [com]mands are great, she clasped ... which was lofty ... was set.

xiii 1–3) Lacuna

xiii 4–5) he (Šū-Sîn[?]) offered to them for his own life.

xiii 6–11) No king had ever made a *magur* boat sailing so (well) for the god Enlil (and) the goddess Ninlil,

xiii 12–16) (but) Šū-Sîn, mighty king, king of Ur, king of the four quarters,

xiii 17–18) [fashioned it] for the [god E]nlil, his [king],

xiii 19–20) (and) for [the goddess Ni]nlil, [h]is [queen],

xiii 21–48) Lacuna

xiv 1–10) (the one who) breaks the [oars], the puntin[g poles], the rudder, the equipment, the things I have made, (and) puts them in (his) storehouse, (or) places them in a forbidden place,

xiv 11–20) when he *calls* the lof[ty] [*m*]*agur* boat for caulking on behalf of the [god E]nlil (and) the [goddess Ni]nlil (and) he ... its ... and equipment which I made, for a different boat, ...

Lacuna

Concluding formula (ex. 2 only)
Lacuna
1′) [xxx] x x [...]
2′) [^{d}ni]n-urta ur-sa[g-gal-^{d}en-líl-lá]
3′) [maš]kim-bi ḫ[é-a]

Concluding formula
Lacuna
xiv 1′–3′) ..., may [the god Ni]nurta, [great] warr[ior of the god Enlil], ser[ve] as its (the curse's) [bail]iff.

Colophon (ex. 2 only)
1–2) [m]u-sar-ra GIŠ.x(?) mu-sar-⌜ra má⌝-[gur$_8$] ⌜^{d}⌝en-líl ^{d}nin-líl-⌜ka⌝-kam

Colophon
1–2) [In]scription (on) a ... Inscription of the *ma*[*gur*] boat of [the god] Enlil and the goddess Ninlil.

10

A seven-line brick inscription of Šū-Sîn was found in excavations at Susa.

CATALOGUE A

Ex.	Museum number	Excavation number	Dimensions (cm)
1	Sb 14730	6082	20×18.5×8
2	Sb 14731	6081	40×19×30
3	Sb 14732	—	38.5×15.5×9.5
4	Sb 14733	—	39.5×19×19
5	Sb 14734	—	39.5×8.5×13
6	Sb 14735	—	20×18.5×8
7	Sb 14736	3157	21×19×9
8	Sb 14737	9846	11×16×9
9	Sb 14738	—	9.6×16×6.5
10	Sb 14739	—	18×16.5×8.5
11	Sb 14740	—	9.5×12×6
12	Sb 14741	1086	23×12×8.5
13	Sb 14742	—	18×9.5×24
14	Sb 14743	—	14.5×9×9
15	Sb 14744	—	11×6×8.5
16	Sb 14745	—	21.5×9×16

CATALOGUE B

Ex.	Publication	Lines preserved	cpn
A	MDP 2 pl. 13 no. 1	1–5	p
B	MDP 2 pl. 13 no. 6	1–2	p
C	MDP 4 pl. 1 no. 5	1–3	p
D	MDP 4 pl. 18 no. 1	2–7	p
E	MDP 10 pl. 6 no. 1	1–7	p

COMMENTARY

The text is arranged in one column. Catalogue A provides the information on the Šū-Sîn bricks according to the records in the Louvre; this material was kindly provided by A. Echalier and B. André-Salvini. The bricks themselves were not collated. Catalogue B gives the data on the published exemplars. As yet, it has not been possible to match up the catalogued pieces to their published counterparts.

BIBLIOGRAPHY

1900 Scheil, MDP 2 p. 56 and pl. 13 nos. 1 (ex. A, photo, edition); p. 82 and pl. 13 no. 6 (ex. B, photo, edition)
1902 Scheil, MDP 4 p. 8, pl. 1 no. 5, and pl. 18 no. 1 (exs. C–D, photo, conflated edition)
1907 Thureau-Dangin, SAK pp. 200–201 Gimil-sin a (exs. C–D, edition)
1908 Scheil, MDP 10 p. 12 and pl. 6 no. 1 (ex. E, photo, edition)
1929 Barton, RISA pp. 292–93 Gimil-Sin 1 (exs. C–E, edition)
1959–60 Borger, AfO 19 p. 163 (exs. A–C, study)
1961 Gelb, MAD 2[2] p. 16 § 1a (study)
1962 Hallo, HUCA 33 p. 37 Šu-Sin 1 (ex. B, study); Šu-Sin 2 (exs. A, C–E, study)
1971 Sollberger and Kupper, IRSA IIIA4a (exs. A–C, translation)
1986 Kärki, KDDU p. 91 Šusuen 2 (exs. A–C, edition)
1990 Gelb and Kienast, Königsinschriften p. 343 Ur 7 (ex. E, edition)
1991 Steible, NSBW 2 p. 253 Šūsuen 1–2 (exs. A–E, edition)

TEXT

1) ^{d}*šu*-^{d}EN.ZU
2) *na-ra-am*-^{d}*en-líl*
3) *šar-ru-um*
4) *dan-núm*
5) *šar* URI$_5$.KI
6) *ù šar ki-ib-ra-tim*
7) *ar-ba-im*

1–7) Šū-Sîn, beloved of the god Enlil, mighty king, king of Ur, and king of the four quarters.

11

A fifteen-line brick inscription from Adab records the Adab governor Ḫabaluge's building of a temple for the deified Šū-Sîn.

COMMENTARY

The brick was found in excavations by Banks at Bismāyā; its exact findspot is unknown. The piece measures 31.7×32.2×5.2 cm and was given the museum number A 1134 (Chicago). The text is arranged in one column. The inscription was collated.

BIBLIOGRAPHY

1930 Luckenbill, Adab no. 43 (copy)
1962 Hallo, HUCA 33 p. 37 Šu-Sin 3 (study)
1966 Falkenstein, Inschriften Gudeas p. 4 n. 9 (study)
1971 Sollberger and Kupper, IRSA IIIC1b (translation)
1986 Kärki, KDDU p. 91 Šusuen 3 (edition)
1991 Steible, NSBW 2 p. 254 Šūsuen 3 (edition)

TEXT

1) ^{d}*šu*-^{d}EN.ZU
2) ki-ág-^{d}en-líl-lá
3) lugal ^{d}en-líl-le
4) ki-ág šà-ga-na
5) in-pà
6) lugal-kala-ga
7) lugal-uri$_5$.KI-ma
8) lugal-an-ub-da-límmu-ba
9) dingir-ki-ág-gá-a-ni

1–9) Šū-Sîn, beloved of the god Enlil, the king whom the god Enlil lovingly chose in his (own) heart, mighty king, king of Ur, king of the four quarters, his beloved god,

10) ḫa-ba(Text: ZU)-lu₅-gé   10–13) Ḫabaluge, governor of Adab, his servant,
11) énsi
12) adab.KI-
13) ìr-da-né
14) é-ki-ág-gá-a-ni   14–15) built for him his beloved temple.
15) mu-na-dù

12

An eighteen-line inscription found on two door sockets records the Ešnunna
governor Itūrīia's construction of a temple dedicated to the deified Šū-Sîn.

CATALOGUE

Ex.	Museum number	Excavation number	Ešnunna provenance	Lines preserved	cpn
1	IM —	As 31-246	Doorway to the cella of the "Gimilsin Temple" 30:18	1–18	n
2	A 8164 (Chicago)	As 31-792	Doorway to the cella of the "Gimilsin Temple" 30:18	1–18	c

COMMENTARY

The text is arranged in one column around the top of the door socket.

For a plan of Šū-Sîn's temple at Ešnunna (conventionally designated by the excavators as the "Gimilsin temple"), see Jacobsen, Gimilsin Temple pl. 12.

BIBLIOGRAPHY

1940 Jacobsen, Gimilsin Temple pp. 134–35 and pl. 13 no. 1 (copy, edition)
1952 Archaeology 5 p. 169 (photo)
1962 Hallo, HUCA 33 p. 38 Šu-Sin 12 (study)
1971 Sollberger and Kupper, IRSA IIID1a (translation)
1986 Kärki, KDDU pp. 97–98 Šusuen 12 (edition)
1991 Steible, NSBW 2 pp. 264–65 Šūsuen 12 (edition)

TEXT

1) šu-ᵈEN.ZU   1–12) Šū-Sîn, the one called by name by the god An,
2) mu-pà-da-   beloved of the god Enlil, the king whom the god Enlil
3) an-na   chose in his pure heart for the shepherdship of the
4) ki-ág-ᵈen-líl-lá   land and of the four quarters, mighty king, king of Ur,
5) lugal ᵈen-líl-le   king of the four quarters, his beloved god,
6) šà-kù-ge pà-da
7) nam-sipa-kalam-ma
8) ù an-ub-da-límmu-ba-šè
9) lugal-kala-ga
10) lugal-uri₅.KI-ma
11) lugal-an-ub-da-límmu-ba
12) dingir-ra-ni-ir
13) i-tu-ri-a   13–16) Itūrīia, governor of Ešnunna, his servant,
14) énsi-

15) áš-nun-na.KI-ka
16) ir_{11}-da-né-e
17) é-a-ni
18) mu-na-an-dù

17–18) built his temple for him.

13

A twenty-nine-line inscription incised on four door sockets found in excavations at Girsu records the governor Ir-Nanna's construction of a temple dedicated to the deified Šū-Sîn.

CATALOGUE

Ex.	Museum number	Excavation number	Dimensions (cm)	Lines preserved	Line arrangement
1	AO 3298 a/b	Excavations of de Sarzec 1898	46 dia. 22 high	1–29	col. i: lines 1–19 col. ii: lines 20–29
2	AO 3298 a/g	Excavations of de Sarzec 1900	—	1–14	—
3	—	Excavations of Cros 1903	18×23×35	1–29	col. i: lines 1–16 col. ii: lines 17–29
4	—	Excavations of Cros 1904	25×33×35	1–29	—

COMMENTARY

The master text is ex. 3. These black stone door sockets were found in two sets (exs. 1–2 and 3–4). Exs. 3–4 were found on either side of a doorway in the area of the Tell-des-Tablets at Girsu. For the location, see Cros, Tello p. 229 Plan F, area N. Exs. 1–2, found earlier by de Sarzec, presumably came from the same general area; apparently it was the locus of a temple at Girsu dedicated to the deified Šū-Sîn. Exs. 3–4 could not be located in the Louvre; perhaps they are in Istanbul. According to Cros (Tello p. 238), the text of ex. 4 is an exact duplicate to that of ex. 3. The texts were entered in the scores from the published copies.

BIBLIOGRAPHY

1902 Thureau-Dangin, RA 5 pp. 99–102 (ex. 1, copy, edition; ex. 2, study)
1907 Thureau-Dangin, RA 6 pp. 67–68 (ex. 3, copy, study)
1907 Thureau-Dangin, SAK pp. 148–51 Arad-nanna(r) a (exs. 1, 3, edition)
1910 Cros, in Cros, Tello pp. 237–38 (exs. 3–4, provenance)
1910 Thureau-Dangin, in Cros, Tello pp. 56–58 (ex. 3, copy, edition; ex. 4, study)
1929 Barton, RISA pp. 268–69 Arad-nannar (exs. 1, 3, conflated edition)
1948 Parrot, Tello p. 227 (exs. 1, 3, translation, study)
1962 Hallo, HUCA 33 p. 38 Šu-Sin 13 (exs. 1–4, study)
1971 Sollberger and Kupper, IRSA IIIB5a (exs. 1, 3, translation)
1986 Kärki, KDDU pp. 98–99 Šusuen 13 (exs. 1, 3, edition)
1991 Steible, NSBW 2 pp. 265–68 Šūsuen 13 (exs. 1, 3, edition)

TEXT

1) ^{d}*šu*-^{d}EN.ZU
2) ki-ág-^{d}en-líl-lá
3) lugal ^{d}en-líl-le
4) ki-ág šà-ga-na
5) in-pà

1–5) Šū-Sîn, beloved of the god Enlil, the king whom the god Enlil lovingly chose in his (own) heart,

Variant for E3/2.1.4.13:
2.3 ki-ág-^{d}en-líl-lá(Text: ME).

6) lugal-kala-ga	6) mighty king,
7) lugal-uri$_5$.KI-ma	7–9) king of Ur, king of the four quarters, his lord,
8) lugal-an-ub-da-límmu-ba	
9) lugal-a-ni-ir	
10) ir$_{11}$-^{d}nanna	10–13) Ir-Nanna, grand-vizier, governor of Lagaš,
11) sukkal-maḫ	
12) énsi-	
13) lagaš.KI-ke$_4$	
14) sanga-^{d}en-ki-ka	14–18) *sanga* priest of the god Enki, military governor of Ušar-Garšana, general of Bašime, governor of Sabum and the land of Gutebum,
15) GÌR.NÍTA *ú-ṣa-ar-gar-ša-na*.KI	
16) GÌR.NÍTA ba-šim-e.KI	
17) énsi-sa-bu-um.KI	
18) ù ma-da-gu-te-bu-um.KI.-ma	
19) GÌR.NÍTA *dì-ma-at*-^{d}en-líl-lá	19–27) general of Dimat-Enlila, governor of Āl-Šū-Sîn, general of Urbillum, governor of Ḫam(a)zi and Karaḫar, general of NI.ḪI, general of Simaški and the land of Karda, his servant,
20) énsi-*a-al*-^{d}*šu*-^{d}EN.ZU	
21) GÌR.NÍTA ur-bí-lum.KI	
22) énsi-ḫa-àm-zí.KI	
23) ù kára(Text: GÁNA)-ḫar.KI	
24) ⌜GÌR.NÍTA⌝ NI.ḪI.KI	
25) GÌR.NÍTA simaški(LÚ.SU).KI	
26) ù ⌜ma⌝-da-kar-da.KI-ka	
27) ir$_{11}$-da-a-né	
28) é-gír-su-KI-ka-ni	28–29) built for him his Girsu temple.
29) mu-na-dù	

14

A fourteen-line inscription incised on a door socket found in excavations at Ur records the military governor [...]-kal-la's construction of a temple dedicated to the deified Šū-Sîn.

COMMENTARY

The door socket measures 41×35×11 cm. It was found in the Gipar-ku at Ur and given the excavation number U 6738, museum number CBS 16566. The text is arranged in one column. The inscription was collated.

Collation reveals that the lightly shaded signs in Gadd's copy in UET 1 are restorations. Line 9 is restored [dingir-ra]-ni-ir following E3/2.1.4.15. Another possibility would be [lugal-a]-ni-ir; both are found in Šū-Sîn's inscriptions. As far as can be determined, the general [x]-kal-la named in line 10 is otherwise unattested.

Variants for E3/2.1.4.13:
13.1 lagaš.KI-<ke$_4$>.
14.1 sanga-^{d}en-ki-<ka>.
16.3 GÌR.NÍTA ba-šim-e(Text: BUR).KI.
25.1 šimaški(LÚ.SU).<KI>.
26.1 kar-da-<KI>-ka.
27.1 ir$_{11}$-da-né.

BIBLIOGRAPHY

1928 Gadd, UET 1 no. 81 (copy, edition)
1929 Barton, RISA pp. 368–69 Gimil-Sin 4 (edition)
1962 Hallo, HUCA 33 p. 38 Šu-Sin 10 (study)
1968 Kärki, KDDU p. 96 Šusuen 10 (edition)
1991 Steible, NSBW 2 pp. 262–63 Šūsuen 10 (edition)

TEXT

1) ^{d}*šu*-^{d}EN.ZU
2) ⸢ki⸣-ág-^{d}en-líl-lá
3) [l]ugal-^{d}en-líl-le
4) ⸢ki⸣-ág šà-ga-na
5) in-pà
6) [l]ugal-kala-ga
7) [lu]gal-uri$_5$.KI-ma
8) [lug]al-an-ub-da-límmu-ba
9) [lugal-a]-ni-ir
10) [x]-kal-la
11) GÌR.NÍTA
12) ir$_{11}$-da-né
13) é-a-ni
14) mu-na-dù

1–5) For Šū-Sîn, beloved of the god Enlil, the [k]ing whom the god Enlil lovingly chose in his (own) heart,

6–7) mighty [k]ing, [k]ing of Ur,

8–9) [ki]ng of the four quarters, his [lord],

10–12) [x]-kal-la, general, his servant,

13–14) built his temple for him.

15

A sixteen-line inscription incised on six door sockets from Ur records the governor Lugal-magure's construction of a temple dedicated to the deified Šū-Sîn.

CATALOGUE

Ex.	Museum number	Excavation number	Registration number	Ur provenance	Dimensions (cm)	Lines preserved	cpn
1	VA 3302	—	—	—	49×37×22	1–16	c
2	IM 915	U 2673	—	LL, doorway to 5	—	1–16	p
3	BM 116761	U 1191	1924-9-20,22	PR, room 1	38×31×19	1–16	c
4	IM 1146	U 6335	—	Loose in soil of EH site (see Woolley, UE 6 p. 42)	31×15	11–16	p
5	IM 1027	U 3102	—	ES Nabonidus level	—	—	n
6	IM —	—	—	—	43×34×13	1–16	p

COMMENTARY

Ex. 1 was purchased from C. Homsy; it was seen by Scheil in Aleppo. Exs. 4 and 6 were last seen at the Nineveh dig house. All texts, as far as can be determined, were arranged in one column.

An Ur III archival text (Spar, Met. Mus. 1 no. 17 line 38) indicates that Lugal-magure was the son-in-law of Amar-Suena. For other references to Lugal-magure in archival sources, see A. Goetze, JCS 17 (1963) pp. 10–12 and Archi and Pomponio, Torino, commentary to text no. 226. He often appears with the title sukkal "vizier." According to a tablet from Ur (FLP 153; Sigrist, MVN 13 no. 17) he had died by xi IS 8; the text records (line 6) a disbursement "for the place of the throne of Lugal-magure" (ki GIŠ.gu-za ^{d}lugal-má-gur$_8$-re).

BIBLIOGRAPHY

1904 Scheil, RT 26 pp. 22–23 (ex. 1, edition)
1907 Messerschmidt, VAS 1 no. 27 (ex. 1, copy)
1907 Thureau-Dangin, SAK pp. 200–203 Gimil-sin c (ex. 1, edition)
1925 Woolley and Legrain, MJ 16 p. 293 (ex. 2, photo)
1928 Gadd, UET 1 p. xxiv (exs. 2–4, study)
1929 Barton, RISA pp. 294–95 Gimil-Sin 4 (ex. 1, edition)
1962 Hallo, HUCA 33 p. 38 Šu-Sin 11 (exs. 1–4, study)
1971 Sollberger and Kupper, IRSA IIIA4h (exs. 1–4, translation)
1986 Kärki, KDDU p. 97 Šusuen 11 (exs. 1–4, edition)
1986 Steible, NSBW 2 pp. 263–64 Šūsuen 11 (exs. 1–5, edition)

TEXT

1) ^{d}*šu*-^{d}EN.ZU
2) ki-ág-^{d}en-líl-lá
3) lugal ^{d}en-líl-le
4) ki-ág šà-ga-na
5) in-pà
6) lugal-kala-ga
7) lugal-uri$_5$.KI-ma
8) lugal-an-ub-da-límmu-ba
9) dingir-ra-ni-ir
10) lugal-má-gur$_8$-re
11) nu-bànda-en-nu-gá
12) énsi-
13) uri$_5$.KI-ma
14) ir$_{11}$-da-né
15) é-ki-ág-gá-ni
16) mu-na-an-dù

1–5) For Šū-Sîn, beloved of the god Enlil, the king whom the god Enlil lovingly chose in his (own) heart,

6–9) mighty king, king of Ur, king of the four quarters, his god,

10–14) Lugal-magure, lieutenant of the watch, governor of Ur, his servant,

15–16) built his beloved temple for him.

16

A thirteen-line inscription found on door sockets and stone blocks records Šū-Sîn's construction of the temple of the god Šara in Umma.

CATALOGUE

Ex.	Museum number	Registration number	Object	Dimensions (cm)	Lines preserved	cpn
1	BM 103353	1911-4-8, 43	Door socket	30×26×20	1–13	c
2	CBS 14550	—	Diorite door socket	31×23.5×10.5 Inscription: 16.1×5.5	1–13	c
3	O 279	—	Diorite door socket	20×27	1–13	n
4	YBC 2369	—	Grey diorite door socket	30×20×14	1–13	c
5	MEL 1924–2	—	Stone block(?)	18.4×10.6×4.6	4–13	n
6	BM 114396	1920-3-15, 7	Granite block	—	—	n

COMMENTARY

As far as can be determined, the text on these door sockets is arranged in one column.

BIBLIOGRAPHY

1912 King, CT 32 pl. 6 BM 103353 (ex. 1, copy)
1922 BM Guide, p. 85 no. 74 (ex. 5, study)
1924 Legrain, MJ 15 pp. 78–79 (ex. 2, photo, edition)
1925 Speleers, Recueil pp. 2 and 47 no. 11 (ex. 3, copy, edition)

1926 Legrain, PBS 15 no. 43 (ex. 2, copy, edition)
1929 Barton, RISA pp. 294–95 Gimil-Sin 3 (exs. 1–2, edition)
1937 Stephens, YOS 9 no. 117 (ex. 4, study)
1962 Hallo, HUCA 33 p. 38 Šu-Sin 8 (exs. 1–4, study)
1981 Grégoire, MVN 10 no. 23 (ex. 5, copy, study)
1986 Kärki, KDDU pp. 94–95 Šusuen 8 (exs. 1–4, edition)
1991 Steible, NSBW 2 pp. 259–60 Šūsuen 8 (exs. 1–5, edition)

TEXT

1) dšára
2) nir-gál-an-na
3) dumu-ki-ág-
4) dinanna
5) ad-da-ni-ir

1–5) For the god Šara, distinguished one of the god An, beloved son of the goddess Inanna, his father,

6) dšu-dEN.ZU
7) lugal-kala-ga
8) lugal-uri5.KI-ma
9) lugal-an-ub-da-límmu-ba-ke4

6–9) Šū-Sîn, mighty king, king of Ur, king of the four quarters,

10) é-šà-ge4-pà-da
11) é-ki-ág-gá-ni
12) nam-ti-la-ni-šè
13) mu-na-dù

10–13) built for him E-šage-pada, his beloved temple, for his (own) life.

17

A thirty-line inscription found on door sockets and stone blocks records Šū-Sîn's construction of the temple of the god Šara in Umma.

CATALOGUE

Ex.	Museum number	Registration number	Object	Dimensions (cm)	Lines preserved	Line arrangement	cpn
1	BM 103354	1911-4-8, 44	Portion of stone block	Block: 55×12.7 Inscription: 45×9.3	1–30	col. i: 1–15 col. ii: 16–30	c
2	YBC 2130	—	Door socket	26×61×19.5	1–30	col. i: 1–15 col. ii: 16–30	c
3	YBC 2129	—	Portion of stone block	31×27.2×4.8	1–30	—	c
4	Draper Collection, New York Public Library	—	?		1–30	—	n
5	EŞ 5856	—	Portion of stone block	53×13×3	1–30	One column	p
6	VA 3855	—	Door socket	42 in dia.	1–30	One column	c
7	HS 2011	—	Portion of stone block	Block: 47.5×15×5.8 Inscription: 42.2×10.7	1–29	One column	c
8	WHM 26.13.1	—	Door socket	42×40×19.5	1–30	col. i: 1–19 col. ii: 20–30	c

COMMENTARY

Information on ex. 8 is provided here through the kind permission of Dr. B. Bohen, Director of the World Heritage Museum, Urbana, Illinois. Its inscription was collated by G. Frame.

Variant for E3/2.1.3.16:
10. 3 é-šà-ge-pà-da.

BIBLIOGRAPHY

1912 King, CT 32 pl. 6 BM 103354 (ex. 1, copy)
1912–13 Prince, AJSL 29 pp. 284–87 (ex. 1, study)
1914 Förtsch, MVAG 19/1 pp. 79–80 n. 2 (ex. 1, edition)
1914 Förtsch, OLZ 17 col. 57 (ex. 1, edition)
1914–15 Unger, ZA 29 pp. 179–81 and pl. 1 (ex. 5, photo, edition)
1915 Clay, YOS 1 pp. 16–17 and pl. 12 no. 20 (exs. 2–4, study; ex. 2, copy)
1915 Förtsch, OLZ 18 cols. 201–203 (exs. 1, 5, study)
1929 Barton, RISA pp. 294–95 Gimil-Sin 5 (exs. 2, 5, edition);

pp. 294–97 Gimil-Sin 7 (ex. 1, edition)
1957 Meyer, FuB 1 p. 38 (ex. 6, photo)
1962 Hallo, HUCA 33 p. 38 Šu-Sin 9 (exs. 1–5, study)
1969 Oelsner, WZJ 18 p. 53 no. 21 (ex. 7, study)
1971 Sollberger and Kupper, IRSA IIIA4d (exs. 1–5, translation)
1975 Borger et al., Die Welt des Alten Orients no. 130 (ex. 6, photo, translation)
1986 Kärki, KDDU pp. 95–96 Šusuen 9 (exs. 1–7 edition)
1991 Steible, NSBW 2 pp. 260–62 Šūsuen 9 (exs. 1–7, edition)

TEXT

1) ᵈšára	1–5) For the god Šara, distinguished one of the god An, beloved son of the goddess Inanna, his (Šū-Sîn's) father,
2) nir-gál-an-na	
3) dumu-ki-ág-	
4) ᵈinanna	
5) ad-da-ni-ir	
6) ᵈšu-ᵈEN.ZU	6–11) Šū-Sîn, purification priest of the god An, anointed priest with clean hands for the gods Enlil, Ninlil, and the great gods,
7) išib-an-na	
8) gudu₄ šu-daddag(UD.UD)-	
9) ᵈen-líl	
10) ᵈnin-líl-ka	
11) ù dingir-gal-gal-e-ne	
12) lugal ᵈen-líl-le	12–19) the king whom the god Enlil lovingly chose in his (own) heart for the shepherdship of the land, mighty king, king of Ur, king of the four quarters,
13) ki-ág	
14) šà-ga-na	
15) in-pà	
16) sipa-kalam-ma-šè	
17) lugal-kala-ga	
18) lugal-uri₅.KI-ma	
19) lugal-an-ub-da-límmu-ba-ke₄	
20) u₄ bàd-mar-dú	20–23) when he built the Amorite wall (called) "It keeps Tidnum at a distance"
21) *mu-ri-iq*	
22) *ti-id-ni-im*	
23) mu-dù-a	
24) ù gìr-mar-dú	24–26) and returned the "foot" of the Amorites to their land,
25) ma-da-né-e	
26) bí-in-gi₄-a	
27) é-šà-ge-pà-da	27–30) he built for him (Šara) and for his (own) life, E-šage-pada, his beloved temple.
28) é-ki-ág-gá-ni	
29) nam-ti-la-ni-šè	
30) mu-na-dù	

18

A stone tablet is incised with an inscription commemorating Šū-Sîn's construction of the temple of the god Šara in Umma.

Variants for E3/2.1.3.17:
23.3 Copy: mu-NI-a; text: mu-dù-a.
30.7 Omits.
Ex. 3 adds (lines 31–32): ki-[bé/ mu-na-gi₄].

COMMENTARY

The tablet, NBC 2519, is made of black serpentine. Its top portion is broken away; the extant fragment measures 7.2×5.4×1.9 cm. Lines 1′–7′ are on the obverse, lines 8′–12′ on the reverse. The inscription was collated.

BIBLIOGRAPHY

1920 Keiser, BIN 2 no. 11 (copy, edition)
1929 Barton, RISA pp. 294–95 Gimil-Sin 6 (edition)
1962 Hallo, HUCA 33 p. 37 Šu-Sin 4 (study)
1986 Kärki, KDDU p. 92 Šusuen 4 (edition)
1986 Steible, NSBW 2 p. 255 Šūsuen 4 (edition)

TEXT

Lacuna
1′) [ᵈ*šu*-ᵈEN.ZU]
2′) ki-ág-ᵈen-líl-lá
3′) lugal ᵈen-líl-le
4′) ki-ág šà-ga-na
5′) in-pà
6′) lugal-kala-ga
7′) lugal-uri$_5$.KI-ma
8′) lugal-an-ub-da-límmu-ba-ke$_4$
9′) šà-ge-pà-da
10′) é-ki-ág-ni
11′) nam-ti-la-ni-šè
12′) mu-na-dù

Lacuna
1′–8′) [Šū-Sîn], beloved of the god Enlil, the king whom the god Enlil lovingly chose in his (own) heart, mighty king, king of Ur, king of the four quarters,

9′–12′) Šage-pada, his beloved temple, he built for his (own) life.

19

A ten-line inscription found on door sockets from the Gipar-ku at Ur commemorates Šū-Sîn's construction of the palace at Ur.

CATALOGUE

Ex.	Museum number	Excavation number	Ur provenance	Dimensions (cm)	Lines preserved	cpn
1	BM 119007	U 3337	Gipar-ku, 50 m below Larsa level, in the W corner of room A 2	45×41×16 Inscription: 9.1 wide	1–10	c
2	IM 1147	U 6722	Gipar-ku, room A 2	—	1–10	p
3	IM 1148	U 6722	Gipar-ku, room A 2	42×32×17	1–8	p
4	Was in Mercer's collection	—	—	—	1–10	n

COMMENTARY

The photo published in MJ 16 shows a door socket *in situ*, encased within a brick box. A comparison of the various exemplars reveals that the door socket shown in the MJ photo cannot be ex. 1 or ex. 3. We have assumed, therefore, that it is ex. 2. Ex. 3 was last seen at the Nineveh dig house. The present whereabouts of ex. 4 are unknown; it is entered in the score from the copy of Mercer. All the texts are arranged in one column.

Steible, NSBW 2 p. 256 sub Šūsuen 5, raises the question whether the "house" mentioned in line 9 refers to a temple dedicated to the divine Šū-Sîn or to the palace in Ur. The normal practice in Ur III times is to name city governors in inscriptions dealing with the construction of temples dedicated to the king (cf. E3/2.1.4.11–15). The king, on the other hand, usually appears in inscriptions dealing with the palace (cf. E3/2.1.2.3 and E3/2.1.6.1001). This inscription, then, likely refers to the palace at Ur.

The fact that at least one of these door sockets (ex. 2) was apparently found in its original context, coupled with the evidence of the inscription itself, suggests that Šū-Sîn moved the royal residence from the E-ḫursag to the Gipar-ku. A reflection of this deed may possibly be seen in two economic tablets. One (Sigrist, Drehem p. 359) records disbursements to Kubātum, Šū-Sîn's queen, and Abī-simtī, his mother, for a "tour of the *gipar*" (nigin gi_6-par_4-šè). A second tablet, dated to x ŠS 7 (PD 431: Salonen, Puzriš-Dagan-Texte no. 431), registers the disbursement of various animals to Kubātum and Abī-simtī "for the inspection of the *gipar*" (IGI.GÁR-gi_6-pàr-šè). We are inclined to see these records as attesting to a visit of the two queens to Ur on the occasion of an inspection of the new royal residence.

BIBLIOGRAPHY

1925 Woolley and Legrain, MJ 16 p. 299 (ex. 2[?], photo [in situ])
1928 Gadd, UET 1 no. 72 (exs. 1–3, conflated copy, edition)
1928 Mercer, JSOR 12 pp. 147 and 149 no. 35 (ex. 4, copy, edition)
1929 Barton, RISA pp. 366–67 Gimil-Sin 1 (exs. 1–3, edition)
1962 Hallo, HUCA 33 p. 37 Šu-Sin 5 (exs. 1–4, study)
1976 Woolley and Mallowan, UE 7 pp. 43, 220, and 225 (exs. 1–3, provenance)
1986 Kärki, KDDU pp. 92–93 Šusuen 5 (exs. 1–4, edition)
1991 Steible, NSBW 2 p. 256 Šūsuen 5 (exs. 1–4, edition)

TEXT

1) ᵈ*šu*-ᵈEN.ZU
2) ki-ág-ᵈen-líl-lá
3) lugal ᵈen-líl-le
4) ki-ág šà-ga-na
5) in-pà
6) lugal-kala-ga
7) lugal-uri_5.KI-ma
8) lugal-an-ub-da-límmu-ba-ke_4
9) é-ki-ág-gá-ni
10) mu-dù

1–8) Šū-Sîn, beloved of the god Enlil, king whom the god Enlil lovingly chose in his (own) heart, mighty king, king of Ur, king of the four quarters,

9–10) built his beloved house.

20

A twelve-line door socket inscription commemorates Šū-Sîn's construction of a temple for the goddess Annunītum.

CATALOGUE

Ex.	Museum number	Excavation number	Ur provenance	Dimensions (cm)	Lines preserved	cpn
1	BM 90844	—	—	47×37×30 Inscription: 11.6×5.1	1–12	c
2	IM 1010	U 3059	SFS doorway to room 7	—	—	n

COMMENTARY

The text, as far as can be determined (ex. 1), is found in one column.

Steible (NSBW 2 p. 257) listed as his exemplar B for this inscription a text discussed by C. Bezold (Festschrift Lehmann-Haupt pp. 115–16 no. 5). The text described by Bezold is in fact a canephor inscription of Amar-Suena; it is edited as inscription E3/2.1.3.14.2 in this volume. A temple of Annunītum at Ur is well attested in Ur III archival texts; for references, see Sallaberger, Kalender 2 p. 190, sub An-nu-ni-tum (Ur).

BIBLIOGRAPHY

1872 Smith, TSBA 1 p. 40 (ex. 1, translation)
1874 Lenormant, Études accadiennes 2 p. 318 (ex. 1, translation)
1875 Lenormant, Choix no. 63 (ex. 1, copy)
1875 Ménant, Babylone p. 81 (ex. 1, translation)
1892 Winckler, KB 3/1 pp. 88–89 Gamil-Sin 1 (ex. 1, edition)
1894 4R^2 35 no. 4 (ex. 1, copy)
1899 Bezold, Cat. 5 p. 2241 (ex. 1, study)
1905 King, CT 21 pl. 28 BM 90844 (ex. 1, copy)
1907 Thureau-Dangin, SAK pp. 200–201 Gimil-sin b (ex. 1, edition)
1922 BM Guide p. 61 no. 90 (ex. 1, study)
1928 Barton, RISA pp. 292–95 Gimil-Sin 2 (ex. 1, edition)
1928 Gadd, UET 1 p. xxiv (ex. 2, study)
1962 Hallo, HUCA 33 p. 37 Šu-Sin 6 (exs. 1–2, study)
1971 Sollberger and Kupper, IRSA IIIA4c (exs. 1–2, translation)
1986 Kärki, KDDU p. 93 Šusuen 6 (exs. 1–2, edition)
1991 Steible, NSBW 2 p. 257 Šūsuen 6 (exs. 1–2, edition)

TEXT

1) ⸢*an*⸣-*nu-ni-tum*
2) dam-a-ni-ir
3) ^{d}*šu*-^{d}⸢EN.ZU⸣
4) ki-ág-^{d}en-líl-lá
5) lugal ^{d}en-líl-le
6) ki-ág šà-ga-⸢na⸣
7) in-pà
8) lugal-[ka]la-ga
9) lugal-⸢uri$_5$⸣.KI-ma
10) lugal-an-ub-d[a]-límmu-ba]-k[e$_4$]
11) é-a-ni
12) mu-n[a-dù]

1–2) For the goddess Annunītum, his spouse,

3–10) Šū-Sîn, beloved of the god Enlil, king whom the god Enlil lovingly chose in his (own) heart, [mi]ghty king, king of Ur, king of the fo[ur] quarte[rs],

11–12) built her temple for h[er].

21

A seventeen-line door socket inscription records Šū-Sîn's construction of Nanna's E-murianabak temple in Ur.

CATALOGUE

Ex.	Museum number	Excavation number	Registrastion number	Ur provenance	Object	Dimensions (cm)	Lines preserved	cpn
1	Philadelphia, museum number unknown	—	—	—	Diorite door socket	—	1–17	c
2	BM 116416	U 838	1923-11-10, 1	Found in situ in the brick door box against NW jamb of the door of the NE wall of room 22 of the E-nun-maḫ = TTB 31	Basalt door socket	47×49×23	1–17	c

COMMENTARY

The text is arranged in one column. No museum number was visible on the Philadelphia exemplar.

BIBLIOGRAPHY

1897 Peters, Nippur 2 photo facing p. 238 (ex. 1, photo)
1900 Radau, EBH pp. 277–78 (ex. 1, edition)
1907 Thureau-Dangin, SAK pp. 202–203 Gimil-sin d (ex. 1, edition)
1928 Gadd, UET 1 no. 80 (ex. 2, copy, edition); pl. M (ex. 2, photo)

1929 Barton, RISA pp. 368–69 Gimil-Sin 3 (ex. 2, edition)
1962 Hallo, HUCA 33 p. 37 Šu-Sin 7 (exs. 1–2, study)
1971 Sollberger and Kupper, IRSA IIIA4b (exs. 1–2, translation)
1986 Kärki, KDDU pp. 93–94 Šusuen 7 (exs. 1–2, edition)
1986 Steible, NSBW 2 pp. 258–59 Šūsuen 7 (exs. 1–2, edition)

TEXT

1)	ᵈnanna	1–4) For the god Nanna, first-born son of the god Enlil, his beloved lord,
2)	dumu-sag-	
3)	ᵈen-líl-lá	
4)	lugal-ki-ág-gá-ni-ir	
5)	ᵈšu-ᵈEN.ZU	5–14) Šū-Sîn, beloved of the god Nanna, the king whom the god Enlil lovingly chose in his (own) heart for the shepherdship of the land and of the four quarters, mighty king, king of the four quarters,
6)	ki-ág-ᵈnanna	
7)	lugal ᵈen-líl-le	
8)	šà-ga-na	
9)	in-pà	
10)	sipa-kalam-ma	
11)	ù an-ub-da-límmu-ba-šè	
12)	lugal-kala-ga	
13)	lugal-uri₅.KI-ma	
14)	lugal-an-ub-da-límmu-ba-ke₄	
15)	é-mu-ri-a-na-ba-AK	15–17) built for him E-murianabak, his beloved temple.
16)	é-ki-ág-gá-ni	
17)	mu-na-dù	

22

A weight stone inscribed with Šū-Sîn's name was found in excavations at Telloh.

COMMENTARY

The black diorite, ovoid-shaped weight stone measures 29 cm in length with a diameter of 9–10 cm; it weighs 2.511 kg. The piece bears the museum number AO 246. The text is arranged in one column. The inscription was collated from the published photo.

BIBLIOGRAPHY

1884–1912 de Sarzec, Découvertes 1 p. 438 (study); Découvertes 2 pl. 26bis no. 5 (photo)
1899 Oppert, RA 5 pp. 57–58 no. 2 (copy, translation, study)
1907 Thureau-Dangin, SAK pp. 202–203 Gimil-sin e (edition)
1929 Barton, RISA pp. 296–97 Gimil-Sin 8 (edition)
1962 Hallo, HUCA 33 p. 38 Šu-Sin 17 (study)

1971 Sollberger and Kupper, IRSA IIIA4i (translation)
1982 André-Leicknam, Naissance de l'écriture p. 79 no. 34 (photo, translation)
1986 Kärki, KDDU p. 101 Šusuen 17 (edition)
1991 Steible, NSBW 2 p. 270 Šūsuen 17 (study)

TEXT

1) 5 ma-na gi-na
2) ^{d}*šu*-^{d}EN.ZU
3) lugal-kala-ga
4) lugal-uri$_5$.KI-ma
5) lugal-an-ub-da-límmu-ba

1–5) Five minas, confirmed: Šū-Sîn, mighty king, king of Ur, king of the four quarters.

23

A four-line stamped brick inscription of Šū-Sîn was found at Tell al-Wilāyah.

COMMENTARY

The brick, which measures 31×32×6.5 cm, was found in the SE area of the mound and given the excavation number WH 147, museum number IM 61279. A duplicate is WH 148 = IM (for study). The text is arranged in one column. The inscription was collated from the published photo.

BIBLIOGRAPHY

1960 Madhlūm, Sumer 16 p. 91 and pl. 11 A [Arabic section] (photo, edition)
1976 Postgate, Sumer 32 p. 88 no. 21 (edition)
1986 Kärki, KDDU p. 90 Šusuen 1 (edition)
1991 Steible, NSBW 2 pp. 273–74 Šūsuen 24 (edition)

TEXT

1) ^{d}*šu*-^{d}EN.ZU
2) lugal-kala-ga
3) lugal-uri$_5$.KI-ma
4) lugal-an-ub-da-límmu-ba

1–4) Šū-Sîn, mighty king, king of Ur, king of the four quarters.

24

A vase fragment in Jena is incised with the end of a Šū-Sîn inscription.

COMMENTARY

The alabaster vase fragment measures 4.2×4.4 cm and the inscription 3.2×3.3 cm; its provenance is unknown. The piece bears the museum number HS 1964. The text is arranged in one column. The inscription was collated.

The inscription ends with line 5′ (collated). It would appear, then, that the text was a simple label rather than a dedicatory inscription.

BIBLIOGRAPHY

1969 Oelsner, WZJ 18 p. 53 no. 23 (edition)
1986 Kärki, KDDU p. 133 Šusuen 25 (edition)
1991 Braun-Holzinger, Weihgaben p. 190 G 367 (edition)
1991 Steible, NSBW 2 p. 277–78 Šūsuen 28 (edition)

TEXT

Lacuna
1′) [lugal ^{d}en-líl-le]
2′) ki-ág šà-ga-na
3′) in-pà
4′) lugal-kala-ga
5′) lugal-uri$_5$.KI-ma

Lacuna
1′–5′) [Šū-Sîn, ..., the king whom the god Enlil] lovingly chose in his (own) heart, mighty king, king of Ur.

25

A bowl fragment found at Nippur is incised with an inscription of Šū-Sîn.

COMMENTARY

The bowl fragment, which measures about 3×3.65×1.2 cm, is made of a translucent white stone. It was found on the surface of the mound near the ziqqurrat and given the excavation number 11 N 129. Its IM number is unknown.

BIBLIOGRAPHY

1975 Civil, in Gibson, OIC 22 pp. 117 and 136 no. 35 (edition, study)
1991 Braun-Holzinger, Weihgaben p. 190 G 368 (edition)
1991 Steible, NSBW 2 p. 278 Šūsuen 29 (edition)

TEXT

1) ^{d}*šu*-^{d}E[N.ZU]
2) [ki]-ág-^{d}en-[líl-lá]
3) [lu]gal ^{d}e[n-líl-le]
Lacuna

1–3) Šū-S[în], [be]loved of the god En[lil], [the ki]ng whom the god E[nlil]
Lacuna

Votive and Seal Inscriptions
(a) Of the King
26–27

26

A fragment of a statue of Šū-Sîn was found in excavations at Ur.

COMMENTARY

The diorite statue fragment was found in the courtyard of the Dublalmaḫ (ES 13) and given the excavation number U 3159. It now bears the museum number IM 1049.

BIBLIOGRAPHY

1928 Gadd, UET 1 no. 73 (copy, edition)
1962 Hallo, HUCA 33 p. 38 Šu-Sin 14 (study)
1986 Kärki, KDDU pp. 99–100 Šusuen 14 (edition)
1991 Braun-Holzinger, Weihgaben p. 274 St 155 (edition)
1991 Steible, NSBW 2 pp. 268–69 Šūsuen 14 (edition)

TEXT

Col. i
Lacuna
1′) lugal-a-[ni-ir]
2′) ^{d}*šu*-^{d}E[N.ZU]
3′) ki-ág-^{d}[en-líl-lá]
4′) lugal-ka[la-ga]
5′) lugal-[uri$_5$.KI-ma]
6′) lugal-an-ub-da-límmu-ba-ke$_4$
Col. ii
Broken away

Col. i
Lacuna
i 1′) [For the god DN, his] lord,
i 2′–6′) Šū-S[în], beloved [of the god Enlil], mi[ghty] king, king [of Ur], king of the four quarters.

Col. ii
Broken away

27

A fragment of a marble mace-head of Šu-Sîn was found in excavations at Ur.

COMMENTARY

The marble mace-head fragment was found in room 3 of the Šulgi mausoleum and given the excavation number U 16272. It now bears the museum number UM 31-43-252. The text is arranged in one column.

BIBLIOGRAPHY

1965 Sollberger, UET 8 no. 35 (copy)
1986 Kärki, KDDU pp. 132–33 Šusuen 24 (edition)
1991 Braun-Holzinger, Weihgaben p. 61 K 85 (edition)
1991 Steible, NSBW 2 pp. 271–72 Šūsuen 21 (edition)

TEXT

Lacuna
1′) ⌜x⌝ [...]
2′) d⌜*šu*-d⌝[EN.ZU]
3′) ki-ág-d⌜en-líl-lá⌝
4′) lu[gal den-líl-le]
5′) ⌜ki⌝-[ág šà-ga-na]
6′) [in-pà]
Lacuna

Lacuna
1′–6′) ..., Šū-[Sîn], beloved of the god Enlil, the k[ing whom the god Enlil] [lov]ingly [chose in his (own) heart]
Lacuna

Votive, Seal, and Label Inscriptions (b) Of the Royal Family 28–33

The data found in the following chart are based on the MS of D. Owen entitled "The Royal Family of Ur [Preliminary List of Sources]" (see page 166).

Šū-Sîn — Royal Family

Item	Royal Name	RIM number	Attestations (A) and Bibliography (B)
Queen			
1	*ku-ba-tum*	E3/2.1.4.28	(B) Falkenstein, OLZ 53 (1958) p. 143, who cites Salonen, Puzriš-Dagan-Texte no. 431; Sollberger, article "Kubātum" in RLA 3 p. 265, where he refers to various texts; Steinkeller, ASJ 3 (1981) p. 80, citing University of Michigan 89075 = Snell, MVN 9 no. 165; Foster, SEL 2 (1985) pp. 37–42, noting a text in the Rosen Collection (attribution to queen Kubātum uncertain); Wilcke, DV 5 (1988) p. 26 n. 14; and finally Sallaberger, Kalender 1 p. 45 n. 190, citing Umma 960, a tablet now published as Waetzoldt and Yıldız, MVN 16 no. 960.
Lukurs			
2	A.AB.BA-*ba-áš-ti*	E3/2.1.4.29	(B) Wilcke, DV 5 (1988) pp. 21 26 (Russian version); ibid., pp. 225–27 (English version); and ibid., NABU 1990 p. 28 no. 36
3	šà-bi-[...]	E3/2.1.4.30	(A) Owen, NATN no. 768 (seal impression) (no date)

Item	Royal Name	RIM number	Attestations (A) and Bibliography (B)
Daughters			
4	géme-^{d}en-líl-lá	See also the discussion under Ibbi-Sîn Family Item 1.	(A) Owen, NATN no. 859 lines 4–6 (30 iv ŠS 7); Sigrist, MVN 13 no. 123 line 5 (3 xii ŠS 7); Yıldız and Gomi, PDT 2 no. 1056 col. iii lines 6 and 11 (- - IS) (offerings for deceased); (B) Michalowski, ASJ 4 (1982) pp. 136–37; Sallaberger, ZA 82 (1992) p. 134, note to no. 1056
5	*ša-at-èr-ra*	E3/2.1.4.31	Possibly a daughter of Šulgi (see commentary to E3/2.1.4.31).
6	*tá-bur-ḫaṭ-ṭum*	—	(A) Keiser, BIN 3 no. 382 line 5 (- xi AS 9) (Tabūr-ḫaṭṭum not named; title "daughter-in-law" of Ur-Iškur appears); de Genouillac, Trouvaille no. 87 = Limet, Textes sumériens no. 41 lines 2–3 (- xii-diri ŠS 2); NCBT no. 1600; Salonen, Puzriš-Dagan-Texte no. 454 (29 x ŠS 7). Although she is not named as princess, the fact that she was betrothed to the governor of Ḫamazi argues for her royal status. She is tentatively listed under Šū-Sîn because of the dates on the tablets — they all postdate the death of Amar-Suena.
Brother			
7	ur-^{d}en-líl-lá	—	(A) Calvot and Pettinato, MVN 8 no. 129 line 12 (5 iv AS 9); tentatively assigned to Šū-Sîn in view of the date — the tablet postdates the death of Amar-Suena.
Uncle			
8	*ba-ba-ti*	E3/2.1.4.32–33	(A) Michalowski, Correspondence pp. 48–56; (B) Whiting, JCS 28 (1976) 178–79.

28

According to archival texts dated to the reign of Šū-Sîn, Kubātum was Šū-Sîn's queen (see Šū-Sîn — Royal Family item 1 above).

Sigrist's attempt to identify a certain Kubātum, wet-nurse for the children of Amar-Suena, with the later queen (see Sigrist, RA 80 [1986] p. 185) is inconclusive, since the PN, while rare, is not unique (see, for example, Owen, MVN 3 no. 278 line 4, where the accompanying seal inscription makes it clear that Kubātum in this case does not refer to a *lukur*).

An agate bead from Uruk, whose inscription is edited below, names Kubātum as Šū-Sîn's *lukur*.

COMMENTARY

The inscribed bead formed the centre-piece of a necklace belonging to the the queen. It was flanked by two smaller beads which were simply inscribed with the label inscription: ^{d}*šu*-^{d}EN.ZU. The necklace was found in the foundation level, in the middle of the doorway leading to room 216, that is, the doorway leading from the ziqqurrat to the suite of rooms to the northwest of it (PaXV4; see UVB 8 pl. 6 — the findspot is marked as a small circle in the middle of the doorway on the plan). It was given the excavation number W 16183. The piece was in the Vorderasiatisches Museum, Berlin, VA 12908. It is now lost. The text is arranged in one column.

BIBLIOGRAPHY

1937 Nöldeke et al., UVB 8 p. 23 and pl. 38 (photo, edition)
1962 Hallo, HUCA 33 p. 43 Family 8 (study)
1971 Sollberger and Kupper, IRSA IIIA4m (translation)
1981 Sollberger, in RLA 6/3 p. 265 sub Kubātum (edition)
1986 Kärki, KDDU p. 132 (Familie 8 =) Šusuen 23 (edition)
1988 Limper, AUWE 2 pp. 63–66 no. 140 and pls. 21–22 (photo, edition, study)
1991 Braun-Holzinger, Weihgaben p. 368 P 17 (edition, study)
1991 Steible, NSBW 2 p. 273 Šūsuen 23 (edition)

TEXT

1) *ku-ba-tum*
2) lukur-ki-ág-
3) ^{d}*šu*-^{d}EN.ZU

1–3) Kubātum, beloved *lukur* of Šū-Sîn.

29

An agate bead found at Uruk names Šū-Sîn's *lukur* Ti'āmat-bāštī (see Šū-Sîn — Royal Family item 2 above).

COMMENTARY

The bead, which formed one link in a necklace belonging to the *lukur*, was found in the same locus as E3/2.1.4.28. It was given the excavation number W 16172 and the museum number IM 26833. The text is arranged in one column.

For references to Ti'āmat-bāštī in Ur III archival texts, see C. Wilcke, DV 5 (1988) pp. 21–26 (Russian version) and pp. 225–27 (English version). See also Wilcke, NABU 1990 p. 28 no. 36. Wilcke points out that two of the three references to Ti'āmat-bāštī in Ur III archival texts link the *lukur* with the goddess Šauška. In turn, the only toponym mentioned in connection with Šauška in the Ur III archival texts is the city of Nineveh. In all likelihood, then, Šū-Sîn's marriage to the foreign princess Ti'amāt-bāštī was connected with the conquest of the city and area of Nineveh, an event which likely did not occur until the beginning of Šū-Sîn's reign (see Whiting, JCS 28 [1976] pp. 177–78).

BIBLIOGRAPHY

1937 Nöldeke et al., UVB 8 p. 23 and pl. 39 (photo, edition)
1962 Hallo, HUCA 33 p. 43 Family 7 (study)
1971 Sollberger and Kupper, IRSA IIIA4n (translation)
1975 Orthmann (ed.), Der alte Orient pl. 123b (photo)
1986 Kärki, KDDU p. 132 (Familie 7 =) Šusuen 22 (edition)
1988 Limper, AUWE 2 pp. 63–66 no. 141 and pls. 2 and 23–25 (photo, edition, study)
1988 Wilcke, DV 5 pp. 21–26 (Russian version) and pp. 225–27 (English version) (study)
1991 Braun-Holzinger, Weihgaben p. 368 P 17 (edition, study)
1991 Steible, NSBW 2 pp. 272–73 Šūsuen 22 (edition)

TEXT

1) A.AB.BA-*ba-áš-ti*
2) lukur-ki-ág-
3) ^{d}*šu*-^{d}EN.ZU
4) lugal-uri$_{5}$.KI-ma-ka

1–4) Ti'āmat-bāštī, beloved *lukur* of Šū-Sîn, king of Ur.

30

A seal impression on a fragment from a Nippur tablet refers to a princess named šà-bi-[x x] as chief *lukur* of Šū-Sîn (see Šū-Sîn — Royal Family item 3 above).

COMMENTARY

The seal impression is found on the undated tablet fragment N 769.

The restoration of the PN of line 1 is uncertain. One may compare, for example, the šà-bi-kù-zu cited in Limet, Anthroponymie p. 525.

BIBLIOGRAPHY

1982 Owen, NATN no. 768 (copy)

TEXT

1) šà-bi-[x x]
2) dumu-munus-lu[gal]
3) lukur-gal-^{d}*šu*-[^{d}EN.ZU]
4) kúr-ra-á-g[ál]
5) rá-gaba ir$_{11}$-zu

1–3) Šabi-[x x], daughter of the king, chief *lukur* of Šū-[Sîn]:

4–5) Kura-agal, dispatch-rider, (is) your servant.

31

A seal inscription attested from impressions found on various Nippur tablets dating to the period vi AS 9–ix ŠS1 names a certain Šāt-Erra as daughter of an unspecified Ur III king. In view of the dates of the tablets, and bearing in mind that Amar-Suena had died by 29 ii AS 9, we have very tentatively assigned Šāt-Erra as a daughter of Šū-Sîn (see Šū-Sîn — Royal Family item 5 above).

An argument against this genealogy may be seen in the appearance of a lady named Šāt-Erra (along with two other princesses, Ninegale-si and Nin-TUR.TUR) in a tablet dated to Š 42 (Crozer 75: Sigrist, Rochester no. 165 lines 16–18). The Crozer tablet, then, suggests that Šāt-Erra may have been a daughter of Šulgi — more data is needed to clarify this question.

CATALOGUE

Ex.	Museum number	TMH NF 1/2 number	Date
1	HS 1192	192	vi AS 9
2	HS 1198	198	vi AS 9
3	HS 1199	199	x AS 9
4	HS 1200	200	i ŠS 1
5	HS 1205	205	iii ŠS 1
6	HS 1206	206	v ŠS 1
7	HS 1207	207	v ŠS 1
8	HS 1208	208	v ŠS 1
9	MAH 16273	—	v ŠS 1
10	HS 1209	209	vii ŠS 1
11	HS 1210	210	ix ŠS 1

BIBLIOGRAPHY

1937 Pohl, TMH NF 1/2 Siegel no. *101 (exs. 1–8, 10–11, copy)
1969 Sauren, WMAH no. 120 (ex. 9, edition)
1974 Sauren, MVN 2 no. 120 (ex. 9, copy)

TEXT

1) *ša-at-èr-ra*
2) dumu-munus-lugal
3) *um-mi*-DU_{10}
4) géme-ni

1–2) Šāt-Erra, daughter of the king:

3–4) Ummī-ṭābat (is) her female servant.

32

A seal inscription of Babati, maternal uncle of Šū-Sîn, is found on three tablets (see Šū-Sîn — Royal Family item 8 above).

CATALOGUE

Ex.	Museum number	Excavation number	Dimensions (cm)	Lines preserved	Date	cpn
1	MLC 1822	—	3.8 high	1–2, 5–10, 17–21	v ŠS 6	c
2	MLC 2339	—	—	1–14, 17–21	—	c
3	—	TA 1931-T615	—	1–14, 16–20	- ŠS 3	p

COMMENTARY

The seal inscription is restored from E3/2.1.4.33, a second Babati inscription. Lines 1–9 of the text are found in col. i, lines 10–20 in col. ii. Ex. 3 is dated to the month ezen-maḫ at Ešnunna.

For literature concerning Babati, see Michalowski, SMS 2/2 (1978) pp. 4 and 13; and ibid., Correspondence pp. 48–56. Of interest is an archival text (Birmingham A.1660-1982: Watson, Birmingham 1 no. 126) that mentions Babati as "brother of the queen" (line 4: ba-ba-ti šeš nin), thus confirming the evidence of the seal inscription edited below. A seal inscription of Babati in which he appears with the simple title "scribe" (dub-sar) and as a servant of Amar-Suena was published in Sauren, New York Public Library no. 354. A seal dedicated to Šū-Sîn in which Babati also appears with the title "scribe" was published in Buchanan and Hallo, Early Near Eastern Seals no. 637.

In line 14, the expression: ma-d[a a-du_{11}-ga] "lan[d of sweet water]" may be an allusion to the Ṭaban River, since Nashef, in a discussion of the etymology of the river name Ṭaban (Bagh. Mitt. 13 [1982] p. 118 n. 7), notes: "Anscheinend wird hier an das Verbum *ṭâbu* gedacht ..." *Ṭâbu(m)*, in turn, can be connected with Sumerian du_{10}-ga.

BIBLIOGRAPHY

1920 Clay, BRM 3 nos. 37–38 (exs. 1–2, copy)
1962 Hallo, HUCA 33 p. 39 Šu-Sin 19ii (study)
1963 Goetze, JCS 17 pp. 22–23 no. 43 (exs. 1–2, edition)
1971 Sollberger and Kupper, IRSA IIIA4j (exs. 1–2, partial translation)
1976 Michalowski, Correspondence p. 49 (exs. 1–3, study)
1976 Whiting, JCS 28 pp. 173–82 (ex. 3, photo, edition)
1977 Franke, in Gibson and Biggs, Seals Fiche C 3 (ex. 3, photo)
1981 Buchanan and Hallo, Early Near Eastern Seals pp. 250–51 and 453 no. 654 (ex. 1, photo, edition)
1986 Kärki, KDDU pp. 105–106 Šusuen 19 (ii) (exs. 1–2, edition)
1987 Winter, in Gibson and Biggs, Bureaucracy pp. 96 IIIb and 97 IVh (exs. 1–3, study)

TEXT

1) [^{d}*šu*]-^{d}EN.ZU 2) [nita]-kala-ga 3) [lugal-ur]i$_{5}$[KI]-ma 4) [lugal-a]n-ub-[da]-límmu-ba-ke$_{4}$	1–4) [Šū]-Sîn, mighty [man], [king of U]r, [king of] the four qu[arters],
5) ba-ba-ti 6) pisan-dub-ba 7) šà-tam-lugal 8) GÌR.NÍTA 9) *maš-kán-šar-um*.KI 10) [é]nsi 11) a-⌈wa-al⌉.[KI]	5–11) to Babati, accountant, royal controller, military governor of Maškan-šarrum, [go]vernor of Awal,
12) šabra [...] 13) kù-[gal] 14) ma-d[a a-du$_{11}$-ga] 15) [šabra nin-min-a-bi] 16) ^{d}*be*-[*la-at šuḫ-nir*] 17) ù ^{d}[*be-la-at*]-*te-ra-ba*-⌈*an*⌉ 18) šeš *a-bí-sí-im*-⌈*ti*⌉ 19) ama ki-ág-gá-na 20) ir$_{11}$-da-ni-ir	12–20) chief administrator of [...], canal-[inspector] of the lan[d of sweet water (= the land of the Ṭaban River?), chief administrator of the two ladies], Be[lat-Šuḫnir] and Be[lat]-Terraban, brother of Abī-Simtī, his (Šū-Sîn's) beloved mother, his servant,
21) in-na-[ba]	21) he (Šū-Sîn) pres[ented] (this seal).

33

An Old Babylonian tablet provides us with the copy of a second Babati inscription (see Šū-Sîn — Royal Family item 8 above).

COMMENTARY

The tablet bearing this inscription, BM 114024 (1914-4-4, 490), was acquired through purchase; its original provenance is unknown. Lines 1–8 are found on the obverse of the tablet, lines 9–17 on the reverse.

As noted by Walker, the text seems to be a conflation by an Old Babylonian editor of two inscriptions: an original seal inscription of Babati and a royal inscription of Šū-Sîn. The title "king of the land of Sumer and Akkad" in line 5 and the designation "wife" in line 16 are obvious mistakes. The toponym in line 10, if it refers to the city of Apiak near Borsippa, is unexpected.

BIBLIOGRAPHY

1983 Walker, JCS 35 pp. 91–96 (copy, edition, study)

TEXT

1) ^{d}*šu*-^{d}EN.ZU ki-ág ^{d}en-líl-le
2) lugal ^{d}en-líl-le
3) ki-ág šà-ga-ni ì-pà
4) lugal-úri.KI-ma
5) lugal-ki-en-gi-ki-uri-ke
6) lugal-an-ub-da-límmu-ba-ke$_4$
7) ⸢ba$_4$⸣-ba$_4$-ti dub-⸢sar⸣ šà-tam
8) [pi]san-dub-ba agrig-l[ugal(?)]
9) énsi-a-wa-al.⸢KI⸣
10) ù a-PI-ak.⸢KI⸣
11) kù-gal ma-da (erasure) a-du$_{10}$-ga
12) šabra nin-min-a-bi
13) sanga ^{d}*be-la-at-ter*(Text: NIR)*-ba-an*
14) ù ^{d}*be-la-at-šuk-nir*
15) šeš *a-bi-sí-im-ti*
16) dam ki-ág-gá-ni
17) ir$_{11}$-zu

1–6) Šū-Sîn, beloved of the god Enlil, the king whom the god Enlil lovingly chose in his (own) heart, king of Ur, king of the land of Sumer and Akkad, king of the four quarters:

7–11) Babati, scribe, accountant, [co]ntroller, *ro[yal]* steward, governor of Awal and A-PI-ak, canal-inspector of the land of sweet water (= the land of the Ṭaban River?),

12–17) chief administrator of the two ladies, *sanga* priest of Bēlat-Terraban and Bēlat-Šuknir, brother of Abī-simtī, his beloved wife (sic!), (is) your servant.

Votive and Seal Inscriptions (c) Of Various City Governors 2001–2015

The information found in the following chart derives from the data found in Keiser, Patesis; Hallo, Ensi's and Ensi's^{2}; Goetze, JCS 17 (1963) pp. 1–31; Edzard, Rép. Géogr. 2; Owen, JCS 33 (1981) pp. 244–70; ibid., JAOS 108 (1988) pp. 116–22; ibid., BiOr 49 (1992) cols. 444–47; T. Maeda, ASJ 14 (1992) pp. 162–63; and ibid., ASJ 16 (1994) pp. 157–62.

The names of governors referred to in seal inscriptions edited in this volume are marked with an asterisk (*). Names appearing in seal inscriptions are indicated with (s); those mentioned in tablets are marked with (t).

We have not listed tablets impressed with the seal inscription of the Umma governor Aa-kala, nor that of Gududu, son of the Umma governor Dadaga.

Year	Adab	Ešnunna	Girsu/Lagaš	Kazallu	Kutha
1	—	—	**ir₁₁-mu** A 3197 (Chicago), see Hallo Ensi's p. 19, (t) (- viii); Dhorme, RA 9 (1912) p. 62 AM 13 line 7 (sukkal-maḫ) (t) (29 xii); de Genouillac, ITT 3 no. 6359 rev. line 1 (t) (- -)	—	**gù-dé-a** Salonen, Puzriš-Dagan-Texte no. 263 lines 2–3 (t) (- i)
2	**ḫa-ba-lu₅-ge** Nies, UDT no. 94 line 1 (Adab not mentioned) (t) (- x); Jones and Snyder, SET no. 68 line 28 (t) (- ix)	**lugal-kù-zu** Boson, Aegyptus 17 (1937) no. 156 rev. line 5 = Archi and Pomponio, Torino no. 72 rev. line 5 (t) (6 viii)	—	—	**gù-dé-a** Oppenheim, Eames Collection, Eames KK 14 = Sauren, New York Public Library no. 203 lines 5–6 (t) (- x)
3	**ḫa-ba-lu₅-ge** Oppenheim, Eames Collection, Eames W 78 = Sauren, New York Public Library no. 307 line 2 (t) (25 v)	—	**gù-dé-a** de Genouillac, ITT 5 no. 9827 line 1 (s) (- -) **(E3/2.1.4.2003)**	**a-pi₅-la-ša*** Kutscher, JCS 22 (1968) pp. 63–65 (general; elsewhere attested as governor, see Goetze, JCS 17 [1963] p. 15 no. 12) (s) (- -) **(E3/2.1.4.2004)**	**gù-dé-a** Sigrist, AUCT 3 no. 496 line 4 (Kutha not mentioned) (t) (- x)
4	—	—	**ir₁₁-mu** Keiser, BIN 3 no. 241 lines 7–8 (t) (- i)	—	—
5	**ḫa-ba-lu₅-ge** Owen, MVN 3 no. 268 line 20 (t) (- -)	—	—	—	—
6	—	—	**gù-dé-a** de Genouillac, ITT 2 no. 4216 line 1 (s) (- xiii) **(E3/2.1.4.2003)**	—	**gù-dé-a** King, CT 32 pl. 25 BM 103439 obv. line 2 (Kutha not mentioned) (t) (- xii)
7	—	—	—	—	—
8	**ur-ᵈašas₇-gi₄*** Myhrman, BE 3/1 no. 13 line 6 (case) (s) (- ii) **(E3/2.1.4.2001)**	—	—	—	—
9	—	**i-tu-ri-a** de Genouillac, TCL 2 no. 4691 rev. 2–3 = de Genouillac, RA 7 (1910) p. 191 rev. 2–3 (t) (-vi)	—	—	—

Year	Marad	Nippur	Simudar	Simurrum	Sippar
1	—	**lugal-me-lám** seal found on Pohl, TMH NF 1/2 no. 231 (**see E3/2.1.3.2004**) (dedicated to Amar-Suena)	**lú-^{d}nanna** Legrain, UET 3 no. 75 lines 2–3 (general) (t) (-i); Owen, NATN no. 776 (s) (- -) (**E3/2.1.4.2010**)	—	—
2	*im-lik-é-a* King, CT 32 pl. 12 BM 103436 col. iv line 8 (t) (28 xi)	—	—	—	^{d}UTU-*ba-ni* Jones and Snyder, SET no. 68 line 18 (t) (-iii)
3	—	—	—	*ṣi-lu-uš-^{d}da-gan* Yıldız and Gomi, PDT 2 nos. 1355 and 1365 (- vi) (s) (**E3/2.1.4.2011**)	^{d}UTU-*ba-ni* LB 2204, see Hallo, Ensi's[2] p. 51 no. 9 (-iii); Fish, Catalogue no. 418 rev. 1 (- iii)
4	—	—	—	*ṣi-lu-uš-^{d}da-gan* Schneider, Orientalia 47–49 (1930) no. 38 lines 11–12 (t), messenger named, no indication of Ṣilluš-Dagān's status	^{d}UTU-*ba-ni* NCBT no. 1413, see Hallo, JCS 14 (1960) p. 114 no. 22 col. iv line 14 (- xii)
5	—	**da-da*** Pohl, TMH NF 1/2 Siegel no. 130* (29 xii) (s) (**E3/2.1.4.2008**)	—	*ṣi-lu-uš-^{d}da-gan* Yıldız and Gomi, PDT 2 nos. 1327 and 1375 (- vi) (s) (**E3/2.1.4.2011**)	—
6	—	—	—	—	[^{d}UTU-*ba*]-*ni* Salonen, Puzriš-Dagan-Texte no. 522 line 12 (t) (16 xi)
7	—	—	—	—	—
8	NE.NE Owen, MVN 3 no. 286 line 4 (t) (-x); Cagni and Pettinato, MVN 4 no. 112 lines 4–5 (t) (- x)	—	—	—	—
9	—	—	—	—	—

Year	Šarrākum	Šuruppak	Ti-WA (A.ḪA)	Umma	Urum
1	—	—	—	**a-a-kal-la** Yıldız and Gomi, Umma-Texte no. 1649 line 6 (t) (15 x); Schneider, Orientalia 47–49 (1930) no. 392 lines 19–20 (- -)	—
2	—	**ur-^{d}nin-kur-ra** Jones and Snyder, SET no. 68 line 23 (t) (- vii)	**^{d}en-líl-zi-šà-gál** Jones and Snyder, SET no. 68 line 39 (t) (- -)	**a-a-kal-la** WHM 957, see Hallo, Ensi's[2] p. 63 no. 68 (- -)	—
3	**ur-mes** A 4516 (Chicago), see Hallo, Ensi's[2] p. 9 no. 11 (t) (-iii); Delaporte, RA 8 (1911) p. 193 no. 15 rev. line 1 (t) (24 iv)	—	—	**a-a-kal-la** A 5687 (Chicago), see Hallo, Ensi's p. 49; ibid., Ensi's[2] p. 63 no. 69 (t) (- vi)	—
4	**ur-mes** Schneider, Orientalia 47–49 (1930) no. 391 lines 4–5 (t) (- -)	**ur-^{d}nin-kur-ra** NCBT no. 1413; see Hallo, JCS 14 (1960) p. 114 no. 22 col. iv line 20 (t) (- vii)	—	**a-a-kal-la** Yıldız and Gomi, Umma-Texte no. 1834 line 11 (t) (- v)	—
5	**ur-mes** Owen, MVN 11 no. 147 line 3 (5 i)	—	—	**a-a-kal-la** Yıldız and Gomi, Umma-Texte no. 2073 lines 5–6 (t) (30 vi)	—
6	**ur-mes** Lambert RA 47 (1953) p. 11 lines 5–7 (t) (- xiii)	**kù-^{d}nanna** Nies, UDT no. 120 line 4 (t) (- vii)	—	—	**ir$_{11}$-^{d}nanna** Keiser, YOS 4 no. 69 lines 9–10 (t) (- vi)
7	—	—	—	**a-a-kal-la** Nikol'skiy, DV 5 no. 528 rev. line 6 (t) (- ii); Keiser, YOS 4 no. 237 lines 229–30 (t) (-ii); MLC 1916 (t) (- i); **da-da-ga** Nikol'skiy, DV 5 no. 528 rev. line 7 (t) (- ii); Keiser, YOS 4 no. 237 lines 231–32 (t) (- ii); MLC 1916 (t)	—
8	—	—	—	—	—
9	—	**kù-^{d}nanna** Schneider, Orientalia 47–49 (1930) no. 124 lines 5–6 (t) (- xii)	—	—	—

2001

Tablets dated to the years ŠS 2–3 and 5 mention Ḫabaluge as governor of Adab. His brick inscription recording the construction of a temple for the divine Šū-Sîn at Adab is edited as inscription E3/2.1.4.11 in this volume.

Ḫabaluge was apparently succeeded by Ur-Ašgi as governor of Adab. The impression of a seal of a son of Ur-Ašgi is found on a tablet envelope dated to ŠS 9.

COMMENTARY

The tablet envelope, which measures 7.5×5.3×3.1 cm, was found in excavations at Nippur. It bears the date ii ŠS 8 (Umma month name). It is registered under the museum number CBS 3593.

BIBLIOGRAPHY

1910 Myhrman, BE 3/1 pl. 7 no. 13 (copy)
1962 Hallo, HUCA 33 p. 39 Šu-Sin 18iii (study)
1986 Kärki, KDDU p. 102 Šusuen 18 (iii) (edition)
1987 Winter, in Gibson and Biggs, Bureaucracy p. 97 IVr (study)
1991 Steible, NSBW 2 p. 271 Šūsuen 18 iii (study)

TEXT

1) ^{d}*šu*-^{d}EN.ZU
2) lugal-kala-ga
3) lugal-uri$_{5}$.KI-ma
4) lugal-an-ub-da-límmu-ba
5) lú-^{d}utu
6) dumu ur-^{d}^{aš}aš$_{7}$-gi$_{4}$
7) énsi-
8) adab.KI
9) ir$_{11}$-zu

1–3) Šū-Sîn, mighty king, king of Ur,

5–9) Lu-Utu, son of Ur-Ašgi, governor of Adab, (is) your servant.

2002

Tablets dated to the years ŠS 4–6 mention a certain Irmu as governor of Girsu. He is almost certainly the same figure who appears as Ir-Nanna, governor of Lagaš, in inscription E3/2.1.4.13 and in this text.

For the equation of Irmu = Ir-Nanna, see E. Sollberger, AfO 17 (1954–56) pp. 36–38; Falkenstein, Neusumerische Gerichtsurkunden 1 p. 37; Hallo, Royal Titles pp. 114–15; C. Wilcke, ZA 60 (1970) p. 62; J.M. Scharashenidze, in Harmatta and Komoróczy, Wirtschaft und Gesellschaft pp. 106–107; P. Steinkeller, in Gibson and Biggs, Bureaucracy p. 35 n. 48; and Sallaberger, Kalender 1 p. 167. Reservations on the equation were expressed by H. Waetzoldt in WO 11 (1980) p. 139 and JAOS 111 (1991) p. 640. If the Ir-Nanna mentioned as a dumu-lugal "prince" in line 4 of the tablet

(Schneider, Strassburg no. 111) refers to this same Ir-Nanna, then the governor was a member of the royal family. Further, according to an unpublished tablet in Chicago (A 5426 line 7, see Michalowski, in Gibson and Biggs, Bureaucracy p. 58 n. 15), Amar-Suena's daughter Geme-Eanna was betrothed to Irmu's son. Irmu is frequently named in the corpus of Ur III "literary letters" edited in part by P. Michalowski (see Michalowski, Correspondence pp. 135–85).

A seal inscription referring to Ir-Nanna as "grand-vizier" (sukkal-maḫ) is found on three undated tablets from Girsu.

CATALOGUE

Ex.	Museum number	Dimensions (cm)	Lines preserved	cpn
1	AOT c: 3 (Paris)	3+ long	1–7, 9	p
2	L 866 (Istanbul)	2.7 long	1–9	p
3	AO 2450 = AOT c: 25 (Paris)	—	1–9	p

COMMENTARY

Ex. 1 belongs to a slightly different seal inscription; it omits line 8. The three inscriptions are edited here for convenience. All the impressions come from undated tablets. Lines 1–4 of exs. 2–3 are found in col. i, lines 5–9 in col. ii.

BIBLIOGRAPHY

1884–1912 de Sarzec, Découvertes 1 p. 310 fig. P (ex. 1, copy); p. 311–12 (ex. 3, study)
1894 Thureau-Dangin, RA 3 p. 124 n. 5 (ex. 3, partial edition)
1897 Thureau-Dangin, RA 4 pl. 31 (ex. 3, copy)
1903 Thureau-Dangin, RTC no. 430 (ex. 1, copy); no. 429 (ex. 3, copy)
1907 Thureau-Dangin, SAK pp. 202–203 Gimil-sin f (exs. 1, 3, edition)
1910 de Genouillac, ITT 2 pl. II no. 866 (ex. 2, photo)
1910 Ward, Seals p. 28 fig. 52b (ex. 3, copy)
1920 Delaporte, Louvre 1 p. 23 and pl. 12, T. 217 and T. 218 (exs. 1, 3, photo, edition); ex. 2 (study)
1929 Barton, RISA pp. 296–97 Gimil-Sin 9 (ex. 1, edition)
1971 Sollberger and Kupper, IRSA IIIB5b (exs. 1, 3, translation)
1986 Kärki, KDDU pp. 102–103 Šusuen 18 (v) (exs. 1, 3, translation)
1987 Winter, in Gibson and Biggs, Bureaucracy p. 97 § IVg (study)
1989 Lafont and Yıldız, TCT 1 p. 113 no. 866 (ex. 2, transliteration)

TEXT

1) ᵈ*šu*-ᵈEN.ZU
2) lugal-kala-ga
3) lugal-uri$_5$.KI-ma
4) lugal-an-ub-da-límmu-ba
5) ir$_{11}$-ᵈnanna
6) sukkal-maḫ
7) dumu ur-ᵈšul-pa-è
8) sukkal-maḫ
9) ir$_{11}$-zu

1–4) Šū-Sîn, mighty king, king of Ur, king of the four quarters:

5–9) Ir-Nanna, grand-vizier, son of Ur-Šulpae, grand-vizier, (is) your servant.

2003

Two tablets from Girsu dating to the reign of Šū-Sîn bear the impressions of a seal of a servant of Gudea, governor of Lagaš. Lines 1–5 are arranged in one column.

CATALOGUE

Ex.	Museum Number	ITT no.	Date
1	L 4216	ITT 2 no. 4216	- xiii ŠS 6
2	L 9827	ITT 5 no. 9827	- ŠS 3

BIBLIOGRAPHY

1910 de Genouillac, ITT 2 pl. 62 no. 4216 (ex. 1, copy)
1921 de Genouillac, ITT 5 no. 9827 (ex. 2, study)

TEXT

1) dgù-dé-a
2) énsi-lagaš.KI
3) ur-dšár-ùr-ra
4) dumu ur-dEN.ZU
5) ir$_{11}$-zu

1–2) Gudea, governor of Lagaš:

3–5) Ur-Šarura, son of Ur-Suena (is) your servant.

2004

The seal inscription of Apillaša, general of Kazallu, is known from a clay bulla dated to ŠS 3 (no month name noted).

COMMENTARY

The bulla, NCBT 2307, is housed in the Yale collections. Lines 1–4 are found in col. i, lines 5–8 in col. ii. The inscription was collated.

BIBLIOGRAPHY

1969 Kutscher, JCS 22 pp. 63–65 (photo, edition)
1974 Wilcke, CRRA 19 p. 182 n. 100 (study)
1981 Buchanan and Hallo, Early Near Eastern Seals no. 648x (study)
1987 Winter, in Gibson and Biggs, Bureaucracy p. 97 § IVf (study)

TEXT

1) ^{d}*šu*-^{d}EN.ZU
2) lugal-kala-ga
3) lugal-uri$_5$.KI-ma
4) lugal-an-ub-da-límmu-ba
5) *a-pi-la-ša*
6) GÌR.NÍTA
7) ka-zal-lu.KI
8) ir$_{11}$-zu

1–4) Šū-Sîn, mighty king, king of Ur, king of the four quarters:

5–8) Apillaša, general of Kazallu, (is) your servant.

2005

The names of four Nippur governors are known for the reign of Šū-Sîn. The first, Lugal-melam, had served in the post during the entire reign of Amar-Suena; he is further mentioned in a tablet dated to ŠS 1 (Pohl, TMH NF 1/2 no. 231). Lugal-melam was apparently followed by Namzi-tara, who, in turn, was succeeded by Ur-Nanibgal. While we have, as yet, no seal inscription for Ur-Nanibgal, he is named as governor of Nippur in the seal inscription of his son Dada (see E3/2.1.4.2007). Dada, in turn, is attested as governor of Nippur in a tablet dated to ŠS 5 (see Keiser, YOS 4 no. 77 line 4) and in inscriptions E3/2.1.4.2007–9 and E3/2.1.5.2007–2010. In view of its broken nature and the fact that it appears on an undated tablet, the seal inscription of Ur-Dumuzi[da], servant of Dada (see Çığ and Kızılyay, NRVN 1 no. 255), is not edited in this volume.

The seal inscription of Namzi-tara is found on an undated tablet from Nippur.

COMMENTARY

A cast of the tablet, CBS 9766, was published by D. Owen (see bibliography); the number of the original in Istanbul is unknown. Lines 1–5 are found in col. i, lines 6–12 in col. ii.

BIBLIOGRAPHY

1973 Owen, in Studies Gordon 1 pp. 131–34 (copy, edition)
1987 Winter, in Gibson and Biggs, Bureaucracy p. 97 IVt (study)

TEXT

1) [^{d}]*šu*-^{d}EN.ZU
2) ki-ág-^{d}en-líl-lá
3) lugal-kala-ga
4) lugal-uri$_5$.KI-ma
5) lugal-an-ub-da-límmu-ba
6) nam-z[i-tar-ra]
7) énsi-
8) nibru.KI

1–5) Šū-Sîn, beloved of the god Enlil, mighty king, king of Ur, king of the four quarters:

6–8) Namz[i-tara], governor of Nippur,

9) dumu ur-^{d}nanibgal(DINGIR over DINGIR.NISSABA)
10) énsi-
11) nibru.KI-ka
12) ir_{11}-[zu]

9–12) son of Ur-Nanibgal, governor of Nippur, (is) [your] servant.

2006

The impression of a seal of Namzi-tara that dates to a time before he was governor is found on an undated tablet inscribed with an Ur III letter order.

COMMENTARY

The tablet was found in the Hilprecht excavations at Nippur; it bears the museum number Ni 372. Ḫabaluge, governor of Adab, is mentioned in line 1 of the letter. Lines 1–4 are found in col. i, lines 5–9 in col. ii.

BIBLIOGRAPHY

1966 Sollberger, Correspondence pp. 26–27 no. 73 (edition)
1986 Kärki, KDDU p. 102 Šusuen 18 (iv) (edition)
1987 Winter, in Gibson and Biggs, Bureaucracy p. 97 IVt (study)

TEXT

1) ^{d}*šu*-^{d}EN.ZU
2) lugal-kala-ga
3) lugal-uri_5.KI-ma
4) lugal-an-ub-da-límmu-ba
5) nam-zi-tar-ra
6) dumu ur-^{d}nanibgal(DINGIR over DINGIR.NISSABA)
7) énsi-
8) nibru.KI-ka
9) ir_{11}-zu

1–4) Šū-Sîn, mighty king, king of Ur, king of the four quarters:

5–9) Namzi-tara, son of Ur-Nanibgal, governor of Nippur, (is) your servant.

2007

The impression of a seal of Dada, governor of Nippur, in which he acknowledges Šū-Sîn as his lord, is found on an undated tablet from the SI.A-a archive.

COMMENTARY

The seal impression is found on IM 43456, a tablet which was written at Nippur, but which apparently came from the (as yet unlocated) site which yielded the tablets of the so-called SI.A-a archive. For this archive, see the comments of Steinkeller in Sale Documents pp. 305–307.

We may note here in connection with the Dada seal inscription an Ur III tablet that mentions the house of Dada, "governor of Nippur" (IM 44369: Calvot and Pettinato, MVN 8 no. 219 obv. line 6′).

BIBLIOGRAPHY

1979 Calvot and Pettinato, MVN 8 no. 151 (copy)
1989 Steinkeller, Sale Documents pp. 247–48 no. 66 (edition)
1990 Maeda, ASJ 12 p. 71 (edition)

TEXT

1) [d]*šu*-dEN.ZU 2) [ki]-ág-[d]en-líl-lá 3) lugal-kala-ga 4) lugal-uri$_5$.KI-ma 5) lugal-an-ub-da-límmu-ba	1–5) Šū-Sîn, [be]loved of the [god] Enlil, mighty king, king of Ur, king of the four quarters:
6) da-[da] 7) én[si]- 8) nibru.[KI]	6–8) Da[da], gov[ernor] of Nippur,
9) dumu ur-dnanib[gal](DINGIR over DINGIR.NI[SSABA] 10) én[si]- 11) nibru.[KI]	9–11) son of Ur-Nanib[gal], gov[ernor] of Nippur:
12) ir$_{11}$-[zu]	12) (is) [your] servant.

2008

The impression of a seal of a servant of Dada is found on a tablet from Nippur dated to i ŠS 5.

COMMENTARY

The seal impression is found on HS 1330; lines 1–3 are found in col. i, lines 4–7 in col. ii.

Line 4 was copied as lú by Pohl, TMH NF 1/2 Siegel no. 130*. Waetzoldt (OrAnt 15 [1976] p. 327) collated the impression and read lugal-[...]/⌈al/ta⌉[x]. Based on the assumption that this seal inscription is the successor of Lugal-magure's seal dedicated to the Nippur governor Lugal-melam during the time of Amar-Suena (see E3/2.1.3.2004), we have restored line 4 as lugal-[má-gur$_8$]-⌈re⌉.

BIBLIOGRAPHY

1937 Pohl, TMH NF 1/2 pl. 94 seal no. 130* (copy)
1976 Waetzoldt, OrAnt 15 p. 327 to no. 130* (study)

TEXT

1) da-da
2) énsi-
3) nibru.KI
4) lugal-[má-gur$_8$]-⌈re⌉
5) dub-sar
6) dumu lugal-gub-ba-ni
7) ir$_{11}$-zu

1–3) Dada, governor of Nippur:

4–7) Lugal-magure, scribe, son of Lugal-gubani (is) your servant.

2009

The seal of a servant of Dada is housed in the Vorderasiatisches Museum, Berlin. Since no Ur III king is named in the seal inscription it could date to the time of either Šū-Sîn or Ibbi-Sîn. The inscription has arbitrarily been edited in this volume under the rubric Šū-Sîn.

COMMENTARY

The haematite seal with this inscription, which measures 2.5 cm in length and 1.3 cm in diameter, was purchased in London in 1890. It now bears the museum number VA 2666. Lines 1–4 are found in col. i, lines 5–7 in col. ii.

BIBLIOGRAPHY

1893 Lehmann, BA 2 pp. 595–96 (copy in typescript, translation)
1908–9 Messerschmidt, Amliche Berichte 20 p. 130 fig. 85 (photo, translation, study)
1940 Moortgat, VAR no. 252 (photo, edition, study)

TEXT

1) da-da
2) énsi-
3) nibru.KI
4) ^{d}nanna-gal-zu
5) dub-sar
6) dumu ^{d}en-líl-dingir-zu
7) ìr-<zu>

1–3) Dada, governor of Nippur:

4–7) Nanna-galzu, scribe, son of Enlil-dingirzu (is) <your> servant.

2010

A seal impression of Lu-Nanna, general of Simudar, appears on a tablet from Nippur that dates to ŠS 1 (no month name preserved).

COMMENTARY

The seal inscription appears on N 798 (Philadelphia). Lines 1–4 are found in col. i, lines 5–8 in col. ii. The inscription was collated.

For the career of Lu-Nanna, general of Simudar, see Goetze, JCS 17 (1963) pp. 16–17 no. 18; Lieberman, JCS 22 (1969) pp. 59–60 and n. 70; Owen, in Studies Gordon 1 p. 136 and n. 53; and Michalowski, Correspondence pp. 56–59. He appears in the "literary letter" of Šarrum-bāni to Šū-Sîn as "governor of the land of Simudar." According to the letter, he was charged (along with Šarrum-bāni — elsewhere known to be the governor of Apiak) with the construction of the wall named Murīq-Tidnim "It keeps Tidnum at a distance" (see Michalowski, Correspondence p. 226 line 28).

There is a Lu-Nanna who is named as a prince (dumu-lugal) in two tablets dated to Š 44 (Legrain, TRU no. 24 line 5 and no. 28 line 10), and in a tablet probably to be dated to AS 7 rather than IS 9 (see Schneider, Strassburg no. 105 lines 9–10), but whether he was the Lu-Nanna of this seal inscription cannot be determined with the evidence at hand. According to Goetze (JCS 17 [1963] p. 16 sub no. 18), Lu-Nanna is attested as the son of Ur-nigin-gar in YBC 13087 (likely date AS 7 or 8) and NBC 91 (Nies, UDT no. 91 line 38 — date broken away). Of interest, then, is the fact that Ur-nigin-gar appears as a prince in a tablet dated to Š 32 (see Hackman, BIN 5 no. 11 line 5). If Lu-Nanna, general of Simudar, was the son of this Ur-nigin-gar, then he likely was Šulgi's grandson. The fact that it was a common practice for the Ur III kings to instal their children in high administrative positions makes this hypothesis an attractive supposition.

Simudar was a major city which, according to the evidence of Legrain, UET 3 no. 75 lines 6–7, lay on the banks of the Diyālā river. The cited text (which dates to i ŠS 1) records a votive gift of Lu-Nanna; perhaps it was made to celebrate Šū-Sîn's accession to the throne.

BIBLIOGRAPHY

1973 Owen, in Studies Gordon p. 136 n. 53 (transliteration)
1976 Michalowski, Correspondence, pp. 57–58 (edition)
1982 Owen, NATN no. 776 (copy, transliteration)
1987 Winter, in Gibson and Biggs, Bureaucracy p. 97 IVp (study)

TEXT

1) [^{d}*š*]*u*-^{d}EN.ZU
2) lugal-kala-ga
3) lugal-uri$_5$.KI-ma
4) lugal-an-ub-[d]a-límmu-ba
5) lú-^{d}[nanna]
6) GÌR.[NÍTA]
7) sí-m[u-dar.KI]
8) ir$_{11}$-[zu]

1–4) [Š]ū-Sîn, mighty king, king of Ur, king of the four quart[ers]:

5–8) Lu-[Nanna], gen[eral] of Sim[udar], (is) [your] servant.

2011

Four Drehem tablets in Istanbul dated to ŠS 3 and ŠS 5 bear impressions of a seal of a servant of Ṣilluš-Dagān, governor of Simurrum. The text is arranged in one column.

CATALOGUE

Ex.	Museum number	Date
1	PD 1327	vi ŠS 5
2	PD 1355	vi ŠS 3
3	PD 1365	vi ŠS 3
4	PD 1375	vi ŠS 5

BIBLIOGRAPHY

1988 Yıldız and Gomi, PDT 2 nos. 1327, 1355, 1365, and 1375 (exs. 1–4, transliteration)
1992 Maeda, ASJ 14 p. 161 n. 39 (exs. 1–4, transliteration)

TEXT

1) *ṣi-lu-uš-*^{d}*da-gan* 2) énsi si-mu-ru-um.KI	1–2) Ṣilluš-Dagān, governor of Simurrum:
3) *i-la-ak-šu-qir* 4) dumu a-lu šabra 5) ir_{11}-zu	3–5) Ilak-šūqir, son of Alu, the chief administrator, (is) your servant.

2012

Archival sources indicate that Aa-kala served as governor of Umma in the period from AS 8 to ŠS 6 (see Maeda, ASJ 12 [1990] p. 75). The governor's seal inscription is known from innumerable examples.

For a seal inscription of Aa-kala dating to the reign of Amar-Suena see E3/2.1.3.2007.

COMMENTARY

Here we list YBC 1500 (YOS 4 no. 193) as being representative of the many exemplars of this seal inscription. Lines 1–4 of the text are found in col. i, lines 5–8 in col. ii. For a list of tablets bearing this seal impression see Bergamini, Mesopotamia 26 (1991) p. 114.

A seal of a supposed *a-a-nu-um*, governor of Umma, is found on a tablet published by Legrain (RA 32 [1935] p. 130). That the reading actually is *a-a-nu-um* has been confirmed by collation; see Borger, HKL 3 p. 2, citing Gelb. Since *a-a-nu-um* is otherwise unattested as governor of Umma, it may be (as Hallo, HUCA 33 [1962] p. 39 suggests) that *a-a-nu-um* is an ancient mistake for Aa-kala.

BIBLIOGRAPHY

1919 Keiser, YOS 4 no. 193 (copy)
1929 Barton, RISA pp. 296–97 Gimil-Sin 13; pp. 300–301 Âkalla (edition)
1962 Hallo, HUCA 33 p. 39 Šu-Sin 18i (study)
1981 Buchanan and Hallo, Early Near Eastern Seals nos. 651–52 (photo, edition, study)
1986 Kärki, KDDU p. 101 Šusuen 18 (i) (edition)
1987 Winter, in Gibson and Biggs, Bureaucracy p. 97 § IVa (study)
1990 Maeda, ASJ 12 p. 75 (transliteration)
1991 Bergamini, Mesopotamia 26 pp. 113–14 (study)

TEXT

1) *šu-*^{d}EN.ZU 2) lugal-kala-ga 3) lugal-uri_5.KI-ma 4) lugal-an-ub-da-límmu-ba	1–4) Šū-Sîn, mighty king, king of Ur, king of the four quarters:
5) a-a-kal-la 6) énsi- 7) umma.KI 8) ir_{11}-zu	5–8) Aa-kala, governor of Umma, (is) your servant.

2013

Two seal inscriptions of Nin-ḫilia, wife of governor Aa-kala, are known from various archival sources. The first inscription is found on twelve tablets.

CATALOGUE

Ex.	Museum number	Date
1	UCBC 668	i ŠS 3
2	BM 106686	- ŠS 1
3	BM 110896	viii ŠS 2
4	BM 106533	- ŠS 2
5	BM 107673	iv ŠS 3
6	BM 106711	- ŠS 3
7	BM 106801	xi ŠS 4
8	BM 112443	ŠS 4
9	BM 107517	- ŠS 4
10	BM 110813	xii ŠS 5
11	BM 107318	xii ŠS 5
12	BM 106830	- ŠS 5

COMMENTARY

The text is arranged in one column.

BIBLIOGRAPHY

1928 Lutz, UCP 9/2 p. 249 no. 68 (ex. 1, copy)
1974 Parr, JCS 26 pp. 90–111 Seal B (exs. 2–12, combined copy, study)

TEXT

1) nin-ḫi-lí-a
2) dam a-a-kal-la
3) énsi
4) umma.KI-ka

1–4) Nin-ḫilia, wife of Aa-kala, governor of Umma.

2014

A second seal inscription of Nin-ḫilia is found on one tablet from Umma.

COMMENTARY

The seal inscription is found on BM 107758. The tablet is dated to vii ŠS 1. The text is arranged in one column.

BIBLIOGRAPHY

1974 Parr, JCS 26 pp. 93 and 111 Seal A (copy, study)

TEXT

1) nin-[ḫ]í-⌜lí⌝-a
2) dam a-a-kal-la
3) énsi
4) umma.KI-ka

1–4) Nin-ḫilia, wife of Aa-kala, governor of Umma.

2015

Archival sources indicate that a certain Dadaga followed Aa-kala as governor at Umma; he is attested in tablets dating to the years ŠS 7–IS 2. While we have, as yet, no seal inscriptions of Dadaga as governor of Umma for the reign of Šū-Sîn (for a seal of the governor during the time of Ibbi-Sîn see E3/2.1.5.2012), we do have a seal inscription of his son, Gududu.

According to Maeda, ASJ 12 (1990) p. 74, the governor Dadaga was likely the son of Ur-nigin-gar, the "groom" (kuš$_7$ = Akkadian *kizû*[*m*]). This hypothesis is supported by the evidence of the tablet Um 2258 (see Yıldız and Gomi, Umma-Texte no. 2258), which mentions the seal of the governor in line 8′ and which is impressed with the seal of "Dadaga, scribe, son of Ur-nigin-gar, the groom."

CATALOGUE

Ex.	Museum number	Date	Lines preserved
1	WHM 619	v AS 7	1–8
2	Um 493	x ŠS 9	1–8

COMMENTARY

Lines 1–4 are found in col. i and lines 5–8 in col. ii. Here we have listed only the earliest and the latest examples of this well-attested seal inscription.

BIBLIOGRAPHY

1973 Kang, SETUA no. 46 seal impression no. 21 (ex. 1, copy, edition)
1988 Yıldız, MVN 14 no. 493 (ex. 2, transliteration)
1990 Maeda, ASJ 12 p. 74 (transliteration)

TEXT

1) ^{d}*šu*-^{d}EN.ZU
2) lugal-kala-ga
3) lugal-uri$_5$.KI-ma
4) lugal-an-ub-da-límmu-ba
5) gu-du-du
6) dub-sar
7) dumu da-da-ga
8) ir$_{11}$-zu

1–3) Šū-Sîn, mighty king, king of Ur,

4) king of the four quarters:
5–8) Gududu, scribe, son of Dadaga, (is) your servant.

(d) Miscellaneous Votive Inscriptions 2016–18

2016

A vase fragment formed from the join of two smaller pieces bears a votive inscription for the life of Šū-Sîn.

COMMENTARY

The vase fragment of dark-grey steatite is formed from the join of BM 15976 (reg. no. 96-6-12, 196) (frgm. 1) + Collection U. Sissa (number unknown) (frgm. 2). Both fragments are purchased pieces whose original provenances are unknown.

BIBLIOGRAPHY

1922 BM Guide p. 86 no. 76 (frgm. 1, study)
1966 Leemans, JCS 20 pp. 35–36 no. 2 (frgm. 2, copy, study)
1972 Sjöberg, JCS 24 p. 73 (frgm. 2, transliteration)
1986 Kärki, KDDU pp. 133–34 Šusuen 26 (frgm. 2, edition)
1991 Braun-Holzinger, Weihgaben p. 189 G 365 (frgm. 1, edition); pp. 189–90 G 366 (frgm. 2, edition)
1991 Steible, NSBW 2 pp. 274, 276–77 Šūsuen 25 and 27 (frgms. 1–2, edition); pl. 24 (frgm. 1, photo)

TEXT

Lacuna
1′) nam-[ti]-
2′) ^{d}*šu*-⌈^{d}⌉[EN.ZU]
3′) išib-an-[na]
4′) gudu$_4$-šu-[daddag]-
5′) ^{d}en-[líl]
6′) ^{d}nin-líl-[ka]
7′) ù dingir-[gal-gal-e-ne]
8′) [lugal ^{d}en-líl-le]
9′) ki-á[g]-
10′) šà-ga-[na]
11′) in-p[à]

Lacuna
1′–13′) for the li[fe]of Šū-[Sîn,] purification priest of the god A[n], anointed priest with [clean] hands for the gods En[lil], Ninlil, and the [great] gods, [the king whom the god Enlil] lovingly chose [in his] (own) heart [for] the shepherdship [of] the land, [mighty ki]ng,
Lacuna

12′) sipa-kalam-[ma-šè]
13′) [lu]gal-[kala-ga]
Lacuna

2017

A marble vase fragment was dedicated to the god Šara for the life of Šū-Sîn.

COMMENTARY

The translucent red-beige marble vase fragment, which has a diameter of 5.5 cm (original diameter 11.2 cm) and a height of 9.2 cm, was acquired through purchase. It bears the museum number YBC 2159. The text is arranged in one column. The inscription was collated.

BIBLIOGRAPHY

1937 Stephens, YOS 9 no. 24 (copy)
1962 Hallo, HUCA 33 p. 38 Šu-Sin 15 (study)
1986 Kärki, KDDU p. 100 Šusuen 15 (edition)
1991 Braun-Holzinger, Weihgaben p. 189 G 364 (edition)
1991 Steible, NSBW 2 p. 269 Šūsuen 15 (edition)

TEXT

1) ⸢d⸣šára
2) [lu]gal-a-ni-ir
3) [n]am-ti-
4) ⸢d⸣*šu*-dEN.ZU
5) [lug]al-kala-ga
6) [luga]l-uri$_5$.KI-ma
7) [lugal-an-ub-d]a-límmu-ba-[ka-šè]
Lacuna

1–2) For the god Šara, his [lo]rd,

3–7) [for] the [l]ife of Šū-Sîn, mighty [ki]ng, [kin]g of Ur, [king of the] four [quart]ers,
Lacuna

2018

A bronze axe was dedicated for the life of Šū-Sîn.

COMMENTARY

The bronze or copper axe, which measures 16×5×5 cm, was acquired through purchase; it bears the museum number O 353 (Brussels). Lines 1–5 are found in col. i, lines 6–9 in col. ii, and lines 10–14 in col. iii.

BIBLIOGRAPHY

1925 Speleers, Recueil no. 13 (copy, edition)
1962 Hallo, HUCA 33 p. 38 Šu-Sin 16 (study)
1986 Kärki, KDDU pp. 100–101 Šusuen 16 (edition)
1991 Braun-Holzinger, Weihgaben p. 90 MW 14 (edition)
1991 Steible, NSBW 2 pp. 269–79 Šūsuen 16 (edition)

TEXT

1) ^{d}šára
2) nir-gál-an-na
3) dumu-ki-ág-
4) ^{d}inanna
5) lugal-a-ni-ir

1–5) For the god Šara, distinguished one of the god An, beloved son of the goddess Inanna, his lord,

6) nam-[t]i-
7) ^{d}*šu*-^{d}EN.ZU
8) lugal-kala-ga
9) lugal-uri$_{5}$.KI-ma
10) lug[al-an-ub]-d[a-límmu-ba-ka-šè]

6–10) for the li[f]e of Šū-Sîn, mighty man, king of Ur, ki[ng of the four quar]te[rs],

11) ur-^{d}[...]
12) àga-ús-lu[g]a[l](?)
13) dumu-ur-ab-ba-ke$_{4}$

11–13) Ur-[...], *royal* soldier, son of Ur-aba,

14) mu-na-⌜dím⌝

14) fashioned (this axe) for him.

Ibbi-Sîn

E3/2.1.5

According to the Weld-Blundell exemplar of the Sumerian King List, Ibbi-Sîn reigned twenty-four years. This is the same figure given in the Ur-Isin King List published by Sollberger (JCS 8 [1954] pp. 135–36). The year names of Ibbi-Sîn are listed here according to the scheme given by Sollberger in RLA 5 [1980] pp. 4–7.

I. Year Names and Events of the Reign

(1) mu ^{d}*i-bí*-^{d}EN.ZU lugal "The year Ibbi-Sîn (became) king." U 3637: L. Legrain, UET 3 no. 950.

Archival texts dating to x ŠS 9, the month after Šū-Sîn died, enable us to follow in some detail the events of the coronation of Ibbi-Sîn. These have been studied by M. Sigrist ("Le deuil pour Šū-Sîn," in Studies Sjöberg pp. 499–505); Th. Jacobsen ("The Reign of Ibbī-Suen," JCS 7 [1953] p. 36 n. 2); E. Sollberger ("Remarks on Ibbīsîn's Reign," JCS 7 [1953] pp. 48–50); ibid. (RLA 5 [1980] p. 2); and W. Sallaberger (Kalender 1 pp. 112–13 and n. 509). On the first day of x AS 9, Ibbi-Sîn was in Nippur. A tablet from Drehem (Schneider, Drehem- und Djoḫatexte no. 108 = Molina, Montserrat no. 108) records (i 1–7) various offerings to the temples of Enlil and Ninlil on the occasion of the royal entry (lugal-ku_4-ra). The tablet follows (i 8–14) with a list of provisions for the king's trip to Ur: "(for) the king going to Ur, loaded on the boat" (lugal-uri_5.KI-šè du-ni má-a ba-a-gar); for the reading du-ni instead of gin-né in this line, see Sallaberger, ZA 82 (1992) p. 139. The tablet MAH 19352 (E. Sollberger, JCS 7 [1953] p. 48) reveals that the king's journey to Ur involved a stop at Uruk. The tablet records the disbursement of various animals which are subsumed by the expression: "(at) the entry of the king in the evening, (during) the king's trip from Nippur to Uruk, when Ibbi-Sîn received the crown" (á-u_4-te-na lugal-ku_4-ra lugal nibru.KI-ta unu.KI-šè du-ni u_4 ^{d}*i-bí*-^{d}EN.ZU àga šu ba-an-ti-a). By 3 x ŠS 9, Ibbi-Sîn was at Ur; a Yale tablet bearing that date (NBC 100: Nies, UDT no. 100) records various offerings for the god Nanna in Ur on the occasion (lines 19–20): "when Ibbi-Sîn received the crown" (u_4 ^{d}*i-bí*-^{d}EN.ZU àga šu ba-an-ti-a). Finally, a tablet dated to 6 x ŠS 9 (Emory 38: Sollberger, JCS 10 [1956] p. 28) also alludes to the coronation (u_4 ^{d}*i-bí*-^{d}EN.ZU àga šu ba-an-ti-a).

The installation ceremonies for a-ra-zu-^{d}*i-bí*-^{d}EN.ZU-ka-šè-pà-da, *en* of Eridu.

An archival text from Drehem (AUAM 73.2209: Sigrist, AUCT 3 no. 489) ends with a broken year name of Šū-Sîn: mu ^{d}*šu*-[^{d}EN.ZU] [...] x [...]. The tablet records the disbursement of various animals for festivities, which apparently took place in Uruk (if the restoration of line 50: [šà-unu].KI-ga is correct), and which involved the installation of a certain a-ra-zu-^{d}*i-bí*-^{d}EN.ZU-ka-šè-pà-da as *en* of Eridu. As far as can be determined, priestly officials whose names were composed with royal names were installed only during the reigns of their royal namesakes. This fact, then, coupled with the evidence of the broken year name, indicates that a-ra-zu-^{d}*i-bí*-^{d}EN.ZU-ka-šè-pà-da must have been installed during ŠS 9. More precisely, her installation likely occurred after the death of Šū-Sîn, that is, sometime after ix ŠS 9.

Of interest in this connection is a Drehem tablet dated to ix ŠS 9 (U 22, National and University Library, Prague: Krušina-Černy, ArOr 25 [1957] p. 562) that records (lines 4–5): "regular offerings for NINLIL*tum-zinušu*, *en* of Eridu, at Kuʾar" (sá-du$_{11}$-^{d}NIN.LÍL-*tum-zi-nu-šu* en-eridu.KI-ga šà-ḪA.A.KI). It appears, then, that ^{d}NIN.LÍL-*tum-zi-nu-šu* was the personal name of a-ra-zu-^{d}*i-bí*-^{d}EN.ZU-ka-šè-pà-da. As far as can be determined, this is the only time we know the actual personal name of a priest or priestess. The already cited Drehem tablet (AUAM 73.2209: Sigrist, AUCT 3 no. 489) gives a detailed account of the ceremonies for the *en*'s installation, which, as it turns out, took place at Uruk, not Eridu. A companion to this tablet is the text UCBC 604: Lutz, UCP 9/2/2 no. 4, which clearly attests to the identical rites in Uruk. Its date of xii ŠS 9 suggests a date for AUCT 3 no. 489. Another tablet (LB 50: Hallo, TLB 3 no. 29), dated to xii ŠS 9, may refer to the same ceremonies. It notes a *ki-utu* held (line 10): "when the *en* of Eridu was installed" (⸢u$_{4}$⸣ en-eridu.KI-ga ba-ḫun). Another tablet (PD 270: Salonen, Puzriš-Dagan-Texte no. 270), dated to 10 xii ŠS 9, records various royal disbursements (zi-ga lugal) on the occasion "when the festival of the god Enki was celebrated" (u$_{4}$ ezem-^{d}en-ki-ka in-na-ak). In view of the date of the tablet, we are inclined to see this as a further reference to ceremonies for the installation of the new *en*. It is not clear, however, whether these last noted observances took place at Uruk or Eridu. Finally, a tablet dated to vi IS 1 (L 10002: de Genouillac, ITT 5 pl. 63 no. 10002) mentions (line 1′) the installation of the new *en* ([a]-ra-zu-[^{d}]-i-bí-^{d}EN.ZU-ka-pà-da ḫun-gá).

In normal circumstances the installation of the new *en* of Eridu would have provided the name of the next year. In this case, it had to be named for the accession of Ibbi-Sîn. Apparently, a-ra-zu-^{d}*i-bí*-^{d}EN.ZU-ka-šè pà-da had a short tenure of office; the name of her successor, en-nam-ti-^{d}*i-bí*-^{d}EN.ZU-ka-šè-[k]ìri-šu-gál x-unu en-^{d}en-ki-ka, appears in the year name for IS 11.

(2) mu en ^{d}inanna máš-e ì-pà "The year the *en* of the god Inanna was chosen by omens." U 3517: L. Legrain, UET 3 no. 1667.

The name of the new *en* of Inanna, who is unnamed in the year name, is known from the year name for IS 4 to have been En-amgal-ana. An archival text in Jerusalem (Ste-Anne no. 374: unpublished, information courtesy R.M. Sigrist) refers to her designation by oracles.

The evidence of an archival text (PD 563: Salonen, Puzriš-Dagan-Texte no. 563) indicates that En-amgal-ana's predecessor had died by 21 x ŠS 9. The text, according to a collation of the tablet by K. Volk (see Sallaberger, Kalender 1 p. 147 n. 696), records an offering for "the throne of the (deceased) *en* of Inanna" ([GIŠ.g]u-za en [^{d}ina]nna[?]-šè).

The installation of the *en* of the god Nanna at Urum.

A tablet in the Eames Collection (housed in the New York Public Library), L 20: Oppenheim, Eames Collection pp. 110–11 L 20 = Sauren, New York Public Library no. 374, contains the remark (lines 8–9): "when the *en* of Nanna of Urum was installed" (u$_{4}$ en-^{d}nanna ÚR×Ú.KI-ka ba-ḫun-gá). See the comments of Steinkeller, JCS 32 (1980) p. 25 who notes this cultic installation and discusses the location of the important Babylonian city of Urum. It was situated somewhere between Kutha and Sippar. See also Frayne, Early Dynastic List pp. 12–13 (citing Green, ASJ 8 [1986] pp. 77–83), where evidence suggesting a location for ancient Urum near modern Tell ʿUqair is given .

(3) mu ^{d}*i-bí*-^{d}EN.ZU lugal-uri$_{5}$.KI-ma-ke$_{4}$ *si-mu-ru-um*.KI mu-ḫul "The year Ibbi-Sîn destroyed Simurrum." U 4607: L. Legrain, UET 3 no. 1664.

The evidence of the archival record would suggest that Ibbi-Sîn's Simurrum campaign had begun already by vii IS 1. A Girsu tablet dated to that time (Telloh 737: de Genouillac, ITT 2 no. 737) notes cattle as a máš-da-ri-a offering "brought from(?) the campaign" (kaskal-la er!-ra).

(4) mu en-am-gal-an-na en-^{d}inanna ba-ḫun "The year En-amgal-ana, *en* of the goddess Inanna was installed." U 6399: L. Legrain, UET 3 no. 856.

A reflection of this cultic installation in the archival record is found in a small tablet dated to the 27 xi IS 3 (AO 27489: B. Lafont, RA 77 [1983] p. 71 = Lafont, Documents no. 273). It records a disbursement of animals "to instal the *en* of the goddess Inanna of Uruk" (en-^{d}inanna-unu.KI-ga ḫun-e-dè).

(5) mu *tu-ki-in*-PA-*mi-ig-ri-ša* dumu-munus-lugal énsi-za-ab-ša-li.KI-ke$_4$ ba-an-tuk "The year the governor of Zabšali married Tukīn-ḫaṭṭi-migrīša, the daughter of the king." U 4708: L. Legrain, UET 3 no. 376.

(6) mu ^{d}*i-bí*-^{d}EN.ZU lugal-uri$_5$.KI-ma-ke$_4$ nibru.KI uri$_5$.KI-ma bàd-gal-bi mu-dù "The year Ibbi-Sîn, king of Ur, built the great walls of Nippur and Ur." U 3968: L. Legrain, UET 3 no. 151.

Ibbi-Sîn's construction of the "wall of Ur" is recorded in inscription E3/2.1.5.1. Now, as noted in our discussion of E3/2.1.1.4 (an Ur-Nammu text dealing with the construction of the "wall of Ur"), the expression "wall of Ur" need not have referred exclusively to the city wall, but may have been a designation as well of the temenos wall. Likewise, the fact that some of the cones with the Ibbi-Sîn "wall of Ur" text came from the area of the Royal Cemetery would indicate that Ibbi-Sîn's construction work did include repair of the temenos wall. On the other hand, the fact that one exemplar (ex. 7) came from the NE city wall suggests that the whole wall compound subsumed by the name "wall of Ur" during the reign of Ibbi-Sîn included *both* the temenos and city walls.

(7) mu-ús-sa ^{d}*i-bí*-^{d}EN.ZU lugal-uri$_5$.KI-ma-ke$_4$ nibru.KI uri$_5$.KI-ma bàd-gal-bi mu-dù "The year after Ibbi-Sîn, king of Ur, built the great walls of Nippur and Ur." U 3724: L. Legrain, UET 3 no. 410.

(8) mu-ús-sa ^{d}*i-bí*-^{d}EN.ZU lugal-uri$_5$.KI-ma-ke$_4$ nibru.KI uri$_5$.KI-ma bàd-gal-bi mu-dù-a mu-ús-sa-bi "The year after Ibbi-Sîn, king of Ur, built the great walls of Nippur and Ur, the year after this." U 3639: L. Legrain, UET 3 no. 395.

(9) mu ^{d}*i-bí*-EN.ZU lugal-uri$_5$.KI-ma-ke$_4$ ḫu-úḫ-nu-ri KA. BAD-ma-da-an-ša-an.KI-šè [á]-dugud ba-ši-in-gin [...-r]a-gin$_7$ á-maḫ [sì-bi sa] bí-[in-gar] "The year Ibbi-Sîn, king of Ur, marched with heavy forces against Ḫuḫnuri, the 'open mouth' of the land of Anšan, and like a ..., his might [having surrounded it, caught it in (his) net]." U 7712: L. Legrain, UET 3 no. 1383.

For the reading of the Ibbi-Sîn year name and the location of Ḫuḫnuri at modern Arrajan, about eight kilometres north of modern Behbehan on the route from Khuzistān to Fars, see J. Duchene, "La localisation de Huhnur," Studies Steve pp. 65–74.

(10) [m]u en-nir-sì-an-na [en]-^{d}nanna(Text: INANNA) máš-e in-pà "The year En-nirsi-ana, [*en*] of the god Nanna, was chosen by omens." U 7755 = IM 85465: C. Gadd, UET 1 no. 292 col. i lines 5–6.

(11) mu en-nam-ti-^{d}*i-bí*-^{d}EN.ZU-ka-šè [k]iri-šu-gál x-unu en-^{d}en-ki-ka máš-e ì-pà "The year En-namti-^{d}Ibbi-Sîn kiri-šu-gal ..., the *en* of the god Enki, was chosen by omens." U 5568: D. Loding, UET 9 no. 97; U 5320: ibid., no. 903; U 5579: ibid., no. 1142; U 5572: ibid., no. 1155; U 5569: ibid., no. 805; U 3845: L. Legrain, UET 3 no. 846; IM 85465: C. Gadd, UET 1 no. 292 col. i lines 7–11.

(12) mu ^{d}*i-bí*-^{d}EN.ZU lugal-uri$_5$.KI-ma-ke$_4$ gu-za an ^{d}nanna-ra mu-na-dím "The year Ibbi-Sîn, the king of Ur, fashioned a divine throne for the god Nanna." U 3680: L. Legrain, UET 3 no. 1384.

(13) mu-ús-sa ^{d}*i-bí*-^{d}EN.ZU lugal-uri$_5$.KI-ma-ke$_4$ gu-za an ^{d}nanna-ra mu-na-dím "The year after Ibbi-Sîn, the king of Ur, fashioned a divine throne for the god Nanna." U 6370: L. Legrain, UET 3 no. 702.

(14) mu ^{d}*i-bí*-^{d}EN.ZU lugal-uri$_5$.KI-ma-ke$_4$ šušin.KI a-dam-dun.KI ma-da a-wa-an.KI-ka u$_4$-gin$_7$ ŠID bí-in-gi$_7$ u$_4$-AŠ-a mu-un-GAM ù en-bi LÚ<×KÁR>-a mi-ni-in-dab$_5$-ba-a "The year Ibbi-Sîn, king of Ur, roared like a storm against Susa, Adamdun, (and) the land of Awan; made them submit in a single day; and took their lord(s) as bound captive(s)." U 6725: L. Legrain, UET 3 no. 45.

Two inscriptions known from an Old Babylonian Sammeltafel copy (E3/2.1.5.2–3) describe Ibbi-Sîn's fashioning of two cult vessels for the god Nanna from the gold plundered at Susa. They both contain a virtually verbatim rendition of this year name. The spectacular rise in the number of documents at Ur for the period IS 14–16 (see Lafont, RA 89 [1995] p. 5 fig. 1) is probably due to a short-lived boom in the economy at Ur brought on by the influx of booty from the campaign against Susa and Adamdum.

While the site of ancient Susa is, of course, well known (modern Šuš-e Daniel, long. 48° 15′, lat. 32° 11′) the locations of the city of Adamdum and the land of Awan have been uncertain.

Recently, F. Vallat has reported (Vallat, Rép. Géogr. 11, p. 4) the find of an inscription of Gudea of Lagaš at the village of Qalʿeh Surkekh about 6 km southwest of modern Šuštar; it apparently mentions the building of a temple in the city of Adamdum. This discovery would argue for a location of ancient Adamdum at, or near, modern Šuštar, that is, about 60 km southeast of Susa.

The data connected with Awan has been collected by M. Stolper (Encyclopaedia Iranica 3/5 pp. 113–14). Awan seems to have been a very important city in Early Dynastic times; indeed a "dynasty" of Awan appears in the Sumerian King List. The city is named in three inscriptions of the Sargonic king Rīmuš (Frayne, RIME 2 pp. 51–58 E2.1.2.6–8 = Gelb and Kienast, Königsinschriften pp. 213ff. Rīmuš C 8, C 10, and C12). All texts refer to a battle fought on the Qablītum River between the cities of Awan and Susa. Normally, the Sargonic inscriptions describe battle sites with some precision, so we would expect that Awan lay not too far from Susa. The Qablītum River of the Rīmuš inscriptions may possibly equate with Greek Coprates; the Coprates, in turn, is generally identified as the modern Diz (see Hansman, Iranica Antiqua 7 [1967] p. 32). If this is true, then we should look for ancient Awan somewhere east of the modern Diz not far from ancient Susa.

Awan does not appear, as yet, in any Ur III archival texts. As Stolper (op. cit. p. 114) notes: "Ibbi-Sin's use of the toponym is merely geographical, and probably already archaic."

(15) mu ^{d}*i-bí*-^{d}EN.ZU lugal-uri$_5$.KI-ma-ra ^{d}nanna-a šà-ki-ág-gá-ni dalla mu-un-na-an-è-a "The year the god Nanna, through the kindness of his heart, let Ibbi-Sîn, king of Ur, come forth magnificently." U 3726: L. Legrain, UET 3 no. 652.

(16) mu ^{d}*i-bí*-^{d}EN.ZU lugal-uri$_5$.KI-ma-ke$_4$ ^{d}nanna-ar ^{d}nun-me-te-an-na mu-na-dím "The year Ibbi-Sîn, king of Ur, fashioned 'Prince, ornament of heaven' for the god Nanna." U 3868: L. Legrain, UET 3 no. 679.

(17) mu ^{d}*i-bí*-^{d}EN.ZU lugal-uri$_5$.KI-ma-ra mar-dú á-IM.ùlu ul-ta uru.KI nu-zu gú im-ma-na-na-gá-ar "The year the Amorites of (the) southern border, who from ancient times have known no cities, submitted to Ibbi-Sîn, king of Ur." U 3862: L. Legrain, UET 3 no. 698.

(18) mu ^{d}*i-bí*-^{d}EN.ZU lugal-uri$_5$.KI-ma-[ke$_4$] ^{d}nin-líl ù ^{d}inanna-[ra é-GI].NA.AB.T[UM-kù mu]-ne-dù "The year Ibbi-Sîn, king of Ur, built a shining [sto]rehou[se] [for] the goddesses Ninlil and Inanna."

(19) mu-ús-sa ^{d}*i-bí*-^{d}EN.ZU lugal-uri$_5$.KI-ma-ke$_4$ ^{d}nin-líl ù ^{d}inanna-ra é-šútum-kù mu-ne-dù "The year after Ibbi-Sîn, king of Ur, built a shining storehouse for the goddesses Ninlil and Inanna." U 16517: L. Legrain, UET 3 no. 41.

(20) mu ^{d}*i-bí*-^{d}EN.ZU lugal-uri$_5$.KI-ma ^{d}en-líl-le [me]-lám-a-ni [kur-kur-r]a bí-in-dul$_4$ "The year Ibbi-Sîn, king of Ur — the god Enlil made his fearful [rad]iance cover the [lan]ds." U 2962: C. Gadd, UET 1 no. 203.

(21) mu ^{d}*i-bí*-^{d}EN.ZU lugal-uri$_5$.KI-ma-ke$_4$ ^{d}nin-igi-zi-bar-ra balag ^{d}inanna-ra mu-na-dím "The year Ibbi-Sîn, king of Ur, fashioned 'Nin-igizi-bara' the lyre/drum of the goddess Inanna." U 6378: L. Legrain, UET 3 no. 1056.

For the divine harp Nin-igizi-bara, see Sallaberger, Kalender 1 p. 88 n. 374.

(22) mu ^{d}*i-bí*-^{d}EN.ZU lugal-uri$_5$.KI-ma-ke$_4$ a-ma-ru nì-du$_{11}$-ga-dingir-re-ne-ke$_4$ zà-an-ki im-sùḫ-sùḫ-a uri$_5$.KI URU×UD.KI tab-ba bí-in-ge-en "The year Ibbi-Sîn, king of Ur, held firm the cities of Ur and URU×UD which had been devastated by the 'flood' which had been commanded by the gods and which shook the whole world." A 5765 (Chicago); U 10625; U 6718: see M. Civil, NABU 1987 no. 2 pp. 27–28 no. 49.

Although this year name was taken by Sollberger (RLA 5 [1980] p. 4) to refer to a natural disaster, the phraseology it employs is strikingly similar to that found in a passage of the literary composition "Lamentation over the Destruction of Sumer and Akkad." It describes an attack on Ur by the Gutians (Michalowski, Lamentation pp. 40–41 lines 75-78β):

u$_4$-ba ^{d}en-líl-le gu-ti-um.KI kur-ta im-ta-an-è
DU-bi a-ma-ru ^{d}en-líl-lá gaba-gi$_4$ nu-tuku-àm
im gal eden-na eden-e im-si igi-šè mu-un-ne-DU
eden níg-dagal-ba sìg ba-ab-dug$_4$ lú nu-mu-ni-in-dib-bé

Enlil then sent down Gutium from the mountains.
Their advance was as the flood of Enlil that cannot be withstood,
The great storm of the plain filled the plain, it advanced before them,
The teeming plain was destroyed, no one moved about there.

In view of this literary parallel, and bearing in mind the political circumstances of IS 22, it seems much more likely that the expression a-ma-ru in the year name should be seen not as a reference to a deluge, but rather as a "métaphore du pays inondé d'ennemis" (van Dijk, JCS 30 [1978] p. 196).

(23) mu ^{d}*i-bí*-^{d}EN.ZU lugal-uri$_5$.KI-ma-ra úgu(A.KA)^{ku}-bi-dugud kur-bi mu-na-e-ra "The year in which the people (of its country) brought a 'stupid monkey' to Ibbi-Sîn, king of Ur." U 17211 R: L. Legrain, UET 3 no. 711.

The mention of the "mountain land" in this year name suggests some connection with the Elamite invasion of Sumer. For another allusion to enemy forces as monkeys see the literary letter of Ibbi-Sîn to Puzur-Numušda (lines 15–17; translation S. Dunham, ZA 75 [1985] p. 242):

u$_4$-na-an-ga-ma ^{d}en-líl-le ki-en-gi ḫul mu-un-gi$_4$
^{úgu}ugu$_4$-bi kur-bi-ta e$_{11}$-dè
nam-sipa-kalam-ma-šè mu-un-íl

Earlier Enlil hated Sumer
and a monkey, who came down from his mountain,
he (= Enlil) raised to shepherdship over Sumer.

The reference in the letter is clearly to Išbi-Erra; see Sjöberg, in Studies Hallo p. 211. For the word úgu^{ku}-bi "monkey" in general, see M. Powell, ZA

68 (1978) pp. 177–79; J. Klein, JCS 31 (1979) pp. 149–60; and S. Dunham, ZA 75 (1985) p. 235.

(24) [mu ...] bí!(Text: GIBIL)-⸢ra⸣ "[The year ...] smote [Ur/Ibbi-Sîn)]." U 7755 = IM 85465: C. Gadd, UET 1 no. 292 col. ii line 1.

The final line of the Ibbi-Sîn section of the Ur date list is so broken that any interpretation of the traces must remain, for the present, a conjecture. Sollberger (RLA 5 [1980] p. 7) suggested that it might refer to a (second) attack on Ur.

II. The Collapse of the Ur III State.

While the evidence of archival texts and year names for the first two years of Ibbi-Sîn give no hint of anything unusual with the accession of the new king, signs of the disintegration of the Ur III state begin to appear already by the year IS 3. Jacobsen (JCS 7 [1953] p. 38) notes:

> Soon, however, serious trouble developed. Documents dated with formulas of Ibbī-Suen are relatively frequent all over the empire in the king's first two years. Then they begin to cease in one part after the other, a clear indication that his authority was no longer recognized there. In Eshnunna(k) the Ibbī-Suen datings stop with his second year, in Susa with his third, in Lagash with his fifth, in Umma with his sixth, and in Nippur, emblem of the kingship over Sumer, with his seventh year.

Thanks to the publication by Sigrist and Gomi of The Comprehensive Catalogue of Published Ur III Tablets, Lafont (RA 89 [1995] pp. 3–13 and especially p. 5 fig. 1) was able to document in concrete terms the huge drop in archival records using Ibbi-Sîn year names at Ur and other major cities of the realm during the period IS 2–5.

The rulers of the new breakaway states soon began to issue their own royal inscriptions. At Girsu, for example, excavations have revealed bricks and alabaster vessels inscribed with the names and titles of the seemingly independent rulers Ur-Ningirsu (E3/2.2.1.1–2) and Ur-Nanše (E3/2.2.2.1). At Ešnunna, seal inscriptions of a certain Šū-ilīia, who styles himself as "king" (lugal), have been found (E3/2.3.1.1).

The loss of the various cities of the empire was a severe blow to the economy of the Ur III state. Gomi ("On the Critical Economic Situation at Ur Early in the Reign of Ibbisin," JCS 36 [1984] pp. 211–12) notes:

> A steep increase in the prices of foodstuffs can be observed in some texts from Ur from Ibbisin's sixth through eighth years: one sila (ca. 0.84 liter) of barley cost from 9 to 36 še (1 še approximates 0.047 gram) of silver, compared with its normal value of 0.6 še per sila earlier in the Ur III period. The high price of barley in the reign of Ibbisin presumably indicates that at that time there was a serious shortage of grain at Ur.

Further, in a separate article ("On Dairy Productivity at Ur in the Late Ur III Period," JESHO 23 [1980] pp. 1–42), Gomi was able to demonstrate (by a detailed study of archival texts connected with the dairy industry) that a marked decrease in dairy production occurred at Ur during the early years of Ibbi-Sîn's reign. He writes (ibid., pp. 35–36):

> 9.2. We do not know either the direct causes for this [decrease in production] or the date when the fall began. Historical material available to us conveys information about a sharp rise in prices at Ur and the difficult political situation of the kingdom. This might have

caused the deterioration of the quality and quantity of fodder, though this fact is not attested to concretely in existing texts.

In addition to the archival texts, the "literary letters" exchanged between Ibbi-Sîn and his governors — these are known from later Old Babylonian tablet copies — shed considerable light on the events that transpired in the period of IS 9–19. They enabled Wilcke to determine three distinct phases in the collapse of the Ur III state (C. Wilcke, "Drei Phasen des Niedergangs des Reiches von Ur III," ZA 60 [1970] pp. 54–69). For the first phase we have the evidence of two letters exchanged between Ibbi-Sîn and Išbi-Erra, the governor of Isin. In the first letter (see Michalowski, Correspondence pp. 243–51 no. 19) Išbi-Erra reports on his expedition to buy grain for the beleaguered capital city of Ur. He writes (lines 1–12, translation Michalowski):

> To Ibbi-Sin, my king, speak,
> thus says Išbi-Erra, your servant:
> You have instructed me to proceed on an expedition to Isin and Kazallu in order to purchase grain.
> The market price of grain has reached one gur (per shekel).
> The twenty talents of silver (which I had been given) for the purchase of the grain has been spent.
> Word having reached me that the hostile Mardu had entered into the midst of your land
> I brought all of the 72,000 gur of grain into Isin.
> And now all of the Mardu have entered into the land.
> One by one they have seized all the fortifications.
> Because of the Mardu I have been unable to thresh the grain.
> They are too strong for me, I am trapped.

In the reply letter of Ibbi-Sîn to Išbi-Erra (see Kramer, in Gurney and Kramer, OECT 5 pp. 15–16), the king of Ur expresses his extreme displeasure at the actions of his servant (lines 1–18, translation Kramer):

> Speak to Išbi-Erra, thus says your king Ibbi-Sin:
> ... You received 20 talents of silver to buy grain (and) you proceed to buy two *gur* grain for each shekel, (but) to me you sent one *gur* for each shekel.
> How is it you permitted the Martu, the enemy, to enter my land against Puzur-Numušda, the commandant of Bad-igihursagga?
> As long as I(?) sent(?) you weapons (with which) to strike, how is it that you(?) sent(?) the "men without heads" who are in the land, to him(?) against(?) the Martu "from above"?

For the second phase of the collapse of the Ur III state we have the evidence of a "literary letter" — it describes events dated to the time around IS 19 — in which Puzur-Šulgi, the faithful governor of Ibbi-Sîn based at Kazallu, reports to his lord on the advances of the king's adversary Išbi-Erra (see Michalowski, Correspondence pp. 253–68 no. 21 lines 42–53, translation Michalowski):

> Išbi-Erra proceeds at the head of his army.
> It was just as he said.
> He captured the bank(s) of the Tigris, Euphrates, the Abgal and Me-Enlila canals.
> He brought in Idin-Malgium.
> He quarreled with Girbubu, the governor of Girkal, cut off his "girdle," and took him (prisoner).
> His (battle) cry lies heavy upon me.
> (Now) he has set his eye upon me.
> I have no ally, no one to go with!

Although his hand has not yet reached me,
should he descend (upon me) I shall have to flee.
May my king know!

In a final letter, Ibbi-Sîn pleads with his governor Puzur-Numušda (an apparent variant in the literary tradition for Puzur-Šulgi) to remain loyal to Ur (translation from Kramer, Sumerians p. 334):

To Puzur-Numushda, the governor of Kazallu, speak; thus says your king Ibbi-Sin:
Since I have selected for you ... troops (and) have put them at your disposal as the governor of Kazallu, are not, as in my case, your troops your renown? Why did you send me thus: "Ishbi-Erra has his eyes on me, and (only) after he has left me will I come." How is it that you did not know when Ishbi-Erra will return to (his) land? Why did not you together with Girbubu, the governor of Girkal, march forth the troops which had been placed in your hand before him? How is it that you delay to turn back the ...?

The final phase in the downfall of the Ur III state saw bands of marauding Elamites and Gutians overwhelming the land of Sumer and Akkad; the deluge of enemy forces is described in vivid terms in the literary composition "Lamentation over the Destruction of Sumer and Ur." Ur having been vanquished, Ibbi-Sîn was taken off in fetters to die in Anšan.

1

As noted, the name of IS 6 commemorates the construction of the great walls at Nippur and Ur. While we do not have as yet a cone inscription dealing with the construction of the wall of Nippur, a twenty-two-line inscription incised on cones, a stone foundation tablet, and an Old Babylonian(?) tablet copy does deal with the erection of a "great wall" at Ur. For the location of this wall at Ur, see the introductory comments above for the year IS 6.

CATALOGUE

Ex.	Museum number	Excavation number	Registration number	Ur provenance	Dimensions (cm)	Lines preserved	cpn
Cones							
1	IM 92974	U 2	—	Trial Trench A	6×8.5	1–5, 13–14	n
2	BM 119040	U 2576	1927-10-3, 35	Trial trench outside the temenos	7.8×5.2	1–5	c
3	CBS 17225	U 7711	—	Area of Larsa houses, SW side of temenos	7.5×10	1–5, 13–17, 21–22	c
4	IM 92973	U 11659	—	Area of Royal Cemetery	6.5 dia.	1–5, 13–22	n
5	IM 92964	U 11672	—	Area of Royal Cemetery	—	6–9, 16–20	n
6	IM 92970	U 13661a	—	Flood pit	—	1–4, 13–14	n
7	IM 92972	U 13661b	—	NE city wall, central section	—	15–17, 21–22	n
8	IM 92959	U 15026	—	Area of Royal Cemetery, inside 3rd Dynasty foundation	—	1–5, 13–18, 21 22	n
9	IM 92773	U 16541	—	Isin-Larsa residential quarter	—	1–22	n
10	IM 22888	U 16542	—	Isin-Larsa residential quarter	—	7–14	n
11	IM 92951	U 18742	—	Extension of Royal Cemetery area, "loose in upper soil below the Neo-Babylonian foundation"	—	1–14	n
12	IM 92951	U 18824	—	Same as ex. 11, "loose in the soil between levels 1600 and 1500"	—	2–7, 15–19	n
13	IM 92965	U 19482	—	Diqdiqqah	—	1–22	n
14	IM 21980	U i	—	Ur—	—	15–22	n
15	IM 22889	U j	—	Ur(?)	—	15–19	n

Ex.	Museum number	Excavation number	Registration number	Ur provenance	Dimensions (cm)	Lines preserved	cpn
Stone tablet							
16	IM 1	U 219	—	Trial Trench B 19, below rammed earth of first burnt brick building	—	7–13, 17–22	n
Tablet copy							
17	IM 85675	U k	—	—	—	11–22	n

COMMENTARY

As far as can be determined, the text is arranged on the cones with lines 1–14 in col. i, and lines 15–22 in col. ii. In the stone tablet the lines are arranged with lines 1–13 on the obverse and lines 14–22 on the reverse.

In line 10 we have taken the verb sa ... gar to be a variant for sá ... gar = Akk. *malāku(m)* "to come to a decision," following Falkenstein, BiOr 23 (1966) p. 166 no. 36. Krecher (ZA 60 [1970] p. 197), following Edzard and Pettinato, had suggested "die Sehne anlegen," taking the expression to be parallel to éš-gar "die Messleine anlegen." Further, there is an uncertainty whether to translate the za-pa-ág of line 15 as "tumult" (following Sollberger and Kupper, IRSA IIIA5a), or to take it as a variant for zi-pa-ág = Akk. *nappāšu(m)* "(archer's) loop-hole" (following Krecher, ZA 60 [1970] p. 197). We have opted for the second possibility. The data found in the scores comes from the collated texts, the published copies, and the notes of Sollberger in UET 8 pp. 7–8 no. 36.

BIBLIOGRAPHY

1928 Gadd, UET 1 nos. 86 and 291 (exs. 2–3, copy, edition); no. 135 (ex. 1, copy)
1929 Barton, RISA pp. 368–69 Ibi-Sin 1 (ex. 2, edition)
1957 Edzard, Sumer 13 pp. 180–81 (exs. 2–4, 10, 14–16 conflated edition); pls. 1–2 (exs. 10, 14–16, copy)
1962 Hallo, HUCA 33 p. 39 Ibbi-Sin 1–2 (exs. 1–4, 10, 14–16, study)
1965 Sollberger, UET 8 no. 36 (exs. 1–17, study; ex. 13, copy)
1966 Falkenstein, BiOr 23 p. 166 (study)
1967 Pettinato, Orientalia NS 36 pp. 453–54 (exs. 1–4, 10, 13, 14–16, edition, study)
1970 Krecher, ZA 60 pp. 197–98 (study)
1971 Sollberger and Kupper, IRSA IIIA5a (exs. 1–17, translation)
1986 Kärki, KDDU pp. 136–37 Ibbisuen 1–2 (exs. 1–17, edition)
1991 Steible, NSBW 2 pp. 279–81 Ibbīsuen 1–2 (exs. 1–17, edition)

TEXT

1) ^{d}*i-bí*-^{d}EN.ZU
2) dingir-kalam-ma-na
3) lugal-kala-ga
4) lugal-uri$_5$.KI-ma
5) lugal-an-ub-da-límmu-ba-ke$_4$
6) nam-gal-ki-ág-
7) ^{d}EN.ZU-na-da
8) uri$_5$.KI
9) dagal-e-dè
10) sa im-ma-ši-gar
11) ur$_5$-ta
12) kalam gi-né
13) sig-nim GAM-e-dè
14) bàd-gal
15) za-pa-ág-ba šu nu-ku$_4$-ku$_4$
16) ḫur-sag-sig$_7$-ga-gin$_7$
17) uru.KI-né im-mi-da$_5$
18) uru$_{18}$ temen-bi
19) ki in-ma-ni-pà
20) bàd-ba
21) ^{d}*i-bí*-^{d}EN.ZU gú-gal-nam-nun-na
22) mu-bi-im

1–5) Ibbi-Sîn, god of his land, mighty king, king of Ur, king of the four quarters,

6–7) on account of the great love of the god Suen,

8–10) reached the decision to expand Ur.

11–13) Therefore, in order to make the land secure and to make the highlands and lowlands bow down (before him),
14–17) he surrounded his city with a great wall, whose *loop-holes* cannot be reached, and which was like a yellow mountain.

18–19) He found places in its (the wall's) footings for foundation deposits.
20–22) The name of that wall (is) "Ibbi-Sîn is the noble canal-inspector."

2

An inscription known from an Old Babylonian Sammeltafel copy records Ibbi-Sîn's fashioning of a golden bur-šagan (= Akk. *būr šikkati*) "a large container used for the storage of oil" (see A. Salonen, Hausgeräte 2 p. 132) from gold that was taken as booty of Susa. The temporal clause found in lines 11–16 of this inscription is a verbatim repetition of the year name for IS 14.

COMMENTARY

The inscription is lines 1–29 of U 7737, a clay tablet that was found in room 5 or 6 of no. 7 Quiet Street. Lines 1–26 are found on obv. col. i, and lines 27–29 on obv. col. ii. The tablet is now housed in the Iraq Museum; its museum number is unknown. Since the tablets UET 1 nos. 285 and 292 bear the museum nos. IM 85462 and IM 85465, respectively, we would expect that U 7737 (UET 1 no. 289) would bear an IM number 8546x. Collations of various signs by J. Black were incorporated in Steinkeller's partial edition of the inscription in OrAnt 23 (1984) pp. 39–41.

For bur "impermeable vessel" ("wasser undurchlässiges Gefäss") of line 17 see Heimpel, WZKM 120 (1970) p. 180. For šagan "Spitzgefäss" of line 17, see H. Waetzoldt, WO 6 (1970–71) p. 21.

The precise nature of the beast of line 19 designated gu$_4$-alim in Sumerian (= Akkadian *kusarikku*[*m*]) is uncertain. Ellis (in Studies Sjöberg pp. 126–27) writes:

> It seems clear from the combination of lexical, faunal, and pictorial evidence that the animal component of the *kusarikku* and its lexical equivalents most commonly must be a wild ox or bison, and as such is associated with the mountainous regions east of Mesopotamia. But it should also be noted that in texts the *kusarikku* is often mentioned in connection with water, be it primordial or ritual. Perhaps, then, the ancient terms, like the modern word "buffalo" could be used to designate both the bison and the water-buffalo.

According to Sallaberger (Kalender 1 pp. 191–92), the "Exalted Festival" of line 23 was an annual celebration held at Ur during the tenth month of the Ur calendar. It apparently involved a ritual bath of the statue of the god Nanna. Consequently, the translation of zà-mu of line 23 as "New Year" would not be appropriate in this context. According to the evidence of this inscription, the ceremony took place at the "place of the (secret) treasure-chest." An allusion to a celebration of the ezen-maḫ during x IS 7 is found in an archival text from Ur (U 3693: Gadd, UET 3 no. 209; see Sallaberger, Kalender 1 p. 191 n. 909); it notes (lines 9–11): "regular offerings, provisions for the bath of the god Nanna and the minor deities and those things needed for the 'Exalted Festival'" (sá-du$_{11}$ nì-dab$_5$ a-tu$_5$ ^{d}nanna dingir TUR.TUR ù nì-gù-dé ezem-maḫ). Of further interest is an archival text from Girsu (A 1176: see M. Civil, in Studies Sjöberg pp. 61–62) that contains a record (iv 5′-8′) of fine quality oil for a *bur-šagan* as provisions for the bath ([N sì]la ì-nun bur-šagan ... ⸢nì⸣-dab$_5$-a-tu$_5$-a). We have followed Sallaberger (Kalender 1 p. 192) in reading the end of line 14 as ka!-duḫ-ḫu-ba and translating "'mouth-opening' ritual." Steinkeller (OrAnt 23 [1984] pp. 39–41) suggested either sag duḫ-ḫu-ba "to anoint (the worshippers') heads" or ka!-duḫ-ḫu-ba "'mouth-opening' ritual." For dub-šen, see the literature cited by P. Michalowski in Lamentation p. 103 notes to line 442.

The three elements of *kusarikku* "bison," snakes, and "radiant dark rain (clouds)" named as the decorations on the vessel can be associated with iconographic elements commonly found on steatite vessels of Iranian manufacture. In particular, a steatite vessel of Early Dynastic date found at Khāfāje (but of clear eastern manufacture — see Frankfort, Art and Architecture p. 41 for a photo and drawing) shows a humped bull, a snake, and rosettes among its various artistic motifs. I intend to discuss this vase in more detail in a separate study and to show connections between the elements of the vase decoration and the constellations of Cetus (= the snake); Taurus (= the *kusarikku*); and the Pleiades and Hyades (= the two [stellar] rosettes). Further, evidence will be put forward suggesting a connection between the "radiant dark rain (clouds)" of the Ibbi-Sîn text and the star clusters of the Hyades or Pleiades.

BIBLIOGRAPHY

1928 Gadd, UET 1 no. 289 (copy, edition)
1962 Hallo, HUCA 33 p. 40 Ibbi-Sin 9 (study)
1971 Sollberger and Kupper, IRSA IIIA5b (translation)
1976 Jacobsen, Treasures p. 124 (partial translation)
1984 Steinkeller, OrAnt 23 pp. 39–41 (lines 17–29, edition)
1986 Kärki, KDDU pp. 146–47 Ibbisuen 9 (edition)
1991 Steible, NSBW 2 pp. 285–91 Ibbīsuen A 9 (edition)
1993 Sallaberger, Kalender 1 p. 191–92 (study)

TEXT

1)	^dnanna	1–5) For the god Nanna, whose radiance spreads over his people, the lord who alone is a luminous god, his lord,
2)	sù-rá-ág	
3)	un-<gá>-na ba-ra-ge	
4)	en AŠ-ni dingir-pa-è-a	
5)	lugal-a-ni-ir	
6)	^di-bí-EN.ZU	6–10) Ibbi-Sîn, god of his land, mighty king, king of Ur, king of the four quarters,
7)	dingir-kalam-ma-na	
8)	lugal-kala-ga	
9)	lugal-uri₅.KI-ma	
10)	lugal-an-ub-da-límmu-ba-ke₄	
11)	u₄ šušin.KI	11–16) when he roared like a storm against Susa, Adamdun, (and) the land of Awan; made them submit in a single day; and took their lord(s) as bound captive(s),
12)	a-dam-dun.KI	
13)	ma-da-a-wa-an.KI-ka	
14)	u₄-gin₇ ŠID bí-in-gi₄	
15)	u₄-AŠ-a mu-un-GAM	
16)	ù en-bi LÚ×KÁR!-a mi-ni-in-dab₅-ba-a	
17)	bur-šagan-kù-GI	17–22) — a golden šikkatu vessel, a masterpiece whose decorations — (depicting) a kusarikku, snakes, and radiant dark rain (clouds) — are of unceasing wonder,
18)	kin-ga-lam-kad₅(Text: PAP)	
19)	gu₄-alim muš-ba	
20)	šèg-gi₆ ní-ÍL	
21)	še-er-ga-an-du₁₁-ga-bi	
22)	u₆-di nu-til-le-dam	
23)	ezen-maḫ zà-mu a-tu₅-a-	23–26) which (during) the "Exalted Festival," the highpoint of the year, (being) the bath of the god Nanna, (performs) without end the "mouth-opening" ritual at the place of the (secret) treasure-chest —
24)	^dnanna-ka	
25)	ki-DUB.ŠEN-e ka!-duḫ-ḫu-ba	
26)	[mu]š nu-túm-mu-dè	
27)	mu-na-d[ím]	27) he fa[shioned] for him (the god Nanna)
28)	nam-ti-[l]a-ni-šè	28–29) (and) dedicated for his (own) life.
29)	a mu-na-ru	

3

A second Ibbi-Sîn inscription found on the aforementioned Sammeltafel records the king's fashioning of a ṣurṣuppu vessel "a container provided with teat-shaped protuberances (CAD)." As in the previous inscription, the temporal clause found in lines 11–16 is a verbatim repetition of the year name for IS 14.

COMMENTARY

The inscription is lines 30–72 of U 7737, a clay tablet that was found in room 5 or 6 of no. 7 Quiet Street. The tablet lines correspond to lines 1–43 of the reconstructed text given here. Tablet lines 30–52 are found on obv. col. ii and tablet lines 53–72 on rev. col. i. The tablet is housed in the Iraq Museum; its museum number is unknown.

The term ne-sag of line 27 is tentatively translated as "sacristy" by Heimpel, NABU 1994 pp. 72–73 no. 83. He notes (p. 73):

As preliminary hypothesis of the meaning of ne-saĝ/nisaĝ I would suggest: it designated something like a sacristy, with the special function to store the wine and the sacred utensils which were needed for the New Year's festival, including canopies and wind screens to accommodate large numbers of participants in the outdoor festivity, forms for special pastries, and images with specific roles at the celebration; and by extension also objects belonging to the ne-saĝ and playing their roles at the New Year's festival, including the female statuette of reference (5), and pitchers of reference (6); and finally the abundant streams of most precious drink, wine,

> which ultimately flow from the sacristy, as in references 9 and 10. In line 47 of the Nanshe Hymn the first meaning seems to fit easily: "the dream interpreter brought (the materials) of the sacristy before Nanshe," and the New Year's festival could begin.

For the object du$_8$-maḫ of line 38, see the study of R. Ellis entitled "Mountains and Rivers," in Levine and Young, Mountains and Lowlands pp. 29–34. Ellis notes various Isin and Old Babylonian year names that name cult objects that are described in terms using river imagery. Of particular interest is a year name of Būr-Sîn of Isin (CBS 3691: Chiera, PBS 8 no. 3) that reads: mu ⸢^{d}*bur*⸣-^{d}EN.ZU lugal-⸢e⸣ URUDU.KI.LUGAL.DU i$_7$-ḫé-⸢gál⸣ URUDU.du$_8$-maḫ nì-dé-a ⸢^{d}nin⸣-in-si-na-ra mu-na-an-dím "The year Būr-Sîn, the king, fashioned for the goddess Ninisina a copper KI.LUGAL.DU, 'a river of abundance,' and a lofty du$_8$, (being) cast metal objects (nì-dé-a = Akk. *pitqu*[*m*])." We may also note the year name for Hammurapi 13 (quoted from an MS. of Old Babylonian year names through the courtesy of M. Horsnell): mu *ḫa-am-mu-ra-pí* URUDU. KI.LUGAL.DU.BA du$_8$-maḫ-bi kur-ra i$_7$ "The year Ḫammu-rāpi (fashioned) a copper KI.LUGAL.DU.BA with its lofty du$_8$ — 'mountains and rivers.'" The fact that the antecedent of the du$_8$-maḫ in the Ibbi-Sîn inscription is identified (in line 23) as a *ṣurṣuppu* vessel suggests that the du$_8$-maḫ was some kind of container for holding liquids. It is generally mentioned in year names along with the KI.LUGAL.DU. The latter object has been discussed by Michalowski, who writes (Lamentation pp. 102–103):

> Usually, KI.LUGAL.GUB has been etymologized as "the place where the king does service (to the gods)" (Steible, *Rīmsîn* 49) or as "royal stand" (Klein, *Three Šulgi Hymns* 162). Note, however, that KI.LUGAL.GUB is frequently mentioned with food; ... Perhaps one should understand KI.LUGAL.GUB as an abbreviation from *ki lugal zú-gub "where the king eats," that is, the place where the ruler shares a cultic meal with the gods. Compare the logogram NÍG.GUB(LUGAL) = *naptan* (*šarrim*), often encountered in the Mari texts.

BIBLIOGRAPHY

1928 Gadd, UET 1 no. 289 (copy, edition)
1962 Hallo, HUCA 33 p. 40 Ibbi-Sin 10 (study)
1971 Sollberger and Kupper, IRSA IIIA5c (translation)
1986 Kärki, KDDU pp. 147–48 Ibbisuen 10 (edition)
1991 Steible, NSBW 2 pp. 286–93 Ibbīsuen A 10 (edition)

TEXT

1) ^{d}nanna
2) en pirig-gal-an-ki
3) lugal-a-ni-ir
4) ^{d}*i-bí*-^{d}EN.ZU
5) dingir-kalam-ma-na
6) nir-g̃ál me-nì-nam-ma
7) si-sá-sá-e-da gal-zu-bi
8) lugal-kala-ga
9) lugal-uri$_5$.KI-ma
10) lugal-an-ub-da-límmu-ba-ke$_4$
11) u$_4$ šušin.KI
12) a-dam-dun.KI
13) ma-da-a-wa-an.KI-ka
14) u$_4$-gin$_7$ ŠID bí-in-gi$_4$
15) u$_4$-AŠ-a mu-un-GAM
16) ù en-bi LÚ×KÁR-a mi-ni-in-dab$_5$-ba-a
17) ^{d}nanna
18) á-gal-la-na ba-an-ku$_4$-ra-ke$_4$-eš
19) kù-GI(Text: ZI) kù-GI$_6$-a dugud-bi de$_6$-a-ni
20) ^{d}*i-bí*-^{d}EN.ZU
21) nun á-maḫ ní-ÍL
22) géštu-dagal-la-ke$_4$

1–3) For the god Nanna, lord, great lion of heaven (and) earth, his lord,

4–10) Ibbi-Sîn, god of his land, prince who wisely knows how to execute all the *me*s, mighty king, king of Ur, king of the four quarters,

11–16) when he roared like a storm against Susa, Adamdun, (and) the land of Awan; made them submit in a single day; and took their lord(s) as bound captive(s);

17–19) since Nanna brought (those lands) under his jurisdiction, and took away (their) weighty gold and ... metal,

20–22) Ibbi-Sîn, the prince with great power, who emanates a fearful radiance, (by) his broad intelligence

23) sursub(DUG.UBUR.IMIN)-kù-GI(Text: ZI)
24) KA-bi ⌈a⌉-làl bar-re
25) gi-kù-GI-bi
26) pa_5-maḫ ga(Text:BI)-lam
27) ⌈ne⌉-sag-e(?) ḫé-du_7(?)
28) ⌈URUDU⌉.kin ^{gur}(?)-ra(?)-bi
29) [x] GI.diri nì-kala-ga
30) ḫur-sag li-sikil mú
31) du_8 nì šár-šár-re
32) šul-^{d}EN.ZU-ka
33) muš nu-tùm-mu-dè
34) nam-ti-la-ni-šè
35) a mu-na-ru

23–35) dedicated to him (Nanna), for his own life, a golden *ṣurṣuppu* vessel, whose *lip* overflows with sweetened water, whose golden (drinking) reed is an artfully (made) main conduit, which is suitable for the *sacristy*, whose copper *sickles*(?) ... a stout object, a mountain with pure juniper trees growing on it, making ... abundant for the hero Suen without end,

36) lú á-nì-ḫul-dím-ma
37) íb-ši-ág-e-a
38) du_8-maḫ únu-gal
39) ù ki-ezem-ma
40) ^{d}nanna-ke_4
41) bí-íb-TAG_4.TAG_4-a
42) dingir-gal-gal-an-ki-ke_4-ne
43) nam ḫa-ba-an-da-$kuru_5$-ne

36–41) As for the one who gives orders to do evil against it (and) abandons the lofty ... of the great dining hall or festival place of the god Nanna,

42–43) may the great gods of heaven and earth curse him.

4

An inscription known from an Old Babylonian tablet copy deals with Ibbi-Sîn's fashioning of an image of some animal, possibly a leopard, for the god Nanna.

COMMENTARY

The tablet is marked with the excavation number U 17899; according to the Ur registry books this should be a "bone object." Sollberger thus reassigned the piece the arbitrary excavation number U 1. The tablet bears the museum number IM 85676. Lines 1–11 are found on the obverse of the tablet, lines 12–18 on the reverse.

For the translation of the term ur-GÙN of lines 9 and 16, see Steinkeller, ZA 72 (1982) p. 253 and Heimpel, ZA 77 (1987) p. 59 § V.A.8d. Steible, NSBW 2 p. 294 indicated that the sign of lines 9 and 16 is clearly dar, not gùn, but an examination of signs 96 and 116 in Schneider, Keilschriftzeichen, reveals that the two signs are so similar as to raise doubts that they were clearly differentiated in Ur III script. Certainly, a reading ur-gùn "speckled 'dog'" makes sense, but ur-dar remains inexplicable.

BIBLIOGRAPHY

1965 Sollberger, UET 8 no. 37 (copy, study)
1966 Falkenstein, BiOr 23 p. 166 no. 37 (study)
1971 Sollberger and Kupper, IRSA IIIA5d (translation)
1972 Pettinato, Mesopotamia 7 p. 64 n. 98 (edition)
1982 Steinkeller, ZA 72 p. 253 and nn. 60–61 (study)
1986 Kärki, KDDU pp. 149–50 Ibbisuen 12 (edition)
1991 Steible, NSBW 2 pp. 293–95 Ibbīsuen A 11 (edition)

TEXT

1) ^{d}nanna amar-bàn-da-an-na
2) en dumu-sag-^{d}en-líl-lá
3) lugal-a-ni-ir

1–3) For the god Nanna, the impetuous young bull of the god An, lord, first-born son of the god Enlil, his lord,

4) ^{d}*i-bí*-^{d}EN.ZU
5) dingir-kalam-ma-na
6) lugal-kala-ga
7) lugal-uri$_{5}$.⸢KI⸣-ma
8) lugal-an-ub-d[a]-límmu-ba-ke$_{4}$
9) ⸢ur-GÙN⸣-a-me-luḫ-ḫa.KI
10) m[ar-ḫ]a-ši.KI(Text: DI)-[ta]
11) ⸢gú⸣-un-šè mu-na-ab-túm-ma-ni
12) ⸢*tam*⸣-*ši-lum*-bi
13) ⸢mu⸣-dím
14) nam-ti-l[a-n]i-šè
15) a mu-na-[r]u
16) ur-GÙN-⸢a⸣-ba
17) ḫé-[d]ab$_{5}$
18) mu-b[i-i]m

4–8) Ibbi-Sîn, king of his land, mighty king, king of Ur, king of the four quarte[rs],

9–13) fashioned an image of a Meluḫḫan speckled "dog" (= leopard?) that had been brought to him as tribute from Marḫaši.

14–15) He [de]dicated (it) for [h]is (own) life.

16–18) The name of that speckled "dog" (is): "May he catch (the enemy)."

Votive and Seal Inscriptions
(a) Of the King
5

An agate bead in the Louvre bears a dedicatory inscription of Ibbi-Sîn.

COMMENTARY

The banded agate bead, which measures 6.8×4.2×0.7 cm, was acquired through purchase in 1907 and given the museum number AO 4621 = AO 27622. The text is arranged in one column. The inscription was collated.

BIBLIOGRAPHY

1910 Ledrain, RA 7 p. 49 (copy, translation)
1923 Delaporte, Louvre 2 p. 179 and pl. 93 fig. 5 no. 816 (photo, edition)
1962 Hallo, HUCA 33 p. 40 Ibbi-Sin 6 (study)
1971 Sollberger and Kupper, IRSA IIIA5e (translation)
1982 André-Leicknam, Naissance de l'écriture pp. 15 and 88 no. 47 (photo, translation)
1986 Kärki, KDDU pp. 138–39 Ibbisuen 6 (edition)
1991 Steible, NSBW 2 p. 284 Ibbīsuen 6 (edition)

TEXT

1) ^{d}nanna
2) lugal-a-ni-ir
3) ^{d}*i-bí*-^{d}EN.ZU
4) dingir-kalam-ma-na
5) lugal-kala-ga
6) lugal-uri$_{5}$.KI-ma
7) lugal-an-ub-da-límmu-ba-ke$_{4}$
8) nam-ti-la-ni-šè
9) a mu-na-ru

1–2) For the god Nanna, his lord,

3–7) Ibbi-Sîn, god of his land, mighty king, king of Ur, king of the four quarters,

8–9) dedicated (this bead) for his (own) life.

Votive and Seal Inscriptions
(b) Of the Royal Family
6–8

Ibbi-Sîn — Royal Family

Item	Royal Name	RIM number	Attestations (A) and Bibliography (B)
Wife			
1	géme-^{d}en-líl-lá	—	(B) Jacobsen, JCS 7 (1953) p. 37 n. 6; Steinkeller, ASJ 3 (1981) pp. 80–81; Michalowski, ASJ 4 (1982) pp. 136–38; Sallaberger, ZA 82 (1992) p. 134 note to no. 1056; Sallaberger, Kalender 1 p. 61 n. 263. Cf. Owen, NATN no. 859 lines 4–6 (see p. 337 above Šū-Sîn — Royal Family Item 4); King, CT 32 pl. 43 col. iii line 25.
Daughter			
2	^{d}šul-gi-*sí-im-ti*	—	(B) Sallaberger, Kalender 1 p. 164 and n. 775
3	*ma-me-tum*	E3/2.1.5.6	(A) Owen, NATN no. 631 (seal) (- x IS 1)
Great uncle			
4	ba-ba-ti	E3/2.1.5.7–8	—

Concerning Ibbi-Sîn's queen Geme-Enlila, we may note the comments of Michalowski (ASJ 4 [1982] pp. 136–37):

> Steinkeller has reopened the debate on the identity of the lady Geme-Enlila who became the wife of the last ruler of the Ur III dynasty, Ibbi-Sin. Steinkeller sides with those who identify the Geme-Enlila who appears as a princess, presumably a daughter of Šu-Sin, with the woman, or girl, by that name who was married to Ibbi-Sin. As Steinkeller points out, brother-sister marriages are otherwise completely unknown from ancient Mesopotamia. In light of the fact that our information on the matter is so slight, I would prefer not to identify the princess Geme-Enlila with the queen who bore the same name. An account text from Nippur may be cited here in partial support for this point of view. In this text [Owen, NATN no. 859] foodstuffs were issued for
>
> | | |
> |---|---|
> | 4. é géme-^{d}en-líl-lá | the estate of Geme-Enlila, |
> | 5. dumu munus lugal | the princess, |
> | 6. lukur ^{d}nin-urta | the lukur-priestess of Ninurta. |
>
> The tablet is dated to the fourth month of ŠS 7. If Geme-Enlila, the princess, was already a lukur-priestess of Ninurta as early as the seventh year of Šu-Sin, then it is quite unlikely that she was still a child at the time. Three texts from the seventh and eighth years of Šu-Sin mention one Eštar-tukulti, the wetnurse of Geme-Enlila, the princess. Steinkeller has proposed that Geme-Enlila, who was Ibbi-Sin's sister, married her brother while she was still a child. Three

solutions are possible. Either there were two princesses by the same name, one a priestess and the other one a child during the last years of the reign of Šu-Sin, or a young daughter of the king was made an 'honorary' lukur of Ninurta, or, finally, the phrase ummeda PN meant not only "nurse (in charge of the child) PN" but also "nurse (to the child of) PN."

6

The impression of a seal naming a certain Mammētum as "daughter of the king" (dumu-munus-lugal) is found on a Nippur tablet dated to vi IS 1. In view of the date, we have tentatively assigned Mammētum as a daughter of Ibbi-Sîn (see Ibbi-Sîn — Royal Family item 3 above).

COMMENTARY

The tablet with this impression was found during the Hilprecht expedition to Nippur and given the museum number UM 29-15-744. For the PN of line 3, see Stamm, Namengebung p. 163 § b.

BIBLIOGRAPHY

1982 Owen, NATN no. 631 (copy)

TEXT

1) *ma*! *-me-tum*
2) dumu-munus-lugal
3) *a-tá-na-aḫ*
4) šabra ⌜ir$_{11}$⌝-[zu]

1–2) Mammētum, daughter of the king:

3–4) Ātanaḫ, chief administrator, (is) [your] servant.

7

A seal that names Aḫam-arši, son of Babati, may refer, in the case of Babati, to the great-uncle of Ibbi-Sîn (see E3/2.1.4.32–33, and Ibbi-Sîn — Royal Family item 4 above).

COMMENTARY

The calcite seal, which measures 3.22×2×1.9 cm was purchased from Gegou; its original provenance is unknown. The seal bears the museum number BM 102510 and the registration number 1908-4-11, 18. Lines 1–5 are found in col. i, lines 6–9 in col. ii. The inscription was collated from the published photo.

BIBLIOGRAPHY

1982 Collon, Cylinder Seals 2 no. 446 (photo, edition, study)
1987 Collon, First Impressions no. 118 (photo, study)
1987 Winter, in Gibson and Biggs, Bureaucracy p. 98 Va (study)
1990 Collon, RA 84 p. 132 n. 5 (study)

TEXT

1) ^{d}*i-bí-*^{d}EN.ZU
2) lugal-kalam-ma-na
3) lugal-kala-ga
4) lugal-uri$_5$.KI-ma
5) lugal-an-ub-da-límmu-ba
6) *a-ḫa-am-ar-ši*
7) dub-sar
8) dumu ba-ba-ti
9) ir$_{11}$-zu

1–5) Ibbi-Sîn, king of his land, mighty king, king of Ur, king of the four quarters:

6–9) Aḫam-arši, scribe, son of Babati, (is) your servant.

8

The impression of a seal of a second son of Babati is found on a tablet dated to ŠS 9; the month name is illegible (see Ibbi-Sîn — Royal Family item 4 above).

COMMENTARY

The impression is found on Eames P 264B. Lines 1–4 are found in col. i, lines 5–8 in col. ii.

In view of the fact that the title pisan-dub-ba "comptroller" forms part of Babati's titles in both this inscription and inscriptions E3/2.1.4.32–33 makes it highly likely that these texts refer to the same person.

BIBLIOGRAPHY

1948 Oppenheim, Eames Collection p. 126 P 4 (partial transliteration)
1978 Sauren, New York Public Library no. 264B (copy)
1987 Winter, in Gibson and Biggs, Bureaucracy p. 98 Vh (study)

TEXT

1) ^{d}*i-bí-*^{d}EN.ZU
2) lugal-kala-ga
3) lugal-uri$_5$.KI-ma
4) lugal-an-ub-da-límmu-ba
5) gìri-ni-ì-sa$_6$
6) dub-sar
7) dumu ba-ba-ti
8) pisan-dub-ba

1–4) Ibbi-Sîn, mighty king, king of Ur, king of the four quarters:

5–8) Girini-isa, scribe, son of Babati, the comptroller.

Votive and Seal Inscriptions
(c) Of City Governors and High Priestly Officials
2001–2013

The information in the following chart derives from the data found in Keiser, Patesis; Hallo, Ensi's and Ensi's2; Goetze, JCS 17 (1963) pp. 1–31; Edzard, Rép. Géogr. 2; Owen, JCS 33 (1981) pp. 244–70; ibid., JAOS 108 (1988) pp. 116–22; ibid., BiOr 49 (1992) cols. 444–47; Maeda, ASJ 14 (1992) pp. 162–63; and ibid., ASJ 16 (1994) pp. 157–62.

The names of governors referred to in seal inscriptions edited in this volume are marked with an asterisk (*). Names appearing in seal inscriptions are indicated with (s); those mentioned in tablets are marked with (t).

We have not included in the chart references to tablets impressed with the seal inscription of Gududu, son of the Umma governor Dadaga.

Year	Adab	Babylon	Ešnunna	Girsu/Lagaš	Kutha
1	—	—	***i-tu-ri-a*** Keiser, YOS 4 no. 73 lines 3–4 (t) (- -)	**ir$_{11}$-^{d}nanna** de Genouillac, ITT 2 no. 937 (s) (- -) **(E3/2.1.5.2003)**	***pí-ša-ah̬*-DINGIR** Jean, ŠA clxiv (tablet actually dates to xi ŠS 9) (s); Scheil, RT 37 (1915) p. 128 (s) (unknown date, seal names Ibbi-Sîn) **(E3/2.1.5.2006)**
2	**ur-^{d}ašaš$_7$-gi$_4$*** A 903, see Yang, Sargonic Inscriptions p. 24 (s) **(E3/2.1.5.2001)**	**⌜puzur$_4$⌝-tu-[tu]** Calvot and Pettinato, MVN 8 no. 139 rev. col. ii line 8 (t) (- vi)	***i-tu-ri-a*** TA 1931-T622 lines 8–9, see Owen, JAOS 108 (1988) p. 120 (t) (- xi)	—	**lú-^{d}šára** Oppenheim, Eames Collection, Eames L 20 lines 10–11 = Sauren, New York Public Library no. 374 lines 10–11 (- i)
3	—	—	—	—	—
4	—	—	—	**ir$_{11}$-mu** Salonen, Puzriš-Dagan-Texte no. 205 line 6 (t) (- xii)	—

Year	Marad	Nippur	Simudar	Šarrākum	Umma
1	**NE-NE** Keiser, BIN 3 no. 592 line 3 (t) (28 iv)	—	—	—	**da-da-ga** Oppenheim, Eames Collection, Eames F 19 = Sauren, New York Public Library no. 86 (s) (- vi) **(E3/2.1.5.2012)**
2	—	**da-da** Delaporte, RA 8 (1911) p. 196 no. 20 (s) (- -) **(E3/2.1.5.2008)**	**lú-^{d}nanna** King, CT 32 pl. 19, BM 103998, col. iii line 1 (Simudar not mentioned) (t) (29 iv)	**ur-mes** de Genouillac, TCL 2 no. 5514 rev. line 20 (t) (- x); Salonen, Puzriš-Dagan-Texte no. 342 line 25 (t) (- x); Jones and Snyder, SET no. 57 line 31 (t) (9 x); Jones and Snyder, SET no. 58 line 24 (t) (24 x)	**da-da-ga** Nikol'skiy, DV no. 399 (s) (- -) **(E3/2.1.5.2012)**
3	—	—	**lú-^{d}nanna** Çığ and Kızılyay, NRVN 1 no. 176 (s) (- vii) **(E3/2.1.5.2011)**	—	—
4	—	**da-da** Nies, UDT no. 37A line 1 (s) (13 iii) **(E3/2.1.5.2008)**; Zettler, Inanna Temple p. 345 n. 1 (s) (15 vi) **(E3/2.1.5.2009)**	—	—	—

The Puzur-Tutu listed in the chart as governor of Babylon for the year IS 2 is likely to be connected with the Puzur-Tutu who appears as governor of Badziabba (= Borsippa) in the literary letter of Puzur-Šulgi to Ibbi-Sîn (see Michalowski, Correspondence pp. 253–68, line 39). Borsippa is located a mere 18 kms SW of Babylon.

2001

A tablet dated to the year IS 2 bears the seal impression of a son of the Adab governor Ur-Ašgi.

COMMENTARY

The seal impression is found on the tablet A 903 (Chicago). It was found in excavations by Banks at Adab. Lines 1–3 are found in col. i, lines 4–6 in col. ii. The inscription was collated.

BIBLIOGRAPHY

1986 Yang, Sargonic Archive p. 42 (transliteration)
1989 Yang, Sargonic Inscriptions p. 24 (transliteration)

TEXT

1)	ur-^{d}aš aš$_{7}$-gi$_{4}$	1–3) Ur-Ašgi, governor of Adab:
2)	énsi-	
3)	adab.KI	
4)	nita-sa$_{6}$-ga	4–6) Nita-saga, scribe, (is) his son.
5)	dub-sar	
6)	dumu-ni	

2002

A tablet dated to IS 1 (YBC 1732 = Keiser, YOS 4 no. 73; no month date) mentions Itūrīia as governor of Ešnunna. The impression of a seal of Šū-ilīia, son of governor Itūrīia, was found in excavations at Ešnunna. Šū-ilīia later became an independent ruler of Ešnunna (see section E3/2.3.1).

COMMENTARY

The tablet bearing this impression was found at locus O 31:5 in the Ilshuilia-Nurahum palace at Ešnunna and was given the excavation number As 31–188. The edition follows the transliteration of Jacobsen. The impression was not available for collation; we expect that lines 1–4 would have been written in col. i and lines 5–9 in col. ii. According to R. Whiting (JAOS 97 [1977] p. 171), the tablet is now missing and cannot be collated. The reading of line 5 is uncertain.

BIBLIOGRAPHY

1940 Jacobsen, Gimilsin Temple p. 143 Seal Legend no. 5 (edition)
1971 Sollberger and Kupper, IRSA IIID1b (translation)
1977 Whiting, JAOS 97 pp. 171–72 (transliteration, study)
1986 Kärki, KDDU p. 142 Ibbisuen 7a (x) (edition)
1987 Winter, in Gibson and Biggs, Bureaucracy p. 99 Vp (study)

TEXT

1)	⸢d⸣*i-bí*-^{d}EN.ZU	1–4) Ibbi-Sîn, mighty [ki]ng, king of Ur, king of the four quarters:
2)	[lu]gal-kala-ga	
3)	lugal-uri$_{5}$.KI-ma	
4)	lugal-an-ub-da-límmu-ba	
5)	^{d}*šu*-⸢*ì-lí-a*⸣	5–9) Šū-ilīia, sc[ribe], son of Itū[rīia], gover[nor], (is) your servant.
6)	dub-[sar]	
7)	dumu *i-tu*-[*ri-a*]	
8)	éns[i]	
9)	ir$_{11}$-zu	

2003

A tablet from Girsu dated to IS 1 (no month named) is impressed with the seal of Ir-[Nanna], the grand-vizier; it acknowledges Ibbi-Sîn as king. For a seal of Ir-Nanna as subject of Šū-Sîn, see E3/2.1.4.2002.

COMMENTARY

The seal impression is found on the undated tablet envelope L 937 (Istanbul), which measures 7.6 cm in height. Lines 1–4 are found in col. i, lines 5–8 in col. ii. The inscription was collated from the published photo.

BIBLIOGRAPHY

1910 de Genouillac, ITT 2/1 no. 937 (copy, translation); pl. II no. 937 (photo)
1925 Scheil, RA 22 pp. 147–48 (edition)
1971 Sollberger and Kupper, IRSA IIIB5c (translation)
1977 Franke, in Gibson and Biggs, Seals p. 62 and Fiche C-4a (photo, study)
1986 Kärki, KDDU p. 146 Ibbisuen 8 (vii) (edition)
1987 Winter, in Gibson and Biggs, Bureaucracy p. 98 Vb (study)

TEXT

1) [^{d}*i*]-*bí*-^{d}EN.ZU
2) lugal-kala-ga
3) lugal-uri$_5$.KI-ma
4) lugal-an-ub-da-límmu-ba-ke$_4$
5) ir$_{11}$-^{d}[nanna]
6) sukkal-ma[ḫ]
7) ir$_{11}$-da-n[i-]i[r]
8) in-na-[ba]

1–4) [I]bbi-Sîn, mighty king, king of Ur, king of the four quarters:

5–8) to Ir-[Nanna], gran[d]-vizier, his servant, he [pres]ented (this seal).

2004

An agate eyestone in a private collection bears a dedicatory inscription of the wife of the Lagaš governor Ir-Nanna for the life of Ibbi-Sîn.

COMMENTARY

The brown and white agate eyestone, which measures 5.7×4.8 cm, was in the collection of A. Mazda, Teheran. The inscription follows the transliteration and copy of W.G. Lambert. The text is arranged in one column.

BIBLIOGRAPHY

1967 Sollberger, RA 61 pp. 69–70 (edition)
1971 Sollberger and Kupper, IRSA IIIB5d (translation)
1979 Lambert, Iraq 41 p. 44 (copy, edition)
1986 Kärki, KDDU p. 150 Ibbisüen 13 (edition)
1991 Steible, NSBW 2 p. 295 Ibbīsuen 12 (edition)

TEXT

1)	^{d}ba-ba$_{6}$	1–2) To the goddess Baba, his lady,
2)	nin-a-ni-ir	
3)	nam-ti-	3–4) for the life of Ibbi-Sîn,
4)	^{d}*i-bí*-^{d}EN.ZU-ka-šè	
5)	ʾ*à-ma-an-ì-lí*	5–8) Aman-ilī, wife of Ir-Nanna, governor of Lagaš,
6)	dam-ir$_{11}$-^{d}nanna	
7)	énsi-	
8)	lagaš.KI-ka-ke$_{4}$	
9)	a mu-na-ru	9) dedicated (this eyestone).

2005

A brown limestone statuette now in Berlin bears an inscription of the priest Ur-Ningirsu in which he dedicates the piece to the god NinDARa for the life of Ibbi-Sîn. NinDARa was the spouse of the goddess Nanše.

COMMENTARY

The headless statuette, which depicts a male figure in an attitude of prayer, was purchased from Gegou in Paris in 1926. It bears the museum number VA 8787. The piece measures 38×21×13 cm and the inscription 16.3×5.2 cm. The inscription, which is on the back of the statue, and which is arranged in one column, was collated.

For a brief discussion of the god NinDARa and his cult cities, see M. Civil, in Studies Sjöberg p. 51.

BIBLIOGRAPHY

1924 Thureau-Dangin, Monuments Piot 27 pp. 108–10 and figs. 2–3 (photo, edition)
1928–29 Meissner, AfO 5 pl. 6 figs. 1–2 (photos)
1948 Parrot, Tello fig. 46 a–a′ and p. 231 (study, drawings)
1962 Hallo, HUCA 33 p. 39 Ibbi-Sin 3 (study)
1967 Renger, ZA 58 p. 115 n. 15 (partial transliteration)
1971 Sollberger and Kupper, IRSA IIIA5f (translation)
1981 Spycket, Statuaire p. 208 n. 124 (study)
1986 Kärki, KDDU p. 137 Ibbisuen 3 (edition)
1987 Marzahn, AoF 14/1 pp. 36–37 and pl. 5 no. 17 (photo, copy, edition)
1991 Braun-Holzinger, Weihgaben p. 275 St 157 (edition)
1991 Cavigneaux, RA 85 pp. 63–66 (study of Ur-Ningirsu and his titles)
1991 Steible, NSBW 2 pp. 281–82 Ibbīsuen 3 (edition)

TEXT

1)	^{d}nin-DAR-a	1–3) For the god NinDARa, the mighty lord, his lord,
2)	lugal-uru$_{16}$	
3)	⸢lugal⸣-a-ni-ir	
4)	⸢nam⸣-ti-	4–8) for the life of Ibbi-Sîn, mighty king, king of Ur, king of the four quarters,
5)	^{d}*i-bí*-^{d}EN.ZU	
6)	lugal-kala-ga	

7)	lugal-uri$_5$.KI-ma	
8)	lugal-an-ub-da-límmu-ba-ka-šè	
9)	ur-^{d}nin-gír-su	9–12) Ur-Ningirsu, EN.ME.ZI.AN.NA, *šennu* priest, belov[ed] *en* priest of the goddess Nanše,
10)	EN.ME.ZI.AN.NA	
11)	šennu(ME.AD.KÙ)	
12)	en-ki-á[g]-^{d}nanše-k[e$_4$]	
13)	mu-na-dím	13) fashioned (this statuette) for him.

2006

A seal inscription known from two tablets names a certain Pišaḫ-ilum as governor of Kutha. If Scheil's reading of ex. 1 of this inscription is correct, the seal acknowledges Ibbi-Sîn as sovereign.

CATALOGUE

Ex.	Museum number	Lines preserved
1	Was in the collection of Kelekian	1–9
2	Was in the collection of Jean	1–4, 6–9

COMMENTARY

Lines 1–4 are arranged in col. i and lines 5–10 in col. ii.

There is some confusion about the correct reading of this seal inscription. In the transliteration of ex. 1 published by Scheil in RT 37 (1915) p. 128, Scheil gives line 1 as [*i*]-*bi*-(*ilu*) *Sin*; this is probably to be interpreted as reflecting an original: [^{d}*i*]-*bí*-^{d}EN.ZU. The line after that was read uš danga (= ? nita-kala-ga) by Scheil, but this is almost certainly a mistake for lugal-kala-ga, since nita-kala-ga is not attested as a title of Ibbi-Sîn (nor of Šū-Sîn, for that matter). In the copy of ex. 2, Jean indicates a lugal sign in the first line. This is probably a mistake. Owen (in ASJ 15 [1993] p. 151) restores the first line of ex. 2 as [^{d}*šu*-^{d}EN.ZU] presumably because the tablet is dated to x ŠS 9. If ex. 1 is indeed a duplicate of ex. 2 and if Scheil's transliteration is correct, then we should probably restore the royal name as Ibbi-Sîn rather than Šū-Sîn. The fact that Ibbi-Sîn is known to have acceded to the throne during x ŠS 9 (see the introductory remarks to the year name for IS 1 on p. 361) would argue that a seal for the new king could have been cut as early as x ŠS 9. Of course, since the whereabouts of both of the two tablets with this seal inscription are unknown, a definitive reading of the text cannot be given.

BIBLIOGRAPHY

1915 Scheil, RT 37 p. 128 (ex. 1, edition)
1923 Jean, ŠA no. 164 (ex. 2, copy)
1962 Hallo, HUCA 33 p. 40 Ibbi-Sin 7iii (ex. 2, study)
1986 Kärki, KDDU p. 139 Ibbisuen 7a (ii) (ex. 1, edition)
1993 Owen, ASJ 15 p. 151 no. 55 (ex. 1, transliteration [inadvertently omits lines 1–4]); p. 151 no. 56 (ex. 2, transliteration)

TEXT

1)	[*i*]-*bí*-^{d}EN.ZU	1–4) [I]bbi-Sîn, mighty king, king of Ur, king of the four quarters:
2)	lugal-kala-ga	
3)	lugal-uri$_5$.KI-ma	
4)	lugal-an-ub-da-límmu-ba	
5)	*é-a-ba*-[*ni*]	5–10) Ea-bā[ni], son of Pišaḫ-ilum, governor of Kutha, (is) your servant.
6)	dub-sar	

7) dumu *pi₅-ša-aḫ*-DINGIR
8) énsi-
9) gú-du₈-a.KI
10) ir₁₁-zu

2007

Impressions of a seal of Dada, governor of Nippur, in which he acknowledges Ibbi-Sîn as sovereign, are found on four clay sealings from Ur and a tablet envelope from Nippur, none of which are dated.

CATALOGUE

Ex.	Museum number	Excavation number	Provenance	Dimensions (cm)	Lines preserved	cpn
1	—	U 4871	Ur —	4.5×3.7	1–2, 6–9	p
2	UM —	U 6706	Ur —	—	1–12	n
3	—	U 6343A	Ur, southern extension of Gipar-ku site, room A3	4.3×3.2	1–12	p
4	—	U 6343B	As ex. 3	5×4.9	1–6, 7–12	p
5	HS 1351b	—	Nippur	5.7×4.75×2.6	1–12	n

COMMENTARY

Lines 1–5 are found in col. i and lines 6–12 in col. ii. Line 9 was read as ur-sa₆-ga by Gadd (UET 1 [text volume] p. 20 no. 89) and Legrain (UE 10 p. 32 nos. 418 and 419), but it is now known to be ur-ᵈnanibgal (DINGIR over DINGIR.NISSABA). The correct reading of the father's name (on the basis of the Nippur exemplar) was pointed out by Waetzoldt in OrAnt 15 (1976) p. 327. The reading was confirmed by the discovery of a seal inscription of Dada in which he acknowledges Šū-Sîn as lord and names Ur-Nanibgal as his father (see Calvot and Pettinato, MVN 8 no. 151 = E3/2.1.4.2007).

BIBLIOGRAPHY

1928 Gadd, UET 1 no. 89 (exs. 3–4, composite copy, edition)
1929 Barton, RISA pp. 368–69 Ibi-Sin 3 (exs. 3–4, conflated edition)
1937 Legrain, UET 3 no. 52 (ex. 2, copy)
1937 Pohl, TMH NF 1/2 Siegel no. 142* (ex. 5, copy)
1951 Legrain, UE 10 nos. 418–19, pl. 25 (exs. 1, 3–4, transliteration, photo)
1962 Hallo, HUCA 33 p. 40 Ibbi-Sin 7i (exs. 1–5, study)
1976 Waetzoldt, OrAnt 15 p. 327 no. 142 (ex. 5, collation)
1984 Zettler, AfO 31 p. 5 n . 27 (exs. 3–4, transliteration)
1986 Kärki, KDDU p. 139 Ibbisuen 7a (i) (exs. 1–5, edition)
1987 Winter, in Gibson and Biggs, Bureaucracy p. 98 Vc (study)
1990 Maeda, ASJ 12 p. 71 (study)

TEXT

1) ᵈ*i-bí*-ᵈEN.ZU
2) dingir-kalam-ma
3) lugal-kala-ga
4) lugal-uri₅.KI-ma
5) lugal-an-ub-da-límmu-ba
6) da-da
7) énsi-

1–5) Ibbi-Sîn, god of the land, mighty king, king of the four quarters:

6–12) Dada, governor of Nippur, son of Ur-Nanibgal, governor of Nippur, (is) your servant.

8) nibru.KI
9) dumu ur-nanibgal(DINGIR over DINGIR.NISSABA)
10) énsi-
11) nibru.KI-ka
12) ir_{11}-zu

2008

The impression of a seal of a servant of Dada is found on two Nippur tablets.

CATALOGUE

Ex.	Museum number	Date	Lines preserved
1	—	viii IS 2	1–7
2	NBC 37A	iii IS 4	1–7

COMMENTARY

Ex. 1 was formerly in the collection of M. Nessonneau. Its present whereabouts are unknown. Ex. 2 was kindly collated by P.-A. Beaulieu.

BIBLIOGRAPHY

1911 Delaporte, RA 8 p. 196 no. 20 (ex. 1, copy, edition)
1920 Nies, UDT no. 37a (ex. 2, copy)

TEXT

1) da-da
2) énsi-
3) nibru.KI
4) gìri-né-ì-sa_6
5) dub-s[ar]
6) dumu lú-ka[l]-la
7) ir_{11}-zu

1–3) Dada, governor of Nippur:

4–7) Girine-isa, sc[ribe], son of Lu-kala, (is) [your] servant.

2009

The impression of a seal of Id(ī)-ilī, servant of Dada, is found on a Nippur tablet dated to 15 vi IS 4.

COMMENTARY

The seal impression is found on the tablet with excavation number 6 N-T 631. It dates to 15 vi IS 4. For Ur III PNs composed with the element *idu*(*m*) "arm," see Gelb, MAD 3 p. 17.

BIBLIOGRAPHY

1984 Zettler, Inanna Temple p. 345 n. 1 (transliteration)

TEXT

1)	da-da	1–3) Dada, governor of Nippur:
2)	énsi-	
3)	nibru.KI	
4)	Á-*ì-lí*	4–7) Id(ī)-ilī, son of [...]-mu, steward, (is) [your] servant.
5)	dumu [...]-mu	
6)	agrig	
7)	ir_{11}-[zu]	

2010

The impression of a seal of a servant of Dada is found on a tablet from Nippur dated to ii IS 8.

COMMENTARY

The seal impression is found on Ni 2109 (Istanbul); it comes from the Hilprecht expedition to Nippur.

BIBLIOGRAPHY

1965 Çığ and Kızılyay, NRVN no. 118 (copy)

TEXT

1)	da-da	1–3) Dada, governor of Nippur:
2)	énsi-	
3)	nibru.KI	
4)	ad-da-kal-la	4–7) Adda-kala, scribe, son of [...] (is) [your] servant.
5)	dub-sar	
6)	dumu-[...]	
7)	ir_{11}-[zu]	

2011

A tablet from Nippur bears the impression of a seal of Ennam-Šulgi, son of governor Lu-Nanna; the latter very likely was the Lu-Nanna, general of Simudar, attested in E3/2.1.4.2010.

COMMENTARY

The impression is found on Ni 11 (Istanbul). The tablet is dated to vii IS 3. The text is arranged in one column.

BIBLIOGRAPHY

1965 Çığ and Kızılyay, NRVN 1 no. 176 (copy)
1976 Michalowski, Correspondence p. 58–59 (edition)

TEXT

1) *en-nam*-^{d}šul-gi
2) dumu lú-^{d}nanna
3) GÌR.NÍTA

1–3) Ennam-Šulgi, son of Lu-Nanna, general.

2012

The seal inscription of Dadaga, governor of Umma, is found on tablets dated to the years IS 1 and 2.

CATALOGUE

Ex.	Museum number	Date	Lines preserved	cpn
1	New York Public Library, Eames Collection F 19	- viii IS 1	1–8	c
2	Moscow Archaeological Museum, Nikol'skiy 399	- - IS 2	1–8	n

COMMENTARY

Lines 1–4 are found in col. i, lines 5–8 in col. ii.

BIBLIOGRAPHY

1915 Nikol'skiy, DV 5 no. 399 (ex. 2, copy)
1948 Oppenheim, Eames Collection p. 60 F 19 (study [seal wrongly ascribed to Aa-kala])
1962 Hallo, HUCA 33 p. 40 Ibbi-Sin 7ii (exs. 1–2, study)
1978 Sauren, New York Public Library no. 86 (ex. 1, copy)
1987 Winter, in Gibson and Biggs, Bureaucracy p. 98 Vd (study)

TEXT

1) ^{d}*i-bí*-^{d}EN.ZU
2) lugal-kala-ga
3) lugal-uri$_5$.KI-ma
4) lugal-an-ub-da-límmu-ba
5) da-da-ga
6) énsi-
7) umma.KI
8) ir$_{11}$-zu

1–4) Ibbi-Sîn, mighty king, king of Ur, king of the four quarters:

5–8) Dadaga, governor of Umma, (is) your servant.

2013

The seal inscription of Gududu, son of the Umma governor Dadaga, is known from several tablets; eight exemplars are given here as being representative.

CATALOGUE

Ex.	Museum number	Lines preserved	Date	cpn
1	Moscow Archaeological Museum, Nikol'skiy 180	1–10	- - IS 1	n
2	Moscow Archaeological Museum, Nikol'skiy 190	1–10	- - ŠS 9	n
3	Moscow Archaeological Museum, Nikol'skiy 380	1–10	- iii IS 1	n
4	MLC 2314	1–10	- - IS 1	c
5	Was in the collection of G. Contenau	1–10	IS 1	n
6	Um 403 (Istanbul)	1–10	- vii IS 2	n
7	Um 855 (Istanbul)	1–10	- - IS 3	n
8	Um 1053 (Istanbul)	1–10	- - IS 3	n

COMMENTARY

Lines 1–4 are found in col. i, lines 5–10 in col. ii.

BIBLIOGRAPHY

1915 Nikol'skiy, DV 5 nos. 180, 190, and 380 (exs. 1–3, copy)
1916 Contenau, Umma p. 51 no. 6 (ex. 5, transliteration)
1920 Clay, BRM 3 no. 32 (ex. 4, copy)
1962 Hallo, HUCA 33 p. 40 Ibbi-Sin 7iv (exs. 1–5, study)
1971 Sollberger and Kupper, IRSA IIIA5i (exs. 1–5, translation)
1986 Kärki, KDDU p. 140 Ibbisuen 7a (iii) (ex. 4, edition)
1987 Winter, in Gibson and Biggs, Bureaucracy p. 98 Vf (study)
1988 Yıldız, MVN 14 no. 403 (ex. 6, transliteration)
1994 Waetzoldt and Yıldız, MVN 16 nos. 855 and 1043 (exs. 7–8, transliteration)

TEXT

1) ^{d}*i-bí-*^{d}EN.ZU
2) lugal-kala-ga
3) lugal-uri$_5$.KI-ma
4) lugal-an-ub-da-límmu-ba
5) gu-du-du
6) dub-sar
7) dumu da-da
8) énsi-
9) umma.KI
10) ir$_{11}$-zu

1–4) Ibbi-Sîn, mighty king, king of Ur, king of the four quarters:

5–10) Gududu, scribe, son of Dada, governor of Umma, (is) your servant.

Seal Inscription of Sîn-abūšu "Childhood Companion of the King"

Although it does not actually belong to the corpus of royal seal inscriptions, a remarkable seal inscription found on the tablets Um 916 (Yıldız and Gomi, PDT 2 no. 916); U 242 (Legrain, UET 3 no. 242); and Sigrist, Syracuse no. 210, should be mentioned in this volume. The text was studied by Wilcke (NABU 1989 no. 4, pp. 4–5), who pointed out that the seal was granted by Ibbi-Sîn to the cup-bearer Sîn-abūšu; the latter is described as being the king's "childhood companion" (du$_{10}$-ús-sa nam-dumu-ka-ni). Now, a cup-bearer named Sîn-abum, possibly a variant of the name Sîn-abūšu, is mentioned in the tablets published by Legrain as UET 3 nos. 229, 281, and 1134. Further, a precursor of Sîn-abūšu's seal granted by Ibbi-Sîn is a seal that was presented by Šū-Sîn to Sîn-abūšu; for the details, see Owen, JAOS 108 (1988) p. 114 and also see below. We may also note in this connection the comments of Sallaberger (ZA 82 [1992] p. 133 notes to 916 and ibid., Kalender 1 p. 179 n. 841 and p. 222). The two seals of Sîn-abūšu are compared below.

Watson, Birmingham 1 p. 152 no. 96	Yıldız and Gomi, PDT 2 no. 916; Sigrist, Syracuse no. 210; Legrain, UET 3 no. 242
1) ⌈^{d}⌉*šu*-^{d}EN.ZU	1) *i-bí*-^{d}EN.ZU
	2) dingir-kalam-ma-na
2) [l]ugal-kala-ga	3) lugal-kala-ga
3) [l]ugal-uri$_5$.KI-ma	4) ^{d}lugal-uri$_5$.KI-ma
4) [l]ugal-an-ub-da-límmu-ba-ke$_4$	5) lugal-an-ub-da-límmu-ba-[ke$_4$]
5) ^{d}EN.[ZU]-*a*-⌈*bu-šu*⌉	6) ^{d}EN.ZU-*a-bu-šu*
6) sag[i](SÌLA.ŠU.[DU$_8$])	7) sagi(SÌLA.ŠU.DU$_8$)
7) ir$_{11}$-da-ni	8) du$_{10}$-ús-[sa]
	9) nam-dumu-ka-ni-i[r]
8) in-na-[ba]	10) in-na-ba

Votive and Seal Inscriptions (d) Of Private Individuals 2014–2016

2014

A mace-head from Ur was dedicated for the life of Ibbi-Sîn.

COMMENTARY

The originally pear-shaped limestone mace-head, which measures 6.3×7.7×2.4 cm, was found on the surface at Ur and given the excavation number U 198. It bears the museum number BM 116434 and the registration number 1923-11-10, 19. The text is arranged in one column. The inscription was collated.

BIBLIOGRAPHY

1928 Gadd, UET 1 pl. M no. 85 (photo, edition)
1962 Hallo, HUCA 33 p. 40 Ibbi-Sin 4 (study)
1968 Solyman, Götterwaffen no. 210 (photo, study)
1986 Kärki, KDDU p. 138 Ibbisuen 4 (edition)
1991 Braun-Holzinger, Weihgaben p. 61 K 86 (edition)
1991 Steible, NSBW 2 pp. 282–83 Ibbīsuen 4 (edition)

TEXT

1) ^{d}⌈mes⌉-l[am-t]a-è-a
2) dingir-⌈ra⌉-a-ni-ir
3) ⌈x⌉-*ku-bu-um*
4) ⌈x x⌉-[t]i-a-ke$_4$
5) [na]m-ti-
6) [^{d}]⌈*i-bí*⌉-^{d}EN.ZU
Lacuna

1–2) For the god Meslamta-e'a, his (personal) god,

3–4) x-kūbum, ...,

5–6) ([for]) the [l]ife of Ibbi-Sîn
Lacuna

2015

A marble bead was dedicated to the goddess Gatumdu for the life of Ibbi-Sîn.

COMMENTARY

The translucent yellowish marble bead, streaked with iron deposits, measures 6.1×2.5×0.9 cm. It was acquired through purchase and is said to have come from Iran. In view of the DN in line 1, a Lagaš provenance for the piece is conceivable. The bead bears the museum number NBC 6106; the text is arranged on one column. The inscription was collated.

One may note the unusual orthography in line 2: nin-na-ni for nin-a-ni.

BIBLIOGRAPHY

1937 Stephens, YOS 9 no. 69 (photo, copy, study)
1962 Hallo, HUCA 33 p. 40 Ibbi-Sin 5 (study)
1986 Kärki, KDDU p. 138 Ibbisuen 5 (edition)
1991 Steible, NSBW 2 pp. 283–84 Ibbīsuen 5 (edition)

TEXT

1) ^{d}gá-tùm-du$_{10}$ 2) nin-na-ni	1–2) For the goddess Gatumdu, his lady,
3) nam-ti-<NI> 4) ^{d}*i-bí*-^{d}EN.ZU	3–4) for the life of Ibbi-Sîn,
5) é-ḫé-gál 6) dumu-AN.ZA 7) a mu-na-ru	5–7) E-ḫegal, son of AN.ZA, dedicated (this bead).

2016

A vessel fragment found in excavations at Nippur bears part of a votive inscription for the life of Ibbi-Sîn.

COMMENTARY

The vessel fragment, which is made of a veined white and tan stone, measures 9.8 cm in height, with a rim diameter of 13 cm and a thickness of 1.5 cm. It was found in level VI in area WA at Nippur, locus 14, fl. 2, near Wall CA, in burned debris near the baulk, and was given the excavation number 12 N 621. Its IM number is unknown. The text, as far as preserved, is arranged in one column. The inscription was collated from the published photo.

According to the Canonical Temple List entry 457 (see George, House Most High p. 66 no. 53) the name of Ninšubur's shrine at Nippur was called é-akkil-du$_{6}$-kù "House of Lamentation, Pure Mound."

BIBLIOGRAPHY

1978 Gibson, OIC 23 pp. 26, 121, and fig. 9 no. 2 (provenance, photo, transliteration)
1991 Braun-Holzinger, Weihgaben p. 190 G 369 (edition)
1991 Steible, NSBW 2 pp. 295–96 Ibbīsuen 13 (edition)

TEXT

1) ^{d}nin-šubur 2) dingir-a-ni-ir	1–2) For the god(dess) Ninšubur, his/her god(dess),
3) nam-ti- 4) ^{d}*i-bí*-^{d}⌈EN.ZU⌉ 5) dingir-ka[lam-ma-na-ka-šè]	3–5) for the life of Ibbi-Sîn, god [of his] la[nd]
Lacuna	Lacuna

Unattributed Ur III

E3/2.1.6

(i) Building Inscriptions
(a) Original Inscriptions
1001–1005

1001

A fragment of a stone foundation tablet was found at Diqdiqqah.

COMMENTARY

The tablet fragment, which measures 6.4×7 cm with a thickness of 2 cm, was found loose at Diqdiqqah and was given the excavation number U 1585, museum number CBS 15611. The text is found on the obverse of the tablet; the inscription was collated.

In view of the preserved titulary, an attribution of this inscription to either Ur-Nammu or Šulgi is likely. It may be a stray piece from Ur that recorded the building of the royal palace (Eḫursag) there, or, alternatively, may be evidence that a palace once stood in Diqdiqqah.

BIBLIOGRAPHY

1928 Gadd, UET 1 no. 82 (copy, edition)
1962 Hallo, HUCA 33 p. 41 Anonymous 1 (study)
1986 Kärki, KDDU p. 150 Anonym 1 (edition)
1991 Steible, NSBW 2 p. 297 Ur 1 (edition)

TEXT

Lacuna
1′) ⌜lugal⌝-[uri$_5$].KI-m[a]
2′) lugal-ki-en-gi-ki-uri-k[e$_4$]
3′) é-gal-ki-ág-g[á]-n[i]
4′) mu-na-[dù]

Lacuna
1′–2′) [RN], king of [Ur], king of the land of Sumer and Akkad,
3′–4′) [built] for him hi[s] beloved palace.

1002

A steatite foundation tablet fragment from Ur records the construction of a temple by a king of Ur.

COMMENTARY

The tablet fragment was found in the courtyard of the ziqqurrat and given the excavation number U 10640 and the museum number IM 92935. Line 1′ is found on the obverse, lines 2′–3′ on the reverse. The inscription was not collated.

BIBLIOGRAPHY

1965 Sollberger, UET 8 no. 40 (copy, study)
1986 Kärki, KDDU pp. 155–56 Anonym 16 (edition)
1991 Steible, NSBW 2 p. 302 Ur 10 (edition)

TEXT

Lacuna
1′) lugal-ki-en-gi-ki-uri-ke$_4$
2′) é-a-ni
3′) ⌜mu-na-dù⌝

Lacuna
1′) king of the land of Sumer and Akkad,
2′–3′) built his/her temple for him/her.

1003

A fragment of a foundation tablet from Ur commemorates the construction of the temple of the goddess Ulmašītum.

COMMENTARY

The steatite tablet fragment was found in the area of the Royal Cemetery at Ur and given the excavation number U 11630 and the museum number IM 92934. The inscription was collated by H. Steible.

BIBLIOGRAPHY

1965 Sollberger, UET 8 no. 43 (copy, study)
1986 Kärki, KDDU p. 157 Anonym 19 (edition)
1991 Steible, NSBW 2 pp. 303–304 Ur 12 (edition)

TEXT

Lacuna
1′) [lugal-uri$_5$.KI-m]a
2′) [lugal-a]n-ub-[da-l]ímmu-ba
3′) [lú é]-^{d}*ul*-[*ma-ši-tu*]*m*-⌜ma⌝
4′) [in-dù-a]

Lacuna
1′–2′) [RN, king] of [Ur], [king of the f]our [qu]arters,
3′–4′) [the one who built the temple] of the goddess Ul[mašītu]m.

1004

A fragment of a black stone foundation tablet from Nippur, of probable Ur III date, records the construction of a storehouse. Unfortunately, both the names of the king who built the storehouse and the god to whom it was dedicated are missing from the extant text.

COMMENTARY

The foundation tablet, which was found by Haynes during the third season of the old American excavations at Nippur, and which measures 7.1×8.8×2.2 cm, was given the museum number CBS 8759. The inscription is edited here for the first time through the kind permission of Å.W. Sjöberg. Lines 1′–3′ are found on the obverse, lines 4′–6′ on the reverse.

TEXT

Lacuna
1′) ⌈nita⌉-[kala-ga]
2′) lu[gal ki-en]-⌈gi⌉-[ki-uri]
3′) lug[al-an-ub-da-límmu-ba]
4′) gá-⌈nun⌉-[...]
5′) é-⌈zì⌉(?)-⌈x⌉-[x-n]i
6′) m[u-na-dù]

Lacuna
1′–3′) [RN, mighty] man, ki[ng of the land of Sum]er [and Akkad], ki[ng of the four quarters],

4′–6′) b[uilt the god/goddess ...] a ... storehouse, [hi]s/[he]r ... house.

1005

A three-line inscription on a brick found in the northwest gate of the Ur III Inanna temple mentions the god Ninurta. It may have been placed by an Ur III king.

COMMENTARY

The brick was given the excavation number 5 N-T 689. Goetze mentions another exemplar found on the floor of the room 1T 21 E. We would expect this brick inscription to name the king responsible for the temple's construction. However, both exemplars appear to be anonymous. Construction work on the Ninurta temple in Ur III times is attested in the name of Š 5. The text is arranged in one column.

BIBLIOGRAPHY

1960 Goetze, Iraq 22 p. 151 n. 3 (transliteration)
1976 Basmachi, Treasures p. 205 no. 10 (study)
1984 Zettler, Inanna Temple p. 478 (transliteration)
1992 Steinkeller, Texts Baghdad p. 39 (transliteration)

TEXT

1) ^{d}nin-urta 2) énsi-gal 3) ^{d}en-líl-lá	1–3) The god Ninurta, great governor of the god Enlil.

(i) Building Inscriptions
(b) Tablet Copy
1006

A school copy from Nippur provides part of the text of a building inscription that mentions a shrine of the goddess Nintinuga at Nippur. The reverse of the tablet mentions Ur-Nammu, and it is possible that the obverse of the tablet also bore an inscription of that king. However, in view of the uncertainties, we have included the text in the "Unattributed" section. In all likelihood, the inscription belongs to an Ur III king.

COMMENTARY

The inscription is found on CBS 8358.

According to Sallaberger (Kalender 1 p. 100 § 1.1.4) Nintinuga belonged to the circle of gods connected with the cult of Ninlil. This accords well with the fact that a number of votive inscriptions to the healing goddess Nintinuga were found in the same area which yielded votive inscriptions to Ninlil (that is, "beneath the rooms of [the] T[emple of Bêl] on the S.E. side of [the] Z[iqqurrat]"; Hilprecht BE 1/1 p. 47 text 1). This shrine to Nintinuga is to be kept distinct from a second Nippur shrine to a healing goddess, namely the temple of the goddess Gula located in area WA west of the ancient mid-city canal (see McC. Gibson, "Nippur, 1990: the Temple of Gula and a Glimpse of Things to Come," Oriental Institute Annual Report 1989–1990 pp. 17–22).

BIBLIOGRAPHY

1922 Legrain, PBS 13 no. 26 (copy, edition)
1924 Poebel, OLZ 27 col. 265 (study)

TEXT

Obverse 1) ^{d}nin-tin-ug$_{5}$-ga 2) nin šim-mú-gal-^{d}en-líl-lá-ra 3) é-a-mir-kù 4) é-NI-gu-la 5) ^{d}en-líl-lá-ka 6) é-dumu-sag(Text: KA) 7) mu-na-ni-dù	obv. 1–2) For the goddess Nintinuga, lady, great incantation priestess of the god Enlil, obv. 3–7) in the E-a-mirku, the great ... temple of the god Enlil, he built for her there (the shrine) E-dumusag.
8) šim-erin-gal-gal 9) [...]-e nin-ki-ib Lacuna	obv. 8–9) Great cedar aromatics, ... Lacuna

Reverse
Col. i
Lacuna
1′) ur-^{d}[nammu]
2′) lugal
3′) ^{d}en-líl-le
4′) ki-ág-⌜ra⌝
Several blank spaces
Col. ii
Lacuna
1′) [...]
2′) [...]-⌜x⌝-a-kam
3′) U.SAG
Blank space
4′) an-gub-ba 7

Lacuna
rev. i 1′–4′) For Ur-[Nammu], the king beloved of the god Enlil

Lacuna
rev. ii 1′–4′) Too broken for translation.

(ii) Stele Inscriptions
(a) Original Inscriptions
1007–1011

1007

Three fragments of a stele were found by Peters in his excavations of the "small shrine" of Enlil at Nippur (see Zettler, JNES 43 [1984] p. 235). The preserved portion of the stele contains part of the concluding formula of a royal inscription. Since bricks found by Peters (see E3/2.1.3.4) indicate that the "small shrine" was constructed by Amar-Suena, it may be that this king was responsible for the fashioning of this stele. However, in view of the uncertainties, the inscription has been edited in the "Unattributed" section.

CATALOGUE

Frgm. number	Museum number	No. of cast in Philadelphia	Dimensions (cm)	Scene depicted	cpn
1	EŞ 453	CBS 4935a	5.5×5	Torso of female	c
2	EŞ 455	CBS 4928a	7×7	Head	c
3	EŞ 454	CBS 4929a	7×9	Torso plus two signs	c

COMMENTARY

The stele is formed, in part, by the join of three fragments. Plaster casts of the three pieces are housed in Philadelphia, the originals are in Istanbul. The inscription was kindly collated in Philadelphia by S. Tinney, and information about the Istanbul pieces was graciously provided by J. Canby.

BIBLIOGRAPHY

1893 Hilprecht, BE 1/1 pl. XII nos. 29–31 (frgms. 1–3, photo)
1897 Peters, Nippur 2 pl. opposite p. 140 [top] (frgms. 1–3, photo)
1984 Zettler, JNES 43 p. 235 (study)

TEXT

Frgm. 1
(Partially preserved torso of female divine figure facing left)
Lacuna
1′) [...]-ba
Lacuna

Lacuna
1′) ...
Lacuna

Frgms. 2+3
1′) mu-sar-ra-ba
(Partially preserved torso of male divine figure facing right)
2′) [šu bí-íb]-ùr-⌈a⌉
3′) [mu-n]i
Lacuna

1′–3′) [As for the one who era]ses its inscription (and) who [writes h]is (own) [name there]
Lacuna

1008

A black stone fragment from Nippur, possibly from a stele, bears part of an inscription of a king of Sumer and Akkad. While this piece may date to the Ur III period, an Isin or Larsa date cannot be excluded.

COMMENTARY

The stone fragment, which measures 4.4×1.7×1.5 cm, was found on the surface of the mound and given the excavation number 9 N 232. It bears the museum number A 32776. The preserved text is arranged in one column. The inscription was collated.

BIBLIOGRAPHY

1969 Buccellati and Biggs, AS 17 no. 47 (copy, study)
1991 Steible, NSBW 2 p. 353 Nippur 3 (edition)

TEXT

Lacuna
1′) [lugal ki-e]n-[gi-ki]-uri-[...]
2′) [...] ⌈x⌉ [...]
Lacuna

Lacuna
1′–2′) [king of the land of S]ume[r] and Akkad, ...
Lacuna

1009

A stone fragment from Nippur bears part of a royal inscription of a king of Sumer and Akkad; it may be of Ur III date.

COMMENTARY

The stone fragment measures 3.7×4×0.2 cm and bears the museum number CBS 13898. The preserved text is arranged in one column. The inscription was collated.

The colour of the stone of CBS 13898 differs from the pieces copied by Legrain as PBS 15 nos. 28–39 (Ur-Nammu Cadastre). It likely belongs to a different monument.

BIBLIOGRAPHY

1926 Legrain, PBS 15 no. 33 (copy)

TEXT

Lacuna
1′) [lugal-ki]-⸢en⸣-g[i-ki]-⸢uri⸣-k[e$_4$]
2′) [...] ⸢x⸣
Lacuna

Lacuna
1′–2′) [king of the lands of S]um[er] and Akkad
Lacuna

1010

A stone fragment from Nippur is inscribed with a list of various offerings; the text may be part of the end of a stele or statue inscription of an Ur III king.

COMMENTARY

The fragment measures 6×5.2 cm and bears the museum number CBS 9563. The inscription was collated.

The colour of the stone indicates that it did not make up part of the monument whose fragments were copied by Legrain as PBS 15 nos. 28–30 and 32–39 (Ur-Nammu Cadastre).

BIBLIOGRAPHY

1926 Legrain, PBS 15 no. 31 (copy)

TEXT

Col. i′
Lacuna
1′) [...]
2′) [...] DI
3′) [...] GAR
4′) [...] ⌈x⌉
Lacuna
Col. ii′
Lacuna
1′) [x] ⌈sìla⌉ [...]
2′) 1 sìla ka[š]
3′) 10 ⌈x⌉ [...]
Lacuna

Lacuna
i′ 1′–4′) Too broken for translation.
Lacuna

Lacuna
ii′ 1′–3′) [so many] *sila* [...], 1 *sila* bee[r], 10 ...
Lacuna

1011

A stone fragment from Ur records offerings that may have been instituted by an Ur III king.

COMMENTARY

The blue stone fragment, which measures 11.1×8×7.3 cm, was found northwest of the ziqqurrat and given the excavation number U 2577. Its present whereabouts are unknown.

BIBLIOGRAPHY

1928 Gadd, UET 1 no. 20 (copy)

TEXT

Col. i′
Lacuna
1′) [...] ⌈2 sìla⌉
2′) [...]-ga [...] ⌈x⌉
Lacuna
Col. ii′
Lacuna
1′) [...]
2′) d[a ...]
Lacuna

Lacuna
i′ 1′ – 2′) Two *sila* ...
Lacuna

Lacuna
ii′ 1′ – 2′) Too broken for translation.
Lacuna

(ii) Stele Inscriptions
(b) Tablet Copy
1012

An Old Babylonian tablet copy of what may be part of a royal inscription, possibly a stele inscription, names various cities in Elam. Since many of the GNs mentioned also appear in year names of Šulgi and Amar-Suena, an attribution of this text to one of the Ur III kings is a distinct possibility.

COMMENTARY

The inscription is found on Ni 9717 (Istanbul). The preserved text is arranged in one column.

The GN Duduli of line 5′ refers to the Duduli located somewhere in Elam. It is frequently mentioned in Ur III texts in connection with its governor Ḫulibar (see Goetze, JNES 12 [1953] pp. 114–23). It is to be kept distinct from the GN NE<du>ḫuli which was also located in Elam (see Lafont, Documents p. 101 no. 377).

BIBLIOGRAPHY

1969 Çığ and Kızılyay, ISET 1 p. 179 no. 9717 (copy)

TEXT

Lacuna
1′) [...].KI ⌈x x⌉ [...]
2′) [...].KI ḫu-úḫ-nu-ri.KI ⌈x⌉ [...]
3′) [...]-⌈x⌉-ri-ni.KI ši-pa-ra.⌈KI⌉ ⌈mu⌉-⌈x⌉- [...]
4′) [...]-ki.KI sa-bu-um.KI-bi-d[a ...]
5′) [...]-⌈x⌉.KI ki-maš.KI du$_8$-du$_8$-lí.K[I ...]
6′) [... ma]-da-an-ša$_4$-an.KI [...]
7′) [...].⌈KI⌉ ⌈x x x⌉ [...]
Lacuna

Lacuna
1′–7′) ..., ..., ..., Ḫuḫnuri, ..., [...]rini, Šipara, ..., ..., an[d] Sabum, ..., Kimaš, Duduli, ..., [the la]nd of Anšan, ...
Lacuna

(iii) Inscriptions on Statues and Other Cult Objects
(a) Original Inscriptions
1013–1015

1013

A statue(?) fragment in the Yale collections is incised with the end of an apparent Ur III royal inscription.

COMMENTARY

The felsite fragment, which measures 5.6×8.2×4.2 cm, is of unknown provenance. It bears the museum number NBC 2524. The inscription was collated.

For the translation "temple oval" for ib-gal, see R. Biggs in D. Hansen, "Al-Hiba, 1968–1969, A Preliminary Report," Artibus Asiae 32 (1970) p. 247.

BIBLIOGRAPHY

1920 Keiser, BIN 2 no. 7 (copy)

TEXT

Lacuna
1′) [...] ⌈x⌉-ni
2′) [z]à-ká-ib-gal
3′) [k]á-ᵈutu
4′) [ḫé]-na-⌈bé⌉
5′) [x]-*na-tu*-UB-*tum*
6′) [mu]-un-dù

Lacuna
1′–4′) [May] he utter his ... beside the gate of the great *temple oval* (and) the gate of the god Utu.

5′–6′) He built a ... (for him/her).

1014

A basalt statue fragment in the Yale collections is incised with an apparent royal inscription; it likely dates to the period Gudea-Ur III.

COMMENTARY

The statue fragment, which is of unknown provenance, measures 9.6×9 cm, and bears the museum number NBC 2525. The inscription was collated.

BIBLIOGRAPHY

1920 Keiser, BIN 2 no. 10 (copy)

TEXT

Col. i′
Lacuna
1′) [...]
2′) [...ki(?)-á]g-[...]-⌈x⌉-gar
3′) [... n]ir-[...-N]E
4′) [...]
Lacuna
Col. ii′
Lacuna
1′) [...]-⌈x⌉ [...]
2′) ^{d}nin-ḫu[r-saga]
3′) dingir-[...]
4′) nin an-kù-g[e] s[a$_4$]
5′) nin sù-ág-⌈x⌉
6′) [...]-⌈x x⌉ [...]
Lacuna

Lacuna
i′ 1′ – 4′) Too broken for translation.
Lacuna

Lacuna
ii′ 1′ – 6′) ..., Ninḫu[rsaga], ... goddess, lady nam[ed] by pur[e] An, lady, radiance of ...
Lacuna

1015

A statuette fragment from Nippur was dedicated to the goddess Inanna, possibly for the life of an Ur III king.

COMMENTARY

The statuette fragment, which is made of ivory, measures 3.8×2.7×1.2 cm. It was found in locus 141, level IV (that is, the Ur III level), of the Inanna temple and given the excavation number 6 N 426. It bears the museum number A 31056. The preserved text is arranged in one column. The inscription was collated.

BIBLIOGRAPHY

1984 Zettler, Inanna Temple p. 132 n. 1 and p. 489 (transliteration, study)
1991 Braun-Holzinger, Weihgaben p. 275 St 161 (study)

TEXT

1) ^{d}inanna
2) nin-a-ni-ir
3) nam-[ti]-
Lacuna

1–2) To the goddess Inanna, his lady,
3) for the li[fe of ...]
Lacuna

(iii) Inscriptions on Statues and Other Cult Objects
(b) Tablet Copy
1016

A fragment of a Nippur tablet provides part of an apparent royal inscription (see Borger, HKL 2 p. 143, notes to ISET 1 p. 212 Ni 13213, where Wilcke is cited). The ductus of the tablet and the language of the text indicate an Ur III date for the composition.

COMMENTARY

The tablet bears the museum number Ni 13213 (Istanbul). It forms part of a collection of Nippur tablets (Ni 13200 to Ni 13224 at least) that apparently date to the Ur III period. The fact that col. iv in Çığ and Kızılyay's copy is followed by a large blank space argues that the text proceeds from left to right on the reverse of the tablet, a practice attested in early tablets. By this understanding, Çığ and Kızılyay's col. iv represents the end of the text. Illegible traces of a colophon(?) appear after the blank space. In the column which is not marked, but which would be col. vi in Çığ and Kızılyay's copy, there is some uncertainty as to the exact location of the line dividers; we have thus given each successive line on the tablet a consecutive line number.

Obv. col. ii′, if interpreted correctly, would seem to refer to the placing of a frieze(?) of animal figurines. It brings to mind Hall's reconstruction of the south-east face of the Ninḫursaga temple at Tell al-ʿUbaid/Nutur (see Hall, UE 1 pl. 38); there recumbent bulls adorn the temple face.

If line 6′ of rev. col. ii′ does indeed refer to the goddess Ninsuna (the reading is uncertain), then KAL.KI-šè in line 3′ of the same column would, in all likelihood, refer to the goddess's cult centre at KI.KAL. See the introductory comments to E3/2.1.1.6 in this connection.

If col. iii′ of the reverse gives the end of the composition, then line 1′ could very well be the end of a curse formula. In this case the expression gu ab-lá-e "he (the god?) will stretch the net (over him)" would refer to the god's snaring the evil-doer who dared to destroy the king's handiwork. Although conventionally translated "thread," gu in this context apparently denotes a net that was made of vegetable fibre (hemp?) as opposed to animal sinews (sa-pàr). A comparable expression is found in line 281 of the literary composition "Enki and the World Order" (see Benito's unpublished dissertation, "Enki and Ninmaḫ" and "Enki and the World Order" pp. 100 and 128): gu-lá-a-na mušen nu-è "(from) the net stretched by him no bird escapes." We may also compare Gudea Cylinder A col. xiv line 24: gu máš-anše eden-na lá "Net that is stretched over the animals in the steppe." See the comments of Falkenstein in ZA 56 (1964) p. 79.

BIBLIOGRAPHY

1969 Çığ and Kızılyay, ISET 1 p. 212 Ni 13213 (copy)

TEXT

Obverse
Col. i′
Lacuna
1′) [...] ⸢x⸣ [x] ⸢x⸣
2′) [...] me x x [x] ⸢x⸣ [... d]ul$_4$(?)
3′) [...-d]ù(?)-a
4′) [...]-ù
5′) [...]

Lacuna
obv. i′ 1′–5′) Too broken for translation.

Col. ii′
Lacuna
1′) é [...]
2′) [...] ⸢x x⸣ [...]

Lacuna
obv. ii′ 1′–4′) The temple ..., after I(?) set recumbent [li]ons(?) and bulls (in) *the dwelling*

3′) [pi]rig(?)-gu$_4$-ná ki(Text: NA)-dúr ⸢ù⸣-gar
4′) [...]
Col. iii′
Lacuna
1′) [...]
2′) ⸢x x⸣ ma-šè

Lacuna
obv. iii′ 1′–2′) Too broken for translation.

Reverse
Col. i′ = Çığ and Kızılyay col. (vi)
Lacuna of three lines
1′) [...]-si(?)
2′) [...-z]i
3′) [...] ⸢x⸣-ḫul-
4′) [...]-e
5′) [...]-⸢x⸣-me
6′) [...-íb]-si
7′) [...] ⸢x⸣
Lacuna

Lacuna of three lines
rev. i′ 1′–7′) Too broken for translation.
Lacuna

Col. ii′ = Çığ and Kızılyay col. v
1) [n]á-bi
2) kur-mar-dú-ta
3) KAL.KI-šè
4) ba-an-tùm
5) KAL.KI D[U(?) x]
6) ^{d}nin-⸢súna⸣(?)-ra
7) [...] ⸢ù⸣ [x] ⸢ab⸣-⸢x⸣ [x]
Lacuna

rev. ii′ 1–4) That [b]ed was brought from the land of Mardu to KAL.KI.

rev. ii′ 5–7) ... KAL.KI, for the goddess *Ninsuna* ...
Lacuna

Col. iii′ = Çığ and Kızılyay col. iv
1) gu ab-lá-e

rev. iii′ 1) he (the god?) will stretch a net (over him).

Blank space
Colophon(?)
1) ⸢x x⸣ [...]
Lacuna

Blank space
Colophon(?)
Too broken for translation.
Lacuna

(iv) Mace-head Inscriptions 1017–1018

1017

A mace-head was dedicated to the god Nanna by a king of Ur.

COMMENTARY

The alabaster or calcite mace-head consists of two fragments, U 247+250, which were found in E-nun-maḫ room 11, and given the museum number BM 116429 and the registration number 1923-11-10, 14. The joined pieces measure 16 cm in height and 17.5 cm in diameter. The large, but slender, mace-head has an oval form. The text is arranged in one column. The inscription was collated.

BIBLIOGRAPHY

1928 Gadd, UET 1 no. 83 (copy, edition)
1962 Hallo, HUCA 33 p. 41 Anonymous 10 (study)
1974 Woolley, UE 6 p. 86 sub U 247 (study)
1986 Kärki, KDDU pp. 154–55 Anonym 10 (edition)
1991 Braun-Holzinger, Weihgaben p. 62 K 87 (edition)
1991 Steible, NSBW 2 p. 299 Ur 5 (edition)

TEXT

1) ^{d}nanna
2) dumu-sag-
3) [^{d}e]n-líl-lá
4) [...] x
Lacuna
1′) [lugal]-uri$_5$.KI-ma-ke$_4$
2′) é-kiš-nu-gál-šè
3′) a mu-na-ru

1–4) For the god Nanna, first-(born) son of the god [E]nlil, ...
Lacuna
1′–3′) [RN, king] of Ur, dedicated (this mace) to the Ekišnugal.

1018

A mace-head fragment bears an inscription likely indicating that it was dedicated to the god Meslamta-eʾa.

COMMENTARY

The chalcedony(?) mace-head fragment was found in EM, loose in the soil, and was given the excavation number U 7709. It now bears the museum number IM 3567. The preserved text is arranged in one column. The inscription was kindly collated by H. Steible.

BIBLIOGRAPHY

1928 Gadd, UET 1 no. 280 (copy, edition)
1991 Braun-Holzinger, Weihgaben p. 62 K 90 (edition)
1991 Steible, NSBW 2 pp. 302–303 Ur 11 (edition)

TEXT

Lacuna
1′) [mu-ni] bí-[í]b-sar-a
2′) [x]-ba
3′) [^{d}mes]-lam-ta-[UD].DU-<a>
4′) [dingir/lugal]-mu
5′) [...] ⸢x⸣

Lacuna
1′) who writes [his (own) name] there,
2′) ...
3′–5′) [May] the god [Mes]lamta-⸢e⸣ʾ<a>, my [god/lord *curse him*].

(v) "Booty Inscriptions" 1019–1022

1019

An alabaster vase fragment from Ur was dedicated as a piece of booty by an Ur III king.

COMMENTARY

The white calcite fragment, which measures 6.7×3 cm, was found in the great Nanna courtyard over ruins of the east corner of the Larsa range and given the excavation number U 2756; for the precise location, see AJ 5 (1925) p. 353 fig. 1b room 1. The piece bears the museum number IM 933. The preserved text is arranged in one column.

BIBLIOGRAPHY

1928 Gadd, UET 1 no. 18 (copy, edition)
1955 Woolley, UE 4 p. 170 (provenance)
1960 Sollberger, Iraq 22 p. 89 (study)
1991 Braun-Holzinger, Weihgaben p. 191 G 374 (edition)
1991 Steible, NSBW 2 p. 300 Ur 7 (edition)

TEXT

Lacuna	Lacuna
1′) [...]-⌈x⌉-a	1′–3′) [The ... object which he to]ok as [bo]oty
2′) [nam-r]a-aš	
3′) [mu-na-a]k-a	
4′) [nam-ti-l]a-ni-šè	4′–5′) he [de]dicated for his (own) [l]ife.
5′) [a mu-n]a-ru	

1020

An alabaster vase from Nippur was dedicated as booty by an Ur III king.

COMMENTARY

The alabaster vase fragment, which measures 13×5.5×4.1 cm, was found during the third season of the old American excavations at Nippur. The preserved text is arranged in one column. It bears the museum number CBS 9592.

BIBLIOGRAPHY

1926 Legrain, PBS 15 no. 24 (copy)
1991 Braun-Holzinger, Weihgaben p. 197 G 411 (edition)
1991 Steible, NSBW 2 pp. 352–53 Nippur 2 (edition)

TEXT

Lacuna	Lacuna
1′) [...]	1′–3′) [the ...] which he took as [bo]oty
2′) [nam-r]a-aš	
3′) [m]u-na-ak-a	
4′) [n]am-ti-la-ni-šè	4′–5′) he [dedic]ated (this vase) for his (own) [l]ife.
5′) [a mu-na-r]u	

1021

A calcite vase fragment from Ur likely formed part of the the spoils of an attack by an Ur III king on Susa.

COMMENTARY

The calcite vessel fragment, which measures 6×5.5×2.4 cm, was found loose in the filling of the Enun-maḫ, and given the excavation number U 439. It bears the museum number CBS 14934. The inscription was collated.

The inscription was tentatively ascribed by Woolley (UE 6 p. 90) to Rīmuš. However, since that Sargonic king's "booty inscriptions" are otherwise all recorded in Akkadian, and in view of the appearance of the title "king of Ur," which is not found in the Sargonic inscriptions, the attribution to Rīmuš is unlikely. The fact that the royal titulary ends with the epithet "[k]ing of Ur" would suggest an attribution of the fragment to Šulgi, since Amar-Suena, Šū-Sîn, and Ibbi-Sîn all used the title "king of the four quarters" after "king of Ur" in their inscriptions. If line 1′ is a royal name, then it cannot be Ur-Nammu; his name never appears with the prefixed DINGIR sign in contemporary royal inscriptions.

A campaign against Elam is alluded to in the hymn Šulgi B line 43 (ms. Haayer): sig-šè elam.KI-ma KA-ba giš ma-ab-ús "In the low(land), on the 'mouth(?)' of Elam, the yoke (literally: wood) was imposed for me"; see the year name for IS 9 quoted in part here: mu ^{d}*i-bí*-EN.ZU lugal-uri$_5$.KI-ma-ke$_4$ ḫu-úḫ-nu-ri KA.BAD-ma-da-an-ša-an.KI-šè [á]-dugud ba-ši-in-gin ... "The year Ibbi-Sîn, king of Ur, marched with heavy forces against Ḫuḫnuri, the 'open mouth' of the land of Anšan ..."

BIBLIOGRAPHY

1974 Woolley, UE 6 p. 90 (provenance)
1991 Braun-Holzinger, Weihgaben p. 167 G 243 (edition, study)

TEXT

Lacuna	Lacuna
1′) ⌈d⌉[...]	1′–4′) [RN, ki]ng of Ur, [when] he destroyed [S]usa
2′) [lu]gal-uri$_5$.[KI-m]a-ke$_4$	Lacuna
3′) [u$_4$ M]ÙŠ.EREN.KI	
4′) [m]u-ḫul-a	
Lacuna	

1022

A fragment of an alabaster vessel may be a piece of booty from Susa.

COMMENTARY

The alabaster vase fragment, which measures 17×7×1.8–2.2 cm, was found in the Enun-maḫ, and given the excavation number U 259. It bears the museum number CBS 14935.

The piece could not be located for collation purposes. The edition follows Braun-Holzinger's transliteration.

BIBLIOGRAPHY

1991 Braun-Holzinger, Weihgaben p. 167 G 244 (edition, study)

TEXT

Lacuna
1′) [...] uri$_5$.KI(?)-ta
2′) MÙŠ.EREN.KI
3′) mu-ḫul-a
4′) nam-ra-ak
Lacuna

Lacuna
1′–4′) from ... Ur(?), he destroyed Susa, booty
Lacuna

(vi) Weight Stones 1023–1026

1023

A fragment of a diorite weight stone bears an inscription of an Ur III king.

COMMENTARY

The weight stone was found at Ur, but its exact findspot is unknown. It was given the arbitrary excavation number U m by Sollberger. It bears the museum number BM 116451 and the registration number 1923-11-10, 37. The text is arranged in one column. The inscription was collated.

While Kärki assigned this inscription to Šulgi, the attribution is not certain. While the title "king of the four quarters" is found in inscriptions dating to the latter part of Šulgi's reign, the epithet also appears as part of the royal titulary of Amar-Suena, Šū-Sîn, and Ibbi-Sîn.

BIBLIOGRAPHY

1965 Sollberger, UET 8 no. 38 (copy, study)
1986 Kärki, KDDU pp. 53–54 Šulgi 51 (iv) (edition)

TEXT

Lacuna
1′) ⌈lugal⌉-[u]ri$_5$.KI-ma
2′) lu[gal-an]-ub-[da-límmu-ba]-ke$_4$
3′) ⌈10⌉+(x) [ma-n]a
4′) [mu-na-gi]-in

Lacuna
1′–2′) king of [U]r, ki[ng] of the [four] [qua]rte[rs],

3′–4′) [confir]med [for him /her (the god DN)] (this weight stone as) ten (+ x) [min]as.

1024

A fragment of a weight stone found in Taylor's excavation at Ur bears the end of an inscription of an Ur III king.

COMMENTARY

The weight stone fragment bears the museum number BM 91148 and the registration number 59-10-14, 31. The text is arranged in one column. The inscription was collated.

As was the case with the previous inscription, Kärki's proposed attribution of this weight stone to Šulgi is not certain.

The é-kišib-ba-^{d}nanna-a-gar-ra was the name of a storehouse at Ur (see Legrain, UET 3 nos. 886, 891, 1044, 1146, and 1149 and Loding, UET 9 no. 927; variant spelling é-kišib-ba-^{d}nanna-e-gar-ra in Legrain, UET 3 no. 1192). For Ur III references to é-kišib-ba = Akkadian *bīt kunukki*(*m*) "storehouse," see Oppenheim, Eames Collection p. 8 note b and Falkenstein, Gerichtsurkunden 2 p. 345 note to line 50.

BIBLIOGRAPHY

1887 Winckler, MAOV 1 p. 18 no. 4 (copy)
1892 Winckler and Böhden, ABK no. 52 (copy)
1907 Thureau-Dangin, SAK pp. 194–95 Dun-gi t (edition)
1929 Barton, RISA pp. 280–81 Shulgi 20 (edition)
1962 Hallo, HUCA 33 p. 42 Anonymous 11i (study)
1971 Sollberger and Kupper, IRSA IIIA2e (edition)
1986 Kärki, KDDU pp. 62–63 (Anonym 11 =) Šulgi 57 (edition)

TEXT

Lacuna
1′) [nita/lugal]-kala-ga
2′) lugal-uri$_5$.KI-ma
3′) lugal-an-ub-da-límmu-ba-ke$_4$
4′) 2 ma-na
5′) é-kišib-ba-^{d}nanna-a-gar-ra
6′) mu-na-gi-in

Lacuna
1′–3′) [RN], mighty [man/king], king of Ur, king of the four quarters,

4′–6′) confirmed for him/her (the god DN) (this weight stone as) two minas in E-kišiba-Nanna-gara.

1025

A fragment of a weight stone found in Woolley's excavations at Ur bears part of an inscription of an Ur III king.

COMMENTARY

The weight stone was found in the courtyard of the Dublal-maḫ and given the excavation number U 3205; its IM number is unknown. As was the case for the previous two inscriptions, this weight stone was ascribed to Šulgi by Kärki, but the attribution is not certain. The text is arranged in one column; as restored, it is identical to the previous inscription.

BIBLIOGRAPHY

1928 Gadd, UET 1 no. 74 (copy, edition)
1962 Hallo, HUCA 33 p. 42 Anonymous 11ii (study)
1986 Kärki, KDDU pp. 62–63 (Anonym 11 =) Šulgi 57 (conflated edition with E3/2.1.6.1024)

TEXT

Lacuna
1′) [nita/lugal]-kal[a]-ga
2′) [lu]gal-uri$_5$.KI-ma
3′) lugal-an-ub-da-límmu-ba-ke$_4$
4′) [N] ma-n[a]
5′) ⌜é⌝-kišib-ba-⌜d⌝[nanna-a-gar-ra]
6′) [mu-na-gi-in]

Lacuna
1′–3′) [RN], migh[ty man/king, k]ing of Ur, king of the four quarters,

4′–6′) [confirmed for him/her (the god DN)] (this weight stone as) [N] minas in E-kišiba-Nanna-gara.

1026

A fragment of a duck weight found in Woolley's excavations at Ur gives part of an inscription of an Ur III king.

COMMENTARY

The duck weight, which measures 22×17×14.8 cm, was found loose near the south corner of the ziqqurrat and was given the excavation number U 1190. Its IM number is unknown. The text is arranged in one column.

BIBLIOGRAPHY

1928 Gadd, UET 1 no. 84 (copy, edition)
1962 Hallo, HUCA 33 p. 42 Anonymous 12 (study)
1986 Kärki, KDDU p. 63 (Anonym 12 =) Šulgi 58 (edition)

TEXT

Lacuna
1′) ni[ta-kala-ga]
2′) lu[gal-uri$_5$.KI-ma]
3′) lugal-a[n-ub-da]-límmu-[ba-ke$_4$]
4′) nam-ti-[la]-ni-[šè]
5′) 30 ma-[na]
6′) mu-na-gi-in

Lacuna
1′–3′) [RN], [mighty] m[an], ki[ng of Ur], king of the four qu[arters],

4′) [for] his (own) li[fe],
5′–6′) confirmed for him/her (the god DN) (this weight stone as) thirty mi[nas].

(vii) Votive Inscriptions on Stone and Clay Vessels
(a) Dedicated by the King
1027–1032

1027

Two fragments of a black and white marble vessel from Ur provide the text of part of an Ur III dedicatory inscription.

COMMENTARY

Fragment 1, a porphyry vessel fragment which measures 8.2×5 cm, was found in the building HT, and given the excavation number U 6956 and the museum number IM 1156. Fragment 2 is said to be black and white marble and was found in the area of the ziqqurrat terrace, "just behind the SW wall of the Neo-Babylonian Boat Shrine, in the stratum of broken bricks lying above the plano-convex brick and bitumen mass." It was given the excavation number U 18224 and the museum number IM 16700.

BIBLIOGRAPHY

1928 Gadd, UET 1 no. 19 (frgm. 1, copy, edition)
1962 Hallo, HUCA 33 p. 41 Anonymous 5 (frgm. 1, study)
1965 Sollberger, UET 8 no. 106 (frgm. 2, copy, study)
1986 Kärki, KDDU p. 152 Anonym 5 (frgm. 1, edition)
1991 Braun-Holzinger, Weihgaben p. 190 G 371 (frgm. 1, edition); p. 192 G 381 (frgm. 2, edition)
1991 Steible, NSBW 2 p. 298 Ur 3 (frgm. 1, edition); pp. 307–308 Ur 19 (frgm. 2, edition)

TEXT

Lacuna
1′) lugal-ki-en-[g]i-[ki]-uri-ke$_4$
2′) [nam]-ti-la-ni-šè
3′) [a] mu-na-ru
4′) lú mu-sar-ra-ba
5′) ⸢šu bí⸣-íb-⸢ùr-a⸣
6′) [mu-ni bí-í]b-sar-a
7′) [lú]-ba

Lacuna
1′) [RN], king of the land of Sum[er] and Akkad,
2′–3′) [de]dicated (this bowl) for his (own) life.

4′–5′) As for the one who erases its inscription

6′) and writes [his (own) name there],
7′) that [man]

8′) [^{d}]nanna
9′) [lug]al(?)-mu
10′) [x]-mu
11′) ⸢^{d}⸣nin-gal-e
12′) [nam ḫa-ba-da-kuru$_5$-ne]

8′–12′) may [the god] Nanna, my [lo]rd , my [...], (and) the goddess Ningal, [curse him].

1028

A fragment of a white calcite vase mentions (a king) of Ur.

COMMENTARY

The vase fragment, which measures 9×4 cm, was found in the E-nun-maḫ area, either rooms 16–17, according to the Field Catalogue, or room 11, according to the catalogue in UE 6. It was given the excavation number U 881. It bears the museum number BM 116440 and the registration number 1923-11-10, 25. The preserved text is arranged in one column. The inscription was collated.

BIBLIOGRAPHY

1965 Sollberger, UET 8 no. 50 (copy, study)
1974 Woolley, UE 6 p. 93 sub U 88 1 (provenance)
1986 Kärki, KDDU p. 157 Anonym 20 (edition)
1991 Braun-Holzinger, Weihgaben p. 192 G 379 (edition)
1991 Steible, NSBW 2 pp. 305–306 Ur 16 (edition)

TEXT

1′) [...] šè(?) [...]
2′) [... u]ri$_5$.KI-ma

1′–2′) ... of [U]r.

1029

An inscription on a fragment of a black steatite bowl gives the title "king of Ur."

COMMENTARY

The bowl fragment, which measures 4.5×3.2×0.6 cm, was found in the E-nun-maḫ area — under the pavement of rooms 16–17, according to the Ur registry books, or in room 11, according to the catalogue in UE 6. It was given the excavation number U 281 and bears the museum number BM 116447 and the registration number 1923-11-10, 33. The preserved text is arranged in one column. The inscription was collated.

No RN is preserved on this fragment. Because the piece was found with a second bowl fragment that bore an inscription of Šulgi (E3/2.1.2.43), Sollberger (UET 8 p. 6 notes to no. 27) assigned it as well to Šulgi. However, since these two bowl fragments were found in a secondary context, the attribution of U 281 to Šulgi is uncertain.

BIBLIOGRAPHY

1965 Sollberger, UET 8 no. 27 (copy, study)
1974 Woolley, UE 6 p. 88 sub U 281 (study)
1986 Kärki, KDDU p. 66 Šulgi 66 (edition)
1991 Braun-Holzinger, Weihgaben p. 187 G 352 (edition)
1991 Steible, NSBW 2 pp. 203–204 Šulgi 58 (edition)

TEXT

1) [...]
2) [nita/lugal-kala-ga]
3) lugal-uri$_5$.KI-ma-ke$_4$

1–3) [RN, mighty man/king], king of Ur.

1030

An alabaster vase known from three fragments was dedicated, probably by an Ur III king, in Sippar.

COMMENTARY

The cylindrical alabaster vase, which measures 11 cm in height, with an outside diameter of 12 cm and an inside diameter of 8 cm, was found in H. Rassam's excavations at Sippar and given the museum number BM 90903 (formerly BM 12031) and the registration number 82-7-14, 1016. The text is arranged in one column. The inscription was collated.

BIBLIOGRAPHY

1893 Winckler, AOF 1 p. 546 no. 6 ([partial] copy)
1899 King, CT 7 pl. 3 BM 12031 (copy)
1967 Borger, HKL 1 p. 224 to CT 7 pl. 3 (study)
1980 Walker, in de Meyer, Tell ed-Dēr 3 p. 98 no. 26 (study)
1986 Kärki, KDDU pp. 63–64 Šulgi 59 (edition)
1991 Braun-Holzinger, Weihgaben p. 192 G 382 (edition)
1991 Steible, NSBW 2 pp. 309–10 Ur 21 (edition)

TEXT

Lacuna
1′) [lugal-ur]i$_5$(?).⌜KI⌝(?)-[ma]
2′) [lugal-an]-ub-⌜da⌝-[límmu-b]a-ke$_4$
3′) [nam-ti]-la-ni-šè
4′) [a mu-n]a-ru
5′) [lú mu-sa]r-ra-na
6′) [šu bí-i]n-ùr
7′) [mu-ni b]í-íb-[sa]r-e-a
8′) ⌜^{d}⌝utu
9′) [lugal(?)]-⌜zimbir.KI⌝-ra-ke$_4$
10′) [numun]-a-ni
11′) [ḫé]-éb-til-e

Lacuna
1′–2′) [king of U]r(?), [king of the four qua]rters,

3′–4′) [ded]icated (this vase) for his (own) [life].

5′–7′) [As for the one who er]ases his (the king's) [inscr]iption (and) [writ]es [his (own) name th]ere,

8′–11′) may the god Utu, [lord] of Sippar, bring his [progeny] to an end.

1031

A fragment of an obsidian cup gives part of an Ur III curse formula.

COMMENTARY

The obsidian cup fragment was found in room C 23 of the Gipar-ku, "near the sanctuary," and was given the excavation number U 6702. It bears the museum number IM 1176. The text is arranged in one column. The inscription was not collated.

For the translation "cupboard" for gú-ne-sag, see Civil apud Cooper and Heimpel, JAOS 103 (1983) p. 79 and Sallaberger, Kalender 1 p. 117 n. 532. See the translation of "sacristy" given for ne-sag in E3/2.1.5.3. We have given lines 5′–7′ of this text following the transliteration of Civil; it differs slightly from the text as copied.

BIBLIOGRAPHY

1928 Gadd, UET 1 no. 15 (copy, edition)
1955 Woolley, UE 4 p. 172 (provenance)
1960 Sollberger, Iraq 22 p. 89 notes to (f) (study)
1976 Woolley and Mallowan, UE 7 pp. 57–58 (provenance)
1983 Civil, apud Cooper and Heimpel, JAOS 103 p. 79 commentary to line 6 (study)
1991 Braun-Holzinger, Weihgaben p. 193 G 388 (edition)
1991 Steible, NSBW 2 pp. 314–16 Ur 28 (edition)

TEXT

Lacuna
1′) numun-na-[ni]
2′) ḫé-éb-[til]-l[e]
3′) tukum-b[i]
4′) gú-ne-sa[g-gá-ta]
5′) íb!-ta-[an-zi-zi]
6′) é-nì-gá-[ra-(ni)]
7′) ⌜ì-íb⌝-k[u_4-ku_4-dè]
Lacuna

Lacuna
1′–2′) May he [bring his] progeny to an e[nd].

3′–7′) If he takes (this cup) out of the cupboard and brings it into (his) storehouse
Lacuna

1032

An alabaster vessel fragment from Nippur bears the inscription of an Ur III king.

COMMENTARY

The fragment was found on the surface of the mound in the SO section of the city and was given the excavation number 4 N-T 15. It bears the museum number IM 58934. The text is arranged in one column. The inscription was not collated.

BIBLIOGRAPHY

1978 McCown, Nippur 2 pp. 76 and 92 no. 49 (copy, study)
1991 Braun-Holzinger, Weihgaben p. 197 G 412 (transliteration)
1991 Steible, NSBW 2 pp. 353–54 Nippur 4 (edition)

TEXT

Lacuna
1′) [lugal-uri$_5$.K]I-⸢ma⸣
2′) lugal-an-ub-da-límmu-ba-⸢ke$_4$⸣
Lacuna

Lacuna
1′–2′) [king of U]r, king of the four quarters,
Lacuna

(vii) Votive Inscriptions on Stone and Clay Vessels (b) Dedicated for the Life of the King 1033–1041

1033

A diorite bowl fragment from Ur was dedicated for the life of a king of Ur.

COMMENTARY

The diorite bowl fragment, which measures 8.7×6 cm, and the inscription 6.2×2.9 cm, was found at Ur in the Gipar-ku (near the Ningal cella) and given the excavation number U 6380. It bears the museum number BM 118556 and the registration number 1927-5-27, 29. The text is arranged in one column. The inscription, which was carved near the edge of the bowl, was collated. In lines 1′–3′ the LUGAL sign is written upside down, as is the ur sign in line 4′.

BIBLIOGRAPHY

1928 Gadd, UET 1 no. 68 (copy, edition)
1962 Hallo, HUCA 33 p. 41 Anonymous 6 (study)
1976 Woolley and Mallowan, UE 7 pp. 57–58 and 223 (provenance)
1986 Kärki, KDDU pp. 152–53 Anonym 6 (edition)
1991 Braun-Holzinger, Weihgaben p. 191 G 372 (edition)
1991 Steible, NSBW 2 pp. 298–99 Ur 4 (edition)

TEXT

Lacuna
1′) lugal-kala-ga
2′) lugal-uri$_5$.KI-ma
3′) lugal-inim-gi-na
4′) dumu-ur-^{d}utu
5′) ir$_{11}$-da-né
6′) a mu-na-ru

Lacuna
1′–2′) [For RN], mighty king, king of Ur,

3′–6′) Lugal-inim-gina, son of Ur-Utu, his servant, dedicated (this bowl).

1034

A fragment of a granite cup found in excavations at Girsu was dedicated for the life of a king of Ur.

COMMENTARY

The granite cup would have had an original diameter of about 30 cm; it now measures 10.5×8.5×1.4 cm. The piece was found in the excavations by Parrot at Telloh during the 1932–33 season. It was given the excavation number T 1218 and the museum number AO 16651. The text is arranged in one column. The inscription was not collated.

BIBLIOGRAPHY

1947 Nougayrol, RA 41 pp. 27–29 (copy, edition)
1962 Hallo, HUCA 33 p. 41 Anonymous 7 (study)
1986 Kärki, KDDU p. 153 Anonym 7 (edition)
1991 Braun-Holzinger, Weihgaben p. 181 G 321 (edition)
1991 Steible, NSBW 1 pp. 421–22 "Lagaš" 54 (edition)

TEXT

Lacuna
1′) [RN]
2′) nita-kala-ga
3′) lugal-uri$_5$.KI-ma-ka-šè
4′) me-nam-nin-a
5′) dam GA.NI-ke$_4$
6′) a mu-ru
7′) bur-ba nin-mu
8′) èn-mu ḫé-tar
9′) [mu-bi-im]

Lacuna
1′–3′) for [RN], mighty king, king of Ur,

4′–6′) Menam-nina, wife of Gani, dedicated (this cup).

7′–9′) [The name] of this cup [is]: "May my lady take care of me."

1035

A calcite vase was dedicated by a "lieutenant of the watch" for an Ur III king.

COMMENTARY

The fragment of a cylindrical calcite vase, which measures 8×5×1.2 cm, was found in room 16–17 of the E-nun-maḫ at Ur, probably from the Kurigalzu level, and was given the excavation number U 255. It bears the museum number BM 116438 and the registration number 1923-11-10, 23. The text is arranged in one column. The inscription was collated.

BIBLIOGRAPHY

1965 Sollberger, UET 8 no. 39 (copy, study)
1974 Woolley, UE 6 p. 87 sub U 255 (provenance)
1986 Kärki, KDDU p. 155 Anonym 15 (edition)
1991 Braun-Holzinger, Weihgaben p. 191 G 375 (edition)
1991 Steible, NSBW 2 p. 301–302 Ur 9 (edition)

TEXT

Lacuna
1′) [lugal]-⌜uri$_5$⌝.KI-ma
2′) [lu]gal-ki-en-[gi]-ki-uri-ka-šè
3′) [^{d}nan]na-kù-zu
4′) [nu-bànda-e]n-nu-ke$_4$
5′) [a mu]-na-ru

Lacuna
1′–2′) [king] of Ur, [ki]ng of the land of Su[mer] and Akkad,
3′–5′) [Nan]na-kuzu, [lieutenant of the w]atch, [ded]icated (this vessel).

1036

A fragment of an alabaster vessel was dedicated to the god Nanna, possibly for the life of an Ur III king.

COMMENTARY

The vessel fragment, which measures 7.2×3.7×0.8 cm, was found in room 11 of the E-nun-maḫ and given the excavation number U 288 and the museum number CBS 14945. The text is arranged in one column. The inscription was collated.

BIBLIOGRAPHY

1974 Woolley, UE 6 pp. 51 and 88 sub U 288 (study)
1991 Braun-Holzinger, Weihgaben pp. 192–93 G 384 (edition)
1991 Steible, NSBW 2 p. 311 Ur 23 (edition)

TEXT

1) [^{d}]nanna
2) [luga]l-a-ni
3) [nam]-t[i]-
4) [...]
Lacuna

1–4) For [the god] Nanna, his [lord], for the [li]fe of ...
Lacuna

1037

An alabaster bowl fragment from Ur bears an inscription dedicated to the goddess Ninkununa, a form of the goddess Inanna.

COMMENTARY

The calcite bowl fragment, which measures 5×5.9×1.2 cm, was found in room 11 of the E-nun-maḫ and given the excavation number U 287 and the museum number CBS 14946. The text is arranged in one column. The inscription was collated.

For building inscriptions of Ur-Nammu dealing with Inanna-Ninkununa, see E3/2.1.1.15–16. For texts from Puzriš-Dagān dated to the period ŠS 1–IS 2 that record offerings for Ninkununa at Ur, see Sallaberger, Kalender 1 p. 208.

BIBLIOGRAPHY

1974 Woolley, UE 6 pp. 51 and 88 sub U 287 (provenance, study)
1991 Braun-Holzinger, Weihgaben p. 193 G 385 (edition)
1991 Steible, NSBW 2 pp. 311–12 Ur 24 (edition)

TEXT

1) ^{d}nin-kù-nun-na
2) nin-a-ni-ir
3) nam-ti-
4) [...]
Lacuna

1–4) For the goddess Ninkununa, his lady, for the life of ...
Lacuna

1038

A mace-head fragment bears a dedicatory inscription for the life of an Ur III king.

COMMENTARY

The provenance of the black basalt mace-head fragment, which was no. 5150 in the Collection Golénišev, is unknown. The inscription was not collated.

Since the title "king of the four quarters" does not appear in this inscription, it was probably dedicated to either Ur-Nammu or Šulgi.

BIBLIOGRAPHY

1921 Shileiko, ZVO 25 p. 143 (transliteration)
1986 Kärki, KDDU p. 64 Šulgi 60 (edition)
1991 Braun-Holzinger, Weihgaben p. 62 K 88 (edition)
1991 Steible, NSBW 2 pp. 313–14 Ur 26 (edition)

TEXT

Lacuna
1′) [lugal-uri$_5$].[K]I-ma
2′) lugal-ki-en-gi-ki-uri-ka-šè
3′) ur-mes
4′) dumu i-lam-<lam-mu>-ma
5) a mu-na-ru

Lacuna
1′–2′) for [the life of RN], [king] of [Ur], king of the land of Sumer and Akkad,
3′–5′) Ur-mes, son of Ilam<lamu>ma, dedicated (this object).

1039

A vase was dedicated for the life of a king of Ur.

COMMENTARY

The white felsite vase fragment, which measures 6.4×6.5 ×1.3 cm, was acquired through purchase; its original provenance is unknown. The piece bears the museum number NBC 2521; the inscription was collated.

The absence of the title "king of the four quarters" suggests a restoration of the RN as either Ur-Nammu or Šulgi.

BIBLIOGRAPHY

1920 Keiser, BIN 2 no. 6 (copy, transliteration)
1962 Hallo, HUCA 33 p. 41 Anonymous 4 (study)
1986 Kärki, KDDU pp. 151–52 Anonym 4 (edition)
1991 Braun-Holzinger, Weihgaben p. 193 G 386 (edition)
1991 Steible, NSBW 2 pp. 312–13 Ur 25 (edition)

TEXT

Col. i′	
1′) [...]	i′ 1′–3′) For [the life] of [RN, migh]ty [man], [king of U]r,
2′) [nita-kala]-ga	
3′) [lugal-u]ri$_5$.KI-[m]a-ka-šè	
4′) [x-àg]a-zi	i′ 4′) [...-àg]a-zi
Col. ii′	
1) [...-SA]R	ii′ 1) ...
Lacuna	Lacuna

1040

A fragment of an alabaster vase from Girsu was dedicated for the life of a king of Ur.

COMMENTARY

The vase, which measures 7.6×11.1 cm with a rim thickness of 1.3 cm and an original diameter of about 14 cm, was found in excavations of de Genouillac at Girsu and given the excavation number TG 697 and the museum number AO 12210. The text is arranged in one column. The inscription was collated from the published photo.

BIBLIOGRAPHY

1936 de Genouillac, FT 2 p. 117 and pls. 85 and XL (photo, copy, study)
1962 Hallo, HUCA 33 p. 41 Anonymous 8 (study)
1986 Kärki, KDDU pp. 153–54 Anonym 8 (edition)
1991 Braun-Holzinger, Weihgaben pp. 181–82 G 322 (edition)
1991 Steible, NSBW 1 pp. 422–23 "Lagaš" 55 (edition)

TEXT

Lacuna
1′) l[ugal-uri$_5$].⌈KI⌉-⌈ma⌉
2′) lugal-an-ub-da-límmu-ba-ka-šè
3′) lú-^{d}utu zadim
4′) bur-sa$_6$-ga
5′) mu-na-dím
6′) bur-ba nin-mu
7′) GIŠ.KAK nì-sa$_6$-ga-ni
8′) ⌈ga⌉-a-ti
9′) igi-sa$_6$-ga-ni ḫu(Text: RI)-mu-SI-ba-re
10′) mu-bi

Lacuna
1′–2′) [To the goddess DN, for the life of RN], k[ing] of [Ur], king of the four quarters,
3′–5′) Lu-Utu, the lapidary, fashioned (this) beautiful bowl for her.

6′–10′) The name of this bowl (is): "May my lady behold with delight her beautiful ... (named) "Let me live."

1041

A bowl fragment from Nippur bears the inscription of a *sanga* priest of the god Enlil.

COMMENTARY

The inscription is found on 3 N 302, a greenish stone bowl fragment that was found at Nippur in the Inanna temple, in Locus 1, in the high floor of level IV (that is the Ur III level of the temple). It measures 6.3×3.7 cm at the base and was given the museum number A 29448 (Chicago). The inscription was kindly collated by R. Biggs.

BIBLIOGRAPHY

1984 Zettler, Inanna Temple p. 469 (provenance, transliteration)

TEXT

1) ^{d}inanna
2) pap-làl
3) [du]mu amar-sumun
4) [(x) s]anga
5) [^{d}en-l]íl
6) [...]
Lacuna(?)

1) To the goddess Inanna,
2–6) Pap-lal, son of Amar-sumun, *sanga* priest of [the god Enl]il ...
Lacuna(?)

(viii) Undated Sources Mentioning Members of the Royal Family

Item	Royal Name	Designation	RIM number	Attestations
1	a-tu	dumu-lugal	—	Thureau-Dangin, RTC no. 254 rev. col. i line 4
2	*a-ḫu-we-er*	dumu-lugal	—	de Genouillac, ITT 2 no. 650 = Lafont and Yıldız, TCT no. 650 line 6
3	lugal-ezem	dumu-lugal	—	Schneider, Orientalia 47–49 (1930) no. 502 lines 14–15
4	lú-^{d}utu	dumu-lugal	—	Schneider, Orientalia 47–49 (1930) no. 502 lines 14–15
5	*ma-ma-ni-ša*	dumu-munus-lugal	**E3/2.1.6.1042**	See RIM edition
6	*na-bí-*^{d}EN.ZU	dumu-lugal	—	Pohl, TMH NF 1/2 no. 154 line 6; Lafont, Documents no. 151 line 3; de Genouillac, ITT 2 no. 939 = Lafont and Yıldız, TCT no. 939 line 23
7	nin-é-gal-e-si	dumu-lugal	—	Delaporte, ITT 4 no. 7254 = Pettinato, MVN 6 no. 7254 rev. line 5
8	puzur$_4$-^{d}nin-súna	dumu-lugal	—	Nies, UDT no. 91 line 114
9	puzur$_4$-^{d}EN.ZU	dumu-lugal	—	Nikol'skiy, DV no. 350 line 8
10	*šar-ru-um-ì-lí*	dumu-lugal	—	de Genouillac, ITT 5 no. 9690

1042

A green jasper seal names Mamma-niša as daughter of an (unnamed) Ur III king.

COMMENTARY

The seal, which measures 2.4×1.1 cm, was purchased by M. Dieulafoy. It is now housed in the Louvre, where it bears the museum number AOD 25. The inscription was collated from the published photo.

The DN ^{d}àš-ki found in the PN puzur$_4$-^{d}àš-ki of line 3 is elsewhere attested in the Ur III period only in the onomastica of tablets: (a) of the archive excavated by Madhloom at Tell al-Wilāyah (see Postgate, Sumer 32 [1976] pp. 89–90: cf. Aški-bāni, Aški-[...], Puzur-Aški, and Ur-Aški); and (b) of the Tūram-ilī archive studied by Van De Mieroop (JCS 38 [1986] pp. 1–80: cf. Aški-ellassu, Aški-liddin, Kurbī-Aški). As noted by Van De Mieroop (JCS 38 [1986] p. 6), the Tūram ilī archive almost certainly came from Tell al-Wilāyah or its vicinity. The fact that ^{d}àš-ki occurs in four PNs from the Tell al-Wilāyah archive led Postgate (Sumer 32 [1976] p. 79) to propose that ^{d}àš-ki was the tutelary deity of the city. Further, Postgate suggested that ^{d}àš-ki might be a variant writing of the divine name ^{d}ašŠIR-gi$_4$ attested as the consort of the goddess Ninḫursaga at the cities of Adab and Šarrākum/Keš. However, the fact that the goddess Mamma/Mammītum, wife of the underworld god Nergal (for a discussion of Mamma/Mammītum see Krebernik, RLA 7 pp. 330–31), is commonly found in the PNs appearing in the archives connected with both Tell al-Wilāyah (cf. Puzur-Mamma, Mammītum) and Tūram-ilī (cf. Būr-Mamma, Šū-Mamma) points to a probable identification of the divine couple of Tell al-Wilāyah as being Mamma/Mammītum and Aški. This theory accords well with the fact that PNs composed with the DN Erra are also commonly found in the PNs of the Tell al-Wilāyah/Tūram-ilī archives. In all likelihood, then, we should see the DN ^{d}àš-ki not as a variant spelling of ^{d}ašŠIR-gi$_4$, but rather as an alternate writing of the DN ḫuš-ki-a (for this god see Lambert, RLA 4 pp. 522–23). Ḫuš-ki-a appears as a name of Nergal in the god list An:*Anum* VI line 5 (MS Litke); it occurs there two lines after a reference to the goddess Mammītum.

BIBLIOGRAPHY

1893 Dieulafoy, L'acropole de Suse fig. 331 (photo, study)
1909 Toscanne, RT 31 pp. 127–28 (copy, edition, study)
1910 Ward, Seals p. 118 no. 340 (copy)
1920 Delaporte, Louvre 1 p. 69 D. 26 (edition, study); pl. 50 no. 8 (photo)

TEXT

1) *ma-ma-ni-ša*
2) dumu-munus-lugal
3) puzur$_4$-^{d}àš-ki
4) dub-sar ir$_{11}$-zu

1–2) Mamma-niša, daughter of the king:

3–4) Puzur-Aški, scribe, (is) your servant.

(ix) Inscriptions Mentioning City Governors 1043–1046

1043

An alabaster vase fragment from Nippur bears the inscription of a son of a Nippur governor. The script indicates an Ur III date for this text.

COMMENTARY

The inscription is found on CBS 9327, which was collated. The text is arranged in one column.

BIBLIOGRAPHY

1914 Poebel, PBS 5 no. 30 (copy)
1984 Gerardi, Bibliography p. 274 (notes to PBS 5 no. 30)
1991 Steible, NSBW 2 p. 352 Nippur 1 (edition)

TEXT

Lacuna
1′) dumu-⌈x⌉-[(x)]-da-⌈x⌉-[x]
2′) énsi-
3′) nibru.KI-ka-ke$_4$
4′) nam-ti-la-ni-šè
5′) a mu-na-ru

Lacuna
1′–5′) [PN], son of ..., governor of Nippur, dedicated (this vase) to him/her for his own life.

1044

Tablets dated to Š 47 and AS 1, 5, and 6 mention a certain Aḫūma as governor of Puš. An Aḫḫū'a, also governor of Puš and possibly the same person, is named in a tablet dating to Š 40.

An impression of a seal of a son of Aḫḫū'a, governor of Puš, is found on a clay sealing from Ur. The RN in the seal inscription is broken away; in all likelihood it is to be restored either as Šulgi or Amar-Suena.

This same Aḫūma/Aḫḫū'a may appear in a tablet dated to AS 1 (see M. Tanret, Akkadica 13 [1979] pp. 28–45). Since he appears elsewhere as governor of Puš, his identification in the Tanret text as governor of Nippur is apparently due to a mistake of the ancient scribe (as is argued by Sallaberger, Kalender 1 p. 32 n. 136).

COMMENTARY

The clay fragment, which measures 4.1×3.5 cm, was found in the Gipar-ku and given the excavation number U 6732. The piece was assigned to the Iraq Museum; its museum number is unknown. Lines 1–4 are found in col. i, lines 5–9 in col. ii. The missing royal name of line 1 was restored by Gadd, without explanation, as Ibbi-Sîn. In this he was followed by Kärki, who lists the seal inscription under the rubric Ibbisuen 7a (xiii).

BIBLIOGRAPHY

1928 Gadd, UET 1 no. 93 (copy, edition)
1937 Legrain, UET 3 no. 1553 (copy)
1951 Legrain, UE 10 no. 417 (photo, transliteration)
1962 Hallo, HUCA 33 p. 42 Anonymous 13 (study)
1986 Kärki, KDDU p. 143 Ibbisuen 7a (xiii) = Anonym 13 (edition)

TEXT

1) [RN]
2) [nita/lugal-kala-ga]
3) [lugal ŠE]Š.[AB.K]I-[m]a
4) [lugal-a]n-ub-[da]-límmu-ba
5) [PN]
6) ⌜dumu⌝ a-⌜ḫu⌝-a
7) énsi-
8) pu-uš.KI-ka
9) ir_{11}-zu

1–4) [RN, mighty man/king, king of U]r, [king] of the four [qu]arters,

5–9) [PN], son of Aḫḫū'a, governor of Puš, (is) your servant.

1045

A magnesite vase was dedicated by the son of a governor of Adab.

COMMENTARY

The cylindrical vase is made of fired calcite (magnesite) and measures 5×4 cm, with a thickness at the rim of 0.8–0.9 cm. It was found under the Kurigalzu flooring in room 11 of the E-nun-maḫ and was given the excavation number U 274. It bears the museum number BM 116444. The text is arranged in one column. The inscription was collated.

BIBLIOGRAPHY

1965 Sollberger, UET 8 no. 52 (copy, study)
1974 Woolley, UE 6 pp. 51 and 88 sub U 274 (findspot)
1991 Braun-Holzinger, Weihgaben p. 192 G 380 (edition)
1991 Steible, NSBW 2 pp. 306–307 Ur 18 (edition)

TEXT

Lacuna
1′) du[mu ...]
2′) én[si]
3′) adab.K[I]
4′) a mu-na-ru

Lacuna
1′–4′) so[n of PN], gov[ernor] of Adab, dedicated (this vase) to him/her.

1046

A tablet envelope from Drehem, whose date is broken away, bears a seal inscription that mentions Ṣilluš-Dagān.

COMMENTARY

An envelope in a private collection is, according to D.I. Owen, a join to Scheil RA 23 (1926) pp. 36–37; it provides the missing column and completes the seal figures. He will publish the seal impression in the near future.

Although the date of the fragment is not preserved, it should be dated to ca. Š 42. Since the information kindly provided by Owen came after these pages had been set, we have maintained the original RIM numbering within the Unattributed section; the seal would otherwise have appeared in the section on Šulgi.

BIBLIOGRAPHY

1926 Scheil, RA 23 pp. 36–37 no. 4 (copy, edition)
1962 Hallo, HUCA 33 p. 42 Anonymous 14 (study)
1977 Franke, in Gibson and Biggs, Seals p. 61 (study)
1978 Hallo, RHA 36 pp. 77–78 (study)
1986 Kärki, KDDU p. 62 (Anonym 14 =) Šulgi 56a (edition)

TEXT

Col. i
1) ^{d}šul gi
2) nita-kala-ga
3) lugal-uri$_5$.KI-ma
4) lugal-an-ub-da-límmu-ba-ke$_4$

i 1–4) Šulgi, mighty man, king of Ur, king of the four quarters,

Col. ii
1) *ṣi-lu-uš-*^{d}*da-gan*
2) énsi-
3) si-mu-ru-⸢um.KI⸣-[ma]
4) ir$_{11}$-da-ni-[ir] in-na-[ba]

ii 1–3) [to] Ṣilluš-Dagān, governor of Simurrum,

ii 4–5) his servant, he (Šulgi) [present]ed (this seal).

GIRSU

E3/2.2

Inscriptions of two apparently independent rulers of Girsu of late Ur III times, Ur-Ningirsu and Ur-Nanše, are known from a handful of inscriptions. Their relative order has not yet been established.

Ur-Ningirsu

E3/2.2.1

A certain Ur-Ningirsu appears as *šennu* and *en* priest of the god Nanše in a statue inscription dedicated to the goddess Ninmarki, for Šulgi (E3/2.1.2.2032), and in a statuette inscription dedicated to the god NinDAR, for Ibbi-Sîn (E3/2.1.5.2005). Further, in an inscription incised on a model wig dedicated to the goddess Lamma for the life of Šulgi (E3/2.1.2.2030), a cup-bearer(?) of Ur-Ningirsu is named.

Now, in a brick building inscription from Girsu, Ur-Ningirsu appears once again, but this time, in contrast to all previous occurrences, without any reference to an Ur III overlord. Since building inscriptions were normally the prerogative of independent rulers, we would expect that this inscription comes from a period of Girsu autonomy. It may be, as Heimpel (JCS 33 [1981] p. 103) suggests, that Ur-Ningirsu became an independent ruler sometime during late Ur III times. The change in the status of the city likely occurred during the reign of Ibbi-Sîn; according to E. Sollberger (RLA 5 p. 2), the latest tablet from Lagaš with an Ur III year name dates to IS 6.

1

A brick stamped with a four-line inscription of Ur-Ningirsu was found by de Sarzec at Girsu.

COMMENTARY

The brick bears the museum number AO 26694. The inscription was collated from the published photo. The text is arranged in one column.

BIBLIOGRAPHY

1884–1912 de Sarzec, Découvertes 2 p. XXXIII Inscriptions d'Our-Nin-ghirsou Brique (1) and pl. 37 no. 8 (photo, translation)
1889 Amiaud, in RP NS 2 p. 106 § VIII Inscriptions of Ur-Nin-gir-su no. 1 (translation)
1892 Winckler, KB 3/1 pp. 66–69 § I Inschriften Ur-Ningirsu's b (edition)
1892 Winckler and Böhden, ABK no. 14 (copy)
1907 Thureau-Dangin, SAK pp. 146–47 Ur-nin-gir-su a (edition)
1969 Sauren, ZDMG Suppl. 1/1 p. 128 (study)
1969 Wilcke, Lugalbandaepos pp. 41–42 n. 96 (study)
1991 Cavigneaux, RA 85 pp. 63–66 (study)
1991 Steible NSBW 1 pp. 395–96 "Lagaš" 11 A (edition)

TEXT

1) ur-^{d}nin-gír-su
2) EN.ME.ZI.AN.NA
3) šennu$_{x}$(ME.AD.KÙ)
4) en-ki-ág-^{d}nanše

1–4) Ur-Ningirsu, EN.ME.ZI.AN.NA, *šennu* (priest), beloved *en* (priest) of the goddess Nanše.

2

A steatite bowl fragment and an alabaster vessel from Girsu bear a four-line inscription of Ur-Ningirsu.

CATALOGUE

Ex.	Museum Number	Excavation Number	Lines preserved	cpn
1	AO 150	(Fouilles de Sarzec 1881)	1–4	p
2	AO 12775G	TG 3886 (Fouilles de Genouillac 1930)	1–4	p

COMMENTARY

The text is arranged in one column.

BIBLIOGRAPHY

1884–1912 de Sarzec, Découvertes 2 pl. 26 no. 5 (ex. 1, photo)
1892 Winckler and Böhden, ABK no. 15 (ex. 1, copy)
1926 de Genouillac, FT 2 pl. XLI (ex. 2, copy)
1981 Heimpel, JCS 33 p. 103 (ex. 2, study [text erroneously cited as Cros, Tello pl. XLI])
1991 Steible, NSBW 1 pp. 395–96 "Lagaš" 11 B–C (exs. 1–2, edition)

TEXT

1) [ur]-⌈d⌉nin-gír-su
2) EN.ME.ZI.AN.NA
3) šennu$_x$(ME.AD.KÙ)
4) en-ki-ág-^{d}nanše

1–4) [Ur]-Ningirsu, EN.ME.ZI.AN.NA, *šennu* (priest), beloved *en* priest of the goddess Nanše.

Ur-Nanše

E3/2.2.2

1

An inscription incised on an alabaster vessel reveals that the object was dedicated to the goddess Nanše, for the life of the *šennu* priest Ur-Nanše. He probably was an independent ruler of Lagaš during late Ur III times.

COMMENTARY

The vase, which entered the Iraq Museum with no indication of its provenance, likely comes from Girsu. It bears the museum number IM 13829. The inscription follows the reading of Cavignaux, who was able to examine the object in 1979 in the Kirkuk Museum. The text is arranged in one column.

Of interest is the fact that Ur-Nanše's titulary (apart from the omission of the epithet EN.ME.ZI.AN.NA) is identical with that found in Ur-Ningirsu's inscriptions.

BIBLIOGRAPHY

1991 Cavigneaux, RA 85 pp. 63–66 (edition, study)

TEXT

1) ^{d}nanše
2) nin-uru$_{16}$(EN)-ra
3) nam-ti-
4) ur-^{d}nanše
5) šennu x(ME.AD.KÙ)
6) en-ki-ág-
7) ^{d}nanše
8) ur-ba-ba$_{6}$-k[e$_{4}$]
9) ù n[am-ti-la-ni-šè]
10) [a mu-na-ru]

1–10) To the goddess Nanše, the strong lady, for the life of Ur-Nanše, the *šennu* priest, beloved *en* priest of the goddess Nanše, and [for his own life], Ur-Baba [dedicated] (this vessel).

Unnamed Ruler Probably of Girsu

E3/2.2.3

1001

A clay bowl rim fragment published by Scheil and Clay gives the beginning lines of a dedicatory inscription to the goddess Nissaba. The ductus of the inscription indicates a Gudea-Ur III date for the text, and the elaborate set of epithets of the goddess Nissaba would seem to be more characteristic of a royal, rather than of a private, dedicatory inscription. The bowl may have been dedicated by a ruler who controlled Girsu during Ur III times.

COMMENTARY

The bowl fragment measures 9.3×3.1×3 cm and bears the museum number MLC 1823 (Yale). The provenance of the bowl is not entirely certain; it came with an assortment of contracts from Girsu that were purchased from an antiquities dealer by Scheil. This suggests a Girsu provenance for the bowl, albeit does not prove it. The text is arranged in one column. The inscription was collated.

Lines 10–13 of this composition may be compared with line 12 of the Nissaba hymn edited by Hallo (CRRA 17 p. 124): munus-zi dub-sar-maḫ-an-na sa$_{12}$-sug$_{5}$-^{d}en-líl-lá "true lady, august scribe of the god An, accountant of the god Enlil." Curiously enough, one exemplar of the Nissaba hymn edited by Hallo is a stone tablet that was found in excavations of Cros at Girsu (see Thureau-Dangin, RA 7 [1909] pp. 107–11 and Thureau-Dangin, in Cros, Tello pp. 171–76). In view of the agreement between this bowl inscription and the aforementioned Nissaba hymn, with respect to their provenance (Girsu), date (Gudea-Ur III), and subject matter (the goddess Nissaba), one wonders if there might have been some special ceremony for Nissaba at Girsu that was celebrated in both a votive(?) inscription and a hymn. As far as can be determined, we have no building inscriptions of either Gudea or of the Ur III kings connected with Nissaba at Girsu, nor, to judge from the index found in Sallaberger, Kalender 2 p. 193, do we have offerings for Nissaba at Girsu attested for the reigns of the five Ur III kings. The bowl could conceivably be connected with one of the independent rulers of late Ur III times such as Ur-Ningirsu or Ur-Nanše. Now, in his discussion of the Nanše hymn, Heimpel (JCS 33 [1981] p. 67) notes:

> If the mention of Gudea is a historic reference, it may be suspected that the text originates from the time of Ur-Ningirsu, the "beloved En of Nanshe." It is remarkable that his titles coincide with those attributed to Urnanše in the text (see comment to lines 34–35).

Of course, Heimpel was unaware of the Ur-Nanše inscription edited as E3/2.2.2.1 in this volume, since it had not yet been published. Had it been known, he would have undoubtedly mentioned it in his discussion. Of interest, then, is the prominent role that the goddess Nissaba plays in the Nanše hymn (lines 96–101, quoted from the edition of Heimpel [p. 89]):

> On the day when the bowls of food allotments
> are inspected
> Nanshe inspects the reviewing of the servants.
> Her chief scribe Nisaba
> places the precious tablets on the knees.
> She takes the golden stylus in the hand.
> She arranges for Nanshe the servants in single
> file.

It may be, then, that two important literary works transmitted in the Nippur canon, namely the "Nanše hymn" (edition Heimpel, JCS 33 [1981] pp. 65–139 — incipit: uru.KI na-nam) and the "Nissaba hymn" (edition Hallo, CRRA 17 pp. 123–34 — incipit nin mul-an-gin$_7$ DAR-a) were both literary creations at Girsu during late Ur III times.

For the reading of the DN of line 1, generally cited in older literature as Nisaba, see the comments in CAD N/2 p. 273 sub nissabu d: "note ^{d}NAGA = ni-is-sà-ba 3N-T270+ iii 11′ (Proto-Diri), and ni-is-sa-a-ba for the parallel's ^{d}Nun.bar.še.gùn-nu ZA 47 195:14." See the discussion of Selz in Studies Sjöberg pp. 491–97 where he proposes (p. 492) the etymology: ^{d}nissaba(k)<^{d}nin-saba-(ak)<^{d}nin-še-ba-(ak) "lady of grain (or barley) allotments."

BIBLIOGRAPHY

1904 Scheil, OLZ 7 cols. 253–55 (copy, edition, study)
1923 Clay, BRM 4 no. 46 (copy)
1989 Selz, in Studies Sjöberg p. 494 (study)

TEXT

1) ^{d}nissa[ba]
2) munus-z[i]
3) munus-sa$_6$-g[a]
4) munus-mul-mul-l[a]
5) ki-ág-an-na
6) munus ḫi-li-kur-kur
7) munus DÚR-imin
8) ga-x-imin
9) gèštu(GIŠ.PI.TÚG) ki-kù
10) [d]ub-sar-maḫ-
11) [an]-na
12) [sag$_{12}$-s]ug$_5$-maḫ-
13) [^{d}]en-lí[l-lá]
Lacuna

1–13) For the goddess Nissa[ba], faith[ful] woman, beautifu[l] woman, astral woman, beloved of the god An, woman (who is) the luxuriance of the mountain lands, woman with seven ... and seven ..., wise one (of) the pure place, august [s]cribe of the god [A]n, august [accou]ntant of the [god] Enli[l],
Lacuna

EŠNUNNA

E3/2.3

According to R. Whiting (AfO 34 [1987] p. 33), tablets from Ešnunna using Ibbi-Sîn year names cease with IS 3. Evidence from various seal inscriptions indicates that Šū-ilīia, who is attested as a son of the Ur III governor Itūrīia in the seal inscription E3/2.1.5.2002, governed as an independent ruler at Ešnunna in late Ur III times.

Šū-ilīia

E3/2.3.1

I. Year Names and Events of the Reign

For the year names of Šū-ilīia, see Jacobsen, Gimilsin Temple pp. 170 and 173–74 Date formulas nos. 40–41 and 46–48, and R. Whiting, JAOS 97 (1977) p. 174 n. 10.

(a) [mu ^{d}*šu-ì-lí-a* lugal "The year Šū-ilīia (became) king."]

The year formula dealing with the accession of Šū-ilīia is not extant; its reconstruction is based on various Ur III parallels.

(b) mu dumu-munus-lugal máš-e ì-pà "The year the daughter of the king was chosen by omens (to be priestess)." Jacobsen, Gimilsin Temple p. 170 Date formula 40.

(c) mu-ús-sa dumu-munus-lugal máš-e ì-pà "The year after the daughter of the king was chosen by omens (to be priestess)." Jacobsen, Gimilsin Temple p. 170 Date formula 41.

(d) mu *i-ku-un-pí-*^{d}*tišpak* DUMU.NÍTA-lugal dur-šub-ba máš-e ì-pà "The year Ikūn-pî-Tišpak, son of the king, was chosen by omens on ..." Jacobsen, Gimilsin Temple pp. 173–74 Date formula 47.

(e) [mu-ús-sa DUMU.NÍTA-lugal máš-e ì-pà "The year after the son of the king was chosen by omens."] Restored on the basis of year name (f).

(f) mu-ús-sa DUMU.NÍTA-lugal máš-e ì-pà mu-ús-sa-bi "The year after the son of the king was chosen by omens, the year after this." Jacobsen, Gimilsin Temple p. 174 Date formula 48.

(g) mu má-gur$_8$-^{d}tišpak ba-ab-du$_8$ "The year the *magur* boat of the god Tišpak was caulked." Jacobsen, Gimilsin Temple p. 173 Date formula 46.

The evidence of the Šū-ilīia year names listed here indicates that the king reigned at least seven years. Information provided by letters, administrative texts, and seal impressions from Ešnunna, coupled with a study of the literary correspondence between Ibbi-Sîn and Puzur-Numušda known from later Old Babylonian tablet copies, enables us to determine, at least in general terms, the date of Šū-ilīia's reign. As noted, the king must have acceded to the throne sometime after IS 2. As for the date of the end of his reign, Date formula no. 42 (Jacobsen, Gimilsin Temple pp. 170–71) provides important information. Whiting (Letters pp. 23–24) writes:

> The date formula records a defeat of Subartu which is attributed to the god Tišpak (mu ^{d}Tišpak lugal-e SAG×DU SU.BAPPIR-a-ke$_4$ tibír-ra bi-in-ra-a). ... Leaving aside the divine intervention of Tišpak as a possibility, the successive mention of the capture of the ensi of Subartu, the plundering of Ḫamazi, and the returning of Nur-aḫum to his place in the Kazallu letter makes it very likely that the defeat of Subartu should be attributed to Išbi-Irra, and that, in fact, the defeat of Subartu reported in the letter and the defeat recorded in the year date represent the same event.
>
> Considerable weight is added to this argument by the conclusion arrived at by Jacobsen, *OIP* 43, p. 172, that Date Formula No. 42 is the first year of Nur-aḫum. Since the Kazallu letter and the Eshnunna year date seem to agree on the fact that Nur-aḫum came to the throne in the wake of a defeat of Subartu, it seems likely that the two sources refer to the same event and that Nur-aḫum was placed on the throne by Išbi-Irra. A corollary to this conclusion is that the reign of Nur-aḫum's predecessor, Šu-ilija, was brought to an end by a defeat at the hands of Subartu and that the city of Eshnunna was in imminent danger of falling into its hands when Išbi-Irra intervened.

Whiting further notes (Letters pp. 25–26):

> If we assume that Išbi-Erra's mission to Puzur-Numušda took place shortly before the building of the wall and that the events enumerated in the letter took place between the visit of Išbi-Irra's messenger and the writing of the letter, we arrive at Išbi-Irra 8 [=IS 18] as the earliest possible date for the accession of Nur-aḫum at Eshnunna. ... Since Ibbi-Sin's reply seems to follow Puzur-Numušda's letter almost immediately, Išbi-Irra 11 [=IS 21] is also the latest possible date for it.

The sum of the evidence, then, points to placing the seven-or-more-year reign of Šū-ilīia sometime within the period IS 4–21.

1

The impression of a seal of Šū-ilīia is found on two jar sealings from Ešnunna.

CATALOGUE

Ex.	Museum number	Excavation number	Ešnunna provenance	Lines preserved	cpn
1	—	As 31–630	Under L 32:2, Ilushuilia-Nur-aḫum palace	—	n
2	—	As 31–670	As ex. 1	1–15	p

COMMENTARY

Lines 1–8 are found in col. i, lines 9–15 in col. ii.

BIBLIOGRAPHY

1940 Jacobsen, Gimilsin Temple p. 143 Seal Legend no. 6 (exs. 1–2, edition); p. 215 fig. 100 (ex. 2, photo)

1955 Jacobsen, Cylinder Seals no. 705, pp. 42, 46, 49–50, and pl. 66 (ex. 2, photo, edition, study)

1961 Hallo, BiOr 18 p. 13 Ešnunna (exs. 1–2, study)

1971 Sollberger and Kupper, IRSA IIID2a (exs. 1–2, translation)

1977 Whiting, JAOS 97 pp. 174 and 177 Seal legend 6 (exs. 1–2, copy, edition)

TEXT

1) [^{d}]*tišpak*
2) [LUGA]L *da-núm*
3) [LUGA]L *ma-at* [*wa*]-*ri-im*
4) LUGAL
5) [*ki-ib*]-*ra-tim*
6) [*a*]*r-ba-im*
7) ⸢^{d}⸣*šu-ì-lí-a*
8) ⸢DUMU(?)⸣-*šu*
9) *na-ra-a*[*m*]
10) ^{d}*be-la-at-t*[*e*]-*ra-ba-an*
11) ^{d}*be-la-at-š*[*uḫ*]-*n*[*ir*]
12) ^{d}⸢IŠKUR⸣
13) *ù* ^{d}⸢x-x⸣-[x]
14) *i-š*[*i*(?)-...]
15) *mu-uš-te-*[*mi-qum*]

1–6) [The god] Tišpak, mighty [kin]g, [kin]g of the land of [Wa]rum, king of the [f]our [qua]rters:

7–15) Šū-ilīia, his *son,* belov[ed] of the goddesses Bēlat-T[e]raban (and) Bēlat-Š[uḫ]n[ir], of Adad and the god/goddess DN, piou[s] ...

2001

A tablet from Ešnunna bears the impression of a seal of a servant of Šū-ilīia. As noted by R. Whiting (JAOS 97 [1977] p. 173), the fact that the tablet with this seal impression bears an Ur III month name suggests a date for the seal inscription relatively early within the reign of Šū-ilīia. The other known seal inscriptions mentioning Šū-ilīia (E3/2.3.1.2002–2003) appear on tablets with Akkadian month names.

COMMENTARY

The impression is found on As 31-715, which was found in locus L 32:3 in the Ilshuillia-Nuraḫum palace. The text is arranged in one column. The inscription was not collated.

BIBLIOGRAPHY

1940 Jacobsen, Gimilsin Temple p. 144 Seal Legend no. 7 (edition)
1961 Hallo, BiOr 18 p. 14 Ešnunna 21 i (study)
1977 Whiting, JAOS 97 pp. 173 and 177 Seal Legend no. 7 (copy, edition)

TEXT

1) ᵈ*šu-i-lí-a*
2) *na-ra-am*
3) ᵈ*tišpak*
4) *še-il-ḫa* LÚ.⌈ÙR.RA⌉
5) IR₁₁.ZU

1–3) Šū-ilīia, beloved of the god Tišpak:

4–5) Šilḫa, *the roofer*, (is) your servant.

2002

A tablet from Ešnunna bears the impression of a seal of another servant of Šū-ilīia. As compared with the previous inscription, this second seal inscription displays a more developed royal titulary. In all likelihood it dates to a later period of Šū-ilīia's reign.

COMMENTARY

The impression is found on As 31-633, which was found in locus N 30:14 in the Ilshuillia-Nuraḫum palace. Lines 1–5 are found in col. i, lines 6–9 in col. ii. The inscription was not collated.

BIBLIOGRAPHY

1940 Jacobsen, Gimilsin Temple p. 144 Seal Legend no. 8 (edition)
1961 Hallo, BiOr 18 p. 14 Ešnunna 21 i (study)
1971 Sollberger and Kupper, IRSA IIID2b (translation)
1977 Whiting, JAOS 97 pp. 174 and 177 Seal Legend no. 8 (copy, edition)

TEXT

1) ^{d}*šu-ì-lí-a*
2) *na-ra-am-*^{d}*tišpak*
3) ^{d}NIN-*te-ra-ba-an*
4) ^{d}NIN-*šuk-nir*
5) LUGAL *da-núm*
6) LUGAL *ma-at wa-ri-im*
7) *at-ta-a-a*
8) ⌈x x x⌉
9) IR_{11}.ZU

1–6) Šū-ilīia, beloved of the god Tišpak, the goddess Bēlat-Terraban, (and) the goddess Bēlat-Šuknir, mighty king, king of the land of Warum:

7–9) Attaia, the ..., (is) your servant.

2003

Impressions of a seal of a third servant of Šū-ilīia are found on a tablet from Ešnunna. The text is arranged in one column.

BIBLIOGRAPHY

1977 Whiting, JAOS 97 pp. 174–75 and 177 Seal Legend no. 8A (copy, edition)

TEXT

1) ^{d}*šu-ì-*[*lí-a*]
2) [DU]MU ^{d}*tišpak* [LUGAL *da-núm*]
3) [LU]GAL *ma-at* [*wa-ri-im*]
4) [l]ú-KA[...]
5) [DU]MU ir_{11}-mu I[R_{11}.ZU]

1–3) Šu-i[līia], [s]on of the god Tišpak, [mighty king], [ki]ng of the land [of Warum]:

4–5) Lu-KA-[...], [s]on of Irmu, (is) [your se]rvant.

Nūr-aḫum

E3/2.3.2

As noted, Šū-ilīia was succeeded by Nūr-aḫum as ruler of Ešnunna sometime in the period IŠ 18–21. Nūr-aḫum appears in his inscriptions with the title "governor" (ÉNSI) rather than "king" (LUGAL); in all likelihood he was an appointee of Išbi-Erra of Isin. His inscriptions have been edited under the rubric E4.5.1 in the volume RIME 4.

MARI

E3/2.4

J.-M. Durand, in an article entitled "La situation historique des Šakkanakku: Nouvelle Approche," MARI 4 pp. 147–72, has used the evidence of two Old Babylonian tablet copies of dynastic lists of Mari *šakkanakku*s to establish a probable sequence of rulers at Mari during the Ur III period. His list is given below.

RIM number	**Mari *šakkanakku* list**	**Length of reign (years)**	**Contemporary Ur III king**
E3/2.4.1	Apil-kīn	35	Ur-Nammu
E3/2.4.2	Iddin-Ilum	5	Šulgi
E3/2.4.3	Ilum-išar	12	Šulgi
E3/2.4.4	Tūram-Dagān	20	Šulgi
E3/2.4.5	Puzur-Eštar	25	Amar-Suena
E3/2.4.6	Ḫitlal-Erra = Itlal-Erra	7	Šū-Sîn
E3/2.4.7	ʾAnun-Dagān	8	Ibbi-Sîn

We have normalized the name of the sixth Mari ruler as Itlal-Erra, assuming that it is a Gt imperative of the verb *alālu* B "to shout *alāla*, to brag, to boast."

Documents from Mari excavated after the period of the French Mandate in Syria are now housed in the Damascus, Aleppo, and Deir ez-Zor museums. Unfortunately, we have been unable to determine which pieces belong to which particular museum. They are simply noted here as being housed in Syria.

Apil-kīn

E3/2.4.1

1

Two bronze foundation plaques of Apil-kīn were found in excavations in the area of the Ninḫursaga temple at Mari.

CATALOGUE

Ex.	Museum number	Excavation number	Mari Provenance	Dimensions (cm)	Lines preserved	cpn
1	—	M 1785	Depot 5, Ninḫursaga Temple, to N of gateway	12.5×12	1–6	p
2	—	M 1786	Depot 6, Ninḫursaga temple, to S of gateway	12×12	1–6	p

COMMENTARY

The plaques were found in two foundation deposits from a building that appears to be an annex to the Ninḫursaga temple constructed by Niwār-Mēr. Their present whereabouts are unknown. The text is arranged in one column.

For an inscription mentioning a daughter of Apil-kīn as é-gi$_4$-a "daughter-in-law" of Ur-Nammu, see E3/2.1.1.52. W. Sallaberger, in an article to appear in AoF 23 (1996), discusses two Ur III archival texts that refer to offerings for the deceased Apil-kīn.

BIBLIOGRAPHY

1940 Dossin, Syria 21 pp. 159–61 (ex. 1, copy; exs. 1–2, edition)
1940 Parrot, Syria 21 pp. 6–7, pl. II, and fig. 5 (exs. 1–2, provenance, photo [in situ], study)
1946 Dossin, Syria 25 pp. 322–23 (exs. 1–2, study)
1961 Gelb, MAD 2^2 p. 16 § 1b (study)
1962 Civil, RA 56 p. 213 (study)
1971 Sollberger and Kupper, IRSA IIIE1b (exs. 1–2, translation)
1985 Durand, MARI 4 p. 151 § 2 c (exs. 1–2, edition)
1990 Gelb and Kienast, Königsinschriften pp. 359–60 MŠ 2 (Apilkīn) (ex. 1, edition)
1992 Gelb, in Young, Mari in Retrospect p. 153 no. 1 (edition, study)

TEXT

1) *a-pìl*-GI
2) *da-núm*
3) GÌR.NÍTA
4) *ma-rí*.KI
5) DÍM
6) *śa-ḫu-rí*

1–6) Apil-kīn, the mighty, general, builder of the *šaḫūru*.

Iddi(n)-Ilum

E3/2.4.2

1

A statue of Apil-kīn's successor, Iddi(n)-Ilum, possibly his son, was found in the Zimrī-Līm palace at Mari.

COMMENTARY

The steatite statue, which measures 41.5 cm in height, was excavated during the fourth campaign at Mari, 1936–37. It was found in two pieces. The first piece, with the inscription, was found on the surface of courtyard 136. The second piece, which bears no inscription, was found on the paving of the great portal 148–210. The joined statue was given the excavation number M 1349 and the museum number AO 19486. The text is arranged in one column around the skirt of the standing figure. The inscription was collated from the published photo.

BIBLIOGRAPHY

1937 Thureau-Dangin, RA 34 pp. 172–75 (photo, edition)
1938 Parrot, Syria 19 pp. 17–18 and pl. VII 1 (provenance, photo, translation)
1953 Parrot, Mari figs. 108–109 (photos)
1959 Parrot, Documents pp. 16–22 § 5 and figs. 12–19 (photo, edition, drawing)
1960 Parrot, Sumer fig. 330 (photo)
1961 Gelb, MAD 2^{2} p. 16 § 1b (study)
1967 Moortgat, Kunst figs. 179–80 (photos)
1971 Sollberger and Kupper, IRSA IIIE2a (translation)
1975 Orthmann (ed.), Der alte Orient pls. 67a–b (photos)
1981 Spycket, Statuaire pp. 241–45, n. 86 and pl. 167 (photo, study)
1985 Durand, MARI 4 p. 151 § 2 d (transliteration)
1990 Gelb and Kienast, Königsinschriften p. 360 MŠ 3 (Iddi[n]ilum) (edition)
1991 Braun-Holzinger, Weihgaben pp. 276–77 St 166 (edition)

TEXT

1) *i-dì*-DINGIR
2) GÌR.NÍTA *ma-rí*.KI
3) *a-na* ^{d}INANNA
4) AN.DÙL-*šu*
5) A.MU.RU
6) *ša* DUB *$šu_4$-a*
7) *ú-sa-sà-ku_8*
8) ^{d}INANNA ŠE.NUMUN-*šu*
9) *lu tal-qù-ut*

1–2) Iddi(n)-Ilum, general of Mari,

3) for the goddess Eštar,
4–5) dedicated a statue of himself.

6–9) As for the one who removes this inscription, may the goddess Eštar destroy his progeny.

2

A cylinder seal of a son of Iddi(n)-Ilum was found in excavations at Mari.

COMMENTARY

The haematite cylinder seal, which measures 2 cm in length and 1.1 cm in diameter, was found in sounding B in a tomb (IV.A.SO.T3) that was identified by the excavator as belonging to a son of Iddin-Ilum. The piece was given the excavation number TH.80.145 (IV.A.17.SO.33) and is now housed in one of the Syrian museums. The text is arranged in one column. The inscription was collated from the published photo.

BIBLIOGRAPHY

1983 Margueron, MARI 2 p. 16 and pl. V a–b (provenance)
1985 Beyer, MARI 4 p. 183 no. 16 (provenance, photo, copy, edition)
1990 Gelb and Kienast, Königsinschriften p. 357 no. 14 (edition)

TEXT

1) *i-din*-DINGIR	1–3) Iddin-Ilum, general of Mari:
2) GÌR.NÍTA	
3) *ma-rí*.KI	
4) *zi-nu-ba*	4–5) Zinuba (is) his son.
5) DUMU-*šu*	

2001

The seal of a servant of Iddi(n)-Ilum was found in excavations at Mari.

COMMENTARY

The haematite seal, which measures 2.75×1.4 cm, was given the excavation number M. 1400. It is now housed in the museum in Aleppo. The text is arranged in one column. The inscription was collated from the published photo.

Iddin-Dagān's title *šabra* "intendant" was carved in the area of the seal design immediately in front of the divine figure with raised hands, The normal practice would be for the title to appear in the field of the main seal inscription.

BIBLIOGRAPHY

1959 Parrot, Documents pp. 146–47, fig. 99, and pl. XXXIX M. 1400 (photo, copy, translation)
1971 Sollberger and Kupper, IRSA IIIE2b (translation)
1985 Durand, MARI 4 pp. 149–50 (transliteration)
1990 Gelb and Kienast, Königsinschriften p. 356 no. 9 (edition)

TEXT

1) *i-dì*-DINGIR
2) GÌR.NÍTA
3) *ma-rí*.KI
4) *i-dì-*^{d}*da-gan*
5) ŠABRA

1–3) Iddi(n)-Ilum, general of Mari:

4–5) Iddin-Dagān, the intendant (is his servant).

Ilum-išar

E3/2.4.3

1

A six-line brick inscription records Ilum-išar's introduction of some object for the god Ḫubur into the town Bāb-Mēr.

COMMENTARY

We have been unable to determine the museum numbers or excavation numbers for the bricks published in a photo by Thureau-Dangin. They do not appear to be in the Louvre. Ex. 1 contains lines 1–6; ex. 2 lines 1–4; and ex. 3 lines 3–6. The entire text was arranged in one column.

BIBLIOGRAPHY

1936 Thureau-Dangin, RA 33 pp. 177–79 (exs. 1–3, photos, edition)
1961 Gelb, MAD 2^{2} p. 16 § 1b (study)
1971 Sollberger and Kupper, IRSA IIIE5a (exs. 1–3, translation)
1985 Durand, MARI 4 p. 151 § 2 e (exs. 1–3, edition)
1990 Gelb and Kienast, Königsinschriften pp. 360–61 MŠ 4 (Ilumišar) (exs. 1–3, edition)

TEXT

1) DINGIR-*i-šar*
2) GÌR.NÍTA
3) *ma-rí*.KI
4) *ù-šu-rí-id*
5) ^{d}*ḫu-bu-ur*
6) *a-na* KÁ-*me-er*.KI

1–3) Ilum-išar, general of Mari,

4–6) brought down a (statue?) of the god Ḫubur into Bāb-Mēr.

Tūra(m)-Dagān

E3/2.4.4

1

An impression of a seal of Puzur-Eštar that apparently dates to the time when his father, Tūra(m)-Dagān, served as general of Mari is found on a jar sealing from Mari.

COMMENTARY

The jar sealing, which is a beige-pink colour and which measures 4.3×3.6 cm, was given the excavation number ME 56. The inscription was collated from the published photo. It is housed in one of the Syrian museums. The text is arranged in one column.

BIBLIOGRAPHY

1959 Barrelet and Parrot, in Parrot, Documents p. 157 *Cylindre II de Tûra-Dagan* and pl. XLV ME 56 (photo, study)
1959 Dossin, in Parrot, Documents p. 251 Cylindre II de *Tûra-Dagan* (edition)
1971 Sollberger and Kupper, IRSA IVF2a (translation [incorrect restoration])
1981 Durand, RA 75 p. 180 ME 56 (transliteration)
1985 Durand, MARI 4 p. 150 ME 56 (transliteration)
1990 Gelb and Kienast, Königsinschriften p. 355 no. 2 (edition)

TEXT

1) *tu-ra-*[d]*da-ga*[*n*]
2) GÌR.[NÍTA]
3) [*ma-rí*.KI]
4) *pu*[*zur*[4]*-eš-tár*]
5) DUMU-*šu*

1–3) Tūra(m)-Dagā[n], gene[ral of Mari]:

4–5) Pu[zur-Eštar] (is) his son.

Puzur-Eštar

E3/2.4.5

1

A diorite statue with an inscription that mentions Puzur-Eštar as general was found during Koldewey's excavations at Babylon.

COMMENTARY

The statue was found in two pieces. The lower portion (frgm. 1 — the torso) was found in excavations in the "museum" of the "Hauptburg" and given the excavation number BE 65774. It now bears the museum number EŞ 7813. The upper portion (frgm. 2 — the head) was acquired through the antiquities trade before the beginning of excavations at Babylon, and was purchased by the Vorderasiatisches Museum. It bears the museum number VA 8748. D. Opitz was the first to realize that these two statue fragments belonged together. The reconstituted statue measures 170 cm in height. The main inscription is arranged in one column around the bottom of the skirt. The "cartouche" is found below the right arm. The inscription was collated from the published photos.

BIBLIOGRAPHY

1906 Meyer, Sumerier und Semiten pl. VI (top) (frgm. 2, photo)
1925 Koldewey, WEB[4] p. 164 and figs. 105 a–b (frgm. 1, photo, study)
1926 Nassouhi, AfO 3 pp. 109–14 and figs. 1–3 (frgms. 1–2, photo, copy, edition)
1926 Nassouhi, Guide Sommaire pp. 27–28 and pl. 5 (frgms. 1–2, photo, study)
1932 Wetzel, Königsburgen p. 20 nos. 6–7 and pls. 22–23 (frgms. 1–2, photo, study)
1940 Dossin, Syria 21 p. 164 n. 3 (frgms. 1–2, study)
1959 Nagel, ZA 53 pp. 261–65 and figs. 1–2 (frgms. 1–2, photo, study)
1960 Parrot, Sumer figs. 334–35 (frgms. 1–2, photo)
1960 Strommenger, Bagh. Mitt. 1 pp. 74–76 and pl. 20, 2 (photo, study)
1961 Gelb, MAD 2[2] p. 16 § 1b (study)
1967 Moortgat, Kunst figs. 181–82 (frgms. 1–2, photo)
1975 Orthmann (ed.), Der alte Orient pls. 159–60a (frgms. 1–2, photo)
1981 Spycket, Statuaire pp. 240–45, nn. 74–75, and pl. 166 (frgms. 1–2, photo, study)
1985 Durand, MARI 4 p. 151 § 2 f–g (partial transliteration)
1990 Gelb and Kienast, Königsinschriften pp. 363–64 MŠ 9–10 (Puzureštar 1) (frgms. 1–2, edition)
1991 Braun-Holzinger, Weihgaben pp. 277–78 St 168 (edition)
1992 Gelb, in Young, Mari in Retrospect pp. 153, 155 no. 4 and p. 157 no. 8 (study)

TEXT

1) *tu-ra-*^{d}*da-gan*
2) GÌR.NÍ[TA]
3) *ma-rí*.[KI]
4) *puzur*$_{4}$*-eš*$_{4}$*-tár*
5) GÌR.NÍTA
6) DUMU-*šu*

1–3) Tūra(m)-Dagān, gen[eral] of Mari:

4–6) Puzur-Eštar, general, (is) his son.

7) *a-na* ⸢^{d}⸣[EN.KI]
8) *be-al* [UNKEN]
9) ⸢AN⸣.[DÙL-*šu*]
10) ⸢*a*⸣-[*na ba-la-ṭi-šu*]
11) [A.MU.RU]
12) [*ša* DUB]
13) [*šu-a-ti*]
14) [*u-š*]*a-sà*-⸢*ku*⸣
15) ^{d}INANNA
16) ^{d}*da-gan*
17) *ú* ^{d}EN.KI
18) *be-al* UNKEN
19) SUḪUŠ-*šu*
20) *li-sú-ḫa*
21) *a-dì* SI-*tár-ki-šu*
Cartouche
1) *puzur*$_{4}$-*eš*$_{4}$-*tár*
2) GÌR.NÍTA
3) *ma-rí*.KI
4) *ṣil-l*[*á-a-k*]*à*
5) NU.[BÀNDA]
6) ŠE[Š-*šu*]

7–11) To the god [Ea], lord of [the assembly], he [dedicated] (this) st[atue of himself] f[or his own life].

12–14) [As for the one who re]moves [this inscription],

15–21) may the gods Eštar, Dagān, and Ea, lord of the assembly, tear out his foundations as far as ...

Cartouche
1–3) Puzur-Eštar, general of Mari:

4–6) Ṣill[akka], lieu[tenant], (is) [his] broth[er].

2

The impression of a seal that mentions Puzur-Eštar is found on a (door?) sealing from Mari. It probably belonged to a son or servant of Puzur-Eštar.

COMMENTARY

The sealing, which measures 2.4×4.6 cm, was found in the palace of Zimrī-līm, and was given the excavation number ME 68. It is housed in one of the Syrian museums. The text is arranged in one column. The inscription was not collated.

BIBLIOGRAPHY

1959 Barrelet and Parrot, in Parrot, Documents p. 158 Cylindre de Puzur-Ishtar(?) (study)
1959 Dossin in Parrot, Documents p. 252 ME 68 (edition)
1981 Durand, RA 75 p. 180 ME 68 (transliteration)
1985 Beyer, MARI 4 pp. 182–83 no. 15 (copy, transliteration)
1985 Durand, MARI 4 p. 150 ME 68 (transliteration)
1990 Gelb and Kienast, Königsinschriften p. 35 no. 5 (edition)
1992 Gelb, in Young, Mari in Retrospect p. 157 no. 8b (study)

TEXT

1) *puzur*$_{4}$-[*eš*$_{4}$-*tár*]
2) GÌR.[NÍTA]
3) [*m*]*a-rí*.[KI]
Lacuna

1–3) Puzur-[Eštar], gen[eral] of [M]ari:
Lacuna

3

A seal legend mentioning Itlal-Erra as son of Puzur-Eštar is known from two slightly variant seal impressions. They were both found in the sondage stratigraphique (chantier A) at Mari. For convenience, the two inscriptions are edited together here. They are housed in one of the Syrian museums.

CATALOGUE

Ex.	Museum number	Excavation number	Mari provenance	Dimensions (cm)	Lines preserved	cpn
1	—	TH.80.142+143	IX.Q.50.SO.16 and 17	3.4 high, 6.6 long (impression)	1–4	p
2	—	TH.82.1	IX.P.50.SE.101	3.1 high (impression)	1–5	n

COMMENTARY

Lines 1–3 are found in col. i, lines 4–5 in col. ii.

BIBLIOGRAPHY

1983 Beyer, MARI 2 pp. 54–55 no. 3 and fig. 11; pl. II fig. 1 (ex. 1, photo, copy, edition)
1985 Beyer, MARI 4 pp. 178–79 nos. 6–7 (exs. 1–2, copy, edition)
1990 Gelb and Kienast, Königsinschriften p. 357 no. 12 (exs. 1–2, edition)

TEXT

1) *puzur$_4$-eš$_4$-tár*
2) GÌR.NÍTA
3) *ma-rí*.KI
4) [*it*]-*làl-èr-r*[*a*]
5) [DUMU]-*šu*

1–3) Puzur-Eštar, general of Mari:

4–5) [It]lal-Err[a] (is) his [son].

Itlal-Erra

E3/2.4.6

1

As noted, the name Ḫitlal-Erra (= Itlal-Erra) appears immediately after Puzur-Eštar in the *šakkanakku* list (ARMT 22 no. 333) studied by Durand (MARI 4 pp. 152–59). He is known with the title nu-bànda "lieutenant" in inscriptions dating to the time before he served as general (see Beyer, MARI 4 pp. 177–79 and 181). In all likelihood, he was Puzur-Eštar's son. A Neo-Babylonian tablet copy of a monument that was originally set up in Sippar by a son of Puzur-Eštar, likely Itlal-Erra, is housed in the British Museum.

COMMENTARY

The inscription is found on BM 38947, a baked light brown tablet that measures 7.5×5.6×2.1 cm. It was found in Rassam's excavations in Babylonia, and was given the registration number 80-11-12, 383. Lines 1–11 are found on the obverse of the tablet, lines 1′–6′ and the colophon on the reverse. The inscription was collated.

Durand (MARI 4 p. 151) suggested a restoration of the RN at the beginning of the text as ʾAnun-Dagān. Gelb and Kienast (Königsinschriften pp. 366–67 MŠC 2), on the other hand, gave a more probable ascription of the text to Itlal-Erra.

BIBLIOGRAPHY

1967 Sollberger, CRRA 15 pp. 104–107 (copy, edition, study)
1985 Durand, MARI 4 pp. 151–52 § 2h (edition)
1990 Gelb and Kienast, Königsinschriften pp. 366–67 MŠ C2 (Itlalerra) (edition)
1992 Gelb, in Young, Mari in Retrospect p. 155 no. 4 (study)

TEXT

Obverse
1) *ḫe-pí* [...]
2) LUGA[L]
3) *<ma>-rí*.KI
4) DUMU *puzur*$_4$-*eš*$_4$-*tár*
5) LUGAL
6) *ì-na maḫ-ri*
7) ^{d}⌈I$_7$⌉
8) *be-lí-*[*š*]*u*
9) ^{d}MAŠ.TAB.[B]A
10) ⌈*ù*⌉ ^{d}K[A.DI]
11) [...]

1) (Broken) [...]
2–3) king of <Ma>ri,

4–5) son of Puzur-Eštar, the king,

6–11) in the presence of the River-God, his lord, and the gods MAŠ.TAB.BA and Iš[tarān, ...]
Lacuna

Lacuna
Reverse
1′) ⌜d⌝[I₇]
2′) d[KA.D]I
3′) ⌜*ù* d⌝MAŠ.TAB.BA
4′) ŠE.NU[MU]N-*šu*
5′) *li-i*[*l*]-*qù-tù*
6′) *a-dì* SI-*tár-ki-šu*

rev. 1′–6′) May the [River-God] and the gods I[štarān] and MAŠ.TAB.BA [d]estroy his prog[en]y as far as ...

Colophon
1) *ki-ma pí-i* NA_4.NA.RÚ.A LIBIR.RA *šá ina* URU.*sip-pár*.KI
2) m*re-mu-tum* DUB.SAR BÀN.DA m*su*-⌜x⌝-[...]
3) *ú-ṣab-bi-ma is-su-*[*uḫ*]

Colophon
1–3) According to the text of an ancient stone monument which Rēmūtum, junior scribe, son of Su-..., examined and *copied out* in Sippar.

ᵓAnun-Dagān

E3/2.4.7

1

A door socket inscription names ᵓAnun-Dagān as king of Mari.

COMMENTARY

The door socket, which measures 37×37×15.5 cm, was found on the west side of vestibule 156, the portal of the palace of Zimrī-Līm, and was given the excavation number M 1572. The inscription itself measures 30.5×10 cm. The door socket is now housed in the museum in Aleppo. The text is arranged in one column. The inscription was collated from the published photo.

The reading of line 2 follows Durand, MARI 4 p. 151 n. 26. Gelb and Kienast, Königsinschriften p. 359 sub MŠ 1 read me-er.⌜KI⌝. The published photo is indistinct.

BIBLIOGRAPHY

1938 Parrot, Syria 19 p. 16 fig. 10 (photo)
1958 Parrot, Architecture pp. 11–12 (provenance)
1959 Parrot, Documents p. 81 and pl. XXXII M 1572 (photo, study)
1968 Dossin in Parrot, Trésor pp. 58–59 and fig. 42 (copy, study)
1971 Kupper, RA 65 pp. 117–18 (study)
1985 Durand, MARI 4 pp. 151–52 § 2 h and n. 26 (transliteration, study)
1990 Gelb and Kienast, Königsinschriften p. 359 MŠ 1 (ᵓAnundagān) (edition)

TEXT

1) *ʾà-nun*$_x$-^{d}*da-gan*
2) LUGAL ⸢*ma-rí*⸣.KI
3) ⸢ZA-x⸣
Cases for lines 4–20 are uninscribed

1–3) ʾAnun-Dagān, king of *Mari*, ...

4–20) Uninscribed

2

Two clay sealings found in the palace of Zimrī-Līm bear a seal inscription (in a restored text) of ʾAnun-Dagān.

CATALOGUE

Ex.	Museum number	Excavation number	Dimensions (cm)	Lines preserved	cpn
1	—	ME 197	2.9×3.4	—	n
2	—	ME 213	2.2×3.0	—	n

COMMENTARY

The reading of the inscription follows that provided by Durand (MARI 4 p. 150). According to Charpin, the impressions come from two distinct, but similar, seals. They are edited here together for convenience. The text is arranged in one column. The sealings are housed in one of the Syrian museums.

BIBLIOGRAPHY

1981 Durand, RA 75 p. 181 (transliteration)
1985 Durand, MARI 4 p. 150 (transliteration)
1990 Gelb and Kienast, Königsinschriften p. 355 no. 7 (edition)

TEXT

1) *ʾà-nun*$_x$(NIM)-[^{d}*da-gan*]
2) DUMU [*it-làl-èr-ra*]

1–2) ʾAnun-[Dagān], son of [Itlal-Erra].

KARAḪAR

E3/2.5

Three campaigns of Šulgi were directed against the important eastern stronghold of Karaḫar; the city appears in the year names for Š 24, 31, and 33. As for the location of Karaḫar, we offer the following brief discussion.

While an Ur III variant spelling ḫar-ḫar for kára-ḫar is known (see Gelb, Hurrians p. 57 n. 72; identification confirmed by R. Whiting, JCS 28 [1976] p. 181 n. 21), this ḫar-ḫar is to be kept distinct from Assyrian Ḫarḫar, which Levine (Iran 12 [1974] pp. 116–17) has indicated is to be located much farther east, namely, on the Great Khorasan Road in the area of the central or eastern Mahidasht. According to my interpretation of the geographical list from Ebla and Abū Ṣalābīkh (see Frayne, Early Dynastic List p. 65), Karaḫar is to be identified with LGN 242: *kak-kà-ra*. It apparently lay close to LGN 244: *ʾà-ir-rìm*; the latter toponym, in turn, I have equated (Early Dynastic List p. 65) with ancient Ḫalman. The location of Ḫalman has been discussed by R. Borger in connection with his study of a *kudurru* found at Sar-i-pūl-Zohāb. Borger (AfO 23 [1970] p. 1) writes:

> Kol. II 4 (vgl. I 14) ist zu entnehmen, dass unser Text aus 'dem Lande der Stadt Halman' stammt. Die Lage des Landes Halman (bzw. Arman) war bis jetzt noch nicht restlos gesichert. Belegstellen und Fachliteratur wurden zuletzt zusammengestellt von Brinkman, *A Political History of Post-Kassite Babylonia 1158–722 B.C.*, S. 195, Anm. 1195. Für die Lokalisierung von Ḫalman und 'its possible identification with modern Holwan' verweist Brinkman auf Albright, JAOS 45, S. 212ff. und Güterbock, ZA 44, S. 73f., vgl. auch Cameron, *History of Early Iran*, S. 115ff. und Goetze, JNES 12, S. 118. Genaueres über Holwan (Ḥulwān) findet sich in *The Encyclopaedia of Islam* III, S. 571f.: eine alte Stadt, deren Lage mit dem heutigen Sarpol-e Zohāb identifiziert worden ist. Das heisst natürlich, dass der neue Grenzstein die Gleichsetzung Ḫalman (Arman) = Ḥulwān = Sarpol-e Zohāb endgültig sichert. Andererseits kann man auf diesem Wege mit Sicherheit feststellen, dass unser Kudurru *in situ* gefunden worden ist.

The combined evidence of the aforementioned *kudurru* found at Sar-i-pūl-Zohāb and the Early Dynastic List of Geographical Names would indicate a location of the ancient cities of Karaḫar and Ḫalman on the modern Alwand River (variant name Cham-i-Ḥalwān) in the greater vicinity of Sar-i-pūl-Zohāb.

Tiš-atal

E3/2.5.1

2001

A seal of a servant of a certain Tiš-atal of Karaḫar is in the Louvre.

COMMENTARY

The seal is made of red jasper and measures 3.3×1.8 cm. It was formerly housed in the de Clercq Collection; it is now in the Louvre, AO 22316. The inscription was collated from the published photo. Lines 1–2 are found in col. i, lines 3–4 in col. ii. It is unclear whether the seal inscription is to be read in Akkadian or Sumerian.

BIBLIOGRAPHY

1888 de Clercq, Collection 1 pp. 82–83 and pl. XIV no. 121 (photo, copy, edition)
1907 Thureau-Dangin, SAK pp. 174–75 XV. Kisâri, König von Ganḫar (edition)
1910 Ward, Seals p. 109 fig. 303 (drawing)
1929 Barton, RISA pp. 168–69 King of Gankhar 1. Kisari (edition)
1936 Ungnad, Subartu p. 146 (study)
1944 Gelb, Hurrians p. 57 and nn. 66–67 (study)
1948 Nougayrol, RA 42 p. 11 no. 1 (study)
1950 Lewy, ArOr 18/3 p. 384–85 n. 86 (study)
1957 Hallo, Royal Titles p. 64 (study)
1961 Gelb, MAD 2² p. 16 § 1d (study)
1963 Hirsch, AfO 20 p. 33 n. 369 (study)
1971 Sollberger and Kupper, IRSA IIIH1a (translation)
1987 Collon, First Impressions no. 122 (photo, translation)
1990 Collon, RA 84 pp. 132–33 and 135 no. 2 (photo, study)
1990 Gelb and Kienast, Königsinschriften p. 386 no. 3 (edition)

TEXT

1) ^{d}*ti*$_{4}$!-*śa-a-tal*
2) LUGAL *kár-ḫar*.KI
3) *ma-ṣi-am-eš*$_{4}$-*tár*
4) IR$_{11}$.ZU

1–2) Tiš-atal, king of Karaḫar:

3–4) Maṣi'am-Eštar (is) your/his servant.

Zardamu

E3/2.5.2

1

A seal bearing an inscription of Zardamu, king of Karaḫar, is housed in the British Museum.

COMMENTARY

The lapis lazuli seal, which is worn and slightly weathered, measures 3.05×1.85 cm. The piece was purchased from Gegou in 1895, and given the museum number BM 89851 and the registration number 95-10-22, 3. Lines 1–12 are found in col. i; lines 13–21 in col. ii.

BIBLIOGRAPHY

1980 Sollberger, AnSt 30 pp. 64–65 and pl. IV (photo, edition, study)
1982 Collon, Cylinder Seals 2 no. 472 (photo, edition, study)
1990 Collon, RA 84 pp. 133 and 135 (photo, study)
1990 Gelb and Kienast, Königsinschriften p. 386 no. 4 (edition)

TEXT

1) ^{d}*za-ar-da-mu*
2) ^{d}UTU *ma-ti-šu*
3) *na-ra-am*
4) ^{d}KIŠ.UNU.GAL
5) *ì-lí-šu*
6) *an-nu-ni-tum*
7) *um-ma-šu*
8) ^{d}[šul]-⸢pa⸣-è
9) ⸢x⸣-*ti*-[x]-⸢AN-*šu*⸣
10) ⸢x⸣-[...]
11) ⸢x⸣-[...]-⸢*šu*⸣
12) ^{d}EN.SIG.NUN
13) *a-li-ik i-mi-ti-šu*
14) ⸢x⸣ ^{d}UTU
15) ^{d}DUMU.ZI-⸢*šu*⸣(?)
16) LUGAL *da-núm*
17) LUGAL *kára-ḫar*.KI
18) *ù* LUGAL
19) *ki-ib-ra-tim*
20) *ar-ba-im*
21) DAM ^{d}INANNA

1–9) Zardamu, sun-god of his land; beloved of the god Nergal, his (personal) deity; Annunītum (is) his mother; Šulpa'e (is) his ...

10–11) Too broken for translation.

12–15) The god EN.SIG.NUN (is the one) who walks at his right side; the ... of Šamaš, (is) his(?) Dumuzi,

16–21) mighty king, king of Karaḫar, and king of the four quarters, spouse of the goddess Eštar.

KIMAŠ

E3/2.6

The year names for Š 46–48 commemorate an apparent ongoing campaign of Šulgi in the mountainous region of Kimaš. Major targets of this war, as attested by the GNs occurring in the year names, were the cities of Kimaš, Ḫurti, and Ḫarši. Another likely conquest, to judge from the evidence of archival texts, was the defeat of the city of Zidānum. Its mention together with Ḫarši in a Drehem text dated to AS 3 (Private collection: L. Delaporte, RA 8 [1911] pp. 188–89 no. 7 lines 5, 7) and with Ḫurti in a tablet dated to AS 9 (Sainte-Anne 200: P.-E. Dhorme, RA 9 [1912] pl. V, SA 200, lines 6, 7) points to Zidānum's location in the Kimaš region. The author (Frayne, Early Dynastic List p. 57) has proposed that the GN Zidānum is to be connected with the GN *gi-d*[*a-n*]*u* that appears in an Early Dynastic list of city names from Abū Ṣalābīkh and Ebla. This correlation would assume a confusion between the GI and ZI signs; the alternation is commonly found in cuneiform texts. Gidānum, in turn, can be plausibly located, according to the author's interpretation of the geographical list from Abū Ṣalābīkh and Ebla (Frayne, Early Dynastic List p. 57), on the mountain road that connected the ancient cities of Awal and Madga. Of further note is a year name of an OB king of Ešnunna (see Greengus, OBTI p. 28 DF no. 25 and n. 34 and pp. 30–31 DF no. 33) that commemorates the defeat of the cities of Kimaš and Ekallātum.

It would appear, then, that the theatre of operations of Šulgi's Kimaš lay in the mountains northwest of the area of the junction of the Diyālā River and Jebel Ḥamrīn.

Three notables of Kimaš are named in Ur III archival sources. A tablet dated to AS 7 (Boson, TCS no. 140) mentions a certain *ḫu-un-ḫi-li* (line 2) and *ra-ši-ši* (line 4) as "'men' of Kimaš" (lú-ki-maš.KI-me). The former name could be a reference to the Ḫunḫili named in the seal inscription edited in this section, or, alternately, could belong to his namesake. As Hallo (RHA 36 [1978] p. 76) has pointed out, the latter name, Rašiši, may be connected with Rabsisi named as a ruler of Kimaš in the apodosis of a Middle Assyrian omen (BM 112643: Walker CT 51 pl. 53 no. 152 rev. line 14′) as well as a Seleucid chronicle from Uruk (W 22289: Hunger, SbTU 1 no. 2 line 5). A third personage of Kimaš is the GÌR-ni(Text: IR) who appears as general (GÌR.NÍTA) of Kimaš in an archival text whose date is broken away (YBC 3633: Keiser, YOS 4 no. 207 line 153). To judge from inscription E3/2.1.6.1012 line 5′, there apparently was another city named Kimaš situated somewhere in Elam.

Ḫunḫili

E3/2.6.1

2001

A seal in the Hermitage Museum, St. Petersburg, bears an Akkadian inscription that names a certain *Ḫu-un*-NI-NI as governor of Kimaš and general of Elam. The name has been normalized here as Ḫunḫili, following Zadok's suggestion to see it as an Elamite PN.

COMMENTARY

The haematite seal was numbered A. vi. 3. no. 7 in the Hermitage collection. The inscription was collated by M. Powell as communicated in the article "Kimaš" in RLA 5 p. 593. The text is arranged in one column.

The GN of line 3 was previously (and erroneously) read as *ma-ad-ga*.KI. For the PN of line 1, we may note the following lemma in Hinz and Koch, Elamisches Wörterbuch p. 719:

hu-un.hi-li N.pr.m. aE (Ur-III-Zeit); s.a. hu-un.ì-lí, das nach R. Zadok (ElOn, 1984, 11) den elamischen Namen akkadisiert, "not Amorite as hesitantly suggested by Edzard/Rollig, RlA 5, g 593." Die Bedeutung könnte sein *Licht durch [Gott] Hili*. Vgl. a. an-na.hi-li und a-ta.d.hi-li.

BIBLIOGRAPHY

1891 Sayce, ZA 6 pp. 161–63 (partial translation, study)
1897 Sayce, PSBA 19 pp. 68–70 (copy [in typescript], transliteration, study)
1907 Thureau-Dangin, SAK pp. 176–77 XVIII. Hunnini, Patesi von Kimaš (edition)
1908 Ward, in Harper Memorial 1 pp. 368–69 and fig. 11 (copy, translation [by Price], study)
1910 Ward, Seals p. 117 fig. 332 (copy)
1929 Barton, RISA pp. 302–303 A Ruler of Kimash 1. Khunini (edition)
1930 Poebel, ZA 39 p. 129 (edition)
1936 Cameron, Iran p. 54 and n. 31 (study)
1961 Gelb, MAD 2^2 p. 57 (study)
1980 Edzard and Röllig, RLA 5 p. 593 (study)
1984 Zadok, Elamite Onomasticon p. 14 (study [of PN of line 1])

TEXT

1) *ḫu-un-ì-lí*
2) ÉNSI *ki-maš*.KI
3) GÌR.NÍTA *ma-at* NIM.KI
4) *tam-gú-gú*
5) ZÉ ÌR ZI MI

1–3) Ḫunḫili, governor of Kimaš, general of the land of Elam:

4–5) Tamgugu, ...

URKIŠ AND NAWAR

E3/2.7

A handful of Ur III archival texts (see Edzard, Rép. Géogr. 2 p. 224 sub Urkiš) refer to a ruler of Urkiš named An-na-tal. Although Urkiš apparently remained outside the political control of the Ur III state during much (or all) of the Ur III period, the archival sources do attest to diplomatic relations between Ur and Urkiš.

The location of Urkiš, a very important ancient city, has been the subject of considerable scholarly discussion. W.J. van Lière, in an article entitled "Urkiš, centre religieux hurrite retrouvé dans la haute jézireh syrienne" (AAAS 7 [1957] p. 91–94), summarized the then available scholarly opinion on the subject:

> Urkiš, centre religieux et siège du panthéon hurrite et du Dieu principal Kummarbi, a été le but de plusieurs recherches dans la haute Jézireh. Nougayrol [A. Parrot et J. Nougayrol, "Un document de fondation hurrite," RA 42 (1948) pp. 1–20] suppose qu'Urkiš se trouve dans la région à l'ouest de Kamichlye; Moortgat [A. Moortgat "Archäologische Forschungen der Max Freiherr von Oppenheim Stiftung im nördlichen Mesopotamien 1955 Arbeitsgem. für Forschung des Landes Nordrhein—Westfalen" abh. 62, 1957] a consacré deux jours pour prospecter la région pendant ses fouilles à Tell Fecharyé; Goetze ["An Old Babylonian Itinerary," JCS 7 (1953) pp. 62–63] exprime l'opinion, qu'Urkiš doit être trouvé facilement dans la partie occidentale de la plaine fertile entre Ras-el-Ain, Hassakeh el Kamichlye. Le point de départ pour Moortgat est la provenance de deux lions en bronze et une tablette de fondation du temple de Kummarbi. Des informations fortuites, que j'ai obtenues récemment, indiquent que ces lions ont été excavés de Tell Amouda.

More recently, G. Buccellati has proposed to identify Urkiš with modern Mozan (near Amouda) in the Ḫabūr plains. He writes (Mozan 1 p. 38):

> On the basis of the information presented in the following chapters, it appears that Mozan is a likely candidate as the site of ancient Urkish. It is a large urban center in the third millennium, it shows more limited evidence of occupation for the early second millennium, and is abandoned thereafter. Given its close proximity to Amuda (some 5 km. to the east), all the arguments which have been adduced in the past in favor of the identification of Amuda (i.e. Tell Shermola) with Urkish apply equally as well to Mozan.

The hypothesis Mozan = Urkiš has now been confirmed by recent discoveries at Mozan (see Buccellati, Orient Express 1995/3 pp. 67–70). Buccellati reports the finding at Mozan of seal inscriptions of Old Akkadian date belonging to a king (endan) of Urkiš named Tupkiš.

The two GNs Urkiš and Nawar appear in the royal title "king of Urkiš and Nawar" found in the foundation inscription of Atal-šen which is edited as inscription E3/2.7.2.1 below. While the Nawar in this title was at first identified by scholars with the east trans-Tigridian land of Namri or Namar, the recent discovery of the GN *na-wa-ar*.KI on a tablet of Middle Babylonian date from Tell Brāk (Oates, Iraq 49 [1987] pp. 188–89 and Finkel, Iraq 50 [1988] pp. 105–108 no. 2) indicates that a town by this name lay at or not too far distant from Tell Brāk. In a recent discussion of ancient Nawar, Matthews and Eidem (Iraq 55 [1993] p. 204) observe:

> The earliest reference to Nawar is found in an Ur III text which mentions a certain Nawar-šen gudu$_4$ of Ninhursag "man" of na-wa-ar^{ki} (see Michalowski 1986, 147). Simultaneously Nawar-šen is an example of the many PNs compounded with Nawar which are found in Mesopotamian texts, often as deified GN and very likely identical with the Habur Nawar. The name also plays a certain role in Hurrian religion and ritual.
>
> Nawar occurs together with Urkiš in the inscription of Atal-šen.

Nawar, in turn, is possibly to be connected with the GN Nagar which appears in various Pre-Sargonic and Sargonic sources. Matthews and Eidem (Iraq 55 [1993] p. 203) note:

> "The land of Nagar" is named after the city called Nagar and it is interesting to note that we have a direct reference to a territorial entity as opposed to the inscriptions of Atal-šen and Tiš-atal where only cities are mentioned.
>
> The earliest references to a city Nagar come from the Ebla archives (see Catagnoti, in press). Here the GN is frequently and almost systematically connected with a specific, but as yet rather obscure, occupational title (hub$_2$.ki), and we also learn about a king of Nagar who travels to Tuttul (Tell Biʾa outside modern Raqqa) to visit the temple of Dagan. In fact it seems likely that Nagar may be the only major city in the Habur region mentioned in the Ebla archives (Catagnoti and Bonechi, pers. comm.). From approximately the same period a place written nagar^{ki} is mentioned in an inscription of IpLULil of Mari (Gelb/Kienast 1990, p. 13: MP 12).
>
> Two Old Akkadian administrative texts CT 1, 91-5-9, 588 and 590, probably from Sippar, both mention a place nagar^{ki} in connection with large quantities of barley.
>
> Nagar, written na-[g]àr?^{ki}, is perhaps listed as the first town in the Old Akkadian tablet from Brak F.1153 (previously read na-[h]ur?^{ki}; see Catagnoti and Bonechi 1992).
>
> The great goddess of Nagar, Bēlet-Nagar, is first mentioned in the curse section of the inscription of Tiš-atal (^{d}nin-na-gàr^{ki}).

The city of Nagar also appears in the recently discovered tablets of Early Dynastic date found at Tell Beydar (according to an oral communication of K. van Lerberghe delivered at the 204th meeting of the American Oriental Society, Madison, Wisconsin, March 1994). As for the location of ancient

Nagar, Charpin (in Eichler, Tall al-Hamīdīya 2 p. 68) writes:

> it is in fact known that Nagar is located on the route between Kaḫat and Mari. J.-M. Durand even advocates — using other sources — locating Nagar at Tell Brak.

This identification has been reiterated by a handful of scholars: A. Catagnoti and A.M. Bonechi, "Le volcan Kawkab, Nagar et problèmes connexes," NABU 1992 no. 65 and J.-M. Durand, "L'emploi des toponymes dans l'onomastique d'époque Amorrite," SEL 8 (1991) p. 93 n. 46.

The tutelary deity of Nagar, the goddess Bēlet-Nagar, has been the subject of a study by M. Guichard entitled "Au pays de la Dame de Nagar" (in Charpin and Durand, Florilegium marianum 2 pp. 235–72; see especially section E: "La dame de Nagar"). She first appears in a pre-Sargonic tablet from Mari published by D. Charpin (MARI 5 pp. 79 and 114–15 no. 20 col. ii line 4). We may recall the appearance of Nawar-šen, anointed priest ($gudu_4$) of Ninḫursaga and "man" of na-wa-ar^{ki} in the Ur III tablet cited in our discussion above. The designation lú-GN "man of GN" in Ur III sources may denote the ruler of a city, and thus it may be that Nawar-šen, devotee of Ninḫursaga, was a ruler at Nagar. Could it be, in turn, that Bēlet-Nagar was simply a local form, at Nagar, of the goddess Ninḫursaga? We may note, in this connection, a finely modelled seal of the Sargonic period that was apparently found at Urkiš. Nougayrol (Syria 37 [1960] p. 213) notes: "Selon le vendeur, il provient, en effet, du même site que le lion de bronze acquis par le Musée du Louvre." In his description of the seal design (Nougayrol, ibid., p. 212) Nougayrol identifies the seated goddess depicted on the seal as being Ninḫursaga:

> Pour en comprendre tout le sens nous devons examiner de plus près la déesse assise. C'est une montagne qui lui sert de trône et de tabouret, mais c'est aussi la cime d'une montagne qui pointe entre les cornes de sa tiare. Le graveur, par ce détail inusité, a pu vouloir suggérer que cette divinité n'était pas *une* déesse-montagne quelconque, mais *la* déesse-montagne par excellence, la "Dame de la Montagne" l'éminente Ninhursag, mère des dieux et accoucheuse du ciel et de la terre.

Of course, the tentative equation of Ninḫursaga with Bēlet-Nagar is, for the present, only a conjecture. Guichard (Florilegium marianum 2 p. 270) notes: "Elle (Bēlet-Nagar) règnait sur ce domaine avec Addu, qui apparaît surtout comme un simple parèdre. L'archétype du couple déese-mère et dieu d'orage, est similaire dans le couple 'Reine d'Apum'-Addu."

In summary, the available data point to the locations of Urkiš (= Mozan) and Nawar (=? Tell Brāk), the two principal cities of Atal-šen's realm, in the Ḫabūr basin, about 45 km apart.

Talpuš-atili

E3/2.7.1

1

A flat strip of unbaked clay now conserved in the Aleppo Museum is impressed with the seal inscription of a certain Talpuš-atili, an apparent ruler of Nagar.

COMMENTARY

The clay strip was found in excavations of Mallowan at Tell Brāk in the so-called "Palace of Narām-Sîn." It bears the museum number Aleppo Museum 6763. The inscription was not collated. Matthews and Eidem (Iraq 55 [1993] pp. 202–203) discuss the date of the inscription and conclude: "In sum therefore we would opt for an early post-Akkadian date."

Lines 1–2 are found in col. i and lines 3–4 in col. ii.

BIBLIOGRAPHY

1993 Matthews and Eidem, Iraq 55 pp. 201–207 (photo, copy, edition, study)

TEXT

1) *tal-pu-za-ti-li*
2) ^{d}UTU *ma-ti*
3) *na-*⌈*gàr*.KI⌉
4) DUMU ⌈x-x-x⌉-[x]

1–4) Talpuš-atili, sun-(god) of the land of Nagar, son of PN.

Atal-šen

E3/2.7.2

1

A copper foundation tablet bears an Akkadian inscription commemorating Atal-šen's construction of the temple of the god Nergal.

COMMENTARY

The foundation tablet, which measures 15×16.7 cm, was found, according to the evidence of its seller, at modern Samarra on the Tigris. It now bears the museum number AO 5678. All text lines are found on the obverse of the tablet. Lines 1–13 are found in the central column, lines 14–17 on the left transverse column, and lines 18–20 on the right transverse column. A colophon is found on the right edge of the tablet. The inscription was collated from the published photo.

The author, in a review article of Gelb and Kienast, Königsinschriften (JAOS 112 [1992] pp. 620–21), has proposed that the shift of *ś* to *š* in the orthography of royal inscriptions took place sometime during the reign of Šulgi. Thus the shift of *ś* to *š* in *šāninūtim* (line 13), *šu'āti* (line 15), and *zēršu* (line 19), would argue for a date of composition of this text to Ur III times.

BIBLIOGRAPHY

1912 Thureau-Dangin, RA 9 pp. 1–4 and pl. 1 nos. 1–2 (photo, edition)
1924 Landsberger, ZA 35 pp. 228–30 (study)
1930 Speiser, Origins p. 144 (study)
1936 Ungnad, Subartu pp. 142–43 (study)
1943 Gelb, Nuzi Personal Names pp. 233–34 (study)
1944 Gelb, Hurrians p. 56 (study)
1961 Gelb, MAD 2^2 p. 16 § 1e (study)
1963 Hirsch, AfO 20 p. 32 sub 3 Arisen (study)
1966 Finet, RA 60 p. 17 (study)
1968 Herzfeld, Persian Empire pp. 155–56 and fig. 10 (copy, edition)
1971 Sollberger and Kupper, IRSA IIH1a (translation)
1990 Collon, RA 84 p. 134 (study)
1990 Gelb and Kienast, Königsinschriften p. 383 Varia 16 (Atalšen von Urkiš und Nawar) (edition)

TEXT

1) ^{d}KIŠ.UNU.GAL
2) LUGAL
3) *ḫa*-WI-*li-im*.KI
4) *a-tal*-SI-*en*
5) ⸢*re-um*⸣ *ep-šum*
6) ⸢LUGAL⸣
7) ⸢*ur-kìš*.KI⸣
8) *ù* ⸢*na-wa-ar*.KI⸣
9) DUMU *sá*-⸢*dar-ma-at*⸣
10) LUGAL
11) ⸢DÍM⸣ É

1–3) O god Nergal, lord of ḪaWIlum:

4–13) Atal-šen, the capable shepherd, king of Urkiš and Nawar, son of Sadar-mat, the king, (is) the builder of the temple of the god Nergal, (the god) who vanquishes opposition.

12) ⌈d⌉KIŠ.UNU.GAL
13) *nir*$_{x}$(GAZ×NIR)⌉ *ša-nin-ú-tim*
14) ŚU$_{4}$ DUB
15) *šu*-⌈*a*⌉-*ti*
16) *ú-šá-sà-ku*
17) ^{d}UTU
18) *ù* ^{d}INANNA
19) ⌈NUMUN-*šu*⌉
20) ⌈*li-il*⌉-*qù-ta*

14–20) As for the one who removes this inscription, may the gods Šamaš and Eštar destroy his progeny.

Tiš-atal

E3/2.7.3

Three Ur III sources mention an important personage (or personages) named Tiš-atal. R. Whiting, JCS 28 (1976) pp. 174–77, notes they were:

1) *Ti-iš-a-tal en-da-an Ur-kèš*.KI in an undated foundation inscription written in Hurrian (RA 42 [1948] pp. 1–20) here edited as inscription E3/2.7.3.1.

2) ^{d}Ti$_{4}$(!)-sa-a-tal LUGAL Kár(a)-ḫar.ki in an Ur III or early Isin-Larsa style seal (de Clercq, Collection 1 no. 121) here edited as inscription E3/2.5.1.2001.

3) Ti-iš-a-tal lú Ni-nu-a.ki in an Ur III administrative text from Eshnunna dated to Šū-Sîn 3 (Tell Asmar 1931-T615).

While it is unlikely that the king of Karaḫar named in item 2 is to be considered as the same person(s) mentioned in items 1 and 3, there is a distinct possibility, as was first suggested by Whiting (JCS 28 [1976] p. 177), that Tiš-atal of Urkiš was the same man as Tiš-atal of Nineveh. It may be, as Whiting suggests, that before the conquest of Nineveh by Šū-Sîn, the city lay within the orbit of Tiš-atal of Urkiš and Nawar. If so, the Hurrian ruler would have controlled a rather extensive kingdom stretching from Urkiš (= Mozan) and Nagar (=? Tell Brāk) in the west to Nineveh in the east. Such a hypothesis may be supported by the fact that Atal-šen, one of Tiš-atal's predecessors as king of Urkiš and Nawar, has given us an inscription (E3/2.7.2.1) that is supposed to have come from the site of modern Samarra. If the provenance is true, it would attest to building activity of a king of Urkiš and Nawar on the middle Tigris. The limits of Tiš-atal's realm may have been roughly comparable to those known for Šalmaneser I of Assyria. One of his building inscriptions (see Frame and Donbaz, ARRIM 1 [1983] pp. 1–5) attests to temple constructions (among others) in the cities of Kaḫat (on the Ḫabūr) and Nineveh.

1

Two copper lion pegs and a limestone tablet of unsure provenance — they may have come from the modern site of Amouda or vicinity — mention a certain Tiš-atal as *endan* of Urkiš. The pieces clearly came from an ancient foundation deposit. They are now housed in museums in New York and Paris.

CATALOGUE

Ex.	Museum number	Dimensions (cm)	Lines preserved	cpn
	Copper lion pegs			
1	AO 19937	Lion: 12.2×8.5 Copper plate: 8.5×5.6	1–5	c
2	MMA 48.180	Lion: 11.7×7.9	Traces only	c
	Grey limestone foundation tablet			
3	AO 19938	10×9×3	1–25	p

COMMENTARY

The text given is that provided by the foundation tablet. Lines 1–12 are found on the obverse of the tablet, lines 13–25 on the reverse.

Both the Paris and New York lion pegs bear a shorter version (it contains only 12 lines) of the tablet inscription. It is arranged on the pegs in two columns, the first column containing ten lines, and the second two lines. Unfortunately, the peg inscriptions are virtually illegible (a transliteration is not given here), and with the exception of a few isolated lines, a match cannot be made between tablet and peg inscriptions. Though they are, strictly speaking, different inscriptions, data on the exemplars of the peg inscription have been included under the rubric E3/2.7.3.1. The text given, however, is only that of the tablet inscription.

Concerning the deity of lines 9 and 13, we may note the comments of Wilhelm (Hurrians p. 53):

> The god Nupatik, who is well-attested in Ugarit and Hattuša but whose nature and genealogy are still unclear, may also have been a member of the most ancient Hurrian pantheon, for he is invoked under the name Lubadaga in Tiš-atal's foundation tablet.

The translation of the deity of line 15 as "(weather)-god(??)" follows that given in Wilhelm, Hurrians p. 11. M. Guichard (in Charpin and Durand, Florilegium marianum 2 p. 270) notes:

> A. Archi a proposé que l'association Déesse de Nagar/Dieu-soleil/Addu dans l'inscription hourite forme une triade. Le-Dieu-soleil serait donc le fils divin.

Ex. 1 was kindly collated by B. André-Salvini and ex. 2 by I. Sparr and D. Fleming. For a detailed bibliography for the Metropolitan piece (which is not repeated here), see Muscarella, Bronze and Iron, p. 377.

BIBLIOGRAPHY

1948 Nougayrol, CRAIB pp. 130–31 (exs. 1, 3, translation, study)
1948 Parrot and Nougayrol, RA 42 pp. 1–20 and figs. 1–3 (exs. 1, 3, photo, edition); p. 6 fig. 4 (ex. 3, copy)
1953 Goetze, JCS 7 p. 62 and n. 81 (exs. 1–3, study)
1954 Parrot, Syria 31 pp. 11–13 and pl. IV 2–3 (exs. 1, 3, photo, study)
1960 Parrot, Sumer p. 182 and fig. 220 (exs. 1, 3, photo, study)
1961 Gelb, MAD 2[2] p. 16 § 1f (exs. 1, 3, study)
1966 Crawford, Ancient Near Eastern Art pp. 10–11 and fig. 15 (ex. 2, photo, study)
1975 Edzard and Kammenhuber, RLA 4 p. 509 § 3. A. 1. (exs. 1–3, study)
1976 Amiet, L'art d'Agadé pp. 111 and 132 no. 64 (a–b) (exs. 1, 3, photo, study)
1982 Wilhelm, Hurriter, p. 15 (exs. 1, 3, translation)
1988 Muscarella, Bronze and Iron pp. 375–77 (ex. 2, photo, [partial] transliteration, study)
1989 Wilhelm, Hurrians p. 11 (exs. 1–3, translation)
1990 Collon, RA 84 pp. 134–35 (exs. 1–3, photo, translation)
1990 Gelb and Kienast, Königsinschriften p. 382 Varia 15 (Tišatal von Urkiš) (exs. 1, 3, edition)
1994 Guichard, in Charpin and Durand, Florilegium marianum 2 p. 269 (exs. 1, 3, translation)

TEXT

1) *ti-iš-a-tal*
2) *en-da-an*
3) *ur-kìš*.KI
4) *pu-ur-li*
5) ^{d}PIRIG.GAL
6) *pá-ʾà-áš-tum*
7) *pu-ru-li*
8) *a-di-ʾà-al-li*
9) ^{d}*lu-ba-da-ga-áš*
10) *ša-ak-ru-in*
11) *e-me-ni*
12) *tá-áš-pí-ʾà-al-li*
13) ^{d}*lu-ba-da-ga-áš*
14) *tá-áš-pu-in*
15) AN
16) *ḫa-wa-ʾà-a*
17) *ḫa-su-e-in*
18) ^{d}NIN *na-gàr*.KI
19) ^{d}UTU-*ga-an*
20) ^{d}IŠKUR
21) *e-me-ni*
22) *tá-áš-bi-ʾà-al-li*
23) *in-u-be*
24) *i-na-u-be*
25) SI(?)-*ti-in*

1–6) Tiš-atal, *endan* of Urkiš, built the temple of the god PIRIG.GAL.

7–10) May the god Lubadaga (Nupatik) protect this temple.

11–14) As for the one who destroys it, may the god Lubadaga (Nupatik) destroy (him).

15–17) May the (weather)-god(?) not hear his prayer.

18–25) May the lady of Nagar, the sun-god, (and) the storm-god(?) ... him who destroys it.

Index of Museum Numbers

Aleppo, Aleppo Museum

No.	E3/2.	No.	E3/2.	No.	E3/2.	No.	E3/2.
6763	7.1.1	—	1.2.68	—	4.7.1	—	4.2.2001

Ann Arbor, Michigan, Kelsey Museum of the University of Michigan

No.	E3/2.	No.	E3/2.
Kelsey 63.6.111	1.1.24.39d	Kelsey —	1.2.9.4

Baghdad, Iraq Museum

No.	E3/2.	No.	E3/2.	No.	E3/2.	No.	E3/2.
IM 1	1.5.1.16	IM 741	1.1.39.12	IM 1140	1.3.8.8	IM 3568/5	1.1.11.64
IM 2	1.2.2	IM 779	1.1.26.2	IM 1141	1.3.8.9	IM 3568/6	1.1.11.65
IM 22	1.1.4.21	IM 780	1.1.26.3	IM 1142	1.3.8.10	IM 3568/7	1.1.11.66
IM 96	1.1.11.21	IM 790	1.1.26.5	IM 1143	1.3.8.11	IM 3568/8	1.1.11.67
IM 97	1.1.45	IM 906A	1.1.11.49	IM 1144	1.3.8.12	IM 3568/9	1.1.11.68
IM 100	1.1.39.5	IM 906B	1.1.11.50	IM 1145	1.3.8.13	IM 3568/10	1.1.11.69
IM 103	1.1.11.23	IM 915	1.4.15.2	IM 1146	1.4.15.4	IM 3568/11	1.1.11.70
IM 114	1.1.11.24	IM 916	1.1.2.32	IM 1147	1.4.19.2	IM 3568/12	1.1.11.71
IM 115	1.1.11.25	IM 929	1.1.2.34	IM 1148	1.4.19.3	IM 3568/13	1.1.11.72
IM 123	1.1.11.28	IM 931	1.1.2.35	IM 1149	1.3.8.3	IM 3568/14	1.1.11.73
IM 134	1.1.11.29	IM 933	1.6.1019	IM 1150	1.3.8.15	IM 3568/15	1.1.11.74
IM 135	1.1.11.30	IM 938	1.1.2.36	IM 1151	1.2.2046	IM 3568/16	1.1.11.75
IM 176	1.1.39.6	IM 939	1.2.57	IM 1156	1.6.1027	IM 3568/17	1.1.11.76
IM 177	1.1.11.31	IM 940	1.1.2.37	IM 1157	1.2.4.3b	IM 3568/18	1.1.11.77
IM 238	1.1.39.9	IM 941	1.1.2.38	IM 1158	1.2.4.4b	IM 3568/19	1.1.11.78
IM 239	1.1.11.40	IM 963	1.1.2.39	IM 1173	1.2.56	IM 3568/20	1.1.11.79
IM 240	1.1.11.41	IM 998	1.2.2048	IM 1174	1.1.43	IM 3568/21	1.1.11.80
IM 288	1.1.39.11	IM 1007	1.1.2.45	IM 1176	1.6.1031	IM 3569	1.1.26.7
IM 376	1.1.11.32	IM 1008	1.3.8.14	IM 1259	1.2.42.2	IM 3572A	1.1.40.6
IM 377	1.1.11.33	IM 1010	1.4.20.2	IM 1351	1.1.11.54	IM 3574	1.1.11.82
IM 378	1.1.11.46	IM 1027	1.4.15.5	IM 1376	1.2.4.1a	IM 3576	1.1.41
IM 380	1.1.11.26	IM 1028	1.1.2.46	IM 1376	1.2.4.2a	IM 3580	1.2.52
IM 384	1.1.39.7	IM 1039	1.1.11.53	IM 1376	1.2.4.3a	IM 9226	1.1.11.83
IM 385	1.1.39.8	IM 1049	1.4.26	IM 1387	1.3.8.17	IM 9425	1.2.83
IM 386	1.1.11.34	IM 1057	1.1.2.47	IM 1388	1.3.8.18	IM 13358	1.3.20
IM 387	1.1.11.35	IM 1087	1.1.2.48	IM 1389	1.3.8.19	IM 13829	2.2.1
IM 388	1.1.11.36	IM 1132	1.1.13.7	IM 2222	1.1.11.55	IM 14322	1.1.47
IM 389	1.1.11.37	IM 1133	1.1.13.4	IM 2412/1	1.1.11.56	IM 16700	1.6.1027
IM 392	1.1.11.38	IM 1134	1.1.13.5	IM 2412/12	1.1.11.57	IM 20864	1.1.28.5
IM 566A	1.1.11.42	IM 1135	1.1.14.3	IM 3567	1.6.1018	IM 20866	1.2.10.26
IM 566B	1.1.11.43	IM 1136	1.1.13.8	IM 3568/1	1.1.11.60	IM 21980	1.5.1.14
IM 566C	1.1.11.44	IM 1137	1.1.13.6	IM 3568/2	1.1.11.61	IM 22846	1.2.10.27
IM 566D	1.1.11.45	IM 1138	1.1.13.9	IM 3568/3	1.1.11.62	IM 22847	1.1.28.6
IM 672	1.1.2.31	IM 1139	1.1.13.10	IM 3568/4	1.1.11.63	IM 22849	1.2.12.9

No.	E3/2.	No.	E3/2.	No.	E3/2.	No.	E3/2
IM 22851	1.2.10.28	IM 56106	1.2.18.1	IM 90943	1.1.40.15	IM 92972	1.5.1.7
IM 22866A	1.1.11.84	IM 58934	1.6.1032	IM 90944	1.1.40.16	IM 92973	1.5.1.4
IM 22866B	1.1.11.85	IM 59586	1.1.24.38a	IM 90945	1.1.11.130	IM 92974	1.5.1.1
IM 22866C	1.1.11.86	IM 59587	1.2.20.3b	IM 90946	1.1.11.131	IM—	1.1.2.A
IM 22866D	1.1.11.87	IM 59588	1.2.20.2b	IM 90947	1.1.11.132	IM—	1.1.2.B
IM 22866E	1.1.11.88	IM 59589	1.2.20.4b	IM 90948	1.1.11.133	IM—	1.1.2.C
IM 22866F	1.1.11.89	IM 59590	1.1.24.40b	IM 90949	1.1.11.134	IM—	1.1.2.D
IM 22866G	1.1.11.90	IM 61278	1.2.47	IM 90950	1.1.11.135	IM—	1.1.2.E
IM 22866H	1.1.11.91	IM 61279	1.4.23	IM 90951	1.1.11.136	IM—	1.1.2.F
IM 22866I	1.1.11.92	IM 61402/1	1.1.24.39a	IM 90952	1.1.11.137	IM—	1.1.10.2
IM 22866J	1.1.11.93	IM 61403/1	1.2.20.6b	IM 90953	1.1.11.138	IM—	1.1.16.2
IM 22866K	1.1.11.94	IM 61766	1.2.20.6a2	IM 90954	1.1.11.139	IM—	1.1.25.2
IM 22866L	1.1.11.95	IM 66433	1.2.3.19	IM 90955	1.1.39.25	IM—	1.1.26.9
IM 22866M	1.1.11.96	IM 66434	1.1.4.25	IM 90961	1.1.39.17	IM—	1.1.26.10
IM 22868	1.1.39.24	IM 66951	1.1.24.31	IM 90962	1.1.40.17	IM—	1.1.26.11
IM 22888	1.5.1.10	IM 77967	1.1.35.9	IM 90963	1.1.40.9	IM—	1.1.26.13
IM 22889	1.5.1.15	IM 85462	1.1.19.12	IM 90964		IM—	1.1.27
IM 22907	1.1.11.97	IM 85674	1.4.1.5	(old IM 3568)	1.1.11.59	IM—	1.1.34.4
IM 22908(?)	1.1.40.1	IM 85675	1.5.1.17	IM 90965	1.1.39.20	IM—	1.1.35.7
IM 23088–1	1.2.10.29	IM 85676	1.5.4	IM 90967	1.1.40.10	IM—	1.1.35.8
IM 23088–2	1.2.10.30	IM 85688+	1.1.20.3	IM 90968	1.1.40.11	IM—	1.1.39.22
IM 23088–3	1.2.10.31	IM 85689+	1.1.20.3	IM 90969	1.1.39.26	IM—	1.1.39.23
IM 23088–4	1.2.10.32	IM 90903	1.1.11.107	IM 92768	1.1.19.11	IM—	1.1.40.14
IM 23088–5	1.2.10.33	IM 90904	1.1.11.98	IM 92771	1.1.19.9	IM—	1.2.18.2
IM 23088–6	1.2.10.34	IM 90905	1.1.11.99	IM 92772	1.1.19.10	IM—	1.2.19.1a
IM 23088–7	1.2.10.35	IM 90906	1.1.11.27	IM 92773	1.5.1.9	IM—	1.2.42.3
IM 23088–8	1.2.10.36	IM 90907	1.1.11.58	IM 92779	1.1.26.1	IM—	1.3.1.63
IM 23088–9	1.2.10.37	IM 90908	1.1.11.100	IM 92781	1.1.19.3	IM—	1.3.1.64
IM 23088–10	1.2.10.38	IM 90909	1.1.11.101	IM 92782	1.1.19.4	IM—	1.3.1.65
IM 23088–11	1.2.10.39	IM 90910	1.1.11.81	IM 92783	1.1.19.6	IM—	1.3.1.66
IM 23088–12	1.2.10.40	IM 90912	1.1.11.108	IM 92788	1.1.39.21	IM—	1.3.1.67
IM 23089	1.1.28.7	IM 90913	1.1.11.109	IM 92792	1.1.11.140	IM—	1.3.1.68
IM 23576–A	1.2.10.41	IM 90914	1.1.11.110	IM 92793	1.1.11.141	IM—	1.3.1.69
IM 23576–B	1.2.10.42	IM 90916	1.1.39.18+19	IM 92794	1.1.40.7	IM—	1.3.1.70
IM 23576–C	1.2.10.43	IM 90917	1.1.11.111	IM 92795	1.1.40.8	IM—	1.3.1.71
IM 23839	1.2.28.1	IM 90918	1.1.11.112	IM 92797	1.1.11.142	IM—	1.3.1.72
IM 26833	1.4.29	IM 90919	1.1.11.102	IM 92798	1.1.11.143	IM—	1.3.1.73
IM 43456	1.4.2007	IM 90920	1.1.11.103	IM 92799	1.1.39.27	IM—	1.3.3
IM 45428	1.1.34.3a	IM 90921	1.1.11.104	IM 92800	1.1.11.144	IM—	1.3.8.A
IM 45429	1.1.34.3b	IM 90922	1.1.11.105	IM 92803	1.1.11.145	IM—	1.3.8.B
IM 45472	1.1.26.8	IM 90923	1.1.11.115	IM 92804	1.1.11.146	IM—	1.3.8.C
IM 45614	1.2.6.3a	IM 90926	1.1.11.120	IM 92805	1.1.11.147	IM—	1.3.8.D
IM 45615	1.2.6.3b	IM 90927	1.1.11.121	IM 92806	1.1.11.148	IM—	1.3.9.2
IM 45765	1.1.24.28	IM 90928	1.1.11.122	IM 92814	1.1.17.5	IM—	1.4.12.1
IM 49857/5	1.1.11.55	IM 90929	1.1.11.114	IM 92925	1.2.39.10	IM—	1.4.15.6
IM 49858–1	1.2.10.44	IM 90930	1.1.11.113	IM 92931	1.2.44	IM—	1.4.25
IM 49858–2	1.2.10.45	IM 90931	1.1.11.123	IM 92934	1.6.1003	IM—	1.5.2
IM 49858–3	1.2.10.46	IM 90932	1.1.11.124	IM 92935	1.6.1002	IM—	1.5.3
IM 52374	1.1.31	IM 90936	1.1.11.125	IM 92940	1.3.8.16	IM—	1.5.2016
IM 52380	1.3.15.35	IM 90937	1.1.11.106	IM 92951	1.5.1.11+12	IM—	1.6.1025
IM 53977	1.2.38	IM 90938	1.1.11.126	IM 92959	1.5.1.8	IM—	1.6.1026
IM 54537	1.3.17.2	IM 90939	1.1.11.127	IM 92964	1.5.1.5	IM—	1.6.1044
IM 54540	1.2.21.2	IM 90940	1.1.11.128	IM 92965	1.5.1.13		
IM 56105	1.1.24.29	IM 90942	1.1.11.129	IM 92970	1.5.1.6		

Barcelona, Museo de la Abadía de Montserrat

No.	E3/2.
MM 54	1.2.71
MM 1101	1.2.71

Berkeley, California, Phoebe Hearst Museum of Anthropology

No.	E3/2.	No.	E3/2.	No.	E3/2.
UCPHMA 9-1777	1.1.39.28	UCPHMA 9-16476	1.2.2032	UCPHMA 9-7953	1.3.15.43

Berkeley, California, University of California, Babylonian Collection

No.	E3/2.
UCBC 668	1.4.2013.1

Berlin, Vorderasiatisches Museum

No.	E3/2.	No.	E3/2.	No.	E3/2.
VA 2666	1.4.2009	VA 12908 (now lost)	1.4.28	VA 14656	1.1.35.10
VA 3040	1.3.1.40	VA 14656	1.1.24.32	VA 14657	1.3.13.6
VA 3119	1.2.10.1	VA 14656	1.1.24.33	VA 14657	1.3.13.7
VA 3302	1.4.15.1	VA 14656	1.1.33.8	VA 14657	1.3.13.8
VA 3324	1.2.2004	VA 14656	1.1.33.9	VA 15192	1.2.6.4a
VA 3855	1.4.17.6	VA 14656	1.1.33.10	VA 15192	1.2.6.4b
VA 5393	1.1.24.34	VA 14656	1.1.33.11	VA 15447	1.1.39.29
VA 8748	4.5.1	VA 14656	1.1.33.12	VA 15448	1.1.26.15
VA 8787	1.5.2005	VA 14656	1.1.33.13	VA 15449	1.2.10.2
VA 10938 (now lost)	1.1.34.1a	VA 14656	1.1.33.14	VA 15450	1.1.34.2b
VA 10945	1.1.34.1b	VA 14656	1.1.33.15		

Berrien Springs, Michigan, Horn Archaeological Museum

No.	E3/2.	No.	E3/2.	No.	E3/2.	No.	E3/2.
AUAM 73.0833	1.2.78	AUAM 73.1039	1.2.80	AUAM 73.2212	1.2.79	AUAM 73.3155	1.2.2006

Birmingham, England, Birmingham City Museum

No.	E3/2.	No.	E3/2.	No.	E3/2.
BCM 63'76	1.1.11.160	BCM 69'76	1.1.50	BCM 287'35	1.1.26.14
BCM 64'76	1.1.11.161	BCM 285'35	1.1.10.3		

Brussels, Musée du Cinquantenaire

No.	E3/2.	No.	E3/2.	No.	E3/2.
O 68	1.2.97	O 279	1.4.16.3	O 353	1.4.2018

Buffalo, Buffalo Museum of Science

No.	E3/2.
C 517b	1.2.74.1

Burlington, University of Vermont, Robert Hull Fleming Museum

No.	E3/2.
A 14948	1.3.15.46

Cambridge, England, Fitzwilliam Museum

No.	E3/2.	No.	E3/2.	No.	E3/2.
FM E 3.48	1.1.11.163	FM E.64.1935	1.1.40.20	FM E.206.1934	1.1.12.9

Cambridge, Massachusetts, Harvard Semitic Museum

No.	E3/2.
HSM 911.10.405	1.2.91
HSM 911.10.460	1.2.67.1

Chicago, Field Museum for Natural History

No.	E3/2..
FMNH 156003	1.1.11.159

Chicago, University of Chicago, Oriental Institute

No.	E3/2.	No.	E3/2.	No.	E3/2.	No.	E3/2.
A 199	1.2.2001.frgm. 1	A 1134	1.4.11	A 8997	1.2.27	A 31069	1.2.20.5a
		A 1135	1.3.1.47	A 29448	1.6.1041	A 31226	1.2.2024
A 202	1.2.2001.frgm. 3	A 1140	1.2.16.4	A 30568	1.2.2025	A 32776	1.6.1008
		A 1141	1.2.16.2	A 30791	1.1.24.37c	A 33656a	1.1.30 frgm. 1
A 438	1.3.1.75	A 1142	1.2.16.3	A 30791	1.1.24.38c	A 33657	1.1.30 frgm. 2
A 438	1.3.2	A 1143	1.2.16.1	A 30792	1.2.20.1a	—	1.2.20.5b
A 903	1.5.2001	A 3700	1.2.34	A 31056	1.6.1015		
A 1133	1.3.1.46	A 8164	1.4.12.2	A 31068	1.1.24.39c		

Durham, England, Gulbenkian Museum of Oriental Art

No.	E3/2.
N 2421	1.2.2040

Erlenmeyer Collection

No.	E3/2.
—	1.1.34.9b

Geneva, Musée d'Art et d'Histoire

No.	E3/2.	No.	E3/2.	No.	E3/2.	No.	E3/2.
MAH 15870	1.2.2019.6	MAH 16273	1.4.31.9	MAH 16522	1.2.2019.5	MAH 19351	1.1.11.158

Glasgow, Burrell Collection

No.	E3/2.
28/75	1.1.34.7a

Haifa, University of Haifa, Brockmon Collection

No.	E3/2.	No.	E3/2.
BT 4+HS 2009+ HS 2985	1.4.3.1	BT 4+HS 2009+ HS 2985	1.4.5.1 1.4.7.1

Hartford, Hartford Theological Seminary

No.	E3/2.
HTS 104	1.2.73

Istanbul, Arkeoloji Müzeleri

No.	E3/2.	No.	E3/2.	No.	E3/2.	No.	E3/2.
EŞ 419	1.2.12.1	EŞ 5562	1.2.10.20	EŞ 8979(?)	1.3.4.4	L 1001	1.2.2020
EŞ 420	1.2.10.14	EŞ 5856	1.4.17.5	EŞ 9625	1.1.33.17	L 4216	1.4.2003.1
EŞ 438 (frgm. 2)	1.2.55	EŞ 6682	1.3.1.2	EŞ 9648	1.3.13.10	L 4312	1.2.2014
EŞ 453	1.6.1007.1	EŞ 6683	1.3.1.3	EŞ 9650	1.3.13.9	L 7220	1.2.2015
EŞ 454	1.6.1007.3	EŞ 7070	1.3.2001	EŞ 13531	1.2.10.21	L 7226	1.2.2019.2
EŞ 455	1.6.1007.2	EŞ 7813	4.5.1	EŞ 13532	1.2.10.22	L 7491	1.2.2019.3
EŞ 489	1.2.11.1	EŞ 8854	1.1.33.16	EŞ 13539	1.1.26.12	L 7497	1.2.2019.4
EŞ 490	1.2.11.2	EŞ 8926	1.1.24.21	EŞ —	1.1.25.1	L 9827	1.4.2003.2
EŞ 1333	1.3.1.1	EŞ 8927	1.1.24.22	EŞ —	1.2.11.3	(Nippur)	
EŞ 3229	1.2.16.5	EŞ 8928	1.1.24.23	EŞ —	1.2.16.9	Ni 11	1.5.2011
EŞ 3232	1.2.16.6	EŞ 8929	1.1.24.24	EŞ —	1.2.51	Ni 372	1.4.2006
EŞ 3233	1.2.16.7	EŞ 8962	1.3.1.4	EŞ —	1.3.4.5	Ni 1199	1.2.2022.2
EŞ 3234	1.2.16.8	EŞ 8963	1.3.1.5	(Lagaš)		Ni 2094	1.2.90
EŞ 5557	1.2.10.15	EŞ 8964	1.3.16.2	L 839	1.3.2002	Ni 2109	1.5.2010
EŞ 5558	1.2.10.16	EŞ 8965	1.3.16.1	L 858	1.3.2002	Ni 2432	1.2.54
EŞ 5559	1.2.10.17	EŞ 8966	1.3.16.3	L 866	1.4.2002.2	Ni 2438	1.1.21.2
EŞ 5560	1.2.10.18	EŞ 8967	1.3.1.6	L 937	1.5.2003	Ni 2464	1.1.21.1
EŞ 5561	1.2.10.19	EŞ 8971	1.3.4.3	L 954	1.3.22	Ni 2760	1.4.5.2

No.	E3/2.	No.	E3/2.	No.	E3/2.	No.	E3/2.
Ni 3191	1.1.20.1	Ni 9662	1.4.1.6	PD 530	1.2.70	(Umma)	
Ni 4375	1.1.1	Ni 9662	1.4.9.2	PD 1327	1.4.2011.1	Um 403	1.5.2013.6
Ni 4394	1.4.1.1	Ni 9717	1.6.1012	PD 1355	1.4.2011.2	Um 493	1.4.2015.2
Ni 6718	1.4.1.1	Ni 13213	1.6.1016	PD 1365	1.4.2011.3	Um 855	1.5.2013.7
Ni 9654	1.4.1.2	Ni 13221	1.4.1.4	PD 1375	1.4.2011.4	Um 1053	1.5.2013.8
Ni 9654	1.4.2	Ni 13222	1.4.1.7	(Sippar)			
Ni 9656	1.4.1.3	(Puzriš-Dagan)		Si 277	1.1.20.2		

Jena, Friedrich-Schiller Universität, Hilprecht Collection of Babylonian Antiquities

No.	E3/2.	No.	E3/2.	No.	E3/2.	No.	E3/2.
HS 1192	1.4.31.1	HS 1208	1.4.31.8	HS 1231	1.3.2004.5	HS 1963	1.2.17
HS 1198	1.4.31.2	HS 1209	1.4.31.10	HS 1240	1.3.2004.6	HS 1964	1.4.24
HS 1199	1.4.31.3	HS 1210	1.4.31.11	HS 1241	1.3.2004.7	HS 1965	1.1.38
HS 1200	1.4.31.4	HS 1226	1.3.2004.1	HS 1330	1.4.2008	HS 1967	1.3.4.2
HS 1205	1.4.31.5	HS 1227	1.3.2004.2	HS 1334	1.3.2003	HS 1991	1.1.24.19
HS 1206	1.4.31.6	HS 1228	1.3.2004.3	HS 1346	1.2.2022.1	HS 2011	1.4.17.7
HS 1207	1.4.31.7	HS 1229	1.3.2004.4	HS 1351b	1.5.2007.5	HS 2014	1.1.24.20

Jerusalem, Bible Lands Museum

No.	E3/2.
BLMJ 1340	1.2.72
BLMJ—	1.3.1.75

Jerusalem, Musée du Studium Biblicum Franciscanum

No.	E3/2.
MSBF —	1.3.1.62

Kelekian Collection

No.	E3/2.
—	1.2.69

Leiden, Netherlands Institute for the Near East, de Liagre Böhl Collection

No.	E3/2.
LB 934	1.2.2001.2
LB 1308a	1.3.15.44

London, British Museum

No.	E3/2.	No.	E3/2.	No.	E3/2.	No.	E3/2.
BM 13016	1.2.2016	BM 90035	1.3.15.4	BM 104744	1.1.18	BM 114274	1.3.1.29
BM 15976	1.4.2016	BM 90036	1.3.10.1	BM 106533	1.4.2013.4	BM 114275	1.3.1.30
BM 17288	1.2.29	BM 90037	1.3.1.11	BM 106686	1.4.2013.2	BM 114297	1.3.15.23
BM 17827	1.2.1	BM 90038	1.3.15.5	BM 106711	1.4.2013.6	BM 114298	1.1.24.10
BM 26256	1.2.8	BM 90039	1.3.10.2	BM 106801	1.4.2013.7	BM 114301	1.2.3.9
BM 30051	1.1.11.1	BM 90040	1.3.1.12	BM 106830	1.4.2013.12	BM 114302	1.2.3.10
BM 30052	1.1.11.2	BM 90042	1.3.1.13	BM 107318	1.4.2013.11	BM 114303	1.2.3.11
BM 30053	1.1.11.3	BM 90043	1.3.1.14	BM 107517	1.4.2013.9	BM 114304	1.2.3.12
BM 30054	1.1.11.4	BM 90044	1.3.15.6	BM 107673	1.4.2013.5	BM 114305	1.2.3.13
BM 30055	1.1.11.5	BM 90056	1.3.15.7	BM 107758	1.4.2014	BM 114306	1.2.3.14
BM 30056	1.1.19.1	BM 90058+	1.3.15.8	BM 110813	1.4.2013.10	BM 114343	1.3.15.24
BM 30057	1.1.11.6	BM 90061	1.3.15.9	BM 110896	1.4.2013.3	BM 114344	1.3.15.25
BM 30065	1.1.39.1	BM 90276	1.2.39.3	BM 112443	1.4.2013.8	BM 114396	1.4.16.6
BM 30068	1.1.11.7	BM 90277	1.2.3.1	BM 113866	1.1.34.6b	BM 114684	1.3.17.3
BM 30075	1.1.11.8	BM 90278	1.2.3.2	BM 113896	1.1.34.6a	BM 115025	1.1.14.2
BM 30076	1.1.11.9	BM 90279	1.3.15.10	BM 114024	1.4.33	BM 115026	1.1.2.29
BM 30077	1.1.11.10	BM 90296	1.1.5.1	BM 114187	1.1.23	BM 116416	1.4.21.2
BM 30078	1.1.11.11	BM 90348	1.3.1.15	BM 114208	1.2.45.1	BM 116418	1.3.8.1
BM 30079	1.1.11.12	BM 90349	1.3.1.16	BM 114216	1.3.15.13	BM 116429	1.6.1017
BM 30080	1.1.11.13	BM 90352	1.3.1.17	BM 114217	1.3.15.14	BM 116430	1.2.85
BM 30081	1.1.11.14	BM 90353	1.3.10.3	BM 114218	1.3.15.15	BM 116433	1.1.46
BM 30082	1.1.11.15	BM 90372	1.3.1.18	BM 114219	1.3.15.16	BM 116434	1.5.2014
BM 30083	1.1.11.16	BM 90374	1.1.24.2	BM 114220	1.3.15.17	BM 116437	1.3.21
BM 30084	1.1.39.2	BM 90379	1.2.39.4	BM 114221	1.3.15.18	BM 116438	1.6.1035
BM 30085	1.1.11.17	BM 90396	1.1.23.3	BM 114222	1.3.15.19	BM 116440	1.6.1028
BM 30086	1.1.17.1	BM 90399	1.3.1.19	BM 114223	1.3.15.20	BM 116441	1.2.40
BM 30087	1.1.11.18	BM 90717	1.3.15.11	BM 114224	1.3.15.21	BM 116442	1.2.89.2
BM 30088	1.1.39.3	BM 90722+	1.1.35.6	BM 114225	1.3.15.22	BM 116444	1.6.1045
BM 30090	1.1.11.19	BM 90767	1.3.1.20	BM 114226	1.1.2.7	BM 116447	1.6.1029
BM 35389	1.2.24	BM 90790	1.1.2.4	BM 114227	1.1.2.8	BM 116448	1.2.43
BM 38947	4.6.1	BM 90791+	1.1.2.5	BM 114228	1.1.4.6	BM 116449	1.2.2045
BM 54722+	1.1.20.4	BM 90792	1.1.24.4	BM 114229	1.1.2.9	BM 116451	1.6.1023
BM 78681+	1.2.26	BM 90793+	1.1.2.5	BM 114230	1.1.2.10	BM 116452	1.3.7
BM 78681+	1.2.35	BM 90794+	1.1.24.5	BM 114231	1.1.4.7	BM 116453	1.3.16.8
BM 78681+	1.2.64	BM 90795	1.1.24.6	BM 114232	1.1.4.8	BM 116719	1.2.2038
BM 78681+	1.2.2043	BM 90796	1.1.24.7	BM 114233+	1.1.4.9	BM 116761	1.4.15.3
BM 80151	1.1.24.1	BM 90797	1.1.4.5	BM 114234	1.1.15.1	BM 116984	1.1.40.2
BM 89126	1.1.2001	BM 90799	1.1.24.8	BM 114235+	1.1.4.9	BM 116985	1.1.40.13
BM 89131	1.2.2039	BM 90800+	1.1.35.6	BM 114236	1.1.2.11	BM 116986	1.1.26.6
BM 89851	5.2.1	BM 90801	1.1.2.6	BM 114237	1.1.2.12	BM 117142	1.1.39.14
BM 90000	1.1.12.1	BM 90802	1.1.24.9	BM 114238	1.1.4.10	BM 118456	1.3.8.7
BM 90001	1.1.35.1	BM 90804	1.2.3.3	BM 114239	1.1.2.13	BM 118547	1.1.6
BM 90002	1.1.2.1	BM 90811	1.3.10.4	BM 114240	1.1.4.11	BM 118548	1.1.13.1
BM 90003	1.1.2.2	BM 90813	1.3.15.12	BM 114241	1.1.4.12	BM 118550	1.1.13.2
BM 90004	1.1.4.1	BM 90821+	1.3.15.8	BM 114242	1.1.4.13	BM 118552	1.2.53
BM 90005	1.2.39.1	BM 90826	1.1.37.1	BM 114243	1.1.15.2	BM 118553	1.2.89.1
BM 90006	1.1.33.1	BM 90844	1.4.20.1	BM 114244	1.1.2.14	BM 118555	1.3.19
BM 90007	1.1.33.2	BM 90846	1.1.2.27	BM 114245	1.1.4.14	BM 118556	1.6.1033
BM 90008	1.1.35.2	BM 90897		BM 114246	1.1.2.15	BM 118560	1.2.4.1b
BM 90009	1.1.4.2	(=BM 12025)	1.2.6.1	BM 114247	1.1.15.3	BM 118729	1.2.42.5
BM 90010	1.1.33.3	BM 90900		BM 114248	1.1.4.15	BM 118730	1.2.42.4
BM 90011	1.1.4.3	(=BM 12028)	1.3.15.51	BM 114249	1.1.4.16	BM 119006	1.3.9.3
BM 90012	1.1.4.4	BM 90901		BM 114250	1.1.4.17	BM 119007	1.4.19.1
BM 90013	1.1.35.3	(=BM 12029)	1.3.15.52	BM 114251	1.1.4.18	BM 119008	1.1.16.1
BM 90014	1.1.33.4	BM 90903		BM 114252	1.2.3.4	BM 119009	1.3.8.4
BM 90015	1.1.33.5	(=BM 12031)	1.6.1030	BM 114253	1.1.4.19	BM 119014	1.3.11
BM 90016	1.1.35.4	BM 90904		BM 114254	1.1.2.16	BM 119017	1.1.11.47
BM 90017	1.2.39.2	(=BM 12032)	1.1.2.25	BM 114255	1.2.3.5	BM 119018	1.1.11.52
BM 90018	1.1.35.5	BM 90911	1.1.11.20	BM 114256	1.2.3.6	BM 119019	1.1.11.48
BM 90019	1.1.33.6	BM 91014		BM 114257	1.2.3.7	BM 119020	1.1.11.51
BM 90020	1.1.2.3	(=BM 12156)	1.3.14.1	BM 114258	1.2.3.8	BM 119026	1.1.39.16
BM 90021	1.1.33.7	BM 91017	1.3.14.2	BM 114265	1.3.1.21	BM 119027	1.1.40.3
BM 90023	1.3.1.7	BM 91074	1.2.2033	BM 114266	1.3.1.22	BM 119029	1.1.17.3
BM 90024	1.3.15.1	BM 91075	1.2.2030	BM 114267	1.3.1.23	BM 119040	1.5.1.2
BM 90025	1.3.1.8	BM 91148	1.6.1024	BM 114268	1.3.1.24	BM 119041	1.1.17.2
BM 90026	1.3.15.2	BM 102510	1.5.7	BM 114269	1.3.1.25	BM 119042	1.1.40.4
BM 90027	1.3.15.3	BM 103352	1.1.37.2	BM 114270	1.3.1.26	BM 119054	1.1.39.15
BM 90030	1.3.1.9	BM 103353	1.4.16.1	BM 114272	1.3.1.27	BM 119055	1.1.40.5
BM 90034	1.3.1.10	BM 103354	1.4.17.1	BM 114273	1.3.1.28	BM 119273	1.1.5.2

No.	E3/2.	No.	E3/2.	No.	E3/2.	No.	E3/2
BM 119275	1.1.5.3	BM 134880	1.1.51	BM 137398	1.1.5.4	BM 138346	1.1.19.8
BM 120520	1.3.12	BM 137338	1.3.15.26	BM 137403	1.3.1.37	BM 139969+	1.2.26
BM 122936	1.2.2042	BM 137339	1.3.15.27	BM 137416	1.1.15.4	BM 139969+	1.2.35
BM 122941	1.3.1.31	BM 137344	1.3.1.33	BM 137417	1.1.4.20	BM 139969+	1.2.64
BM 123119	1.1.19.7	BM 137348	1.3.1.34	BM 137418	1.1.5.5	BM 139969+	1.2.2043
BM 124349	1.1.12.2	BM 137357	1.1.2.17	BM 137419	1.3.1.38	BM —	1.3.15.53
BM 124352	1.1.11.116	BM 137358	1.1.24.11	BM 137420	1.3.15.29	BM —	1.3.15.54
BM 124353	1.1.11.117	BM 137359	1.3.1.35	BM 137421	1.3.15.30	BM —	1.3.15.55
BM 124354	1.1.11.118	BM 137382	1.3.1.36	BM 137422	1.3.15.31		
BM 124355	1.1.11.119	BM 137386	1.3.16.4	BM 137423	1.3.1.39		
BM 132804	1.3.1.32	BM 137387	1.3.15.28	BM 137495	1.1.2.18		

Luxemburg, Musées de l'Etat, Musée d'Histoire et d'Art, Cabinet des Médailles

No.	E3/2.
MEL 1924–2	1.4.16.5

Montreal, Redpath Museum, Ethnological Collections

No.	E3/2.
RM 15	1.1.26.16

Moscow, Moscow Archaeological Museum, Nikol'skiy Collection

No.	E3/2.	No.	E3/2.	No.	E3/2.	No.	E3/2.
No. 180	1.5.2013.1	No. 190	1.5.2013.2	No. 380	1.5.2013.3	No. 399	1.5.2012.2

New Haven, Yale University

No.	E3/2.	No.	E3/2.	No.	E3/2.	No.	E3/2.
EAH 26	1.3.14.3	NBC 1934	1.2.96	NCBT 2307	1.4.2004	YBC 2159	1.4.2017
MLC 1822	1.4.32.1	NBC 2519	1.4.18	YBC 528	1.2.2029.1	YBC 2369	1.4.16.4
MLC 1823	2.3.1001	NBC 2521	1.6.1039	YBC 1381	1.2.2029.3	YBC 2376	1.3.15.33
MLC 2075	1.1.33.20	NBC 2524	1.6.1013	YBC 1482	1.2.2029.2	YBC 2382	1.1.24.25
MLC 2314	1.5.2013.4	NBC 2525	1.6.1014	YBC 1500	1.4.2012	YBC 2384	1.1.2.24
MLC 2339	1.4.32.2	NBC 2530	1.3.2009	YBC 1755	1.2.2029.4	YBC 2387	1.2.13.4
MLC 2357	1.2.94	NBC 5613	1.3.2005	YBC 2129	1.4.17.3	YBC 11864	1.2.77
MLC 2629	1.1.34.5b	NBC 6105	1.2.2034	YBC 2130	1.4.17.2	YBC 16435	1.2.10.25
NBC 37A	1.5.2008.2	NBC 6106	1.5.2015	YBC 2156	1.1.44	YBC 16573	1.2.2008
NBC 1316	1.2.2007	NBC 11412	1.3.16.7	YBC 2158	1.2.2044	YBC 16948	1.3.15.34

New York, Collection E.S. David

No.	E3/2.
—	1.3.15.45

New York, Metropolitan Museum of Art, Department of Ancient Near Eastern Art

No.	E3/2.	No.	E3/2.	No.	E3/2.
MMA 41.160.184	1.1.21.3 frgm. 11	MMA 48.180	7.3.1.2	MMA 59.41.87	1.2.20.6a1
MMA 41.160.334	1.2.59	MMA 59.4.1	1.2.20.1b	MMA L 1983 95a-b	1.2.2031
MMA 47.49	1.1.34.8a	MMA 59.41.86	1.1.24.30		

New York, New York Public Library, Rare Books and Manuscripts Division

No.	E3/2.	No.	E3/2.	No.	E3/2.
D-28	1.1.40.19	Eames Collection F-19	1.5.2012.1	Eames Collection P 264B	1.5.8
Draper Collection	1.4.17.4	Eames Collection FF-1	1.2.10.23	Eames Collection S10	1.2.2026

New York, Pierpont Morgan Library Collection

No.	E3/2.	No.	E3/2.	No.	E3/2.	No.	E3/2.
MLC 2310	1.3.2006	MLC 2334	1.3.2007	MLC 2628	1.1.24.35a	MLC 2628	1.1.24.35b

Oxford, Ashmolean Museum

No.	E3/2.	No.	E3/2.	No.	E3/2.
Ash 1922-9	1.2.15	Ash 1935-774	1.1.11.39	Ash 1980-126	1.3.1.50
Ash 1924-625	1.3.1.49	Ash 1967-1504	1.1.24.26	(on loan	
Ash 1925-663	1.1.11.162	Ash 1971-346	1.2.75	to Ashmolean)	1.1.32

Paris, Musée du Louvre, Département des Antiquités Orientales

No.	E3/2.	No.	E3/2.	No.	E3/2.	No.	E3/2.
AO 36 (frgm. 1)	1.2.55	AO 4621	1.5.5	AO 21051a	1.2.10.11	Sb 2883	1.2.30.1
AO 44	1.2.2012	AO 5678	7.2.1	AO 21051b	1.2.10.12	Sb 2884	1.2.30.9
AO 150	2.1.2	AO 9063	1.2.58	AO 21051c	1.2.10.13	Sb 2885	1.2.30.2
AO 191	1.2.2010	AO 11924	1.2.10.6	AO 22187	1.2.50	Sb 2886	1.2.30.10
AO 246	1.4.22	AO 11925	1.2.10.7	AO 22312	1.2.2023	Sb 5634	1.2.49
AO 557	1.2.10.3	AO 11926	1.2.10.8	AO 22316	5.1.2001	Sb 6627	1.2.58
AO 768	1.2.12.2	AO 12210	1.6.1040	AO 22992	1.2.23	Sb 6847	1.2.30.11
AO 840	1.2.12.3	AO 12227	1.2.46	AO 26688	1.1.2.23	Sb 6848	1.2.30.12
AO 841	1.2.12.4	AO 12775	2.1.2	AO 26694	2.1.1	Sb 6849	1.2.30.13
AO 842	1.2.10.4	AO 12776	1.1.28.2	AO 27622	1.5.5	Sb 6850	1.2.30.14
AO 843	1.2.10.5	AO 12777	1.2.14	AO 27907	1.2.11.4a	Sb 6851	1.2.30.15
AO 2418	1.2.86	AO 15302	1.2.12.5	AO 27910	1.2.11.4b	Sb 6852	1.2.30.16
AO 2450	1.4.2002.3	AO 15304	1.1.28.3	AO —	1.3.1.48	Sb 6853	1.2.30.17
AO 3142	1.3.17.6	AO 15305	1.1.28.4	AOD 25	1.6.1042	Sb 6854	1.2.32.11
AO 3143	1.3.17.1	AO 15306	1.1.17.6	AOTc:25	1.4.2002.3	Sb 6855	1.2.32.12
AO 3298	1.4.13.1+2	AO 16650	1.2.2011	AOTc:3	1.4.2002.1	Sb 6856	1.2.32.13
AO 3545	1.2.2013	AO 16651	1.6.1034	MNB 1363	1.2.9.2	Sb 6857	1.2.32.14
AO 3546	1.2.2017	AO 19486	4.2.1	MNB 1371	1.2.9.1	Sb 6858	1.2.32.15
AO 3548	1.2.2018.	AO 19937	7.3.1.1	MNB 1970	1.2.7	Sb 6859	1.2.32.16
AO 3549	1.2.2018.	AO 19938	7.3.1.3	Sb 7	1.1.20.5	Sb 6860	1.2.32.17
AO 3550	1.2.2020.1	AO 210xx	1.2.12.8	Sb 2745	1.2.2036	Sb 11455	1.2.32.3
AO 4164	1.2.2028	AO 21046	1.2.12.6	Sb 2879	1.2.32.1	Sb 11456	1.2.32.4
AO 4194	1.1.28.1	AO 21048c	1.2.12.7	Sb 2880	1.2.32.9	Sb 11457	1.2.32.5
AO 4359	1.2.2037	AO 21049	1.2.10.9	Sb 2881	1.2.32.2	Sb 11458	1.2.32.6
AO 4392	1.2.2047	AO 21050	1.2.10.10	Sb 2882	1.2.32.10	Sb 11459	1.2.32.7

No.	E3/2	No.	E3/2.	No.	E3/2.	No.	E3/2.
Sb 11460	1.2.32.8	Sb 14726	1.2.31.3	Sb 14735	1.4.10.6	Sb 14743	1.4.10.14
Sb 11461	1.2.30.3	Sb 14728	1.2.31.5	Sb 14736	1.4.10.7	Sb 14744	1.4.10.15
Sb 11462	1.2.30.4	Sb 14729	1.2.31.6	Sb 14737	1.4.10.8	Sb 14745	1.4.10.16
Sb 11463	1.2.30.5	Sb 14730	1.4.10.1	Sb 14738	1.4.10.9	Sb—	1.2.31.1
Sb 11464	1.2.30.6	Sb 14731	1.4.10.2	Sb 14739	1.4.10.10	Sb—	1.2.31.2
Sb 11465	1.2.30.7	Sb 14732	1.4.10.3	Sb 14740	1.4.10.11		
Sb 11466	1.2.30.8	Sb 14733	1.4.10.4	Sb 14741	1.4.10.12		
Sb 14272	1.2.31.4	Sb 14734	1.4.10.5	Sb 14742	1.4.10.13		

Philadelphia, Free Library, John Frederick Lewis Collection

No.	E3/2.	No.	E3/2.	No.	E3/2.	No.	E3/2.
FLP 217	1.2.2005.1	FLP 243	1.2.2005.4	FLP 1349	1.2.2003.3	FLP 1380	1.2.2005.8
FLP 218	1.2.2003.1	FLP 250	1.2.2003.2	FLP 1350	1.2.2005.7	FLP 2640	1.2.10.24
FLP 224	1.2.2005.2	FLP 808	1.2.2005.5	FLP 1362	1.2.2003.4	FLP —	1.2.9.5
FLP 242	1.2.2005.3	FLP 1158	1.2.2005.6	FLP 1377	1.2.2003.5		

Philadelphia, University of Pennsylvania, University Museum, Babylonian Section

No.	E3/2.	No.	E3/2.	No.	E3/2.
CBS 841	1.1.36	CBS 14939	1.1.49	CBS 16537a	1.3.1.54
CBS 842	1.2.5	CBS 14940	1.1.54.2	CBS 16537b	1.3.1.55
CBS 2489	1.2.48	CBS 14943	1.1.42	CBS 16538	1.3.15.40
CBS 3593	1.4.2001	CBS 14944	1.2.41	CBS 16564	1.1.14.1
CBS 4928a	1.6.1007.2	CBS 14945	1.6.1036	CBS 16565	1.3.8.5
CBS 4929a	1.6.1007.3	CBS 14946	1.6.1037	CBS 16566	1.4.14
CBS 4935a	1.6.1007.1	CBS 15323	1.1.2.28	CBS 16567	1.1.13.3
CBS 5005	1.1.53	CBS 15327	1.1.4.22	CBS 16568	1.3.8.6
CBS 8105	1.2.93	CBS 15329	1.3.15.36	CBS 16676	1.1.9
CBS 8358	1.6.1006	CBS 15331	1.3.1.52	CBS 16676	1.1.22
CBS 8598	1.2.66	CBS 15334	1.3.15.37	CBS 17225	1.5.1.3
CBS 8638	1.1.24.12	CBS 15338	1.1.2.19	CBS 19704	1.1.11.156
CBS 8647	1.1.24.13	CBS 15339	1.3.1.53	CBS 19928	1.1.21.3 frgm. 5
CBS 8648	1.1.24.14	CBS 15346	1.1.15.5	N 2230+N4006	1.1.52
CBS 8653	1.3.4.1	CBS 15501	1.2.65	N 2230+N4006	1.2.36
CBS 8759	1.6.1004	CBS 15611	1.6.1001	N 2230+N4006	1.2.37
CBS 8838	1.3.5	CBS 15885	1.3.9.1	N 2230+N4006	1.2.81
CBS 9327	1.6.1043	CBS 16209	1.3.18	N 2230+N4006	1.2.84
CBS 9332	1.1.24.36b	CBS 16216	1.2.4.4a	N 2230+N4006	1.2.2049–59
CBS 9540	1.2.2022.3	CBS 16217	1.2.4.2b	N 769	1.4.30
CBS 9557	1.1.21.3 frgm. 1	CBS 16231	1.1.17.4	N 798	1.4.2010
CBS 9558	1.1.21.3 frgm. 10	CBS 16458	1.1.12.3	N 6264	1.4.3.2
CBS 9559	1.1.21.3 frgm. 9	CBS 16459	1.1.15.6	UM 29-15-556+	
CBS 9560	1.1.21.3 frgm. 3	CBS 16461	1.1.4.23	UM 29-16-611+	
CBS 9561	1.1.21.3 frgm. 4	CBS 16462	1.1.5.6	N 3152+N 3180+	
CBS 9563	1.6.1010	CBS 16463	1.2.39.5	N 4240+N 4241+	
CBS 9564	1.1.21.3 frgm. 7	CBS 16464	1.2.3.15	N 5144+N 6718+	
CBS 9592	1.6.1020	CBS 16465	1.3.15.39	Ni 4394	1.4.1.1
CBS 9766	1.4.2005	CBS 16466	1.3.10.5	UM 29-15-556+	
CBS 9908	1.1.21.3 frgm. 8	CBS 16525	1.2.42.1	UM 29-16-611+	
CBS 12694	1.4.6	CBS 16527	1.1.2.20	N 3152+N 3180+	
CBS 13148	1.1.11.157	CBS 16528a	1.1.12.4	N 4240+N 4241+	
CBS 13893	1.1.21.3 frgm. 2	CBS 16528b	1.1.12.5	Ni 4394+N 5144+	
CBS 13898	1.6.1009	CBS 16529	1.1.15.7	N 6435+N 6718	1.4.8.1
CBS 13899	1.1.21.3 frgm. 6	CBS 16530	1.1.4.24	N 6435+N 6718	1.4.9.1
CBS 14177	1.2.2009	CBS 16531a	1.1.5.7	UM 29-15-744	1.5.6
CBS 14193	1.2.2021	CBS 16531b	1.1.5.8	UM 29-16-42	1.4.4
CBS 14549	1.2.21.1	CBS 16532	1.1.5.9	UM 31-43-249	1.1.7
CBS 14550	1.4.16.2	CBS 16533	1.2.39.6	UM 31-43-252	1.4.27
CBS 14934	1.6.1021	CBS 16535a	1.2.3.16	UM 31-43-253	1.1.48
CBS 14935	1.6.1022	CBS 16535b	1.2.3.17	UM 33-35-194	1.1.11.149
CBS 14938	1.1.54.1	CBS 16536a	1.2.3.18	UM 33-35-195	1.1.11.150

No.	E3/2.	No.	E3/2.	No.	E3/2.
UM 35-1-148	1.1.40.18	UM 35-1-397	1.1.5.10	UM 84-26-33	1.2.39.8
UM 35-1-149	1.1.11.151	UM 84-3-1	1.1.11.155	UM 84-26-34	1.2.39.9
UM 35-1-150	1.1.11.152	UM 84-26-2	1.3.1.57	UM 84-26-35	1.1.24.15
UM 35-1-151	1.1.11.153	UM 84-26-3	1.3.1.58	UM 84-26-36	1.1.24.16
UM 35-1-152	1.1.11.154	UM 84-26-4	1.3.1.59	UM 84-26-37	1.1.24.17
UM 35-1-394	1.1.12.6	UM 84-26-5	1.3.1.60	UM 84-26-38	1.1.24.18
UM 35-1-395	1.1.12.7	UM 84-26-6	1.3.15.38	UM —	1.5.2007.2
UM 35-1-396	1.1.12.8	UM 84-26-32	1.2.39.7		

Pittsburgh, Pittsburgh Theological Seminary

No.	E3/2.
03-45	1.3.1.77

Rome, Hechich Collection

No.	E3/2.
—	1.3.15.47

Rome, Museo Barracco

No.	E3/2.
—	1.1.2.21
No. 44	1.2.6.2

St Petersburg, Russia, State Hermitage

No.	E3/2.
MA 9612	1.2.74.2
MA 14933	1.2.82
A vi.3 no.7	6.1.2001

Strasbourg, Bibliothèque Nationale et Universitaire de Strasbourg

No.	E3/2.
146	1.3.1.61

Toronto, Royal Ontario Museum, West Asian Department

No.	E3/2.	No.	E3/2.	No.	E3/2.
ROM 961.162	1.2.21.3	ROM 961.162.1	1.2.19.1b	ROM 961.162.2	1.2.19.1c

Tübingen, Galling Collection

No.	E3/2.
—	1.3.15.42

Turin, Museo di Antichità di Torino

No.	E3/2.
—	1.1.2.22

Urbana, University of Illinois, World Heritage Museum

No.	E3/2.
WHM 26.13.1	1.4.17.8
WHM 619	1.4.2015.1

Vancouver, University of British Columbia, Museum of Anthropology

No.	E3/2.
MOA 4.29	1.3.15.49
MOA 4.30	1.3.15.50

Washington D.C., Smithsonian Institution

No.	E3/2.
SI 344992	1.2.76

Werl, Germany, Missionsmuseum der Franziskaner

No.	E3/2.
105	1.2.2027

Index of Excavation Numbers

Aššur (Qalʿat Širqāt)

No.	E3/2.
Ass 21982	1.3.2001

Babylon

No.	E3/2.
BE 65774	4.5.1

Eridu (Abū Šahrein)

No.	E3/2.
E 733	1.2.26.13

Ešnunna (Tell Asmar)

No.	E3/2.
As 31-188	1.5.2002
As 31-246	1.4.12.1
As 31-615	1.4.32
As 31-630	3.1.1.1
As 31-633	3.1.2002
As 31-670	3.1.1.2
As 31-715	3.1.2001
As 31-736	1.2.28.1
As 31-737	1.2.28.2
As 31-765	1.2.27
As 31-792	1.4.12.2

Girsu (Telloh)

No.	E3/2.
T 31 (?)	1.1.17.6
T 1218	1.6.1034
TG 70	1.2.10.7
TG 697	1.6.1040
TG 1027	1.2.10.6
TG 1382	1.2.46
TG 1459	1.2.2011
TG 2528	1.1.28.2
TG 3886	2.1.2
TG —	1.1.28.1
TG —	1.1.28.3
TG —	1.1.28.4

Isin (Išān Baḥrīyāt)

No.	E3/2.
IB 205	1.3.1.63
IB 206	1.3.1.64
IB 262	1.3.1.65
IB 293	1.3.1.66
IB 294	1.3.1.67
IB 593	1.3.1.68
IB 687	1.3.1.69
IB 689(?)	1.3.1.70
IB 1537	1.1.29
IB —	1.3.1.71
IB — various exs.	1.3.1.72
IB — 17 exs.	1.3.1.73

Larsa (Senkereh)

No.	E3/2.
L 7090	1.1.35.8
L 7425	1.1.35.9
L 7989	1.1.35.7

Mari (Tell Harīrī)

No.	E3/2.
M 1349	4.2.1
M 1400	4.2.2001
M 1572	4.7.1
M 1785	4.1.1.1
M 1786	4.1.1.2
ME 56	4.4.1
ME 68	4.5.2
ME 197	4.7.2.1
ME 213	4.7.2.2
TH.80.142+143	4.5.3.1
TH.80.145	4.2.2
TH.82.1	4.5.3.2

Nippur (Nuffar)

No.	E3/2.
3 N 302	1.6.1041
3 N 407	1.2.21.2
5 N 200	1.1.24.37a
5 N 200	1.1.24.37b
5 N 201	1.1.24.38a
5 N 202	1.1.24.38b
5 N 202	1.2.20.1b
5 N 202	1.2.20.1c
5 N 203	1.2.20.2b
5 N 203	1.2.20.2c
5 N 204	1.2.20.3b
5 N 204	1.2.20.3c
5 N 204	1.2.20.4b
5 N 204	1.2.20.4c
5 N 236	1.2.2025
5 N 251	1.2.19.1b
5 N 251	1.2.19.1c
6 N 250	1.2.20.5b
6 N 250	1.2.20.5c
6 N 250	1.2.20.5d
6 N 300	1.2.20.6b
6 N 300	1.2.20.6c
6 N 300	1.2.20.6d
6 N 351	1.4.7.2
6 N 426	1.6.1015
6 N —	1.1.24.39a
6 N —	1.1.24.39b
9 N 232	1.6.1008
11 N 129	1.4.25
12 N 621	1.5.2016
2 N-T 46	1.1.24.29
2 N-T 487	1.1.24.29a
2 N-T 734b	1.3.1.56
2 N-T 738	1.2.18.1
4 N-T 15	1.6.1032
5 N-T 595	1.2.22.1
5 N-T 678	1.2.21.3
5 N-T 679	1.2.21.4
5 N-T 680	1.2.21.5
5 N-T 681	1.1.24.37c
5 N-T 683	1.2.18.2
5 N-T 683	1.1.24.38c
5 N-T 685	1.2.20.1a
5 N-T 686	1.2.20.2a
5 N-T 687	1.2.20.3a
5 N-T 688	1.2.19.1a
5 N-T 689	1.6.1005
5 N-T 690	1.3.3
6 N-T 630	1.2.2024
6 N-T 631	1.5.2009
6 N-T 688	1.2.22.2
6 N-T 908	1.1.30.3
6 N-T 908	1.1.30.4
6 N-T 908a	1.1.30.1
6 N-T 909	1.1.30.2
6 N-T 1125	1.1.24.30
6 N-T 1126	1.1.24.39d
6 N-T 1127	1.1.24.39c
6 N-T 1128	1.2.20.5a
6 N-T 1129	1.2.20.6a1
6 N-T 1130	1.2.20.6a2
6 N-T 1146	1.2.21.6
6 N-T 1147	1.2.21.7
8 N-T 20	1.1.24.31

Susa

No.	E3/2.	No.	E3/2.	No.	E3/2.
1086	1.4.10.12	7616	1.2.32.8	7629	1.2.32.16
3157	1.4.10.7	7617	1.2.32.1	7630	1.2.32.14
6081	1.4.10.2	7618	1.2.30.3	7631	1.2.32.12
6082	1.4.10.1	7621	1.2.30.1	7632	1.2.32.9
7610	1.2.32.3	7622	1.2.30.6	7633	1.2.32.10
7611	1.2.32.4	7623	1.2.30.7	7636	1.2.30.9
7612	1.2.32.5	7624	1.2.30.2	7638	1.2.30.15
7613	1.2.32.6	7625	1.2.30.8	7639	1.2.30.16
7614	1.2.32.7	7626	1.2.32.13	7640	1.2.30.12
7615	1.2.32.2	7628	1.2.32.17	9846	1.4.10.8

Tell al-Wilāyah

No.	E3/2.
WH 147	1.4.23
WH 148	1.4.23

Ur (Tell al-Muqayyar)

No.	E3/2.	No.	E3/2.	No.	E3/2.	No.	E3/2.
U 2	1.5.1.1	U 297	1.1.11.24	U 1165	1.3.9.1	U 2750	1.1.2.35
U 32(?)	1.1.4.21	U 300	1.1.11.25	U 1190	1.6.1026	U 2756	1.6.1019
U 65(?)	1.1.2.19	U 328	1.1.11.26	U 1191	1.4.15.3	U 2757	1.3.11
U 73	1.3.1.53	U 331	1.1.11.27	U 1357	1.1.2.31	U 2768	1.1.2.36
U 88	1.6.1028	U 345	1.1.11.28	U 1516	1.1.39.12	U 2770	1.2.57
U 111(?)	1.3.15.37	U 404	1.1.50	U 1517	1.1.39.13	U 2771	1.1.2.37
U 169	1.1.39.4	U 422	1.1.2.28	U 1585	1.6.1001	U 2772	1.1.2.38
U 198	1.5.2014	U 423	1.1.2.29	U 1595	1.1.26.2	U 2795	1.1.39.16
U 201	1.1.11.21	U 436	1.1.11.29	U 1596	1.1.26.3	U 2855	1.1.2.39
U 208	1.1.45	U 437	1.1.11.30	U 1597	1.1.26.4	U 2861	1.3.10.5
U 209	1.1.54.1	U 439	1.6.1021	U 1597	1.1.39.14	U 2878a	1.1.15.6
U 219	1.5.1.16	U 520	1.1.39.6	U 1632	1.1.26.5	U 2878b	1.1.15.7
U 220	1.3.7	U 522	1.1.39.7	U 1634	1.1.40.2	U 2880a	1.2.3.16
U 222	1.2.2	U 526	1.1.39.8	U 1649	1.1.26.6	U 2880b	1.2.3.17
U 228	1.1.11.22	U 527	1.1.11.31	U 1727	1.3.8.3	U 2880c	1.2.3.18
U 229	1.1.39.5	U 529	1.1.11.34	U 2437	1.1.11.46	U 2881a	1.2.39.5
U 243a	1.1.11.23	U 530	1.1.11.35	U 2520	1.1.17.2	U 2881b	1.2.39.6
U 246	1.1.49	U 531	1.1.11.36	U 2521	1.1.40.3	U 2891	1.3.15.39
U 247+	1.6.1017	U 533	1.1.11.37	U 2521	1.1.40.4	U 2996	1.2.2048
U 248+	1.2.85	U 551	1.1.11.39	U 2521	1.1.40.5	U 3031	1.3.8.4
U 249+	1.1.54.2	U 615x	1.3.8.7	U 2576	1.5.1.2	U 3031	1.3.8.14
U 250+	1.6.1017	U 652	1.2.2045	U 2577	1.6.1011	U 3032	1.1.2.45
U 252	1.1.42	U 722	1.1.39.9	U 2595	1.1.39.15	U 3037	1.3.8.14
U 254	1.2.89.2	U 747	1.1.11.40	U 2624a	1.1.4.22	U 3059	1.4.20.2
U 255	1.6.1035	U 748	1.1.11.41	U 2624b	1.1.4.23	U 3081	1.1.5.2
U 257+	1.2.85	U 838	1.4.21.2	U 2624c	1.1.4.24	U 3081	1.1.5.3
U 259	1.6.1022	U 872	1.1.26.1	U 2648	1.1.11.47	U 3081a	1.1.5.6
U 260+	1.2.85	U 872	1.1.39.10	U 2648A	1.1.11.48	U 3081b	1.1.5.7
U 267	1.1.46	U 874	1.3.16.8	U 2648B	1.1.11.49	U 3081c	1.1.5.8
U 269	1.2.41	U 901	1.3.8.2	U 2648C	1.1.11.50	U 3081d	1.1.5.9
U 270+	1.1.54.2	U 908	1.3.21	U 2648D	1.1.11.51	U 3102	1.4.15.5
U 274	1.6.1045	U 917	1.1.39.11	U 2648E	1.1.11.52	U 3103	1.1.2.46
U 280	1.2.43	U 918	1.1.40.1	U 2673	1.4.15.2	U 3132	1.1.2.20
U 281	1.6.1029	U 975	1.3.1.33	U 2675	1.1.2.32	U 3133a	1.1.12.3
U 287	1.6.1037	U 1116a	1.1.11.42	U 2701	1.1.17.3	U 3133b	1.1.12.4
U 288	1.6.1036	U 1116b	1.1.11.43	U 2736	1.1.16.1	U 3133c	1.1.12.5
U 295	1.3.8.1	U 1116c	1.1.11.44	U 2749	1.1.2.33	U 3134	1.1.11.53
U 296	1.2.40	U 1116d	1.1.11.45	U 2749a	1.1.2.34	U 3135	1.3.1.34

No.	E3/2.	No.	E3/2.	No.	E3/2.	No.	E3/2.
U 3135a	1.3.1.54	U 6357	1.3.8.11	U 7713s	1.1.11.77	U 13613a	1.1.39.21
U 3135b	1.3.1.55	U 6357	1.3.8.12	U 7713t	1.1.11.78	U 13613b	1.1.39.22
U 3159	1.4.26	U 6357	1.3.8.13	U 7713u	1.1.11.79	U 13661a	1.5.1.6
U 3172	1.1.2.47	U 6357	1.3.8.15	U 7713v	1.1.11.80	U 13661b	1.5.1.7
U 3205	1.6.1025	U 6364	1.1.13.10	U 7717	1.1.11.81	U 15024	1.1.19.6
U 3215	1.1.9	U 6364	1.1.13.7	U 7722	1.1.17.5	U 15026	1.5.1.8
U 3224	1.3.9.2	U 6364	1.1.13.8	U 7724	1.1.26.7	U 16008	1.2.2042
U 3224	1.3.9.3	U 6364	1.1.13.9	U 7737	1.5.2	U 16272	1.4.27
U 3261	1.1.2.48	U 6366	1.1.43	U 7737	1.5.3	U 16528	1.1.7
U 3265	1.1.22	U 6380	1.6.1033	U 7739+	1.1.20.3	U 16530	1.1.47
	frgm. 2	U 6702	1.6.1031	U 7740+	1.1.20.3	U 16533	1.1.48
U 3328	1.1.22	U 6706	1.5.2007.2	U 7746	1.1.19.12	U 16539	1.2.83
	frgm. 1	U 6722	1.4.19.2	U 7771	1.1.40.6	U 16541	1.5.1.9
U 3337	1.4.19.1	U 6722	1.4.19.3	U 7771	1.1.40.7	U 16542	1.5.1.10
U 4871	1.5.2007.1	U 6726	1.3.19	U 7778	1.1.19.2	U 17821	1.1.19.7
U 6019	1.1.17.4	U 6732	1.6.1044	U 7779	1.1.11.82	U 18224	1.6.1027
U 6081	1.1.11.58	U 6736	1.2.2046	U 7799	1.1.41	U 18742	1.5.1.11
U 6157	1.2.4.1b	U 6738	1.4.14	U 7825	1.2.52	U 18769	1.1.11.114
U 6158	1.2.4.1a	U 6744	1.1.16.2	U 7847	1.2.39.10	U 18786	1.1.11.115
U 6300	1.2.4.2b	U 6746	1.2.2002	U 10101	1.1.19.3	U 18807	1.2.2041
U 6301	1.2.4.2a	U 6954	1.2.53	U 10102	1.1.11.98	U 18824	1.5.1.12
U 6302	1.2.4.3b	U 6956	1.6.1027	U 10102	1.1.11.99	U 19482	1.5.1.13
U 6303	1.2.4.3a	U 6967	1.3.18	U 10102	1.1.11.100	U k	1.5.1.17
U 6304	1.2.4.4b	U 6970	1.3.8.17	U 10102	1.1.11.101	U l	1.5.4
U 6305	1.2.4.4a	U 6971	1.3.8.18	U 10102	1.1.11.102	U m	1.6.1023
U 6306	1.2.56	U 6972	1.3.8.19	U 10102	1.1.11.103	U na	1.1.40.13
U 6307	1.1.39.17	U 7024	1.2.87	U 10102	1.1.11.104	U oa	1.1.40.14
U 6334	1.3.8.5	U 7701	1.1.39.18	U 10102	1.1.11.105	U ob	1.1.19.9–11(?)
U 6335	1.4.15.4	U 7701	1.1.39.19	U 10102	1.1.11.106	U pb	1.1.19.9-11 (?)
U 6336	1.1.6	U 7704	1.3.12	U 10135a	1.1.39.20	U pa	1.1.39.23
U 6337a	1.2.42.1	U 7709	1.6.1018	U 10135b	1.1.40.8	U qa	1.1.26.9
U 6337b	1.2.42.2	U 7711	1.5.1.3	U 10613	1.3.8.16	U ra	1.1.26.10
U 6337c	1.2.42.3	U 7713a	1.1.11.59	U 10615	1.2.44	U rb	1.1.11.116
U 6337d	1.2.42.4	U 7713b	1.1.11.60	U 10640	1.6.1002	U sa	1.1.26.11
U 6337e	1.2.42.5	U 7713c	1.1.11.61	U 11630	1.6.1003	U sb	1.1.11.117
U 6343A	1.5.2007.3	U 7713d	1.1.11.62	U 11659	1.5.1.4	U tb	1.1.11.118
U 6343B	1.5.2007.4	U 7713d	1.1.11.63	U 11672	1.5.1.5	U ub	1.1.11.119
U 6353	1.1.13.1	U 7713e	1.1.11.64	U 11673a	1.1.19.4	U—	1.1.39.24
U 6353	1.1.13.2	U 7713f	1.1.11.65	U 11673b	1.1.19.5	U—	1.1.39.25
U 6353	1.1.13.3	U 7713h	1.1.11.66	U 13001	1.1.40.9	U—	1.1.39.26
U 6353	1.1.13.4	U 7713i	1.1.11.67	U 13602	1.1.40.10	U—	1.1.39.27
U 6353	1.1.13.5	U 7713j	1.1.11.68	U 13603a	1.1.40.11	U—	1.1.2.A
U 6353	1.1.13.6	U 7713k	1.1.11.69	U 13603b	1.1.40.12	U—	1.1.2.B
U 6354	1.1.14.1	U 7713l	1.1.11.70	U 13604a	1.1.11.107	U—	1.1.2.C
U 6354	1.1.14.3	U 7713m	1.1.11.71	U 13604b	1.1.11.108	U—	1.1.2.D
U 6355	1.2.89.1	U 7713n	1.1.11.72	U 13604c	1.1.11.109	U—	1.1.2.E
U 6357	1.3.8.6	U 7713o	1.1.11.73	U 13604d	1.1.11.110	U—	1.1.2.F
U 6357	1.3.8.8	U 7713p	1.1.11.74	U 13604e	1.1.11.111		
U 6357	1.3.8.9	U 7713q	1.1.11.75	U 13604f	1.1.11.112		
U 6357	1.3.8.10	U 7713r	1.1.11.76	U 13604g	1.1.11.113		

Uruk (Warka)

No.	E3/2.	No.	E3/2.	No.	E3/2.
W 433	1.3.13.1	W 6434	1.1.39.29	W 17922a	1.1.34.3a
W 877	1.3.13.2	W 12117	1.1.24.32	W 17922b	1.1.34.3b
W 1162	1.1.33.9	W 13201	1.1.26.15	W 17945a	1.2.6.4a
W 1253a	1.3.13.3	W 13936a	1.1.34.1a	W 17945b	1.2.6.4b
W 1253c	1.3.13.4	W 13936b	1.1.34.1b	W—	1.1.34.4
W 1830	1.1.33.14	W 16172	1.4.29	W—	1.3.13.10
W 3210	1.3.13.5	W 16183	1.4.28	W—	1.3.13.8
W 3772	1.1.35.10	W 16956	1.1.34.2b	W—	1.3.13.9
W 4268	1.3.13.6	W 17303	1.2.6.3a	W—	1.3.16.6
W 4557	1.3.13.7	W 17304	1.2.6.3b		
W 5766	1.2.10.2	W 17715	1.3.16.5		

Concordances of Selected Publications

Barton, RISA

P.	No.	E3/2.
152–53	Kallamu 1	1.2.2009
166–67	Dur-ili (Der) 1	1.2.63
168–69	Kisari	5.1.2001
266–67	Lukani 2	1.2.2013
	Lukani 3	1.2.2014
	Ur-Lama 1	1.2.2018
268–69	Arad-nannar	1.4.13
	Alla 1	1.2.2019
270 ff.	Ur-Nammu 1	1.1.2
	Ur-Nammu 2	1.1.4
	Ur-Nammu 3	1.1.12
	Ur-Nammu 4	1.1.33
	Ur-Nammu 5	1.1.35
	Ur-Nammu 6	1.1.5
	Ur-Nammu 7	1.1.24
	Ur-Nammu 8	1.1.11
	Ur-Nammu 9	1.1.28
	Ur-Nammu 11	1.1.37
	Ur-Nammu 12	1.1.2
	Ur-Nammu 14	1.1.16
	Ur-Nammu 15	1.1.36
	Ur-Nammu 16	1.1.24
	Ur-Nammu 17	1.1.44
	Ur-Nammu 18	1.1.2001
274 ff.	Shulgi 1	1.2.39
	Shulgi 2	1.2.3
	Shulgi 3	1.2.31
	Shulgi 4	1.2.12
	Shulgi 5	1.2.13
	Shulgi 6	1.2.21
	Shulgi 7	1.2.24
	Shulgi 8	1.2.23
	Shulgi 9	1.2.9
	Shulgi 10	1.2.11
	Shulgi 11	1.2.5
	Shulgi 12	1.2.17
	Shulgi 13	1.2.1
	Shulgi 14	1.2.6
	Shulgi 15	1.2.29
	Shulgi 16	1.2.32
	Shulgi 17	1.2.2033
	Shulgi 18	1.2.66
	Shulgi 19	1.2.50
	Shulgi 20	1.6.1024
	Shulgi 22	1.2.2010
	Shulgi 23	1.2.2044
	Shulgi 24	1.2.2012
	Shulgi 25	1.2.2030
	Shulgi 26	1.2.58
	Shulgi 27	1.2.61
	Shulgi 28	1.2.2035
	Shulgi 29	1.2.2036
	Shulgi 30	1.2.2039
	Shulgi 31	1.2.2023
	Shulgi 34	1.2.2028
	Shulgi 36	1.2.2037
	Shulgi 37	1.2.2036
	Shulgi 38	1.2.2020
286 ff.	Bur-Sin 1	1.3.4
	Bur-Sin 2	1.3.1
	Bur-Sin 3	1.3.10
	Bur-Sin 4	1.3.15
	Bur-Sin 5	1.3.16
	Bur-Sin 6	1.3.17
	Bur-Sin 7	1.3.5
	Bur-Sin 8	1.3.6
	Bur-Sin 9	1.3.9
	Bur-Sin 10	1.3.14
	Bur-Sin 11	1.3.17
	Bur-Sin 13	1.3.22
292 ff.	Gimil-Sin 1	1.4.10
	Gimil-Sin 2	1.4.20
	Gimil-Sin 3	1.4.16
	Gimil-Sin 4	1.4.15
	Gimil-Sin 5	1.4.17
	Gimil-Sin 6	1.4.18
	Gimil-Sin 7	1.4.17
	Gimil-Sin 8	1.4.22
	Gimil-Sin 9	1.4.2002
	Gimil-Sin 13	1.4.2012
300–301	Âkalla	1.4.2012
	Ur-Negun 1	1.2.2029
302–303	Lishalu	1.2.2021
	Khunini	6.1.2001
360 ff.	Ur-Nammu 1	1.1.6
	Ur-Nammu 2	1.1.43
	Ur-Nammu 3	1.1.13
	Ur-Nammu 4	1.1.16
	Ur-Nammu 5	1.1.14
	Ur-Nammu 6	1.1.15
	Ur-Nammu 9	1.1.40
	Ur-Nammu 10 (a)	1.1.9
	Ur-Nammu 10 (b)	1.1.22
	Ur-Nammu 11	1.1.39
	Ur-Nammu 12	1.1.26
	Ur-Nammu 13	1.1.23
	Ur-Nammu 14	1.1.54
	Ur-Nammu 15	1.1.17
364 ff.	Shulgi 1	1.2.89.1
	Shulgi 2	1.2.89.2
	Shulgi 3	1.2.56
	Shulgi 4	1.2.57
	Shulgi 5	1.2.2046
	Shulgi 6	1.2.53
	Shulgi 8	1.2.85
	Shulgi 9	1.2.9
	Shulgi 10	1.2.2
	Shulgi 11	1.2.4
366–67	Bur-sin 1	1.3.8
366 ff.	Gimil-Sin 1	1.4.19
	Gimil-Sin 3	1.4.21
	Gimil-Sin 4	1.4.14
368 ff.	Ibi-Sin 1	1.5.1
	Ibi-Sin 3	1.5.2007

Braun-Holzinger, Weihgaben

P.	No.	E3/2.
59 ff.	K 78	1.1.45
	K 79	1.1.46
	K 80	1.2.2033
	K 81	1.2.2034
	K 82	1.2.61
	K 83	1.2.2036
	K 84	1.2.2035
	K 85	1.4.27
	K 86	1.5.2014
	K 87	1.6.1017
	K 88	1.6.1038
	K 90	1.6.1018
90	MW 12	1.2.49
	MW 13	1.2.48
	MW 14	1.4.2018
167	G 243	1.6.1021
	G 244	1.6.1022
	G 321	1.6.1034
	G 322	1.6.1040
183 ff.	G 336	1.1.41
	G 337	1.1.43
	G 338	1.1.44
	G 339	1.1.54
	G 340	1.1.48
	G 341	1.1.49
	G 342	1.1.42
	G 343	1.2.46
	G 344	1.2.2004
	G 345	1.2.2010
	G 346	1.2.2001
	G 347	1.2.2044
	G 348	1.2.2046
	G 349	1.2.40
	G 350	1.2.83
	G 351	1.2.43
	G 352	1.6.1029
	G 353	1.2.44
	G 354	1.2.2042
	G 355	1.2.2045
	G 356	1.2.2041
	G 357	1.2.85
	G 358	1.2.89
	G 359	1.2.89
	G 360	1.2.2047
	G 361	1.2.41
	G 362	1.3.18
	G 363	1.3.21
	G 364	1.4.2017
	G 365	1.4.2016 frgm. 1
	G 366	1.4.2016 frgm. 2
	G 367	1.4.24
	G 368	1.4.25
	G 369	1.5.2016
	G 371	1.6.1027 frgm. 1
	G 372	1.6.1033
	G 373	1.3.19
	G 374	1.6.1019
	G 375	1.6.1035
	G 379	1.6.1028
	G 380	1.6.1045
	G 381	1.6.1027 frgm. 2
	G 382	1.6.1030
	G 384	1.6.1036
	G 385	1.6.1037
	G 386	1.6.1039
	G 388	1.6.1031
197	G 410	1.2.2001
	G 411	1.6.1020
	G 412	1.6.1032
217–18	Ständer 8	1.1.54
	Ständer 9	1.1.47
272–73	St 147	1.2.55
	St 150	1.2.56
	St 151	1.2.57
	St 152	1.2.2031
	St 153	1.2.2012
	St 154	1.2.55
	St 155	1.4.26
	St 156	1.4.7
	St 157	1.5.2005
	St 158	1.2.2032
	St 161	1.6.1015
276–78	St 166	4.2.1
	St 168	4.5.1
316–17	W 31	1.3.2001
340	Stele 25	1.1.9/1.1.22
340–41	Stelen 26–28	1.3.8
356	S 6	1.2.2039
	S 7	1.2.2037
	S 8	1.2.2023
357	S 9	1.2.2038
366-67	P 7	1.1.50
	P 9	1.2.66
	P 10	1.2.72
	P 11	1.2.58
	P 13	1.2.60
	P 14	1.2.88
	P 15	1.3.2009
	P 17	1.4.28/1.4.29

Calmeyer, Datierbare Bronzen

P.	No.	E3/2.
38	§ 18a	1.2.49

Gelb, MAD 2[2]

P.	No.	E3/2.	P.	No.	E3/2.
16	No. 1a	1.2.23	16	No. 1b	4.2.1
	No. 1a	1.2.27		No. 1b	4.3.1
	No. 1a	1.2.65		No. 1b	4.5.1
	No. 1a	1.3.2001		No. 1d	5.1.2001
	No. 1a	1.4.10		No. 1e	7.2.1
	No. 1b	4.1.1		No. 1f	7.3.1

Gelb and Kienast, Königsinschriften

P.	No.	E3/2.	P.	No.	E3/2.
Die Akkadischen Inschriften der Könige von Ur III				no. 7	4.7.2
339 ff.	Ur 1	1.2.27		no. 9	4.2.2001
	Ur 2	1.2.23		no. 12	4.5.3
	Ur 3	1.2.29		no. 14	4.2.2
	Ur 4	1.2.65	359 ff.	MŠ 1	4.7.1
	Ur 5	1.2.33		MŠ 2	4.1.1
	Ur 6	1.3.2001		MŠ 3	4.2.1
	Ur 7	1.4.10		MŠ 4	4.3.1
	Ur C 1	1.2.38		MŠ 9	4.5.1
	Ur C 2	1.4.5		MŠ 10	4.5.1
				MŠ C 2	4.6.1
Die Inschriften der Šakkanakkum-Periode aus Mari			382 ff.	Varia 15	7.3.1
355 ff.	no. 2	4.4.1		Varia 16	7.2.1
	no. 5	4.5.2	386	no. 4	5.2.1

Grayson, RIMA 1

P.	No.	E3/2.
9	Zarriqum	1.3.2001

Hallo, HUCA 33

P.	No.	E3/2.	P.	No.	E3/2.
24 ff.	Ur-Nammu 1	1.1.2		Ur-Nammu 25	1.1.11
	Ur-Nammu 2	1.1.6		Ur-Nammu 26	1.1.17
	Ur-Nammu 3	1.1.24		Ur-Nammu 27	1.1.19
	Ur-Nammu 4	1.1.10		Ur-Nammu 28	1.1.28
	Ur-Nammu 5	1.1.5		Ur-Nammu 29	1.1.22/1.1.9
	Ur-Nammu 6	1.1.15		Ur-Nammu 30	1.1.41
	Ur-Nammu 7	1.1.33		Ur-Nammu 31	1.1.43
	Ur-Nammu 9	1.1.4		Ur-Nammu 32	1.1.44
	Ur-Nammu 10	1.1.12		Ur-Nammu 33	1.1.45
	Ur-Nammu 11	1.1.35		Ur-Nammu 34	1.1.46
	Ur-Nammu 12	1.1.31		Ur-Nammu 35	1.1.54
	Ur-Nammu 13	1.1.34		Ur-Nammu 36	1.1.2001
	Ur-Nammu 14	1.1.36	28 ff.	Šulgi 1i, iv	1.2.39
	Ur-Nammu 15	1.1.23		Šulgi 1v	1.2.49
	Ur-Nammu 16	1.1.25		Šulgi 1ii	1.2.42
	Ur-Nammu 17	1.1.16		Šulgi 1iii	1.2.45
	Ur-Nammu 18	1.1.14		Šulgi 3	1.2.27
	Ur-Nammu 19	1.1.13		Šulgi 4i	1.2.23
	Ur-Nammu 21	1.1.37		Šulgi 4ii	1.2.24
	Ur-Nammu 22	1.1.39		Šulgi 5	1.2.3
	Ur-Nammu 23	1.1.26		Šulgi 6	1.2.31
	Ur-Nammu 24	1.1.40		Šulgi 7	1.2.28

P.	No.	E3/2.	P.	No.	E3/2.
	Šulgi 8	1.2.16		Amar-Sin 13	1.3.8
	Šulgi 9	1.2.17		Amar-Sin 14	1.3.13
	Šulgi 10	1.2.1		Amar-Sin 15	1.3.2001
	Šulgi 11	1.2.6		Amar-Sin 16	1.3.2008
	Šulgi 12	1.2.32		Amar-Sin 17	1.3.2009
	Šulgi 13i–iv	1.2.9		Amar-Sin 18ii	1.3.2006
	Šulgi 14	1.2.29		Amar-Sin 18i	1.3.2007
	Šulgi 15	1.2.11	37 ff.	Šu-Sin 1	1.4.10
	Šulgi 16	1.2.2		Šu-Sin 2	1.4.10
	Šulgi 17	1.2.5		Šu-Sin 3	1.4.11
	Šulgi 18	1.2.4		Šu-Sin 4	1.4.18
	Šulgi 19	1.2.34		Šu-Sin 5	1.4.19
	Šulgi 20	1.2.21		Šu-Sin 6	1.4.20
	Šulgi 21	1.2.13		Šu-Sin 7	1.4.21
	Šulgi 22	1.2.10		Šu-Sin 8	1.4.16
	Šulgi 23	1.2.12		Šu-Sin 9	1.4.17
	Šulgi 24	1.2.14		Šu-Sin 10	1.4.14
	Šulgi 25	1.2.56		Šu-Sin 11	1.4.15
	Šulgi 26	1.2.2031		Šu-Sin 12	1.4.12
	Šulgi 27	1.2.57		Šu-Sin 13	1.4.13
	Šulgi 28	1.2.2012		Šu-Sin 14	1.4.26
	Šulgi 29	1.2.2030		Šu-Sin 15	1.4.2017
	Šulgi 30	1.2.46		Šu-Sin 16	1.4.2018
	Šulgi 31	1.2.2004		Šu-Sin 17	1.4.22
	Šulgi 32	1.2.2010		Šu-Sin 18i	1.4.2012
	Šulgi 33	1.2.2001		Šu-Sin 18iii	1.4.2001
	Šulgi 34	1.2.2044		Šu-Sin 19ii	1.4.32
	Šulgi 35	1.2.2046		Šu-Sin 20i	1.4.3/1.4.5/1.4.7
	Šulgi 36	1.2.65		Šu-Sin 20ii	1.4.1/1.4.8
	Šulgi 37	1.2.2033	39 ff.	Ibbi-Sin 1	1.5.1
	Šulgi 38	1.2.2034		Ibbi-Sin 2	1.5.1
	Šulgi 39	1.2.61		Ibbi-Sin 3	1.5.2005
	Šulgi 40	1.2.2036		Ibbi-Sin 4	1.5.2014
	Šulgi 41	1.2.66		Ibbi-Sin 5	1.5.2015
	Šulgi 42	1.2.72		Ibbi-Sin 6	1.5.5
	Šulgi 43	1.2.58		Ibbi-Sin 7i	1.5.2007
	Šulgi 44	1.2.59		Ibbi-Sin 7ii	1.5.2012
	Šulgi 45	1.2.60		Ibbi-Sin 7iii	1.5.2006
	Šulgi 46	1.2.88		Ibbi-Sin 7iv	1.5.2013
	Šulgi 47	1.2.2039		Ibbi-Sin 9	1.5.2
	Šulgi 48	1.2.2037		Ibbi-Sin 10	1.5.3
	Šulgi 49	1.2.2023	41 ff.	Anonymous 1	1.6.1001
	Šulgi 51i	1.2.50		Anonymous 2	1.3.18
	Šulgi 51ii	1.2.51		Anonymous 3	1.2.2001
	Šulgi 51iii	1.2.52		Anonymous 4	1.6.1039
	Šulgi 52	1.2.53		Anonymous 5	1.6.1027
	Šulgi 53i	1.2.2008		Anonymous 6	1.6.1033
	Šulgi 53ii	1.2.2020		Anonymous 7	1.6.1034
	Šulgi 53iv	1.2.2021		Anonymous 8	1.6.1040
	Šulgi 53v	1.2.2028		Anonymous 9	1.2.2035
	Šulgi 53vi	1.2.2029		Anonymous 10	1.6.1017
	Šulgi 54	1.2.38		Anonymous 11i	1.6.1024
34 ff.	Amar-Sin 1	1.3.4		Anonymous 11ii	1.6.1025
	Amar-Sin 2	1.3.1		Anonymous 12	1.6.1026
	Amar-Sin 3	1.3.10		Anonymous 13	1.6.1044
	Amar-Sin 4	1.3.12		Anonymous 14	1.3.2005/1.6.1046
	Amar-Sin 5	1.3.15	42 ff.	Family 1	1.2.85
	Amar-Sin 6	1.3.16		Family 2	1.2.89
	Amar-Sin 7	1.3.14		Family 3	1.2.87
	Amar-Sin 8	1.3.17		Family 4	1.3.19
	Amar-Sin 9	1.3.5		Family 5	1.2.94
	Amar-Sin 10	1.3.6		Family 6	1.3.22
	Amar-Sin 11	1.3.16		Family 7	1.4.29
	Amar-Sin 12	1.3.9		Family 8	1.4.28

Kärki, KDDU

P.	No.	E3/2.
1 ff.	Urnammu 1	1.1.2
	Urnammu 2	1.1.6
	Urnammu 3	1.1.24
	Urnammu 4	1.1.10
	Urnammu 5	1.1.5
	Urnammu 6	1.1.15
	Urnammu 7	1.1.33
	Urnammu 9	1.1.4
	Urnammu 10	1.1.12
	Urnammu 11	1.1.35
	Urnammu 12	1.1.31
	Urnammu 13	1.1.34
	Urnammu 14	1.1.36
	Urnammu 15	1.1.23
	Urnammu 16	1.1.25
	Urnammu 17	1.1.16
	Urnammu 18	1.1.14
	Urnammu 19	1.1.13
	Urnammu 21	1.1.37
	Urnammu 22	1.1.39
	Urnammu 23	1.1.26
	Urnammu 24	1.1.40
	Urnammu 25	1.1.11
	Urnammu 26	1.1.17
	Urnammu 27	1.1.19
	Urnammu 28	1.1.28
	Urnammu 29	1.1.9/1.1.22
	Urnammu 30	1.1.41
	Urnammu 31	1.1.43
	Urnammu 32	1.1.44
	Urnammu 33	1.1.45
	Urnammu 34	1.1.46
	Urnammu 35	1.1.54
	Urnammu 36a	1.1.2001
	Urnammu 36b	1.1.51
	Urnammu 38	1.1.52
	Urnammu 39	1.1.7
	Urnammu 40	1.1.48
	Urnammu 41	1.1.47
	Urnammu 42	1.1.38
	Urnammu 43	1.1.50
	Urnammu 44	1.1.32
27 ff.	Šulgi 1a	1.2.40
	Šulgi 1b	1.2.39/1.2.45/1.2.49
	Šulgi 1c	1.2.42/1.2.47
	Šulgi 3	1.2.27
	Šulgi 4a	1.2.23
	Šulgi 4b	1.2.24
	Šulgi 5	1.2.3
	Šulgi 6	1.2.31
	Šulgi 7	1.2.28
	Šulgi 8	1.2.16
	Šulgi 9	1.2.17
	Šulgi 10	1.2.1
	Šulgi 11	1.2.6
	Šulgi 12	1.2.32
	Šulgi 13	1.2.9
	Šulgi 14	1.2.29
	Šulgi 15	1.2.11
	Šulgi 16	1.2.2
	Šulgi 17	1.2.5
	Šulgi 18	1.2.4
	Šulgi 19	1.2.34
	Šulgi 20	1.2.21
	Šulgi 21	1.2.13
	Šulgi 22	1.2.10
	Šulgi 23	1.2.12
	Šulgi 24	1.2.14
	Šulgi 25	1.2.56
	Šulgi 26	1.2.2031
	Šulgi 27	1.2.57
	Šulgi 28	1.2.2012
	Šulgi 29	1.2.2030
	Šulgi 30	1.2.46
	Šulgi 31	1.2.2004
	Šulgi 32	1.2.2010
	Šulgi 33	1.2.2001
	Šulgi 34	1.2.2044
	Šulgi 35	1.2.2046
	Šulgi 36	1.2.65
46 ff.	Šulgi 37	1.2.2033
	Šulgi 38	1.2.2034
	Šulgi 39	1.2.61
	Šulgi 40	1.2.2036
	Šulgi 41	1.2.66
	Šulgi 42	1.2.72
	Šulgi 43	1.2.58
	Šulgi 44	1.2.59
	Šulgi 45	1.2.60
	Šulgi 46	1.2.88
	Šulgi 47	1.2.2039
	Šulgi 48	1.2.2037
	Šulgi 49	1.2.2023
	Šulgi 51i	1.2.50
	Šulgi 51ii	1.2.51
	Šulgi 51iii	1.2.52
	Šulgi 51iv	1.6.1023
	Šulgi 52	1.2.53
	Šulgi 53a (i)	1.2.2008
	Šulgi 53a (ii)	1.2.2020
	Šulgi 53a (iv)	1.2.2021
	Šulgi 53a (v)	1.2.2028
	Šulgi 53a (vi)	1.2.2029
	Šulgi 53b	1.2.67
	Šulgi 53c	1.2.69
	Šulgi 53d	1.2.74
	Šulgi 53e	1.2.87
	Šulgi 54	1.2.38
	Šulgi 55	1.2.94
	Šulgi 56a	1.6.1046
	Šulgi 56b	1.2.75
	Šulgi 57	1.6.1024/1.6.1025
	Šulgi 58	1.6.1026
	Šulgi 59	1.6.1030
	Šulgi 60	1.6.1038
	Šulgi 61	1.2.85
	Šulgi 62	1.2.89
	Šulgi 63	1.3.19
	Šulgi 64	1.2.83
	Šulgi 65	1.2.43
	Šulgi 66	1.6.1029
	Šulgi 67	1.2.44
	Šulgi 68	1.2.2042
	Šulgi 69	1.2.2045
	Šulgi 70	1.2.2041
	Šulgi 71	1.2.33
	Šulgi 72	1.2.30
	Šulgi 73	1.2.62
	Šulgi 74	1.2.2038
	Šulgi 75	1.2.2040
70 ff.	Amarsuena 1	1.3.4
	Amarsuena 2	1.3.1
	Amarsuena 3	1.3.10
	Amarsuena 4	1.3.12
	Amarsuena 5	1.3.15
	Amarsuena 7	1.3.14
	Amarsuena 8	1.3.17
	Amarsuena 9	1.3.5

P.	No.	E3/2.
	Amarsuena 10	1.3.6
	Amarsuena 11	1.3.16
	Amarsuena 12	1.3.9
	Amarsuena 13	1.3.8
	Amarsuena 14	1.3.13
	Amarsuena 15	1.3.2001
	Amarsuena 16	1.3.2008
	Amarsuena 17	1.3.2009
	Amarsuena 18 (i)	1.3.2007
	Amarsuena 18 (ii)	1.3.2006
	Amarsuena 19	1.3.22
90 ff.	Šusuen 1	1.4.23
	Šusuen 2	1.4.10
	Šusuen 3	1.4.11
	Šusuen 4	1.4.18
	Šusuen 5	1.4.19
	Šusuen 6	1.4.20
	Šusuen 7	1.4.21
	Šusuen 8	1.4.16
	Šusuen 9	1.4.17
	Šusuen 10	1.4.14
	Šusuen 11	1.4.15
	Šusuen 12	1.4.12
	Šusuen 13	1.4.13
	Šusuen 14	1.4.26
	Šusuen 15	1.4.2017
	Šusuen 16	1.4.2018
	Šusuen 17	1.4.22
	Šusuen 18 (i)	1.4.2012
	Šusuen 18 (iii)	1.4.2001
	Šusuen 18 (iv)	1.4.2006
	Šusuen 18 (v)	1.4.2002
	Šusuen 19 (ii)	1.4.32
	Šusuen 20a 1–2	1.4.3
	Šusuen 20a 3–5	1.4.5
	Šusuen 20b	1.4.1/1.4.2/1.4.8/1.4.9
	Šusuen 21	1.4.6
	Šusuen 22	1.4.29
	Šusuen 23	1.4.28
	Šusuen 24	1.4.27
	Šusuen 25	1.4.24
	Šusuen 26	1.4.2016
	Šusuen 27	1.4.4

P.	No.	E3/2.
136 ff.	Ibbisuen 1–2	1.5.1
	Ibbisuen 3	1.5.2005
	Ibbisuen 4	1.5.2014
	Ibbisuen 5	1.5.2015
	Ibbisuen 6	1.5.5
	Ibbisuen 7a (i)	1.5.2007
	Ibbisuen 7a (ii)	1.5.2006
	Ibbisuen 7a (iii)	1.5.2013
	Ibbisuen 7a (x)	1.5.2002
	Ibbisuen 7a (xiii)	1.6.1044
	Ibbisuen 8 (vii)	1.5.2003
	Ibbisuen 9	1.5.2
	Ibbisuen 10	1.5.3
	Ibbisuen 12	1.5.4
	Ibbisuen 13	1.5.2004
150 ff.	Anonym 1	1.6.1001
	Anonym 2	1.3.18
	Anonym 3	1.2.2001
	Anonym 4	1.6.1039
	Anonym 5	1.6.1027
	Anonym 6	1.6.1033
	Anonym 7	1.6.1034
	Anonym 8	1.6.1040
	Anonym 9	1.2.2035
	Anonym 10	1.6.1017
	Anonym 11	1.6.1025
	Anonym 12	1.6.1026
	Anonym 13	1.6.1044
	Anonym 14	1.6.1046
	Anonym 15	1.6.1035
	Anonym 16	1.6.1002
	Anonym 17	1.3.7
	Anonym 18	1.3.21
	Anonym 19	1.6.1003
	Anonym 20	1.6.1028
	Anonym 21	1.2.3
158 ff.	Familie 1	1.2.85
	Familie 2	1.2.89
	Familie 3	1.2.87
	Familie 4	1.3.19
	Familie 5	1.2.94
	Familie 6	1.3.22
	Familie 7	1.4.29
	Familie 8	1.4.28

Sollberger and Kupper, IRSA

P.	No.	E3/2.
128	IIH1a	7.2.1
129	IIJ3a	1.1.53
135 ff.	IIIA1b	1.1.2
	IIIA1c	1.1.4
	IIIA1d	1.1.12
	IIIA1c	1.1.40
	IIIA1f	1.1.17
	IIIA1g	1.1.28
	IIIA1h	1.1.19
	IIIA1i	1.1.13
	IIIA1j	1.1.5
	IIIA1k	1.1.47
139 ff.	IIIA1l	1.1.54
	IIIA1m	1.1.2001
	IIIA1n	1.1.51
	IIIA2a	1.2.40
	IIIA2b	1.2.39/1.2.45/1.2.49
	IIIA2c	1.2.47

P.	No.	E3/2.
	IIIA2d	1.2.50
	IIIA2e	1.6.1024
	IIIA2f	1.2.88
	IIIA2g	1.2.21
	IIIA2h	1.2.29
	IIIA2i	1.2.11
	IIIA2j	1.2.28
	IIIA2k	1.2.27
	IIIA2l	1.2.24
	IIIA2m	1.2.23
	IIIA2n	1.2.31
	IIIA2o	1.2.34
	IIIA2p	1.2.33
	IIIA2q	1.2.89
	IIIA2r	1.2.85
	IIIA2s	1.2.66
	IIIA2t	1.2.72
	IIIA2u	1.2.2030

P.	No.	E3/2.	P.	No.	E3/2.
	IIIA2v	1.2.2023	156 ff.	IIIA5a	1.5.1
	IIIA2w	1.2.2039		IIIA5b	1.5.2
146 ff.	IIIA2x	1.2.94		IIIA5c	1.5.3
	IIIA2y	1.2.2008		IIIA5d	1.5.4
	IIIA2z	1.2.69		IIIA5e	1.5.5
	IIIA3a	1.3.4		IIIA5f	1.5.2005
	IIIA3b	1.3.1		IIIA5i	1.5.2013
	IIIA3c	1.3.9	162 ff.	IIIB4a	1.2.2010
	IIIA3d	1.3.16/1.3.17		IIIB4b	1.2.2011
	IIIA3e	1.3.10		IIIB4c	1.2.2012
	IIIA3e n. 1	1.3.11		IIIB5a	1.4.13
	IIIA3f	1.3.6		IIIB5b	1.4.2002
	IIIA3g	1.3.13		IIIB5c	1.5.2003
	IIIA3h	1.3.15		IIIB5d	1.5.2004
	IIIA3i	1.3.2008		IIIC1a	1.2.2004
151 ff.	IIIA3j	1.3.22		IIIC1b	1.4.11
	IIIA4a	1.4.10		IIID1a	1.4.12
	IIIA4b	1.4.21		IIID1b	1.5.2002
	IIIA4c	1.4.20		IIID2a	3.1.1
	IIIA4d	1.4.17		IIID2b	3.1.2002
	IIIA4e	1.4.3		IIIE1a	1.1.52
	IIIA4f	1.4.3		IIIE1b	4.1.1
	IIIA4g	1.4.6		IIIE2a	4.2.1
	IIIA4h	1.4.15		IIIE2b	4.2.2001
	IIIA4i	1.4.22		IIIE5a	4.3.1
	IIIA4j	1.4.32		IIIF1a	1.3.2001
	IIIA4m	1.4.28		IIIH1a	5.1.2001
	IIIA4n	1.4.29	242	IVF2a	4.4.1

Steible, NSBW 2

P.	No.	E3/2.	P.	No.	E3/2.
93ff.	Urnammu 1	1.1.2		Urnammu 36	1.1.2001
	Urnammu 2	1.1.6		Urnammu 38	1.1.7
	Urnammu 3	1.1.24		Urnammu 39	1.1.48
	Urnammu 4	1.1.10		Urnammu 40	1.1.47
	Urnammu 5	1.1.5		Urnammu 41	1.1.51
	Urnammu 6	1.1.15		Urnammu 42	1.1.49
	Urnammu 7	1.1.33		Urnammu 43	1.1.50
	Urnammu 9	1.1.4		Urnammu 44	1.1.42
	Urnammu 10	1.1.12		Urnammu 45	1.1.38
	Urnammu 11	1.1.35		Urnammu 46	1.1.32
	Urnammu 12	1.1.31		Urnammu 47	1.1.18
	Urnammu 13	1.1.34	153 ff.	Šulgi 1a	1.2.39/1.2.45/1.2.49
	Urnammu 14	1.1.36		Šulgi 1b	1.2.42/1.2.47
	Urnammu 15	1.1.23		Šulgi 3	1.2.27
	Urnammu 16	1.1.25		Šulgi 4a	1.2.23
	Urnammu 17	1.1.16		Šulgi 4b	1.2.24
	Urnammu 18	1.1.14		Šulgi 5	1.2.3
	Urnammu 19	1.1.13		Šulgi 6	1.2.31
	Urnammu 21	1.1.37		Šulgi 7	1.2.28
	Urnammu 22	1.1.39		Šulgi 8	1.2.16
	Urnammu 23	1.1.26		Šulgi 9	1.2.17
	Urnammu 24	1.1.40		Šulgi 10	1.2.1
	Urnammu 25	1.1.11		Šulgi 11	1.2.6
	Urnammu 26	1.1.17		Šulgi 12	1.2.32
	Urnammu 27	1.1.19		Šulgi 13	1.2.9
	Urnammu 28	1.1.28		Šulgi 14	1.2.29
	Urnammu 29	1.1.9/1.1.22		Šulgi 15	1.2.11
	Urnammu 30	1.1.41		Šulgi 16	1.2.2
	Urnammu 31	1.1.43		Šulgi 17	1.2.5
	Urnammu 32	1.1.44		Šulgi 18	1.2.4
	Urnammu 33	1.1.45		Šulgi 19	1.2.34
	Urnammu 34	1.1.46		Šulgi 20	1.2.21
	Urnammu 35	1.1.54		Šulgi 21	1.2.13

P.	No.	E3/2.
	Šulgi 22	1.2.10
	Šulgi 23	1.2.12
	Šulgi 24	1.2.14
	Šulgi 25	1.2.56
	Šulgi 26	1.2.2031
	Šulgi 27	1.2.57
	Šulgi 28	1.2.2012
	Šulgi 29	1.2.2030
	Šulgi 30	1.2.46
	Šulgi 31	1.2.2004
	Šulgi 32	1.2.2010
	Šulgi 33	1.2.2001
	Šulgi 34	1.2.2044
	Šulgi 35	1.2.2046
	Šulgi 36	1.2.65
	Šulgi 37	1.2.2033
	Šulgi 38	1.2.2034
	Šulgi 39	1.2.61
	Šulgi 40	1.2.2036
	Šulgi 41	1.2.66
	Šulgi 42	1.2.72
	Šulgi 43	1.2.58
	Šulgi 44	1.2.59
	Šulgi 45	1.2.60
	Šulgi 46	1.2.88
	Šulgi 47	1.2.2039
	Šulgi 48	1.2.2037
	Šulgi 49	1.2.2023
	Šulgi 51	1.2.50
	Šulgi 52	1.2.53
	Šulgi 53	1.2.2028
	Šulgi 54	1.2.38
	Šulgi 55	1.2.40
	Šulgi 56	1.2.83
	Šulgi 57	1.2.43
	Šulgi 58	1.6.1029
	Šulgi 59	1.2.44
	Šulgi 60	1.2.2042
	Šulgi 61	1.2.2045
	Šulgi 62	1.2.2041
	Šulgi 63	1.2.33
	Šulgi 64	1.2.2035
	Šulgi 65	1.2.85
	Šulgi 66	1.2.89
	Šulgi 67	1.2.7
	Šulgi 68	1.2.15
	Šulgi 69	1.2.55
	Šulgi 70	1.2.62
	Šulgi 71	1.2.2047
	Šulgi 72	1.2.41
	Šulgi 73	1.2.30
	Šulgi 74	1.2.8
	Šulgi 75	1.2.20
218 ff.	Amarsuen 1	1.3.4
	Amarsuen 2	1.3.1/1.3.2
	Amarsuen 3	1.3.10/1.3.11
	Amarsuen 4	1.3.12
	Amarsuen 5	1.3.15
	Amarsuen 6	1.3.16
	Amarsuen 7	1.3.14
	Amarsuen 8	1.3.17
	Amarsuen 9	1.3.5
	Amarsuen 10	1.3.6
	Amarsuen 11	1.3.16
	Amarsuen 12	1.3.9
	Amarsuen 13	1.3.8
	Amarsuen 14	1.3.13
	Amarsuen 15	1.3.2001
	Amarsuen 16	1.3.2008

P.	No.	E3/2.
	Amarsuen 17	1.3.2009
	Amarsuen 19	1.3.7
	Amarsuen 20	1.3.18
	Amarsuen 21	1.3.16
	Amarsuen 22	1.3.21
253 ff.	Šūsuen 1–2	1.4.10
	Šūsuen 3	1.4.11
	Šūsuen 4	1.4.18
	Šūsuen 5	1.4.19
	Šūsuen 6	1.4.20
	Šūsuen 7	1.4.21
	Šūsuen 8	1.4.16
	Šūsuen 9	1.4.17
	Šūsuen 10	1.4.14
	Šūsuen 11	1.4.15
	Šūsuen 12	1.4.12
	Šūsuen 13	1.4.13
	Šūsuen 14	1.4.26
	Šūsuen 15	1.4.2017
	Šūsuen 16	1.4.2018
	Šūsuen 17	1.4.22
	Šūsuen 18 iii	1.4.2001
	Šūsuen 20A	1.4.3
	Šūsuen 20B	1.4.1
	Šūsuen 20C	1.4.4
	Šūsuen 21	1.4.27
	Šūsuen 22	1.4.29
	Šūsuen 23	1.4.28
	Šūsuen 24	1.4.23
	Šūsuen 25	1.4.2016
	Šūsuen A 26	1.4.6
	Šūsuen 27	1.4.2016
	Šūsuen 28	1.4.24
	Šūsuen 29	1.4.25
279 ff.	Ibbīsuen 1–2	1.5.1
	Ibbīsuen 3	1.5.2005
	Ibbīsuen 4	1.5.2014
	Ibbīsuen 5	1.5.2015
	Ibbīsuen 6	1.5.5
	Ibbīsuen A 9	1.5.2
	Ibbīsuen A 10	1.5.3
	Ibbīsuen A 11	1.5.4
	Ibbīsuen 12	1.5.2004
	Ibbīsuen 13	1.5.2016
297 ff.	Ur 1	1.6.1001
	Ur 3	1.6.1027
	Ur 4	1.6.1033
	Ur 5	1.6.1017
	Ur 6	1.3.19
	Ur 7	1.6.1019
	Ur 9	1.6.1035
	Ur 10	1.6.1002
	Ur 11	1.6.1018
	Ur 12	1.6.1003
	Ur 16	1.6.1028
	Ur 18	1.6.1045
	Ur 19	1.6.1027
	Ur 21	1.6.1030
	Ur 23	1.6.1036
	Ur 24	1.6.1037
	Ur 25	1.6.1039
	Ur 26	1.6.1038
	Ur 28	1.6.1031
335–36	Lugirizal 1 (Šulgi)	1.2.2011
349–50	Adab 2	1.2.2001
352 ff.	Nippur 1	1.6.1043
	Nippur 2	1.6.1020
	Nippur 3	1.6.1008
	Nippur 4	1.6.1032

Thureau-Dangin, SAK

P.	No.	E3/2.
146–47	Ur-nin-gir-su a	2.1.1
148–49	Galu-ka-zal c	1.2.2013
	Ur-lama	1.2.2018
	Al-la	1.2.2019
148–51	Arad-nanna(r)	1.4.13
174–75	Kisâri	5.1.2001
176–77	Ḫunnini	6.1.2001
186 ff.	Ur-engur a	1.1.2
	Ur-engur b	1.1.4
	Ur-engur c	1.1.12
	Ur-engur d	1.1.33
	Ur-engur e	1.1.35
	Ur-engur f	1.1.5
	Ur-engur g	1.1.24
	Ur-engur h	1.1.11
	Ur-engur i	1.1.28
	Ur-engur k	1.1.25
	Ur-engur l	1.1.37
	Ur-engur m	1.1.36
	Ur-engur n	1.1.2001
190 ff.	Dun-gi a	1.2.39
	Dun-gi b	1.2.3
	Dun-gi c	1.2.31
	Dun-gi d	1.2.12
	Dun-gi e	1.2.13
	Dun-gi f	1.2.24
	Dun-gi g	1.2.23
	Dun-gi h	1.2.9
	Dun-gi i	1.2.11
	Dun-gi k	1.2.5
	Dun-gi l	1.2.17
	Dun-gi m	1.2.1
	Dun-gi n	1.2.6
	Dun-gi o	1.2.29
	Dun-gi p	1.2.32
	Dun-gi q	1.2.2033
	Dun-gi r	1.2.66
	Dun-gi s	1.2.50
	Dun-gi t	1.6.1024
	Dun-gi v	1.2.2010
	Dun-gi w	1.2.2012
	Dun-gi x	1.2.2030
	Dun-gi y	1.2.58
	Dun-gi z	1.2.2039
196 ff.	Dun-gi a′	1.2.2023
	Dun-gi d′	1.2.2028
	Dun-gi f′	1.2.2037
	Pûr-sin a	1.3.4
	Pûr-sin b	1.3.1
	Pûr-sin c	1.3.15
198 ff.	Pûr-sin d	1.3.10
	Pûr-sin e	1.3.16
	Pûr-sin f	1.3.5
	Pûr-sin g	1.3.6
	Pûr-sin h	1.3.14
	Pûr-sin i	1.3.17
	Pûr-sin l	1.3.22
200 ff.	Gimil-sin a	1.4.10
	Gimil-sin b	1.4.20
	Gimil-sin c	1.4.15
	Gimil-sin d	1.4.21
	Gimil-sin e	1.4.22
	Gimil-sin f	1.4.2002

Winter, in Gibson and Biggs, Bureaucracy

P.	No.	E3/2.
95	Ia	1.1.2001
	IIb	1.2.2021
96	IIi	1.2.94
	IIl	1.2.2028
	IIn	1.2.2029
	IIo	1.2.2022
	IIIa	1.3.2007
	IIIb	1.4.32
	IIIg	1.3.2006
97	IVa	1.4.2012
	IVf	1.4.2004
	IVg	1.4.2002
	IVh	1.4.32
	IVp	1.4.2010
	IVr	1.4.2001
	IVt	1.4.2005/1.4.2006
98	Va	1.5.7
	Vb	1.5.2003
	Vc	1.5.2007
	Vd	1.5.2012
	Vf	1.5.2013
	Vh	1.5.8
99	Vp	1.5.2002

Scores of Inscriptions

1	0	ur-^{d}nammu
1	27	ur-^{d}nammu
1	28	...
1	29	ur-^{d}nammu
1	30	...
1	31	...
1	32	...
1	33	ur-^{d}nammu
1	34	...
1	A	ur-^{d}nammu
1	B	ur-^{d}nammu
1	C	[u]r-^{d}nammu
1	D	ur-^{d}nammu
1	E	[...]
1	F	ur-^{d}nammu

2	0	lugal-uri$_5$.KI-ma
2	27	lugal-uri$_5$.KI-ma
2	28	...
2	29	lugal-uri$_5$.KI-ma
2	30	...
2	31	...
2	32	...
2	33	lugal-uri$_5$.KI-ma
2	34	...
2	A	lugal-uri$_5$.KI-ma
2	B	lugal-uri$_5$.KI-ma
2	C	[l]ugal-uri$_5$.KI-ma
2	D	lugal-uri$_5$.KI-ma
2	E	[lugal]-uri$_5$.[KI]-ma
2	F	lugal-uri$_5$.KI-ma

3	0	lú é-^{d}nanna
3	27	lú é-^{d}nanna
3	28	...
3	29	lú é-^{d}nanna
3	30	...
3	31	...
3	32	...
3	33	lú é-^{d}nanna...
3	34	...
3	A	lú é-^{d}nanna
3	B	lú é-^{d}nanna
3	C	lú é-^{d}nanna
3	D	lú é-^{d}nanna
3	E	[...]
3	F	[...]

4	0	in-dù-a
4	27	in-dù-a
4	28	...
4	29	in-dù-a
4	30	...
4	31	...
4	32	...
4	33	in-dù-a
4	34	...
4	A	in-dù-a
4	B	in-dù-a
4	C	in-dù-a
4	D	in-dù-a
4	E	i[n]-⸢dù⸣-a
4	F	in-dù-a

1	0	^{d}nin-gal
1	1	...
1	2	⸢^{d}⸣nin-gal
1	3	⸢^{d}nin-gal⸣
1	4	...
1	5	...
1	6	...
1	7	...
1	8	...
1	9	...
1	10	...
2	0	nin-a-ni
2	1	...
2	2	nin-a-ni
2	3	nin-a-ni
2	4	...
2	5	...
2	6	...
2	7	...
2	8	...
2	9	...
2	10	...
3	0	ur-^{d}nammu
3	1	...
3	2	ur-^{d}nammu
3	3	ur-^{d}nammu
3	4	...
3	5	...
3	6	...
3	7	...
3	8	...
3	9	...
3	10	...
4	0	nita-kala-ga
4	1	...
4	2	nita-kala-ga
4	3	nita-kala-ga
4	4	....
4	5	...
4	6	...
4	7	...
4	8	...
4	9	...
4	10	...
5	0	lugal-uri$_5$.KI-ma
5	1	...
5	2	lugal-uri$_5$.KI-ma
5	3	lugal-uri$_5$.KI-ma
5	4	...
5	5	...
5	6	...
5	7	...
5	8	...
5	9	...
5	10	...
6	0	lugal-ki-en-gi-ki-uri-ke$_4$
6	1	...
6	2	lugal-ki-en-gi-ki-uri-ke$_4$
6	3	lugal-ki-en-gi-ki-uri-ke$_4$
6	4	...
6	5	...
6	6	...
6	7	...
6	8	...
6	9	...
6	10	...

7	0	gi_6-par_4-kù-ga-ni
7	1	...
7	2	gi_6-par_4-kù-ga-ni
7	3	gi_6-par_4-kù-ga-ni
7	4	...
7	5	...
7	6	...
7	7	...
7	8	...
7	9	...
7	10	...

8	0	mu-na-dù
8	1	...
8	2	mu-na-dù
8	3	mu-na-dù
8	4	...
8	5	...
8	6	...
8	7	...
8	8	...
8	9	...
8	10	...

1	0	^{d}nin-é-gal
1	1	^{d}nin-é-gal
1	2	^{d}nin-é-gal
1	3	...
2	0	nin-a-ni
2	1	nin-a-ni
2	2	nin-a-ni
2	3	...
3	0	ur-^{d}nammu
3	1	ur-^{d}nammu
3	2	ur-^{d}nammu
3	3	...
4	0	nita-kala-ga
4	1	nita-kala-ga
4	2	nita-kala-ga
4	3	...
5	0	lugal-uri$_5$.KI-ma
5	1	lugal-uri$_5$.KI-ma
5	2	lugal-uri$_5$.KI-ma
5	3	...
6	0	lugal-ki-en-gi-ki-uri-ke$_4$
6	1	lugal-ki-en-gi-ki-uri-ke$_4$
6	2	lugal-ki-en-gi-ki-uri-ke$_4$
6	3	...
7	0	é-a-ni
7	1	é-a-ni
7	2	é-a-ni
7	3	...
8	0	mu-na-dù
8	1	mu-na-dù
8	2	⸢mu-na-dù⸣
8	3	...

1	0	^{d}inanna
1	1	^{d}inanna
1	2	^{d}inanna
2	0	nin-kù-nun-na
2	1	nin-nun-na
2	2	nin-kù-nun-na
3	0	nin-a-ni
3	1	nin-a-ni
3	2	nin-a-ni
4	0	ur-^{d}nammu
4	1	ur-^{d}nammu
4	2	ur-^{d}nammu
5	0	lugal-kala-ga
5	1	lugal-kala-ga
5	2	lugal-kala-ga
6	0	lugal-uri$_{5}$.KI-ma
6	1	lugal-uri$_{5}$.KI-ma
6	2	lugal-uri$_{5}$.KI-ma
7	0	lugal-ki-en-gi-ki-uri-ke$_{4}$
7	1	lugal-ki-en-gi-ki-uri-ke$_{4}$
7	2	lugal-ki-en-gi-ki-uri-ke$_{4}$
8	0	èš-bur
8	1	èš-bur
8	2	èš-bur
9	0	é-ki-ág-a-ni
9	1	é-ki-ág-a-ni
9	2	é-ki-ág-a-ni
10	0	mu-na-dù
10	1	mu-na-dù
10	2	⸢mu-na-dù⸣

1	0	^{d}nanna
1	1	[^{d}]nann[a]
1	2	[...]
1	3	[...]
1	4	[^{d}nan]na
1	5	...
1	6	^{d}nanna
2	0	dumu-sag-
2	1	[dumu]-sa[g]-
2	2	[...]
2	3	[...]
2	4	[dumu-s]ag-
2	5	...
2	6	dumu-sag-
3	0	^{d}en-líl-lá
3	1	[...]
3	2	[...]
3	3	[...]
3	4	[^{d}en-l]íl-lá
3	5	...
3	6	^{d}en-líl-lá
4	0	lugal-a-ni
4	1	[...]
4	2	[...]
4	3	[lugal-a-n]i
4	4	[lugal]-a-ni
4	5	...
4	6	lugal-a-ni
5	0	ur-^{d}nammu
5	1	[...]
5	2	[...]
5	3	[ur-^{d}]nammu
5	4	[ur]-⸢^{d}⸣nammu
5	5	...
5	6	ur-^{d}nammu
6	0	nita-kala-ga
6	1	[...]
6	2	[...]
6	3	[nita-kala-g]a
6	4	[nita-k]ala-ga
6	5	...
6	6	nita-kala-ga
7	0	lugal-uri$_5$.KI-ma
7	1	[...]
7	2	[...]
7	3	[lugal-ur]i$_5$.KI-ma
7	4	[lugal]-⸢ŠEŠ⸣.AB.KI-ma
7	5	...
7	6	lugal-uri$_5$.KI-ma
8	0	lugal-ki-en-gi-ki-uri-ke$_4$
8	1	[lugal-ki-en-g]i-⸢ki-uri-ke$_4$⸣
8	2	[...]
8	3	[...]
8	4	[lug]al-ki-en-gi-[ki]-uri-ke$_4$
8	5	...
8	6	lugal-ki-en-gi-ki-uri-ke$_4$
9	0	lú é-^{d}nanna
9	1	[l]ú ⸢é⸣-^{d}nanna
9	2	[...]
9	3	[...]
9	4	[lú] é-[^{d}nanna]
9	5	...
9	6	lú é-^{d}nanna
10	0	in-dù-a
10	1	[i]n-dù-a
10	2	[...]
10	3	[...]
10	4	[in-d]ù-a
10	5	...
10	6	in-dù-a

11	0	nì-ul-lí-a-ke$_4$ pa mu-na-è
11	1	[...]
11	2	[nì-ul]-lí-a-ke$_4$ [pa mu]-na-è
11	3	[n]ì-ul-lí-a-ke$_4$ ⸢pa⸣ mu-na-è
11	4	nì-ul-lí-a-ke$_4$ pa mu-na-è
11	5	... pa mu-na-ni-è
11	6	nì-ul-lí-a-ke$_4$ pa mu-na-è
12	0	gaba-a-ab-ka-ka
12	1	[...]
12	2	[gaba]-⸢a⸣-ab-ka-ka
12	3	gaba-a-ab-ka-ka
12	4	gaba-a-ab-ka-ka
12	5	...
12	6	gaba-a-ab-ka-ka
13	0	ki-SAR-a nam-ga-eš$_8$ bí-sá
13	1	[...]
13	2	[ki-S]AR-a nam-[ga-eš$_8$] bí-sá
13	3	ki-SAR-a nam-ga-eš$_8$ bí-s[á]
13	4	ki-⸢SAR⸣-a nam-ga-eš$_8$ bí-sá
13	5	...
13	6	ki-SAR-a nam-ga-eš$_8$ bí-sá
14	0	má-má-gan šu-na mu-ni-gi$_4$
14	1	[...]
14	2	[má]-má-gan [šu-na mu-n]i-gi$_4$
14	3	má-má-gan šu-n[a] mu-⸢ni⸣-g[i$_4$]
14	4	má má-gan.šu-na mu-ni-gi$_4$
14	5	...
14	6	má má-gan.šu-na mu-ni-gi$_4$

1	0	^{d}nanna
1	1	[...]
1	2	[...]
1	3	...
1	4	...
1	5	...
1	6	...
1	7	⸢^{d}⸣nanna
1	8	^{d}nanna
1	9	...
1	10	...
1	11	...
1	12	^{d}nanna
2	0	dumu-sag-
2	1	[...]
2	2	[...]
2	3	...
2	4	...
2	5	...
2	6	...
2	7	[d]umu-sag-
2	8	dumu-sag-
2	9	...
2	10	...
2	11	...
2	12	dumu-sag-
3	0	^{d}en-líl-lá
3	1	[...]
3	2	[...]
3	3	...
3	4	...
3	5	...
3	6	...
3	7	⸢^{d}⸣en-líl-lá
3	8	^{d}en-líl-lá
3	9	...
3	10	...
3	11	...
3	12	⸢^{d}⸣[...]
4	0	lugal-a-ni
4	1	[...]
4	2	[...]
4	3	...
4	4	...
4	5	...
4	6	...
4	7	[l]ugal-a-ni
4	8	lugal-a-ni
4	9	...
4	10	...
4	11	...
4	12	lugal-a-ni-⸢ir⸣
5	0	ur-^{d}nammu
5	1	[...]
5	2	[...]
5	3	...
5	4	...
5	5	...
5	6	...
5	7	[u]r-^{d}nammu
5	8	^{d}ur-^{d}nammu
5	9	...
5	10	...
5	11	...
5	12	ur-^{d}nammu
6	0	nita-kala-ga
6	1	[...]
6	2	[...]
6	3	...
6	4	...
6	5	...
6	6	[...]
6	7	<...>
6	8	nita-kala-ga
9	9	...
6	10	...
6	11	...
6	12	nita-ka[la-ga]

7	0	lugal-uri$_5$.KI-ma
7	1	[...]
7	2	[...]-m[a]
7	3	...
7	4	...
7	5	...
7	6	[...]
7	7	[l]ugal-uri$_5$.KI-ma
7	8	lugal-uri$_5$.KI-ma
7	9	...
7	10	...
7	11	...
7	12	lugal-uri$_5$.KI-[ma]
8	0	lugal-ki-en-gi-ki-uri-ke$_4$
8	1	[...]
8	2	[lu]gal-ki-e[n-gi]-ki-uri-k[e$_4$]
8	3	...
8	4	...
8	5	...
8	6	...
8	7	[lu]gal-ki-en-[gi]-⸢ki-uri⸣-ke$_4$
8	8	lugal-ki-en-gi-ki-uri-ke$_4$
8	9	...
8	10	...
8	11	...
8	12	lugal-ki-en-gi-ki-[uri-ke$_4$]
9	0	sug-peš-dù-a
9	1	[...]
9	2	sug-peš-dù-[a]
9	3	...
9	4	...
9	5	...
9	6	[...]
9	7	[sug]-⸢peš-dù⸣-a
9	8	sug-peš-dù-a(Text: MIN)
9	9	...
9	10	...
9	11	...
9	12	sug-peš-dù-⸢a⸣
10	0	sug ḫé-me-àm
10	1	[...]
10	2	sug ḫé-me-⸢àm⸣
10	3	...
10	4	...
10	5	...
10	6	...
10	7	[sug] ḫé-me-⸢àm⸣
10	8	sug ḫé-me-àm
10	9	...
10	10	...
10	11	...
10	12	sug ḫé-me-àm
11	0	a-šà-bi
11	1	[...]
11	2	a-šà-b[i]
11	3	...
11	4	...
11	5	...
11	6	...
11	7	[a]-šà-[bi]
11	8	a-šà-bi
11	9	...
11	10	...
11	11	...
11	12	a-šà-bi
12	0	ŠÁR.GAL GÁNA-àm
12	1	[...]
12	2	[ŠÁR.GA]L GÁNA-⸢àm⸣
12	3	...
12	4	...
12	5	...
12	6	...
12	7	[ŠÁR.G]AL <GÁNA>-[àm]
12	8	ŠÁR.GAL GÁNA-àm
12	9	...
12	10	...
12	11	...
12	12	ŠÁR.GAL <GÁNA>-àm

13	0	a-ta
13	1	⸢a⸣-ta
13	2	[...]
13	3	...
13	4	...
13	5	...
13	6	...
13	7	a-[ta]
13	8	a-[ta]
13	9	...
13	10	...
13	11	...
13	12	a-ta
14	0	ḫa-mu-na-ta-DU
14	1	⸢ḫa⸣-mu-na-ta-⸢è⸣
14	2	[...]
14	3	...
14	4	...
14	5	...
14	6	...
14	7	ḫa-[...]
14	8	ḫa-mu-na-[ta-DU]
14	9	...
14	10	...
14	11	...
14	12	⸢ḫa⸣-ma-na-ta-DU
15	0	e-bi 4 da-na 260 nindan
15	1	⸢e⸣-bi 4 ⸢da-na⸣ ⸢x⸣ ⸢nindan⸣
15	2	[...]
15	3	...
15	4	...
15	5	...
15	6	... 270 nindan
15	7	e-b[i ...]
15	8	e-bi 4 d[a-na] 260 nind[an]
15	9	...
15	10	...
15	11	...
15	12	e-bi 4 da-na 260 nindan
16	0	ḫé-na-AK
16	1	[ḫé]-⸢na-AK⸣
16	2	[...]
16	3	...
16	4	...
16	5	...
16	6	...
16	7	ḫ[é-...]
16	8	ḫé-na-[AK]
16	9	...
16	10	...
16	11	...
16	12	ḫé-na-AK
17	0	uri$_5$.KI-e gi$_{16}$-sa-aš
17	1	⸢uri$_5$.KI-e gi$_{16}$-sa-aš⸣
17	2	[...]
17	3	...
17	4	uri$_5$.KI-a; a over an erased ma
17	5	...
17	6	...
17	7	u[ri$_5$.KI ...]
17	8	uri$_5$.K[I ...]
17	9	...
17	10	...
17	11	...
17	12	uri$_5$.KI-ma ⸢gi$_{16}$⸣-sa
18	0	ḫé-mi-AK
18	1	⸢ḫé-mi-AK⸣
18	2	[...]
18	3	...
18	4	...

18	5	...
18	6	ḫé-mi-na
18	7	[...]
18	8	ḫé-m[i-AK]
18	9	...
18	10	...
18	11	...
18	12	ḫé-mi-AK
19	0	e-ba a-ba-^{d}nanna-gin$_7$
19	1	[e-ba a]-ba-⌈^{d}nanna-gin$_7$⌉
19	2	[...]
19	3	[...]
19	4	...
19	5	...
19	6	...
19	7	[...]
19	8	e-ba a-[...]
19	9	...
19	10	...
19	11	...
19	12	e-ba a-ba-^{d}nanna-gin$_7$
20	0	mu-bi
20	1	[m]u-⌈bi⌉
20	2	[...]
20	3	...
20	4	...
20	5	...
20	6	...
20	7	[...]
20	8	mu-[bi]
20	9	...
20	10	...
20	11	...
20	12	mu-bi

1	0	ur-^{d}nammu	4	0	lú é-^{d}en-líl-lá
1	35a	ur-^{d}nammu	4	35a	lú é-^{d}en-líl-lá
1	35b	ur-^{d}nammu	4	35b	lú é-^{d}en-líl-lá
1	36b	ur-^{d}nammu	4	36b	lú ⌈é⌉-en-líl-lá
1	37a	...	4	37a	...
1	37b	...	4	37b	...
1	37c	ur-^{d}nammu	4	37c	lú é-^{d}en-líl-lá
1	38a	ur-^{d}nammu	4	38a	...
1	38b	...	4	38b	...
1	38c	ur-^{d}nammu	4	38c	lú é-^{d}en-líl-lá
1	39a	...	4	39a	...
1	39b	...	4	39b	...
1	39c	ur-^{d}nammu	4	39c	lú ^{d}é-^{d}en-líl-lá
1	40b	...	4	40b	...
2	0	lugal-uri$_{5}$.KI-ma	5	0	in-dù-a
2	35a	lugal-uri$_{5}$.KI-ma	5	35a	in-dù-a
2	35b	lugal-uri$_{5}$.KI-ma	5	35b	in-dù-a
2	36b	lugal-uri$_{5}$.KI-ma	5	36b	in-dù-a
2	37a	...	5	37a	...
2	37b	...	5	37b	...
2	37c	lugal-uri$_{5}$.KI-ma	5	37c	in-dù-a
2	38a	lugal-uri$_{5}$.KI-ma	5	38a	...
2	38b	...	5	38b	...
2	38c	lugal-uri$_{5}$.KI-ma	5	38c	in-dù-a
2	39a	...	5	39a	...
2	39b	...	5	39b	...
2	39c	lugal-uri$_{5}$.KI-ma	5	39c	in-dù-a
2	40b	...	5	40b	...
3	0	lugal-ki-en-gi-ki-uri			
3	35a	lugal-ki-en-gi-ki-uri			
3	35b	lugal-ki-en-gi-ki-uri			
3	36b	lugal-ki-en-gi-ki-⌈uri⌉			
3	37a	...			
3	37b	...			
3	37c	lugal-ki-en-gi-ki-uri			
3	38a	lugal-ki-en-gi-ki-uri			
3	38b	...			
3	38c	...			
3	39a	...			
3	39b	...			
3	39c	lugal-ki-en-gi-ki-uri			
3	40b	...			

1	0	^{d}en-líl
1	1	^{d}en-líl
1	2	^{d}en-líl
2	0	lugal-kur-kur-ra
2	1	lugal-kur-kur-ra
2	2	lugal-kur-kur-ra
3	0	lugal-a-ni
3	1	lugal-a-ni
3	2	lugal-a-ni
4	0	ur-^{d}nammu
4	1	ur-^{d}nammu
4	2	ur-^{d}nammu
5	0	nita-kala-ga
5	1	nita-kala-ga
5	2	nita-kala-ga
6	0	lugal-uri$_5$.KI-ma
6	1	lugal-uri$_5$.KI-ma
6	2	lugal-uri$_5$.KI-ma
7	0	lugal-ki-en-gi-ki-uri-ke$_4$
7	1	lugal-ki-en-gi-ki-uri-ke$_4$
7	2	lugal-ki-en-gi-ki-uri-ke$_4$
8	0	é-kur
8	1	é-kur
8	2	é-kur
9	0	é-ki-ág-gá-ni
9	1	é-ki-ág-gá-ni
9	2	é-ki-ág-gá-ni
10	0	mu-na-dù
10	1	mu-na-dù
10	2	mu-na-dù

1	0	^{d}en-líl
1	1	...
1	2	...
1	3	...
1	4	...
1	5	...
1	6	^{d}en-líl
1	7	...
1	8	...
1	9	...
1	10	...
1	11	...
1	12	...
1	13	...
1	14	...
1	15	^{d}e[n-líl]
1	16	⸢^{d}en-líl⸣
2	0	lugal-kur-kur-ra
2	1	...
2	2	...
2	3	...
2	4	...
2	5	...
2	6	lugal-kur-kur-ra
2	7	...
2	8	...
2	9	...
2	10	...
2	11	...
2	12	...
2	13	...
2	14	...
2	15	lugal-kur-[...]
2	16	⸢lugal-kur-kur-ra⸣
3	0	lugal-a-ni
3	1	...
3	2	...
3	3	...
3	4	...
3	5	...
3	6	lugal-a-ni
3	7	...
3	8	...
3	9	...
3	10	...
3	11	...
3	12	...
3	13	...
3	14	...
3	15	lugal-⸢a⸣-[ni]
3	16	⸢lugal-a-ni⸣
4	0	ur-^{d}nammu
4	1	...
4	2	...
4	3	...
4	4	...
4	5	...
4	6	ur-^{d}nammu
4	7	...
4	8	...
4	9	...
4	10	...
4	11	...
4	12	...
4	13	...
4	14	...
4	15	ur-[...]
4	16	⸢ur-^{d}nammu⸣

5	0	lugal-uri$_5$.KI-ma	7	0	é-a-ni
5	1	...	7	1	...
5	2	...	7	2	...
5	3	...	7	3	...
5	4	...	7	4	...
5	5	...	7	5	...
5	6	lugal-uri$_5$.KI-ma	7	6	é-a-ni
5	7	...	7	7	...
5	8	...	7	8	...
5	9	...	7	9	...
5	10	...	7	10	...
5	11	...	7	11	...
5	12	...	7	12	...
5	13	...	7	13	...
5	14	...	7	14	...
5	15	lugal-ur[i$_5$.KI-ma]	7	15	é-a-[ni]
5	16	⌜lugal⌝-[uri$_5$].⌜KI-ma⌝	7	16	[...]
6	0	lugal-ki-en-gi-ki-uri-ke$_4$	8	0	mu-na-dù
6	1	...	8	1	...
6	2	...	8	2	...
6	3	...	8	3	...
6	4	...	8	4	...
6	5	...	8	5	...
6	6	lugal-ki-en-gi-ki-uri-ke$_4$	8	6	mu-na-dù
6	7	...	8	7	...
6	8	...	8	8	...
6	9	...	8	9	...
6	10	...	8	10	...
6	11	...	8	11	...
6	12	...	8	12	...
6	13	...	8	13	...
6	14	...	8	14	...
6	15	lugal-ki-[en-gi]-ki-[uri$_5$-ke$_4$]	8	15	mu-n[a-dù]
6	16	[...]	8	16	m[u-n]a-dù

9	0	I$_{7}$.EN.ÉREN.NUN
9	1	I$_{7}$.EN.x.NUN
9	2	...
9	3	...
9	4	...
9	5	...
9	6	I$_{7}$.EN.ÉREN.NUN
9	7	...
9	8	...
9	9	...
9	10	...
9	11	...
9	12	...
9	13	...
9	14	...
9	15	I$_{7}$.⌈EN⌉.ÉREN.NUN
9	16	⌈I$_{7}$.EN.ÉREN.NUN⌉
10	0	i$_{7}$-nidba-ka-ni
10	1	...
10	2	...
10	3	...
10	4	...
10	5	...
10	6	i$_{7}$-nidba-ka-ni
10	7	...
10	8	...
10	9	...
10	10	...
10	11	...
10	12	...
10	13	...
10	14	...
10	15	i$_{7}$-⌈nidba-ka-ni⌉
10	16	⌈i$_{7}$-nidba-ka⌉-ni
11	0	mu-na-ba-al
11	1	...
11	2	...
11	3	...
11	4	...
11	5	...
11	6	mu-na-ba-al
11	7	...
11	8	...
11	9	...
11	10	...
11	11	...
11	12	...
11	13	...
11	14	...
11	15	mu-n[a-...]
11	16	mu-⌈na-ba-al⌉

1	0	^{d}nanna
1	1	^{d}nanna
1	2	^{d}nann[a]
1	3	^{d}nanna
1	4	^{d}⸢nanna⸣
1	5	...
1	6	...
1	7	...
2	0	dumu-sag-^{d}en-líl-lá
2	1	dumu-sag-^{d}en-líl-lá
2	2	dumu-sa[g]-^{d}en-líl-[lá]
2	3	dumu-sag-^{d}en-líl-lá
2	4	dumu-⸢sag⸣-^{d}en-líl-lá
2	5	...
2	6	...
2	7	...
3	0	lugal-a-ni
3	1	lugal-a-ni
3	2	lugal-a-[ni]
3	3	lugal-a-ni
3	4	lugal-a-⸢ni⸣
3	5	...
3	6	...
3	7	...
4	0	ur-^{d}nammu
4	1	ur-^{d}nammu
4	2	⸢ur-^{d}⸣na[mmu]
4	3	ur-^{d}nammu
4	4	ur-^{d}nammu
4	5	...
4	6	...
4	7	...
5	0	nita-kala-ga
5	1	nita-kala-ga
5	2	⸢nita⸣-kal[a-ga]
5	3	nita-kala-ga
5	4	nita-kala-ga
5	5	...
5	6	...
5	7	...
6	0	lugal-uri$_5$.KI-ma
6	1	lugal-uri$_5$.KI-ma
6	2	⸢lugal⸣-u[ri$_5$].⸢KI⸣-ma
6	3	lugal-uri$_5$.<KI>-ma-ke$_4$
6	4	lugal-uri$_5$.KI-ma
6	5	...
6	6	...
6	7	...
7	0	lugal-ki-en-gi-ki-uri-ke$_4$
7	1	lugal-ki-en-gi-ki-uri-ke$_4$
7	2	⸢lugal-ki-en-gi⸣-[ki-uri-ke$_4$]
7	3	lugal-ki-en-gi-ki-uri-ke$_4$
7	4	lugal-ki-en-gi-ki-uri-ke$_4$
7	5	...
7	6	...
7	7	...
8	0	u$_4$ é-^{d}en-líl-lá-
8	1	u$_4$ <é>-^{d}en-líl-lá
8	2	⸢u$_4$ é-^{d}en-líl⸣-[lá]
8	3	u$_4$ é-^{d}en-líl-lá-
8	4	u$_4$ é-^{d}en-líl-lá-
8	5	...
8	6	...
8	7	...

9	0	in-dù-a
9	1	in-dù-a
9	2	⌈in-dù-a⌉
9	3	in-dù-<a>
9	4	in-dù-a
9	5	...
9	6	...
9	7	...
10	0	i$_7$-da
10	1	i$_7$-da
10	2	⌈i$_7$-da⌉
10	3	i$_7$-da
10	4	i$_7$-da
10	5	...
10	6	...
10	7	...
11	0	^{d}nanna-gú-gal mu-bi
11	1	^{d}nanna-gú-gal mu-bi
11	2	⌈^{d}nanna-gú-gal mu-bi⌉
11	3	^{d}nanna-gú-gal mu-bi
11	4	^{d}nanna-gú-gal mu-bi
11	5	...
11	6	...
11	7	...
12	0	i$_7$-ki-sur-ra-kam
12	1	i$_7$-ki-sur-ra-kam
12	2	⌈i$_7$-ki-sur-ra⌉-[kam]
12	3	i$_7$-ki-sur-ra-kam
12	4	i$_7$-ki-sur-ra-kam
12	5	...
12	6	...
12	7	...
13	0	mu-ba-al
13	1	mu-ba-al
13	2	⌈mu-ba⌉-[al]
13	3	mu-ba-al
13	4	mu-ba-al
13	5	...
13	6	...
13	7	...
14	0	kun-bi a-ab-ba-ka ì-lá
14	1	kun-bi a-ab-ba-ka ì-lá
14	2	kun-bi ⌈a-ab⌉-[ba]-ka ⌈ì⌉-[lá]
14	3	kun-<bi> a-ab-ba-ka-NI ì-lá
14	4	kun-bi a-ab-ba-ka ì-lá
14	5	...
14	6	...
14	7	...
15	0	di-nì-gi-na-
15	1	di-nì-gi-na-
15	2	di-nì-⌈gi⌉-na-
15	3	di-nì-gi-na
15	4	⌈di-nì-gi-na⌉
15	5	...
15	6	...
15	7	...
16	0	^{d}utu-ta
16	1	^{d}utu-ta
16	2	^{d}utu-[ta]
16	3	^{d}utu-ta
16	4	^{d}utu-ta
16	5	...
16	6	...
16	7	...

17	0	bar bí-tam
17	1	bar bí-tam
17	2	bar ⸢bí⸣-[tam]
17	3	bar bí-tam
17	4	bar bí-tam
17	5	...
17	6	...
17	7	...
18	0	KA bí-gi-in
18	1	KA bí-gi-in
18	2	[...]
18	3	KA bí-gi-in
18	4	⸢KA⸣ [b]í-gi-in
18	5	...
18	6	...
18	7	...
19	0	lú
19	1	l[ú]
19	2	[...]
19	3	lú
19	4	lú
19	5	...
19	6	...
19	7	...
20	0	^{d}nanna-a
20	1	^{d}nanna-⸢a⸣
20	2	[...]
20	3	^{d}nanna-a
20	4	^{d}nanna-a
20	5	...
20	6	...
20	7	...

21	0	in-da$_{5}$-kúru-a
21	1	in-da$_{5}$-kúru-[a]
21	2	[...]
21	3	in-da$_{5}$-kúru-a
21	4	in-da$_{5}$-kúru-a
21	5	...
21	6	...
21	7	...
22	0	lugal ḫé-a
22	1	lugal ḫé-[a]
22	2	[...]
22	3	lugal ḫé-a
22	4	lugal ḫé-a
22	5	...
22	6	...
22	7	...
23	0	énsi ḫé-a
23	1	énsi ḫé-[a]
23	2	[...]
23	3	énsi ḫé-a
23	4	énsi ḫé-a
23	5	...
23	6	...
23	7	...
24	0	lú-áš-du$_{11}$-ga-
24	1	lú-áš-du$_{11}$-g[a]-
24	2	[...]
24	3	lú-áš-du$_{11}$-ga-
24	4	lú-áš-du$_{11}$-ga-
24	5	...
24	6	...
24	7	...

25	0	^{d}nanna-gin$_{7}$
25	1	^{d}nanna-g[in$_{7}$]
25	2	[...]
25	3	^{d}nanna-gin$_{7}$
25	4	^{d}nanna-gin$_{7}$
25	5	...
25	6	...
25	7	...
26	0	ḫé-na
26	1	ḫé-[na]
26	2	[...]
26	3	ḫé-na
26	4	ḫé-⸢na⸣
26	5	...
26	6	...
26	7	...
27	0	ki-tuš-^{d}nanna-ka
27	1	ki-tuš-^{d}nanna-k[a]
27	2	[...]
27	3	ki-tuš-^{d}nanna-ka
27	4	ki-tuš-^{d}nanna-⸢ka⸣
27	5	...
27	6	...
27	7	...
28	0	ḫé-éb-GIBIL
28	1	ḫé-éb-GIBI[L]
28	2	[...]
28	3	ḫé-éb-GIBIL
28	4	ḫé-éb-[GIBIL]
28	5	...
28	6	...
28	7	...
29	0	uru-ni gi-suḫur$_{x}$(KA)-ta
29	1	uru-ni gi-suḫur$_{x}$(KA)-t[a]
29	2	[...]
29	3	uru-ni gi-suḫur$_{x}$(KA)-ta
29	4	uru-ni gi-suḫur$_{x}$(KA)-ta
29	5	...
29	6	...
29	7	...
30	0	ḫé-ta-DAG.DAG-ge
30	1	ḫé-ta-DAG.DAG-ge
30	2	[...]
30	3	ḫé-ta-DAG.DAG-ge
30	4	ḫé-ta-DAG.DAG-ge
30	5	...
30	6	...
30	7	...
31	0	nam-ti-il nì-gig-ga-ni
31	1	nam-ti-il nì-gig-ga-ni
31	2	[...]
31	3	nam-ti-il nì-gig-ga-ni
31	4	nam-ti-⸢il⸣ nì-gig-ga-ni
31	5	...
31	6	...
31	7	...
32	0	ḫé-a
32	1	ḫé-na
32	2	[...]
32	3	ḫé-a
32	4	ḫé-a
32	5	ḫé-a(over erased -na)
32	6	...
32	7	...

1	0	^{d}inanna
1	1a	...
1	1b	^{d}inanna
1	2b	[...]
1	3a	^{d}inanna
1	3b	^{d}inanna
1	4	...
1	5b	^{d}inanna
1	6a	^{d}inanna
1	6b	^{d}inanna
1	7a	...
1	8a	^{d}inanna
1	9b	^{d}inanna
2	0	nin-é-an-na
2	1a	...
2	1b	nin-é-an-na
2	2b	[...]
2	3a	nin-é-an-na
2	3b	nin-é-an-na
2	4	...
2	5b	nin-é-an-na
2	6a	nin-é-an-na
2	6b	nin-é-an-na
2	7a	...
2	8a	nin-é-an-na
2	9b	nin-é-an-na
3	0	nin-a-ni
3	1a	...
3	1b	nin-a-ni
3	2b	[...]
3	3a	nin-a-ni
3	3b	nin-a-ni
3	4	...
3	5b	nin-a-ni
3	6a	nin-a-ni
3	6b	nin-a-ni
3	7a	...
3	8a	nin-a-ni
3	9b	nin-a-ni
4	0	ur-^{d}nammu
4	1a	...
4	1b	ur-^{d}nammu
4	2b	[...]
4	3a	ur-^{d}nammu
4	3b	ur-^{d}nammu
4	4	...
4	5b	ur-^{d}nammu
4	6a	ur-^{d}nammu
4	6b	ur-^{d}nammu
4	7a	...
4	8a	ur-^{d}nammu
4	9b	ur-^{d}nammu
5	0	nita-kala-ga
5	1a	...
5	1b	nita-kala-ga
5	2b	⸢nita⸣-k[ala-ga]
5	3a	...
5	3b	nita-kala-ga
5	4	...
5	5b	nita-kala-ga
5	6a	nita-kala-ga
5	6b	nita-kala-ga
5	7a	...
5	8a	nita-⸢kala⸣-ga
5	9b	nita-kala-ga
6	0	lugal-uri$_5$.KI-ma
6	1a	...
6	1b	lugal-uri$_5$.KI-ma
6	2b	lugal-Š[EŠ.AB].KI-[ma]
6	3a	...
6	3b	lugal-uri$_5$.KI-ma
6	4	...
6	5b	lugal-uri$_5$.KI-ma
6	6a	lugal-uri$_5$.KI-ma
6	6b	lugal-uri$_5$.KI-ma
6	7a	...
6	8a	lugal-uri$_5$.KI-ma
6	9b	lugal-uri$_5$.KI-ma

7	0	lugal-ki-en-gi-ki-uri-ke$_4$
7	1a	...
7	1b	lugal-ki-en-gi-ki-uri-ke$_4$
7	2b	lugal-k[i-en]-gi-ki-u[ri-ke$_4$]
7	3a	...
7	3b	lugal-ki-en-gi-ki-uri-ke$_4$
7	4	...
7	5b	lugal-ki-en-gi-ki-uri-ke$_4$
7	6a	lugal-ki-en-gi-ki-uri-ke$_4$
7	6b	lugal-ki-en-gi-ki-uri-ke$_4$
7	7a	...
7	8a	lugal-ki-en-gi-ki-uri-ke$_4$
7	9b	lugal-ki-en-gi-ki-uri-ke$_4$

8	0	é-a-ni
8	1a	...
8	1b	é-a-ni
8	2b	é-a-[ni]
8	3a	é-a-ni
8	3b	...
8	4	...
8	5b	é-a-ni
8	6a	é-a-ni
8	6b	é-a-ni
8	7a	...
8	8a	é-a-⸢ni⸣
8	9b	...

9	0	mu-na-dù
9	1a	...
9	1b	mu-na-dù
9	2b	[...]
9	3a	mu-na-dù
9	3b	...
9	4	...
9	5b	mu-na-dù
9	6a	mu-na-dù
9	6b	mu-na-dù
9	7a	...
9	8a	mu-na-⸢dù⸣
9	9b	...

10	0	ki-bé mu-na-gi$_4$
10	1a	...
10	1b	ki-bé mu-na-gi$_4$
10	2b	[...]
10	3a	ki-bé mu-na-gi$_4$
10	3b	...
10	4	...
10	5b	ki-bé mu-na-gi$_4$
10	6a	ki-bé mu-na-gi$_4$
10	6b	ki-bé mu-na-gi$_4$
10	7a	...
10	8a	⸢ki-bé mu-na-gi$_4$⸣
10	9b	...

1	0	^{d}nin-líl
1	1	^{d}nin-líl
1	2	^{d}nin-líl
2	0	nin-a-ni
2	1	nin-a-ni
2	2	nin-a-ni
3	0	ur-^{d}nammu
3	1	ur-^{d}nammu
3	2	ur-^{d}nammu
4	0	nita-kala-ga
4	1	nita-kala-ga
4	2	nita-kala-ga
5	0	lugal-uri$_5$.KI-ma
5	1	lugal-uri$_5$.KI-ma
5	2	lugal-uri$_5$.KI-ma
6	0	lugal-ki-en-gi-ki-uri-ke$_4$
6	1	lugal-ki-en-gi-ki-uri-ke$_4$
6	2	lugal-ki-en-gi-ki-uri-ke$_4$
7	0	é-šu-tum-ki-ág-gá-ni
7	1	é-šu-tum-ki-ág-gá-ni
7	2	é-šu-tum-ki-ág-gá-ni
8	0	mu-na-dù
8	1	mu-na-dù
8	2	mu-na-dù

1	0	^{d}en-líl
1	1	⸢^{d}en-líl⸣
1	2	[^{d}en]-líl
1	3	[^{d}e]n-⸢líl⸣
1	4	...
1	5	...
1	6	...
1	7	...
1	8	...
1	9	...
1	10	...
1	11	...
1	12	...
1	13	...
1	14	[^{d}]⸢en-líl⸣
1	15	[...]
1	16	[^{d}e]n-líl
1	17	...
1	18	...
1	19	...
1	20	...
1	21	...
1	22	...
1	23	...
1	24	...
1	25	...
1	26	...
1	27	...
1	28	^{d}en-líl
1	29	⸢^{d}en-líl⸣
2	0	lugal-kur-kur-ra
2	1	⸢lugal-kur-kur-ra⸣
2	2	lugal-kur-kur-[ra]
2	3	<...>
2	4	...
2	5	...
2	6	...
2	7	...
2	8	...
2	9	...
2	10	...
2	11	...
2	12	...
2	13	...
2	14	[lug]al-⸢kur-kur-ra⸣
2	15	[...]
2	16	[...][lugal-ku]r-kur-ra
2	17	...
2	18	...
2	19	...
2	20	...
2	21	...
2	22	...
2	23	...
2	24	...
2	25	...
2	26	...
2	27	...
2	28	lugal-kur-kur-ra
2	29	⸢lugal-kur-kur-ra⸣
3	0	lugal-a-ni
3	1	⸢lugal-a-ni⸣
3	2	lugal-a-n[i]
3	3	[l]ugal-a-n[i]
3	4	...
3	5	...
3	6	...
3	7	...
3	8	...
3	9	...
3	10	...
3	11	...
3	12	...
3	13	...
3	14	[lug]al-⸢a-ni⸣
3	15	[...]
3	16	[lugal]-⸢a⸣-ni
3	17	...
3	18	...
3	19	...
3	20	...
3	21	...
3	22	...
3	23	...
3	24	...
3	25	...
3	26	...
3	27	...
3	28	lugal-a-ni
3	29	⸢lugal-a⸣-[ni]

4	0	ur-^{d}nammu
4	1	⌈^{d}ur⌉-[nammu]
4	2	ur-^{d}[nammu]
4	3	[u]r-^{d}[nammu]
4	4	...
4	5	...
4	6	...
4	7	...
4	8	...
4	9	...
4	10	...
4	11	...
4	12	...
4	13	...
4	14	[u]r-⌈^{d}nammu⌉
4	15	[...]
4	16	[ur]-⌈^{d}⌉[nammu]
4	17	...
4	18	...
4	19	...
4	20	...
4	21	...
4	22	...
4	23	...
4	24	...
4	25	...
4	26	...
4	27	...
4	28	ur-⌈^{d}⌉[nammu]
4	29	⌈ur⌉-[^{d}nammu]
5	0	nita-kala-ga
5	1	[ni]ta-kala-ga
5	2	<...>
5	3	[nita]-kala-g[a]
5	4	...
5	5	...
5	6	...
5	7	...
5	8	...
5	9	...
5	10	...
5	11	...
5	12	...
5	13	...
5	14	[nita]-⌈kala-ga⌉
5	15	[...]
5	16	[nita-kala-g]a
5	17	...
5	18	...
5	19	...
5	20	...
5	21	...
5	22	...
5	23	...
5	24	...
5	25	...
5	26	...
5	27	...
5	28	nita-ka[la]-⌈ga⌉
5	29	⌈nita-kala-ga⌉
6	0	lugal-uri$_5$.KI-ma
6	1	[lu]gal-⌈uri$_5$.KI-ma⌉
6	2	lugal-ur[i$_5$.KI]-m[a]
6	3	[lugal]-u[ri$_5$.KI-ma]
6	4	...
6	5	...
6	6	...
6	7	...
6	8	...
6	9	...
6	10	...
6	11	...
6	12	...
6	13	...
6	14	[l]ugal-⌈uri$_5$.KI-ma⌉
6	15	[...]
6	16	[lugal-uri$_5$].KI-[m]a
6	17	...
6	18	...
6	19	...
6	20	...
6	21	...
6	22	...
6	23	...
6	24	..
6	25	...
6	26	...
6	27	...
6	28	lugal-⌈uri$_5$⌉.[KI]-⌈ma⌉
6	29	Traces

7	0	lugal-ki-en-gi-ki-uri-ke$_4$
7	1	[...]
7	2	⸢lugal-ki-en⸣-[...]
7	3	[...]
7	4	...
7	5	...
7	6	...
7	7	...
7	8	...
7	9	...
7	10	...
7	11	...
7	12	...
7	13	...
7	14	[lu]gal⸢ki-en⸣-[gi-ki]-⸢uri-ke$_4$⸣
7	15	[luga]l-⸢ki-en-gi-ki-uri-ke$_4$⸣
7	16	[...-g]i-[...-k]e$_4$
7	17	...
7	18	...
7	19	...
7	20	...
7	21	...
7	22	...
7	23	...
7	24	...
7	25	...
7	26	...
7	27	...
7	28	⸢lugal⸣-ki-⸢en-gi⸣-ki-uri-ke$_4$
7	29	Traces
8	0	i$_7$-uri$_5$.KI-ma
8	1	⸢i$_7$-uri$_5$.KI-ma⸣
8	2	[...]
8	3	[...]
8	4	...
8	5	...
8	6	...
8	7	...
8	8	...
8	9	...
8	10	...
8	11	...
8	12	...
8	13	...
8	14	[...]-⸢ma⸣
8	15	[i$_7$]-⸢uri$_5$.KI-ma⸣
8	16	[...-K]I-ma
8	17	...
8	18	...
8	19	...
8	20	...
8	21	...
8	22	...
8	23	...
8	24	...
8	25	...
8	26	...
8	27	...
8	28	⸢i$_7$-uri$_5$⸣.KI-ma
8	29	Traces
9	0	i$_7$-nidba-ka-ni
9	1	⸢i$_7$-nidba-ka-ni⸣
9	2	[...]
9	3	[...]
9	4	...
9	5	...
9	6	...
9	7	...
9	8	...
9	9	...
9	10	...
9	11	...
9	12	...
9	13	...
9	14	[i$_7$-nid]ba-⸢ka-ni⸣
9	15	[i$_7$]-⸢nidba-ka-ni⸣
9	16	[i$_7$]-[n]idba-[k]a-ni
9	17	...
9	18	...
9	19	...
9	20	...
9	21	...
9	22	...
9	23	...
9	24	...
9	25	...
9	26	...
9	27	...
9	28	⸢i$_7$⸣-nidba-⸢ka⸣-ni
9	29	Traces

10	0	mu-na-ba-al
10	1	⸢mu-na-ba-al⸣
10	2	[...]
10	3	[...]
10	4	...
10	5	...
10	6	...
10	7	...
10	8	...
10	9	...
10	10	...
10	11	...
10	12	...
10	13	...
10	14	[...]-⸢al⸣
10	15	[mu-n]a-⸢ba-al⸣
10	16	[...]-al
10	17	...
10	18	...
10	19	...
10	20	...
10	21	...
10	22	...
10	23	. .
10	24	...
10	25	...
10	26	...
10	27	...
10	28	mu-na-ba-al
10	29	Traces

1	0	^{d}nanna
1	1	...
1	2	^{d}nan[na]
1	3	[^{d}nan]na
1	4	⸢^{d}nanna⸣
1	5	[...]
1	6	...
1	7	...
1	8	...
1	9	...
1	10	...
1	11	...
1	12	...
1	13	^{d}nanna
1	14	...
1	15	...
1	16	...
1	17	...
1	18	...
1	19	[^{d}]⸢nanna⸣
1	20	^{d}nanna
2	0	lugal-a-ni
2	1	...
2	2	lugal-a-ni
2	3	[lugal-a]-ni
2	4	⸢lugal-a-ni⸣
2	5	[...]
2	6	...
2	7	...
2	8	...
2	9	...
2	10	...
2	11	...
2	12	...
2	13	lugal-a-ni
2	14	...
2	15	...
2	16	...
2	17	...
2	18	...
2	19	⸢lugal-a-ni⸣
2	20	[lu]gal-a-ni

3	0	ur-^{d}nammu
3	1	...
3	2	ur-^{d}nammu
3	3	[ur]-^{d}nammu
3	4	⸢ur-^{d}nammu⸣
3	5	[...]
3	6	...
3	7	...
3	8	...
3	9	...
3	10	...
3	11	...
3	12	...
3	13	ur-^{d}nammu
3	14	...
3	15	...
3	16	...
3	17	...
3	18	...
3	19	ur-^{d}nammu
3	20	[u]r-^{d}nammu
4	0	nita-kala-ga
4	1	...
4	2	nita-kala-ga
4	3	[nita-k]ala-ga
4	4	⸢nita-kala-ga⸣
4	5	[nita-ka]la-g[a]
4	6	...
4	7	...
4	8	...
4	9	...
4	10	...
4	11	...
4	12	...
4	13	nita-kala-ga
4	14	...
4	15	...
4	16	...
4	17	...
4	18	...
4	19	nita-kala-ga
4	20	[ni]ta-kala-ga

5	0	lugal-uri$_5$.KI-ma	7	0	i$_7$-nun
5	1	...	7	1	...
5	2	lugal-uri$_5$.KI-ma	7	2	i$_7$(Text: ENGUR)-nun
5	3	lugal-ur[i$_5$.KI-ma]	7	3	[i$_7$-n]un
5	4	lugal-uri$_5$.KI-ma	7	4	⸢i$_7$⸣-nun
5	5	⸢lugal⸣-uri$_5$.KI-[ma]	7	5	[...]
5	6	...	7	6	...
5	7	...	7	7	...
5	8	...	7	8	...
5	9	...	7	9	...
5	10	...	7	10	...
5	11	...	7	11	...
5	12	...	7	12	...
5	13	lugal-ur[i$_5$].KI-ma	7	13	i$_7$-nun
5	14	...	7	14	...
5	15	...	7	15	...
5	16	...	7	16	...
5	17	...	7	17	...
5	18	...	7	18	...
5	19	lugal-uri$_5$.KI-ma	7	19	i$_7$-nun
5	20	lugal-uri$_5$.KI-ma	7	20	i$_7$-nun
6	0	lugal-ki-en-gi-ki-uri-ke$_4$	8	0	i$_7$-ki-ág-ni
6	1	...	8	1	...
6	2	lugal-ki-en-gi-ki-uri-ke$_4$	8	2	i$_7$(Text: ENGUR)-ki-ág-ni
6	3	[...]	8	3	[i$_7$-ki-á]g-ni
6	4	lugal-ki-⸢en⸣-[gi]-ki-uri-⸢ke$_4$⸣	8	4	i$_7$-[...]
6	5	[lug]al-ki-en-[gi-ki]-uri-k[e$_4$]	8	5	[i$_7$-k]i-ág-ni
6	6	...	8	6	...
6	7	...	8	7	...
6	8	...	8	8	...
6	9	...	8	9	...
6	10	...	8	10	...
6	11	...	8	11	...
6	12	...	8	12	...
6	13	lugal-ki-en-gi-⸢ki⸣-uri-ke$_4$	8	13	i$_7$-ki-ág-gá-ni
6	14	...	8	14	...
6	15	...	8	15	...
6	16	...	8	16	...
6	17	...	8	17	...
6	18	...	8	18	...
6	19	lugal-ki-en-gi-ki-uri-ke$_4$	8	19	i$_7$-ki-ág-ni
6	20	lugal-ki-en-gi-ki-uri-ke$_4$	8	20	i$_7$-ki-ág-ni

9	0	mu-na-ba-al
9	1	...
9	2	mu-na-ba-al
9	3	[mu-na]-ba-al
9	4	⸢mu-na⸣-[...]
9	5	[mu]-na-⸢ba⸣-a[l]
9	6	...
9	7	...
9	8	...
9	9	...
9	10	...
9	11	...
9	12	...
9	13	mu-na-ba-al
9	14	...
9	15	...
9	16	...
9	17	...
9	18	...
9	19	mu-na-ba-al
9	20	mu-na-ba-al

1	0	⸢^{d}⸣nin-gal
1	1	⸢^{d}⸣nin-gal
1	2	[...]
2	0	[ni]n-a-ni
2	1	[ni]n-a-ni
2	2	[...]
3	0	[na]m-ti-
3	1	[na]m-ti-
3	2	[...]
4	0	⸢ur⸣-^{d}nammu
4	1	⸢ur⸣-^{d}nammu
4	2	[...]
5	0	[nita-k]ala-ga
5	1	[nita-k]ala-ga
5	2	[...]
6	0	[luga]l-uri$_{5}$.KI-ma
6	1	[luga]l-uri$_{5}$.KI-ma
6	2	[...]
7	0	lugal-ki-en-gi-ki-uri
7	1	[luga]l-ki-en-gi-ki-uri
7	2	⸢lugal-ki⸣-e[n]-gi-⸢ki-uri⸣
8	0	ad-da-na-šè
8	1	[ad-d]a-na-šè
8	2	ad-da-na-[šè]
9	0	en-nir-gál-⸢an⸣-na
9	1	[en-n]ir-gál-⸢an⸣-na
9	2	en-nir-⸢gál⸣-[an-na]
10	0	[e]n-^{d}nanna
10	1	[en]-⸢^{d}⸣nanna
10	2	[e]n-^{d}n[anna]
11	0	[dum]u ki-ág-ni
11	1	[dum]u ki-ág-ni
11	2	[dumu] ki-á[g-...]
12	0	⸢a⸣ mu-na-ru
12	1	⸢a⸣ mu-na-ru
12	2	[a mu]-⸢na⸣-[ru]

1	0	^{d}nimin-tab-ba
1	1a	...
1	1b	^{d}nimin-tab-ba
1	2a	...
1	2b	^{d}nimin-tab-ba
1	3a	...
1	3b	^{d}nimin-tab-ba
1	4a	^{d}nimin-tab-ba
1	4b	^{d}nimin-tab-ba
2	0	nin-a-ni
2	1a	...
2	1b	nin-a-ni
2	2a	...
2	2b	nin-a-ni
2	3a	...
2	3b	nin-a-ni
2	4a	nin-a-ni
2	4b	nin-a-ni
3	0	šul-gi
3	1a	...
3	1b	šul-gi
3	2a	...
3	2b	šul-gi
3	3a	...
3	3b	šul-gi
3	4a	šul-gi
3	4b	šul-gi
4	0	nita-kala-ga
4	1a	nita-kala-ga
4	1b	nita-kala-ga
4	2a	...
4	2b	nita-kala-ga
4	3a	...
4	3b	nita-kala-ga
4	4a	nita-kala-ga
4	4b	nita-kala-ga
5	0	lugal-uri$_5$.KI-ma
5	1a	...
5	1b	lugal-uri$_5$.KI-ma
5	2a	...
5	2b	lugal-uri$_5$.KI-ma
5	3a	...
5	3b	lugal-uri$_5$.KI-ma
5	4a	lugal-uri$_5$.KI-ma
5	4b	lugal-uri$_5$.KI-ma
6	0	lugal-ki-en-gi-ki-uri-ke$_4$
6	1a	...
6	1b	lugal-ki-en-gi-ki-uri-ke$_4$
6	2a	...
6	2b	lugal-ki-en-gi-ki-uri-ke$_4$
6	3a	...
6	3b	lugal-ki-en-gi-ki-uri-ke$_4$
6	4a	lugal-ki-en-gi-ki-uri-ke$_4$
6	4b	lugal-ki-en-gi-ki-uri-ke$_4$
7	0	é-a-ni
7	1a	...
7	1b	é-a-ni
7	2a	...
7	2b	é-a-ni
7	3a	...
7	3b	é-a-ni
7	4a	é-a-ni
7	4b	é-a-ni
8	0	mu-na-dù
8	1a	...
8	1b	mu-na-dù
8	2a	...
8	2b	mu-na-dù
8	3a	...
8	3b	mu-na-dù
8	4a	mu-na-dù
8	4b	mu-na-dù

1	0	^{d}inanna
1	1	^{d}ina[nna]
1	2	^{d}inanna
1	3a	^{d}inanna
1	3b	^{d}inanna
1	4a	^{d}inanna
1	4b	^{d}inanna
2	0	nin-é-an-na
2	1	nin-é-an-na
2	2	nin-é-an-na
2	3a	nin-é-an-na
2	3b	nin-é-an-na
2	4a	nin-é-an-na
2	4b	nin-é-an-na
3	0	nin-a-ni
3	1	nin-a-ni
3	2	nin-a-ni
3	3a	nin-a-ni
3	3b	nin-a-ni
3	4a	nin-a-ni
3	4b	nin-a-ni
4	0	šul-gi
4	1	šul-gi
4	2	⌈šul⌉-gi
4	3a	šul-gi
4	3b	šul-gi
4	4a	šul-gi
4	4b	šul-gi
5	0	nita-kala-ga
5	1	nita-kala-ga
5	2	nita-kala-ga
5	3a	...
5	3b	nita-kala-ga
5	4a	nita-kala-⌈ga⌉
5	4b	nita-kala-⌈ga⌉
6	0	lugal-uri$_{5}$.KI-ma
6	1	lugal-uri$_{5}$.KI-ma
6	2	⌈lugal⌉-uri$_{5}$.KI-ma
6	3a	...
6	3b	lugal-uri$_{5}$.KI-ma
6	4a	⌈lugal-uri$_{5}$.KI-ma⌉
6	4b	lugal-uri$_{5}$.KI-ma
7	0	lugal-ki-en-gi-ki-uri-ke$_{4}$
7	1	lugal-ki-en-gi-ki-uri-ke$_{4}$
7	2	⌈lugal⌉-ki-en-⌈gi⌉-ki-uri-ke$_{4}$
7	3a	...
7	3b	lugal-ki-en-gi-ki-uri-ke$_{4}$
7	4a	⌈lugal-ki-en-gi-ki-uri-ke$_{4}$⌉
7	4b	lugal-ki-en-gi-ki-uri-ke$_{4}$
8	0	é-an-na
8	1	é-an-na
8	2	é-⌈an-na⌉
8	3a	...
8	3b	é-an-na
8	4a	é-an-na
8	4b	é-an-na
9	0	ki-bé-mu-na-gi$_{4}$
9	1	ki-bé-mu-na-gi$_{4}$
9	2	ki-⌈bé⌉-[mu-na]-⌈gi$_{4}$⌉
9	3a	ki-bé-mu-na-gi$_{4}$
9	3b	ki-bé-mu-na-gi$_{4}$
9	4a	⌈ki-bé⌉-mu-na-gi$_{4}$
9	4b	ki-bé-mu-na-gi$_{4}$
10	0	bàd-gal-bi
10	1	bàd-gal-bi
10	2	bàd-gal-bi
10	3a	bàd-gal-bi
10	3b	bàd-gal-bi
10	4a	b[àd-gal-bi]
10	4b	bàd-gal-bi

11	0	mu-na-dù
11	1	mu-na-dù
11	2	mu-na-dù
11	3a	mu-na-dù
11	3b	mu-na-dù
11	4a	m[u-na-dù]
11	4b	mu-na-dù

Šulgi E3/2.1.2.9 page 35

1	0	^{d}nanše
1	1	⸢^{d}nanše⸣
1	2	^{d}nanše
1	3	^{d}nanše
1	4	...
1	5	...
2	0	nin-uru$_{16}$
2	1	⸢nin-uru$_{16}$⸣
2	2	nin-uru$_{16}$
2	3	^{d}nanše
2	4	...
2	5	...
3	0	nin-in-dub-ba
3	1	⸢nin⸣-i[n...]
3	2	nin-in-dub-ba
3	3	nin-in-dub-ba
3	4	...
3	5	...
4	0	nin-a-ni
4	1	nin-a-ni
4	2	nin-a-ni
4	3	nin-a-ni
4	4	...
4	5	...
5	0	šul-gi
5	1	šul-gi
5	2	šul-gi
5	3	šul-gi
5	4	...
5	5	...
6	0	nita-kala-ga
6	1	nita-kala-ga
6	2	nita-kala-ga
6	3	nita-kala-ga
6	4	...
6	5	nita-kala-ga
7	0	lugal-uri$_5$.KI-ma
7	1	l[ugal-...]
7	2	lugal-uri$_5$.KI-ma
7	3	lugal-uri$_5$.KI-ma
7	4	...
7	5	...
8	0	lugal-ki-en-gi-ki-uri-ke$_4$
8	1	[...]
8	2	lugal-ki-en-gi-ki-uri-ke$_4$
8	3	lugal-ki-en-gi-ki-uri-ke$_4$
8	4	...
8	5	...
9	0	é-šeš-šeš-e-gá-ra
9	1	[...]
9	2	é-šeš-šeš-e-gá-ra
9	3	é-šeš-šeš-e-gá-ra
9	4	...
9	5	...
10	0	é-ki-ág-gá-ni
10	1	[...]
10	2	é-ki-ág-gá-ni
10	3	é-ki-ág-gá-ni
10	4	...
10	5	...
11	0	mu-na-dù
11	1	[...]
11	2	mu-na-dù
11	3	mu-na-dù
11	4	...
11	5	...

1	0	^{d}nanše
1	1	^{d}nanše
1	2	[^{d}nan]še
1	3	^{d}nanše
1	4	^{d}nanše
1	5	^{d}nanše
1	6	^{d}nanše
1	7	^{d}nanše
1	8	^{d}nanš[e]
1	9	⌈^{d}⌉nanše
1	10	^{d}nanše
1	11	^{d}nanše
1	12	⌈^{d}nanše⌉
1	13	^{d}[na]nše
1	14	...
1	15	...
1	16	...
1	17	...
1	18	...
1	19	...
1	20	...
1	21	...
1	22	...
1	23	^{d}nanše
1	24	^{d}nanše
1	25	^{d}nanše
2	0	nin-in-dub-ba
2	1	nin-in-dub-ba
2	2	[nin-in-du]b-ba
2	3	nin-in-dub-ba
2	4	nin-in-dub-ba
2	5	nin-in-dub-ba
2	6	nin-in-dub-ba
2	7	nin-in-dub-ba
2	8	nin-in-dub-ba
2	9	[nin-i]n-dub-ba
2	10	nin-in-dub-ba
2	11	nin-in-dub-ba
2	12	⌈nin-in-dub-ba⌉
2	13	nin-in-dub-b[a]
2	14	...
2	15	...
2	16	...
2	17	...
2	18	...
2	19	...
2	20	...
2	21	...
2	22	...
2	23	nin-in-dub-ba
2	24	nin-in-dub-ba
2	25	nin-in-dub-ba
3	0	nin-a-ni
3	1	nin-a-ni
3	2	[nin-a]-ni
3	3	nin-a-ni
3	4	nin-a-ni
3	5	nin-a-ni
3	6	nin-a-ni
3	7	nin-a-ni
3	8	nin-a-ni
3	9	[nin-a]-ni
3	10	nin-a-ni
3	11	nin-a-ni
3	12	⌈nin-a-ni⌉
3	13	nin-a-ni
3	14	...
3	15	...
3	16	...
3	17	...
3	18	...
3	19	...
3	20	...
3	21	...
3	22	...
3	23	nin-a-ni
3	24	nin-a-ni
3	25	nin-a-ni

4	0	šul-gi
4	1	šul-gi
4	2	[šul]-gi
4	3	šul-gi
4	4	šul-gi
4	5	šul-gi
4	6	šul-gi
4	7	šul-gi
4	8	šul-gi
4	9	⸢šul⸣-gi
4	10	šul-gi
4	11	šul-gi
4	12	⸢šul-gi⸣
4	13	šul-gi
4	14	...
4	15	...
4	16	...
4	17	...
4	18	...
4	19	...
4	20	...
4	21	...
4	22	...
4	23	šul-gi
4	24	šul-gi
4	25	šul-gi
5	0	nita-kala-ga
5	1	nita-kala-ga
5	2	[nita-ka]la-ga
5	3	nita-kala-ga
5	4	nita-kala-ga
5	5	nita-kala-ga
5	6	nita-kala-ga
5	7	nita-kala-ga
5	8	nita-kala-ga
5	9	⸢nita-kala⸣-ga
5	10	nita-kala-ga
5	11	nita-kala-ga
5	12	⸢nita-kala-ga⸣
5	13	nita-kala-ga
5	14	...
5	15	...
5	16	...
5	17	...
5	18	...
5	19	...
5	20	...
5	21	...
5	22	...
5	23	nita-kala-ga
5	24	nita-kala-ga
5	25	nita-kala-ga
6	0	lugal-uri$_5$.KI-ma-ke$_4$
6	1	lugal-uri$_5$.KI-ma-ke$_4$
6	2	[lugal-ur]i$_5$.[KI]-ma
6	3	lugal-uri$_5$.KI-ma-ke$_4$
6	4	lugal-uri$_5$.KI-ma-ke$_4$
6	5	lugal-uri$_5$.KI-ma-ke$_4$
6	6	lugal-uri$_5$.KI-ma-ke$_4$
6	7	lugal-uri$_5$.KI-ma-ke$_4$
6	8	lugal-uri$_5$.KI-ma-ke$_4$
6	9	lugal-uri$_5$.KI-ma-ke$_4$
6	10	lugal-uri$_5$.KI-ma-ke$_4$
6	11	lugal-ur[i$_5$].KI-ma-ke$_4$
6	12	⸢lugal⸣-uri$_5$.KI-ma-ke$_4$
6	13	lugal-uri$_5$.KI-ma-ke$_4$
6	14	lugal-uri$_5$.KI-ma-ke$_4$
6	15	lugal-uri$_5$.KI-ma-ke$_4$
6	16	...
6	17	...
6	18	...
6	19	...
6	20	...
6	21	...
6	22	...
6	23	lugal-uri$_5$.KI-ma-ke$_4$
6	24	lugal-uri$_5$.KI-ma-ke$_4$
6	25	lugal-uri$_5$.KI-ma-ke$_4$

7	0	é-šeš-šeš-gar-ra-ka-ni
7	1	é-šeš-šeš-gar-ra-ka-ni
7	2	[... še]š-gar-ra-[ka]-ni
7	3	é-šeš-šeš-gar-ra-ka-ni
7	4	é-šeš-šeš-gar-ra-ka-ni
7	5	é-šeš-šeš-gar-ra-ka-ni
7	6	é-šeš-šeš-gar-ra-ka-ni
7	7	é-šeš-⌜šeš⌝-gar-ra-ka-ni
7	8	é-šeš-šeš-gar-ra-ka-ni
7	9	é-šeš-šeš-gar-ra-ka-ni
7	10	é-šeš-šeš-gar-ra-ka-ni
7	11	é-šeš-šeš-gar-[ra]-ka-ni
7	12	⌜é⌝-šeš-šeš-gar-ra-ka-ni
7	13	é-šeš-šeš-gar-r[a]-ka-ni
7	14	...
7	15	...
7	16	...
7	17	...
7	18	...
7	19	...
7	20	...
7	21	...
7	22	...
7	23	é-šeš-šeš-gar-ra-ka-ni
7	24	é-šeš-šeš-gar-ra-ka-ni
7	25	é-šeš-šeš-gar-ra-ka-ni
8	0	mu-na-dù
8	1	mu-na-dù
8	2	[mu-na]-dù
8	3	mu-na-dù
8	4	mu-na-dù
8	5	mu-na-dù
8	6	mu-na-dù
8	7	mu-na-dù
8	8	mu-na-dù
8	9	mu-na-dù
8	10	mu-na-dù
8	11	mu-na-dù
8	12	mu-na-dù
8	13	mu-na-dù
8	14	...
8	15	...
8	16	...
8	17	...
8	18	...
8	19	...
8	20	...
8	21	...
8	22	...
8	23	mu-na-dù
8	24	mu-na-dù
8	25	mu-na-dù

1	0	^{d}nin-gír-su
1	1	^{d}nin-gír-su
1	2	^{d}nin-gír-su
1	3	...
1	4a	^{d}nin-gír-su
1	4b	^{d}nin-gír-su
2	0	ur-sag-kala-ga
2	1	ur-sag-kala-ga
2	2	ur-sag-kala-ga
2	3	...
2	4a	ur-sag-kala-ga
2	4b	ur-sag-kala-ga
3	0	^{d}en-líl-lá
3	1	^{d}en-líl-lá
3	2	^{d}en-líl-lá
3	3	...
3	4a	^{d}en-líl-lá
3	4b	^{d}en-líl-lá
4	0	lugal-a-ni
4	1	lugal-a-ni
4	2	lugal-a-ni
4	3	...
4	4a	lugal-a-ni
4	4b	lugal-a-ni
5	0	^{d}šul-gi
5	1	^{d}šul-gi
5	2	^{d}šul-gi
5	3	...
5	4a	^{d}šul-gi
5	4b	^{d}šul-gi
6	0	nita-kala-ga
6	1	nita-kala-ga
6	2	nita-kala-ga
6	3	...
6	4a	nita-kala-ga
6	4b	nita-kala-ga
7	0	lugal-uri$_5$.KI-ma
7	1	lugal-uri$_5$.KI-ma
7	2	lugal-uri$_5$.KI-ma
7	3	...
7	4a	lugal-uri$_5$.KI-ma
7	4b	lugal-uri$_5$.KI-ma
8	0	lugal-ki-en-gi-ki-uri-ke$_4$
8	1	lugal-ki-en-gi-ki-uri-ke$_4$
8	2	lugal-ki-en-gi-ki-uri-ke$_4$
8	3	...
8	4a	lugal-⸢ki-en⸣-gi-ki-uri-ke$_4$
8	4b	lugal-ki-en-gi-ki-uri-ke$_4$
9	0	é-ninnu
9	1	é-ninnu
9	2	é-ninnu
9	3	...
9	4a	é-⸢ninnu⸣
9	4b	é-ninnu
10	0	é-ki-ág-gá-ni
10	1	é-ki-ág-gá-ni
10	2	é-ki-ág-gá-ni
10	3	...
10	4a	é-[ki-ág]-g[á-ni]
10	4b	é-ki-ág-gá-ni
11	0	mu-na-dù
11	1	mu-na-dù
11	2	mu-na-dù
11	3	...
11	4a	mu-⸢na-dù⸣
11	4b	mu-na-dù

1	0	^{d}nin-gír-su
1	1	...
1	2	^{d}nin-gír-su
1	3	^{d}nin-gír-su
1	4	^{d}nin-gír-su
1	5	^{d}nin-[gír-s]u
1	6	^{d}nin-gír-su
1	7	^{d}nin-g[ír-su]
1	8	^{d}nin-gír-su
1	9	...
2	0	ur-sag-kala-ga
2	1	...
2	2	ur-sag-kala-⌈ga⌉
2	3	ur-sag-kala-ga
2	4	ur-sag-kala-ga
2	5	ur-sag-⌈kal⌉-ga
2	6	ur-sag-kala-ga
2	7	ur-sag-kal[a-ga]
2	8	ur-sag-kala-ga
2	9	...
3	0	^{d}en-líl-lá
3	1	...
3	2	^{d}en-líl-lá
3	3	^{d}en-líl-lá
3	4	^{d}en-líl-lá
3	5	^{d}en-líl-lá
3	6	^{d}en-líl-lá
3	7	^{d}en-líl-[lá]
3	8	^{d}en-líl-lá
3	9	...
4	0	lugal-a-ni
4	1	...
4	2	lugal-a-ni
4	3	lugal-a-ni
4	4	lugal-a-ni
4	5	lugal-a-ni
4	6	lugal-a-ni
4	7	lugal-a-n[i]
4	8	lugal-a-ni
4	9	...
5	0	^{d}šul-gi
5	1	...
5	2	^{d}šul-gi
5	3	^{d}šul-gi
5	4	^{d}šul-gi
5	5	⌈^{d}⌉šul-gi
5	6	^{d}šul-gi
5	7	^{d}šul-g[i]
5	8	^{d}šul-g[i]
5	9	...
6	0	nita-kala-ga
6	1	...
6	2	nita-kala-ga
6	3	nita-kala-ga
6	4	nita-kala-ga
6	5	nita-kala-ga
6	6	nita-kala-ga
6	7	nita-kala-g[a]
6	8	nita-kala-ga
6	9	...
7	0	lugal-uri$_5$.KI-ma
7	1	...
7	2	lugal-uri$_5$.KI-ma
7	3	lugal-uri$_5$.KI-ma
7	4	lugal-uri$_5$.KI-ma
7	5	lugal-uri$_5$.KI-ma
7	6	lugal-uri$_5$.KI-ma
7	7	lugal-u[ri$_5$].KI-m[a]
7	8	lugal-uri$_5$.KI-ma
7	9	...
8	0	lugal-ki-en-gi-ki-uri-ke$_4$
8	1	...
8	2	lugal-ki-en-gi-ki-uri-ke$_4$
8	3	lugal-ki-en-gi-ki-uri-ke$_4$
8	4	lugal-ki-en-gi-ki-uri-ke$_4$
8	5	lugal-ki-en-gi-ki-uri-ke$_4$
8	6	lugal-ki-en-gi-ki-uri-ke$_4$
8	7	lugal-k[i-en]-gi-ki-uri-[ke$_4$]
8	8	lugal-ki-en-gi-ki-uri-ke$_4$
8	9	...

9	0	é-a-ni
9	1	...
9	2	[é]-⌈a⌉-ni
9	3	é-a-ni
9	4	é-a-ni
9	5	é-a-ni
9	6	é-a-ni
9	7	é-a-ni
9	8	é-a-ni
9	9	...

10	0	mu-na-dù
10	1	...
10	2	[m]u-na-dù
10	3	mu-na-dù
10	4	mu-na-dù
10	5	⌈mu⌉-na-[dù]
10	6	mu-na-dù
10	7	mu-na-[dù]
10	8	mu-na-dù
10	9	...

1	0	^{d}nin-mar-ki
1	1	^{d}nin-mar-ki
1	2	^{d}nin-mar-ki
1	3	^{d}nin-mar-ki
1	4	^{d}nin-mar-ki
2	0	nin-a-ni
2	1	nin-a-ni
2	2	nin-a-ni
2	3	nin-a-ni
2	4	nin-a-ni
3	0	^{d}šul-gi
3	1	^{d}šul-gi
3	2	^{d}šul-gi
3	3	^{d}šul-gi
3	4	^{d}šul-gi
4	0	nita-kala-ga
4	1	nita-kala-ga
4	2	nita-⸢kala⸣-ga
4	3	nita-kala-ga
4	4	nita-kala-ga
5	0	lugal-uri$_5$.KI-ma
5	1	lugal-uri$_5$.KI-ma
5	2	lugal-uri$_5$.KI-ma
5	3	lugal-uri$_5$.KI-ma
5	4	lugal-uri$_5$.KI-ma
6	0	lugal-ki-en-gi-ki-uri-ke$_4$
6	1	lugal-ki-en-gi-ki-uri-ke$_4$
6	2	lugal-ki-en-gi-ki-uri-ke$_4$
6	3	lugal-ki-en-gi-ki-uri-ke$_4$
6	4	lugal-ki-en-gi-ki-uri-ke$_4$
7	0	é-munus-gi$_{16}$-sa
7	1	é-munus-gi$_{16}$-s[a]
7	2	é-munus-gi$_{16}$-sa
7	3	é-munus-gi$_{16}$-sa
7	4	é-munus-gi$_{16}$-sa
8	0	gír-su.KI-ka-ni
8	1	gír-su.KI-ka-ni
8	2	gír-su.KI-ka-ni
8	3	gír-su.KI-ka-ni
8	4	gír-su.KI-ka-ni
9	0	mu-na-dù
9	1	mu-na-dù
9	2	mu-na-dù
9	3	mu-na-dù
9	4	mu-na-dù

1	0	^{d}inanna
1	1a	^{d}inanna
1	2a	...
1	3a	...
1	4a	...
1	5a	^{d}inanna
1	6a1	^{d}[i]nanna
1	6a2	...
2	0	nin-a-ni
2	1a	nin-a-ni
2	2a	...
2	3a	...
2	4a	...
2	5a	nin-a-ni
2	6a1	nin-⸢a⸣-[n]i
2	6a2	...
3	0	šul-gi
3	1a	šul-gi
3	2a	...
3	3a	...
3	4a	...
3	5a	šul-gi
3	6a1	[š]ul-[g]i
3	6a2	...
4	0	nita-kala-ga
4	1a	nita-kala-ga
4	2a	...
4	3a	...
4	4a	...
4	5a	nita-kala-ga
4	6a1	nita-kala-ga
4	6a2	...
5	0	lugal-uri$_5$.KI-ma
5	1a	lugal-uri$_5$.KI-ma
5	2a	...
5	3a	...
5	4a	...
5	5a	lugal-uri$_5$.KI-ma
5	6a1	lugal-ŠEŠ.[A]B.ki-m[a]
5	6a2	...
6	0	lugal-ki-en-gi-ki-uri-ke$_4$
6	1a	⸢lugal-ki-en-gi-ki-uri-ke$_4$⸣
6	2a	...
6	3a	...
6	4a	...
6	5a	lugal-⸢ki⸣-en-gi-⸢ki-uri⸣-ke$_4$
6	6a1	lugal-ki-en-[g]i-ki-uri-k[e$_4$]
6	6a2	...
7	0	é-dur-an-ki-ka-ni
7	1a	é-dur-an-ki-ka-ni
7	2a	...
7	3a	...
7	4a	...
7	5a	é-dur-an-ki-⸢ka⸣-ni
7	6a1	é-dur-an-k[i]-ka-ni
7	6a2	...
8	0	mu-na-dù
8	1a	mu-na-dù
8	2a	...
8	3a	...
8	4a	...
8	5a	mu-na-dù
8	6a1	mu-na-[dù]
8	6a2	...

1	0	^{d}inanna
1	1	^{d}inanna
1	2	^{d}inanna
1	3	^{d}inanna
2	0	nin-a-ni
2	1	nin-a-ni
2	2	nin-a-ni
2	3	nin-a-ni
3	0	šul-gi
3	1	šul-gi
3	2	šul-gi
3	3	šul-gi
4	0	nita-kala-ga
4	1	nita-kala-ga
4	2	nita-kala-ga
4	3	nita-kala-ga
5	0	lugal-uri$_5$.KI-ma
5	1	lugal-uri$_5$.KI-ma
5	2	lugal-uri$_5$.KI-ma
5	3	lugal-uri$_5$.KI-ma
6	0	lugal-ki-en-gi-ki-uri-ke$_4$
6	1	lugal-ki-en-gi-ki-uri-ke$_4$
6	2	lugal-ki-en-gi-ki-uri-ke$_4$
6	3	lugal-ki-en-gi-ki-uri-ke$_4$
7	0	é-dur-an-ki-ka-ni
7	1	⌈é-dur-an-ki-ka⌉-ni
7	2	é-dur-an-ki-ka-ni
7	3	é-dur-an-ki-ka-ni
8	0	mu-na-dù
8	1	mu-na-dù
8	2	mu-na-dù
8	3	mu-na-dù
9	0	ki-bé mu-na-gi$_4$
9	1	ki-bé mu-na-gi$_4$
9	2	ki-bé mu-na-gi$_4$
9	3	ki-bé mu-na-gi$_4$
10	0	nam-ti-la-ni-šè
10	1	nam-ti-la-ni-šè
10	2	nam-ti-la-ni-šè
10	3	nam-ti-la-ni-šè
11	0	a mu-na-ru
11	1	a mu-na-ru
11	2	a mu-na-ru
11	3	a mu-na-ru

1	0	^{d}nin-ḫur-saga
1	1	^{d}nin-ḫur-saga
1	2	^{d}nin-ḫur-saga
1	3	^{d}nin-ḫur-saga
1	4	^{d}nin-ḫur-saga
1	5	^{d}nin-ḫur-saga
1	6	^{d}nin-ḫur-saga
1	7	^{d}nin-ḫur-saga
1	8	^{d}nin-ḫur-saga
1	9	^{d}nin-ḫur-saga
1	10	...
1	11	^{d}nin-ḫur-saga
1	12	^{d}nin-ḫur-saga
1	13	...
1	14	...
1	15	...
1	16	^{d}nin-ḫur-saga
1	17	...

2	0	šušin.KI-na
2	1	šušin.KI-na
2	2	šušin.KI-na
2	3	šušin.KI-na
2	4	šušin.KI-na
2	5	šušin.KI-na
2	6	šušin.KI-na
2	7	šušin.KI-na
2	8	šušin.KI-na
2	9	šušin.KI-na
2	10	...
2	11	šušin.KI-na
2	12	šušin.KI-na
2	13	...
2	14	...
2	15	...
2	16	šušin.KI-na
2	17	...

3	0	nin-a-ni
3	1	nin-a-ni
3	2	nin-a-ni
3	3	nin-a-ni
3	4	nin-a-ni
3	5	nin-a-ni
3	6	nin-a-ni
3	7	nin-a-ni
3	8	nin-a-ni
3	9	nin-a-ni
3	10	...
3	11	nin-a-ni
3	12	nin-a-ni
3	13	...
3	14	...
3	15	...
3	16	nin-a-ni
3	17	...

4	0	^{d}šul-gi
4	1	^{d}šul-gi
4	2	^{d}šul-gi
4	3	^{d}šul-gi
4	4	^{d}šul-gi
4	5	^{d}šul-gi
4	6	^{d}šul-gi
4	7	^{d}šul-gi
4	8	^{d}šul-gi
4	9	^{d}šul-gi
4	10	...
4	11	^{d}šul-gi
4	12	^{d}šul-gi
4	13	...
4	14	...
4	15	...
4	16	^{d}šul-gi
4	17	...

5	0	nita-kala-ga
5	1	nita-kala-ga
5	2	nita-kala-ga
5	3	nita-kala-ga
5	4	nita-kala-ga
5	5	nita-kala-ga
5	6	nita-kala-ga
5	7	nita-kala-ga
5	8	nita-kala-ga
5	9	nita-kala-ga
5	10	...
5	11	nita-kala-ga
5	12	nita-kala-ga
5	13	...
5	14	...
5	15	...
5	16	nita-kala-ga
5	17	...

6	0	lugal-uri$_5$.KI-ma
6	1	lugal-uri$_5$.KI-ma
6	2	lugal-uri$_5$.KI-ma
6	3	lugal-uri$_5$.KI-ma
6	4	lugal-uri$_5$.KI-ma
6	5	lugal-uri$_5$.KI-ma
6	6	lugal-uri$_5$.KI-ma
6	7	lugal-uri$_5$.KI-ma
6	8	lugal-uri$_5$.KI-ma
6	9	lugal-uri$_5$.KI-ma
6	10	...
6	11	lugal-uri$_5$.KI-ma
6	12	lugal-uri$_5$.KI-ma
6	13	...
6	14	...
6	15	...
6	16	lugal-uri$_5$.KI-ma
6	17	...

7	0	lugal-ki-en-gi-ki-uri-ke$_4$
7	1	lugal-ki-en-gi-ki-uri-ke$_4$
7	2	lugal-ki-en-gi-ki-uri-ke$_4$
7	3	lugal-ki-en-gi-ki-uri-ke$_4$
7	4	lugal-ki-en-gi-ki-uri-ke$_4$
7	5	lugal-ki-en-gi-ki-uri-ke$_4$
7	6	lugal-ki-en-gi-ki-uri-ke$_4$
7	7	lugal-ki-en-gi-ki-uri-ke$_4$
7	8	lugal-ki-en-gi-ki-uri-ke$_4$
7	9	lugal-ki-en-gi-ki-uri-ke$_4$
7	10	...
7	11	lugal-ki-en-gi-ki-uri-ke$_4$
7	12	lugal-ki-en-gi-ki-uri-ke$_4$
7	13	...
7	14	...
7	15	...
7	16	lugal-ki-en-gi-ki-uri-ke$_4$
7	17	...

8	0	é-a-ni
8	1	é-a-ni
8	2	é-a-ni
8	3	é-a-ni
8	4	é-a-ni
8	5	é-a-ni
8	6	é-a-ni
8	7	é-a-ni
8	8	é-a-ni
8	9	é-a-ni
8	10	...
8	11	é-a-ni
8	12	é-a-ni
8	13	...
8	14	...
8	15	...
8	16	é-a-ni
8	17	...

9	0	mu-na-dù
9	1	mu-na-dù
9	2	mu-na-dù
9	3	mu-na-dù
9	4	mu-na-dù
9	5	mu-na-dù
9	6	mu-na-dù
9	7	mu-na-dù
9	8	mu-na-dù
9	9	mu-na-dù
9	10	...
9	11	mu-na-dù
9	12	mu-na-dù
9	13	...
9	14	...
9	15	...
9	16	mu-na-dù
9	17	...

1	0	šul-gi
1	1	[šu]l-gi
1	2	šul-gi
1	3	...
1	4	...
1	5	...
1	6	...
2	0	nita-kala-ga
2	1	[nita]-kal-ga
2	2	nita-kala-ga
2	3	...
2	4	...
2	5	...
2	6	...
3	0	lugal-uri$_5$.KI-ma
3	1	[lugal]-uri$_5$.[KI]-ma
3	2	lugal-uri$_5$.KI-ma
3	3	...
3	4	...
3	5	...
3	6	...
4	0	lugal-ki-en-gi-ki-uri-ke$_4$
4	1	[lugal-ki]-en-[gi-ki]-uri-ke$_4$
4	2	lugal-ki-en-gi-<ki>-uri-ke$_4$
4	3	...
4	4	...
4	5	...
4	6	...
5	0	^{d}NIN-šušin-KI-ra
5	1	[...]
5	2	^{d}NIN.šušin.KI-ra
5	3	...
5	4	...
5	5	...
5	6	...
6	0	é-a-ni
6	1	[...]
6	2	é-a-ni
6	3	...
6	4	...
6	5	...
6	6	...
7	0	mu-na-dù
7	1	[...]
7	2	mu-na-dù
7	3	...
7	4	...
7	5	...
7	6	...
8	0	ki-bé mu-na-gi$_4$
8	1	[...]
8	2	ki-bé mu-na-gi$_4$
8	3	...
8	4	...
8	5	...
8	6	...

Šulgi E3/2.1.2.32 page 49

1	0	^{d}NIN-šušin
1	1	...
1	2	^{d}NIN-šušin
1	3	⸢^{d}NIN-šušin⸣
1	4	^{d}NIN-šušin
1	5	^{d}NIN-šušin
1	6	^{d}NIN-šušin
1	7	^{d}NIN-šuš[in]
1	8	^{d}NIN-šušin
1	9	^{d}NIN-šušin
1	10	...
1	11	^{d}NIN-šušin
1	12	^{d}NIN-šušin
1	13	^{d}NIN-šušin
1	14	^{d}NIN-šušin
1	15	^{d}NIN-šušin
1	16	^{d}NIN-šušin
1	17	[^{d}NIN]-šušin
2	0	lugal-a-ni
2	1	...
2	2	lugal-a-ni
2	3	[lugal]-a-ni
2	4	[lug]al-a-ni
2	5	lugal-a-ni
2	6	lugal-a-ni
2	7	lugal-a-ni
2	8	lugal-a-ni
2	9	lugal-a-ni
2	10	...
2	11	lugal-a-ni
2	12	lugal-a-ni
2	13	lugal-a-ni
2	14	lugal-a-ni
2	15	lugal-a-ni
2	16	lugal-a-ni
2	17	[l]ugal-a-ni
3	0	^{d}šul-gi
3	1	...
3	2	^{d}šul-gi
3	3	^{d}[šul-gi]
3	4	⸢^{d}šul⸣-gi
3	5	^{d}šul-gi
3	6	^{d}šul-gi
3	7	^{d}šul-gi
3	8	^{d}šul-gi
3	9	^{d}šul-gi
3	10	...
3	11	^{d}šul-gi
3	12	^{d}šul-gi
3	13	^{d}šul-gi
3	14	^{d}šul-gi
3	15	^{d}šul-gi
3	16	^{d}šul-gi
3	17	^{d}šul-gi
4	0	nita-kala-ga
4	1	...
4	2	nita-kala-ga
4	3	[...]
4	4	⸢nita-kala⸣-[g]a
4	5	nita-kala-ga
4	6	nita-kala-ga
4	7	nita-kala-ga
4	8	⸢nita⸣-kala-ga
4	9	nita-kala-ga
4	10	...
4	11	nita-kala-ga
4	12	nita-kala-ga
4	13	nita-kala-ga
4	14	nita-kala-ga
4	15	nita-kala-ga
4	16	nita-kala-ga
4	17	nita-kala-ga

5	0	lugal-uri$_5$.KI-ma	7	0	a-ar-ke$_4$-éš
5	1	...	7	1	...
5	2	lu[gal]-⸢uri$_5$⸣.KI-⸢ma⸣	7	2	a-ar-ke$_4$-éš
5	3	[...]	7	3	[a-ar]-⸢ke$_4$⸣-éš
5	4	lugal-⸢uri$_5$.⸣KI-ma	7	4	a-ar-ke$_4$-éš
5	5	⸢lugal-uri$_5$.KI-ma⸣	7	5	a-ar-ke$_4$-éš
5	6	lugal-uri$_5$.KI-ma	7	6	a-ar-ke$_4$-éš
5	7	lugal-uri$_5$.KI-ma	7	7	⸢a⸣-[...]
5	8	lugal-uri$_5$.KI-ma	7	8	a-ar-ke$_4$-éš
5	9	lugal-uri$_5$.KI-ma	7	9	a-ar-ke$_4$-éš
5	10	...	7	10	...
5	11	lugal-uri$_5$.KI-ma	7	11	a-ar-ke$_4$-éš
5	12	lugal-uri$_5$.KI-ma	7	12	a-ar-ke$_4$-éš
5	13	lugal-uri$_5$.KI-ma	7	13	a-ar-ke$_4$-éš
5	14	lugal-uri$_5$.KI-ma	7	14	a-ar-ke$_4$-éš
5	15	lugal-uri$_5$.KI-ma	7	15	a-ar-ke$_4$-éš
5	16	lugal-uri$_5$.K[I-ma]	7	16	a-ar-ke$_4$-éš
5	17	lugal-uri$_5$.KI-ma	7	17	a-ar-ke$_4$-éš
6	0	lugal-ki-en-gi-ki-uri-ke$_4$	8	0	é-ki-ág-gá-ni
6	1	...	8	1	...
6	2	lugal-ki-en-gi-ki-uri-ke$_4$	8	2	é-ki-ág-gá-ni
6	3	⸢lugal⸣-ki-en-⸢gi⸣-uri-ke$_4$	8	3	⸢é⸣-[ki]-ág-⸢gá-ni⸣
6	4	lugal-ki-en-gi-ki-uri-ke$_4$	8	4	é-[ki-ág]-g[á-n]i
6	5	lugal-ki-en-gi-ki-uri-ke$_4$	8	5	é-ki-ág-gá-ni
6	6	⸢lugal-ki⸣-en-[g]i-ki-uri-ke$_4$	8	6	é-ki-ág-gá-ni
6	7	[...]	8	7	⸢é⸣-[...]
6	8	lugal-ki-en-gi-ki-uri-ke$_4$	8	8	é-ki-ág-gá-ni
6	9	lugal-ki-en-gi-ki-uri-ke$_4$	8	9	é-ki-ág-gá-ni
6	10	...	8	10	...
6	11	lugal-ki-en-gi-ki-uri-ke$_4$	8	11	é-ki-ág-gá-ni
6	12	lugal-ki-en-gi-ki-uri-ke$_4$	8	12	é-ki-ág-gá-ni
6	13	lugal-ki-en-gi-ki-uri-ke$_4$	8	13	é-ki-ág-gá-ni
6	14	lugal-ki-en-gi-ki-uri-ke$_4$	8	14	é-ki-ág-gá-ni
6	15	lugal-ki-en-gi-ki-uri-ke$_4$	8	15	é-ki-ág-gá-ni
6	16	lugal-[ki-en]-gi-ki-⸢uri-ke$_4$⸣	8	16	é-ki-ág-gá-ni
6	17	lugal-ki-en-gi-ki-uri-ke$_4$	8	17	é-ki-ág-gá-ni

9	0	mu-na-dù
9	1	...
9	2	mu-na-dù
9	3	mu-na-dù
9	4	mu-n[a-dù]
9	5	[mu-na]-dù
9	6	mu-na-dù
9	7	[...]
9	8	mu-na-dù
9	9	mu-na-dù
9	10	...
9	11	mu-na-dù
9	12	mu-na-dù
9	13	mu-na-dù
9	14	mu-na-dù
9	15	mu-na-dù
9	16	mu-na-dù
9	17	mu-na-dù

1	0	^{d}šul-gi
1	1	^{d}šul-gi
1	2	^{d}šul-⸢gi⸣
2	0	nita-kala-ga
2	1	nita-kala-ga
2	2	nita-kala-⸢ga⸣
3	0	lugal-uri$_5$.KI-ma
3	1	lugal-uri$_5$.KI-ma
3	2	lugal-uri$_5$.KI-ma
4	0	lugal-an-ub-da-límmu-ba
4	1	lugal-an-ub-da-límmu-ba
4	2	lugal-an-ub-da-límmu-ba
5	0	*simat*(ME)-^{d}*en-líl*
5	1	*simat*(ME)-^{d}*en-líl*
5	2	*simat*(ME)-^{d}*en-líl*
6	0	dumu-munus-a-ni
6	1	dumu-munus-a-ni
6	2	dumu-munus-a-ni

1	0	^{d}nin-gal
1	1	^{d}nin-gal
1	2	...
1	3	...
1	4	^{d}nin-gal
1	5	^{d}nin-gal
1	6	^{d}nin-gal
1	7	^{d}nin-gal
1	A	^{d}nin-gal
1	B	^{d}nin-gal
1	C	[...]
1	D	[...]
2	0	nin-a-ni-ir
2	1	nin-a-ni-ir
2	2	...
2	3	...
2	4	nin-a-ni-ir
2	5	nin-a-ni-ir
2	6	nin-a-ni-ir
2	7	nin-a-ni-ir
2	A	nin-a-ni-ir
2	B	nin-a-ni-ir
2	C	[...]
2	D	[...]
3	0	^{d}amar-^{d}EN.ZU
3	1	^{d}amar-^{d}EN.ZU
3	2	...
3	3	...
3	4	^{d}amar-^{d}EN.ZU
3	5	^{d}amar-^{d}EN.ZU
3	6	^{d}amar-^{d}EN.ZU
3	7	^{d}amar-^{d}EN.ZU
3	A	^{d}amar-^{d}EN.ZU
3	B	^{d}amar-^{d}EN.ZU
3	C	[...]
3	D	[...]
4	0	nita-kala-ga
4	1	nita-kala-ga
4	2	...
4	3	...
4	4	nita-kala-ga
4	5	nita-kala-ga
4	6	nita-kala-ga
4	7	nita-kala-ga
4	A	nita-kala-ga
4	B	nita-kala-ga
4	C	[nita-kala-g]a
4	D	[...]
5	0	lugal-uri$_5$.KI-ma
5	1	lugal-uri$_5$.KI-ma
5	2	...
5	3	...
5	4	lugal-uri$_5$.KI-ma
5	5	lugal-uri$_5$.KI-ma
5	6	lugal-uri$_5$.KI-ma
5	7	lugal-uri$_5$.KI-ma
5	A	lugal-uri$_5$.KI-ma
5	B	lugal-uri$_5$.KI-ma
5	C	[lugal-ŠEŠ].AB.[KI]-ma
5	D	[lugal-ŠEŠ].AB.[KI]-⌈ma⌉
6	0	lugal-an-ub-da-límmu-ba-ke$_4$
6	1	lugal-an-ub-da-límmu-ba-ke$_4$
6	2	...
6	3	...
6	4	lugal-an-ub-da-límmu-ba-ke$_4$
6	5	lugal-an-ub-da-límmu-ba-ke$_4$
6	6	lugal-an-ub-da-límmu-ba-ke$_4$
6	7	lugal-an-ub-da-límmu-ba-ke$_4$
6	A	lugal-an-ub-da-límmu-ba-ke$_4$
6	B	lugal-an-ub-da-límmu-ba-ke$_4$
6	C	[lugal-an]-⌈ub⌉-[da-límmu-ba-ke$_4$]
6	D	[lugal-an-ub]-da-[límmu-ba]-ke$_4$

7	0	gi$_6$-par$_4$-kù é-ki-ág-gá-ni
7	1	gi$_6$-par$_4$-kù-ga-ni
7	2	...
7	3	...
7	4	gi$_6$-par$_4$-kù é-ki-ág-gá-ni
7	5	g[i$_6$]-par$_4$-⌈kù⌉ é-ki-⌈ág⌉-gá-ni
7	6	gi$_6$-par$_4$-kù-ga-ni
7	7	gi$_6$-par$_4$-kù é-ki-ág-gá-ni
7	A	gi$_6$-pàr-kù-ga-ni
7	B	gi$_6$-pàr-kù-ga-ni
7	C	[...]
7	D	gi$_6$-pàr-⌈kù⌉-g[a]-⌈ni⌉
8	0	mu-na-dù
8	1	mu-na-dù
8	2	...
8	3	...
8	4	mu-na-dù
8	5	mu-na-dù
8	6	mu-na-dù
8	7	mu-na-dù
8	A	mu-na-dù
8	B	mu-na-dù
8	C	[...]
8	D	[mu-na-d]ù
9	0	nam-ti-la-ni-šè
9	1	nam-ti-la-ni-šè
9	2	...
9	3	...
9	4	nam-ti-la-ni-šè
9	5	[na]m-ti-la-ni-šè
9	6	nam-ti-la-ni-šè
9	7	nam-ti-la-ni-šè
9	A	nam-ti-la-ni-šè
9	B	nam-ti-la-ni-šè
9	C	[...]
9	D	[nam-ti-la]-ni-šè
10	0	a mu-na-ru
10	1	a mu-na-ru
10	2	...
10	3	...
10	4	a mu-na-ru
10	5	[a m]u-na-ru
10	6	a mu-na-ru
10	7	a mu-na-ru
10	A	a mu-na-ru
10	B	a-mu-na-ru
10	C	[...]
10	D	[...]

1	0	^{d}nanna
1	1	[...]
1	2	^{d}nanna
1	3	^{d}nanna
2	0	lugal-ki-ág-gá-ni-ir
2	1	[...]
2	2	lugal-ki-ág-gá-ni-ir
2	3	lugal-ki-ág-gá-ni-ir
3	0	dub-lá-maḫ
3	1	[...]
3	2	dub-lá-maḫ
3	3	dub-lá-maḫ
4	0	u$_{4}$-ul-lí-a-ta
4	1	[u$_{4}$]-ul-lí-a-ta
4	2	u$_{4}$-ul-lí-a-ta
4	3	u$_{4}$-ul-lí-a-ta
5	0	ki-šu-tag
5	1	[ki]-šu-tag
5	2	ki-šu-tag
5	3	ki-šu-tag
6	0	šuku-UD šub-ba
6	1	[šuku]-UD šub-ba
6	2	šuku-UD šub-ba
6	3	šuku-UD šub-ba
7	0	ì-me-a-na-an-na
7	1	[ì-me]-a-na-an-na
7	2	ì-me-a-na-an-na
7	3	ì-me-a-na-an-na
8	0	é-bi nu-dù-àm
8	1	⸢é⸣-bi nu-dù-àm
8	2	é-bi nu-dù-àm
8	3	é-bi nu-dù-àm
9	0	^{d}amar-^{d}EN.ZU
9	1	⸢^{d}⸣amar-^{d}EN.ZU
9	2	^{d}amar-^{d}EN.ZU
9	3	^{d}amar-^{d}EN.ZU
10	0	ki-ág-^{d}nanna
10	1	⸢ki⸣-ág-^{d}nanna
10	2	ki-ág-^{d}nanna
10	3	ki-ág-^{d}nanna
11	0	nibru.KI-a
11	1	nibru.KI-a
11	2	nibru.KI-a
11	3	nibru.KI-a
12	0	^{d}en-líl-le
12	1	^{d}en-líl-le
12	2	^{d}en-líl-le
12	3	^{d}en-líl-le
13	0	mu-pà-da
13	1	mu-pà-da
13	2	mu-pà-da
13	3	mu-pà-da
14	0	sag-ús-
14	1	sag-ús-
14	2	sag-ús-
14	3	sag-ús-
15	0	é-^{d}en-líl-ka
15	1	é-^{d}en-líl-ka
15	2	é-^{d}en-líl-ka
15	3	é-^{d}en-líl-ka
16	0	nita-kala-ga
16	1	nita-kala-ga
16	2	nita-kala-ga
16	3	nita-kala-ga

17	0	lugal-uri$_5$.KI-ma
17	1	lugal-uri$_5$.KI-ma
17	2	lugal-uri$_5$.KI-ma
17	3	lugal-uri$_5$.KI-ma
18	0	lugal-an-ub-da-límmu-ba-ke$_4$
18	1	lugal-an-ub-da-límmu-ba-ke$_4$
18	2	lugal-an-ub-da-límmu-ba-ke$_4$
18	3	lugal-an-ub-da-límmu-ba-ke$_4$
19	0	dub-lá-maḫ
19	1	dub-lá-maḫ
19	2	dub-lá-maḫ
19	3	dub-lá-maḫ
20	0	é-u$_6$-di-kalam-ma
20	1	é-u$_6$-di-kalam-ma
20	2	é-u$_6$-di-kalam-ma
20	3	é-u$_6$-di-kalam-ma
21	0	ki-di-ku$_5$-da-ni
21	1	ki-di-ku$_5$-da-ni
21	2	ki-di-ku$_5$-da-ni
21	3	ki-di-ku$_5$-da-ni
22	0	sa-bar-a-ni
22	1	sa-bar-a-ni
22	2	sa-bar-a-ni
22	3	sa-bar-a-ni
23	0	lú-NE.RU-
23	1	lú-NE.RU-
23	2	lú-NE.RU-
23	3	lú-NE.RU-
24	0	^{d}amar-^{d}EN.ZU-ka
24	1	^{d}amar-^{d}EN.ZU-ka
24	2	^{d}amar-^{d}EN.ZU-ka
24	3	^{d}amar-^{d}EN.ZU-ka
25	0	nu-è
25	1	nu-è
25	2	nu-è
25	3	nu-è
26	0	é-bi mu-na-dù
26	1	é-bi mu-na-dù
26	2	é-bi mu-na-dù
26	3	é-bi mu-na-dù
27	0	pa mu-na-an-è
27	1	pa mu-na-an-è
27	2	pa mu-na-an-è
27	3	pa mu-na-an-è
28	0	kù-GI kù-babbar NA$_4$.za-gìn-na
28	1	kù-GI kù-babbar NA$_4$.za-gìn-na
28	2	kù-GI kù-babbar NA$_4$.za-gìn-na
28	3	kù-GI kù-babbar NA$_4$.za-gìn-na
29	0	mí mu-na-ni-du$_{11}$
29	1	mí mu-na-ni-du$_{11}$
29	2	mí mu-na-ni-du$_{11}$
29	3	mí mu-na-ni-du$_{11}$
30	0	^{d}amar-^{d}EN.ZU-ke$_4$
30	1	^{d}amar-^{d}EN.ZU-ke$_4$
30	2	^{d}amar-^{d}EN.ZU-ke$_4$
30	3	^{d}amar-^{d}EN.ZU-ke$_4$
31	0	u$_4$-im-da-ab-sù-re$_6$
31	1	u$_4$-im-da-ab-sù-re$_6$
31	2	u$_4$-im-da-ab-sù-re$_6$
31	3	u$_4$-im-da-ab-sù-re$_6$

32	0	lú é a-ba-sumun
32	1	lú é a-ba-sumun
32	2	lú é a-ba-sumun
32	3	lú é a-ba-sumun
33	0	ù-un-dù
33	1	ù-un-dù
33	2	ù-un-dù
33	3	ù-un-dù
34	0	mu-sar-ra-bi
34	1	mu-sar-ra-bi
34	2	mu-sar-ra-bi
34	3	mu-sar-ra-bi
35	0	ù GIŠ.šu-kár-bi
35	1	ù GIŠ.šu-kár-bi
35	2	ù GIŠ.šu-kár-bi
35	3	ù GIŠ.šu-kár-bi
36	0	ki-gub-ba-bé
36	1	ki-gub-ba-bé
36	2	ki-gub-ba-bé
36	3	ki-gub-ba-bé
37	0	nu-ub-da-ab-kúr-re-a
37	1	nu-ub-da-ab-kúr-re-⌜a⌝
37	2	nu-ub-da-ab-kúr-re-a
37	3	nu-ub-da-ab-kúr-re-a
38	0	igi-^{d}nanna-ka
38	1	igi-^{d}nanna-ka
38	2	igi-^{d}nanna-ka
38	3	igi-^{d}nanna-ka
39	0	ḫé-en-sa$_6$
39	1	ḫé-⌜en⌝-sa$_6$
39	2	ḫé-en-sa$_6$
39	3	ḫé-en-sa$_6$
40	0	lú mu-sar-ra-ba
40	1	lú ⌜mu⌝-sar-ra-ba
40	2	lú mu-sar-ra-ba
40	3	lú mu-sar-ra-ba
41	0	šu bí-íb-ùr-re-a
41	1	šu bí-íb-ùr-[re]-⌜a⌝
41	2	šu bí-íb-ùr-re-a
41	3	šu bí-íb-ùr-re-a
42	0	ù GIŠ.šu-kár-bi
42	1	ù ⌜GIŠ⌝.šu-kár-bi
42	2	ù GIŠ.šu-kár-bi
42	3	ù GIŠ.šu-kár-bi
43	0	ki-gub-<ba>-bi-šè
43	1	ki-[g]ub.<ba>-bi-šè
43	2	ki-gub-<ba>-bi-šè
43	3	ki-gub-<ba>-bi-šè
44	0	nu-ub-ši-íb-gi$_4$-gi$_4$-a
44	1	⌜nu⌝-[ub]-ši-íb-gi$_4$-g[i$_4$-a]
44	2	nu-ub-ši-íb-gi$_4$-gi$_4$-a
44	3	nu-ub-ši-íb-gi$_4$-gi$_4$-a
45	0	muš-^{d}nanna
45	1	⌜muš-^{d}nanna⌝
45	2	muš-^{d}nanna
45	3	muš-^{d}nanna
46	0	ḫé-en-gar
46	1	[...]
46	2	ḫé-en-gar
46	3	ḫé-en-gar
47	0	numun-na-ni
47	1	[...]
47	2	numun-na-ni
47	3	numun-na-ni

48	0	^{d}nanna
48	1	[...]
48	2	^{d}nanna
48	3	^{d}nanna

49	0	ḫé-eb-til-le
49	1	[...]
49	2	ḫé-eb-til-le
49	3	ḫé-eb-til-le

1	0	^{d}inanna
1	1	^{d}inanna
1	2	⸢^{d}⸣inanna
1	3	^{d}inanna
2	0	^{d}nin-^{d}si$_{4}$-an-na
2	1	^{d}nin-^{d}si$_{4}$-an-na
2	2	^{d}⸢nin-^{d}si$_{4}$-an⸣-na
2	3	^{d}[nin-^{d}s]i$_{4}$-an-na
3	0	nin-a-ni-ir
3	1	nin-a-ni-ir
3	2	nin-a-ni-ir
3	3	⸢nin⸣-a-[ni]-ir
4	0	^{d}amar-^{d}EN.ZU
4	1	^{d}amar-^{d}EN.ZU
4	2	^{d}⸢amar-^{d}ENZU⸣
4	3	^{d}ama[r-^{d}]⸢EN⸣.ZU
5	0	nita-kala-ga
5	1	nita-kala-ga
5	2	[nita]-kala-ga
5	3	nita-k[ala]-ga
6	0	lugal-uri$_{5}$.KI-ma
6	1	lugal-uri$_{5}$.KI-ma
6	2	[lu]gal-uri$_{5}$.KI-ma
6	3	[l]ugal-[ur]i$_{5}$.KI-[ma]
7	0	lugal-an-ub-da-límmu-ba-ke$_{4}$
7	1	lugal-an-ub-da-límmu-ba-ke$_{4}$
7	2	lu[gal]-⸢an⸣-[ub-da]-⸢límmu⸣-[ba-ke$_{4}$]
7	3	[lugal-an-ub]-⸢da⸣-límmu-[b]a-ke$_{4}$
8	0	é-a-ni
8	1	é-a-ni
8	2	⸢é⸣-[a]-⸢ni⸣
8	3	é-[a]-ni
9	0	mu-na-dù
9	1	mu-na-dù
9	2	m[u-na-dù]
9	3	mu-[n]a-dù

1	0	^{d}nanna
1	1	^{d}nanna
1	2	...
1	3	...
1	4	[...]
1	5	^{d}nanna
1	6	...
1	7	[...]
1	8	[...]
2	0	kar-zi-da
2	1	kar-zi-d[a]
2	2	...
2	3	...
2	4	[...]
2	5	kar-zi-da
2	6	...
2	7	[...]
2	8	[...]
3	0	lugal-ki-ág-gá-ni-ir
3	1	lugal-ki-ág-gá-ni-ir
3	2	...-ir
3	3	...
3	4	[...]
3	5	lugal-ki-ág-gá-ni-ir
3	6	...
3	7	[...]
3	8	[...]
4	0	^{d}amar-^{d}EN.ZU
4	1	^{d}amar-^{d}EN.ZU
4	2	...
4	3	...
4	4	[...]
4	5	^{d}amar-^{d}EN.ZU
4	6	...
4	7	[...]
4	8	[...]
5	0	nibru.KI-a
5	1	nibru.KI-a
5	2	...
5	3	...
5	4	[...]
5	5	[n]ibru.KI-a
5	6	...
5	7	[...]
5	8	[...]
6	0	^{d}en-líl-le
6	1	^{d}en-líl-le
6	2	...
6	3	...
6	4	[...]
6	5	([EN.L]ÍL.KI)-a
6	6	...
6	7	[...]
6	8	[...]
7	0	mu pà-da
7	1	mu pà-da
7	2	...
7	3	...
7	4	[...]
7	5	⸢mu⸣ pà-da
7	6	...
7	7	[...]
7	8	[...]
8	0	sag-ús-
8	1	sag-ús-
8	2	...
8	3	...
8	4	[...]
8	5	sag-ús-
8	6	...
8	7	[...]
8	8	[...]

9	0	é-^{d}en-líl-ka
9	1	é-^{d}en-líl-ka
9	2	...
9	3	...
9	4	[...]
9	5	é-^{d}en-líl-ka
9	6	...
9	7	[...]
9	8	[...]
10	0	dingir-zi
10	1	dingir-zi
10	2	...
10	3	...
10	4	[...]
10	5	dingir-zi
10	6	...
10	7	[...]
10	8	[...]
11	0	^{d}utu-kalam-ma-na
11	1	^{d}utu-kala[m]-ma-na
11	2	...
11	3	...
11	4	[...]
11	5	^{d}utu-kalam-ma-na
11	6	...
11	7	⸢^{d}⸣[...]
11	8	[...]
12	0	lugal-kala-ga
12	1	lugal-kala-ga
12	2	...
12	3	...
12	4	[...]
12	5	lugal-kala-ga
12	6	...
12	7	lu[gal-kala-ga]
12	8	[...]

13	0	lugal-uri$_5$.KI-ma
13	1	lugal-uri$_5$.KI-ma
13	2	...
13	3	...
13	4	[...]
13	5	lugal-uri$_5$.KI-ma
13	6	...
13	7	lug[al-uri$_5$.KI-ma]
13	8	[...]
14	0	lugal-an-ub-da-límmu-ba-ke$_4$
14	1	lugal-an-[ub]-da-límmu-ba-ke$_4$
14	2	...
14	3	...
14	4	[...]
14	5	[l]ugal-an-ub-da-límmu-ba-ke$_4$
14	6	...
14	7	luga[l-an-ub-da-límmu-ba-ke$_4$]
14	8	[...]
15	0	kar-zi-da
15	1	kar-zi-d[a]
15	2	...
15	3	...
15	4	kar-zi-da
15	5	kar-zi-da-a
15	6	...
15	7	kar-zi-[da]
15	8	[...]

16	0	u$_4$-ul-lí-a-ta
16	1	u$_4$-ul-lí-a-[ta]
16	2	...
16	3	...
16	4	u$_4$-ul-lí-a-ta
16	5	u$_4$-ul-lí-a-ta
16	6	...
16	7	u$_4$-ul-l[í]-[a-ta]
16	8	[...]
17	0	gi$_6$-par$_4$-bi nu-dù-àm
17	1	gi$_6$-par$_4$-bi [nu]-dù-⌈àm⌉
17	2	...
17	3	...
17	4	gi$_6$-par$_4$-bi nu-dù-àm
17	5	gi$_6$-par$_4$-bi nu-dù-àm
17	6	...
17	7	[g]i$_6$-⌈par$_4$-bi⌉ [...]
17	8	[...]
18	0	en nu-un-ti-la-àm
18	1	en nu-u[n]-ti-⌈la⌉-à[m]
18	2	...
18	3	...
18	4	en nu-un-ti-la-àm
18	5	en nu-un-ti-la-àm
18	6	...
18	7	[...]
18	8	[...]
19	0	^{d}amar-^{d}EN.ZU
19	1	^{d}amar-^{d}E[N.ZU]
19	2	...
19	3	...
19	4	^{d}amar-^{d}EN.ZU
19	5	^{d}amar-^{d}EN.ZU
19	6	...
19	7	[...]
19	8	[...]

20	0	ki-ág-^{d}nanna-ke$_4$
20	1	⌈ki-ág⌉-^{d}nanna-ke$_4$
20	2	...
20	3	...
20	4	ki-ág-^{d}nanna-ke$_4$
20	5	ki-ág-^{d}nanna-ke$_4$
20	6	...
20	7	[...]
20	8	[...]
21	0	gi$_6$-par$_4$-kù-ga-ni
21	1	gi$_6$-par$_4$-kù-ga-ni
21	2	...
21	3	...
21	4	gi$_6$-par$_4$-kù-ga-ni
21	5	gi$_6$-par$_4$-kù-ga-ni
21	6	...
21	7	[...]
21	8	[gi$_6$-par$_4$-kù]-ga-ni
22	0	mu-na-dù
22	1	mu-na-dù
22	2	...
22	3	...
22	4	mu-na-dù
22	5	mu-na-dù
22	6	...
22	7	[...]
22	8	[mu-na]-dù
23	0	en ki-ág-gá-ni
23	1	en ki-⌈ág⌉-gá-ni
23	2	...
23	3	...
23	4	en ki-ág-gá-ni
23	5	en ki-ág-gá-ni
23	6	...
23	7	[...]
23	8	[en-ki-á]g-gá-ni

24	0	mu-na-ni-ku$_4$
24	1	mu-na-ni-ku$_4$
24	2	...
24	3	...
24	4	mu-na-ni-ku$_4$
24	5	mu-na-ni-ku$_4$
24	6	...
24	7	[...]
24	8	[mu-na]-⸢ni⸣-ku$_4$
25	0	^{d}amar-^{d}EN.ZU-ke$_4$
25	1	^{d}amar-^{d}EN.Z[U]-ke$_4$
25	2	...
25	3	...
25	4	^{d}amar-^{d}EN.ZU-ke$_4$
25	5	⸢^{d}⸣amar-^{d}EN.ZU-ke$_4$
25	6	...
25	7	[...]
25	8	[...]
26	0	u$_4$ im-da-ab-sù-re$_6$
26	1	u$_4$ im-da-ab-sù-re$_6$
26	2	...
26	3	...
26	4	u$_4$ im-da-ab-su$_{13}$-re$_6$
26	5	u$_4$ im-da-ab-su$_{13}$-re$_6$
26	6	...
26	7	[...]
26	8	[...]
27	0	nam-ti-la-ni-šè
27	1	nam-ti-⸢la⸣-ni-⸢šè⸣
27	2	...
27	3	...
27	4	nam-ti-la-<ni>-šè
27	5	nam-ti-la-ni-šè
27	6	...
27	7	[...]
27	8	[...]
28	0	a mu-na-ru
28	1	a mu-na-[ru]
28	2	...
28	3	...
28	4	a mu-na-ru
28	5	a mu-na-ru
28	6	...
28	7	[...]
28	8	[...]

1	0	^{d}nanna-	5	0	nibru.KI-a
1	1	^{d}nanna-	5	1	nibru.KI-⸢a⸣
1	2	^{d}nanna-	5	2	nibru.KI-a
1	3	^{d}nanna-	5	3	nibru.KI-a
1	4	^{d}nanna-	5	4	nibru.KI-a
1	5	^{d}nanna-	5	5	nibru.KI-a
1	6	[^{d}nann]a-	5	6	nibru.KI-a
1	7	^{d}nanna-	5	7	nibru.KI-a
2	0	kar-zi-da	6	0	^{d}en-líl-le
2	1	kar-zi-da	6	1	^{d}en-líl-l[e]
2	2	kar-zi-da(Text: GUR)	6	2	^{d}en-líl-le
2	3	kar-zi-da	6	3	^{d}en-líl-le
2	4	kar-zi-da	6	4	^{d}en-líl-le
2	5	kar-zi-da	6	5	^{d}en-líl-le
2	6	⸢kar⸣-zi-da	6	6	^{d}en-líl-le
2	7	kar-zi-da	6	7	^{d}en-líl-le
3	0	lugal-a-ni-ir	7	0	mu pà-da
3	1	lugal-a-ni-ir	7	1	mu pà-d[a]
3	2	lugal-a-ni-ir	7	2	mu pà-da
3	3	lugal-a-ni-ir	7	3	mu pà-da
3	4	lugal-a-ni-ir	7	4	mu pà-da
3	5	lugal-a-ni-ir	7	5	mu pà-da
3	6	[l]ugal-a-ni-ir	7	6	mu pà-da
3	7	lugal-a-ni-ir	7	7	mu pà-da
4	0	^{d}amar-^{d}EN.ZU	8	0	sag-ús-
4	1	^{d}amar-^{d}EN.Z[U]	8	1	sag-ús-
4	2	^{d}amar-^{d}EN.ZU	8	2	sag-ús-
4	3	^{d}amar-^{d}EN.ZU	8	3	sag-ús-
4	4	^{d}amar-^{d}EN.ZU	8	4	sag-ús-
4	5	^{d}amar-^{d}EN.ZU	8	5	sag-ús-
4	6	^{d}amar-^{d}EN.ZU	8	6	sag-ús-
4	7	^{d}amar-^{d}EN.ZU	8	7	sag-ús-

9	0	é-^{d}en-líl-ka
9	1	é-^{d}en-líl-ka
9	2	é-^{d}en-líl-ka
9	3	é-^{d}en-líl-ka
9	4	é-^{d}en-líl-ka
9	5	<é>-^{d}en-líl-ka
9	6	é-^{d}en-líl-ka(Text: SAG)
9	7	é-^{d}en-líl-ka
10	0	dingir-zi-kalam-ma-na
10	1	dingir-zi-kalam-ma-na
10	2	dingir-zi-kalam-ma-na
10	3	dingir-zi-kalam-ma-<na>
10	4	dingir-zi-kalam-ma-na
10	5	dingir-zi-kalam-ma-na
10	6	dingir-zi-kalam-ma-[na]
10	7	dingir-zi-⸢kalam-ma-na⸣
11	0	lugal-uri$_5$.KI-ma
11	1	lugal-uri$_5$.KI-ma
11	2	lugal-uri$_5$.KI-ma
11	3	lugal-uri$_5$.KI-ma
11	4	lugal-uri$_5$.KI-ma
11	5	lugal-uri$_5$.KI-ma
11	6	[lu]gal-uri$_5$.⸢KI⸣-[ma]
11	7	lugal-ŠEŠ.A[B.KI-ma]
12	0	lugal-an-ub-da-límmu-ba-ke$_4$
12	1	lugal-an-ub-da-límmu-ba-ke$_4$
12	2	lugal(Text:LÚ)-⸢an⸣-ub-da-límmu-ba (Text:UD)-ke$_4$
12	3	lugal-an-ub-da-límmu-ba-ke$_4$
12	4	lugal-an-ub-da-límmu-ba-ke$_4$
12	5	<...>
12	6	[l]ugal-an-u[b]-da-límmu-ba-ke$_4$
12	7	lugal-an-ub-da-límmu-ba-ke$_4$

13	0	u$_4$-ul-lí-a-ta
13	1	u$_4$-ul-lí-a-ta
13	2	u$_4$-ul-lí-a-ta
13	3	u$_4$-ul-lí-a-ta
13	4	u$_4$-ul-lí-a-ta
13	5	<...>
13	6	u$_4$-ul-lí-a-ta
13	7	⸢u$_4$-ul-lí-a-ta⸣
14	0	kar-zi-da
14	1	kar-zi-da
14	2	kar-zi-da
14	3	kar-zi-da
14	4	kar-zi-da
14	5	<...>
14	6	kar-⸢zi⸣-da
14	7	⸢kar-zi-da⸣
15	0	gi$_6$-par$_4$ nu-dù
15	1	gi$_6$-par$_4$ nu-dù
15	2	gi$_6$-par$_4$ nu-dù
15	3	gi$_6$-par$_4$ nu-dù
15	4	gi$_6$-par$_4$ nu-dù
15	5	<...>
15	6	[g]i$_6$-par$_4$ n[u-dù]
15	7	gi$_6$-par$_4$ nu-[dù]
16	0	en nu-un-tìl-a
16	1	en nu-un-tìl-a
16	2	en nu-un-tìl-a
16	3	en nu-un-tìl-⸢a⸣
16	4	en nu-un-tìl-a
16	5	<...>
16	6	⸢en⸣-nu-un!(written on two lines!)-tìl-a
16	7	⸢en nu-un⸣-tìl-a

17	0	^{d}amar-^{d}EN.ZU
17	1	^{d}amar-^{d}EN.ZU
17	2	^{d}amar-^{d}EN.ZU
17	3	^{d}amar-^{d}EN.ZU
17	4	^{d}amar-^{d}EN.ZU
17	5	<...>
17	6	^{d}amar-^{d}EN.ZU
17	7	^{d}amar-^{d}EN.ZU
18	0	dumu-ki-ág-^{d}nanna-ke$_4$
18	1	dumu-ki-ág-^{d}nanna-ke$_4$
18	2	dumu-ki-ág-^{d}EN.ZU
18	3	[d]umu-ki-ág-^{d}nanna-ke$_4$
18	4	dumu-ki-ág-^{d}nanna-ke$_4$
18	5	<...>
18	6	⸢dumu-ki⸣-ág-^{d}[nann]a-ke$_4$
18	7	dumu-ki-[á]g-^{d}nanna-⸢ke$_4$⸣
19	0	^{d}nanna
19	1	^{d}nanna
19	2	^{d}nanna
19	3	^{d}nanna
19	4	^{d}nanna
19	5	<...>
19	6	^{d}[nan]na
19	7	^{d}nanna
20	0	ki-ág-gá-ni-ir
20	1	ki-ág-gá-ni-ir
20	2	ki-ág-gá-ni-ir
20	3	ki-ág-gá-ni-ir
20	4	ki-ág-gá-ni-ir
20	5	<...>
20	6	ki-á[g-g]á-ni-ir
20	7	[k]i-ág-gá-ni-ir
21	0	kar-zi-da-a
21	1	kar-zi-da-a
21	2	kar-zi-da-a
21	3	kar-zi-da-a
21	4	kar-zi-da-a
21	5	<...>
21	6	[kar-z]i-da-[a]
21	7	⸢kar-zi⸣-d[a-a]
22	0	gi$_6$-par$_4$ mu-na-dù
22	1	gi$_6$-par$_4$ mu-na-dù
22	2	gi$_6$-par$_4$ mu-na-dù
22	3	gi$_6$-par$_4$ mu-na-dù
22	4	gi$_6$-par$_4$ mu-na-dù
22	5	[...]
22	6	gi$_6$-par$_4$ mu-na-dù
22	7	gi$_6$-par$_4$ [mu-na-dù]
23	0	en àga-zi-an-na
23	1	en àga-zi-an-na
23	2	en àga-zi-an-na
23	3	en àga-zi-an-na
23	4	en àga-zi-an-na
23	5	<...>
23	6	e[n]-⸢àga⸣-zi-an-⸢na⸣
23	7	⸢en-àga-zi⸣-an-n[a]
24	0	en ki-ág-gá-ni
24	1	en ki-ág-gá-ni
24	2	en ki-ág-gá-ni
24	3	en ki-ág-gá-ni
24	4	en ki-ág-gá-ni
24	5	<...>
24	6	en ki-ág-gá(Text: UŠ)-ni (Text: DÙ)
24	7	⸢en ki⸣-[ág-gá-ni]

25	0	mu-un-na-ni-in-ku$_4$
25	1	mu-un-na-ni-in-k[u$_4$]
25	2	mu-un-na-ni-<in-ku$_4$>
25	3	mu-un-na-ni-<in-ku$_4$>
25	4	mu-un-na-ni-<in-ku$_4$>
25	5	<...>
25	6	[m]u-un-[n]a-<ni-ku$_4$>
25	7	mu-un-[na]-ni-⸢in⸣-k[u$_4$]
26	0	^{d}amar-^{d}EN.ZU-ke$_4$
26	1	^{d}amar-^{d}EN.ZU-k[e$_4$]
26	2	^{d}amar-^{d}EN.ZU-ke$_4$
26	3	^{d}amar-^{d}EN.ZU-k[e$_4$]
26	4	^{d}amar-^{d}EN.ZU-ke$_4$
26	5	<...>
26	6	^{d}amar-^{d}EN.ZU-ke$_4$
26	7	⸢amar-^{d}EN.ZU⸣-[ke$_4$]
27	0	nam-ti íb-sù-re$_6$
27	1	nam-ti íb-sù-re$_6$
27	2	RI!+ŠE-ti bi-sù!-u$_5$(?)
27	3	nam-ti íb-x-[x]
27	4	nam-ti íb-sù-re$_6$
27	5	<...>
27	6	nam-ti íb-sù-re$_6$
27	7	⸢nam-ti⸣ [íb]-sù-⸢x⸣

Ex. 7, which contains 17 lines near the end of the inscription, has not been included in the score.

Lacuna of 24 lines

i 25	0	[...]-lá
	1	[...]-lá
	2	[...]
	3	[...]
	4	[...]
	5	[...]
	6	[...]
i 26	0	[...]-ni
	1	[...]-ni
	2	[...]
	3	[...]
	4	[...]
	5	[...]
	6	[...]
i 27	0	[...]-⸢x⸣-a-ba
	1	[...]-⸢x⸣-a-ba
	2	[...]
	3	[...]
	4	[...]
	5	[...]
	6	[...]
i 28	0	[nin mè]-šen-šen-na
	1	[nin mè]-šen-šen-na
	2	[...]
	3	[...]
	4	[...]
	5	[...]
	6	[...]
i 29	0	[am-gi]n$_7$(?) du$_7$-du$_7$
	1	[am-gi]n$_7$(?) du$_7$-du$_7$
	2	[...]
	3	[...]
	4	[...]
	5	[...]
	6	[...]
i 30	0	[in-ni]n(?) nam-ur-sag-šè
	1	[in-ni]n(?) nam-ur-sag-šè
	2	[...]
	3	[...]
	4	[...]
	5	[...]
	6	[...]
i 31	0	[t]u-da
	1	[t]u-da
	2	[...]
	3	[...]
	4	[...]
	5	[...]
	6	[...]
i 32	0	⸢x⸣ GIŠ.tukul ti mar-uru$_5$
	1	⸢x⸣ GIŠ.tukul ti mar-uru$_5$
	2	[...]
	3	[...]
	4	[...]
	5	[...]
	6	[...]
i 33	0	[s]ag-éš RIG$_7$-a
	1	[s]ag-éš RIG$_7$-a
	2	[...]
	3	[...]
	4	[...]
	5	[...]
	6	[...]
i 34	0	[m]ud$_5$-me-gar dul$_4$(Text: dul$_4$ without *šeššig*)-dul$_4$-la
	1	[m]ud$_5$-me-gar dul$_4$(Text: dul$_4$ without *šeššig*)-dul$_4$-la
	2	[...]
	3	[...]
	4	[...]
	5	[...]
	6	[...]

i 35	0	[du]mu-gal-^{d}EN.ZU-na
	1	[du]mu-gal-^{d}EN.ZU-na
	2	[...]
	3	[...]
	4	[...]
	5	[...]
	6	[...]
i 36	0	[m]e-ninnu šu-du$_{8}$
	1	[m]e-ninnu šu-du$_{8}$
	2	[...]
	3	[...]
	4	[...]
	5	[...]
	6	[...]
i 37	0	⸢kù⸣-^{d}inanna-ke$_{4}$
	1	⸢kù⸣-^{d}inanna-ke$_{4}$
	2	[...]
	3	[...]
	4	[...]
	5	[...]
	6	[...]
i 38	0	^{d}*šu*-^{d}EN.ZU
	1	^{d}*šu*-^{d}EN.ZU
	2	[...]
	3	[...]
	4	[...]
	5	[...]
	6	[...]
i 39	0	⸢MÍ⸣.ÚS ki-ág-gá-ni-ir
	1	[MÍ].ÚS ki-ág-gá-ni-ir
	2	[...]
	3	[MÍ].ÚS ki-ág-gá-ni-ir
	4	[...]
	5	[...]
	6	[...]
i 40	0	kur gú-érim-gál
	1	kur gú-érim-gál
	2	[...]
	3	kur g[ú-...]
	4	[...]
	5	[...]
	6	[...]
i 41	0	nu-še-ga-na
	1	nu-še-ga-na
	2	[...]
	3	[...]
	4	[...]
	5	[...]
	6	[...]
i 42	0	mè giš-giš-šè-lá-a-ba
	1	mè giš-giš-šè-lá-a-ba
	2	[...]
	3	mè g[iš-...]
	4	[...]
	5	[...]
	6	[...]
i 43	0	a-ma-ru ùlu(GIŠGAL)-maḫ
	1	a-ma-ru ùlu(GIŠGAL)-maḫ
	2	[...]
	3	a-ma-ru [...]
	4	[...]
	5	[...]
	6	[...]
i 44	0	zi-ga-gin$_{7}$
	1	zi-ga-gin$_{7}$
	2	[...]
	3	[...]
	4	[...]
	5	[...]
	6	[...]
i 45	0	un-ba ùr-ùr-dè
	1	un-ba ùr-ùr-dè
	2	[...]
	3	[...]
	4	[...]
	5	[...]
	6	[...]

i 46	0	á-tuku ḫul-gál
	1	á-tuku ḫul-gál
	2	[...]
	3	á-tuku ḫ[ul-gál]
	4	[...]
	5	[...]
	6	[...]
i 47	0	érim-DU-bi-ne
	1	érim-DU-bi-ne
	2	[...]-bi-⌈ne⌉
	3	[...]
	4	[...]
	5	[...]
	6	[...]
i 48	0	[t]u_{10}-tu_{10}-bé ak-dè
	1	[t]u_{10}-tu_{10}-bé ⌈ak-dè⌉
	2	[t]u_{10}-tu_{10}-bé ak-dè
	3	[...]
	4	[...]
	5	[...]
	6	[...]
ii 1	0	sag-gi_6 zi-gál
	1	[...]
	2	[sag-g]i_6 zi-gál
	3	sag-gi_6 z[i-gál]
	4	[...]
	5	[...]
	6	[...]
ii 2	0	mu-tuku-ba
	1	[...]
	2	mu-tuku-ba
	3	[...]
	4	[...]
	5	[...]
	6	[...]
ii 3	0	mu-bi ḫa-lam-e-dè
	1	[...]
	2	mu-bi ḫa-lam-e-dè
	3	[...]
	4	[...]
	5	[...]
	6	[...]
ii 4	0	ḫur-sag-gal-gal
	1	[...]
	2	ḫur-sag-gal-gal
	3	ḫur-sag-gal-[...]
	4	[...]
	5	[...]
	6	[...]
ii 5	0	á-sù-rá-bi
	1	[...]
	2	á-sù-rá-bi
	3	[...]
	4	[...]
	5	[...]
	6	[...]
ii 6	0	gú ki-šè gá-gá-dè
	1	[...]
	2	gú ki-šè gá-gá-dè
	3	[...]
	4	[...]
	5	[...]
	6	[...]
ii 7	0	^{d}inanna ^{d}en-líl-le
	1	[...]
	2	^{d}inanna ^{d}en-líl-le
	3	^{d}inanna ^{d}en-l[íl-le]
	4	[...]
	5	[...]
	6	[...]
ii 8	0	^{d}*šu*-^{d}EN.ZU
	1	[...]
	2	^{d}*šu*-^{d}EN.ZU
	3	[...]
	4	[...]
	5	[...]
	6	[...]

ii 9	0	lugal-kala-ga
	1	[...]
	2	lugal-kala-ga
	3	[...]
	4	[...]
	5	[...]
	6	[...]
ii 10	0	lugal-úri.KI-ma
	1	[...]
	2	lugal-úri.KI-ma
	3	[...]
	4	[...]
	5	[...]
	6	[...]
ii 11	0	lugal-an-ub-da-límmu-ba-ra
	1	[...]
	2	lugal-an-ub-da-límmu-ba-ra
	3	[...]
	4	[...]
	5	[...]
	6	[...]
ii 12	0	á-daḫ-a-na
	1	[...]
	2	á-daḫ-a-na
	3	⌈á⌉-[da]ḫ-[a-na]
	4	[...]
	5	[...]
	6	[...]
ii 13	0	mu-na-ni-in-ku_4-ku_4
	1	[...]
	2	mu-na-ni-in-ku_4-ku_4
	3	[...]
	4	[...]
	5	[...]
	6	[...]
ii 14	0	mìn-na-ne-ne
	1	[...]
	2	mìn-na-ne-ne
	3	mìn-n[a-ne-ne]
	4	[...]
	5	[...]
	6	[...]
ii 15	0	zi-da-gùb-bu-na
	1	[...]
	2	zi-da-gùb-bu-na
	3	[...]
	4	[...]
	5	[...]
	6	[...]
ii 16	0	⌈an-ta mu-è⌉-e[š]
	1	[...]
	2	⌈an-ta mu-è⌉-e[š]
	3	[...]
	4	[...]
	5	[...]
	6	[...]
ii 17	0	lugal-[^{d}*šu*]-^{d}EN.[ZU]
	1	[...]
	2	[...]
	3	lugal [^{d}*šu*]-^{d}EN.[ZU]
	4	[...]
	5	[...]
	6	[...]
ii 18	0	[...]
	1	[...]
	2	[...]
	3	[...]
	4	[...]
	5	[...]
	6	[...]
ii 19	0	[...]
	1	[...]
	2	[...]
	3	[...]
	4	[...]
	5	[...]
	6	[...]

ii 20	0	é-kur-za-gìn
	1	[...]
	2	[...]
	3	é-kur-za-gìn
	4	[...]
	5	[...]
	6	[...]
ii 21	0	[...]
	1	[...]
	2	[...]
	3	[...]
	4	[...]
	5	[...]
	6	[...]
ii 22	0	[...]
	1	[...]
	2	[...]
	3	[...]
	4	[...]
	5	[...]
	6	[...]
ii 23	0	[...]
	1	[...]
	2	[...]
	3	[...]
	4	[...]
	5	[...]
	6	[...]
ii 24	0	⸢inim(?)-^{d}en-líl⸣
	1	[...]
	2	[...]
	3	⸢inim(?)-^{d}en-líl⸣
	4	[...]
	5	[...]
	6	[...]
ii 25	0	⸢^{d}⸣[nin-líl-lá-ta]
	1	⸢^{d}⸣[nin-líl-lá-ta]
	2	[...]
	3	[...]
	4	[...]
	5	[...]
	6	[...]
ii 26	0	^{d}[...]
	1	^{d}[...]
	2	[...]
	3	[...]
	4	[...]
	5	[...]
	6	[...]
ii 27	0	x [...]
	1	x [...]
	2	[...]
	3	[...]
	4	[...]
	5	[...]
	6	[...]
ii 28	0	⸢x⸣ [...]
	1	⸢x⸣ [...]
	2	[...]
	3	[...]
	4	[...]
	5	[...]
	6	[...]
ii 29	0	zà [...]
	1	zà [...]
	2	[...]
	3	[...]
	4	[...]
	5	[...]
	6	[...]
ii 30	0	^{d}[...]
	1	^{d}[...]
	2	[...]
	3	[...]
	4	[...]
	5	[...]
	6	[...]

ii 31 0 ^{d}[...]
1 ^{d}[...]
2 [...]
3 [...]
4 [...]
5 [...]
6 [...]

ii 32 0 sig-[...]
1 sig-[...]
2 [...]
3 [...]
4 [...]
5 [...]
6 [...]

ii 33 0 x [...]
1 x [...]
2 [...]
3 [...]
4 [...]
5 [...]
6 [...]

ii 34 0 NI [...]
1 NI [...]
2 [...]
3 [...]
4 [...]
5 [...]
6 [...]

ii 35 0 kur [...]
1 kur [...]
2 [...]
3 [...]
4 [...]
5 [...]
6 [...]

ii 36 0 x [...]
1 x [...]
2 [...]
3 [...]
4 [...]
5 [...]
6 [...]

ii 37 0 [lugal-bi]
1 [...]
2 [...]
3 [...]
4 [...]
5 [...]
6 [...]-ba(?)

ii 38 0 [mè šen-še]n-ba
1 [mè šen-šen]-ba
2 [...]
3 [...]
4 [...]
5 [...]
6 [mè šen-še]n-ba

ii 39 0 ⸢x⸣ [^{d}e]n-líl
1 ⸢x⸣-[^{d}e]n-líl
2 [...]
3 [...]
4 [...]
5 [...]
6 [...]

ii 40 0 ^{d}[ni]n-líl-lá-ta
1 ^{d}[ni]n-líl-lá-ta
2 [...]
3 [...]
4 [...]
5 [...]
6 [^{d}nin-líl-lá]-ta

ii 41 0 ^{d}*šu*-^{d}EN.ZU
1 ^{d}*šu*-^{d}EN.ZU
2 [...]
3 [...]
4 [...]
5 [...]
6 [...]

ii 42 0 lugal-kala-ga
1 lugal-kala-ga
2 [...]
3 [...]
4 [...]
5 [...]
6 [...]

ii 43 0 lugal-úri.KI-ma
1 lugal-úri.KI-ma
2 [...]
3 [...]
4 [...]
5 [...]
6 [lugal-úr]i.KI-ma

ii 44 0 lugal-an-ub-da-límmu-ba-ke$_4$
1 lugal-an-ub-da-límmu-ba-ke$_4$
2 [...]
3 [...]
4 [...]
5 [...]
6 [...]

ii 45 0 TÙN.KÁR bí-sè-sè
1 TÙN.KÁR bí-sè-sè
2 [...]
3 [...]
4 [...]
5 [...]
6 [... b]í-sè-sè x

ii 46 0 kur ⸢bala⸣(?) [x x]
1 kur ⸢bala⸣(?) [x x]
2 [...]
3 [...]
4 [...]
5 [...]
6 [...]

ii 47 0 ⸢gú⸣(?)-[érim-gál]
1 ⸢gú⸣(?)-[érim-gál]
2 [...]
3 [...]
4 [...]
5 [...]
6 [...]

ii 48 0 x [...]
1 x [...]
2 [...]
3 [...]
4 [...]
5 [...]
6 [...]

Col. iii
Lacuna of 18 lines

iii 19 0 ⸢lugal⸣ x [x x]
1 [x] x x x
2 [...]
3 [...]
4 ⸢lugal⸣ x [x x]
5 [...]
6 [...]

iii 20 0 [a-m]a-ru
1 [a-m]a-ru
2 [...]
3 [...]
4 [a-ma-ru]
5 [...]
6 [...]

iii 21 0 ki-bal-a ùr-ùr
1 [ki-b]al-a ùr-ùr
2 [...]
3 [...]
4 ki-bal-a ùr-[ùr]
5 [...]
6 [...]

iii 22	0	á-ág-gá-ni
	1	[á-á]g-gá-ni
	2	[...]
	3	[...]
	4	á-⌈ág⌉-gá-ni
	5	[...]
	6	[...]
iii 23	0	kur-tuk$_4$-tuk$_4$-e
	1	[kur-tuk$_4$]-tuk$_4$-e
	2	[...]
	3	[...]
	4	kur-tuk$_4$-tuk$_4$-⌈e⌉[...]
	5	[...]
	6	[...]
iii 24	0	kala-ga-ni
	1	[kala-g]a-ni
	2	[...]
	3	[...]
	4	kala-ga-ni
	5	[...]
	6	[...]
iii 25	0	sag-bi-šè è-a
	1	[sag-b]i-šè è-a
	2	[...]
	3	[...]
	4	sag-bi-šè ⌈è⌉-[a]
	5	[...]
	6	[...]
iii 26	0	dumu-munus-a-ni
	1	[dumu-munus]-a-ni
	2	[...]
	3	[...]
	4	dumu-munus-a-ni
	5	[...]
	6	[...]
iii 27	0	si-ma-núm.KI-e
	1	[si-ma-nú]m-KI-e
	2	[...]
	3	[...]
	4	si-ma-núm.KI
	5	[...]
	6	[...]
iii 28	0	⌈nam-é⌉-gi$_4$-a-bi-šè
	1	[nam-é-gi$_4$]-a-bi-šè
	2	[...]
	3	[...]
	4	⌈nam-é⌉-gi$_4$-a-bi-[šè]
	5	[...]
	6	[...]
iii 29	0	[...]-sum
	1	[...]-sum
	2	[...]
	3	[...]
	4	[...]-x
	5	[...]
	6	[...]
iii 30	0	[si-ma-nú]m.KI
	1	[si-ma-nú]m.KI
	2	[...]
	3	[...]
	4	[...]
	5	[...]
	6	[...]
iii 31	0	[ḫa-bu-r]a.KI
	1	[ḫa-bu-r]a.KI
	2	[...]
	3	[...]
	4	[...]
	5	[...]
	6	[...]
iii 32	0	[ù ma-da m]a-da-bi
	1	[ù ma-da-m]a-da-bi
	2	[...]
	3	[...]
	4	[...]
	5	[...]
	6	[...]

iii 33 0 [lugal-da gú-ér]im
1 [lugal-da gú-ér]im
2 [...]
3 [...]
4 [...]
5 [...]
6 [...]

iii 34 0 [ba-an-da-ab]-gál
1 [ba-an-da-ab]-gál
2 [...]
3 [...]
4 [...]
5 [...]
6 [...]

iii 35 0 [dumu-munus-a]-ni
1 [dumu-munus-a]-ni
2 [...]
3 [...]
4 [...]
5 [...]
6 [...]

iii 36 0 é-[ki-tuš-a-ni]-ta
1 é-[ki-tuš-a-ni]-ta
2 [...]
3 [...]
4 [...]
5 [...]
6 [...]

iii 37 0 ság [im-ta]-eš
1 ság [im-ta]-eš
2 [...]
3 [...]
4 [...]
5 [...]
6 [...]

iii 38 0 mar-dú l[ú (?) x x] x [...] x
1 mar-dú l[ú (?) x x] x [...] x
2 [...]
3 [...]
4 [...]
5 [...]
6 [...]

iii 39 0 *ti-id-nu*-[*um*.K]I
1 *ti-id-nu*-[*um*.K]I
2 [...]
3 [...]
4 [...]
5 [...]
6 [...]

iii 40 0 *ià-a-ma-d*[*ì-um*.K]I
1 *ià-a-ma-d*[*ì-um*.K]I
2 [...]
3 [...]
4 [...]
5 [...]
6 [...]

iii 41 0 im-ma-da-U[D.DU-eš]
1 im-ma-da-U[D.DU-eš]
2 [...]
3 [...]
4 [...]
5 [...]
6 [...]

iii 42 0 lugal-b[i]
1 lugal-b[i]
2 [...]
3 [...]
4 [...]
5 [...]
6 [...]

iii 43 0 mè šen-š[en-ba gaba]
1 mè šen-š[en-ba gaba]
2 [...]
3 [...]
4 [...]
5 [...]
6 [...]

iii 44	0	im-m[a-na-d]a
	1	im-m[a-na-d]a
	2	[...]
	3	[...]
	4	[...]
	5	[...]
	6	[...]
iii 45	0	-r[i]-eš
	1	-r[i]-eš
	2	[...]
	3	[...]
	4	[...]
	5	[...]
	6	[...]
iii 46	0	[á-^{d}en]-líl-
	1	[á-^{d}en]-líl-
	2	[...]
	3	[...]
	4	[...]
	5	[...]
	6	[...]
iii 47	0	[lugal-n]a-ta
	1	[lugal-n]a-ta
	2	[...]
	3	[...]
	4	[...]
	5	[...]
	6	[...]
iii 48	0	[mè šen-šen]-ba
	1	[mè šen-šen]-ba
	2	[...]
	3	[...]
	4	[...]
	5	[...]
	6	[...]
iv 1	0	[TÙN.KÁR bí-sè-sè]
	1	[...]
	2	[...]
	3	[...]
	4	[...]

	5	[...]
	6	[...]

Lacuna

iv 1′	0	[x] pà [...]
	1	[...]
	2	[...]
	3	[...]
	4	[...]
	5	[x] pà [...][...]
	6	[...]
iv 2′	0	[š]ul-^{d}utu [...]
	1	[...]
	2	[...]
	3	[...]
	4	[...]
	5	[š]ul-^{d}utu [...]
	6	[...]
iv 3′	0	dumu-munus-a-[ni]
	1	[...]
	2	[...]
	3	[...]
	4	[...]
	5	dumu-munus-a-[ni]
	6	[...]
iv 4′	0	si-ma-núm.KI
	1	[...]
	2	[...]
	3	[...]
	4	[...]
	5	si-ma-núm.KI
	6	[...]
iv 5′	0	ḫa-bu-ra.K[I]
	1	[...]
	2	[...]
	3	[...]
	4	[...]
	5	ḫa-bu-ra.K[I]
	6	[...]

iv 6′	0	ù ma-da-ma-da-bi
	1	[...]
	2	[...]
	3	[...]
	4	[...]
	5	ù ma-da-ma-da-bi
	6	[...]

iv 7′	0	lugal-da gú-érim-gál ba-an-da-ab-gál
	1	[...]
	2	[...]
	3	[...]
	4	[...]
	5	lugal-da gú-érim-gál ba-an-da-ab-gál
	6	[...]

iv 8′	0	dumu-munus-a-ni
	1	[...]
	2	[...]
	3	[...]
	4	[...]
	5	dumu-munus-a-ni
	6	[...]

iv 9′	0	é-ki-tuš-a-ni-ta
	1	[...]
	2	[...]
	3	[...]
	4	[...]
	5	é-ki-tuš-a-ni-ta
	6	[...]

iv 10′	0	[s]ág im-ta-eš-àm
	1	[...]
	2	[...]
	3	[...]
	4	[...]
	5	[s]ág im-ta-eš-àm
	6	[...]

iv 11′	0	*šu*-^{d}EN.ZU lugal-kala-ga
	1	[...]
	2	[...]
	3	[...]
	4	[...]
	5	*šu*-^{d}EN.ZU lugal-kala-ga
	6	[...]

iv 12′	0	[lu]gal-úri.KI-ma
	1	[...]
	2	[...]
	3	[...]
	4	[...]
	5	[lu]gal-úri.KI-ma
	6	[...]

Lacuna

iv 14	0	ḫur [...]
	1	[...]
	2	ḫur [...]
	3	[...]
	4	[...]
	5	[...]
	6	[...]

iv 15	0	am TAR [...]
	1	[...]
	2	am TAR [...]
	3	[...]
	4	[...]
	5	[...]
	6	[...]

iv 16	0	⸢x⸣ [...]
	1	[...]
	2	⸢x⸣ [...]
	3	[...]
	4	[...]
	5	[...]
	6	[...]

iv 17 0 du$_{10}$-tuku-bi ⸢LÚ×GÁNA *tenû*-a⸣
1 [...]
2 du$_{10}$-tuku-bi ⸢LÚ×GÁNA *tenû*-a⸣
3 [...]
4 [...]
5 [...]
6 [...]

iv 18 0 [mi-ni-(in)]-da[b$_5$]
1 [mi-ni-(in)]-da[b$_5$]
2 [...]
3 [...]
4 [...]
5 [...]
6 [...]

iv 19 0 nam-lú-ùlu(GIŠGAL)-ba
1 nam-lú-ùlu(GIŠGAL)-ba
2 nam-lú-ùlu(GIŠGAL)-ba
3 [...]
4 [...]
5 [...]
6 [...]

iv 20 0 saḫar im-mi-⸢dul⸣
1 [s]aḫar im-mi-⸢dul⸣
2 saḫar i[m-...]
3 [...]
4 [...]
5 [...]
6 [...]

iv 21 0 si-ma-núm.KI
1 si-ma-[n]úm.KI
2 si-ma-núm.KI
3 [...]
4 [...]
5 [...]
6 [...]

iv 22 0 ḫa-bu-ra.KI
1 ḫa-⸢bu⸣-ra.KI
2 ḫa-bu-ra.KI
3 [...]
4 [...]
5 [...]
6 [...]

iv 23 0 ù [m]a-da-ma-da-bi
1 ù [m]a-da-ma-da-bi
2 ⸢ù⸣ [...]
3 [...]
4 [...]
5 [...]
6 [...]

iv 24 0 sag-du-bi
1 sag-du-bi
2 sag-du-bi
3 [...]
4 [...]
5 [...]
6 [...]

iv 25 0 tíbir im-mi-ra
1 tíbir im-mi-ra
2 tíbir [...]
3 [...]
4 [...]
5 [...]
6 [...]

iv 26 0 dumu-munus-a-ni
1 dumu-munus-a-ni
2 dumu-munus-a-ni
3 [...]
4 [...]
5 [...]
6 [...]

iv 27	0	é-ki-tuš-a-ni-a
	1	é-ki-tuš-a-ni-a
	2	é-ki-[tuš-a-ni-a]
	3	[...]
	4	[...]
	5	[...]
	6	[...]
iv 28	0	im-ma-ši-in-gi$_4$
	1	im-ma-ši-in-gi$_4$
	2	i[m-...]
	3	[...]
	4	[...]
	5	[...]
	6	[...]
iv 29	0	si-ma-núm.KI
	1	si-ma-núm.KI
	2	[...]
	3	[...]
	4	[...]
	5	[...]
	6	[...]
iv 30	0	ḫa-bu-ra.KI
	1	ḫa-bu-ra.KI
	2	[...]
	3	[...]
	4	[...]
	5	[...]
	6	[...]
iv 31	0	ù ma-da-ma-da-bi
	1	ù ma-da-ma-da-bi
	2	[...]
	3	[...]
	4	[...]
	5	[...]
	6	[...]
iv 32	0	nam-ìr(?)-da-ni-šè
	1	nam-ìr(?)-da-ni-šè
	2	[...]
	3	[...]
	4	[...]
	5	[...]
	6	[...]
iv 33	0	sag-šè mu-ni-rig$_7$
	1	sag-šè mu-ni-rig$_7$
	2	[...]
	3	[...]
	4	[...]
	5	[...]
	6	[...]
iv 34	0	sag-érim-gál
	1	sag-érim-gál
	2	[...]
	3	[...]
	4	[...]
	5	[...]
	6	[...]
iv 35	0	nam-ra-aš-ak-ni
	1	nam-ra-aš-ak-ni
	2	[...]
	3	[...]
	4	[...]
	5	[...]
	6	[...]
iv 36	0	^{d}en-líl ^{d}nin-líl-r[a]
	1	^{d}en-líl ^{d}nin-líl-r[a]
	2	[...]
	3	[...]
	4	[...]
	5	[...]
	6	[...]

iv 37	0	ki-sur-r[a]
	1	ki-sur-r[a]
	2	[...]
	3	[...]
	4	[...]
	5	[...]
	6	[...]
iv 38	0	nibru.KI-ka [(x)]
	1	nibru.KI-ka [(x)]
	2	[...]
	3	[...]
	4	[...]
	5	[...]
	6	[...]
iv 39	0	si-ma-nú[m.KI]
	1	si-ma-nú[m.KI]
	2	[...]
	3	[...]
	4	[...]
	5	[...]
	6	[...]
iv 40	0	ki m[u-ne]-gar
	1	ki m[u-ne]-gar
	2	[...]
	3	[...]
	4	[...]
	5	[...]
	6	[...]
iv 41	0	[... mu-n]e-dù
	1	[... mu-n]e-dù
	2	[...]
	3	[...]
	4	[...]
	5	[...]
	6	[...]
iv 42	0	[... t]a mu-ne-
	1	[... t]a mu-ne-
	2	[...]
	3	[...]
	4	[...]
	5	[...]
	6	[...]
iv 43	0	[x-t]a-an-gub
	1	[x-t]a-an-gub
	2	[...]
	3	[...]
	4	[...]
	5	[...]
	6	[...]
iv 44	0	uru.KI-ba
	1	uru.KI-ba
	2	[...]
	3	[...]
	4	[...]
	5	[...]
	6	⸢uru.KI-ba⸣
iv 45	0	^{d}*šu*-^{d}EN.ZU
	1	^{d}*šu*-^{d}EN.ZU
	2	[...]
	3	[...]
	4	[...]
	5	[...]
	6	⸢^{d}⸣[šu-^{d}EN.ZU]
iv 46	0	dingir-bi-im
	1	dingir-bi-im
	2	[...]
	3	[...]
	4	[...]
	5	[...]
	6	[dingir]-⸢bi-im⸣-ma(?)

iv 47	0	u$_4$-nam-tar-ra-ta
	1	u$_4$-nam-tar-ra-ta
	2	[...]
	3	[...]
	4	[...]
	5	[...]
	6	u$_4$-nam-tar-ra-ta
iv 48	0	lugal-na-me
	1	lugal-na-me
	2	[...]
	3	[...]
	4	[...]
	5	[...]
	6	⸢lugal⸣-na-me
v 1	0	sag-nam-ra-aš-ak-ni-ta
	1	sag-nam-ra-aš-ak-ni-ta
	2	[...]
	3	[...]
	4	[...]
	5	[...]
	6	sag-nam-ra-aš-ak-ni-ta
v 2	0	^{d}en-líl ^{d}nin-líl-ra
	1	^{d}en-líl ^{d}nin-líl-ra
	2	[...]
	3	[...]
	4	[...]
	5	[...]
	6	^{d}en-líl ^{d}nin-líl-ra
v 3	0	ki-sur-ra
	1	ki-sur-ra
	2	[...]
	3	[...]
	4	[...]
	5	[...]
	6	ki-sur-ra
v 4	0	nibru.KI-ka
	1	nibru.KI-ka
	2	[...]
	3	[...]
	4	[...]
	5	[...]
	6	nibru.KI-ka
v 5	0	uru.KI
	1	uru.KI
	2	[...]
	3	[...]
	4	[...]
	5	[...]
	6	uru.KI
v 6	0	ki nu-ne-gar
	1	ki nu-ne-gar
	2	[...]
	3	[...]
	4	[...]
	5	[...]
	6	ki nu-ne-gar
v 7	0	^{d}*šu*-^{d}EN.ZU
	1	^{d}*šu*-^{d}EN.ZU
	2	[...]
	3	[...]
	4	[...]
	5	[...]
	6	^{d}*šu*-^{d}EN.ZU
v 8	0	lugal-kala-ga
	1	lugal-kala-ga
	2	[...]
	3	[...]
	4	[...]
	5	[...]
	6	lugal-kala-ga

v 9
0 lugal-úri.KI-ma
1 lugal-úri.KI-ma
2 [...]
3 [...]
4 [...]
5 [...]
6 lugal-úri.KI-ma

v 10
0 lugal-an-ub-da-límmu-ba-ke₄
1 lugal-an-ub-da-límmu-ba-ke₄
2 [...]
3 [...]
4 [...]
5 [...]
6 lugal-an-ub-da-límmu-ba-ke₄

v 11
0 si-ma-núm.KI
1 si-ma-núm.KI
2 [...]
3 [...]
4 [...]
5 [...]
6 si-ma-núm.KI

v 12–18 Lacuna

v 19
0 ᵈen-l[íl ᵈnin-líl-ra]
1 ᵈen-l[íl ᵈnin-líl-ra]
2 [...]
3 [...]
4 [...]
5 [...]
6 [...]

v 20
0 ki-su[r-ra]
1 ki-su[r-ra]
2 [...]
3 [...]
4 [...]
5 [...]
6 [...]

v 21
0 ni[bru.KI-ka]
1 ni[bru.KI-ka]
2 [...]
3 [...]
4 [...]
5 [...]
6 [...]

v 22
0 si-ma-n[úm.KI]
1 si-ma-n[úm.KI]
2 [...]
3 [...]
4 [...]
5 [...]
6 [...]

v 23
0 ki mu-ne-[gar]
1 ki mu-ne-[gar]
2 [...]
3 [...]
4 [...]
5 [...]
6 [...]

v 24
0 u₄-bi-t[a]
1 u₄-bi-t[a]
2 [...]
3 [...]
4 [...]
5 [...]
6 [...]

v 25	0	mar-dú lú-ḫa-lam-m[a]
	1	mar-dú lú-ḫa-lam-m[a]
	2	[...]
	3	[...]
	4	[...]
	5	[...]
	6	[...]
v 26	0	dím-ma-ur-ra-gin_7
	1	dím-ma-ur-ra-gin_7
	2	[...]
	3	[...]
	4	[...]
	5	[...]
	6	[...]
v 27	0	ur-bar-ra-gin_7
	1	ur-bar-ra-gin_7
	2	[...]
	3	[...]
	4	[...]
	5	[...]
	6	[...]
v 28	0	tùr ⸢x⸣ [x] ⸢x⸣
	1	tùr ⸢x⸣ [x] ⸢x⸣
	2	[...]
	3	[...]
	4	[...]
	5	[...]
	6	[...]
v 29	0	lú [še nu]-zu
	1	lú [še nu]-zu
	2	[...]
	3	[...]
	4	[...]
	5	[...]
	6	[...]
v 30	0	lú [...]-ga
	1	lú [...]-ga
	2	[...]
	3	[...]
	4	[...]
	5	[...]
	6	[...]
v 31	0	[...] silim-ma
	1	[...] silim-ma
	2	[...]
	3	[...]
	4	[...]
	5	[...]
	6	[...]
v 32	0	[...]-da
	1	[...]-da
	2	[...]
	3	[...]
	4	[...]
	5	[...]
	6	[...]
v 33	0	⸢bára(?)⸣-[...]-ke_4
	1	⸢bára(?)⸣-[...]-ke_4
	2	[...]
	3	[...]
	4	[...]
	5	[...]
	6	[...]
v 34	0	⸢mu⸣-[un]-sì-sì
	1	⸢mu⸣-[un]-sì-sì
	2	[...]
	3	[...]
	4	[...]
	5	[...]
	6	[...]

v 35–39 Lacuna

v 40	0	u_4 uru.KI
	1	u_4 uru.KI
	2	[...]
	3	[...]
	4	[...]
	5	[...]
	6	[...]
v 41	0	an-ta nam-m[i-...]
	1	an-ta nam-m[i-...]
	2	[...]
	3	[...]
	4	[...]
	5	[...]
	6	[...]
v 42	0	ḫur-sag-gal-ga[l]
	1	ḫur-sag-gal-ga[l]
	2	[...]
	3	[...]
	4	[...]
	5	[...]
	6	[...]
v 43	0	ḫu-rí-in-g[in_7]
	1	ḫu-rí-in-g[in_7]
	2	[...]
	3	[...]
	4	[...]
	5	[...]
	6	[...]
v 44	0	gú ki-[šè]
	1	gú ki-[šè]
	2	[...]
	3	[...]
	4	[...]
	5	[...]
	6	[...]
v 45	0	ba-an-da-ab-[gar]
	1	ba-an-da-ab-[gar]
	2	[...]
	3	[...]
	4	[...]
	5	[...]
	6	[...]
v 46	0	uru.KI á-dam
	1	uru.KI á-dam
	2	[...]
	3	[...]
	4	[...]
	5	[...]
	6	[...]
v 47	0	ki gar-gar-ra-b[i]
	1	ki gar-gar-ra-b[i]
	2	[...]
	3	[...]
	4	[...]
	5	[...]
	6	[...]
v 48	0	du_6-du_6-rá mi-ni-[gar]
	1	du_6-du_6-rá mi-ni-[gar]
	2	[...]
	3	[...]
	4	[...]
	5	[...]
	6	[...]

For the remainder of the text, cols. vi–vii, see pp. 299–300 of the text edition.

Shoulder inscription

1 0 ^{d}*šu*-^{d}EN.ZU
1 1 ^{d}*šu*-^{d}EN.ZU
1 2 [...]

2 0 ki-ág-^{d}en-⸢líl⸣-lá
2 1 ki-ág-^{d}en-⸢líl⸣-lá
2 2 [...]

3 0 lugal ^{d}en-líl-le
3 1 lugal ^{d}en-líl-le
3 2 [...]

4 0 šà-ga-na
4 1 šà-ga-na
4 2 [...]

5 0 in-pà
5 1 in-pà
5 2 [...]

6 0 lugal-kala-⸢ga⸣
6 1 lugal-kala-⸢ga⸣
6 2 [...]

7 0 lu[gal]-ú[ri].KI-⸢ma⸣
7 1 lu[gal]-ú[ri].KI-⸢ma⸣
7 2 [...]

8 0 lugal-an-ub-da-límmu-ba
8 1 lugal-an-ub-da-límmu-ba
8 2 [...]

9 0 nam-ti-la-ni-šè
9 1 nam-ti-la-ni-šè
9 2 [...]

10 0 a mu-n[a-ru]
10 1 a mu-n[a-ru]
10 2 [...]

Colophon 1

1 0 mu-sar-ra
1 1 mu-sar-ra
1 2 [...]

2 0 zag-zi-da-ni
2 1 zag-zi-da-ni
2 2 [...]

3 0 alan-na$_4$
3 1 alan-na$_4$
3 2 [...]

Socle inscription

1 0 2 sìla ninda
1 1 2 sìla ninda
1 2 [...]

2 0 2 sìla làl
2 1 2 sìla làl
2 2 2 ⸢sìla⸣ [...]

3 0 1 sìla kurun
3 1 1 sìla kurun
3 2 1 sì[la ...]

4 0 1 sìla kaš
4 1 1 sìla kaš
4 2 [...]

5 0 1 *ma-la-kum*$_x$ (GÚM) udu
5 1 1 *ma-la-kum*$_x$ (GÚM) udu
5 2 [...]

6	0	[nì-d]ab$_5$ itu-da-ka
6	1	[nì-d]ab$_5$ itu-da-ka
6	2	[...]
7	0	[GI]Š.banšur
7	1	[GI]Š.banšur
7	2	[...]
8	0	^{d}en-lí1
8	1	^{d}en-lí1
8	2	[...]
9	0	lugal-[gá-ta]
9	1	lugal-[gá-ta]
9	2	[...]
10	0	⸢1⸣ gín ⸢x (x)⸣
10	1	⸢1⸣ gín ⸢x (x)⸣
10	2	[...]
11	0	1 sìla ì-du$_{10}$-ga
11	1	1 sìla ì-du$_{10}$-ga
11	2	1 sì[la ...]
12	0	nì-dab$_5$ itu-da-ka
12	1	nì-dab$_5$ itu-da-ka
12	2	ni-dab$_5$-itu-da
13	0	é-^{d}nin-lí1
13	1	é-^{d}nin-lí1
13	2	é-^{d}nin-lí1
14	0	nin-gá-t[a]
14	1	nin-gá-t[a]
14	2	nin-gá-t[a]
15	0	^{d}*šu*-^{d}EN.ZU
15	1	^{d}*šu*-^{d}EN.ZU
15	2	^{d}*šu*-^{d}EN.ZU

16	0	ki-ág-^{d}en-lí1-lá
16	1	ki-ág-^{d}en-lí1-lá
16	2	ki-ág-^{d}en-lí1-lá
17	0	lugal ^{d}en-lí1-le
17	1	lugal ^{d}en-lí1-le
17	2	lugal ^{d}en-lí1-l[e]
18	0	ki-ág šà-ga-na
18	1	ki-ág šà-ga-na
18	2	ki-ág šà-ga-n[a]
19	0	in-pà
19	1	in-pà
19	2	[i]n-p[à]
20	0	lugal-kala-ga
20	1	lugal-kala-ga
20	2	lugal-kala-ga
21	0	lugal-úri.KI-ma
21	1	lugal-úri.KI-ma
21	2	lugal-úri.KI-ma
22	0	lu[ga]l-an-ub-[da-límmu-ba]-ke$_4$
22	1	lu[ga]l-an-ub-[da-límmu-ba]-ke$_4$
22	2	[luga]l-an-ub-[da-límmu-b]a-ke$_4$
23	0	ì-ba
23	1	ì-ba
23	2	[...]
24	0	lú u$_4$-na-me
24	1	lú u$_4$-na-me
24	2	[...]

25 0 nì-⸢dab$_5$⸣-e
25 1 nì-⸢dab$_5$⸣-e
25 2 [...]

26 0 ì-⸢ku$_5$⸣-re$_6$-[a]
26 1 ì-⸢ku$_5$⸣-re$_6$-[a]
26 2 [...]

27 0 lú-bi
27 1 lú-bi
27 2 [...]

28 0 lugal ḫé-a
28 1 lugal ḫé-a
28 2 [...]

29 0 en ḫé-a
29 1 en ḫé-a
29 2 [...]

30 0 énsi ḫé-a
30 1 énsi ḫé-a
30 2 [...]

31 0 sanga ḫé-a
31 1 sanga ḫé-a
31 2 [...]

32 0 gudu$_4$ máš-e pà-da ⸢ḫé-a⸣
32 1 gudu$_4$ máš-e pà-da ⸢ḫé-a⸣
32 2 [...]

33 0 lú-ba
33 1 lú-ba
33 2 [...]

34 0 ^{d}en-líl
34 1 ^{d}en-líl
34 2 [...]

35 0 ^{d}nin-líl-e
35 1 ^{d}nin-líl-e
35 2 [...]

36 0 nam ḫa-ba-da-kuru$_5$-ne
36 1 nam ḫa-ba-da-kuru$_5$-ne
36 2 [...]

37 0 DUMU.NITA na-an-ni-TUK.TUK-ne
37 1 DUMU.NITA na-an-ni-TUK.TUK-ne
37 2 [...]

38 0 mu-ni kalam-ma na-an-ni-gá-gá-ne
38 1 mu-ni kalam-ma na-an-ni-gá-gá-ne
38 2 [...]

39 0 lú inim(Text: SAG)-bi
39 1 lú inim(Text: SAG)-bi
39 2 [...]

40 0 nu-ub-da-ab-kúr-r[e-a]
40 1 nu-ub-da-ab-kúr-r[e-a]
40 2 [...]

41 0 igi-^{d}e[n-l]íl
41 1 igi-^{d}e[n-l]íl
41 2 [...]

42 0 ^{d}ni[n-l]íl-lá-ka
42 1 ^{d}ni[n-l]íl-lá-ka
42 2 [...]

43 0 ḫé-en-sa$_6$
43 1 ḫé-en-sa$_6$
43 2 [...]

Colophon

1	0	mu-sar-ra
1	1	mu-sar-ra
1	2	[...]
2	0	ki-gai ^{d}[*šu*-^{d}EN].ZU
2	1	ki-gal ^{d}[*šu*-^{d}EN].ZU
2	2	[...]
3	0	alan-na$_4$-kam
3	1	alan-na$_4$-kam
3	2	[...]

1	0	^{d}*šu*-^{d}EN.ZU
1	1	^{d}*šu*-^{d}EN.⸢ZU⸣
1	2	...
1	3	^{d}*šu*-^{d}EN.ZU
1	4	...
2	0	ki-ág-^{d}en-líl-lá
2	1	ki-ág-^{d}en-líl-lá
2	2	...
2	3	ki-ág-^{d}en-líl-lá(Text: ME)
2	4	...
3	0	lugal ^{d}en-líl-le
3	1	lugal ^{d}en-líl-le
3	2	...
3	3	lugal ^{d}en-líl-le
3	4	...
4	0	ki-ág šà-ga-na
4	1	ki-ág šà-ga-na
4	2	...
4	3	ki-ág šà-ga-na
4	4	...
5	0	in-pà
5	1	in-pà
5	2	...
5	3	in-pà
5	4	...
6	0	lugal-kala-ga
6	1	lugal-kala-ga
6	2	...
6	3	lugal-kala-ga
6	4	...
7	0	lugal-uri$_{5}$.KI-ma
7	1	lugal-uri$_{5}$.KI-ma
7	2	...
7	3	lugal-uri$_{5}$.KI-ma
7	4	...
8	0	lugal-an-ub-da-límmu-ba
8	1	lugal-an-ub-da-límmu-ba
8	2	...
8	3	lugal-an-ub-da-límmu-ba
8	4	...
9	0	lugal-a-ni-ir
9	1	lugal-a-ni-ir
9	2	...
9	3	lugal-a-ni-ir
9	4	...
10	0	ir$_{11}$-^{d}nanna
10	1	ir$_{11}$-^{d}nanna
10	2	...
10	3	ir$_{11}$-^{d}nanna
10	4	...
11	0	sukkal-maḫ
11	1	sukkal-maḫ
11	2	...
11	3	sukkal-maḫ
11	4	...
12	0	énsi-
12	1	énsi-
12	2	...
12	3	énsi-
12	4	...
13	0	lagaš.KI-ke$_{4}$
13	1	lagaš.KI-<ke$_{4}$>
13	2	...
13	3	lagaš.KI-ke$_{4}$
13	4	...
14	0	sanga-^{d}en-ki-ka
14	1	sanga-^{d}en-ki-<ka>
14	2	...
14	3	sanga-^{d}en-ki-ka
14	4	...

15	0	GÌR.NÍTA *ú-ṣa-ar-gar-ša-na*.KI
15	1	GÌR.NÍTA ⸢*ú*⸣-*ṣa-ar-gar-ša-na*.KI
15	2	...
15	3	GÌR.NÍTA *ú-ṣa-ar-gar-ša-na*.KI
15	4	...
16	0	GÌR.NÍTA ba-šim-e KI
16	1	GÌR.NÍTA ba-šim-e KI
16	2	...
16	3	GÌR.NÍTA ba-šim-e (Text: BUR).KI
16	4	...
17	0	énsi-sa-bu-um.KI
17	1	énsi-sa-bu-um.KI
17	2	...
17	3	énsi-sa-bu-um.KI
17	4	...
18	0	ù ma-da-gu-te-bu-um.KI-ma
18	1	ù ma-da-gu-te-bu-um.KI-ma
18	2	...
18	3	ù ma-da-gu-te-bu-um.KI.-ma
18	4	...
19	0	GÌR.NÍTA dì-ma-at-^{d}en-líl-lá
19	1	GÌR.NÍTA dì-ma-at-^{d}en-líl-lá
19	2	...
19	3	GÌR.NÍTA dì-ma-at-^{d}en-líl-lá
19	4	...
20	0	énsi-*a-al*-^{d}*šu*-^{d}EN.ZU
20	1	énsi-*a-al*-^{d}*šu*-^{d}EN.ZU
20	2	...
20	3	énsi-*a-al*-^{d}*šu*-^{d}EN.ZU
20	4	...
21	0	GÌR.NÍTA ur-bí-lum.KI
21	1	GÌR.NÍTA ur-bí-lum.KI
21	2	...
21	3	GÌR.NÍTA ur-bí-lum.KI
21	4	...
22	0	énsi-ḫa-ma-zí.KI
22	1	énsi-ḫa-ma-zí.KI
22	2	...
22	3	énsi-ḫa-àm-zí.KI
22	4	...
23	0	ù kára (Text: GÁNA)-ḫar.KI
23	1	⸢ù⸣ kára (Text: GÁNA)-ḫar.KI
23	2	...
23	3	ù kára (Text: GÁNA)-ḫar.KI
23	4	...
24	0	⸢GÌR.NÍTA⸣ NI.ḪI.KI
24	1	⸢GÌR.NÍTA⸣ NI.ḪI.KI
24	2	...
24	3	GÌR.NÍTA NI.ḪI.KI
24	4	...
25	0	GÌR.NÍTA simaški(LÚ.SU).KI
25	1	GÌR.NÍTA simaški(LÚ.SU)<KI>
25	2	...
25	3	GÌR.NÍTA simaški(LÚ.SU).KI
25	4	...
26	0	ù ma-da-kar-da.KI-ka
26	1	ù ma-da-kar-da.<KI>-ka
26	2	...
26	3	ù ma-da-kar-da.KI-ka
26	4	...

27	0	ir_{11}-da-a-né
27	1	ir_{11}-da-né
27	2	...
27	3	ir_{11}-da-a-né
27	4	...
28	0	é-gír-su-KI-ka-ni
28	1	é-gír-su-KI-ka-ni
28	2	...
28	3	é-gír-su-KI-ka-ni
28	4	...
29	0	mu-na-dù
29	1	⸢mu⸣-na-dù
29	2	...
29	3	mu-na-dù
29	4	...

1	0	^{d}*šu*-^{d}EN.ZU
1	1	^{d}*šu*-^{d}EN.ZU
1	2	^{d}*šu*-^{d}EN.ZU
1	3	^{d}*šu*-^{d}EN.ZU
1	4	[...]
1	5	[...]
1	6	[...]
2	0	ki-ág-^{d}en-líl-lá
2	1	ki-ág-^{d}en-líl-l[á]
2	2	ki-ág-^{d}en-líl-lá
2	3	ki-ág-^{d}en-líl-lá
2	4	[...]
2	5	⸢ki-ág-^{d}en-líl-lá⸣
2	6	[ki]-⸢ág⸣-^{d}en-líl-lá
3	0	lugal-^{d}en-líl-le
3	1	lugal-^{d}en-líl-le
3	2	⸢lugal⸣-^{d}en-líl-le
3	3	lugal-^{d}en-líl-le
3	4	[...]
3	5	⸢lugal-^{d}en-líl-le⸣
3	6	[lu]gal-^{d}en-líl-⸢le⸣
4	0	ki-ág šà-ga-na
4	1	ki-ág šà-ga-na
4	2	ki-[á]g šà-ga-na
4	3	⸢ki⸣-ág šà-ga-na
4	4	[...]
4	5	[ki-á]g šà-ga-[na]
4	6	[ki]-á[g] šà-ga-n[a]
5	0	in-pà
5	1	in-pà
5	2	in-pà
5	3	in-pà
5	4	[...]
5	5	[i]n-pà
5	6	⸢in⸣-pà
6	0	lugal-kala-ga
6	1	lugal-kala-ga
6	2	lugal-kala-ga
6	3	lugal-kala-ga
6	4	[...]
6	5	[lu]gal-kala-ga
6	6	lugal-kala-ga
7	0	lugal-uri$_5$.KI-ma
7	1	lugal-uri$_5$.KI-ma
7	2	lu[gal-u]ri$_5$.KI-ma
7	3	lugal-uri$_5$.KI-ma
7	4	[...]
7	5	[lu]gal-ur[i$_5$].KI-ma
7	6	lugal-uri$_5$.KI-ma
8	0	lugal-an-ub-da-límmu-ba
8	1	lugal-an-ub-da-límmu-⸢ba⸣
8	2	⸢lugal⸣-an-ub-da-límmu-ba
8	3	lugal-an-ub-da-límmu-ba
8	4	[...]
8	5	[lu]gal-an-ub-⸢da-límmu-ba⸣
8	6	lugal-an-ub-da-límmu-ba
9	0	dingir-ra-ni-ir
9	1	dingir-ra-ni-ir
9	2	[ding]ir-⸢ra⸣-ni-ir
9	3	dingir-ra-ni-ir
9	4	[...]
9	5	dingir-⸢ra⸣-ni-ir
9	6	dingir-ra-ni-ir
10	0	lugal-má-gur$_8$-re
10	1	lugal-má-gur$_8$-re
10	2	⸢lugal⸣-má-gur$_8$-re
10	3	lugal-má-gur$_8$-re
10	4	[...]
10	5	lugal-má-gur$_8$-re
10	6	lugal-má-gur$_8$-re

11	0	nu-bànda-en-nu-gá
11	1	nu-bànda-en-nu-gá
11	2	nu-bànda-en-nu-gá
11	3	nu-bànda-en-nu-gá
11	4	Traces
11	5	nu-bànda-en-nu-gá
11	6	nu-bànda-en-nu-gá

12	0	énsi-
12	1	énsi-
12	2	énsi-
12	3	énsi-
12	4	⸢énsi⸣-
12	5	énsi-
12	6	énsi-

13	0	uri$_5$.KI-ma
13	1	uri$_5$.KI-ma
13	2	uri$_5$.KI-ma
13	3	uri$_5$.KI-ma
13	4	[u]ri$_5$.KI-ma
13	5	uri$_5$.KI-ma
13	6	uri$_5$.KI-m[a]

14	0	ir$_{11}$-da-né
14	1	ir$_{11}$-da-né
14	2	ir$_{11}$-da-né
14	3	[i]r$_{11}$-da-né
14	4	⸢ir$_{11}$-da⸣-né
14	5	ir$_{11}$-da-n[é]
14	6	ir$_{11}$-da-n[é]

15	0	é-ki-ág-gá-ni
15	1	é-ki-ág-gá-ni
15	2	é-ki-ág-gá-⸢ni⸣
15	3	[é-ki]-ág-gá-ni
15	4	[é]-⸢ki-ág-gá-ni⸣
15	5	é-⸢ki⸣-ág-gá-ni
15	6	é-ki-ág-gá-ni

16	0	mu-na-an-dù
16	1	mu-na-an-dù
16	2	mu-na-an-dù
16	3	[mu]-⸢na-an-dù⸣
16	4	[m]u-⸢na-an-dù⸣
16	5	m[u-n]a-an-d[ù]
16	6	m[u]-[n]a-an-d[ù]

1	0	^{d}šára
1	1	^{d}šára
1	2	^{d}šára
1	3	^{d}šára
1	4	^{d}šára
1	5	[...]
1	6	...
2	0	nir-gál-an-na
2	1	nir-gál-an-na
2	2	nir-gál-an-na
2	3	nir-gál-an-na
2	4	nir-gál-an-na
2	5	[...]
2	6	...
3	0	dumu-ki-ág-
3	1	dumu-ki-ág-
3	2	dumu-ki-ág-
3	3	dumu-ki-ág-
3	4	dumu-ki-ág-
3	5	[dumu-ki-á]g-
3	6	...
4	0	^{d}inanna
4	1	^{d}inanna
4	2	^{d}inanna
4	3	^{d}inanna
4	4	^{d}inanna
4	5	[^{d}]inanna
4	6	...
5	0	ad-da-ni-ir
5	1	ad-da-ni-ir
5	2	ad-da-ni-ir
5	3	ad-da-ni-ir
5	4	ad-da-ni-ir
5	5	ad-da-ni-ir
5	6	...
6	0	^{d}*šu*-^{d}EN.ZU
6	1	^{d}*šu*-^{d}EN.ZU
6	2	^{d}*šu*-^{d}EN.ZU
6	3	^{d}*šu*-^{d}EN.ZU
6	4	^{d}*šu*-^{d}EN.ZU
6	5	^{d}*šu*-^{d}EN.ZU
6	6	...
7	0	lugal-kala-ga
7	1	lugal-kala-ga
7	2	lugal-kala-ga
7	3	lugal-kala-ga
7	4	lugal-kala-ga
7	5	lugal-kala-ga
7	6	...
8	0	lugal-uri$_5$.KI-ma
8	1	lugal-uri$_5$.KI-ma
8	2	lugal-uri$_5$.KI-ma
8	3	lugal-uri$_5$.KI-ma
8	4	lugal-uri$_5$.KI-ma
8	5	lugal-uri$_5$.KI-ma
8	6	...
9	0	lugal-an-ub-da-límmu-ba-ke$_4$
9	1	lugal-an-ub-da-límmu-ba-ke$_4$
9	2	lugal-an-ub-da-límmu-ba-ke$_4$
9	3	lugal-an-ub-da-límmu-ba-ke$_4$
9	4	lugal-an-ub-da-límmu-ba-ke$_4$
9	5	lugal-an-ub-da-límmu-ba-ke$_4$
9	6	...

10	0	é-šà-ge$_4$-pà-da
10	1	é-šà-ge$_4$-pà-da
10	2	é-šà-ge$_4$-pà-da
10	3	é-šà-ge$_4$-pà-da
10	4	é-šà-ge$_4$-pà-da
10	5	é-šà-ge$_4$-pà-da
10	6	...
11	0	é-ki-ág-gá-ni
11	1	é-ki-ág-gá-ni
11	2	é-ki-ág-gá-ni
11	3	é-ki-ág-gá-ni
11	4	é-ki-ág-gá-ni
11	5	é-ki-ág-gá-ni
11	6	...
12	0	nam-ti-la-ni-šè
12	1	⸢nam-ti-la-ni⸣-šè
12	2	nam-ti-la-ni-šè
12	3	nam-ti-la-ni-šè
12	4	nam-ti-la-ni-šè
12	5	nam-ti-la-ni-šè
12	6	...
13	0	mu-na-dù
13	1	⸢mu⸣-na-d[ù]
13	2	mu-na-dù
13	3	mu-na-dù
13	4	mu-na-dù
13	5	mu-na-dù
13	6	...

1	0	^{d}šára
1	1	^{d}šára
1	2	^{d}šára
1	3	^{d}šára
1	4	...
1	5	^{d}šára
1	6	^{d}šára
1	7	⸢^{d}⸣šára
1	8	^{d}šára
2	0	nir-gál-an-na
2	1	nir-gál-an-na
2	2	nir-gál-an-na
2	3	nir-gál-an-na
2	4	...
2	5	nir-gál-an-na
2	6	nir-gál-an-na
2	7	nir-gál-an-na
2	8	nir-gál-an-na
3	0	dumu-ki-ág-
3	1	dumu-ki-ág-
3	2	dumu-ki-ág-
3	3	dumu-ki-ág-
3	4	...
3	5	dumu-ki-ág-
3	6	⸢dumu⸣-ki-ág-
3	7	dumu-ki-ág-
3	8	dumu-ki-ág-
4	0	^{d}inanna
4	1	^{d}inanna
4	2	^{d}inanna
4	3	^{d}inanna
4	4	...
4	5	^{d}inanna
4	6	⸢^{d}inanna⸣
4	7	^{d}inanna
4	8	^{d}inanna
5	0	ad-da-ni-ir
5	1	⸢ad-da⸣-ni-ir
5	2	ad-da-ni-ir
5	3	ad-da-ni-ir
5	4	...
5	5	ad-da-ni-ir
5	6	ad-da-ni-ir
5	7	ad-da-ni-ir
5	8	ad-da-ni-ir
6	0	^{d}*šu*-^{d}EN.ZU
6	1	⸢^{d}⸣[*šu*-^{d}EN.ZU]
6	2	^{d}*šu*-^{d}EN.ZU
6	3	^{d}*šu*-^{d}EN.ZU
6	4	...
6	5	^{d}*šu*-^{d}EN.ZU
6	6	^{d}*šu*-^{d}EN.ZU
6	7	^{d}*šu*-^{d}EN.ZU
6	8	^{d}*šu*-^{d}EN.ZU
7	0	išib-an-na
7	1	[išib-an]-na
7	2	išib-an-na
7	3	išib-an-na
7	4	...
7	5	išib-an-na
7	6	išib-an-⸢na⸣
7	7	išib-an-na
7	8	išib-an-na
8	0	gudu$_4$ šu-daddag(UD.UD)-
8	1	[gudu$_4$ šu]-daddag(UD.UD)-
8	2	gudu$_4$ šu-daddag(UD.UD)-
8	3	gudu$_4$ šu-daddag(UD.UD)-
8	4	...
8	5	gudu$_4$ šu-daddag(UD.UD)-
8	6	gudu$_4$ šu-daddag(UD.UD)-
8	7	gudu$_4$ šu-daddag(UD.UD)-
8	8	gudu$_4$ šu-daddag(UD.UD)-

9	0	^{d}en-líl
9	1	⸢^{d}en-líl⸣
9	2	^{d}en-líl
9	3	^{d}en-líl
9	4	...
9	5	^{d}en-líl
9	6	^{d}en-líl
9	7	^{d}en-líl
9	8	^{d}en-líl
10	0	^{d}nin-líl-ka
10	1	^{d}nin-⸢líl-ka⸣
10	2	^{d}nin-líl-ka
10	3	^{d}nin-líl-ka
10	4	...
10	5	^{d}nin-líl-ka
10	6	^{d}nin-líl-ka
10	7	^{d}nin-líl-ka
10	8	^{d}nin-líl-ka
11	0	ù dingir-gal-gal-e-ne
11	1	⸢ù⸣ dingir-gal-gal-⸢e-ne⸣
11	2	ù dingir-gal-gal-e-ne
11	3	ù dingir-gal-gal-e-ne
11	4	...
11	5	ù dingir-gal-gal-e-ne
11	6	ù dingir-gal-gal-e-ne
11	7	ù dingir-gal-gal-e-ne
11	8	ù dingir-gal-gal-e-ne
12	0	lugal-^{d}en-líl-le
12	1	lugal-^{d}en-líl-le
12	2	lugal-^{d}en-líl-le
12	3	lugal-^{d}en-líl-le
12	4	...
12	5	lugal-^{d}en-líl-le
12	6	lugal-^{d}en-líl-le
12	7	lugal-^{d}en-líl-le
12	8	lugal-^{d}en-líl-le

13	0	ki-ág
13	1	⸢ki⸣-ág
13	2	ki-ág
13	3	ki-ág
13	4	...
13	5	ki-ág
13	6	ki-ág
13	7	⸢ki⸣-ág
13	8	ki-ág
14	0	šà-ga-na
14	1	šà-⸢ga⸣-na
14	2	šà-ga-na
14	3	šà-ga-na
14	4	...
14	5	šà-ga-na
14	6	šà-ga-na
14	7	⸢šà⸣-ga-na
14	8	šà-ga-na
15	0	in-pà
15	1	in-pà
15	2	in-pà
15	3	in-pà
15	4	...
15	5	in-pà
15	6	in-pà
15	7	[i]n-pà
15	8	in-pà
16	0	sipa-kalam-ma-šè
16	1	sipa-kalam-ma-šè
16	2	sipa-kalam-ma-šè
16	3	sipa-kalam-ma-šè
16	4	...
16	5	sipa-kalam-ma-šè
16	6	⸢sipa⸣-kalam-ma-šè
16	7	sipa-kalam-ma-šè
16	8	sipa-kalam-ma-šè

17	0	lugal-kala-ga
17	1	lugal-kala-ga
17	2	lugal-kala-ga
17	3	lugal-kala-ga
17	4	...
17	5	lugal-kala-ga
17	6	lugal-kala-ga
17	7	lugal-kala-ga
17	8	lugal-kala-ga
18	0	lugal-uri$_5$.KI-ma
18	1	lugal-uri$_5$.KI-ma
18	2	lugal-uri$_5$.KI-ma
18	3	lugal-uri$_5$.KI-ma
18	4	...
18	5	lugal-uri$_5$.KI-ma
18	6	[lu]gal-uri$_5$.KI-ma
18	7	[l]ugal-uri$_5$.KI-ma
18	8	lugal-uri$_5$.KI-ma
19	0	lugal-an-ub-da-límmu-ba-ke$_4$
19	1	lugal-an-ub-da-límmu-ba-ke$_4$
19	2	lugal-an-ub-da-límmu-ba-ke$_4$
19	3	lugal-an-ub-da-límmu-ba-ke$_4$
19	4	...
19	5	lugal-an-ub-da-límmu-ba-ke$_4$
19	6	lugal-an-ub-da-límmu-ba-ke$_4$
19	7	lugal-an-ub-da-límmu-ba-ke$_4$
19	8	lugal-an-ub-da-límmu-ba-ke$_4$

20	0	u$_4$ bàd-mar-dú-
20	1	u$_4$ bàd-mar-dú-
20	2	u$_4$ bàd-mar-dú-
20	3	u$_4$ bàd-mar-dú-
20	4	...
20	5	u$_4$ bàd-mar-dú-
20	6	u$_4$ bàd-mar-dú-
20	7	u$_4$ bàd-mar-dú-
20	8	u$_4$ bàd-mar-dú-
21	0	*mu-ri-iq-*
21	1	*mu-ri-iq-*
21	2	*mu-ri-iq-*
21	3	*mu-ri-iq-*
21	4	...
21	5	*mu-ri-iq-*
21	6	*mu-ri-iq-*
21	7	*mu-ri-iq-*
21	8	*mu-ri-iq-*
22	0	*ti-id-ni-im*
22	1	⸢*ti*⸣-*id-ni-im*
22	2	*ti-id-ni-im*
22	3	*ti-id-ni-im*
22	4	...
22	5	*ti-id-ni-im*
22	6	*ti-id-ni-im*
22	7	*ti-id-ni-im*
22	8	*ti-id-ni-im*
23	0	mu-dù-a
23	1	mu-dù-a
23	2	mu-dù-a
23	3	mu-dù-a
23	4	...
23	5	mu-dù-a
23	6	mu-dù-a
23	7	mu-dù-a
23	8	mu-dù-a

24	0	ù gìr-mar-dù
24	1	ù gìr-mar-dù
24	2	ù gìr-mar-dù
24	3	ù gìr-mar-dù
24	4	...
24	5	ù gìr-mar-dù
24	6	ù gìr-mar-dù
24	7	ù gìr-mar-dù
24	8	ù gìr-mar-dù
25	0	ma-da-né-e
25	1	ma-da-né-e
25	2	ma-da-né-e
25	3	ma-da-né-e
25	4	...
25	5	ma-da-né-e
25	6	ma-da-né-e
25	7	ma-da-né-e
25	8	ma-da-né-e
26	0	bí-in-gi$_4$-a
26	1	bí-in-gi$_4$-a
26	2	bí-in-gi$_4$-a
26	3	bí-in-gi$_4$-a
26	4	...
26	5	bí-in-gi$_4$-a
26	6	[b]í-in-gi$_4$-a
26	7	bí-in-gi$_4$-a
26	8	bí-in-gi$_4$-a
27	0	é-šà-ge-pà-da
27	1	é-šà-ge-pà-da
27	2	é-šà-ge-pà-da
27	3	é-šà-ge-pà-da
27	4	...
27	5	é-šà-ge-pà-da
27	6	⌈é-šà-ge-pà⌉-da
27	7	é-šà-g[e]-pà-da
27	8	é-šà-ge-pà-da
28	0	é-ki-ág-gá-ni
28	1	é-ki-ág-gá-ni
28	2	é-ki-ág-gá-ni
28	3	é-ki-ág-gá-ni
28	4	...
28	5	é-ki-ág-gá-ni
28	6	é-ki-ág-gá-ni
28	7	é-ki-⌈ág⌉-gá-ni
28	8	é-ki-ág-gá-ni
29	0	nam-ti-la-ni-šè
29	1	nam-ti-la-ni-šè
29	2	nam-ti-la-ni-šè
29	3	nam-ti-la-ni-šè
29	4	...
29	5	nam-ti-la-ni-šè
29	6	⌈nam⌉-ti-la-ni-šè
29	7	nam-⌈ti⌉-la-ni-šè
29	8	nam-ti-la-ni-šè
30	0	mu-na-dù
30	1	mu-na-dù
30	2	mu-na-dù
30	3	mu-na-dù
30	4	...
30	5	mu-na-d[ù]
30	6	m[u]-⌈na⌉-dù
30	7	Blank line
30	8	mu-na-dù

Ex. 3 adds ki-[bé mu-na-gi$_4$]

1	0	^{d}šu-^{d}EN.ZU
1	1	^{d}šu-^{d}EN.ZU
1	2	^{d}šu-^{d}EN.ZU
1	3	^{d}šu-^{d}EN.ZU
1	4	^{d}šu-^{d}EN.ZU
2	0	ki-ág-^{d}en-líl-lá
2	1	ki-ág-^{d}en-líl-lá
2	2	ki-ág-^{d}en-líl-lá
2	3	ki-ág-^{d}en-líl-lá
2	4	ki-ág-^{d}en-líl-lá
3	0	lugal-^{d}en-líl-le
3	1	lugal-^{d}en-líl-le
3	2	lugal-^{d}en-líl-le
3	3	lugal-^{d}en-líl-le
3	4	lugal-^{d}en-líl-le
4	0	ki-ág šà-ga-na
4	1	ki-ág šà-ga-na
4	2	ki-ág šà-ga-na
4	3	ki-ág šà-ga-na
4	4	ki-ág šà-ga-na
5	0	in-pà
5	1	in-pà
5	2	in-pà
5	3	in-pà
5	4	in-pà
6	0	lugal-kala-ga
6	1	lugal-kala-ga
6	2	lugal kala-ga
6	3	lugal-kala-ga
6	4	lugal-kala-ga
7	0	lugal-uri$_{5}$.KI-ma
7	1	lugal-uri$_{5}$.KI-ma
7	2	lugal-uri$_{5}$.KI-ma
7	3	lugal-uri$_{5}$.KI-ma
7	4	lugal-uri$_{5}$.KI-ma
8	0	lugal-an-ub-da-límmu-ba-ke$_{4}$
8	1	lugal-an-ub-da-límmu-ba-ke$_{4}$
8	2	lugal-an-ub-d[a]-límmu-ba-ke$_{4}$
8	3	lugal-an-ub-da-límmu-ba-ke$_{4}$
8	4	lugal-an-ub-da-límmu-ba-ke$_{4}$
9	0	é-ki-ág-gá-ni
9	1	é-ki-ág-gá-ni
9	2	é-ki-ág-gá-ni
9	3	[...]
9	4	é-ki-ág-gá-ni
10	0	mu-dù
10	1	mu-dù
10	2	mu-dù
10	3	[...]
10	4	mu-dù

1	0	^{d}nanna
1	1	^{d}nanna
1	2	^{d}nanna
2	0	dumu-sag-
2	1	dumu-sag-
2	2	dumu-sag-
3	0	^{d}en-líl-lá
3	1	^{d}en-líl-lá
3	2	^{d}en-líl-lá
4	0	lugal-ki-ág-gá-ni-ir
4	1	lugal-ki-ág-gá-ni-ir
4	2	lugal-ki-ág-gá-ni-ir
5	0	^{d}*šu*-^{d}EN.ZU
5	1	^{d}*šu*-^{d}EN.ZU
5	2	^{d}*šu*-^{d}EN.ZU
6	0	ki-ág-^{d}nanna
6	1	ki-ág-^{d}nanna
6	2	ki-ág-^{d}nanna
7	0	lugal ^{d}en-líl-le
7	1	lugal ^{d}⸢en⸣-lí[l]-l[e]
7	2	lugal ^{d}en-líl-le
8	0	šà-ga-na
8	1	[šà]-ga-n[a]
8	2	šà-ga-na
9	0	in-pà
9	1	in-p[à]
9	2	in-pà
10	0	sipa-kalam-ma
10	1	sipa-kalam-⸢ma⸣
10	2	sipa-kalam-ma
11	0	ù an-ub-da-límmu-ba-šè
11	1	ù an-ub-da-límmu-ba-šè
11	2	ù an-ub-da-límmu-ba-šè
12	0	lugal-kala-ga
12	1	lugal-kala-ga
12	2	lugal-kala-ga
13	0	lugal-uri$_{5}$.KI-ma
13	1	[lu]gal-uri$_{5}$.KI-ma
13	2	lugal-uri$_{5}$.KI-ma
14	0	lugal-an-ub-da-límmu-ba-ke$_{4}$
14	1	[lug]al-an-ub-[d]a-límmu-ba-ke$_{4}$
14	2	lugal-an-ub-da-límmu-ba-ke$_{4}$
15	0	é-mu-ri-a-na-ba-AK
15	1	é-mu-ri-a-na-ba-AK
15	2	é-mu-ri-a-na-ba-AK
16	0	é-ki-ág-gá-ni
16	1	é-ki-ág-⸢gá⸣-ni
16	2	é-ki-ág-gá-ni
17	0	mu-na-dù
17	1	[m]u-⸢na⸣-dù
17	2	mu-na-dù

1	0	^{d}*i-bí*-^{d}EN.ZU
1	1	[...]
1	2	^{d}*i-b*[*í*]-^{d}EN.[ZU]
1	3	^{d}*i-bí*-^{d}EN.ZU
1	4	...
1	5	[...]
1	6	^{d}*i-bí*-^{d}EN.ZU
1	7	[...]
1	8	^{d}*i-bí*-^{d}EN.ZU
1	9	...
1	10	[...]
1	11	^{d}*i-bí*-^{d}EN.ZU
1	12	...
1	13	^{d}*i-bí*-^{d}EN.ZU
1	14	[...]
1	15	[...]
1	16	[...]
1	17	[...]
2	0	dingir-kalam-ma-na
2	1	[...]
2	2	dingir-kalam-[...]
2	3	dingir-kalam-ma-na
2	4	...
2	5	[...]
2	6	dingir-kalam-ma-na
2	7	[...]
2	8	dingir-kalam-ma-na
2	9	...
2	10	[...]
2	11	dingir-kalam-ma-na
2	12	dingir-kalam-ma-na
2	13	dingir-kalam-ma-na
2	14	[...]
2	15	[...]
2	16	[...]
2	17	[...]
3	0	lugal-kala-ga
3	1	[...]
3	2	lugal-[...]
3	3	lugal-kala-ga
3	4	...
3	5	[...]
3	6	...
3	7	[...]
3	8	lugal-kala-ga
3	9	lugal-kala-ga
3	10	[...]
3	11	lugal-kala-ga
3	12	...
3	13	lugal-kala-ga
3	14	[...]
3	15	[...]
3	16	[...]
3	17	[...]
4	0	lugal-uri$_5$.KI-ma
4	1	[...]
4	2	lu[gal-...]
4	3	lugal-uri$_5$.KI-ma
4	4	...
4	5	[...]
4	6	...
4	7	[...]
4	8	lugal-uri$_5$.KI-ma
4	9	lugal-uri$_5$.KI-ma
4	10	[...]
4	11	...
4	12	lugal-uri$_5$.KI-ma
4	13	lugal-uri$_5$.KI-ma
4	14	[...]
4	15	[...]
4	16	[...]
4	17	[...]

5	0	lugal-an-ub-da-límmu-ba-ke$_4$
5	1	luga[l-an-ub]-da-límmu-⸢ba⸣-[ke$_4$]
5	2	lu[gal-...]
5	3	luga[al]-⸢an-ub⸣-[...]
5	4	...
5	5	[...]
5	6	...
5	7	[...]
5	8	...
5	9	lugal-an-ub-da-límmu-ba-ke$_4$
5	10	[...]
5	11	...
5	12	lugal-an-ub-da-límmu-ba-ke$_4$
5	13	lugal-an-ub-da-límmu-ba-ke$_4$
5	14	[...]
5	15	[...]
5	16	[...]
5	17	[...]
6	0	nam-gal-ki-ág-
6	1	nam-gal-ki-á[g]-
6	2	[...]
6	3	[...]
6	4	[...]
6	5	[...]
6	6	[...]
6	7	[...]
6	8	[...]
6	9	nam-gal-ki-ág-
6	10	[...]
6	11	...
6	12	nam-gal-ki-ág-
6	13	nam-gal-ki-ág-
6	14	[...]
6	15	[...]
6	16	[...]
6	17	[...]

7	0	^{d}EN.ZU-na-da
7	1	^{d}EN.ZU-na-d[a]
7	2	[...]
7	3	[...]
7	4	[...]
7	5	[...]
7	6	[...]
7	7	[...]
7	8	[...]
7	9	...
7	10	[^{d}E]N.ZU-⸢na⸣-[da]
7	11	...
7	12	^{d}EN.ZU-na-da
7	13	^{d}EN.ZU-na-da
7	14	[...]
7	15	[...]
7	16	⸢^{d}⸣EN.Z[U]-n[a-da]
7	17	[...]
8	0	uri$_5$.KI
8	1	uri$_5$.K[I]
8	2	[...]
8	3	[...]
8	4	[...]
8	5	[...]
8	6	[...]
8	7	[...]
8	8	[...]
8	9	uri$_5$.KI
8	10	[u]ri$_5$.[KI]
8	11	...
8	12	[...]
8	13	uri$_5$.KI
8	14	[...]
8	15	[...]
8	16	u[ri$_5$.KI]
8	17	[...]

9	0	dagal-e-dè	11	0	ur$_5$-ta
9	1	dagal-e-d[è]	11	1	ur$_5$-[ta]
9	2	[...]	11	2	[...]
9	3	[...]	11	3	[...]
9	4	[...]	11	4	[...]
9	5	[...]	11	5	[...]
9	6	[...]	11	6	[...]
9	7	[...]	11	7	[...]
9	8	[...]	11	8	[...]
9	9	dagal-e-dè	11	9	ur$_5$-ta
9	10	dagal-e-d[è]	11	10	ur$_5$-[ta]
9	11	...	11	11	...
9	12	[...]	11	12	[...]
9	13	dagal-e-dè	11	13	ur$_5$-ta
9	14	[...]	11	14	[...]
9	15	[...]	11	15	[...]
9	16	dagal-⸢e-dè⸣	11	16	ur$_5$-ta
9	17	[...]	11	17	...
10	0	sa im-ma-ši-gar	12	0	kalam gi-né
10	1	sa im-ma-š[i-gar]	12	1	k[alam...]
10	2	[...]	12	2	[...]
10	3	[...]	12	3	[...]
10	4	[...]	12	4	[...]
10	5	[...]	12	5	[...]
10	6	[...]	12	6	[...]
10	7	[...]	12	7	[...]
10	8	[...]	12	8	[...]
10	9	sa im-ma-ši-gar	12	9	kalam gi-né
10	10	sa im-ma-[...]	12	10	kalam g[i-né]
10	11	...	12	11	...
10	12	[...]	12	12	[...]
10	13	sa im-ma-ši-gar	12	13	kalam gi-né
10	14	[...]	12	14	[...]
10	15	[...]	12	15	[...]
10	16	sa ⸢im⸣-ma-ši-gar	12	16	kalam gi-né
10	17	[...]	12	17	...

13	0	sig-nim GAM-e-dè
13	1	[...]
13	2	[sig]-nim G[AM-e-dè]
13	3	[...]
13	4	...
13	5	[...]
13	6	...
13	7	[...]
13	8	...
13	9	sig-nim GAM-e-dè
13	10	sig-nim GAM-[...]
13	11	sig-nim GAM-e-dè
13	12	[...]
13	13	sig-nim GAM-e-dè
13	14	[...]
13	15	[...]
13	16	⸢sig⸣-igi GAM-e-dè
13	17	...

14	0	bàd-gal
14	1	[...]
14	2	[b]àd-g[al]
14	3	[...]
14	4	...
14	5	[...]
14	6	bàd-gal
14	7	[...]
14	8	bàd-gal
14	9	...
14	10	bàd-[gal]
14	11	bàd-gal
14	12	[...]
14	13	bàd-gal
14	14	[...]
14	15	[...]
14	16	[...]
14	17	...

15	0	za-pa-ág-ba šu nu-ku$_4$-ku$_4$
15	1	[...]
15	2	[...]
15	3	za-pa-ág-b[a šu] nu-ku$_4$-k[u$_4$]
15	4	za-pa-ág-ba šu nu-ku$_4$-ku$_4$
15	5	[...]
15	6	[...]
15	7	...
15	8	za-pa-ág-ba šu nu-ku$_4$-ku$_4$
15	9	za-pa-ág-ba šu nu-ku$_4$-ku$_4$
15	10	[...]
15	11	[...]
15	12	...
15	13	za-pa-ág-ba šu nu-ku$_4$-ku$_4$
15	14	[za]-pa-ág-ba šu [n]u-ku$_4$-ku$_4$
15	15	[za-pa-á]g-b[a] [šu n]u-ku$_4$-ku$_4$
15	16	[...]
15	17	...

16	0	ḫur-sag-sig$_7$-ga-gin$_7$
16	1	[...]
16	2	[...]
16	3	ḫur-sag-sig$_7$-[ga]-gi[n$_7$]
16	4	ḫur-sag-sig$_7$-ga-gin$_7$
16	5	...
16	6	[...]
16	7	...
16	8	...
16	9	ḫur-sag-sig$_7$-ga-gin$_7$
16	10	[...]
16	11	[...]
16	12	ḫur-sag-sig$_7$-ga-gin$_7$
16	13	ḫur-sag-sig$_7$-ga-gin$_7$
16	14	[ḫur-sa]g-sig$_7$-ga-gin$_7$
16	15	[ḫur-s]ag-sig$_7$-ga-⸢gin$_7$⸣
16	16	[...]
16	17	...

17	0	uru.KI-né im-mi-da$_5$
17	1	[...]
17	2	[...]
17	3	uru.KI-n[é im]-m[i-da$_5$]
17	4	uru.KI-né im-mi-da$_5$
17	5	uru.KI-né im-mi-da$_5$
17	6	[...]
17	7	...
17	8	...
17	9	uru.KI-né im-mi-da$_5$
17	10	[...]
17	11	[...]
17	12	uru.KI-né im-mi-da$_5$
17	13	uru.KI-né im-mi-da$_5$
17	14	[uru]-⸢né⸣ im-mi-da$_5$
17	15	[uru.K]I im-mi-⸢da$_5$⸣
17	16	[uru.K]I im-mi-da$_5$
17	17	...

18	0	uru$_{18}$ temen-bi
18	1	[...]
18	2	[...]
18	3	[...]
18	4	...
18	5	uru$_{18}$ temen-bi
18	6	[...]
18	7	[...]
18	8	...
18	9	uru$_{18}$ temen-bi
18	10	[...]
18	11	[...]
18	12	uru$_{18}$ temen-bi
18	13	uru$_{18}$ temen-bi
18	14	[uru$_{18}$] temen-bi
18	15	[uru$_{18}$-t]emen-[bi]
18	16	[uru$_{18}$ te]men-bi
18	17	...

19	0	ki in-ma-ni-pà
19	1	[...]
19	2	[...]
19	3	[...]
19	4	...
19	5	ki in-ma-ni-pà
19	6	[...]
19	7	[...]
19	8	[...]
19	9	ki in-ma-ni-pà
19	10	[...]
19	11	[...]
19	12	ki in-ma-ni-pà
19	13	ki in-ma-ni-pà
19	14	[ki] in-ma-ni-pà
19	15	[ki] in-[ma]-ni-[pà]
19	16	[ki in]-⸢ma⸣-[n]i-pà
19	17	...

20	0	bàd-ba
20	1	[...]
20	2	[...]
20	3	[...]
20	4	...
20	5	...
20	6	[...]
20	7	[...]
20	8	[...]
20	9	bàd-ba
20	10	[...]
20	11	[...]
20	12	[...]
20	13	bàd-ba
20	14	[bà]d-ba
20	15	[...]
20	16	[bàd]-ba
20	17	...

21	0	^{d}*i-bí*-^{d}EN.ZU gú-gal-nam-nun-na
21	1	[...]
21	2	[...]
21	3	[...]
21	4	^{d}*i-bí*-^{d}EN.ZU gú-gal-nam-nun-na
21	5	[...]
21	6	[...]
21	7	...
21	8	...
21	9	^{d}*i-bí*-^{d}EN.ZU gú-gal-nam-nun-na
21	10	[...]
21	11	[...]
21	12	[...]
21	13	^{d}*i-bí*-^{d}EN.ZU gú-gal-nam-nun-na
21	14	^{d}*i-bí*-^{d}EN.ZU gú-gal-nam-nun-na
21	15	[...]
21	16	[^{d}]⌈*i*⌉-*bí*-⌈^{d}EN⌉.ZU ⌈gú⌉-gal-nam-nun-na
21	17	^{d}*i-bí*-^{d}EN.ZU gú-gal-nam-nun-na

22	0	mu-bi-im
22	1	[...]
22	2	[...]
22	3	...
22	4	mu-bi-im
22	5	[...]
22	6	[...]
22	7	...
22	8	mu-bi-im
22	9	mu-bi-im
22	10	[...]
22	11	[...]
22	12	[...]
22	13	mu-bi-im
22	14	mu-bi-im
22	15	[...]
22	16	mu-bi-im
22	17	...